TANTRARĀJA TANTRA

प्राचीनभारतीयतन्त्रशास्त्रशेखरीभूतं

तन्त्रराजतन्त्रम्

तच्च

"महामहोपाध्याय" इति विरुदभाजैः

श्रीलक्ष्मणशास्त्रिमहोदयैः

सम्पादितम्

तत्रभवद्भिः

श्री आर्थर अवलॉन महाभागैश्च

सारगर्भितयाऽऽङ्ग्लभाषाभूमिकया

सन्दृब्धम्

मोतीलाल बनारसीदास इंटरनेशनल

दिल्ली

Tantrarāja Tantra

Edited by
MAHĀMAHOPĀDHYĀYA LAKSHMANA SHASTRI

Introduction by
ARTHUR AVALON

MOTILAL BANARSIDASS INTERNATIONAL
DELHI

Delhi, 2026
First Edition : Calcutta, 1926

ISBN : 978-93-47683-13-8

Also available at
MOTILAL BANARSIDASS INTERNATIONAL
H.O. : 41 U.A. Bungalow Road, (Back Lane) Jawahar Nagar, Delhi - 110 007
4261 (Basement) Lane #3, Ansari Road, Darya Ganj, New Delhi - 110 002
203 Royapettah High Road, Mylapore, Chennai - 600 004
12/1A, 2nd Floor, Bankim Chatterjee Street, Kolkata - 700 073
Stockist : Motilal Books, Ashok Rajpath, Near Kali Mandir, Patna - 800 004

Printed in India
MOTILAL BANARSIDASS INTERNATIONAL

INTRODUCTION.

The Tantrarâja, as its name implies, is an important work of its class which is, in one of its parts, here published for the first time with a commentary called Manoramâ by Subhagânandanâtha of (as Bhâskararâya in his commentary on the Nityâ*shod*ashikâr*n*ava says) the Kashmir school.

There are three sections of this Tantra each dealing with a separate Mata, that is way of regarding and worshipping the Devatâ, namely Kâdi, Hâdi, and Kahâdi, terms alluded to in my "Shakti and Shâkta" and explained later. The last portion is also I am told called Shaktisanggama which has four parts. The first is here published, namely the Kâdimata part of Tantrarâja consisting of 36 Chapters of 100 verses each.

The manuscripts which have been used for the preparation of this Edition belong to the Asiatic Society of Bengal, the Sanskrit College and Pandit Yajnapuru*sh*a respectively. To the last I am indebted for help in the preparation of this and other works. Ha is Bîja of Shiva. Ka is the first letter of the Bîja mantra of Kâlî or Krîng. In the Bîjâbhidânam quoted at page 321 of Pandit Jaganmohana Tarkâlangkâra's Edition of Mahânirvâna it is said :—

> Ka Kâlî Brahma ra proktam mahâmâyârthakashcha Î
> Vishvamâtrarthako nâdo bindur du*h*khâpahâraka*h*
> Tenaiva kâlikâng devîng pûjayed du*h*khashântaye

When Devî asks (vv. 7, 8) "what is Kâdi" Shiva replies, that Kâlî and Kâdi are Shakti and that "Thy form is the meaning of Kâdi" (Kâdisangjnâ bhavadrûpâ). The meaning of this is that the triangle is the form of the Devî. The letter Ka written in Bengali (ক) and generally in earlier Devanâgara forms of the letter shows a triangle in the left. According to the Var*n*oddhâra and Kâmadhenu Tantras (see Shabdakalpadruma *Sub. voc.* Ka) the left line of the triangle is red Brahmâ, the right line white Vi*sh*nu and the bottom line is dark green (Marakata) Rudra. The Mâtrâ is the white Sâk*sh*ât Sarasvatî. The crooked portion on the right like a goad is the lightning-like Ku*nd*alinî. The empty space in the triangle is the white Sudarshana shining like millions of moons and with Him is Kâlî the grantor of Kaivalya and in the three corners are Jye*shth*â, Vâmâ, and Raudrî Shaktis. This Triko*n*a is known as the Yonima*nd*ala which is the seat (Âsana) of Tripurâ Devî. She is Jnânâtmâ in whom are the four Kalâs and as the collectivity of Jnâna, Ichchhâ, Kriyâ, She is the Mûrtimân Prakriti. From Kakâra comes Kâma. It is the Mûlaprak*ri*ti of all Var*n*as and the imperishable Power of Blossom (Sphuradavyaya) the Mother of all Devas and the Giver of Liberation. In Chhândogya Upani*sh*ad (4-10-5) it is said "Kang Brahma"; "Ka is Brahma." It is that Shakti Which being spread by means of the nine Nâthas (the means of experience—ears (2) mouth, eyes (2), nostrils (2), penis and anus) manifests throughout the earth Kalpa after Kalpa, and at the end of the Kalpa they and She return to Him (Sâ tai*h* sârddham brajechchamâm). Shiva and Shakti are one and where one is worshipped the other is worshipped. Sammohana Tantra (Chapter I) says Kâdimata is that Mata in which the Mantras begin with Ka. In Hâdi they begin with Ha. It is also called Hangsarâja. Kahâdi is formed by the union of Kâdi and Hâdi which is Uttarâmnâyagochara. Kulâr*n*ava which is Ûrddhvâmnâya is I have been told the highest Tantra in Kahâdi-mata.

The Tantras of the Kâdi class are according to the present Text nine in number and are according to the Manoramâ :— Sundarîh*ri*daya, Nityâ*shod*ashikâr*n*ava, (published in Vol. 56 of Ânandâshrama Sanskrit Texts) Chandrajnâna, Mât*ri*kâ, Sammohana, Vâmakeshvara, Bahurûpâ*sht*aka, Prastârachintâma*n*i, and Meruprastâra.

Bhâskararâya, the learned Commentator on various Tântrik and Aupani*sh*âdic texts, questions the accuracy of the Manoramâ on this point in his Setubandha which is a Commentary of his on the Nityâ*shod*ashikâr*n*ava. He there says that the Nityâ*shod*ashikâ is part of the Vâmakeshvara Tantra and the Sundarî or Yoginîh*ri*daya is a part of the former. The three therefore make one Tantra. He also says in the same Commentary that the Bahurûpâ*sht*aka is not one Tantra but eight named after the seven Mât*ri*s beginning with Brâhmî and Shivadûtî. I may here observe that if the Sammohana Tantra be counted as one of the nine it cannot be the Tantra of that name published by Rasika Mohana Chattopâdhyâya for that is a Vai*sh*n*ava Tantra and a fragment of a work consisting of 40,000 verses. A copy of another work of the same name was supplied to me from the collection of Mahâmahopâdhyâya Vindhyeshvarîprasâda Divedî and copies are said to be available in Nepal of this Tantra which is a Kâdi Tantra, and therefore it must be to this and not to the published Sammohana that the Manoramâ refers.

The Kâdi Tantras give detailed injunctions touching the worship of Shakti in Her various forms : such worship being either gross (Sthûla) subtle (Sûk*sh*ma) or supreme (Para). Naturally the Sâdhaka begins with the first and the ritual takes the Sâdhaka up to the highest. The aim and object is the practical realization of the truths of the Advaita Vedânta.

Tripurasundarî or Lalitâ has three aspects (Rûpa), Sthûla, Sûk*sh*ma, Para. The ritual of Her worship is also of three kinds, Kâyika by body, Vâchika by speech and Mânasa by mind, also ca led Bâhyayâga, Antaryâga, and Bhâvanâ.

This Tantra gives all the three forms whereby the Sâdhaka is led by his Guru through ascending stages to Advaita Siddhi. The Guru is one with Âdyâ Shakti Vimarshamayî the cause of all. The ninefoldness of his body is seen in the nine apertures.

> Gururâdyâ bhavechchhakti*h* sâ vimarshamayî matâ
> Navatvang tasya dehasya randhratvenâvabhâsate

The nine Gurus are in the form of the nine apertures. The body of the Sâdhaka is the Shrîchakra which consists of nine Chakras. The object of worship of the Shrîchakra is the realisation of the inseparateness (Abhedabhâvanâ) of Jnâtâ which is Hotâ, of Jnâna which is Arghya and of Jneya which is Havi*h*.

> Jnâtâ svâtmâ bhavejjnânam arghyang jneyang havi*h* sthitam
> Shrîchakrapûjanang te*sh*âm ekîkara*n*am îritam.

The scheme of Sâdhanâ and the different parts of the Shrîchakra are explained in the Vâsanâ Pa*t*ala (Ch. XXXV) of this work. The Tripurâtâpinî Upani*sh*ad deals with Kâyika and Vâchika Karma and the Bhâvanopani*sh*ad with Bhâvanâ or Mânasa Karma. This last Upani*sh*ad summarises in the main the Vâsanâ Pa*t*ala of the Tantrarâja and begins with the Sûtra "Shrîguru*h* sarvakâra*n*abhûtâ shakti*h*" ending with "Bhâvanâparo jîvanmukto bhavati."

In order to follow the ritual of this work it is necessary to understand the Shrîyantra figured on the cover of this volume. This celebrated Yantra represents the human body and the whole universe and man (for what is in the former is in the latter and *vice versa*) as also the Shiva-Shakti Svarûpa or Âtmâ It is thus the symbol of the Devî as She is in Her own form (Svarûpa) and as She is in the form of the universe

(Vishvâtmâ). The account here given is taken from the Text, which account agrees with that given in other Kâdi Tantras such as Yoginîhṛidaya and Nityâṣhoḍashikârṇava and with the Bhâvanopaniṣhed which is an Upaniṣhad of the Kâdimata.

The Yantra is composed of nine triangles and Chakras one within the other until the central point or Bindu is reached. In each of the nine Chakras the Devî is worshipped in its centre under one of Her nine names united with the Pâdukâ Mantra of seven letters. The nine triangles are four with points upwards that is the Shrîkaṇṭhas or Shiva element, and the five downward pointed triangles or Shivayuvatîs, the Shakti element. All are formed by the Mûlaprakṛiti of the Shivabindu, the ninth being the Mûlaprakṛiti, and the eight the Vikṛitis which in relation to their productions are Prakṛiti. The nine Chakras also represent Sṛiṣhṭi (Creation) Sthiti (Maintenance) and Sanghâra, (Absorbtion) each set of three being formed of the combinations Sṛiṣhṭi-Sṛiṣhṭi, Sṛiṣhṭi-Sthiti, Sṛiṣhṭi-Sanghâra ; Sthiti-Sṛiṣhṭi, Sthiti-Sthiti, Sthiti-Sanghâra ; Sanghâra-Sṛiṣhṭi, Sanghâra-Sthiti, Sanghâra-Sanghâra. The object of the worship is, as the Bhâvanopaniṣhad says (Sûtra 10), the realisation of the unity of Jnâtâ, Jnâna, Jneya (Jnâtṛijṇâna-jneyânâmabhedabhâvanam) which is the aim and object of every Advaitin. The nine Chakras are (1) Bhûpura (2) sixteen petals (3) eight petals (4) first set of fourteen angles (5) second set of ten inner angles (6) third set of ten angles within these (7) fourth set of eight angles within these (8) three angles within these and (9) the point or Bindu. These are called (commencing with the first above named or outermost) Trailokyamohana, Sarvâshâparipûraka, Sarvasangkṣhobhaṇa, Sarvasaubhâgyadâyaka, Sarvârthasâdhaka, Sarvarogahara, Sarvarakṣhâkara, Sarvasiddhiprada and Sarvânandamaya.

There are two ways in which the Shrîyantra may be described. We may start from the outer Chakra and work inwards which is called Layakrama, or commence with the Bindu and work outwards. The latter which is called Sṛiṣhṭi-krama, is here adopted. The central Bindu or the Supreme united Kâmeshvara and Kâmeshvarî is the Devî Tripurâ or Lalitâ Who is Âtmâ whether as Jîvâtmâ in bodies or as the bodiless Paramâtmâ. For Kâmeshvara is the Supreme Samvit without Upâdhi and Kâmeshvarî is His Shakti. This Bindu is in the innermost triangle or All-blissful (Sarvânandamaya) Chakra. The word Yoni in this worship does not mean the generative organ of a woman but means Kâraṇam or Cause, the Womb of the Universe. This Bindu is threefold (Bindutraya) one above being the face of the Devî and the two below Her Breasts. This is symbolism of worship in which in India as elsewhere anthropomorphic forms are employed, those forms being those seen by the worshippers of the race. More abstractedly the three Bindus are Sun, Moon and Fire ; not the luminaries or element so called but names given to the Prakâsha and Vimarsha aspects of the Parabindu differentiating to create the Universe, such aspects being again symbolised by the single and double Bindus the Anusvâra and Visarga breathings respectively. The worship of Lalitâ is a part of Shrîvidyâ. Lalitâ is also called the Âdyâ or Angginityâ Devatâ Who is Sat and Ânanda and Pur*n*â and around Her as Angga or Âvara*n*a Devatâs are the fifteen Nityâ Devatâs or Devîs representing the five Bhûtas with their fifteen Gu*n*as or (as one account goes) the three Gu*n*as Sattva, Rajas, Tamas.

The number '15' is got by dealing with each of the Bhûtas from their Sattva, Rajas, Tamas aspects or by addition of the Gu*n*as of the Bhûtas themselves. In the triangle surrounding the Devî are the nine Lords or Nâthas. These are the nine apertures which exist both in the cosmic and individual bodies namely the two Eyes and Mouth (Divyaugha) the two ears and Penis (Siddhaugha) and the two Nostrils and Anus (Mânavaugha).

Lalitâ is the Vimarsha Shakti of Prakâsha Shiva. Lalitâ is red ; for in the 28th Sutra of the Bhâvanopani*sh*ad it is said "Redness is the Vimarsha of all this (Lauhityam etasya sarvasya vimarsha*h*). By 'Sarvasya' is meant, as Bhâskararâya says in his commentary on the Bhâvanopanishad, Kâmeshvara, Lalitâ, and the Sâdhaka's self. Râga and redness are one. It is said that "One's Âtmâ is Devî Lalitâ Whose body is the universe (Vishvavigrahâ). Redness is Her Vimarsha and worship is the meditation on this." The Bindu is surrounded by a triangle or the Siddhiprada Chakra. At the corners of this triangle which is the Second Chakra are the Shaktis (distinct from the Nityâs of that name) Kâmeshvarî (to be distinguished both from Supreme Kâmeshvarî and the Nityâ Kâmeshvarî) Vajreshvarî and Bhagamâlinî who are Avyakta or Prak*ri*ti, Mahat the Cosmic Buddhi and Ahangkâra. The three corners are the Pî*th*as Kâmarûpa, Pûr*n*agiri, Jâlandhara. In the centre is Au*dd*îyâna Pîtha the Shrîpâdukâ Mantra being "Hûng, Shrîng, Samastâm Mûlavidyâm, Au*dd*îyânapî*th*e Shrîmahâtripurasundarî-Devî Shrîpâdukâm pûjayâmi Nama*h*." In the spaces outside this triangle are the five Tanmâtras which are the five arrows of

Kâma, Manas, the sugar-cane bow of Kâma, Râga which is his noose and Dve*sh*a which is his goad.

The third Chakra (Sarvarak*sh*âkara) is composed of eight angles being the first eight angles formed by the intersection of the triangles other than that already described which are Vashinî, Kâmeshvarî, Mohinî, Vimalâ, Aru*n*â, Jayinî, Sarveshvarî and Kaulinî which are Devatâs of Cold (Shîta) Heat (U*shn*a) Happiness (Sukha) Pain (Du*h*kha) Desire (Ichchhâ) and Sattva, Rajas, Tamas. At this stage the Sâdhaka strives to control the Gu*n*as and to be unaffected by the Dvandvas.

The fourth or Sarvarogahara Chakra is composed of ten angles presided over by the ten Shaktis Sarvajnâ, Sarvashaktipradâ, Sarvaishvaryyapradâ, Sarvajnânamayî, Sarvavyâdhivinâshinî, Sarvâdhârâ, Sarvapâpaharâ Sarvânandamayî, Sarvarak*sh*â, Sarvepsitaphalapradâ. These are the Devatâs of the functions of the vital fire (Vahnikalâ) which are Rechaka (elimination) Pâchaka (Digestion) Sho*sh*aka (that which removes the Do*sh*a of Ja*th*arâgni) Dâhaka (burning) Plâvaka (flooding, that is, spreading of Rasa which helps Ja*th*arâgni) K*sh*âraka (bile secreting) Udgâraka (belching). K*sh*obhaka (churning of the food) J*ri*mbhaka (yawning) Mohaka that which causes pain and fainting.

The fifth outer Chakra Sarvârthasâdhaka of ten angles is presided over by the Devîs Sarvasiddhipradâ, Sarvasampatpradâ, Sarvapriyangkarî, Sarvamangalakârinî, Sarvakâmapradâ, Sarvadu*h*khavimochanî, Sarvam*ri*tyuprashamanî, Sarvavighnanivâri*n*î, Sarvângasundarî, Sarvasaubhâgyadâyinî. These are the Devîs of the ten Prâ*n*as which are controlled by their worship.

The sixth Chakra (Sarvasaubhâgyadâyaka) has fourteen angles in which are the Shaktis Sarvasangk*sh*obhi*n*î, Sarvavidrâvi*n*î, Sarvâkar*sh*i*n*î, Sarvâhlâdinî, Sarvasammohanî, Sarvastambhinî, Sarvajambhinî, Sarvavashangkarî, Sarvaranjanî, Sarvonmâdinî, Sarvârthasâdhanî, Sarvasampattipûra*n*î, Sarvamantramayî, Sarvadvandvak*sh*ayangkarî, who are the Âdhidevatâs of the fourteen principal Nâ*d*îs *viz.* : Alambu*sh*â, Kuhû Vishvodarâ, Vâra*n*â, Hastijihvâ, Yashovatî, Payasvinî, Gândhârî, Pû*sh*â, Shangkhinî, Sarasvatî, Î*d*â, Pinggalâ and Su*sh*umnâ.

The seventh Chakra is the eight petalled Sarvasang*sh*obha*n*a Chakra which surrounds the circle in which the other triangles mentioned are placed. The Devîs here are Anangga-kusumâ, Ananggamekhalâ, Ananggamadanâ, Ananggamada-nâturâ, Ananggarekhâ, Ananggaveginî, Ananggamadanâng-kushâ, Ananggamâlinî, which are Devatâs of the Buddhi of speech (Vachana) grasping (Âdâna) walking (Gamana) excreting or rejecting (Visarga) pleasurable feeling (Ânanda) relinquishment (Hâna) concentration (Upâdâna) and detachment (Upek*sh*â).

Outside this again is a lotus of sixteen petals which is the Sarvâshâparipûraka Chakra. Here are sixteen Shaktis namely :— Kâmâkar*sh*a*n*î, Buddhyâkar*sh*a*n*î, Ahangkârâkar-*sh*a*n*î, Shabdâkar*sh*a*n*î, Sparshâkar*sh*a*n*î, Rûpâkar*sh*a*n*î, Rasâ-kar*sh*a*n*î, Gandhâkar*sh*a*n*î, Chittâkar*sh*a*n*î, Dhairyâkar*sh*a*n*î, Sm*ri*tyâkar*sh*a*n*î, Nâmâkar*sh*a*n*î, Bîjâkar*sh*a*n*î, Âtmâkar*sh*a*n*î, Am*ri*tâkar*sh*a*n*î, Sharîrâkar*sh*a*n*î, who are Devatâs of the attainment of the object of desire by, in particular, the acquisition and strengthening (as regards the self) and the control (as regards others) of powers over Buddhi, Ahangkâra, Shabda (such as hearing at a distance) Sparsha, Rûpa, Rasa, Gandha, Chitta, stead-fastness, memory ; name (attraction by saying), growth, the subtle body, revivification, and the gross body. These Siddhis are acquired by worship in the Chakra.

Outside the sixteen petals in the surrounding space of the Bhûpura are (see Bhâvanopani*sh*ad S. 12) the ten Mudrâshaktis namely Sarvasang*sh*obhi*n*î, Sarvavidrâvi*n*î, Sarvâkar*sh*a*n*î, Sarvâveshakâri*n*î, Sarvonmâdinî, Mahângkushâ, Khecharî, Bîjamudrâ, Mahâyoni, and Trikha*nd*ikâ. The first nine Mudrâs belong to the nine Chakras of the Shrî-Yantra respectively, the tenth being above all. The nine Mudrâ Shaktis represent, that is are shaped into the form of, the nine Âdhâras other than the last which is above all. Bhâskararâya says : the nine Âdhâras are the six Chakras Mûlâdhâra and the rest, and the two Lotuses of a Thousand Petals and Lambi-kâgra, a centre approximately below the eyes and behind the nose.

Outside the sixteen petals are four circular lines containing three circular spaces. The outer circle is on the same level with the sixteen petalled, eight petalled, and first outer fourteen-angled Chakras and connected with these Chakras. The middle circle is on the level and connected with these Chakras. The middle circle is on the level and connected with the two sets of ten angles and the eight angles ; and the innermost circle is on the same level and connected with the inner Chakra of three angles.

Outside these and on the outermost line of the Bhûpura are worshipped the ten Siddhis, *A*nimâ and the rest. These in the Manoramâ are said to be not different from (Abheda) Niyati and the nine Rasas. Four are at the doors, one at each; four at the corners, one at each, and one is above and one below. At the middle line the eight Mât*ri*kâs are worshipped, four at the doors and four at the corners. These are Brâhmî, Mâheshvarî, Kaumârî, Vai*shn*avî, Vârâhî, Indrâ*n*î, Châmu*nd*â, and Mahâlak*sh*mî, considered as constituted of Kâma (Kâmamaya) Krodha, Lobha, Moha, Mada, Mâtsaryya, Pâpa and Pû*n*ya. Brâhmî is conjoined with Kâma because She creates, Mâheshvarî with Krodha because She 'destroys,' Kaumâri with Lobha because, being youthful, She is full of longing, Vai*shn*avî with Moha because She fascinates the Universe by Her Moha, Vârâhî with Mada because the boar is an obstinate and proud animal ('pigheaded'), Indrâ*n*î with Mâtsaryya because Indra Her consort is a jealous Devatâ, Châmu*nd*â with Pâpa because by and through Her mediation injury is done, Lak*sh*mî with Pû*n*ya because She is benign and leads the Sâdhaka to all virtuous acts. On the inner line of the Bhûpura the ten Dikpâlas are worshipped, placed in the same way as the Siddhis. These Mudrâ Shaktis, Dikpâlas Mât*ri*kâs, and Siddhis constitute the ninth Chakra called Trailokyamohana. The Siddhis are first worshipped for self-protection during Sâdhanâ. The Mât*ri*kâs are worshipped to suppress all evil inclinations associated with each of their names and to gain virtue, and the Dikpâlas for protection of the Sâdhaka and his Sâdhanâ. The Bhûpura is that in which the whole Yantra is placed. The Tantrarâja says that after worship in manner enjoined let the Sâdhaka consider himself as like unto Devî (Svâtmânang tatsamang smaret) and one with Devî (Devyâtmâ). He is then happy.

Let us then consider the principle involved in this worship. Tântrik Sâdhana is based on a very profound knowledge of the principles of psychology. The object here is the realization of the unity of the Jîvâtmâ with the Mother or Devî. Now one may tell a Chela that this is the fact without anything more following from such mere instruction. The truth is not realised by mere oral instruction but by action following it. If the Chela were to call the statement in question the answer of the Guru would not be a mere philosophical argument though reasoning has its place, but a direction to do certain things with the statement that the achievement of them will produce both capacity for the actual knowledge required. How? No one can really know any spiritual truth except he personally experiences it. Until then it merely remains an instruction for the mind which, though based on Scriptural authority is evidence of a secondary character. What is sought is not a mere statement of fact however true it may be but that actual experience which it indicates and to which it leads. The mind must then be first prepared to fully receive and then realise the truth taught. Such preparation consists in placing before it successively and continuously the idea that every thing which exists in nature and therefore in the human body is, from the Devatâ aspect, a Shaktî. The universe is the Body of the Mother as the Lord of all. But all is Shaktî whether as the Mother in Her Supreme Self (Svarûpa) or in the form of every object in the universe. Matter is not something wholly apart from Spirit or God. It is an aspect assumed by Spirit. Further as "all this is Brahman" every single thing or person is Brahman in that particular form. The Brahman Svarûpa is pure Spirit and its Power or Shakti which manifests as the Universe is that same Spirit in material forms. But the matter also of these forms is Shakti for there is nothing but Shakti anywhere in anything which is apparent to us. Therefore Mind and Senses in their varying forms are each in their Devatâ aspect particular Shaktis, that is the whole Universe is informed by, and is the manifestation of, Spirit, but a particularly named Devatâ is that Spirit in the particular manifestation to which the name is given. Thus the Brahman or Shiva-Shakti is the name of the Universal Spirit. But Shakti in that aspect in which It exists at rest in the Mûlâdhâra as the static centre round which all the bodily forces revolve is called Ku*nd*alinî Devî. Shakti as the source of, and manifesting as, the vital functions is Prâ*n*ashakti and each again of these functions is a separate Shakti, that is the general Shakti manifesting Herself in that particular way. The Sâdhaka is taught to realise this in his worship. He looks upon each part of and function of his body as a Shakti or Devatâ, or more simply in earlier stages as presided over by a Devatâ (Adhi*shth*âtrî Devatâ). An elementary view is to regard, say, the Mind as something apart, over and governing which is a Devatâ or Shakti. The more experienced and correct view is that the Mind *is* Shakti, that is a particular manifestation of It. By continual and repeated practice in Chakra after Chakra everything thus become *divinised*. It is seen not as gross and so-called inert matter but as what it is, namely Brahman or Shakti, in that form. It is so seen because the Mind by constant and earnest association of the Divine with the Universe familiarises itself with, and then realises, the fact. Everything is thus a particular Shakti. The next step is to realise that all these particu.ar Shaktis are, as it were, fragments of the one Power which is the Primordial Divine Power (Âdyâ shakti), and thirdly that the Sâdhaka himself both in his essential nature (Âtmâ or Spirit) and in his mind and body (particular aspects of Shakti) is one with that Supreme Shakti which is the end of all Vedântic monistic teaching (Advaitavâda). Sâ, ham "She I am." The Sâdhaka worships all forms as particular Shaktis. He is then led up from lower to higher forms of Shakti until he places before himself for worship the Supreme Power Who is both the Mother of all these particular Shaktis and Who appears in, and as, them. For there is nothing but the one Mother. As the human father is reborn in his son so the Mother Who creates the Universe Herself enters into it. She makes and is the form in which She in Her formless aspect abides. Thus to take the particular example under discussion the Sâdhaka in the outermost Chakra meditates (in connection with Devatâ) upon forms of sin and virtue, the emotions and then desire, the mind and senses, the Nâ*d*îs, the vital airs and fires, the Manas, Tanmâtra, Râga, Dve*sh*a, Ahangkâra, Buddhi, Prak*ri*ti and the Bhûtas of which the Devîs are the fifteen Nityâs who are parts of the body (as indeed are all the rest) of the Supreme Shakti Tripurasundarî or Lalitâ Devî from Whom they emanate. The Devî as Kâmeshvarî is one with Kâmeshvara and the Sâdhaka thinks of himself as one with Devî. The Chhândogya Upani*sh*ad says that as one thinks so he becomes. Practice of the ritual transforms the mind itself and what is at first seen merely as external Yantra with lines, curves and petals becomes a pure mental state in the Sâdhaka himself. He too is a Shrî-Yantra and he realises himself as such. This realisation is not to be had by mere discussion (Vichâra) but by the practical methods of the spiritual discipline enjoined. In the same way (for the Tântrik methods are everywhere substantially the same though the forms vary) the Sâdhaka in the Buddhist Demchog (Mahâsukha) Tantra, which I am about to publish, meditates on the Ma*nd*ala of the Devatâ. He the Devatâ as method (Thabs or Upâya) which is compassion (Karu*n*â) is united with His spouse the Mahâyoginî Who is wisdom (Shesrab or Jnâna) which is the Void or Shûnyatâ. Around these "two in one" are Âvara*n*a Devatâs which form part of the Body of the Supreme Devatâ in whom by meditation they are merged and the Sâdhaka unites himself with them and Him according to the doctrines of the "not two" wisdom (Nyismed yeshes) that is Advaita. So also the object of worship of the Indian Shrî-Chakra is the realisation of the inseparateness of Jnâtâ which is Hotâ, of Jnâna which is Arghya, and of Jneya which is Havi*h*.

The following is a short analysis of the Chapters of the work here published.

Chapter I. This begins with a prayer followed by a request made by Devî of Shiva that He should declare to Her an independent Tantra of the sixteen Nityâ Devatâs, because the nine then existing Tantras, through their interdependence, were the cause of confusion. That is none of these Tantras were complete and Devî wished to have a Tantra which should be all-inclusive. There would then be no necessity to have recourse to any other. Shiva in reply gives the meaning of Kâdi, a summary of the contents of the Tantra, the marks of the right Guru and Shi*sh*ya, the mode of worshipping the Guru and the manner of selection of a Mantra, though He adds that this is not necessary in the case of Mantras of the Nityâs. Vv. 68-71 speak of the men who are qualified to gain Siddhi. V.72 defines the terms Yoga, Pallava, Sampu*t*a, Grathana, and Vidarbha as applied to Japa of Mantra. This is followed by nine verses enumerating twenty-five defects (Do*sh*a) of Mantras which it is the duty of the Guru to remove before giving the Mantra to the disciple. Vv. 82, 83 state the duty of the Guru to be to teach the disciple the making of the Yonimudrâ and to give him Vîryyayojanâ of Mantra. This means imparting to the disciple the power (Vîryya) of the Mantra: a process which is given in some detail in Ch. XXXV but can be only fully learnt of the Guru. The latter should (the verses continue) protect the disciple and teach him the meaning of the first and last letters of the Mât*ri*kâs. Without this the letters are like the autumn clouds which come and go without fruit of useful rain. V 84 says that the knowledge of this is Ahangk*ri*ti, from which Ahangkâra man becomes like unto Shiva (Matsamo jâyate nara*h*). Ahangk*ri*ti or Ahangkâra literally means the making of or realization of "I". The union of A the first letter and Ha the last letter makes Aham = I, which contains within it all the letters of the alphabet and is therefore in the terms of Mantra the full expression of the Self. The union of the first and last letters of the Mât*ri*kâ is Tâdâtmya-siddhi the receptacle of the sense of all Mantras. Through it is realised the identity of the Sâdhaka with the Mât*ri*kâ and the Devatâs who are the Artha thereof. VV. 96-100 contain the following :—

HYMN TO THE GURU.

Obeisance to Thee Oh Lord Oh Bhagavân
Thou art Shiva Whose nature is auspicious (Shiva)
It is Thou who hast devised the various modes
Whereby knowledge (Vidyâ) descends.
Thou art ever nine
Thy form is of nine aspects
Thou art the Sun which dispels the darkness of ignorance
Thou art free (Svatantra) and Massive Consciousness (Chidghana)
Mercy is Thy form
And Thou art all good (Shivâtmâ)
Thou art the support of the devotee
And the being of all that are
Thou art the Viveka of the Vivekins
And the Vimarsha of the Vimarshins (1)
Thou art the revelation of all revelations
And the Jnâna of all Jnânins
I bow to Thee as in front of me, as on either side of me
As behind me, as below me, and as above me
Grant me this that Thou hast Thy abode ever in my mind.

Chapter II. This deals with the Ma*nd*ala of the nine Nâthas or Lords who are enumerated in vv. 2-5. The Divyaugha (two ears and mouth) are Prakâshânanda, Vimarshânanda and Ânandânanda. The Siddhaugha (eyes and penis) are Shrî Jnânânanda, Shri Satyânanda and Shrî Pûr*n*ânanda. The Mânavaugha (two nostrils and anus) are Svabhâva, Pratibha and Subhaga. The first class ever abide with Shiva (Madantike nityam) the second both near Him and on earth (Bhûmâvihâpi cha) and the third on earth (Bhûmâveva satatang nivasanti). They are all Shiva (Madâtmaka) in varying aspect. By their help the Kâdishakti Who is inseparate from Shiva revealed the fullness of the Tantrashâstra on earth in the K*ri*ta Yuga. They are described as beautiful forms having two arms, two eyes, smiling and of gracious mien, making with their hands the gestures (Mudrâ) of granting favours and dispelling fear. So they should be worshipped in their respective Ma*nd*alas (v. 8).

---

(1) That is the knowledge of the difference of the "I" and "This" (Ahantâ and Idantâ) and of the manner in which they are yet one. Vimarsha is the object and Vimarshin is the "I" which perceives it.

VV. 12-16 give the Pâdukâ mantra of seven letters. Then follow the names of sixteen letters of the nine Nâthas who are one with the sixteen Nityâ Devatâs (*Shod*ashanityâtmâ). Instructions follow for the drawing of the Ma*nd*ala and worship of the Guru. Vv. 37-38 state the length of time a disciple should be tested before initiation is given to him. Vv. 39-43 speak of the three modes of Prati*shth*â (placing of the Devî) which may be in the Chakra (that is the Lalitârchâchakra), in the disciple, or in the image of Devî: as also of the time when this should be done. It is the Siddhâtmâ (*i.e.* Tattvavit) and not the man proud of his knowledge (Jnânagarbita) who should do this. He who performs it without the permission of his Guru either in ignorance or prompted by hope of gain goes with wife and child to Hell. Vv. 44-51 speak of the Prati*shth*â of the Shrîchakra and other connected rites. (The above are followed by 25 verses which occur in one of the Texts but are not noticed or commented upon by the Manoramâ. These have not been numbered). Vv. 52-57 lay down the rules for instructing a good disciple. Fifteen verses beginning with v. 58 describe two kinds of Abhi*sh*eka and their respective merits. In these nine gems are put into medicated water of one Khâri (=4096 pala) namely ruby (Padmarâga) pearl (Muktâ) coral (Pravâla) cat's-eye (Vaiduryya) topaz (Pu*sh*parâja) diamond (Vajra) sapphire (Nîla) cow's fat stone called Gomeda, emerald (Marakata). These gems represent the nine component parts of the human body namely, chyle (Rasa) flesh (Mângsa) skin (Tvak) blood (Rudhira) semen (Shukra) marrow (Majjâ) bone (Asthi) fat (Meda). Vv. 73-74 enjoin that daily worship be performed thrice (Sandhyâtraya-bhajana) and speak of Kâmya-nyâsavidhi. Vv. 75-79 prescribe the auspicious periods for Abhi*sh*eka, and the following four verses the worship of the Guru and other rites. Vv. 84-85 give the articles to be used in the making of the Guru Ma*nd*ala. Vv. 88-98 contain a Stotra of Mât*ri*kâ Devî which also occurs in Chapter I of the Nitya-*shod*ashikâr*n*ava. In its interpretation of this Stotra the Manoramâ follows the Kashmir School. Bhâskararâya differs from it in some particulars.

Chapter III. From the Sâdhaka's standpoint this is of great importance for it gives the Mantras of the sixteen Nityâs. These are Âdyâ or Angginityâ Devatâ and the other fifteen or Anggas are described by Bhâskararâya as like unto, and rays of, the Âdyâ Nityâ Herself. She alone is united with Kâmeshvara, in this differing from the remaining Nityâs, who in other respects resemble Her (see p. 25 Nityâ*shod*ashikâr*n*ava). Kâmeshvara is defined in the 26th Sûtra of Bhâvanopani*sh*ad as 'Nirupâdhika-sangvideva Kâmeshvara*h*,' that is Samvit without Upâdhis; and Lalitâ as the supreme Kâmeshvarî is 'Sadânandapûr*nah* svâtmaiva paradevatâ Lalitâ,' that is one's self is Pûr*n*a, Sat and Ânanda (ib 27). She is in the centre of the Shrî Yantra which is Sarvânandamaya. The Mantra of Âdyâ Nityâ is (vv. 3-5) H*ri*t (=S) Prâ*n*a (=K) Ilâ (=L) Hangsa (=H) Dâha (=R) Vahni (=Î) Khang (=Bindu). H can be placed in the beginning, middle or end. By changing its position the other Mantras are obtained. H at the end is appropriate for Mukti and elsewhere for prosperity (Sampat). The Mantras of the other Nityâs are given in vv. 6-72.

Âdyâ Nityâ is Vimarsha Shakti that is the Shakti of Prakâsha Shiva. Shiva is Prakâsha and Vimarsha Shakti is in the language of the Kâmakalâvilâsa "the pure mirror in which He reflects Himself." (Pratiphalati vimarshadarpa*n*e vishade). It is in this mirror which is another aspect of Himself that He knows Himself as the universe. It is this supreme "I" (Parâhantâ) which is the seed of all multiple world experience. According to this Tantra, the Âdyâ Nityâ or Vimarsha Shakti becomes fivefold in the Bhûtas, ether, air, fire, water, earth, and by association of each of these with the three Gu*n*as, there are the fifteen Nityâs which are rayed forth from Her (Ekaikagu*n*ab*ri*ddhyâ tu tithisangkhyâtvamâgatâ). The number 15 is also got in another way that is by Vyavakara*n*a or arithmetical progression of the number of the Gu*n*as of the five Bhûtas, Âkâsha having one, Vâyu two, and so on until we get to P*ri*thîvî which has five. The addition of these gu*n*as makes fifteen. In the Subhagodaya it is said that the fifteen minor Nityâs are the Kalâs of the fifteen Tithis beginning with Pratipat of the light half of the lunar month and ending with the Pûr*n*imâ and the sixteenth that is Âdyâ is Sachchidânandarûpi*n*î. The 33rd Sûtra of the Bhâvanopani*sh*ad says "Panchadashatithirûpe*n*a kâlasya pari*n*âmâvalokanam." Bhâskarâya in his commentary on this Sûtra says that the Prapancha or Universe is of three kinds, Kâla (Time) and De*sh*a (Space) and that which is the union of both. "Realising the evolution of time through the fifteen letters" is thus the dissolution of the external world in one's Âtmâ, as is shown in Ch. XXXV of the present work.

Tithirûpe*n*a kâlasya pari*n*âmâvalokanam
Nityâ*h* panchadashaitâ*h* syur iti proktâscha vâsanâ*h*

Verses 73-87 give the Mantras of Vârâhî and verse 88 the five names of Vârâhî which are Vârâhî, Panchamî, Vishvavijayâ

Bhadrakaumadî and Vârtâlî. In vv. 89-93 is found the Mantra of Kurukullâ.

Vârâhî is fatherhood (Pit*ri*rûpâ) and Kurukullâ is motherhood. They are outside the Nityâs and a Chapter is devoted to them.

Bhâvanopani*sh*ad says (5):—

"Vârâhî pit*ri*rûpâ kurukullâvalî devatâ mâtâ"; and this Tantra says:

Balidevya*h* svamâyâ*h* syu*h* panchamî janakâtmikâ
Kurukullâ bhaven mâtâ puru*sh*ârthâstu sâgarâ*h*

Panchamî here mentioned is Vârâhî who is Janakâtmikâ and Kurukullâ is mother. Though Vârâhî is female she is yet Pit*ri*rûpâ Her aspect being male (Pungrûpâ). She is the Devatâ of Bone Asthi) which a child gets from its father and Kurukullâ is the Devatâ of flesh (Mângsa) which it receives from its mother.

Vv. 94-95 give the Prapanchayâga Mantra and v. 96 the Mantras of each of the five Bhûta.

Chapter IV. This and the two following Chapters dea with the rites relating to the Âdyâ Nityâ Lalitâ. The Compiler of the Catalogue of Mss in Nepal seems to have been insufficiently acquainted with the Mss he described. Thus he incorrectly says that the third Chapter is devoted to this subject. In his summary of the sixteen Nityâs he leaves out three of them (namely Vahnivâsinî, Sarvamangalâ, and Jvâlâmâlinî and wrongly includes Vârâhî and Kurukullâ amongst the Nityâs and repeats the name of Nityâ twice as the first and eleventh. He makes no mention of the Shrîchakra the important part of this work nor deals with the XXXVth Chapter which gives its philosophy. He states, in some cases incorrectly, the names of the nine Nâthas on the authority of the late Librarian, Nepal Darbar though the names are correctly given in the Ms. described. He confuses the nine Nâthas here described with Âdinâtha, Ka*nth*anâtha and other recognised Avatâras of Shiva.

The fourth Chapter begins with Karashuddhividyâ, *Shada*-ngganyâsavidyâ Devyâtmâsanavidyâ, Chakrâsanavidyâ, Sarvamantrâsanavidyâ, Sâdhyasiddhâsanavidyâ, Âvâhanavidyâ.

Some of the rites such as *Shad*anggányâsa are common to all the Nityâs. Vv. 14-20 give the names of eight Shaktis namely, Vashinî, Kâmeshvarî, Mohinî, Vimalâ, Aru*n*â, Jayinî, Sarveshvarî and Kaulinî as also their Mantras and Nyâsakrama the performance of which renders the Sâdhaka Devyâtmaka. These eight Shaktis represent cold (Shîta) heat (U*shn*a) pleasure (Sukha) pain (Du*h*kha) desire (Ichchhâ) and the three Gu*n*as Sattva, Rajas and Tamas. The places in which Nyâsa is done with these Shaktis are given in v. 21. Cf. Bhâvanopani*sh*ad Sûtra 20. Vv. 22-25 give the Bîja Mantras of the nine Mudrâs. Cf. Âdhâranavakam mudrâshaktaya*h* in Bhâvanopani*sh*ad 12. Vv. 30, 31 enumerate twenty Mudrâs. They are Âvâhanî, Sthâpanî, Sannirodhanî, Avagu*nth*anî, Sannidhâpanî, Heti, (*i. e.* the four Mudrâs Vâ*n*a, Dhanu*h*, Pâsha, Angkusha) Namaskriyâ, Sangk*sh*obha*n*î, Drâvi*n*î, Âkar*sh*a*n*î, Vashyâ, Unmâdanî, Mahângkushâ, Khecharî, Bîja, Yoni, and Shaktyutthâpanî also called Trikha*nd*â. Heti above described is fourfold as the five Arrows (Vâ*n*a) Bow (Dhanu*h*) Noose (Pâsha) and Goad (Angkusha). The five arrows are the five Tanmâtras. The Mind as Manas is the Bow of Sugarcane. Attachment to objects is bondage or the noose (Râgâ*h* pâshâ*h*) and Aversion to objects is the goad (Dve*sh*o'ngkusha*h*). See Bhâvanopani*sh*ad 21-24. Vv. 34-54 describe the Mudrâs which in vv. 55-59 are said to be of three kinds, Sthûla, Sûk*sh*ma, Para, according as they are made with the hands or body, thought of in Mantras, and understood as they really are (Tattvarûpe*n*a). The last ten Mudrâs are alluded to in the Sûtra cited. Trikha*nd*â or Shaktyutthâpanî is so called because it cuts the three which are Jnâtâ, Jnâna, Jneya from the Sangsâra (Tribhi*h* jnât*ri*jnânajneyâtmabhi*h* sangsârakha*nd*anât). This is the Mudrâ by which Lalitâ is invoked (Lalitâvahâ). V. 58 defines Mudrâ (Mudang râtîti Mudrâ) as that which causes pleasure (to the Devatâ). The least little mistake it says might produce displeasure where pleasure was intended. The meaning of the Sûtra in the Bhâvanopani*sh*ad is that the last ten Mudrâs are associated with (Abheda) nine Âdhâras namely the six Chakras beginning with Mûlâdhâra, the Lambikâgra and two lotuses of a thousand petals one of which is in the head and the other below the Mûlâdhâra, the tenth being the collectivity of all these.

Vv. 60, 61 speak of the five kinds of Arghyapâtra.

Lalitâ should be meditated upon as being red in colour. In the 28th Sûtra of Bhâvanopani*sh*ad it is said "Redness is the Vimarsha of all this" (Lauhityametasya sarvasya vimarsha*h*). Bhâskararâya says that by "of all" (Sarvasya) is meant Kâmeshvara, Lalitâ, and the Sâdhaka's self. The Vimarsha of these is the redness of the Devî Who is object of worship. This is so because of the welding (Âtmanyanurâgât) of these three in one, and this attachment (Râga) or welding and Redness (Lauhitya) are one (see also Ch. XXXV) Cf. "One's Âtmâ is the Devatâ Lalitâ Whose body is the universe (Vishvavigrahâ). Redness is Her Vimarsha (as mere Prakâsha She is white and redness indicates Ichchhâ and Rajas) and worship is the Meditation on this". She is of blissful mien, carries in Her hands arrows, bow, noose and goad. She is seated and united with Kâmarâja and is surrounded by Shaktis. These are of the same colour, are decked in the same ornaments and carry the same weapons but are not (as Lalitâ is) united with Kâmarâjâ.

Vv. 66-71 enumerate the eighteen Shaktis who should be worshipped in the first or Trailokyamohana Chakra. These again are divided into two groups. The first of ten beginning with A*n*imâ and the second of eight begins with Brâhmî. The places of worship are given in Chapters I and VIII of Nityâ*sho*-*d*ashikâr*n*ava (See also Bhâvanopani*sh*ad S. 1.1 and Ch. XXV of this book). The first group of ten are associated with Niyati and the nine Rasa beginning with Sh*ri*nggâra, and the second group of eight represent Kâma, Krodha, Lobha, Moha, Mada, Mâtsaryya, Pû*n*ya and Pâpa. (See Bhâvanopani*sh*ad S. 11).

Vv. 72, 73 name the Shaktis to be worshipped on the sixteen petalled lotus. These are Kâmâkar*shin*î and others. These Shaktis are Adhidevatâs of Earth (P*ri*thivî) Water (Ap) Fire (Tejas) Air (Vâyu) Ether (Âkâsha) Hearing (Shrotra) Touch (Tvak) Sight (Chak*sh*u), Taste (Jihvâ) Smell (Ghrâ*n*a) Speech (Vâk) Feet (Pâda) Hands (Pâ*n*i) Anus (Pâyu) Genitals (Upastha). There is then Manovikâra which some read as applying to all sixteen and others to Manas alone. The sixteen (See Bhâvanopani*sh*ad) are enumerated not only in the Tantrarâja but in the Nityâ*shod*ashikâr*n*ava, Yoginîh*ri*daya and other works.

Vv. 75, 76 give the names of the eight Shaktis to be worshipped on the petals of the eight-petalled lotus (third Chakra). They are Ananggakusumâ and others. These are the Buddhi of Speech (Vachana), Taking (Âdâna), Motion (Gamana) Elimination (Visarga), Bliss (Ânanda) relinquishment (Hâna), concentration (Upâdâna) and Detachment (Upek*sh*â) (See Ch. XXXV) Bhâ Up. 14 Nityâ*shod*asikâr*n*ava I 177-178 VIII 140-143).

The fourteen Shaktis to be worshipped in the Saubhâgya-dâyaka Chakra of fourteen angles are given in vv. 77-79. They are Sarvasangkshobhinî and others. They are the Devîs of the fourteen Nâdîs (See Ch. XXXV Bhâ, Up. 15).

Vv. 80-83 give the ten Shaktis Sarvasiddhipradâ and others to be worshipped in the Dashâra called Sarvârthasâdhana. These are the Devatâs of the ten "airs" in the body, Prâna and the rest (Ch. XXXV Bha. Up. 16-18) Nityâshodashikârnava I. 184-186, VIII 151-155. The first five belong to the Pentad commencing with Prâna and the second to that commencing with Nâga.

Vv. 84-86 name ten Shaktis to be worshipped in the inner Dashâra called Sarvarogahara. These are Sarvajnâ and others and the Kalâs of fire. These are Rechaka Pâchaka Shoshaka, Dâhaka, Plâvaka, Kshâraka, Udgâraka, Kshobhaka, Jrimbhaka, and Mohaka. Some say that the vital fire is tenfold because it is in the seven Dhâtus and the three Dosha. (See Introduction Prapanchasâra Tantra vol. III Tantrik Texts Ed. A. Avalon); but this is not apparently so according to the Tantrarâja (See Ch. XXXV also Bhâ, Up. 19). Nityâshodashikârnava 187-190 VIII 156-159 Yoginîhridaya III.

V. 87 gives the Mantra and rules of worship of the eight Shaktis Vashinî and others to be worshipped in the eight angles (Ashtâra) or Sarvarakshâkara Chakra. These, though not named in this Chapter, are Vashinî, Kâmeshî, Modinî, Vimalâ, Arunâ, Jayinî, Sarveshî, and Kaulinî (vv. 14-20). Between this Chakra and the next which is a triangle called Sarvasiddhimaya are worshipped the arrows, the bow, the noose and the goad representing the Tanmâtras, Manas, Râga and Dvesha. The second line of v. 89 gives the place of worship of the nine Nâthas at the back of the Devî (Devyâh prishthatah) in the inner triangle. V. 90 says that inasmuch as the Devî in the centre manifests Herself in sixteen different forms (*Shodashâkâratah* sthitâ), the other fifteen should be worshipped in Her body (Tasyâh tanau). The three Shaktis Kâmeshvarî, Vajreshvarî, and Bhagamâlinî are to be worshipped in the three corners beginning with the western, that is lower, angle and going round on the right. That is wherever the Sâdhaka faces is regarded as the east. Therefore the lower point of the triangle is the west. These are not the Nityâs so called but Âvarana Devatâs bearing the same name. These three corners are the Pîthas Kâmrûpa, Pûrnagiri, and Jâlandhara. These Shaktis are Avyakta, Mahat and Ahangkâra that is Prakriti, the cosmic

Buddhi and Ahangkâra (See Bhâvanopani*sh*ad 25) Then the Devî should be worshipped in the middle that is in the middle of the ninth Chakra which is Au*dd*yânapî*th*a. This is the Sthûlapûja. Her Pâdukâ Mantra is "Hrîng Shrîng Samastâm mûlavidyâm au*dd*yânapî*th*e shrîmahâtripurasundarî-devîshrî-pâdukâm pûjayâmi". In each of the nine Chakras the Devî is worshipped in the centre under one of Her nine names (given in the following Chapter vv. 14-15) united with the Pâdukâ Mantra of seven letters.

Her worship again is of three kinds :—Sthûla (as where She is thought of as red) Sûk*sh*ma (in the mantra-body or mantra-tanu) and Para when the Pûjâ and the fruit thereof is offered to Her. The Sthûla worship is Samastavidyâ, the Sûk*sh*ma worship in the form of the letters is Nâmarûpavidyâ and the Para worship is Arpa*n*a vidyâ.

Vv. 98-100 speak of Meditation on the identity of Guru, Devatâ and Mantra which (says the Manoramâ) is very secret (Rahasya) and should not be disclosed and is only to be learnt from the Guru. The highest (Turîya) form of the Devî is the three Bindus (Bindutraya) which are also the form of the fourth vowel. This Chakra has one Bindu above and two below. The former is the face and the two below are the breasts and the lines of the fourth vowel (I) are Her lower limbs. By meditation on these the Sâdhaka becomes one (Tadâtmaka) with Devî.

Chapter V. This continues the worship of Lalitâ. After worshipping Her in manner enjoined the Sâdhaka considers himself as the Devî (Svâtmânang tatsamang smaret) and one with Devî (Devyâtmâ). He is then happy (v. 5).

There are nine Chakras which Bhâskararâya (p. 40) says fall under three heads *Srisht*i, Sthiti and Sanghâra, creation, maintenance and withdrawal. The first three (1, 2, 3,) are *Srisht*i of which the first is *Srisht*i-*srisht*i, the second *Srisht*i-sthiti the third *Srish*ti-sanghâra. The second group of three (4, 5, 6) of the nine are Sthiti of which the first is Sthiti-*srisht*i, the second Sthiti-sthiti and the third Sthiti-sanghâra. The last group of three (7,8,9) of the nine are Sanghâra of which the first is Sanghâra-*Srisht*i the second Sanghâra-Sthiti and the third Sanghâra-Sanghâra. In the Tantrântara Tantra these three primary groups are called Moon (Soma or *Srisht*i) Sun (Sûryya or Sthiti) and Fire (Anala or Sanghâra). The names of the nine Chakras are (1) Trailokya-mohana (*Srisht*i-*Srisht*i), (2) Sarvâshâ-paripûraka (Sr*isht*i-Sthiti), (3) Sarvasangk*sh*obha*n*a (Sr*isht*i-Sanghâra), (4) Sarvasaubhâgyadâyaka (Sthiti-Sr*isht*i), (5) Sarvârthasâdhaka (Sthiti-Sthiti), (6) Sarvarogahara (Sthiti-Sanghâra), (7) Sarvaraksh*â*-kara (Sanghâra-Sr*isht*i), (8) Sarvasiddhiprada (Sanghâra-Sthiti), (9) Sarvânandamaya (Sanghâra-Sanghâra). This last is the place of the Central Bindu and is Shivâtmaka (vv. 9 and 10). The Yoginîs in these Chakras are (1) Praka*t*â (2) Guptâ (3) Guptatarâ (4) Sampradâyâ (5) Kulakaulâ (6) Nigarbhâ (7) Rahasyâ (8) Parâpararahasyâ (9) Atirahasyâ. These are in the Middle of the Chakras and are gross forms (Sthûlavigrahâ) being the covering (Âvara*n*a) of the Sûk*sh*ma or Mantra form. The Para is unconditioned by time or space and is immanent in the last. The nine names of the Devî are Tripurâ, Tripureshî, Tripurasundarî, Tripuravâsinî, Tripurashrî, Tripuramâlinî, Tripurasiddhâ, Tripurâmbâ, and Mahâtripurasundarî (v. 14). In each of these nine forms the Devî is worshipped in the nine different Chakras with the prescribed Mantra (v. 15). Vv. 17, 18 say that as soon as the Sâdhaka rises from his sleep in the early morning he should think of himself as Tripurâ (Tripurâtmânam) and meditate on Her lustrous Light form (Jyotîrûpa) in the head.

Vv. 19-21 enjoin that during worship the Sâdhaka should wear a red cloth, smear himself with red sandal, wear red garlands and red ornaments. He should be in a pleasant frame of mind, scented with camphor. He should sit in Padmâsana facing East and keep himself and his vital airs (Prâ*n*â*h*) under control.

Vv. 23-25 enjoin the worship of the nine gems, the garden of Kalpa trees (Kalpakodyâna) the six seasons, the senses, which are compared to horses and the the objects of the senses which are likened to elephants. V. 26 also refers to the nine gems. In this connection may be noted Bhâvanopani*sh*ad (6-8) which says that the body is the island of nine gems (Deho navaratnadvîpa*h*) which are Pu*sh*parâga (topaz) Nîla (sapphire) Vaidûrya (catseye) Vidruma (coral) Mauktika (pearl) Marakata (emerald) Vajra (diamond) Gomeda, Padmarâga (ruby). Tvagâdisaptadhaturomasangyukta*h*. These gems in the body are Tvak (touch) the seven Dhâtus namely Rasa (chyle) Mângsa (flesh) Rudhira (blood) Shukra (semen) Majjâ (marrow) Asthi (bone) and Meda (fat) together with Roma (hair). Time is divided into nine parts *viz.* Gha*t*ikâ (24 minutes) Yâma (3 hours) Ahorâtra (day and night) Vâra (day of a week) Tithi (lunar day) Pak*sh*a (lunar fortnight) Mâsa (solar month) *R*itu (season or two months) and Abda (year).

The principal Mudrâs beginning with Sangkshobhinî are nine. The Mâtrikâs are divided into nine groups. There are nine Gurus. The Tattvas are nine (obtained by combinations of Jnâtri, Jnâna, Jneya). The planets are nine as are also the Dhâtus (Tvak, Asrik, etc.) V. 47 speaks of the worship of the arrows (Vâna) bow (Châpa) noose (Pâsha) and goad (Angkusha). The arrows are either Sthûla, Sûkshma or Para. As being the first they are made of flowers, as being second they are in the form of Mantra (Mantrâtmânah) and as Para they are (as described in the Chapter dealing with Vâsanâ) the five Tanmâtras. As Sthûla they are of the following flowers, Lotus (Kamala) Red Night-Lotus (Rakta kairava) water lily (Kalhâra) blue lotus (Indîvara) and mango flower (Sahakâraja). The Bow, Noose and Goad are similarly Sthûla, Sûkshma and Para.

The bow is sugarcane (Sthûla), made of Mantra, and the Manas. The noose and the goad are of material, or Mantra form, and their Para form is Râga (desire : noose) and Dvesha (hostility : goad).

Then follows description of the Nityapûjâ.

Vv. 78-79 direct that when doing Purashchârana the company of an unbeliever (Nâstika) should be avoided and vv. 79-80 enjoin the avoidance of desire for, or decrying, the land, house and wife of another, and being angry with and beating women even if they be wicked.

In v. 81 it is said that in the Vâsanâ Chapter (XXXV) the signs which indicate the attainment of the state of a Siddha are given ; the following indicate that a man is moving to that state ; dreams of association with women, or of riding on an elephant, of enjoyment in a palatial house or on a mountain top, the seeing of kings, procession of elephants, singing and dancing of women in dream, the seeing of festivals in dream, the seeing and taking of wine and meat in dream. Some other signs are mentioned which indicate that a man is straying from the path of Siddhi *viz.* Seeing black soldiers, beating, smearing of oil (which is not done by Brahmachârîs), sexual connection with others' wives, state of anarchy, fear of fire, air, water, death of a friend, slighting a Guru, accumulation of wealth, disease and worshipping with other mantras than the Sâdhaka's own.

He (v. 88) who does Japa without knowing Kûrmasthiti not only fails to get the fruit thereof but he meets with destruction. Therefore should Kûrma be first known. Kûrma is of four kinds namely firstly Para Kûrma. This which is steady (Sthira) and extends to 50 Koti (500,000,000) of Yojanas (between 8 and 9 miles) supports Prithivî. The others are Deshagata, Grâmaga and Grihaga. That is just as the Supreme Tortoise supports the whole universe, the others support particular countries, villages, and dwellings.

Chapter VI. Naimittika and Kâmya Pûjâ are here dealt with; the first in verses 1-32. Here the rites are described which are to be performed from Chaitra to Fâlguna. The *Shat*karma of those devoted to Naimittika rites are Yantra, Homa, K*ri*yâ, Dhyâna, Yoga and Tarpa*n*a which are described in the rest of the Chapter. The six Kâmya Karmas are Rak*sh*â, Shânti, Jaya, Lâbha, Nigraha and Nidhana, *i.e.*, protection and peace giving, victory and gain giving, punishing and destruction (v. 35). For the first worship should be done in the Bhûpura; for the second in the Vârima*nd*ala, for the third in the Dahanâgâra, for the fourth in the Anilaman*nd*ala and for the fifth and sixth in the Vyomama*nd*ala (v. 37). Onward to v. 51 details are given of worship in the five Bhûta Ma*nd*alas as regards the appropriate season, month, letter, day of the week and the articles of worship. Then follow the fruits gained by worship in different parts of the Shrîchakra (vv. 52-57); how to control Apsarâ and Yak*shin*î (vv. 58-70); worship productive of knowledge of past, present and future (vv. 73-74) worship to gain four kinds of proficiency (Pâ*nd*itya) (vv. 75-77) which (according to the Manoramâ) are Vâditva, Kavitva, Vâgmitva and Vyâkhyât*ri*tva or the power to speak clearly, literary ability, eloquence, and power of explanation. Then follows worship for the avoidance of all ailments (vv. 78-80); the names of the seven articles for making Shrîchakra, to wit, saffron, vermilion, red ochre (Gairika) Lac, red lead (Darada) and sandal both red and white (v. 78). Each of verses 93-98 give a different form of worship (Bhajana) and v. 99 states the final aim of worship namely the realisation of the unity of the Devî, the self, Chakra, the Devatâs therein and the surrounding Shaktis.

Chapter VII. This is devoted to the second Nityâ, Kâmeshvarî who (III. v 8) is fulfiller of Desire (Kâmadâ). After speaking of Nyâsa-krama (in vv. 3-6) verses 8-10 give the following Dhyâna of this Devî. She is (lustrous red) like ten million rising suns, wears a bright crown of rubies and is adorned with throat ornament (Graiveya), necklaces, waistchains and rings on Her hands and feet. Her ornaments are set with gems. Her raiment is red. She is six-armed and three-eyed and carries the crescent (Kalâ) of the Moon on Her head. Her face is lit up with a soft smile and Her eyes are merciful. She is in Her Chakra or Yantra which is on a lotus. She carries in Her hands a bow of sugarcane, arrows of flowers, noose and goad and a cup made of gems filled with nectar. She makes the gesture granting boons. The five arrows are to be worshipped in each of the petals of the five petalled lotus which is Kâmeshvarî's Yantra. Their names are Madana, Unmâdana, Dipana, Mohana and Sho*shana* the five effects of desire, longing maddening, kindling, enchanting, wasting (v. 13). The eight Shaktis in the eight petalled lotus are Ananggakusumâ; Ananggamekhalâ, Ananggamadanâ, Ananggamadanâturâ, Madaveginî, Bhuvanapâlâ, Shashirekhâ, Gaga*n*arekhâ (vv. 14-15). In the lotus of sixteen petals the following Shaktis are to be worshipped :— Shraddhâ, Prîti, Rati, Dh*ri*ti, Kânti, Manoramâ, Manoharâ, Manorathâ, Madanonmâdinî, Mohinî, Dîpanî, Sho*shan*î, Vashangkarî, Sinjinî, Subhagâ, Priyadarshanâ. Each of these is to be worshipped with one of the vowels before Her name (vv. 16-18) In the outer lotus of sixteen petals sixteen Kalâs of the Mooon are to be worshipped. These are Pû*sh*â, Âveshâ, Shrimanasâ, Rati, Prîti, Dh*ri*ti, Buddhi, Saumyâ, Marîchi, Angshumâlinî, Shashinî, Anggirâ, Chhâyâ, Sampû*rn*ama*nd*alâ, Tu*sht*i, Am*ri*tâ (vv. 19-20). In the corners of the outer Hexagon is worshiped *D*âkinî and others (v. 21). Outside this and round the square Ba*t*uka Ga*n*apa, Durgâ and K*sh*etresha should be worshipped. The Supreme Devî first created the five Kâmas or Desire-Devatâs which are Jnânâtmaka and which the Commentary explains to be Her five Jnânend*ri*yas. The former are of bewildering power and can move and agitate the three worlds (Loka) (vv. 27-28). These Kâmas are Kâmarâja (King of Desire) Manmatha (Agitator) Kandarpa (Inflamer) Makaraketana (whose banner bears a Makara) and Manobhava (Mind-born, for desire is born there). These agitate the world (vv. 29-30). They are of five colours, yellow, white, red, purple (Dhûmra the colour of smoke) and blue. They have two eyes and arms and are of smiling countenance and carry sugarcane bow and flowery arrows. They are Bhautika (Bhûtâtmaka) and exist in the form of all things (Vishvavigraha) (vv. 31-33). The concluding verses give the Mantras, Nyâsa, and Yantras and so forth in the worship of this Devî.

Chapter VIII. This deals with the third Nityâ, Bhagamâlinî through whose worship (III-31) the Sâdhaka charms his wife and the whole world (Vanitâ-janamohinî). Her Dhyâna is given as follows :—

She is beautiful and red, of smiling countenance, three-eyed, six-armed, seated on a lotus. She carries the night-water-lily, noose, sugarcane bow in Her left hands, in the right hands She holds a lotus, a goad, and flowery arrows. She is surrounded by Shaktis on all sides like Herself. The Devî is worshipped as surrounded by two classes of Âvara*n*a Shaktîs twenty in all, namely Madanâ, Mohinî Lolâ, Jambhinî, Udyamâ, Shubhâ, Hlâdinî, Drâvi*n*î, Prîti, Ratî, Raktâ, Manoramâ, Sarvonmadâ, Sarvasukhâ, Ananggâ, Amitodyamâ, Analpâ, Vyaktavibhavâ, Vividhavigrahâ, K*sh*obhavigrahâ, (vv. 9-11). The next eighteen verses describe the Pûjâkrama of the Devî and the fruit gained thereby. Then follows description of articles for making of the Yantra (vv. 30-32); the making of the fourteen petalled Yantra (vv. 33-38); the fourteen fruits gained by worship of the Yantra (vv. 39-40); the making of the Yantra of thirty-three sections (vv. 43-45); the thirty-three fruits gained thereby (vv. 46-49); the method of drawing the complete Chakra and the complete Pûjâ ritual (vv. 52-71). The Mantra which is given in the third Chapter is one of the longest known, being of 135 Kû*t*as.

Then follow nineteen verses (72-90) of disordered letters (Vyâkulitâk*sh*ara). This is a cryptic style of writing adopted to keep the contents concealed and which can only be read by those who have the key. The notes to the verses are also in the same character. As here printed the words have been wrongly arranged as the Texts consulted are at fault. Whilst reproducing the texts I add here a correct reading :

वं षु ते स ष्वे रे तु वा वेत् त्ता कं र्व्वा पि प र स ।
य जा धा हि ना पू वि ब्र तु ष्वा व ल्प स्य न स क ॥१॥
च्च्रे मि णु थ प्रा या शृ क नं स क म्य ल्प गा व स ।
ध्वौ ष्टौ था ड़ौ मा पै त गौ तं त्त्रि धं वं स्म्रृ त वि त्वे ॥२॥
च ड़ौ मा षु ध्वौ गौ च ते जं दु पै णु ष्टौ स्वा च शृ ।
व्यं स्वा दो ड़ षा म दु गौ णु त यं था शृ प्ये त्त्र त ॥३॥
म्रा ष्यो षी ड़ च्चि मु द गु पेत् ध्य नि मा च्चि लो वि स ।
स्मिन् च ये टे त का म घ जः सु नो त र की म धा ॥४॥
स्तु मौ न्ध्य त्वा यो भू स खा सा चो भू रैः य सं भ्य क ॥
स्मिन् व ते स त मा ग मा तं र सि म द्र म्ने ज नि ॥५॥

न पू ये ग्रो त्ते ध्य ज सं तः गु यो ड़ी ग सा ड़ गी ।
गात् धु मा वं यो म स ए ये ष्टौं ग्गु व्वौं प्रि पै शृ मा ॥६॥

ये ह्वि ग्गो ध्य तो ह्ब गु ष्प नैः त्त लान् प ग्र ये ग्ड्ड त्त्र ।
स्मिन् यो ते न त त्व षि दि पेत् र जः त्स्य च्चिं च्छु र ग्रा ॥७॥

ते कं ते न वा मे ध्रु दि तः स्था ये व्वीं त्त ते प नि ।
च्चात् र्लौं तं द प कै लि उ घु पै जं लि म तं ष्टि गा ॥८॥

ति फ ज च्च स्व्रे जं ल द्व धु क्ति ते वि म धं य ह्वि ॥९॥

ज्ञे गां ग्गु न्नि प्रा र्म्मा शृ त यः दा नो दा ल स्वा न्म य ।
रं वा खा ह्वि र्जु कं थ न्मृ वा ष्प था ल पि पु म फ ॥१०॥

म्रा स्या सि धु च्चि क भ्र म तम् र्द्धा श्री त षि म व शृ ।
न स ली शृ श्री ता व प्राक् यात् दि स लि ह्व तं व मौ ॥११॥

हैं स्वा पू लि जा तं दु गा भम् य रं नो ग्रु ल क म ।
स्यात् ना क्षी ग्रं लं तु रि ब्रा तः स्था ता न्ता ल ल ग्र ह्वि ॥१२॥

गधं ग्डात् तं ल दु क्का स्तु फ हं द्यो ला तं व स व नौ (पौ) ।
स्थ ल ला रि न्तः क्षी फ ना ते ग्र ना लि यु ली ग्धि स ॥१३॥

थं ग ल न्ध प्रो पू फ ग्मा येत् च्चि ता सं प नि प्य र ।
त स ए त वै पे द्य ग्मा व द ते स त वं द दा ॥१४॥

तै रे रु स दि वै भि ग्मा येत् वा वे र्घ्या द थैं नि र ।
द्यो त्वा तः व्यै स क्त त दे यम् सि ये द्यात् त्व तत् ह्व द ॥१५॥

रः नि ता ध ह्रा को य सा यम् स्थः वेत् मा स्व धि पि स ।
ह्वो चित् वेत् क सि दा पि न तम् म वे व्य दि र्घ्यं नि दे ॥१६॥

त ता क्रु न वीं स्व वत् पा यः स्यान् नो व ल ता म या ।
द्यः रो चेत् तः स क ति त वं भ ति त भ्रु कौ व पा ॥१७॥

न्यत् गु सि व वा ता क दे या स मा व श न्ना व पि ।
श्चा रा द त ण्ड्य की ज पा च स ए द्यो व पा क वि ॥१८॥
तत् ध यो ध्य रे सा क सा तम् व मौ म्य रि मे स का ।
तां स दा ह प्रो स्य व्वं सि वेत् (त) त्व यो तो भ सौ न्म य ॥१९॥

The key is as follows 8, 4, 6, 2, 7, 3, 5, 1, that is the first letter is given as the eighth and so on. These verses describe only the different kinds of wine to be used in the worship, how to make and how to drink them. There is no mention here or in the rest of the volume of Maithuna. It states that the Siddha should never drink wine unless it has been first offered as Arghya to the Devî on whom as the object of worship the Mind must be kept. Wine should be drunk until the Mind is wholly absorbed in the Devî. To drink more than that is to sin. He, who drinks without offering and for the satisfaction of his desire, is a sinner, a worshipper of ignorance and should be punished by the King. The following verses of which the above is a translation should be noted by those who criticise this Shâstra,

Na kadâchit pivet siddho devyarghyamaniveditam.
Pânancha tâvat kurvîta yâvatâ syân manolaya*h*.
Tata*h* karoti chet sadya*h* pâtakî bhavati dhruvam.
Devatâgurusevânyat pîvannâsavamâshayâ.
Pâtakî râjada*nd*yashchâvîdyopâsaka eva cha.

V. 91 and following describe the Yantra called Yonyar*n*ava, the worship thereof and the fruits gained thereby.

Chapter IX. This deals with the fourth Nityâ, called Nityaklinnâ. Her Dhyâna is as follows :—

She is red with red raiment and smeared with red sandal-paste. She smiles. Three eyes enhance the beauty of Her face. On Her forehead are beads of sweat shining like pearls. Above it is the half-moon. In Her four hands She holds the noose, goad, drinking cup, and with the last hand makes the gesture dispelling fear. She is seated in the middle of the Lotus, listless with desire (Madâlasâ) (vv. 7-9). She should be worshipped with all Her Shaktîs. In the corner of the triangle are K*sh*obhi*n*î, Mohinî, Lîlâ (v. 10). In the eight petals are Nityâ, Niranjanâ, Klinnâ, Kledinî, Madanâturâ, Madadravâ,

Drâvinî and Vidhânâ (v. 11); in the Square (Chaturasra) are also worshipped Madâvilâ, Manggalâ, Manmathârtâ, Manasvinî, Mohâ, Âmodâ, Mânamayî, Mâyâ, Mandâ, Manovatî (v. 13). Then follows a description of the Chakra of the Devî and the Pûjâ-krama (vv. 14-23); the method of Vidyâpurashcharana, articles of Homa and Tarpana, and the different fruits gained from Homa done with different articles (vv. 23-26). (Vv. 61-71) describe the Yantra of the Devî and (vv. 72-74) another kind of Yantra. The rest of the Chapter is devoted to Prayoga of the Mantra and Yantra. In praise of this Devî it is said (III. 34) that he, who attains Siddhi of Her Mantra, becomes more beautiful than Kandarpa and makes his wives do what he wills.

Chapter X. This deals with the fifth Nityâ or Bherundâ whose Dhyâna and that of Her Shaktis is given (vv. 16-19) as follows :—

Her body is like molten gold. She has three eyes and Her face is lit with smiles. She is adorned with ornaments of celestial beauty, with earrings, necklace, armlets, waist-chain and rings on hands and feet. She carries the noose, goad, shield, sword, mace and thunderbolt (Vajra) and bow. Her Shaktis are given (vv. 6 10) as follows : Brâhmî and others who are the Yoga Shaktis, should be worshipped on the outer part of the Yantra and Vijayâ, Vimalâ, Shubhâ, Vishvâ Vibhûtî, Vinatâ, Vividhâ and Viratâ in the lotus of eight petals. In the eight corners (within the lotus) are to be worshipped Kamalâ, Kâminî, Kirâtâ, Tîrti, Kuttanî, Kulasundarî, Kalyânî, and Kâlakolâ. In the corners of the six-angled figure are to be worshipped *D*âkinî, Râkinî, Lâkinî, Kâkinî, Shâkinî, and Hâkinî; in the corners of the triangle Ichchhâ, Jnânâ, Kriyâ ; and in the spaces outside the figure of eight angles the eight weapons should be worshipped. The Chakra is described (vv. 11-13); a second Yantra (vv. 25-35); a third Yantra (vv. 36-46) and a fourth (51-63). Japa of the name of Bherundâ frees from the evil effects of the three kinds of poison (v. 80 and see III. 37). These are according to the Manoramâ, Sthâvara (from treesand herbs) Janggama (serpents and other animals) and Kritrima (prepared by the mixing of various ingredients). Verses 81-85 speak of Trailokya-mohana-vidyâ yoga.

Chapter XI. This speaks of the sixth Nityâ or Vahnivâsinî, whose Dhyâna (vv. 9-13) is as follows :—

With the beauty of early youth She is lustrous like burning gold. Her lotus face with three eyes is lit by a gentle smile.

She is eight-armed and dressed in yellow silk with ruby ornaments. Such is the strength of the rays of the rubies on Her diadem that they make ruddy the surrounding region. Her radiance is enhanced by anklets and waist-chain of gems, pearls and other ornaments making clusters of jewels. In Her left hands She holds a red lotus, a conch, a bow of red sugarcane and the full moon and in Her right hands a white water lily, a golden horn, flowery arrows and a citron (Mâtulungga). She is surrounded on all sides by Shaktis like unto Her. So should She the Fire-dweller (Vahnivâsinî) Who assumes the form of the Universe (Vishva-vigrahâ) be meditated upon and worshipped. According to Pandit Yajna Puru*sh*a the right reading is Vishvaghasmarâ (She Who devours the universe) and not Vishvavigrahâ.

Her Shaktis are (vv. 14-22) Jvâlinî Visphulinggini Manggalâ, Sumanoharâ, Kanakâ, Angkitâ, Vishvâ and Vividhâ who are worshipped in the eight corners. The Râshi Shaktis Me*sh*â, B*rish*â and the others are to be worshipped in the twelve petals. Her Nityapûjâ Chakra is described (vv. 22-27). The Tithis beginning with Pratipat and ending with Panchadashî are the fifteen Devîs beginning with Kâmeshvarî and ending with Chitrâ (vv. 34-35). General rules for the attainment of Vidyâ (Vidyâprâptividhi) are given (vv. 39-57). Vidyâ and Mantra are distinguished (vv. 61-62) and some Yantras and their worship is described (vv. 63-67). He who is Siddha in the Mantra of this Nityâ can by its utterance subject the three worlds (III. 46).

Chapter XII. Vajreshvarî the seventh Nityâ is here spoken of. Her Dhyâna is given (vv. 6-10) as follows :—

She is seated at Her ease on Her chakra (Yantra) consisting of a triangle, hexagon, lotuses and Mahîpura (Bhûpura) placed on a throne (Singhâsana). She is seated on this throne in a golden boat flowing in an ocean of blood. She has four arms and three eyes. She is red, attired in red raiment, surrounded with red unguent and garlanded with red flowers. On Her head is a diadem of lustrous rubies. In Her hands She carries noose, goad, sugarcane bow and arrows of pomegranate flowers. She looks upon Her Sâdhaka with the cooling gaze of mercy. Her lotus face being in smiles. She is surrounded in the boat, which is swaying, by Shaktis unto Her.

Ichchhâ, Jnânâ, Kriyâ are in the corners of the triangle and Dâkinî and others in the corner of the hexagonal figure (v. 11). In the twelve petals of the lotus are the twelve Shaktis

H*ri*llekhâ, Kledinî, Klinnâ K*sh*obhi*n*î, Madanâturâ, Niranjanâ, Râgavatî, Madanâvatî, Mekhalâ, Drâvi*n*î and Vegavatî (vv. 12-13). In the lotus of sixteen petals the following sixteen Shaktis are to be worshipped. Kamalâ, Kâminî, Kalpâ, Kalâ, Kalitâ, Kautukâ, Kirâtâ, Kâlâ, Kadanâ, Kaushikâ, Kambuvâhinî, Kâtarâ, Kapa*t*â, Kîrtî, Kumârî and Kungkumâ (vv. 14-15). The Shaktis in the Square Jambhikâ. Veginî, Nâmnî, Chapalâ, Peshalâ, Satî, Rati, Shradhâ, Bhogalobhâ (?) Madâ, Unmattâ, Manasvinî. Injunctions for the Sâdhanâ of this Devî are given (vv. 23-35) ; a list of the articles required for doing Homa are given (vv. 36-62) and rules are given for the drawing of the Yantras Mahâvajra, Vajra and others (vv. 63-73). The rest of the Chapter deals with Yantras of various kinds and the purposes for which they are made. This Nityâ is Kântâra-sâgara-krûra-du*h*kha-sangghâta-târi*n*î or the Destructress of the cruel Evils dense as boundless forests or the wide ocean. This Evil is Aviveka, for from want of discrimination all evils arise. The Siddha in the Mantra of this Nityâ is freed of Aviveka (see III. 43).

Chapter XIII. This Chapter give details of the Pûjâ, Dhyâna, Nyâsa, Chakra and so forth of the eight Nityâ, Shivadûtî whose Dhyâna (vv. 14-17) is as follows :—

She has eight arms and three eyes and is bright like the midday sun in summer. She is garbed in red raiment and wears various kinds of ornaments on different parts of Her body, which enhance its beauty. There are nine gems in Her diadem. Her face smiles gently. The great *Rish*is are hymning Her praise. In Her left hands She carries a horn, shield (Kheta), mace, and cup (Cha*sh*aka) made of gems. In Her right hands She holds a goad, sword (Kha*d*ga) axe (Ku*th*âra) and a lotus. She is the Destroyer of wickedness and is eager to grant the pleasing objects of desire.

Her Âvara*n*a Shaktis are given in vv. 7 to 22 and are as follows :—

In the Bhûpura Vihvalâ, Kar*sh*a*n*î, Lolâ, Nityâ, Madanâ Mâlinî, Vinodâ, Kautukâ, Pu*n*yâ, and Purâ*n*â. In the figure of eight anglesare Vâgîshâ, Varadâ, Vishvâ, Vibhavâ, Vighnakâri*n*î Vîrâ, Vighnaharâ, Vidyâ. In the lotus of eight petals are Sumukhî, Sundarî, Sârâ, Samarâ, Sarasvatî, Samayâ, Sarvagâ and Siddhâ. *D*âkinî and others are in the lotus of six petals. Shivâ, Vâ*n*î, Dura-siddhâ, Tyaivigrahâ, Nâdâ and Manomayî should be worshipped in the six petals. Ichchhâ, Jnânâ and

Kriyâ are to be worshipped in the corners of the triangle. In the middle is to be worshipped the eight (Nityâ) who has assumed a supreme form (Parâ tanu) for the saving of Her devotees.

Directions are given for the drawing of Yantra (vv. 62-68) ; the Prâ*n*apratis*hth*â Vidyâ is given (vv. 62-68) ; as also a Dhyâna of Prâ*n*ashakti (which may be compared with that set out in the Prapanchasâra Tantra in the third volume of this series) and her ten Parivârashaktis are stated. These are the ten vital airs Prâ*n*a, Apâna, and so forth. In praise of this Nityâ it is said (III. 46) that her Vidyâ or Mantra is Samastâpattâri*n*î Âpat according to the Manoramâ = Aviveka. It destroys this and therefore all evils, makes the Sâdhaka pleasing to all (Vishvaranjanî) gives him prosperity (Shrîkâri) and granting all Siddhis leads the Sâdhaka to the Shiva-state (Shivatâvâptikâri*n*î).

Chapter XIV. This deals with Tvaritâ or Totalâ Devi, the ninth Nityâ, so called because (v. 12) She is quick (Tvarita) to grant fruit to the Sâdhaka and whose Dhyâna is given as follows (vv. 6-10) :—

She is of auspicious form in the first flush of youth and dark of colour. She has three eyes and four hands and Her beautiful lotus-like face smiles gently. She is clad in new leaves She is adorned with eight fierce and great serpents, of four kinds, and with waist chain and anklets. They are the four castes Vipra, K*sh*atriya, Vi*t* (Vaishya) and Shûdra. (The Manoramâ says that there are two of each castes and the ornaments should be understood as following the origination of each caste) On Her head is a crystal crown with a crest of peacock's feather. Her arms are adorned with bangles made of beautiful peacock's tail feathers. These are also made up into an umbrella and banner. Strings of gunjâ berries are round and on Her throat and breasts which are smeared with red (sandal). Smiling gently She holds in Her four hands noose and goad and makes the gesture (Mudrâ) of granting boon and dispelling fear,

Vv. 13-16 give the names of Her attendants who are as follows :—

Her Shaktis are Hungkâri, Khecharî, Cha*nd*â, Chhedinî, K*sh*epa*n*î, Strîkârî, Hungkârî, (?), K*sh*emakârî. These which are like the Lokapâlas and are the Shaktis of the Mantra-letters, should be worshipped in the eight petals. In front of the Devî is a black servitor carrying a mace who should be worshipped for the attainment of the desired fruit. On either side should be worshipped the Shaktis Jayâ and Vijayâ who are like Her and who carry and swing canes of gold.

The rest of the Chapter gives rules of Pûjâ, directions for the drawing of Yantra, lists of Pûjâ articles and the benefits to be gained by these various acts of worship. Ch. III. v. 47 says that the Siddha in this Vidyâ gains prosperity, beauty, fame, learning, wealth, health, long life and what he desires. He is affected neither by poverty nor poison.

Chapter XV. This deals with the tenth Nityâ called Kulasundarî, whose Sâdhaka (III. 52) becomes all-knowing (Sarvajna and Whose Dhyâna is given (vv. 3-11) as follows :—

She is propitious, supremely kind, and blissful with twelve arms and six lotus-like faces which smile sweetly and three eyes in each face. She is red, seated on a red lotus and is smeared with blood. Her raiment and ornaments are red and is surrounded by Shaktis who are also red. Her crown is bright with gems beyond all price and rubies, earrings, neck-chains, armlets, waist chains and anklets highten Her own brightness. On Her beautious breasts are clusters of red gems. In Her are all the words of the Vedas. In Her right hands She carries a rosary of coral beads, a lotus, a Ka*nd*kâ (Kama*nd*alu) made of gems a drinking cup (Cha*sh*aka) made of gems, full of wealth, a citron or lemon (Mâtulungga) and with one hand She makes the gesture of explanation (Vyâkhyânamudrâ). In the left hands are a book, red lotus, a golden pen, a garland of gems, a conch shell. She makes the gesture of granting boons (Varamudrâ) She is surrounded by Devas, Gandharvas, Kinnaras who sing Her praises as also by Yak*sh*as, Râk*sh*asas and the like. So should She be meditated upon for the attainment of learning wealth and beauty. When worshipped for the attainment of learning She is thought of as white, and when wealth is sought of Her, She is meditated upon as being of a golden colour.

Her eleven Parivâra Shaktis are (vv. 17-20 as follows :—

Bhâ*sh*â, Sarasvatî, Vâ*n*î, Sangskr*i*tâ, Prâkr*i*tâ, Parâ, Kha*d*garûpâ, Vittarûpâ, Ramyâ, Ânandâ, Kautukâ who should be worshipped in the Navayonis. In the eight petals of the outer lotus should be worshipped (the eight Mâtr*i*kâs) Brâhmî and others. In the square the Lokapâlas and their Shaktis (or in their Shakti form) should be worshipped.

The four following verses give directions for drawing Her Nityapûjâ Chakra and as to the scents to be used in the worship of this Devî (17-24).

The Tantra then deals with the three Kû*t*as or parts of or divisions of the Mantra "Aing, Klîng, Hsau*h*." The Vidyâ of Kulasundarî is Trayîmayî or Vedamayî and is when its vowels are united with the consonants, the cause of the Prapancha which is both Shabdamaya and Arthamaya (Vâchya-Vâchakarûpa) Sâmaveda is Akârâdi and so is *R*igveda. Yajurveda is Ikârâdi. By the union of these Aikâra is produced (a+i=e and a+e=ai). Aikâra or Shuchi is therefore Trayîmaya (vv. 33-38). This is the meaning of Aing the first Kû*t*a. The meaning of the second Kû*t*a "Klîng" is given in vv. 39 & 40. This Mantra denotes Her as cause of the Vâchya-vâchakarûpa Prapancha. The consonants between Ka and Ha signify the five Bhûtas and as such they are Jneya, just as vowels are Jnâna (Veda). Hsau*h* the last Kû*t*a is Jnât*ri*rûpa (v. 41). The first Kû*t*a is Vâk-svarûpa; the second is Vahni that is the union of Shiva and Shakti for in it is the fourth vowel (î) and Bindu and Visarjanîya, the origin of all the Mât*ri*kâs. By the last Bîja She is Vishvâtmarûpâ whether united with Bindu (=Kha) or Visarga (=Mâyâ). This is Tripurâkanda which is the united-state of Jnât*ri*, Jnâna, Jneya, Vâta, Pitta, Shle*sh*mâ, Agni, Sûryya, Soma. Therefore She pervades the whole Universe.

Vv. 45-55 speak of the effects of the Mantra according as it is united with other Bîjas. V. 68 speaks of the making of Vi*sh*nu Gh*ri*ta which gives powers of speech.

Chapter XVI. This Chapter speaks of the Eleventh Nityâ called Nityâ Nityâ All moving bodies are controlled by Her and by Her all Jîvas dwell in their respective bodies. According to Her Dhyâna (vv. 6-10) She is beneficient and pervades all beings (Sarvâtmikâ) for She is the Chaitanya in all. According to the Manoramâ She is the presiding Devatâ over *D*âkinî and others who are the Shaktis of the bodily Dhâtus. Coloured like the rising sun She bears on Her head a luminous crown. Her face is lit by a soft smile. She is dressed in red raiment and adornod with rubies. She has three eyes and twelve hands. With her right hands She carries the noose, the white lotus, sugar-cane bow, shield and trident and makes the gesture of granting favours (Varamudrâ); and in the left hands She carries the goad, book, flowery arrows, sword, skull and makes the gesture of dispelling fear (Abhayamudrâ). Her Shaktis are countless and form a complete circle. Chapter XXV speaks of them and includes amongst the principal *D*âkinî and others (vv. 11-15). Then the Tantra describes three different kinds of Pûjâ in three different Chakras (vv. 16-21) the Yantra (vv. 27-35) six Yantras shaped like Vajra (vv. 37-45) the Ma*nd*apa and Vedî and so forth under and on which the same are kept and the fruit to be gained (vv. 46-58); and the six Âdhâras or Chakras (vv. 59-71). It is to be noted that the Shaktis *D*âkinî and others are not placed in the same order as in the *Shat*chakranirûpa*n*a and the Dhyâna differs. They are described as being like unto Nityâ Nityâ. Then follows an account of the external Chakra and Pûjâ thereof (vv. 72-75), the same subject being continued in the following verses (vv. 76-87) and in verses 88-94. In v. 91 it is said that seven youthful women should be placed in the seven Chakras and worshipped with presents of food, clothes, scents and jewels. By worship of the fifty couples who preside over the divisions of Time the desired end is gained vv. 95-100). In praise of this Nityâ it is said (III. 55) the Sâdhaka becomes Khechara (*i.e.* Shiva) and blissful. By his mere wish he can favour or punish.

Chapter XVII. This Chapter deals with the twelfth Nityâ called Nîlapatâkâ. After describing the Nyâsa of Her Mantra (vv. 5-7) Her Dhyâna is given (vv. 8-12) as follows. She is sapphire-blue in colour with five faces and three eyes in each, and ten hands. Her face is sweet and smiling. She is clad in red raiment and Her hand is adorned with lustrous gems. She is decked mostly with pearls. Clusters of gems are on various parts of Her body. In her left hands She carries a noose, banner, shield, a bow made of horn and makes the gesture of granting gifts. In Her right hands She carries the goad, the Shakti weapon, sword, arrows, and makes the gesture of dispelling fear. She is seated on a lotus and surrounded by a number of Shaktîs resembling Herself. Vv. 13-17 describe the Ma*nd*ala of Her daily worship. In the three corners of the Yantra are worshipped Ichchhâ, Jnânâ, Kriyâ and round about the triangle the five Âv*ri*ttis and in the six corners of the *Shat*ko*n*a, *D*âkinî and others should be worshipped, and in the corners of the A*sht*ako*n*â the Shaktis Brâhmî and the rest. The verses which follow up to v. 49 give details of the ritual and the fruit gained thereby. They speak of Vetâla, Pishâcha, Yak*sh*i*n*î and other similar Siddhis. The Yak*sh*i*n*îs are described as young and beautiful women Spirits in fine raiment who give to the Sâdhaka all worldly good he may desire. Then follow the names of thirty-six Yak*sh*i*n*îs (vv. 50-53) and of sixty-four Che*t*akas (vv. 60-67). After some verses dealing with Mantras of Che*t*akas and with Yantras the Tantra speaks

(vv. 96-100) of the fruit which is gained by one who is Siddha in the worship of the sixteen Nityâs. He is ever honoured and worshipped by the Pitris, Devarshis, Râkshasas, Pishâchas, Uragas, Siddhas, Kinnaras, Apsarâs, Vâyus, Vasus, Seven *Rishis*, Yakshas, Dânavas, Eleven Rudras, Sâdhyas, nine Grahas, twelve Suns, the Lokapâlas, ten Prajâpati Devatâs, Kings, Women, Men and Wild Animals. He becomes the abode of all desired Siddhis and happiness. He is cheerful of mind, charitable, merciful and pleasing of mien, forgiving and contented, ever happy and free from all anxiety (Nirapekshaphalânvita) wealthy, enjoying his possessions and averse to injuring others. Such an one is "the abode of Our Love" that is the love of Shiva and Shakti. Ch. III. vv. 59, 60, speak of various Siddhis obtained by worship of this Vidyâ such as Khadga Siddhi, Pâdukâ Siddhi, Anjana Siddhi, Nidhi Siddhi, Bila Siddhi and control over Vetâlas, Yakshinîs, Chetakas Pishâchas and so forth. Similarly in the same Chapter (vv. 62, 63, 71, 72) it is said that Siddhi in the Nityâ Vijayâ Vidyâ gives victory in battle and success in trade and in the Sarvamangalâ Nityâ makes the Sâdhaka Khechara Siddha, in the Jvâlâmâlinî Vidyâ gives the Siddhis Vedha, Âkarshana, Santâpa, Vashya and Âvesha and by Siddhi in the Chitrâ Vidyâ, wealth and self-knowledge (Âtmalâbha) is attained.

Chapter XVIII. The last Chapter in this volume deals with the thirteen Nityâ called Vijayâ Nityâ whose Dhyâna (vv. 5-10) is given as follows :—Her body is lustrous red like that of the rising sun. She has five smiling faces in each of which are three eyes and She has ten hands Her raiment is yellow. She bears a brilliant crown and on Her forehead a crescent moon She is decked with all kinds of ornaments. In Her left hands She carries conch, noose, shield, bow, and white lily (Kahlâra) and in Her right hands discus (Chakra), goad (Angkusha), arrows (Sâyaka) and a citron (Mâtulunga) fruit. According to the Prayoga when She is invoked for the purpose of victory in war and the like She is of terrific aspect but in daily worship Her aspect is benignant. In Samaraprayoga She is meditated upon as seated on a lion and surrounded by Shaktis who are mounted on Tigers. In other kinds of Prayoga She is to be meditated upon as seated at her ease (Sukhâsana) surrounded by Shaktis similarly seated. Her Shaktis all resemble this Nityâ and carry the same weapons. Vv. 11-25 describe the Yantra of Her daily worship and name the Shaktis who are in the different angles of Her Chakra. The self-controlled (Vashî) man who daily worships the Devî in the Chakra in manner enjoined becomes happy in every way. Then are described (vv. 26-27) the rules of Purashcharana and the following verses give details of the worship: then in vv. 55-58 is described the ritual with a Mantra of eighty letters. The fifteen verses which follow describe the drawing of a Yantra of nine chambers and the mode of worship therein. Verses 74 to the end of the Chapter give an account of Vajra Yantra with Mantra of eightyone letters and of its worship.

The author of the Manoramâ whilst commenting on the passage in the Tantrarâja "Concerning the sixteen Nityâs there are nine complete Tantras," counts the Nityâ*sh*o*d*ashikâr*n*ava Tantra (published as Volume 56 of the Ânandâshrama Series, Poona,) the Sundarîh*ri*daya (the name given by some to the Second Part of the Nityâ*sh*o*d*ashikâr*n*ava) and Vâmakeshvara Tantras, separately. Bhâskararâya contests this view citing a passage from the Yoginîh*ri*daya itself "In this Vâmakeshvara Tantra are many matters the meaning of which is unknown" (Vâmakeshvaratantrê'sminnajnâtârthâstvanekasha*h*) and the *Ri*ju-vimarshinî which says "The Shâstra named Shrî Vâmakeshvara Tantra is revealed. In it is the Nityâ*sh*o*d*ashikâr*n*ava and in this latter are two parts of 400 verses each."

He also discusses the question whether the Vâmakeshvara Tantra with its parts or the Tantrarâja is the 65th independent (Svatantra) Tantra referred to in the 31st verse of the Ânandalahari (See "Wave of Bliss" by Arthur Avalon). "Pashupati Who knows all things in the universe, promulgated by means of the 64 Tantras the special Siddhis mentioned therein. Thereafter at Thy entreaty He brought down to this world Thy Svatantra (Tantra indedendent of others) which contains the means of accomplishment of all the Puru*sh*ârthas." Those, who support the claim of the Tantrarâja to be the Svatantra here referred to, say that it does show in fact independence. They cite the passage (1-3) in the Tantrarâja :—"the interdependence (Anyonyasâpek*sh*ya) of the Tantras produces confusion. Therefore Oh Lord speak to me that Tantra relating to the sixteen Nityâs which is independent (Nirapek*sh*a = Svatantra) of all other Tantras. According to the Commentator Gaurîkânta, by Svatantra in the verse cited is meant the Jnânâr*n*ava Tantra (Vol. 69 Ânandâshrama series). Bhâskararâya supports the claim of the Vâmakeshvara Tantra. He says that the Sundarî Tantras such as Kulâr*n*ava, Jnânâr*n*ava Svachchhanda, Parânanda, Bhairavî, Dak*shin*âmûrti and other Tantras are full of Bahiryâga rites and contain but litt'e of Antaryâga, whilst the reverse is the case as regards the Vâmakeshvara. He claims that it is the most excellent of Tantras since its characteristic is inner worship (Ântaropâsti). It is he says Upâsakamûrdhni. The Devî in the Nityâshodashikârnava (1. 13-22) enumerates 64 Tantras by name, and therefore, he says, it must be the 65th. It is true he says that the Tantrarâja takes no notice of other Tantras as regards external rites (Bahiryâga) for the attainment of Moksha yet he says that it is the Nityâshodashikârnava (part of Vâmakeshvara) which has independence as regards Antaryâga

Bhâskararâya also relies on the statement in the Tantrarâja that Nityâhridaya is another name for Yoginîhridaya and this latter is the second part of the Nityâshodashikârnava which is a portion of the Vâmakeshvara Tantra. As regards this contention however it is to be noted that when the Tantrarâja says that Nityâhridaya is another name for Yoginîhridaya, it is not referring to any Tantra at all but giving an equivalent name for Yoginîhridaya. Bhâskararâya admits that there is not much said as to Bâhyayâga in the Nityâshodashikârnava. He meets this however by quoting the precept "He has done all things who has done according to the true intention of the Shâstra that which he is enjoined to do by his own Grihya, be it much or little." As a matter of fact the Tantrarâja contains both Bâhyayâga and Antaryâga rites whereas the Nityâshodashikârnava is for the most part a selection of Antaryâga ritual. Moreover it is to be noted that Bhâskararâya himself, when commenting on the Bhâvanopanishad of the Kâdimata, cites more largely from the Tantrarâja and he commences the commentary by saying that the Bhâvanopanishad deals with Antaryâga. To the statement of the Tantrarâja 'that all other Tantras are interdependent' he replies that the texts which speaks of interdependence (Sâpekshyavachana) merely say that those who are initiated according to some other Tantra will, by doing to the best of their ability the rites prescribed in such Tantras, attain great fruit, whereas those who are initiated according to the Dîkshâ prescribed in Tantrarâja will by such Dîkshâ alone, that is without reference to rites prescribed in other Tantras, gain abundant fruit. Moreover if indispensable rites are lacking in this or any other Tantra they ought to be sought in Kalpasûtras—it being a settled fact that the Kalpasûtras were composed with the sole object of supplying what was wanting in any particular case. (Tattachchhâkhâpekshitârtha samarpanârthatvena): Therefore he says the objection against the independence (Svâtantrya) of these two parts constituting the Nityâshodashikâ on the ground that there is nothing said therein about Dîkshâ, Purashcharana, and the like is not maintainable. His argument however touching the Kalpasûtra would, if sound, be applicable to establish the independence of any Tantra. He proceeds to say that as a fact Dîk*sh*â and the like are alluded to in the Nityâ*shod*ashikâ. However this question of pre-eminence may be decided, there is no doubt as to the authority and importance of the Tantrarâja here published. This is shown intrinsically by its contents as also by the claim made on its behalf that it is the 65th Tantra and Bhâskararâya's arguments on such contention.

It is hoped to publish the second and last volume of the Tantrarâja text, now in preparation, during the course of the years 1919, 1920.

INTRODUCTION

Chapter XIX deals with the fourteenth Vidyâ or Nityâ named Sarvamangalâ (All-beneficent) whose Bîja is (as given in Ch. III. v. 63) Svaung. By Sâdhanâ of this Nityâ the Sâdhaka becomes Khechara (One who moves across the firmament; Shiva). Vv. 4-8 give the Dhyâna of the Devî and some rules of worship (Saparyâ). She is of golden colour, decked with pearls and rubies and bears a ruby crown on her head. Her eyes full of mercy are Sun and Moon. She has two arms and is seated on a lotus which has (in its inner circle) eight petals (then in the middle circle) sixteen petals and (in its outer circle) thirty-two petals. This is surrounded by a Bhûpura, square in shape with a door in each of the four sides. In her right hand she holds a Mâtulunga (pomegranate or may be lemon) and with her left hand she gives wealth and the like to her devotees (*i. e.* by Vara-mudrâ). She is surrounded on all sides by her Shaktis who are like herself and by others 76 in number who have originated from the solar, lunar, and fiery letters.

Vv. 9-17. There are eight Shaktis, one on each of the eight petals of the lotus. They are Bhadrâ (Propitious) Bhavânî (Existence), Bhavyâ (Futurity), Vishâlâk*sh*î (Large-eyed or whose senses are great), Suvismitâ (Wonder-struck), Karu*n*â (Pity), Kamalâ (Desireful), Kalpâ (Competency). Similary there are sixteen Shaktis in the lotus of sixteen petals. They are Kalâ, Pûri*n*î, Nityâ, Am*ri*tâ, Jîvitá, Dayâ, Ashokâ, Amalâ, Pûr*n*â, Pu*n*yâ, Bhâgyâ, Udyatâ, Vivekâ, Vibhavâ, Vishvâ, Vitatâ. They are to be worshipped on the petals in the order of Dak*shin*âvarta. On the petals of the lotus of 32 petals the 32 Shaktis are to be worshipped. Their names are :—Kâminî, Khecharî, Sarvâ, Purâ*n*â, Parameshvarî, Gaurî, Shivâ, Ameyâ, Vimalâ, Vijayâ, Parâ, Pavitrâ, Padminî, Divyâ, Vishveshî, Shivaballabhâ, Ashe*sh*arûpâ, Ânandâ, Ambujâk*sh*î Anînditâ, Varadâ Vâkpradâ, Vâ*n*î, Vividhâ, Vedavigrahâ, Vidyâ, Vâgîshvarî, Sandhyâ, Sangyâtâ, Sarasvatî, Nirmalâ, Dânarûpâ. These Shaktis in the three lotuses are "what their names signify" (Anvartha-samjnakâ), that is, represent the impulses of the human mind implied by their several names. The Shaktis Brâhmî and others who are Lokapâla Shaktis (Protecting Powers) are to be worshipped at the doors.

Vv. 18-20 deal with Purashcharan*a*.

Vv. 21-33 give the names of the 38 Kalâs in couples (Kalârûpa-mithunîbhûtâ) which are the Shaktis of the Mât*ri*kâ letters previously spoken of.

There are sixteen of these which belong to the lunar letters, *i. e.* the vowels. These are with very slight variation as given in Mahânirvâ*n*a Tantra (VI. 25).

There are twelve solar Shaktis of the Consonants (See Mahânirvâ*n*a Tantra) and ten of the Fiery letters from Ya to K*sh*a which are U*sh*mâ (Dipthong) letters. Each of these thirty-eight Shaktis has her Consort making seventy-six Devatâs in all. There are thus not 76 Shaktis but seventy-six attendants of Sarvamangalâ who have originated from the letters. The mode of worship is similar to that which is laid down in the Mahânirvâ*n*a Tantra. But the number 76 has importance as will appear in Chapters xxv and xxvi.

Vv. 34-36 say that the Mûlavidyâ of Sarvamangalâ undergoes 9216 variations. These are got in the following way The 36 consonants multiplied by the 16 vowels = 576 letters. By substituting in turn, in place of the vowel Au all the 16 vowels, 9216 variations result (576 x 16 = 9216).

Vv. 37-42 show how 144 Yantras can be formed with these 9216 letters.

Vv. 43-46 describe how the Yantras of the other fifteen Nityâs can similarly be multiplied by arrangement of the letters forming their respective Vidyâs or Mantras.

Vv. 47-59 speak of the application (Viniyoga) of the Yantras previously mentioned. Verse 49 is missing from all the three MSS. consulted. The Commentary however gives the sense of the verses including that missing.

Vv. 60-63 refer to shortened forms of ritual.

Vv. 64-66 describe how a Chakra of 12 triangles (Dvâdashâsraka) should be made.

Vv. 67, 68 contain instructions about shortened ritual (Laghupûjâ).

Vv. 69-85 give further instructions relating to same subject.

The rest of the chapter (vv. 86-100) contains further and similar details together with the fruits gained by such ritual.

Chapter XX. This chapter deals with the 15th Nityâ Jvâlâmâlinî (Garlanded with Flames). Her Vidyâ (given in Chapter III vv. 64-71) consists of 63 letters and runs thus :— Ong Namo (Obeisance) Bhagavati (All-powerful) Jvâlâmâlini Devadevi (Devi of the Devas) Sarvabhûta-samhârakârike

(Who withdraws all creation into Herself) Jâtavedasi (Origin of Veda) jvalanti (Kindling) jvala jvala (Kindle Kindle) prajvala prajvala Hrîng Hrîng Hûng Rang Rang Rang Rang Rang Rang Rang Jvâlâmâlini Hûm Pha*t* Svâhâ.

V. 3 speaks of Nyâsa with her Mantra.

Vv. 4-6 give her Dhyâna. She is lustrous like flaming fire and resplendent with her ruby crown. She has six faces and twelve arms and is decked with all kinds of adornment. She holds in her hands the Pâsha (Noose), Angkusha (Goad), Kha*d*ga (Sword), Khe*t*aka (Shield), Châpa (Bow), Vâ*n*a (Arrow), Gadâ (Mace), Dhara (Tortoise), Shûla (Spear), and Vahni (Fire). With two hands she makes the gestures of granting boons (Vara) and dispelling fears (Abhîti = Abhaya). She is surrounded by her attendant Devatâs who are like herself. Her lotus-like faces, each of which has three eyes, are illumined by a sweet smile.

Vv. 7 and 8 describe her Chakra. The Bhûpura consists of two squares, one inside the other and has four doors with projecting buttresses on either side. Inside it is a lotus of eight petals and inside it again is a figure of eight triangles (A*sht*âsra) and inside this again is a hexagon (*Shat*ko*n*a) and inside this last a triangle within which the Devî should be worshipped.

Verses 9-13 speak of the surroundiug (Âvara*n*a) Shaktis of five classes.

Ichchhâ, Jnâna, Kriyâ Shaktis are to be worshipped in the corners of the triangle.

*D*âkinî and five other Shaktis namely, Râki*n*î, Kâkinî, Lâkinî, Shâkinî and Hâkinî are to be worshipped in the the corners of the *Shat*-ko*n*a (Figure of six angles).

Ghasmarâ (Devourer), Vishvakavalâ (Universe-swallower), Lolâk*sh*î (Hungry-eyed), Lola-jihvikâ (Hungry-tongued), Sarvabhak*sh*â (All-devouring), Sahasrâk*sh*î (Thousand-eyed), Ni*h*sangâ (Companionless), Samh*ri*tipriyâ (Who delights to Destroy) are to be worshipped in the A*sht*âsra (Figure of eight angles).

Achintyâ (Incomprehensible) and seven other Shaktis namely, Aprameyâ (Immeasureable), Pûr*n*arûpa (All-comprehending), Durâsadâ (Difficult of attainment), Sarvagâ (All-pervading), Siddhirûpâ (Image of Success), Pâvanâ (Purifying) and Ekarûpi*n*î (Whose form is one) are to be worshipped in the lotus of eight petals.

In the corners and doors of the squares are to be worshipped the eight Shaktis Brâhmî and others.

After giving the rules relating to Purashcharana in verse 14 the text proceeds to give directions concerning ten kinds of Yantra in Vv. 15-21.

Vv. 22-80 deal with the different uses (Prayoga) of the Yantras. For instance Vv. 28-34 describe how the Devî can be invoked into a child (boy or girl) who is well formed and of propitious signs,and how she speaks through the mouth of the child and answers questions relating to past, present and future. Vv. 35-36 describe how a person suffering from any ailment may be made to tell its cause and the remedy therefor. Vv. 41-50 speak of Vedhadîkshâ,

V. 81 says that by drinking water into which the Vidyâ of Jvâlâmâlinî has been invoked the digestive fire (Kukshigo-'nala) is increased.

The rest of the chapter is devoted to an account of Homa and other rituals done for the physical welfare of the devotee.

Chapter XXI. This chapter deals with rites relating to Chitrâ the sixteenth Nityâ. Her Vidyâ given in Chapter III is not quite intelligible owing to corruption of the text.

Her Dhyâna is given in Vv. 5-7. She is herself lustrous like the rays of the rising sun, and is decked with jewels made of nine kinds of gems which are set also in her crown. She has four arms and three eyes and is clothed with a wonderful silken garment of variegated colour. A pure smile illumines her face. She is all-bliss (Sarvânandamayî) and ever-existent (Nityâ) and she grants all desires. In her four arms she holds the noose (Pâsha) the goad (Angkusha) and makes the gestures of granting boons and dispelling fear.

Vv. 8 and 9 speak of her as seated inside a figure of nine triangles, which is again within the triangle of a Yantra like that of Sarvamangalâ. This is where she should be invoked for the purposes of worship. The Nine Nâthas (see Chapter II) and her attendant Shaktis are to be worshipped in different parts of the Yantra.

Vv. 10-11 speak of the worship of the Nâthas and attendant Devatâs and V. 12 of Purashcharana.

Vv. 12-29 describe Kâmyahoma, that is, Homa for the attainment of one's desire.

Vv. 30-37 speak of Nigrahahoma, i. e. Homa to punish an enemy.

Vv. 38 and 39 caution the man who practises magic with a view to injure another (Abhichâra) that he should protect himself and explain how this is necessary.

V. 40 gives the very important and proper injunction that Abhichâra should neither be done to satisfy one's anger (Svasya ro*sh*âta*h*) nor for hope of gain (Vittâshayâ).

Vv. 42-47 and the first line of V. 48 speak of the formation of 25 Yantras which may be formed in different ways according as the 576 letters above referred to are arranged. The second line of V. 48 and Vv. 49-53 speak of the other 27 Yantras which may be formed. They are called Vajrayantras and are shaped like a Greek cross. The arrangement of the letters in different order in the "houses" or compartments within the Yantra gives it a different character.

Vv. 54-69 show the connection between these 27 Yantras with the 27 Nak*sh*atras or Constellations. (V. 55 is missing). Directions are given as to the ritual with each of these Yantras in its relation to the Nak*sh*atras (Constellations).

In the eleven verses 70-80 it is said that the names of the Lords of the Vâras (Days of the week) have already been given (Ch. XV. v. 70). Here the names of the Lords of the Tithis or lunar days are given. The Devatâs of the Nak*sh*atras are also here stated. Here are also given (vv. 76-78) the names of 27 trees which are the trees of the 27 Constellations (Nak*sh*atra-v*ri*k*sh*â*h*). In Vv. 79 and 80 are given the names of 27 animals which are Nak*sh*atra-yoni (literally meaning 'originated from the Nak*sh*atras'). The commentary however says that the correct interpretation of this can only be known from the mouth of the Guru.

V. 81 says that by knowing the time of origin of an ailment the right time to begin a rite for its removal is determined.

Four verses (82-85) describe how the 27 Yantras are to be intently meditated upon in the six centres (Mûlâdhâra etc.) to attain the desired fruit.

Vv. 86 and 87 give an alternative method for those who are incapable of this intense meditation (Paribhâvanâ).

Vv. 88-96 speak of the sacrificial offering (Vali) to the Devî and the fifty couples (Panchâshan-mithuna) and the fruit gained thereby.

Vv. 97-100 describe what the offerings to the Mithunas should be.

Chapter XXII. This chapter speaks of the rites relating the Validevatâ (Receiver of Offerings) of the sixteen Nityâs. This Devî, Kurukullâ, is inseparate from each of the Nityâs. Her Mantra which has been given in Chap. III (Vv. 89-93) is of 25 letters. This Mantra of 25 letters can be made into two others one of 7, another of 13 letters, by dropping out some of the letters—there are thus three Mantras of Kurukullâ. Her Vidyâ is therefore called Trikha*nd*â. Her Dhyâna is given in verses 10-12. Her hair is loose and dishevelled (Vikîr*na*-kuntalâ). She is naked. She is red and the embodiment of Bliss (Ânandavigrahâ). She holds in her four hands an arrow, a bow, a noose and a quiver (Tû*n*a). She is surrounded by Shaktis who, as in the case of the Nityâs, resemble herself in form and colour and carry the same weapons. They have just had the first bath after cessation of Pu*sh*pa (*Ri*tusnâtâ) and are quick with desire (Sphurad-yoni). Their eyes are red with the excitement of Bliss (Madânandâru*n*ek*sh*a*n*â).

The commentary says that by Naked (Nagnâ), we are to understand that she is Digambarâ, that is, she is clothed with space (Dik=the points of the compass). She is Ânanda-vigrahâ because she is blissful Consciousness (Smvid). The Devî also has just bathed and she too is passionate. She is so described as she is Sat Chit Ânanda, (Being Consciousness Bliss).

Vv. 13-18 describe the worship of the Devî and her four attendants (Âvara*n*a-devatâs). All these and others are to be worshipped in the Yantra described in Vv. 7 and 8.

The second line of V. 18, and Vv. 19 and 20 speak of the worship of Kurukullâ considered as part or limb (Anga) of Lalitâ the first (Pradhâna) of the Nityâs, and Vv. 21 and 22 state the fruit obtained by such worship.

Vv. 24 to 27 give the daily worship of, and specific to, Kurukullâ. The Mantra to be used is the same as that of Târâ.

Vv. 28 to 30 set out the Dhyâna of Târâ-shakti. She is dark hued (Shyâma-var*n*â), has three eyes and two hands with one of which she makes the gesture of granting boons and with the other she holds a lotus. She is surrounded by Shaktis of various colours and forms. She has a smiling face and is adorned with gems and pearls. Her lotus feet rest on two jewelled footstools. This is apparently also the Dhyâna of Kurukullâ in her daily specific worship.

V. 31 speaks of the articles to be used in daily Homa, and 32 and the first line of v 33 deal with Purashcharana. The second line of 33 and V. 34 say that it is only those who have done Purashcharana who are qualified for any ritual (Prayoga) for the attainment of any desire.

Vv. 35 to 50 speak of different rituals for different specifie purposes such as, obtaining control over man and animals, obtaining a good wife and so forth.

Vv 51-54 describe how a Yantra is to be drawn wherein the Mantra of 25 letters is to be used.

Vv. 54-61 state the five different purposes for which the Yantra may be used.

Ten verses (62-71) describe how a Yantra may be drawn wherein the Mantra of 13 letters is to be used and the four different purposes for which the Yantra may be employed.

Vv. 72-81 treat of the Yantra in which the Mantra or Vidyâ of 7 letters is to be used as above and the purposes for which the same may be employed.

Vv. 82 and 83 speak of eight other Yantras which may be formed by the help of the 13 letters varied by the addition of the vowel letters. By adding the different vowels (16) they can be made into 208 (16 × 13) letters.

Vv. 84-89 state the different purposes for which the Yantras may be employed; such as Shànti, Krûra and other rites previously spoken of.

Vv. 90-95 speak of the Vajra Yantra of 221 "Houses" and its uses.

Chapter XXIII. This chapter is devoted to Vârâhî. The Mantra of Vârâhî which is of 110 letters, is given in Chap. III, Vv. 73-88.

Vv. 13-15 give her Dhyâna in Nityapûjâ (daily worship). She should be meditated upon along with her attendants (Parivâra). She has the head of a boar (Kolâsyâ) and her body which from her throat downward is that of woman, is of the colour of molten gold. Her hair is of a burning tawny colour. She has three eyes and eight arms. She holds in her hands the Discus (Chakra), the Conchshell (Shangkha) the Lotus (Ambuja), the Noose (Pâsha), the Mace (Mus*h*ala), the Plough (Shîra) and makes the gesture of Dispelling Fear (Abhaya) and Granting Boons (Vara) She is seated on the back of Garu*d*a. Her Shaktis or attendants are to be meditated upon as like herself. In her worship (vv. 16-18) for the attainment of any specific object she must be meditated upon as seated on a lion, a tiger, an elephant, a horse or Garu*d*a. She is to be meditated upon according to the Sâdhaka's aim as being of a dark green, red, yellow, black or smoky purple hue. Her attendants are also to be meditated upon in the same way.

V. 19 says that she is to be meditated upon as yellow in colour when Paralysing (Stambhana) as of dark green hue and seated on a lion (vv. 20-24) in a difficult pass (Durga-ma-mârga).

Vv. 25-29 give her Dhyâna for rites done to gain victory in battle. There is a serious printer's mistake in the notes in the last line of page 416. For "Pralâpanâma jalpavish*shah*" should be read "Palâyanadyapajayavishe*shah*." The other verses up to verse 43 give different other Dhyânas for different purposes.

Verses 44 and 45 state what are the "poisonous hours' (Vi*sh*a-nâ*d*î) and other times such as M*ri*ti-yoga (Death-dealing moment) and so on. The calculation is based on the position of the Constellations. The commentary quotes a text which is to some extent corrupt but of which correct copy has since been obtained. It is given in the errata.

Verses 46-60 describe propitious rites.

Verses 61-100 describe eight different Yantras for Stambhana (Paralysing) and other magical rites. These Yantras are formed by drawing diagrams and placing the different letters of the Mantra of Vârâhî in different "houses" therein.

Chapter XXIV This chapter gives various Dhyânas of the 16 Nityâs.

Verse 3 says that for the attainment of Wealth (Shrî), Fame (Kîrti), Conquest (Jaya), powers of Subjugation (Vashya) and Attracting (Âkar*shana*) the Devîs should be meditated upon as red, clothed in red and decked with red adornments.

Similarly (v. 4) for the acquisition of Learning (Vidyâ), Peace (Shânti) and Liberation (Mukti, they should be meditated upon as white like the moon and camphor. Whereas (v. 5) they should be thought of as black or of a smoky purple hue in the doing of rites to cause harm to an enemy In every case the attendant Shaktis should also be meditated upon in the same way.

In verses 6 and 7 it is said that there are countless minor or subsidiary Shaktis which originate from the five "elements"

(Bhûta) Kshiti and others and the Gunas Sattva and others. They are in them individually or in their combinations and in this way are countless. It is only a few of them who are dealt with in this chapter.

In verses 8-11 it is said that the Earthy Ones (Bhaumâkârâ) are yellow in colour, raiment and ornament and paralyze (Stambhanakârikâ). The Water-produced Ones (Âpyâ) who are Sâttvikâ, are white and grant Knowledge (Jnâna), Peace (Shânti), Wealth (Shrî), Fame (Kîrti), Good Fortune (Saubhâgya) and Liberation (Moksha). The Fiery Shaktis are red and Râjasâ and grant the powers of Subjugation (Vashya), Attraction (Âkarshana) and Peace (Shânti). The Aerial Shaktis are smoky purple (Dhûmrâ) and the Etherial Shaktis (Nâbhasâ) are blue.

Verses 12 and 13 say that some of them have one face, some four, some nine, sixteen, twenty-five, thirty-six, forty-nine sixty-four, eighty-one and a hundred faces respectively. The number depends upon the proportion of the Gunas and Bhûtas. The commentary says that the number of arms is double that of the faces in each case.

Verses 16 to 18 speak of the relation of Lalitâ who is the Pradhânâ (chief) with the other 15 Nityâs. It is further said here that all this is the gross form of Meditation (Sthûladhyâna).

Verses 19-21 speak of subtle Meditation (Sûkshmadhyâna). By this also the Sâdhaka attains his desire. In this Sûkshma-dhyâna he meditates on the Devî in the six bodily centres (Mûlâdhâra and others), as red in colour and inseparate from himself.

Verse 22 speaks of the supreme form of Meditation (Para-dhyâna). This is done by meditating on the Parâ Shakti as one, impartite and impartible whole and visualising the Âtmâ as a steady, motionless flame in a windless place.

Verses 23 to 24 say that good or evil aimed at is accomplished by Sthûla-dhyâna in manner described in this book. The Adept (Siddha) attains his aim by Sûkshma-dhyâna. Para-dhyâna is for the attainment of the highest End, the Place of Rest (Vishrântibhûmi).

The rest of the chapter gives different Dhyânas appropriate for the attainment of different aims. In propitiary rites (Shubhakarma) the Devî appears with a smiling face and in rites in which evil to others is aimed at (Ashubhakarma) she appears fearsome of aspect and everything about her awakens fear.

Chapter XXV. In this Chapter it is stated that the 16 Nityâs along with the (36 consonant) letters which are the manifested 36 Tattvas, and the Mantras which are formed by the letters, as also the Yantras are one with Time (Kâla). The Prayogas with these are also given.

In verse 3 it is said that the vowels are the 16 Nityâs and the 35 consonants Ka to Ks*h*a along with the first vowel A (अ) (which is both vowel and consonant) are the thirty-six Tattvas. The nine groups into which the letters are divided are the nine Nâthas or Gurus. The 16 vowels are divided (v. 4) into two groups of 8 letters each. But the vowels make one group when they are considered in connection with the Mât*ri*s Vashinî and others. The consonant letters are divided into seven groups of five each.

Three verses (5-7) say that by uniting each of the different Nityâs with each of the different Tattvas, the number of letters obtained is 576 (= 16 × 36). This is the complete number of letters, the complete number of Yantras and of years (i. e. they represent a cycle). Multiples of this number represent Yuga, Kalpa and other periods of time. Multipled by 3,000 we get the duration of K*ri*ta-yuga (Satya Yuga). That is, 1,728,000 years is the duration of Satya Yuga. Three-fourths of this period (1,296,000) is the duration of Tretâ Yuga. Half of the duration of Satya (864,000) is the duration of Dvâpara and a fourth of it (432,000) is the duration of Kali Yuga.

Verses 8-10 give the letters of the four Yugas, which are Mâyâ (A*h*), Dharâ (Um), Agni (Im) and Vâta (Am), as also directions as to the way the letters of the alphabet are to be placed in the Time Yantras (Gha*t*ikâyantras).

Verse 11 states the purposes for which these Gha*t*ikâ-yantras may be employed.

Verses 12 and 13 say that Mât*rî*kâvar*n*a-chakra (Chakra of the Alphabets) being based upon measures of time (Gha*ti*-kâtmakatvena) is identical with the Jyotis*h*chakra (Sidereal Chakra).

Verses 14 to 16 contain directions for drawing the Gha*t*ikâ-yantra and for the writing therein of the Vidyâ in the order of the Yugas and so forth.

Verses 17 and 18 classify the 576 letters into three sections representing three parts of Tripurâ Mantra.

After giving some rituals (verses 19-24), verses 25 and 26 give some particulars about the mode of calculation of time which is explained at great length by the commentary. It is there said on the authority of an older text that the duration of the year is 365 days, 15 Da*nd*as, 30 Palas and 22½ Vipalas, (A Da*nd*a = 24 minutes). The same authority says that the duration of the Kali age is 157,791,645 days, The duration in days of the other Yugas are also given by the commentator.

Verses 27 and 28 speak of the necessity of worshipping the Lords of Dhâtus (constituent parts of the body) who are *D*âkinî and others and of the K*sh*etra (the Soil) and verses 29-37 of the way the 576 Yantras, one for each of the 576 years, are to be drawn with the aid of the 576 letters.

The uses to which these Yantras may be put is given in Verses 38-40.

Verses 41-48 give directions as to the performance of Abhi*sh*eka and state the fruits gained thereby.

Verses 49-53 speak of four kinds of worship (Upâsti) and of the fruits to be derived therefrom.

Verses 54 and 55 fix the time for particular kinds of worship according to the phase of the Moon and Verses 56-60 give some details about rituals for avoiding evils, etc.

Verses 59 and 60 hymn the greatness of the man versed in these Mantras.

Verse 61 is in praise of the Yantra. It is said here that in establishing a city and the like in any place this Yantra should be first placed there. For as verse 62 says, even the City of the Devas (Amarâvatî) may, without this Chakra, be annihilated.

Verses 72-78 speak of the merit or benefit gained by the repetition mentally of these Vidyâs a certain stated number of times. Verse 79 gives Anganyâsa and Verse 80 some directions about Meditation (Dhyâna) and Verses 81 to 88 give some directions about worship in the Yantras. Verse 89 speaks of the fruit obtained thereby.

Chapter XXVI. This Chapter deals with the world-pervading nature of the Mantras (Mantra-vyâpti) and of the oneness of the 16 Nityâs with the Mât*ri*kâs. It deals first (verses 5-10) with the origin of sound as Nâda (See "Garland of Letters") and how from its Parâ stage it changes into Vaikharî. This passage has been quoted in the *Shat*chakra-nirûpa*n*a and translated in the "Serpent Power" (P. 31).

Verses 11-16 say that by uniting each of the 16 vowels with each of the 36 consonants we get 576 letters (16×36). By uniting these letters in different ways all the Mantras, words, sentences and languages are formed. There is no one who can fully describe the greatness (Mâhâtmya) of Sound.

Verse 17 says that in each section of the nine-sectioned Chakra of Lalitâ there are 64 Ko*t*is Shaktis (Ko*t*i = ten million). Verses 18-20 speak of the formation of the Mantras (Mantrod-dhâra) of the Gupta-yoginîs.

In verses 30-31 it is said that bodily evils and impurities are removed by Abhi*sh*eka. By steadfast gazing (Vîk*sh*a*n*a), as described in connection with Vedha-dîk*sh*â (spoken of in Chapter xx), all false knowledge (Ayâthârthyam—Atasmin tad-buddhi*h*) is removed and by spiritual instruction (Upadesha) which teaches the disciple self-communion (Svâtmavimarsha) all the unconquerable longings are destroyed.

In verse 32 it is said that when all this is done then all attachment to Sangsâra arising from Mâyâ is removed and the eternal (Nitya) and pure (Shuddha) Âtmâ is realised.

Verses 36-43 show that all letters, words and sentences are Mantras.

Verses 44-48 establish the identity of all Vai*shn*ava, Shaiva and Vaidika Mantras with the Mantra of Lalitâ. The commentator, among other Mantras, quotes the well-known eight-lettered Vai*shn*ava Mantra :—Ong Namo Nârâya*n*âya and says that Nâra means collective humanity (Nara-samûha) and Nârâya*n*a is He who pervades Humanity. Humanity is not thus worshipped as such, as a Comtist might do, but as the Body of the Lord who informs it. That being so, this Mantra means the same thing as the Mantra of Lalitâ Some other Mantras are also quoted and discussed by the Commentator.

Verses 49-53 speak of the necessity of Faith, Devotion (Bhakti) in worship.

Verses 54 and 55 begin the subject of Am*ri*teshvarî Devî and verse 56 gives her Vidyâ or Mantra. Verses 57-62 speak of the six aspects of Am*ri*teshvarî-vidyâ. The Dhyâna of Am*ri*teshvarî is given in Verses 64-65. She is like pure crystal. Her body is moist with the nectar flowing from the Moon on her forehead. She is dressed in pure (white) raiment, and holds in her hands a water lily, a lotus, the full moon and a jar of nectar. She is seated, decked with jewels set with pearls, in the middle of a lotus of 16 petals and is surrounded by 160 attendant Shaktis. It is to be noted that in the text all the adjective words are in the plural because the Devî has six aspects.

Verses 67-70 give some rituals and 71 and 72 the mode of worship with her Mantra (Vidyâsâdhanâ). Verses 73 and 74 speak of the mode of formation of Lotus-shaped Yantras (Padma-yantras), and Verses 75-82 of 6 kinds of Vajra-yantras and their rites. The rest of the Chapter deals with formation of other Yantras and rituals.

Chapter XXVII. This Chapter treats of the identity of Prâ*n*a (Life) with the Shrîchakra, the Shaktis and Time (Kâla).

The first three verses speak of the division of time into Lava and so forth as given in Prapanchasâra (See Introduction Vol. III of these Texts.)

Verses 4 and 5 say that the "Air" (Vâyu) which originates from the Mûlâdhâra is given different names such as Prâ*n*a, Apâna etc. (See "World as Power, Life"). It assumes the character of the different elements (K*sh*iti etc.) according to the place in which it is experienced.

Verses 6 to 12 demonstrate how the vital breath (Shvâsa) assumes the characteristics of those of or are influenced by the eight planets respectively. Râhu is left out here. Verse 13 speaks of the effect of these different characters.

Verses 14 to 17 notify what should, or should not be done, according to the characteristics of the vital breath. Verses 18 and 19 determine the time of initiation (Upadesha) according to the character of the vital breath.

Verses 20 and 21 state that a man breathes 360 times in one Nâ*d*ikâ (= Da*nd*a = 24 minutes) and as there are 60 Nâ*d*ikâs in a day he breathes 21,600 times daily.

Verses 22 to 24 describe how man's breathing affects and is affected by the five Bhûtas during the day. The verses which follow to verse 34 deal with the same subject of breathing and in greater detail.

Verses 35 to 44 have as their subject the Nâ*d*îchakra and the place of Ku*nd*alinî therein.

Verses 45 to 47 speak of the 38 vital junctions (Marma) in the human body and the fruit gained by the operation of vital activity (Vâyu-dhâra*n*a) in these places. By this, it is said, a man may go-out of his own body and enter that of another.

Verses 48 to 52 give the names of the ten Vâyus in the body and their functions.

Verse 53 defines Yoga. It says that the union (Yoga) of the Mind which sees no distinction between the Jîva and Âtmâ with the Paramâtmâ is Yoga. Yoga has eight limbs (Anga).

Verses 54 and 55 speak of the eight limbs of Yoga which are Yama, Niyama, Âsana and others (See "Serpent Power"),

Verses 56 and 57 speak of the six obstacles of Yoga. They are Kâma (Lust), Krodha (Anger), Lobha (Greed), Moha (Delusion), Mâna (Jealousy, Envy), Mada (Pride)

The first line of verse 56 defines Yama and says that restraint from all effort to gain objects of sense is Yama The second line of verse 56 and verse 57 define Niyama. It consists of Ahimsâ (Harmlessness), Satya (Truth), Âstikya (Faith), Arjava (Absence of Duplicity), Samatâ (Equanimity), Dh*ri*tî (Firmnes), Ks*h*amâ (Forgiveness), Dayâ (Mercy), Threefold Purity (Tridhâ Shaucham), Santos*h*a (Contentment) and Gurusevana (Service of the Guru). By threefold purity is meant purity in mind, body and action. (See "Serpent Power").

Verse 59 speaks of four kinds of Âsana (Padma, Svastika, Vîra and Bhadra) and says that these are necessary to attain steadfastness of the mind (Mana*h*-sthairya-karam).

Verses 60-63 describe the Âsanas. Verses 64-69 speak of Prâ*n*âyâma (See "Serpent Power") and describe the three stages therof. Verse 70 speaks of Pratyâhâra and verse 71 of Dhâra*n*â. Verses 72 to 80 state the fruits of Dhâra*n*â.

Verses 75 to 77 describe the mode of leaving one's body at will (Svechchhotkrânti) and verses 78-80 the mode of entering another body. The first is done by restraining the vital airs and taking same through the Sus*h*um*n*â to the Brahmarandhra through which the escape is made.

Verses 81 and 82 give the signs of a Siddha.

Verses 83 to 100 describe the signs of approaching death so that men may prepare themselves for it when it comes. The Gaurî-kânchalikâ Tantra which is a Medical Tantra give the signs more fully.

Among other signs given in this book the following may be noted. If a man without cause changes his nature such as a miser becomes liberal and so on; when a man cannot see the polar star, when a man on the eye balls being pressed on either side of the bridge of his nose does not see the half-moon-like lights, when on closing his ears he does not hear the sound of Ku*nd*alinî and so on.

Chapter XXVIII. This Chapter shows the identity of the Universe with the 16 Nityâs (S*hod*asha-nityânâm lokâtmatvam).

In the first four verses the reader is reminded that the oneness of the 16 Nityâs with the Letters (Mât*r*ikâs) and Time (Kâla) has been dealt with in the previous Chapters (xxvi, xxvii)

In verses 7 and 8 it is said that in the middle of Bhûmi (Bhûloka) is the Meru of gold round which Bhûmi extends to a distance of 5000 Yojanas and outside this, in their order, are the seven oceans of salt-water, sugar-cane juice, wine, ghee, curd, milk and water. These are of varying width. A Yojana is four Kroshas which is 8000 cubits.

Verses 9-11 say that envelvoping these is the wheel of Time (Kâlachakra) moving round and round in the direction of the hands of a clock (Prâdak*sh*i*n*yakramât) which is put in motion by the Will of the Supreme Power (Ichchhâshakti of Parâshakti). This circle is divided into twelve sections by twelve shining spokes (Tejomayadvâdashâra).

Verse 12 speaks of the planets (Grahas) which are all within this circle.

In verse 13 it is said that Lalitâ is in the Meru in the middle with Her Light spread over all; and the fourteen from Kâmeshvarî to Jvâlâmâlinî are in the seven Islands (Dvîpas) and the seven Oceans and outside these is Chitrâ, the sixteenth Nityâ The abode of Chitrâ is spoken of as the supreme Ether (Parama-vyoma.)

Verses 17 to 22 give other details on this matter

Verses 23 to 30 relate to some rituals. Verses 31 to 33 describe the order in which Bhûmi, Kâlachakra and Mahâvyoma are, and of the places of the planets in Kâlachakra.

Verses 34 to 42 describe Nityâloka and the place there of the Devî and her attendants as also of Vârâhî and Kurukullâ

Verses 37 to 41 contain a Dhyâna of Lalitâ. She is in the garden of Kalpa trees where all the six seasons prevail. She is surrounded by countless Shaktis of Music (Sangîta-shakti) who are singing, playing on musical instruments and dancing. She is seated on a throne set with gems and in her eyes are seen her enjoyment of the dancing and music. Her face is illumined with a pure smile, Her body shows the bliss which is had on partaking of the "Natural Wine" (Sahajâsava). She regards with a kindly gaze good Sâdhakas. Around her are elephants and horses decked with variegated clothing, golden fly whisks and the like. She is surrounded by other Nityâs who are like unto Herself.

Verses 43 to 51 speak of the extent of the place where the Nityâs are and the fruit to be gained by doing Pûjâ there. Verses 52 to 71 speak of the protective amulet (Nityâ-kavacha) and the benefits derived therefrom.

Verses 72-75 deal with the identity of the planets (Grahas) with the letters (Mâtr*i*kâs) and verses 76-89 with the Ma*nd*ala necessary for the worship of the Nine planets.

Verses 90-98 give directions as to the time of worship and then of the separate Ma*nd*alas for the worship of the Moon (Chandra) and Sun (Arka) and of the materials with which the same is to be made.

Verses 99 and 100 give general rules regarding the Ma*nd*ala or Chakra or Yantra of the nine planets (Navagrahama*nd*ala).

Chapter XXIX. In this chapter are given directions for making Ma*nd*apa, Ku*nd*a and the like in the daily Homa of the 16 Nityâs.

Verses 5-9 contain rules for finding out the directions (Dikparijnâna) by the position of Sun. Instruction is given here for the drawing of a diagram by which with the help of the shadow of a peg placed in its middle the point of the compass can be ascertained.

Verses 10-12 give general rules regarding the making of the Ma*nd*apa and also the places where the altar (Vedî) and Ku*nd*a are to be made and verses 20-22 give the measurements.

Verses 23-27 speak of the making of the square-shaped Ku*nd*a and other Ku*nd*as within it and verses 28-31 give other details. Verses 32 and 33 describe the semicircular, verses 34 and 35 the triangular, verses 36-39 the Yoni Ku*nd*a, verses 40-41 the five-sided (pentagonal), verses 42-43 the six-sided (hexagonal), verses 44-46 describe the seven-sided and verses 47-51 the octagonal (A*sht*âsra) Ku*nd*as respectively.

Verses 52-57 give the dimension of the Ku*nd*a for making ten million Homas (Ko*t*ihomaku*nd*a), the number of priests required therefor and other details and Verse 58 speaks of the depth (Khâta-mâna) of the Ku*nd*as and verses 59-61 give the measure of the sacrificial String (Mekhalâ-mâna). Verses 62-66 speak of the Svarûpa of the Yoni-ku*nd*a and how to make it The Yoni is in shape like the leaf of the Ashvattha tree (*Ficus relegiosa*). It is said here that the Yoni is the great place (Pada) of the Tattva which is the Cause (Kâra*n*a-bhûta) and therefore the oblations should be made into it. The word Pada is defined by the Commentator to mean the place of origin (Udaya) and absorption or rest (Vishrânti) and he says it is great (Mahat) because it is complete (Pûr*n*a). By offering oblations into the Yoni full fruit is obtained within a short time.

Verses 66-68 speak of the Navel (Nâbhi) within the Ku*nd*a and how to make it and verse 69, of the two kinds of Dhyâna of Fire (Agni). It is either placid, kind (Saumya) or wrathful, cruel (Kraurya).

Verses 70-72 give the wrathful (Krûra) Dhyâna, In this he has two heads and seven hands, three feet and seven tongues. He has three aspects varying according to the Gu*n*as: Sattva, Rajas, Tamas. He has six cruel red eyes. In his four right hands he is holding the Shakti (his weapon) a garland of Ak*sh*a seeds, the sacrificial Spoon (Sruk) and sacrificial Ladel (Sruva) In his three left hands he holds a Javelin (Tomara), a Palm Leaf and a golden Vessel full of Ghee. His mouths are ever wide open longing to destroy.

The rest of the Chapter deals with details of Homa sacrifice —the fruits to be gained thereby and the consequences of mistakes and omissions.

Chapter XXX.—This chapter deals with the Vâstudevatâs (Devatâs of the homestead) of the sixteen Nityâs, with their Chakra and mode of worship therein of the Devî.

Verses 4-10 give their origin. Of old there was an Asura by name Vâstupuru*sh*a whose form was a square (Chaturasrâk*r*iti).

He was all-destructive (Sarva-nâsha-k*r*it). All the Devas tried to kill him. But by reason of the boon (Vara) granted by Shakti and Shiva he could not be destroyed by them. Then the Devas came to Shiva for his destruction. They said: Tell us now of how the pride, born of the sense of indestructability, of this Asura can be destroyed. Unless you do this the universe (Vishva) will be distressed by him. They having said this Shiva replied: His destruction is difficult. He should be buried underground and fifty-three Devas should remain on him; then only will he not be able to move. From those who are averse to the worship of these Devas, they will take (the fruits of) their good acts and do them evil. Therefore these Devatâs should daily be worshipped.

Verses 11-14 describe the Chakra of the Vâstudevatâs.

Verses 15-26 enumerate the names of the 53 Vâstudevatâs The first of these is Brahmâ. Verses 27-29 describe how the Yuga and other letters are to be placed in the Vâstu-chakra and verses 30 and 31 give the Homa to the Vâstudevatâs.

Verse 32 describes the offerings and verses 33-39 the proper time for doing Vâstupûjâ every year Verses 40-42 contain directions about the making of Vâstuchakra and the materials to be used therefor.

Verses 43 and 44 briefly allude to Subtle (Sûk*sh*ma) and Transcendent (Para) Homa Here it is said Sûk*sh*ma Homa is the offering as oblation, into the fire in the mouth of Ku*nd*alini in one's Mûlâdhâra, of the manifested universe (Prapancha) objective and subjective (Vâchya-vâchaka-rûpa). By this one becomes like unto Shiva aud Shakti.

In Verses 47-50 it is said that this rite is what is spoken of as Prâ*n*âgni-hotra in the Vedas. By knowledge of this a man becomes freed from re-birth. It does not involve expenditure and labour and a man is not dependent on other's help. It is the means whereby the troubles of the mind find rest (Mana*h*-klesha-vishrânte*h* sthânam) It ends all sin (Ni*h*-she*sh*a-kalma*sh*am). It is all happiness (Sukhâspada). It is so, says the Commentary, because it completely dissolves the mind. It is held within one's Self (Svaga: because it has disappeared in one's Self) and because it is Knower (Chit = Jnât*ri*), Object of Knowledge (Vedya = Jneya) and Knowledge (Vedana = Jnâna.) It pervades the universe (Vishva-maya). This is fully dealt with in the thirty-sixth chapter.

In verses 51-55, however, something on this matter is said. It is here stated that in the Mûlâdhâra of all animals is Fire

(Pâvaka) and in the heart is Sun (Prabhâkara). In the head below the Brahmarandhra is the Moon (Chandramâ) The First (Âdyâ) Nityâ (i. e. Lalitâ) pervades these three (Trayâtmaka). The oneness of these three along with their Lights (Tejas,) with the Mind should be meditated upon. The letters of Sun, Moon and Fire should then be offered as oblation into the Light (Tejas) which has been kindled in manner stated above.

Verses 56-60 show how this oblation should be made.

Verses 61 and 62 say that the imperishable body of Shiva and Shakti is composed of the three aforementioned forms or Tejas Other bodies (consisting of the five Bhûtas) are assumed by the will of Shiva-Shakti By Liberation (Mukti) is meant steadiness in the realisation of one's own oneness with the aforementioned three Lights. (Tanmayî-bhâvasthairya = Proktatejastraya-tâdâtmya-bhâva-sthairya)

Verses 64-69 describe Ku*nd*alî It is here said that She is within the Light (Tejas) of Fire. She is the Power which constitutes the individual (Jîvashakti), sleeping like a serpent thrice-coiled. She is of boundless effulgence as she makes the universe manifest (Vishva-prakâshakatvât). Her head is Mâyâ (= Visarjanîya). Uttering a sound she moves up and up along the channel of Sus*h*um*n*â When Ku*nd*alinî moved by her own desire uncoils and straightens herself then the individual realises the whole Universe otherwise the Universe is to him like the darkness of night. He who knows Her as such knows Parama Brahma and Shiva and Shakti. It is here parenthetically stated that if a man does not hear, on closing his ears, the sound made by Ku*nd*alinî then his death is imminent.

Verses 70-72 say that such a man is liberated while living (Jîvanmukta) and then give the traits (Laks*h*a*n*a) of a Jîvanmukta: He cannot be affected by Merit (Pu*n*ya) or Demerit or Sin (Pâpa), he is beyond Sorrow and Joy; he neither loves nor hates; he has abandoned the desire for the fruits of his action; he has all contentment; he is not moved to anything by the wish of others; he merely abides in his body; to him praise and blame are the same; to him enemy and friend are the same; he is merciful and beneficent (Kalyâ*n*agu*n*a).

In Verses 73-80 it is said that others also may attain Siddhi after many births who worship the Devî with devotion, but fools who are proud of their learning and wealth go the downward path, birth after birth. When all sin arising from ignorance and wicked longings is destroyed then there arises devotion

(Bhakti) for the Nityâs. It is by the power of that Bhakti that a man becomes a Jîvanmukta. Even Devatâs are what they are by the power of that Bhakti. The Lokapâlas derive their respective places from this. Even Shiva meditates upon Her. All Devatâs owe their existence to Her and their bodies are but of Her substance.

Verse 81 says that Supreme (Para) Homa is possible only for the Siddhas and in verse 82 it is stated that Bhakti in the Nityâs is possible only for those whose sins are all destroyed and who serve the knowers of Tat, that is, the Gurus who realise the Supreme Essence (Viditaparamârtha).

Verses 83-88 describe the character of those who are Bhaktas of Nityâ-vidyâ. They are not uncertain as regards the future life; they are contented (as for them there is nothing unattained); they are always complete (Pûr*n*a: because time and space do not limit them); they are blissful and not dependent, always seek the True and the Good and are devoted to the feet of the Guru; they covet nothing and seek not to hoard anything; they are free from meanness and busy themselves not in other's affairs. They are merciful towards all creatures, large-heatrd, undisturbed in mind whether there be gain or loss. They are pleased with, and free from anger towards all creatures and by nature they tend towards doing good and sing the praise of the good. They are averse from speaking of those who are addicted to sinful ways They stay where and when they wish; they are not afraid of kings, thieves, wicked men or enemies; they possess the full power of enjoying life, and have all devotion towards all Devatâs and Holy Places; they are free from crookedness and helpful towards all. They are fond of music (as it is Nâda) and are the possessors of all they desire (as there is nothing separate from themselves.) Being possessed of the power of pleasing all they are honoured by women, kings, rulers and the wise. They have no envy for there are none better than they. Their desire is to be one with the Devatâ which is the highest of all desires.

In Verse 89 it is said that Para Homa is the dissolution of the mind which now accepts and now rejects (Sangkalpa-vikalpa-kâra*n*a-bhûta) into that which vascillates not (Nirvikalpa) and which is the common aim of both Gross (Sthûla) and Subtle (Sûk*sh*ma) Homas.

Verses 90-93 establish the oneness of Sthûla and Sûk*sh*ma Homa with Para Homa. It is here said that the articles of

Homa offered in Sthûla Homa when burnt become one with the Fire into which they are offered: Sûks*h*ma Homa, it is said, is the realisation of the oneness of all sound and whatever is signified thereby with the object of Knowledge, the Knower, and the act of Knowing. Para Homa is that whereby is effected the total absorption, into the Changeless (Avikâri*n*i) Pure Being (Paramârthâtmani = Sattâmâtrasvarûpe), which is the Mahâshakti inseparate from one's Self and is the Light which shines without being fed by any fuel.

The remaining seven verses contain directions about Homa.

Chapter XXXI. This chapter deals with Sthûla Homa done with the object of punishing an enemy (Nigraha-homa). Verses 3-6 speak of certain things which should be known regarding the enemy before a Homa is begun.

Verse 7 tells of appropriate time for performance and verses 8 and 9 of the position of the 12 signs of the Zodiac (Râshis). Verse 10 says that Homa should be done after knowing the position of the Râshis. Verses 11 and 12 speak of the influence of the Sun on the Râshis and the influence of the Râshis on all animate beings.

In verse 14 is to be found the preliminaries of rites to be done with a doll representative of the person aimed at, and

Verses 15-21 speak of the manner of performance.

Verses 15-17 relate the position of Vis*h*akalâ (Poisonable or Vulnerable point) which changes according to the phase of the moon.

Verse 22 speaks of the Lords or Regents of the houses of the Zodiac, and verse 23 deals with the Constellations (Naks*h*atras).

Verses 24-26 speak of the size of the doll to be used, and

Verses 27-29 of the materials to be used.

Verses 30 and 31 give other details about the size of the doll.

Verses 32-34 state the appropriate times for the doing of injurious acts. The times are Pâtâlayoga, Nîchayoga, Vis*h*ayoga and so on The commentary makes quotations from a number of astronomical authorities some of which are not intelligible and it has not been possible to trace the books from which they have been taken.

The rest of the Chapter gives details of different kinds

of Homa and of the times when the same should be done and of the materials to be used therein.

Here there are a number of trees mentioned by name.

Chapter XXXII. This Chapter deals with Homa done for one's own or another man's benefit. This is called Saumya Homa. Verses 2 and 3 describe ordinary Homa (Sâmânya Homa). This is done with lotuses. Verses 4-10 describe Homa for the attainment of power and dominion (Aishvarya) and Verses 11-19, Homa for the attainment of wealth and prosperity and Verses 20 and 21 Homa for the acquisition of cows, lands, gold and so forth.

Verses 22-28 speak of articles of Homa. Other Verses to 41 deal with the same matter, verses 42 and 43 speaking of Homa for the propitiation of the Planets (Graha).

Verses 44 to the end of the book deal with details as to time of performance, articles of Homa and so on.

Chapter XXXIII deals with the Yantras of the Âdyâ Nityâ Lalitâ. There are, it is said here, 960 such Yantras.

The chapter describes the different Yantras and the different fruits gained by worshipping in the different Yantras. The principal Yantras or Chakras named are Shrî Yantra, Pûjâ-kamala Chakra, Amr*i*tagha*t*a, Siddhavajra, Ko*shth*a-vajra, Vajra-linga, Merulinga, Mahâlinga, Yoni Vajra-vajraka, Mahâ-vajravajra.

Chapter XXXIV This describes some rites of a "wonderful" character (Loka-chamatkârakara).

These are done by worshipping the different aspects of the Devîs. There are the names of twenty-four Vidyâs given in Verses 2-4. They are Siddha-sârasvata, M*ri*tyunjaya, Tripû*t*â, Gâru*d*a, Ashvârû*dh*â, Annapûr*n*â, Navâtmâ, Navâtmikâ, Devîh*ri*daya, Gaurî, Lak*sh*adâ, Ni*sh*katrayapradâ, I*sht*adâyinî, Mâtanginî, Râjyalak*sh*mî, Mahâlak*sh*mî, Siddhalak*sh*mî, and seven aspects of Gopâla or Kris*h*na.

Verses 5 and 6 give ihe Siddha-sârasvata-vidyâ

In Verses 8-10 it is said that if this Vidyâ be infused into water in the manner prescribed, and a little girl with faultless limbs be made to drink it then she speaks like Sarasvatî herself of the past, present and future.

Verse 11 gives the M*ri*tyunjayavidyâ (M*ri*tyunjaya is Shiva as Conqueror of Death). His Dhyâna is given in

Verses 13 and 14. He is seated on a lotus the stalk, the petals and the pericarp of which are respectively, the first, second and third letters of his Vidyâ. His body is bathed with nectar. On his forehead is a Kalâ of the Moon. He is white in colour and is holding in his hands a deer, a rosary of Ak*sh*a seeds, and a noose (Pâsha) and is making the gesture of Exposition (Chin*t*â = Vyâkhyâna-mudrâ). He should be meditated upon upon as one with the meditator (Svaikyena bhâvayet).

Verse 15 gives the Vidyâ of Tripu*t*â and verses 15-20 her rituals and Dhyâna She is red and gracious of aspect, carrying in her six hands a flowery arrow, a goad, two lotuses (one in each) a noose and a sugar cane bow. She has a bright gem-set crown on her head. She is surrounded by Shaktis singing sweetly, decked in love-provoking fashion (Sh*ri*ngâra-bhû*sh*â) and carrying fly whisks (Châmara), mirrors, and so forth.

Verses 21 and 22 give the Gâru*d*a Mantra. Verse 27 gives the Vidyâ of Ashvârû*dh*â and 28-30 give the rituals. Verses 31-33 give her Dhyâna. She is red and seated on a red horse and gracious of aspect. In her right hand is a spear with a crescent-like head and in her left a leathern stick (or whip), with one of her other two hands she holds the enemy of the Sâdhaka tied by a golden rope and with the other strikes him with a cane of gold.

Verse 35 gives the Vidyâ of Annapûr*n*â. Her Dhyâna is related in verse 37. She is smilingly looking at Shiva dancing the Tâ*nd*ava dance whereby the serpents are frightened, holding in her hand a golden vessel full of custard (Pâyasa).

Verses 41 and 42 give the Vidyâs of Navâtmâ and Navâtmikâ.

Verse 43 gives the Vidyâ of Devîh*ri*daya. Her Dhyâna is the same as that of Sarvamangalâ The following verses give her ritual.

Verse 48 gives Gaurî-vidyâ and the following verses the ritual.

Verses 53 and 54 give the Vidyâ of Lak*sh*asuvar*n*adâ.

In this way the different Vidyâs mentioned above are given.

Verse 84 makes the important statement that Lalitâ assumed a male form (Pungrûpa) as K*rishn*a and by enveloping all women (Sarva-nârî-samârambhât) enchanted the whole world.

Krishna was surrounded by his Shaktis (i. e. the Shaktis of Lalitâ). He assumed six different forms (*Shodhâ*'kalpayad vapu*h*).

The names of the six forms are Siddhagopâla, Kâmarâja gopâla, Manmatha-gopâla, Kandarpa-gopâla, Makaraketana-gopâla and Manobhava-gopâla. The last five, namely, Kâmarâja, Manmatha, Kandarpa, Makaraketana, Manobhava were, it is stated in Chapter VII, vv. 23-33, created by the Dêvi Lalitâ. They are Her five arrows of desire representing Her five senses of knowledge. (Jnânâtmakân = panchendriya-jnânavigrahân).

Verse 95 gives their Dhyâna

Verses 96 to 99 speak of ceratin herbs by the use of which in manner prescribed Devatâs may be visualised.

Chapter XXXV. This is called the Vâsanâ-patala or the Chapter dealing with the Vâsanâ of words The word Vâsanâ has various meanings, but in the sense it is used here and in the last Chapter of the Kulâr*n*ava Tantra it means not the etymological meaning of a particular word but what the Sâdhaka does or ought to understand by it.

The Chapter begins by speaking (V. 1) of the Vâsanâ which shows the oneness of the sixteen Nityâs with the Sâdhaka's Self (Svâtmatve vâsanâm) The latter visualizes his oneness with them (Pratyak*sh*â tanmayatâ-siddhi*h*) The Guru is the Âdyâ Shakti who is Vimarsha. His ninefold character (Navatva) appears in the nine apertures of the body. [The Commentary adds that as through these apertures we take in what is good (Upâdeya) and throw out what is bad (Anupâdeya) so by the mercy of the Guru the Sâdhaka's mind tends towards the Truth (Artha) and abstains from untruth (Anartha). The two ears and the mouth are the Divya, the two eyes and genitals are the Siddha, the two nostrils and the anus are the Mânava Gurus respectively].

The Validevîs are (verse 3) the Shaktis who lead us astray (Unmârgapravartikâ*h* shaktaya*h*) by making us believe that which is not *That* to be *That* (Atasmin tadbuddhing janayitvâ). Panchamî (= Vârâhî) occupies the place of the Father (Janakâtmikâ) as she (as the commentary says) protects us from evil (Anabhimata) and Kurukullâ is Mother as she gives us what is good (Abhimata). The aims of human existence (Pura-*sh*ârthâ*h*) are ocean-like on account, as the Commentary says, of their greatness and boundlessness. The body is an island of (nine) gems (verse 5). The nine gems are Ojas, Shukra, Majjâ, Asthi, Medas, Mângsa, Roma, Tvak, Rudhira. Resolutions (Sangkalpâ*h*) are like the wish-granting trees, for any action undertaken with resolution is fruitful. The Âdhâras (that is, the Six Chakras or centres in the body) are the Seasons. [This is so because by the Union of Su*sh*um*n*â with I*d*â and Pingalâ, which are Moon and Sun, time may be measured in the Chakras]. Time which is Âtmâ (Kâlâtmâ = Kâlasvarûpâtmâ) along with the Planets, the Constellations, the Zodiac (Râshichakra) move west (*lit.* faces west), therefore the Sâdhaka faces East (when he is doing Sâdhanâ).

The Tâttvika aspect (Svarûpa) of Kâla is dealt with in the 36th. Chapter. In verse 6 it is said the Knower (Jnâtâ) is one's Self (Svâtmâ) i. e. the worshipper; Knowledge (Jnâna) is the offering (Arghya); the Object of Knowledge (Jneya) which is the Shrîchakra (See Tantrik Texts, vol. X) is outside the Knower. The worship of the Shrîchakra is the unification of these three (viz. the Knower, the Knowledge and the Object of Knowledge). Here is shown the identity of different parts of the Sâdhaka's Self with different parts of the Shrîchakra for which see pp. 5-8 of Introduction to Part I (vol. VIII of T. T.). Verses 7-11 say that the Siddhis (A*n*imâ etc.) in the Shrîchakra are the Rasas Sh*ri*ngâra and others together with Niyati; the six Ûrmis (Hunger, Thirst, Sorrow, Delusion Decay and Death) together with Pu*n*ya (Virtue or Merit) and Pâpa (Sin) are the eight mothers Brâhmî and others. The (five) Bhûtas, the (ten) Indriyas (Senses) and Mind (Manas) are the (16) Kalâs of Nityâ. The functions of the five Organs (Indriyas) of Action (Karma) such as Speech (Vachana), Taking (Âdâna), Walking (Gamana), Emission (Visarga) and Bliss (Ânanda) together with the three Do*sh*as namely Vâyu, Pitta and Kapha, (See Introduction to Vol III of Tantrik Texts) are the eight Shaktis Ananga-kusumâ and others. The fourteen Nâ*d*îs mentioned in the 27th Chapter are the fourteen Shaktis K*sh*obhi*n*î and others. The ten Vâyus (Prâ*n*a, Apâna, Samâna, Vyâna, Udâna; Nâga, Kûrma, K*ri*kara, Devadatta, Dhananjaya) are the ten Shaktis Sarva-siddhi-pradâ and others. The ten Fires (seven of which are in the Dhâtus and three in the Do*sh*as) are the Shaktis Sarvajnâ and others; Heat and Cold, Happiness and Pain, Wish or Desire (Ichchhâ) and the three Gu*n*as (Sattva, Rajas, Tamas) are the Shaktis Vashinî and others. The (five) flowery Arrows are (five) Tanmâtras. The Mind (Manas) is the Sugar cane Bow (Ik*sh*udhanu*h*). Attachment (Râga) is the Noose

(Pâsha). Repulsion (Dve*sh*a) is the Goad (Ankusha). The Text in Verse 12 then proceeds to state that Avyakta, Mahat, Ahamk*ri*ti (Prak*ri*ti-tattva, Buddhi-tattva, Ahamkâra-tattva) are the Devîs Kâmeshvarî, Vajreshvarî and Bhagamâlinî, and Samvit (= Sakalâtmaka-chaitanya = the supreme, all-embracing Consciousness) is Kâmeshvara. One's own Âtmâ [which remains as the one Sat after having absorbed within itself all the Vikalpas which is the world (Vishva-vikalpa)] is the Devî Lalitâ whose body is the Universe (Vishva-vigrahâ). Meditation on Her which is the same as meditation on one's Self (Tadvimarsha = Svâtma-vimarsha) is Redness (Lauhitya). Bhâskararâya in his commentary to the Bhâvanopai*sh*ad, *Ri*k 29 (See Tantrik Text Vol. XI pp. 54, 55) has dealt with this. Kâmeshvara he says is like crystal and therefore the part which is white (Shuklachara*n*a). The Commentator says that attachment of mind to anything (Râga) is Redness. The Consummation of worship (Upâsti) is meditation on one's Self. Siddhi is attained when thought does not wander (from the contemplation of the identity of one's Self with the Object of worship). The Mudrâs (Yoni Mudrâ and others) signify (verse 14) faith (Bhâvanâ) in the greatness (Vaibhava) of the object of worship. For the attainment of this Bhâvanâ, what is necessary is action (Kriyâ). Though action passes (Chalatve'pi), it yet produces steadiness. Prayogas (Rites done to avert evil and induce what is good) help in the dissolution of indiscrimination (Aviveka) which is the cause of all distinctions (Vikalpa) into Vimarsha. Yantras and Mantras (verse 16) help to produce steadiness in the belief of one's unity or oneness with the Âtmâ (Svâtmatve). Worshipping or saying prayers thrice daily (Sandhyâ) rids man of the notion of beginning, middle and end (Âdimadyânta-majjana, i. e. it leads one into Timelessness). The other Shaktis (i. e. the Guptayoginîs) who dwell in the Chakra produce the belief in the multifariousness of the Universe. By Nyâsa (v. 18) the body is made like that of the Devatâs. [Nyâsas tu devatâtvena svâtmano dehakalpanam]. Japa produces a sense of identity with the Devatâ. [Japas tanmayatâ-rûpabhâvanam]. By Homa is destroyed the sense of multifariousness. [The Commentator here says:—there are different kinds of ornaments made of gold but they are all gold. The Bhâvanopani*sh*ad, *Ri*k 32, T. T. Vol. X, p. 59 says that Homa is the dissolution into the Âtmâ of all Vikalpas or Distinctions such as "Thou" and "I," "Is" "Is not," "Should be done" and "Should not be done" and the like]. Tarpa*n*a is the Contentment (T*ri*pti) caused by the realisation of the identity of all things with one's Self. (i. e. Tarpa*n*a leads to this realisation). [E*sh*âm anyonyasambheda-bhâvanang tarpa*n*ang sm*ri*tam]. The Bhâvanopani*sh*ad says that the Contemplation on the object thereof as one with one's Self (Abheda-bhâvanâ) is Tarpa*n*a. Abhi*sh*eka is (i. e. leads to) the final removal of the pain arising from Moha, Ajnâna and the like. [Moha is defined in the Commentary to mean "the absence of the knowledge of the rightness and wrongness (Kartavyâkartavyajnânâbhâva) of action arising out of overwhelming desire]. Vidyâ is Âtmâ which is the abode of all (Sarvâshraya) as all things are one with It. This is Great (Mahân) as it is All-pervading (Vibhu). Upadesha (instruction i. e. spiritual instruction) is (i. e. leads to) the removal of all attributes (Upâdhi). Dak*sh*i*n*â (to the Guru) is (implies) inseparateness (Bheda-shûnyatvam) between the two (Guru and Shi*sh*ya). Service (of the Guru) is (i. e. causes) steadfastness (Sthairya) of Self-knowledge. The fifteen Nityâs are the fifteen lunar days (Tithis) in the evolution (Pari*n*âma) of Time. The five fingers are the five Elements (Panchabhûtas). Their intimate connection with one another is (as appearing in Kara-mudrâ or Mudrâ made with the hands and fingers) indicative of the manifoldness (Prapanchatâ = *lit* five-foldness) of the Âtmâ.

Verses (24-25) which are in a wilfully disordered (Vyâkulita) form to ensure secrecy give the meaning of the Bîja (Hrîm), of Lalitâ, which is the Rûpa of the Devî. "H" stands for Prakâsha, because it is (the Bîja of) Âkâsha which is Sphura*n*âtmaka, "R" which is (the Bîja of) Agni means Devouring (Grâsa) because Fire devours ; "Î" is the Vimarsha (as it leads to oneness in the Supreme sense : Tâdâtmya-paramârtha-melana). By the Bindu (M) is effected the Niphâlâna of Realisation of oneness of the Sâdhaka with these.

In verses 27-30 it is said that a Mantra of one letter is called a Pi*nd*a, of two letters Kartarî, of three to nine letters Bîjaka, of 10 to 20 letters Mantraka, and one which exceeds this number is called a Mâlâ.

Verses 31-33 show in how many different ways the Mantras can be arranged. A Mantra of three letters can be arranged in six ways, one of four letters in twenty-four, and so on.

Verses 34-43 show how the Mantras can be arranged in a Yantra. The Commentary deals with this in very great detail.

Verses 44-45 contains six questions by the Devî (1) relating to the meaning of the five kinds of Mantras—as Sthûla, Sûk*sh*ma and Para ; (2) how the Sâdhanâ of these Mantras can be adequately carried out ; (3) wherein lies the in-efficacy of their

Sâdhanâ; (4) how inefficacy may be rectified; (5) what are signs of the Siddha; (6) what is Siddhi.

Verses 46-48 state how for the ascertainment of the meaning of Mantras a diagram with fifty 'houses' therein should be drawn for the purpose of placing therein each group of letters of the alphabet classified according to the Bhûtas (Elements) to which they belong.

Verses 49 to 53 give the names of each of the ten letters in the five groups. The verses are in Vyâkulitâk*sh*ara or disordered form. Verses 54-55 says that this is done to keep the names secret. The letters belonging to Air, (v. 49), Fire (v. 50), Earth (v. 51), Water (v. 52), Ether (v. 53) respectively are given in the verses stated. These verses have been set right though with some difficulty owing to incorrectness of the Text.

Verse 56 is also in Vyâkulitâk*sh*ara. The second half of the second line of the verse is indecipherable. In this and the following verse Shiva says that the Deshika (Guru) makes countless verses unintelligible to the ordinary reader. The Commentator explains how these verses are to be read.

Verses 57-60 state how a Yantra may be drawn to enable the man versed in this Tantra and Vidyâ to attain the state of the Devatâ whose Sâdhanâ he is doing.

Verses 62-63 say that Mantras are either cruel (Krûra) or benevolent (Saumya) or they are mixed (Mishra). This depends on the character of the letters they are composed of. Mantras in which the letters of Ether (Nabha*h*) Fire (Agni) and Air (Vâyu) are in excess are cruel. Mantras in which Earth (Bhû) and Water (Toya) letters are the greater in number are benevolent.

In Verse 64-66 it is said that the meanings of Mantras are of three kinds. Upâsakas also are of three kinds. The Siddhas know the oneness of Mantras with Parâ rising as they do through different stages such as Pashyantî and the like and returning again by the very nature of their oneness (Tâdâtmya) to Parâ. The Sâdhyas seek to know the meanings of Mantras according to the rules of grammar and the like. The Sâdhakas meditate on the identity in the Mantras of, on the one hand, the five Bhûtas which are that which is denoted by speech (Vâchya) and are aspects of Avyakta (Avyaktâtmaka) with, on the other hand, the letters (Ak*sh*aras), which are that which denotes (Vâchaka) as they are the Shaktis of Avyaktanâda.

Verses 67-69 speak of the transcendental significance of Mantras (Mantra-vîryam = Mantrâ*n*âm paramârtha-svarûpam). By a knowledge of this man becomes liberated whilst living (Jîvan-mukta). By a knowledge of this, Mantras may be made efficacious. Verses 70-72 give the thirteen causes whereby a Mantra becomes inefficacious and verses 73-75 note the traits of a man who has attained Siddhi in Mantra. He neither hates nor is attached to anything greatly. He is neither over-sorrowful nor over-joyful. He is neither over-affectionate nor envious. He is not overcome by any calamity. He makes others happy and avoids giving pain. His body is merely a vehicle for his Self. He meddles not in the affairs of others To him loss and gain are the same and he is always contented. He can enjoy a thing and yet give it away. Verses 76-79 describe other powers of a man who is Mantra-siddha. It is here said that it is only a man of this kind who should do any rite (Prayoga). Verses 80-83 say that just as between men and men and Devas and Devas there exists enmity—so also is it between Mantras and Mantras. It shows how such enmity arises and between what Mantras. Verses 84-86 explain how owing to the fault of the Upâsaka a Mantra may become inimical and if so how this evil can be remedied. Verses 87-88 state how a Mantra may be made propitious. Verse 89 gives direction about the making of amulets and verse 90 instructs as to how to use the same. Verses 91 to 100 give the names of fifty Herbs (O*sh*adhi) one for each of the fifty letters of the alphabet These are classified in five groups of ten each. Each of such groups belongs to one of the five elements (Bhûtas).

Chapter XXXVI. This is the last Chapter. It begins with twenty questions (Vv. 1-6) by the Devî. She asks Shiva about (1) The true nature (Svarûpa) of the sixteen Nityâs, of Shiva himself, of Her own Self and of the other Devatâs. (2) How the same can be known. (3) What is the form of the Universe (Kimâkâram vishvam). (4) What are the merits (Pu*n*yas) and demerits (Pâpas) of creatures. (5) How or by what acts are they caused. (6) What are the causes which lead to their being born. (7) What is Liberation, (Mukti). (8) What is the world of birth and death (Samsâra). (9) Who gets Mukti. (10) What is the cause of bondage. (11) How is one liberated thereform. (12) What is the root of Samsâra. (13) What are the Tattvas. (14) What is intelligence (Dhî) (15) What are the Indriyas (Senses.) (16) What are Prâ*n*as. (17) What is Jîva. (18) What is Para, (i. e. what is beyond Jîva). (19) What is Time

(Kâla) and (20) What are the planets (Graha) The Devî ends Her questions by asking that Her questions may be answered in a manner authorised by the Vedas, the (Dharma) Shâstras, the Purâ*n*as and the Âgamas.

In verses 7 to 10 Shiva says that though these matters are of a secret character He will yet answer Her questions clearly. By listening thereto and controlling the wild longings one will fully know one's own true nature (Svasvarûpa) and conquer the evil proclivities with which one is born and thus participate in the true, pure, manifest and boundless Becoming. [Satya-shuddha-sphu*t*âshe*sh*a-sphurattâtmâ bhavet]. This is very secret and can be understood by the mercy of the Guru alone and should always and in every way be kept secret.

In verses 11 and first line of verse 12 he answers the first question. He says—there is the knowledge (Jnâna) of "This" and there is the knowledge (Jnâna) of "I". The transcendent Knowledge (Jnâna) which is Chaitanya and wherein both these are united is My Body. [The commentater says that Shiva pervades the universe as its Consciousness (Châitanya), like heat in a bar of hot iron, in the bodies consisting of the Bhûtas the Indriyas &c.] "This Body of Mine," the text proceeds, "is the Chaitanya of the sixteen Nityâs, of Thee and of other beings."

The second line of verse 12 and verse 13 answer the second question. It is here said that by the annihilation of evil desires (Durvâsanâ), the unchanging (Sthira) Âtmâ manifests Itself. This Âtmâ is eternal (Nitya) true and therefore without a second and great (Mahân i. e. not limited by time and space). It may also be attained by means laid down in Nityâ-h*ri*daya Tantra (i. e. Yoginî-h*ri*daya). Verse 14 answers the 3rd question Here Shiva says :—Shabda and Buddhi are of two kinds transcendental (Paramârtha-rûpa) and non-transcendental (Aparamârtha-rûpa) ; the latter pervades truth and untruth. The universe therefore appears to be so. Shiva answers the 4th question in the first line of verse 15 by saying "It is on account of the two fold character of Shabda and Buddhi that creatures become virtuous and sinful. Shabda and Buddhi and the Prapancha are the same in that which is true (Satya) and what is untrue".

In the second line of verse 15 and verse 16 He answers the 5th and 6th questions. He says: "That the exercise or functioning (Vyâpâra) of the senses (Indriyas) of a man who is prompted by true Jnâna is Pu*n*ya. It is Pâpa when the mind takes that to be right which is not so It is from the latter that various kinds of birth emanate." In verse 17 He answers four questions. True knowledge (Yâthârthye jnânam arthânâm) is Mukti. The reverse of this (Tadviparîtatâ) is Samsriti (= Samsâra). Liberation therefrom is by Buddhi. Desire is bondage.

In verse 18 the 11th question is answered, It is here said that by the destruction of Karma effected by Vedhadîkshâ by the Guru and by his word of instructions (Ukti) and also by meditating thereon (Vimarsha) is Liberation from bondage gained. In verse 19 the twelfth question is answered. The root (Kanda) of Samsriti (Samsâra) is Non-discrimination (Aviveka)—which is defined by the Commentary to mean the absence of a true knowledge of the difference between the body (Deha) and Âtmâ. This Aviveka the Text says is great for it pervades and rules all creation.

Verse 20 answers the thirteenth question. The Tattvas, it is said here, have been so called in all Tantras because they as Jnâtri, Jnâna, Jneya (Jnâtri-jnâna-jneya-mayâni) are in all bodies. They are so, says the commentary, as they are manifestations of and are one with Chaitanya (Chaitanyasya tâdâtmyena sphuranatvât).

The seventeen verses after this (vv. 21-37) in answering the 16th question describes the 107 qualities (Gunas) of Buddhi (Dhî) and how same are recognised After saying that Manas, Buddhi, Ahangkâra and Chitta are but different forms of Dhî the Text proceeds to give all the other different forms such as Sthûla, Sûkshma and others. In verse 35 Shiva says: "That aspect which is Tvanmayî (Shaktimayî) is Dhî and that aspect which is Manmayi (Shivamayî) is Chit. [The commentator says that it is Dhî or Buddhi when Chit has apprehension (Upalabdhi) of objects. It may be compared to fire actually seizing and consuming a piece of wood. Chit is the state (of Consciousness) in which there is no such apprehension. It may be compared to fire not acting upon but latent in a piece of wood.]

Verse 38 answers the 15th question. The Indriyas, it is said here, are the five Bhûta-shaktis whereby the mind functions on such objects as it wishes.

Verse 39 answers the 16th, 17th and 18th questions. The different manifestations (Vijrimbhana) of Chaitanya caused by the action thereon of Buddhi and the five Bhûtas are the Prânas (i. e. the Vâyus,—Prâna, Apâna, Samâna, Vyâna, Udâna). Jiva is the witness thereof (Tat-sâkshibhûta) [The Commentary says Jîva is that which goes not the way suggested by the body and senses (Deha and Indriya)]. Para is Tattva (Tattvâtmaka) because Tat is Truth. [The Commentary says that when Buddhi which in itself is apprehension of objects (Upalabdhi-svarûpinî) knows that the body and the senses are not the Self and is not affected thereby and thus resumes its true nature—as it were a fire which does not burn—then it is called Para].

Verses 40-47 answer the 19th question. Kâla, it is said, possesses all the qualities above enumerated as regards Buddhi. Shiva says: "Whatever the two letters in the word Kâla signify that is My Body. I cannot easily describe or show it to Thee, but will try to do so by illustration. Day succeeds night because of the movements by rotation of the sun, the moon and the other heavenly bodies. Therefore it is not right to speak of Time (Kâla) as identical with night and day (Tan-mayatâ-rûpam). Lava, Truti and other divisions of time are merely fractions of universal Time. The one nature (Rûpa) of Kâla is that Chit which has neither beginning nor end. Lava, Truti and the like are merely measures of (Anumîyate) Kâla. That is the true nature (Svarûpa) of Kâla, which is gained or known (Yat tu labhyate) by meditating thereon (Bhâvanât) according to the capacity of one's intelligence (Svabuddhyâ) Nothing more can be said about this."

Verses 48 and 49 answer the 20th question. The Grahas (Planets) are forms of Chit inseparate from Kâla (Kâlâprithag-rûpa-chid-rûpa). They go round and round at different times and in different places in continuous circles. By reason of this they make the Bhûtas (Elements) and others, undergo many changes. These many variations appear as the universe (Prapancha). It is by these Planets again that the Bhûtas and their modifications are destroyed.

In verses 50 to 54 the Devî says: "Lord though Thou hast answered my queries yet I have not gained a complete knowledge of the universe (Prapanchâtma-viveka)." Then She proceeds to ask twelve more questions. Who is born and who dies? Why is one born and why does he die? If the Jîva is of the formless omnipresent Âtmâ, then how and where does it exist (Kathang sthitih)? How and where do Kâla and Paramâtmâ abide? Is it the Liberated or the others who are born? Where are the five Bhûtas? Are they in the bodies (Deheshu) or outside them? How does the Jîva enter the body and how does it leave the body? To these Shiva replies (Vv. 55-56) that as a result of the actions (Karma-vipâkatah) caused by the variety of Buddhi (Buddhivaividhyena) about which I have spoken both birth and death take place. [The Commentater adds that the cause of birth and death (Janana-marana-kâranam) of the Jîva is the Egoism (Abhimâna) that the body is the Self]. The relation between Supreme (Para) and the Universe (Vishva) is like fire in a piece of heated metal. Kâla and Para are one with the other (Tâdâtmya). The Liberated (Muktâh) never become Jîvas on any account, nor are any born who have not previously been born (Apûrvâh). Buddhi makes its individualising impress on the form of Jîva, just as a seal (Mudrikâ) makes its mark on a bit of bees' wax (Madhûchchhishta).

The Text (Vv. 59, 60) then deals with Earth, Water, Fire, Air and Ether, the last of which is all pervading (Sarvaga) and one with Time (Kâla-tâdrûpyatah). They are in bodies.

The coming (Âgati) of the Jîva (V. 61), into the body composed of the five Elements, is the result of the union of the Vîryas (Seeds), that is, Shukra and Shonita of the father and mother. Their union (Tâdâtmyam sangatam) manifests as the individualised Chit. When, as in the case of the Siddhas, there is a cessation (Viramana) of that which produces the sense of I-ness (Ahamiti upalabdhih) which is the result of Prârabdhakarma, death is like sleep and there is no change when they leave the body. [The Commentator says :—By the Will (Svechchhayâ) of the impartite Chit (Anavachchhinnachit), that which is the Svarûpa of Buddhi which is apprehension (Upalabdhisvarûpa) in bodies, becomes Jîva and goes out through the senses (Indriya-dvârâ vahirgatâ) and experiences (Anubhavati) the things of the Objective World (Vishayân). This is the Wakeful State (Jâgradavasthâ). When it detaches itself from the senses and remaining in the heart experiences whatever is therein, it is said to be in a Dreamful State (Svapnâvasthâ). When it detaches itself from the heart also and rests (Vishrâmyati) in the Consciousness (Chaitanya) which is the Paramârtha, it is said to be in a state of Dreamless Sleep (Sushuptyavasthâ). To the Siddha who is Chitsvarûpa, to whom birth and death are like the reflection of the Moon in water, the latter is therefore like dreamless sleep]. For they know the true relation of body and Self by the initiation (i. e. by Vedha or Drig Dîkshâ) of the good Guru. In the case of the ordinary man, (Itara = Pâmara), the Sâdhyas and the Sâdhakas this is not so. [The Commentary says that the Sâdhyas, though they are initiated by a good Guru (Sad-guru-katâkshe satyapi), are yet by reason of their propensities occupied in ritual and averse from making any attempt to know the true nature of the body and the Âtmâ. The Sâdhakas although they, by the initiation of the Sad-guru, have attained some apprehension of the Paramârtha, are not fully rid of their natural propensities]. These three classes only lose their attachment for the body when severed therefrom (by death).

Death during the six months (Vv 65, 66) beginning with Paus*h*a (mid December to mid January), between the 8th day of the light half of the lunar months and the 8th day of the dark half, indicates that the person so dying has gone upon a Good Path (Sugati). The Siddha has previously (to death) been freed from (attachment to) the body, the senses and the mind and whenever, wherever, and howsoever he may leave the body he goes the Good Path, for he was liberated whilst living (Jîvanmukta).

In verse 67 the Devî asks :—Lord, all creatures have bodies but why are their Buddhis so multiform ? In verse 68 Shiva says :—The taste (Rasa) of water depends on the nature of the soil on which it is. The same is the case with Buddhi. This again is the result of Karma.

Verses 69-71 state, that without the help of the Sadguru and one's own efforts nothing can be gained. Through the aid of both, man realises his Svarûpa. The Devî then (V. 72) asks :—What is gained by the service of the Sad-guru ? Verses 73-81 give in reply the forty-seven qualities acquired by the service of the Sad-guru which produces Self-knowledge (Âtmajnâna). Such a man looks upon all as himself (Âbhirûpya = Sarvâtmabhâva). He is free from all doubts in spite of conflicting Shrutis. He is full of contentment as he has realized himself and has a feeling of his Completeness (Paripûr*n*atâ). He is always merciful and free from both attachment (Râga) and hatred (Dves*h*a). He is easily accessible and free from pride, and is self-controlled (Niyata-shîla). He is grateful. His concern is Truth and not the affairs of others. He is honest and humble (Ârjava). He seeks not wealth. His attachment, to anything outside himself, is only to the extent necessary for the preservation of his body. He is free from procrastination and meanness and excessive longings.

He does not indulge in idle converse and useless pursuits, nor in harmful enjoyment. He avoids the society of the deceitful. He delights in talking of the aims of humanity (Purus*h*ârtha) and in thought of the same. It is not in him to take what belongs to another. He is full of faith (Âstikya) and ever thinks of the world to come (Paraloka). He is constantly engaged in worshipping, singing hymns of praise of, and in conversation regarding the greatness (Vaibhava) of, the Devatâs. He avoids sin and seeks merit. He is indifferent to the praise and censure of others, and is free from all attachment. He desires nothing and is never agitated. He regrets nothing (Anâk*sh*epa or, if the variant reading Anapek*sh*a be taken, he depends on no one or is free from partiality), He is always alert. He conceals nothing (the Âgamas and the like) from the believers, but, does conceal them from the non-believers. He praises and upholds the Guru, the Vidyâ (Mantra), the Âgamas and the customs. These are the signs of Siddhas. The ignorant calumniate them.

Verses 82 to 90 describe the daily practice of those who have realised the Âtmâ (Âtmavatâm).

Verses 91-96 explain how the Jîvanmuktas who have realised the Âtmâ do ritual worship

In verse 97 to 99 Shiva says :—By a complete knowledge of this Tantra a man attains union with Thee (i. e. Shakti) and Me (Shiva). It should not be communicated to a non-believer (Abhakta), who is not a disciple, to a hypocrite, to one who does wrong in secret, to one who does not beg for it, to an atheist (Nâstika), nor to a covetous, proud, idle or sinful man, or one who cannot keep a secret. It should not on any account be communicated for gain.

In verse 100 Shiva says, that the man who worships in manner enjoined herein becomes one with Himself, that is, becomes Chitsvarûpa.

Each Chapter, Thirty-six in number, of the Tantrarâja is named after one of the thirtysix Tattvas. At the end of the first chapter which deals with Descent or Revelation of the Tantra and the like (Tantrâvatârâdi), it is said that the Vyâpti herein is "Earth" (Bhûmitattva). Vyâpti means "Omnipresence" "Universal pervasion." It here means that Bhûmitattva is that which this chapter signifies and so with the other Tattvas. The text further says that, by the full understanding (Niphâlana) of this Vyâpti, complete mastery or control is obtained (Svâtma-sât-k*ri*tam) over that Tattva (i. e. Bhûmîtattva).

The second chapter which deals with the Nâthas (i. e. the Gurus of the three classes namely the Divya, the Siddha and the Mânava—see Chapter 36) ends with a verse stating that the Vyâpti of this chapter is "Water" (Toyatattva). By its Niphâlana, that Tattva is completely mastered (Svâtma-sât-k*ri*tam). The third chapter which deals with Nityoddhâra (i. e. gives the formation of the Vidyâs or Mantras of the sixteen Nityâs and of Vârâhî and Kurukullâ) in its last verse states that the Vyâpti is "Fire" (Vahnitattva). The Vyâpti of the fourth chapter, which speaks of the identity of Lalitâvidyâ with the Gurus and so forth, is "Air" (Vâyutattva) ; and the Vyâpti of chapter V., which speaks of the daily worship (Nityapûjâ) of Lalitâ, is "Ether" (Vyomatattva). Chapter VI deals with the rites which are Naimittaka (occasional) and Kâmya (i. e. for gaining objects of desire). The Vyâpti of this chapter is "Smell" (Gandhatattva) which is the Guṇa of Bhûmi or Prithivî. Chapter VII contains ritual rules relating to the worship of Kâmeshvarî, the second Nityâ, who is the first of the Nityâs who are the limbs of Lalitâ. This chapter is "Fluidity" (Rasatattva). The eighth chapter which gives the ritual of the third Nityâ, Bhagamâlinî, is "Form" (Rûpatattva). The ninth chapter describes the rituals of Nitya-klinnâ. Its Vyâpti is "Touch" (Sparsha-tattva) The tenth chapter relates to Bheruṇḍâ. The Vyâpti is "Sound" (Shabdatattva). The eleventh chapter deals with Vahnivâsinî. The Vyâpti is the "Genital Organ" (Yonitattva) The twelfth chapter gives the rules of worship of the seventh Nityâ Mahâvajreshvarî. The Vyâpti of this is "Anus" (Pâyutattva). The thirteenth chapter relates to the eighth Nityâ named Dûtî. The Vyâpti is "Feet" (Pâdatattva). The fourteenth chapter gives the rules relating to the worship of the ninth Nityâ, Tvaritâ. The Vyâpti is "Hands" (Pâṇitattva). The tenth Nityâ is Kûlasundarî. The fifteenth chapter contains the rules (Vidhâna) relating to her worship. The Vyâpti is "Speech" (Vâktattva). The eleventh Nityâ is Nityâ. The sixteenth chapter contains the rituals relating to her worship. The Vyâpti of this is "Vital" Function (Prâṇatattva). The seventeenth chapter deals with twelfth Nityâ named Nîlapatâkâ the Vyâpti of which is "Tongue" (Jihvâtattva). The thirteenth Nityâ is Vijayâ. The eighteenth chapter contains the rules relating to her Sâdhanâ and the Vyâpti here is "Eye" (Netratattva). The nineteenth chapter contains the rituals of Sarvamangalâ. The Vyâpti of this chapter is sense of "Smell" (Ghrâṇatattva). The twentieth chapter relates to Jvâlâmâlinî. The Vyâpti of this chapter is "Sense of Hearing" (Shrotratattva). The next chapter deals with the last of the sixteen Nityâs by name Chitrâ. The Vyâpti is "Egoism.' (Ahangkâratattva). The twenty-second chapter contains details of the rituals relating to Kurukullâ. The Vyâpti is Buddhitattva. The twenty-third chapter relates to Vârâhî. The Vyâpti is "Mind" (Manastattva). The twenty-fourth chapter contains various meditations (Dhyâna) of the sixteen Nityâs and the Vyâpti of this chapter is Prakrityâtmamayî. The twenty-fifth is the Mâtrikâpti chapter and describes how the thirty six consonant (Vyanjana) letters are thirty-six Tattvas and how the Mantras and Yantras are formed and in this way demonstrates the identity of the sixteen Nityâs with the Mâtrikâs and

Time (Mâtrikâtmakatva and Kâlâtmakatva). The Vyâpti of this chapter is Purushâtmamayî. The twenty-sixth speaks of the Greatness (Vaibhava) of Mantra The Vyâpti is Niyamâtmamayî. The twenty-seventh chapter demonstrates the identity of the sixteen Nityâs as also of the Mâtrikas, the Nâthas, the Shrîchakra and the Shaktis with Prâna. The Vyâpti is Kâlatattvamayî. The twenty-eighth chapter speaks of the identity of the sixteen Nityâs with Time and Space (Kâla and Loka). The Vyâpti is Râgatattvamayî. The twenty-ninth chapter contains directions relating to the mode of making of Mandapas and Kundas for doing Homa to the sixteen Nityâs and the Vyâpti of this chapter is Vidyâtattva. The Vyâpti of the thirtieth chapter which describes Vâstu-Devatâ-chakra of the sixteen Nityâs is Kalâtattvamayî. The thirty-first chapter contains rituals relating to crushing an enemy (Arimardana Homa) and the Vyâpti of this chapter is Mâyâtattvamayî. The Vyâpti of the thirty-second chapter is Shuddhavidyâ. The subject of the chapter is Saumya Homa, that is, Homa done with the object of attaining wealth, prosperity, a life free from trouble and the like. The thirty-third chapter speaks of some Yantras by which objects of desire may be gained. The Vyâpti is Îshvarâtmamayî. The next chapter speaks of certain rites whereby extraordinary results are obtained. The Vyâpti is Sadâshivamayî The thirty-fifth chapter speaks of the identity of the sixteen Nityâs with the Sâdhaka. It is called the Vâsanâpatala. The Vyâpti is Shaktitattvamayî. The thirty-sixth chapter says that the Siddha in the Vidyâs of the sixteen Nityâs is one with the Paramârtha or supreme Brahman. The Vyâpti is Shivatattvamayî.

The commentary on Chapter I—XXII is by Subhagânandanâtha and that on the rest of the book is by his disciple Prakâshânanda Deshika.

OXFORD,
25th January, 1926.

ARTHUR AVALON.

सूचीपत्रम् ।

विषयः	पृष्ठायाम्

प्रथमपटले ।

द्वितीयपटले ।

तृतीयपटले ।

चतुर्थपटले ।

पञ्चम पटले ।

षष्ठपटले ।

सप्तमपटले ।

अष्टमपटले ।

नवम पटले ।

दशम पटले ।

एकादशपटले ।

द्वादशपटले ।

त्रयोदशपटले ।

चतुर्द्दशपटले ।

——

पञ्चदशपटले ।

——

षोडशपटले ।

——

सप्तदशपटले ।

अष्टादशपटले ।

ऊनविंशपटले ।

विंशपटले ।

एकविंशपटले ।

द्वाविंशपटले ।

त्रयोविंशपटले ।

——

चतुर्विंशपटले ।

पञ्चविंशपटले ।

षड् विंशपटले ।

सप्तविंशपटले ।

—

अष्टाविंशपटले ।

एकोनत्रिंशपटले ।

त्रिंशपटले ।

एकविंशपटले ।

द्वात्रिंशपटले ।

त्रयस्त्रिंशपटले ।

चतुस्त्रिंशपटले ।

पञ्चत्रिंशपटले ।

षट्त्रिंशपटले ।

समाप्तमिदं सूचीपत्रम् ।

शुद्धिपत्रम् ।

एतत् पुस्तकमुद्राङ्कणानन्तरं प्राप्तपुस्तकान्तरे ये ये अधिका न्यूना विभिन्नाकारा वा पाठा लभ्यन्ते तेऽप्यत्र शुद्धिपत्रे सन्निवेशिता इति ।

अशुद्धः ।	शुद्धः	पत्रे	पङ्क्तौ
पूज्यं	पूज्ये	६	४
सिद्धे	सिद्धः	१०	१
नि: फालना	निफालना*	१८	१
वपृण	वस्त्र	३२	८
पयसाचरवगिनीं	पयश्चाचरवर्गिणीम्	३८	१
मात्राष्टकं	मात्रष्टकं	३८	१
न्ये नैका	येनैका	७६	८
निष्फालना	निफालना	८५	४
सुर	पुर	८८	८
श्रोमा	श्रोम्मा	८८	१०
मेवच	मे वद	८९	४
मूर्त्तिष्टे न्यस्तविग्रहा:	मुक्तिष्ठेन्न्यस्तविग्रहः	८९	६
योगिनो	योगिनी:	९२	१०
स्त्रोस्व	स्त्रोषु	१०२	८
स्वेचि	स्वेति	१०४	६
जेष्ठे	ज्येष्ठे	१०८	७
पीताश्वेता	पीतश्वेता	११४	७
स्वकीयविवेकैः	स्वकीयाविवेकैः	१२३	१८
द्वितीय तृतीया	द्वितीया	१२७	२४
विघोधः	विश्रो:	१२८	२३
दुक्रमेण	दुत्क्रमेण	१६४	१४
सन्देहेत्ये	सन्देहति	१८९	११

* प्रतिपटलं पटलसमाप्तिकाले "निफालनात्" इति पाठो ज्ञेयः ।

न्यासन्नेव समीरितम्	न्यासएव समीरित:	१८३	४
दधाना माधुकाभीष्ट	दधानां साधकाभीष्ट	२२२	७
साधकम्	साधक:	२३१	१
मातृकाचरा:	मातृकाचरजा:	३३८	१५
मतानी	मतान्यम्निदेवतानी	३३८	१७
तेषु स्थानेषु	अत: परम् "अस्खौं आ स्खौं इ स्खौं इत्यादि ऋ: स्खौं इत्यन्तं ५७६ अस्खं अस्खां अस्खिं अस्खीं अस्खुं अस्खूं अस्खृं अस्खॄं अस्खॢं अस्खॣं अस्खें अस्खैं अस्खों अस्खौं अस्खं अस्ख: आस्खां आस्खिं इत्यादि क्षा स्ख: ८२१६" इत्यधिक: ।	३४०	१८
एवं पूर्वोक्त	एवं पूर्वपूर्वोक्त	३४१	१८
तथा लक्ष्मी	तथा यथा लक्ष्मी	३४४	२१
ग्रत्यधिक	ग्रत्याद्यधिक	३४८	१न
चित्ते	क्षिप्ते	३५४	८
अष्टास्त्र:	अष्टास्रत:	३५६	१८
कोणि	कोणेषु	३५६	२४
षड्ष्टास्नान्तरालेषु	अत: परम् "षट्कोणान्तरालेषु अष्टकोणान्तरालेषु" इत्यधिक:	३६०	२२
साध्या	सा साध्या	३६३	१८
मत:	मन:	३६४	१३
लोहैर्विरचितपट्टे	त्रिलोहविरचिते पट्टे	३६६	१८
इदमेव	दरदमेव	३६७	१७
मप्युक्त:	मप्युच्च:	३६८	१८
कूला	कूलेत्र	३७०	१८
वासम्	वासरम्	३७१	२५
मूलदेवताया	मूलदेवतया	३७२	१४
प्रोक्ते	प्रोत्थे	३७३	१३
परितना	परितनोपरितना	३७५	१४
योन्येव	योन्येव	३७७	१४
कोण	त्रिकोण	३८३	८
हृतं	ह्रुतं	३८३	१६

समरेखं	समत्रिरेखं	३८३	१८
शतिस	शतिस्	३८४	१३
वज्ञ	वर्जं	३८५	८.
इत्येकस्य	इत्येकैकस्य	३८८	२१
भिन्नान्न	मुद्गभिन्नान्न	३९२	१७
मिथुनानां	प्रयोगवलिप्रदाने च मिथुनानां	३९३	६
तन्मध्यस्थल	तन्मध्ये वृत्त	३९५	२४
मन्त्रा	अंशा	३९७	१६
यद्वा	यष्ट्वा	३९७	१८
संख्येषु कोष्ठेष्वित्यर्थ:	संख्यानि कोष्ठानि मार्जयेदित्यथ:	४०८	२७
ध्यानं	प्रयोगेषु च ध्यानं	४१४	२६
रत्नाभि:	रनत्नाभि:	४१६	४
प्रलापनाम जल्पविशेष:	पलायनाख्यपजय विशेष:	४१६	२६
दामै:	वामै:	४१७	१४
चतुर्थजस्य	चतुर्थभुजस्य	४१७	२२
सहित	यामसहित	४२०	१४
पदा३२दष्टादशा१८त् खाग्ने ३०नेखा१०स्तत:	पदात्३२खाग्ने३०नेखा१० दष्टादशा१८स्तत:	४२०	१८
कहोम	करहोम	४२३	११
अष्टकोणि	अष्टकोण कोणे	४२५	१८
त्मकं	ष्टकं	४२५	२२
कृत्वा	अत:परं 'तदन्तरालेप्राग्वत् समत्रिरेखं त्रिकोणं कृत्वा-पुनस्त्रिकोणवाह्य वृत्तादहिस्तवृत्तविष्कम्भार्द्ध-मानेन वृत्तं कृत्वा" इत्यधिक:	४२६	११
स्तम्भय	स्तम्भय स्तम्भय	४२८	२४
वीथ्यां	अत:परं "प्राङ् मध्यकोष्ठात् रेखाग्राणि वाह्यवृत्त-गतैकादशसंख्यानीतिशेष:। साध्यञ्च मध्यत: इत्यत्र चकारेण कर्णिकायां सर्ववाह्यवीथि" इत्यधिक:	४३३	१०
सर्वा: परि	सर्वा: सपरि	४३५	२७

सुष्ठ्वा	स्वच्छा	४३६	८
स्थयोः प्राग्	स्थयोः वामदक्षक्रमेण चापसायकौ तदधः स्थयोः प्राग्	४४०	१२
शेषः ।	अतःपरं "कोदण्डनिवहमित्यनेन प्रतिभुजं कोदण्डमित्यर्थः । अन्यैर्दक्षिणभुजैर्नवभिरिति शेषः । शरभिन्नकलेवरां शरभिन्न शरीरां । प्रोक्तां प्राग्वदरिसेनाविनाशादिप्रकारेण । अथवा पक्षान्तरे । नवभिर्भुजैरिति शेषः । अन्यैर्दक्षिणभुजैर्नवभिरिति शेषः ।" इत्यधिकः	४४२	२६
शक्र	चन्द्र	५८१	१३
वर्गं	वर्गेषु	५८८	२१
दिगक्ताः	द्विग्वक्ताः	५८७	२३
लग्न	लग्ने	६००	२१
स्थित्य	स्थिति	६८२	२०
व्यन्यक्तोरव	व्यनक्तोरव	७३२	२

———

समाप्तमिदं शुद्धिपत्रम् ।

श्रीश्रीतन्त्रराजतन्त्रम् ।

श्रीश्रीतन्त्रराजतन्त्रम् ।

श्रीआर्थार् एवलनेन प्रवर्त्तितं पर्य्यवेक्षितञ्च ।

महामहोपाध्यायश्रीलक्ष्मणशास्त्रिणा सम्पादितम् ।

कलिकातानगर्य्यां

महामायायन्त्रे

श्रीसिद्धेश्वरचतुर्धुरिणा मुद्रितम् ।

लण्डनराजधान्यां लुज्याक् एण्ड् कों कर्त्तकेण

प्रकाशितम् ।

खृः १९१८ ।

श्रीगणेशाय नमः ।

अथ तन्त्रराजः

मनोरमाटीकासहितः ।

प्रथमः पटलः ।

अनाद्यन्तोऽपराधीनः स्वाधीनभुवनत्रयः ।
जयत्यविरतो (१) व्याप्तविश्वः कालो विनायकः ॥ १ ॥

मनोरमाटीका प्रारभ्यते ।

श्रीगणेशाय नमः ।

आद्यश्लोकेन प्रबन्धवाक्यार्थगर्भं विनायकस्तुतिः क्रियते । तत्र अनाद्यन्तः (२) कालस्याऽऽद्यन्तरहितत्वात् । अपराधीनः—इतरप्रेरणाविधुरः । स्वाधीनभुवनत्रयः—स्वायत्तमातृमानमेयात्मभुवनत्रयः । जयति—विश्वोत्कृष्टोभवतीत्यर्थः (३) अविरतः—कालस्य सन्तन्यमानत्वात् । व्याप्तविश्वः—देशरूपाभ्यामनवच्छिन्नत्वात् । कालइति विशेषणस्य नाम । विनायकः विघ्नेश्वरो विगतनायक इति च । एतदुक्तं भवति-एवमुक्तः कालरूपो विनायकः सर्वोत्कृष्टो भवतीति तथाविधो विगतनायकः कालो विश्वोत्कृष्टो भवतीति च । तेन कालरूपपरमार्थाया ललितानित्याया विश्वमयत्वं साधकानां तादात्म्यं च प्रबन्धवाक्यार्थत्वेनात्र सूचितमित्युपदिशन्ति पूज्यपादाः ॥ १ ॥

---

(१) जयत्यपुरत इति मूलपुस्तकपाठः ।

(२) अनाद्यन्तस्तु इति १ पु० पा० ।

(३) इत्यर्थ इति १ पु-नास्ति ।

भगवन् ! सर्व्वं तन्त्राणि भवतोक्तानि मे पुरा ।
नित्यानां षोड़शानां च नवतन्त्राणि कृत्स्नशः ॥ २ ॥
तेषामन्योन्यसापेक्ष्या(१)ज्जायते मतिविभ्रमः ।
तस्मात्तु निरपेक्षं मे तन्त्रं तासां वद प्रभो ! ॥ ३ ॥
शृणु कादिमतं तन्त्रं पूर्णमन्यानपेक्षया ।
गोप्यं सर्वप्रयत्नेन गोपनं तन्त्रचोदितम् ॥ ४ ॥
कथं कादिमतं नाम्ना तन्त्रं ब्रूहि महेश्वर ! ।
कादिकालीतिशक्तौ स्तः (२) पुरा तत्तन्मते मया ॥ ५ ॥
प्रोक्ते तन्त्रे कादिकालीमताख्ये तेन नामतः ।
शृणु तत्सर्वतन्त्राणां राजानं सर्वसिद्धिदम् ॥ ६ ॥
कादिसंज्ञा भवद्रूपा सा शक्तिः सर्वसिद्धये ।
तन्त्रं मदुक्तं भुवने नवनाथैरकल्पयत् ॥ ७ ॥
तया तैर्भुवने तन्त्रं कल्पे कल्पे विजृम्भते ।
अवसानेषु कल्पानां सा तैः सार्द्धं व्रजेच्च माम् ॥ ८ ॥

अथ भगवन्नित्यादिभिः व्रजेच्च मामित्यन्तैः सप्तभिः श्लोकैस्तन्त्रावतार क्रममुपदिशति। तत्र सर्वतन्त्राणि नित्याषोड़शकार्णवोक्तरुद्रयामलादिचतुःषष्टिमुखानि तन्त्राणि। नवतन्त्राणि—सुन्दरीहृदयनित्याषोड़शकार्णवचन्द्रज्ञानमातृकातन्त्रसंमोहनतन्त्रवामकेश्वरबहुरूपाष्टकप्रस्तारचिन्तामणिमेरु(३)प्रस्ताराख्यानि इति। अन्योन्यसापेक्ष्यात्—तन्त्रान्तरोक्तार्थपूजाङ्गीकारेणोक्तत्वात्। विभ्रमः—व्यामोहः। तासां—षोड़शानां नित्यानाम्। अन्यानपेक्षया—इतरतन्त्रोक्तार्थपूजाङ्गीकारमकृत्वोपदेशात्। गोपनं तन्त्रचोदितमिति—पञ्चविंशे पटले षट्पञ्चाशत्श्लोकोक्तसङ्केतविधानेनेत्यर्थः। नवनाथैः—द्वितीयपटले प्रतिपादितस्वरूपैः। अकल्पयत्—प्रसारयति स्म। तया—कादिशक्त्या। तैः—नवनाथैः। सा तैः सार्द्धं व्रजेच्च मां—कल्पावसानेषु सा

---

(१) सापेक्षादिति मू० पु० पा०। (२) कादिकालीतिशक्त्यास्तां इति मो० पु० पा०। कालिकादितिशक्तौस्तः पुरा तत्तन्मतान्मया इतिमू लपुस्तकपाठः। (३) मरु इति मो० पु० पा०।

आद्ये तन्त्रावतारादि द्वितीये नाथमण्डलम् ।
नित्योद्धारस्तृतीये स्यात् ललितार्चा तयोर्द्वयोः ॥ ९ ॥
नैमित्तिकं तथा काम्यमर्चनं षष्ठके भवेत् ।
कामेश्वरी सप्तमके परतो भगमालिनी ॥ १० ॥
नित्यक्लिन्ना तु नवमे भेरुण्डा दशमे स्मृता ।
एकादशे वह्निवासिन्यथ वज्रेश्वरी मता ॥ ११ ॥
त्रयोदशे भवेद्दूती त्वरिता स्याच्चतुर्दशे ।
कुलसुन्दर्य्यतोऽन्यस्मिन् नित्यानित्या तु षोड़शे ॥ १२ ॥
ततो नीलपताका स्यात् विजयाऽष्टादशे (१) परे ।
सर्वमङ्गलनित्याऽतो (२) ज्वालामालिनिसंज्ञिका (३) ॥१३॥
एकविंशतिमे चित्रा कुरुकुल्ला त्वनन्तरे ।
त्रयोविंशे तु वाराहीध्यानानि तदनन्तरे ॥ १४ ॥
पञ्चविंशे मातृकाप्तिः (४) षड्विंशे मन्त्रवैभवाः ।
सप्तविंशे (५) श्वासरूपा अष्टाविंशे तु लोकता ॥ १५ ॥
अनन्तरे कुण्डक्लृप्तिस्तदूर्द्ध्वं होमकर्म्म च (६) ।

कादिशक्तिर्नवनाथैस्तन्त्रेण च सार्द्धं मयि विलीना तिष्ठतीत्यर्थः । ॥ २ ॥ ३ ॥
॥ ४ ॥ ५ ॥ ६ ॥ ७ ॥ ८ ॥

आद्य इत्यादिभिः सङ्गृह इत्यन्तैः दशभिः श्लोकैस्तत्पटलान् तदर्थांश्चोपदिशति । तयोर्द्वयोः—चतुर्थपञ्चमयोः (७) । परतः—अष्टमे । अथ द्वादशे (८)

---

(१) षोड़शे इति मूलपुस्तकपाठः ।　　(२) नित्यान्त इति सो० पु० पा० ।

(३) संज्ञिता इति मू० पु० पा० ।　　(४) मातृकोक्ता इति सो० पु० पा० ।

(५) षड्विंशे इति मू० पु० पा० ।　　(६) स्तदूर्द्ध्वं होमकर्मैव च इति मूलपुस्तकपाठः ।

(७) तत्र द्वये चतुर्थपञ्चमके इति सो० पु० पा० । तत्र द्वये चतुर्थपञ्चके इति व० पु० पा० ।

(८) अत ऊर्द्ध्वं विंशे इति सो० अधिकः पाठः ।

एकत्रिंशे तदूर्द्ध्वं च होमाः काम्या महोदयाः (१) ॥ १६ ॥
त्रयस्त्रिंशे तु पटले यन्त्राणि फलभेदतः ।
चतुस्त्रिंशे तु नामानि (२) पञ्चत्रिंशेऽस्य वासना ॥ १७ ॥
षट्त्रिंशे स्वात्मकथनमध्यायास्तत्वविग्रहाः ।
प्रत्यध्यायं शतश्लोकाः स्यादेवं तन्त्रसंग्रहः ॥ १८ ॥
सुन्दरः सुमुखः स्वच्छः सुलभो बहुतन्त्रवित् ।
असंशयः संशयच्छिन्निरपेक्षो गुरुर्मतः ॥ १९ ॥
सौन्दर्यमनवद्यत्वं रूपे सौमुख्यता पुनः ।
स्मेरपूर्वाभिभाषित्वं स्वच्छताऽजिह्मवृत्तिता ॥ २० ॥
सौलभ्यमपरागर्वित्वं सन्तोषो बहुतन्त्रता ।
असंशयस्तत्वबोधे तच्छक्तिप्रतिपादनात् ॥ २१ ॥
नैरपेक्ष्यमवित्तेच्छा गुरुत्वं हितवादिता ।
एवंविधो गुरुर्ज्ञेयस्त्वितरः शिष्यदुःखदः ॥ २२ ॥
चतुर्भिरांद्यैः संयुक्तः श्रद्धावान् सुस्थिराशयः ।

अन्यस्मिन्—पञ्चदशके । ततः—सप्तदशे । परं—एकोनविंशे । अतः—विंशे । अनन्तरे—द्वाविंशे । तदनन्तरे—चतुर्विंशे । अनन्तरे—एकोनत्रिंशे । तदूर्द्ध्वे—त्रिंशत्तमे । तदूर्द्ध्वे—द्वात्रिंशे । अस्य—उपासनादेः । तत्वविग्रहाः—षट्त्रिंशत्सङ्ख्याविशिष्टत्वात्, ॥ ८ ॥ १० ॥ ११ ॥ १२ ॥ १३ ॥ १४ ॥ १५ ॥ १६ ॥ १७ ॥ १८ ॥

सुन्दर इत्यादिभिः दुःखद इत्यन्तैश्चतुर्भिः श्लोकैर्देशिकलक्षणमुपदिशति । तत्र सन्तोषः पूर्णता । प्रतिपादनात्(३)तत्त्वस्य । इतरः उक्तलक्षणविहीनो-देशिकः । शिष्यदुःखदः—शिष्यस्य वित्तापहारशरीरक्लेशबुद्धिव्यामोहादिभिरित्यर्थः ॥ १९ ॥ २० ॥ २१ ॥ २२ ॥

---

(१) होमात्काम्यफलोदयं इति मो० पु० पा० । (२) नमोंणि इति मू० पु० पा० ।
(३) प्रतिपादनात्त्वस्येति मो० व० पु० पा० ।

अलुब्धः स्थिरगात्रश्च प्रेक्षाकारी जितेन्द्रियः ॥२३॥
आस्तिको दृढभक्तिश्च गुरौ मन्त्रे सदैवते ।
एवंविधो भवेच्छिष्यस्त्वितरो दुःखकृद्गुरोः ॥२४॥
गुरूच्यमाने वचने दद्यादित्थं वचः सदा ।
प्रसीद नाथ ! देवेति तथेति च कृतादरम् ॥२५॥
प्रणम्योपविशेत्पार्श्वे तथा गच्छेदनुज्ञया ।
मुखावलोकी सेवेत कुर्य्यादादिष्टमादरात् ॥२६॥
असत्यं न वदेदग्रे न बहु प्रलपेदपि ।
कामं क्रोधं तथा लोभं मानं प्रहसनं स्तुतिम् ॥२७॥
चापलानि च जिह्मानि नर्माणि (१) परिदेवनम् (२)।
ऋणादानं तथाऽऽदानं वस्तूनां क्रयविक्रयम् ॥२८॥
न कुर्याद्गुरुणा सार्द्धं शिष्यो भूष्णुः कदाचन ।
यतो गुरुः शिवः साक्षात्तं स्तुवन् प्रणमन् भजेत् ॥२९॥
यथा देवे तथा मन्त्रे यथा मन्त्रे तथा गुरौ ।

चतुरिभिरित्यादिना गुरोरितग्न्तेन श्लोकद्वयेन शिष्यलक्षणमुपदिशति, तत्र चतुर्भिराद्यैः संयुक्तः—गुरोर्लक्षणत्वेनोक्तैः सुन्दरत्वादिभिश्चतुर्भिर्विशेषणैः उपेतः। इतरः—उक्तगुणविहीनः (३) दुःखकृत् गुरोः—अकीर्त्यनर्थचित्तदेहक्लेशाद्यैः ॥ २२ ॥ २३ ॥ २४ ॥

गुरूच्यमान इत्यादिभिः प्रणमन् भजेदित्यन्तैः पञ्चभिः श्लोकैः शिष्याचारक्रममुपदिशति। तत्र स्तुतिः—स्वात्मपरयोः। जिह्मानि—कुटिलानि। परिदेवनं—प्रलापः। भूष्णुः—जिजीविषुः। भजेत् सेवेत ॥ २५॥२६॥२७॥२८॥

यथा देवे इत्यादिभिर्भक्तिसमन्वित इत्यन्तैर्दशभिःश्लोकैः पूज्यपादो-

---

(१) कार्याणि इति सो० पु० पा०।

(२) परिवेदनमिति मू० पु० पा०।

(३) उक्तलक्षणविहीन इति सो० व० पु० पाठः।

यथा गुरौ तथा स्वात्मन्येवं भक्तिक्रमः प्रिये ! ॥३०॥
गुरोस्तु जन्मदिवसे कुर्यादुत्सवमादरात् ।
विशेषपूजां योगिभ्यो भोजनं तत्पदार्चनम् ॥३१॥
व्याप्ते दूरगते पूज्यं पूजयेदग्रजादिषु ।
एकदेशे नितरांसेवा दूरस्थे योजनक्रमात् ॥३२॥
एकादि ऋतुसंख्या वर्षे षड्योजनान्तरे ।
ततोऽदूरगते सेवा तदाज्ञापरिपालनम् ॥३३॥
आसनं शयनं वस्त्रं भूषणं पादुकां तथा ।
छायां कलत्रमन्यच्च यत्तस्येष्टं (१) तु पूजयेत् ॥३४॥
एकग्रामे पृथक्पूजां न कुर्यादननुज्ञया ।
पूजामध्ये समायाते पूज्ये नत्वा स्थितिं वदेत् ॥३५॥
विधेर्हि शेषमित्युक्तः कुर्यान्नो चेत्तदाज्ञया ।
वर्तेत सोऽपि तच्छेषं कुर्यान्निश्चलमानसः ॥३६॥
पूजामध्ये गुरौ पूज्ये त्वन्ये वाऽपि समागते ।
कृत्यमेवं समुद्दिष्टं मौनं तैर्न समाचरेत् ॥३७॥
गुरुं न मर्त्यं बुध्येत यदि बुध्येत तस्य तु ।

पास्तिक्रममुपदिशति। तत्र व्याप्ते—लोकान्तरं गते। दूरगते—वक्ष्यमाणषड्योजनादुपरिसङ्ख्याविशिष्टयोजनदेशं गते। अग्रजादिषु गुरुं तदग्रज (२) इत्याद्युपरिष्टात् वक्ष्यमाणानुपदिशत्यादिशब्देन। एकदेशे-ग्रामनगरमण्डलखेटखर्वटपत्तनादिषु गुरुशिष्ययोः स्थितौ। योजनक्रमात्-दूरस्थ इत्यन्वयः। एकग्राम इति पूर्वोक्तनगरादीनामुपलक्षणम्। पृथक्पूजां—गुरुमन्तरेणान्येषां

---

(१) यत्तत्स्पृष्टं तु इति सी० पु० पा० ।
(२) तदग्रत इति टी० पु० पाठः ।

न कदापि भवेत्सिद्धिर्मन्त्रैर्वा देवपूजनैः ॥३८॥
मन्त्रेण तस्य नियतं पूजां कुर्य्याद्यथोदिताम्।
तां च तत्पटले सम्यक् ज्ञात्वा भक्तिसमन्वितः ॥३९॥
नित्यानां त्वैपुराणां च नाविच्छ्यास्त्वंशकादयः।
तथाप्यत्रोच्यते किञ्चिदभिचारादिसिद्धये ॥४०॥
अश्विन्यादिषु ऋक्षेषु * विन्दुसर्गान्त्यवर्जितम्।
चतुरो + योजयेदाद्यान् विन्दुसर्गौ तु सर्वगौ ॥४१॥
तेन मन्त्रादिवर्णेन नाम्नश्चाद्याक्षरेण च।
गणयेदत्र ‡ षष्ठं वाऽप्यष्टमं द्वादशं तु वा ॥४२॥
रिपोर्मन्त्राद्यवर्णं स्यात् तेन तस्याहितं भवेत्।
राशिष्वनात्र ऋक्षेषु सप्तपञ्चत्वतीयमैः ॥४३॥
साध्यानामपि विज्ञेयमंशकाद्यमनुग्रहे।

देवतानां वा पूजां स्वयं न कुर्यात् इति। पूज्ये त्वन्ये वा तदग्रतः प्राप्तविध्यमित्यादिष्वन्यतमे। तत्पटले-द्वितीयपटले ॥ २८ ॥ ३० ॥ ३१ ॥ ३२ ॥ ३३ ॥ ३४ ॥ ३५ ॥ ३६ ॥ ३७ ॥ ३८ ॥ ३९ ॥

नित्यानामित्यादिभिः सर्वत इत्यन्तैर्द्वाविंशत्या श्लोकैर्मन्त्राणामंशकादिकमुपदिशति। तत्र अंशकादय इत्यत्र अंशकशब्दो राश्यादिवाचकः। आदिशब्देन सिद्धादिचक्रगणन ऋणऋणि (१) प्रभृतय उच्यन्ते। अश्विन्यादिषु ऋक्षेषु मेषादिषु राशिष्वित्यर्थः। विन्दुविसर्गान्त्यवर्जितं— विन्दुविसर्जनीयक्षकाररहितम्। चतुर इति पुंलिङ्गद्वितीयाबहुवचनम्। आद्यान्—अकाराद्यान् वर्णानितिशेषः। विन्दुसर्गौ तु सर्वगौ—विन्दुसर्गयोः शिवशक्तिरूपत्वात् सर्वात्मता। तेन राशिषु योजिताक्षरक्रमेण। एतदुक्तं भवति - प्रत्यक्षरं सन्निपादास्त्रयस्त्रिंशद्घटिकाः सम्भवन्ति ताभिः साध्यसाधकयोरंशकं जानीयात्

---

* अश्विन्यादिक ऋक्षेषु इति मू० पु० पा०। + चत्वारि इति सो० मू० व० पुस्तके पाठः।
‡ गणयेच्च इति मू० पु० पा०। (१) धन इति व० पु० पाठः।

यतस्ते तत्त्वविज्ञानरहितास्तेन चोदितम् ॥४४॥
प्राक्प्रत्यग्दक्षिणोदक् च सूत्रपञ्चकयोगतः ।
कोष्ठानि षोडशाऽत्र स्युस्तेषु वर्णान् क्रमाल्लिखेत् ॥४५॥
चतुश्चतुर्विभागेन कल्पयेत्तानि वै क्रमात् ।
प्रथमप्रथमे * त्वाद्यं द्वितीयप्रथमे + तथा ॥४६॥
द्वितीयमन्यतश्चान्यत् तथाऽन्यदपि कल्पयेत् ।
तत्तकोष्ठेषु ‡ विलिखेत् तत्तत्पञ्चममक्षरम् ॥ ४७ ॥
एवं चतुर्षुकोष्ठेषु ज्ञान्तावधि समालिखेत् ।

इति । गणयेत्—रिपुनामाद्यक्षरराशिमारभ्य मन्त्राद्यक्षरराश्यन्तं गणिते षष्ठाष्टमद्वादशराशिगताक्षरादिकैर्मन्त्रैररातेरभिचारादिकं कुर्यादित्यर्थः । राशिषु प्रोक्तमितिशेषः । ऋक्षेषु—अश्विन्यादिषु नक्षत्रेषु । सप्तपञ्चतृतीयगैः—प्राग्वत् रिपुनामाद्यक्षरनक्षत्रमारभ्य मन्त्राद्यक्षरराश्यन्तं गणिते सप्तपञ्चतृतीयनक्षत्रगताद्यवर्णैर्मन्त्रैस्तस्याभिचारादिकं कुर्यादित्यर्थः । साध्यानामित्यादि उपरिष्टाद्वक्ष्यमाणसाध्यसाधकसिद्धाख्येषु त्रिषूपासकेषु प्रथमस्य तत्वज्ञानरहितत्वात् प्रागुक्तांशकाद्यमनुग्रहेष्वविचक्षणीयमितार्थः ॥ ४० ॥ ४१ ॥ ४२ ॥ ४३ ॥ ४४ ॥ ४५ ॥

वर्णान् क्रमाल्लिखेदितात्र क्रमशब्दार्थः प्रदर्श्यते—चतुश्चतुर्विभागेन षोडशकोष्ठानि प्रादक्षिण्येन चत्वारि चत्वारि वक्ष्यमाणसाध्यसिद्धसुसिद्धारिवर्गेषु सङ्कल्प्य । प्रथमप्रथमे—प्रथमचतुष्कप्रथमकोष्ठे आद्यमक्षरं लिखेत् । द्वितीयप्रथमे—द्वितीयचतुष्कप्रोक्तक्रमप्रथमकोष्ठे(१) तथा—यथा पूर्वचतुष्टयस्य प्रथमकोष्ठः कल्पितः अत्रापि तथा कुर्यादित्यर्थः । द्वितीय—माकारं लिखेत् । अन्यतश्च—तृतीयचतुष्कप्रोक्तक्रमपृथमकोष्ठे । अन्यत्—तृतीयमिकारं लिखेत् । तथाऽन्यदपि कल्पयेत्—तथा—यथा पूर्वचतुष्कत्रयम् । अन्यत्—चतुर्थचतुष्कम् । अपिः समुच्चये । कल्पयेत्—विलिखेत् । चतुर्थमीकारं चतुर्थचतुष्क (२) प्रोक्त-

---

* प्रथमः प्रथमे इति मू० पु० पाठः । + द्वितीयं प्रथमे इति मूलपुस्तके पाठः ।

‡ तत्कोष्ठेषु इति मूलपुस्तके पाठः । (१) द्वितीयचतुष्कप्रथमेकोष्ठे १ पुस्तके पाठः ।

(२) चतुर्थचतुष्टय इति मो० पुस्तके पाठः ।

स्वनामाद्यक्षरं यत्र कोष्ठे सन्दृश्यते ततः ॥ ४८ ॥
सिद्धादीन् गणयेद्यावन्मन्त्राद्यक्षरदर्शनम्।
सिद्धसिद्धो जपात्सिद्ध्येत् द्विगुणात्सिद्धसाध्यकः (१) ॥४९॥

प्रथमप्रथमकोष्ठे लिखेदित्यर्थः। तत्तत्कोष्ठेषु—उक्तचतुष्कचतुष्टयद्वितीयकोष्ठेषु। तत्तत्पञ्चमं—प्रथमप्रथमद्वितीयतृतीयकोष्ठलिखिताक्षराणां (२) पञ्चमाक्षराणि विलिखेदित्यर्थः। एवं—प्राग्वत्। द्वितीयकोष्ठाक्षराणां पञ्चमाक्षराणि तृतीयकोष्ठेषु विलिखेत्। तृतीयकोष्ठाक्षराणां पञ्चमाक्षराणि चतुर्थकोष्ठेषु विलिखेत्। उक्ते चतुष्कचतुष्के प्रत्येकं कोष्ठे पुनः पुनः पञ्चमाक्षरलेखनतः क्षान्तावधि चतुष्कचतुष्टयेऽपि समालिखेत्। एवं लिखिते सति प्रथमचतुष्कप्रथमकोष्ठे अकथह इति चत्वार्यक्षराणि। तद्द्वितीयकोष्ठे उङप इति त्रीणि। तत्तृतीयकोष्ठे लृझम इति त्रीणि। तच्चतुर्थकोष्ठे ओडव इति त्रीणि। द्वितीयचतुष्कप्रथमकोष्ठे आखदल इति चत्वारि अक्षराणि। तद्द्वितीयकोष्ठे ऊचफ इति त्रीणि। तत्तृतीयकोष्ठे लॄञय इति त्रीणि। तच्चतुर्थकोष्ठे औढश इति त्रीणि। तृतीयचतुष्कप्रथमकोष्ठे इगधक्ष इति चत्वारि। तद्द्वितीयकोष्ठे ऋछब इति त्रीणि। तत्तृतीयकोष्ठे एटर इति त्रीणि। तच्चतुर्थकोष्ठे अंणष इति त्रीणि। चतुर्थचतुष्कप्रथमकोष्ठे ईघन इति त्रीणि। तद्द्वितीयकोष्ठे ॠजभ इति त्रीणि। तत्तृतीयकोष्ठे ऐठल इति त्रीणि। तच्चतुर्थकोष्ठे- अः त स इति त्रीणि। एवं लिखिते प्रथमचतुष्ककोष्ठाक्षराणामुपरितनाक्षराणि द्वितीयचतुष्ककोष्ठेषु यथाक्रमं दृश्यन्ते। अकारादिक्षकारान्तान्येकपञ्चाशदक्षराणि तेषु षोडशकोष्ठेषु व्याकुलक्रमाणि दृश्यन्त इति प्रथमप्रोक्तक्रमशब्दस्यार्थः॥ ४६ ॥ ४७ ॥ ४८ ॥ ४९ ॥

सिद्धसिद्ध इत्यादिभिः सुनिश्चितमित्यन्तैरर्द्धैः षड्भिः श्लोकैस्तेषां षोडशकोष्ठाक्षराणां फलान्युपदिशति। तत्र अतोऽन्यथा—सुसिद्धसाध्यादन्यः अनन्तरभूतः सुसिद्ध इत्यर्थः। अभिचारे रिपोरेवं यदि स्वात्मविपत्तये—रिपोरभिचारकाले तस्य सुसिद्धसुसिद्धश्चेदभिचारमन्त्रस्तस्याभिचारकस्यैव निधनाय भवतीत्यर्थः।

ऋणसिद्धादियोगेषु मन्त्रदाने विशेषतः।

---

(१) सिद्ध्यसाधक इति मू० पु० पा०।

(२) प्रथमप्रथमकोष्ठलिखिताक्षराणां पञ्चमपञ्चमाक्षराणि इति १ पुस्तके पाठः।

सिद्धे सुसिद्धः सम्प्राप्त्या सिद्धारिर्हन्ति गोत्रजान् ।
साध्यसिद्धेऽतिसंक्लेशात् साध्यसाध्योऽतिदुःखकृत् ॥ ५० ॥
साध्ये सुसिद्धो भजनात्साध्यारिः स्वां श्रियं हरेत् ।
सुसिद्धसिद्धोऽध्ययनात् फलं दद्यादाशेप्सितम् ॥५१॥
सुसिद्धसाध्यो (१) जापाद्यैः सिद्धये स्यादतोऽन्यथा ।
सुसिद्धे तु प्रसिद्धस्तु पूर्वजन्मकृतश्रमः ॥५२॥
तस्मात् तु सर्वसिद्धीनां साधने यो जपेन्मनुम् ।
अभिचारे रिपोरेवं यदि स्वात्मविपत्तये ॥५३॥
सुसिद्धोरिरशेषेण स्वकुलान्नाशयेद्ध्रुवम् ।
अरिसिद्धः सुतं हन्यादरिसाध्यः स्वयोषितम् ॥५४॥
अरिः सुसिद्धोमन्त्रस्तु कुलोत्सादनकृच्छ्नैः ।
अर्यरिः स्वात्महा मन्त्रः सम्प्राप्त्यैव सुनिश्चितम् ॥५५॥
नामाद्यक्षरमारभ्य यावन्मन्त्रादिवर्णकम् ।
त्रिधा कृत्वा स्वरैर्भिन्द्यात् (२) तदन्यद्विपरीतकम् ॥५६॥

प्रसिद्धं नाम गृह्णीयात् प्रसुप्ता येन जाग्रति ॥ ५० ॥ ५१ ॥ ५२ ॥ ५३ ॥ ॥ ५४ ॥ ५५ ॥

नामाद्यक्षरमित्यादिभिः सर्वत इत्यन्तैः षड्भिः श्लोकैः साधकमन्त्रयोरुत्तमर्णाधमर्णत्वं तत्फलानि चोपदिशति। तत्र यावमन्त्रादिवर्णकं—मातृकाक्षरक्रमेण स्वनामाद्यक्षरमारभ्य मन्त्राद्यक्षरावधि गणयेदित्यर्थः। त्रिधा कृत्वा—तां सङ्ख्यां त्रिगुणीकुर्यात्। स्वरैः स्वरशब्देन षोड़शसप्तत्रिसङ्ख्या उच्यन्ते। तत्र सम्प्रदायात् सप्तसङ्ख्याऽङ्गीकृता। भिन्द्यात्—तया तां सङ्ख्यामाहरेत्। तदन्यत्—मन्त्राद्यक्षरमारभ्य स्वनामाद्यक्षरावधि मातृकाक्षराणि। विपरीतकं—सप्तभिः संवर्द्ध्य त्रिभिरा हरेदित्यर्थः। एतदुक्तं भवति—सर्वेषां विद्यामन्त्राणां सर्वेषां साध्यादीनां च उत्तमर्णाधमर्णत्वं ज्ञातुमुपायः मातृकाक्षरपाठक्रमेण स्वनामाद्यक्षरमारभ्य उद्देश्यस्य

---

(१) सुसाध्यसाध्योऽति मू० पु० पा०।

(२) भिन्नात् इति सो० मू० पुस्तके पाठः।

कृत्वाऽधिको ऋणी ज्ञेयो ऋणी चेन्मन्त्रमुत्तमम् ।
स्वयं ऋणी चेत्तन्मन्त्रं त्यजेत् पूर्वं ऋणी यतः ॥५७॥
कथं ऋणित्वं मन्त्राणां साधकानां च मे वद ! ।
पूर्वजन्मकृताभ्यासि (१) पापादस्याफलाप्तिकृत् ॥५८॥
पापे नष्टे फलावाप्तिः काले देहक्षयादृणी ।
मन्त्रः सम्प्राप्तिमात्रेण प्राक्तनः सिद्ध्यै भवेत् ॥५९॥
सिद्धम त् गुरोर्लब्धमन्त्रो यः सिद्धिभाङ्नरः ।
लक्ष्मीमदादनादृत्य मन्त्रे भोगमवाप्तवान् (२) ॥६०॥
सन्मन्त्रस्य (३) ऋणी ज्ञेयो भजनं तस्य पूर्वगम् ।
तस्मादृणविशुद्धिस्तु कार्या सर्वैस्तु सर्वतः ॥६१॥
रुद्राक्षैरपि पद्माख्यैः पुत्रजीवैः कुचन्दनैः ।
स्फाटिकैश्च प्रवालैश्च मौक्तिकैर्हेमनिर्मितैः ॥६२॥

आद्यक्षरात् पूर्वाक्षराणि गणयित्वा तां सङ्ख्यां त्रिगुणीकृत्य सप्तभिराहृत्य शिष्ट-सङ्ख्यां विज्ञाय तथा मन्त्राद्यक्षरादि स्वनामाद्यक्षरावधि गणयित्वा तां सङ्ख्यां सप्तभिर्वर्धयित्वा त्रिभिराहृत्य शिष्टं च जानीयादिति। कृत्वेत्यादिना एतदुक्तं भवति—पूर्व-श्लोकोक्तशिष्टसङ्ख्ययोरधिकसङ्ख्यायुक्तोऽधमर्णः हीनसङ्ख्यायुक्त उत्तमर्णः। तत्र मन्त्रस्य अधमर्णत्वे फलभूयस्त्वं स्वस्याधमर्णत्वे नैष्फल्यं, तेनोत्तमर्णविद्यादीन् परित्यज्य अधमर्णानेव स्वीकुर्यादिति। सर्वैः साधकैः साधैश्च। सर्वतः—मन्त्रेषु विद्यासु चेत्यर्थः ॥ ५६ ॥ ५७ ॥ ५८ ॥ ५९ ॥ ६० ॥ ६१ ॥ ६२ ॥

रुद्राक्षैरित्यादिभिर्जपमित्यन्तैश्चतुर्भिः श्लोकैरक्षमालादिकमुपदिशति। तत्र कुचन्दनैः रक्तचन्दनैः ॥ ६३ ॥ ६४ ॥ ६५ ॥

---

(१) भ्यासात् इति मू० पु० पा० ।

(२) मवाप्नुयात् इभि मूलपुस्तकी पाठः ।

(३) स मन्त्रस्य इति मूलपुस्तकी पाठः ।

राजतैर्जपमाला (१) स्यात् पूर्वं पूर्वं फलेद्गुरुः ।
आदिक्षान्तैरक्षरैः स्यादक्षमाला यथार्थतः ॥६३॥
अनुलोमविलोमाभ्यां मातृकान्तरितां जपेत् ।
एवं सर्वगुणोपेतो जायते सर्वसिद्धिमान् ॥६४॥
तर्जनीरहितैः कुर्यादङ्गुल्यग्रैर्जपक्रियाम् ।
अङ्गुलीपर्वसंस्पर्शादपि वा गणयेज्जपम् ॥६५॥
अबुद्धिपूर्वं विहिते निषिद्धे कर्म्मणि द्रुतम् ।
विद्यां जपेच्छतं तेन तत्पापान्मुच्यते ध्रुवम् ॥६६॥
नित्यातिक्रमदोषाणां शान्त्यै विद्यां शतं जपेत् ।
नैमित्तिकातिक्रमणे सहस्रं प्रजपेत्तदा ॥६७॥
विशुद्धदेहवदनः शुक्लाम्बरधरः शुचिः ।
विमुखः परनिन्दासु देवतादर्शनेषु च ॥६८॥
परार्थवनिताभूमिपीड़ासु विगतस्पृहः ।
दयान्वितः सर्वजने प्रेक्षाकारी गतस्पृहः ॥६९॥
आस्तिको गुरुभक्तश्च नित्यशो नियमान्वितः ।
यः स सर्वगुणोपेतो विद्यासिद्धिमवाप्नुयात् ॥७०॥
अन्यथा वर्तमानो यो विद्याभजनवांश्चिरम् ।
न तस्य सिद्धिः कुत्रापि कदाचिच्च कथञ्चन ॥७१॥

अबुद्धीत्यादिना तदेत्यन्तेन श्लोकद्वयेन प्रायश्चित्तमुपदिशति ॥ ६६ ॥६७॥

विशुद्धेत्यादिभिः कथञ्चनेत्यन्तैश्चतुर्भिः श्लोकैः साधकसमाचारमुपदिशति । तत्र देवतादर्शनेषु—देवतासु दर्शनेषु च निन्दासु विमुखः । दर्शनेषु—वैदिकवैष्णवशैवादिषु ॥ ६८ ॥ ७० ॥ ७१ ॥ ७२ ॥

---

(१) राजतैर्वाऽक्षमाला इति मू० पु० पा० ।

आदौ योगो भवेदन्ते पल्लवः सम्पुटो(१)द्वयोः ।
एकान्तरं तु ग्रथनं विदर्भो व्यन्तरीकृतः ॥७२॥
मन्त्रदोषांस्तु विज्ञाय गुरुः परिहरेत् क्षणात् ।
अन्यथा स गुरुः शिष्यं निहन्त्यैवाचिरात् ध्रुवम् ॥७३॥

आदौ योगेत्यादिना श्लोकेन मन्त्रेषु साध्यकर्मयोजनप्रकारमुपदिशति । तत्र एतदुक्तं भवति—मन्त्रविद्ययोरादौ साधकसाध्यकर्मणां योजने योग इति संज्ञा । मन्त्रविद्ययोरन्ते पूर्वोक्तयोजनात् पल्लव इति संज्ञा । मन्त्रविद्ययोराद्यन्तयोः पूर्वोक्तयोजनात्संपुट इति संज्ञा । मन्त्रविद्ययोः प्रागुक्तानाञ्च एकैकाक्षरतोऽन्योन्यसम्मेलनात् ग्रथनमिति संज्ञा । मन्त्रविद्ययोः पूर्वोक्तानां च अन्योन्यमक्षरद्वययोजनात् विदर्भ इति संज्ञा । स च त्रिविधः मन्त्राक्षरद्वयान्तरे साध्याक्षरमेकमेकं योजयेत् इत्येकः प्रकारः । साध्याक्षराणां द्वयान्तरे मन्त्रादीनामक्षरमेकं योजयेत् सोऽपरः । मन्त्रादीनामक्षरद्वयान्तरे साध्यादीनामक्षरं द्वयं द्वयं योजयेदेषोऽन्यः । एवं त्रैविध्यमिति ॥ ७३ ॥

मन्त्रदोषानित्यादिभिर्गुरुरित्यन्तैर्नवभिः श्लोकैर्मन्त्रदोषादिकमुपदिशति । तत्र स गुरुरित्यत्र सशब्दो मन्त्रविषयः । षट्कर्णगः—स्वव्यतिरिक्तयोर्द्वयोर्युगपत्पठनात् । अधिकैर्जपात्—अधिकदेवतामन्त्रैः सार्द्धं क्षुद्रदेवतामन्त्रजपात् क्षुद्रस्य त्रासः । गर्वितः—साधकस्यानभिमुखः । अविधिप्राप्तः—दीक्षादिविधिमन्तरेण सम्प्राप्तः । वैरिकोष्ठगाः—पूर्वोक्तवैरिवर्गचतुष्ककोष्ठगाः । निर्जिताः—पराजिताः । कर्म्मबाहुल्यात्—साधकस्य प्राग्जन्मदुष्कृतबाहुल्यात् । अहसाः—हकारसकाररहिताः । सत्त्ववर्जिताः—बलहीनाः । अपूर्णरूपाः—वाच्यस्य अपुष्कलाक्षराः । छिन्नाः—महावयविन एकदेशत्वात् । स्तम्भिताः—साधकाभिमतप्रदानेषु । सानुनासिकाः—स्पर्शवर्गेष्वन्त्याक्षरप्रायाः । अकालविनियोगेन—मन्त्रस्य स्वापकालेषु प्रयोगादिषु विनियोगेन । मन्त्राणां स्वापप्रबोधयोर्लक्षणमुच्यते । प्रणवक्षकाररेफहकाराक्षरप्रायान्त्याद्या आग्नेयाः । इन्द्वक्षरप्राया मन्त्राः सौम्याः । साधकस्य श्वासे दक्षिणनासापुटे परिपूर्णं प्रवहति सति आग्नेय-

---

(१) सम्पुटं इति मू० पु० पा० ।

तेन तत्परिहारश्च शृणु देवि ! समाहिता ।
परिहारप्रकारन्तु वक्ष्ये योगेषु (१) तत्त्वतः ॥७४॥
दग्धः षट्कर्णगो मन्त्रः त्रस्तः (२) स्यादधिकैर्जपात् ।
गर्वितस्त्ववधिप्राप्तः शत्रवो वैरिकोष्ठगाः ॥७५॥
बाला लघ्वक्षरप्राया वृद्धा गुर्वक्षरान्विताः ।
निर्जिता कर्मबाहुल्यादहसाः सत्ववर्जिताः ॥७६॥

मन्त्रादीनां प्रबोधकालः । इतरेषां सौम्यादीनां तदा स्वापकाल एव । वामनासापुटे श्वासे प्रवहति सति सौम्यमन्त्रादीनां प्रबोधकालः । इतरेषामाग्नेयानामन्त्राणां तदा स्वापकालश्च । एतत्सकलमविज्ञाय मन्त्रान् मनीषितेषु कार्येषु विनियोजकः साधकस्तेषाम्मूर्छाक्लेशकारी भवतीत्यर्थः । मूर्छिताः निर्व्यापाराः । साधकसमीहितसंपादने निर्व्यापारा इत्यर्थः । स्वापगाः—सुप्तवत् साधकानभिमुखाः । अजपात्—गुरोर्विद्याधिगमदिवसमारभ्य तदुक्तक्रमभजनानङ्गीकारात् । अत्र सन्धिर्दिव्यत्वादचिन्त्यः । मत्ता मन्त्राः—समीचीनभजनशीलस्य साधकस्यार्थानर्थौ समं साधयन्तीत्यर्थः । पत्रेषु पठनात्—यथाविधि गुरुमुखादधिगममन्तरेण यतः कुतश्चित् पत्रेषु मन्त्रादीन् दृष्ट्वा तत्र पठित्वा जपादित्यर्थः । अन्यवर्णैः मन्त्राक्षरेभ्या बहिर्भूतैः । तेषां तत्र नाम साधकस्यानवधानपठनाद्वा सम्भवः । कीलिताः—यथा कालाख्यः शङ्कुर्द्रुमकुड्यादिषु भिन्नरूपः तद्वन्नामसाम्यसाधकानवधानसंपादितैरक्षरैः कीलिता इत्यर्थः । रुद्धाः—निरुद्धाः—निवारिता इत्यर्थः । विसन्धिकाः—विगतसन्धिकाः—गुणवृद्धियणादेशादिप्राप्तौ सत्यां अकृतसन्धिकाः । प्राप्तदुःखा—प्राप्तक्लेशाः । वैरिसमन्विताः—वैरिमन्त्राद्यैः सहोपासिताः । मन्त्राङ्गमन्योन्यं वैरलक्षणमुपरिष्टात् वासनापटले वक्ष्यमाणत्वादिह नोक्तम् । खण्डीभूताः—भिन्नविग्रहाः । अंशजापात्—मन्त्रविद्यानामेकदेशजापात् । अङ्गहीनाः—अङ्गन्यासमन्त्रहीनाः । असंवृताः—अगोपिताः । गोपितेन गौरवं प्रकाशनेन नैष्फल्यं

---

(१) योगन्तु इति सो० पु० पा० ।

(२) मन्त्रस्त्रस्तश्चस्यादिति इति सो० पु० पा०

अपूर्णरूपाश्छिन्नाः स्युः स्तम्भिता: मातृनामिकाः ।
अकालविनियोगेन प्रबोधः (१) स्वापगा जपात् ॥७७॥
मत्ताः पर्वेषु (२) पठनादन्यवर्णैस्तु कीलिताः ।
रुद्धा विसन्धिकाः प्राप्तदुःखा वैरिसमन्विताः ॥७८॥
खण्डीभूतास्त्वंशजापादङ्गहीनास्त्वसंवृताः ।
अपूर्णेनोपदिष्टा ये हीनवीर्यास्तु ते मताः ॥७९॥
सदा प्रयोगात् कुण्ठत्वं क्लिष्टताऽतिविलम्बनात् ।
रुग्णा प्रलपनैर्जापादन्यमन्त्रैः सहाविलाः ॥८०॥
उपेक्षावस्थया जापात् वैषम्यादवमानिताः ।
पञ्चविंशतिरुद्दिष्टा दोषांस्तान् शमयेद्गुरुः ॥८१॥

च सर्व्वमन्त्रदेवतानां सर्वत्रोच्यते। अपूर्णेन —अनुग्रहविधौ पूर्णाभिषेकादिगुर्वाज्ञामन्तरेण प्रवृत्तेन। हीनवीर्याः—क्षीणबलाः अनुक्तकरणात्संजातशक्तिना प्रतिपादितत्वात् अस्मिन् शिष्ये त्वकार्य्यकरादभजन्नादनर्थकरास्त्वित्यर्थः। कुण्ठत्वम्—अकार्य्यकरत्वम्। सुसिद्धा अपि मन्त्रादयः सर्वदा विनियोक्तुस्तीक्ष्णशस्त्रवत्कुण्ठाः निस्तेजसा भवन्तीत्यर्थः। क्लिष्टता—क्लेशार्दितत्वम् अतिविलम्बनात् उक्तकालादधिकं विलम्ब्य मन्त्रादीनामच्चरावर्तनात्। रुग्णाः—पीड़िताः। प्रलपनैर्ज्जापात्—अयोग्यैरालप्यालप्य जापात्। अन्यमन्त्रैः—जप्यमानादन्यमन्त्रैः। आविलाः—व्याकुलाः—एकस्मिन्मन्त्रे जप्यमाने अन्यमन्त्रस्य मध्ये मध्ये जपत उभयोरपि मन्त्रयोर्व्याकुलता भवति तयोर्नैष्फल्यानर्थादयः सम्भवन्तीत्यर्थः। उपेक्षा – परित्यागः। अनवस्थया जापात्—गुरूक्तकल्पोक्तस्वकल्पितमार्गेष्वन्यतममपहाय यथोक्तितक्रमजापादित्यर्थः। वैषम्यात्—मन्त्राणां देवतानां च जपपूजाहोमादिषु वैषम्यात्। विषमभावात् हीनाधिक्यत इत्यर्थः। अवमानिताः—परिभूताः। शमयेद् गुरुः—वक्ष्यमाणोपायेनेत्यर्थः॥ ७४ ॥ ७५ ॥ ७६ ॥ ७७ ॥ ७८ ॥ ७९ ॥ ८० ॥ ८१ ॥ ८२॥

---

(१) मूर्च्छिताः स्वा इति मौ० पु० पाठः

(२) मन्त्रपर्वेषु इति मु० पु० पा०।

बन्धनं योनिमुद्राया मन्त्राणां वीर्ययोजनम् ।
उभयं बोधयन् शिष्यं संरक्षेद्‌गुरुरात्मवान् ॥८२॥
गुरोर्लक्षणमेतावदादिमान्त्यन्तु वेदयेत् ।
आदिमान्त्यविहीनास्तु वर्णाः स्युः शरदभ्रवत् ॥८३॥
तस्मादादित एवासौ कुर्यात्तत्तदहङ्कृतिः ।
यदहङ्कारविज्ञानान्मत्समोजायते नरः ॥८४॥
अनादिक्रमसंसिद्धमातृकाद्यन्तयोजनात् ।
तादात्म्यसिद्धिं तां विद्धि सर्वमन्त्रार्थविग्रहाम् ॥८५॥
द्विजातीनां तु संस्कारं वेदोक्तं समुदाहृतम् ।
तेषां च तत्र तत्रापि विद्यया विधिमाचरेत् ॥८६॥
स विद्यास्मरणं कुर्यात् क्रियां सर्वत्र चोदिताम् ।
तेन तन्मयतासिद्धिः सर्वत्र भवति ध्रुवम् ॥८७॥

बन्धनमित्यादिभिर्विग्रहाम् इत्यन्तैश्चतुर्भिः श्लोकैर्देशिकस्य कर्तव्यमुपदिशति। तत्र बन्धनम्—अनुसन्धानम्। योनिमुद्राया उत्तरत्र होमपटले प्राणमानसयोर्मूलाधारादिब्रह्मरन्ध्रावधि सुषुम्णान्तरालेन गमागमरूपा योनिमुद्रा तदनुसन्धानं-योनिमुद्राबन्ध इत्यर्थः। वीर्ययोजनम्—उत्तरत्र वासनापटले प्रोक्तस्य मन्त्र-वीर्यस्य मन्त्रेण साधकेनच योजनं मन्त्रवीर्ययोजनमित्यर्थः। एतदाराधगमुखात् स्फुटतरमवगन्तव्यम्। आदिमान्त्यम् आदिममन्त्यञ्च। आदिमान्त्रविहीनाः—आदिमान्तग्रज्ञानसम्बन्धविहीनाः। वर्णाः—केवलमक्षरविग्रहा मन्त्रा इत्यर्थः। तत्तदहंकृतिम् मातृकाया आद्यन्ताक्षरद्वयात्मिकाम्॥ ८३ ॥ ८४ ॥ ८५ ॥ ८६ ॥

अनादीत्यादिना श्लोकेनैतदुक्तं भवति। अनादिसिद्धक्रमाणामक्षराणां समुदायरूपाया मातृकायाः प्रथमचरमाक्षयोरकारहकारयोर्योजनात् संजातरूपमहं शब्दं तदर्थं च आद्यन्तप्रत्याहृतिन्यायेन स्वात्मनो मातृकात्मतां तत् वाऽच्यरूपं सर्वदेवतात्मतां चेति॥ ८७ ॥

अन्येषामपि वर्णानां विद्यया समुपाचरेत्।
निधने विद्यया दाहो विद्ययाऽन्यत् समाचरेत् ॥८८॥
सम्पूज्य भोजयेदेकमनेकं वा स्वशक्तितः।
योगिनं विद्यया सिद्धं पूर्वतस्च निमन्त्रितम् ॥८९॥
उर्मिकावसनाद्यैस्तं पूजयित्वा (१) प्रणम्य च।
विद्यया विसृजेन्मन्त्री स्वविद्यासिद्धये शिवे! ॥९०॥
गुरोस्तु जन्मदिवसं विद्याप्राप्तिदिनं तथा।
स्वजन्मदिवसं नाथव्याप्तिवासरमेव च ॥९१॥
अक्षरत्रयसम्पातदिनं पूर्णादिनं तथा।
षट् पर्वाणि विशिष्टानि सदर्शं (२) सप्तपर्वकम् ॥९२॥
मासतो वर्षतो वाऽपि कुर्यादेतेषु पूजनम्।
गुरोस्तु जीविते नित्यव्याप्ते तत्पुत्रकादिकम् (३) ॥९३॥
पूजयेत्तत्समं तं च प्रणामाद्यैरुपाचरेत्।
तदभावे तत्कुलीनं तद्भक्तं वा समर्चयेत् ॥९४॥

द्विजातीनामित्यादिभिः शिवे इत्यन्तैः पञ्चभिः श्लोकैर्नाथकृत्यमुपदिशति। तत्र—द्विजातीनां—ब्राह्मणक्षत्रियवैश्यानाम्। संस्कारं—जातकर्मादिकम्। अन्येषां वर्णानाम्—शूद्राणाम् अनुलोमप्रतिलोमसङ्करात्मनां च ॥८६॥८७॥८८॥८९॥९०॥

गुरोरित्यादिभिर्भवेदित्यन्तैः पञ्चभिः श्लोकैः पर्वादिकमुपदिशति। तत्र—अक्षरत्रयसंपातदिनम्—उत्तरत्र मातृकापटले वक्ष्यमाणाक्षरात्मकदिनेषु वर्णाक्षरद्वयं घटिकाक्षरं च त्रीण्यक्षराणि यस्मिन् दिने संगतानि भवन्ति तदक्षरत्रयसम्पातदिनम्। तत्प्रकारस्य तत्रैव स्फुटतरं वक्ष्यमाणत्वादिह न प्रपञ्चितम् ॥९१॥९२॥९३॥९४॥९५॥

---

(१) रचयित्वेति मू॰ पु॰ पा॰ (२) संदर्शमिति मू॰ सो॰ पु॰ पा॰
(३) गुरोस्तु जीवतो दूरे व्याप्ते तत्पूर्वकादिकमिति मू॰ पु॰ पा॰।

स्तुवीत पञ्चभिः श्लोकैस्तन्नित्यं सर्वसिद्धये ।
प्रातः प्रबोधसमये जपात्सुदिवसं भवेत् (१) ॥९५॥
नमस्ते नाथ ! भगवन् ! शिवाय (२) शिवरूपिणे ।
विद्यावतारसंसिध्यै स्वीकृतानेकविग्रह ! ॥९६॥
नवाय नवरूपाय परमार्थैकरूपिणे ।
सर्वाज्ञानतमोभेदभानवे चिद्घनाय ते ॥९७॥
स्वतन्त्राय दयाक्लृप्तविग्रहाय शिवात्मने ।
परतन्त्राय भक्तानां भव्यानां भव्यरूपिणे ॥९८॥
विवेकिनां विवेकाय विमर्शाय विमर्शिनाम् ।
प्रकाशानां प्रकाशाय ज्ञानिनां ज्ञानरूपिणे ॥९९॥
पुरस्तात्पार्श्वयोः पृष्ठे नमस्कुर्यादुपर्यधः ।
सदा मे चित्तरूपेण विधेहि भवदासनम् ॥१००॥
भूमितत्वमयो व्याप्तिरिति सम्यक्समीरिता ।

नम इत्याद्यैरासनमित्यन्तैः पञ्चभिः श्लोकैर्नाथस्तोत्रमुपदिशति । तत्र—नवाय—सर्वदा नवनवत्वस्पृहणीयाय । नवरूपाय—नवसङ्ख्याविशिष्टविग्रहाय । परमार्थैकरूपिणे—शिवत्वेनैकविग्रहायेत्यर्थः । विवेकविमर्शयोरिदन्ताहन्तयोर्यथात्म्यज्ञानमर्थः । प्रकाशानाम्—मतररूपाणाम् ॥ ९६ ॥ ९७ ॥ ९८ ॥ ९९ ॥ १०० ॥

पुरस्तादित्यादिना श्लोकेनैतदुक्तं भवति । देशकालाकारैस्त्वन्मयतां मे विधेहीति शिवम् ॥ १०१ ॥

---

(१) व्रजेत् इति मृ० पु० पा० ।
(२) गुरुरूपिणे इति स्तो० पु० पा० ।

अस्या निःफालनाच्चित्ते तत्तत्त्वं स्वात्म(१)सात्कृतम् ॥१०१॥

इति षोडशनित्यातन्त्रे श्रीकादिमते प्रथमं पटलम् (२) ।

इति षोडशनित्यातन्त्रेषु श्रीकादिमताख्यस्य परिपूर्णस्य तन्त्रस्य प्रपञ्चसार-सिंहराजप्रकाशाभिधानेन सुभगानन्दनाथेन विरचितायां मनोरमाख्यायां व्याख्यायां तन्त्रावतारादिप्रकाशनपरं प्रथमं पटलं परिपूर्णं परामृष्टम् ॥ ग्रन्थसंख्या ।

प्रथमे यन्त्रमेकं स्यात् ग्रन्थसंख्या शतात्परम् ।
त्रिषष्टिरिति निर्दिष्टं व्याख्यानं सम्यगीक्षणात् ॥

---

(१) ततत्त्वं स्वात्म इति मूलपुस्तके पाठः । (२) प्रथमः पटल इति खं० पु० पाठः ।

अथ द्वितीयं पटलम् ।

अथ नाथान् प्रवक्ष्यामि मद्रूपान् नित्यविग्रहान् ।
विद्यावतारसोपानभूतांस्तत्पूजनं तथा ॥ १ ॥
प्रकाशोऽथ विमर्शोऽन्यस्त्वानन्दोऽपर इत्यपि ।
नामभेदादहं लोके कल्पयन् दिव्यरूपतः ॥२॥
त्रयस्तेभ्यः समुत्पन्नाः सिद्धाश्च त्रय एव ते ।
ज्ञानः सत्यः पूर्ण इति श्रीमुखास्ते समीरिताः ॥३॥
दिव्या मदन्तिके नित्यं सिद्धा भूमाविहापि च ।
निवसन्ति ततस्तेभ्यः समुत्पन्नास्त्रयस्तथा ॥४॥
(१) स्वाभावः प्रतिभस्तद्वत् सुभगश्चेति नामतः ।
ते भूमाविव सततं निवसन्ति मदात्मकाः ॥५॥
एवं तैर्नवभिस्तन्त्वं लोके प्रथितवैभवम् ।
अकल्पयत् कादिशक्तिस्त्वदनन्या कृते युगे ॥६॥
एते द्विनेत्रा द्विभुजा ललिताकारसंयुताः ।
प्रसन्नवदनाः स्मेरा वराभयकरान्विताः ॥७॥

द्वितीयं पटलम् ।

पूर्वस्मिन् प्रथमे पटले तन्त्रावतारादिकमुपदिश्यानन्तरं सकलपुरुषार्थप्रकाशकानां तन्त्रावतारकाणां नवानां नाथानां स्वरूपं तत्सपर्याविशेषादिकमुपदिशति

(१) स्वभावप्रतिभस्तद्वत इति सं० पु० पा० ।

पूज्या एवंविधाः स्वस्वमण्डलादिषु पूजने ।
देवी श्रीचक्रसंस्थास्तु (१) देव्याकारास्तदाज्ञया ॥८॥
(२) प्रियाक्षराभिधानास्ते सर्वेऽप्यानन्दसंयुताः ।
स्वमण्डलेषु नाथान्ताः शक्त्यन्ता देवि ! मण्डले ॥९॥
माया लक्ष्म्यादिकास्तद्वन्नवार्णाख्यास्तथा भवेत् ।
नवानां सर्वशक्तीनां देवतानां च पूजने ॥१०॥
या विद्या सर्वसन्तोषकारिणी सर्वसिद्धिदा ।
सप्ताक्षर्या तया देवि ! (३) पूजयेन्नामपूर्वकम् ॥११॥
तां मे कथय विद्यां तु या सर्वप्रियकारिणी ।
शृणु देवि ! महासिद्धिकरी सर्वप्रियंकरी ॥१२॥

अथ नाथानित्यादिना तद्यत इत्यन्तश्लोकशतात्मना द्वितीयेन पटलेन । तत्र अथ नाथानित्यादिभिर्नामपूर्वकमित्यन्तै रेकादशभिः श्लोकैर्नवानां नाथानामुत्पत्तिक्रमं तत्कार्यं तैर्विद्याप्रसारणं तन्मन्त्रांश्चोपदिशति । तत्र—मद्रूपानित्युक्त्या नित्यविग्रहत्वम् । तथेति समुच्चये । श्रीमुखाः—श्रीशब्दाद्यसंज्ञाः । मदात्मकाः—शिवरूपिणः । एते असाधारणाः (४) त्र्यक्षरनामानः । सर्वसाधारणाः त्र्यक्षरसंज्ञा नव । त्रिविक्रमेण दिव्याः सिद्धा मानवाश्च वेदितव्या इत्यर्थः । एतेषां नवानां नाथानामसाधारणत्र्यक्षरनामार्थप्रतिपादनेनाखण्डविग्रहशिवरूपत्वमाराध्यमुखादेवाऽवगन्तव्यम् । स्वस्वमण्डलादिष्वित्यत्र मण्डलान्युत्तरत्र वक्ष्यति । आदिशब्दः स्वशीर्षादिविषयः । आनन्दसंयुता इति—आनन्दशब्दोपेतसंज्ञा इत्यर्थः । नवानाम्—नाथानामिति शेषः । नामपूर्वकम्—तत्तन्नामपूर्वकम् ॥ १ ॥ २ ॥ ३ ॥ ४ ॥ ५ ॥ ६ ॥ ७ ॥ ८ ॥ ९ ॥ १० ॥ ११ ॥

ताम्मे इत्याद्यैर्नमसास्थितिरित्यन्तैः पञ्चभिः श्लोकैः सकलशक्तितन्त्रसाधारणसप्ताक्षरं मन्त्रमुपदिशति । तत्र या—सप्ताक्षरी विद्या ! जवी—पकारः । मरुत्

---

(१) संस्थात् इति सो० पु० पा० । (२) वर्णयक्षरा इति सो० पु० पा० ।
(३) देवीमिति मू० पु० पा० । (४) रत्नाक्षर इति व० पु० पा० ;

जवी मरुत्समोपेतो गोत्रा च धरया युता ।
प्राणोऽपि मरुता युक्तः स नभः स्यात् तृतीयकम् ॥१३॥
पुनर्जवी क्षमयोपेतो ज्या च वातसमन्विता ।
व्याप्तं मरुत्सखं षष्ठं नभोऽग्निः सप्तमाक्षरम् ॥१४॥
एवं सप्ताक्षरी प्रोक्ता शक्तितन्त्रेषु सिद्धिदा ।
सर्वासामपि शक्तीनां देवतानां च नामभिः ॥१५॥
योजयेन्नामपूर्वा सा सिद्ध्यै साधारणं तथा ।
शक्तितन्त्राद्बहिर्भूततन्त्रेषु नमसा स्थितिः ॥१६॥
नवानां नव नामानि नवार्णानि पृथक् पृथक् ।
तानि सप्ताक्षरीयोगात्प्रत्येकं षोड़शाक्षरम् ॥१७॥
नित्याषोड़शरूपाणि तानि ज्ञेयान्यनुक्रमात् ।
तेषां नवानां नामानि मण्डलीकरणं प्रिये ! ॥१८॥
पारम्पर्य्यमिति प्रोक्तमाप्तिर्विद्यान्वयस्थितौ ।
तेन शुद्धेन शुद्धिः स्याद्विद्यायामन्यथाऽन्यथा ॥१९॥

आकारः । गोत्रा—दकारः । धरया—उकारेण । प्राणः—ककारः । मरुता प्राग्वत् । नभः—मकारः—विन्दुरित्यर्थः । तृतीयकम्—अक्षरमिति शेषः । जवी—प्राग्वत् । क्षमया—उकारेण । ज्या—जकारः । वातः—अकारः । व्याप्तम्—यकारः । मरुत्—प्राग्वदाकारः । नभः—प्राग्वत् । अग्निः—ईकारः । देवतानामि-त्युक्तिः पुंविषया ॥ १२ ॥ १३ ॥ १४ ॥ १५ ॥ १६ ॥

नवानामित्यादिना नामानीत्यन्तेन सत्रिपादेन श्लोकेन षोड़शनित्यात्मनां तेषां नवानां नाथानां षोड़शाक्षराणि नामान्युपदिशति । तत्र । षोड़शाक्षरम्—नामेति शेषः ॥ १७ ॥ १८ ॥

मण्डलीकरणमित्यादिना अन्यथा इत्यन्तेन पादादिना श्लोकेन पारम्पर्य-स्याविच्छिन्नत्वमुपदिशति । तत्र मण्डलीकरणं आद्यन्तयोः संबन्धतः । आप्तिः—प्रामाण्यम् । अन्वयः—सन्ततिः ॥ १८ ॥

साधकानां तु नामानि दिनपर्यायतोऽपि वा ।
दिनाक्षराण्यपि तथा ऽमायोऽनन्त्यमेव च (१) ॥२०॥
नाम पर्यायतः प्राप्तं कालावाप्तमिति द्वयम् ।
प्रसिद्धं बाह्यतो यच्च त्रीणि नामानि साधकि ! ॥२१॥
तस्मात् सम्प्राप्तविद्यास्तु साधकास्तैस्त्रिभिः स्तुतम् ।
पूजाश्लोकस्तुतीः कुर्यात् पारम्पर्यप्रसिद्धये ॥२२॥
गुरुमण्डलपूजां तु कुर्यात्सप्तसु पर्वसु ।
पूर्णायां षोड़शार्णानि नामान्यालिख्य पूजयेत् ॥२३॥
अन्यत्र पर्वषट्के तु नवार्णान्येव लेखयेत् ।
पूजयेत्तत्र तत्रापि वदन् सप्ताक्षरीं शिवे ! ॥२४॥
गुरुमण्डलपूजासु सर्वत्र नव चोदिताः ।
उपचारास्ततस्तांस्तैः पूजयेत् शृणु तान्यपि ॥२५॥

साधकानामित्यादिभिः प्रसिद्धये इत्यन्तैस्त्रिभिः श्लोकैर्मर्त्यानां त्रयाणां श्रोतव्यानि त्रीणि नामान्युपदिशति। तत्र वा—समुच्चये। तेन नामद्वयं भवतीत्यर्थः। दिनाक्षराणि—पञ्चविंशपटले वक्ष्यमाणानि। तथा—द्विप्रकाराणि। अमायः—अविसर्जनीयः। अनन्त्यः—अन्त्येन चकारेण रहितः प्रकार इति शेषः। एतदुक्तं भवति उपरिष्टाद्वक्ष्यमाणेषु घटिकाक्षरेषु विसर्जनीयचकारयोरेकमङ्गीकृत्य एकमपास्य पञ्चाशदक्षराणि भवन्तीति। पर्यायतः प्राप्तम्—स्वगुरोर्नामान्तरतः प्राप्तम्। कालावाप्तम्—युगादिदिवसमारभ्य विद्याप्राप्तिदिवसावधि नव नवसंख्यया हृतेषु युगदिवसेषु शिष्टदिनसंख्यया प्राप्तं नाम। बाह्यतः सिद्धम्—मातापितृदत्तम्। तैस्त्रिभिः—नामभिरिति शेषः। पूजाश्लोकस्तुतीरित्यत्र मण्डलादिषु पूजां पर्यायप्राप्तेन नाम्नैव कुर्यात् ॥ २० ॥ ॥ २१ ॥ २२ ॥

गुरुमण्डलपूजामित्यादिभिः समीरिता इत्यन्तैश्चतुर्भिः श्लोकैः पूजामण्डले नामाक्षरलेखनक्रमादिकमुपदिशति। तत्र सप्तपर्वाण्याद्यपटलोक्तानि। तत्र तत्रापि

---

(१) वा इति मो० पु० पा०।

गन्धं पुष्पं तथा धूपं दीपं नैवेद्यकं तथा ।
ताम्बूलं नमनं स्तोत्रं स्वात्मनेति समीरिता: ॥२६॥
गुरुमण्डलनिर्माणं पीठे कुर्यान्महेश्वरि ! ।
फलकायां स्थले वापि सुशुद्धे सुसमे स्थिरे ॥२७॥
प्राक्प्रत्यगदक्षिणोदक च सूत्राणि दश विन्यसेत् ।
पश्चाङ्गुलान्तरालानि ततो देवेशि ! जायते ॥२८॥
एकाशीतिपदोपेतं चतुरस्रन्तु मण्डलम् ।
तत्सर्वमध्ये प्रथमं द्वितीयन्तु पुरोगते ॥२९॥
तद्वामे (१) तत्तृतीयं चालिखेन्नवनवस्वपि ।
एवं नवनवोपेतं मण्डलं सप्तपर्वसु ॥३०॥
नवकं नवधा कृत्वा मध्ये सूत्रद्वयार्पणात् ।
तेषु नामार्णनवकमालिख्याभ्यर्चयेत् क्रमात् ॥३१॥
पूर्णा पर्वणि तन्मध्ये कृत्वा सूत्रत्रयं त्रयम् ।

वक्ष्यमाणेषु मण्डलेषु सम्प्रदायोक्तैर्नामभि: पूजयेदित्यर्थ: । स्वात्मना—स्वात्मसमर्पणात् ॥ २३ ॥ २४ ॥ २५ ॥ २६ ॥

गुरुमण्डलेत्यादिभि: क्रमादित्यन्तै: पञ्चभि: श्लोकै: षट्सु पर्वसु पूजनीयगुरुमण्डललेखनपूजादिकमुपदिशति । तत्र—आलिखेन्नवनवस्वपि—नवसु नवकेषु नाथानां नवनवकान्यालिखेदिति । एतदुक्तं भवति । एकाशीतिकोष्ठेषु मध्यनवकमारभ्य तत्पूर्वादिगतनवकादिषु अन्येषु नवकेषु प्रादक्षिण्येन नवानां नाथानां क्रमेण (२) तत्तन्मध्यकोष्ठावस्थानं, इतरेषामुक्तक्रमेणाभितोऽवस्थानञ्च जानीयादिति । तेषु नामार्णनवकं मध्यमुपक्रम्य पूर्वादिप्रादक्षिण्येन लिखेदित्यर्थ: ॥ २७ ॥ २८ ॥ २९ ॥ ३० ॥ ३१ ॥

पूर्णेत्यादिभि: सिद्धये इत्यन्तै: पञ्चभि: श्लोकै: पूर्णासु पूजनीयगुरुमण्डलविशे-

---

(१) तद्वामे तत्तृतीयं इति को० पु० पा० ।

(२) तत्र मध्ये ति ख० पु० पा० ।

षोड़शीकृत्य तेष्वेवं लिखेन्नामानि तानि वै ॥३२॥
एवं पूजा गुरौ जीवत्युपेते मामभूनि वै ।
स्थानानि मण्डलीकृत्य तत्र चाऽऽलेखने मते ॥३३॥
एवं यः पूजयेन्नाथान् पर्वस्ववहितः शिवे ।।
स देशिकवरः सिद्धः तस्माद्विद्याप्नि(१)रुत्तमा ॥३४॥
अन्यथाऽवाप्तिरुभयोरनर्थाय सुनिश्चितम् ।
व्याधिशस्त्रादिपीड़ा वा चित्तभ्रान्तिर्जले मृतिः ॥३५॥
इत्यादिव्यसन(२)प्राप्तिर्नृपादशनितो मृतिः ।
तस्मादुक्तक्रमेणैव कुर्यात्सर्वार्थसिद्धये ॥३६॥
एकद्वित्रिचतुःपञ्चवर्षाण्यालोच्य योग्यताम् ।
भक्तियुक्तान् गुणांश्चापि क्रमाद्वर्णेषु सङ्करे ॥३७॥
पश्चादुक्तक्रमेणैव वदेद्विद्यामनन्यधीः ।
अन्यथा चेद्वदेन्नाशं सशिष्यो गुरुराप्नुयात् ॥३८॥

षादिकमुपदिशति । तत्र—तेष्वेवं लिखेदित्यत्र एवमिति—पारम्पर्यप्राप्तसम्प्रदायक्रमेण लिखेदित्यर्थः । तद्यथा—मध्यचतुष्टये वामाधःस्थितं कोष्ठमारभ्य मध्यचतुष्टयं प्रादक्षिण्येन परीतग्रामुक्तक्रमं बहिरपि तथा परीयात् । मामुपेते—मुक्ते । मण्डलीकृत्य—वृत्तमालिख्य । अन्यथा—गुरुमण्डलार्चाविरहिता इत्यर्थः । इत्यादिरित्यत्रादिशब्दः सर्वानर्थनिवारणादीनामुपलक्षणम् ॥ ३१ ॥ ३२ ॥ ३३ ॥ ३४ ॥ ३५ ॥ ३६ ॥

एकद्वीत्यादिना गुरुराप्नुयात् इत्यन्तेन श्लोकद्वयेन वर्णानुरूपतः शिष्यस्य परीक्षाकालादिकमुपदिशति । तत्र योग्यता—प्रोक्तसमाचारशुद्धवत्वादि ॥ ३७ ॥ ३८ ॥

---

(१) विद्या निरुत्तमा इति मू० पु० पाठः ।

(२) व्याप्तिर्नृपादिति मू० पु० पा० ।

चक्रे देव्यां तथा शिष्ये प्रतिष्ठा त्रिविधोच्यते ।
सा तु तत्त्वविदा कार्या सम्प्रदायानुरोधिना ॥३९॥
स्थिरे शुभग्रहोपेतेऽनुकूले गुणशालिनि ।
मुहूर्ते कारयेद्विद्वान् पूर्णायां वा शुभोदये ॥४०॥
अक्षरत्रयसम्पातदिने पूर्णादिनत्रये ।
प्रोक्तेषु पञ्चस्वन्येषु सर्वदा वा शुभोदये ॥४१॥
कुर्यात्प्रतिष्ठां सिद्धात्मा (१) नत्वन्यो (२) ज्ञानगर्वितः ।
गुर्वनुज्ञामृते मोहाल्लोभाद् वा कुरुते यदि ॥४२॥
सपुत्रदारो निधनं प्राप्नुवन्निरयं व्रजेत् ।
तस्मात् पूर्णाभिषेकेण प्राप्तानुज्ञः समाचरेत् ॥४३॥
क्षौद्राज्यदुग्धैः प्रथमं नालिकेराम्भसा ततः ।

चक्रे देव्यामित्यादिभिः समाचरेदित्यन्तैः पञ्चभिः श्लोकैः प्रतिष्ठेयत्रैविध्यादिकमुपदिशति। तत्र चक्रे—ललितार्चाचक्रे । देव्याम्—देवीमूर्त्तौ। सम्प्रदायानुरोधिना—विदिततत्त्वेनापि नित्यनैमित्तिकोपास्तिनिरतेन। स्थिरे—राशाविति शेषः। अनुकूल—इति दिनादिविषयस्य। गुणशालिनीति—मुहूर्त्तविशेषणम्। यद्वा तदसिद्धौ। वा—अवधारणे। पूर्णायां—विशेषतः श्वासे शुभोदये कुर्यात्। तदितरत्रेतेत्यर्थः। अक्षरत्रयसम्पातदिने—पञ्चविंशपटलोदिताक्षरक्रमेण दिननित्याघटिकाक्षरे(३)ष्वेकाक्षरस्य त्रिस्थानदर्शनं यस्मिन् दिने तस्मिन्नित्यर्थः। पूर्णादिनत्रये पञ्चमीदशमीपञ्चदशीषु तिथिषु। प्रोक्तेषु पञ्चस्वन्येषु—प्रागुक्तेषु सप्तसु पर्वसु अत्रोदितं पर्वद्वयं वर्जयित्वा अन्येषु पञ्चस्वित्यर्थः। सर्वदा वा शुभोदये वा पक्षान्तरे। तिथिवारयोगनक्षत्रपूर्णादिवत् प्रोक्तमखिलमनवेक्ष्य स्वात्मनः श्वासस्य शुभोदय एव कुर्यादित्येकः पक्षः सिद्धविषयः। सिद्धात्मा तत्त्ववित्। मोहः—अज्ञानम्। लोभः—वित्तेच्छा। निरयं—क्लेशस्थानम्॥ ३९ ॥ ४० ॥ ४१ ॥ ॥ ४२ ॥ ४३ ॥

क्षौद्रेत्यादिभिर्भविष्यतीत्यन्तैरष्टभिः श्लोकैः श्रीचक्रप्रतिष्ठादिकमुपदिशति।

---

(१) शुद्धात्मा इति मू० पु० पा०। (२) ज्ञानवर्जित इति मो० पु० पा०।

(३) क्षरयोरेका इति १ पु० पा०।

अभिषिच्याथ तोयेन क्वथितेना(१)ष्टरौषधैः ॥४४॥
आवाह्याभ्यर्च्य तल्लग्ने चक्रे संस्थाप्य पूजयेत् ।
नित्यातत्त्वाग्निकालोत्थविद्ययाऽभ्यर्च्य ताः क्रमात् ॥४५॥
स्पृशन् जपेत् कराग्रेण श्रीचक्रं पूजयेदपि ।
एवं दिनत्रयं कृत्वा ततो नित्यक्रमं भजेत् ॥४६॥
गन्धैः पुष्पैर्नैवेद्यैर्धूपैर्दीपैर्नैवेद्यतर्पणैः ।
त्रिरात्रं पूजयेद्देवीं (२) योगिनीयोगिभिः समम् ॥४७॥
एवं देवीप्रतिष्ठायां क्रमः सान्निध्यकारकः ।
गुरवे दक्षिणां दद्यात् प्रत्यक्षाय शिवात्मने ॥४८॥
सर्वस्वं वा तदर्धं वा तदर्धं वा तदाज्ञया ।
न चेत्तच्छक्तिसङ्क्रान्तिः कथमस्य भविष्यति ॥४९॥
गजाश्वमहिषीमेषपशुदासीमहीयुतम् ।
सुवर्णं भूषणं वासो भवनं वाऽन्यदीप्सितम् ॥५०॥

तत्र क्वथितेनाष्टरौषधैः—पञ्चत्रिंशपटलोक्तैः पंचाशदष्टरौषधैः । नित्यातत्त्वाग्निकालोत्थविद्यया—पञ्चविंशपटलप्रोक्तकालावाप्ततद्दिननित्याविद्यया । ताः क्रमात्—तत्पटलप्रोक्तषट्त्रिंशत्सप्तशताधिकविंशतिसहस्राणि नित्या विद्याः । अपिर्भिन्नक्रमः । अपि वा स्पृशन् जपेदित्यर्थः । एतदुक्तं भवति—आवाहनानन्तरन्तद्दिननित्याविद्यया मूलविद्यातार्तीयखण्डेन मूलविद्यया च प्रत्येकं त्रिवारमभ्यर्च्य क्रमसपर्यानन्तरं ताभिः पूजयेत् । अपि वा स्पृष्टश्रीचक्रः प्रोक्तसङ्ख्याविशिष्टाः कालनित्यास्ता जपेदिति । तर्पणैः—प्रीतिदायकैरमृतैः । एवं देवीति । पूर्वोक्तक्रमादिति शेषः । तदाज्ञया—गुरोरिच्छया । भवनं वेत्यत्र वाशब्दः समुच्चये । स्वशक्तितः—यथाविभवम् । तदायत्तः—समस्तं स्वव्यापारन्तदनुमतमेव कुर्यादित्यर्थः ॥ ४४ ॥ ४५ ॥ ४६ ॥ ४७ ॥ ४८ ॥ ४९ ॥ ५० ॥ ५१ ॥

---

(१) क्वथितैरष्टरौषधैरिति सो० पु० पा० ।

(२) दैशो इति मा० मु० पु० पा० ।

दद्यात्स्वशक्तितो भक्त्या त्वशक्तो यदि सर्वथा (१) ।
सर्वदासौ तदाऽऽयत्तस्तेन सिद्धिर्भविष्यति ॥५१॥
(२) (वामेशनापि संपूज्य तत्तत्फलमवाप्नुयात् ।
कार्या योगेषु योगेषु वाऽऽन्तरेष्वितरेष्वपि ॥
वारर्क्षतिथिसंप्रोक्तमन्त्रैर्वा चैश्च दैवतैः ।
आवृत्तामर्चयेदग्निरक्षोवाय्वीशदिग्गतैः ॥
रोगशान्तिसमुद्योगफलानि समवाप्नुयात् ।
वाराणामित्यधिया प्रोक्ता तिथिनक्षत्रदेवताः ॥
ऋक्षऋक्षांस्तिथीनां च वद मे परमेश्वर ! ।
वह्निदस्राम्बुमाविघ्नो भुजगा षण्मुखो रविः ॥
मातरश्च तथा दुर्गा दिशो यक्षेश्वरो हरिः ।
यमो हरः शशी चेति तिथीशाः परिकीर्तिताः ॥
नक्षत्रदेवताश्चापि शृणु वक्ष्ये यथाविधि ।
अश्विनौ च यमो वह्निर्धाता चन्द्रः शिवोऽदितिः ॥
गुरुसर्पाश्च पितरः अर्यमा भग एव च ।
दिनकृच्च तथा त्वष्टा मरुतेन्द्राग्निमित्रकाः ॥
इन्द्रनिरृति यत्नानि विश्वे देवा हविस्तथा ।
वसवो वरुणः पश्चादज एकपदस्तथा ॥
अहिर्बुध्नस्तथा पूषा प्रोक्ता नक्षत्रदेवताः ।
कारस्करश्चामलकोदुम्बरो जम्बुकस्तथा ॥
खदिरः कृष्णवंशौ च पिप्पलौ नागरोहिणौ ।
पलाशः प्लक्षकाम्बष्टः बिल्वार्जुनविकङ्कताः ॥

---

(१) सर्वदा इति मू० पु० पा० ।

(२) ( ) एतदन्तर्गतो ग्रन्थो मूलपुस्तक एकस्मिन्नेव वर्तते तस्य व्याख्या च नास्ति ।

बटलः सरलः सर्जबकुलः पनसस्तथा ।
अर्कः शमी कदम्बश्चाभूतो निम्बस्तथातिमः ॥
मधुकश्चेति सम्प्रोक्ता वृक्षाभानां क्रमाद्दमी ।
अश्वं गजमदं मजं सर्पं सर्पिणी च विड़ालिका ॥
अत्तमाश्चरीमुखा मूषकी वृषमाहिषी ।
व्याघ्रश्च महिषो व्याघ्री मृगी मृगशुनी कपिः ॥
गोखण्डवानरा नारी तुरङ्गी च जगो गजाः ।
यदा रोगादिदुःखार्त्तिः भवेत्तत्पूर्वमे सुतैः ॥
मुहूर्त्तैः संख्यया चेति शान्तिः स्याद्विगुणेनधीः ।
आधारे पञ्च चक्राणि स्वाधिष्ठाने चतुष्टयम् ॥
प्रोक्तेषु भावयेत्तानि तावन्ति मणिपूरके ।
अनाहते ततः पञ्च यन्त्राणि परिभावयेत् ॥
विशुद्धाख्ये तु चत्वारि पञ्चाज्ञायोमिति क्रमात् ।
तत्तत्तिथिदिनेष्वेवं भावयेत् षोड़शीं शिवाम् ॥
तत्तच्चक्रगतां देवीं पूजयेत् सर्वसम्पदे ।
आधारादिषु चक्राणि भावयेद्ध्यानयोगतः ॥
ननु सर्वत्र सर्वाणि भावन्न कदाचन ।
भावयानामशक्तानां तत्तद्यन्त्राद्बहिस्तथा ॥
प्रोक्तान्याधारपद्मानि कृत्वा तत्रार्चयेद्विधिम् ।
एवं दिनेषु वारेषु पूजयेच्चक्रगतां शिवाम् ॥
संपूज्य देवीमिष्टानि प्राप्नुयात् प्रोक्तवासरैः ।
बलिं च दद्यात्तेष्वेव वासरेषु यथाविधि ॥
पञ्चाशन्मिथुनान्यत्र प्रोक्ते चक्रेऽङ्गराचके ।
मध्याह्ने सन्ध्ययोश्चापि चक्रस्थानामपीश्वरी ॥

शक्तिचक्रं मन्त्रचक्रमानिनां गामिनां—— ।
कूटानां मन्त्ररूपाणि प्रोक्तानि स्फुटमीश्वरी ॥
वैस्तेषां तेषु कालेषु बलिं दद्यात्तथोत्तरैः ।
देव्यास्त्वनुग्रहप्रोक्तः निवेद्यौ मिकथकं महत् ॥
निधाय तस्य मध्ये तु कृत्वा दीपं घृतप्लुतम् ।
निधाय तत्र तन्मन्त्रैस्तु मिथुनानामनुक्रमात् ॥
प्रत्येकं देव्यानां स्तेन सिद्धिर्भविष्यति ।) (१)
उक्तलक्षणसम्पन्नं शिष्यमाचारभूषणम् ।
पञ्चषट्कूटविद्याभ्यां शोधितं बहुवासरैः ॥५२॥
कलशैरभिषिच्याशु श्रीचक्रे सन्निवेश्य च ।
आधारे हृदये मूर्ध्नि चक्रं सञ्चिन्त्य मध्यतः ॥५३॥
स्वान्तादावाह्य संस्थाप्य संपूज्य न्याससंयुताम् ।
विंशो विद्यां वदेत् कर्णे देव्यात्मा पूर्णमानसः ॥५४॥
देवतागुरुमन्त्रात्मतत्त्वैक्यं भावयेद्धिया (२)।
शतं जपेत्तदग्रस्थो निकटे त्रिदिनं वसेत् ॥५५॥

उक्तेत्यादिभिर्दनादिभिरित्यन्तैः षड्भिः श्लोकैः सच्छिष्योपदेशक्रममुपदेशानन्तरं शिष्यकृत्यं चोपदिशति। तत्र --शोधितं बहुवासरैः—आस्तिक्योपास्तिभक्तीनां स्थैर्यज्ञानार्थं बहुवासरशोधनम् । कलशैः—नवभिश्चतुर्भिरेकेन वा । मध्यतः—श्रीचक्रत्रयमध्यतः । स्वान्तात्--देशिकस्य स्वात्मनः । अत्रास्य पकारोर्थो देशिकमुखादेवाचार्याभिषेकसमये लभ्यत्त्वादिह नोक्तः । देव्यात्मा पूर्णमानसः—स्वरूपं देवीरूपं विभाव्य स्वात्मानं तन्मयं बुद्ध्वा । एतदुक्तं भवति—केवलं देवतारूपो दयामयेन चित्तेनेतरनिरपेक्षेण विश्वाकारेणोपदिशेदिति । देवतागुरुमन्त्रात्मतत्त्वैक्यम्—देवतागुरुमन्त्राणां स्वात्मना तत्वतः चतुर्थपटलावसानश्लोकोक्तप्रकारेण । संचारिणी--

---

(१) ( ) एतन्मध्यगता: श्लोका यथाऽऽदर्शमेव मुद्रिता इति नात्र सुधीभिर्दोषदृष्टिः कार्या ।

२) भावयन्मुदा इति मू० पु० पा० ।

नोचेत् संचारिणी शक्तिर्गुरुमेति न संशयः ।
तस्मात् तदन्तिके तस्य पूजादेशादिकृद्भवेत् (१) ॥५६॥
तादात्म्यमात्मनो लब्धं गुरोर्मन्त्रात्मनो यतः ।
ततस्तदा समारभ्य तदायत्तोधनादिभिः ॥५७॥
अथाभिषेकं द्विविधं समवाप्य तदाज्ञया ।
अनुग्रहादि कुर्वीत सिद्धये नान्यथा भवेत् ॥५८॥
विधाय चक्रं तन्मध्ये योन्यां कुम्भं निधाय तु ।
क्वाथोदकैः समापूर्याभिषिच्याभिर्वदेन्मनुम् ॥५९॥
क्रमागतसमाचारनिरते शक्तिशालिनि ।
द्वितीयमभिषेकन्तु कुर्याद्देव्यात्मसिद्धये ॥६०॥
विरच्य विपुलं चक्रं प्रतियोनि च षोड़श ।
त्रिकोणानि विधायात मध्ये कुम्भं तु विन्यसेत् ॥६१॥

चंचला । मन्त्रात्मनः—चतुर्थपटलावसानोक्तप्रकारेण । धनादिभिरित्यत्रादिशब्देन गृहक्षेत्रादीन्युच्यन्ते ॥ ५२ ॥ ५३ ॥ ५४ ॥ ५५ ॥ ५६ ॥ ५७ ॥

अथाभिषेकं द्विविधमित्यादिभिः समाचरेदितयन्तैः पञ्चदशभिः श्लोकैः साधकानां द्विविधमभिषेकं तत्प्रकारादिकं चोपदिशति । तत्र—अनुग्रहादीत्यत्रादिशब्देन प्रयोगा उच्यन्ते । विधाय चक्रम्—त्रयस्त्रिंशत्पटलोक्तं पूजायन्त्रम् । क्वाथोदकैः—वक्ष्यमाणाश्वरौषधिभिः क्वथितशीतैरुदकैः । क्रमो—नित्यक्रमः । द्वितीयम्—पूर्णाभिषेकम् । विपुलं चक्रं—प्रागुक्तं ललितापूजाचक्रं वक्ष्यमाणकुम्भनिधानयोग्यप्रमाणं विरच्येत्यर्थः । तत्प्रमाणन्तु तत्रैव वक्ष्यामः । प्रतियोनि च षोड़श त्रिकोणानि विधाय—प्रतित्रिकोणं त्रयस्त्रिंशत्पटले वक्ष्यमाणेन प्रमाणेन तिर्यग्रूपा नवरेखा यथासम्प्रदायं विलिखेत् । तेन षोड़श त्रिकोणानि सम्भ-

---

(१) लभेत् इति मू० पु० पा० ।

सौवर्णं राजतं ताम्रं काचं मार्तिकमेव वा ।
पूरितं खारितोयेन क्वथितेनाखरौषधैः ॥६२॥
निक्षिप्य नवरत्नानि धान्यानि विविधानि च ।
हिरण्यानि सतामाणि वासोभ्यामभिवेष्टयेत् ॥६३॥
रक्ताभ्यां चन्दनैश्चूतपनसाश्वत्थपल्लवैः ।
शतक्रतुलताबद्धैः मातुलुङ्गफलान्वितैः ॥६४॥
विधाय कलशानन्यानन्येष्वेकैकशोन्यसेत् ।
सार्द्धं सहस्रं षट्त्रिंशत् पञ्चसंख्याः क्रमोदिताः ॥६५॥
मध्ये चक्रेषु तोयादि कृत्वाऽऽवाह्याभिपूज्य च ।
कालात्मनित्यामन्त्रांश्च जपित्वा पूर्ववासरे ॥६६॥

वन्ति। एतदुक्तं भवति—श्रीचक्रे चतुरस्रपद्मदलदेवतास्थानेषु हेतिस्थानेषु च त्रिकोणानि षोडश त्रिकोणगर्भाण्यालिखेदिति। मध्ये—सर्व्वमध्यमध्ये (१)। (खारीतोयेन—(२) खारीप्रमाणतोयेन। खारी च पल ४०९६। उक्तञ्च—पलाश्च कुड़वः प्रस्थ आढ़की द्रोण एव च। धान्यादिमाने बोद्धव्याः। द्रोणी षोड़शभिः खारी कुम्भः कार्यश्च विंशतिः।) नवरत्नानि—वक्ष्यमाणानि पद्मरागमुक्ताप्रवाल-वैडूर्यपुष्पराजवज्रनीलगोमेदमरकताख्यानि। धान्यानि—व्रीहितिलमुद्गमाषयवगोधूमादीनि। पल्लवविधानं सुरद्रुमशाखावासनया। मातुलुङ्गफलोक्त्या नारिकेरफलादिकमुपलक्षयति। लतापल्लवादीनां देशीसंज्ञा च स्वरूपे मुखागमविषये। सार्द्धं सहस्रं षट्त्रिंशत्पञ्चेत्येषासंख्या पञ्चनवतिसंख्यानानां श्रीचक्रस्थानामावरणशक्तीनां प्रत्येकं मूलदेवतावत्षोड़शविग्रहवत्वात्। (३) (तेनं पञ्चनवतिशक्तीनां षोड़शभेदैः पञ्चदशशतानि विंशत्यधिकानि भवन्ति। षोड़शभेदा मूलदेवतायाः। एवं षट्त्रिंशदधिकानि पञ्चदशशतानि शक्तीनामतस्तावन्त एव कुम्भाः पूर्वोक्तप्रकारेण पञ्चविधकुम्भसङ्ख्याक्रमेण जाता इत्यर्थः।) एतदुक्तं भवति—आयुधानां द्वैविध्यात् अष्टौ षोड़शत्र्यस्र(४)गर्भवन्ति वज्राकारेणान्योन्यमभिमुखानि

---

(१) सर्वमध्ययोन्यां इति सो० पु० पा०। (२) एतदन्तर्गतो ग्रन्थः सो० पुस्तक एव वर्तते।
(३) एतदन्तर्गतो ग्रन्थः सो० पुस्तक एव वर्तते। (४) षोड़शास्रगर्भं इति मू० पु० पा०।

जन्मर्क्षे प्रातरुत्थाय स्वनित्यां तत्र (१) पूजयेत् ।
सहस्रं प्रजपेत्पश्चाद्धोमं कृत्वा समन्ततः ॥६७॥
शृङ्गकाहलशङ्खादिवाद्यसङ्गीतनर्तनैः ।
मुदितैर्योगिनीवृन्दैरेकैकं देवतात्मभिः ॥६८॥
वृत्तैः (२) सम्पूजितैः सार्द्धमभिषिञ्चेद्‌गुरुः स्वयम् ।
स्वक्रमं तस्य कथयेत्तदा प्रभृति सोऽपि तम् ॥६९॥
अनुतिष्ठेदविच्छिन्नं पर्यायं तस्य विच्युतौ ।
सहस्रं प्रजपेद्विद्यामभिषेकसमन्वितम् ॥७०॥
अथवा षष्ठ्यावत्यस्तु कलशांस्तत्र विन्यसेत् ।
तेषु शक्तीः समावाह्य सम्पूज्यैवाभिषेचयेत् ॥७१॥
एकं वा कलशं जन्मदिने कृत्वाऽभिषेचयेत् ।
एवं नैमित्तिकं नित्यमविच्छिन्नं समाचरेत् ॥७२॥

समालिख्य सर्वमध्यत्रिकोणस्य कोणत्रये तिर्यग्रेखात्रयेण त्रीणि त्रिकोणानि षोडशत्रिकोणगर्भाणि कृत्वा तेषामन्तराले वृत्तमालिख्य तदधः योनिषोड़(३)शत्र्यस्रगर्भवह्नि वज्राकारेणान्योन्यमभिमुखमालिखेदिति । कालात्मनित्यामन्त्रान्-पञ्चविंशे पटले वक्ष्यमाणान् तद्दिननित्यामन्त्रान् । एतदुक्तं भवति—सर्वत्राभिषेकेषु पूर्वस्मिन् दिवसे अधिवासनपूर्वमन्येद्युरभिषेकं कुर्यात् । अथवा सद्योधिवासं विदधीत । जन्मर्क्षे—शिष्यस्य जन्मदिने पूर्णाभिषेकं कुर्यादित्यर्थः । होमं कुर्यात्—नित्यहोमोक्तक्रमतः इति शेषः । समन्तत इत्यस्योपरिष्टादन्वयः । वृत्तैः—देवतात्मत्वेन पूर्वाभिमन्त्रितैः । स्वं क्रमम्—अचरक्रमम् । अविच्छिन्नपर्यायम्—पर्यायशब्देन षट्त्रिंशद्दिनान्युच्यन्ते । एतदुक्तं भवति—गुर्वाज्ञामृते पर्यायविच्छित्तौ साभिषेकं ससहस्रं प्रायश्चित्तमुक्तम् । विच्छिन्नदिनानां प्रत्येकं सन्ध्यात्रयषष्टिघटिका जप-

---

(१) नित्यान्ते प्र इति सो० पु० पा० । (२) एतैः सु इति सो० पु० पा० ।
(३) षोडशास्रगर्भ इति ब० पु० पा० ।

नाथैस्तत्त्वैश्च नित्याभिः कालनित्या (१) तु विद्यया ।
आधारे हृदये शीर्षे वह्नौ सूर्ये निशाकरे ॥७३॥
ध्यायंस्त्रिसन्ध्यं प्रजपेत् सवर्गं व्यञ्जनस्वरम् ।
न्यसेच्च मातृकास्थाने तदा तद्देहसिद्धये ॥७४॥
ग्रहाणां वैपरीत्येषु जन्मर्क्षे ग्रहणे द्वयोः ।
क्लेशप्राप्तौ रिपुक्लेशे कुर्याद्देवाभिषेचनम् ॥७५॥
तेन दोषाः स्पृशन्त्येनं न कदाचन तद्बलात् ।
क्षुद्राणि क्रूरकर्माणि कृत्याश्च रिपुकल्पिताः ॥७६॥

प्रायश्चित्तं शतवारञ्च कृत्वा तद्दिनादि भजेत् । तत्र—इति केवल एव श्रीचक्रे । एकं वेति पक्षः (२) काम्यविषयः ॥ ५८ ॥ ५९ ॥ ६० ॥ ६१ ॥ ६२ ॥ ६३ ॥ ६४ ॥ ६५ ॥ ६६ ॥ ६७ ॥ ६८ ॥ ६९ ॥ ७० ॥ ७१ ॥ ७२ ॥

नाथैरित्यादिना सिद्धय इत्यन्तेन श्लोकद्वयेन सन्ध्यात्रयभजनं काम्यन्यासविशेषं चोपदिशति । तत्र एतदुक्तं भवति—आत्मज्ञानस्य नाथोपक्रमत्वात्तैः प्रातः सन्ध्या, विश्वस्य षट्त्रिंशत्तत्त्वात्मनाऽवस्थानात् माध्यन्दिनसन्ध्या, नित्याविद्यास्वरूपपरामर्शेन पारिपूर्ण्यात् सायं सन्ध्याऽनुष्ठीयते इति । सवर्गं व्यञ्जनस्वरमित्यस्यार्थस्य पञ्चविंशपटले वक्ष्यमाणत्वादिह न प्रपञ्चितः । न्यसेच्च मातृकास्थाने—पञ्चदशपटले वक्ष्यमाणमातृकान्यासस्थानेषु सर्वेषु क्रमागततत्तदक्षरैः सार्द्धं तत्तद्दिननित्याद्योपेतां श्रीविद्यां न्यसेदित्यप्युपकारः—सम्प्रदायः ॥ ७३ ॥ ७४ ॥

ग्रहाणामित्याद्यैरभिषेचनमित्यन्तैः पञ्चभिः श्लोकैरभिषेककालविशेषं (३) तदनुभावं चोपदिशति । ग्रहणे द्वयोः—चन्द्रसूर्ययोः । क्षुद्राणि—विद्वेषणोच्चाटनादीनि । क्लेशाः—आध्यात्मिकाधिदैविकाधिभौतिकाः । अशेषदुःखार्त्तिः—चित्तस्य संकुचितत्वदुःखार्त्तिः ॥ ७५ ॥ ७६ ॥ ७७ ॥ ७८ ॥ ७९ ॥

---

(१) काला नित्या इति सो० पु० पा० ।

(२) काम्यविषय इति सो० वं० पु० पा० ।

(३) विशेषां तदनु इति वं० १ पु० पा० ।

बलं कथं भवेत् तस्य सेकस्य परमेश्वर ! ।
ब्रूहि मे तद्बलं येन क्लेशा नश्यन्त्यशेषतः ॥७७॥
सोमसूर्याग्निरूपेण जलेन स्पर्शमात्रतः ।
नश्यन्त्यशेषतो दोषाः तस्मात्सेकसमो न हि ॥७८॥
सोमसूर्याग्निरूपत्वं जलस्योपरि कीर्तितम् ।
तस्मादशेषदुःखार्तिशान्त्यै स्यादभिषेचनम् ॥७९॥
सप्तसूत्रेषु कालेषु पुण्येष्वन्येषु चादरात् ।
कुर्यात्सदक्षिणां पूजां गुरोः प्रत्यब्दमेव वा ॥८०॥
उक्तेषूत्पातजातेषु पूजयेत् स्वर्णपुष्पकैः ।
अभिषिक्तस्तु विधिना प्रदद्याद्दक्षिणां गुरोः ॥८१॥
गुरुं तदग्रतः प्राप्तविद्यं तदनुजं तथा ।
गुरोर्गुरुं तद्गुरुं च स्वाग्रतो लब्धविद्यकात् ॥८२॥
प्रणामपूजास्तवनसेवादिभिरुपासनैः ।
तोषयेदन्यथा शक्तिः स्वीया तद्गामिनी भवेत् ॥८३॥
चन्द्रचन्दनकाश्मीरलघुकस्तूरिकायुतैः ।
पङ्कैर्विदध्यात्सर्वत्र गुरुमण्डलकल्पनम् ॥८४॥

सप्तस्वित्यादिभिर्भवेदितान्तैश्चतुर्भिः श्लोकैर्गुरुपूजादिकमुपदिशति । तत्र प्रत्यब्दमेव वा इत्यत्र एवकारोऽवश्यकरणीयत्वप्रतिपादकः वाशब्दोऽधमसूचकः । वित्तादिभिः प्रतिमासपूजनं मध्यमः पक्षः । सप्तसु च पर्वस्वन्येषु पुण्यसमयेषु वित्तादिभिः पूजनमुत्तमः पक्षः । उत्पातजातेषु—दिव्यान्तरिक्षभौमत्रैविध्य-जातेषु विकारविशेषेषु । उपासनम्—चित्तानुवृत्तिः । स्वीया—शिष्यगता । तद्गा-मिनी—गुरुगामिनी ॥ ८० ॥ ८१ ॥ ८२ ॥ ८३ ॥

चन्द्रेत्यादिना परमेश्वरीत्यन्तेन श्लोकद्वयेन गुरुमण्डलनिर्म्माणद्रव्यादिकमुपदिशति । तत्र—चन्द्रं—कर्पूरम् । लघुः—अगुरुः । भाल इत्यादिना अवश्यधार्यत्वं कथयति । सर्वतः—सर्वत्र सिद्ध्यति ॥ ८४ ॥ ८५ ॥

पूजान्ते मार्जयित्वा तद्भाले चोरसि चांसयोः ।
धारयेत्सर्वतो लक्ष्मीं रसस्यात्परमेश्वरी ॥ ८५ ॥
पूर्वोक्तिमण्डलेष्वेव यानि स्थानानि पूजने ।
प्रोक्तानि तानि सर्वाणि पद्मानि (१) परिकल्पयेत् ॥८६॥
पूजादाववसाने च पञ्चश्लोकान् जपेत्ततः ।
देव्यात्मत्वं गुरोर्लब्ध्वा श्लोकद्वादशकं जपेत् ॥८७॥
गणेशग्रहनक्षत्रयोगिनीं राशिरूपिणीम् ।
देवीं मन्त्रमयीं नौमि मातृकां पीठरूपिणीम् ॥८८॥
प्रणमामि महादेवीं मातृकां परमेश्वरीम् ।
कालहल्लोहलोल्लोलकलनाशमकारिणीम् ॥८९॥

पूर्वेत्यादिना श्लोकेन प्रागुक्तगुरुमण्डलविशेषविधानमुपदिशति। एतदुक्तं भवति - नवभिर्नवभिः कोष्ठैः सकर्णिकमष्टदलपद्मं यथाविधि विधाय तेषु नामाक्षराणि पङ्क्तिक्रमेणालिखेदिति। तन्मानं तन्निर्माणप्रकारं च यन्त्रपटले सुव्यक्तं वक्ष्यामः ॥ ८६ ॥

पूजादावित्यादिना श्लोकेन नाथदेवतयोः स्तोत्रद्वयजपकालमुपदिशति। तत्र—नाथ एव देवतास्वरूपेण भासत इति परमार्थं बुध्वेत्यर्थः ॥ ८७ ॥

अतःपरं देवीस्तोत्रश्लोकद्वादशकस्य पूर्वमेव नित्याषोड़शकार्णवे महात्मभिः काश्मीरिभिर्व्याख्यातत्वात्तेषां द्वादशानां श्लोकानामत्र व्याख्या सैव लिख्यते। गणेशेति। गणेशो—विनायकः। स च कालरूपी कथितः। ग्रहाः—सूर्यादयः। नक्षत्राणि—अश्विन्यादीनि। तन्मन्त्रादि च तन्नाम चाग्रे वक्ष्यति। योगिन्यो—वशिन्याद्याः। राशिः—मेषादिः। रूपिणीम्—एषां कारणत्वात्। देवीमिति पूजोक्तिः। मन्त्रमयीम्—अक्षरमयत्वात्। नौमि—नमनं तादात्म्यमुक्तम्। मातृकां—मातृवन्मातृकाम्—विश्वप्रसवित्रीम्। पीठरूपिणीम्—उक्तप्रकारैः सर्वाधाररूपाम्। एतदुक्तं भवति--शब्दराशेः कालस्य च स्वात्मत्वेन भावनास्थैर्यं जीवन्मुक्तिरिति। प्रणमामीति। कालहल्लोहलोल्लोलकलनाशमकारिणीम्—कालस्य

---

(१) यन्त्राणि इति मू० पु० पा०।

यदक्षरैकमात्रेऽपि संसिद्धे स्पर्द्धते नरः ।
रवितार्क्ष्येन्दुकन्दर्पशङ्करानलविष्णुभिः ॥९०॥
यदक्षरशशिज्योत्स्नामण्डितं भुवनत्रयम् ।
वन्दे सर्वेश्वरीं देवीं महाश्रीसिद्धमातृकाम् ॥९१॥
यदक्षरमहासूत्रप्रोतमेतज्जगत्त्रयम् ।
ब्रह्माण्डादिकटाहान्तं तां वन्दे सिद्धमातृकाम् ॥९२॥
यदेकादशमाधारं बीजं कोणत्रयोद्भवम् ।
ब्रह्माण्डादिकटाहान्तं जगदद्यापि दृश्यते ॥९३॥

हल्लोहलो — वेगः । उल्लोलकलना — पूर्वोत्तरसम्बन्धः । एतदुक्तं भवति — पूर्वोक्तभावनामन्त्रसंसिद्धौ कालपारवश्यात् क्लेशो न भवतीति । यदक्षरेति । एकमात्र इत्यस्यार्थ आराध्यपादमुखादवगन्तव्यः । संसिद्धे — पूज्यपादैरुक्तप्रकारेण । रविणा — प्रकाशादिना स्पर्द्धते । तार्क्ष्येण चक्रविषहरणादिना । इन्दुना चामृतमयत्वादिना । कन्दर्पेण सौभाग्यादितः । शङ्करेण चानन्दमयत्वादितः । अनलेन च प्रतापादितः । विष्णुना च विश्वात्मत्वादितः । एतदुक्तं भवति — मातृकायामेकाक्षरेऽपि संसिद्धे तत्तथा सिद्ध्यतीति ॥ ८८ ॥ ८९ ॥ ९० ॥

यदक्षरेति । शशी — अमृतमयत्वात् । ज्योत्स्ना — प्रकाशरूपवाचकत्वम् । मण्डितं — तत्सम्बद्धम् । भुवनत्रयं — ज्ञातृज्ञानज्ञेयात्मरूपम् । सिद्धमातृकां — सर्वेषां शब्दादेवार्थप्रतिपत्तेः । एतदुक्तं भवति — शब्दार्थयोर्निरवशेषाहन्ताश्रिरात्मनः सिद्धेति । यदक्षरेति । महासूत्रप्रोतं — महत्त्वमनाद्यत्वात् । सूचनात् विशेषाणामर्थानां सूत्रम् । प्रोतं — नियतसम्बन्धः । एतदिति — प्रत्यक्षत्वम् । ब्रह्माण्डादिकटाहान्तं — ब्रह्माण्डमित्यपश्चिमं ब्रह्मत्वं, कटाहमितरवरं सौक्ष्म्यम् । एतदुक्तं भवति — प्रागवच्छब्दार्थयोर्निरवशेषव्याप्तौ सत्यां प्रतिनियतावान्तरसम्बन्धत्वमुपदिश्य तन्मयता चात्मनः सिद्धेति ॥ ९१ ॥ ९२ ॥

यदेकेति । आधारः — अधिकरणम् । बीजं — कारणम् । कोणत्रयोद्भवं यत् — कोणत्रयाकारतामेकादशाक्षरस्योक्त्वा तदुद्भूतत्वं जगत्प्रत्यक्षसिद्धं दृश्यत इत्यर्थः प्रागुक्तप्रपञ्चस्य प्रत्यक्षमिति दर्शयति । एतदुक्तं भवति — मातृकायामेकाक्षरस्याऽपि जगत्कारणत्वमस्तीत्युपदिश्य तन्मयता स्वात्मनः सिद्धेति शेषः ॥ ९३ ॥

अकचादिटतोन्नद्धपयसाक्षरवर्गिणीम् ।
ज्येष्ठाङ्गबाहुहृत्पृष्ठकटिपादनिवासिनीम् ॥८४॥
तामीकाराक्षरोद्धारां सारात्सारां परात्पराम् ।
प्रणमामि महादेवीं परमानन्दरूपिणीम् ॥८५॥
अद्यापि यस्या जानन्ति न मनागपि देवताः ।
केयं कस्मात् क्व केनेति (१) सरूपारूपभावनाम् ॥८६॥
वन्दे तामहमक्षय्यमातृकाक्षररूपिणीम् ।
देवीं कुलकलोल्लोलप्रोल्लसन्तीं परां शिवाम् ॥८७॥

अकचेति। वक्ष्यमाणवशिन्यादिशक्त्यष्टकरूपेण समस्तेन। ज्येष्ठाङ्गेति—व्यस्तरूपैश्च मातृकाक्षरैः सर्वतः शरीरित्वेनावभासमानाम्। एतदुक्तं भवति—मातृकायाः समसव्यासरूपेण शरीरिणां शरीरितामुपदिश्य तन्मयता स्वात्मनः सिद्धेति शेषः। उद्धारो—लिपिरूपः। सारात्सारां—स्वयं च। उभयसारशब्दविषयं दर्शयति परात्परामिति। परमानन्दरूपिणीम्। इकारस्य विन्दुविसर्गात्मनः। शिवशक्त्योः सामरस्यरूपत्वात्। एतदुक्तं भवति—मातृकायाः कारणभूतयोर्विन्दुविसर्जनीययोरैक्यरूपस्य इकारस्य विन्दुसंकल्पेति वक्ष्यमाणस्य स्वात्मत्वेन भावनायां परमानन्दानुभव इति ॥ ८४ ॥ ८५ ॥

अद्यापीति पूर्वोक्तं रहस्यं स्तौति। देवताः—इन्द्रियाणि। केयं—स्वरूपतः। कस्माद्धेतोः। क्व—कुत्रस्थाने। केनोपायेनेति। सरूपभावनामरूपभावनां च। एतदुक्तं भवति—अदेशिककटाक्षविद्धैः षड्भिरिन्द्रियैः किंरूपा कस्माद्धेतोः कुत्रस्थाने केनोपायेनेति सरूपभावनामरूपभावनां चाद्यापि सर्वदा मनागीषदपि न जानन्तीति। अत्र प्रश्नचतुष्टयमाराध्यपादमुखादवगन्तव्यम्। अतिरहस्यत्वादिह नोद्घाटितम् ॥ ८६ ॥

वन्दे इति। अहम्। आद्यन्तप्रत्याहृत्या मातृकारूप आत्मा। अक्षयाम्। अकारक्षकारयोर्मध्यजाम्—मातृकाक्षररूपिणीम्। सप्तमसूत्रप्रकाशितेन वर्त्मनाकुल-

---

(१) स्वरूपेति मू० पु० पा०।

(१) वर्गानुक्रमयोगेन यस्या मात्राष्टकं स्थितम् ।
वन्दे तामष्टवर्गोत्थमहासिद्ध्यष्टकेश्वरीम् ॥९८॥
कामपूर्णं (२)जकाराद्यश्रीपीठान्तर्निवासिनीम् ।
चतुराज्ञाकोशभूतां नौमि श्रीत्रिपुरामहम् ॥९९॥
इति द्वादशभिः श्लोकैः स्तवनं सर्वसिद्धिकृत् ।
देव्यास्त्वखण्डरूपायाः स्तवनं तव तद्यतः ॥१००॥

कलोल्लोलप्रोल्लसन्तीम्—कुलं शरीरं पृथिव्यां लीयमानत्वात्। कला—एकदेशः। उल्लोलं उर्द्ध्वोर्द्ध्वं प्रोल्लसन्तीम्—वैश्वर्यापरां अचिन्त्यस्वभाववैभवाम्। चिन्तयतः। एतदुक्तं भवति। अव्यक्तरूपं व्यक्तरूपं च मातृकाया रूपमुद्दिश्य तन्मयता स्वात्मनः सिद्धेति ॥ ८७ ॥

वर्गेति। अनुक्रमयोगेन—सप्तमसूत्रोपदिष्टेन। मातृकाष्टकं तदपि तत्रोक्तम्। अष्टवर्गोत्थमहासिधयष्टकेश्वरीम्—प्रतिवर्गोत्थाणिमादिसिद्ध्यष्टकेश्वरीम्। एतदुक्तं भवति। मातृकाया अष्टौ वर्गास्तदधिष्ठात्र्योऽष्टमातरस्तासां प्रत्येकोत्थाणिमाद्यष्ट—सिद्धयश्च संभूय चतुःषष्टिः। तासां व्यष्टिशक्तीनां कारणभूता समष्टिशक्तिः स्वात्मत्वेन सिद्धेति। अत्रापि रहस्यमस्ति तदवगन्तव्यमाराध्यचरणमुखात् ॥९८॥

कामेति। जकाराद्यं—जकारो यस्य पीठस्याद्यं तत् जकाराद्यम्—जालंधरपीठम्। श्रीपीठं श्रीड्याणपीठं देव्यावासत्वात्। भूजलाग्निवायुरूपपीठचतुष्टयं वियद्रूपेण सर्वत्र निवासिनीम्। चतुराज्ञा कोशभूतां—आज्ञा—पूर्वाम्नायादिः। कोशभूतां—समस्तकारणत्वात्। त्रिपुरा—मातृका—मातृकाभिः ज्ञातृज्ञानज्ञेयाभिरात्मस्वरूपतत्त्वज्ञातैरखण्डतं पूरयतीति। एतदुक्तं भवति—एकादशभिरुक्तसूत्रैरुपदिष्टवैभवमातृकादेशविशेषेषु तत्त्वविशेषेषु च व्याप्ता विश्वप्रपञ्चरूपा शक्तिः स्वात्मत्वेन सिद्धेति। इतः परमस्मद्व्याख्या ॥ ९९ ॥

इति इत्यादिना श्लोकेन स्तोत्रजपफलमुपदिशति। तत्राखण्डरूपायाः देशाकारैरनवच्छिन्नाया मातृकायास्तादात्म्यादिति शिवम् ॥ १०० ॥

---

(१) उर्वनु इति मू० पु० पा० ।

(२) जकाराख्य इति मू० पु० पा०

तोयतत्वमयी व्याप्तिरिति सम्यक् प्रदर्शिता ।
अस्या निःफालनाच्चित्ते तत्तत्त्वं स्वात्मसात्कृतम् ॥१०१॥

इति षोड़शनित्यातन्त्रेषु श्रीकादिमते
द्वितीयं पटलम् ।

इति श्रीषोड़शनित्यातन्त्रेषु श्रीकादिमताख्यस्य परिपूर्णस्य तन्त्रस्य प्रपञ्चसारसिंहराजप्रकाशाभिधानेन सुभगानन्दनाथेन विरचितायां मनोरमायां व्याख्यायां नवनाथवैभवपूजाभिधानादिप्रकाशनपरं द्वितीयं पटलं परिपूर्णं परामृष्टम् ॥२॥

अथ तृतीयं पटलम् ।

अथ षोड़शनित्यानां क्रमाद्विद्यास्तु (१) षोड़श ।
वाराद्या कुरुकुल्लाया आत्मनोऽष्टाक्षरस्य च ॥१॥
भूतानां च बलेश्चैव क्रमान्मन्त्रांश्छृणु प्रिये ! ।
प्राच्यते साधुसङ्केतैर्लिपीनां प्रागुदीरितैः ॥२॥
हृत्प्राणेलाहंसदाहवह्निस्वैर्ललितेरिता ।
त्रिविधा हंसभेदेन शृणु ताश्च यथाक्रमम् ॥३॥

अथ तृतीयं पटलम् ।

पूर्वस्मिन् द्वितीये पटले नवनाथवैभवपूजाविधानादिकमुपदिश्यानन्तरं षोड़शनित्यानां षोड़शमन्त्रांस्तदङ्गमन्त्रानव च, सम्भूय पञ्चविंशतिमन्त्रानुपदिशति, अथ षोड़शेत्यादिना बलेर्मनुरित्यन्तेन श्लोकशतरूपेण तृतीयेन पटलेन । तत्र— अथ षोड़शेत्यादिना प्रागुदीरितैरित्यन्तेन श्लोकद्वयेन पटलार्थोद्देशादिकमुपदिशति । तत्र सङ्केतैः—सामयिकैर्नामभिः । प्रागुदीरितैः पूर्वतन्त्रे (२) पञ्चत्रिंशत्पटले प्रोक्तैः ॥ १ ॥ २ ॥

हृदित्याद्यैः समीरितेत्यन्तैस्त्रिभिः श्लोकैराद्याया अङ्गिनित्याया ललिता—विद्यायाः स्वरूपं तत्प्रभेदादिकमुपदिशति । तत्र—हृत्—सकारः । प्राणः—ककारः । इला—लकारः । हंसः—हकारः । दाहः—रेफः । वह्निः—ईकारः । स्वं—बिन्दुः । हंसेत्यादिना स्वमित्यन्तेन ह्रूस्वोच्यते क्लीं इति । ललिता—विद्येति शेषः । हंसभेदेन—हंकारयोजनाभेदेन ॥३॥ हंसाद्यया—हकाराद्यया । ललिता-

---

(१) विद्या तु षो इति म० पु० पा० । (२) पञ्चविंश इति ख० पु० पा० ।

हंसाद्ययाऽऽद्या मध्या(१)स्यादादिमध्यस्थहंसया ।
तृतीया प्रकृतिः सैव तुर्या तैरन्त्यमायया (२) ॥४॥
आसु तुर्या भवेन्मुक्त्यै तिस्रोऽन्याः स्युश्च सम्पदे ।
इति त्रिपुरसुन्दर्या विद्या सम्यक् समीरिता (३) ॥५॥
शुचिः स्वेन युतस्त्वाद्यो ललिता स्याद्द्वितीयकः ।
शून्यमग्नियुतं पश्चाद्रयो व्याप्तेन संयुतः ॥६॥
प्राणो रसाग्निसहितः शून्ययुग्मं चरान्वितम् ।
नभो गोत्रा पुनश्चैषा दाहेन समयोजिता ॥७॥
अम्बु स्याच्चरसंयुक्तं (४) वनशक्तियुतं च हृत् ।

विद्ययेति शेषः । आदिमध्यस्थहंसयेत्यत्र मध्येऽपि ककारस्योपरि । सैव — ललिताविद्यैव । तुर्या — चतुर्थी । तैरन्त्यमायया — तैः कूटत्रयगतैरक्षरैः । अन्त्यमायया — अन्तस्थहृल्लेखया । एतदुक्तं भवति — प्रोक्तकूटत्रयाक्षरैः प्रोक्तक्रमगतैः प्रथमद्वितीयकूटचरमगतहृल्लेखाविरहितैस्तृतीयकूटचरमगतहृल्लेखासहितैः समस्ताऽऽद्या तुरीया विद्येति ॥ ४ ॥ आसु — चतसृषु विद्यासु ॥ ५ ॥

शुचिरित्यादिभिरेकादशाक्षरेत्यन्तैस्त्रिभिः श्लोकैर्द्वितीयायाः कामेश्वरीनित्याया एकादशाक्षरीं (५) विद्यामुपदिशति। तत्र — शुचिः ऐकारः। स्वेन युतः — स्वं — विन्दुः। तेन युक्तः ऐं इति। आद्यो — वर्ण इति शेषः। ललिता — प्रागभिहिता विद्या। शून्यं — नकारः। अग्नियुतं — अग्निरिकारः तेन सहितं नि इति। रयः — तकारः। व्याप्तेन संयुतः — व्याप्तं — यकारस्तेन संयुक्तः त्य इति॥६॥ प्राणः ककारः। रसाग्निसहितः — रसा — लकारः। अग्निरिकारः ताभ्यां सहितः क्लि इति। शून्ययुग्मं — नकारद्वयम्। चरान्वितं — चरः — एकारस्तेन सहितं न्ने इति। नभो —

---

(१) हंसाद्ययाममध्या इति मू० पु० पा० ।

(२) अयं श्लोकः पुनरपि मू० पुस्तके लिखितः ।

(३) प्रचक्षते इति मू० पु० पा० ।

(४) नवशक्ति इति मू० पु० पा० । (५) चरां इति १ पु० पा० ।

एषा कामेश्वरी नित्या कामदैका दशाक्षरा (१) ॥८॥
कामेश्वर्यादिरादिः स्याद्रसश्चाथ स्थिरा रसः।
धरायुक् सचरा पश्चात् स्थिरा पश्चाद्रसः स्मृतः ॥९॥
स्थिराशून्येऽग्निसंयुक्ते रसः स्यात्तदनन्तरम्।
स्थिरा भूःसहिता गोत्रा सदाहोऽग्नी रसः स्थिरा ॥१०॥
नभश्च मरुता (२) युक्तं रसा चरसमन्विता।

मकारः। गोत्रा—दकारः। पुनश्चैषा—पुनरपि दकारः। दाहेन समयोजिता—दाहो—रेफः तेनाऽपृथक् योजिता ॥७॥ अम्बु—वकारः। चरसंयुक्तं—चर—एकारः तेन सहितं वे इति। वनशक्तियुतं—वनं—औकारः, शक्ति—विसर्जनीयः ताभ्यां सहितम्। हृत्—सकारः सौः इति। एवमुक्तप्रकारेणैकादशाक्षरेत्यर्थः ॥ ८ ॥

कामेश्वर्येत्यादिभिः मोहिनीत्यन्तैस्त्रयोविंशतिभिः श्लोकैः तृतीयाया भगमालिनीनित्यायाः पञ्चत्रिंशत्छताक्षरीं (३) विद्यामुपदिशति। तत्र कामेश्वर्यादिः—विन्दुसहित ऐकारः ऐं इति। रसः—भकारः। स्थिरा—गकारः। रसो—भकारः। धरायुक्—धरा—उकारः तेन युक्तः भु इति। सचरा—एकारसहिता। स्थिरा—गकारः गे इति। रसः—भकारः ॥९॥ स्थिराशून्ये—गकारनकारौ। अग्निसंयुक्ते—इकारेण प्रत्येकं संयुक्तौ गिनि इति। रसः—भकारः। स्थिरा—गकारः। भूःसहिता—भू—ऊकारः तेन सहिता। भूःसहितेति संज्ञाशब्दस्वरूपोपादानं भूः इति (४) संज्ञोपेतेनाक्षरेणेत्यर्थः। एवमस्मिन् प्रकरणेऽन्यत्र सर्वत्रापि निर्वाहः। गो इति। गोत्रा—दकारः। सदाहः—रेफसहितः। अग्निः—इकारः रि इति। रसो—भकारः। स्थिरा—गकारः ॥१०॥ नभः—मकारः। मरुता युक्तं—मरुत्—आकारः तेन युक्तं मा इति। रसा—लकारः। चरसमन्विता—

---

(१) चरी इति मू० पु० पा०।
(२) संयुक्तं इति मू० पु० पा०।
(३) चरां इति १ पु० पा०।
(४) संज्ञायेत्यक्षरं इति २ पु० पा०।

ततो रसः स्थिरा पश्चान्मरुता सह योजिता ॥११॥
अम्बु हंसश्च सचरो रसोऽथ स्यात्स्थिरायुतः ।
स्थिरा धरान्विता हंसो व्याप्तेन च चरेण च ॥१२॥
रसः स्थिरा ततो व्याप्तं भूयुतं शून्यमग्नियुक् ।
रसः स्थिरा ततः साग्निः शून्यं जवियुतो मरुत् ॥१३॥
रयः शून्यं चाग्नियुतं हृद्दाहः साम्बुतः परम् ।
रसः स्थिराऽम्बु च वियत् खयुतं प्राण एव च ॥१४॥
दाहोग्नियुग्रसस्तस्मात् स्थिरा क्ष्मा दाहसंयुता ।

एकारेण सहिता लेइति। रसः—भकारः। स्थिरा गकारः। मरुता सह योजिता —आकारेण सह(१) पृथग्योजिता गा इति ॥११॥ अम्बु—वकारः। हंसो—हकारः। सचर—एकारेण सहितः हे इति। रसो—भकारः। स्थिरा—गकारः। धरान्विता —उकारेण सहिता गु इति। हंसो—हकारः। व्याप्तेन—यकारेण। चरेण—एकारेण ताभ्यां युक्तः ह्ये इति ॥१२॥ रसो—भकारः। स्थिरा—गकारः। व्याप्तं—यकारः। भूयुतं—ओकारसहितं यो इति। शून्यं—नकारः। अग्नियुक्—इकारेण सहितं नि इति। रसो—भकारः। स्थिरा गकारः। साग्निः—इकारेण सहितम्। शून्यं—नकारः। साग्निरिति संज्ञिविशेषणपरोऽयं निर्देशः शून्याख्योवर्ण इकारसहितः स्यादित्यर्थः। अस्मिन् प्रकरणे सर्वत्र संज्ञासंज्ञिपरत्वेन विशेषणलिङ्गानां निर्देशनियमो बोद्धव्यः। तत्र संज्ञिपरो लिङ्गनिर्देशनियमस्त्रिविधः वर्णशब्दापेक्षया—अक्षरशब्दापेक्षया—लिपिशब्दापेक्षया च। तेन नि इति। जवियुतः—पकारेण सहितः। मरुत्—आकारः पा इति॥१३॥ अथ रयः तकारः। शून्यं नकारः। अग्नियुतं—इकारेण सहितं एतत् शून्यस्यैव विशेषणं नि इति। हृत्—सकारः। दाहः—रेफः। साम्बु—वकारेण सहितं भवति र्व इति। रसः—भकारः। स्थिरा—गकारः। अम्बु—वकारः। वियत्—सकारः। खयुतं—विन्दुना सहितं सं इति। प्राणः—ककारः ॥१४ दाहः—रेफः। अग्नियुक् —इकारेण सहितः रि इति। रसः भकारः। स्थिरा—गकारः। क्ष्मा—ऊकारः।

---

(१) आकारेणापृथग्योजिता इति १ पु० पा०।

सचरश्च जवी पूर्वविद्यातार्तीयतः क्रमात् ॥१५॥
चतुष्टयमथार्णानां रसस्तदनु च स्थिरा ।
हृदम्बुयुक् क्ष्मया दाहः सचरः स्याज्जवी च हृत् ॥१६॥
दाहोऽम्बुमरुता युक्तो व्योम साग्नी रसस्ततः ।
स्थिरा (तु) ऽपि मरुता युक्ता शून्यं साग्नि नभश्चरी ॥१७॥
हंसो व्याप्तमरुद्युक्तः शून्यं व्याप्तमतोऽम्बु च ।
दाहो गोत्रा चरयुता तथा दाहस्तथा रयः ॥१८॥
हृद्धरासहितं दाहरयौ चरसमन्वितौ ।
रसः स्थिरा ततः प्राणो रसाग्निसहितो भवेत् ॥१९॥

दाहसंयुता - दाहः - रेफः तेन संयुता रेफसहिता रु इति । सचरः - एकारेण सहितः । जवी - पकारः पे इति । पूर्वविद्यातार्तीयतः क्रमात् चतुष्टयमथार्णानां— तृतीयादिवर्णानां चतुष्टयमित्यर्थः । एतदुक्तं भवति— कामेश्वरीनित्याविद्यायास्तृतीयचतुर्थपञ्चमषष्ठान्यक्षराणि चत्वारि (न पे इत्यस्मात्परं) नित्यक्लिन्ने एतद्रूपाणि ज्ञेयानि ॥१५॥ रसो भकारः । स्थिरा - गकारः । हृत्—सकारः । अम्बु—वकारः । क्ष्मया—जकारेण सहितः । दाहो रेफः रु इति । जवी—पकारः । चरेण एकारेण सहितः पे इति । हृत्—सकारः॥१६॥ दाहोऽम्बुमरुता युक्तः—वकाराकाराभ्यां युक्तो दाहस्तेन स्वा इति । व्योम—णकारः । साग्निः—इकारेण सहितः णि इति । रसो —भकारः । स्थिरा—गकारः । अस्मिन् प्रकरणे सर्वोऽपि शब्दः समुच्चये । मरुता युक्ता—आकारेण युक्ता गा इति । शून्यं—नकारः । साग्नि—इकारेण सहितः नि इति । नभश्चरी—नभो—मकारः चर—एकारः एकारसहितो मकार इत्यर्थः ॥१७॥ हंसो—हकारः । व्याप्तमरुद्युक्तः—व्याप्त—यकारः । मरुत्—आकारः ताभ्यां युक्तः ह्या इति । शून्यं—नकारः । व्याप्तं—यकारः । अतः—परमिति शेषः । अम्बु —वकारः । दाहो—रेफः । गोत्रा - दकारः । चरयुता—एकारसहिता दे इति । तथा दाहः—रेफः एकारसहित इत्यर्थः रे इति । तथा रयः—एकारसहितस्तकार इत्यर्थः ते इति ॥१८॥ हृत्—सकारः । धरासहितं—उकारसहितं सु इति । दाहरयौ—रेफतकारौ । चरसमन्वितौ—एकारसहितौ । रेफतकारौ प्रत्येकमेकारेण सहितावित्यर्थः रेते इति । रसो—भकारः । स्थिरा—गकारः ।

शून्ययुग्मं चरयुतं ततः पूर्वमतः परम् ।
शून्ययुग्मं च गोत्रा स्यात् दाहयुक्ताम्बुना चरः ॥२०॥
प्राणो रसाचरयुतो गोत्रा व्याप्तमतःपरम् ।
गोत्रा दाहमरुद्युक्ता त्वम्बु व्याप्तमतो भवेत् ॥२१॥
वातो नभश्च भूयुक्तं वाश्चरेण समन्वितम् ।
रसः स्थिराऽम्ब्वग्नियुतं वायुयुग्मं चरान्वितम् ॥२२॥
ग्रासोधरायुतः पश्चाद्रसः शक्त्या समन्वितः ।
ग्रासो भूःसहितो देवि ! रसो व्याप्तं ततश्च हृत् ॥२३॥
दाहेनाम्बु च हृत्पश्चात् रयोऽम्बुमरुदन्वितः ।
शून्यं च केवलं भद्रे ! रसश्च सचरा स्थिरा ॥२४॥

प्राणः—ककारः । रसाग्निसहितः—रसा—लकारः । अग्निरिकारः ताभ्यां सहितः क्लि इति ॥१८॥ शून्ययुग्मं—नकारद्वयं—चरयुतम्—एकारेण सहितं न्ने इति । ततः पूर्वमतःपरं—अस्याक्षरस्य पूर्वाक्षरमेवोत्तराक्षरमित्यर्थः । क्लि इति । शून्ययुग्मं—नकारद्वयं न्न इति । गोत्रा -दकारः । दाहसहितः— द्र इति । अम्बुना—वकारेण सहितः । चर—एकारः ॥२०॥ प्राणः—ककारः । रसा —लकारः । चर—एकारस्ताभ्यां सहितः क्ले इति । गोत्रा—दकारः । व्याप्तं यकारः । गोत्रा—दकारः । दाहमरुद्युक्ता - दाहः--रेफः । मरुत्—आकारः द्रा इति । अम्बु - वकारः । व्याप्तं —यकारः ॥२१॥ वातः —अकारः । नभो— मकारः । भूयुक्तं—ऊकारयुक्तं मो इति । वाः —घकारः । चरेण समन्वितं --एकारेण सहितं घे इति । रसो —भकारः । स्थिरा --गकारः । अम्बु—वकारः । अग्नियुतं—इकारेण युक्तं वि इति । वायुयुग्मं-- चकारद्वयम् । चरान्वितं---एकारसहितं चे इति ॥२२॥ ग्रासः—चकारः । धरायुतः --उकारयुतः चु इति । रसो—भकारः । शक्त्या समन्वितः—विसर्जनीयेन सहितः भः इति । ग्रासः —चकारः । भूः सहितः—ओकारेण सहितः भूः सहितः इत्यत्रापि संज्ञाशब्दस्वरूपोपादानं भू इति संज्ञोपेतेनेत्यर्थः चो इति । देवीति सम्बुद्धिः । रसो —भकारः । व्याप्तं—यकारः । हृत्—सकारः ॥२३॥ दाहेन —रेफेण सहितमिति शेषः । अम्बु—वकारः वं इति । हृत्—सकारः । रयः—तकारः । अम्बुमरुदन्वितः—अम्बु --वकारः मरु-दाकारः त्वा इति । शून्यं—नकारः ।

वियदम्बुयुतं दाहस्त्वग्नियुक् खयुतः शुचिः ।
भूमौ रसाच्छमाखयुता पञ्चैकान्तरिताः स्थिताः ॥२५॥
तदन्तरितबीजानि खसंयुक्तानि पञ्च वै ।
तानि क्रमात् ज्या सचरो रसो भूश्च नभोयुता ॥२६॥
हंसश्चरयुतो द्विःस्यात् ततः प्राणो रसाग्नियुक् ।
शून्ययुग्मं चरयुतं हृद्दाहोऽम्बु मरुद्युतः ॥२७॥
व्योमाग्निसहितं पश्चाद्रसश्च मरुता स्थिरा ।
शून्यं साग्नि नभः कुर्याच्चरेण सहितं प्रिये ! ॥२८॥

केवलं च स्वररहितं न् इति । भद्रे इति देवीसम्बोधनं मन्त्रानन्तरितम् । रसः—भकारः । स चरा—एकारेण सहिता, स्थिरा—गकारः गे इति ॥२४॥ वियत्—सकारः । अम्बयुतं—वकारयुतम्—स्व इति । दाहो—रेफः अग्नियुक्—इकारेण सहितः रि इति । खं—विन्दुस्तेन युतः । शुचिः—एकारः ऐं इति । भूमिः—बकारः । रसाच्छमाखयुता—रसा—लकारः । च्छमा—उकारः । खं—विन्दुः तैः संयुक्ता ब्लूं इति । पञ्चैकान्तरिता स्थिताः—ब्लूं इत्येतत्कूटाक्षरं एतदाद्यमेकैकाक्षरान्तरितं पञ्चकृत्वः प्रयोज्यमित्यर्थः । तदन्तरितबीजानि खसंयुक्तानि पञ्च वै—प्रोक्तस्य ब्लूं इति बीजस्यान्तरालेषु—उपरिस्थितानि सविन्दूनि बीजानि पञ्च तानि क्रमात् कथयामीति शेषः । ज्या—जकारः जं इति । सचरः—एकारसहितो, रसः—भकारः भें इति । भूः ओंकारः । नभोयुता—नभो—मकारः तेन सहिता मों इति ॥२६॥ हंसो—हकारः । चरयुतः एकारसहितः हें इति । ब्लूमिति प्रोक्तस्य पञ्चमस्य बीजस्यान्ते च स्यात् हेमिति बीजं वारद्वयं स्यादित्यर्थः । यथा—ब्लूं जं ब्लूं मों ब्लूं हें ब्लूं हें एवं प्रकारेण । प्राणः—ककारः । रसाग्नियुक् रसा लकारः । अग्नि—रिकारः ताभ्यां सहितः क्लि इति । शून्ययुग्मं—नकारद्वयम् । चरयुतं—एकारेण सहितं न्ने इति । हृत्—सकारः । दाहो—रेफः । अम्बु—मरुद्युतः—अम्बु—वकारः । मरुत्—आकारः ताभ्यां सहितः वा इति ॥२७॥ व्योम—णकारः । अग्निसहितं—णि इति । रसो—भकारः । मरुता—आकारेण सहितेति शेषः । स्थिरा—गकारः गा इति । शून्यं—नकारः । साग्नि—इकारेण सहितं नि इति । नभो—मकारः । चरेण सहितं—एकारेण सहितं मे इति

अम्बु पश्चाद्वियत्तस्मान्नभस्तु मरुदन्वितम् ।
शून्यं व्याप्तं च हृद्युक्तं रयदाहखवह्निभिः ॥२९॥
हंसः सदाहोऽम्बुरसाचरखैः संयुतो भवेत् ।
हंसः स्याद्दाहवह्निखैर्युक्तमन्त्यमुदीरितम् ॥३०॥
पञ्चविंशच्छतार्णैः स्यान्नित्याऽसौ भगमालिनी ।
कथिता परमेशानि ! वनिताजनमोहिनी ॥३१॥
हंसस्तु दाहवह्निखैर्युक्तः प्रथममुच्यते ।
कामेश्वर्यास्तृतीयादिवर्णानामष्टकं भवेत् ॥३२॥
हृदम्बु मरुता युक्तं हंसश्च मरुता युतः ।
एकादशाक्षरी नित्यक्लिन्ना नित्या समीरिता ॥३३॥

प्रिये इति देवी सम्बोधनम् ॥२८॥ अम्बु—वकारः । वियत्-सकारः । नभः—मकारः । तुशब्दः समुच्चये । मरुदन्वितं—आकारेण सहितं—मा इति । शून्यं—नकारः । व्याप्तं—यकारः । हृत्—मकारः । युक्तं रयदाहखवह्निभिः—रयस्तकारः । दाहो—रेफः । खं—विन्दुः । वह्निः—इकारः । तैर्युक्तं स्त्रीं इति ॥२९॥ हंसो—हकारः । सदाहः—रेफसहितः । अम्बुरसाचरखैः संयुतः—अम्बु—वकारः रसा—लकारः चर—एकारः खं—विन्दुः एतैः संयुक्तः । एतदुक्तं भवति—हकाररेफवकारलकारएकारविन्दुभिरेकं कूटमिति ह्व्लूं इति । हंसो—हकारः । दाहवह्निखैः संयुतम्—दाहो—रेफः । वह्निः—इकारः । खं—विन्दुः । तैः संयुतम् । अन्त्यं—बीजमिति शेषः । ह्रींकारमित्यर्थः । भगमालिनी नित्या विद्येति शेषः । परमेशानीति देवीसम्बुद्धिः ॥ ३० ॥ ३१ ॥

हंसेत्यादिभिः सुन्दरीत्यन्तैस्त्रिभिः श्लोकैः चतुर्थ्या नित्यक्लिन्नाया नित्याया एकादशाक्षरीं विद्यां तज्जपादिफलं चोपदिशति । तत्र हंसो—हकारः । दाहवह्निखैर्युक्तः—दाहो—रेफः वह्निः—इकारः खं—विन्दुः तैः संयुक्तः—ह्रीं इत्यर्थः । ह्रीं इति प्रथमं बीजमिति शेषः । कामेश्वर्यास्तृतीयादिवर्णानामष्टकं भवेत्—कामेश्वर्यादि नित्या विद्या तृतीयमक्षरमारभ्य दशमाक्षरपर्यन्तं अत्र द्वितीयाक्षरादीन्यष्टाक्षराणि तेन नवाक्षराणि सम्पन्नानि । हृत्—सकारः । अम्बु मरुता युक्तः—

वनितानवनीतानां द्रावकोऽग्निर्जपादिना ।
जायते साधको नित्यं कन्दर्पाधिकसुन्दरः ॥३४॥
भूः खेन युक्ता प्रथमं प्राणो दाहेन तद्युतम् ।
रसो दाहेन तद्युक्तं प्राणो दाह-वन-ख-युक् ॥३५॥
कं च दाहेन तद्युक्तं प्रभा दाहेन तद्युता ।
ज्या च दाहेन तद्युक्ता नित्यक्लिन्नान्तता द्वयम् ॥३६॥
एषा नवाक्षरी नित्या भेरुण्डा सर्वसिद्धिदा ।
यस्याः स्मरणतो नश्येद्गरलं त्रिविधं क्षणात् ॥३७॥

अम्बु—वकारः । मरुत्—ओकारः । ताभ्यां युक्तं स्वा इति । हंसो—हकारः । मरुता—ओकारेण युक्तः ह्रों इत्यर्थः । वनितानवनीतानां द्रावकोऽग्निः । एतदुक्तं भवति—एतस्य विद्यासिद्धस्य दर्शनादेव वनिताः अर्थ-प्राणाद्युपकारिका (१) वश्या भवन्ति ॥ ३२ ॥ ३३ ॥ ३४ ॥

भूः खेनेत्यादिभिः क्षणादित्यन्तैस्त्रिभिः श्लोकैः पञ्चम्या भेरुण्डानित्याया नवाक्षरीं विद्यामुपदिशति । तत्र—भूः-ओकारः । खेन युक्ता-विन्दुना सहिता, ओमिति । प्रथमं—बीजमिति शेषः । प्राणः—ककारः । दाहेन—रेफेण । तद्युतं—ओंकारयुक्तं ककाराक्षरमित्यर्थः क्रौं इति । रसो-भकारः । दाहेन-रेफेण । तद्युक्तं—ओंकारयुक्तं भकाराक्षरमित्यर्थः भ्रों इति । प्राणः—ककारः । दाहवनखयुक्—दाहो—रेफः । वनं-ओकारः । खं—विन्दुः एतैः संयुतः क्रों इति ॥ ३५ ॥ कं च—झकारः । दाहेन—रेफेण । तद्युक्तं ओंकारयुक्तं झकाराक्षरमित्यर्थः झ्रों इति । प्रभा—छकारः । दाहेन—रेफेण, तद्युक्तं—ओंकारयुक्तं छकाराक्षरमित्यर्थः छ्रों इति । ज्या-जकारः । दाहेन-रेफेण । तद्युक्तं ओंकारयुक्तं जकाराक्षरमित्यर्थः ज्रों इति । नित्य-क्लिन्नाऽन्ततोद्वयं—नित्यक्लिन्ना (नित्या) विद्याया अन्त्यः अक्षरद्वयं स्वाहा इत्यर्थः ॥ ६२ ॥ नित्या-भेरुण्डा—नित्या विद्येति शेषः । गरलं—विषं त्रिविधं—स्थावरजङ्गमकृत्रिमभेदेन । तत्र स्थावरं—कारस्करकरवीरादि, जङ्गमं—फणिगोनासादि । कृत्रिमं—लिकुचरसकर्पूरादि ॥३७॥

---

(१) अर्थप्रणामाद्युपकारिका इति टी० पु० पा० ।

भेरुण्डाद्यमिहाद्यं स्यान्नित्यक्लिन्नाद्यनन्तरम् ।
ततोऽम्बु शून्यं हंसाग्नियुक्तमम्बु मरुद्गतम् ॥३८॥
हृदग्निना युतं शून्यं व्याप्तेन शुचिना च युक् ।
शून्यं नभःशक्तियुतं नवार्णेयमुदीरिता ॥३९॥
नित्या सर्वार्थदा वह्निवासिनी विश्वघस्मरा ।
यस्याः स्मरणतो वश्यं जायते भुवनत्रयम् ॥४०॥
द्वितीयं वह्निवासिन्या नित्यक्लिन्ना चतुर्थकम् ।
पञ्चमं भगमालाद्यं भेरुण्डाया द्वितीयकम् ॥४१॥

भेरुण्डाद्येत्यादिभिस्त्रयमित्यन्तैस्त्रिभिः श्लोकैः षष्ठ्या वह्निवासिनीनित्याया नवाक्षरीं विद्यामुपदिशति। तत्र 'भेरुण्डाद्यमिहाद्यं स्यात्'—भेरुण्डानित्याविद्याया आद्यमक्षरं वह्नि-वासिनीनित्याविद्याया आद्यमक्षरं भवतीत्यर्थः तेन ओमिति सिद्धम्। 'नित्यक्लिन्नाद्यनन्तरं'—नित्यक्लिन्ना नित्याविद्याया आद्यमक्षरं क्लींकारोऽस्या द्वितीयमक्षरमित्यर्थः। ततः—अनन्तरम्। अम्बु—वकारः। शून्यं—नकारः। हंसाग्नियुक्तं—हकारेकाराभ्यां सहितं वह्नि इत्यर्थः। अम्बु—वकारः। मरुद्युतं—आकारयुक्तं वा इति ॥३८॥ हृत्—सकारः। अग्निना युतं—इकारेण सहितं सि इति। शून्यं—नकारः। व्याप्तेन—यकारेण शुचिना च एकारेण च युक्—युतं आभ्यां द्वाभ्यां युक्तमित्यर्थः न्ये इति। शून्यं—नकारः। नभो—मकारः। शक्तियुतं—विसर्जनीयसहितं मः इति ॥ ३९ ॥ विश्वघस्मरा-प्रलये विश्वग्रासकरी ॥ ४० ॥

द्वितीयमित्यादिभिः तारिणीमित्यन्तैस्त्रिभिः श्लोकैः सप्तम्या महावज्रेश्वरीनित्याया द्वादशाक्षरीं विद्यामुपदिशति। तत्र द्वितीयं वह्निवासिन्याः—वह्निवासिनीनित्याविद्यायाः द्वितीयमक्षरं अस्या आद्याक्षरं क्लीं इति। नित्यक्लिन्ना चतुर्थकं पञ्चमस्य (१) नित्यक्लिन्नेत्यर्थः। भगमालाद्यं—ऐंकारः। भेरुण्डाया द्वितीयकं—क्रोंकारः ॥४१॥ नित्यक्लिन्नाद्वितीयं च तृतीयं च—नित्य इत्यक्षरद्वयम्। षष्ठसप्तमौ तस्या एव (मद) इत्यर्थः। अष्टमं नवमं पश्चात्—तस्या एवाष्टमाक्षरं नवमाक्षरं च स्याताम् (द्रवे) इत्यर्थः। एतदाद्यं—अस्या महावज्रेश्वर्या आद्यं क्लींकार इत्यर्थः। दुःखसङ्घाततारिणी—अविवेकतारिणीत्यर्थः ॥ ४२ ॥

---

(१) चतुर्थकं पञ्चमं क्लि इति क्लिन्ने इत्यर्थः इति टी०पु०पा०। चतुर्थकं पञ्चपञ्चक्लिन्नेत्यर्थ इति वङ्ग पु०पा०।

नित्यक्लिन्नाद्वितीयं च तृतीयं षष्ठसप्तमौ ।
अष्टमं नवमं पश्चादेतदाद्यमितीरितम् ॥४२॥
महावज्रेश्वरी नित्या द्वादशार्णा समीरिता ।
कान्तारसागरक्रूरदुःखसङ्घाततारिणी ॥४३॥
वज्रेश्वर्यन्त्यमाद्यं (१) स्याद्वियदग्नियुतं ततः ।
अम्बु स्यान्मरुता युक्तं गोत्रा क्ष्मासंयुता ततः ॥४४॥
रयो व्याप्तेन शुचिना युतं स्यात् तदनन्तरम् ।
अन्त्यार्णौ वह्निवासिन्या दूती नित्या समीरिता ॥४५॥
सप्ताक्षरी समस्तापत्तारिणी विश्वरञ्जिनी ।
श्रीकारी शिवतावाप्तिकारिणी सर्वसिद्धिदा ॥४६॥
आद्यन्तु वह्निवासिन्या दूत्यादिस्तदनन्तरम् ।
हंसो धराखसंयुक्तः तेजस्वरसमन्वितम् ॥४७॥

वज्रेश्वरीत्यादिभिः सिद्धिदेत्यन्तैः त्रिभिः श्लोकैः अष्टम्या दूतीनित्यायाः सप्ताक्षरीं विद्यामुपदिशति । तत्र वज्रेश्वर्यन्त्यमाद्यं स्यात्—वज्रेश्वरीनित्यायाः अन्त्यमक्षरं अस्यां दूतीनित्यायामाद्यमक्षरं भवति क्रों इत्यर्थः । वियदग्नियुतं—वियत्—शकारः । अग्नि-युतं—इकारसहितम् । ततः—द्वितीयमित्यर्थः शि इति । अम्बु स्यान्मरुता युक्तं-अम्बु—वकारः । मरुता युक्तं—आकारेण सहितं वा इति तृतीयमक्षरम् । गोत्रा क्ष्मासंयुता ततः – गोत्रा-दकारः । क्ष्मया युता—ऊकारेण सहिता दू इति चतुर्थमक्षरम् ॥ ४४ ॥ रयो व्याप्तेन शुचिना युतं स्यात् तदनन्तरं—रयस्तकारः । व्याप्तेन—यकारेण, शुचिना—ऐकारेण युतं त्यै इति । अन्त्यार्णौ वह्निवासिन्याः—नम इत्यर्थः ॥ ४५ ॥ समस्तापत्तारिणी—अविवेकापन्नाशकरी ॥ ४६ ॥

आद्यमित्यादिभिः कारिणी इत्यन्तैश्चतुर्भिः श्लोकैर्नवम्यास्त्वरितानित्याया द्वादशाक्षरीं विद्यामुपदिशति । तत्र—आद्यन्तु वह्निवासिन्याः—ॐ इत्यर्थः । दूत्यादि तदनन्तरम्—क्रोंकारो द्वितीयं बीजम् । हंसोधराखसंयुक्तः—हंसो—हकारः । धरा—ऊकारः—खं विन्दु स्ताभ्यां युक्तः हूंकारः तृतीयं बीजम् । तेजस्वर-

---

(१) वज्रेश्वर्यन्तमाद्यं इति पुस्तकान्तरपाठः ।

वायुः प्रभा चरयुता ग्रासः शक्ति-समन्वितः ।
हृदा रयेण दाहेन वह्निः स्यादष्टमं प्रिये ! ॥४८॥
हंसः क्ष्माखयुतो ग्रासस्वरयुक्तो द्वितीयकम् ।
द्युतिर्नादयुता नित्या त्वरिता द्वादशाक्षरी ॥४९॥
लक्ष्मीकान्तियशोविद्याधनारोग्यायुराप्तिकृत् ।
विषदुःखप्रशमनी सर्वाभीष्टाप्तिकारिणी ॥५०॥
शुचिः खेन युतस्त्वाद्यो रसा वह्नि-समन्वितः ।
प्राणो द्वितीयः खयुतो वनहृच्छक्तिभिः परः ॥५१॥
इतीरिता त्र्यक्षरी स्यान्नित्याऽसौ कुलसुन्दरी ।
यस्याः स्मरणमात्रेण सर्वज्ञत्वं प्रजायते ॥५२॥

समन्वितम्—तेजः—खकारः । चरेण—एकारेण समन्वितः खे इति चतुर्थम् ॥४७॥ वायुः—चकारः । (पदाम्) (१) प्रभा—छकारः । चरयुता—एकारयुक्ता छे इति षष्ठम् । ग्रासः शक्तिसमन्वितः—ग्रासः—चकारः । शक्त्या—विसर्जनीयेन समन्वितः चः इति सप्तमम् । हृदा रयेण दाहेन वह्निः—सकार-तकार रेफ-ईकारैः स्त्री इत्यष्टमं बीजम् । प्रिये ! इति देवीसम्बुद्धिः ॥४८॥ हंसः क्ष्माखयुतः ह्लूँ (२) इति नवमम् । ग्रासस्वरयुतः—चे इति दशमम् । द्वितीयकं—अस्या एव द्वितीयं बीजं क्लीँ इत्येकादशम् । द्युतिर्नादयुता—द्युतिः—फकारः । नादः—टकारः तेन युक्ता फट् इति द्वादशं बीजम् ॥ ४९ ॥ विषदुःखप्रशमनी—विषं—सर्पादिजं, दुःखं—दारिद्र्यादिजं द्वयो र्नाशकरी ॥ ५० ॥

शुचिरित्यादिना जायत इत्यन्तेन श्लोकद्वयेन दशम्याः कुलसुन्दरीनित्यायाः त्र्यक्षरां विद्यामुपदिशति—तत्र—शुचिः खेन युतः—विन्दुना सहित ऐकारः ऐँ इति प्रथमं बीजम् । रसावह्निसमन्वितः—रसा—लकारः, वह्निरीकारः ताभ्यां समन्वितः । प्राणः—ककारः, खयुतः—विन्दुयुतः—क्लीँ इति द्वितीयम् । वनहृच्छक्तिभिः परः—सौः इति तृतीयं बीजम् ॥ ५१ ॥ यस्याः स्मरणमात्रेण—जपाराधनादिवैगुण्येनापीत्यर्थः ॥ ५२ ॥

---

(१) ( ) एतत्पदं केवलं टीकापुस्तक एव वर्त्तते । (२) ह्लौमिति टी० पु० पा० ।

हंसस्य हृत्प्राणरसादाहकुभिः समन्वितः ।
विद्यया कुलसुन्दर्या योजितः सम्प्रदायतः ॥५३॥
नित्या नित्या त्वचरा स्यात् षड्भिः कूटाचरैर्युता ।
प्रतिलोमादिभी रूपै र्द्वासप्ततिभिराहता ॥५४॥
यस्या भजनतः सिद्धो नरः स्यात् खेचरः सुखी ।
निग्रहानुग्रहौ चास्य जायते स्वेच्छयाऽनिशम् ॥५५॥
त्वरितोपान्त्यमाद्यं स्यात् द्यु तिर्दाहचरस्वयुक् ।
हृच्च दाहद्मास्वयुतं वज्रेशी पञ्चमं ततः ॥५६॥

हंस इत्यादिभिः अनिशमित्यन्तैस्त्रिभिः श्लोकैरेकादश्या नित्यायास्त्र्यक्षरां विद्यां तद्भेदसङ्ख्यां चोपदिशति । तत्र हंसस्य हृत्प्राणरसादाहकुभिः समन्विता—हंसो—हकारः । हृत्—सकारः । प्राणः—ककारः । रसा—लकारः । दाहः—रेफः । कुः—उकारः । पञ्चभिः हंसाख्यो हकारः सहितः स्यात् । एतदुक्तं भवति एतैर्हकारादिभिः (१) उकारान्तैः षड्भिरक्षरैः प्रत्येकमनुलोमक्रमेणाद्यन्तक्रमयोजितैरेवं षड्भेदभिन्नैस्तदनु उकारादिभि र्हकारान्तैः प्रत्येकं प्रतिलोमक्रमेण चाद्यन्तक्रमयोजितैरेवं षड्भेदभिन्नैस्तदनुकूलसुन्दरीनित्याविद्यायाः प्रकृतिभूतया सङ्केतविद्यया षट्प्रकारभिन्नया सम्प्रदायतो योजितैः नित्याविद्याया द्वासप्ततिर्भेदाः सम्भवन्ति, तेष्वाद्या प्रधाना सेयमिति ॥ ५३ ॥ नित्यानित्येत्यादिना श्लोकेन नित्यानित्याविद्याया उपरिष्टाद्वक्ष्यमाणेषु विंशत्यधिक(२)शतभेदेषु द्वासप्ततिभिदेत्युक्तिः तेषु क्रमागतानां विभवभेदानां प्रयोगप्राधान्यदर्शनायेत्यर्थः ॥ ५४ ॥ यस्या भजनत इत्यादिना श्लोकेन विद्यासिद्धस्य सामर्थ्यं कथयति । तत्र स्वेच्छया—उपरिष्टान्नित्यानित्यापटलोक्तनिग्रहानुग्रहस्य योगबलादित्यर्थः ॥ ५५ ॥

त्वरितेत्यादिभिः कामदोदितेत्यन्तैः पञ्चभिः श्लोकैर्द्वादश्या नीलपताकानित्यायाः सप्तदशाक्षरां विद्यामुपदिशति, तत्र त्वरितोपान्त्यं - उपान्त्यं अन्त्याक्षरात्पूर्वम् ग्र्ह१ स्ह २ ल्क् ३ ल्वह ४ ल्वस्द्र ५ ड्ल्स्फ ६एवं अनुलोमक्रमेण

---

(१) अत्र "ऐईं ओ १ईंऐ ओ २ईं ओऐ ३ ऐओई ४ओ ऐईं ५ओ ईंऐ ६ एते मू" इत्यधिकः पाठः टी० पु० ।

(२) अधिकसप्तशतेषु टी० पु० पा० ।

मरुत् स्वयुक्तो मध्याद्ये दशम्याः क्रमशः स्मृते (१)।
भूमी रसाच्छास्वयुता वज्रेशी षष्ठतः क्रमात् ॥५७॥
षड्क्षराणि त्वरिता तृतीयं तदनन्तरम्।
द्युतिर्दाहचरस्वेन अस्या आद्यमनन्तरम् ॥५८॥
उक्ता नीलपताकाख्या नित्या सप्तदशाक्षरी।
समरे विजयं खड्गपादुकाञ्जनसिद्धिदा ॥५९॥
वेतालपक्षिणीचेटपिशाचादिप्रसाधनी।
निधानबिलसिद्धान्नसाधनी कामदोदिता ॥६०॥

षड्भेदाः। ह्रं १द्र २लु ३क्लु ४स्लु ५स्लु ६(२) एवं प्रतिलोमक्रमेण षड्भेदाः। एवं द्वादशभेदेषु (३) षड्विधसङ्केतविद्यायोजनात् द्वासप्ततिभेदाः सम्भवन्ति। ऐईऔँ१ ईऐऔँ २। ईऔँऐ ३। ऐऔँई ४। औँ ईऐ५। ओईऐ ६। एतेमूलसङ्केतविद्या षड्भेदाः। (४) साध्याक्षरा हृल्लेखा क्रीं इति प्रथमं बीजमितिशेषः। द्युतिर्दाहचरस्वयुक्—फकाररेफएकारविन्दुभिर्युक्तः फ्रें इति द्वितीयम्। दहन दाहच्छास्वयुतं - सकाररेफऊकारविन्दुभिर्युक्तं तृतीयं स्रूं इति। वज्रेशो पञ्चमं ततः ओंकारश्चतुर्थमित्यर्थः ॥ ५६ ॥ ततः मरुत्स्वयुक्तः—विन्दुसहित आकारः। आँ इति पञ्चमम्। मध्याद्ये दशम्याः क्रमशः स्मृते - दशम्याः कुलसुन्दरीनित्यायाः मध्याद्यं बीजद्वयं क्लीं ऐं इति अस्याः षष्ठं सप्तमं चाक्षरद्वयं स्यादित्यर्थः। भूमीरसाच्छास्वयुता— वकारः लकारऊकारविन्दुभिर्युक्तः व्लूं इति अष्टमं बीजम् वज्रेशी षष्ठतः क्रमात् ॥ ५७ ॥

षड्क्षराणि (ऽ)तानि नित्यमदद्रवे। इति। एभिः षड्भिर्मन्त्रस्य चतुर्दशाक्षराणि त्वरिता तृतीयं तदनन्तरं—हुं इति पञ्चदशं बीजम्। द्युतिर्दाहचरस्वेन-फकार रेफएकारविन्दुभिर्युक्तमस्याःद्वितीयं कूटं फ्रें इति षोडशमक्षरम्। अस्या आद्यमनन्तरं - क्रींकारः सप्तदशमित्यर्थः ॥ ५८ ॥

---

(१) दशम्या-परतः शिवे इति सो० पु० पा०।

(२) अत्रा(वराद्)ियारभ्य स्लु इत्यन्तोग्रन्थः सो० पुस्तके नास्ति। (३) षु त्रिधाभेदाः षड् इति सो० पु० पा०।

(४) ऐईऔं—भेदाः इत्यन्त पाठः टीकापुस्तके नास्ति।

रसो नभस्तथा दाहो व्याप्तं क्षमा वनपूर्विका।
खेन युक्ता भवेन्नित्याविजयैकाक्षरी मता ॥६१॥
वादेषु समरे कृच्छ्रे व्यवहारे सदा जयम्।
विधत्ते स्मरणादेव विजया विश्ववैभवा ॥६२॥
हृदम्बुवनयुक्तं खं नित्या स्यात् सर्वमङ्गला।
एकाक्षर्याऽनया सिद्धो जायते खेचरः क्षणात् ॥६३॥
भूःशून्ये नभसा भूश्च रसश्चाथ स्थिराम्बु च।
रयोऽग्निना युतो ज्याऽम्बु मरुद्युक्ता रसा मरुत् ॥६४॥
नभश्च मरुता युक्तं रसाशून्येऽग्निसंयुते।

खड्गपादुकेत्यादीनि उपरिष्टान्नीलपताकानित्याविधानपटलेषु व्यक्तं वक्ष्यमाणान्यत्र प्रस्तौति ॥ ५८ ॥ ६० ॥

रस इत्यादिना वैभवेत्यन्तेन श्लोकद्वयेन त्रयोदश्या विजयानित्याया एकाक्षरीं विद्यां तदनुभावं चोपदिशति—तत्र रसो—भकारः। नभः मकारः। दाहो—रेफः। व्याप्तं—यकारः। क्षमा—ऊकारः। वनपूर्विका औकारयुक्ता। खेन युक्ता—विन्दुना सहिता। एतदुक्तम्भवति—भकारमकाररेफयकारौकारविन्दुभिः कूटरूपा एकाक्षरी विद्येति। भ्म्र्यौं इति कूटम् ॥ ६१ ॥ समरे कृच्छ्रे युद्धे दुर्जये ॥ ६२ ॥

हृदम्बु इत्यादिना श्लोकेन चतुर्दश्याः सर्वमङ्गलानित्याया एकाक्षरीं विद्यां तदनुभावं चापदिशति। तत्र हृदम्बुवनयुक्तं खं—सकारवकारऔकारविन्दुभिर्युक्तं कूटं स्वौं इत्येकाक्षरी ॥ ६३ ॥

भूःशून्येइत्यादिभिर्भवेदित्यन्तैरष्टभिः श्लोकैः पञ्चदश्याः ज्वालामालिनीनित्यायास्त्रिषष्ठ्यक्षरां विद्यामुपदिशति—तत्र भूः ओकारः (१)। शून्ये—नकारद्वयं चेति। नभसा भूः—मकारसहित ओकारः मो इति। रसो—भकारः। स्थिरा—गकारः। अम्बु—वकारः। रयः—तकारः। अग्निना युतः—इकारसहितः ति इति। ज्या—जकारः। अम्बुमरुद्युक्ता—वकाराकारयुक्ता ज्वा इति। रसामरुत्—लाइति ॥ ६४ ॥

नभो—मकारः। मरुता—आकारेण युक्तः माइति। रसाशून्ये—लकारो नका-

---

(१) ऊकार इति टी० पु० पा०।

गोत्रा चरेण सहिता अम्बु पूर्वाक्षरं तथा ॥६५॥
अम्बुग्नी हृत् सदाहाम्बु रसक्ष्मारयहृत्खयुक् ।
हंसश्च मरुता दाहः प्राणश्च मरुता युतः ॥६६॥
दाहः साग्निः प्राणचरौ ज्या मरुत्सहिता रयः ।
चरेणाम्बु च गोत्रा हृत्साग्नि ज्याम्बुरसा खयुक् ॥६७॥
रयः साग्नि ज्याम्बु रसा पुनरेतौ जवी ततः ।
दाहेनानेन ते द्विः स्यात् हंसो दाहमरुत्खयुक् ॥६८॥
हंसश्च दाहवह्निखैर्दाहक्ष्माखयुतश्च सः ।
सप्त दाहास्ततोऽस्याः स्युरष्टमाद्यास्तु पञ्च वै ॥६९॥

रश्च। अग्निसंयुते—इकारसहितौ लिनि इति। गोत्रा—दकारः। चरेण सहिता—एकारेण सहिता दे इति। अम्बु—वकारः। पूर्वाक्षरं तथा—वकारपूर्वाक्षरं देइति ॥ ६५ ॥

अम्बुग्नी—अम्बु—वकारः अग्निरिकारः विइति। हृत्—सकारः। दाहाम्बु—रेफवकारौ र्वं इति। रस—क्ष्मा—रसः—भकारः क्ष्मा—जकारः भू इति। रयः—तकारः। हृत्—सकारः। खयुक् विन्दुयुक्तम्। खयुगितिसकारस्यैव विशेषणं संइति। हंसश्च मरुता युत इति सम्बन्धः—हा इति। दाहोरेफः रइति। प्राणश्च मरुता युतः का इति॥६६॥ दाहः साग्निरिति। रेफः ईकारसहितः रिइति। प्राणचरौ—केइति। ज्या मरुत्सहिता—जाइति। रयः—तकारः चरेणाम्बु च वे इति। गोत्रा—दकारः। हृत्—सकारः। साग्निः—सि इति। ज्यांबु—ज्वइति। रसा खयुक् लं इति ॥६७॥ रयः—अग्निना सहितः ति इति। ज्यांबु—ज्वइति। रसा—लकारः। पुनरेते एतत्पूर्वोक्ताक्षरद्वयं पुनरपि स्यात् ज्वलइति। जवीदाहेन युतः पकारोरेफेण युतः प्र इति। अनेन ते द्विः स्यात्—अनेन प्रत्यक्षरेण ते इति पूर्ववीप्सितमक्षरद्वयं द्विः ज्वलज्वल इति प्रज्वल त्रीण्यक्षराणि द्विरुच्चरेदित्यर्थः। स्यादित्यस्योपरिष्टात् इत्यन्वयः। हंसोदाहमरुत्खयुक्स्यादिति क्रीं इत्यर्थः ॥६८॥ हंसश्च दाहवन्हिखैरिति—क्रीं इत्यर्थः। दाहक्ष्माखयुतश्चस इति—हंसः हकारएव ह्रूँ इति। सप्तदाहाः रइति सप्तकृत्व उच्चरेदित्यर्थः। ततः—अनन्तरम्। अस्याः—विद्याया इतिशेषः। स्युरिति काकाक्षिगोलकन्यायवत्पूर्वापरयोरन्वेति। अष्टमाद्यास्तु पञ्चवै—अस्या विद्याया

उपान्त्याधःस्थितं नीलपताकाया अनन्तरम्।
त्वरितान्त्यश्च भेरुण्डा अष्टमं नवमं तथा ॥७०॥
ज्वालामालिनिनित्याऽसौ विषष्ठार्णसमीरिता।
वेधाकर्षणसन्तापवश्यावेशकरी भवेत् ॥७१॥
वायुप्राणवनस्वैः सा चित्रा स्यादक्षरद्वया।
या सिद्धिधनधान्यात्मनिधिलाभाय कल्पते ॥७२॥
शुचिः स्वेनाथ शून्यं स्यान्नभसा भूरसः स्थिरा।
अम्बु पश्चाद्रयः साग्निर्मरुताऽम्बुरयौ तथा ॥७३॥
इलायुतोऽग्निरेतानि पुनरम्बु मरुद्युतम्।
दाहश्च मरुता हंसस्त्वग्निरेतत्त्रयं पुनः ॥७४॥

अष्टमाक्षरमारभ्य द्वादशाक्षरावधि पञ्चाक्षराणि ज्वालामालिनी इति स्युरित्यर्थः ॥६८॥ उपान्त्याधःस्थितं नीलपताकाया अनन्तरं—नीलपताका नित्याविद्याया अन्त्याद्याक्षरात् पूर्वाक्षरं पूर्वस्थितमक्षरमित्यर्थः हुं इति। त्वरितान्त्यं—त्वरिताविद्यायाश्चरमाक्षरं फट्कारमित्यर्थः। भेरुण्डा अष्टमं नवमं तथा—भेरुण्डाविद्याया अष्टमनवमाक्षरद्वयं स्वाहा इत्यर्थः ॥ ७० ॥

ज्वालामालिनीत्यादिना श्लोकेन अस्या अक्षरसङ्ख्यामसाधारणानि पञ्चफलानि चोपदिशति ॥ ७१ ॥

वायुरित्यादिना श्लोकेन षोडश्याश्चित्रानित्याया द्व्यक्षरीं विद्यां तत्सिद्धिफलं चोपदिशति। तत्र वायुप्राणवनस्वैः-चकारककारऔकारविन्दुभिरित्यर्थः। तत्र चकारः प्रथमाक्षरम्। आत्मलाभः - स्वरूपज्ञानम् ॥ ७२ ॥

शुचीत्याद्यखिलेष्टदेत्यन्तैः षोडशभिः श्लोकैर्वाराह्या दशोत्तरशताक्षरीं विद्यां तन्नामादिकं चोपदिशति—तत्र शुचिः स्वेन—ऐं इति। शून्यं—नकारः। नभसा भूः—मो इति। रसो—भकारः। स्थिरा—गकारः। अम्बु—वकारः। रयः साग्निः - ति इति। मरुताम्बु—वाइति। रयौ—तकारद्वयम्। तथा—मरुदन्वितं त्वा इति ॥७३॥ इला युतोऽग्निः—इला—लकारः। अग्निः—इकारः लि इति। एतानि पुनः—उक्तानि त्रीण्यक्षराणि पुनरप्युच्चरेदित्यर्थः। अम्बु

अम्बु दाहो मरुद्युक्तो हंसोऽथ धरया नभः ।
तेजोऽग्निना पुनः पञ्च वातः स्वेन समायुतः ॥७५॥
तोयं चरेण तत्पूर्वं तोयमग्नियुतं ततः ।
शून्यं व्याप्तेन शुचिना शून्यं शक्त्या नभोयुतम् ॥७६॥
दाहोधरास्वसहितस्तोयं चरसमन्वितम् ।
एतत्पूर्वमधः प्रोक्तचतुष्टयमतः परम् ॥७७॥
ज्या स्वेन युक्ता सचरो रसश्चैतस्य पूर्वकम् ।
रसोऽग्निना पुनः प्रोक्तचतुष्कात् त्रयमन्ततः ॥७८॥
नभो भुवा चरेणापि हंसस्त्वेतस्य पूर्वकम् ।
हंसोऽग्निना प्राक्त्रितयं हृदयं स्वसमायुतम् ॥७९॥

मरुद्युतं—वाइति। दाहश्च मरुता—राइति। हंसस्त्वग्नियुतः—ह्रि इति। एतत्त्रयं पुनः—एतानि त्रीण्यक्षराणि पुनरपि वदेदित्यर्थः ॥७४॥ अम्बु—वकारः। दाहो मरुद्युक्तः—राइति। हंसो—हकारः। धरया—उकारेण। नभो–मकारः मु इति। तेजोऽग्निना—तेजः—खकारः खि इति। पुनः पञ्च—प्रोक्तानि वाराहमुखीपञ्चाक्षराण्येव पुनश्चास्याः। वातः स्वेन समायुक्तः—वातः अकारः ॐ इति ॥७५॥ तोयं चरेण तोयं—धकारः (१) धेइति। तत्पूर्वं—अक्षरमिति शेषः। धं इति। तोयमग्नियुतं—धिइति। ततः–उपरि। शून्यं—नकारः। व्याप्तेन शुचिना—युतमिति शेषः न्यै इति। शून्यं—नकारः। शक्त्या नभोयुतं—शक्तिर्विसर्जनीयः मः इत्यर्थः ॥७६॥ दाहो धरास्वसहितः—रूं इति। तोयं चरसमन्वितं—धे इति। एतत्पूर्वं—रूं इत्यर्थः। अधःप्रोक्तचतुष्टयमतः परं—रूं धे इत्यस्मात्पूर्वस्थितं धिन्यै नम इत्यक्षरचतुष्टयमस्योपरिष्टाद्योजयेदित्यर्थः ॥७७॥ ज्या स्वेन युक्ता—विन्दुयुक्तो जकारः जं इति। सचरो रसः—भे इति। एतस्य पूर्वकं—उक्ताक्षरस्य पूर्वमक्षरं जं इत्यर्थः। रसोऽग्निना—युत इति शेषः भि इति। पुनः प्रोक्तचतुष्कात्त्रयमन्ततः—पूर्वोक्तधिन्यै नम इति चतुष्के–प्रथमाक्षरवर्जं न्यै नमः इत्यक्षरत्रयं उपरिष्टाद्योजयेदित्यर्थः ॥७८॥ नभो भुवा—युतमिति शेषः मो इति। चरेणापि हंसः—अपिः समुच्चये हे इति।

---

(१) चकारः चे इति ब० पु० पा०।

रसस्वरेण तत्पूर्वमग्निना च रसो युतः ।
पश्चात्प्रागुक्तत्रयं वातो धरया च नभः प्रिये ! ॥८०॥
प्राणः स्वेन युतः पश्चाद्धृदयं स्वयुतं रसः ।
व्याप्तमेतत्त्रयं पश्चाद्धृद्दाहेनाम्बुसंयुतम् ॥८१॥
गोत्रा धरायुता स्पर्शो नादयुक्तो जवी युतः ।
दाहेन पूर्वं पूर्वं च पूर्वं च मरुता युतम् ॥८२॥
शून्यं मरुत्स्वसहितं हृद्दाहेनाम्बुना चरः ।
स्पर्शो मरुत्स्वसहितो हृद्दाहेनाम्बुसंयुतम् ॥८३॥
ज्याग्निः स्वसंयुतो हंसः तथाम्बु मरुता सह ।
हृदयेन स्वेन युतं रसश्च स्वेन संयुतः ॥८४॥
प्राणदाहौ धरायुक्तौ पुनस्तौ वह्निना वियत् ।
वार्दाहयुक्तमम्बु स्यादियद्व्याप्तस्वसंयुतम् ॥८५॥

एतस्य पूर्वकं—हे इत्यस्य पूर्वं मो इत्यर्थः । हंसोऽग्निना—हि इति । प्राक्त्रितयं—प्रागुक्तं न्येनमः इत्यक्षरत्रयम् । हृदयं स्वसमायुतं—स्तं इति ॥७९॥ रसस्वरेण—भे इति । तत्पूर्वं—भे इत्येतस्य पूर्वमक्षरं स्तं इति । अग्निना च रसो युतः—चकारः समुच्चये भि इति । पश्चादुक्तत्रयं—प्रागुक्तं न्येनम इति त्रितयम् । वातः अकारः । धरया च नभः—यु इति । प्रिये इति देवीसम्बुद्धिः ॥८०॥ प्राणः स्वेन युतः—कं इति । हृदयं स्वयुतं—स्तं इति । रसो—भकारः । व्याप्तं—यकारः । एतत्त्रयं पश्चात्-प्रोक्तं स्तं भय इत्यक्षरत्रयं पुनरपि स्यादिति । हृत् सकारः । दाहेनाम्बुना संयुक्तं र्वे इति ॥ ८१ ॥ गोत्रा—दकारः । धरान्विता—दु इति । स्पर्शो नादयुक्तः—स्पर्शः—षकारः । नादः—टकारः ष्ट इति । जवी दाहेन युतः—पकारो रेफेण युतः प्र इति । पूर्वं प्र इत्यस्मादक्षरात्पूर्वाक्षरस्य पूर्वमक्षरं दुइति । पूर्वं च मरुता युतम्—अत्र पूर्वशब्दः दु इत्येतस्य पूर्वाक्षरविषयः ष्टा इत्यर्थः ॥८२॥ शून्यं मरुत्स्वसहितं—नां इति । हृत्—सकारः । दाहेनाम्बुना चरः—र्वे इति । स्पर्शो मरुत्स्वसहितः—षां इति । हृत्—सकारः । दाहेनाम्बुसंयुतं—र्व इति ॥८३॥ ज्याग्निः स्वसंयुतः—जिं इति । हंसस्तथाम्बु मरुता सह—तथा इति सर्वत्रात्र प्रकरणे समुच्चयार्थः ह्वा इति । हृदयेन स्वेन युतं—स्तं इति । रसश्च स्वेन संयुतः—भं इति ॥८४॥ प्राण-

पूर्वद्विरुक्तवर्णौ च शुचिः स्वेन युतस्तथा ।
स्थिरा रसा वनस्वेन दावौ हंसो धरास्वयुक् ॥८६॥
द्युतिर्नादवती पश्चाद्धृदम्बु मरुता युतम् ।
हंसश्च मरुता विद्या दशोत्तरशताक्षरी ॥८७॥
वाराही पञ्चमी विश्वविजया भद्रकौमुदी ।
वार्ताली चेतिविख्याता स्तम्भनाद्यखिलेष्टदा ॥८८॥
प्राणदाहौ धरायुक्तौ पुनराद्यं रसे मरुत् ।
व्याप्तं मरुच्छक्तियुतं भूःस्वयुक्ता ततस्त्वयम् ॥८९॥
अस्यादौ तु रसायुग्मं चरेण समयोजितम् ।
दाहेन वह्निशक्तिभ्यां युतो हंसस्ततःपरम् ॥९०॥
नभो द्विर्हृत्सदाहाम्बु ज्या शून्यं स्वनसंयुतम् ।

दाहौ धरायुक्तौ—प्रत्येकमिति शेषः कुरु इति। पुनस्तौ पुनरपि कुरु इति वर्णौ। वह्निना वियत्—श्री इति। वाः दाहयुक्तं—वाः—धकारः ध्र इति। अम्बु—वकारः। वियत्व्याप्तस्वसंयुतं—श्यं इति ॥८५॥ पूर्वद्विरुक्तवर्णौ—वश्यं इत्येतदारभ्य पूर्वस्माद्वतुष्टयाक्षरात् पूर्वं कुरु इत्यर्थः। शुचिः स्वेन युतः ऐं इति। स्थिरा रसावनस्वेन—युक्तेति शेषः ठलौं इति। दावौ – ठकारद्वयं ठठ इति। हंसो धरास्वयुक्—हुं इति ॥ ८६ ॥ द्युतिर्नादवती पश्चात् – अनन्तरं—फट् इति। हृदम्बु मरुता युतं—स्वा इति। हंसश्च मरुता—युक्त इति शेषः हा इति ॥ ८७ ॥

वाराहीत्यादिना श्लोकेन देव्या नामपञ्चकं कथयति ॥८८॥

प्राणेत्यादिभिः क्रमादित्यन्तैः पञ्चभिः श्लोकैः कुरुकुल्लायाः पञ्चविंशत्यक्षरीं सप्ताक्षरीं त्रयोदशाक्षरीं च विद्यामुपदिशति। तत्र प्राणदाहौ धरा युक्तौ – प्रत्येकमिति शेषः कुरु इति। पुनराद्यं—पुनरपि तत्रो राद्यं कु इति। रसे लद्वयं मरुत् आकारः ला इति। व्याप्तं मरुच्छक्तियुतं—याः इति। भूः स्वयुक्ता ॐ इति। ततस्त्वयम् ॥८९॥ अस्यादौ तु ॐ—मित्यस्योपरि अस्य मन्त्रस्यादिभूतं कुरु कु इत्यक्षरत्रयं भवेदित्यर्थः। रसायुग्मं चरेण समयोजितं—ल्ले इति। दाहेन वह्निशक्तिभ्यां युतो हंसस्ततः परम्—क्रोः इति ॥९०॥ नभो द्विः—स्यादिति शेषः मम इति।

अम्बु पश्चाद्वियद्युक्तं मरुता तु नभः प्रिये ! ॥८१॥
शून्यं व्याप्तं भुवा हंसः पूर्वान्त्यौ स्यान्मनुत्रयम् ।
अस्य षष्ठादिपञ्चार्णादन्त्यौ स्यादाद्य ईरितः ॥८२॥
एकादशाक्षरादन्त्यौ द्वितीयः समुदीरितः ।
तृतीयः पञ्चविंशार्णः प्रोक्ता मन्त्रा इति क्रमात् ॥८३॥
भूःखेन हंसो दाहवह्निस्वयुतः खेन हंसकः ।
हृन्मायया भुवा हृत्स्यात् खेन हंसः समन्वितः ॥८४॥
कुरुकुल्लान्त्यवर्णौ च स्यादात्माष्टाक्षरः स्मृतः ।
सर्वाभीष्टार्थसंसिद्ध्यै सुलभोऽयं सुरद्रुमः ॥८५॥
सङ्केतोदीरितैर्वर्णैर्दशभिर्दशभिः पृथक् ।

हृत्–सकारः। सदाहाम्बु–दाहसहितं म इत्यर्थः वं इति। व्याप्त–जकारः। शून्यं खेन युतं–न इति। अम्बु पश्चात्–अनन्तरं वकारः। वियत्–सकारः। (युक्तं) मरुता युक्तं नभ इति यावत् मा इति। प्रिये इति देवीसम्बुद्धिः ॥८१॥ शून्यं—नकारः। व्याप्तं–यकारः। भुवा हंस इति शेषः ह्रो इति। पूर्वान्त्यौ पञ्चमोविद्याक्षरमाक्षरद्वयं स्वाहा इत्यर्थः। स्यान्मनुत्रयं—अयमेव मन्त्रः अक्षरविभागयोगक्रमान्मन्त्रत्रयं भवतीत्यर्थः। अस्य षष्ठादि पञ्चार्णादन्त्यौ स्यादाद्य ईरितः। एतदुक्तं भवति—अस्य पञ्चविंशाक्षरमन्त्रस्य षष्ठाक्षरमारभ्य दशमाक्षरान्तमुच्चार्य ततः परं स्वाहा इति वदेत्। तेन सप्ताक्षरी प्रथमा विद्या भवतीति ॥८२॥ एकादशाक्षरादन्त्यौ द्वितीयः समुदीरितः। एतदुक्तं भवति—अस्यैव पञ्चविंशाक्षरस्याद्याक्षरमारभ्य एकादशाक्षरान्तमुच्चार्य ततःपरं तच्चरमभूतस्वाहा इत्यक्षरद्वययोजनात् त्रयोदशाक्षरी विद्या भवतीति। तृतीयः पञ्चविंशार्णः प्रागेवाभिहितः प्रथमद्वितीययोः प्रकृतिभूतः सप्तपञ्चविंशार्णो मन्त्रः तृतीय इत्यर्थः ॥ ८३ ॥

भूःखेनेत्यादिना सुरद्रुम इत्यन्तेन श्लोकद्वयेनात्माष्टाक्षरीं प्रपञ्चयागविद्यामुपदिशति। तत्र भूः खेन–ॐ इति। हंसो दाहवह्निखेन क्ष्रौंकारःखेन हंसकः—हं इति। हृन्मायया–युक्त इति शेषः स इति। भुवा हृत्स्यात्–सो इति। खेन हंसः समन्वितः–हं इति। कुरु कुल्लान्त्यवर्णौ च—स्वाहा इत्यर्थः ॥ ८५ ॥

सङ्केतेनेत्यादिना चराचरमित्यन्तेन श्लोकद्वयेन पञ्चभूतानां प्रत्येकमेक-

प्राणाग्नीलाऽऽम्बुशाखाभिः शक्तिसमाचरीयुतैः ॥९६॥
भूतमन्त्राः समुद्दिष्टाः पञ्च सर्वार्थसिद्धिदाः ।
येषामालोकतो विश्वं वर्तते सचराचरम् ॥९७॥
पूर्वस्याद्यौ च तत्पूर्वं चतुर्दशतदन्त्यकौ ।
अम्बुनाग्निर्वाः स शून्यं प्राणो जलरयान्वितः ॥९८॥

विंशत्यक्षरान् मन्त्रानुपदिशति । तत्र सङ्केतोदीरितैर्वर्णैरिति । एतदुक्तं भवति—वातो मरुदित्यादिभिः पञ्चत्रिंशत्पटलोक्तैः श्लोकैर्भूतेषु विभक्तानां मातृकाक्षराणां संज्ञाभिरुदोरितैः । प्राणाग्नीलाम्ब शाखाभिः प्रत्येकं दशभिरक्षरैरुपेता स्वाख्याशक्तिशब्दसमाचर्यन्ताः एवं प्रत्येकमेकविंशत्यक्षरास्त्वारो विंशत्यक्षरव्योममन्त्रसहिता एवं पञ्चमन्त्राः । प्रोक्तक्रमेण पञ्चानां भूतानां स्युरिति । ते यथा—तेषां पञ्चानामपि मन्त्राणां स्वरूपं ललितानित्यासपर्याक्रमे मन्त्रमलिखितमपि अत्र तेषां स्वरूपं प्रकटं प्रकाश्यते—प्राक् प्रत्यक् दक्षिणोदक् च एकादश षट् रेखाः समान्तरालं विलिख्य तासु दशदशकोष्ठात्मसु पञ्चसु पंक्तिषु ऊर्ध्वाधः क्रमेण अकारादीनि अइउ ऋऌ इति ह्रस्वपञ्चाक्षराणि प्रथमपङ्क्तौ समालिख्य तद्द्वितीयपङ्क्तौ आईऊ ॠ ॡ इति दीर्घाक्षरपञ्चकं क्रमादालिख्य तृतीयपङ्क्तौ एऐ ओ औ अं इति वर्णपञ्चकं समालिख्य चतुर्थ्यादिषु पङ्क्तिषु प्रोक्तक्रमेण ककारादोन् शकारान्तान् षड्वर्गान् पञ्चशः समालिख्य सर्वान्त्यपङ्क्तौ षचलसह इति पञ्चाक्षराणि—चालिख्य पश्येत् । सर्वोर्ध्वपङ्क्तिकोष्ठदशाक्षराणि प्राणात्मकानि । तदधःस्थितद्वितीयपङ्क्तिकोष्ठदशकस्थानि दशाक्षराणि अग्न्यात्मकानि । तदधःस्थिततृतीयपङ्क्तिकोष्ठदशकस्थितदशाक्षराणि इलात्मकानि । तदधःस्थितचतुर्थपङ्क्तिकोष्ठदशकस्थितानि अबात्मकानि । तदधः—स्थितपञ्चमपङ्क्तिकोष्ठदशकस्थानि दशाक्षराणि खात्मकानि । तेषां दशानामन्ते तत्तन्नामद्व्यक्षराणि व्योम्नः एकाक्षरं च सर्वत्र शक्तीति द्व्यक्षरं तदुपरि समाक्षरीं च योजयेत् ॥७६॥ एवं कृते एकविंशा दशाक्षराः पञ्चभूतमन्त्रा भवन्ति । तेषामालोकतः प्रभावादित्यर्थः । वर्तते—अद्यापि क्रियते इत्यर्थः ॥९७॥

पूर्वेत्यादिभिर्मनुरित्यन्तैस्त्रिभिः श्लोकैः षोडशनित्यानां साधारणं षोडशाक्षरं बलिमन्त्रमुपदिशति । तत्र पूर्वस्याद्यौ च—प्रागुक्तस्यात्माष्टार्णमन्त्रस्यादिभूतौ प्रणवक्षकारावर्णौ अस्य प्रथमद्वितीयवर्णौ स्यातामित्यर्थः । तत्पूर्वं चतुर्दशत-

रसः स्याद्व्याप्तमायाभ्यां तृतीयोऽस्य चतुर्थकः ।
रसः क्ष्मया रयो युक्तस्वरेण परमेश्वरि ! ॥९९॥
रसो युक्तो व्याप्तभूम्यां हंसः क्ष्मास्वयुतस्ततः ।
पूर्वान्त्यवर्णावित्युक्तः षोड़शार्णो बलेर्मनुः ॥१००॥
वह्नि तत्त्वमयी व्याप्तिरिति सम्यक् समीरिता ।
अस्या निःकालनात् चित्ते तत्तत्त्वं स्वात्मसात्कृतम् ॥१०१॥

इति षोड़शनित्यातन्त्रेषु श्रीकादिमते
तृतीयं पटलम् ।

दन्त्यकौ—आत्माष्टाक्षरमन्त्रस्य पूर्वभूतायाः कुरुकुल्लाविद्यायाः चतुर्दशपञ्चदशाक्षरे सर्वं इति हे अस्य तृतीयचतुर्थाक्षरे स्यातामित्यर्थः । अम्बु नाम्निः—युत इति शेषः वि इति । वाः सशून्यं—म्र इति । प्राणो जलरयान्वितः—ककारो ऋकारतकाराभ्यां सहितः क्रृत् इति ॥९८॥ रसः स्यात् व्याप्तमायाभ्यां-भ्य इति । मायाशब्दः शक्तिशब्दश्चास्मिन् तन्त्रे हृल्लेखा विसर्जनीयोरेकैकस्याभिधायकौ, एवं स्थिते अन्यतरयोजनं सम्प्रदायबलादित्यर्थः । तृतीयोऽस्य चतुर्थकः सर्वं इति नवमदशमाक्षरे । रसः क्ष्मय—युक्त इति शेषः भू इति एकादशमक्षरम् । रयो युक्तस्वरेण—ते इति द्वादशम् । परमेश्वरीति सम्बुद्धिः ॥९९॥ रसो युक्तो व्याप्तभूभ्यां भ्यो इति त्रयोदशम् । हंसः क्ष्मा स्वयुतस्ततः—क्ष्ं इति चतुर्दशमक्षरम् । पूर्वान्त्यवर्णौ—आत्माष्टाक्षरमन्त्रौ स्वाहा इति पञ्चदश । षोड़शार्णौ इत्युक्तः षोड़शार्णौ बलेर्मनुः—एवं षोड़शाक्षरः सर्वासां षोड़शनित्यानां बलिमन्त्र उक्त इत्यर्थः ॥१००॥

इति श्रीषोड़शनित्यातन्त्रेषु श्रीकादिमताख्यस्य परिपूर्णस्य
तन्त्रस्य प्रपञ्चसारसिंहराजप्रकाशाभिधानेन सुभगानन्द-
नाथेन विरचितायां मनोरमाख्यायां व्याख्यायां नित्या-
विद्यास्वरूपप्रकाशनपरं तृतीयपटलं परिपूर्णं
परामृष्टम् ॥

ग्रन्थसंख्या तृतीये यन्त्रमेकं स्याद्व्याख्यानं ग्रन्थसंख्यया
शतद्वयं सप्तनवतिसहितं सार्द्धमीरितम् ।

अथ चतुर्थपटलारम्भः ।

अथ षोड़शनित्यानामाद्यायाः पूजनं प्रिये ! ।
कथयामि क्रमेणैव नित्यं सर्वार्थसिद्धिदम् ॥१॥
नैमित्तिकं तथा काम्यं शृणु त्वं पटलैस्त्रिभिः ।
येनातिपापयुक्तोऽपि सिद्धिमेति सुनिश्चितम् ॥२॥
न्यासत्रयस्य मन्त्रांश्च आसनानां चतुष्टयम् ।
आवाहनमनुं पश्चात् समस्तार्चामनुं तथा ॥३॥
मुद्रायुधानां बीजानि मुद्रारचनवासने ।
ध्यानं सपरिवाराया नित्यपूजाविधिक्रमौ ॥४॥
नवावरणशक्तीनां नामान्यर्चाक्रमं तथा ।
मन्त्रात्मयोगमर्चाया उपचारान् जपक्रमम् ॥५॥
वातः खसंयुतस्त्वाद्यं मरुत्खेन द्वितीयकम् ।
हृद्वनेन समायेन तृतीयं प्रथमा त्वसौ ॥६॥

अथ चतुर्थपटलारम्भः ।

पूर्वस्मिन् तृतीयपटले षोड़शनित्याविद्यादिकमुपदिश्यानन्तरमङ्गिनित्यायाः प्रधानाया ललिता विद्यायानित्यनैमित्तिकाभ्यां समाराधनक्रममुपदिशति । अथ षोड़शनित्येत्यादिभिस्तन्मयो भवेदित्यन्तैस्त्रिभिः पटलैः प्रत्येकं श्लोकशतरूपैः । तत्र अथ षोड़शनित्येत्यादिभिः क्रममित्यन्तैः पञ्चभिः श्लोकैश्चतुर्थपञ्चमषष्ठपटलार्थानुद्दिशति । तत्र नित्यं—पूजनमित्यर्थः । नैमित्तिकं तथा काम्यं—पूजनमित्यस्य विशेषणम् । अतिपापयुक्तोऽपि—विवेकद्वेषी ॥२॥ न्यासत्रयस्येत्यादिना बीजानीत्यन्तेन पादाधिकेन द्वाविंशन्मन्त्रोद्देशकः कृतः तत्र न्यासत्रयत्येत्युक्तिरुद्देश क्रमोल्लङ्घिन्यपि श्लोकसौकर्यार्थेति सम्प्रदायः । समस्तार्चामनुं — बीजद्वयरूपम् ॥५॥

वातेत्यादिना मार्जनादित्यन्तेनार्द्धाधिकेन श्लोकेन करशुद्धिविद्यां शोधनप्रकारं चोपदिशति । तत्र वातः खसंयुक्तस्त्वाद्यं ॐ इति प्रथमं बीजमंरुत्खेन

अनयाः करयोः शुद्धिं कुर्यादन्योन्यमार्जनात् ।
हृच्छिरश्च शिखावर्म नेत्रमस्त्रं षडङ्गकम् ॥ ७ ॥
द्वितीयया सा विज्ञेया या नित्या कुलसुन्दरी ।
तृतीया सैव शक्त्याद्या देव्यात्मासनमेतया ॥८॥
त्रिषु हंससमायोगाच्चक्रासनमुदीरितम् ।
हंसहृद्वां पञ्चमी च सर्वमन्त्रासनं तथा (१) ॥९॥

द्वितीयकं—ऐं इति द्वितीयकम् । इदनेन समायेन तृतीयं—सौः इति तृतीयम् । प्रथमा त्वसौ—विद्येति शेषः ॥६॥ शुद्धिमिति । शुद्धिः—सपर्योपकरणस्पर्शार्हताकरणम् । अन्योन्यमार्जनात्—वामदक्षिणकरतलस्पृष्टयोरिति शेषः ।

हृदित्यादिना सुन्दरीत्यन्तेनार्द्धद्वयेन षडङ्गं षडङ्गन्यासविद्यां चोपदिशति । तत्र द्वितीयया—उद्दिष्टद्वात्रिंशत्सु द्वितीयया विद्ययेति शेषः ॥७॥

तृतीयेत्यादिना एतया इत्यन्तेन उत्तरार्द्धेन देव्यात्मासनविद्यामुपदिशति । तत्र तृतीया सैव—षडङ्गन्यासे प्रोक्ताकुलसुन्दरी विद्यैव । शक्त्याद्या । अत्र शक्तिः—हृल्लेखा । उत्तरश्लोकाद्यगतं त्रिष्विति पदमावाहनविद्यान्तमन्वेति । तेनैतदुक्तं भवति—त्रीणि बीजानि प्रत्येकं हृल्लेखापुरःसराणि कुर्यादिति । ह्रीं ऐं ह्रीं क्लीं ह्रीं सौः इति । देव्यात्मासनं—परिच्छिन्नविग्रहाणां देव्यात्मनां सर्वशक्तीनामासनं—उपलब्धिस्थानं सर्वासां देवतानामुपलब्धिस्थानमित्यर्थः । अत्र उद्देशक्रममपहाय कथनमासनविद्याचतुष्टयस्य द्वितीयविद्यानुबन्धित्वात् सौकर्यार्थम् । तृतीयेति परिगणनक्रमस्य सौकर्यार्थः ॥ ८ ॥

त्रिष्वित्यादिना श्लोकपूर्वार्द्धेन चक्रासनविद्यामुपदिशति—तत्र हंससमायोगात्—बालायास्त्रिषु बीजेषु प्रत्येकं हकारोपक्रममुच्चारणं(२) हैं ह्क्लीं ह्सौः चतुर्थी चक्रासनविद्येत्यर्थः । चक्रासनमिति । सर्वेषां मन्त्रदेवतात्म (३) भूतानां यन्त्राणामासनं उपलब्धिस्थानम् ।

हंसेत्यादिनोत्तरार्द्धेन सर्वमन्त्रासनविद्यामुपदिशति । तत्र हंसहृद्वयां समेतेति शेषः । प्राग्वत्त्रीणि बीजानि प्रत्येकं हकारसकारोपक्रमोच्चारणात् ह्सैं

---

(१) तथा इति सौ० पु० पा० ।

(२) मुच्चारणात् इति टी० पु० पा० । (३) मन्त्रदेवता वासभूतानामिति टी० पु० पा० ।

ततोम्बु च रसोपेतं चरखसहितं च तत् ।
तस्य शक्तेश्च मध्यस्था या सा षष्ठी समीरिता ॥१०॥
साध्यसिद्धासनं दद्यात् तया देव्यै समर्चनात् ।
सप्तम्याऽऽवाहनं कुर्यान्नमसोक्तत्रिखण्डया ॥११॥

ह्स् क्लीँ ह्सौः पञ्चमो सर्वमन्त्रासनविद्या। सर्वमन्त्रासनमिति – श्रीचक्रस्य कथनम्। अकथादिमातृकात्मकत्वेन त्रिकोणरेखाणां च वक्ष्यमाणत्वात् सर्वेषां मन्त्राणामुपलब्धिस्थानमित्यर्थः ॥ ८ ॥

तत इत्यादिना समर्चनादित्यन्तेनाध्यर्द्धेन श्लोकेन साध्यसिद्धासनविद्यामुपदिशति। तत्र ततोऽम्बु च रसोपेतं चरखसहितं च तत्—अम्बु—वकारः। चकारः समुच्चये। रसा—लकारः। चर – एकारः। ख – विन्दुस्ताभ्यां सहितम्। चकारः समुच्चये। तच्छब्दो विशिष्टरूपं परामृशति। एतदुक्तं भवति—वकारलकारविन्दभिर्युक्तं व्लेँ इति कूटाक्षरं स्यादिति। तस्य शक्तेश्च मध्यस्था या सा षष्ठी समीरिता—तस्य—प्रोक्तस्य व्लेँकारस्य। शक्तेः—ह्स्क्लेँ खायाः। मध्यस्था एतयोर्द्वयोर्मध्यस्थेत्यर्थः। एतदुक्तं भवति—तस्यास्तु बालायास्त्रीणि बीजानि – ह्रींकारोपक्रमाणि व्लेँ कारावसनानि च भवेयुः ह्रीँ ऐँ ह्रीँ क्लीँ सौः व्लेँ एवंरूपा सा बाला साध्यसिद्धासनविद्यास्यादिति ॥१०॥ साध्यसिद्धासनमिति। सर्वेषां साध्यानामभिमतानां सिद्धीनामुपलब्धिस्थानं अखण्डात्मकस्वरूपविमर्श (१) सिद्धेरित्यर्थः। अत्र देव्यै समर्चनादिति – आसनचतुष्टयेऽप्यन्वेति। एतस्याऽऽसनचतुष्टयस्य मन्त्रयोजनाप्रकारं पञ्चमे पटले वक्ष्यति।

सप्तम्येत्यादिना समीरित इत्यन्तेनार्द्धाद्येनैकेन श्लोकेन सप्तमीमावाहनविद्यामुपदिशति। तत्र सप्तम्या—विद्ययेति शेषः। नमसा—युक्तयेति शेषः। नमःशब्दान्तयेत्यर्थः। उक्तत्रिखण्डया – मुद्रयेति शेषः। उत्तरत्र वक्ष्यमाणामपि उक्तमिति सर्वत्र कथयति। हंसह्रद्दाहसंयुक्ता सैव स्यात् सप्तमो मता—एतदुक्तं भवति—हकारसकाररेफाक्षरैः प्रत्येकं त्रिषु बीजेषु युक्ता कुलसुन्दरीविद्या आवाहनविद्येत्यर्थः। मध्यमे दाहयोगस्तु व्यञ्जनान्ते समीरितः—मध्यमबीजस्य हकारसकारौ पुरस्तात् संयोज्य रेफं लकारान्ते योजयेदित्यर्थः। तेन हकारसकारककारलकाररेफईकारविन्दुभिर्मध्यमं बीजं मायान्तम्। इतरस्मिंस्तु

---

(१) विमर्शात् सिद्धेरिति सौ० व० पु० पा०।

हंसहृद्दाहसंयुक्ता सैव स्यात् सप्तमी मता ।
मध्यमे दाहयोगस्तु व्यञ्जनान्ते समीरितः ॥१२॥
वियत् सदाहं वह्निस्वशक्त्याद्यं स्यात् स्वयं (१)भवेत् ।
तदादिकाः सर्वशक्तीश्चक्रस्था नामभिर्जपेत् ॥१३॥
दाहभूमीरसाच्छास्वैर्वशिनीबीजमीरितम् ।
प्राणोरसाशक्तियुतः कामेश्वर्यक्षरं महत् ॥१४॥
शून्यमम्बुरसावह्निस्वयोगान्मोहिनी मनुः ।
व्याप्तं रसाच्छास्वयुतं विमलाबीजमीरितम् (२) ॥१५॥
ज्या नभोवह्निदाहस्वयोगैः स्यादरुणा मनुः ।

सकारस्वरयोर्मध्ये रेफं योजयेदित्यर्थः । तेन हकारसकारद्वयरेफश्रौकारविसर्जनीयै(३)रन्त्यबीजं मायान्तं ह्सौं ह्स्क्लृीं ह्स्रौः नमः इति ॥ १२ ॥

वियदित्यादिना श्लोकेन ललितायाः श्रीचक्रावस्थितानां शक्तीनां पूजानामरूपमन्त्राणां प्रणवभूतं बीजद्वयमुपदिशति । तत्र वियत्—सकारः । सदाहवह्निस्वं रेफईकारविन्दुसहितं स्रीं इति । शक्त्याद्यं—ह्स्क्लेखाद्यम् । एतदुक्तं भवति । ह्स्क्लेखाश्रीबीजोपक्रमैः पूजानाममन्त्रैः सर्वाः शक्तीः पूजयेदिति ॥१३॥

दाहभूमीत्यादीना श्लोकेन वशिनीकूटाक्षरविद्यां कामेश्वरीकूटाक्षरविद्यां चोपदिशति । दाहभूमीरसाच्छास्वैः—रेफवकारलकारऊकारविन्दुभिः व्लूं इति । प्राणो रसाशक्तियुतः—प्राणः । ककारः । रसा—लकारः । शक्तिः—ह्स्क्लेखा । तैर्युक्तः ककार लकार ह्स्क्लेखाभिः कूटं क्ल्ह्रीं इति ॥ १४ ॥

शून्यमित्यादिना श्लोकेन मोहिनीविमलयोः कूटाक्षरीविद्याद्वयमुपदिशति । तत्र शून्यं—नकारः । अम्बुरसावह्निस्वयोगात्—वकारलकारईकारविन्दुयोगादित्यर्थः व्लीं इति । व्याप्तं—यकारः । रसाच्छास्वयुतं लकारउकारविन्दुसहितं य्लूं इति ॥१५॥

ज्या नभो इत्यादिना श्लोकपूर्वार्द्धेन अरुणाकूटाक्षरीविद्यामुपदिशति ।

---

(१) शक्त्याद्यं यद्वयं भवेत् इति मू० पु० पा० ।

(२) वशिनी बीजमीरितम् । प्राणोरसाशक्तियुतं विमलाबीजमीरितम् इति सो० पु० पा० ।
प्राणोरसा इत्यादि सो० पु० विहाय कुत्रापि न वर्त्तते ।

(३) तेन हकारसकाररेफश्रौकारविसर्जनीयैरिति व० पु० पा० ।

हंसः सहृद्रसाम्बुः स्याद्व्याप्तच्छास्वैर्युतो मनुः ॥१६॥
जयिन्यास्तु समुद्दिष्टः सर्वत्र जयदायकः ।
वादेषु व्यवहारेषु समरेषु च निश्चितम् ॥१७॥
कं नभोदाहसहितं व्याप्तच्छास्वयुतं मनुः ।
सर्वेश्वर्याः समाख्यातः सर्वसिद्धिकरः सदा ॥१८॥
ग्रासो नभोदाहवह्निस्वैर्युक्तः कौलिनीमनुः ।
एतैर्मनुभिरष्टाभिः शक्तिभिर्वर्गसंयुतैः ॥१९॥
वाग्देवतान्तैर्न्यासः स्याद्येन देव्यात्मको भवेत् ।
मर्त्योऽपि पूज्यते देवैः सर्वैः सर्वत्र सर्वदा ॥२०॥

तत्र ज्या नभोदाहवह्निस्वयोगैः—जकारमकाररेफईकारविन्दूनामन्योन्यमुक्तक्रमयोगात् ज्म्री॑ इति ॥ १६ ॥

हंसेत्यादिना निश्चितमित्यन्तेनार्द्धाद्येनैकेन श्लोकेन जयिनीं कूटाक्षरविद्यां तत्सामर्थ्यं चोपदिशति । तत्र हंसो—हकारः । सहृद्रसाम्बुः—सकारलकारवकारसहितः । व्याप्तच्छास्वैर्युतः—(१)यकारजकारविन्दुभिश्च युक्तः । एतदुक्तं भवति—हकारसकारलकारवकारयकारजकारविन्दुभिः कूटं ह्स्व्ल्यूं॑ इति ॥ १७ ॥

कमित्यादिना सदा इत्यन्तेनार्धाद्येनैकेन श्लोकेन सर्वेश्वरीकूटाक्षरविद्यां तदनुभावं चोपदिशति । कं—लकारः(२) । नभोदाहसहितम्—मकाररेफसहितम् । व्याप्तच्छास्वयुतं—यकार जकारविन्दुसहितम् । एतदुक्तं भवति—लकारमकाररेफयकारजकारविन्दुभिः ल्म्र्यूं॑(३)इति ॥ १८ ॥

ग्रासेत्यादिना श्लोकपूर्वार्द्धेन कौलिनीकूटाक्षरविद्यामुपदिशति-तत्र ग्रासः—क्षकारः । नभोदाहवह्निस्वैः—मकाररेफईकारविन्दुभिः क्ष्म्रीं॑ इति ।

एतैरित्यादिना सर्वदा इत्यन्तेनार्द्धाद्येनैकेन श्लोकेन वशिन्यादीनां न्यासक्रमं तत्फलं चोपदिशति । तत्र मनुभिरष्टाभिः—प्रोक्तकूटाक्षरैरिति शेषः । शक्तिभिः—

---

(१) कं पकारञ्ज इति वं० पु० पा० ।

(२) सकारञ्ज इति व० टी० पु० पा० ।

(३) रम्र॑ इति वं० पु० पा० । इ—म्यूं॑ इति टी० पु० पा० ।

रन्ध्रे भाले तथाऽऽज्ञायां गले हृदि तथा न्यसेत्।
नाभावाधारके पादद्वये मूलाग्रकावधि(१) ॥२१॥
गोत्रादाहमरुत्खैः स्यादाद्योऽन्यो व्यत्ययादसौ।
मरुद्दक्षोः प्राणरसावह्निखैः स्यात्तृतीयकः ॥२२॥
भूमी रसाद्यमाखयुता चतुर्थः शक्तिहृत्परः।
प्राणेन दाहभूखेनानन्तरः सप्तमः पुनः ॥२३॥
हंसो हृदा तेजसा च दुग्धया दाहचरखयुक्।
अष्टमो हंसहृत्प्राणवनखैः समुदीरितः ॥२४॥
शुचिः खेन युतस्तद्वन्नवमः परिकीर्तितः।
एते एकाक्षरा मन्त्रा मुद्रारूपा महेश्वरि ! ॥२५॥

प्रोक्तैर्वशिन्याद्यष्टशक्तिभि(२)र्युक्तैरिति शेषः। वर्गसंयुतैः—अकचटतपयशाक्षराद्यैः वाग्देवतान्तैः प्रत्येकम्॥१८॥ वाग्देवतेति। चतुरक्षरनामान्तैर्न्यसेन। देव्यात्मकः—देवविग्रहः देव्यास्तु अक्षरैरेव विग्रहवत्त्वादित्यर्थः। एतदुक्तं भवति—अकारादिविसर्जनीयान्तान् षोडश स्वरान् सविन्दूनुच्चार्य तदुपरि क्ष्म्ल्व्र्यूं इति कूटाक्षरमुच्चार्य वशिनी वाग्देवतायै नम इत्युच्चरन्न्यसेत्। एवमन्यान्यसहमन्त्रान् वर्गबीजनामवाग्देवतानमोन्तैर्न्यसेत् प्रोक्तविग्रहान् कुर्यादित्यर्थः। अत्र नमःशब्दयोजनमुत्तरत्र पूजायां नमः पदे इत्याक्षेपपूर्वं विधानात् ॥२०॥

रन्ध्रेत्यादिना श्लोकेन वशिन्याद्यष्टशक्तिमन्त्रन्यासस्थानान्युपदिशति। तत्र रन्ध्रे—ब्रह्मरन्ध्रे। आज्ञायां-भ्रुवोर्मध्ये। मूलाग्रकावधि—पादयोर्मूलादारभ्याग्रकावधि करतलद्वयेन समं मन्त्रोच्चारं परामृशेदित्यर्थः। अनन्तरं मूलविद्यायाः प्रथमखण्डेन मूर्धादिहृदयान्तं, द्वितीयखण्डेन हृदादिप्रपदान्तं, तृतीयखण्डेन प्रपदादिहृदयान्तं, करद्वयेन देशिकप्रदर्शितप्रक्रियया अङ्गन्यस्तं, व्यापकन्यासं त्रिःकुर्यात्। अस्य वासना गुरुमुखादेवावगन्तव्या ॥२१॥

गोत्रेत्यादिभिर्महेश्वरीत्यन्तैश्चतुर्भिः श्लोकैः नवानां मुद्राणां नवबीजमन्त्रान् क्रमेणोपदिशति। तत्र गोत्रा—दकारः। दाहमरुत्खैः—रेफअकारविन्दुभिः

---

(१) पादद्वयोर्मूलाग्रकावधिः इति सो० पु० पा०।

(२) शक्तिनामभिरिति टी० पु० पा०।

बाणाक्षराणि देवेशि ! शृणु सौभाग्यदानि वै ।
व्याप्तं दाहो रसात्वम्बु हृन्मरुत्खयुतं पृथक् ॥२६॥
मुद्राक्षराणि पञ्चादौ बाणाः स्युः सर्वजृम्भणाः ।
शाक्ताः शैवाश्च विज्ञेयाः पञ्चपञ्च समीरिताः ॥२७॥
शिखितोये खसंयुक्ते धनुषी सर्वमोहने ।

द्राँ इति । अन्यः—द्वितीयः । मरुदङ्ग्योर्व्यत्ययादसौ द्रीँ इति मन्त्रः । एतदुक्तं भवति । पूर्वबीजस्यैव आकारस्थाने ईकारं योजयेत् इति । प्राणरसावह्निखैः—ककारलकारईकारविन्दुभिः क्लीँ इति ॥२२॥ भूमी—वकारः । रसाम्भास्खयुता—लकारऊकारविन्दुभिर्युक्तावब्लूँ इति । शक्ति हृत्सकारो विसर्जनीययुक्त इत्यर्थः । परः—पञ्चम सः इति । प्राणेन—ककारेण । दाहभूखेन—रेफः—औकारविन्दुसहितः । अनन्तरः—षष्ठः क्रौँ इति ॥२३॥ हंसो हृदा तेजसा च द्युत्या दाहचरस्वयुक् । हंसो—हकारः । हृदा – सकारेण । तेजसा—खकारेण । द्युत्या—फकारेण युत इति शेषः । दाहचरस्वयुक्—रेफ एकारविन्दुयुक्तः । एतदुक्तं भवति—हकारःसकारेण खकारेण फकारेण एकारेण विन्दुना युक्तः कूटाक्षररूपः सप्तमो मन्त्रः स्यादिति । ह्स्ख्फ्रेँ इति । अष्टमो हंस हृत्प्राप्तवनखैः—मन्त्र इति शेषः । हकारसकार औकारविन्दुभिर्युक्तोऽष्टमः – ह्सौँ इति ॥२४॥ शुचिः स्वेन युतः ऐँ इति । मुद्रारूपाः—मुद्राणां स्थूलसूक्ष्मपरत्वेन त्रैविध्यात्मकाः (१) स्थलाः अक्षरात्मिकाः सूक्ष्माः वास-नात्मिका परा इत्युक्तत्वात् ॥ २५ ॥

बाणेत्यादिना समीरिता इत्यन्तेन श्लोकद्वयेन द्विविधानि बाह्याक्षराणि दशतद्वैविध्यं(२)चोपदिशति । तत्र—व्याप्तं दाहो रसात्वम्बु हृन्मरुत्खयुतं पृथक्—यकाररेफ लकारवकारसकाराक्षराणि पञ्च प्रत्येकं आकारविन्दुभिर्युक्तानि शक्तेः नव बाणाक्षराणि याँ राँ लाँ वाँ साँ इति पञ्च मुद्राक्षराणि । पञ्चादौ प्रोक्तेषु मुद्राक्षरेषु आदितः द्राँ द्रीँ क्लीँ ब्लूँ सः इति पञ्चाक्षराणि । कामत्मनः शिवस्य सर्वजृम्भणाः सर्व्वकामिनोवशंकराः । बाणानां स्थूलसूक्ष्मपरत्वेन तत्त्रैविध्यं पञ्चमे पटले वक्ष्यति ॥२६॥२७॥

शिखेत्यादिना श्लोकपूर्वार्द्धेन चापाक्षरद्वयमुपदिशति । तत्र शिखितोये

---

(१) मुद्राणां स्थलसूक्ष्मरूपाणां स्थलसूक्ष्मपरत्वेन त्रैविद्यात्मकाः न त्रैविद्यात्मका इति वं० पु० पा० ।

हंसगैर्दाहवह्निखैः सखेन मरुता तथा ॥२८॥
पाशौ तयोः समुद्दिष्टौ तथा सर्ववशङ्करी ।
सर्वस्तम्भकरस्त्वेको मुद्रा षष्ठोऽङ्कुशस्तयोः ॥२९॥
आवाहनं स्थापनं च सन्निरोधोऽवगुण्ठनम् ।
सन्निधापनसंज्ञं च हेतिमुद्रा नमस्क्रिया ॥३०॥
संक्षोभद्रावणाकर्षवश्योन्मादमहांकुशाः ।
खेचरी बीजयोन्याख्या शक्त्युत्थापनमित्यपि ॥३१॥
मुद्रा विंशतिरुद्दिष्टास्तासां विरचनं शृणु ।
याभिर्विरचिताभिस्तु मन्त्राः सिद्ध्यन्ति यत्नतः ॥३२॥
कृताञ्जली करौ कृत्वा व्यत्यस्येत्तदनामिके ।
तन्नखे तर्जनीग्रस्ते त्रिखण्डा ललितावहा ॥३३॥

स्वसंयुक्तौ—थकारधकाराक्षरे विन्दुसंयुक्ते थं धं इति क्रमेण शिवयोश्चापाक्षरद्वयम् । चापयोस्त्रैविध्यं पञ्चमे पटले वक्ष्यति ।

हंसेत्यादिभ्यां च वशङ्करावित्यन्ताभ्यां श्लोकोत्तरार्द्धपूर्वार्द्धाभ्यां पाशयोरक्षरद्वयमुपदिशति । तत्र हंसगैर्दाहवह्निखैः—क्रीं इति । सखेनमरुता—आं इति । पाशौ तयोः समुद्दिष्टौ प्राग्वदुभयोः पाशाक्षर एते ।

सर्व्वस्तम्भेत्यादिनोत्तरार्द्धेनोभयसाधारणमङ्कुशाक्षरमेकमुच्यते । तत्र मुद्रा-षष्ठः क्रौंकारः ॥ २८ ॥ २९ ॥

आवाहनमित्यादिभिः प्रयत्नत इत्यन्तैस्त्रिभिः श्लोकैर्विरचनीयमुद्राविंशति-नामान्युपदिशति । तत्र-सन्निधापनं—सन्निधापनसंज्ञा मुद्रेत्यर्थः । हेतिपदेन बाण-धनुःपाशाङ्कुशा उच्यन्ते, तेन चतस्रोमुद्राः ॥ ३० ॥ ३१॥१२॥

कृतेत्यादिना श्लोकेन आवाहनार्थं त्रिखण्डामुद्राविरचनप्रकारमुपदिशति । त्रिखण्डाकारत्वात् त्रिभिः ज्ञातृज्ञानज्ञेयात्मभिः संसारखण्डनाच्च । ललितावहा—आह्वानकरी । अत्र विश्वात्मिकाया ललिताया आह्वानं नाम परिच्छिन्नया वेष्टण-(१) मिति सम्प्रदायः । अन्यत् सुगमम् ॥ ३३ ॥

---

(१) परिच्छिन्ना वेष्टणमिति वं० पु० पा० ।

अधोमुखौ करौ श्लिष्टौ प्रसृताङ्गुलिसंयुतौ ।
विदध्यात् स्थापनी मुद्रा सर्वा संस्थापनी मता ॥३४॥
अंगुष्ठाग्रनखाऽऽश्लिष्टकनिष्ठामध्यमुष्टिकौ ।
करौ सुश्लिष्टनखरौ मुद्रैषा सन्निरोधिनी ॥३५॥
ऋजुतर्जनिमुष्टिभ्यां कराभ्यां पार्श्वभूमितः ।
व्यत्यस्यौपकराभ्रान्त्योपक्रमे तौ निवेशयेत् (१) ॥३६॥
एषाऽवगुण्ठनी मुद्रा सन्निधानकरी पुनः ।
मुद्राञ्जलिस्तु विज्ञेया प्रसृता मुकुलापि वा (२) ॥३७॥
बाणकोदण्डमुद्रा स्यादृज्वङ्गुष्ठेन मुष्टिना ।
पाशमुद्रा तु तेनैव तर्जन्यङ्गुष्ठयोगतः ॥३८॥
कनिष्ठानामिकयोः पृष्ठे स्यादङ्गुष्ठस्तु तर्जनी ।
कुटिला ऋजुमध्यस्था (३) मुद्रासावङ्कुशाभिधा ॥३९॥

अधोमुखावित्यादिना सन्निरोधिनीत्यन्तेन श्लोकद्वयेन सर्वासां देवतानां साधारणस्थापनतन्निरोधनमुद्राद्वयविरचनक्रममुपदिशति । तत्र सन्निरोधनं नाम—देवताया अनन्यचित्तत्वप्रार्थनम् ॥३४॥३५॥

ऋज्वित्यादिना मुकुलापि वा इत्यन्तेन श्लोकद्वयेनावगुण्ठनमुद्राविरचनक्रमं सन्निधापनमुद्राविरचनक्रमं चोपदिशति । तत्र उपक्रमे-दक्षिणकरोपक्रमे वामकरस्य विश्रान्तिः वामकरोपक्रमे दक्षिणकरस्य विश्रान्तिश्चेत्यर्थः । अवगुण्ठनं नाम अयोग्यदृष्ट्यविषयत्वापादनपरम् । सन्निधापनं नामाभिमुख्येनोपचाराङ्गीकरणप्रार्थनपरम् ॥३६॥३७॥

बाणेत्यादिना श्लोकेन बाणमुद्राविरचनक्रमं पाशमुद्राविरचनक्रमं चोपदिशति । तत्र तर्जन्यङ्गुष्ठ योगतः—तर्जन्यङ्गुष्ठयोरग्रयोगत इत्यर्थः ॥३८॥

कनिष्ठेत्यादिना श्लोकेन अङ्कुशमुद्राविरचनक्रममुपदिशति—तत्र ऋज्वाकारमध्यमाङ्गुलिश्लिष्टेत्यर्थः । एतास्वतस्रो हेतिमुद्राः देवतायाः स्वरूपस्वप्रति-

---

(१) व्यात्यास्योपक्रमोद्भ्रान्तोपक्रमे तौ निवेशयेत् इति मू० पु० पा० ।

(२) प्रसृता मुकुला शिवा इति मू० पु० पा० ।

(३) मुद्रा सर्वाङ्कुशाभिधा इति मू० पु० पा० ।

खेचर्या वक्ष्यमाणाया मध्यमे करपृष्ठगे (१) ।
तर्जन्यौ ऋजुसंश्लिष्टे मुद्रैषोक्ता नमस्कृतौ ॥४०॥
कनिष्ठाऽनामिका मध्या नखैरन्योन्यसङ्गता ।
कृत्वाऽङ्गुष्ठौ कनिष्ठास्थौ ऋजू कुर्याच्च तर्जनी ॥४१॥
सर्वसंक्षोभणी मुद्रा त्रैलोक्यक्षोभकारिणी ।
एतस्या मध्यमे देवि ! तर्जनीवत्कृते सति ॥४२॥

पत्तौ तत्तत्करस्थानेषु तत्तदायुधानां परिभावनम् । एताः स्वात्मनो देवता-भावेनैव (२) विरचनीयास्तत्तत्स्थानेषु । समन्त्रविरचने तन्मन्त्रोपेतं विरचयेदिति सम्प्रदायार्थः ॥३८॥

खेचर्या इत्यादिना श्लोकेन नमस्कारमुद्राविरचनक्रममुपदिशति । तत्र नमस्कृतिर्नाम वन्दनीयस्याङ्गत्वेन स्वात्मपृथग्भावेनाभिनयप्रदर्शनमिति । अत्युपस्कारः (३) सम्प्रदायार्थः । तेनैव सर्वत्र प्रणामस्य प्रसादापादकत्वम् । स्थापननमस्कारान्तानां पञ्चानां मुद्राणां प्रदर्शनं मूलविद्यातृतीयखण्डेन कुर्यादिति सम्प्रदायः॥४०॥

कनिष्ठेत्यादिना कारिणीत्यन्तेनार्द्धाधिकेन श्लोकेन संक्षोभणीमुद्राविरचनक्रममुपदिशति । तत्र तर्जनी—तर्जन्यावित्यर्थः । त्रैलोक्यक्षोभकारिणी—सुखकारिणी (४) । सर्वदेवतानां सर्वयोषितां च एतद्दर्शनात् हृदयोल्लासो भवतीत्यर्थः ॥४१॥

एतस्या इत्यादिना योषितामित्यन्तेनार्द्धद्वयेन श्लोकेन सर्वविद्रावणीमुद्राविरचनक्रममुपदिशति । तत्र एतस्याः—संक्षोभणीमुद्रायाः । मध्ये—अङ्गुली इति शेषः । देवीति संबुद्धिः । तर्जनीवत्कृते—ऋजूकृते स्यातामित्यर्थः । सति—एवं कृते सति इत्यध्याहरणीयम् ॥४२॥ सर्वविद्रावणी—सर्वासां देवतानां वशीकरणात्—सर्वासां योषितां योनेश्च विद्रावणात् ।

---

(१) करपृष्ठके इति मू० पु० पा० ।
(२) भावने इति सो० पु० पा० । भावने च इति टी० पु० पा० ।
(३) पंस्कारः इति सो० पु० पा० ।
(४) प्रथा कारिणी इति टी० पु० पा० ।

सर्वविद्रावणी मुद्रा सर्वासामपि योषिताम् ।
ताभ्यामङ्कुशरूपाभ्यां संश्लिष्टाऽऽकर्षणी मता ॥४३॥
परिवृत्ताङ्गुली कृत्वा नखाश्लिष्टतली करौ ।
अङ्गुष्ठौ तर्जनीश्लिष्टौ नखैरावेशकारिणी ॥४४॥
कराग्रे प्रसृते कृत्वा व्यत्यस्येत् तत्कनिष्ठिके ।
तदग्राश्लेषतो भुग्ने मध्यमेऽनामिके ऋजू ॥४५॥
तन्नखस्थे तु तर्जन्यावङ्गुष्ठौ मध्यमोपरि ।
इयमुन्मादिनी मुद्रा सर्वोन्मादनकारिणी ॥४६॥
अस्यास्त्वनामिके भुग्ने तर्जन्यावङ्कुशाकृती ।
एषा महाङ्कुशा मुद्रा स्तम्भनाऽऽकर्षकारिणी ॥४७॥
सव्यदक्षकरौ सम्यक् व्यत्यस्येत्कूर्परोपरि ।
मणिबन्धे च बध्नीयादङ्गुली मध्यपृष्ठयोः ॥४८॥

ताभ्यामित्यादिना श्लोकोत्तरार्द्धेनाकर्षणीमुद्राविरचनक्रमम् पदिशति । तत्र ताभ्यां अङ्कुशरूपाभ्यां—प्राग्वदङ्कुशरूपेण युक्ताभ्यां मध्यमातर्जनीभ्यां संश्लिष्टा अनामिकयोरिति शेषः । एतदुक्तं भवति—प्रागुक्तद्राविणीमुद्रैवानामिकाद्वये अङ्कुशाकारमध्यमातर्जनीसंश्लेषात् - आकर्षणी मुद्रा स्यात् । आकर्षः समीपानयनम् । आगत्य निजवाञ्छा(याः) कारित्वे स्थैर्यमित्यर्थः ॥४३॥

परिवृत्तेत्यादिना श्लोकेनाऽऽवेशनमुद्राविरचनक्रममुपदिशति । तत्र परिवृत्ताङ्गुली व्यत्यस्ताङ्गुली । आवेशकारिणी—देवताभावोद्बोधनकारिणी ॥४४॥

कराग्रेत्यादिना कारिणीत्यन्तेन श्लोकद्वयेनोन्मादिनीमुद्राविरचनक्रममुपदिशति । तत्र सर्वोन्मादकारिणी—सर्वयोषितामुन्मादकरी क्लेदनकरीत्यर्थः ॥४६॥

अस्या इत्यादिना श्लोकेन महाङ्कुशमुद्राविरचनक्रममुपदिशति । तत्र अस्याः—उन्मादिनीम् द्रायाः । भुग्ने – अङ्गुष्ठाग्राश्लेषतः ॥४७॥

सव्येत्यादिभिर्देवता इत्यन्तैस्त्रिभिः श्लोकैः खेचरीमुद्राविरचनक्रमम् पदिशति । तत्र मध्यपृष्ठयोः—मध्यमाङ्गुलिपृष्ठयोः । खेचरी—खेचरत्वसिद्धिकरी । अत्र मुद्राविरचनप्रतिपादकेषु ग्रन्थेषु सुगमत्वात् व्याख्या न लिख्यते ॥४८॥४९॥५०॥

विधाय भुग्ने तर्जन्यावङ्गुष्ठौ कारयेदृजू ।
कनिष्ठाऽनामिके कुर्याद्व्यत्यस्ते करपृष्ठगे ॥४९॥
इयं सा खेचरी मुद्रा ललिताप्रीतिकारिणी ।
अस्या विरचनेनैव सर्वाः सिद्ध्यन्ति देवताः ॥५०॥
मध्यमा मध्यपार्श्वाधः कनिष्ठाग्रे विपर्ययात् ।
अनामिकेऽधोव्यत्यस्ते तर्जन्यावङ्कुशाकृती ॥५१॥
इतरे तन्नखाग्राग्रे बीजमुद्रेयमीरिता ।
कनिष्ठाङ्गुष्ठसंश्लेषा महायोनिस्त्रिखण्डिका ॥५२॥
कनिष्ठाऽनामिकामध्या व्यत्यस्ताः पृष्ठतः क्रमात् ।
वलितावूर्ध्वयोगेन (१) ऋजुतर्जनिकौ करौ ॥५३॥

मध्यमेत्यादिना त्रिखण्डिका इत्यन्तेन श्लोकद्वयेन बीजमुद्रारचनाक्रमं महायोनिमुद्रारचनाक्रमं चोपदिशति। तत्र विपर्ययात्—विपरीते स्यातामित्यर्थः। बीजमुद्रा—सर्वसिद्धिकारणत्वात् ॥५२॥

कनिष्ठेत्यादिना समीरितमित्यन्तेन श्लोकद्वयेन शक्त्युत्थापनमुद्राविरचनक्रममुपदिशति। तत्र समाधिः—सम्यगाधीयते इति समाधिः स्वात्मनि देवताऽहंभाव इत्यर्थः। मूर्तीकरणं—देवताया मूर्तित्वेन स्वदेहस्य कल्पनमित्यर्थः ॥५४॥

मुद्रा इत्यादिभिः शिवेत्यन्तैः पञ्चभिः श्लोकैर्मुद्राणां त्रैविध्यं तद्वासनां मुद्राशब्दनिर्वचनं तदुपपत्त्यादिकं चोपदिशति। तत्र तत्त्वं—तद्भावः याथार्थ्यमित्यर्थः। अङ्गुष्ठतः क्रमात्—अङ्गुष्ठमारभ्य व्योमादिपृथिव्यन्तक्रमात्। माया—स्वस्वरूपस्य प्रपञ्चस्वात्मज्ञानतिरोधानं(२) त्वत्प्रसादात्—त्वदात्मसिद्धेः रातीति रादाने इति धातोर्निष्पन्नः ददातीत्यर्थः। स्वल्पभेदात् कोपहर्षावित्यत्र प्रहारप्रणामयोर्मुष्टेरैकरूप्ये मणिबन्धे किञ्चिद्वक्रता आर्जवं स्वल्पभेद इत्युच्यते, हर्षविपरीतं कोपं कोपविपरीतं हर्षं स्वेत्थे तदुक्तं भवति। प्रहारप्रणामयोर्वक्रावक्ररूपाया एकस्या मुष्टेः कोपप्रसादयोरुद्भावकत्वे प्रसादप्रतिपादिका मुष्टिर्मुद्रासंज्ञिका कोपप्रतिपादिका मुष्टिरेवेति ॥५९॥

---

(१) ऊर्ध्वयोगेन इति सो० पु० पा०।

(२) प्रपञ्च स्वात्मज्ञान निरोधनमिति सो० पु० पा०।

भक्तोत्थापनमुद्रैषा जपपूजासमाधिषु ।
मूर्त्तीकरणमेतस्या रचनेन समीरितम् ॥५४॥
मुद्राः स्युस्त्रिविधा देवि ! रचनामन्त्रतत्त्वतः ।
स्थूलसूक्ष्मपराख्याता स्तत्त्रैविध्यं शृणु प्रिये ! ॥५५॥
रचनामन्त्रयोरूपं कथितं तव साम्प्रतम् ।
तत्त्वरूपाण्यङ्गुलयो भूतान्यङ्गुष्ठतः क्रमात् ॥५६॥
तत्तद्व्यत्यासरचना दर्शनेन तु कथ्यते ।
तव मायाबहिर्भूतस्त्वत्प्रसादादहन्त्विति ॥५७॥
मुदं रातीति मुद्रा स्यात्न्येनैका (?) मुष्टिरेव तु ।
स्वल्पभेदात् कोपहर्षौ प्राणिनां जनयत्यतः ॥५८॥
तेनैव सर्वदेवानां मुद्रा हर्षप्रदा मता ।
पूजाकाले दर्शनीया मुद्रास्ताः सर्वदा शिवे ! ॥ ५९ ॥

त्रिलोहेत्यादिना शिवेत्यन्तेन श्लोकद्वयेन पञ्चविधमर्घ्यपात्रमर्घ्यकल्पनप्रकारादिकं चोपदिशति । तत्र त्रिलोहशब्देन सुवर्णरजतताम्राण्युच्यन्ते । एकस्मिन्नन्यतमे । अर्घ्यकल्पनं—पञ्चमपटले वक्ष्यमाणप्रकारेण कल्पिते तस्मिन्नर्घ्यजले धेनुयोनिमुद्रे दर्शयेत् । धेनुमुद्राबन्धस्तु व्यत्यस्ताङ्गुलिकममञ्जलिं बध्वा वामदक्षिणतर्जनीद्वयं दक्षिणवाममध्यमाङ्गुलिभ्यां दण्डवत्संश्लेष्य तद्वद्वामदक्षिणे कनिष्ठाद्वयं दक्षिणवामानासिकाभ्यां (दण्डवत्संश्लेष्य तद्वामदक्षिणे कनिष्ठाद्वयं दक्षिणवामानामिकाभ्यां) दण्डवत्संश्लेषयेत् । एषा सुरभिमुद्रा । तद्दर्शनप्रकारं गुरुमुखादवगच्छेत् । तद्दर्शनानन्तरं षडङ्गनित्यातातीरैरेकैकं दशवारतः जपेनेति (१)। षडङ्गनित्यामन्त्राणामेकवारं मूलविद्यातृतीयखण्डस्य दशवारं जपे क्रमो वा समर्चनं वेत्यर्थः । तदनु तद्दिननित्याविद्यया त्रिखण्डरूपया मूलविद्यया च त्रिवारमभ्यर्चयेत् जपेद्वेत्यानुश्रविकोऽर्थः । विद्यारूपेण—प्रोक्तक्रमतः एतदर्घ्यजलस्य विशेषणम् । विद्यया—ललितया त्रिखण्डेनेत्यर्थः । अभ्यर्चनेन विद्यात्मतापादनम् ।६०॥६१॥

---

(१) जपेनेति इति व० पु० पा० । जपेत् इति सो० पु० पा० ।

त्रिलोहकाचमृत्पात्रे ष्वेकस्मिन्नर्घ्यकल्पनम् ।
षडङ्गनित्यातार्तीयैरेकैकं दशवारतः ॥६०॥
जपेन विद्यारूपेण प्रोक्षयेदर्घ्यवारिणा ।
स्वात्मपूजोपकरणान्यशेषं विद्यया शिवे ! ॥६१॥
लोहितां ललितां बाणचापपाशसृणीः करैः ।
दधानं कामराजाङ्कीं यन्त्रितां मुदितां स्मरेत् ॥६२॥
काम्यध्यानोक्तरूपेण (१) समेतां शक्तिभिर्वृताम् ।
नित्यार्चनेषु सर्वत्र प्रोक्तं नैमित्तिकार्चने ॥६३॥
मध्यप्रधानदेव्यास्तु समुल्लासात्मकत्वतः ।
नवावरणशक्तीनां ध्यानं देव्या समं भवेत् ॥६४॥
कामाङ्कयन्त्रादन्यत्र भूषावर्णायुधादिकम् ।
तत्समं परमेशानि ! चक्रस्थानामशेषतः ॥६५॥
अणिमा लघिमा पश्चान्महिमा तदनन्तरम् ।

लोहितां (२) इत्यादिना अर्चने इत्यन्तेन श्लोकद्वयेन ललिताया नित्यनैमित्तिकयोर्ध्यानमुपदिशति । तत्र बाणचापपाशसृणीः करैः—दक्षिणाधोभुजादि-दक्षिणोर्ध्वभुजान्तं अप्रादक्षिण्येन चतुर्षु भुजेषु प्रोक्तक्रमेणायुधानां स्थितिः । यन्त्रि—तामित्यस्यार्थो गुरुमुखादेवावगन्तव्यः । मुदितां—आनन्दशतविग्रहत्वात् । काम्यध्यानोक्तरूपेणेति—नूपुरवीरवलयांशुकरचनास्वस्तिकहारग्रैवेयकाङ्गदवलय-मुद्रिकाकर्णाभरणमुकुटाद्युपेतरूपा च नित्यनैमित्तिकार्चनयोर्ध्यातव्येत्यर्थः ॥ ६२॥६३॥

मध्येत्यादिनाऽशेषत इत्यन्तेन श्लोकद्वयेन परिवारशक्तिवृन्दध्यानमुपदिशति । तत्र समुल्लासात्मकत्वतः । देव्यास्तु बहुस्यां प्रजायेय इति समुद्योगात् । कामाङ्कयन्त्रादन्यत्रेत्यत्र रहस्यार्थो गुरुमुखादेवावगन्तव्यः ॥६४॥६५॥

अणिमेत्यादिभिः प्रथमावृतावित्यन्तैः पञ्चभिः श्लोकैः प्रथमावरणे चतुरस्रे

---

(१) काम्यार्चनोक्तरूपेण इति सो० पु० पा० ।

(२) लोहितमिति व० पु० पा० ।

तथेशित्वं वशित्वं च प्राकाम्या भुक्तिसंयुता ॥६६॥
इच्छारसयुताः सर्वाः कामाः स्युः सिद्धयो दश ।
बीजद्वयाद्याः सिद्ध्यन्ताः सम्प्राचर्या च संयुताः ॥६७॥
ब्राह्मी माहेश्वरी पश्चात् कौमारी वैष्णवी तथा ।
वाराही च तथेन्द्राणी चामुण्डा तदनन्तरम् ॥६८॥
महालक्ष्मीति कथिताः शक्तयश्चतुरस्रगाः ।
एताश्चाष्टौ तद्वयाद्याः सम्प्राचर्यन्तगाः क्रमात् ॥७०॥
द्वारकोणदिगासीना अध ऊर्ध्वं च संस्थिताः ।
प्रादक्षिण्येन ताः सर्वाः पूजयेत्प्रथमावृतौ ॥७१॥
कामं बुद्धिमहंकारं शब्दं स्पर्शं ततः परम् ।
रूपं रसं तथा गन्धं चित्तं धैर्यं स्मृतिं तथा ॥७२॥
नाम बीजं तथात्मा च अमृतं सशरीरकम् ।
बीजद्वयस्वराद्याश्च आकर्षिण्यन्तकाः क्रमात् ॥७३॥

शक्त्यष्टादशकस्य मन्त्रांस्तत्पूजाक्रमं चोपदिशति । तत्र तेषां श्लोकानां सुगमत्वात्तासां मन्त्रेष्वेकं प्रदर्श्यान्यानप्येवं योजयेदित्युच्यतेऽस्माभिः । यथा ऐं८ ह्रीं८ अणिमासिद्धिपादुकां पूजयामीत्यादि । द्वारे—पूर्वपश्चिमे । कोणाः—विदिशः दिशौ दक्षिणोत्तरौ, अधऊर्ध्वकल्पनं पूर्वपश्चिमद्वारोपकण्ठयोः । प्रथमावृतौ चतुरस्रे ॥६६॥६७॥६८॥६९॥७०॥७१॥

काममित्यादिभिः सुन्दरि इत्यन्तैस्त्रिभिः श्लोकैः षोडशदले द्वितीयावरणे शक्तिषोडशकस्य पूजनमन्त्रांस्तत्पूजाक्रमं चोपदिशति । तत्र आत्मा—आत्मानमित्यर्थः । सशरीरकं—शरीरमित्यर्थः । अत्रापि गूढानां सुगमार्थत्वात् एकस्य मन्त्रस्वरूपं प्रदर्श्य एवमन्यदपि कल्पनीयमित्युच्यतेऽस्माभिः ग्रन्थविस्तृतिभीत्या । पश्चाद्दलं—देव्याः अग्रदलमित्यर्थः । ऐं८ह्रीं८ (१)अं कामाकर्षिणीनित्या—कलापादुकां पूजयामि । एवमन्येपि पञ्चदशमन्त्रा ऊहनीयाः ॥७२॥७३॥७४॥

---

(१) अं कामा इति टी० पु० पा० ।

नित्या कलेति च ततः सप्ताचर्याऽर्चयेत् क्रमात् ।
पश्चाद्दलं समारभ्य वामावर्तेन सुन्दरि ? ॥७४॥
कुसुमा मेखला पश्चान्मदना मदनातुरा ।
रेखा च वेगिनी पश्चादङ्कुशा मालिनीति च ॥७५॥
इयानङ्गादिकाः सर्वाः सप्ताचर्यन्तगा अपि ।
प्राच्यादिदिक्षु स्वाग्न्यादिकोणेष्वर्च्याः प्रदक्षिणम् ॥७६॥
अष्टस्वपि च पत्रेषु तृतीयावरणे स्थिताः ।
अन्तश्चतुर्दशारादौ पश्चिमादप्रदक्षिणम् ॥७७॥
संक्षोभणी तु प्रथमा विद्राविण्यप्यनन्तरा ।
आकर्षिण्याह्लादनिका ततः सम्मोहिनीति च ॥७८॥
स्तम्भिनी जम्भिनी पश्चाद्वशङ्करी च रञ्जनी ।
उन्मादिनी ततोऽज्ञेया ततः स्यादर्थसाधनी (१) ॥७९॥

कुसुमेत्यादिना स्थिता इत्यन्तेनाध्यर्द्धेन श्लोकद्वयेन तृतीयावरणे अष्टदलशक्त्यष्टकमन्त्रा॰ स्तत्पूजाक्रमं चोपदिशति। तत्राप्येकमन्त्रप्रदर्शनेनान्ये सप्तमन्त्रा योज्याः—क्लीं॰ श्रीं॰ अनङ्गकुसुमापादुकां पूजयामि इत्यादि ॥७५॥७६॥

अन्तरित्यादिना अन्वर्थसंज्ञिका इत्यन्तेनार्धाद्यन्तेन श्लोकत्रयेण चतुर्थावरणे चतुर्दशारे शक्तिचतुर्दशकमन्त्रान् दशा(च)रद्वयशक्तिपूजाक्रमं चोपदिशति। तत्र चतुर्दशा(च)रादावित्यत्रादिशब्देन दशा(च)रद्वयेपि देव्याः अग्रमारभ्य अप्रादक्षिण्येन पूजयेदित्युच्यते। वशङ्करि—वशङ्करी इत्यर्थः। इयसर्वादिकाः उक्तबीजद्वयोपरि सर्वशब्दं चतुर्दशानामादौ योजयेत्। शक्तिसप्ताचरी इत्यत्र शक्ति इत्यक्षरद्वयमेव गृह्यते न तु विसर्जनीयक्लींकाराविति सम्प्रदायः। क्रमेण—उद्दिष्टक्रमेण। शक्तिप्रत्येकं प्रतिकोणं देव्यग्रकोणमारभ्य पूजयेदित्यर्थः। क्लीं॰ श्रीं॰सर्वसंक्षोभणीशक्तिपादुकां पूजयामि। एवमन्यान् त्रयोदशमन्त्रान् योजयेत् ॥७७॥७८॥७९॥

---

(१) साधिनी इति मू॰ पु॰ पा॰ ।

सम्पत्तिपूरणी(१) मन्त्रमयी द्वन्द्वक्षयङ्करी ।
इयसर्वादिकाः सर्वा शक्तिसम्प्राचरीयुताः ॥७९॥
पूज्याः क्रमेण देवेशि ! सर्वास्त्वन्वर्थसंज्ञिकाः (२) ।
अन्तर्दशारयुग्मे तु देवी सम्प्राचरात्मिका ॥८०॥
सिद्धिसम्पत्प्रदे पश्चात्तृतीया तु प्रियङ्करी ।
चतुर्थी शक्तिराख्याता तथा मङ्गलकारिणी ॥८१॥
कामप्रदा ततो दुःखात्परतश्च विमोचनी ।
मृत्युप्रशमनी पश्चात्तथा विघ्ननिवारिणी ॥८२॥
अङ्गसुन्दरिका पश्चात्तथा सौभाग्यदायिनी ।
दशैताः शक्तयः पूज्या इयसर्वादिकाः क्रमात् ॥८३॥
ज्ञानशक्तिः तथैश्वर्यप्रदा ज्ञानमयी मता ।
प्रोक्ता सा पञ्चमी शक्ति स्तथा व्याधिविनाशिनी ॥८४॥
प्रोक्ताऽऽधारस्वरूपाऽन्या तथा पापहराऽपरा ।
उक्तैवमानन्दमयी तथा रक्षास्वरूपिणी ॥८५॥

अन्तर्दशारेत्यादिना क्रमादित्यन्तेनार्द्धादिना श्लोकत्रयेण पञ्चमावरणे पूज्यशक्तिदशकमन्त्रानुपदिशति। तत्र देवी सम्प्राचरात्मिकाः देवी इति अक्षरद्वयम् तदनु सम्प्राचरीं दशसु मन्त्रेषु। अन्तर्दशा(क्ष)रमन्त्रदशके च योजयेत् ॥८०॥ सिद्धिसम्पत्प्रदे—सर्वसिद्धिप्रदा सम्पत्प्रदा च। दुःखात्परतश्च विमोचनी—दुःखविमोचिनी इत्यर्थः। अन्यत् सुगमम् ॥८२॥ अङ्गसुन्दरिका—अङ्गसुन्दरीत्यर्थः। इयसर्वा(मा)दिकाः—उक्तबीजद्वयात्परं सर्वशब्द एतद्दशारशक्तिमन्त्राणामादितो योजयेत् क्लीं श्रीं सर्वसिद्धिप्रदादेवीपादुकां पूजयामि। एवमन्येऽपि नवमन्त्रा योजनीयाः ॥८३॥

ज्ञानेत्यादिना यजेदित्यन्तेन श्लोकत्रयेण षष्ठावरणे द्वितीयदशारे पूज्यशक्ति-

---

(१) सम्पत्प्रपूरणी इति मू० पु० पा०।
(२) सर्वा तत्त्वार्थसंज्ञिता इति मू० पु० पा०।

दशमी शक्तिरुदिता स्यादीप्सितफलप्रदा ।
इयसर्वादिकाश्चैताः षष्ठाऽऽवरणगा यजेत् ॥८६॥
अन्तरष्टस्वपि तथा पश्चिमाद्प्रदक्षिणम् ।
वशिन्यादीन् (१) यजेत् प्राग्वत् सप्ताक्षर्या नमः पदे ॥८७॥
मध्यं त्रिकोणमभितः शरांश्चापमथार्चयेत् ।
पाशमङ्कुशमित्येतच्चतुष्कं तद्बीजान्विकी ॥८८॥
बीजान्युक्तानि नामानि नमान्तानि महेश्वरि ! ।
नाथाँश्च पृष्ठतो देव्या जयिनीविमलान्तरे ॥८९॥

दशकमन्त्रानुपदिशति । तत्र सर्वा—सर्वज्ञेत्यर्थः । प्राग्वत् क्लीँ श्रीँ सर्वज्ञा—देवीपादुकां पूजयामि । एवमन्यानपि नवमन्त्रान् योजयेत् ॥८४॥८५॥८६॥

अन्तरित्यादिना श्लोकेन सप्तमावरणे अष्टारे पूज्यशक्त्यष्टकस्य मन्त्राँस्तत्—पूजाक्रमं चोपदिशति । तत्र पश्चिमात्—अग्रमारभ्य प्राग्वदिति वर्गबीजादि-योजनविषयः सप्ताक्षर्या सार्द्धमिति शेषः । नमःपदे—न्यासक्रमप्रोक्तनमः—शब्दमपास्य तत्स्थाने सप्ताक्षरीमष्टसु मन्त्रेषु योजयेदित्यर्थः । क्लीँ श्रीँ अँ आँ इँ ईँ उँ ऊँ ऋँ ॠँ ऌँ ॡँ एँ ऐँ ओँ औँ अँ अः व्लूँ वशिनीवाग्देवतापादुकां पूजयामि (२) । एवमन्येपि मन्त्रा योजनीयाः । अत्रापि बीजद्वययोजनं प्रथमविधानात्—अन्यत्रानुविधानात् सर्वत्र ॥८७॥

मध्येत्यादिना महेश्वरीत्यन्तेनाध्यर्द्धेनैकेन श्लोकेनायुधानां पूजामन्त्रान् पूजा-क्रमं चोपदिशति । तत्र मध्यं त्रिकोणमभित इत्येतदुक्तं भवति । प्रधानदेवता—वाससर्वमध्यत्रिकोण मभितः तत्तद्भुजस्थानेषु (३) तत्तदायुधानि बाणाद्यङ्कुशान्तमर्च-येत् । बीजान्युक्तानीति । एतदुक्तं भवति—क्लीँ श्रीँ इति पूर्वोद्दिष्टबीज—द्वयान्ते याँ राँ लाँ वाँ शाँ द्राँ द्रीँ क्लीँ व्लूँ सः सर्वजृम्भनेभ्यो बाणेभ्यो नमः इति बाणमन्त्रः । ततोऽपि क्लीँ श्रीँ इति प्रोक्तबीजद्वयान्ते थँ धँ सर्वमोहनाय धनुषे नम इति धनुर्मन्त्रः । तदनु च क्लीँ श्रीँ इति प्रोक्तबीजद्वयान्ते

---

(१) वशिन्यादि यजेत् इति मू० पु० पा० ।

(२) इत्येवमन्यानपि सप्तमन्त्रानपि योजयेत् इति टी० पु० पा० ।

(३) तत्तद्गुरुस्थानेषु इति टी० पु० पा० ।

मध्यस्थदेवी त्वेकैव षोड़शाकारतः स्थिता ।
यतस्तस्मात्तनौ तस्या अन्याः पञ्चदशार्चयेत् ॥९०॥
मध्यत्रिकोणकोणेषु पश्चिमादप्रदक्षिणम् ।
कामेश्वरीं सवज्रेशीं तथाच भगमालिनीम् ॥९१॥
पूर्वद्वयं ततो विद्या त्वेकैकं पीठनाम च ।
ततो नामानि शक्तीनां देवीसप्ताक्षरीयुतम् ॥९२॥
तैस्ताः समर्चयेत् पश्चात् मध्ये देवीं तथाऽर्चयेत् ।
द्वयं समस्तां विद्यां च पीठदेव्यभिधायुताम् ॥९३॥
देवीसप्ताक्षरोपेतमित्युक्तं तव पूजनम् ।
प्रतिचक्रं च मध्यस्थां विद्यया नवनामभिः ॥९४॥

क्रों आं सर्ववशीकरणाय पाशाय नमः इति पाशमन्त्रः । ततोऽपि च श्रीं क्रों इति प्रोक्त बीजद्वयान्ते सर्वस्तम्भनाय अङ्कुशायनमः इत्यङ्कुशमन्त्रः । अत्रापि बीजद्वययोजनं प्राग्वत् ।

नाथानित्यादिना श्लोकोत्तरार्द्धेन नवानां नाथानामर्चनस्थानमुपदिशति॥८८॥

मध्यस्थेत्यादिना श्लोकेन देव्याः षोड़शनित्यात्मकत्वं तेन तस्या विग्रहे अन्यासां पञ्चदशोनां तिथिनित्यानामर्चनं चोपदिशति ॥९०॥

मध्यत्रिकोणेत्यादिना समर्चयेदित्यन्तेन षड़क्षराधिकेन श्लोकद्वयेनाष्टमावरणे मध्यत्रिकोणकोणत्रये पूजनीयशक्तित्रयं तन्मन्त्रांस्तत्पूजाक्रमं चोपदिशति। तत्र पश्चिमाद्देव्यग्रकोणमारभ्य विद्याया एकमेकं खण्डं एकैकस्याः शक्तेरित्यर्थः। पीठानि कामरूपपूर्णगिरिजालंधराख्यानि त्रीणि, नामानि शक्तीनां कामेश्वरीवज्रेश्वरीभगमालिनीति त्रीणि। देवीसप्ताक्षरीयुतं—देवी इत्यक्षरद्वयात् परं (१) श्रीपूर्वां सप्ताक्षरीं योजयेत् इति। श्रीं क्रीं(२) मूलविद्याप्रथमखण्डं कामरूपपीठे कामेश्वरीदेवीश्रीपादुकां पूजयामि। एवमन्यौ द्वौ मन्त्रौ योजनीयौ। अत्र श्रीशब्दप्रयोगः सम्प्रदायात् ॥९२॥

---

(१) देवीपादानान्तरं इति सो० पु० पा०।

(२) क्रीं श्रीं इति टी० पु० पा०।

सप्ताक्षर्या समेतं तु पूजयेच्च तथाऽर्चयेत्।
द्वयमेता इति प्रोक्ता गुणान्योगिन्य इत्यपि ॥९५॥
अभिधामावृतेरुक्ता पूजां गृह्णन्त्विति क्रमात्।
देव्या गृह्णन्त्विति (१) भवेत्तत्त्वैविध्यं शृणु प्रिये ॥९६॥

पश्चादित्यादिना पूजनमित्यन्तेन दशाक्षराद्येनार्धद्वयेन नवमावरणे सर्वमध्ये देव्याः स्थूलरूपपूजनमुपदिशति। तत्र समस्तां विद्यां—प्रागुक्तां तुरीयां विद्याम्। पीठदेव्यभिधायुतां—पीठाभिधा देव्यभिधा चेति। तत्र पीठाभिधां श्रोड्यानपीठे इति। देव्यभिधा श्रीमहात्रिपुरसुन्दरी इति। देवीसप्ताक्षरोपेतं—प्राग्वद्देवी इत्यक्षरद्वयमुच्चार्य श्रीपूर्वां सप्ताक्षरीमुच्चरेदित्यर्थः। क्लीँ श्रीँ समस्तां मूलविद्यां श्रोड्यानपीठे श्रीमहात्रिपुरसुन्दरीदेवीश्रीपादुकां पूजयामि, अत्रापि श्रीशब्दद्वयप्रयोगः प्राग्वत् सम्प्रदायात् ॥८३॥

प्रति चक्रमित्यादिना भवेदित्यन्तेनार्द्धादिना त्रिपादान्तेनैकेन श्लोकेन देव्याः नवस्वावरणेषु प्रत्येकं नवनामभिस्तत्पूजनमन्त्रानेव तत्पूजार्पणमन्त्रानेव चोपदिशति। तत्र नवनामभिः—पञ्चमे पटले चतुर्दशपञ्चदशश्लोकाभ्यामुक्तैस्त्रिपुरे—त्यादिभिर्नामभिरुपेतैस्तत्रोक्तयोजनाप्रकारैश्च मन्त्रैः पूजयेदित्यर्थः। तत्र योजनाप्रकारो यथा—मूलविद्यात्रिपुरानित्यापादुकां पूजयामि। (२) इत्येवं क्रमेणान्या—नष्टौ योजयेत्। अत्र मन्त्रनवकेऽपि बीजद्वययोजनं न स्यादिति सम्प्रदायः। नवमे च श्रीशब्दद्वयप्रयोगः स्यात् सम्प्रदायतः। तत्—तदिति द्विविधं पूजनं द्वयमिति बीजयद्वयं। गुणान्—प्रकटादिकान्। श्रीशक्तिसंज्ञागुणान्। तेऽपि पञ्चमे पटले द्वादशत्रयोदशाभ्यां श्लोकाभ्यां प्रोक्ताः। योगिन्य इति प्रोक्ता इत्यत्रान्वेति। प्रोक्तेति दिव्यत्वात्। अभिधामावृते (३) र्नवानामावरणचक्राणां त्रैलोक्यमोहनादिकाः संज्ञाः। ताश्च पञ्चमे पटले नवदशमाभ्यां अभिहिताः। ते यथा—क्लीँ श्रीँ एताः प्रकटयोगिन्यस्त्रैलोक्यमोहने चक्रे पूजां गृह्णन्त्विति। एवमन्यानप्यष्टौ

---

(१) गृह्णात्विति सो० पु० पा०।

(२) इदं क्रमेणान्यान्यदौ यो इति सो०पु० पा०। एवं क्रमेणेत्यादौ श्री० इति वं० पु० पा०।

(३) अभिधानावृते रिति सो० पु० पा०। अभिधानावृतेरिति वं० पु० पा०।

स्थूलं समस्तया नाम्ना सूक्ष्मं मन्त्रतनुं तथा ।
पररूपं त्वर्पणेन विदितं पूजनं शिवे ॥८७॥
विद्या बीजत्रयं देवि तुरीयस्वरशेखरम् ।
तत्तुरीयस्वरूपं तु विन्दुत्रयवदीरितम् ॥८८॥
तदात्मकत्वं देव्यास्ते साधकस्य च यद्भवेत् ।
तद्भावनां शृणु प्राज्ञे ! महोदयकरीं शुभाम् ॥८९॥

मन्त्रान् योजयेत् । तत्र चरमस्तु—ऐं ह्रीं श्रीं एषा अतिरहस्ययोगिनी सर्वानन्दमये महाचक्रे महापूजाफलं गृह्णात्विति । अत्रापि महाशब्दप्रयोगः सम्प्रदायात् ॥८४॥८५॥

तत्रे विधमित्यादिना शिवे इत्यन्तेन पादाधिकेन मध्यस्थाया देव्याः स्थूलसूक्ष्मपरत्वेन त्रिरूपत्वमुपदिशति, तत्र स्थूलं—लोहितमित्यादिनोक्तं रूपम् । समस्तया—विद्यया तुरीयया विद्यया पूजयेदित्यर्थः । नामनाम्ना नामरूपया विद्यया सूक्ष्मं रूपं पूजयेदिति यावत् । मन्त्रतनुं—अक्षरविग्रहमित्यर्थः । एतत् सूक्ष्मरूपमित्यनेनान्वेति । देव्याः सूक्ष्मरूपमित्यक्षरात्मकमित्यर्थः । पररूपं—देशकालादिभिरनवच्छिन्नम् । अर्पणेन—पूजानिवेदनेन पूजयेदिति शेषः । देव्याः पररूपं पूजानिवेदनमन्त्रेण पूजयेदित्यर्थः । मङ्गलानि सर्वाणि देव्यै निवेदनीयान्येव । अतएव मङ्गलतरं तत्पूजनं च तस्यैव (१) निवेदनीयमिति न्यायेन सर्वत्र देवताभ्रस्तत्पूजनं च निवेदनीयमित्यर्थः । विदितं—पूजितं भवेदिति शेषः । विदित्वा पूजयेदित्यर्थः । एतदुक्तं भवति—देव्याः स्थूलं रूपं समस्ताख्यया तुरीयया विद्यया, सूक्ष्ममक्षरात्मकं रूपं नामरूपया विद्यया, परं रूपमर्पणविद्यया च पूजयामीति विदित्वा पूजयेत् । एवमन्येष्वष्टस्वपि बोद्धव्यम् ॥८६॥८७॥

विद्येत्यादिभिः भावयेदित्यन्तैस्त्रिभिः श्लोकैः गुरुमन्त्रदेवतात्मैक्ययोग—भावनामुपदिशति । अस्यार्थस्यातिरहस्यत्वादप्रकाश्योऽपि नाथाज्ञया विविच्योच्यते, विद्या बीजत्रयं—मूलविद्याखण्डत्रयं, तुरीयस्वरशेखरं—चतुर्थस्वरावसानं ईका-

---

(१) तस्यैव इति सो० पु० पा० ।

ऊर्ध्वं विन्द्वात्मकं चक्रमधोविन्दुद्वयात्मकम् ।
कुचरूपञ्च (३) तच्छेषैः शेषाङ्गानि च भावयेत् ॥१००॥
वायुतत्त्वमयी व्याप्तिरिति सम्यक् समीरिता ।
अस्या निष्फालनाच्चित्ते तत्तत्त्वं स्वात्मसात्कृतम् ॥१०१॥

इति श्रीषोड़शनित्यातन्त्रे कादिमते ललितार्चनं
नाम चतुर्थं पटलम् ॥

रावसानं इत्यर्थः। तत्तुरीयस्वरूपं तस्य तुरीयस्वरूपस्य ईकारस्य स्वरूपमित्यर्थः। स्वरूपमिति लिपिरूपमुच्यते, विन्दुत्रयवदीरितं—सर्वासु लिपिषु तुरीयस्वरूपस्य विन्दुत्रयात्मता विद्यत एव, तेन चैतदात्मकत्वं गुरुदेवतासाधकानां प्रतिपादयति। तद्भावनां तदात्मत्वभावनाम्। महोदयकरीं—अखण्डात्मस्वरूपलाभात् ॥९८॥

ऊर्ध्वेत्यादिना श्लोकेन गुरुमन्त्रदेवतानां स्वात्मैक्यसिद्धिकरयोगभावनाक्रममुपदिशति। तत्र ऊर्ध्वं विन्द्वात्मकमिति। एतदुक्तं भवति—मूलविद्यायाः खण्डत्रयस्यापि (१) चतुर्थस्वरैकावसानत्वात् तत्स्वरूपस्य च विन्दुत्रयवत्वात्तदूर्ध्वं विन्दुनावदनं (२) अधःस्थितविन्दुद्वयेन कुचद्वयं, तदक्षरशेषरेखया तस्या देव्याः परिपूर्णानवयवांश्च। एवं देवतामन्त्रयोरैकरूप्यं तेन गुरुस्वात्मनोश्च तत्स्वरूपस्थितं भावयन्निमां विद्यां जपेत्तेन तादात्म्यसिद्ध्या प्रोक्तानि फलानि सिद्ध्यन्त्येवेति। गुरोर्मन्त्रात्मकत्वं तन्मुखादवगन्तव्यम् ॥१०१॥

इति श्रीषोड़शनित्यातन्त्रेषु श्रीकादिमताख्यस्य परिपूर्णस्य
तन्त्रस्य प्रपञ्चसारसिंहराजप्रकाशाभिधानेन सुभगानन्द-
नाथेन विरचितायां मनोरमाख्यायां व्याख्यायां ललिता-
नित्यानित्यसपर्याक्रमप्रकाशनपरं चतुर्थपटलं परि-
पूर्णं परामृष्टम्।

---

(१) त्रयस्यापि इति वं० पु० पा०।

(२) अस्थितं विन्दु इति सो० पु० पा०। अथ विस्थितितविन्दु इति टी० पु० पा०।

(३) कम्बुद्वयञ्च इति मू० पु० पा० टीकानुसारेण कुचद्वयमित्येव पाठः।

अथ पञ्चमं पटलम् ।

भावनेन तु तेनैव जपेद्विद्यासमाहितः ।
मन्त्रात्मनस्ते सायुज्यं सिद्ध्यत्येव न संशयः ॥१॥
विद्यातृतीयखण्डेन कुर्यात्पूज्योपचारकान् ।
पाद्यार्घ्याचमनं स्नानं वसनाभरणानि च ॥२॥
गन्धपुष्पं धूपदीपौ नैवेद्याचमनं पुनः ।
ताम्बूलमर्चनास्तोत्रं तर्पणं च नमस्क्रियाम् ॥३॥

ग्रन्थसङ्ख्या—चतुर्थे पटले यन्त्रं नास्ति व्याख्यानगामिनो ।
ग्रन्थसङ्ख्याऽष्टसप्तत्याऽभ्यधिकं द्विशतं भवेत् ॥

अथ पञ्चमं पटलम् ।

पूर्वस्मिंश्चतुर्थे पटले ललितानित्याविद्यायाः गुरुमन्त्रदेवतात्मैक्ययोगभावनातन्नित्यपूजामुपदिश्यानन्तरं तस्या ललितादेव्याः नित्याराधनक्रमे प्रोक्तशेषादिकं कूर्मविभागात्तमुपदिशति—भावनेत्यादिना तथेत्यन्तश्लोकशतरूपेण पञ्चमेन पटलेन। तत्र भावनेनेत्यादिना श्लोकेन मन्त्रजपप्रकारं सिद्धेरव्यभिचारित्वं चोपदिशति। तत्र—तेनैव तु भावनेन—पूर्वं पटलावसाने गुरुमन्त्रदेवतास्वात्मनामैक्यरूपभावनायोगेनैवेत्यर्थः। सायुज्यं—तादात्म्यम् ॥१॥

विद्येत्यादिना श्लोकपूर्वार्द्धेन देवताया उपचारनिवेदनमन्त्रमुपदिशति। तत्र—तृतीयखण्डेनेत्युक्तोऽपि तद्दिननित्यया (१) समेतेन तेन तेकुर्यादिति, नाथाज्ञया तथा कर्तव्यमिति सम्प्रदायः ॥२॥

पाद्येत्यादिना नमस्क्रियामित्यन्तेनार्धाद्येन श्लोकेन तन्त्रसाधारणान् (२) षोड़शोपचारानुपदिशति। तत्र निवेद्याङ्गत्वात् द्वितीयमाचमनमुपचारत्वेन न गण्यते। तर्पणमिति क्षौद्रदुग्धनालिकेराम्बुफलद्रवार्घ्योदकेषु यथालाभं निवेदनमुक्तम्। नमस्क्रियां—मुद्रासमयप्रोक्तमुद्राः। एवं षोड़शसङ्ख्याकान् पूजोपचारान् कुर्यादित्यन्वयः ॥३॥

---

(१) नित्याविद्यासमेतेन इति टी० पु० पा०।

(२) तत्र साधारणानिति सो० पु० पा०।

एवं सम्पूज्य पुरतः प्रोक्तयोगसमन्वितम् ।
जपेत्सहस्रमथवा शतं तद्दिनजन्तु वा ॥४॥
ततो देव्याः प्रसादेन स्वात्मानं तत्समं स्मरेत् ।
न्यासत्रयं विधायाथ देव्यात्मा विहरेत्सुखी ॥५॥
एवं नित्यक्रमं यस्तु कुर्वन् गुरुपरो नरः ।
न तस्य कुवचित् कश्चित् कदाचित् क्लेशसम्भवः ॥६॥
यस्तस्यामङ्गलं क्लेशमुपेक्षां वा समाचरेत् ।
तस्यावयोः प्रसादेन तानि स्युर्लक्षणं हि तत् ॥७॥
नवावरणनामानि तत्तच्छक्त्याभिधास्तथा ।
शृणु यैरतुला सिद्धिस्तत्तच्चक्रेषु पूजनात् ॥८॥
त्रैलोक्यमोहनं चाद्यं सर्वाशापरिपूरकम् ।
सर्वसंक्षोभणं सर्वसौभाग्यपरिदायकम् ॥९॥

एवमित्यादिना सुखीत्यन्तेन श्लोकद्वयेन पूजावसानकृत्यमुपदिशति। तत्र पुरतः—देव्यग्रे तद्दिनजं—तत्पूजादिनजम् । वा अवधारणे । प्रातःसन्ध्योक्त—नववारं, मध्यन्दिनसन्ध्योक्तषड्त्रिंशद्वारं, सायंसन्ध्योक्तषोडशवारं तद्दिन-घटिकासङ्ख्योक्तषष्ठिवारं चैवं एकविंशत्यधिकशतवारं जपेदित्यर्थः ॥४॥ प्रसादेन—देवभाववितीर्णतादात्म्यभावनासामर्थ्येन। देव्यात्मन्यासानन्तरं—देवताऽहम्भावयुक्तः सदा विचरेदित्यर्थः (१) ॥५॥

एवमित्यादिना तदित्यन्तेन श्लोकद्वयेन नित्यक्रमोपासकस्यानुभावमुपदिशति। तत्र गुरुपरः तदायत्तसर्वव्यापारः ॥६॥ लक्षणं हि तत्—नित्यक्रमोपासकस्येति शेषः। एतदुक्तं भवति—नित्यक्रमोपासकस्यानुकूल्यप्रातिकूल्योपेक्षा (नवावरणनित्यक्रमैकोपासकस्याप्युपेक्षा कारिणी) (२) अस्मदानुकूल्योपेक्षास्तवाभ्यां कृतेन प्रसादेन सम्भवन्तीति ॥७॥

नवेत्यादिना श्लोकेन नवावरणनानि तच्छक्तिनामानि च प्रस्तौति। तत्र यैः—नामभिः ॥८॥

---

(१) विरचयेदित्यर्थः इति टी० पु० पा० ।

(२) ( ) एतदन्तर्गतो ग्रन्थः सो० पुस्तक एव वर्तते ।

सर्वार्थसाधनं सर्वरोगतो हरमेव च ।
सर्वरक्षाकरं सर्वसिद्धिप्रदमतः परम् ॥१०॥
सर्वानन्दमयं मध्यविन्दुस्थानं शिवात्मकम् ।
एवं नवानि नामानि गुणयोगीनि पार्वति ! ॥११॥
प्रकटा बाह्यगा गुप्तास्ततो गुप्ततरास्तदा ।
सम्प्रदायास्तदन्तस्थाः कुलकौलनिगर्भिकाः ॥१२॥
रहस्याः स्युस्तदन्ताश्च परापररहस्यकाः ।
अतिपूर्वरहस्यास्तु मध्यस्थाः स्थूलविग्रहाः ॥१३॥
त्रिपुरा त्रिपुरेशी स्यात्सुन्दरी सुरवासिनी ।
श्रीमालिनी च सिद्धाम्बा महात्रिपुरसुन्दरी ॥१४॥

त्रैलोक्येत्यादिभिः पार्वतीत्यन्तैः त्रिभिः श्लोकैर्नवावरणचक्राणां अन्वर्थानि नवनामान्युपदिशति । तत्र सर्वसंक्षोभणं—सर्वसंक्षोभकरम् सम्यक् प्रथाकरं—प्रसिद्धिकरमित्यर्थः । परिदायकमित्यत्र परि इत्युपसर्गः श्लोकपूरणार्थः । सर्वसौभाग्यदायकमित्यर्थः ॥९॥ सर्वरोगतो हरं—सर्वरोगशब्दात् परं हरशब्दं योजयेत्—सर्वरोगहरमित्यर्थः । सर्वसिद्धिप्रदं—सर्वसिद्धिमयत्वात् सर्वसिद्धिप्रदं सर्वसिद्धिमयमिति सम्प्रदायः ॥१०॥ विन्दुस्थानं—मध्यमविन्दुस्थानम् । सर्वानन्दमयं—शिवात्मकमित्यन्वयः । विन्दुस्थानं—ब्रह्मवत् सर्वमध्यमित्यर्थः । गुणयोगीनि—अन्वर्थानि । पार्वतीति सम्बुद्धिः ॥११॥

प्रकटा इत्यादिना विग्रहा इत्यन्तेन श्लोकद्वयेन नवावरणशक्तीनामन्वर्थानि नवनामान्युपदिशति । तत्र तासां विशेषणानि निरुपाधिकस्वभावानीति सम्प्रदायः । तत्र तृतीयचरमावरणशक्त्योर्व्यत्यस्तगुणसंज्ञाशब्दाः यथा गुप्ततरा—योगिन्य इत्यादि । अतिरहस्या योगिनी इति । अन्यास्तु समस्तगुणसंज्ञाशब्दाः यथा गुप्तयोगिन्य इत्यादि । कुलकौलाः—कुलोत्तीर्णा इति चोभयं सम्प्रदायवत् यथा नाथादेशमनुष्ठेयमित्यर्थः । निगर्भिकाः—निगर्भा इत्यर्थः ॥१२॥ परापररहस्यकाः—परापररहस्या इत्यर्थः । अतिपूर्वरहस्या—अतिशब्दपूर्वरहस्याः अतिरहस्या इत्यर्थः । मध्यस्थाः स्थूलविग्रहाः—मध्यस्थाः सविग्रहाः अतिरहस्या इत्यर्थः । अत्र स्थूलं रूपं सूक्ष्मरूपस्य मन्त्रस्यावरणं परं रूपं देशकालाकारे

मध्यषट्के तु पुरतस्त्रिपुरेतिपदान्वितैः ।
विद्यासप्ताक्षरीमध्ययोजितैरेभिरर्चयेत् ॥१५॥
पूजाक्रमं तद्विशेषान् विद्यासाधनकर्म च ।
साधकव्रतचर्यां च सिद्धिचिह्नानि मेव (?) च ॥१६॥
त्रिपुरात्मानमात्मानं भावयेन्मूर्ध्नि रन्ध्रगम् ।
ज्योतिरूपं च नाथाङ्घ्रिमूर्तिष्टे (?) न्यस्तविग्रहाः ॥१७॥
नानावर्णाऽऽयुधाकारवाहनाभरणाः स्त्रियः ।
सर्वदा सर्वगाः सर्वसिद्धिदा बलिदानतः ॥१८॥

रनियन्त्रितम् । स्थूलसूक्ष्मरूपे पररूपस्य प्रापके मप्यवच्छिन्नतया (१) भावरक्षणात (२) इत्यावरणमितुग्रपञ्चरः सम्प्रदायार्थः ॥१३॥

त्रिपुरेत्यादिनाऽर्चयेदित्यन्तेन श्लोकद्वयेन देव्याः नवस्वावरणेषु प्रत्यावरणं प्रतिनियतानि नवनामानि च तैस्तत्र तत्र पूजार्थं मन्त्रयोजनाक्रमं चोपदिशति । तत्र त्रिपुरेशी—त्रिपुरेश्वरी इत्यर्थः । मध्यषट्के—सुन्दर्याद्यम्बान्तेषु षट्सु नामसु । तत्र पुरवासिनो इत्यत्र त्रिपुरवासिनो इतरार्थः । त्रिशब्दमेव योजयेदिति च सम्प्रदायः । विद्या—श्रीविद्या । मनुयोजनाप्रकारः पूर्वस्मिन् पटलेऽभिहितोऽस्माभिः ॥१४॥१५॥

पूजाक्रमित्यादिना श्लोकेनाथ पञ्चप्रश्नान् करोति । तत्र तद्विशेषान्—सङ्कोचक्रमरूपान् । सिद्धिचिह्नानि—विद्यासिद्धिचिह्नानि ॥१६॥

त्रिपुरात्मानमित्यादिना दानत इत्यन्तेन श्लोकद्वयेन साधकस्य प्रातः प्रबोधसमयविधातव्यमुपदिशति । तत्र उत्थानसमये । मूर्ध्नि भावनानन्तरं तदनन्तरं न्यासः त्रिपुरात्मानं—वक्ष्यमाणगमागमानुसन्धानपुरःसरं देवीस्वरूपं स्वस्वरूपं भावयेदित्यर्थः । बलिदानतः—षोडशाक्षरमन्त्रेणेति शेषः । पुष्पान्तव्यञ्जनसहितो बलिः तद्दानतः सर्वसिद्धिदा भवेयुरिति शेषः । एवं ध्यात्वा सर्वसिद्धये प्रातर्बलिं दद्यात् इति शेषः ॥ १७॥१८ ॥

---

(१) मप्यावच्छिन्नतया इति सो० वं० पु० पा० ।

(२) ज्ञानः इति सो० पु० पा० । ज्ञावः इति वं० पुस्तके पाठः ।

रक्तगन्धाम्बरः स्रग्वी रक्तभूषादिभूषितः (१) ।
प्रसन्नचेताः कर्पूरवासिता स्यावराङ्गवान् (२) ॥१९॥
पद्मासनः प्राग्वदनः प्राणानायम्य संयतः ।
षोड़शाक्षरमन्त्रेण बलिं दत्त्वाऽर्चयेद्गुरून् ॥२०॥
मूर्ध्नि तस्याज्ञया पश्चात् पूजां कुर्याद्यथाविधि ।
नाथं च तन्मयीभूतं ध्यात्वाऽऽत्मानं तदात्मकम् ॥२१॥
नवरत्नमयं द्वीपं नवखण्डविराजितम् ।
मातृकाद्येन तन्नाम्ना नमोन्तेन समर्चयेत् ॥२२॥

रक्तेत्यादिभिस्तदात्मकमित्यन्तैस्त्रिभिः श्लोकैः सपर्यासमारम्भक्रममुपदिशति । तत्र—पद्मासनः । उपरिष्टाद्वक्ष्यमाणत्वादिह नोच्यते । प्राणानायम्य—प्राणायामं कृत्वा । उपरिष्टाद्वक्ष्यमाणमपि प्राणायामं किञ्चिदत्र व्याकरोमि दक्षिणनासारन्ध्रेण वामनासारन्ध्रनिरोधेन श्वासं मारुतं यथा शक्त्या निर्गमय्य अनन्तरं दक्षिणनासारन्ध्रनिरोधेन वामनासारन्ध्रेण यथाबलं प्रवेश्य श्वासमारुतं, पुनरप्येवं रेचकं पूरकं च कृत्वा यथाबलं तमन्तर्विधाय पश्चाच्छनैः शनैः तं मुञ्चेदिति । एवं सर्वत्र प्राणायामक्रमः । संयतः—सकलान्यविषयनिवृत्तबाह्यान्तःकरणः । षोड़शाक्षरमन्त्रेण—तृतीयपटलावसानोपदिष्टस्वरूपेण बलिं दत्त्वा प्राग्वदर्चयेत् । गुरून् मूर्ध्नि—ब्रह्मरन्ध्रे स्थितान् यथासम्प्रदायं पूजयेदित्यर्थः । तस्येति स्वनाथविषयः । यथा विधि—वक्ष्यमाणप्रकारेण । नाथं च तन्मयीभूतं—नाथ एव देवीरूपेण स्थित इति बुद्ध्वेत्यर्थः ॥ १९ ॥२०॥२१॥

नवरत्नेत्यादिभिर्मीतर इत्यन्तैरष्टभिः श्लोकैर्देवीनिवासस्थानार्चनक्रमं तन्मन्त्रांश्चोपदिशति । तत्र मातृकाद्येनेति । अकारादिक्षकारान्तान्येकपञ्चाशदक्षराणि सबिन्दूनि बीजद्वयपुरस्सरमुच्चार्य तदुपरि तन्नाम तदनु च नमः शब्दं योजयेदित्यर्थः । यथा—क्लीँ ब्लूँ अँ आँ इँ ईँ उँ ऊँ ऋँ ॠँ ऌँ ॡँ एँ ऐँ ओँ औँ अँ अः कँ खँ गँ घँ ङँ चँ छँ जँ झँ ञँ टँ ठँ डँ ढँ णँ तँ थँ दँ धँ नँ पँ फँ बँ भँ मँ यँ रँ

---

(१) भूषाविभूषिता इति सो० पुस्तके पाठः । (२) वसिताख्यां वाराङ्गवान् इति सो०पु० पा० ।

पुष्पं नीलं च वैडूर्य्यं विद्रुमं मौक्तिकं तथा ।
ईशान्मरकतं वज्रं गोमेदं पद्मरागकम् ॥२३॥
कल्पकोद्यानमन्त्रैश्च ऋतूँश्चापि समर्चयेत् ।
इन्द्रियाण्यश्वरूपाणि तत्र पश्चिमतो यजेत् ॥२४॥
इन्द्रियार्थान् गजान् (१) पूर्वे तन्नाम्नैव समर्चयेत् ।
पश्चिमादि तु मध्यान्तं विलोमान्नवरत्नकम् (२) ॥२५॥
कालो मुद्रा मातृका च रत्नं देशो गुरुस्तथा ।
तत्त्वं ग्रहाश्च मूर्तिश्च चक्रेश्वर्यन्तनामकः (३) ॥२६॥

लँ वँ शँ षँ सँ हँ लँ क्षँ नवरत्नद्वीपाय नमः इत्यनेन । अत्र प्रकरणे इन्द्रियार्थावधि नमोन्तेनैव तत्तन्नाम्ना पूजयेत् ॥२२॥

पुष्पमित्यादिना श्लोकेन नवरत्ननामान्युपदिशति—तत्र ईशान्मरकतमित्युक्तिः पश्चिमं पुष्परागमिति कुरुकुल्लापटले वक्ष्यमाणत्वात्(४)प्रादक्षिण्यक्रमं (५) प्रदर्शयति, ईशात्—ईशानदेशे इत्यर्थः ॥२३॥ कल्पकोद्यानं—क्लीँ श्रीँ कल्पकोद्यानाय नमः । अत्रैव रत्नद्वीपे क्लीँ श्रीँ ऋतुभ्यो नमः । इन्द्रियाणि—श्रोत्रत्वक्चक्षुर्जिह्वाघ्राणवाक्पाणिपादपायूपस्थानि दश । पश्चिमतः—देवीमण्डपस्याग्रतः क्लीँ श्रीँ इन्द्रियाश्वेभ्यो नमः । इन्द्रियार्थान्—शब्दस्पर्शरूपरसगन्धवचनादानगतिविसर्गानन्दाख्यान् क्रमेण दश । पूर्वे देवीमण्डपस्य पृष्टभागतः क्लीँ श्रीँ इन्द्रियार्थगजेभ्यो नमः । नवरत्नकमर्चयेदिति ॥२४॥२५॥

कालो मुद्रा इत्यादिना श्लोकेन कालादिरूपनवरत्नमयानां नवानां खण्डानां प्रत्येकं नवनाथात्मनां पूजामन्त्रानुपदिशति । गुरुर्नाथ इत्यर्थः । तत्र कालस्य नवधात्वं घटिकायामाहोरात्रवारतिथिपक्षमासऋत्वब्दरूपतः । मुद्राया नवधात्वं प्रागुक्तसंक्षोभणादिभिः । मातृकाया नवधात्वं उपरिष्टाद्वक्ष्यमाणवर्गक्रमतः । रत्नस्य नवधात्वं प्रोक्तरूपतः । देशस्य नवधात्वं रत्ननवधात्ववत् । नाथानां नवधात्वं प्रोक्तक्रमतः । तत्त्वानां नवधात्वं ज्ञातृज्ञानज्ञेयरूपस्य त्रिकस्य पञ्चीकरणप्रक्रियया । एतन्नित्यत्वाङ्गीकारतः । ग्रहाणां नवधात्वं सुप्रकटमेव । मूर्तीनां नवधात्वं त्वगसृङ्मांसमेदोस्थिमज्जाशुक्रौजःप्राणात्मतः चक्रेश्वर्यन्तनामकाः ॥२६॥

---

(१) गतापूर्वे इति मू० पु० पा० ।
(२) विलोमानवरत्नकम् इति मू० पु० पा० ।
(३) नामका इति मू० पुस्तके पाठः ।
(४) त्वादप्रा इति सौ० पुस्तके पाठः ।
(५) क्रमेप्र इति वं० पुस्तके पाठः ।

उक्तक्रमेण सम्पूज्य (१) तत्तच्चक्रेश्वरी प्रिये ! ।
करुणातोयपरिखं मध्येमाणिक्यमण्डपम् (२) ॥२७॥
देशं कालं तथाऽऽकारं शब्दं कोणेषु पूजयेत् ।
रूपिणीशक्तिसहितं ततः संगीतियोगिनीः ॥२८॥
समस्तगुप्तप्रकटसिद्धयोगिनि (३) चक्रयुक् ।
सप्ताचरैरुपेतास्तु पूजयेत् सर्वमातरः ॥२९॥
रोचनाचन्द्रकाश्मीरलघुकस्तूरिकायुतम् ।
हेमादिपात्रे साधारे स्थापयेदर्घ्यमम्बुना ॥३०॥
भावयेद्वह्निसूर्येन्दुभूतानि परमेश्वरि ! ।
जपेच्च दशवारं तत्तर्पयेत्तेन योगिनी ॥३१॥

क्रमेणेति—प्रोक्ता एता नव चक्रेश्वरीः शक्तिस्वस्वनामान्ते चक्रेश्वरीं इति वदन् पूजयेदित्यर्थः। क्रों श्रीं कालचक्रेश्वरीशक्तिपादुकां पूजयामि। एवमत्र (४) शक्तिशब्दः पारम्पर्यप्राप्तः। नवानां प्रत्येकं नवरूपत्वाद्बहुवचनम्। प्रिये इति देवीसम्बुद्धिः। करुणातोयपरिखमिति—देव्याः करुणामयतोयपरिपूर्णपरिखापरिवृतं माणिक्यमण्डपमित्यर्थः। क्रों श्रीं करुणातोयपरिखाय नमः क्रों श्रीं माणिक्यमण्डपाय नमः अत्रापि नमःशब्दयोजनं सम्प्रदायात् ॥२७॥

देशमित्यादिना सङ्कोचकारिकाः शक्तीरुपदिशति। तत्र—क्रों श्रीं देशरूपिणीशक्तिपादुकां पूजयामि। एवमन्ये मन्त्रास्त्रयः तथा निऋर्त्यादिविलोमतः। अत्र देशकालाकारशब्दानां द्विरुपादानं कार्यकारणानुरूपत्वेन, तत्र कार्यरूपं नवधाभूतं प्रथमं, कारणरूपं द्वितीयम्। संगीतयोगिनीः—नृत्यगीतवाद्यविनोदिकाः शक्तीः क्रों श्रीं संगतयोगीनीशक्तिपादुकाः पूजयामि। अत्रापि शक्तिशब्दयोजनं बहुवचनं च प्राग्वत् ॥२८॥

समस्तगुप्तेत्यादिश्लोकपूर्वार्द्धस्य अन्त्याक्षरवर्जं मन्त्ररूपमित्यर्थः। तत्र योगिनि—योगिनी इत्यर्थः। क्रों श्रीं समस्तगुप्तप्रकटसिद्धियोगिनीचक्र—

---

(१) सम्पूज्यास्तत्र इति मू० पु० पा०।

(२) प्रियो करुणातोयेस्थिं मध्ये माणिक्यमण्डपे इति सो० पुस्तके पाठः।

(३) योगिनीं इति मू० पु० पा०। (४) मन्यत्रेति टी० पु० पाठः।

आधारे हृदये रन्ध्रे विद्याखण्डत्रयं स्मरेत्।
लोहितं तत्प्रभावेधाल्लोहितं (१) च निजं वपुः ॥३२॥
प्राणायामं विधायाथ कृत्वोक्तकरशोधनम्।
आद्ययाऽथ तृतीयादिषष्ठान्ताभिः तथासनम् ॥३३॥

श्रीपादुकाः पूजयामि। अत्रापि बहुत्वाद्बहुवचनं श्रीशब्दप्रयोगश्च प्राग्वत्। सर्वमातरः—सर्वशक्तीरित्यर्थः। एतत्समाचरोयोजनं तत्तच्छक्तिसाधारणमिति यावत्। अष्टभिरेतैः श्लोकैरेतदुक्तं भवति। देहेन्द्रियरूपस्वविग्रहोदितशब्द-कल्पितस्वरूपप्रादुर्भावा प्रतिपत्तव्या देवी इति ॥२८॥

हूँमित्यादिना योगिनीरित्यन्तेन श्लोकद्वयेन देवतायाः सपर्यार्थमर्घ्यकल्पन-प्रकारं तद्विनियोगं चोपदिशति। तत्र चन्द्रः—कर्पूरम्। लघुः—अगुरुः ॥३०॥

परमेश्वरीति देवीसम्बुद्धिः। जपेच्च दशवारं तत्—तदिति विद्यायास्तृतीयखण्ड-मुच्यते, तेन—अर्घ्याम्बुना। योगिनी इति देव्याः परिवारभूताः शक्तीः कथयति। एतदुक्तं भवति—आधारचषकाम्बुनि वह्निसूर्यसोमात्मविद्याखण्डत्रयात्मकं (२) बुद्ध्वा तस्मिन् न्यस्तानि पञ्चद्रव्याणि क्रमेण पृथिव्यादिपञ्चभूतात्मकान्याकलय्य प्रागुक्तक्रमेण धेनुयोनिमुद्रे प्रदर्श्य अम्बुमध्ये श्रीचक्रं च विभाव्य तत्र नित्य-क्लिन्नापटले वक्ष्यमाणबाह्यादिक्रमात् षडङ्गमन्त्रैः षोडशनित्यामन्त्रैश्चैकैकवारं विद्यातृतीयखण्डेन दशवारं मूलविद्यादिननित्याभ्यां प्रतित्रिवारं चाभ्यर्च्य जपित्वा अर्घ्योदकेन प्रोक्तकार्याणि कुर्यात् ॥३१॥

आधार इत्यादिना विधायाथ इत्यन्तेन पादाधिकेन श्लोकेन प्राणायामकाल-भावनीयमुपदिशति—तत्र रन्ध्रे—ब्रह्मरन्ध्रे। तत्प्रभावेधात् तेषां प्रभावे-धात्। वेधः—तन्मयीभावः। आधारब्रह्मरन्ध्रगतयोरग्नीषोमात्मविद्याप्रथम—चरमखण्डयोस्तयोस्तेजसी क्रमेण ऊर्ध्वाधोमुखप्रसरं हृदयगतसूर्यात्ममध्यमखण्डे-तेजस्तूर्ध्वाधःप्रसरणेन ताभ्यां सम्मीलितं भवति, एतदुक्तं भवति—मूलाधारस्थ-प्रथमखण्डवह्नितेजसा खचितं हृदयगतं द्वितीयखण्डसूर्यतेजः प्रसरं तेनानुषक्तं ब्रह्मरन्ध्रगततृतीयखण्डचन्द्रमस्तेजःप्रसरं च त्रीणि तेजांसि अविभक्ताकार-मिलितरूपं अन्तर्बहिर्भावयेदिति। प्राणायामं प्राग्वत्, ललिताविद्याजपपूजा-

---

(१) तत्प्रभावेन लोहितं इति मू० पु० पा०।

(२) त्मकां बुद्ध्वेति सो० पु० पा०।

पूजयेद्बीजनमसोर्मध्यस्थैर्नामभिर्युतम् ।
ततो द्वितीयया प्रोक्तषडङ्गानि समाचरेत् ॥३४॥
प्रसारिततलेनैव पाणिना हृदयं शिरः ।
प्रोक्ता शिखा तथा सम्यगधोङ्गुष्ठेन मुष्टिना ॥३५॥
तथाविधाभ्यां पाणिभ्यां वर्मस्कन्धादिनाभिगम् ।
तर्जनीमध्यमानामा प्रोक्ता नेत्रत्रये (च) क्रमात् ॥३६॥
प्रसारिततलाभ्यान्तु तालत्रयमुदीरितम् ।
सशब्दं तर्जनीज्येष्ठायोगादस्त्रमुदीरितम् ॥३७॥
दिग्विदिक्चोपरि तथा स्वाधो मध्ये च विघ्नहृत् ।
ततः कृत्वा वशिन्यादि न्यासं प्रागुक्तयोगतः ॥३८॥

समाधिषु प्राणायाम एवं विद्याखण्डत्रयरूपं तेजस्त्रयं भावनीयम्। अन्यत्र केवलं तेजस्त्रयं आधारत्रयगतं भावनीयम् ॥३२॥

कृत्वेत्यादिभिर्योगत इत्यन्तैस्त्रिपादाधिकैः पञ्चभिः (१) श्लोकैर्न्यासत्रयादिकमुपदिशति, तत्र आद्यया—पूर्वपटले वातः खसंयुत इत्याद्युक्तया। तृतीयादिषष्ठ्यन्ताभिस्ततस्तृभिर्विद्याभिरासनचतुष्टयं समर्चयेदित्यर्थः। बीजनमसोर्मध्यस्थैर्नामभिर्युतम्। प्रोक्तानां विद्याकूटाक्षराणामुपरि प्रत्येकं तत्तदासननाम चतुर्थ्यन्तमुक्त्वा ततो नमःशब्दं च योजयेदित्यर्थः। क्रों ऎं क्रीं क्लीं क्रौं सौः देव्यात्मासनाय नमः। क्रैं क्र्स् क्लीं ह्सौः चक्रासनाय नमः। ह्सैं ह्स्क्लीं ह्सौं सर्वमन्त्रासनाय नमः। क्रीं ऐं क्लीं सौः व्लूं साध्यसिद्धाय नमः इत्यत्रासनमन्त्रचतुष्टये आदौ बीजद्वयं न संयोज्यते सम्प्रदायात्। द्वितीयया—पूर्वस्मिन् पटले हृच्छिर इत्यत्र प्रोक्तकुलसुन्दरीविद्यया। ऐं क्लीं सौं हृदयाय नमः ऐं क्लीं सौः शिरसे स्वाहा ऐं क्लीं सौः शिखायै वषट् ऐं क्लीं सौः कवचाय हुम् ऐं क्लीं सौः नेत्रत्रयाय वौषट् ऐं क्लीं सौः अस्त्राय फट् ॥३३॥३४॥

प्रसारिततलेत्यादिभिर्हृदित्यन्तैस्त्रिभिरर्ध्यर्द्धैः श्लोकैः षडङ्गन्यासप्रकारमुपदिशति। तत्र तालत्रयं सशब्दं करतलयोः त्रिरास्फालनम्। त्रिः प्रोक्तया कुल-

---

(१) त्रिभिः पादाधिकैः इति सं० पु० पा०।

सप्तम्याऽऽवाहनं कुर्याद्विद्ययाऽथ त्रिखण्डया ।
अग्रस्थमध्यचक्रस्थयोनिमध्ये निवेश्य ताम् ॥३९॥
तथाविधां सावरणां ध्यात्वा मुद्रां प्रदर्शयेत् ।
प्रोक्ताः सप्तदशार्थैनामुपचारैः समर्चयेत् ॥४०॥
जयिनीविमलामध्ये नाथान् नव यजेत्त्रिशः (१) ।
ततो देव्याः स्वमूर्तित्वान्नित्याः पञ्चदशापि च ॥४१॥
देवीमूर्तौ जपेत्तत्तद्वि(२)द्याभिस्तन्मयी क्रमात् ।
आरभ्य पश्चिमद्वारदक्ष(३)शाखामथार्चयेत् ॥४२॥
अभितश्चाष्टसु तथा दिक्ष्वधोर्ध्वं तथेरिताः ।
तथा ब्राह्म्यादिका अष्टौ पूजयेत् प्रथमावृतौ ॥४३॥

सुन्दरीविद्ययेति शेषः । सर्वत्र न्यासत्रये बीजत्रयाद्यता (४) न भवति । प्रागुक्त-योगतः—पूर्वपटलप्रतिपादितवर्ग्कूटाक्षरादियोगतः ॥३५॥३६॥३७॥३८॥

सप्तम्यावाहनमित्याद्यैः सुखोत्यन्तैः पञ्चविंशत्या श्लोकैर्देव्या नित्यपूजां नित्यहोमविधिं पूजावसानं (५) चोपदिशति, तत्र सप्तम्या विद्ययेति सम्बन्धः । पूर्वस्मिन् पटले हंसहृदित्याद्युक्तया त्रिखण्डया मुद्रयेतिशेषः । तथाविधां—पूर्वस्मिन् पटले लोहितामित्यादिश्लोकोक्तवैग्रहां मुद्राः प्रदर्शयेत् । प्रोक्ताः सप्तदशस्थापनादि-हेतिचतुष्टयान्ताः पूर्वपटलोक्ताः सप्तदश मुद्राः प्रदर्शयेदित्यर्थः । उपचारैः—षोड़शभिः पञ्चभिर्वा, पञ्चोपचारास्तु गन्धपुष्पधूपदीपनैवेद्यानि ॥ ८३ ॥ ४० ॥

त्रिशः--त्रीन् त्रीन् दिव्यसिद्धमानुषान् देवीवामभागादि दक्षिणभागान्तं त्रिपङ्क्त्युपविष्टान् देव्यवेक्षिणः । तन्मयी - तत्तत्स्वरूपेणाप्यवस्थानमेतस्या एवे-त्यर्थः । क्रमात्—एकादिवृद्धिक्रमात्, दक्षशाखां द्वारस्य देव्याः सव्येतरभाग-शाखाम् ॥४१॥४२॥ अभित इति, अत्र प्रथमं दिक्षु, ततो विदिक्षु, तत्र तत्रापि देव्याः दक्षिणभागे, तथा अणिमादिवत् ब्राह्म्यादिकास्तत्र तत्र देवीसव्यभागे

(१) नाथान्वर्जयेत्त्रिश इति मू० पु० पा० ।

(२) यजेत्तत्तदिति सो० पु० पा० ।

(३) दन्तशाखामिति मू० पु० पा० ।

(४) बीजत्रयाख्यता इति टी० पुस्तके पाठः ।

मूलविद्यायुतैः प्रोक्तनामभिर्मध्यतो यजेत् ।
नवस्वावृत्तिषु प्रोक्तैर्नवभिर्मनुभिः क्रमात् ॥४४॥
निवेदयेच्च तत्पूजां मुद्राः कुर्यान्नवैकशः ।
षोड़शारे त्वष्टदले तथा तच्चतुरावृतौ ॥४५॥
प्रोक्ताभिः शक्तिभिः प्रोक्तक्रमात्पूजां समाचरेत् ।
मध्ययोनेरग्रमूले पार्श्वयोर्बहिरर्चयेत् ॥४६॥
बाणान् पञ्च तथा चापं पाशमङ्कुशमीश्वरि ! ।
(१)बाह्यादीशान्तमभितो वामावर्त्तेन संस्थिताः ॥ ४७ ॥
बाणाः स्युस्त्रिविधाः प्रोक्ताः स्थूलसूक्ष्मपरत्वतः ।
स्थूलाः पुष्पमयाः, सूक्ष्माः मन्त्रात्मानः समीरिताः ॥४८॥
पराश्च वासनायां तु प्रोक्ताः स्थूलान् शृणु प्रिये ! ।
कमलं कैरवं रक्तं कह्लारेन्दीवरं तथा ॥ ४९ ॥
सहकारज(२)मित्युक्तं पुष्पपञ्चकमीश्वरि ! ।
मान्मथक्षोभजनकं पूजाहोमविधानतः ॥ ५० ॥

प्रोक्तनामभिस्त्रिपुरेत्याद्युक्तैः । प्रागुदीरितक्रमतःप्रोक्तैःप्रागेवास्माभिरपि प्रकटीकृतै-र्पणमन्त्रैः ॥४३॥४४॥ तत्पूजां—स्थूलसूक्ष्मरूपं पूजां प्रागुक्ताम् । एकैकशः—प्रत्यावरणमितिशेषः ॥४५॥ प्रोक्तक्रमादित्याद्युक्तमस्माभिरपि प्रागेव प्रोक्तमेव अग्रमूलपार्श्वयोर्बहिः—मध्ययोनेर्वहिः । वशिन्याद्यष्टकोष्ठानां मध्यस्थावकाश इत्यर्थः ॥४६॥४७॥४८॥ रक्तशब्दः कैरवविशेषणम्॥४९॥ सहकारजं पुष्पमिति शेषः । मान्मथं—कामसम्बन्धि क्षोभजनकं स्त्रीपुंसयोरितरेतरप्रयोगः चित्ताकर्षक-मित्यर्थः । पूजाहोमविधानतः—उक्तेन पुष्पपञ्चकेन पूजादिविधानात् क्षोभकरं तदित्यर्थः । मन्त्रैस्तु पञ्चभिः—शैवबाणसम्बन्धिभिरित्यर्थः । सर्वत्र शैवैः पञ्चभिर्बाणमन्त्रैः जपपूजादि कुर्यादित्यर्थः॥५०॥तथाविधं स्थूलसूक्ष्मभेदेन पुण्ड्रेक्षु-काण्डजश्चापमित्यन्वयः । यथा पाशाङ्कुशयोः स्थूलं रूपंसौवर्णमयमिति सम्प्रदायः । सूक्ष्मपररूपे प्राग्वत् । प्रोक्तक्रमात्-प्रागुक्तक्रमतः प्रागभिहितक्रमात् चत्वारि

(घ) वायव्यादीशां मभितो इति मू० पु० पा० ।

(ङ) सहकारमिति मू० पु० पाठः ।

जपमन्त्रप्रयोगादौ सिद्धमन्त्रैश्च* पञ्चभिः।
तथाविधं स्यात्तच्चापं स्थूलं पुण्ड्रेक्षुकाण्डजम् ॥ ५१ ॥
मध्ययोन्यग्रकोणादिसंख्याः (१) प्रोक्तक्रमात् यजेत्।
कामेश्वर्य्यादिकाः शक्तीः (२)तथा मध्ये शिवां यजेत् ॥५२॥
प्रदर्श्य मुद्रानवकं चत्वारि च ततः क्रमात्।
उपचारान् विधायाथ (३) प्रोक्तयोगसमन्वितम् (४) ॥५३॥
जपित्वा दशवारञ्च स्वात्मानं देवतातनुम्।
स्मरेत्स्वात्मनि(५) ताः पञ्चदश नित्याः समर्चयेत् ॥ ५४ ॥
ततो भूतात्मभिः पञ्चमन्त्रैरभ्यर्च्य भक्तितः।
आत्माष्टाक्षरमन्त्रेण पूजयित्वा ततो जपेत् ॥ ५५ ॥
सहस्रं पुरतो देव्याः शतं तद्दिनजं तु वा।
सन्ध्यात्रयं षष्ठिसङ्ख्यमुक्तं (६) वा प्रोक्तरूपतः ॥ ५६ ॥

इति मुद्राचतुष्टयम्। (७)क्रमात्—उक्तक्रमात्। उपचारान्—प्रागुक्तान्। क्रमात्—विद्यातातीर्यखण्डदिननित्याविद्याभ्यां षोड़शोपचारान् विदध्यादित्यर्थः। प्रोक्तयोगसमन्वितं—पूर्वपटलावसाने प्रोक्तम् ॥५२॥५३॥ पञ्चदशेतिकथनं स्वात्मनः षोड़शीललिताविद्याऽऽत्मकत्वसिद्धेरित्यर्थः ॥५४॥ भूतात्मभिः—तृतीयपटलोपदिष्टैः। आत्माष्टाक्षरमन्त्रेण—सोऽपि तृतीयपटलोपदिष्टरूपः। भूतात्ममन्त्राणां बीजद्वयाद्यता भवति, आत्ममन्त्रस्य सप्ताक्षरीयोजनं च न भवेत् सम्प्रदायात् ॥ ५५ ॥

सहस्रमित्यादिना श्लोकेन जपस्य मुख्यगौणपक्षावुपदिशति। तत्र शतमित्युक्तिः प्रायश्चित्तरूपत्वात्पक्षद्वयगामिनी। उक्तं वा प्रोक्तरूपत इत्युक्तिः पञ्च-

---

* सिद्धिर्मन्त्रैस्तु इति सो० पु० पा०।

(१) संस्थाः इति मू० पु० पाठः।
(२) कामेश्वर्यादिकाशक्तिस्तथाइति मू० पु० पाठः।
(३) विदयाथ इति मू० पु० पाठः।
(४) प्रोक्तएव समन्वितं इति सो० पु० पा०।
(५) स्मरन्स्वात्मनि इति मू० पु० पा०।
(६) षष्ठिसङ्ख्यासुक्तां इति मू० पु० पाठः।
(७) हेतिमुद्राचतुष्टयं इति सो० व० पुस्तके पाठः।

ततः पुष्पाञ्जलिं कृत्वा मूलेनाभ्यर्च्य होमयेत् ।
कुण्डे स्थण्डिलमध्ये वा सम्प्रोक्ष्यार्घ्याम्बुना कुशैः ॥ ५७ ॥
रेखास्तिस्रः प्रागग्रा उत्तराग्राश्च संलिखेत् ।
मध्ये तथाऽग्निमाधाय क्रव्यादांशं परित्यजेत् ॥ ५८ ॥
परिषिंच्य परिस्तीर्य वह्निवीर्ये(१) विभावयेत् ।
प्रत्येकं सप्तजिह्वासु कुर्यान्नव घृताहुतीः ॥ ५९ ॥
ततः पूजाक्रमेणैव हुत्वा षोड़श मूलतः ।
ततस्तां विन्दुगे(२) धाम्नि विलीनां परिभावयेत् ॥ ६० ॥
बलिं दद्यात्ततस्त्वग्रे कुरुकुल्लामनुत्रयात् ।
अन्नव्यञ्जनपुष्पाम्बुदानेनोक्तस्वरूपतः(३) ॥ ६१ ॥

विंशत्पटलोक्तार्थस्य सदा हृदये वर्तमानत्वात् । वा शब्दोऽवधारणार्थः । एतदुक्तं भवति प्रोक्तक्रियया तद्दिनजभूतां सन्ध्यात्रयसङ्ख्यां (४) षष्टिघटिकासङ्ख्यां च एवं सम्भूयोक्तामिव सङ्ख्यां जपेदिति ॥५६॥ ततः—जपानन्तरम् । मूलेन—मूलविद्यया । अभ्यर्च्य—वह्नौ सन्निधेयमिति । कुण्डे—एकोनत्रिंशत्पटलोक्तस्वरूपे । स्थण्डिलमध्ये वा—स्थण्डिलमिति—हस्तायामविस्तारं एकाङ्गुलोत्सेधं वालुकाकल्पितं चतुरस्ररूपं धिष्ण्यविशेषमभिधत्ते ॥५७॥ मध्ये—कुशैर्विलिखितेषु नवसु कोष्ठेषु मध्यकोष्ठे इत्यर्थः । सर्वत्रात्र मन्त्रानुक्तौ विद्यात्टतीयखण्डतद्दिननित्याविद्ये मन्त्रौ ज्ञेयाविति शेषः । क्रव्यादांशं परित्यजेत्—क्रव्यादेभ्यो नम इति अङ्गारशकलं दक्षिणस्यां दिश्यपास्येत्यर्थः ॥ ५८॥ परिषिंच्य—परिषेचनं प्रादक्षिण्यक्रमतः कुशैर्दर्भैर्वा इति शेषः । सप्तजिह्वासु—एकोनत्रिंशत्पटलवक्ष्यमाणहिरण्याख्यादिषु । तत्तज्जिह्वास्मरणपूर्वं विद्यात्टतीयखण्डदिननित्याभ्यां आहुतीः कुर्यादिति सम्प्रदायः । अन्यत्र सर्वत्र तत्तज्जिह्वानामभिः ॥५९॥ मूलतः—मूलेन । होमान्ते हुतसङ्ख्यां सर्वत्र जपेदिति सम्प्रदायः । विन्दुगे धाम्नि—भ्रुवोर्मध्ये इत्यर्थः ॥६०॥ अग्रे—देवतायाः । मनुत्रयात्—त्रिभिर्मन्त्रैः कुरुकुल्लाया बलिं दद्यात् इति । उक्तस्वरूपतः—गुरूक्तस्वरूपया

---

(१) वह्निदेवी इति मू० पु० पा० ।
(२) ततस्तद्बिन्दुगे इति मू० पु० पा० ।
(३) क्तास्वरूपत इति सो० वं० पु० पा० ।
(४) ध्यानत्रयसङ्ख्यामिति सो० पुस्तके पाठः ।

अभ्यर्च्य देवीं चक्रस्थां तथा(१) तद्रूपवान् स्वयम् ।
स्वमुद्रया शक्तिचक्रं खेचर्यात्मनि योजयेत् ॥ ६२ ॥
ततोन्यासत्रयं कृत्वा प्राणायामपुरस्सरम् ।
जपित्वा स्तोत्रयुगलं देव्यात्मा विचरेत् सुखी ॥ ६३ ॥
पूजाविशेषान् देवेशि ! शृणु नित्यं क्रमोदितान् ।
अशक्तानां तु विस्तारे तथाऽऽपत्सु च शस्यते ॥ ६४ ॥
अन्यथाऽनर्थकारी स्यात् सङ्कोचार्चनमीश्वरी (?) ।
हेतिभिर्मध्यमाद्यं स्यात् द्वितीयं नवयोनिषु ॥ ६५ ॥
चतुर्दशारान्मध्यान्ताच्चतुर्थं(२) प्रोक्तरूपतः ।
पञ्चमं सर्वदुःखार्तिनाशनं वाञ्छितप्रदम् ॥ ६६ ॥

मुद्रया। सा च करतलयोस्त्रिभिरास्फालनपूर्वं प्रसारिततर्जनीद्वयाभ्यां उभयकरमुष्टिभ्यां ऊर्ध्वाधःस्थितिरूपाभ्यां देवताया निवेदितबलिद्रव्यदर्शनपररूपेत्युक्ता ॥ ६१॥ तया तद्रूपवान्—देवताविस्तीर्णलब्धप्रसादसारूप्यवान्। स्वमुद्रया—मूलाधारहृदयब्रह्मरन्ध्रेषु भावितविद्याखण्डत्रयरूपया—प्रागुदीरितया महात्रिपुरमुद्रया। शक्तिचक्रम्—शक्तिवृन्दम्। खेचर्या—प्रागुपदिष्टविरचनात्मिकया मुद्रया। स्वतन्त्रस्मरणम्। आत्मनि योजनाप्रकारोगुरुमुखादवगन्तव्यः ॥६२॥ स्तोत्रयुगलम्—नाथदेवयोः। देव्यात्मा—न्यासत्रयादितः सुखीकृताखिलकर्तव्यत्वात् ॥६३॥

पूजेत्यादिभिः सिद्धिदा इत्यन्तैश्चतुर्भिः श्लोकैः सङ्कोचविकासरूपतः पञ्चविधां सपर्याप्रक्रियामुपदिशति। तत्र अशक्तादीनां—राजवनितादीनाम्। आपत्सु—अग्निपातज्वरादिषु ॥६४॥ अन्यथाऽनर्थकारी—विस्तृतसपर्यासमर्थस्य स्वैरतः सङ्कोचार्चनम्। अनर्थकारी इति—स्वातन्त्र्यात् अनर्थकारीत्यर्थः। हेतिभिर्मध्यमाद्यं स्यात्—हेतिचतुष्टयार्चनसहितं मध्यदेवताचतुष्टयस्यार्चनं, सङ्कुचितेच्छाद्यम्। द्वितीयं नवयोनिषु—नवयोन्यादिमध्यमान्तं अर्चनं द्वितीयमित्यर्थः ॥ ६५॥ चतुर्दशारावधरान्या—चतुर्दशारादिमधरांता सपर्या तृतीयेत्यर्थः। चतुर्थं

---

(१) तया इति सो० पु२ पा०

(२) चतुर्दशारवध्यन्या च इति सो० पुस्तके पाठः।

तत्प्रकारन्तु देवेशि ! कुरुकुल्लार्चने शृणु ।
इति पञ्चप्रकाराऽर्चा प्रोक्ता सर्वार्थसिद्धिदा ॥ ६७ ॥
विद्यायाः साधनं सिद्धिं तद्व्रतं वर्ज्यमेव च ।
तदाभिमुख्यचिह्नानि विघ्नानि प्राक्तनाद्यतः ॥ ६८ ॥
शृणु क्रमेण देवेशि ! सर्वदा प्रीतिकारकम् ।
येन मर्त्योऽपि सिद्धः स्यात् जीवन्मुक्तो भवन्मयः ॥ ६९ ॥
स्नातः सुगन्धसलिलैः प्राक्पूजाप्रोक्तरूपवान् ।
गुरुं वित्तेन सन्तोष्य रत्नागारे क्रमं भजेत् ॥ ७० ॥
सन्ध्याचर्येऽपि जपवान् सहस्रं मौनसंयुतः ।
मोचागुडसितोपेतं पयःपायसमर्पयेत् ॥ ७१ ॥

प्रोक्तरूपताः,—चतुरस्रादिमध्यमान्तमर्चनं चतुर्थमित्यर्थः । पञ्चमं—अर्चनमिति शेषः ॥ ६६॥तत्प्रकारमिति । पञ्चमसपर्याप्रक्रिया द्वाविंशे कुरुकुल्लापटले वक्ष्यते । तत्रैव तां शृणु इत्यर्थः ॥ ६७ ॥

विद्याया इत्यादिना भवन्मय इत्यन्तेन श्लोकद्वयेन षडर्थप्रस्तावनां (१) सिद्धिफलं चोपदिशति । तत्र विद्यायाः साधनं—पुरश्चरणम् । सिद्धिं—पुरश्चरणसिद्धिम् । तद्व्रतं—विद्यापुरश्चरणव्रतम् । वर्ज्यं—विद्यासाधनसमये सर्वकाले च । तदाभिमुख्यचिह्नानि—विद्याभिमुख्यचिह्नानि विघ्नानि—आभिमुख्यविघ्नानि । प्राक्तनाद्यतः—दुर्वासनातिसङ्गात् ॥६८॥ येषु प्रीतिकारकं येषां एषां फलरूपं स्वात्मानुसन्धानं भवति तानि शृण्विति । येन—फलरूपेण भवन्मयः देवीविग्रहः ॥६९॥

स्नातइत्यादिभिः क्रममित्यन्तैरधार्धैः सप्तभिः श्लोकैः विद्यायाः साधनप्रकारं तत्पुरश्चरणसिद्धिं चोपदिशति । तत्र प्राक्पूजाप्रोक्तरूपवान्—नित्यापूजा—प्रोक्तविग्रहः । सन्तोष्य—वित्तादिभिः । सन्तुष्टेन गुरुणा अनुशिष्ट एव कुर्यात् । क्रमं—नित्यक्रमम् ॥७०॥ सहस्रं—प्रतिसन्ध्यं सहस्रमित्यर्थः । मोचा—कदलीफलम् । सिताः—शर्कराः । अर्पयेत्—निवेदयेत् प्रतिसन्ध्यमिति शेषः ॥७१ ॥

---

(१) षडर्थप्रस्तावान् इति वं० पुस्तके पाठः ।

नीराजनं च कर्पूरैः कुर्यात्सन्ध्यासु तास्वपि।
होमं दशांशतः कुर्यात्तर्पणं (१)चेन्दुमज्जलैः ॥ ७२ ॥
स्वनित्यादूर्ध्वताजाप्यं द्विसहस्रं(२) दिनं प्रति।
कुर्यात्तेन भवेत् पूर्णं लक्षं(३) पूर्णान्तमीश्वरि ! ॥ ७३ ॥
एवं लक्षत्रयं प्रोक्तं प्रथमे तु कृते युगे।
त्रेतायां द्विगुणं तद्वत् द्वापरे त्रिगुणं स्मृतम् ॥ ७४ ॥
कलौ चतुर्गुणं प्रोक्तमक्षराणां च संख्यया।
तार्तीयसप्तसङ्ख्या सा तेन स्यादेकविंशतिः ॥ ७५ ॥

दशांशं जपसङ्ख्यायाः। इन्दुमज्जलैः—कर्पूरवासितजलैः। तर्पणं च। चकारेण दशांशतः इत्याकृष्यते ॥७२॥ स्वनित्यादूर्ध्वतः—स्वनित्योक्तसन्ध्यात्रयषष्टिघटिकाजपसङ्ख्यापुरश्चरणजपसङ्ख्यायाः पृथग्भूता इत्यर्थः। लक्षं पूर्णान्तमित्युक्त्या प्रतिदिनं चतुस्त्रिंशदधिकं त्रिशतं त्रिसहस्रादूर्ध्वं जपेदित्यर्थः। एतदुक्तं भवति—पुरश्चरणं चिकीर्षुः गुरुं स्वशक्त्यानुरूपं वित्तैराराध्य तदनुज्ञातो लोहितमित्यादिकपूजामण्डपवर्त्ती अयोग्यप्रलापरहितः नियताहारः स्त्रीसङ्गवर्जी अव्याकुलचेताः सुगन्धिसलिलैः स्नातः परार्द्ध्यकर्णाम्बरलेपनस्रगाभरणः सन्ध्यासु तिसृषु स्वनित्यक्रमानन्तरं प्रोक्तरूपां क्रमपूजां कृत्वा प्रतिसन्ध्यं द्वादशाधिकशतं सहस्रवारं जपं तद्दशांशसङ्ख्यं च तर्पणं तावत्त्रिमध्वक्तैः पलाशपुष्पैः कुसुम्भकुसुमैः कह्लारैर्वा दशांशक्रमहोमं च कृत्वा तत्सङ्ख्ययाऽरुणैः कुसुमैः सौरभाद्यैर्वा समर्चनं जपं च तत्पूर्णादि, पूर्णान्तं लक्षसङ्ख्यां पूरयन्नुक्तलक्षसङ्ख्यां जपेत् सर्वत्रेति ॥७३॥एवं लक्षत्रयमिति। एतदुक्तं भवति—सर्वेषु पिण्डकर्त्तरीबीजमन्त्रेषु अपुनरुक्ताक्षराणि प्रत्येकमक्षरत्रिलक्षं कृतयुगे जपेत्। त्रेताद्वापरकलियुगेषु त्रिषु पादार्द्धत्रिपादक्षयाज्जपसंख्या प्रागुक्ता द्विगुणा त्रिगुणा चतुर्गुणा चेति। एकादिनवाक्षरान्तानां मन्त्राणां पिण्डकर्तरीबीजसंज्ञकानामपुनरुक्ताक्षरलक्षेण प्रोक्तयुगक्रमाभिवृद्ध्या जपः। दशाक्षरादिविंशाक्षरान्तानां मन्त्राणां प्राग्वत् युगानुरूपमक्षरलक्षं जपः। एकविंशादिशताक्षरान्तादीनां मन्त्राणां

---

(१) सेन्दुसज्जलैरिति मू० पुस्तके पाठः। (२) त्रिसहस्रं इति मू० पु० पाठः।
(३) लक्ष्यं इति सो० पुस्तके पाठः।

तेनान्येषु युगेषु स्यात् संख्या वृद्धिरुदीरिता ।
वनिताक्षोभतोभोगान्न विघ्नं जायते यदि ॥ ७६ ॥
तासु संख्यासु पूर्णासु सम्प्रार्थ्य स्वाश्रयेत्क्रमम्(१) ।
वर्ज्यानि शृणु देवेशि ! तद्दिनेषु (२)सदापि च ॥ ७७ ॥
नास्तिकैः सह संलापा मैथुनं परनिन्दितम्(३) ।
निद्राशोकौ(४) तथाऽऽलापं देशान्तरपरिभ्रमम् ॥ ७८ ॥
तद्वासरेषु वर्ज्यानि प्रोक्तान्यन्यानि शाङ्करि !
शृणु सर्वत्र सर्वेषां सर्वदा नाशकानि च(५) ॥७९॥
परक्षेत्रगृहस्त्रीस्ववाञ्छातन्निन्दनानि च ।
स्त्रीषु रोषं प्रहारं च दुष्टास्वपि न योजयेत् ॥८०॥

केवलं लक्षमात्रं जपः, । तदूर्ध्वं सङ्ख्याविशिष्टाक्षराणां मन्त्राणां दशसहस्रो जपः । इत्येवं मन्त्रतन्त्रप्रकाशिकोक्तः । एतत्सर्वस्मिंस्तन्त्रे पुरश्चरणजपसङ्ख्याविशेषानुक्तावेवाङ्गीकरणीयम् ॥७४॥ तार्तीयसप्तसङ्ख्या सा—विद्यायास्तार्तीयखण्डे सप्ताक्षराणामपुनरावृत्तित्वात् । एकविंशतिः लक्षमिति शेषः । प्रथमे कृतयुगे सम्भूय जपसङ्ख्या एकविंशतिलक्षमित्यर्थः ॥७५॥ तेन—क्रमेण । अन्येषु युगेषु—त्रेतादिषु । वनिताक्षोभतो भोगात्—युवतिजनानुज्ञातो भोगतः । प्रोक्तपुरश्चरणजपसाङ्ख्यायाः युवतिजनभोगविघ्नरहितम् ॥७६॥ सम्पूर्तिः—सिद्धिः । स्वक्रमं—नित्यानुष्ठानप्रोक्तम् ॥

वर्ज्यानीत्यादिनाश्लोकोत्तरार्द्धेन विद्याजनपराणि भवर्ज्यानि प्रस्तौति । तत्र तद्दिने—पुरश्चरणदिनेषुसर्वदा—सर्वस्मिन् काले च ॥७७॥

नास्तिकैरित्यादिभिर्योजयेदित्यन्तैस्त्रिभिः श्लोकैः पुरश्चरणकाले सर्वकाले च वर्जनीयान्युपदिशति ॥७८॥ तत्र तद्वासरेषु पुरश्चरणादिदिनेषु—अन्यानि । सर्वकालवर्ज्यानि॥७९॥तन्निन्दनानि—परनिन्दनानि। दुष्टास्वपि—अविधेयास्वपि॥८०॥

---

(१) स्वभजेत्क्रमं इति मू० पु० पाठः ।
(२) तद्दिने सर्वदापिचेति मू० पुस्तके पाठः ।
(३) परिनिन्दित मिति सी० पु० पा० ।
(४) चिन्ताशोकं इति मू० पु० पा० ।
(५) सर्वनाशकराणि च इति मू० पुस्तके पाठः ।

सिद्धचिह्नानि चोक्तानि वासना कथने(१) मया ।
आनुकूल्यस्य चिह्नानि शृणु साधयतस्तदा(२) ॥८१॥
स्वप्ने पोतेषु वनितावृन्दैः संमेलनं निशि ।
गजाद्रिसौधशृङ्गेषु विहारो राजदर्शनम् ॥८२॥
गजानामङ्गनानां च दर्शनं नृत्यगीतयोः ।
उत्सवं ससुरामांसदर्शनं स्पर्शनं तथा ॥८३॥
निन्द्यानि शृणु देवेशि ! विघ्नानर्थकराणि च ।
कृष्णवर्णैर्भटैः स्वप्ने प्रहारस्तैललेपनम् ॥८४॥
मैथुनं परनारीभिरिन्द्रियच्यवनं तथा ।
राष्ट्रक्षोभो वह्निवायुजलभीबन्धुनाशनम् ॥८५॥
गुरावुपेक्षाऽसम्पत्तिर्वस्तूनां व्याधिबाधनम् ।
अन्यमन्त्रार्चनश्रद्धा(४) विघ्नो नित्यार्चनेऽनिशम् ॥८६॥
नराणां यच्च दुष्पुण्यैः(४) कृतैर्बहुषु जन्मसु ।
श्रद्धास्थैर्यं सम्प्रदायसिद्धिर्नित्यार्चनं(५) भवेत् ॥८७॥

सिद्धेत्यादिभिस्तथा इत्यन्तैस्त्रिभिः श्लोकैः साधकस्य देवतामुख्यचिह्नान्युपदिशति। तत्र वासना कथने पञ्चत्रिंशे पटले । साधयतः—साधनपरस्य । तदा—प्रागुक्ते सर्वकाले॥८१॥ नृत्यगीतयोर्दर्शनमित्यन्वयः। स्पर्शनं तथा तयोरिति शेषः ॥८२॥८३॥

निन्द्यानीत्यादिभिः अनिशमित्यन्तैस्त्रिभिः श्लोकैः प्राक्तनपापबाहुल्याद्देवताभिमुख्यप्रत्यूहचिह्नान्युपदिशति। तत्र विघ्नानर्थकराणि च—विघ्नकराणि अनर्थकराणि वस्तूनामसम्पत्तिरित्यन्वयः। एतदुक्तं भवति अत्र कृष्णवर्णभटतैलाभ्यङ्गेन्द्रियच्यवनदर्शनगुरूपेक्षामन्त्रान्तरभजनश्रद्धा चेत्येतानि पञ्चानर्थकराणि। इतराणि विघ्नकराणीति ॥८४॥८५॥८६॥

नराणामित्यादिना श्लोकेन सङ्क्तिस्थैर्यसम्प्रदायनित्यार्चनप्राप्तिकारणमुप-

---

(१) कथ्यते इति मू० पुस्तके पाठः। (२) तः सदा इति मू० पुस्तके पाठः
(३) र्चनं श्रद्धाविघ्नो इति मू० पुस्तके पाठः। (४) नराणां बहुभिः पुण्यैरिति मू० पुस्तके पाठः।
(५) शुद्धनित्यर्चनं इति पुस्तके पाठः।

कूर्म्मस्थितिमविज्ञाय योजपादिविधिस्थित: ।
स नाप्नोति फलान्युक्तान्यन्यथा नाशमेति च ॥८८॥
तस्मात् कूर्म्मविभागं तु विज्ञायाऽखिलमाचरेत् ।
स चतुर्द्धा ततोलोक्ये तत्प्रकारान् शृणु प्रिये ! ॥ ८९ ॥
प्रथमस्तु पर: कूर्म्मस्ततो देशगतस्तथा ।
ग्रामगोगृहगश्चेति चतुर्धा तद्व्यवस्थिति: ॥ ९० ॥
देशं ग्रामं गृहं वास्तु नवधा विभजेत्तत: ।
प्रागादि पश्चिमान्तं तु कादिमान्तानि विन्यसेत् ॥ ९१ ॥
अक्षराणि समान्येव चत्वारि परयोर्न्यसेत् ।
ईशे द्वयमथोमध्ये स्वरात्प्रागादि विन्यसेत् ॥ ९२ ॥

दिशति। बहुषु जन्मसु-चिरकालम्। सम्प्रदायसिद्धिरित्यत्र सम्प्रदायशब्दस्य अर्थ निर्वाहे अभियुक्तोक्ति: ।

"समा सम्यक्त्वमुदितं प्रेणोत्कर्षश्च दायत: ।
वस्तु, तेनोत्तमा विद्या साऽस्तुन: सम्प्रदायत" इति ॥

एतदुक्तं भवति सद्गुरो: सम्प्रदाय-लब्धा मनीषितार्थ प्राप्तिकरीविद्या सत्-सम्प्रदायवतीति ॥८७॥

कूर्मेत्यादिभि: सदा इत्यन्तैरेकादशभि: श्लोकै: सर्वतन्त्रसाधारणं कूर्मस्थिति—विभागं तज्ज्ञानफलं तदनङ्गीकरणे प्रत्यवायं चोपदिशति। उक्तानि-देवता-भजनादीनि प्रोक्तानि। अन्यथा—न केवलं प्रोक्तफलानाप्ति: अखिलं गृह-मण्डलग्रामनगरपत्तनखेटखर्वटादिकरणम् ॥८८॥ स—कूर्म: । तत्प्रकारं—कूर्म-स्थितिप्रकारम् ॥८९॥ पर: कूर्म: पञ्चाशत्कोटियोजनविस्तीर्णाया: पृथिव्या धारक:स्थिर: कूर्म: । तत: द्वितीय इति—उक्तप्रकारेण। तद्व्यवस्थिति:—कूर्मव्यवस्थिति: ॥९०॥ नवधा विभजेदिति, एतदुक्तं भवति। प्राक्प्रत्यग्द-क्षिणोदक् च समान्तरालेन रेखाचतुष्टयेन नवकोष्ठानि भवन्ति। तेषु प्राक्दिक्पङ्क्तिकोष्ठमारभ्य पश्चिमदिक्पङ्क्तिमध्ये कोष्ठान्तेषु पञ्चसु कोष्ठेषु प्रतिकोष्ठं प्रादक्षिण्येन पञ्च पञ्चक्रमेण कादि मान्तान्यक्षराणि वर्गश: समा लिख्य तदनु यादि हकारान्तान्यक्षराणि चत्वारि चत्वारि वायूत्तरदिग्गतयो: (१)

---

(१) दिगायतोरिति वं० पुस्तके पाठ: दिगयमयोरिति सो० पुस्तके पाठ: ।

ईशान्ते (१) द्विद्विशः पश्चान्नामाद्यर्णं(२) यतो भवेत् ।
तन्मुखं पार्श्वयोः पाणी कुक्षी पादौ ततस्ततः ॥९३॥
पुच्छमेकमथो (३) मध्ये पृष्ठमेवं षडङ्गवत् ।
मुखे सर्वार्थसिद्धिः स्यात्करयोर(४)ल्पसिद्धिकृत् ॥९४॥
कुक्षौरुनित्यनैष्फल्यं पादयोः सर्वदुःखकृत् ।
पुच्छे मृत्युस्तु नियतं पृष्ठे सर्वार्थदायकम् ॥९५॥
तस्मात्तत् साधु विज्ञाय कुर्यात् सर्वं समीरितम् ।
व्यञ्जनं देशकूर्मे* स्यात् गृहकूर्मे स्वरास्तथा ॥९६॥
ग्रामादिकूर्मे द्वितयं परकूर्मे न तत्त्रयम् (५) ।
नित्यं पूर्वमुखो यस्मात्तेन तत्सिद्धिरीरिता ॥९७॥

कोष्ठयोर्विलिख्य अवशिष्टं लक्ष इत्यक्षरद्वयं ईशकोष्ठे समालिखेदिति । सर्वमध्यकोष्ठे प्रागादिषु ईशान्तास्वष्टसु दिक्षु प्रत्येकं अकारादिविसर्जनीयान्तान् षोडश स्वरान् प्रादक्षिण्येन द्वयं द्वयं समालिखेत् । एवं कृते प्रागुक्तानां गृहादीनां नामाद्यक्षरं प्रोक्ते चक्रे यस्मिन् कोष्ठे दृश्यते तत्कोष्ठं तस्य कूर्मस्य मुखं ज्ञेयम्, तत्कोष्ठपार्श्वयोः स्थितं कोष्ठद्वयं तस्य कूर्मस्य करयुगं. तदनन्तरं कोष्ठद्वयं तस्य जठरम् ॥९३॥ तदनन्तरमेकं कोष्ठं तस्य पुच्छं, सर्वमध्यं स्वराक्षरोपेतं तन्नवमकोष्ठं तस्य पृष्ठं, एवं मुखकरजठरपादपुच्छपृष्ठाख्यषडङ्गवत्तस्य कूर्मस्य स्वरूपं, सर्वत्र नामाक्षरकोष्ठमारभ्य तस्य कूर्मस्य मुखादिकल्पनमिति ॥ ९४ ॥ सर्वार्थदायकं—भजनमिति शेषः ॥९५॥ सर्वं समीरितं(६) भजनप्रयोगादिति शेषः । व्यञ्जनं—नामाक्षरगतम् । स्वराः—नामाद्यक्षरगताः ॥९६॥ द्वयं—स्वराक्षरं(७) व्यञ्जनाक्षरं च । एतदुक्तं भवति । प्रोक्ते चक्रे देशकूर्मस्य नामाद्यक्षरे व्यञ्जनाक्षरं यत्र कोष्ठे दृश्यते तत्तस्य मुखं गृहकूर्मस्वनामाद्यक्षरे स्वराक्षरं यस्य कोष्ठे दृश्यते तत्तस्य

---

(१) ईशान्तामुदिशः पश्चादिति मू० पु० पा० ।
(२) दार्ण्यं यतो इति सो० पु० पा० ।
(३) मधोमध्यं इति मू० पु० पाठः ।
(४) करयोश्चाल्प इति मू० पु० पाठः ।
(५) न तद्द्वयमिति सो० पु० पा० ।
(६) समीहितं इति टी० पु० पा० ।
(७) नामाक्षरमितिटी० पु० पा० ।
* दशकूर्मे इति सो० पु० पा० ।

एवं कूर्मविभागोऽयमीरितस्ते चतुर्विधः ।
मन्त्राणां तेन सिद्धिः स्यात्सर्वेषां सर्वतस्तदा ॥९८॥
सम्वर्ध्यायामविस्तारं (१) हृत्वाऽष्टाभिस्तु शेषतः ।
विस्राय वर्गं तेष्वेकमाद्यं (२) नाम्नि प्रकल्पयेत् ॥९९॥
वास्तुष्वज्ञातरूपेषु(३) प्रसिद्धं नामतो भवेत् ।
तत्तत्स्थानेषु नियतमनर्थं शून्यता तथा(४) ॥१००॥
व्योमतत्त्वमयी व्याप्तिरिति सम्यक् समीरिता ।
अस्या निष्कालनाच्चित्ते तत्तत्त्वं स्वात्मसात्कृतम् ॥१०१॥

मुखम्. ग्रामादीनां कूर्मस्य नामाद्यक्षरे स्वरव्यञ्जनाक्षरे यत्र कोष्ठे दृश्येते तत्तस्य मुखं तद्द्वयानुगुणे अङ्गे उक्तानि कुर्यात् । तद्द्वयस्यान्योन्याननुगुणेष्वङ्गेषु यथेष्टमन्यतरानुगुणे अङ्गे कुर्यात् । देशकूर्मस्य नामाद्यक्षरे केवलं स्वराक्षरे सति तत्कोष्ठदिग्गतबाह्यकोष्ठं मुखं तस्य कल्पयेत् । पूर्वाभिमुखः—परकूर्मं इति शेषः । तेन—नियतस्थितित्वात्—तत्सिद्धिरीरिता—तदवयवावस्थानाधीना ॥ ९७ ॥ येन—कूर्मविभागज्ञानेन ॥ ९८ ॥

सम्वर्धेत्यादिना तथेत्यन्तेन श्लोकद्वयेन ग्रहादीनां प्रोक्तवास्तुविशेषाणामज्ञातसंज्ञानां नामकल्पनप्रकारमुपदिशति । तत्र आयामेन—दैर्घ्यमानेन । अष्टाभिः—अष्टसङ्ख्याभिः । शेषतः—आवाहनशेषतः । वर्ग—अष्टस्वेकम् । तेषु—वर्गाक्षरेषु एकं अक्षरं—आद्यमक्षरम् ॥९९॥ अज्ञातरूपेषु—अज्ञातनामसु । एतदुक्तं भवति—अज्ञातनामकस्य स्वमनीषितस्य वास्तोः आयामेन विस्तारं संवर्ध्य तां सङ्ख्यां अष्टसङ्ख्यया आहृत्य अवशिष्टसङ्ख्यायाः स्वरेषु—अकचटतपयशरूपवर्गेषु अन्यतमं ज्ञात्वा तद्वर्गजेष्वक्षरेषु अन्यतमाद्यक्षराद्यन्तस्य नाम कल्पयेदिति । प्रसिद्धं नामतः ५) ज्ञातनामसु वास्तुष्विति शेषः । तेन कूर्मावयवान् कल्पयेत् तत्स्थानेषु—पादपुच्छकुक्षिस्थानेषु । शून्यता निष्फलता ॥१००॥

---

(१) संवध्यायोगविस्तारं इति मू० पु० पा० । (२) तेष्वेके नामाद्यं नाम्नि कल्पयेत् इति सो० पु० पाठः (३) अज्ञानरूपेष इति मू० पु० पा० । (४) मता इति मू० पु० पा० ।
(५) प्रसिद्धान् नामत इति टी पु० पा० ।

इति श्रीषोड़शनित्यातन्त्रेषु श्रीकादिमते(१) पञ्चमं पटलं परिपूर्णं परामृष्टम् ।

इति श्रीषोड़शनित्यातन्त्रेषु श्रीकादिमताख्यस्य परिपूर्णस्य तन्त्रस्य प्रपञ्चसारसिंहराजप्रकाशाभिधानेन सुभगानन्दनाथेन विरचितायां मनोरमाख्यायां व्याख्यायां ललितानित्यार्चनक्रमादिप्रकाशनपरं पञ्चमं पटलं परिपूर्णं परामृष्टम् ।

ग्रन्थसङ्ख्या—

पञ्चमे यन्त्रमेकं स्यात् ग्रन्थव्याख्यानगामिनः ।
शतद्वयं पञ्चषष्ट्या समेतमितिवोच्चितम् ॥

---

(१) नैमित्तिकार्चनं नाम इत्यधिकं मूलपुस्तके ।

(२) ग्रन्थसङ्ख्यानगामिनः इति सो० पु० पा० ।

अथ षष्ठं पटलम् ।

अथ षोडशनित्यानां नित्यार्चानिरतात्मनाम् ।
नैमित्तिकं च काम्यं च वक्ष्येऽहं शृणु सुन्दरि ! ॥१॥
नित्यं नैमित्तिकं काम्यं सापेक्षं पूर्वपूर्वतः ।
अन्यथा भजनं चेच्छन् (१) करोत्यापत्परम्पराम् ॥२॥
नित्यार्चनरतैः सिद्धैः कार्यं नैमित्तिकार्चनम् ।
तद्विधानमतो वक्ष्ये चैत्राद्यं फाल्गुनावधि ॥३॥
चैत्रे दमनकैः कुर्यात् समूलैर्वाऽथ गुच्छकैः ।
पूर्वपक्षचतुर्दश्यां निशि संस्थाप्य विद्यया ॥४॥

अथ षष्ठं पटलम् ।

पूर्व्वस्मिन् पटले ललिताया नित्यपूजाविधानमुपदिश्यानन्तरं तन्निष्ठानां सर्वनित्यासाधारणं नैमित्तिककाम्यपूजाक्रममुपदिशति—अथ षोडशनित्येत्यादिना तन्मयोभवेदित्यन्तेन श्लोकशतरूपेण षष्ठेन पटलेन । तत्र अथ षोडशेत्यादिभिः तेष्वपोत्यन्तैर्द्वात्रिंशत्श्लोकैर्नैमित्तिकार्चनक्रममुपदिशति । तत्र अथ षोडशेत्यादिना आपत्परम्परामित्यन्तेन श्लोकद्वयेन पटलार्थोद्देशान्नैमित्तिककाम्ययोरप्राप्तक्रमानुष्ठाने प्रत्यवायं चोपदिशति । तत्र नैमित्तिकं काम्यं च—अर्चनमिति शेषः ॥ १ ॥ सापेक्षं पूर्वपूर्वतः—पूर्वपूर्वतः सापेक्षम्—एतदुक्तं भवति-नित्यार्चानिरतानामेव नैमित्तिकार्चासु योग्यता, उभयार्चानिरतानां काम्यार्चायोग्यतेति । अन्यथा भजनं—उक्तक्रमविपर्यासभजनम्, एतत्सर्वसाधारणम् ॥२॥

नित्यार्चन इत्यादिना श्लोकेन सर्वासां नैमित्तिकार्चाविधानेन गुणविधानं तत्प्रकारं च प्रस्तौति ॥ ३ ॥

चैत्रे इत्यादिना पूजनमित्यन्तेनार्द्धाधिकेन श्लोकेन दमनकार्चनक्रममुपदिशति, समूलैः—दमनकैरितिशेषः । गुच्छकैः—शाखाभिः तेषां एष गौणपक्षः । संस्थाप्य विद्यया, एतदुक्तं भवति—सर्वत्र नैमित्तिकार्चासु प्रोक्तानि पूजाद्रव्याणि पूर्वेद्युर्निशि पवित्रे पात्रे विद्याभ्युक्षिते निधाय तद्दिननित्याविद्यया च गन्धपुष्पधूपदीपनैवेद्य-

---

(१) भाजमं चेच्छन् इति भू० पु० पा०

परेद्युर्नित्यपूजान्ते कुर्यादेतैस्तु पूजनम् ।
अस्मिन्मासि च पूर्णायां वसन्तोत्सवपूजनम् ॥५॥
कुर्यात्तत्कालसम्भूतैः प्रसूनैश्चन्द्रचन्दनैः ।
सौगन्धिकैः सकाश्मीरैः पूजां पूर्ववदुज्ज्वलाम् ॥६॥
वैशाखे मासि पूर्णायां पूजयेद्धेमपुष्करैः (१) ।
अपि वा चन्द्रकस्तूरीचन्दनैः शिशिरोदकैः ॥७॥
जेष्ठे मासि च पूर्णायां कदलीपनसाम्रजैः ।
फलैस्तु पूजयेद्देवीं पूर्ववत् सर्वसिद्धये ॥८॥
आषाढ़े मासि पूर्णायां चन्दनैः कुङ्कुमान्वितैः ।
(२)एला कक्कोलजातीभिरुपेतैः पूजयेच्छिवाम् ॥९॥
श्रावणे मासि पूर्णायां पवित्रैः पूजयेच्छिवाम् ।
तद्विधानमिदं भद्रे ! शृणु सौभाग्यदायकम् ॥१०॥

नमस्कारैः पञ्चभिरुपचारैः समभ्यर्च्य क्वचित्सपर्यास्थाने निधाय ॥ ४ ॥ परेद्युः स्वनित्याक्रमार्चनान्ते तैः सविशेषं पूजनं यथाशक्ति वित्तैर्गुरुपूजनं च कुर्यादिति ॥५॥

अस्मिन्नित्यादिना उज्ज्वलमित्यन्तेनार्द्धाद्येन श्लोकेन वसन्तोत्सवपूजनमुपदिशति। अस्मिन् मासे—चैत्रमासे। चन्दनकर्पूरसौगन्धिकैः सकलह्लारैः सकाश्मीरैः कुङ्कुमोपेतैः पूर्ववत्—प्रागुक्ताधिवासपूर्वकम् ॥६॥

वैशाखेत्यादिना श्लोकेन वैशाखमासपूजामुपदिशति। तत्र हिमपुष्करैः हिमजलैरपि चेति पाठान्तरम्। अशक्तविषयः। चन्द्रकस्तूरीचन्दनैः—वासितैरिति शेषः। अत्राप्यधिवासपूर्वकं कर्तव्यम् ॥७॥

ज्येष्ठेत्यादिना श्लोकेन ज्येष्ठमासपूजामुपदिशति। तत्र तत्र पूर्ववत्—साधिवासम् ॥७॥

आषाढेत्यादिना श्लोकेनाषाढ़पूजामुपदिशति—अत्रापि साधिवासं पूजयेत् ॥८॥

श्रावणेत्यादिभिर्विनश्यतीत्यन्तैर्दशभिः श्लोकैः श्रावणे मासे पवित्रारोप-

---

(१) हिमपुष्करैः इति सो० पु० पा०। (२) एलाकंकोल इति मू० पु० पा०।

(३) पवित्रारोहणो इति सो० पु० पा०।

सौवर्णै राजतैर्वापि सूत्रैः पट्टसमुद्भवैः ।
कार्पाससम्भवै रक्तैर्नवधा गुणितैः शुभैः ॥११॥
कुर्यात्पवित्रं शक्तीनां सर्वासां षोडशाङ्गुलैः ।
नवाङ्गुलैर्वा तत्सङ्ख्यं (१) सरग्रन्थ्यादिसंयुतम् ॥१२॥
अथवा वृत्तिशक्तीनां तत्तत्सङ्ख्याङ्गुलादिकम् ।
कृत्वाऽधिवासपूर्वं तु पूजयेत्तैर्यथाक्रमम् ॥१३॥
होमे त्वेकसरग्रन्थि तन्मानं स्यात्पवित्रकम् ।
अष्टोत्तरशतैः सूत्रैः कुर्याच्छक्त्या* च तारकम् ॥१४॥
पूजा विष्टरमानेन वितानादवलम्बयेत् ।
वाराहीकुरुकुल्लादिशक्तीनां मूलशक्तिवत् ॥१५॥

णोत्सवार्चनक्रममुपदिशति। तत्र—पवित्रैर्वक्ष्यमाणैः तत्त्वात्मभिः। तद्विधानं—पवित्रविधानम् ॥१०॥ वा पक्षान्तरे। रक्तैः—कुङ्कुमचन्दनाद्यरुणितैः ॥११॥ नवाङ्गुलैः—सूत्रैरित्यन्वयः। वा पक्षान्तरे, तत्सङ्ख्यासरग्रन्थ्यादिसंयुतम् (२) षोडशाङ्गुलायामपक्षे षोडशसरं षोडशग्रन्थिकं च कुर्यात्। नवङ्गुलायामपक्षे नवसरं नवग्रन्थिकं च कुर्यात्। अत्रादिशब्दो रञ्जनविषयः प्रतिग्रन्थि रञ्जनं कुर्यात् इत्यर्थः ॥१२॥ अथवेति पक्षान्तरं परम्। तत्सङ्ख्याङ्गुलादिकम्—अत्रादिशब्दः सरग्रन्थ्यादिविषयः। एतदुक्तं भवति—यस्मिन्यस्मिन्नावरणे या या शक्तिसङ्ख्या तावत्सङ्ख्याङ्गुलायामसरग्रन्थिसंयुतं पवित्रं कुर्यादित्येकः पक्षः। इत्यस्मिन् पक्षे हेतीनामष्टाङ्गुलायाममष्टसरग्रन्थिकं, नवानां नाथानां नवाङ्गुलायामं नवसरग्रन्थिकं, कामेश्वर्यादीनां तिसृणां त्र्यङ्गुलायामं त्रिसरग्रन्थिकं, मध्यस्थायाः प्रधानायाः षोडशनित्यात्मकत्वात् षोडशसरग्रन्थिकं, अन्यासां पञ्चदशनित्यानां ललिताङ्गभूतानां पञ्चदशाङ्गुलायामं पञ्चदशसंरग्रन्थिकं पवित्रं कुर्यादिति। कृत्वेति अधस्तादन्वयः। अधिवासपूर्वं—प्राग्वत्। तैः—पवित्रैः ॥१३॥ तन्मानं—पक्षत्रये(३) यदङ्गीकृतं तन्मानायामं, तैरष्टोत्तरशतैः सरग्रन्थियुक्तैरिति शेषः ॥१४॥ वाराहीकुरुकुल्लादिशक्तीनां—आदिशब्देन पञ्चदशनित्या उच्यन्ते। मूलशक्तिवत् प्रधानदेव-

---

(१) तत्सङ्ख्यारसग्रन्थ्यादिसंयुताम् इति सो॰ पु॰ पा॰।
(२) तत्सङ्ख्यारसग्रन्थ्यादिसंयुतं इति सो॰ पु॰ पा॰
(३) पक्षद्वये इति टी॰ पु॰ पा॰।
* च्छक्त्यावतारकम् इति मु॰ पु॰ पा॰

स्वमानेनात्मनः कुर्यात् पवित्रं (१) प्रोक्तसङ्ख्यया ।
क्रमागममन्त्रशिष्याणामात्मवत्समुदीरितम् ॥१६॥
अन्येषां योगिशक्तीनामेकग्रन्थिसरं न च (२) ।
परिधानप्रमाणेन मण्डपस्यैकसूत्रतः ॥१७॥
सग्रन्थ्यङ्गुलैर्युक्तं षण्णवत्या तु सङ्ख्यया ।
कृत्वा पवित्रत्रितयं तानि देव्यै समर्पयेत् ॥१८॥
उक्त(३) मानत्रयेप्येकं ग्राह्यं भवति सर्वतः ।
न कुर्यान्मानसाङ्कर्यं यदि कुर्याद्विनश्यति ॥१९॥
अथ भाद्रपदे मासि पूर्णायां श्वेतकोद्भवैः ।
प्रसूनैरर्चयेद्देवीं पूर्वोक्तविधिना युतम् ॥ २० ॥
आश्वयुज्यां विशेषस्तु दर्शान्तप्रतिपत्तिथिम् ।
आरभ्य पूजयेद्देवीं गन्धपुष्पोपहारकैः ॥ २१ ॥
होमे शतादि तद्वृद्ध्या पूर्णायां षट्शताधिकम् ।
सहस्रं जुहुयान्नित्यं जपं चैव समाचरेत् ॥ २२ ॥

तायाः प्रोक्तपक्षत्रये यः पक्षोऽङ्गीकृतस्तद्वत्। अङ्गनित्यानां चतुर्दशसरादिकं, मध्यस्थायाः पञ्चदशसरादिकम् ॥१५॥ स्वमानेन—स्कन्धादिनाभ्यवधिना। क्रमः अक्षरक्रमः। आगमः—कादिमतादि ॥१६॥ परिधान प्रमाणेन - शक्तियोगिनीनां मानेन ॥१७॥ सग्रन्थ्यङ्गुलैरित्याद्युक्तः पक्षःपूर्वोक्तपक्षत्रयानुष्ठानाशक्तविषयः ॥१८॥ मानसाङ्कर्यं उक्तानां पक्षत्रयाणामन्योन्यमानसाङ्कर्यम् ॥१९॥

अथ भाद्रपदेत्यादिना श्लोकेन भाद्रपदमासपूजामुपदिशति, तत्र पूर्वोक्तविधिना युतं—अधिवासपूर्वम् ॥२०॥

आश्वयुज्यामित्यादिभिरर्चनमित्यन्तैश्चतुर्भिः श्लोकैराश्वयुजमासपूजाक्रममुपदिशति। तत्र दर्शान्तप्रतिपत्तिथिं—अमावास्यानन्तरप्रतिपत्तिथिम्। उपहारः—निवेद्यम् ॥२१॥ शतादितद्वृद्ध्या—शतादिशतवृद्ध्या। एवं पूर्णायां षट्शताधिकं

---

(१) तूक्तसङ्ख्यया इति मू० पु० पा०। (२) योगशक्तीनामेकोग्रन्थिसरानव इति मू० पु० पा०।
(३) उक्तं इति म० ए० पा०।

कन्यकायां समावाह्य देवीं सम्पूज्य भक्तितः ।
दत्वा भूषणवस्त्रादि दक्षिणां च समुद्धरेत् ॥ २३ ॥
एव(१)मेकादिसंवृद्ध्या पूर्णान्तं पूजयेत् प्रिये ! ।
तेन विद्वान् भवेत्सिद्धो नृपतिं कुरुतेऽर्चकम् ॥२४॥
कार्तिके मासि पूर्णायां कुङ्कुमेन समर्चयेत् ।
रात्रौ प्रदीपकैर्होमैः कुर्यात् घृतसमेधितैः ॥२५॥
देव्यग्रे स्थापयेद्दीपान् विद्यया षोडश क्रमात् ।
शक्तीनामेकमेकं तु स्थापयेत्तत्तदग्रतः ॥२६॥
अथवा भाजने मध्ये त्वेकं तमभितो नव ।
कृत्वा निवेदयेन्मूलविद्यया सप्रसूनकम् ॥२७॥
मार्गशीर्षे च पूर्णायां नालिकेराम्बु चन्द्रयुक् !
निवेद्याभ्यर्चयेन्माषपिष्टापूपैर्यथाविधि ॥२८॥

मूलविद्यया जुहुयादित्यर्थः। जपं चैवम्—शतादितद्वृद्ध्या जपं च समाचरेदित्यर्थः। सम्पूज्य—नित्योक्तक्रमेण ॥२३॥ एवमेकादिसंवृद्ध्या पूर्णायां षोडश [कन्याः समर्चयेत्। तेन—यजनेन। एतदुक्तं भवति—देवीशेषार्चाहोमाद्यनन्तरं कन्यकापूजनं कुर्यादिति ॥२४॥

कार्त्तिकेत्यादिभिः प्रसूनकमित्यन्तैस्त्रिभिः श्लोकैः कार्त्तिकदीपोत्सवपूजाक्रममुपदिशति, तत्र होमं कुर्यात्—नित्योक्तमन्त्रतइति, (२) ॥२५॥ विद्यया—श्रीविद्यया। शक्तीनां—वाराहीकुरुकुल्लादीनां परिवारशक्तीनां तत्तन्मन्त्रेणेति शेषः। अस्मिन् पक्षे पञ्चदशनित्यानां पृथक् पूजायां पञ्चदशदीपान् स्थापयेत् तत्तद्विद्याभिरिति सम्प्रदायः। वाराहीकुरुकुल्लयोर्देवीवत् ॥२६॥ अथवा पक्षान्तरं एष गौणः पक्षः ॥२७॥

मार्गशीर्षेत्यादिना श्लोकेन मार्गशीर्षमासपूजामुपदिशति। तत्र चन्द्रयुक्—कर्पूरयुतम्। नारिकेलाम्बु निवेद्य तदर्घ्योपेतं माषपिष्टापूपैः पूजयेदित्यर्थः। यथाविधि—अधिवासपूर्वम् ॥२८॥

---

(१) एकमेकादि इति सो॰ पु॰ पा॰। (२) नित्योक्तक्रमेणेति व॰ पु॰ पा॰।

पुष्ये मासि च पूर्णायां शर्कराभिर्गुडेन वा ।
पूजयेदिष्टसंसिद्ध्यै गव्यं दुग्धं निवेदयेत् ॥२६॥
माघे मासि च पूर्णायां तिलैः शुक्लैस्तथेतरैः ।
पूजयेद्दुग्धनैवेद्यसितापूपादिभिः सदा ॥३०॥
फाल्गुने मासि पूर्णायां पङ्कजैः स्वर्णराजतैः ।
चूतसौगन्धिमधुकैः पूजयेदीप्सिताप्तये ॥३१॥
विषुवायनदर्शासु युगादिषु समर्चनम् ।
कुर्याद्वैशेषिकं पुण्येष्वागमोक्तेषु तेष्वपि ॥३२॥
नित्यनैमित्तिकार्चासु निरतानां यतात्मनाम् ।
प्रोच्यन्ते काम्यरूपाणि षट्कर्माणि समर्चनैः ॥३३॥
यन्त्रहोमक्रियाध्यानयोगतर्पणपूजनैः ।
प्रोक्तानि काम्यकर्माणि प्रयोगेऽन्यत्समर्चयेत् ॥ ३४ ॥

पुष्ये मासीत्यादिना श्लोकेन पुष्यमासपूजामुपदिशति—तत्र वा पक्षान्तरे। गव्यं—गोसम्बन्धि । गव्यग्रहणं अजमहिष्यादिक्षीरव्यावृत्त्यर्थम् ॥२६॥

माघे मासीत्यादिना श्लोकेन माघमासपूजामुपदिशति—तत्र—शुक्लैः—श्वेतैः। इतरैः—कृष्णैः। तथेति—पक्षान्तरे। सिता—शर्करा। आदिशब्दः फलादिविषयः। सदा—सर्वदिनार्चनेषु ॥३०॥

फाल्गुने मासीत्यादिना श्लोकेन फाल्गुनमासपूजामुपदिशति। तत्र स्वर्णराजतैः—पुष्पैरिति शेषः ॥३१॥

विषुवेत्यादिना श्लोकेन पुण्येषु दिवसेषु पूजाविशेषानुपदिशति। तत्र युगादिषु—युगादिसंज्ञासु वैशाखादिमासोक्तासु तिथिषु। वैशेषिकं—द्विःक्रमार्चनं त्रिरर्चनं नैमित्तिकार्चनं च। आगमोक्तेषु—गुरुजन्मदिवसादिषु ॥ ३२ ॥

अनन्तरं नित्येत्यादिभिरष्टषष्ठ्या श्लोकैः काम्यपूजाविधानमुपदिशति । तत्र नित्येत्यादिना समर्चनादित्यन्तेन श्लोकद्वयेन काम्यपूजाकरणयोग्यान् पूजयैव कामावाप्तिं चोपदिशति । तत्र—यतात्मनां—विवेकिनाम्। काम्यरूपाणि—यष्टव्यानि अभिमतानीत्यर्थः। समर्चनैः—यन्त्रहोमादिविकारैः। क्रिया—पुत्तलिकासु कण्टक-

रक्षा शान्तिर्जयो लाभो निग्रहो निधनं तथा ।
षट्कर्माणि तदङ्गत्वादन्येषां न पृथक् स्थितिः ॥३५॥
तानि(१) चैत्रादि चैत्रान्तं तिथिवारैश्च पार्वति !
पूजाद्रव्यैर्देशकालैः कथ्यन्ते साध्वनुक्रमात् ॥३६॥
रक्षायै भूपुरे शान्त्यै पूजयेद्वारिमण्डले ।
जयाय दहनागारे लाभायानिलमण्डले ॥३७॥
शेषयोर्व्योमगेहेऽस्याः पीताश्वेतारुणासितैः ।
द्रव्यैः षोढा विभज्याहः क्रमाद्राचिं च पूजयेत् ॥३८॥
तानि चैत्रादिकस्तत्र खण्डानि समुदीरिताः ।
तानि(२) पूजाविधौ प्रोक्तैर्द्रव्यास्तैर्नवनामभिः ॥३९॥
ललिता कामदा कामेत्येताभिर्द्वादश(३) क्रमात् ।
चैत्रादिमासनामानि तेषु तैर्दानपूजनैः ॥४०॥

वेधनादिः । ध्यानं—भूतोदयसमयस्मरणम् । योगः—साध्यस्वात्मनोरैक्यभावनम् । ॥३३॥ प्रयोगोऽन्यत् समर्चनात् । एतदुक्तं भवति—स्वस्वकाम्यावाप्त्युपायभुतेषु प्रोक्तेषु सप्तसु चरमभूतात् सप्तमात् पूजनादन्यदुपरिष्टाद्वक्ष्यते । अत्र केवलं सप्तमेन सपर्याविशेषेणैव वाञ्छिताप्तिकथनमिति ॥ ३४ ॥

रक्षेत्यादिना श्लोकेन षट्कर्मस्वरूपमुपदिशति—तत्रान्येषां—वश्याकर्षणविद्वेषणादीनाम् ॥ ३५ ॥

तानीत्यादिना श्लोकेन काम्यपूजाविधानक्रमकथनप्रकारमुपदिशति । तत्र—तानि—षट्कर्माणि । देशकालैरित्यत्र कालशब्दोमुहूर्तादिवाचो ॥३६॥

रक्षेत्यादिभिः समग्रु त इत्यन्तैः पञ्चदशभिः श्लोकैः भूतमण्डलेषु पूजया ऋतुमासतिथिवारेषु द्रव्यविशेषैः पूजया च फलविशेषानुपदिशति । तत्र भूपुरे—रेखाग्राष्टकशूलोपेते चतुरस्रे । वारिमण्डले—अर्द्धचन्द्राकारे शृङ्गद्वयपद्मोपेते मण्डले । दहनागारे—प्रतिकोणं स्वस्तिकोपेते त्रिकोणे । अनिलमण्डले—एकान्तरितमन्तर्बहिर्विरचितबिन्दुषट्कयुक्ते वृत्ते ॥३७॥ शेषयोः—निग्रहनिधनयोः । व्योमगेहे-केवले

---

(१) एतौ श्लोकौ सो० पुस्तके न स्तः । (२) नित्यपूजा इति मू० पुस्तके पाठः ।
(३) एतानि द्वा इति सो० पुस्तके पाठः ।

अभीष्टं समवाप्नोति बलारोग्यादिसिद्धिभिः ।
व्रीहिमाषयवक्षौद्रघृततैलपयोम्बरैः(१) ॥४१॥
हेम रत्नं तिलं मुद्गमिति द्रव्याण्यनुक्रमात् ।
चैत्रादिषु ऋतं नादं(२) दद्याद्विद्याविदेऽर्चयेत् ॥४२॥
श्लेष्मान्तककरञ्जाक्षनिम्बाश्वत्थकदम्बकाः* ।
बिल्वोवटश्च मातॄणां पादपाः समुदीरिताः ॥४३॥
चन्दनद्वयकर्पूरचूता व्युत्क्रमपीठगाः ।
तेषु चैत्रादिषु यजेदाज्ञासिद्धिर्दृढा भवेत् ॥४४॥
चैत्रादिऋतुसम्भूतैः प्रसूनैर्नित्यमर्चयेत् ।
आयुः कान्तिं श्रियं भूमिं विजयं शश्वदश्नुते ॥४५॥
प्रतिपत्तिथिमारभ्य क्रमादेकाभिवृद्धितः ।
मोचां गुडं नारिकेलं पूर्णान्तं(३) होमयेदपि ॥४६॥
ततः(४) प्रतिपदारभ्यदिनमेकैकशः क्रमात् ।
दर्शे त्वेकमथैवं स्यात् कृते लक्ष्म्या नृपो भवेत् ॥४७॥

वृत्ते। पीतश्वेतारुणासितैः--वायुनाभसोरसितवर्णैः। एतानि द्रव्याणि भूतमण्डलपूजायामेव। षोढाविभज्याहः—पञ्चभिः पञ्चभिर्घटिकाभिः रात्रिं च उक्तक्रमेण विभिद्य ॥३८॥ खण्डानि—घटिकाः। पञ्चपातिकेषु विषयेषु(?)। अहश्च रात्रिं च पञ्चभिर्घटिकाभिः षोढ़ा विभिद्य तेषु षड्ऋतुभूतेषु क्रमात्तद्रव्यादीनि कुर्यात् इति। नवनामभिः त्रिपुरेत्यादिभिः ॥३९॥ क्रमात्—उक्तानीतिशेषः ॥४०॥ सिद्धिभिः—सममिति शेषः। पयः—क्षीरम् ॥४१॥ हेम इति पदच्छेदः। अर्चयेत् तामिति शेषः ॥४२॥ मातॄणां वशिन्यादिपरमार्थानाम्॥४३॥ व्युत्क्रमपीठगा इति। एतदुक्तं भवति। चूतकर्पूररक्तचन्दनचन्दनाख्याः—कामरूपपूर्णगिरिजालन्धरोड्यानपीठगा इति। तेषु—द्वादशसु विष्टरेषु ॥४४॥ नित्यं—नित्यकर्म्म ॥४५॥ होमयेत्—नित्यहोमान्ते विद्यया प्रोक्तद्रव्यसङ्ख्यायुक्तया जुहुयात्॥४६॥ ततः—पूर्णादिनात्। एवं कृते लक्ष्म्या नृपोभवेदित्य-

---

(१) पयो नरैः इति सो० पुस्तके पाठः। * कदम्बकैरिति मू० पु० पाठः।
(२) चैत्रादिषु ऋतनाम्ना दद्याविद्या इति मू० पुस्तके पाठः।
(३) चूर्णान्तं इति सो० पुस्तके पाठः। (४) प्रतिपदारभ्याधीरमी इति सो० पुस्तके पाठः।

रविवारेऽरुणाम्भोजैः (१) कुमुदैः सोमवारके (२) ।
भौमे रक्तोत्पलैः सौम्ये वारे तगरसम्भवैः ॥४८॥
गुरुवारेषु कल्हारैः शुक्रवारे सिताम्बुजैः ।
उत्पलैः शनिवारेषु पूजयेदब्दमादरात् ॥४९॥
निवेदयेत् क्रमात्तेषु(३) रविवारादिसप्तसु ।
पायसं दुग्धकदलीनवनीतं सिते घृतम् ॥५०॥
एवमब्दं समाराध्य देवीं गन्धादिभिः क्रमात् ।
ग्रहपीडां विजित्याशु सुखानि च समश्नुते ॥५१॥
चतुरस्रं समारभ्य नव(४) चक्राण्यनुक्रमात् ।
उन्नतोन्नतमामध्याच्चक्रं स्यान्निधनं धनम्(५) ॥५२॥
त्रित्रिक्रमादुन्नतं तत् सुप्रजत्वं श्रियं(६) लभेत् ।
एक द्विषट्क्रमोन्नामः श्रियै कीर्त्यै च कल्पते ॥५३॥
नवानि समरूपाणि(७) सर्वाभीष्टार्थसिद्धये ।
रत्ने हेमनि रूप्ये च ताम्रे दृषदि च क्रमात् ॥५४॥

न्वयः ॥४७॥ तगरसम्भवैः—जलजविशेषैः नन्द्यावर्तैर्वा ॥४८॥४९॥ सिते—पिण्डसिकताविग्रहे ॥५०॥ गन्धादिभिरित्यत्र आदिशब्देन उपचारान्तराण्युच्यन्ते ॥५१॥

चतुरस्रमित्यादिभिः सर्वथा इत्यन्तैः षड्भिः श्लोकैः श्रीचक्रनिर्माणस्वरूपविशेषेण फलसिद्धिविशेषानुपादानद्रव्यविशेषैः फलविशेषान्निषिद्धाधिकरणानि तेषु करणे प्रत्यवायं चोपदिशति । तत्र आमध्यात् देवतानिवासत्रिकोणमध्यावधि निधनं धनावाप्त्यनन्तरं निधनं भवति ॥५२॥ त्रित्रिक्रमादुन्नतं—चतुरस्रपद्मद्वयरूपात् चतुर्दशारदशारद्वयमुन्नतं तस्मान्नवयोनिकम् । तत्—श्रीचक्रमितिशेषः । एकद्विषट्क्रमोन्नामः—चतुरस्रात् पद्मद्वयमुन्नतं तस्माच्चतुर्दशारादिकं समुन्नतम् ॥५३॥ नवानि इति

---

(१) रविवारेरुणां भोजौ इति सो० पुस्तके पाठः । (२) सोमकारकैः इति सो० पुस्तके पाठः ।
(३) निवेदयन् कामां नेष इति मू० पुस्तके पाठः । (४) पञ्चवक्रान्य इति मू० पुस्तके पाठः ।
(५) धनं धने इति सो० पुस्तके पाठः । (६) त्रित्रिक्रमादुन्नत्तं तत्र सुप्रजत्त्वं श्रयं इति मू० पु० पा० तदप्रजत्त्वं इति सो० पु० पा० । (७) समरूपाणि इति मू० पुस्तके पाठः ।

कृत्वा श्रीचक्रनिर्माणं स्थापयेत् पूजयेदपि ।
लक्ष्मीकान्तियशःपुत्रधनारोग्यादिसिद्धये ॥५५॥
सीसकांस्यादिषु पुनः पूर्वोक्तविपरीतकृत् ।
फलकायां पटे भित्तौ स्थापयेन्न कदाचन ॥५६॥
स्थापितं यदि लोभेन मोहेना ऽज्ञानतोऽपि वा ।
कुलवित्तमपत्यं च निर्मूलयति सर्वथा ॥५७॥
पर्वताग्रे यजेद्देवीं पलाशकुसुमैर्निशि ।
सिद्धद्रव्यैश्च(१) सप्ताहात् खेचरीमेलनं भवेत् ॥५८॥
अरण्ये वटमूले वा कुञ्जे(२) वा धरणीभृताम् ।
कदम्बजातीपुष्पाभ्यां सिद्धद्रव्यैः शिवां यजेत् ॥५९॥
मासेन सिद्धा यक्षिण्यः प्रत्यक्षा वाञ्छितप्रदाः ।
केतकीकुसुमैः सिद्धाश्चेटका वारिधेस्तटे ॥६०॥
आज्ञामभीष्टां वनितां रणे मायां महाद्भुतम् ।
वसूनि मालाभूषादि दद्यादस्येच्छयाऽनिशम् ॥६१॥

दिव्यत्वान्नवेत्यर्थः । समरूपाणि — नवचक्राणि इत्यर्थः । समस्थलानि । रत्ने — षोडशस्वन्यतमे । दृषदि — शिलायाम् । एतान्यधिकरणानि सर्वनित्यार्चनप्रस्तारसाधारणानि ॥ ५४ ॥ स्थापयेत् — प्रतिष्ठां कुर्यात् ॥ ४५ ॥ सीसकांस्यादीत्यत्रादिशब्देन नागमायसं च गृह्णाति । पूर्वोक्तविपरीतकृत्-अलक्ष्म्यादिकरमित्यर्थः ॥ ५६ ॥ लोभेन — वित्तेच्छया । मोहेन — अविवेकात् । अज्ञानतः निषेधाज्ञानतः ॥ ५७ ॥

पर्वताग्रे इत्यादिभिर्विनोदवानित्यन्तैः पञ्चदशभिः श्लोकैः सप्तविधसिद्ध्युपायमुपदिशति । तत्र सिद्धद्रव्यैः — सिद्धद्रव्यं गुरुमुखादेवावगन्तव्यम् । खेचरीमेलनं — अप्सरोमेलनम् ॥५८॥ कुञ्जे — कन्दरायाम् ॥५९॥ यक्षिण्यः — नीलपताकापटले वक्ष्यमाणाः षट्त्रिंशत्विग्रहाः । चेटकाः — चेटकानाम चतुःषष्टिविग्रहाः देवतास्तत्पटले वक्ष्यमाणाः ॥६०॥ मायां — इच्छाधीनान् कृत्रिमविग्रहान् दर्शयितुं सामर्थ्यं

---

(१) सिद्धिद्रव्यैरिति सी० मू० पुस्तके पाठः ।

(२) आरण्ये वटमूलेन वा वज्रे वा इति सी० पुस्तके पाठः ।

पीठमन्त्रद्रुमैः कृत्वा तत्र देवीं यजेन्निशि ।
शाल्मलीकुसुमैः सिद्धद्रव्यैर्मासं तु निर्भयः ॥६२॥
श्मशाने(१) देवदेवेशि ! सिद्ध्यन्त्यस्य पिशाचिकाः ।
अश्मपातप्रहाराद्यैरस्य(२) घ्नन्ति द्विषश्चिरम् ॥६३॥
निर्जने विपिने रात्रौ मासमात्रं तु निर्भयः ।
यजेद्देवीं चक्रगतां सिद्धद्रव्यसमन्विताम् ॥६४॥
मालतीजातिपुन्नागकेतकीमनुभिः(३) क्रमात् ।
तेन सिद्ध्यन्ति वेतालास्ता नारुह्य स्वेच्छया चरेत् ॥६५॥
श्मशाने चण्डिकागेहे निर्जने विपिनेऽपिवा ।
मध्यरात्रे यजेद्देवीं कृष्णवस्त्रादिभूषणः ॥६६॥
कृष्णचक्रे तिकृष्णां तामतिक्रुद्धाशयो जपेत्(४) ।
(५)साध्ययोनिं तदग्रे तु बलिं(६) दद्यान्निवेदयेत् ॥६७॥
सिद्धद्रव्यसमोपेतं मासं तद्भाललोचनात् ।
जायन्ते भीषणाः कृत्यास्ताभ्यः साध्यं निवेदयेत् ॥६८॥
विश्वसंहारसन्तुष्टाः पुनर्यान्ति निजेच्छया ।
देव्या ललाटनेत्राः स्युः प्रार्थनेन तिरोहिताः ॥६९॥

दद्यात्, एकैक इति शेषः ॥६१॥ निर्भयः—पिशाचादिदर्शनात् अचकितचित्तः ॥६२॥ पिशाचिकाः—पिशाचिका नाम काश्चन भीमविग्रहा देवताः ॥६३॥ चक्रगतां—नित्यसपर्याप्रोक्तचक्रे तदुक्तप्रकारेण समस्तु प्रोक्तसिद्धुपायेषु समर्चयेदित्यर्थः । अन्यासामपि तत्तन्नित्यपूजाचक्रे नैमित्तिककाम्यार्चनम् ॥६४॥ वेतालाः ते च विरूपाः । भीषणाकाराः असङ्ख्याताः काश्चन देवताः ॥६५॥ कृष्णवस्त्रादिभूषणः—आदिशब्देन गन्धमाल्यानुलेपनादिकम् ॥६६॥ कृत्यचक्रे अञ्जनद्रवागुरुपङ्काभ्यां निर्मिते । साध्ययोनिं—उत्तरत्र वक्ष्यमाणां साध्यनक्षत्रयोनिम् । तासां

---

(१) श्मशानदेशे देवेशि इति मू० पुस्तके पाठः । (२) दौर्जीयात्ताभिर्द्विष इति मू० पुस्तके पाठः ।
(३) मरुभिः इति सो० पुस्तके पाठः । (४) कृष्णचक्रे प्रतिकृष्णां तामति क्रुध्वाशयो यजेत् इति मू० पु० पा० ।
(५) मध्ययोनिमिति मू० पुस्तके पाठः । (६) बलिं छिन्दन्निवे इति मू० पुस्तके पाठः ।

रक्तभूषाम्बरालेपमालाभूषितविग्रहः।
उद्याने निर्जने देवीं चक्रे सञ्चिन्त्य पूजयेत् ॥७०॥
कह्लारचम्पकाशोकपाटलाशतपत्रकैः।
सिद्धद्रव्यसमोपेतैर्माया: सिद्ध्यन्ति मासतः ॥७१॥
यासां प्रसादलाभेन कामरूपोभवेन्नरः।
याभिर्विश्वमयोविश्व चारी विश्वविनोदवान् ॥७२॥
षड़ाधाराब्जमध्ये तु चक्रं सञ्चिन्त्य पूजयेत्।
चन्द्रचन्दनकस्तूरीमृगनाभिर्महोदयैः ॥७३॥
त्रिकालज्ञो भवेद्देवीं तेषु सम्यग्विचिन्तयेत्।
पूर्णप्रतीतौ भव्यानि विकलेऽभव्यमीरितम् ॥७४॥
देवीं चक्रेण सहितां चुलुके सलिले स्मरेत्।
मातृकासहितां विद्यां त्रिरावृत्त्यामृतात्मकम्(१) ॥७५॥
नाड़ीं सारस्वतीं जिह्वां दीपाकारां स्मरन् पिबेत्।
अब्दाच्चतुर्विधं तस्य पाण्डित्यं भुवि जायते ॥७६॥

विग्रहानुपरिष्टाद्वक्ष्यति ॥ ६७ ॥ प्रार्थनेन—युष्मत्प्रसादात् सिद्धमस्मत्समो—हितम्, यथागतं गच्छत इति प्रार्थनेन ॥६८॥६९॥ मालाभूषितविग्रहः—साधकः इति शेषः ॥ ७० ॥ कल्हारादिभिः समस्तैरन्यतमेन वा। एवं सर्वत्रापि ॥७१॥ विश्वविनोदवान् इन्द्रजालादिप्रदर्शनेन ॥ ७२ ॥

षड़ाधारेत्यादिना ईरित इत्यन्तेन श्लोकद्वयेन भविष्यद्वर्तमानार्थपरोक्षो पायमुपदिशति। तत्र षड़ाधाराब्जादीनि उत्तरत्र वक्ष्यति। चक्रं सञ्चिन्त्य—तेष्व न्यतमे। महोदयः—गुरुमुखादवगन्तव्यः॥७३॥ देवीं—ललिताम्। सम्यक्—नित्य पूजोक्तविग्रहतः। पूर्णप्रतीतौ—प्रोक्तरूपभावनासिद्धौ। भव्यानि—मङ्गलानि सिध्य न्तीति शेषः। विकले—आयुधवर्णावयवादिवैकल्यस्फुरणे। अभव्यं—अमङ्ग लम् ॥७४॥

देवीमित्यादिभिरात्मविदित्यन्तैस्त्रिभिः श्लोकैश्चतुर्विधपाण्डित्यादिसिद्ध्युपाय

---

(१) मृतात्मिकाम् इति मू० पु० पा०।

एवं नित्यमुषःकाले यः कुर्याच्छुद्धमानसः ।
स योगी ब्रह्मविज्ज्ञानी शिवयोगी तथाऽऽत्मवित् ॥७७॥
अनुग्रहोक्तचक्रस्थां देवीं ताभिर्वृतां यजेत् ।
चम्पकेन्दीवरैर्मासादारोग्यमुपजायते ॥७८॥
ज्वरभूतग्रहोन्मादशीतिकाकामलाक्षिरुक् (१) ।
दन्तकर्णज्वरशिरःशूलगुल्मादिकुक्षिजाः ॥ ७९ ॥
व्रणप्रमेहकुष्ठार्शोग्रहण्यन्यत्रिदोषजाः ।
सर्वे तया समं यान्ति पूजया परमेश्वरि ! ॥८०॥
द्रव्यं चक्रस्य निर्माणे काश्मीरं समुदीरितम् ।
सिन्दूरं गैरिकं लाक्षा दरदं चन्दनेऽपि वा ॥८१॥
बिलद्वारे लिखेच्चक्रं षोड़शत्र्यस्रसंयुतम् ।
दरदेनास्य मध्यस्थां पूजयेत्परमेश्वरीम् ॥८२॥

मुपदिशति । तत्र अमृतात्मकं सलिलमिति शेषः ॥७५॥ जिह्वां—एतदुक्तं भवति—सरस्वतीनाड़ीविग्रहां जिह्वां स्वात्मतेजोविग्रहां विभाव्य तत्तेजसि तदमृतं होमबुद्ध्या पिबेदिति। चतुर्विधं पाण्डित्यं वादित्वकवित्ववाग्मित्वव्याख्यातृत्वरूपम् ॥७६॥ नित्यं—यावज्जीवम् । सयोगीत्याद्युक्तस्य पञ्चप्रकारस्यैकरूप्येऽपि एवं नानारूपकथनं लोकोक्त्यनुमत्यर्थम् ॥७७॥

अनुग्रहोक्तेत्यादिना परमेश्वरीत्यन्तेन श्लोकत्रयेण सर्वव्याधिपरिहारपूजामुपदिशति । तत्र अनुग्रहोक्तचक्रस्थां—नित्यानित्यापटलोक्तानुग्रहचक्रस्थाम्। ताभिः—तत्रोक्ताभिर्डाकिन्यादिभिरष्टचत्वारिंशच्छक्तिभिर्यजेत् । तत्रोक्तविधानत इति शेषः । इन्दीवरैर्नीलोत्पलैः ॥७८॥ ज्वर इत्यादि षोड़शविधव्याधिकथनं सर्वेषां व्याधीनामुपलक्षणार्थम् । तत्र दन्तकर्णज्वर इत्यत्र ज्वरशब्दः पीड़ावाची । शिरःशूलं - शिरोरोगः । त्रिदोषजाः वातपित्तश्लेष्मणां एकैकव्याधिसङ्कीर्णजनिता रोगाः सर्वरोगाइति शेषः ॥७९॥८०॥

द्रव्यमित्यादिना श्लोकेन अभिषेकादिषु श्रीचक्रनिर्माणद्रव्यसप्तकमुपदिशति । तत्र चन्दने—शीतरक्ते ॥८१॥

(क) शान्तिकाकामलाक्षियुक् इति मू० पाठः ।

ताभिस्तच्छक्तिभिःसाकं सिद्धद्रव्यैः सुगन्धिभिः ।
कुसुमैर्मासमात्रेण नागकन्याः समेत्य तम् ॥८२॥
पातालादिषु लोकेषु रमयन्ति प्रियाश्चिरम् ।
यक्षराक्षसगन्धर्वसिद्धविद्याधराङ्गनाः ॥ ८३ ॥
पिशाचा गुह्यका वीराः किन्नरा उरगाः प्रिये !
सिद्ध्यन्ति पूजनात्तत्र तथा तत्प्रोक्तकालतः ॥ ८४ ॥
किंशुकैर्भूषणावाप्त्यै (१) पाटलैर्गजसिद्धये ।
रक्तोत्पलैरश्वसिद्ध्यै (२) कुमुदैः खरसिद्धये ॥८५॥
उत्पलैरुष्ट्रसंसिद्ध्यै तगरैः पशुसिद्धये ।
जम्बीरैर्महिषावाप्त्यै (३) लकुचैरजसिद्धये ॥८६॥
दाड़िमैर्निधिसंसिद्ध्यै मधुकैर्नागसिद्धये (४) ।
बकुलैरङ्गनासिद्ध्यै कल्हारैः पुत्रसिद्धये ॥८७॥
शतपत्रैर्जयावाप्त्यै केतकैर्वाहनाप्तये ।
सौरभाद्यैः प्रसूनैस्तु नित्यं सौभाग्यसिद्धये ॥८८॥

बिलद्वारे इत्यादिभिः कालतः इत्यन्तैश्चतुर्भिः श्लोकैर्नागकन्याद्येकादशसिद्ध्युपायमुपदिशति । तत्र बिलद्वारे--पातालप्रवेशमार्गद्वारोपकण्ठतः । षोड़शवर्णसंयुतं—पूर्णाभिषेकप्रोक्तप्रक्रियया ॥८१॥ ताभिः—षण्णवतिसङ्ख्याताभिः । तच्छक्तिभिः--सचत्वारिंशच्चतुःशताधिकसहस्रसङ्ख्याताभिः । एतच्चक्रार्चनं ललितानित्याया एव, नान्यासाम् । तं—साधकम् ॥८२॥ यक्षेत्यादयो देवताविशेषाः ॥८३॥ तत्र वीरा—मनुष्यसिद्धरूपाः ॥८४॥

किंशुकैरित्यादिभिः सौभाग्यसिद्धये इत्यन्तैश्चतुर्भिः श्लोकैः पञ्चदशविधैः प्रसूनैरर्चनात् पञ्चदशविधवाञ्छितसिद्धिमुपदिशति । तत्र रक्तोत्पलैः—रक्तकुसुमैः । तगरैः—प्राग्वत् । जम्बीरैः—नारङ्गैः । वाहनाप्तये—स्यन्दनान्दोलिकादिसिद्धये ॥८५॥८६॥८७॥८८॥

(१) व्याप्तं पालाशैरिति मू० पु० पा० ।
(२) रक्तसिद्ध्यै इति सो० पु० पा० ।
(३) व्याप्तैरिति मू० पु० पा० ।
(४) नागसिद्धये इति मू० पु० पा० ।

पूजयेन्मासमात्रं वा द्विगुणं त्रिगुणं तु वा ।
यावत्फलाप्ति वा क्षीरशर्कराघृतपायसैः ॥८९॥
सचक्रपरिवारां तां देवीं सलिलमध्यगाम् ।
तर्पयेत् कुसुमैः साघ्यैः (१) सर्वोपप्लवशान्तये ॥९०॥
घृतैः पूर्णायुषः सिद्ध्यै क्षौद्रैः सौभाग्यसिद्धये ।
दुग्धैरारोग्यसंसिद्ध्यै त्रिभिरैश्वर्यसिद्धये ॥९१॥
नालिकेरोदकैः प्रीत्यै हिमतोयैर्नृपाप्तये ।
सर्वार्थसिद्धये तोयैरभिषिञ्चेन्महेश्वरीम् ॥९२॥
पूगोद्याने यजेद्देवीं सिद्धद्रव्यैर्दिवाऽनिशम् ।
निवसंस्तत्र तत्पुष्पैर्जायते मन्मथोऽपरः ॥९३॥
पूर्णासु नियतं देवीं कन्यकायां समर्चयेत् (२) ।
कृत्याः परेरिता मन्त्रा विमुखास्तान् ग्रसन्ति वै ॥९४॥

पूजयेदित्यादिना श्लोकेन काम्यफलावाप्तिकालान् सर्वत्र निवेद्यद्रव्याणि चोपदिशति । तत्र क्षीरादीनि चत्वारि द्रव्याणि सर्वनैवेद्यानीत्यर्थः ॥८९॥

सचक्रेत्यादिना श्लोकेन सर्वोपद्रवशान्त्यै साद्र*क्रमतर्पणादिकमुपदिशति । तत्रै तदुक्तं भवति – राजक्रोधविविधोत्पातवैरिपीडाग्रहवैकृतरोगार्त्यादिषु जलाशये स्नातः धौताम्बरः पद्मविष्टरोपविष्टः कृतन्यासः कृतार्चो नाथाज्ञया श्रीचक्रं सलिलोपरि विभाव्य तन्मध्यगां देवीं स्वर्णरूप्यताम्रेष्वन्यतमचषकपूरितं सलिलं अर्घ्यं कर्पूरादिभिः सुरभिप्रसूनजुष्टं प्रतिशक्तिकं नित्यपूजामन्त्रैस्तत्क्रमेण दद्यात्. तेन सर्वोपप्लवशान्तिर्भवति ॥९०॥

घृतैरित्यादिना महेश्वरीमित्यन्तेन श्लोकद्वयेन देव्याः षड्भिरभिषेकद्रव्यैः सप्तविधाभिषेकं तत्फलानि चोपदिशति । तत्र त्रिभिः—प्रोक्तैः (३)॥ ९१ ॥ प्रोत्यै—स्वनिर्वृत्तये ॥ ९२ ॥

पूगेत्यादिभिः घोरतरैरपीत्यन्तैः षड्भिः श्लोकैः प्रतिश्लोकमेकैकप्रकारेण

---

(१) साद्रैरिति सां० पु० पा० ।
(२) समर्चनात् इति मू० पु० पा० ।
(३) श्रोक्तैरिति सां० पु० पा० ।
* साद्र इति टी० पु० पा० ।

लिङ्गत्रयगतां देवीं चक्रस्थाभिः (१) स्वशक्तिभिः ।
पूजयन्निष्ट(२)मखिलं लभतेऽत्र परत्र च ॥९५॥
शतमानकृतैः स्वर्णपुष्पैः सौरभ्यवासितैः ।
पूजयेन्मासमात्रेण प्रागजन्माघैर्विमुच्यते ॥९६॥
तथा रत्नैश्च नवभिः मासं मासन्तु पूजयेत् ।
विमुक्तः सर्वपापौघैस्तां पश्यति च चक्षुषा ॥९७॥
अंशुकैरर्चयेद्देवीं मासमात्रं सुगन्धिभिः ।
मुच्यते पापकृत्यादिदुःखैर्घोरतरैरपि ॥९८॥
देवीरूपं स्वमात्मानं चक्रं शक्तीः समंततः ।
भावयन्विषयैः पुष्पैः पूजयंस्तन्मयो भवेत् (३) ॥९९॥

षट्प्रकारभजनमुपदिशति । तत्र तत्पुष्पैः—पूगप्रसूनैः ॥९३॥९४॥ लिङ्गत्रयगतां स्वयम्भुबाणेतरलिङ्गस्थां मूलाधारहृदयब्रह्मरन्ध्रगताम् । चक्रस्थाभिः—अणिमादिभिः । अत्र इदन्ताविषये । परत्र—पराहन्ताविषये । एतदुक्तं भवति—मूलाधारहृदयब्रह्मरन्ध्रेषु अन्यतमे नित्यसपर्याप्रोक्तचक्रस्थां तत्रस्थाभिरणिमादिभिः परिवृतां विभाव्य पूजयन् इष्टफलं लभेतेति ॥९५॥ प्रागजन्माघैः—चिरन्तनाभिर्दुर्वासनाभिः ॥९६॥ मासंमासं—प्रतिरत्नमेकैकं मासम् । पापौघैः—सङ्कोचभावैः । चक्षुषा इत्युक्त्या मनसाऽनुभवसिद्धं कथयति ॥ ९७ ॥ पापकृत्यादिदुःखैः—पापैः—स्वकीयविवेकैः । कृत्यादिदुःखैररातिभिर्दुष्प्रयोगोत्थाभिः ताभिः कृत्यादिभिः आदिशब्देन यन्त्रचूर्णौषधनिक्षेपा उच्यन्ते तैश्च जनितैर्दुःखैरित्यर्थः ॥ ९८ ॥

देवीरूपमित्यादिना श्लोकेन अखण्डविश्वरूपतादेवताभावनाज्जीवन्मुक्तरूपं परिपूर्णं फलमुपदिशति । तत्र चक्रं—सकलदेवतावासभूतं श्रीचक्रम् । शक्तीः—आवरणशक्त्याद्यनन्तसङ्ख्यात्मशक्तीः । विषयैः—शब्दादिरूपैः । तन्मयोभवेत्—तदहङ्कारे स्वाहङ्कारं विलापयेदित्यर्थः (५) ॥ ९९ ॥

---

(१) चक्रस्थाभिश्च इति म० पु० पा० । (२) पूजयेन्नित्यमिति सो० पु० पा० ।

(३) लभ्यते इति म० पु० पा० । (४) पूजयेन्मन्त्रयोजपेत् इति सो० पु० पा० ।

(५) प्रत्येकं पटलेषु श्लोकानां शतं वर्तते परमस्मिन् पटले बहुवारमादर्शपुस्तकानुसन्धाने कृतेऽपि श्लोकस्यैकस्यादर्शनात् प्रमादादेकः श्लोकः प्रभ्रष्ट इत्यनुमीयते ।

गन्धतत्त्वमयी व्याप्तिरिति सम्यक् समीरिता ।
अस्या निष्कालनाच्चित्ते तत्तत्त्वं स्वात्मसात्कृतम् ॥१०१॥

इति श्रीषोडशनित्यातन्त्रेषु कादिमते षष्ठं
पटलम् ।

इति श्रीषोडशनित्यातन्त्रेषु श्रीकादिमते प्रपञ्चसारसिंहराजप्रकाशाभिधानेन सुभगानन्दनाथेन विरचितायां मनोरमाख्यायां व्याख्यायां षोडशनित्यानैमित्तिककाम्यार्चनप्रकाशनपरं षष्ठं पटलं परिपूर्णं परामृष्टम् ॥ ६ ॥

ग्रन्थसङ्ख्या—

षष्ठे यन्त्राणि सप्त स्युर्व्याख्या ग्रन्थशतात्परम् ।
षट् त्रिपादास्त्रिषष्टिः स्युरिति सम्यक् समीरितम् ॥

अथ सप्तमं पटलम् ।

अथ षोड़शनित्यासु द्वितीया या समीरिता ।
कामेश्वरीति ताः सर्वकामदाः (१) शृणु तत्त्वतः ॥१॥
तत्त्वन्यासं ध्यानभेदांस्तच्छक्तीस्तत्प्रपूजनम् ।
तद्योगभेदांस्तद्यन्त्राण्यभीष्टार्थप्रदानि च ॥२॥
विद्यारूपं तु (२) ते देवि ! प्रोक्तं प्रागेव तत्स्फुटम् ।
मूलविद्याक्षरैरेवं कुर्यादङ्गानि षट्क्रमात् ॥३॥
एकेन हृदयं शीर्षं तावताथोऽद्वयं(३) द्वयात् ।
चतुर्भिर्नयनं तद्वदस्त्रमेकेन चोदितम् ॥४॥

अथ सप्तमं पटलम् ।

पूर्वं प्रथमाया अङ्गिनित्याललितायाः नित्यपूजां सर्वनित्यासाधारणनैमित्तिककाम्यसपर्यादिक्रमं चतुर्थपञ्चमषष्ठपटलैरुपदिश्यानन्तरं द्वितीयायाः कामेश्वरीनित्याया विधानमुपदिशति—अथ षोड़शेत्यादिना क्वचिदित्यन्तेन श्लोकशतरूपेण सप्तमपटलेन। तत्र अथ षोड़शेत्यादिना अर्थप्रदानि च इत्यन्तेन श्लोकद्वयेन पटलार्थानुपदिशति। तत्र—तत्वतः—यथावत्॥ १ ॥ तच्छक्तीः—तदावरणभूताः शक्तीरित्यर्थः ॥ २ ॥

विद्यारूपमित्यादिना क्रमेण वै इत्यन्तैश्चतुर्भिः श्लोकैर्विद्यान्यासक्रममुपदिशति। ऐं स्क्लीं नित्यक्लिन्ने मदद्रवेसौः। तत्र प्रागेव—तृतीयपटले ॥३॥ एकेन हृदयमिति। तावता—एकेन। एतदुक्तं भवति—कामेश्वरीमूलविद्यायाः प्रथमाक्षरेण हृदयं, द्वितीयेन शीर्षं, तृतीयचतुर्थाभ्यां शिखा, पञ्चमषष्ठाभ्यां कवचं, सप्तमाष्टमनवमदशमैश्चतुर्भिर्नेत्रं, एकादशेनान्तेनास्त्रम्। एवं षोढा विभिन्नेन जातियुक्तेन मूलमन्त्रेण षड़ङ्गन्यासं करायोः कुर्यादिति, उत्तरत्र नवमे पटले

---

(१) तान् सर्वं कामदां इति सो॰ पु॰ पा॰। (२) देवेशि इति मू॰ पु॰ पा॰।

(३) तावताथोद्वयं इति सो॰ पु॰ पा॰।

हृक्श्रोत्रनासाद्वितये जिह्वाहृन्नाभिगुह्यके ।
व्यापकत्वेन सर्वाङ्गे मूर्द्धादि प्रपदावधि ॥५॥
न्यसेद्विद्याक्षराख्येषु स्थानेषु तदनन्तरम् ।
समस्तेन व्यापकन्तु कुर्यादुक्तक्रमेण वै ॥६॥
अथ ध्यानं प्रवक्ष्यामि नित्यपूजासु चोदितम् ।
येन देवी सुप्रसन्ना ददातीष्टमयत्नतः(१) ॥७॥
बालार्ककोटिसङ्काशां माणिक्यमुकुटोज्ज्वलाम् ।
हारग्रैवेयकाञ्चीभिरूर्मिकानूपुरादिभिः ॥८॥
मण्डितां रक्तवसनां रत्नाभरणशोभिताम् ।
षड्भुजां त्र्यक्षणामिन्दुकलाकलितमौलिकाम् ॥९॥
पञ्चाष्टषोड़शद्वन्द्वषट्कोणचतुरस्रगाम् ।
मन्दस्मितोल्लसद्वक्त्रां दयामन्थरवीक्षणाम् ॥१०॥

स्वयमेव वक्ष्यति—यथा—अङ्गुष्ठादिकनिष्ठान्तं* अधजर्द्धं क्रमेण हृदयादिभिर्नें त्रान्तैः उभयकरपञ्चाङ्गुलीषु अस्त्रेणान्योन्यमार्जनात् करतलद्वये(न च न्यसेदिति। ऐं हृदयाय नमः इत्यादिभिः ॥ ४ ॥

दृगित्यादिना क्रमेण वै इत्यन्तेन श्लोकद्वयेन विद्याया एकादशाक्षरेण स्वमूर्द्धादिपादद्वयांगुलिनखावधि स्वकरतलाभ्यां परामृश्य पादद्वयाग्रादारभ्य हृदयान्तमूर्द्धं परामृशेत्। हृदये अञ्जल्यन्तं नाथदर्शितप्रक्रियया व्यापकं न्यासं कुर्यादिति। एवं सर्वेषां मन्त्राणां सर्वन्यासान्ते व्यापकं न्यासं कुर्यादित्यर्थः। मन्त्राक्षरन्यासक्रममुपदिशति। तत्र गुह्यके-मूलाधारे। मूर्द्धादिप्रपदावधि। एतदुक्तं भवति—एषु प्रोक्तेषु दशसु स्थानेषु सर्वाङ्गे च समस्तेन मूलमन्त्रेणेतिशेषः। व्यापकं च पूर्ववत् पुनरपि कुर्यादित्यर्थः ॥ ६ ॥

अथ ध्यानमित्यादिभिः तत्र वै इत्यन्तैः षड्भिः श्लोकैर्देव्या नित्यसपर्याध्यानमुपदिशति। तत्र येन—ध्यानेन॥७॥ ऊर्मिका—अङ्गुलीयकम् ॥८॥ इन्दुकलाकलितमौलिकां—चन्द्रकलावतंसत्वं पञ्चदशानां नित्यानां साधारणं नाम ॥ ९ ॥ पञ्चाष्टषोड़शद्वन्द्वषट्कोणचतुरस्रगाम्। एतदुक्तं स्यात्—समान्तरालं सूत्रद्वयमन्त

(१) तदाभोष्टमिति सो॰ पु॰ पा॰।   * अङ्गुष्टादिकवियन्तं इति वं॰ पु॰ पा॰।

पाशाङ्कुशौ च पुण्ड्रेक्षुचापं पुष्पशिलीमुखम्।
रत्नपात्रं सुधापूर्णं वरदं बिभ्रतीं करैः ॥११॥
एवं ध्यात्वाऽर्चयेद्देवीं नित्यपूजासु सिद्धये।
प्रयोगादिषु सर्वत्र वक्ष्ये ध्यानानि तत्र वै ॥१२॥
मदनोन्मादनौ पश्चात्तथा दीपनमोहनौ।
शोषणश्चेति कथिता बाणाः पञ्च पुरोदिताः ॥१३॥
कुसुमा मेखला पश्चान्मदना मदनातुरा।
अनङ्गपदपूर्वास्ताः पञ्चमी मदवेगिनी ॥१४॥
ततो भुवनपाला स्यात् शशिरेखा त्वनन्तरा।
रेखा गगनपूर्वाऽन्या पूज्या पत्रेषु चाष्टसु ॥१५॥

बहिर्विभागेन समचतुरस्राकारं कृत्वा तदन्तर्वृत्तद्वयं कृत्वा तत्र च वक्ष्यमाणक्रमेण षट्कोणं विधाय तदन्तर्वृत्तद्वयं एकाङ्गुलान्तरालं विधाय तदन्तश्चतुरङ्गुलान्तरालं वृत्तं कृत्वा तदन्तरेकाङ्गुलमानेन वृत्तं कृत्वा एवं प्रवेशगत्या त्रिः कृत्वा (१) समान्तर्वृत्तवीथ्यां पञ्च दलानि कृत्वा तद्बहिः वृत्तवीथ्यां * अष्टदलानि कृत्वा तद्बहिरपि वृत्तवीथ्यां षोडशपत्राणि कुर्यात्। एवं पञ्चदलाष्टदलषोडशदलषट्कोणचतुरस्रगामित्यर्थः। एतेषां मानविशेषश्च उपरिष्टाद्वक्ष्यमाणत्वादिह न प्रपञ्चितः ॥१०॥ पाशाङ्कुशाविति। एतान्यायुधादिवामोर्ध्वहस्तादि वामाधरहस्तान्तं वामदक्षिणक्रमेणाधरहस्तयोर्दक्षिणवामक्रमेण च कल्पयेत् ॥११॥ तत्र वै—प्रयोगोपदेशस्थानेषु ॥१२॥

मदनोन्माद इत्यादिना श्लोकेन पञ्चसु दलेषु पूज्याः पञ्चबाणशक्तीरुपदिशति। तत्र—पुरोदिताः– प्रागुदीरिताः। पञ्चबाणशक्तीः। एतदुक्तं—स्यात्—(२) चतुर्थपटलोक्तशैवबाणपञ्चकैः एकैकाक्षरमन्त्रपूर्वैः मदनोन्मादनेत्यादिभिर्नामभिः पञ्चबाणशक्तीः पूजयेत् ॥१३॥

कुसुमेत्यादिना अष्टस्वित्यन्तेन श्लोकद्वयेन द्वितीयतृतीयावरणे अष्टसु दलेषु

---

(१) सर्वान्तर्वृत्तवीथ्यां इति टी० पु० पा० सर्वान्तर्वृत्तवीथ्यामिति सो० पु० पा०।

(२) भवति इति टी० पु० पा०।

* षोडश इति सो० पु० पा०।

श्रद्धा प्रीती रतिश्चैव धृतिः कान्तिर्मनोरमा ।
मनोहराऽष्टमी प्रोक्ता देवी साऽत्र मनोरथा ॥१६॥
मदनोन्मादिनी पश्चान्मोहिनी दीपनी ततः ।
शोषणी च वशंकारी सिंजिनी सुभगा ततः ॥१७॥
सस्वराः षोडश प्रोक्ताः प्रियदर्शन (१) कान्तिकाः ।
पूज्यास्ताः प्रतिपत्त्रं तु प्रत्येकं षोड़शच्छदे ॥१८॥
पूषाविशा (२) सुमनसा रतिः प्रीतिर्धृतिस्तथा ।
वह्निसौम्या (३) मरीचिश्च परतस्त्वंशुमालिनी ॥१९॥
शशिनी चाङ्गिरा छाया ततः सम्पूर्णमण्डला ।
तुष्ट्याऽमृताख्यया कथिताः कलाः स्युः सस्वरा विधोः ॥२०॥
षोड़शेष्वपि पत्रेषु पूजयेत्ता यथाक्रमम् ।
वह्निः षट्कोणकोणेषु डाकिन्याद्यास्तथाऽर्चयेत् ॥२१॥

पूज्याः शक्तीरुपदिशति। तत्र अनङ्गपदपूर्वास्ता इति पूर्वोक्ताश्चतस्रः एतदुक्तं स्यात्—अनङ्गकुसुमा अनङ्गमेखला अनङ्गमदना अनङ्गमदनातुरा इति ॥१४॥ रेखा गगनपूर्वा—गगनरेखेत्यर्थः। अन्या – अष्टमो ॥१५॥

श्रद्धेत्यादिभिः षोड़शच्छदे इत्यन्तैः तृतीयावरणे षोड़शदलपूज्याः शक्तीरुपदिशति। तत्र अष्टमी मनोरथेत्यन्वयः ॥१६॥ मदनोन्मादिनीत्येका। वशंकारी-वशंकरीत्यर्थः ॥१७॥ सस्वराः—षोड़शस्वराक्षरेषु एकैकाक्षरपूर्विकाः। प्रियदर्शन-कान्तिकाः—षोड़श प्रियदर्शना इत्यर्थः ॥१८॥

पूषेत्यादिना यथाक्रममित्यन्तेनाध्यर्द्धेन श्लोकद्वयेन चतुर्थावरणे वह्निः षोड़शपत्रेषु पूज्याः शक्तीरुपदिशति ॥१९॥ तुष्ट्यामृता—तुष्ट्या सह अमृता तुष्टिरित्येका अमृता इत्येकेत्यर्थः। सस्वरा—एताश्च प्राग्वत्। स्वराक्षरेषु एकैकाक्षरपूर्विकाः विधोधः—चन्द्रस्य ॥

वह्निरित्यादिना श्लोकोत्तरार्द्धेन पञ्चमावरणे षट्कोणेषु पूज्याः शक्तीरुप-

---

(१) प्रियदर्शिनि इति सो० पु० पा०। (२) पूषाविशा इति सो० पु० पा०।
(३) वह्निसौम्या मरीचीश्च इति म० पु० पा०।

तद्बहिः चतुरस्रस्थां लोकेशां तत्समां यजेत् (१) ।
बटुकं गणपं दुर्गां क्षेत्रेशं चाभितो यजेत् ॥२२॥
अग्न्याद्यस्रेषु (२) विद्यादि सप्ताक्षर्यन्तराश्रितैः ।
तन्नामभिर्बलिं तेभ्यो दद्याद्गन्धादि चोदितैः ॥२३॥
ततस्तामङ्गविद्याभ्यां क्लृप्तार्घ्यैः पूजयेच्छिवाम् ।
प्रागुक्तैरुपचाराद्यैर्होमं कुर्यात्ततस्तथा (३)॥२४॥

दिशति । तत्र तथाऽर्चयेत्—एतदुक्तं स्यात्—उपरिष्टान्नित्यानित्यापटलप्रोक्त-क्रमेण निर्ऋतिवायुवासवकोणेषु प्रोक्तक्रमेण, डाकिनीराकिनीलाकिनी शक्तित्रयमभ्यर्च्य वह्नीशवरुणकोणेषु त्रिषु प्रोक्तक्रमेण काकिनीशाकिनी—हाकिनीति शक्तित्रयमर्चयेत् इति ॥२१॥

तद्बहिरित्यादिना चोदितैरित्यन्तेन श्लोकद्वयेन षष्ठावरणे चतुरस्रे तदन्तःकोणचतुष्टये पूज्यशक्त्यादिकमुपदिशति । तद्बहिः—षट्कोणाद्बहिः । लोकेशान्(?)—शक्तीरिति शेषः । तत्समाः—प्रधानदेवतासमानवर्णाभरणकरायुधधराः । एतत्सर्वावरणशक्तिसाधारणं यजेत् । प्रागादीशान्तमष्टसु दिक्षु अध ऊर्ध्वं च प्रादक्षिण्येन, अन्यांस्तु षट्कोणमन्तरेणावरणशक्तीर्देव्यग्रादारभ्य प्रादक्षिण्येनार्चयेदिति सम्प्रदायार्थः ॥२२॥ अग्न्याद्यस्रेषु—चतुरस्रषट्कोणबाह्यवृत्तान्तरालस्थेषु । विद्यादिसप्ताक्षर्यन्तराश्रितैः—तत्तन्नामभिः । एतदुक्तं स्यात्—प्रोक्तानामावरणशक्तीनां सर्वासां मूलविद्याद्यक्षरपुरस्सरैः तत्तन्नामभिः सप्ताक्षर्यन्तैः षोडशच्छदद्वयेपि विद्याक्षरानन्तरं षोडशस्वराक्षरसहितं प्रोक्तक्रमेण पूजयेत् । तेभ्यः—बटुकगणपतिदुर्गाक्षेत्रपालेभ्यः । गन्धादिचोदितैः—वक्ष्यमाणैर्द्रव्यैरिति शेषः ॥२३॥

तत इत्यादिभिः सिद्ध्यन्तीत्यन्तैः पादाधिकैस्त्रिभिः श्लोकैर्देव्या नित्यपूजाक्रमं तत्फलं चोपदिशति । तत्र अङ्गविद्याभ्यां क्लृप्तार्घ्यैः—एतदुक्तं स्यात्—प्राग्वदाधारचषकसलिलानि वह्निसूर्य्यसोमा[illegible]नि बुद्ध्वा तत्षडङ्गमन्त्रैः प्रोक्तक्रमेणाभ्यर्च्य सृष्टार्घ्यो(४) मूलविद्यामेकादशवारं जपित्वा साधितेनार्घ्येण प्राग्वत् सपर्यां कुर्यात् इति । एवं—सर्वासां वक्ष्यमाणानां नित्यानामर्घ(५)क्लृप्तिर्विधेये-

---

(१) तत्समा जपेत् इति मू० पुस्तके पाठः ।
(२) अग्न्याद्यस्त्रिषु इति मू० पुस्तके पाठः ।
(३) दतस्तथा मू० पुस्तके पाठः ।
(४) स्पष्टार्घ्यौ इति टी० पु० पा० ।
(५) मर्घं क्लृप्ति रिति सो० पु० पा० ।

घृताक्तैर्मधुराक्तैर्वा प्रसूनैररुणैः शुभैः ।
अन्नाद्याभ्यां प्रजुहुयात्ततः प्राग्वत् समापयेत् ॥२५॥
एवं नित्यं पूजयितुरायुरारोग्यसम्पदः ।
लोकानुरञ्जनं नारीनृपावर्जनकर्म च ॥२६॥
अपृथक्त्वेन सिद्ध्यन्ति तद्योगान् शृणु सुन्दरि ! ।
महाचमत्कारकरांस्त्रैलोक्यक्षोभणक्षमान् ॥२७॥
पुरा देवी पञ्च कामान् पञ्च ज्ञानात्मकान्निजान् ।
ससर्ज (१) बाणानुक्तांश्च त्रिविधान् प्रागुदीरितान् ॥२८॥

त्यर्थः । प्रागुक्तैरुपचाराद्यैः—सपर्याविशेषैरिति शेषः । तथा—ललिताविद्याहोम-प्रोक्तक्रमवत् ॥२४॥ प्राग्वत् समापयेत् । एतदुक्तं स्यात्—देवतातनौ तत्परिवारशक्तो स्तेजोरूपाः समाविष्टा बुद्ध्वा तां च तेजोरूपिणीं प्रवहन्नासामार्गेण खेचर्या मुद्रया स्वान्तं नीत्वा प्राग्वत् समापयेत् इति । पञ्चदशानां नित्यानां विशेषानुपदेशे सपर्यारम्भे षोडशाक्षरमन्त्रेण बलिप्रदानम् । अवसाने कुरुकुल्लाममाक्षर्यो बलिप्रदानं सर्वावरणादौ देवतापश्चिमभागे प्राग्वत् त्रिपङ्क्तिकस्य नाथ-नवकस्य पूजनं च(२)कुर्यादित्यर्थः ॥२५॥ आवर्जनं—वशीकारः ॥२६॥ अपृथ-क्त्वेन—अनवाप्तत्वेनेत्यर्थः । अत्रापि युगानुरूपमक्षरलक्षं जपित्वा तद्दशांशं तर्पण-होमादिकं च कुर्यादिति ।

तद्योगानित्यादिना प्रागुदीरितानित्यन्तेन त्रिपादाद्येन श्लोकेन पञ्चकामस्त-वनमुखेनैतान् प्रस्तौति । तत्र तद्योगान्—पञ्चकामात्मदेवीमन्त्रयन्त्रयोगान् । महा-चमत्कारकरान्-मनीषितार्थप्रापकत्वतः । चमत्कार—आश्चर्यम् । त्रैलोक्यक्षोभण-क्षमान्—अशेषभुवनप्रथाकरान्, एतत्तद्योगानित्यस्य विशेषणम् ॥२७॥ देवो—कामेश्वरीसम्प्रदायः । मदनोन्मादनेत्यादिशक्तित्वेनोक्तान् पञ्चज्ञानात्मकान् पञ्चे-न्द्रियज्ञानविग्रहान्, सर्वेषां ज्ञानेन्द्रियज्ञानात्मकत्वात् । ससर्ज—तद्रूपेण परिण-तेत्यर्थः । त्रिविधान्—स्थूलसूक्ष्मपरत्वेन । प्रागुदीरितान्—पञ्चमे पटले बाणाः स्युरित्यादिभिः प्रोक्तान् ॥२८॥

---

(१) बहुवक्राख्य इति सो० पुस्तके पाठः ।

(२) तद्योगात् पञ्चकामान् इत्यधिकं टी० पु० पा० ।

तेषां नामानि रूपाणि मन्त्रांश्च क्रमतः शृणु ।
यैर्विश्वं वशमायाति क्षणात्तद्भावनादिना ॥२९॥
प्रथमः कामराजाख्यो द्वितीयोमन्मथस्तथा ।
कन्दर्पस्तत्तृतीयोऽभूत्ततो मकरकेतनः ॥३०॥
मनोभवः पञ्चमः स्यात् नामान्येतानि वै क्रमात् ।
ध्यानं (१)तेषां शृणु प्राज्ञे ! विश्वविक्षोभकारिणाम् ॥३१॥
पीतश्वेतारुणाकारास्त्रयोऽन्यौ धूम्रनीलकौ(२) ।
सर्वे द्विनेत्रा द्विभुजाः स्मेरवक्त्रसरोरुहाः ॥३२॥
पुण्ड्रेक्षुचापपुष्पेषुधरा भूतात्मकाः क्रमात् ।
विश्वाकारा विश्वमनोविक्षोभनियतात्मकाः ॥३३॥
एषां मन्त्रान् शृणु प्राज्ञे ! क्रमादेकाक्षरानपि ।
यैरेकैकैः सङ्गतैश्च(३) यन्त्राणि स्युः पृथक् पृथक् ॥३४॥
सहंसदाहवह्निस्वैः कामराजः समीरितः ।
प्राणोरसावह्नियुतस्तथा स्वेनापि मन्मथः ॥३५॥

तेषां नामानीत्यादिना क्रमादित्यन्तेनार्द्धाधिकेन श्लोकद्वयेन तेषां कामानां नामरूपमन्त्रप्रस्तावपूर्वं नामान्युपदिशति। तत्र तेषां—पञ्चानां कामानाम्। यैः—नामरूपमन्त्रैः। तद्भावनादिना—तेषां नाममन्त्ररूपाणाम्। आदिशब्दोऽभिषेकन्यासादिविषयः ॥२९॥ तत्तृतीयः—तेषु तृतीयः ॥३०॥

ध्यानं इत्यादिना नियतात्मका इत्यन्तेन तेषां ध्येयस्वरूपाण्युपदिशति ॥३१॥ तत्र पीतश्वेतारुणाकारास्त्रयः। द्वौ धूम्रनीलकौ। पञ्चभूतशक्तिरूपत्वात्तत्तद्भूतवर्णाः ॥३२॥ भूतात्मकाः—भूतसामर्थ्यविग्रहाः। विश्वाकाराः—भूतसामर्थ्यरूपत्वात्। विश्वमनोविक्षोभकरत्वं च भूतात्मकत्वादेव ॥३३॥

एषामित्यादिना श्लोकेन तेषां मन्त्रान् यन्त्राणि च प्रस्तौति—तत्र एकैकैः—एकैकाक्षरतः एकैकयन्त्रसङ्गतैः समुदितैः पञ्चभिस्त्रीणि यन्त्राणि ॥३४॥

सहंसेत्यादिना मनोभव इत्यन्तेनार्द्धार्द्धेन श्लोकद्वयेन तेषामेकाक्षरान् पञ्चमन्त्रा-

---

(१) मेषां इति सो० पु० पा०। (२) धूम्रनन्तकौ इति सो पु० पा०।
(३) यैरेकैकस्य मन्त्रैश्च इति मू० पुस्तके पाठः।

शुचिः खसंयुतः प्रोक्तः कन्दर्पोऽम्बुरसायुतम् ।
क्ष्मया स्वेन च सम्प्रोक्तः सोऽयं मकरकेतनः ॥३६॥
सहृद्रयैर्दा(१)हवह्निस्वैरुक्तोभून्मनोभवः(२) ।
भालवक्त्र(३)सहृन्नाभिगुह्येष न्यासतस्त्वमी ॥३७॥
समस्तान्वशगान् कुर्युर्बाणानेष्वेव मूलतः ।
भालान्तं(४) विन्यसेन्नित्यं यः स सर्वाङ्गनास्मरः ॥३८॥
एषां यन्त्राणि सर्वाणि त्रैलोक्यक्षोभणानि च ।
तानि क्रमेण कथयाम्याकर्णय समाहिता ॥३९॥

मुपदिशति। तत्र सहंसदाहवह्निस्वैः—क्लीँकारः कामराजमन्त्र इत्यर्थः। प्राणो-रसावह्नियुतःस्वेनापि-ककारलकारईकारविन्दुभिः क्लीँकारः मन्मथमन्त्रः ॥३५॥ शुचिः खसंयुतः—विन्दुसहितद्वादशस्वरः कंदर्पमन्त्रः। अंबुरसात्क्ष्मया स्वेन च—वकारलकारऊकारविन्दुभिः मकरकेतनः ॥३६॥ हृद्रयैर्दाहवह्निस्वैः—सकारतकाररेफईकारविन्दुभिः स्त्रीँ मनोभवमन्त्रः।

भाल इत्यादिना स्मर इत्यन्तेनार्द्धद्येनैकेन श्लोकेन तन्मन्त्राणां बाणमन्त्राणां च न्यासस्थानक्रममुपदिशति। तत्र भालं—ललाटम्। गुह्यमितिमूलाधारस्थानमुच्यते। अमी—पञ्चकाममन्त्राः ॥३७॥ बाणान्—बाणानां शैवानामेकैकाक्षरान् कूटमन्त्रान्। एष्वेव—उक्तेषु स्थानेषु एव। मूलतः—मूलाधारमारभ्य। एतदुक्तं भवति—पञ्चानां तेषां कामानां प्रत्येकमेकाक्षरभूतान् प्रोक्तान् कूटरूपान् पञ्चमन्त्रान् तत्तन्नाम्नाऽन्वितान् ललाटादिमूलाधारान्तं प्रोक्तेषु पञ्चसु स्थानेषु न्यस्य मूलाधारादिललाटान्तं च प्रोक्तेषु विन्यस्य चतुर्थपटलोक्तानेकाक्षरान् कूटरूपान् पञ्चसङ्ख्यान् शैवबाणमन्त्रान् तत्तत्स्थानादि नमोऽन्तान् विन्यसेदिति ॥३८॥

एषामित्यादिभिः शिवे इत्यन्तैरर्द्धाधिकैः पञ्चभिः श्लोकैस्तेषां कामानां प्रत्येकं क्रमेण पञ्च यन्त्राण्युपदिशति। तत्र—क्रमेण—प्रोक्तकूट(५)मन्त्रक्रमेण ॥३९॥

---

(१) सहृद्यैर्दाह इति सो० पुस्तके पाठः।

(२) स्वैरुक्तो इति सो० पुस्तके पाठः।

(३) भालचक्र स इति सो० पुस्तके पाठः।

(४) लाभान्तं वि इति सो० पुस्तके पाठः।

(५) कूटतन्त्र इति टी० पु० पा०।

तेषु पञ्चसु बीजेषु पुनरुक्तिविवर्जितैः ।
योजयेदष्टभिस्तैस्तैः स्वरान् षोड़श मायया ॥४०॥
अष्टाविंशतिसंयुक्तं शतं तेन(१) भवन्ति वै ।
तैर्यन्त्राणि विधेयानि पञ्चानां क्रमतः शिवे ! ॥४१॥
वृत्तत्रयस्थं(२) षट्कोणं कृत्वा मध्ये स्वमक्षरम् ।
लिखेत् साध्याख्ययोपेतं षट्सु कोणेषु तत् पुनः ॥४२॥

पुनरुक्तिविवर्जितैः—अपुनरावृत्तिरूपैः । अष्टभिः—हकाररेफककारलकार-ऐकारवकारसकारतकारैः तथाविधैरक्षरैरितिशेषः। अत्र ऐकारस्वरयोजनं नाम अकारादिविसर्जनीयान्तानां षोड़शस्वराणां यथाक्रममुच्चारणम्। एवं सर्वत्र स्वरेषु स्वरयोजनमेतच्च स्वराणां स्वातन्त्र्यात्। मायया—विसर्जनीयेन तेषां षोड़शस्वरयोजनेन। एतदुक्तं भवति—तेषु पञ्चसु काममन्त्रेषु अपुनरुक्तैर्हकारादिभिरष्टभिरक्षरैः प्रत्येकं विसर्जनीयान्तान् षोड़श स्वरान् योजयेत् तेनोक्तसङ्ख्याक्षराणि भवन्तीति। ते यथा—हः हाः इत्यादयः। पञ्चत्रिंशदक्षरेषु पुनर्विसर्जनीययोजनम् ॥४०॥ तैः—स्वरविकृताक्षरैः ॥४१॥

वृत्तत्रयस्थमित्यादिना शिवेइत्यन्तेनार्द्धाधिकेन श्लोकद्वयेन पञ्चानां यन्त्राणां स्वरूपमुपदिशति। तत्र स्व—मक्षरम्—पञ्चसु कामकूटाक्षरेषु स्वाभिहितमेकमक्षरम्। एतदुक्तं भवति—इष्टप्रमाणेन भ्रमणेन मध्यसूत्रपुरःसरं वृत्तं निष्पाद्य तद्व्यासार्द्धमानेन ब्रह्मसूत्रवृत्तसन्धिद्वयावष्टम्भेन वृत्तपार्श्वयोर्लाञ्छनानि कृत्वा तेषु वृत्तावधिकं दक्षिणोत्तरं सूत्रद्वयमास्फाल्य तयोः पूर्वसूत्राग्रद्वयवृत्तसन्धिमवलम्ब्य मध्यसूत्रपश्चिमाग्रवृत्तसन्ध्यन्तं सूत्रद्वयमास्फाल्य तद्वत् पश्चिमसूत्रपर्यन्तं तद्द्वयात् मध्यसूत्रपूर्वाग्रवृत्तसन्ध्यवधिसूत्रद्वयमास्फाल्य एवं षट्कोणं कृत्वा तत् षट्कोणं तिर्यग्रेखास्पृष्टास्पृष्टिकया मध्यतोवृत्तं कृत्वा पूर्वलिखितषट्कोणबाह्यवृत्ताद्बहिरेकाङ्गुलान्तरालं क्रमेण वृत्तद्वयं निष्पाद्य सर्वमध्यवृत्तमध्ये कामकूटाक्षर(३)मन्त्रेषु पञ्चसु प्रथमाक्षरभूतां ह्स्क्लें खां सबिन्दुकामालिख्य तस्या रेफगर्भं साध्याख्यां चतुर्थस्वरगर्भं साधकाख्यया मुभयोरन्तरा कर्म च समालिख्य बहिः षट्सु कोणेषु अध-

---

(१) भविष्यति इति मू० ०स्तके पाठः। (२) त्रयस्थ इति सो० पुस्तके पाठः।
(३) क्षरं तन्त्रेषु इति टी० पु० पा०।

विभज्य बिन्दुमायाभ्यामध ऊर्ध्वं लिखेत् क्रमात् ।
वृत्तान्तरालयोर्बाह्ये चतुःषष्ट्या द्विरालिखेत् ॥४३॥
एवं यन्त्राणि पञ्च स्युः पञ्चानां क्रमतः शिवे ! ।
पञ्चभिश्चैकमस्त्यन्यद्यन्त्रं सुमहदद्भुतम् ॥४४॥
द्वितीय जठरे (१)त्वाद्यं सनाम विलिखेत्तयोः ।
बहिस्तृतीयरूपेण षट्कोणेन प्रवेष्टयेत् ॥४५॥
चतुर्थं विलिखेत् कोणेष्वेषु षट्स्वपि पार्वति ! ।
वेष्टयेत् पञ्चमेनैव तद्यन्त्रं सर्वमोहनम् ॥४६॥

स्तनेषु त्रिषु कोणेषु तां ह्स्लें खां सबिन्दुकामालिख्य उपरितनेषु त्रिकोणेषु तामेव विसर्जनीयान्तां समालिख्य षट्कोणबाह्यवृत्तवीथ्यां प्रोक्तस्वरविकृताक्षराणि क्रमेण अग्रात् प्रादक्षिण्येन प्रथमचतुःषष्टिं तद्बाह्यवृत्तवीथ्यां (२ तृतीयचतुःषष्टिमक्षराणि च समालिख्य मनोषितेषु कर्मसु नियुञ्ज्यात् । एवमन्यान्यपि कूटाक्षराणि चत्वारि तथाविधे यन्त्रे प्रोक्तक्रमेण समालिख्य प्रागवत्तत्तद्गर्भाक्षरषोडशकादिकं बाह्य-चतुःषष्टिकद्वयमालिखेत् । एवं पञ्च यन्त्राणि मनीषितेष्वर्थेषु विनियुञ्ज्यात् ॥४२॥४३॥

पञ्चभिरित्यादिना सर्वमोहनं इत्यन्तेनार्द्धाद्येन श्लोकद्वयेन प्रोक्तकूटमन्त्रपञ्चक-समुदायात्मकं षष्ठं यन्त्रमुपदिशति ॥४४॥ तत्र द्वितीयकूटजठरे—मन्मथकूटजठरे । आद्यं—कामराजकूटम् । सनाम—साध्यसाकनामकर्मसहितं साधकनामकर्म-सहितम् । तृतीयरूपेण—कन्दर्पकूटरूपेण । षट्कोणेन—कन्दर्पमन्त्ररूपस्य द्वादश स्वरस्य लिपिवशात् त्रिकोणात्मकत्वं, तद्युगलयोगतः षट्कोणत्वम् ॥४५॥ चतुर्थं—मकरकेतनकूटम् । पञ्चमेन - मनोभवकूटेन । तद्यन्त्रं—एवं निर्मितमितिशेषः । एतदुक्तं स्यात्—ह्स्लें खां प्रागवन्नामसहितां समालिख्य तां प्रथमभूतां द्वितीयस्य कूटाक्षरस्य गर्भगां कृत्वा तद्द्वितीयतृतीयेन एकाक्षररूपेण ३ त्रिकोणपुटितरूप-षट्कोणेनावेष्ट्य तस्य षट्सु कोणेषु चतुर्थं मकरकेतनकूटाक्षरमालिख्य तत्षट्-कोणं पञ्चमकूटाक्षरवह्निस्थानगं यथा स्यात्तथा(कोणं) गुरूक्तक्रमतः समालिख्य वाञ्छितार्थेषु विनियुञ्ज्यादिति ॥४६॥

---

(१) चापं न नाम इति मू० पुस्तके पाठः । (२) द्वितीय इति टी० पु० पा० ।
(३) एकाक्षररूपेण इति बं० पु० पा० ।

तस्यापि परतो बाह्ये तैरावेष्ट्य पुरोदितैः।
यन्त्रान्तरं तु जनयेद्बहिर्मातृकयाऽपि च ॥४७॥
यन्त्राण्यष्टौ भवन्त्येवं पञ्च कामात्मकानि वै।
तैरसाध्यं जगत्स्वेषु न(१) किञ्चिन्न कदाचन ॥४८॥
मनुजं मनुजेशं वा महिलां वा मदाविलाम्।
अष्टसूत्रेषु मध्यस्थं भावयेत् स्वेन तेजसा ॥४९॥
एकीभूतं जपेदेतान्यक्षराण्यपि पञ्च तैः।
तेन ते वशगाः क्षिप्रं यावज्जीवं(२)सुनिश्चितम् ॥५०॥

तस्यापीत्यादिना कदाचन इत्यन्तेन श्लोकद्वयेन सप्तममष्टमं च यन्त्रद्वयं तत्सङ्ख्यानिगमनं तदनुभावं चोपदिशति। तत्र तस्य—प्रोक्तरूपस्य षष्ठस्य महायन्त्रस्य। परतः—परं सप्तमं यन्त्रमित्यर्थः। पुरोदितैः—तैः स्वरवर्ज्जितैरष्टभिरक्षरैरित्यर्थः। एतदुक्तं भवति—षष्ठयन्त्रबाह्याक्षरस्पृष्टास्पृष्टं वृत्तं कृत्वा। तद्बहिः—प्रागवदेकैकाङ्गुलान्तरालं वृत्तद्वयं विधाय यन्त्रबाह्यवृत्तत्रयवीथीद्वये पूर्ववत् चतुःषष्टिद्वयं समालिखेत्। एतत् सप्तमं यन्त्रं, यन्त्रान्तरं—अष्टमं यन्त्रम्। बहिः प्रोक्तचतुःषष्टिद्वयवेष्टनादितिशेषः। मातृकया अकारादिक्षकारान्तैरेकपञ्चाशदक्षरैरावेष्टनादित्यर्थः। अपिचेति (च) समुच्चये। एतदुक्तं भवति—सप्तमयन्त्रस्वरूपस्य बहिरप्येकाङ्गुलान्तरालं वृत्तं विधाय तस्यां वीथ्यां प्रागवदादिक्षान्तान्यक्षराणि समालिखेदेतदष्टमं यन्त्रमिति॥४७॥ तेषां पञ्चानां कामानां प्रोक्तध्येयविग्रहेण स्थूलत्वं, प्रोक्तमन्त्रपञ्चकविग्रहेण सूक्ष्मत्वं, प्रोक्तपञ्चभूतसामर्थ्यरूपपञ्चेन्द्रियप्रभवज्ञानपञ्चकविग्रहेण पररूपत्वं च बुद्ध्वा तैरसाध्यकथनमित्यादि सम्प्रदायरहस्यार्थः ॥४८॥

मनुजं इत्यादिभिर्मुद्रया इत्यन्तैः पञ्चभिः श्लोकैः प्रोक्तानामष्टानां यन्त्राणां मनोषितार्थयोगेन ज्ञानान्तरभावनया फलावाप्तिमुपदिशति। तत्र मदाविलां—गन्धगजवत्। अष्टसूत्रेषु—प्रत्येकमितिशेषः। स्वेन तेजसा—स्वात्मस्वरूपेण ॥४९॥

---

(१) न किञ्चन इति मू० पुस्तके पाठः।

(२) निश्चितमिति मू० पु० पा०।

तेषु(१) मध्यस्थमाध्यस्थमात्मसाध्ये जपारुणम् ।
तन्मन्त्रार्णप्रकाशैश्च तथाऽरुणतरैर्वृतम् ॥५१॥
भावयन्नात्मना ग्रस्तं जपेत्तान्यक्षराण्यपि ।
तेन ते वशगाः क्षिप्रं दद्युः प्राणान् धनानि च ॥५२॥
तस्य षष्ठस्य मध्यस्थबीजे मन्त्रेण वेष्टयेत् ।
प्राग्वन्निजसुषुम्णान्तर्भावयेद्योनिमुद्रया ॥५३॥
एवं(२) तदष्टमध्यस्थं कुम्भं कृत्वा यथाविधि ।
तेनाभिषिञ्चेत्(३) दौर्भाग्यरोगदारिद्र्यमुक्तये ॥५४॥
कुचन्दनैर्वा सिन्दूरैर्गैरिकैर्दरदैस्तु वा ।
कृत्वा चक्राष्टकं भूमौ फलकायां शिलासु च ॥५५॥

एकीभूतमित्यत्र भावनाप्रकारोगुरुमुखादवगन्तव्यः। तैर्मन्त्रैरेकीभूतमित्यन्वयः। मन्त्रतेजोभिरेकीभूतमित्यर्थः। तेन - प्रयोगेण ॥५०॥ तेष्वित्यादिः श्लोकः स्पष्टार्थः ॥५१॥ प्राणान् धनानि च—किमुतान्यवस्तूनीत्यर्थः ॥५२॥ मध्यस्थबीजे—कामराजमन्मथकूटद्वयमित्यर्थः। मन्त्रेण—कामेश्वरीविद्यया। अत्र गुरुमुखावाप्तार्थविशेषस्तु मयोच्यते। यथा षष्ठस्य मध्यबीज इत्युक्त्या प्रोक्तानामष्टानां यन्त्राणां मध्यस्थं बीजं कामेश्वरीनित्याविद्यया वेष्टयेत्, तेनाप्यष्टौ यन्त्राणि भवन्ति। एवं सम्भूय षोड़श यन्त्राणि स्युः। अत्र पञ्चकामप्रसङ्गात् कामेश्वरीविद्यया वेष्टनसम्बन्धो ज्ञापित इति प्राग्वत्—मन्त्रार्णप्रकाशैरित्याद्युक्तप्रकारेण। योनिमुद्रया—उपरिष्टाद्वक्ष्यमाणया सुषुम्णान्तर्मूलाधारादि ब्रह्मरन्ध्रान्तं वह्निसूर्यसोमात्मकतेजस्त्रयात्मकस्वरूपेण गमागमानुसन्धानस्य योनिमुद्राबन्ध इति सामयिकी संज्ञा, तया एषां षोड़शानामन्येषां च यन्त्राणां साधारणरूपतेति सम्प्रदायः ॥५३॥

एतदित्यादिना श्लोकेन प्रोक्तेष्वष्टसु यन्त्रेषु सम्प्रदायप्राप्तेष्वष्टसु यन्त्रेषु च कुम्भस्थापनं तेनाभिषेकं तत्फलं चोपदिशति, तत्र यथाविधि—एतदुक्तं भवति। तन्तुवेष्टनत्रिलोहधान्यनवरत्नप्रदीपमूलपल्लवमुखपिधानवासोयुगलवेष्टनाष्टत्रिंशत्कलावर्तनपूर्वकं उद्देश्यं तत्क्रमेणार्चयेदिति ॥ ५४ ॥

---

(१) षष्ठस्य मध्यमात्मसाध्यं इति मू० पुस्तके पाठः।

(२) एतदष्टकम इति मू० पुस्तके पाठः।

(३) भिषिंच्य इति सो पु पा।

मध्ये विद्यावृतं कृत्वा तत्राऽऽवाह्याभिपूज्य ताम् ।
कामेश्वरीतद्व्यस्थो जपेल्लक्षं पयोव्रतः ॥५६॥
तेनास्य पूर्वजन्मान्त(१) दुष्कृतान्यपयान्ति वै ।
अस्मिन् जन्मनि सल्लक्ष्मीमवाप्य सुखमेधते ॥५७॥
नरं नारीं नृपं चान्यं नगरं वाऽथ पत्तनम् ।
देशं जनपदं विश्वं तन्मध्ये प्रविलिख्य तत् ॥५८॥
पूजयेदरुणैः पुष्पैर्गन्धैः काश्मीरसंयुतैः(२) ।
नैवेद्यैः कदलीदुग्धशर्करापायसादिभिः ॥५९॥
मण्डलं वा तदर्द्धं (३) वा सप्तवासरमेव वा ।
कन्दर्पसमसौभाग्यो जायते नियतं नरः ॥६०॥
सुवर्णादिषु संलिख्य धारणा(४)द्धरणीतले ।
लक्ष्मीकान्तिधनारोग्यैरायुः पूर्णमवाप्नुयात् ॥६१॥

कुचन्दनैरित्यादिभिरेधते इत्यन्तैस्त्रिभिः श्लोकैर्यन्त्रलेखनद्रव्यविशेषैस्तेषु कामेश्वरीनित्यार्चनक्रमतः फलान्युपदिशति। तत्र चक्राष्टकमित्यनेन रहस्ययन्त्रात्मकमप्युक्तं भवति ॥५५॥ मध्ये विद्यावृतं—प्राग्वत् । तत्र - प्रत्येकं यन्त्रषोडशकस्य मध्येषु। अभिपूज्य- उक्तक्रमतः। पयोव्रतः—क्षीराहारी ॥५६॥ पूर्वजन्मान्तदुष्कृतानि—चिरकालोपात्तानि दुष्कर्माणि इत्यर्थः। अस्मिन् जन्मनि—तादात्विककाले ॥५७॥

नरमित्यादिभिराप्नुयादित्यन्तैश्चतुर्भिः श्लोकैस्तैरेव यन्त्रैर्विश्ववशीकरणोपायमुपदिशति। तत्र तन्मध्ये—प्रोक्तयन्त्रषोडशकस्य मध्ये। तत्—यन्त्रम् ॥५८॥ पायसादिभिः—अत्रादिशब्देनापूपादिकं कथयति ॥५९॥ मण्डलं- मण्डलमिति सप्तानां वाराणां प्रत्येकमङ्गाङ्गिभावेन सप्तविधत्वादेकोनपञ्चाशद्दिनानि सर्वैरुच्यन्ते ॥६०॥ सुवर्णादिष्वित्यत्रादिशब्देन रजतताम्रभूर्जपत्रादीन्युच्यन्ते। संलिख्य—यन्त्रषोडशकमिति शेषः ॥६१॥

---

(१) जन्मपूर्वान्त इति सो० पु० पाठः ।　　(२) संभवैः इति सो० पु० पा० ।

(३) तदूर्ध्वं इति मू० पु० पाठः ।　　(४) धारणाधर इति म० पु० पा० ।

अनावृत्तैस्तु विद्यार्णैः षोड़शस्वरयोजनात् ।
ज्ञानवल्या शतं वर्णा जायन्ते मन्त्रसम्भवाः ॥६२॥
स्वराणां सर्वमन्त्रेषु योजनं केन हेतुना ।
क्रियते परमेशान ! तन्मे कथय साम्प्रतम् ॥६३॥
स्वराः षोड़श देवेशि ! व्यञ्जनानि तथा पुनः ।
पञ्चविंशत् समाख्यातं तयोरन्योन्यसङ्गतेः ॥६४॥
भारत्या देहभूतैस्तैर्व्यञ्जनैः स्वरयोजनम् ।
तत्प्राणयोजनं विद्धि रहस्यं परमेश्वरि (१) ! ॥६५॥
भारत्या वर्णरूपाया हसौ नेत्रे समीरिते ।
प्राणाः स्वराः समाख्याता विन्दुसर्गौ तु चेतना ॥६६॥
अन्यान्यवयवानि(२) स्युरन्यानि परमेश्वरि ! ।
तेन तद्युक्तितो वर्णाः प्रसीदन्ति न चाऽन्यथा ॥६७॥
विन्दुसर्गौ हसौ तुर्यस्वरश्चेति च पञ्चमम् (३) ।
भारत्या मातृकादेहे विद्धि चैतन्यजृम्भणम् ॥६८॥

अनावृत्तैरित्यादिभिः सिद्धिदा इत्यन्तैर्दशभिः श्लोकैः कामेश्वरीमन्त्रे(४) अनावृत्तैरेकारादिभिर्द्वादशभिरक्षरैः षोड़शस्वरयोजनं अन्येषामपि सर्वेषां मन्त्राणां तथा स्वरयोजनं तद्वासनां चोपदिशति। तत्र—अनावृत्तैः— अपुनरावृत्तैः। विद्यार्णैः कामेश्वरीनित्याविद्याक्षरैर्द्वादशभिरिति शेषः। तानि कानि। ऐं सकलहरनतयमदव इति। अत्र पूर्वलकाराङ्गीकारात् लकार उपेक्षितः ललयोरभेदात् ॥६२॥ योजनं—अपुनरावृत्तैरक्षरैरिति शेषः। तत्—कारणं कथयेत्यन्वयः ॥६३॥ व्यञ्जनानि—कादिक्षान्तानि। पञ्चविंशदिति व्यञ्जनविशेषणम्। समाख्यातं—तयोः स्वरव्यञ्जनयोरन्योन्यसङ्गतेरेव समाख्यातमित्यर्थः ॥६४॥ कथमित्यपेक्षायामाह—भारत्याः इति। भारत्या—मातृकायाः। देहभूतैः—अवयवभूतैः। तत्प्राणयोजनं—भारत्याः प्राणयोजनम् ॥६५॥ हसौ—हकारसकारौ। नेत्रे—शिवशक्तिरूपत्वात्। चेतना—चिद्रूपम् ॥६६॥ तेन—कारणेन। तद्युक्तितः—हकारसकारस्वरैर्योगतः ॥६७॥

---

(१) परमं शिवे इति मू० पु० पाठः। (२) अन्योन्यावयवानि इति सो० पु० पा०।
(३) ऽस्वकं इति मू० पु० पा०। (४) यन्त्रे इति व० पु० पा०।

तेन तैर्हीनरूपास्तु मन्त्रा विद्यास्तथाऽपरे।
निष्प्राणदेहवत् कार्यकारणेष्वक्षमाः स्मृताः ॥६९॥
तेन सर्वत्र तु मया स्वरैर्योग उदीर्यते।
ये ये मन्त्राः प्रोक्तवर्णविहीनास्तेषु योजयेत् ॥७०॥
तेन ते बलवन्तः स्युः कार्येषु च फलान्विताः।
तस्मात् सर्वत्र संयोगात् स्वरैः सर्वार्थसिद्धिदाः ॥७१॥
एवं तैरेव जायन्ते यन्त्राणि सबलानि वै।
द्वात्रिंशद्विनियोगाऽंस्य वच्ये तेषामनुक्रमात् ॥७२॥
वृत्तद्वयान्तः षट्कोणं कृत्वा मध्ये निजेप्सितम्।
मायागर्भं समालिख्य वेष्टयेन्मातृकाक्षरैः ॥७३॥

विन्दुसर्गावित्यादिना श्लोकेन उक्तमर्थं निगमयति। चैतन्यजृम्भणं—चैतन्यप्रसरः ॥६८॥६९॥ तैः—पञ्चभिः परतेजोरूपदेवतायाः। प्रोक्तवर्णविहीनाः - प्रोक्तवर्णपञ्चकविहीनाः। योजयेत्तद्वर्णपञ्चकमितिशेषः ॥७०॥ ते—मन्त्राद्याः। अत्र दशभिः श्लोकैरेतदुक्तं भवति—आदिक्षान्ताक्षररूपमातृकाविग्रहायाः भारत्याः सर्वावयवभूतेषु सर्वाक्षरेषु स्थितेष्वपि तुरीयस्वरविन्दुस्वरा हकारसकारषोड़शस्वराक्षराणां देहिनां देहेषु प्राणचैतन्यादिविजृम्भणवत् कार्यकारणस्वाहर्णपञ्चकविहीनेषु तत्पञ्चकयोजनात् सर्वत्र स्वरयोगेन च सर्वेषां बलयोजनं च भवति ॥७१॥

एवमित्यादिना श्लोकेन कामेश्वरीविद्यायाः स्वरविकृते(२)रक्षरैर्द्वात्रिंशद्यन्त्राणि प्रस्तौति। तत्र तैः - कामेश्वरीविद्यायाः स्वरवर्द्धितैर्द्वानवत्यधिकशतसङ्ख्याक्षरैरित्यर्थः ॥७२॥

वृत्तद्वयेत्यादिना श्लोकेन द्वात्रिंशद्यन्त्रसाधारणं स्वरूपमुपदिशति। तत्र मायागर्भं—ह्रींलेखामध्ये। समालिख्य प्राग्वत्। एतदुक्तं भवति—प्राग्वद्भ्रमेण(३) वृत्तं निष्पाद्य तत्र प्राग्वत् षट्कोणं कृत्वा तन्मध्ये ह्रींलेखां प्रोक्तक्रमेण वाञ्छितार्थलिपिगर्भामालिख्य षट्कोणकोणेषु षट्सु अग्रादारभ्य प्रादक्षिण्येन कामेश्वरीविद्यायाः स्वरविकृतेषु द्वानवत्यधिकशतसङ्ख्याक्षरेषु आदि-

---

(१) सर्वते इति सो० पु० पा०। (२) स्वरवर्द्धितैरिति वं० पु० पा०।

(३) क्रमेण इति० वं० पु० पा०।

प्रथमे कनकावाप्तिर्द्वितीये भूषणोदयः ।
तृतीये कन्यकासिद्धिश्चतुर्थे भूपरिग्रहः ॥७४॥
पञ्चमे वाहनावाप्तिः षष्ठे स्त्रीवश्यमीरितम् ।
सप्तमे भवनावाप्तिरष्टमे धेनुसङ्गमः ॥७५॥
नवमे वशयेद्भूपं दशमे वारणं हयम् ।
एकादशेन विजयी नरः समरसीमनि ॥७६॥
वादेषु व्यवहारेषु द्यूतेषु विविधेष्वपि ।
द्वादशेऽभीप्सिताऽऽवाप्तिः परेणारिविनाशनम् ॥७७॥
गजवाजिखरोष्ट्राणां नरगोमृगपक्षिणाम् ।
भुजङ्गमेषमहिषवाजिनान्त्वाशु (१)नाशनम् ॥७८॥
तत्तत्त्वचि (२) च तद्रक्तैर्लिखितं तत्र तत्र च ।
स्थापितं मण्डलान्मासात् सप्तराचाद्थापि वा ॥७९॥
चतुर्दशेन वृष्टिः स्यात् परेण जृम्भणं रिपोः ।
क्रोधवैरसमुद्योगगमनादेरपि ध्रुवम् ॥८०॥

षट्कमालिख्य वृत्ताद्बहिरेकाङ्गुलान्तरालं वृत्तं निष्पाद्य तद्वीथ्यां प्राग्वदादिक्षान्तान्यक्षराणि लिखेत्। एतत् प्रथमं यन्त्रम्। अस्यैव यन्त्रस्य षट्सु कोणेषु पूर्वयन्त्रलिखिताक्षरषट्कादुपरितनाक्षरषट्कमालिखेत्। एतत् द्वितीयं यन्त्रम्(१)। एवं तेषु षट्सु कोणेषु क्रमेण षडक्षरत आसमाप्ति लेखनात् सम्भूय द्वात्रिंशद्यन्त्राणि क्रियन्त इति ॥७३॥

प्रथमइत्यादिभिर्यन्त्रशक्तय इत्यन्तैरष्टादशभिः श्लोकैर्द्वात्रिंशद्यन्त्राणामसाधारणानि फलान्युपदिशति। तत्र सर्वाणि यन्त्राणि प्रत्येकं सर्वाभीष्टप्रदानि। अमितावाप्तिरित्यादीनि अमितावाप्तिरित्यादिनियमात्तदसाधारणत्वात्। विविधेषु सजीवनिर्जीवभेदतः। ॥७४—७६॥ परेण—त्रयोदशेन। गजादीनां नाशनं त्रयोदशेन यन्त्रेण ॥७७॥७८॥

---

(१) वाजिनां पशुनाशनं इति म० पु० पा० (२) तत्तद्विच: इति सो० पु० पा०

षोड़शेन घृतेनाम्नौ (१) भूताद्यैर्नैव बाध्यते ।
ततः परेण यन्त्रेण खातेन धरणीतले (२) ॥८१॥
रक्षा भवति सर्वत्र प्राणिनां भवति ध्रुवम् ।
अनन्तराभ्यां खननात् कलहोद्वेगयोर्द्वयोः (३) ॥८२॥
सस्यानां (४) बहुभिः क्लेशैर्नाशः स्याद्भूरुहामपि ।
देशानामपि चान्योन्यकलहात् पीड़नं भवेत् ॥८३॥
अनन्तरेण यन्त्रेण विरोधो भूभुजां भवेत् ।
राष्ट्रसन्धितले तस्य खननेनाल्पकालतः ॥८४॥
एकविंशेन यन्त्रेण रोगार्ता वैरिणो ध्रुवम् ।
द्वाविंशेन गवां रोगस्त्रयोविंशेन दन्तिनाम् ॥८५॥
चतुर्विंशेन वाहानां पञ्चविंशेन भूभुजाम् ।
षड्विंशेन प्रधानानां रोगावाप्तिर्दृढ़ं भवेत् ॥८६॥
सप्तविंशेन तेषान्तु प्रोक्तानां क्लेशनाशनम् ।
अष्टाविंशेन यन्त्रेण कृत्या प्रतिनिवर्तते ॥८७॥
धारणाद्भूषु खननात् वृक्षाग्रादिषु बन्धनात् ।
तड़ागकूपवाप्यादिष्वर्पणाद्याति सा ध्रुवम् ॥८८॥
ततः परेण यन्त्रेण वाग्मी मूकोऽपि जायते ।
तत ऊर्ध्वेन यन्त्रेण वैरिवाक्स्तम्भनं भवेत् ॥८९॥
एकत्रिंशेन यन्त्रेण वाहानां दन्तिनामपि ।
रक्षा भवति तद्भूषु खननाद्धारणादपि ॥९०॥

तत्रतत्र — गजादीनामालानस्थानेषु । मण्डलात् — प्रागवत् ॥७९॥८०॥८१॥ खननात् । सस्यादीनां स्थानेष्वित्यर्थः ॥८२॥ प्रोक्तानामत्र प्रकरणे क्लेशनाशनम् ॥८३॥८४॥८५॥

---

(१) घृतेनाश्नी इति मू० पु० पा० ।   (२) शतेन धरणीतलम् इति मू० पु० पा० ।

(३) अन्येन्तरानन्तराभ्यां खननात् भृतर्गं द्वयम् इति मू० पु० पा० ।

(४) संख्यापनामिति मू० पु० पा० ।

द्वाविंशेनाम्बुधौ पोता न क्लिश्यन्ति कदाचन ।
पारं प्रयान्ति(१) चाऽक्लेशाद्दिचिवा यन्त्रशक्तय: ॥९१॥
षोड़शानां तु नित्यानां प्रत्येकं तिथिषु क्रमात् ।
तत्तत्तिथौ तद्भजनं जपहोमार्चनादिना ॥९२॥
घृतं च शर्करा दुग्धमपूपं कदलीफलम् ।
क्षौद्रं गुड़ं नालिकेरं फलं लाजां तिलं दधि ॥९३॥
पृथुकं चणकं मुद्गं पायसं च निवेदयेत् ।
प्रतिपत्तिथिमारभ्य क्रमात्पञ्चदशस्वपि ॥९४॥
कामेश्वर्यादिशक्तीनां सर्वासामपि चोदिताम् (२) ।
आद्याया ललितायास्तु सर्वाण्येतानि सर्वदा ॥९५॥
निवेदयेच्च जुहुयाद्दद्यात् दद्यान्नृणामपि ।
विद्याशक्तिमतां नित्यमभीष्टावाप्तयेऽनिशम् ॥९६॥
तत्तद्दिद्याचरप्रोक्तमौषधं तत्प्रमाणत: ।
संपिष्य गुटिकां कृत्वा ताभि: सर्वत्र साधयेत् ॥९७॥

८६॥८७॥ प्रोक्तानां धारणादिति । सर्वत्र यन्त्राणि धारणस्थापनार्चनाद्यै: फलप्रदानीत्यर्थ: ॥८८॥८९॥९०॥९१॥

षोड़शानामित्यादिना श्लोकेन प्रतिपदादिपञ्चदश्यन्तासु तिथिषु तत्तत्तिथिनित्याभजनक्रममुपदिशति । तत्र जपहोमार्चनादिना – आदिशब्देन तर्पणाऽभिषेका उच्यन्ते ॥९२॥

घृतमित्यादिभिरनिशमित्यन्तैश्चतुर्भि: श्लोकै: पञ्चदशसु तिथिषु पञ्चदशनिवेद्यद्रव्याणि तद्दिनयोगप्रकारांश्चोपदिशति । तत्र क्रमादिति । शक्तितिथिनिवेद्यद्रव्याणां प्रत्येकं क्रमं दर्शयति । सर्वाण्येतानि—निवेद्यद्रव्यादीनि । सर्वदासर्वा– अपि पञ्चदशनित्यामयत्वात् ॥९३॥९४॥९५॥९६॥

---

(१) प्रयान्ति वै इति सो० पुस्तके पा० ।

(२) चोदितमिति सो० पु० पा० ।

अर्घ्यंवत्तर्पणं नित्यं स्नानं पानं च भोजनम् ।
पटीरसंयुतं भाले धारणं सर्वसिद्धिकृत् ॥९८॥
राज्ञां विशेषतो रक्षां कुर्यादेतैस्तु नित्यशः ।
स्नाने पाने धारणे च गुलिकायोजनेन वै ॥९९॥
रोगापमृत्युकृत्यादिदोषा ग्रहसमुद्भवाः ।
न बाधन्ते ततो नित्यमर्चयेत् स्वगृहे क्वचित् ॥१००॥
एषा रसमयी व्याप्तिरिति सम्यक्समीरिता ।
अस्या निष्कालनाच्चित्ते(१) तत्तत्त्वं स्वात्मसात्कृतम् ॥१०१॥

इति श्रीषोडशनित्यातन्त्रेषु श्रीकादिमते सप्तमं पटलं परिपूर्णं परामृष्टम् ॥ ७ ॥

तत्तदित्यादिभिः क्वचित् इत्यन्तैः श्लोकैः सर्वासां विद्यानां तत्तदक्षरौषधिभिर्गुलिकानिर्माणं तद्विनियोगं तत्फलं चोपदिशति । तत्र—तत्प्रमाणतः—तत्तदक्षरावृत्तिसंख्यामानतः ॥९७॥ पटीरं—चन्दनम् ॥९८॥ एतैः—गुलिकाकृतैरौषधैः ॥९९॥ क्वचिद्—देवतासपर्यास्थाने ॥१००॥१०१॥

इति श्रीषोडशनित्यातन्त्रेषु श्रीकादिमते प्रपञ्चसारसिंहराजप्रकाशाभिधानेन सुभगानन्दनाथेन विरचितायां मनोरमाख्यायां व्याख्यायां कामेश्वरीनित्याभिधानप्रकाशपरं सप्तमं पटलं परिपूर्णं परामृष्टम् ॥ ७ ॥

ग्रन्थसङ्ख्या—

यन्त्राणि स्युः सप्तमेऽष्टौ चत्वारिंशच्च सङ्ख्यया ।
व्याख्याग्रन्थाः सत्रिपादाः चतुर्दशशतद्वयम् ॥ १ ॥

---

(१) तस्या निष्कालनाच्चित्ते इति मू० पु० पा० ।

अथ अष्टमं पटलम् ।

अथ षोड़शनित्यासु तृतीयां भगमालिनीम् ।
शृणु देवि ! प्रवक्ष्यामि साङ्गां सावरणां क्रमात् ॥१॥
तदङ्गान्यथ तद्ध्यानं तदावरणदेवताः ।
तत्पूजायाः क्रमं होमं यन्त्राणि विविधानि च ॥२॥
तन्मन्त्रोद्धार उदितः पूर्वमेव मया तव ।
अङ्गानि मन्त्रवर्णैः स्यादाद्येन हृदुदीरितम् ॥३॥
ततश्चतुर्भिः शीर्षं स्यात् शिखा त्रिभिरुदीरिता ।
चतुष्टयत्रयैः शेषाण्यङ्गानि षडिति क्रमात् ॥४॥
अरुणामरुणाकल्पां सुन्दरीं सुस्मितान‍नाम् ।
त्रिनेत्रां बाहुभिः षड्भिरुपेतां कमलासनाम् ॥५॥

अथ अष्टमं पटलम् ।

पूर्वस्मिन् सप्तमे पटले द्वितीयायाः कामेश्वरीनित्याया विधानमुपदिश्यानन्तरं तृतीयाया भगमालिनीनित्याया विधानक्रममुपदिशति। अथ षोड़शेत्यादिना अस्य सा इत्यन्तेन श्लोकशतरूपेणाष्टमेन पटलेन । तत्राऽथ षोड़शेत्यादिना विविधानि चेत्यन्तेन श्लोकद्वयेन पटलार्थानुद्दिशति ॥ २ ॥

तन्मन्त्रोद्धारइत्यादिना क्रमादित्यन्तेन श्लोकद्वयेन षड़ङ्गन्यासक्रममुपदिशति । तत्र पूर्वं तृतीयपटले । अङ्गानि—षट् न्यसेदिति शेषः । आद्येन—मूल विद्याया आद्येनाक्षरेण ॥३॥ चतुष्टयत्रयैः—चतुर्भिश्चतुर्भिरक्षरैः । शेषाण्यङ्गानि कवचनेत्रास्त्राणि । अत्रापि प्राग्वज्जातियोजनं कुर्यात् ॥४॥

अरुणामित्यादिभिर्मदालसाभिरित्यन्तैस्त्रिभिः श्लोकैर्देव्याः सपरिवाराया नित्यपूजाध्यानमुपदिशति, तत्र कमलासनाम्—अम्बुजासने स्थिताम् । वामबाहुभिरूर्ध्वादि-

कल्हारपाशपुण्ड्रेचुकोदण्डान्वामबाहुभिः।
दधानां दक्षिणैः पद्ममङ्कुशं पुष्पसायकम् ॥६॥
तथाविधाभिः(१) परितो वृतां शक्तिगणैस्तुतैः।
अक्षरोत्थाभिरन्याभिः स्मरोन्मादमदात्मभिः ॥७॥
पञ्चत्रिंशच्छतार्णैस्तै रूपिणीशक्तिपञ्चकम्(२)।
सप्ताक्षरीं च संयोज्य शक्तीस्तत्सङ्ख्यका यजेत् ॥८॥
मदनां मोहिनीं लोलां जम्भिनीमुद्यमां शुभाम्।
ल्हादिनीं द्राविणीं प्रीतिं रतिं रक्तां मनोरमाम् ॥९॥
सर्वोन्मादां सर्वसुखामनङ्गा(३)मभितोद्यमाम्।
अनल्पां व्यक्तविभवां विविधक्षोभविग्रहे ॥१०॥
एताः स्युः शक्तयः पञ्चपञ्चाशद्भिः शतंद्वयम्।
ताभिर्वृतां तु तां देवीं पूजयेद्वाञ्छिताप्तये ॥११॥

क्रमतः ॥६॥ तथाविधाभिः शक्तिगणैरित्युक्तिः स्वातन्त्र्यात्। अन्याभिः—मदनामित्याद्याभिरक्षरशक्तिव्यतिरिक्ताभिः। स्मरोन्मादमदात्मभिः स्मरोन्मादश्च मदश्च येषां एतद्विशेषणं सर्वशक्तिगणसाधारणम् (४) ॥ ७ ॥

(एवं) पञ्चत्रिंशदित्यादिना श्लोकेन देव्याः परिवारभूता मन्त्राक्षरात्मिकाः पञ्चत्रिंशच्छतसङ्ख्याताः शक्तीस्तावत्सङ्ख्यास्तद्विद्याश्चोपदिशति। एतदुक्तं भवति—सबिन्दुकं द्वादशस्वरमुच्चार्य तदनु मन्त्राक्षराणि पञ्चत्रिंशच्छतसङ्ख्याकानि क्रमतः प्रत्येकमुच्चार्य तदुपरि रूपिणीशक्तिपादुकां पूजयामीत्युच्चरेत् तेन पञ्चत्रिंशदधिकशतविद्याक्षरसङ्ख्याका विद्यास्तावत्सङ्ख्याः शक्तयश्च सम्भवन्ति ॥८॥

मदनामित्यादिभिर्वाञ्छिताप्तय इत्यन्तैस्त्रिभिः श्लोकैर्विंशतिशक्तिभिर्मन्त्राक्षरशक्तिभिश्चावरणद्वयमुपदिशति। तत्र विविधक्षोभविग्रहे—विविधविग्रहा क्षोभविग्रहा च ॥९॥१०॥ एताः स्युः शक्तय इति। मदनाद्याभिर्विंशतिशक्तिभिरक्षरो-

(१) तथाविधापि इति मू० पु० पा०।
(२) शक्तिपञ्चमम् इति मू० पु० पा०।
(३) सुखासीना मभङ्गामिति मू० पु० पा०।
(४) सर्वशक्तिगावरण साधारणमिति मो० पु० पा०।

अथ पूजाक्रमं देवि ! शृणु सर्वार्थदायकम् ।
येन विश्वं वशी भूयादपि स्थावरजङ्गमम् ॥१२॥
चतुरस्रद्वयं कृत्वा कुर्याद्द्वारं तु पश्चिमे ।
तन्मध्येऽब्जं पञ्चदलं कृत्वा तत्कर्णिकागतम् ॥१३॥
योनिद्वयं(१) तयोर्मध्ये तिर्यग्रेखाविधानतः ।
पञ्चत्रिंशच्छतं सङ्ख्यायोनयः(२) परितःस्थिताः ॥१४॥
अग्रादिलोमगास्तास्तु शक्तीः संस्थाप्य पूजयेत् ।
मध्ये वृत्तत्रयं कुर्यात्†तत्र विंशतिरेखया ॥१५॥
निष्पाद्य तावतीर्योनीर्मदनाद्याः समर्चयेत् ।
वृत्तान्तराले त्वभितो यजेदङ्गानि षट् क्रमात् ॥१६॥

त्याभिः शक्तिभिश्च पञ्चपञ्चाशच्छतं शक्तय इत्यर्थः । (३)द्वयं – आवरणयोरितिशेषः । प्रोक्तसङ्ख्याः शक्तयः—प्रोक्तक्रमेण आवरणद्वयमित्यर्थः ॥११॥

अथ पूजेत्यादिभिर्नराधिपानित्यन्तैरर्द्धाधिकैस्त्रयोदशभिः श्लोकैर्देव्या नित्यपूजाक्रमं तत्फलानि चोपदिशति । तत्र येन – पूजाक्रमेण ॥१२॥ चतुरस्रद्वयमित्यादिभिः क्रमादित्यन्तैश्चतुर्भिः श्लोकैरेतदुक्तं भवति—अन्तर्बहिर्विभागेन चतुरङ्गुलान्तरालां समचतुरस्रां वीथीं कृत्वा तस्याः पश्चिमदिग्भागतः मध्ये द्वारं कृत्वा तस्य चतुरस्रस्य मध्ये पञ्चदलकमलं विधाय वृत्तद्वययुक्तायां तत्कर्णिकायां समत्रिरेखां कर्णिकामध्यवृत्तस्पृष्टास्रत्रयां यथामानं योनिं कृत्वा (तस्य एकां रेखां चतुर्विंशतिधा विभज्य तैरंशैस्त्रयोविंशतिचिह्नानि कृत्वा तस्यास्तिसृषु रेखासु तथा कृत्वा तेषु एकांशमानमभितस्त्यक्त्वा तदन्तः प्राग्वत् समत्रिरेखां योनिं विधाय) तस्या योन्या एकां रेखामेकविंशतिधा विभज्य तेषु विंशतिचिह्नानि रेखासु प्रत्येकं कृत्वा तेषु बाह्याभ्यन्तरचिह्नेषु चिह्नाच्चिह्नमिति क्रमेण पञ्चचत्वारिंशद्रेखास्तिर्यग्रूपाः प्रतिपार्श्वं विलिखेत् । एवं कृते बाह्यरेखाग्राणि आन्तररेखाग्राणि च त्रिकोणानि पञ्चत्रिंशदधिकशतसंख्याकानि भवन्ति । तदन्त

---

(१) योनिध्येयमिति मू० पु० पा० ।
(२) योनिं कृत्वाथतत्सङ्ख्यायोनय इति मू० पु० पा० पञ्चत्रिंशच्छत सङ्ख्या इति सो० पु० पा० ।
(३) द्वयोरावरणयोरिति वं० पु० पा० ।
† कृत्वा इति मू पु० पा० ।
( ) एतच्चिन्हान्तर्गतोग्रन्थः टी० पु० नास्ति ।

तन्मध्ये भगमालां तामावाह्योक्तस्वरूपिणीम्(१) ।
संस्थापनादिभिर्युक्तामर्चयेदुपचारकैः ॥१७॥
अर्घ्यमङ्गैश्च मूलेन संसाध्याभ्युक्ष्य मूलतः ।
द्वारस्य पार्श्वयोरागद्वे षशक्तीस्तथाऽर्चयेत्(२) ॥१८॥
शब्दस्पर्शौ तथा रूपं रसं गन्धं च पूर्ववत् ।
तदन्तवृत्तयोर्मध्ये षडङ्गानि तथाऽर्चयेत् ॥१९॥
तदन्तर्भगमालायां मदनाद्यास्तथाऽर्चयेत् ।
मध्ये च देवीमभितो (षड्) यजेतान्यायुधान्यपि(३) ॥२०॥
ततो देवीं षोडशभिरुपचारैरुदीरितैः ।
पूजयेदाद्यवर्णेन विदध्यात्तद्बलिद्वयम् ॥२१॥

स्त्र्यस्त्ररेखात्रयस्पृष्टरेखं भ्रमेण वृत्तं निष्पाद्य तदन्तरेऽपि तद्व्यासपञ्चमांशमानभ्रमेण वृत्तं निष्पाद्य तयोर्विष्कम्भषोडशांशसहितं विष्कम्भमानं त्रिगुणीकृत्य तत् समुदायमानं दशधा विभज्य तेषु एकैकांशचिह्नानि परितस्तद्वृत्तद्वये दश दश विधाय तेषु क्रमेण बाह्यादाभ्यन्तरं तस्माद्बाह्यमिति गोमूत्रिकाक्रमेण तिर्यग्रूपा विंशतिरेखा विलिखेत्। एवं कृते बाह्यवृत्तस्पृष्टाग्राणि आन्तरवृत्तस्पृष्टाग्राणि च त्र्यस्त्राण्यभितो विंशतिसङ्ख्यानि सम्भवन्ति। अन्तर्बहिर्विभागेन चतुरङ्गुलान्तरालां समचतुरस्त्रां वीथीं तेषु सर्वेषु उक्तक्रमेण उक्ताः शक्तीः पूजयेदिति ॥१३॥१४॥१५॥१६॥१७॥ अभ्युक्ष्य— स्वात्मादीनि। मूलतः—मूलविद्यया। पूर्ववत् स्वरूपिणीति त्र्यक्षरसहितम्॥१८॥ तदन्तवृत्तयोर्मध्ये—पञ्चदल पद्मस्य कर्णिकावृत्तद्वयवीथ्याम्। तथाच वायव्यादिक्रमेण तदन्तर्योन्योर्मध्यस्थपञ्चत्रिंशत्कृतसङ्ख्यात्रिकोणमध्येषु,अग्राद्यप्रादक्षिण्येन॥१९॥ तदन्तर्भगमालायां—वृत्त(द्व)योर्मध्यस्थविंशतित्रिकोणेषु मध्येऽथ देवीमभितः एतदुक्तं भवति—तदन्तर्वृत्तवीथीमध्ये देव्याः षडायुधानि। तां वृत्तवीथीं तिर्यग्रेखाषट्कोणं षोढा विभज्य देव्या वामाधरहस्तस्थादीनि दक्षिणाधरहस्तस्थान्तानि(४) अग्राद्यप्रादक्षिण्येन क्रमेणार्चयेदिति ॥२०॥ आद्यवर्णेन—मन्त्राद्येनाक्षरेण सार्द्धमिति शेषः। मूलमन्त्राद्यक्षरं सविन्दुकं द्वादश-

---

(१) स्वरूपतामिति मू० पु० पा० ।
(२) रागद्वे षशक्तीमथार्चयेत् इति मू० पु० पा० ।
(३) आयुधानि षट इति मू० पु० पा० ।
(४) हस्तादीनि इति टी० पु० पा० ।

जपेदष्टोत्तरशतमग्रे देव्यास्तु नित्यशः ।
प्राग्वदग्निमुखं कृत्वा होमं * कुर्याद्दशांशतः ॥२२॥
संयोज्य बिन्दौ तां प्रायो(१) मूलेनाभ्यर्च्य तां तथा ।
स्वात्मन्युद्वासयेदुक्तप्रकारेण महेश्वरीम् ॥२३॥
देव्यात्मा वशयेद्विश्वं नरनारीनराधिपान् ।
काम्यहोममथो वक्ष्ये नानाभीष्टाप्तिदायकम्(२) ॥२४॥
त्रिमध्वक्तैः पुण्डरीकैर्होमाद्विप्रा वशं नयेत् ।
आरग्वधैस्तु राजानं करवीरैस्तु वैश्यकम् ॥२५॥
उत्पलैर्वशयेच्छूद्रं वनितां जपया हुतैः ।
बिल्वैर्लक्ष्मीर्भवेद्धोमैर्भूम्याद्यैः कमलैर्हुतात् ॥२६॥
कैरवैर्वाहनावाप्तिर्व(र्द)रपुष्पैर्महद्यशः ।
सौभाग्यं चम्पकैः सिद्धै(३) रक्तसौगन्धिकं हुनेत् ॥२७॥
तगरैर्वस्त्रसंसिद्ध्यै पुन्नागैर्भूषणाप्तये ।
मधुकैः कन्यकासिद्ध्यै पलाशैः स्वर्णसिद्धये ॥२८॥

स्वरं सर्वासामावरणशक्तीनां मन्त्राक्षरं कुर्यात् इत्यर्थः । बलिद्वयं—पूजारम्भे षोडशाक्षरमन्त्रेण पूजावसाने कुरुकुल्लासमाचर्या च । सर्वत्र पूजादाववसाने च नाथार्चनं कुर्यादिति सम्प्रदायार्थः ॥२१॥ दशांशतः क्रमहोमानन्तरं जपदशांशमूलमन्त्रेण होमं कुर्यात् । एतत् सर्वासां साधारणम् ॥२२॥ (४ उक्तप्रकारेण प्रधानदेव्याः पूजावसाने उक्तेन क्रमेण ॥२३॥ देव्यात्मा – प्राग्वन्न्यासदेवीरूपाद्वयभावनयेत्यर्थः । अत्रापि पुरश्चरणार्थं केवलं दशसाहस्रं विद्या जपित्वा तद्दशांशं तर्पणादिकं कुर्यादिति सम्प्रदायार्थः ॥२४॥

काम्यहोममित्यादिभिः परमेश्वरोत्यन्तैरर्द्धाद्यैः पञ्चभिः श्लोकैः नानाविधद्रव्यहोमैर्नानाफलावाप्तिमुपदिशति । तत्र त्रिमध्वक्तैः—त्रिमधूनि—क्षौद्राज्यदुग्धानि

---

* कृत्वा इति मू० पु० पा० ।

(१) बिन्दौ तां प्राग्वन्मू इति मू० पु० पा० ।
(२ भीष्टाविधायिकाम्इति मू० पु० पा० ।
(४) उक्तक्रमेण इति व० पुस्तके पाठः ।
(३) सिद्ध्यै हुतसौगन्धिकैर्हुतैरिति मू पु० पा० ।

किंशुकैरंशुकावाप्तौ पाटलैः पशुसिद्धये।
रक्तोत्पलैः सर्वसिद्ध्यै होमयेत्परमेश्वरि! ॥२९॥
अथ यन्त्राणि वक्ष्यामि वाञ्छितार्थप्रदानि तु।
चन्दनागुरुकर्पूरकस्तूरीकुङ्कुमैर्लिखेत् ॥३०॥
सर्वाणि सर्वतो यन्त्राण्यभीष्टावाप्तिकामुकः।
सुवर्णे रजते ताम्रे त्वंशुके भूर्जपत्रके ॥३१॥
धारणं मूर्ध्नि बाह्वोर्वा कण्ठे कट्यां प्रकोष्ठके।
निधाय क्वापि पूजां वा कुर्याद्यन्त्राण्यशेषतः ॥३२॥
षट्कोणं वृत्तयोर्मध्ये कृत्वा तन्मध्यतस्तथा।
योनिं विलिख्य तन्मध्ये मायां† साध्यसमन्विताम् ॥३३॥
विलिख्य कोणचितये (१)वह्निं षट्कोणेऽपि संलिखेत् (२)।
एकैकवृत्तयोर्मध्ये शेषार्णानि समालिखेत् ॥३४॥
बहिर्मातृकया वे(३)ष्ट्यवृत्तान्तविन्दुयुक्तया।
एवं यन्त्राणि मन्त्राणां दशभिर्दशभिर्भवेत् ॥३५॥

क्षौद्रदुग्धदधीनि वा। अस्मिन् प्रकरणे सर्वाणि प्रोक्तानि होमद्रव्याणि त्रिमध्वक्ता-न्येव जुहुयादित्यर्थः। सर्वत्र काम्यहोमेषु पूर्वं स्वनित्यक्रमं निर्वर्त्यानन्तरं वह्नौ तत्तद्विद्यायाः परिवाराहुतीर्हुत्वा पश्चात् प्रोक्तद्रव्यैः प्रोक्तसंख्यं तत्तन्मूलमन्त्रेण प्रोक्तफलावाप्तये जुहुयात्। होमेषु सर्वत्र होमान्ते हुतसंख्यं मूलमन्त्रं जपे-दिति सर्वत्रसमयः ॥२५॥२६॥२७॥२८॥ रक्तोत्पलैः—रक्तकुमुदैः ॥२९॥

अथ यन्त्राणीत्यादिभिरशेषत इत्यन्तैस्त्रिभिः श्लोकैर्यन्त्रकथनप्रस्तावपूर्वं (४)तन्त्र-साधारणं यन्त्रलेखनद्रव्यं यन्त्राधिकरणानि यन्त्रधारणप्रकारांश्चोपदिशति ॥३०॥ ॥३१॥३२॥

षट्कोणमित्यादिभिर्विधीयत इत्यन्तैः (त्रिभिः) षड्भिः श्लोकैश्चतुर्दशयन्त्र-निर्माणक्रममुपदिशति। तत्र मायां ह्रीं ह्रीं खाम्। साध्यसमन्विताम्—प्राग्वत्तत्र

---

† मध्य इति म० पा०। (१) बहिः इति सो० पु० पा०। (२) त्वालिखेत् इति सो० पु० पा०।
(३) वेष्ट इति म० पु० पा०। (४) तत्र इति वं० पुस्तके पाठः।

चरमेऽमृतषष्ट्यैव शेषं संपूजयेच्छिवे ।
ज्या कंदावोऽम्बु ह्रत्खेन माययाऽमृतपञ्चकम् ॥३६॥
तत्पञ्चकं स्वरैर्भेदादशीतिर्माययया तथा ।
तैः षण्ढहीनैः (१) षष्टिः स्यान्माययया च तथा भवेत् ॥३७॥
षष्ट्या शतं समुद्दिष्टं वर्णेष्वमृतविग्रहम् ।
तेषां सर्वत्र तन्त्रेऽस्मिन् विनियोगोविधीयते ॥३८॥

मायामध्ये एकमेकं मन्त्राक्षरं च लिखेदिति सम्प्रदायः ३३॥३४॥ शेषार्णानि क्रमेण पञ्चविंशत्यधिकशतसंख्यानि॥३५॥ चरमे—चतुर्दशयन्त्रे। अमृतषष्ट्या—वक्ष्यमाणया ज्याकं दावोम्बुह्रत्खेनेति। ज्या—जकारः। कं— सकारः। दावः ठकारः। अम्ब— वकारः। ह्रत् - सकारः। खेन— विन्दुना। मायया -- विसर्जनीयेन ॥३६॥ मायया तथा। बिन्दुसहितेषु—स्वरभेदादशीतिसंख्यातेष्वमृताक्षरेषु विन्दुमपास्य सर्वत्र विसर्जनीययोजनात् तान्येवाक्षराणि अशीत्यक्षराणि भवन्तीत्यर्थः। षंढहीनैः—ऋॠ- लृॡ इत्यक्षरविहीनैः। मायया च तथाभवेत् षण्ढचतुष्टयहीनैर्विसर्जनीय- योजितैरपि षष्ट्यक्षराणि स्युरित्यर्थः॥ ३७॥ षष्ट्याशतं समुद्दिष्टमित्युक्तिः षण्ढचतुष्टयोपेतत्वात्। वर्णेषु—मातृकायाम्। अमृतविग्रहं—वर्णपञ्चकमिति- शेषः। अत्र चतुर्दश षण्ढान् विनाऽमृताक्षराणां सङ्ख्या विंशत्यधिकं शतमेव। तेषां षण्ढयुक्तानां षष्टिशतसंख्यानाममृताक्षराणां चतुर्दशानां यन्त्राणां विरचनाक्रमोयथा- एकैकाङ्गुलान्तरालानि त्रीणि वृत्तानि क्रमेणान्तर्बहिर्विभागेन कृत्वा तेषु अन्तस्थतृतीयवृत्तमध्ये यथामानं षट्कोणं विधाय तन्मध्ये समत्रिरेखां स्वाभिमुखां योनिं विलिख्य तन्मध्ये नामोपेतां हृल्लेखामालिख्य तदन्तर्मायांशे मन्त्राद्यक्षरमालिख्य बहिस्त्रिकोणेषु मन्त्रस्य द्वितीयतृतीय- चतुर्थाक्षराण्यालिख्य बहिः षट्सु कोणेषु अग्न्यादिप्रादक्षिण्येन पञ्चमादिदश- मान्तानि वर्णान्यालिख्य तद्बहिर्वृत्तवीथ्यां (२ एकादशाक्षरादीनि पञ्चविंशत्यधिक- शतसंख्यानि मन्त्रशेषाक्षराणि प्राग्वत् समालिख्य तद्बहिर्वृत्तवीथ्यां तथैव सविन्दु- कान्यक्षराणि प्राग्वत् समालिख्य तद्बहिर्वृत्तवीथ्यां तथैव सविन्दुकान्यक्षराणि आदिक्षान्तानि समालिखेत् एतत् प्रथमं यन्त्रम्। द्वितीयादित्रयो-

---

(१) षंडिहीनैरिति मू० पु० पा०।
(२) एकविंशाक्षरादीनि इति त्रं० पु० पा०।

चतुर्दशानां यन्त्राणां विनियोगं शृणु प्रिये!।
वश्यमाकर्षणं स्तम्भमारोग्यं विजयं श्रियम् ॥३९॥
रक्षां गजाश्वगोमेषमहिषाणामनुक्रमात्।
नरनारीनृपाणां च प्रोक्तयोगेन साधयेत् ॥४०॥
अमृतार्णैः (१) स्वमूलार्णैः ललितारहितैस्तु तैः।
नित्याचतुर्दशार्णैश्चाप्येकषष्टिशतेन च ॥४१॥
षटपञ्चाशत्समोपेतं चतुःशतमुदीरितम।
तैर्यन्त्ररचनायोगं फलानि च शृणु प्रिये! ॥४२॥

दशान्तेषु द्वादशसु यन्त्रेषु प्रथमयन्त्रलिखिताक्षरदशकोपरिस्थं दशकं द्वितीये तृतीये तुर्यस्तृतीयदशकं एवं क्रमेण द्वादशसु समालिख्य बहिः शेषाक्षरवेष्टने पञ्चविंशत्यधिकशतसंख्याक्षरसिद्ध्यर्थं तन्मध्यलिखिताक्षरदशकदशमाक्षरादुपरितनमुपरितनमन्त्राक्षरमारभ्य द्वन्नेखा म ध्यलिखिताक्षरपूर्वाक्षरपूर्वाक्षरावधि अक्षराणि समालिखेत्। चरमे चतुर्दशे यन्त्रे षट्कोणद्वितीयकोणादिषु पञ्चसु पञ्चामृताक्षराणि सविन्दुकान्यालिख्य बहिर्मन्त्रशेषाक्षरस्य वोथ्यां विषण्ढस्वराक्षरविकृतानि सविन्दूनि तदमृतषष्ठ्याक्षराणि ततस्तान्येव विसर्जनीययुक्तानि, ततः सविसर्जनीयान्यमृतपञ्चाक्षराणि चैवं पञ्चविंशत्यधिकशताक्षराणि समालिखेदिति ॥३८॥

चतुर्दशानामित्यादिना साधयेदित्यन्तेन श्लोकद्वयेन तेषां चतुर्दशयन्त्राणां यथाक्रमं चतुर्दशफलान्युपदिशति। तत्र—प्रोक्तयोगेन साधयेत्—धारणनिक्षेपादिना ॥३९॥४०

अमृतार्णैरित्यादिना उदोरितमित्यन्तेनार्द्धाधिकेन श्लोकेन त्रयस्त्रिंशद्यन्त्रनिर्माणार्थं मन्त्राक्षराणां संख्याविशेषान् संभूय संख्यां चोपदिशति। तत्रैतदुक्तं भवति-षष्ठ्यधिकशतसंख्यैरमृतार्णैः पञ्चत्रिंशदधिकशतसंख्यैः स्वमूलविद्यार्णैः ललितां विना मूलविद्यारहितैरन्यैश्चतुर्दशनित्याविद्याक्षरैरेकषष्टिशतसङ्ख्यातैश्च संभूय संख्या षट्पञ्चाशत्समोपेतं चतुःशतमुदोरितमिति ॥४१॥

तैरित्यादिना श्लोकोत्तरार्द्धेन तैर्यन्त्राणि तत् फलानि च प्रस्तौति। तत्र—तैः—प्रोक्तसंख्यैरक्षरैः ॥४२॥

(१) चमूलार्णै इति मू॰ पु॰ पा॰।

त्रिकोणमष्टपत्राब्जं बहिर्वृत्तद्वयं तथा ।
(१) विधाय मध्ये मायास्थं कृत्वा नामत्रिकोणगम् ॥४३॥
अन्तरालत्रयं त्रिस्थं वह्निः पत्राष्टगामिव ।
चतुर्दशार्णमालिख्य वृत्तमध्ये तु मातृकाम् ॥४४॥
विलिख्यार्चाहुतजपसेकसिद्धानि योजयेत् ।
त्रयस्त्रिंशत्तमं यन्त्रं सशक्त्यमृतपञ्चकैः ॥४५॥
ज्वरे घोरे शीतिकायां तथा चातुर्थिके गदे ।
स्फोटे मसूरिकायां च नेत्राभ्यां कुक्षिसंभवे ॥४६॥

त्रिकोणमित्यादिभिः पञ्चकैरित्यन्तैस्त्रिभिः श्लोकैः प्रोक्तैः षट्पञ्चाशच्चतुःशतवर्णैरमृतपञ्चाक्षरैः शक्त्याख्यया ह्रल्लेखया च त्रयस्त्रिंशद्रूपयन्त्रविरचनाक्रममुपदिशति । तत्र चैतदुक्तं भवति इष्टमानेन भ्रमेण वृत्तद्वयमन्तर्बहिर्विभागेन एकाङ्गुलान्तरालं निष्पाद्य तदस्थाङ्गुलान्तरालेन वृत्तेन कर्णिकां तद्बहिस्त्र्यंगुलान्तरालेन वृत्तेन कर्णिकां तद्बहिस्त्र्यङ्गुल्यन्तवीथ्यामष्टपत्राणि च कृत्वा कर्णिकामध्ये समत्रिरेखां कर्णिकावृत्तस्पृष्टास्त्रत्रयां योनिं कृत्वा तन्मध्ये प्राग्वन्नामोपेतां ह्रल्लेखामालिख्य तदस्त्रेषु त्रिषु प्रोक्तसङ्ख्येष्वक्षरेषु आदितः त्रयं कर्णिकावृत्तयोन्यस्त्रान्तरालत्रये त्रयं बहिरष्टसु पत्रेषु अग्न्यादिप्रादक्षिण्येनाष्टाक्षराणि चैवं चतुर्दशाक्षराण्यालिख्य बाह्यवृत्तवीथ्यामकारादिक्षकारान्तां मातृकां तथैवाभिलिखेत् एतेष्वक्षरेष्वादितः चतुर्दशभिरक्षरैः प्रथमं यन्त्रम् एवं प्रोक्तचतुर्दशाक्षरादुपरितनैश्चतुर्दशभिरक्षरैर्द्वितीयं यन्त्रम् । एवमुपरिस्थैश्चतुर्दशभिश्चतुर्दशभिरक्षरैः क्रमेणान्यानि च त्रिंशद्यन्त्राणि चरमयन्त्रम् । त्रयस्त्रिंशद्यन्त्रविनियुक्तावशिष्टाक्षराष्टकेनामृतपञ्चाक्षरेण ह्रल्लेखया च एवं चतुर्दशभिरक्षरैः कुर्यात्, एवं त्रयस्त्रिंशद्यन्त्राणि कृत्वा पूजाहोमजपाभिषेकैर्विनियुंज्यादिति । अत्रार्चाजपादिकं मातृकया तत्तल्लिखिताक्षरैश्च, एवं सर्वत्राक्षरयन्त्रेषु विधानम् ॥४५॥

ज्वरेत्यादिभिरीश्वरीत्यन्तैश्चतुर्दशभिः श्लोकैस्त्रयस्त्रिंशद्यन्त्राणां क्रमेण त्रयस्त्रिंशत्फलान्युपदिशति । तत्र चातुर्थिके—चतुर्थादिवसेषु पीड़ाकरशान्ति

---

(१) त्रिधास्थमध्यमायास्थ इति म० पु० पा०

यक्षराक्षसगन्धर्वपिशाचोरगपीड़ने ।
बालग्रहार्त्तौ दौर्भाग्ये वन्ध्यात्वे वैरिपीड़ने ॥४७॥
वादे चोन्मादने(१) राजक्रोधे चोरभये तथा ।
डाकिन्यादिगणैः षड्भिराक्रान्त्यां ब्रह्मराक्षसैः ॥४८॥
प्रमेहकामलाछर्दिदोषजेषु त्रिषु क्रमात् ।
योजयेदुक्तविधिना त्र्यस्त्रिंशदितीश्वरि ! ॥४९॥
कामेश्वर्यादिनित्यानां साधारणसमर्चनम् ।
शृणु देवि ! प्रवक्ष्यामि सर्वाङ्गाङ्गित्वयोगतः (२)॥५०॥
तासां पञ्चदशानान्तु मन्त्रवर्णाः समीरिताः ।
शतद्वयं पञ्चनवतिं तैश्चक्रं तत्र पूजनम् ॥५१॥
प्राक्प्रत्यग्दक्षिणोदक्च रेखाविंशतिमालिखेत् ।
तेन कोष्ठानि जायन्ते चतुरस्राणि पार्वति ! ॥५२॥

कागदे ॥ ४६॥४७ ॥ षड्भिराक्रान्त्यामिति षड्विधानि फलान्युच्यन्ते ॥ ४८ ॥ दोषजेषु त्रिषु—वातपित्तश्लेष्मजेषु रोगवर्गेषु त्रिविधेषु । उक्तविधिना—अर्चाजपादिना ॥४९॥

कामेश्वर्यादीत्यादिना श्लोकेन ललिताया अङ्गभूतानामन्यासां (पञ्चदशानां नित्यानामन्योन्याङ्गित्वेन तासां) पञ्चदशप्रकारं साधारणमर्चनं प्रस्तौति । तत्र—कामेश्वर्यादिनित्यानां—पञ्चदशानामिति शेषः ॥५०॥

तासामित्यादिना श्लोकेन ललितादीनां पञ्चदशानां तासां सम्भूय मन्त्राक्षरसङ्ख्यामुपदिश्य तैरक्षरैस्तासां साधारणं काम्यपूजाचक्रं च प्रस्तौति । तत्र—तैः—प्रोक्तसङ्ख्यैरक्षरैः ॥५१॥

प्राक्प्रत्यगित्यादिभिः पूजयेदित्यन्तैर्विंशत्या श्लोकैः परिपूर्णपूजाचक्रनिर्माणं पूजाक्रमं पूजोपकरणविशेषादिकं चोपदिशति । तत्र प्राक्प्रत्यक् इत्यादिभिः क्रमेण वै इत्यन्तैरेकादशभिः श्लोकैस्तच्चक्रनिर्माणं तत्र पञ्चदशनित्यानां पूजाक्रमं

(१) न्मादके इति मू० पा० ।
(२) सर्वाङ्गानि पञ्चीगत इति मू० पु० पा० ।

शतत्रयं त्वेकषष्ठ्या तेष्वीशादिप्रदक्षिणम् (१)।
प्रदेशगत्या(२) विलिखेद्यावत्सङ्ख्यं यथान्तरम् ॥५३॥
पञ्चषष्टिस्तेषु दिक्षु प्रागादिषु* चतुष्टयम् ।
(३) अवशिष्टं भवेत्तेषु दिक्स्थेष्वेकीकृतेषु च†॥५४॥
(४) मायां चतुष्टयान्तस्थमालिखेद्वाङ्कितं क्रमात् ।
एकोनपञ्चाशत्कोष्ठेष्वेकीभूते(न)षु तत्र वै ॥५५॥
पद्मं चतुर्दशदलं बहिर्वृत्तद्वयं तथा ।
लिखित्वा कर्णिकामध्ये योनिं मायोदरां लिखेत् ॥५६॥
दलेष्वपि तथा शक्तिं चतुर्दशसु संलिखेत् ।
भगमालां मध्यशक्त्यामावाह्याभ्यर्चयेद्बहिः ॥५७॥
पश्चिमादि तु वाय्वन्तमन्या आवाह्य पूजयेत् ।
यथाक्रममिदं चक्रमासां साधारणं भवेत् ॥५८॥
मध्ये मध्ये (तथा) तु या पूज्या शेषास्तत्र दलाश्रिताः ।
यथाक्रमेण चित्रान्ताः पूजयेदुक्तविग्रहाः ॥५९॥

चोपदिशति--तत्र यथान्तरा—पञ्चषष्टिरवशिष्टानि कोष्टानि भवेयुस्तथेत्यर्थः॥५२॥ ॥५२॥तेषु—पञ्चषष्टिषु। प्रागादिष्विति। यथा प्रागादिदिक्षु चतुष्टयं चतुष्टयं मध्यतोऽवशिष्टं स्यात्। तेषु—चतुष्कचतुष्टयेषु एकीकृतेषु, मध्यरेखात्रयमार्जनेति शेषः ॥५४॥ एकोनपञ्चाशत्कोष्ठेषु—एकीभूतेषु तत्र वै ॥५५॥ पद्मं चतुर्दशदलं—समचतुरस्रस्वरूपेण मध्यतः एकीकृतदिग्गतचतुरस्रचतुष्कान्तसूत्रावधि एकोनपञ्चाशत्कोष्ठानि एकीकृत्य तत्र प्रोक्तरूपं पद्मं कुर्यादित्यर्थः ॥५६॥ मध्यशक्त्यां—मध्यशक्तिश्च हृल्लेखा ॥५७॥ अन्याः-चतुर्दशनित्याः। आसां-

---

(१) चिणाम् इति मू० पु० पा०।
(२) प्रवेशगत्येति मू० पु० पा०।
* प्राणादिषु इति सो० पु० पा०।
(३) अष्टविंशं इति मू० पु० पा०।
† तु इति मू० पु० पा०।
(४) माया चतु इति मू० पु० पा०।

चतुरस्रद्वयं बाह्ये कृत्वा द्वाराणि दिक्षु च ।
द्वाराणां पार्श्वयोः कोणे प्रचर्चयेद्द्वादश क्रमात् ॥६०॥
ब्राह्मी माहेश्वरीं द्वारे पश्चिमे सव्यदक्षिणे ।
कौमारीं वैष्णवीं सौम्ये वाराहीन्द्रीं च पूर्वगे ॥६१॥
चामुण्डासु महालक्ष्मी याम्ये वायुादिकोणगाः ।
देशकालौ तथाकारशब्दौ प्रोक्तक्रमेण वै ॥६२॥
पूजयेत्प्रोक्तरूपैस्तु (श)प्रोक्तरूपाश्च ताः क्रमात् ।
उपचारैरासवैश्च मांसैर्मत्स्यैः सुसंस्कृतैः ॥६३॥

चतुर्दशनित्यानाम् ॥५८॥५९॥६०॥ पूर्वगे—द्वारे इति शेषः ॥६१॥६२॥ एवमेतैरेकादशभिः श्लोकैरेतदुक्तं भवति—पञ्च(त्रिं)विंशत्यंगुलान्तरालं समचतुरस्रं कृत्वा तस्माद्द्व्यङ्गुलादन्तः समचतुरस्रं विलिख्य तद्द्व्यङ्गुलवीथ्यां चतुर्दिक्षु द्वाराणीति। अङ्गुलमानेन (समचतुरस्रं चत्वारि सूत्राणि) कृत्वा तत्र मध्ये दक्षिणोत्तराणि प्राक्पश्चिमान्तानि चैकैकाङ्गुलान्तरालानि अत्राष्टादशाष्टादशसूत्राण्यास्फाल्य सर्वमध्ये एकोनपञ्चाशत्कोष्ठान्येकीकृत्य तत्र वृत्तद्वयं चतुरस्रसूत्रस्पृष्टास्पृष्टिकया भ्रमेण निष्पाद्य तन्मध्ये सकर्णिकं चतुर्दशदलपद्मं विधाय तत्कर्णिकामध्ये वृत्तत्रस्रस्पृष्टां समत्रिरेखां योनिं कृत्वा तन्मध्ये हल्लेखामालिख्य तद्बहिः पश्चिमादिवाय्वन्तं (बाह्यान्तं) वामावर्तेन चतुर्दशसु दलेषु प्रतिदलं हल्लेखां समालिख्य तत्पद्मचतुरस्राद्बहिः प्रागादिचतुर्दिक्षु मध्यतश्चत्वारि कोष्ठान्यन्तर्बहिर्विभागेनैकीकृत्य तत्र हल्लेखां प्राग्वद्वाञ्छितार्थगर्भां समालिख्य बहिः सर्वबाह्यपङ्क्तिस्थशिवादिकोष्ठमारभ्य प्रादक्षिण्यक्रमेण प्रवेशगत्या अनुक्तक्रमं षसवत्यधिकशतद्वयसङ्ख्येषु कोष्ठेषु तत्सङ्ख्यानि पञ्चदशनित्याविद्याक्षराणि कामेश्वर्यादिचित्रान्तं क्रमेण समालिख्य चतुर्षु सर्वबाह्यचतुरस्रद्वारेषु पश्चिमादिदक्षिणान्तं प्रादक्षिण्येन ब्राह्म्याद्यष्टशक्तीः सव्यदक्षिणशाखयोर्द्विद्विशो मेणाभ्यर्च्य (वायु)बाह्यादिषु निर्ऋत्यन्तेषु कोणेषु देशकालाकाशशब्दं शक्तीः समभ्यर्च्य तदन्तः प्रागुक्तेषु कोष्ठेषु ईशकोष्ठादिप्रवेशगत्या प्रादक्षिण्येन पञ्चदशनित्याविद्याक्षराणि तैस्तैरक्षरैरभ्यर्च्य पश्चिमादिषु चतसृषु वाञ्छितगर्भहल्लेखासु भगमालामभ्यर्च्य सर्वमध्ये च तामेव तद्विद्ययाऽभ्यर्च्य पश्चिमादिवाय्वन्तं (बाह्यान्तं)

अपूपैः पायसैर्दुग्धैः सुशृतैः सितसंयुतैः ।
कदलीपनसाद्यैश्च फलैर्मधुभिरेव च ॥६४॥
नैवेद्यैः प्रीणयेद्देवीं नृत्यगीतादिभिस्तथा ।
एकरात्रं त्रिरात्रं वा पञ्चरात्रं तु सप्त वा ॥६५॥
नवरात्रं तथा पक्षं मासं पूर्व्वादिकं तु वा ।
वर्षं वा फाल्गुनान्तं वा स्यात्समस्तार्तिनाशनम् ॥६६॥
ग्रहाणां प्रातिकूल्येषु दीर्घरोगेषु वैकृते ।
देवतानामथोत्पाते विविधे त्वभिचारके ॥६७॥
दारिद्र्याविजयप्राप्तौ दुर्भिक्षे शत्रुपीड़ने ।
कृच्छ्रेष्वन्येषु घोरेषु पूजैषा सर्वकामदा ॥६८॥
पीठे वा सुसमे कृत्वा वेदिकामण्डले तु वा(१) ।
कृत्वैतत्प्रोक्तरूपं च प्रोक्तद्रव्यै(२)स्तथाऽर्चयेत् ॥६९॥

तत्तद्बाह्यदलेषु नित्यक्लिन्नादिकामेश्वर्यन्ताश्चतुर्दशनित्याः समर्चयेत् एवमन्यासु चतुर्दशनित्यास्वपि मध्यस्थाया अनन्तरनित्यादि तत्पूर्व्वनित्यान्तं तथाऽर्चयेत् इति ॥ ६२ ॥

पूजयेदित्यादिभिः पूजयेदित्यन्तैर्नवभिः श्लोकैः निवेद्यद्रव्यविशेषांस्तत्र पूजाकालावधिं पूजाविधानसमयादिकं चोपदिशति । तत्र प्रोक्तरूपैः—रक्तगन्धेत्यादिना । साधक इति शेषः । प्रोक्तरूपाः—तत्र मध्यनित्यासमानविग्रहाभरणायुधाः बाह्यदलस्थाश्चतुर्दशनित्याः अत्र प्रोक्तनिवेद्यद्रव्यविशेषाः । अस्मिन् पञ्चदशानां अङ्गाङ्गिभावकाभ्यर्चनक्रमप्रोक्तेषु पञ्चदशसु चक्रेषु निवेदनीयाः । सर्वत्र सर्वासां षोड़शनित्यादीनां नैमित्तिककाम्ययोरेव एतैर्द्रव्यविशेषैः पूजादिकं कुर्य्यादित्युत्तरत्र स्वयमेव वक्ष्यति ॥६३॥ मधुभिः—क्षौद्रैः ॥६४॥६५॥६६ ॥ दीर्घरोगेषु—वाताद्यष्टमहारोगेषु । कृते—देवतानाम् । देवताप्रातिकूल्यत्वात् समोक्ष्य क्रिय-

---

(१) वेदिकां मण्डले तथेति मू० पु० पा०

(२) प्रोक्तं द्रव्यैरिति सो० पु० पा० ।

नमेरुचम्पकाशोकपुन्नागबकुलाम्बुजैः
मल्लिकामालतीजातीशतपत्रोत्पलादिभिः ॥७०॥
सुगन्धिभिस्तथाऽन्यैश्च पूजयेत्पूर्णमानसः ।
एतद्विद्याभक्तिरूपास्तियुतानन्यांश्च पूजयेत् ॥७१॥
वंषुते सष्वरे तु वा चेतत्ताकं वांपि(त)परस ।
यजाधाह्नीना पूविव्र्‌ु तु(वा) चावल्पश्चनं (सका) शकं ॥
च्चे मिथुथप्राया श्र्‌ कां न(म) स कम्पल्पगावसें(ब)ध्वी
ध्वाथाड़ी (ध्वीष्ठीस्थाली) मायैतगै ।
तिचिविधंवं (त्वे) तस्म्‌ त(वित्यो)
वितवलौं माषुध्वीगौचते ॥ ७४ ॥
जंह्विपिष्टे ष्टस्वाचसेद्य दान्दोडं (स्वादोल-
कामादु) षामत्वगौरड्डुतनायश्टप्री
(स्तोवील) मतत्त्वाचि(त)मुदयपेत् द्याह्निमाचिलोविसस्मिक्
चपेटेतकामध्वजः सुनोतरकोमधास्तु ।
(मौध्यात्वथो)त्यायो भूसंरवासाचोमूरेयसम्यकश्चिन् ।

मासेष्वपि सर्वत्र वैपरीत्ये उत्पाते—त्रिविधे दिव्यान्तरिक्षभौमत्वेन प्रोक्ते ॥६७॥ दुर्भिक्षे—अन्नह्रासे । कष्टेषु—देशग्रामसमार्यादिषु । पूजैषा पञ्चदशविधा ॥६८॥ प्रोक्तरूपं—पञ्चदशनित्यासाधारणार्चनचक्रम् । सर्वत्र प्रोक्तेषु ग्रहप्रातिकूल्यादिषु प्रोक्तद्रव्यविशेषैः तत्तन्नित्यपूजाचक्रेषु (न) पूजयेदिति सम्प्रदायः । अन्यांश्च—स्वसम्प्रदायबहिर्भूता नपि ॥७०॥७१॥

अतःपरं नवत्यन्तं श्लोकरूपेण व्याख्यायते ।
चतुःषष्ठितमोपेताखिलःसप्तत्यादयोऽष्टमे ॥
नवत्यन्तानेकविंशाः श्लोका व्याकुलिताक्षराः ॥
देवीतन्त्रार्थगामी यस्तत्पादाम्बुजशेखरः ।

वेतेसतमागमातंरसिमदुम्ने जनिन ।
पूयेषोन्ते ध्वज(श)सन्तः गुयो
(लीगलालपैः)गशालुगीगात् धु ।
(गानधूमांचंसंशय)मावयोमस एष्टीगडध्वी प्रियैश्नायेद्विगे ।
धातोर्धगु अनैःस्लं पशयेडुश्रस्मिन् योते ।
न तत्वषिदिपित् रजः (यं)षिकुरसातेकतम् ।
न वामे धूदितः स्थाये वां तने पनिश्वात् लोतं ॥
दयकीलि(ज्ञ)डधुपैकं लिमतं ष्टिगानि स्फ़ूर्जं ।
च्चे जंलवृधुविते विमधंदाद्विग्ने वांगडं ।
(रोसागुवि) निप्रार्माश्नृतंयदानालस्वात्मयरंवाषाद्दी ।
जूझ्रथम्र्वा(प्यथा)ष्कलालं पिषुमफेस्वास्योसिधू ।
च्चिकभमतं धीशेतषिम(वश्रि)चश्नृन(शै)सलीसि ।
(से)शेध्वाच प्राकया(न्)त् दिसलिहतं व मिहं स्वापुलि ।
जातं दुगाभं यरं नोशुल्कामस्यनाकीर्च्चं ।
रन्तु लिवातः स्यातातालथहिंधड़ाततम् ।
लदुकां सप्तर्हंद्योसाभंवसरनिस्थरलां ।
लितक्षीफना तेशनालियुतेशिसथंगल ।

साधको वाचयेत् श्लोकानष्टमे व्याकुलक्रमान् ॥
एष वाचनाश्लोकः—त्रिसप्तत्यादयः श्लोका नवत्यन्ता दशाष्ट च ।
सुबोधार्था अपि स्वल्पं व्याक्रियन्ते ततस्ततः ।
व्याख्यानमपि तेषां तु श्लोकैर्व्याकुलिताक्षरैः ।
षड्भिर्विलिख्यते तैस्तु वाचयेत्प्रोक्तरूपतः ।

णं सनिस्सर्मात्रावतेः रःपमेवो ख्रतीरव्रर्थमिकाम्यर्चानैमित्तिकाः कं रमान्-स्वादिका क्रतः ॥१॥ त्यगुयोतस्तु कीलधारणंस्तुतुगग(गुंगुं)योचना । ह्याशन्तः लिखिलतसतनः घनः मापुलो पुस ॥२॥

द्रंक्षापूफ श्रायेत् च्नितासयनिरप्यतसए ।
तवैद्यश्रावदतं शतं वपि टाते रेगुस ।
दिवेभि श्रायेत् वाविर्ध्यादथँ निरधग्रोत्वातव्यै ।
स्मकृतदेयं द्वातद्यात् द्वसियदानिरताध ।
ह्याकोयसास्थचेत्मास्वधिपिसद्वोचित् चेल्कसि ।
दापिनतन्नग्रवेवेदित्तनिपितताकुर्नवी ।
चवत्त्याय: त्तनोवलन्ममयाद्य: रोचैत्तत्स ।
कति नवं भवति तभ्रुकी चपान्यत् गुसिवष्ठा ।
नारुदेया समावसन्नावपि स्वरादन्तड़य: ।
कीजपा च सएद्याचपांनवितत्धयोधग्र ।
रेसाकसान्तं च मीम्परिमिसकात्तं सदाह्व ।
प्रोस्यवंशिवेत् त्वयोतोभसो न्मया(१)॥९०॥
अथान्यं शृणु देवेशि ! चक्रमङ्गुतदर्शनम् ।
योन्यर्णवाख्यं वनितागवपर्वतवज्रकम् ॥९१॥

यं लमंह्वातो गुसयज: धाकोर्तिरयं तु तत् ।
नसलेसि श्रेह्वाव प्राक्तर्च चोग: दिशप्रं सत्वयो ॥३॥
शस्य तडुर्यां लतु तं येत् वियोकुष्ज्रंर निर्मलम् ।
दिशह्वोलिका स्मृतं णदोतुरिर्गुमुचम् ॥४॥
योपूफपूंलं रगत: यो इक्तिरितो गत्र्युंव्या ।
लारैत्वंहृ ह्रावत: दाससिद्दिर्यावस: ॥५॥
तृस्वातस्वास्वदारप्राक् चर्दकत्त्यास्य देशगौ ।
स्याज एधो वयत् वा क्षत् क्ष कान्यमथा सद ॥६॥

अथान्यदित्यादिभिरस्य सा इत्यन्तैर्दशभि: श्लोकै: योन्यर्णवाख्यमभंगुर

---

(१) एतावत्पर्यन्तं श्लोका मूलपुस्तके सो० पुस्तके चाऽन्यथावर्तन्ते एषामर्थोनावबुध्यते कुत्रवा श्लोकपूर्तिस्तदपि न ज्ञायते आदर्शपुस्तके यादृशान्यक्षराणि लिखितानि तादृशान्येवाऽत्र मुद्रितानि इति ध्येयम् ।

षड्विंशाङ्गुलमानेन कृत्वा योनि(१)समे तले।
तत्र द्वाङ्गुलमानेषु सूत्राण्येकादशार्पयेत् ॥९२॥
तेनात्र योन्योजायन्ते त्रिकोणानि शतात्परम्।
चत्वारिंशच्च चत्वारि तेषु मन्त्राक्षराणि तु ॥९३॥
प्रादक्षिण्यप्रवेशे(न) तु विलिखेत्तु निरन्तरम्।
मध्येऽवशिष्टनवके नववर्गसमन्विते ॥९४॥
नाथान्नव लिखेत् पश्चात्साध्याख्याकर्मसंयुतम्।
सर्वत्र विलिखेद्भूयो(२) भूयोस्त्वावर्तनेन तु ॥९५॥
मध्ये रात्रे तु तां साध्यां स्मरन्मदनवह्निना।
दह्यमानां हृतस्वांतां मस्तकस्थापिताञ्जलिम् ॥९६॥
विकीर्णकेशीमालोललोचनामरुणारुणाम्।
वायुप्रेङ्खत्पताकाख्यपटोपमकलेवराम् ॥९७॥
विवेकविधुरां मत्तां मानलज्जाभयातिगाम्।
(३)चिन्तयेन्नार्चयेच्चक्रमध्ये देवीं दिगम्बराम् ॥९८॥
जपादाडिमबन्धूककिंशुकाद्यैः समर्चयेत्।
अन्यैः सुगन्धिशे(षत्)फालि कुसुमाद्यैः सुगन्धिभिः ॥९९॥
त्रिसप्तरात्रादायाति प्रोक्तरूपा मदाकुला ।।।५५॥
यावच्छरीरपातन्तु छायेवाऽनपगाऽस्य सा ॥१००॥

वनितासङ्कुलनं यन्त्रं तद्ध्यानं तत्पूजाजपक्रमं तत्फलस्वरूपं चोपदिशति। तत्र मन्त्राक्षराणि भगमालिनीविद्यायाः पञ्चत्रिंशदधिकशताक्षराणि ॥९१॥९२॥९३॥ नववर्गसमन्वितम्। अकारादीनि षोडश स्वराक्षराणि द्विधा विभज्यान्यानि कादिक्षान्तानि अक्षराणि पञ्चशो विभजेत्। एवं कृते लकचटतपयसा इत्या-

---

(१) योनिं म इति को॰ पु॰ पा॰।
(२) भूय आवर्तते इति मू॰ पु॰ पा॰।
(३) विचिन्त्यमर्चयेदिति मू॰ पु॰ पा॰।

रूपतत्त्वमयी व्याप्तिरिति सम्यक् समीरिता ।
अस्या निष्फालनाच्चित्ते तत्तत्त्वं स्वात्मसात्कृतम् ॥१०१ ॥

इति श्रीषोडशनित्यातन्त्रेषु श्रीकादिमतेऽष्टमं पटलम् ॥८॥

दयो नववर्गा नवनाथात्मका: ॥८४॥८५॥८६॥ कलेवरं-- शरीरम् ॥८७॥८८॥८९॥ प्रोक्तरूपा—मदनवह्निना दह्यमानमित्यादिना । अनपगा—अनन्यगा । अत्र एभिः दशभिः श्लोकैरेतदुक्तं भवति, वृत्तान्तः षड् विंशाङ्गुलमानरेखात्रयां योनिं स्वाभिमुखीं तस्याः कृत्वा तस्या एकां रेखां द्वादशधा विभज्य तेषु चिह्नान्येकादश कृत्वा एवमन्यस्मिन्नपि रेखाद्वये चिह्नानि कृत्वा चिह्नात् चिह्नमिति क्रमेण एकादश सूत्राण्यास्फालयेत् । एवं कृते चतुश्चत्वारिंशदधिकं शतं त्र्यस्राणि सम्भवन्ति । तेषु स्ववामोर्द्ध्वादिप्रादक्षिण्यप्रवेशगत्या भगमालिनीविद्यायाः पञ्चत्रिंशदधिकशताक्षराणि समालिख्य मध्ये ऽवशिष्टनवके प्रोक्तनववर्गार्पितनाथनवकस्य प्रत्येकं नवाक्षराणि समालिख्य सर्वत्र चतुश्चत्वारिंशदधिकशतत्रिकोणेष्वपि साध्यसाधककर्माख्याः प्रोक्तक्रमेण प्राग्वत् समालिख्य तन्मध्ये देवीमावाह्य प्रोक्तक्रमेण देवीं ध्यात्वा अभ्यर्च्य प्रोक्तकालात् प्रोक्तफलमवाप्नुयादिति ॥१००॥

इति श्रीषोडशनित्यातन्त्रेषु श्रीकादिमताख्यस्य परिपूर्णस्य तन्त्रस्य प्रपञ्चसारसिंहराजप्रकाशाभिधानेन श्रीसुभगानन्दनाथेन विरचितायां मनोरमाख्यायां व्याख्यायां भगमालिनीनित्याविद्याविधानप्रकाशनपरं अष्टमं पटलं परिपूर्णं
परामृष्टम् ॥ ८ ॥

ग्रन्थसङ्ख्या ।

त्रिषष्टिरष्टमे यन्त्राण्यथ व्याख्यानवर्तिनः ।
ग्रन्थाः शतात्परं सार्द्धमशीतिरिति वोच्चितम् ॥

अथ नवमं पटलम् ।

अथ षोड़शनित्यासु चतुर्थीं शृणु पार्वति !
नित्यक्लिन्नाविधानानां तन्मन्त्रं प्रागुदीरितम्(१) ॥१॥
तदङ्गानि च तद्ध्यानं तच्छक्तीस्ताभिरर्चनाम्(२) ।
होमतर्पणभेदांश्च यन्त्राणि फलभेदतः ॥२॥
निर्दिष्टं क्रमतो वच्ये समस्तं परमेश्वरि !
आद्येन मन्त्रवर्णेन हृदयं समुदीरितम् ॥३॥
ततो द्वाभ्यां पुनर्द्वाभ्यां द्वाभ्यां द्वाभ्यां द्वयेन च ।
कुर्याच्छेषाणि चाङ्गानि करयोश्च न्यसेत् क्रमात् ॥४॥
तन्त्रे षड़ङ्गमन्त्रोक्तं(३) तत्र तत्र करद्वये ।
न्यसेदङ्गुष्ठमूलादि कनिष्ठाग्रान्तमूर्ध्वगम्(४) ॥५॥
शेषं तलद्वये (५)न्यस्त्वा हृद्वत्स्त्रोतेण सार्द्धयोः ।
त्वचि ध्वजे च पायौ च पादयोर्वर्णकं(६) न्यसेत् ॥६॥

अथ नवमं पटलम् ।

पूर्वस्मिन्नष्टमे पटले तृतीयाया भगमालिनीनित्याविद्याया विधानमुपदिश्यानन्तरं चतुर्थ्या नित्यक्लिन्नानित्याविद्याया विधानमुपदिशति । अथ षोड़शेत्यादि-विग्रहादित इत्यन्तेन श्लोकशतरूपेण नवमपटले । तत्र अथ षोड़शेत्यादिना परमेश्वरीत्यन्तेनाध्यर्द्धेन श्लोकद्वयेन पटलार्थानुद्दिशति । तत्र तन्मन्त्रं प्रागुदी-रितं—तृतीयपटल इति शेषः । ताभिः—परिवारशक्तिभिः सार्द्धमितिशेषः । निर्दिष्टं—अर्थजातमिति शेषः ॥२॥

आद्येनेत्यादिभिर्न्यसेदित्यन्तैरर्द्धाधिकैस्त्रिभिः श्लोकैः षड़ङ्गन्यासक्रममुपदिशति । तत्र द्वाभ्यां—विद्याक्षराभ्याम् । शेषाणि—पञ्च क्रमात्॥३॥४॥ तत्र षड़ङ्गमित्यादिना

---

(१) नित्यक्लिन्नाभिधानं तु तन्मन्त्रोद्धारमीरिता इति मू० पु० पा० ।
(२) तच्छक्तिःस्ताभिरर्चनम् इति मू० पु० पा० ।
(३) षड़ङ्गयन्त्रोक्तमिति मू० पु० पा० ।
(४) कनिष्ठान्तस्वभूर्धगमिति मू० पु० पा० ।
(५) न्यस्यहृद्दृक्श्रोत्रनसोर्द्वयेति मू० पु० पा० ।
(६) पादयोर्वर्णकान्न्यसेत् इति मू० पु० पा० ।

अरुणामा(१)रुणाकल्पामरुणांशुकधारिणीम् ।
अरुणास्रग्विलेपां तां चारुस्मेरमुखाम्बुजाम् ॥७॥
नेत्रत्रयोल्लसद्वक्त्रां भाले घर्माम्बुमौक्तिकैः ।
विराजमानां मन्दारलसदर्द्धेन्दुशेखराम् ॥८॥
चतुर्भिर्बाहुभिः पाशमङ्कुशं पानपात्रकम् ।
अभयं बिभ्रतीं पद्ममध्यासीनां मदालसाम् ॥९॥
ध्यात्वैवं पूजयेन्नित्य क्लिन्नानित्यां(२) स्वशक्तिभिः ।
क्षोभिणीमोहिनीलीलाविकोणाग्रिषु शक्तयः ॥१०॥
नित्या निरञ्जना क्लिन्ना क्लेदिनी मदनातुरा ।
मदद्रवा द्राविणी च(३) विधानाचाष्टपत्त्रगा ॥११॥
मदाविला मङ्गला च मन्मथार्ता मनस्विनी ।
मोहाऽऽमोदा मानमयी मायामन्दामनोवतीः(४) ॥१२॥
चतुरस्रगताः पूज्या मदारुणचलेक्षणाः(५) ।
मध्यनित्या समाकारवर्णवाह्ययुधान्विताः(६) ॥१३॥

न्यस्त्वा इत्यन्तपादाधिकश्लोकोक्तार्थः प्रागेवास्माभिरभिहितः। त्वचि--सर्वाङ्गे। ध्वजे—मेहने। पायौ—गुदे। पादयोरेकमक्षरमिति शेषः ॥५॥६॥

अरुणामित्यादिभिर्मदालसां इत्यन्तैस्त्रिभिः देव्या नित्यसपर्याध्यानं श्लोकैः (षड़ङ्गन्यासक्रमसु) पदिशति। तत्र चतुर्भिर्बाहुभिः—वामोर्ध्वादिवामदक्षिण-क्रमेण ॥७॥८॥९॥

ध्यात्वैवमित्यादिभिरन्विता इत्यन्तैश्चतुर्भिः श्लोकैस्तदावरणशक्तीरुपदिशति। तत्र मोहेत्येकाशक्तिः आमोदा इति च ॥१०॥११॥१२॥१३॥

---

(१) मरुणाकल्पामिति मू० पु० पा०।
(२) नित्यंक्लिन्नां इति सो पु० पा०।
(३) द्रविणीचाष्टेति मू० पु० पा०।
(४) मयामन्द्रस्विता च इति मू० पु० पा।
(५) विलीचणा इति सो० पु० पा०।
(६) वर्णवाह्यायुवानिचैति मू० पु० पा०।

चतुरस्रद्वयं कृत्वा प्राक्प्रत्यग्द्वारसंयुतम् ।
तन्मध्येऽष्टदलं(१)पद्मं तन्मध्ये त्र्यस्रकं तथा ॥१४॥
अर्घ्यं षडङ्गमूलाभ्यां कृत्वा तां प्राङ्मुखोऽर्चयेत् ।
चतुरस्रे पश्चिमादिनिरृत्यन्तं यजेच्च ताम् ॥१५॥
द्वारपार्श्वेषु कोणेषु दिक्षु ता दश पूजयेत् ।
तदन्तराऽष्टपत्रेषु पश्चिमादिप्रदक्षिणम् ॥१६॥
अर्चयेदष्टशक्तीस्तास्तदन्तर्योनिकोणगाः ।
अग्रात् प्रदक्षिणं तिस्रः शक्तीश्चोक्तविधानतः ॥१७॥
कर्णिकायोनिमध्यस्थदेशे वायूशवह्निषु ।
निरृत्यां पुरतोदिक्षु यजेदङ्गानि षट् क्रमात् ॥१८॥
ततो देवीं तु तां नित्यक्लिन्नानित्यामुदीरयेत् ।
उपचारैरर्चयेच्च बलिं दद्याच्च पूर्ववत् ॥१९॥
तदग्रतो जपेद्विद्यां सहस्रं यदि वा शतम् ।
ततोऽभ्यर्च्य शिवां होमं कुर्यादुक्तमेण तु ॥२०॥

चतुरस्रद्वयमित्यादिना श्लोकेन देव्या नित्यसपर्याचक्रमुपदिशति। तत्र चक्रनिर्माणं सुकरं कृत्वाऽर्चयेदितिशेषः ॥१४॥

अर्घ्यमित्यादिभिश्चरैदित्यन्तैरष्टभिः श्लोकैर्देव्या नित्यसपर्याक्रममुपदिशति। तत्र प्राङ्मुख इति सर्वत्र साधारणम् ॥१५॥ द्वारपार्श्वेष्विति, एतदुक्तंस्यात्—मदाविलाद्याः दशशक्तीः चतुरस्रे पश्चिमद्वारदक्षिणदिग्गतकक्षामारभ्य वायु-सोमेशानदिक्षु पूर्वद्वारस्य उत्तरदक्षिणपार्श्वयोर्वह्नियमनिरृतिदिक्षु च पूजयेदिति। पश्चिमादिप्रदक्षिणं—देव्या अग्रमारभ्य प्रादक्षिण्येन। एतदत्र सर्वपरिवारशक्तिसाधारणम् ॥१६॥ ताः—नित्याद्यास्तिस्रः क्षोभिण्याद्याः। उक्तविधानतः—एवमुक्तक्रमेणेत्यर्थः॥१७॥ वायूशेत्यादिषडङ्गावरणार्चनक्रमः सर्वत्रार्घ्यादिषडङ्गार्चनविधाने साधारणः। पुरतो—देवतायाः॥१८॥ उपचारैः—षोडशभिरितिशेषः। पूर्ववत्—षोडशा-

---

(१) मध्ये षड्दलं इति मू०

आज्यसिक्तांधसाऽऽज्येन पुष्पैर्वा सौरभान्वितैः।
जुहुयात्प्राग्वदुदितसङ्ख्यं प्राग्वत्समाप्य तत् ॥२१॥
अभ्यर्च्य देवीमथ तां स्वात्मन्युद्वास्य पूर्ववत्।
न्यासं कृत्वा स्तोत्रयुगं जपित्वा तन्मयश्चरेत् ॥२२॥
विद्यायाः साधनं(१) सम्यक् समीहितफलप्रदम्।
शृणु देवि! प्रवक्ष्यामि प्रयोगार्हो यतो भवेत् ॥२३॥
जितेन्द्रियो हविष्याशी त्रिसन्ध्यार्चारतो जपेत्।
प्राग्वल्लक्षं तद्दशांशं कुर्याद्धोमं च तर्पणम् ॥२४॥
मधूकपुष्पैर्मध्वक्तैर्बकुलोत्थैरथापि वा।
चन्द्रचन्दनकस्तूरीवासितैस्तर्पयेज्जलैः ॥२५॥
ततोनित्या(२)प्रयोगार्होनित्यार्चानिरतस्तथा।
सहस्रजापी तद्भक्तः कुर्य्यादुक्तं न चाऽन्यथा ॥२६॥

चरमन्त्रकुरुकुल्लाविद्याभ्यां बलिदानमाद्यन्तयोरित्यर्थः ॥१८॥ उक्तक्रमेण। प्राग्वत् —अग्निमुखादिकं कृत्वेत्यर्थः ॥२०॥ अन्धसा —अन्नेन। प्राग्वत्—नित्यपूजाक्रमेण। उदितसङ्ख्यं—जपदशांशसङ्ख्यम्। तत्—हवनम् ॥२१॥ अभ्यर्च्य—मूलविद्यया। पूर्ववत्—तेजःस्वरूपेण स्वान्तर्योजनम्। स्तोत्रयुगं—पञ्चश्लोकरूपं द्वादशश्लोकरूपं च। एष स्तोत्रयुगजपः सर्वनित्यासाधारणः। तन्मयः—प्राग्वत् ॥२२॥

विद्याया इत्यादिभिरन्यथा इत्यन्तैश्चतुर्भिः श्लोकैर्विद्यापुरश्चरणप्रकारमुपदिशति। तत्र यतः—साधनतः ॥२३॥ त्रिसन्ध्यार्चारतः—त्रिसन्ध्यासु ललितासाधनवत् भजनपरः। प्राग्वत् लक्षं विद्याया युगानुरूपमक्षरलक्षक्रमेण ॥२४॥

मधूकपुष्पैरित्यादिना श्लोकेन यथाक्रमं पुरश्चरणहोमतर्पणद्रव्याणि कथयति। तत्र (त्रि)मध्वक्तैः—त्रिमधुसिक्तैर्मधूकपुष्पैर्जुहुयादितिशेषः ॥२५॥ उक्तान् प्रयोगान्। नित्यार्चनानिरत इत्यादिना एतदुक्तं भवति—पुरश्चरणानन्तरमपि नित्यार्चानिरतः प्रतिदिनं सहस्रजापो विद्यागुरुभक्तः साधकः प्रयोगाद्यभिज्ञः नान्यमिति (नान्यथेति) सर्वदेवतासाधारणम् ॥२६॥

---

(१) विद्याया साम्प्रतं इति मू० पु० पा। (२) विप्रप्रयोगार्हो इति सो० पु० पा०।

पद्मै रक्तैस्त्रिमध्वक्तैर्होमाल्लक्ष्मीमवाप्नुयात् ।
तथैव कैरवै रक्तैरङ्गनास्तु वशं नयेत् ॥२७॥
समानरूपवत्साया: शुक्लायाश्च पय:स्रुतै: ।
मल्लिकामालतीजातीशतपत्रैर्हुतैर्भवेत् ॥२८॥
कीर्तिविद्याधनारोग्यसौभाग्यविजयादिकम् ।
आरग्वधप्रसूनैस्तु क्षौद्राक्तैर्हवनाद्भवेत् ॥२९॥
स्वर्णाप्ति: स्तम्भनं शत्रो: नृपादीनां क्रुधोऽपि वा ।
आज्याक्तै: करवीरोत्थै: प्रसूनैररुणैर्हुतै: ॥३०॥
रक्ताम्बराणि वनिताभूपमर्त्यं वशं तथा ।
भूषावाहनवाणिज्यसिद्धयश्चास्य वाञ्छिता: ॥३१॥
लवणै: सर्षपैर्गौरैरितरैर्वा(स्य)ऽथ होमत: ।
तत्तैलाक्तैर्निशामध्ये त्वानयेद्वाञ्छितां वधूम् ॥३२॥
तैलाक्तैर्जुहुयात्कृष्णा(१)दरपुष्पैर्निशान्तरा ।
मासादराति:(२) तीव्रार्तिज्वरेण भवति ध्रुवम् ॥३३॥
आरुष्करध्रुताभ्यक्तैस्तद्बीजैर्निशि होमत: ।
शत्रोर्देहे व्रणानि स्युर्दु:साध्यानि चिकित्सकै: ॥३४॥
तैरेव ज्वलिताङ्गस्तु रिपुर्याति यमालयम् ।
तथा तत्तैलसंसिक्तैर्बीजैरङ्गारकैरपि(३) ॥३५॥

पद्मैरित्यादिवधूमित्यन्तै: षड्भि: श्लोकैर्नानाविधहोमतोनानाफलावाप्तिमुपदिशति। तत्र समानरूपवत्साया:—शुक्लवत्साया इत्यर्थ: ॥२७॥२८॥२९॥३०॥३१॥ इतरै:—कृष्णै:। वा पक्षान्तरे। तत्तैलाक्तै:—सर्षपद्वयतैलाक्तै: ॥३२॥ तैलाक्तैरित्यादिभिरपीत्यन्तै: त्रिभि: श्लोकै: शत्रुनिग्रहार्थं होममुपदिशति। तत्र तद्बीजै: आरुष्करबीजैर्होमेन यथोक्तफलप्राप्ति: ॥३३॥३४॥३५॥

---

(१) यादृक्षाद इति मू० पु० पा०। (२) मासादारातिस्ती इति मू० पु० पा।
(३) रङ्गोलङ्गैरपीति मू० पु० पा०।

मरीचैः सर्षपाज्याक्तैर्निशि होमात्तु मासतः ।
वाञ्छितां वनितां कामज्वरार्तामानयेद् ध्रुवम् ॥३६॥
मरीचैः सर्षपोपेतैः सप्तवाराहुतैर्निशि ।
धैर्यमानकुलैर्नित्यं दुष्प्रापामानयेद्वधूम् ॥३७॥
अन्नाज्यैर्जुहुयान्नित्यं शतमष्टोत्तरं तु वा ।
तेनान्नपूर्णभुवनोभोक्ता च भवति प्रिये ! ॥३८॥
शालीभिराज्ययुक्ताभिर्होमात्छालीमवाप्नुयात् ।
मुद्गैः मुद्गं घृतैराज्यमिष्टैरिष्टं हुतैर्भवेत् ॥३९॥
साध्यर्क्षवृक्षसंभूतां पिष्टपादरजःकृताम् ।
राजीमरीचलोणोत्थां पुत्तलीं जुहुयान्निशि ॥४०॥
प्रपदाभ्यां च जङ्घाभ्यां जानुभ्यामूरुयुग्मतः ।
नाभेरधस्ताद्धृदयाच्छिन्नेनाकण्ठतस्तथा ॥४१॥
शिरसा च सुतीक्ष्णेन छित्वा शस्त्रेण वै क्रमात् ।
एवं द्वादशधा होमान्नरनारीनराधिपाः ॥४२॥
वश्या भवन्ति सप्ताहाज्ज्वरार्ता चास्य वाञ्छया ।
प्रयान्ति निधनं चास्य वाञ्छयाऽनन्ययोगतः ॥४३॥

मरीचैरित्यादिना वधूमित्यन्तेन श्लोकद्वयेन वनिताकर्षणहोममुपदिशति। तत्र सुगमोऽर्थः ॥३६॥३७॥

अन्नाज्यैरित्यादिना भवेदित्यन्तेन श्लोकद्वयेन अन्नादिद्रव्यहोमविधानात्तत्फलाप्तिमुपदिशति। तत्र तु वाक्यार्थः। चःसमुच्चये ॥३८॥३९॥ साध्यर्क्षं—वृक्षः। अश्विन्यादीनां सप्तविंशतिनक्षत्राणां वृक्षानुत्तरत्र स्वयमेव वक्ष्यति। राजी सर्षपः। लोणं—लवणम्। एतदुक्तं भवति—साध्यजन्मनक्षत्रप्रोक्तवृक्षेण साध्यांशकप्रोक्तमार्गेणोपेतां पुत्तलिकां वा साध्यपादरजःसमेतपिष्टमयीं तथाविधां वा सर्षपमरीचिलवणैर्मस्तृणपेषितैः कृतां वा प्रोक्तक्रमेण जुहुयादिति ॥४०॥ प्रपदाभ्यां—पार्ष्णिसन्धिच्छिन्नाभ्यां अग्रपादाभ्यां जङ्घाभ्यां जानोरधस्ताच्छिन्नाभ्यां जानुभ्यां

पिष्टेन गुड़युक्तेन मरीचैर्जीरकैर्युताम् ।
कृत्वा पुत्तलिकां साध्यनामयुक्तामथो हृदि ॥४४॥
सनामहोमसंपातघृते संपाच्य तां पुनः ।
स्पृशन्निजकराग्रेण सहस्रं प्रजपेन्मनुम् ॥४५॥
अभ्यर्च्य तत् घृताभक्तां भक्षयेत्तद्धिया जपन् ।
नरनारीनृपास्तस्य वश्याः स्युर्मरणावधि ॥४६॥
तैरेव पिष्टैर्वृत्तं तु कृत्वा तन्मध्यतस्तथा ।
साध्यनाम स्फुटं कृत्वा प्राग्वत् संपाच्य भक्षणात् ॥४७॥
वश्यास्ते वत्सरं भूयुः तन्नामार्णान्वितैस्तथा ।
कृत्वाऽभिपाच्य(१) भक्ष्यात्तु वशयेत्तांस्तदर्द्धकम् ॥४८॥

तत्सन्धेरुपरिच्छिन्नाभ्याम् । (जरु)युग्मतः कटीसन्धिच्छिन्ननाभेरधस्तात् नाभिदेशच्छिन्नेन खण्डेनेत्यर्थः । आहृदयात् भिन्नेन—खण्डेनेतिशेषः । आकण्ठतः—कण्ठात् छिन्नेनेत्यर्थः॥४१॥ शिरसा-कण्ठात् उपरिस्थेन । क्रमात्—उक्तक्रमेणैतानि छित्वा एतैर्जुहुयादित्यर्थः ॥४२॥ अनन्ययोगतः—स्वात्मैक्यभावनयेत्यर्थः ॥४३॥

पिष्टेत्यादिभिर्मरणावधि इत्यन्तैस्त्रिभिः श्लोकैः पुत्तलिकाभक्षणे नरनारीनृपादिवश्यमुपदिशति । तत्र पुत्तलिकां—प्राग्वदुक्तमानोपेताम् । हृदि—पुत्तलिकाहृदये, प्राग्वल्लिखितसाध्यसंज्ञामित्यर्थः ॥४४॥ सनामहोमसंपातघृते—साध्यनामसहितविद्याहोमप्रत्याहुत्यवशेषितघृते इत्यर्थः । तां पुत्तलिकाम् ॥४५॥ अभ्यर्च्य—प्राणप्रतिष्ठाविद्यया तत् घृताभक्तां—संपातघृताभक्ताम् । तद्धिया—साध्यभक्षणधिया ॥४६॥

तैरित्यादिना तदर्धकमित्यन्तेन श्लोकद्वयेनापूपविशेषभक्षणेन वशीकरणमुपदिशति । तत्र तैरेव पूर्वोक्तगुडादियुक्तैः । वृत्तं—मण्डलं अपूपमित्यर्थः । प्राग्वत्—संपातातघृतपाचनादिभिः ॥४७॥ते—नरादयः । वत्सरं—अत्यन्तसंयोगे द्वितीया । वत्सरेणेत्यर्थः । भूयुरित्यस्य दिव्यत्वात् स्वरूपं न चिन्त्यं भूयासुरित्यर्थः । तन्नामार्णान्वितैः—संस्कृतैः प्रागुक्तैः पिष्टैः साध्यनामाभिरूपं

---

(१) खादंस्तु वशयेत्तां तदर्धकम् इति मू० पु० पा०

नालिकेरफलाम्भोभिस्तर्पणाद्वनिता वशाः ।
कर्पूरवासितैस्तोयैर्मनुष्याः स्युर्वशे स्थिताः ॥४९॥
तर्पणाल्लवणाम्भोभिः सर्वे स्युस्तस्य किङ्कराः(१) ।
तथा लवणयुक्तेन तोयेन वनिता वशाः ॥५०॥
शुद्धेन वारिणा मासं तदर्द्धं सप्तरात्रकम् ।
तर्पयेद्यस्य नाम्नैव स तस्य स्याद्वशोऽनिशम् ॥५१॥
(२)केतकीवासितैश्चेन्दुयुक्तैः क्षीरफलोदकैः ।
तर्पणाद्वनिता वश्या दद्युः प्राणान्निजं धनम् ॥५२॥
नमेरुवासितैस्तोयैस्तर्पणात् भूमिपा वशाः ।
चम्पकैर्वासितजलैः तर्पणं सर्वरञ्जनम् ॥५३॥
पाटलीशतपत्राभ्यां वासितैस्तर्पणैर्जलैः ।
सर्वलोकचमत्कारकारी भवति नित्यशः ॥५४॥
कस्तूरीवासिताम्भोभिस्तर्पणं सर्वसिद्धिकृत् ।
इन्दुचन्दनसौरभ्यवासिताम्भःप्रतर्पणम् ॥५५॥
वाञ्छितार्थस्य संसिद्धिं मण्डलात् कुरुते ध्रुवम् ।
सक्तुमिश्रजलैराढ्यो धनधान्यादिभिश्चिरम् ॥५६॥

क्त्वेत्यर्थः। तथा—प्रागवत्। संपातघृतादिना वीक्षितान्*। तान्—नरादीन्। तदर्धकं—षण्मासम्। प्रागवत् द्वितीया षण्मासेनेत्यर्थः ॥४८॥

नालिकेरेत्यादिभिर्विघ्ननाशकमित्यन्तैः सार्द्धैरष्टभिः श्लोकैर्नानाकाम्यतर्पण-प्रयोगमुपदिशति। तत्र नालिकेरफलाम्भोभिः—नालिकेरफलोदकैः ॥४९॥५०॥ ॥५१॥५२॥ नमेरुः—सुरपर्णी ॥५३॥५४॥ इन्दुः—कर्पूरम् ॥५५॥ मण्डलात्—मण्डलं नाम एकोनपञ्चाशद्दिनानि। आढ्यः—धनधान्यादिभिरित्यर्थः॥५६॥

---

(१) म्भोधिजलैः सर्वस्य किन्नरा इति खो० पु० पा०। (२) केतकैर्वासितैरिन्दु इति खो पु० पा०।

* वाञ्छितान् नरादीन् इति व० पु० पा०

गुड़मिश्रजले रात्रौ तर्पणं विघ्ननाश(क)नम् ।
चिञ्चाफलरसोपेतैर्जलैर्द्वेषाय तर्पयेत्(१) ॥५७॥
उष्णोदकैः समरिचैस्तर्पयेद्वैरिमृत्यवे ।
केवलोष्णोदकैस्तस्य(२)तीव्रज्वरसमुद्भवः ॥५८॥
निम्बपत्ररसोपेतैरम्बुभिस्तर्पणाद् द्विषाम् ।
जायतेऽन्योन्यवैरस्यं तेन ते नाशमाप्नुयुः ॥५९॥
तथैव सर्षपतिलैस्तर्पणाद्वैरिणोभृशम् ।
अतिसारादिभिर्दोषैरौदरैः क्लेशमावहेत् ॥६०॥
अथ यन्त्राणि देवेशि ! शृणु वाञ्छाप्रदानि वै ।
यैः कृतैः सिद्धयो हस्ते भवन्ति भजनादपि ॥६१॥
षट्कोणं वृत्तयोर्मध्ये कृत्वा मध्ये सनामकम् ।
विद्याद्यवर्णं विलिखेद्द्वितीयादीनि षट् क्रमात् ॥६२॥
षट्सु कोणेषु विलिखेच्छिष्ट(३)वर्णचतुष्टयम् ।
वृत्तयोरन्तरा दिक्षु लिखेत्कोणान्तरालतः ॥६३॥
भूताक्षराणि क्रमशो दश द्विचिक्रमेण तु ।
एवमेकादशविधं मध्येऽन्येषां निवेशनात् ॥६४॥

चिञ्चेत्यादिभिरावहेदित्यन्तैरर्द्धाद्यैस्त्रिभिः श्लोकैर्वैरिनिग्रहतर्पणमुपदिशति । तत्र चिञ्चाफलं—तिन्तिड़ीफलम् ॥५७॥५८॥५९॥ अतिसारादिभिः—रक्तश्लेष्मादिभिः ॥६०॥

अथ यन्त्राणीत्यादिभिः तथा इत्यन्तैरेकादशभिः श्लोकैरविकृतमूलविद्याक्षरैः पञ्चपञ्चाशद्यन्त्राणि तत्फलानि चोपदिशति । तत्र – भजनादपीत्युक्तिर्यन्त्राणां फलप्राप्तौ द्रौत्यप्रतिपादनपरा ॥६१॥६२॥ कोणान्तरालतः—उक्तबन्धचतुष्टयस्य

---

(१) कल्पयेत् मू० पु० पा । (२) तस्यातीव्रेति सो० पु० पा० ।
(३) मर्णचतु इति सो० पु० पा० ।

भूताक्षराणां प्रत्येकं योगात्पञ्चाशताऽन्वितम्।
पञ्चकं परमेशानि! शृणु तानि यथाक्रमम् ॥६५॥
एषु सर्वत्र तद्बाह्ये वृत्तं कृत्वा च मातृकाम्।
विलिखेदभितः पश्चाद्विनियोगमथोच्यते ॥६६॥
वश्ये त्रयमथाकर्षे द्वयं शान्त्यां द्वयं तथा।
मध्ये नामाक्षरन्यासभेदात्तद्भेदकल्पनम् ॥६७॥
एवं तत्फलभेदस्तु सप्तविंशतिधा भवेत्।
शेषाणि शृणु देवेशि! क्रमेण विनियोगतः ॥६८॥
स्तम्भनं मोहनं पश्चाद्विद्वेषोच्चाटनं तथा।
मारणं व्याधिभिः क्लेशं कुलोत्सादकरं तथा ॥६९॥

मध्यस्थकोणदिक्षु ॥६३॥ भूताक्षराणि क्रमशो दश—तानि उद्धारसङ्केतोक्तदशाक्षराणि॥६४॥ षट्कोणमित्यादिभिः पश्चादित्यन्तैस्त्रिपादाधिकैश्चतुर्भिः श्लोकैरेतदुक्तं स्यात्—अभीष्टमानेन वृत्तं कृत्वा तन्मध्ये प्रोक्तक्रमेण षट्कोणं विधाय तद्वृत्तात् बहिरेकैकाङ्गुलमानेन वृत्तद्वयं भ्रमेण निष्पाद्य सर्वबाह्यवृत्तवीथ्यामकारादिक्षकारान्तान्येकपञ्चाशदक्षराणि सविन्दुकानि अग्न्यात्प्रादक्षिण्येनाऽऽलिख्य सर्वमध्ये मूलविद्यादिभूतां ह्रल्लेखां प्राग्वत् सनामाक्षरामालिख्य विद्याद्वितीयाक्षरादि—सप्तमाक्षरान्तानि षडक्षराणि षट्सु कोणेषु अग्न्यादिप्रादक्षिण्येनाऽऽलिख्य विद्यायाः शिष्टाक्षरचतुष्टयं षट्कोणबाह्यवृत्तवीथ्यामग्न्यादिप्रादक्षिण्येन चतसृषु दिक्षु समालिख्य तद्वीथ्यां कोणदिक्षु चतसृषु च वायव्यादिनिर्ऋत्यन्तं भूताक्षराणि दशकर्मानुरूपाणि द्वयं त्रयं इति क्रमेणाऽऽलिखेत् एतत् प्रथमं यन्त्रम्। अस्यैव सर्वमध्ये विद्याद्वितीयाक्षरं—अभितः क्रमेण शिष्टाक्षराणि च मध्यलिखित—पूर्वान्तमालिखेदेतद्द्वितीयं यन्त्रम्। अस्यैव सर्वमध्ये एवमेकादशनामाक्षराणां विद्यागतानां तृतीयादि चरमान्तं प्रत्येकमुक्तक्रमेण विलेखनादुक्ताभ्यां सार्धमेकादश यन्त्राणि सम्भवन्तीति। एष्वेव प्रत्येकं प्रोक्तक्रमात् पञ्चभूताक्षरदशकविन्यासभेदात्पञ्चपञ्चाशद्यन्त्राणि भवन्ति इति॥६५॥ विनियोगः। पञ्चपञ्चाशद्यन्त्राणामितिशेषः ॥६६॥ वश्ये त्रयं—स्त्रीपुरुषराजविषयतस्त्रिविधे वश्ये यन्त्रत्रयम्।

गजाश्वोष्ट्रखराणां च रक्षा महिषमेषयोः ।
गवां नराणां नारीणां विजयः समरद्विषाम् ॥७०॥
द्वन्द्वयुद्धे तथा वादे व्यवहारेषु सर्वतः ।
द्यूते च रक्षानगरग्राममङ्गलकी तथा ॥७१॥
विद्यायां पुनरुक्तानि हित्वा वर्णानि तान्यपि ।
एकादश स्युस्तैः प्राग्वत् स्वरयोगान्महेश्वरि !॥७२॥
षट्सप्तत्या शतं प्रोक्तं वर्णानां मन्त्रगामिनाम् ।
प्रोक्तयन्त्रेषु विलिखेदेकादशविभागतः ॥७३॥
मातृकाविद्यया ऽऽवेष्ट्य कुर्यात्तन्नामयोजनम् ।
षोडशानां च यन्त्राणां विनियोगमथोच्यते ॥७४॥

आकर्षे—स्त्रीपुरुषयोरन्योन्यविषयतो द्विविधे आकर्षे द्वयम् । शान्त्यां—उपद्रवोत्पातविषयतो द्विविधायां शान्त्यां यन्त्रद्वयम् । तद्भेदकल्पनं—यन्त्रभेदकल्पनम्॥६७॥ एवम्—उक्तप्रकारेण । तत्फलभेदः—यन्त्रफलभेदः । सप्तविंशतिधा—वश्याकर्षणशान्तिभिस्तिसृभिः स्तम्भनादिभिश्चतुर्विंशतिभिश्च । वश्यं त्रयमित्यादिभिः तथेत्यन्तैः पञ्चभिः श्लोकैरेतदुक्तं भवति —प्रोक्तानि पञ्चपञ्चाशद्यन्त्राणि वश्यविषये त्रीणि । आकर्षणविषये च द्वयम् । शान्तिविषये च द्वयम् । अन्येषां—स्तम्भनादीनां मङ्गलरक्षान्तानां चतुर्विंशतिविधानां प्रयोगानां प्रत्येकं द्वयं द्वयं एवं पञ्चपञ्चाशद्यन्त्राणां सप्तविंशतिविधफलयोजनं तेषु सर्वत्र नामाक्षरविन्यास—प्रकारकौशलेन तत्र तत्र त्रैविध्यादिकल्पनं, तेन सर्वाण्येतानि पञ्चपञ्चाशद्यन्त्राणि एकैकं सप्तविंशतिविधफलप्रदानि इति ६८॥६९॥७०॥७१॥

विद्यायामित्यादिना योजनमित्यन्तेनार्द्धाधिकेन श्लोकद्वयेन स्वरविकृतमूलविद्याक्षरैः षोडशयन्त्राण्युपदिशति । तत्र—एकादश—हकाररेफनकारतकारयकारककारलकारमकारदकारवकारसकाराः । नात्रासंयुक्तस्वराभावात्स्वरोपादानम् ॥७२॥ प्रोक्तयन्त्रेषु—पञ्चाशत्प्रोक्तयन्त्ररेखाविन्यासत इत्यर्थः । एकादशविभागतः । प्रोक्तस्वरविकृताक्षराणि एकादशैकादशत इत्यर्थः ॥७३॥ तत्रैतदुक्तं

---

(१) मङ्गला इति सो० पु०पा॥

प्रथमेन तु यन्त्रेण कन्यकाः स्ववशं नयेत् ।
तेनैव तासामार्त्तिं च शमयेत्सेकधारणैः ॥७५॥
स्वस्यावेशं च तेनैव कुर्यान्मन्त्रजपं तथा ।
तन्मयीं(तत्स्थां च) भावयेत्कन्यां धूपैः सर्ज्जरसैर्दहेत्(१)॥७६
आविष्टे तां समभ्यर्च्य प्रोक्तैस्तैरुपचारकैः ।
(२)पृच्छेत्स्ववाञ्छितानर्थानाचष्टे साऽऽत्मनः सदा ॥७७॥
ततोऽभ्यर्च्यात्मना योज्यं तां तदात्मा भवेत्स्वयम् ।
तासामवस्थामन्यैश्च शमयेदस्य धारणात् ॥७८॥
द्वितीयेन तु यन्त्रेण कर्पटे गैरिकद्रवैः ।
लिखेत्तेन जयेद्वादे प्रतिवादिनमन्तरा ॥७९॥
स्थापनात्तस्य नियतमतिप्रौढोऽपि तत्क्षणात् ।
स्तब्धजिह्वो निरुद्योगः शुष्कास्यो लोललोचनः ॥८०॥

भवति—प्रोक्ते तस्मिन् यन्त्रे मध्यषट्कोणषट्के अन्तर्वृत्तवीथीमध्यस्थचतुर्दिक्षु यथाक्रमं तत्तदेकादशाक्षराण्यालिख्य बाह्यवृत्तवीथ्यां मातृकामन्ते विद्ययोपेतां तदङ्गतयाऽभिधया सहाग्रादिप्रादक्षिण्येनालिख्य सर्वमध्याक्षरमध्ये च प्राग्वन्नाम समालिखेदिति । एवं तदक्षरैर्विलिखितैरेकादशवर्णोपरिस्थैरेकादशभिरेकादशभिरक्षरैः षोडशयन्त्रकल्पनम् । मातृकान्ते मूलयोजनं तदन्ते नामाक्षरयोजनं कृत्वा तेन वेष्टनमिति सम्प्रदायार्थः ।

षोडशानामित्यादिभिः शहादित इत्यन्तैरर्द्धाधिकैः पञ्चविंशत्या श्लोकैस्तेषां विनियोगक्रममुपदिशति ॥७४॥ तत्र तेनैव—प्रथमेन यन्त्रेण । तासां—कन्यकानाम्॥७५॥ स्वस्यस्य देवतावेशनं तेनैव कुर्यात् तस्मिन् प्रथमे यन्त्रे कन्यकां स्थापयित्वेत्यर्थः । मन्त्रं—मूलविद्यां । तन्मयीं—देवतामयीम् । सर्ज्जरसैः—सर्ज्जरसोनाम धूपद्रव्यविशेषः ॥७६॥ आविष्टे—देवताया आवेशे सति । तां—देवताविष्टां कन्यकाम् । आचष्टे सा देवताऽऽविष्टकन्यकेतिशेषः ॥७७॥ अभ्यर्च्य—मूलविद्यया । तां—

---

(१) दहेत् इति सो० पु० पा० ।

(२) पृच्छेत्तां वाञ्छितं देवि आचष्टे इति सो० पु० पा० ।

विलोकयन् दशदिशस्त्यक्तलज्जः पलायते ।
पतेद्वा पादयोः क्षिप्रं जितोऽस्मीति त्वया वदन् ॥८१॥
तृतीयेन निशापिष्टतोयेन लिखितेन तु ।
कर्पटे खर्परे वापि स्थापितेनोषाभूतले ॥८२॥
चुल्ल्यधो वा दिनैर्द्वित्रैः स्तम्भयेत्सुदृढं रिपोः ।
रोषं गतिं मतिं जिह्वां समरं सर्वमेव च ॥८३॥
आयान्तमग्रतोरातौ मार्गमध्ये खनन्निदम् ।
बलिं दद्यात्तु तद्योन्या तन्त्रचक्रोक्तया पुनः ॥८४॥
तेन तत्पृतना भ्रष्टा रुग्णा गतसमुद्यमा ।
भीता न तन्मुखा जातु घटते यन्त्रवैभवात्(१) ॥८५॥
चतुर्थेनारिनक्षत्रवृक्षोत्थफलकातले ।
लिखितेन पुरोक्तेन स्थापितेन पुरं रिपोः ॥८६॥
नाशमेति रिपुः कृच्छ्रैर्वैरिरोगादिसम्भवैः ।
तेषु तेषु प्रयोगेषु कुर्य्याद्रक्षामथात्मनः(२) ॥८७॥
पञ्चमेनाथ षष्ठेन सप्तमेनाष्टमेन च ।
नवमेन च कुर्वीत रक्षां राष्ट्रपुरालये ॥८८॥

देवताम् । तदात्मा—देवतात्मा । तासां—कन्यकानाम् । अन्यैरपि -पिशाचादिभिः । अस्य—प्रथमस्य यन्त्रस्य धारणादभिषेकपुरःसरादितिशेषः ॥७८॥ अन्तरा स्थापनादित्यन्वयः । तयोरितिशेषः ॥६८॥ तस्य—द्वितीययन्त्रस्य ॥८०॥८१॥ निशापिष्टेन तोयेन—पिष्टहरिद्रारसेनेत्यर्थः । कर्पटे—वस्त्रे । खर्परे—मृण्मये कपाले ॥८२॥ वा—पक्षान्तरे । चुल्ल्यधः । अश्मन्तकाधः वा प्राग्वत् ॥८३॥ आयान्तं—रिपुं ज्ञात्वेतिशेषः । इदं—तृतीययन्त्रम् ॥८४॥ घटते—चेष्टते ॥५८॥ पुरोक्तेन हरिद्रारसेन॥८६॥ तेषु तेषु—अमङ्गलरूपेषु । रक्षां—अभिषेकादितः॥८७॥

पञ्चमेत्यादिभिः प्रयोजकमित्यन्तैश्चतुर्भिः श्लोकैरेतदुक्तं भवति—प्रोक्तेषु

---

(१) मन्त्रवैभवादिति सो० पु० पा० ।   (२) द्रक्षर्थमात्मन इति सो० पु० पा० ।

प्रागादिषु चतुर्दिक्षु बाह्यादिष्वष्टदिक्ष्वपि।
मध्ये च स्थापयेद्यन्त्रं ताम्रपट्टेषु कल्पितम् ॥८९॥
क्रमेण पञ्चमं मध्ये स्थापयेत्तत्प्रयोगतः।
स्वराष्ट्रे नगरे राजगृहे प्रोक्तक्रमात् खनेत् ॥९०॥
तेन वैरिकृताः कृत्याप्रयोगाः क्रूरविग्रहाः।
प्रवेष्टुमशक्तास्ते नाशयन्ति प्रयोजकम् ॥९१॥
दशमे राजते पट्टे विलिख्य कवचं दधत्।
रणं वीरः प्रविश्याशु नाशयेद् द्रावयेच्च तत् ॥९२॥
एकादशं निशातोये घृष्टगैरिकलेखनात्।
कर्पटे स्थापितं शीघ्रं शमयेद्धृतां रणम् ॥९३॥
द्वादशेनेन्दुकाश्मीरलिखितेन धृतेन तु।
भूर्जपत्रपुटे सम्यक् सर्वरक्षा भवेन्नृणाम् ॥९४॥
त्रयोदशेन यन्त्रेण तालपत्रकृतेन तु।
ताललिप्तेन कुड्यान्तः स्थापितेनार्चितेन च ॥९५॥
गृहरक्षा भवेद्व्याधिचोरग्रहभुजङ्गमात्।
राजतो वैरितो बाधादन्यक्षुद्रादितस्तथा ॥९६॥
चतुर्दशेन यन्त्रेण भूर्जपत्रे स्थितेन वै।
धृतेन कामिनीनां तु सौभाग्यमतुलं भवेत् ॥९७॥

पञ्चयन्त्रेषु पञ्चमादि अष्टमान्तं यन्त्रचतुष्कं प्रागादिषु दिक्षु पुनस्तच्चतुष्कं बाह्यादिषु कोणदिक्षु च सर्वमध्ये प्रोक्तानां पञ्चमं नवमं यन्त्रम्। प्रोक्तक्रमेण—स्थापनतः प्रोक्तफलानि स्युरिति। प्रयोजकं—प्रयोक्तारं वैरिपक्षस्थं तत्प्रतिबलमित्यर्थः ॥८८॥८९॥९०॥९१॥९२॥ निशा—प्राग्वत् ॥९२॥९३॥ इन्दुः—कर्पूरम्। काश्मीरं—कुङ्कुमम्। भूर्जपत्रे—भूर्जत्वचि ॥९४॥ ताललिप्तेन—हरिताललिप्तेन। कुड्यान्तः—भित्तिमध्यतः ॥९५॥ राजतः बाधात्—राजकृतात् बाधात्। एवं

तथा पञ्चदशेनापि स्वर्णपट्टधृतेन तु ।
वन्ध्यापि लभते पुत्रं गुणाढ्यं दीर्घजीविनम् ॥९८॥
षोड़शेनोक्तरूपेण साभिषेकं धृतेन वै ।
सपत्नीष्वपि कान्तेन भर्तुः साऽत्यन्तवल्लभा ॥९९॥
भूर्जस्थेन धृतेनैवं सर्वेषामपि सर्वदा ।
रक्षा भवति मर्त्यानां राजचौरग्रहादितः ॥१००॥
स्पर्शतत्त्वमयी व्याप्तिरिति सम्यक्समीरिता ।
अस्या निष्फालनात्चित्ते तत्तत्त्वं स्वात्मसात्कृतम् ॥१०१॥
इति श्रीषोडशनित्यातन्त्रेषु श्रीकादिमते नवमं पटलम् ॥९॥

वैरित इत्यादावपि । क्षुद्रादितः—वैरिकृतक्षुद्रप्रयोगादितः ॥९६॥९७॥९८॥ उक्तरूपेण—स्वर्णपट्टादिषु—विलिखितेन ॥९९॥ धृतेनैवं—एवं धृतेन षोड़शेन यन्त्रेणेत्यर्थः । राजचौरग्रहादित इत्यत्र ग्रहः देवतागणविशेषाः । आदिशब्दः शत्रुकृतक्षुद्रप्रयोगादिविषयः ॥१०१॥

इति श्रीषोड़शनित्यातन्त्रेषु श्रीकादिमताख्यस्य परिपूर्णस्य तन्त्रस्य प्रपञ्चसारसिंहराजप्रकाशाभिधानेन श्रीसुभगानन्दनाथेन विरचितायां मनोरमाख्यायां व्याख्यायां भगमालिनीनित्याविद्याविधानप्रकाशनपरं नवमं पटलं परिपूर्णं परामृष्टम् ॥ ९ ॥

ग्रन्थसङ्ख्या ।

एकसप्ततिसंख्यानि यन्त्राणि नवमे तथा ।
व्याख्या ग्रन्थशतं सत्रिपादमेकोनविंशकम् ॥

अथ दशमपटलम् ।

अथ षोड़शनित्यासु भेरुण्डा पञ्चमी तु या ।
तद्विधानं शृणु प्राज्ञे ! कथयामि यथाविधि ॥१॥
मन्त्रोद्धारः तृतीयेऽभूदङ्गान्याहृतिदेवताः ।
पूजाक्रमं च यन्त्राणि तथैव रिपुनिग्रहम् ॥२॥
कीलप्रयोगान्विजयं समरेषु महीभृताम् ।
रक्षां पुरगजाश्वानां राज(ज्य)रक्षां च वै क्रमात् ॥३॥
आद्यन्तद्वयमध्यस्थैः षड्भिः कुर्यात् षडङ्गकम् ।
रन्ध्राज्ञामुखकण्ठेषु हृन्नाभ्याधारपद्द्वये(१) ॥४॥
न्यसेन्मन्त्रार्णनवकं मातृकान्यासपूर्वकम् ।
ततः शक्तीराहृतिस्था ध्यानं च शृणु पार्वति ! ॥५॥

अथ दशमं पटलम् ।

पूर्वस्मिन्नवमे पटले चतुर्थ्या नित्यक्लिन्नानित्याया विद्यामुपदिश्यानन्तरं पञ्चम्या भेरुण्डानित्याया विधानमुपदिशति । अथ—षोड़शेत्यादिना तन्मयइत्यन्तेन श्लोकशतरूपेण दशमेन पटलेन । तत्र—अथ षोड़शेत्यादिभिः क्रमादित्यन्तैस्त्रिभिः श्लोकैः पटलार्थानुद्दिशति । तत्र—कीलप्रयोगान् त्) साध्यनक्षत्रवृक्षादिकीलकस्थापनेन वैरिनिग्रहविशेषान्(त्) ॥१॥२॥३॥

आद्यन्त·इत्यादिना पा॑तीत्यन्तेन श्लोकद्वयेन न्यासजा(ता)लादिकमुपदिशति । तत्र—आद्यन्तद्वयमध्यस्थैः—आद्यमेकमक्षरं अन्ततोद्वयं च हित्वाऽवशिष्टैर्वर्णैः षड़ङ्गानि कुर्यादित्यर्थः । रन्ध्रं—ब्रह्मरन्ध्रम् । आज्ञा—भ्रुवोर्मध्यम् । पदद्वये—पादद्वये अक्षरद्वयम् ॥४॥ मातृकान्यासपूर्वकं—उपरिष्टाद्वक्ष्यमाणमातृकान्यासपुरःसरमित्यर्थः ॥५॥

---

(१) नाभ्याधारपदद्वये इति सौ० पु० पा० ।

बाह्यावृत्तौ तु ब्राह्माद्या युगशक्तीस्तु पूजयेत्(१) ॥
तदन्तरष्टपत्रेषु विजयां विमलां शुभाम् ॥६॥
विश्वां विभूतिं विनतां विविधां विरतां (२)क्रमात् ।
तदन्तरष्टकोणेषु(३) कमलां कामिनीं तथा ॥७॥
किरातां तीर्तिसहितां कुट्टनीं कुलसुन्दरीम् ।
कल्याणीं कालकोलां च पूजयेदुक्तयोगतः ॥८॥
डाकिनीं राकिनीं तद्वल्लाकिनीं काकिनीं तथा ।
साकिनीं लाकिनीं(४) षट्सु कोणेषु परितोऽर्चयेत् ॥९॥
इच्छाज्ञानक्रियाशक्तीरर्चयेदन्तरावृतौ ।
अष्टकोणान्तरालेषु पूजयेदायुधाष्टकम् ॥१०॥
चतुरस्रद्वयं कृत्वा दिक्षु द्वारसमन्वितम् ।
तदन्तरष्टपत्राब्जं वृत्तयुग्ममथान्तरा ॥११॥

(बाह्ये)बाह्येत्यादिभिरष्टकमित्यन्तैः पञ्चभिः श्लोकैरावरणशक्तीरुपदिशति— तत्र युगशक्तीः—कृतयुगशक्तिः त्रेतायुगशक्तिः द्वापरयुगशक्तिः कलियुगशक्तिरित्येताः। अत्र—ब्राह्म्याद्यष्टशक्तीः पश्चिमादिदिक्षु स्थितेषु द्वारेषु देवीदक्षिणभागादिपार्श्वयोः, पार्श्वयोश्च कृतयुगादिशक्तीः वाय्वादिकोणेषु प्रादक्षिण्येनेत्यर्थः॥६॥७॥ उक्तयोगतः—बीजद्वयसमाक्षरीमध्ये तत्तन्नामयोजनप्रादक्षिण्यादियोगतः। सर्वत्र परिवारशक्तीनां विशेषानुक्तौ सामान्योक्तं बीजद्वयमादावन्ते समाक्षरीं योजयेदिति सम्प्रदायः॥८॥ तथा—नैरृतदिगादि ॥९॥१०॥

चतुरस्रद्वयमित्यादिभिरावृत्तामित्यन्तैस्त्रिभिः श्लोकैः देव्या नित्यसपर्याचक्रमुपदिशति। तत्र अष्टास्रं भूपुरद्वन्द्वात्। एतदुक्तं भवति—प्राक्प्रत्यक् सूत्रं कृत्वा तस्य सूत्रस्य मानं दशधा विभज्य तेषु पूर्वाग्रात्तृतीयांशावसाने पश्चिमाग्राच्च तन्मानेन चिह्नं(५) कृत्वा तस्य सूत्रस्य पूर्वाग्रमवष्टभ्य तयोः पश्चिमचिह्नमानेन तत्पश्चिमा-

---

(१) सञ्चयेत् इति सो० पु० पा०।
(२) विविधाविनतामिति सो पु० पा०।
(३) रष्टपत्रेषु इति मू० पु० पा।
(४) हाकिनीमिति मू० पु० पा०।
(५) पश्चिमाग्राच्चतयोर्जनेन च्छिन्नं कृत्वेति वं० पु० पा०।

अष्टास्रं भूपुरद्वन्द्वात्तच्च वृत्तसमन्वितम् ।
तदन्तस्तादृशं कुर्यात् षट्कोणं वा तु विग्रहम् ॥१२॥
तदन्तस्तादृशीं कुर्याद्योनिं तन्मध्यतोयजेत् ।
भेरुण्डां पञ्चमीं नित्यामुक्तशक्तिभिरावृताम् ॥१३॥
अर्घ्यं षड़ङ्गमूलाभ्यां संसाध्य प्राङ्मुखो यजेत्(१) ।
बलिं च षोड़शार्णेन दद्यादाद्यन्तयोः क्रमात् ॥१४॥
अथ ध्यानं प्रवक्ष्यामि देव्याः सर्वार्थसिद्धिदम् ।
तदावृत्तिस्थशक्तीनां क्रमेण शृणु पार्वति ! ॥१५॥
तप्तकाञ्चनसङ्काशदेहां नेत्रत्रयान्विताम् ।
चारुस्मिताञ्चितमुखीं दिव्यालङ्कारभूषिताम् ॥१६॥

ग्रमवष्टभ्य तयोः पूर्वचिह्नमानेन च भ्रमणात् दक्षिणोत्तरयोः पार्श्वयोः मत्स्यद्वयं निष्पाद्य तन्मत्स्यद्वयमध्यावष्टम्भेन दक्षिणोत्तरं सूत्रमास्फाल्य पश्चात्तन्मध्यहंसपदमारभ्याभीष्टमानेन चतुर्षु पार्श्वसूत्रेषु चिह्नानि कृत्वा तत्तच्चिह्नमवष्टभ्य मध्यहंसपदावधिकमानेन चतुर्षु कोणेषु मत्स्यान्विधाय तेषु मत्स्यान्मत्स्यमिति क्रमेण सूत्रचतुष्टयमास्फालयेत् । एवं कृते चतुष्कोष्ठोपेतं समचतुरस्रं भवति । तत्र मध्यहंसपदमध्यमवष्टभ्य चतुरस्रकोणमानेन बहिर्भ्रमेण वृत्तं कृत्वा मध्यसूत्रद्वयाग्रचतुष्टयं तद्वृत्तावधि विकास्य प्रागग्राद्दक्षिणाग्रं दक्षिणाग्रात्पश्चिमाग्रं पश्चिमाग्रादुत्तराग्रमुत्तराग्रात्प्रागग्रं च सूत्रचतुष्टयमास्फालयेत् । एवं कृते चतुरस्रद्वयेनाष्टसु दिक्षु अष्टकोणानि सम्भवन्तीति । एवं सर्वत्राष्टकोणनिर्माणक्रमः । तादृशं — वृत्तसहितम्॥११॥१२॥ तादृशीं—वृत्तसहिताम् । चक्रविरचनाक्रमो यथा—चतुर्दिक्षु द्वारयुक्तं चतुरस्रद्वयं यथामानं कृत्वा तदन्तर्वृत्तं विधाय तदन्तरष्टदलपद्मं कृत्वा तदन्तर्यथामानमष्टास्रं कृत्वा तदन्तर्वृत्तं तदन्तः प्राग्वत् षट्कोणं कृत्वा तदन्तर्वृत्तसहितां समत्रिरेखां योनिं निष्पाद्य तत्र देवीमुक्तक्रमेण पूजयेदिति ॥१३॥

अर्घ्यमित्यादिना श्लोकेनार्घ्यकल्पनं बलिदानादिकं चोपदिशति । तत्राद्यन्तयोरपि षोड़शार्णेनैव बलिं दद्यादित्यर्थः । क्रमा — बलिद्रव्यं मुद्रासहितम् ॥१४॥

अथ ध्यानं इत्यादिभिः सदा इत्यन्तैः पञ्चभिः श्लोकैः सपरिवाराया देव्या

---

(१) भवेत् इति मू० पु० पा०

ताटङ्कहारकेयूररत्नवस्त्र(१)कमण्डिताम् ।
रसनानूपुरोर्म्यादिभूषणैरतिसुन्दरीम् ॥१७॥
पाशाङ्कुशौ चर्मखड्गौ गदावज्रधनुःशरान् ।
करैर्दधानामासीनां पूजायामन्यदा स्थिताम् ॥१८॥
शक्तीश्च तत्समाकारतेजोहेतिभिरन्विताः ।
पूजयेत्तद्वदभितः स्मितसौम्यमुखः सदा ॥१९॥
एवं देवीमावृतिभिरावृतामर्चयेत्तथा ।
बलिमाद्यन्तयोर्दद्यात् पूर्वोक्तविधिना युतम् ॥२०॥
स्नातोमौनी पयोभक्षः प्रजपेन्नवलक्षकम् ।
तद्दशांशं हुनेदग्नौ त्रिमध्वक्तैः कुशेशयैः ॥२१॥
तावच्च तर्पये(२) त्तोयैरिन्दुचन्दनवासितैः ।
अर्चयेन्नित्यशो देवीं सहस्रं प्रजपेदपि ॥२२॥
ततः स्वगुरुणोद्दिष्टप्रयोगान्विधिना चरेत् ।
अन्यथा निष्फलं भूयात् प्रत्युतैनं निहन्ति च ॥२३॥

नित्यसपर्याध्यानमुपदिशति। तत्र वामोर्ध्वहस्तादि दक्षिणाधोहस्तान्तं वामादिदक्षिणक्रमेणायुधानि कल्पयेत् ॥१५॥१६॥१७॥ अन्यदा—प्रयोगेषु ॥१८॥ तद्वत्—पूर्वोक्तवत् ॥१९॥

एवमित्यादिना श्लोकेन पूजानिगमनमुपदिशति। तत्र तथेति प्रादक्षिण्यं बीजद्वय सप्ताक्षरीसमेतत्वं चोच्यते। पूर्वोक्तविधिनेति—अत्र व्यञ्जनादिकं कथयति ॥२०॥

स्नात इत्यादिभिः निहन्ति चेत्यन्तैस्त्रिभिः श्लोकैर्विद्यासाधनप्रकार तद्विनियोगक्रममन्यथा क्रमकरणे प्रत्यवायं चोपदिशति। तत्र नवलक्षकमिति विशेषविधानेन केवलमक्षरसङ्ख्य लक्षमित्यर्थः ॥२१॥२२॥ प्रत्युत न केवलं नैष्फल्यं स्वविनाशमपीत्यर्थः ॥२३॥

---

(१) रत्नकनकमण्डितामिति सो पु० पा०। (२) तर्पणं इति मू० पु० पा०।

द्वितीयाद्यैस्त्रिभिर्बीजैः षष्ठेन च समीरितम् ।
निग्रहार्थमथान्यैस्तु(१) त्रिभिरन्त्यद्वयेन च ॥२४॥
षट्कोणं वृत्तयुग्मं च कृत्वा तन्मध्यतोलिखेत् ।
द्वितीयार्णं साध्ययुतं कोणेष्वन्यत्त्रयं लिखेत् ॥२५॥
अधरेषु(२) समायानि तानि लेख्यानि सर्वदा ।
वृत्तयोरन्तरा साध्यसमेतैः पवनार्णकैः ॥२६॥
संवेष्ट्य तानि† संजप्य रिपोरष्टमराशिगे ।
श्मशाने स्थापयेत्तत्र लग्ने विद्वेषणं भवेत् ॥२७॥
निम्बपत्ररसे पिष्टा(३) श्मशानाङ्गारलेखनात् ।
पृषदाखुत्वचि च वतत्सहस्रद्वयजायत (?) ॥२८॥
द्वीपिवक्त्रत्वचि लिखेत्तद्यन्त्रं गोमुखत्वचि ।
समालिख्य स्वसंज्ञां तु पूर्वस्मिन्नुत्तरे रिपोः ॥२९॥

द्वितीयाद्यैरित्यादिना श्लोकेन विद्याया निग्रहानुग्रहयोर्द्दिग्याक्षराणि विभजति। तत्र अथान्यैस्तु त्रिभिः अन्त्यद्वयेन च– शान्तिकं कुर्यादिति शेषः ॥२४॥

षट्कोणमित्यादिभिर्यममित्यन्तैरेकादशभिः श्लोकैर्विद्याया द्वितीयाक्षराद्धि- प्रधानं यन्त्रं, तेन यन्त्रेण विद्वेषणं वादविजय उच्चाटनं मारणं चेति चतुरः प्रयोगा- नुपदिशति। तत्र द्वितीयार्णं—क्रोंकारः। अन्यत्त्र त्रयं—मन्त्रस्य तृतीयचतुर्थ- षष्ठाक्षराणि त्रीणि ॥२५॥ अधरेषु समायानि(५) षट्कोणेषु अधस्थेषु त्रिषु तान्यक्ष- राणि विसर्जनीयसहितान्यालिखेदित्यर्थः। तेन उपरितनानां विन्दुयुक्तत्वमुक्त मेव। प्रादक्षिण्येन पवनाक्षरदशकलेखनानन्तरं साध्याक्षरलेखनं कुर्यात् ॥२६॥ तानि—द्वितीयतृतीयचतुर्थषष्ठाक्षराणि चत्वारि। तत्र→अष्टमलग्नोदये ॥२७॥ पृषत्—बिड़ालः। आखुः—मूषकः। (जायते इत्यन्तेन विद्वेषणप्रयोगक-

---

(१) निग्रहाद्यमथोन्यैस्तु इति मू० पु० पा०। (२) अन्तरेषु इति मू० पु० पा०।

(३) पिष्ट श्मशाना इति मू० पु० पा०

(४) समाग्राम्नानि इति वं० पु० पा०। समाग्रातानि इति सो० पु० पा०।

† संवेष्टितानि इति म पु० पा ।

उत्तराधरमाधाय शिलाधः सन्ध्ययोर्जपेत् ।
जपित्वा प्रोक्तसङ्ख्यां च जयेत्तं प्रतिवादिनम्(१) ॥३०॥
एतन्मुखावलोकेन प्रतिवादी हतोद्यमः ।
निरुत्तरः पलायेत जितोऽस्मीति वदेत्तु वा ॥३१॥
हरितालेन घृष्टेन निशारसयुतेन तु ।
विलिखेद्वा(द)रविजये(द्यु) युक्तमुक्तमेण वै ॥३२॥
रुरुचर्मणि(रक्तेन) तद्रक्तलिखितं तद्रिपोर्गृहे ।
प्रोक्तकाले खनेदुक्तक्रमपूजाजपान्वितः ॥३३॥
उच्चाटयेद्रिपुं मासान्नियतं यन्त्रवैभवात् ।
नृचर्मणि च तद्रक्तलिखितं तच्छ्मशानके ॥३४॥
पूजाजपक्रमोपेतं निखनेदुक्तकालतः ।
मासेन याति वैरी तु दाहज्वरयुतो यमम् ॥३५॥
तृतीयं मध्यतः कृत्वा त्वितरान् परितो लिखेत् ।
साध्यर्क्षयोनेस्त्वचितन्मधूच्छिष्टेन पीड़ितम् ॥३६॥
श्मशानभस्मलिखितं निक्षिप्तं नष्टकूपके ।
प्रोक्तकालसमोपेतं(२) नाशयेत्सलिले रिपुम् ॥३७॥

थनम् ॥२८॥ तद्यन्त्रं—पूर्वं विद्वेषणस्योक्तं यन्त्रम् । द्वीपिवक्त्रत्वचि गोमुखत्वचि च । लेखनद्रव्यमुपरिष्टाद्वक्ष्यमाणं हरितालम् । पूर्वस्मिन्—व्याघ्रमुखचर्मणि ॥२८॥ उत्तरे—गोमुखचर्मणि—*उत्तराधरं स्वसंज्ञोपेतं चर्म—उत्तरस्थं रिपुसंज्ञोपेतं (चर्म) अधःस्थितं च । सन्ध्ययोः—प्रातस्तनसायन्तन्योः ॥३०॥३१॥ उक्तक्रमेण वै वादविजये स्तम्भनप्रोक्तपार्थिवदशाक्षरैर्वेष्टयेत् ॥३१॥३३॥३४॥ उक्तकालतः—प्राग्वदष्टमे राशावित्यर्थः ॥३५॥

तृतीयमित्यादिभिर्वैभवात् इत्यन्तैरेकादशभिः श्लोकैर्विद्यायां तृतीयाक्षरादि-

---

(१) जयेत्तान्प्रतिवादिन इति मू० पु० पा० ।
(२) प्रोक्तक्रमसमोपेतं मू० पु० पा० ।
* नतु इति टी० पु० पा० अधिकः पाठः ।

तद्देव वह्निमूलेन पिष्टेन मनुजासृजा।
लिखितं गोत्वचि क्षिप्तं चुल्ल्यामुपरि वह्निना ॥३८॥
ज्वलितेनानिशं मासादग्निनाऽग्नौ पतेद्रिपुः।
तृतीयेन तु मध्येन वेष्टितैरितरैरपि ॥३९॥
उलूककाकपक्षाभ्यां प्रथमोक्तेन संलिखेत्।
गर्दभत्वचि तत् खात्वा कुण्डमध्ये तदूर्ध्वतः ॥४०॥
साध्यनक्षत्रेऽग्नौ वह्नौ बीजैरुन्मत्तसम्भवैः।
कद्रुतैलप्लुतैर्होमान्मत्तोऽरिर्म्रियते(५) ध्रुवम् ॥४१॥
साध्यर्क्षवृक्षकीलं तु प्रोक्तयन्त्रसमन्वितम्।
खरस्नायुभिराबद्धं खातं वैरिपुरे निशि ॥४२॥
राशौ तदष्टमे मासात्तत्पुरं पितृकाननम्।
काकोलूकबकश्येनकङ्कतित्तिरिपादयोः ॥४३॥
विलिख्य यन्त्राण्युक्तानि प्रेतचीरे निबध्य तत्।
खनेन्मङ्गलवारे तु प्रोक्तकाले चतुष्पथे ॥४४॥
त्रिसप्ताहात् व्रजेद्वैरी स्यादुन्मत्तो दिशो दश।
तान्येव तत्तच्चर्मस्थं तदालयभुवि स्थितम् ॥४५॥
नाशयेद्गजमर्त्याश्वगोखरोष्ट्राजसैरिभान्।
सप्ताहात्तद(द्व)यान्मासा (?) नियतं यन्त्रवैभवात् ॥४६॥

प्रधानयन्त्र विधानं तत्प्रयोगांस्त्रयोदश चोपदिशति। तत्र इतरान्—द्वितीय-चतुर्थषष्ठान् विलिखेत्। साध्यनक्षत्रयोनेः—प्राग्वत् उन्मत्तः स्यादित्यन्वयः। दिशोदश व्रजेदित्यन्वयः। तान्येव यन्त्राणीतिशेषः ॥३६॥३७॥३८॥३९॥४०॥४१॥ ॥४२॥४३॥४४॥४५॥ सैरिभान्—महिषान्। अस्मिन् प्रकरणे यन्त्रनिर्माणं सुकरम् ॥४६॥

---

(५) होमादरातिर्म्रियते इति म० पु० पा०।

तच्छान्तिं शृणु देवेशि ! यन्त्रध्यानाभिषेकतः ।
तन्मन्त्रवर्णैर्यन्त्रस्थैश्चिन्तामन्त्रार्थवैभवात् ॥४७॥
पद्ममष्टदलं कृत्वा मध्ये त्वाद्यं सनामकम् ।
लिखित्वाऽष्टसु पत्रेषु चतुष्कं तद्बहिरालिखेत् ॥४८॥
बहिर्वृत्तान्तरा कुर्यान्मातृकाक्षरवेष्टनम् ।
प्रागुक्तैरेव तैर्द्रव्यैः संपूज्य विनियोगतः ॥४९॥
तत्तत्क्लेशविनाशः स्यात् तथा मन्त्रानुभावतः ।
विजयं समरे राज्ञां शृणु वैरिविनाशतः ॥५०॥
मन्त्राक्षराणि प्रत्येकं योजयेत्षोडशस्वरैः ।
तेन मन्त्राक्षराणि स्युः सङ्ख्यया च शतं पुनः (१)॥५१॥
चत्वारिंशच्च चत्वारि तैर्यन्त्ररचनं शृणु ।
येन सर्वत्र समरे विजयोभवति ध्रुवम् ॥५२॥

तच्छान्तिमित्यादिभिरनुभावत इत्यन्तैरर्धाधैस्त्रिभिः श्लोकैर्विद्यायां प्रथमपञ्चमसप्तमाष्टमनवमाक्षरैः पञ्चयन्त्राणि तैरुक्तक्रूरप्रयोगाणां शान्तिप्रयोगं चोपदिशति। तत्र ध्यानं—ध्यानपटले वक्ष्यमाणम्। अभिषेकतः—यन्त्रमध्ये निवेशितैः प्राग्वत्तदक्षरपञ्चकजपादिनेत्यर्थः॥४७॥४८॥ प्रागुक्तैः—शान्तिकर्मणि प्रोक्तसितचन्दनकर्पूरादिलेखनद्रव्यसितप्रसूनाद्यैः। विनियोगतः—साधारणैकादितः। एतदुक्तं भवति—यथामानमष्टदलं पद्मं तद्बहिर्वृत्तद्वयं च विधाय तत्कर्णिकामध्ये प्रथमाक्षरं ससाध्यमालिख्य बहिरग्न्यादिप्रादक्षिण्येनाष्टसु दलेषु पञ्चमसप्तमाष्टमनवमाक्षराणि द्विरालिख्य बाह्यवृत्तवीथ्यामग्न्यादिप्रादक्षिण्येनादिक्षान्तां मातृकामालिखेदित्येतत् प्रथमं यन्त्रम्। एवमन्येषामपि चतुर्णामक्षराणां प्रत्यकं मध्यतोनिवेशनात् तदितरवेष्टनतश्चत्वारि सम्भूय पञ्च यन्त्राणि प्रागुक्तोपद्रवशान्तिकारीणीति ॥४९॥

विजयमित्यादिभिर्भवेदित्यन्तैरर्धाधैस्त्रयोदशभिः श्लोकैर्विद्यायां स्वरविकृताक्षराणि तत्सङ्ख्यां तैर्यन्त्रनिर्माणं तत्प्रयोगांश्चोपदिशति। तत्र—मन्त्राक्षराणि प्रत्येकमित्युक्त्या अपुनरुक्ताक्षरयोजनं नात्र विवक्षितम् ॥५०॥५१॥५२॥

---

(१) पुरा इति मो० पु० पा०

प्राक्प्रत्यगदक्षिणोदक्च कुर्याद्रेखास्त्रयोदश।
तेन तावन्ति कोष्ठानि सम्भवन्ति समन्ततः ॥५३॥
कृत्वाऽष्टास्रं ततो बाह्ये वृत्तयुग्मं ततोलिखेत्।
अक्षराणि शिवाद्यन्तु निऋर्त्यन्तमनुक्रमात् ॥५४॥
तत्र मन्त्रार्णकोष्ठेषु नवस्वाख्यां समालिखेत्।
बहिरष्टसु कोणेषु द्वितीयार्णादि सँल्लिखेत् ॥५५॥
अन्तरालेषु विलिखेदाद्यं वृत्तद्वयान्तरा(न्) ।
तान्येव मातृकाख्याभिर्विदर्भितमथो न्यसेत्(१) ॥५६॥
एतत् पटे समालिख्य ध्वजीकृत्य रणोद्यमे।
दर्शयेत्तेन रिपवः पलायन्ते दिशो दश ॥५७॥

तावन्ति—यावदक्षरसंख्यानि चतुश्चत्वारिंशदधिकशतसंख्यानीत्यर्थः। समन्ततः—समचतुरस्ररूपतः ॥ ५३ ॥ अष्टास्रं—प्राग्वत् ॥५४॥५५॥ तानि--विद्याक्षराणि। नवमातृकाख्याभिः—मातृकाक्षरसाध्याक्षरैः। विदर्भितं—द्व्यन्तरोक्तम्। लिखेत्। प्रागित्यादिभिर्न्यसेदित्यन्तैश्चतुर्भिः श्लोकैरेतदुक्तं भवति--समान्तरालानि प्राक्प्रत्यगग्राणि दक्षिणोत्तराग्राणि च त्रयोदशकोणसूत्राण्यास्फाल्य तद्बहिः कोणस्पृष्टास्पृष्टिकया भ्रमेण वृत्तं कृत्वा तद्बहिः प्राग्वच्चतुरस्रं कृत्वा तद्बहिरेकाङ्गुलान्तरालं वृत्तद्वयं विधाय तत्कोष्ठेषु शिवादिनिऋर्त्यन्तं तानि स्वरविकृतान्यक्षराणि प्रतिपङ्क्ति उत्तरारम्भं दक्षिणावसानं च समालिख्य तत्र मन्त्राक्षरनवकोपेतनवकोष्ठेषु साध्यनाम विलिख्य तद्बहिरग्रादिप्रादक्षिण्येनाष्टसु कोणेषु विद्याद्वितीयाक्षरादीन्यष्टाक्षराणि विलिख्य प्रथमाक्षरं तदष्टकोणान्तरालेष्वष्टस्वालिख्य बहिर्वृत्तवीथ्यां मातृकाक्षरसाध्याक्षरैर्विदर्भितानि विद्याक्षराण्यालिखेदिति। यस्य (य)मन्त्रस्य वर्णस्य स्वरयोजने कृते यस्मिन् स्वरे योजिते मन्त्राक्षरं भवति तदक्षरं यस्मिन् कोष्ठे पतति तत्र साध्यं लिखेत्। एवं मन्त्रस्थनववर्णाश्रयकोष्ठेषु। अत्र नवस्वित्युक्तेर्मन्त्रस्थद्वितीयवर्णस्य ओँकारयोजने मन्त्रस्थचतुर्थवर्णस्य ॐकार-

---

(१) विदर्भितद्वयोन्यन्यसेत् इति मू० पु० पा०। मथोलिखेत् इति सो० पु० पा०।

प्रणमेयुर्निजां लक्ष्मीं प्राभृतीकृत्य तत्क्षणात् ।
तदेव वैरिशिबिरे निखनेदुदये शनेः ॥५८॥
सद्यस्त्वन्योन्यकलहान्नाशमेति सुनिश्चितम् ।
तदेव स्वपुरे मध्ये स्थापयेद्धिषणोदये ॥५९॥
पराभिचारकृत्यादिदुरितानि न तत्र वै ।
संस्पृशन्ति पुरान्तस्थाद्यन्त्रशक्त्यनुभावतः ॥६०॥
तद्यन्त्रं ताम्रपट्टे तु विलिख्याऽभ्यर्च्य तत् पुनः ।
स्थापयेत् साध्यभूभर्तुरेकादशसमुद्यमे ॥६१॥
गजवाजिगृहेष्वस्य(स्वस्य)भाण्डागारेऽस्त्र(स्व)मण्डपे ।
अन्तःपुरे नगर्यास्तु दिक्षु मध्ये च तत् खनेत् ॥६२॥
यत्र संस्थापितं यन्त्रं तत्रार्चा नित्यशोऽनृप ।
कारयेत्तेन तत् सर्वं शाश्वतं वृद्धये भवेत् ॥६३॥
बीजानि तानि प्रत्येकमष्टपत्रसरोरुहे ।
मध्ये दलेषु परितो लिखेदेकैकशः क्रमात् ॥६४॥
बहिर्मातृकयाऽऽवेष्ट्य सञ्जप्याभ्यर्च्य नित्यशः ।
स्वजन्मर्क्षादिनवके कुर्याच्छान्तिमनुक्रमात् ॥६५॥
यन्नाशवे भवेदस्य ग्रहतो राजतोऽथ(पि) वा ।
रोगतो वैरितो वाऽपि तस्मिन् तत्तेन शामयेत् ॥६६॥

योजने मन्त्रवर्णत्वपर्यवसानेपि तत्र न साध्यलिखनमिति ॥५६॥५७॥ तदेव—तद्यन्त्रमेव । शनेरुदये—शनिस्थितराश्युदयकाले ॥५८॥ तदेव—यन्त्रं । धिषणोदये—धिषणो बृहस्पतिस्तस्योदयः प्राग्वत् ॥५९॥ पुरान्तःस्थान्—जनानिति शेषः ॥६०॥ तद्यन्त्रं—पूर्वोक्तम् । एकादशसमुद्यमे—साध्यस्य जन्मलग्नराशेश्चन्द्रलग्नराशेर्वा एकादशे राशौ लग्नगते ॥६१॥ दिक्षु मध्ये चेति गजगृहादिसामान्यम् ॥६२॥ तत्सर्वं—प्रोक्तगजादिकम् । वृद्धये—वृद्ध्यै भवेदित्यर्थः ॥६३॥

मन्त्रार्चीऽप्यथ भस्मस्थं यन्त्रं कृत्वा तु तेन तु ।
रक्षां कुर्वीत सर्वेषां सर्वापत्तारणाय वै ॥६७॥
तत्तद्यन्त्रं तद्दिनेषु स्नानपानासनादिना ।
ग्रहजं वैरिजं दुःखं शाम्यत्येव न संशयः ॥६८॥
क्रमेण नवयन्त्राणि नवग्रहमयानि तु ।
तस्मात्तत्तद्‌ग्रहक्लेशं तत्तद्यन्त्रं (न) (च) शामयेत् ॥६९॥
सङ्काशते (सेकासन) विभूत्यादिप्रयोगैरुदितैः क्रमात् ।
विविधानि विषाण्येभिर्यन्त्रैर्जलनिवे(शितैः)शनैः ॥७०॥
नाशयेत्पान(से)काभ्यां धारणेनार्चनेन च ।
एभिस्तु नवभिर्यन्त्रैर्य(त्तत्)न्न साध्यं न कुत्रचित् ॥७१॥
देशे वा नगरे ग्रामे मङ्गले पर्वतादिके(१) ।
प्रथमं मध्यतः खात्वा प्रागादिषु ततोऽष्टसु ॥७२॥
द्वितीयादीनि तु खनेत् तत्र लक्ष्मीरिति स्थिरा ।
धर्मार्थौ चातिसंवृद्धौ भवेतामुक्तयोगतः ॥७३॥
द्वितीयं मध्यतः खात्वा त्वितराण्यभितः खनेत् ।
धार्मिकास्तेन तत्रस्थाः प्रसीदन्ति च देवताः ॥७४॥
सप्तस्वन्येषु च तथा कान्त्यारोग्ययशोधनैः ।
पुत्रज्ञानधनैश्चाढ्याः प्रभवन्ति च नित्यशः ॥७५॥
दृष्टेषु घोरैः फणिभिः नवभिर्नवरन्ध्रगैः ।
ध्यानैर्मृतोऽपि माहात्म्यान्मन्त्रस्योत्तिष्ठते ध्रुवम् ॥७६॥

बीजानीत्यादिभिस्तत्सिद्धये इत्यन्तैः षोडशभिः श्लोकैर्विद्याक्षरैर्नवभिर्नवयन्त्रविरचनं तद्दिनियोगांस्तत्फलानि चोपदिशति । तत्र स्वजन्मर्क्षं—जन्मत्रयं

---

(१) खर्वटादिके इति मू० पु० पा० ।

अश्विन्यादिषु ऋक्षेषु नवानि नवसु क्रमात् ।
विलिख्य देवीं तत्रस्थां नवाकारां नवस्वपि ॥७७॥
पूजयेदुपचारैस्ता(१) नित्यशोभक्तिसंयुतः ।
प्रागुक्तपरिवारादिरहितां पूजयन्नपि ॥७८॥
सिद्धिमेति नरो भक्त्या परया चेत्समन्वितः ।
स्त्रीबालवृद्धाशक्तानां गतिरेषा च (स्व)सिद्धये ॥७९॥
भेरुण्डा कर्णयोर्जप्याद्विषार्तस्य तदैव सः ।
निर्विषो जायतेऽचिन्त्या(२) मन्त्राणां शक्तयः शिवे ! ॥८०॥
त्रैलोक्यमोहनी विद्या सर्वतो भवतास्तुता(३) ।
न कदाचित्तु सा प्रोक्ता तां मे ब्रूहि महेश्वर ! ॥८१॥
सर्वेषामेव मन्त्राणां विद्यानां च यशस्विनि ! ।
व्याप्तरूपं प्रवक्ष्यामि शृणु त्वमिदमद्भुतम् ॥८२॥
येन नारीनरन्टपदेवताः सर्वजन्तवः ।
भजन्त्येनं यथा मां त्वं तत्प्रयोगबलाद्ध्रुवम् ॥८३॥
अकारादिक्षकारान्तैर्मातृकार्णैः सबिन्दुभिः ।
प्रत्येकं पुटितान् कृत्वा मन्त्रान्विद्या अथापि च(वा) ॥८४॥
विद्यया मातृकावर्णान् पुटयेन्मन्त्रतोऽपि वा ।
प्रोक्तं तद्यन्त्रनवकं कुम्भे संस्थाप्य चैतया ॥८५॥

नवकमित्युक्त्या एकैकनक्षत्रेण चाभिषेकोऽप्यभिहितः । एषामन्यार्थः सुगमः ॥६४॥
६५॥६६॥६७॥६८॥६९॥७०॥७१॥७२॥७३॥७४॥७५॥७६॥७७॥७८॥७९॥

भेरुण्डामित्यादिना श्लोकेन विषापहरणमुपदिशति—तत्राऽर्थः सुगमः ॥८०॥

---

(१) स्तैः इति मू० पु० पा० । (२) जायते चिन्ता इति मू० पु० पा० ।

३ सर्वतोप्रभवास्तुता इति सो० पु० पा ।

जपतर्पणहोमार्चासिद्धया सेक ईरित:(१)।
कुचन्दनैर्गैरिकैर्वा दरदैश्चन्दनैस्तथा ॥८६॥
सिन्दूरैस्तण्डुलैर्मुद्गैस्तिलैः कृष्णैः सितैरपि।
नवानां नवभिः कुर्यादेभिर्यन्त्रप्रकल्पनम् ॥८७॥
चैत्रादिविषुवद्वन्द्वे तथैवायनयोर्द्वयोः।
(२)रक्षोत्तराख्ययोर्जन्मत्रितये वर्षयोः क्रमात् ॥८८॥
राजा वा राजमहिषी सेनापत्याधिपोऽथवा(३)।
अन्योवाथ(भ)क्तिशीलाढ्यः कारयेदभिषेचनम् ॥८९॥
दक्षिणामभिषेके तु दद्याद्भूरि स्वशक्तितः।
वित्तशाठ्यं न कुर्वीत यदि कुर्वीत लोभतः ॥९०॥
(४)संदहेत्येपावकवत्पुत्रलक्ष्मीकलत्रकैः(?)।
तस्मात्सर्वंच तन्त्रेऽस्मिन् वित्तशाठ्यं न चिन्तयेत् ॥९१॥
अभिषेकफलं देवि! शृणु वक्ष्ये यथाविधि।
सोमसूर्याग्निरूपेण जलेनैप्सितमन्त्रतः ॥९२॥

त्रैलोक्येत्यादिभिरपिवा इत्यन्तैरध्यर्द्धैश्चतुर्भिः श्लोकैस्त्रैलोक्यमोहनविद्यायोगमुपदिशति। तत्र व्याप्तरूपं—अशेषमन्त्रसाधारणत्वात् ॥८१॥८२॥एनं—साधकम्। एतद्विद्याभजनपरं सर्वे श्वावामिव भजन्तीत्यर्थः॥८३॥८४॥विद्याया मातृकावर्णान्पुटयेन्मन्त्रतोपि वा—मातृकाक्षराणि प्रत्येकं विद्यया मन्त्रेण वा संपुटीकुर्यादित्यर्थः।

प्रोक्तमित्यादिना प्रकल्पनमित्यन्तेनार्द्धाद्येन श्लोकद्वयेन त्रैलोक्यमोहनविद्यया अभिषेकं नवयन्त्राणां विलेखनद्रव्याणि यथाक्रमं नव चोपदिशति। तत्र एतया—त्रैलोक्यमोहनीविद्यया ॥८५॥८६॥ नवानां यन्त्रप्रकल्पनमिति—स्वातन्त्र्यात् ॥८७॥

चैत्रेत्यादिभिश्चिन्तयेदित्यन्तैश्चतुर्भिः श्लोकैर्नवानां यन्त्राणां नवाभिषेक-

---

(१) चौक्रियासेकं इतीरित इति मू० पु० पा०।
(२) दक्षोनराख्ययो इति मू० पु० पा०।
(३) तत्तद्दाहेत्पावकवत् इति पा० मू० पु०।
(४) सेनापत्याधिकाऽऽतथा इति मू० पु० पा०।

जपपूजादिना सिद्धवैभवेनाभिषेकतः ।
दुर्लक्षणसमुत्थानि तथा दुष्कर्मजानि च ॥९३॥
तद्वद्दुर्नीतिजनितान्यन्यानि दुरितानि च ।
नाशयेत्तत्क्षणाद्देवी सलिलैरिव पावकः ॥९४॥
अपुत्रोवित्तविद्यायुरारोग्यादिसमन्वितान् ।
लभते च बहून् पुत्रान् सुखी च चिरमेधते ॥९५॥
केमद्रुमादियोगेषु जन्म तत् प्राक्तनाद्यतः ।
योभृशं नित्यदा विद्यात् क्लिष्टः सोऽपि श्रियैधते ॥९६॥
प्रागजन्मसञ्चितैः पापैरपथ्यादिनिषेवणैः ।
अनीत्या वैरिविहितैरभिचारादिभिस्तु वा ॥९७॥
ये रोगाः पीड़यन्त्येनं ते विनश्यन्त्यशेषतः ।
कान्तिलक्ष्मीधनारोग्यविद्याविजयकीर्तिभिः ॥९८॥
सुचिरं जीवति ख्यातः पुत्रपौत्रादिभिर्युतः ।
नवाभिषेकं नवसु प्रोक्तेषु विधिना चरन् ॥९९॥
अपमृत्युं विजित्याशात् भक्तः शुद्धान्तमानसः ।
जीवन्मुक्तश्चिरं योगी भुवि जीवति मन्मथः ॥१००॥
शब्दतत्त्वमयो व्याप्तिरिति सम्यक् समीरिता ।
अस्या निष्फालनात् चित्ते तत्तत्वं स्वात्मसात्कृतम् ॥१०१॥

कालानभिषेकयोग्यानभिषेककर्तुर्दक्षिणाप्रदानमप्रदानेन प्रत्यवायं चोपदिशति। तत्र वित्तशाठ्यं—वित्तनिगूहनम्। अन्यत् सुगमं तत् ॥ ८८ ॥ ८९ ॥ ॥९१॥

अभिषेकफलं इत्यादिभिर्मन्मथ इत्यन्तैर्नवभिः श्लोकैरभिषेकफलमुपदिशति। तत्र—पावकः नश्यते इतिशेषः। केद्रुममोनाम नित्यदारिद्र्यकरोयोगविशेषः। नवसु कालेष्वितिशेषः। मन्मथः—शिवात्मा ॥१००॥

इति श्री षोडशनित्यातन्त्रेषु श्रीकादिमते दशमं पटलम् ।

इति श्रीषोडशनित्यातन्त्रेषु श्रीकादिमताख्यस्य परिपूर्णस्य तन्त्रस्य प्रपञ्च-
सारसिंहराजप्रकाशाभिधानेन श्रीसुभगानन्दनाथेन विरचितायां
मनोरमाख्यायां व्याख्यायां भगमालिनीनित्याविद्याविधान-
प्रकाशनपरं नवमं पटलं परिपूर्णं
परामृष्टम् ॥ १० ॥

ग्रन्थसङ्ख्या ।

दशमे पटले सन्ति यन्त्राण्येकोनविंशतिः ।
षण्णवत्यष्टोत्तरशतं व्याख्यानं ग्रन्थसङ्ख्यया ॥

एकादशपटलम् ।

अथ षोड़शनित्यासु या षष्ठी समुदीरिता ।
सा विद्या वह्निवासिन्याः कथिता ते नवाक्षरा ॥१॥
तदङ्गानि लिपिन्यासं ध्यानं शक्तिभिरर्चनम् ।
तत्साधनविधिं तस्याः प्रयोगान्विविधानपि ॥२॥
होमयन्त्रविभेदैश्च कथयामि शृणु प्रिये ! ।
विद्याद्वितीयबीजेन स्वरान् दीर्घान्नियोजयेत् ॥३॥
मायान्तान् षड् भिरेवाङ्गान्याचरेत् खकराङ्गयोः ।
नवाक्षराणि विद्याया नवरन्ध्रेषु विन्यसेत् ॥४॥
व्यापकं च समस्तेन कुर्याद्देव्यात्मसिद्धये ।
सर्वास्वपि च विद्यासु व्यापकं तत् समाचरेत् ॥५॥
तेन तत्तन्मयो भूयात्साधकस्तेन सिद्धयः ।
तस्याचिरेण देवानां प्रसादात् सम्भवन्ति च ॥६॥

अथ एकादशपटलं प्रारभ्यते ।

पूर्वस्मिन् दशमे पटले पञ्चम्या भेरुण्डानित्याविद्याया विधानमुपदिश्यानन्तरं षष्ठ्या वह्निवासिनोनित्याविद्याया विधानमुपदिशति। अथ षोड़शेत्यादि भुवि इत्यन्तेन श्लोकशतरूपेणैकादशेन पटलेन। अथ षोड़शेत्यादिना प्रियेत्यन्तेनार्द्धाधिकेन श्लोकद्वयेन पटलार्थानुद्दिशति। तत्र कथिता—तृतोये पटले। अन्यत् सुगमम् ॥१॥२॥

विद्येत्यादिभिः समीरित इत्यन्तैरर्द्धाद्यैः पञ्चभिः श्लोकैश्चतुर्विंधन्यासादिकमुपदिशति। तत्र स्वरान् दीर्घान्नियोजयेत्। मायान्तान्—सर्वविषण्ढान् आ ई ऊ (ऐ) औ (औ) अः इत्येतान् षट्दीर्घस्वरान् कथयति ॥३॥नवरन्ध्रेषु—दृक्श्रोत्र-नासाद्वन्द्वेषु। षट्वर्णान् आस्यमेहनपायुषु त्रिषु त्रयं इतिक्रमेण नवरन्ध्रेषु

मातृकायाः षड़ङ्गं च मातृकान्यासमेव च ।
सर्वासां प्रथमं कृत्वा पश्चात्तत्रोदितं न्यसेत् ॥७॥
ललितायास्तु वर्गैस्तत्प्रोक्तमष्टाभिरेव च ।
तेन तस्यास्तु लिपिशो न्यासन्नैव(?) समीरितम् ॥८॥
तप्तकाञ्चनसङ्काशां नवयौवनसुन्दरीम् ।
चारुस्मेरमुखाम्भोजां विसलन्नयनत्रयाम् ॥९॥
अष्टाभिर्बाहुभिर्युक्तां माणिक्याभरणोज्ज्वलाम् ।
पद्मरागकिरीटांशुसम्भेदारुणिताम्बराम् ॥१०॥
पीतकौशेयवसनां रत्नमञ्जीरमेखलाम् ।
रत्नमौक्तिकसंभिन्नस्तबकाभरणोज्ज्वलाम्(१) ॥११॥
रक्ताब्जकम्बुपुण्ड्रेक्षुचापपूर्णेन्दुमण्डलाम्(२) ।
दधानां बाहुभिर्वामैः कह्लारं हेमशृङ्गकम् ॥१२॥
पुष्पेषु मातुलिङ्गं(३) च दधानां दक्षिणैः करैः ।
स्वसमानाभिरभितः शक्तिभिः परिवारिताम् ॥१३॥
एवं ध्यात्वाऽर्चयेद्वह्निवासिनीं विश्वविग्रहाम् ।
ज्वालिनीविस्फुलिङ्गिन्यौ(४) मङ्गला सुमनोहरा ॥१४॥

नवाक्षराणि दक्षिणपूर्वं न्यसेत् । व्यापकं प्राग्वत् ॥३॥४॥५॥६॥ मातृकायाः षड़ङ्गमिति । मातृकान्यासं तत्षड़ङ्गन्यासं च पञ्चदशे कुलसुन्दरीपटले वक्ष्यमाणत्वादिह न व्याकरोमि ॥७॥८॥

तप्तकाञ्चनेत्यादिभिर्विश्वविग्रहामित्यन्तैः पञ्चभिः श्लोकैर्देव्याः सपरिवाराया नित्यसपर्याध्यानमुपदिशति । तत्रायुधानि—ऊर्ध्वादिवामदक्षिणयोः कल्पयेत् ॥९॥१०॥११॥१२॥१३॥

---

(१) सम्भिन्नवक्षे काभरणो इति मू० पु० पा० ।
(२) रक्ताब्जकं च पुण्ड्रे क्षुचापं पूर्णेन्दुतण्डलमिति मू० पु० पा० ।
(३) पुष्पे च मातुलुङ्गे इति सौ० पु० पा० । (४) ज्वालिनीविस्फुलिङ्गिन्यौ इति मू० पु० पा० ।

कनकाङ्कितवाविस्त्राविविधाचेतिशक्तयः ।
अष्टकोणेषु सम्पूज्यास्तदग्रात्तु(त्सु) प्रदक्षिणम् ॥१५॥
दलेषु द्वादशस्वेता राशिशक्तीः समर्चयेत् ।
मेषां वृषाह्वयां शक्तिं मिथुनां कर्कटीमपि ॥१६॥
सिंहां कन्यां तुलां कीटां चापां च मकरामपि ।
कुम्भां मीनां यजेत्प्राग्वदग्रादारभ्य शाङ्करि ! ॥१७॥
चतुरस्रेषु द्वारेषु(१) पार्श्वयोः कोणदिक्षु च ।
अन्ययोश्च दिशोः शक्तीः प्रोक्ता दश समर्चयेत् ॥१८॥
मायासप्ताक्षरीमध्ये गतैर्नामभिरीरितैः ।
घस्मरा सर्वभक्षा (२)च विश्वासा विविधोद्भवा ॥१९॥
चित्ररूपा निःसम्पन्ना निरातङ्का च पावनी ।
अचिन्त्यवैभवा रक्ता दशमी परिकीर्तिता ॥२०॥
बलिदेवीति सम्प्रोक्ता कुरुकुल्लाद्यविद्यया ।
यत्र नोक्ता देवता तु बलिकर्मणि तत्र ताम् ॥२१॥
सप्ताक्षर्या समोपेतां विदध्याद्बलिदेवताम् ।
वृत्तयोर्नवयोनिं तु कृत्वा तद्बहिरम्बुजम् ॥२२॥
द्वादशच्छदसंयुक्तं विदध्याद्वृत्तयुग्मकम् ।
तद्बहिश्चतुरस्रे द्वे द्वारद्वयसमन्विते(३) ॥२३॥

ज्वालिनीत्यादिभिर्देवतां इत्यन्तैरष्टभिः श्लोकैर्देव्या आवरणशक्तीस्तत्पूजनप्रकारं तत्तन्मन्त्रयोजनाप्रकारं चोपदिशति । तत्र कीटं—वृश्चिकमित्यर्थः॥१४॥१५॥१६॥१७॥ कोणदिक्षु—वायव्यादिषु ॥१८॥ माया – ह्रल्लेखा ॥१९॥२०॥२१॥ सप्ताक्षर्या—कुरुकुल्लाद्यविद्यया ॥

वृत्तयोरित्यादिभिः व्रतमित्यन्तैः पञ्चभिः श्लोकैः देव्या नित्यसपर्याचक्रं तत्र

---

(१) चतुरस्रद्वारयुगे इति मू० पु० पा० ।
(२) सर्वभक्ता इति मू० पु० पा० ।
(३) समन्वितं इति मू० पु० पा० ।

पूर्वपश्चिमयोरत्र* देवीं चक्रे तथाऽर्चयेत् ।
अनुक्तेष्वङ्गमूलाभ्यामर्घ्यं संसाधयेत्तथा ॥२४॥
द्रव्यानुक्तौ होमविधौ घृतमन्नाद्यमेव च(१) ।
सङ्ख्यानुक्तौ सहस्रं स्याच्छतं वा तन्त्रचोदितम् ॥२५॥
पूजासमाप्तिरप्येवमनुक्ता प्राग्वदीरिता ।
विद्यायाः साधनं तद्वत्तन्त्रेऽस्मिन् परमेश्वरि ! ॥२६॥
अन्य(२)मन्त्रानपेक्षित्वात्पूर्णत्वं नामुना व्रतम्(३) ।
काम्यहोमविधिं वक्ष्ये शृणु वाञ्छितदायकम् ॥२७॥
शालितण्डुलमादाय प्रस्थं भाण्डे नवे क्षिपेत् ।
समानवर्णवत्साया रक्ताया गोपय(?)स्तथा ॥२८॥
द्विगुणं तत्र निक्षिप्य श्रपयेत् संस्कृतेऽनले ।
घृतेन सिक्तं सिक्थं तु(४) कृत्वा तत्ससितं करे ॥२९॥
निधाय विद्यामष्टोर्ध्वं शतं जप्त्वा हुनेत्ततः ।
एवं होमो महालक्ष्मीमावहेत्प्रतिपत्कृतः(५) ॥३०॥
शुक्रवारेष्वपि तथा वर्षान्नृपसमोभवेत् ।
पञ्चम्यां तु विशेषेण प्राग्वद्धोमं समाचरेत् ॥३१॥

नित्यसपर्याक्रमं चोपदिशति । तत्र चक्रनिर्माणं सुगमम् । जपहोमयोः ॥२२॥ ॥२३॥२४॥४५॥ प्राग्वत्—ललितापूजावसानवत् । तद्वत्—ललितासाधनवत् । एत- देकाक्षरादिनवाक्षरान्तानां मन्त्राणां सङ्ख्यानुक्तौ एषापि नवार्णत्वात् ललितावदि- त्यर्थः । अमुना—अस्मिन् तन्त्रे पूर्वापरप्रोक्ताङ्गीकारेण ॥२६॥

काम्यहोमं विशेषपूजाफलं चोपदिशति । तत्र संस्कृतेऽनले—होमार्थं विधानप्रतिष्ठिते । सिक्थकं—अन्नपिण्डम् । ससितं शर्करासहितम् ॥२७॥२८॥२९॥

---

(१) घृतमन्नाज्यमेव वा इति मू० पु० पा० ।
(२) तन्त्रान इति मू० पु० पा० ।
(४) सिक्थं सिक्थं तु इति मू० पु० ।
* पश्चिमयोस्तस्मिन् इति मू० पु० पा० ।
(३) व्रतिरिति मू० पु० पा० ।
(५) प्रतिप्रक्तित इति मू पु० पा० ।

तस्यां तिथौ विमध्वक्तैर्मल्लिकाद्यैः सितैर्हुतैः(१) ।
अन्नाज्याभ्यां तु नियतं हुत्वान्नाद्यो(२)भवेन्नरः ॥३२॥
यद्यद्धि वाञ्छितं वस्तु तानि सर्वाणि सर्वदा ।
घृतहोमादवाप्नोति तथैव तिलतण्डुलैः ॥३३॥
पञ्चमीषु(३) विशेषेण पूजां कुर्याद्व्रती भवेत् ।
प्रतिपत्तिथिमारभ्य पञ्चदश्यन्तमम्बिके ! ॥३४॥
कामेश्वर्यादिचित्रान्ता देव्यस्त्वेकैकविग्रहाः ।
यतस्तेन स्वस्वतिथौ तास्ता पूज्या हुतादिभिः ॥३५॥
प्रीणयेद्व्रतसङ्कल्पसमेतो भक्तिसंयुतः ।
तेनायुःश्रीधनारोग्यविद्याकीर्तिसमन्वितः ॥३६॥
जीवेद्वर्षशतं भूमौ स्वकुल्यायाश्च तद्वली(४) ।
यत्तिथौ या समाख्याता सुता सममवाप्नुयात्(५) ॥३७॥
विद्याविधिवद्दैवताः प्रोक्ताः पञ्चदशापि च ।
सम्प्राप्य जपहोमार्चायोगतर्पणसेकतः(६) ॥३८॥

॥३०॥ तथा—प्रतिपद्धोमवत् । विशेषेण—वह्निवासिन्याः असाधारणतिथित्वात् । प्राग्वत्—प्रतिपद्धोमवत् ॥३१॥ तस्यां—पञ्चम्याम् । सितैः—पुष्पैरितिशेषः ॥३२॥ तानि सर्वाणि सर्वदा घृतहोमादवाप्नोति—घृतहोमात्सर्वाणीष्टानि वस्तूनि अवाप्नोतीत्यन्वयः ॥३३॥ व्रती भवेत्—स्वसङ्कल्पसहितः ॥३४॥

प्रतिपदित्यादिभिराचरेदित्यन्तैः पञ्चभिः श्लोकैः पञ्चदशानां नित्यानां यथाक्रमं पञ्चदशतिथिमयत्वं तत्तिथिषु तत्तद्विद्याप्राप्तिं भजनविशेषं चोपदिशति। तत्र एकैकविग्रहाः—एकैकतिथिरूपाः । व्रतसङ्कल्पः प्राग्वत् ॥३५॥३६॥ यत्तिथौ—यासु तिथिष्वित्यर्थः ३७॥३८॥ अखिलं—प्रयोगादि ।

---

(१) सितैर्हनेत् इति मू० पु० पा० ।
(२) हुत्वान्नाढ्यो पु० पा० ।
(३) तु इति मू० पु० पा० ।
(४) तत्त्ववित् इति मू० पु० पा० ।
(५) सामुतासमवाप्नुयात् इतिमू० पा० पु० ।
(६) जपहोमेन पूजातर्पणसेकत इति मू० पु० पा० ।

विद्यया देवतात्मानं(१) सम्प्राप्याऽखिलमाचरेत् ।
विद्याप्राप्तिविधिं देव ! ब्रूहि सम्यक् ममाधुना ॥३९॥
आसां पञ्चदशानां च येनैताः साधकोन्मुखाः ।
शृणु वक्ष्यामि ते देवि ! विद्याप्राप्तिविधिं शुभम् ॥४०॥
येन विद्यादेवताभ्यामैक्ययोगेन सिद्ध्यति ।
तद्भावमाययोरैक्यरूपमानन्दविग्रहम् ॥४१॥
यदवाप्तुं यतन्तेऽद्याप्यनेके मुनयोऽम्बिके ! ।
कुचन्दनैः कुङ्कुमैर्वा सिन्दूरैर्गैरिकैः शुभैः ॥४२॥
विदध्याद्विपुलं चक्रं व्यक्तरेखं सुशोभनम् ।
यस्या यच्चक्रमाख्यातं नित्यपूजाविधिक्रमे ॥४३॥
तत्र कुम्भं निधायान्तर्जले सम्पूज्य देवताः ।
प्रोक्तक्रमसमोपेतं पूर्वेद्युर्गीतनृत्यकौ ॥४४॥
कृत्वोत्सवमथान्येद्युः प्राग्वदभ्यर्च्य तां तथा ।
तत्तिथौ प्राङ्मुखं शिष्टमुक्तलक्षणसंयुतम् ॥४५॥
तथाविधो गुरुः कुम्भजलैस्तमभिषेचयेत् ।
तज्जलं प्रागुदङ्मध्यदिग्गं सर्वसिद्धिदम् ॥४६॥
अन्यासु क्रमतोऽनिष्टान्यवाप्नोति सुनिश्चितम् ।
वह्निदाहं मृतिं रोगं दारिद्र्यं देशमोचनम् ॥४७॥
क्रमाद्वह्न्यादि वाय्वन्तं फलानि स्युरिमानि वै ।
ततोऽसौ परिधायासु शुभ्रे शुद्धे च वाससी ॥४८॥

विद्याप्राप्तिविधिमित्यादिभिः समोरितमित्यन्तैरष्टादशभिः श्लोकैरस्मिंस्तन्त्रे सर्वासां विद्यानां साधारणं विद्याप्राप्तिप्रकारं प्रश्नपूर्वकमुपदिशति । तत्र येन- विधिना ॥३९॥४०॥४१॥४२॥४३॥ प्रोक्तक्रमसमोपेत—मष्टत्रिंशत्कलार्चनादि ॥४४॥

---

(१) विद्याशादेवतात्मत्व' इति मु० पु० पा० ।

समाचम्य निजैस्त्रित्तैः समस्तैर्वा पुरोदितैः ।
अभ्यर्च्य पादयोर्नाथं पञ्चश्लोकैः स्तुवंस्त्रिशः(१) ॥४९॥
प्रणम्योत्थाय पुरतोबद्धाञ्जलिकरोभवेत् ।
ततोगुरुस्तमाहूय चक्रमध्ये निवेश्य च ॥५०॥
मनसा भावयन्नैक्यमात्मानं देवतात्मना ।
प्रोक्तक्रमेण तां देवीं विद्यारूपां महाद्युतिम् ॥५१॥
समावाह्यास्य मूर्द्धादित्रिषु स्थानेषु तु क्रमात् ।
संस्थाप्य प्रोक्तरूपां तां ध्यात्वाऽभ्यर्च्य वदेन्मनुम् ॥५२॥
जीवकर्णे त्रिशः पूर्णो देवतात्मा समाहितः ।
ततस्तत्रैव तां विद्यां शतं जप्यात्तदात्मवान् ॥५३॥
पुनस्तदाज्ञयोत्थाय पुष्पैरभ्यर्च्य तं स्तुवन् ।
प्रणम्य विरुपासीत मूर्द्धबद्धाञ्जलिः स्तुवन्(२) ॥५४॥
आहूय क्रममाचारं प्रोक्ता सम्यक् भजेति तम् ।
आदिशेद्देशिकस्तस्माद्दिनादारभ्य सोऽपि ताम् ॥५५॥
नित्यशोजपपूजाद्यै रुपासीत शिवां गुरुम् ।
एवं पञ्चदशानां च नित्यानां क्रम ईरितः ॥५६॥
विद्याप्राप्तिविधौ देवि ! सर्वं सम्यक्समीरितम् ।
तासां नैमित्तिकं काम्यं ललितोक्तविधानतः(३) ॥५७॥

प्राग्वत् – नित्यक्रमेण ॥४५॥ मध्यमित्यत्र ईशानदिगुच्यते ॥४६॥४७॥४८॥४९॥५०॥ ५१॥५२॥५३॥५४॥५५॥ तैः षड्भिः श्लोकैः ॥५६॥

तासामित्यादिना श्लोकेन पञ्चदशानां नित्यानां नैमित्तिककाम्यविधानमुपदिशति। तत्र प्रतिष्ठाद्यं—तत्तन्नित्यसपर्याचक्रमूर्त्यौः। काम्यशब्देन पूर्णाभिषेक उच्यते। पूर्णाभिषेकस्य तत्तन्नित्यसपर्याचक्रेण ॥५७॥

---

(१) स्वयंस्तुत्य इति मू० पु० पा०। (२) बद्धाञ्जलिं तु तम् इति मू० पु० पा०।
(३) तत्तन्नोक्तविधानत इति म० पु० पा०।

कुर्यात्प्रतिष्ठाद्यमेवं यत एतास्तु तन्मया(१) ।
आसामन्योन्यमङ्गानि पूजासु परमेश्वरि ॥५८॥
एकाङ्गित्वे स्थिताऽन्यास्तत्परिवारास्तथाविधाः !
अन्यदा प्रोक्तरूपास्तास्तत्तत्वार्चने मताः ॥५९॥
तासां काम्यकलावाप्तिध्यानं तत्पटलोदितम् ।
एवं सर्वं समाख्यातं साधारणविधानकम् ॥६०॥
विद्यामन्त्रा इति प्रोक्तं यत्तद्भेदं वद प्रभो ! ।
शृणु देवि ! विशेषन्तु सन्दर्भे वै समेऽपि वा ॥६१॥
वर्णानां देवताभेदा द्विधाः स्युस्ते त्वशेषतः ।
त्वद्दैवत्याः स्मृता विद्या मद्दैवत्यास्तु मन्त्रकाः ॥६२॥
पुनरस्यास्तु यन्त्राणि तत्फलानि शृणु प्रिये ! ।
विद्याक्षरैश्चनावृत्तान्यक्षराण्यष्ट तैस्तथा ॥६३॥
स्वराणां सङ्गमा द्दष्टविंशत्या शतमीरितम् ।
विधाय वृत्तयोर्मध्ये त्वष्टकोणे ततोद्वयम् ॥६४॥

आसामित्यादिना विधानकमित्यन्तेनार्द्धाधिकेन श्लोकद्वयेन पञ्चदशानां नित्यानामन्योन्याङ्गित्वेन नित्यनैमित्तिककाम्येषु च ध्यानोपदेशं प्रोक्तनिगमनं च करोति। तत्र तथाविधाः—अङ्गनित्यासमानरूपाः। अन्यदा—पृथक् पृथक् स्वस्वाङ्गित्वपूजासु ॥५८॥५९॥ तत्पटलोदितं—ध्यानपटलोदितम्। एवं—उक्त प्रकारेण ॥६०॥

विद्या इत्यादिना मन्त्रका इत्यन्तेनार्द्धाधिकेन श्लोकेन प्रश्नपूर्वकं विद्यामन्त्रयोर्भेदमुपदिशति। तत्र-त्वद्दैवत्याः—स्त्रीदैवत्याः। मद्दैवत्याः--पुन्दैवत्याः ॥६१॥ ॥६२॥

पुनरित्यादिभिरशेषतः इत्यन्तैरध्यर्द्धैः पञ्चभिः श्लोकैः षोडश यन्त्राण्युपदिशति। तत्र अस्याः—वह्निवासिनीनित्याविद्यायाः। अनावृत्तान्यक्षराणि अष्टौ ॐकार-

---

(१) तन्मयं इति मू० पु० पा०।

कृत्वा तेषु न्यसेद्वर्णानष्टस्वष्टौ तु मध्यतः ।
मायां नामान्वितां कृत्वा तां तारेण प्रवेष्टयेत् ॥६५॥
अन्तर्वृत्तान्तराले(१) तांल्लिखेद्वर्णान् दशक्रमात् ।
कर्मानुरूपान् पञ्चाशल्लिखेदुक्तक्रमेण वै ॥६६॥
वृत्तान्तरा प्राग्वदादिरादिक्षान्ताक्षराणि(२) च ।
एवं षोड़श यन्त्राणि जायन्ते तैर्यथाक्रमम् ॥६७॥
तैर्यन्त्रैः साधयेन्नित्यं मनीषितमशेषतः ।
प्रथमं खर्परे रक्तवह्निमूलेन संयुतम् ॥६८॥
सिन्दुरं तद्रसे पिष्ट्वा धत्तूररससंयुते ।
लिखित्वा खदिराङ्गारे तापयेन्निशि जापवान् ॥६९॥
नारी नरोन्नृपोऽन्योवा समायाति च तद्बलात् ।
तद्दैवतेन ताम्रे वा वा कांस्ये वा प्राग्वदालिखेत् ॥६८॥

हकाररेफवकारनकारसकारपकारमकाराः अपुनरुक्तान्यक्षराण्यष्टेत्यर्थः । सर्वत्रासंयुक्तस्वरोपादानं भवति। स्वराणां चापुनरुक्तत्ववगंतः। व्यञ्जनानामक्षरत इति सर्वत्र समयः ॥६३॥ ततो द्वयं—अष्टकोणान्तर्वृत्तयोर्द्वयं कृत्वेत्यर्थः ॥६४॥ तारेण-प्रणवेन ॥६५॥ तान्—प्राग्वत् । प्रादक्षिण्येन तैः स्वरविकृताक्षरैः । यन्त्रविरचनाक्रमोयथा—इष्टमानेन भ्रमेण एकाङ्गुलान्तरालं वृत्तद्वयं निष्पाद्य तन्मध्ये प्राग्वदष्टकोणं कृत्वा तदन्तरापि वृत्तद्वयं विधाय तेषु अष्टसु कोणेषु अग्न्यादिप्रादक्षिण्येन आदितः अष्टौ समालिख्य सर्व्वमध्ये हृल्लेखां प्राग्वन्नामसहितां प्रणवेन वेष्टितामालिख्य अन्तर्वृत्तान्तरा कर्मानुरूपाणि पञ्चभूताक्षराणि दशदशसमालिख्य बहिर्वृत्तवीथ्यामग्न्यादिप्रादक्षिण्येन अकारादिक्षकारान्तान्येकपञ्चाशदक्षराण्यालिखेत् एतत्प्रथमं यन्त्रम् । अस्यैवाष्टसु कोणेषु पूर्व्वपूर्व्वलिखितविद्यास्वरविकृताक्षराष्टकादुपरितनमक्षराष्टकमक्षराष्टकं विलिखेत् । तेन षोड़शयन्त्राणि सम्भवन्ति तैर्मनीषितं साधयेदिति ॥६८॥

---

(१) अन्तर्वृत्तान्तराभूमान् इति मू० पु० पा० । (४) बहिर्वृत्तान्तरा प्राग्वदादिक्षान्ताक्षराणि इति मू० पु० पा०

तत्तापनादपि भवेत् पूर्वोक्तं फलमीश्वरि!।
द्वितीयं खर्परे तेन विलिख्य निशि तापयेत् ॥७१॥
नारी वश्या समायाति जन्माचारविलङ्घिनी।
तृतीयं तेन तत्रैव लिखित्वा निशि तापयेत्* ॥७२॥
श्मशानाग्नौ मुक्तकेशा(१) त्वगाद्वैरिज्वरातुरा(२)।
तदेव दम्पती दग्धवन्ह्यागारं तु निम्नजे(३) ॥७३॥
रसे पिष्ट्वा लिखित्वाऽग्नौ संताप्य निखनेत्ततः।
श्मशाने वैरिणां प्रोक्तकाले क्रुद्धाशयो जपेत् ॥७४॥
मनुं तदेव संभ्रान्तः पिशाचार्तोरिपुर्भवेत्।
चतुर्थं विलिखेत्कृष्णपट्टचीरेऽसिताम्बरे ॥७५॥
पूर्ववत्तत्र निखनेद्रात्रावुक्तक्रमेण च।
दाहज्वरेण सप्ताहाद्रिपुर्याति यमालयम् ॥७६॥
पञ्चमेऽप्यथ वा षष्ठे द्वयोर्नाम लिखेद्द्वयोः।
कालोलूकजपक्षोत्थलेखन्या खर्परद्वये ॥७७॥
श्मशाने निखनेत् प्राग्वन्नदीतीरद्वये द्वयम्।
नद्यांतु वारिणा पूर्णा यां द्वेषास्यात्तयोर्मिथः(४) ॥७८॥

प्रथममित्यादिभि र्भुविइत्यन्तैरर्द्धाद्यैः स्त्रयस्त्रिंशद्भिः श्लोकैः प्रोक्तेषु षोड़श-यन्त्रेषु तृतीयचतुर्थपञ्चमषष्ठसप्तमाष्टमैः षड्भिर्यन्त्रैर्निग्रहान् एकादशेन निग्रहानुग्रहान् शेषैः शुभाशुभानि चोपदिशति। तत्र तद्रसे—रक्तवह्निरसे। रक्तवह्निर्नाम रक्तचित्रकम्। खदिराङ्गारे—खदिरेन्धनाङ्गारे ॥६८॥ तेन—पूर्वोक्त-द्रव्येण। अस्मिन् प्रकरणे सर्वत्र द्रव्यानुक्तौ तापनं खादिराङ्गारे। ॥७०॥७१॥ ७२॥७३॥ प्रोक्तकाले प्राग्वत्॥७४॥ असिताम्बरे इति पूर्वसम्बन्धः ॥७५॥ पूर्ववत्—

---

* नारी वश्या समायाति जन्माचारविलङ्घिनी। तृतीयं तेन तत्रैव लिखित्वा निशि तापयेत् इत्ययं श्लोकः पुनरपि सो० पुस्तके लिखितः मू० पुस्तके नास्ति।

(१) मुक्तकेशः इति मू० पु० पा०।

(२) ज्वरातुरः इति मू० पु० पा०।

(३) दग्धवन्ह्यङ्गारंतु निम्नजैः इति सो पु० पा०।

(४) नद्यातुवारपूर्णायें विद्वेष स्याद्दयोर्मिथ इति मू० पु० पा०।

सप्तमे नाम संलिख्य सीसपट्टे यथाविधि ।
शिरःकपाले निःक्षिप्य श्मशाने निखनेन्निशि ॥७९॥
रिपोः पुरोक्तकाले तु पिशाचैर्ग्रस्यते(१) रिपुः ।
अष्टमं खर्परे कृत्वा रिपुद्वारे खनेन्निशि ॥८०॥
सप्ताहात्तद्गृहाद्वैरी प्रयात्युच्चाटितोऽन्यतः ।
नवमं हेम्नि कृत्वा तदूर्मिकायां वरे दिने(२) ॥८१॥
सिद्धयोगे शुभे लग्ने धिषणोदय एव वा ।
कृत्यापमृत्युरोगादिदुःखेभ्योमुच्यते नरः ॥८२॥
दशमं राजते पट्टे कृत्वा वेश्मनि कुत्रचित् ।
निधाय पूजयेद्वेश्मन्यश्मपातादिशान्तये ॥८३॥
तथा भूतग्रहार्तांश्च रक्षेदेतस्य धारणात् ।
एकादशे लिखेद्भूर्जे पाटीरेन्दुद्रवैस्तु तत् ॥८४॥
उक्तक्रमसमोपेतं गुलिकीकृत्य तां पुनः ।
सितसिक्थमये लिङ्गे संस्थाप्याभ्यर्च्य तत् पुनः ॥८५॥
स्थापयेत् क्षौद्रमध्ये तु पूजयेन्नित्यशश्च तत् ।
सन्ध्यासु सुसितैः पुष्पैः सौरभाद्यैर्विधानतः ॥८६॥
मासात्तदर्द्धात्सप्ताहाद्वशे स्युः शत्रवो ध्रुवम् ।
भवेयुर्व्याधितास्तेन(३) घृतेनारोग्यमाप्नुयुः ॥८७॥
ज्वरार्तास्तु विशेषेण सुखिताः स्युरयत्नतः ।
अम्लसौवीरमध्यस्थे विद्वेषयति वैरिणौ(४) ॥८८॥

निम्बरसादिना ॥७६॥ द्वयोः—यन्त्रयोः । द्वयोः—विद्वेष्ययोः ॥७७॥ अत्रापि लेखनद्रव्यं निम्बरसादि । एतदेवास्मिन्निग्रहप्रकरणे द्रव्यानुक्तौ द्रव्यम् ॥७८॥७९॥

---

(१) गृह्यते इति सो पु० पा० । (२) कृत्वा तु ऊर्मिकायां वरेऽह्नि इति मू० पु० पा० ।
(३) स्तेन तेन रोग मवाप्नुयुरिति सा० पु० पा०
(४) अमलं सौवीरमध्यस्थं विद्वेषयति वै रिपौ इति मू० पु० पा० ।

तत्रैव कथनाद्रोगं तयोरुत्पादयेदपि ।
शुण्ठीमरीचपिप्पल्यः सुसूक्ष्माः परिचूर्णिताः ॥८९॥
लकुचस्य रसोपेताः तन्मध्ये तद्विनिक्षिपेत् ।
तापयेत् त्रिषु सन्ध्यासु यन्त्रारातिस्तु(१) तन्मुखम् ॥९०॥
प्रोक्तकाले ज्वरैरार्तस्तापतृष्णासमन्वितः ।
द्वादशं खर्परे(२) रात्रिरसेनालिख्य तत्पुनः ॥९१॥
*इष्टकायुगमध्यस्थं कृत्वा तत् श्लेषयेद्दृढम् ।
स्थापयेच्चण्डिकागेहे शास्तुरायतनेऽपि(३) वा ॥९२॥
स्वगृहे भित्तिमध्ये वा शयनस्थापनतोऽपि(४) वा ।
स्तम्भयेद्वै रिपोरोषमुद्योगं वाऽथ चिन्तनम् ॥९३॥
व्यवहारं स्वयं चान्यद्यद्यदस्याहितात्मकम्(५) ।
त्रयोदशेन भूर्जस्थे नाम्नि धारणतोऽङ्गना ॥९४॥
वन्ध्यापि लभते पुत्रं विचित्रा यन्त्रशक्तयः ।
चतुर्दशगतं नाम कृत्वा(६) भूर्जे चतुष्पथे ॥९५॥
सिक्थमध्यगतं कृत्वा तन्निशीथेऽभितापयेत् ।
सप्ताहाद्वशमायान्ति स्त्रियो वा पुरुषा नृपाः ॥९६॥
गजा हया मृगास्त्वन्ये ये जीवा भूतलाश्रयाः ।
परेण नाम्ना युक्तेन फलकालिखितेन वै ॥९७॥

॥८०॥ धिषणोदयः प्राग्वत् । वा पक्षान्तरे ॥८२॥८३॥८४॥ सितसिक्थमये—सितमधूच्छिष्टमये । तत्—लिङ्गमितिशेषः ॥८५॥८६॥८७॥८८॥ तत्रैव—अम्लसौवीरे ॥८९॥९०॥ रात्रिरसेन—हरिद्रारसेन ॥९१॥९२॥९३॥९४॥९५॥९६॥

---

(१) यन्त्रं रात्रौ च तन्मुखम् इति मू० पु० पा० । * इष्टिका इति मू० पु० पा० ।
(२) कर्पटे रात्रीरसेन इति मू० पु० पा० । (३) गोस्तु इति मू० पु० पा० ।
(४) स्थापनोऽपि वा इति सो पु० पा० । (५) व्यवहारं वा नवान्यदस्याभिमतमात्मन इति सो पु० पा० ।
(६) तद्भूर्जके सवा इति मू० पु० पा० ।

सुखप्रसूतिः स्यात् स्त्रीणां तत्पूजाप्रेक्षणादिना ।
षोड़शि नाम संलिख्य धारणात्प्राणिनां तथा ॥९८॥
रक्षा भवति सर्वत्र ग्रहरोगभयादिषु ।
तदेव स्वर्णपट्टस्थं विधाय विधिना युतम्(१) ॥९९॥
ऊर्मिकाङ्गदभूषादौ मूर्ध्नि वा बिभृयात्ततः ।
आधिव्याधिविनिर्मुक्तो निःसपत्नो जितेन्द्रियः ॥१००॥
भोक्ता भक्तश्च(२) पुण्यानां जीवेद्वर्षशतं भुवि ।
योनितत्त्वमयी व्याप्तिरितिसम्यक्समीरिता ॥१०१॥
अस्या निष्कालनाच्चित्ते तत्तत्त्वं स्वात्मसात्कृतम् ।

इति श्रीषोड़शनित्यातन्त्रेषु श्रीकादिमताख्यस्य परिपूर्णस्य-
तन्त्रस्य एकादशपटलं परिपूर्णम् ॥११॥✻

परेण—पञ्चदशेन ९७॥ अत्रानुग्रहप्रकरणे द्रव्यानुक्तौ पटीरादिस्वर्णपदस्थम् । हैमपट्टोत्कीर्णम् ॥९८॥९९॥ आधिः—मानसी पीड़ा । अत्र द्वादशतमः श्लोकः षट्चरणगाथा ॥१०१॥

इति श्रीषोड़शनित्यातन्त्रेषु श्रीकादिमताख्यस्य तन्त्रस्य परिपूर्णस्य तन्त्रस्य प्रपञ्च-
सारसिंहराजप्रकाशाभिधानेन श्रीसुभगानन्दनाथेन विरचितायां
मनोरमाख्यायां व्याख्यायां भगमालिनीनित्याविद्याविधान-
प्रकाशनपरं एकादशपटलं परिपूर्णं
परामृष्टम् ॥ ११ ॥

ग्रन्थसङ्ख्या—
यन्त्राणि षोड़श व्याख्या ग्रन्थे स्वार्द्धाधिका भवेत् ।
चतुःषष्टिरितिप्रेक्ष्य प्रोक्तमेकादशेऽखिलम् ॥०॥

---

(१) शुभम् इति मू० पु० पा० । (२) भोक्ता कर्ता च इति मू० पु० पा० ।
अस्मिन्पटले द्वादशतमः श्लोकः षट्चरणगाथा इत्यधिकम् ।

द्वादशपटलम् ।

अथ षोड़शनित्यासु सप्तमी या समीरिता ।
तस्या विधानं वक्ष्यामि शृणु सर्वार्थसाधकम् ॥१॥
प्रोक्तैव विद्या प्रागेव द्वादशाक्षरविग्रहा ।
तदङ्गानि लिपिन्यासं ध्यानं शक्तिभिरर्चनम् ॥२॥
साधनं होमकर्माणि (सर्वतो) यन्त्राणि फलभेदतः ।
प्रोक्तक्रमेण सकलं कथयामि यथाविधि ॥३॥
द्वयमेकैकमथ च द्वयं द्वयमथो द्वयम् ।
मायया पुटितं कृत्वा कुर्यादङ्गानि षट्क्रमात् ॥४॥
प्रत्येकं शक्तिपुटितैर्मन्त्रार्णैर्दशभिर्न्यसेत् ।
दृक्श्रोत्रनासावाग्वक्षोनाभिगुह्येषु च क्रमात् ॥५॥
रक्तां रक्ताम्बरां रक्तगन्धमालाविभूषणाम् ।
चतुर्भुजां त्रिनयनां माणिक्यमुकुटोज्ज्वलाम् ॥६॥

अथ द्वादशपटलम् ।

पूर्वस्मिन्नेकादशे पटले षष्ठ्या वह्निवासिनीनित्या(या)विद्याविधानमुपदिश्यानन्तरं सप्तम्या महावज्रेश्वरीनित्याविद्याया विधानमुपदिशति । अथ षो .शेत्यादिना अवाप्नुये इत्यन्तेन श्लोकशतरूपेण द्वादशेन पटलेन । तत्र अथ षोड़शेत्यादिभि र्यथाविधि इत्यन्तैस्त्रिभिः श्लोकैः पटलार्थानुद्दिशति । तत्र प्रागेव-तृतीयपटले ॥ ॥१॥२॥३॥

द्वयमित्यादिना क्रमादित्यन्तेन श्लोकद्वयेन न्यासक्रममुपदिशति । तत्र एकैकं शिरः शि(व)खयोरिति शेषः । मायया—ह्स्रैं खया । अङ्गानि— हृदयादीनि । क्रमाज्जातियुक्तानि शक्तिपुटितैः ह्स्रैं खापुटितैः दशभिः । ह्स्रैं खा द्वयवर्जवाग्वक्षोनाभिगुह्येषु । एकैकमितिशेषः । गुह्यं नाम मेहनम् ॥४॥५॥

रक्तामित्यादिभिर्नायिकामित्यन्तैः पञ्चभिः श्लोकैर्देव्याः सपरिवाराया नित्य-

पाशाङ्कुशाविक्षुचापं दाडिमीसायकं तथा ।
दधानां बाहुभिर्नेत्रैः दया (पर) दमसुशीतलैः ॥७॥
पश्यन्ती साधकं त्र्यस्रषट्कोणाब्जमहीपुरे ।
चक्रमध्ये सुखासीनां स्मेरवक्त्रसरोरुहाम् ॥८॥
शक्तिभिः स्वस्वरूपाभिरावृतां पोतमध्यगे ।
सिंहासनेऽभितः प्रेङ्खत्प्रोतस्थाभिः स्वशक्तिभिः ॥९॥
वृत्तान्ताभिर्विनोदानि यातायातादिभिः सदा ।
कुर्वाणामरुणाम्भोधौ चिन्तये (द्व्र ज)न्मन्त्रनायिकाम् ॥१०॥
इच्छाज्ञानक्रियास्तत्र त्रिकोणस्थाश्च शक्तयः ।
डाकिन्याद्याः षडस्रस्थाः पद्मद्वादशपत्रगाः ॥११॥
हृल्लेखा क्लेदिनी क्लिन्ना क्षोभिणी मदनातुरा ।
निरञ्जना रागवती तथैव मदनावती ॥१२॥
मेखला द्राविणी वेगवती द्वादशशक्तयः ।
ततः षोडशपत्रस्थाः शक्तीराकर्णयाम्बिके ! ॥१३॥
कामलां कामिनीं कल्यां कलां कलितकौतुके ।
किरातां कालकदने कौशिकां कम्बुवाहिनीम् ॥१४॥

पूजाध्यानमुपदिशति ! आयुधकल्पनं—वामोर्ध्वहस्तादिदक्षिणाधरहस्तान्तं वामदक्षिणवामदक्षिणक्रमेण ॥६॥७॥ त्र्यस्रषट्कोणाब्जमहीपुरे चक्रमध्ये । एतदुक्तं भवति—समत्रिरेखां योनिं विधाय तद्बहिर्यथामानं षट्कोणं कृत्वा तद्बाह्ये द्वादशयन्त्रं द्वादशपद्मं विधाय तद्बाह्ये षोडशदलं पद्मं कृत्वा तद्बहिश्चतुर्दिक्षु द्वारोपेतं समचतुरस्रद्वयं कुर्यात् तत्र चक्रे सुखासीनां तां चिन्तयेदिति ॥८॥९॥ अरुणाम्भोधौ—शोणाम्भोधौ ॥१०॥

इच्छेत्यादिभिर्यजेदित्यन्तैः सप्तभिः श्लोकैर्देव्याः परिवारशक्तीरुपदिशति—तत्र षडस्रस्थाः नैर्ऋत्यादिक्रमेण ॥११॥ मदनातुरा—मदना इति मदनातुरा इति च द्वे शक्ती ॥१२॥१३॥ कलिताकौतुके—कलिता कौतुका इति च द्वे शक्ती ।

कातरां कपटां कीर्तिकुमारीं कुङ्कुमामपि।
चतुरस्रस्थितां(१) चापि शक्तीराकर्णय क्रमात् ॥१५॥
जृम्भिका वेगिनी नाम्नी चपला पेशला सती।
रतिः श्रद्धा भोगलोभमदोन्मत्ते मनस्विनी ॥१६॥
दिक्षु द्वारेषु(पार्श्वेषु) कोण(ादि) दिक्षु च संस्थिताः(नताः)।
द्वादशैता महादेवि! चतुरस्रेऽभितोजपेत् ॥१७॥
कृत्वाऽर्घ्यमङ्गमूलाभ्यां प्रोक्तरूपं ततोऽर्चयेत्।
शोणाब्धिं हेमपोतं च सिंहासनमनन्तरम् ॥१८॥
तत्र चक्रं ततो देवीं प्राग्वदावाह्य शक्तिभिः।
मायासमाचरीमध्यंगतैर्नामभिरर्चयेत् ॥१९॥
बलिं च दद्यात्तदनु समाचर्या पुरोक्तया।
देव्यास्तु कुरुकुल्लाया होमं कुर्याद्यथाविधि ॥२०॥
घृताक्तैररुणैः पुष्पैर्घृतैर्वा होममाचरेत्।
प्राग्वत् समापयेदित्थमर्चनं ते समीरितम् ॥२१॥

कालकदने—कालाकदना इति च द्वे ॥१४॥१५॥ मदोन्मत्ते—मदा उन्मत्ता च इति द्वे ॥१६॥ दिक्षु स्थितेषु द्वारेष्वित्यर्थः। पार्श्वेषु द्वाराणामितिशेषः। प्रथमं पश्चिमादिचतुर्दिक्द्वारपार्श्वेषु पश्चात् वाय्वादिकोणदिक्षु प्रादक्षिण्येनार्चयेत्। सर्वत्रावरणेषु अग्रात्प्रादक्षिण्येन पूजयेत् ॥१७॥

कृत्वेत्यादिभिः समीरितं इत्यन्तैश्चतुर्भिः श्लोकैर्देव्या नित्यपूजाक्रममुपदिशति। तत्र प्रोक्तरूपं—अग्निसोमसूर्यात्मकभावनादियुतम्। शोणाब्धिः—शोणसागरः॥१८॥ तत्र—सिंहासने स्थितायामितिशेषः। प्राग्वत्—त्रिखण्डामुद्रादिभिः। मायासमाचरीमध्यगतैः—ह्रूं क्लीं खासमाचरीमध्ययोजितैः। शोणसागरादीनामपि एवमेव मन्त्रयोजनक्रमः। (माया)समाचर्या कुरुकुल्लाद्य(विद्य)या सर्वत्र अ(न्य)न्यबलेर्विशेषानुक्तौ कुरुकुल्लाद्यविद्यया बलिं दद्यात्। यथाविधि अत्राभ्युपेतम् ॥२०॥ प्राग्वत्—तेजोरूपया स्वात्मयोजनादिति ॥२१॥

(१) स्थापि इति मू० पु० पा०।

वसन्तकाले ग्रीष्मे वा पूर्णामारभ्य साधयेत् ।
हविष्याशी पयोभक्षः फलमूलाशनोऽथ वा ॥२२॥
स्नातः सुगन्धिसलिलैररुणांशुकवान् शुचिः ।
चन्द्रचन्दनकाश्मीरचर्चालोहितविग्रहः ॥२३॥
अञ्जनाक्ताक्षियुगलस्ताम्बुलारुणवक्त्रवान् ।
मुखार्पितेन्दुशकलो हृष्टचेता जितेन्द्रियः ॥२४॥
मौनी त्रिकालपूजासु कृतसङ्कल्पसाधनः ।
नक्ताशी हुतशिष्टेन जपेद्विद्यां समाहितः ॥२५॥
नित्यशोभो (१)जपेद्विद्याभक्तान् भजनकौतुकान् ।
तयाद्हीना(२) मधुरं पायसं भोज्यभक्तिमान् ॥२६॥
प्रणम्याभ्यर्च्य विसृजेन्नित्यशस्तद्दिनेषु तु ।
गुरुजीवं समासाद्य प्रणम्याऽसकृदात्मवान् ॥२७॥
धनधान्याम्बराद्यैस्तं सन्तोष्य तदनुज्ञया ।
कृतारम्भो नित्यशश्च पूजयेत्तं च भक्तितः ॥२८॥
अन्ते च चित्रैः स्तोत्रैश्च तं संतोष्य कृती भवेत् ।
वित्तशाठ्यं च दर्पं च दम्भं चासत्यमेव च ॥२९॥
न कदाचिच्च कुर्वीत विशेषाद्गुरुसन्निधौ ।
एवं लक्षत्रयं जप्त्वा तद्दशांशं हुनेत् घृतैः ॥३०॥

वसन्तकाले इत्यादिभिः साधकइत्यन्तैरध्यर्द्धैरेकादशभिः श्लोकैः सर्वविद्यासाधनसाधारणं गुणविधानमुपदिशति। तत्र हविष्याशो—निर्लवणपक्वव्रीहितण्डुलाहारी ॥२२॥२३॥२४॥ कृतसङ्कल्पसाधनः—कृतस्वसङ्कल्पयोग्यक्रमः ॥२५॥ भजनकौतुकान्—नित्यभजननिरतान् ॥२६॥ तद्दिनेषु—पुरश्चरणदिनेषु ॥२७॥२८॥ अन्ते—पुरश्चरणावसाने। स्तोत्रैः—पञ्चभिः श्लोकैः। तं—गुरुम्। दम्भं—

---

(१) यजेद्विद्या इति मू० पु० पा०। (२) हीनाम्मधुरप्रायं संभोज्यं इति मू० पु० पा०।

आरग्वधप्रसूनैश्च(१) प्रसूनैर्बकुलाद्भवैः ।
मधूकजैश्चम्पकैर्वा त्रिमध्वक्तैश्च नित्यशः ॥३१॥
चन्द्रचन्दनकस्तूरीकाश्मीरसुरभीकृतैः ।
तर्पयेत्सलिलैस्तावद्दिनशोभक्तिमान् दृढः ॥३२॥
एवं संसिद्धमन्त्रस्तु कुर्यात्काम्यानि(२) साधकः ।
गुरुभक्तोनित्यकृत्यकृ(३) तसङ्कल्पसंयुतः ।
सहस्रजापी स्थिरधीर्मन्त्रवीर्यविदात्मवान् ।
यः सोऽपि काम्यान् कुर्वीत प्रयोगान्नान्यथा शिवे ! ॥३४॥
यद्यज्ञानेन मोहेन चापलेनापि वाऽऽचरेत् ।
अनर्थान् क्लेशनाशादि(४) पीड़ां प्राप्नोति निश्चितम् ॥३५॥
अरुणैः पङ्कजैर्होमं कुर्यात्त्रिमधुराप्लुतैः ।
मण्डलाल्लभते लक्ष्मीं महतीं श्लाघ्यविग्रहम्(हाम्) ॥३६॥
कह्लारैः क्षौद्रसंसिक्तैः पौर्णाद्य(त्रि)तद्दि दिनावधि ।
जुहुयान्नित्यशोभक्त्या सहस्रं विकचैः शुभैः ॥३७॥
तत्तद्दिनेषु पूर्वोक्तान् (पू)भोजयेदुक्तरूपतः(५) ।
तावच्च जप्याद्धोमान्ते यावत्सङ्ख्याहुतं(६) कृतम् ॥३८॥

मिथ्यास्वरूपनिर्वहणम् ॥२८॥ लक्षत्रयमितिविशेषविधानात्केवलं लक्षत्रयं जपेदित्यर्थः ॥३०॥३१॥ तावत्-दशांशतः। दिनशः–प्रतिदिनम्। अत्र पुरश्चरणविधौ प्रोक्तमखिलं सकलविद्यापुरश्चरणम् ॥३२॥ एवं—उक्तप्रकारेण ॥३३॥

गुरुभक्त(मि)इत्यादिना निश्चितमित्यन्तेनार्द्धाधेन श्लोकद्वयेन पुरश्चरणमन्तरेणापि प्रयोगयोग्यतामन्यथाकरणे प्रत्यवायं चोपदिशति। तत्र–अन्यथा (अन्यथा) अन्यः नैवंविधगुण इत्यर्थः ॥३४॥३५॥

अरुणैरित्यादिभिर्भवेदित्यन्तैः सप्तविंशत्या श्लोकैर्नानाविधैर्द्रव्यैर्होमादिना

---

(१) प्रसूनैर्वा इति मू० पु० ना०
(२) काम्यादि इति सो० पु० पा०।
(३) नित्यपूजाकृत इति मू० पु० पा०
(४) क्लेशराशादि इति मू० पु० पा०।
(५) भोजयेदुक्तदेवतामिति मू० पु० पा०।
(६) यावत्सङ्ख्यं हुतक्रतं मिति म० पु० पा०।

चम्पकैः क्षौद्रसं(सि)युक्तैः सहस्रहवनाद्ध्रुवम् ।
लभते स्वर्णनिष्काणां शतं मासेन पूर्ववत् ॥३९॥
पाटलैर्घृतसंसिक्तैः त्रिसहस्रं हुतैः(१) तथा ।
(२)दर्शादिमासाँल्लभते चित्राणि वसनानि च ॥४०॥
कर्पूरचन्दनादीनि सुगन्धीनि च मासतः ।
वस्तूनि लभते हव्यैरन्यैर्भोगोप(भो)योगिभिः ॥४१॥
शालिभिः क्षीरसिक्ताभिः सप्तमीषु शतं हुनेत् ।
तेन शालिसमृद्धिः स्यात् मासैः षड्भिरसंशयम् ॥४२॥
तिलैर्हुतैस्तद्दिवसे वर्षादारोग्यमाप्नुयात् ।
स्वजन्मसु त्रिषु(३) तथा दूर्वाभिर्जुहुयात्तथा ॥४३॥
निरातङ्को महाभोगः शतं वर्षाणि जीवति ।
गुडूचीतिलदूर्वाभिस्त्रिषु जन्मसु वा हुनेत् ॥४४॥
तेनायुःश्रीर्यशोभोगापुण्यनिध्या(४)दिभाग्भवेत् ।
घृतपायसदुग्धैस्तु हुतैस्तेषु त्रिषु क्रमात् ॥४५॥
आयुरारोग्यविभवैर्नृपमान्योभवेत्तथा ।
सप्तम्यां कदलीहोमात् सौभाग्यं लभते द्रुतः ॥४६॥

नानाविधफलावाप्तिमुपदिशति । तत्र मण्डलान् प्राग्वत् ॥३६॥ तद्दिनावधि—पूर्णादिनावधि ॥३७॥ तत्तद्दिनेषु—सर्वप्रयोगदिनेषु । पूर्वोक्तान्—विद्याविदः । उक्तरूपतः—मधुरसप्रायादि । एतत्सर्वप्रयोगसाधारणम् । तावदित्याद्युक्तं सर्वहोमसाधारणम् ॥३८॥३९॥ दर्शाऽदिमासान्—दर्शादि दर्शान्तमित्यर्थः ॥४०॥४१॥ सप्तमीषु—तिथिषु अस्य वासना गुरुमुखादवगन्तव्या । एकादशे पटले स्वस्वतिथिषु नित्यानां विशेषतः पूजाहोमादिविधानात् अत्र षष्ठीष्वपि विशेषविधानं कर्तव्यम् ॥४२॥ तद्दिवसे—सप्तम्याम् । स्वजन्मर्क्षेषु त्रिषु—स्वजन्मनक्षत्र-

---

(१) हुतं इति सो० पु० पा० । (२) वर्षादि इति मू० पू० पा० । (३) नृषु इति मू० पु० पा० ।
(४) निध्यासभाग्भ इति मू० पु० पा० ।

दूर्वात्रिकैस्तु प्रादेशमात्रैस्त्रिस्वादुसंयुतैः ।
जुहुयाद्दिनशोघोरे सन्निपातज्वरे गदे(१) ॥४७॥
महारोगेषु दूर्वाभिः तिलैश्छिन्नोद्भवैस्तथा(२) ।
त्रिभिर्वा नित्यशोहोमं कुर्यात्त्रिस्वादुसंयुतैः ॥४८॥
षण्मासादब्दतो वाऽपि रोगान्मुक्तः सुखी भवेत् ।
तद्दिनेषु जपेद्विद्यां नित्यशः सलिलं स्पृशत् ॥४९॥
सहस्रवारं तत्तोयैः स्नानं पानं समाचरेत् ।
पाकाद्यमपि तैरेव कुर्याद्रोगविमुक्तये ॥५०॥
साध्यचर्मत्वच संचूर्ण्य लवङ्गं(३) सर्षपं तिलम् ।
पिष्टं च साध्यपादोत्थ(४) रजसा च समन्वितम् ॥५१॥
कृत्वा पुत्तलिकां तैस्तु हृदये नाम संयुताम् ।
प्राग्वच्छित्त्वाऽऽयसैस्तीक्ष्णैः शस्त्रैः पुत्तलिकां हुनेत् ॥५२॥
एवं दिनैः सप्तभिर्वा त्रिभिर्वैकदिनेन वा ।
साध्यो वशो भवेच्छीघ्रमपि दूरस्थितो दृढः(५) ॥५३॥
तथाविधां पुत्तलिकां कुण्डमध्ये खनेद्भुवि ।
उपर्यग्निं निधायात्र विद्यया दिनशो(वं) हुनेत् ॥५४॥

तद्दशमैकोनविंशतिनक्षत्रेषु । तथा—शतम् । तथा—अरोगः ॥४३॥ निरातङ्कः अव्याकुलः । गुडूची—अमृता । गुडूच्यादीनि त्रीणि द्रव्याणि जन्मत्रये यथाक्रमं जुहुयात् । वा पक्षान्तरे त्रिषु जन्मस्वितिशेषः । क्रमात्—यथाक्रमम् ॥४५॥४६॥ दूर्वात्रिकैः—त्रिसङ्ख्याभिः दूर्वाभिरित्यर्थः । त्रिस्वादुसंयुतैः—त्रिमधुरसंयुक्तैः ॥४७॥ महारोगेषु—महारोगा नाम वातादयोऽष्टौ । छिन्नोद्भवैः—अमृतालताभिः एकै-

---

(१) सन्निपातिगदेज्वरे इति मू० पु० पा० । (२) स्नुवा इति सो पु० पा० ।
(३) त्वचसंचूर्ण्य पूषणं सर्षपं तिलमिति सो० पु० पा० । (४) पादोऽस्य इति सो०पु० पा० ।
(५) दूरस्थितं दृढमिति सो० पु० पा० ।

त्रिसहस्रं त्रियामायां सर्षपैस्तद्रसप्लुतैः ।
शतयोजनदूरादप्यानयेद्वनितां बलात् ॥५५॥
तां तु पुत्तलिकामर्द्धमधूच्छिष्टसमन्विताम् ।
कृतप्राणप्रतिष्ठां च श्मशाने निखनेन्निशि ॥५६॥
साध्ययोनिं च तत्रैव छित्वा दत्वा बलिं ततः ।
कृताभिषेकस्तां विद्यां प्रजपेच्च शतत्रयम् ॥५७॥
अरातेरष्टमे राशौ मासान्नानाविधैरपि ।
रोगैर्भूतादिसंक्लेशैर्नाशमेति सुनिश्चितम् ॥५८॥
यद्यन्तरा समुद्धृत्य सलिले तां खनेन्निशि ।
क्लेशैस्तैः स विनिर्मुक्तः सुखी जीवति भूतले ॥५९॥
साध्यवृक्षेण कृत्वा तां सर्षपाज्ये निवेशिताम् ।
तोयमध्ये निधायैतत्क्राथयेदुक्तवासरैः ॥६०॥
वैरी तीव्रज्वरेणार्तः कृते प्राग्वत् सुखी भवेत् ।
तामेव चण्डिकागेहे तथा बलियुतं खनेत् ॥६१॥
साध्यो नरश्चेत् नारी चेत् शास्तुरायतने खनेत् ।
तद्विधानेन सहितं शत्रुरुन्मादवान् भवेत् ॥६२॥

कैरितिशेषः । त्रिभिः—दूर्वादिभिः समुदितैः । वा-पक्षान्तरे । तद्दिनेषु—महा-रोगप्रतीकारप्रयोगदिनेषु ॥४९॥ तत्तोयैः—अभिमन्त्रितजलैः ! पाकाद्यं अन्नाद्यम् । तैरेव—जलैरेव ॥५०॥५१॥ तैः—साध्यर्क्षवृक्षचूर्णादिभिः समुदितैः ॥५२॥५३॥ ॥५४॥५५॥ अर्द्धमधूच्छिष्टसमन्विताम्—अर्द्धांशमधूच्छिष्टसहितैः प्रागुक्तैः कृताम् ॥५६॥ कृताभिषेक इत्यादि सर्वक्रूरप्रयोगानन्तरकृत्यम् । अभिषेकस्तु तत्तद्देवता नित्यसपर्याचक्रेण ॥५७॥ अष्टमे राशौ निखनेदिति सम्बन्धः । सर्वत्र क्रूर-प्रयोगान् साध्यस्य अष्टमे राशौ कुर्यात् ॥५८॥५९॥ तां—पुत्तलिकां श्मशाने निखाताम् । एतत्—सर्षपाज्यपात्रम् । उक्तवासरैः—मासादिभिः॥६०॥ प्राग्वत्कृते-सलिलस्थापने कृते । तामेव—साध्यनक्षत्रवृक्षकृताम् । तथा बलियुतं—साध्ययो-

महावज्रं च वज्रं च यन्त्राण्यन्यान्यनुक्रमात्।
प्रयोगानपि वक्ष्यामि समाहितधिया शृणु ॥६३॥
प्राक्प्रत्यक्दक्षिणोदिक् च विंशत्सूत्राणि पातयेत्।
तेन कोष्ठानि जायन्ते त्वेकषष्ट्या शतत्रयम् ॥६४॥
तेषु कोण(उपान्तेषु)चतुष्के ऽपि मार्जयेत् पञ्चकेन च।
चत्वारिंशत्तत शेषं वज्राकारं यथा भवेत् ॥६५॥
दिक्षु चत्वारि चत्वारि मार्जयित्वा त्रिकोणकम्।
कुर्याच्छेषाणि कोष्ठानि पञ्चषष्ट्या शतं भवेत् ॥६६॥
तेषु पूर्वादिपरितो लिखे(दा)द्विद्याक्षराणि तु।
प्राग्वत्स्वरविभिन्नानि प्रागुक्तविधिना तथा(तः) ॥६७॥
चत्वारिचत्वारिंशच्च शतं तेषां तु मध्यतः।
एकविंशतिकोष्ठानि शिष्टानि पुनरम्बिके! ॥६८॥

निबलियुतम् ॥६१॥ नरनार्यैर्यथाक्रमं चण्डिकाशास्त्रोर्गृहे। तद्विधानेन—अष्टमराज्यादि ॥६२॥

महावज्रमित्यादिभिः कार्यानुरूपत इत्यन्तैरेकादशभिः श्लोकैर्महावज्रादि यन्त्रनिर्माणक्रममुपदिशति। तत्र प्राग्वत् एकादशानाद्यन्ताक्षराणि प्रागुक्तविधिना प्रादक्षिण्यप्रवेशगत्या तेषां षट्सप्तत्यधिकशतसङ्ख्यास्वरविकृतविद्याक्षराणां समन्वितं शिष्टविकृताक्षरेषु षट्कमितिशेषः। चकाराद्विकृतविद्याक्षरसहितमितिशेषः। अन्यत्सुगमम्। लेखनक्रमस्य सम्प्रदायप्राप्यत्वात् अयमत्र विलेखनक्रमः—यथा—प्राक्प्रत्यक् दक्षिणोदक् च समान्तरालानि विंशतिविंशतिसूत्राणि पातयेत्। एवं कृते एकषष्ठ्यधिकशतत्रयं कोष्ठानि सम्भवन्ति ॥६३॥६४॥ तेषु चतुर्दिक्षु सर्वमध्यकोष्ठचतुष्टयवर्जम्। बाह्यवीथ्यां कोष्ठान्यन्यान्यभितः प्रतिकोणं सप्तदशसप्तदश मार्जयेत्। तदन्तः द्वितीयवीथ्यां प्राग्वत् पूर्वपरित्यक्तकोष्ठपार्श्वेषु एकमेकं कोष्ठं परित्यज्य अन्यानि त्रयोदश त्रयोदश कोष्ठानि प्रतिकोणमभितोमार्जयेत्। तदन्तरेपि तृतीयवीथ्यां प्राग्वत् एकमेकं त्यक्त्वा प्रतिकोणं नव कोष्ठानि मार्जयेत्। तदन्तश्चतुर्थवीथ्यां प्राग्वदेकैकं त्यक्त्वा प्रति-

तेषु पर्यायनित्याद्यवर्णषट्कसमन्वितम् ।
घटिकायुगवर्णौ च लिखेत् प्रागुक्तयोगतः ॥६९॥
शिष्टेषु विद्यावर्णांश्च लिखेद्द्वादशशेषयोः ।
साध्याख्यमालिखेदुक्तक्रमेण पुटयोर्द्वयोः ॥७०॥
चतुर्दिक्षु लिखेत्कोणेष्वभितो भौतिकार्णकान् ।
द्वित्रिक्रमेण प्राक्प्रत्यक्कोणयोस्तु त्रयं त्रयम् ॥७१॥
एतत् प्रोक्तेषु संलिख्य संपूज्य विधिना युतम् ।
स्पृशन् जपेन्मनुं पश्चात्त्रिसहस्रं ततस्तु तत्(तम्) ॥७२॥
विनियुंज्याद्यथोक्तेषु कार्येषु क्रमतः शिवे ! ।
भूताक्षराणि च पुनर्लिखेत्कार्यानुरूपतः ॥७३॥

कोणं पञ्चपञ्चकोष्ठानि मार्जयेत् । तदन्तः पञ्चवीथ्यां प्रागवच्चैकैकमेकं परित्यज्य प्रतिकोणमेकं एकं कोष्ठं मार्जयेत् । एवं कृते एकाशीत्यधिकशतकोष्ठरूपं प्रतिदिशं एकादिप्रतिपङ्क्ति प्रतिपार्श्वं एकैककोष्ठाभिवृद्ध्या वज्राकारं दृश्यते । तेषु चतुर्दिक्षु प्रथमद्वितीयपङ्क्तिस्थकोष्ठचतुष्टयं मार्जयित्वा तत्रोपान्त्यरेखा-द्वयावष्टम्भेन त्रिकोणं कुर्यात् । एवं कृते पञ्चषष्ट्यधिकशतकोष्ठानि दृश्यन्ते । तेषु पूर्वपङ्क्तिस्थकोष्ठपञ्चकमध्यस्थकोष्ठमारभ्य सर्वबाह्यवीथ्यां प्रादक्षिण्येन षट्-सप्तत्यधिकशतसङ्ख्येषु स्वरविकृतविद्याक्षरेष्वादितः षट्त्रिंशदक्षराण्यालिख्य तदन्त-र्द्वितीयवीथ्यामपि मध्यमकोष्ठमारभ्य पूर्वलिखिताक्षरोर्ध्वं द्वात्रिंशदक्षराणि प्रागव-दालिख्य तदन्तस्तृतीयवीथ्यामपि लिखिताक्षरोपरितनान्यष्टाविंशत्यक्षराण्यालिख्य तदन्तश्चतुर्थवीथ्यामपि अमुनाक्षरक्रमं चतुर्विंशत्यराणि प्रागवदालिख्य तदन्तः पञ्च-मवीथ्यां तद्वत् विंशत्यक्षराण्यालिख्य तदन्तः षष्ठवीथ्यां चत्वारि सम्भूय चतुश्चत्वारिंश-दधिकशताक्षराण्यालिख्य ततः शेषाक्षरद्वात्रिंशत्कोष्ठेषु क्रमेणैकविंशतिवर्णैः सह पञ्चविंशपटलवक्ष्यमाणपर्यायनित्यावर्णषट्कं षट्सु समालिख्य तदनु युगघटिका वर्णद्वयं यथा सम्प्रदायमेकस्मिन् कोष्ठे समालिख्य ततो द्वादशसु कोष्ठेषु विद्याया अ(वि)धिकृतानि द्वादशाक्षराणि समालिख्यावशिष्टयोर्द्वयोः कोष्ठयोर्लिखिताक्षर-द्वयमध्ये प्रागवदधस्तात्साध्यमुपरिष्टात् साधककर्मणी च समालिख्य चतुर्दिक्षु त्रिकोणेषु प्रागादिप्रादक्षिण्येन भूताक्षराणि द्वित्रिक्रमादालिख्यावशिष्ट-

महावज्रमितिख्यातं सर्वत्रैवापराजितम् ।
विजयस्तम्भविद्वेषवश्योच्चाटनकर्मसु ॥७४॥
रक्षयेत् पुष्टिशान्त्यै(१) च तथैव रिपुनिग्रहे(२) ।
देशराष्ट्रपुरग्रामनिवेशादेर्विशेषतः ॥७५॥
घोरेषूत्पातजातेषु भूमौ संलिख्य गैरिकैः ।
मध्ये देवीं समावाह्य पूजयेन्नित्यशः शिवाम् ॥७६॥
सन्ध्यासु तिसृषु प्रोक्तक्रमान्नीराजनं तथा ।
कुर्यात् त्रिरात्रं द्विगुणं त्रिगुणं काम्यरूपतः ॥७७॥
राज्ञां वैरिविरोधेन पुरीमात्रावशेषिते ।
विभवे मण्डपे तस्य प्रोक्तवज्रं लिखेन्महत् ॥७८॥
दरदेनार्चयेत्तस्य मध्ये देवीं शुचिस्मिताम् ।
नृत्यगीतादिभिः सार्द्धं सन्ध्यासु च विशेषतः ॥७९॥
एवं प्राग्वद्दिनैरुक्तैर्विजयी नृपतिर्भवेत् ।
वैरिनाशेन वा तस्य भङ्गाद्वासनतोऽपि वा ॥८०॥
ततस्तन्मार्जयित्वा तु भाले कृत्वा पुरीं बलैः ।
प्रतीया(परीया)द्देशिकं त्वग्र्ये गजे जीवेच्चिरं सुखी(म्) ॥८१॥
निःसपत्नो निरातङ्कः षडङ्गः ख्यातवैभवः ।
एवमेतस्य वज्रस्य वैभवं कोनु वर्णयेत् ॥८२॥

विज्ञातविद्याक्षरैकादशकं प्राक्पश्चिमयोस्त्रयं त्रयं दक्षिणोत्तरयोर्द्वयं त्रयं चाऽऽलिखेदिति ॥६३॥६४॥६५॥६६॥६७॥६८॥६९॥७०॥७१॥७२॥७३॥

महावज्रमित्यादिभिर्वर्णयेदित्यन्तैर्नवभिः श्लोकैर्महावज्रयन्त्रप्रयोगविशेषांस्तत्फलानि चोपदिशति। तत्र प्रोक्तक्रमात्—ललिताप्रोक्तक्रमतः ॥७४॥७५॥७६॥७७॥७८॥७९॥ प्राग्वत्—दिनैः मासादिभिः । गजे स्थापयित्वेति शेषः ॥८०॥८१॥

---

(१) रक्षां पुष्टिं च शान्तिं च इति मू० पु० पा० ।   (२) विग्रहम् सो पु० पा० ।

अथान्यद्वज्रनिर्माणं विधानं च शृणु प्रिये ! ।
येन हस्तगतेन स्युः सिद्धयोऽपि स्वहस्तगाः ॥८३॥
प्राक्प्रत्यग्दक्षिणोदक् च दशसूत्राणि पातयेत् ।
तेनैकाशीतिकोष्ठानि जायन्ते त(च्च)दपूर्ववत् ॥८४॥
मार्जयेद्दशकोणेषु शिष्टेषु विलिखेत्तथा ।
त्रिकोणानि चतुर्दिक्षु तेषु ता(न्येव)वच्च पूर्ववत् ॥८५॥
विलिखेदवशिष्टेषु मन्त्रार्णास्त्रिशस्तथा ।
एकस्मिन्मध्यमे शक्तिः जठरे साध्यमालिखेत् ॥८६॥
एतच्च पूर्वमुक्तेषु विनियुञ्ज्यान्निजेच्छया ।
न भेदस्त्वनयोरस्ति प्रयोगेषु तु सर्वतः ॥८७॥
एतद्वज्रस्य मध्यस्थं नाम कृत्वा महीभुजः ।
दशकी हृदये शीर्षे संस्थाप्य समरे कृते ॥८८॥

निरातङ्कः षड्ङ्गः षडङ्गानि नाम अमात्यराष्ट्रदुर्गकोशबलसुहृत्संज्ञानि स्वाम्युपसर्जनानि । अन्यत्सुगमम् ॥८२॥

अथेत्यादिभिरालिखेदित्यन्तैश्चतुर्भिः श्लोकैर्वज्रान्तरनिर्माणमुपदिशति । तत्र पूर्ववत् । वज्राकारेण दशकोणेषु तेषु कोष्ठेषु चतुर्षु कोणेषु प्रतिकोणं दश कोष्ठानि मार्जयेदित्यर्थः । शिष्टेषु कोष्ठेषु । तथाप्रतिदिशं एकं कोष्ठं मार्जयेदित्यर्थः । त्रिकोणानि विलिखेदिति सम्बन्धः । तानि कर्मानुरूपाणि भूताक्षराणि । अवशिष्टेषु सप्तत्रिंशत्सङ्ख्येषु कोष्ठेषु मन्त्रार्णान् द्वादशेति शेषः । त्रिशः द्वयं द्वयम् । तथा—प्रागादि प्रादक्षिण्येन । शक्तिजठरे—ह्रीं खामध्ये । लिखनक्रमो यथा—प्राक् प्रत्यग्दक्षिणोदक् च समान्तरालानि दशदशसूत्राण्यास्फाल्य तत्र पूर्ववत्प्रतिकोणं बाह्यवीथ्यां सप्तकं तदन्तर्द्वितीयवीथ्यां द्वयं तदन्तस्तृतीयवीथ्यामेकमेवं क्रमेण दशकोष्ठान्यभितोमार्जयित्वा चतुर्दिगतकोष्ठचतुष्टयं मार्जयित्वा तत्र त्रिकोणानि विधाय त्रिकोणेषु तेषु प्राग्वत् भूताक्षराण्यालिख्य ततस्तेषु सप्तत्रिंशत्कोष्ठेषु द्वयं द्वयं मन्त्राक्षराणि प्राग्वत् षडावृत्त्या विलिखेत् सर्वमध्यगते कोष्ठे ह्रीं कां ससाध्यां लिखेदिति ॥८३॥८४॥८५॥८६॥

निहत्य वाहिनीं शत्रोश्चतुरङ्गां महीभुजः ।
अक्षतारोगसर्वाङ्गो यशोलक्ष्मीधनान्वितः ॥८९॥
निर्वर्त्य सुचिरं जीवेद्भोगी भूमौ निजेच्छया ।
एतत्ताम्रतले(१) कृत्वा स्थापयेदभिवृद्धये ॥९०॥
विधाय वृत्तयोर्मध्ये षट्कोणं तस्य मध्यतः ।
बाह्ये कृत्वा च विद्याया बीजमाद्यमथान्तिमम्(२) ॥९१॥
षट्सु कोणेषु तु पुनरग्रपश्चिमयोर्लिखेत् ।
एकैकं पार्श्वकोणेषु द्वे द्वे(३)वृत्तान्तरा पुनः ॥९२॥
मातृकां विलिखेदादिक्षान्तां(४) बिन्दुसमन्विताम् ।
मध्यबीजस्य मध्यस्थं लिखित्तं निजवाञ्छितम् ॥९३॥
भर्तुर्दमनभीतानां(५) कुमारीणामिदं भुजे ।
कण्ठे वा धारयेत्सद्यो वल्लभा तस्य जायते ॥९४॥
स्वरप्रसारितैर्मन्त्रवर्णैः पद्मानि कारयेत् ।
वृत्ताष्टपत्रयुक्तानि षोडशानि मनोहरम्(६) ॥९५॥

एतदित्यादिभिः अभिवृद्धये इत्यन्तैश्चतुर्भिः श्लोकैस्तत्प्रयोगान् तत्फलानि चोपदिशति । तत्र दंशकः—कवचः । अन्यत् सुगमम् ॥८७॥८८॥८९॥९०॥

विधायेत्यादिभिर्जायत इत्यन्तैश्चतुर्भिः श्लोकैः सौभाग्यकरं यन्त्रमुपदिशति । तत्र एतदुक्तं भवति—यथामानं षट्कोणं कृत्वा तदन्तवृत्ताद्बहिरेकैकाङ्गुला- (माना)न्तरालं वृत्तद्वयं कृत्वा तत्रान्तर्वीथ्यां यथासम्प्रदायं मन्त्रेणावेष्टनं तद्बाह्यवीथ्यां मातृकाक्षरवेष्टनं अकारादिप्रादक्षिण्येन कुर्यात् इति । अन्यत् सुगमम् । अत्र तन्त्रे सर्वत्र मन्त्रेणावेष्टनं क्रूरेषु कर्मसु रेफांशेन कुर्यात्, अन्यत्र चतुर्थस्वरांशेन कुर्यात् ॥९१॥९२॥९३॥९४॥

स्वरप्रसारितैरित्यादिभिरवाप्तये इत्यन्तैः षड्भिः श्लोकैः षोडश पद्मान्युप

---

(१) ताम्रदले इति मू० पु० पा ।
(२) आद्यं तथान्तिकाम् इति सो० पु० पा० ।
(३) द्वौ द्वौ इति मू० पु० पा० ।
(४) दादिक्षान्तां इति सो० पु० पा० ।
(५) भर्तुर्दमनभीतानामिति म० प० पा०
(६) मनोहराम् इति सो० पु० पा० ।

२८

कर्णिकासु च पत्रेषु लिखेदेकैकमक्षरम् ।
कर्णिकार्णस्य मध्यस्थं कुर्यान्नाम निजेप्सितम् ॥९६॥
घटिकाक्षरसंयुक्तं विनियुञ्ज्यात्तु नित्यशः ।
अहोरात्रं षोडशधा कृत्वा तां तेषु* योजयेत् ॥९७॥
समस्तं वाञ्छितं तत्तत्तन्मध्ये विलिखेत्तदा ।
धारयेदभिषिञ्चेच्च ज(युर्ज)पेदिष्टार्थसिद्धये ॥९८॥
प्राक्प्रत्यक्दक्षिणोदक्च पञ्च सूत्र निपातनात् ।
कोष्ठानि षोडशानि स्युस्तेषु पद्मानि कारयेत् ॥९९॥
प्रागुक्तेषु विधायैवमर्चयेद्यामतः(१) क्रमात् ।
देवीं तु स्थापयेद्भूमौ सर्वसम्पदवाप्तये ॥१००॥
(२)पायुतत्त्वमयी व्याप्तिरिति सम्यक् समीरिता ।
यस्या निष्फालनाच्चित्ते तत्तत्त्वं स्वात्मसात्कृतम् ॥१०१॥

दिशति। तत्र प्रागुक्तेषु—सुवर्णादिष्वधिकरणेषु। एतदुक्तं भवति—विद्याया अनाहतान्येकादशाक्षराणि स्वरप्रसारणात् षट्सप्तत्यधिकशतसङ्ख्यानि भवन्ति। तेष्वक्षरेष्वादितः प्रथममक्षरं कर्णिकामध्ये विलिख्य तदक्षरमध्ये द्वितीयमक्षरं, तत्र तदधोघटिकाक्षरस्थाने तृतीयमक्षरं, बहिरष्टसु दलेषु अग्न्यादिप्रादक्षिण्येन अष्टाक्षराणि, एवमेकादशाक्षराणि अहोरात्रस्य षोडशात्मकेषु खण्डेषु प्रथमखण्डस्य तत्तद्घटिकाक्षरं तत्र तदातदा विलिखेत्। एतत् प्रथमं पद्मम्। अनन्तरं पूर्वलिखिताक्षरैकादशकादुपरितनं एकादशकं प्राग्वद्विलिख्य अहोरात्रस्य द्वितीयखण्डस्य तत्तद्घटिकाक्षरं प्राग्वद्विलिखेत्। एतद्द्वितीयं पद्मम्। एवं क्रमेणान्यानि चतुर्दश पद्मानि कृत्वा तत्र तत्र तदा तदा देवीपूजनादिष्टावाप्तिः। तानि षोडशपद्मानि स्वर्णादिषोडशकोष्ठात्मके मण्डले प्रतिकोष्ठमेकैकं प्राग्वद्विलिख्य पूजनाच्च प्रागुक्ता सिद्धिरिति ॥९५॥९६॥९७॥९८॥९९॥१००॥१०१॥

---

(१) यामनुक्रमात् इति मू० पु० पा०। (२) वायुतत्त्वेति मू० पु० पा०।

* तांस्तेषु इति मू० पु० पा०।

इति श्रीषोडशनित्यातन्त्रेषु श्रीकादिमते द्वादशपटलं परिपूर्णं परामृष्टम् ॥१२॥

इति श्रीषोडशनित्यातन्त्रेषु श्रीकादिमताख्यस्य तन्त्रस्य परिपूर्णस्य तन्त्रस्य प्रपञ्च-
सारसिंहराजप्रकाशाभिधानेन श्रीसुभगानन्दनाथेन विरचितायां
मनोरमाख्यायां व्याख्यायां महावज्रेश्वरीनित्याविद्याविधान-
प्रकाशनपरं द्वादशपटलं परिपूर्णं
परामृष्टम् ॥ १२ ॥

ग्रन्थसङ्ख्या—

एकोनविंशत्यन्यानि व्याख्याग्रन्थाः शतात्परम् ।
द्वादश स्युरितीत्थं द्वादशे पटले स्मृताः ।

अथ त्रयोदशपटलम् ।

अथ षोड़शनित्यासु या प्रोक्ता त्वष्टमी तदा ।
तद्विधानं शृणु प्राज्ञ ! समीहितफलप्रदम् ॥१॥
विद्योद्धारः कृतः पूर्वमथ न्यासक्रमं तथा ।
तदावरणशक्तिश्च तद्ध्यानं तत्प्रपूजनम् ॥२॥
तत्साधनं तत्प्रयोगान् होमयन्त्रादिभिस्तथा ।
प्राणप्रतिष्ठां विद्यां च तद्विधानं च तत्फलम् ॥३॥
क्रमेण वच्ये संप्रोक्तान्यशेषेण महेश्वरि ! ।
यैर्मन्त्रैर्भुवने ख्यातो निग्रहानुग्रहक्षमः ॥४॥
कुर्यात् प्राग्वत् षड़ङ्गानि विद्याद्येनोक्तमार्गतः ।
तेनैव पुटितैर्वर्णैर्न्यसेच्छ्रोत्रादिपञ्चसु* ॥५॥
षष्ठं मनसि विन्यस्य व्यापकं विद्यया न्यसेत् ।
प्राग्वदर्घ्यं समुद्दिष्टं तच्छक्ती शृणु पार्वति ! ॥६॥

अथ त्रयोदशपटलम् ।

पूर्व्वस्मिन् द्वादशे पटले सप्तम्या महावज्रेश्वरीनित्या विद्याया विधानमुपदिश्यानन्तरमष्टम्या शिवदूतीनित्याविद्याया विधानमुपदिशति । अथ षोड़शेत्यादिविधानकमित्यन्तेन श्लोकशतरूपेण त्रयोदशेन पटलेन । तत्र अथ षोड़शेत्यादिभिः क्षम इत्यन्तैः चतुर्भिः श्लोकैः पटलार्थानुद्दिशति । तत्र पूर्वं—तृतीये पटले । अन्यत् सुगमम् ॥१॥२॥३॥४॥

कुर्यादित्यादिना पार्वतीत्यन्तेन श्लोकद्वयेन न्यासविधिं अर्घ्यसाधनादिकं(१) चोपदिशति । तत्र उक्तमार्गतः—दीर्घस्वरषट्कजातियुक्तेनेत्यर्थः । तेनैव—शक्तेश्वया । श्रोत्रादिपञ्चसु—यथाक्रमं श्रोत्रत्वक्चक्षुर्जिह्वाघ्राणाख्येषु इति शेषः ॥५॥ तत्र त्वचि सर्वाङ्गेषु उक्तेषु स्थानेषु शक्तेश्वापुटितेनैकैकेन वर्णेन न्यसेदित्यर्थः ॥६॥

---

(१) अर्घ्यस्थापनादिकमिति वं पु॰ पा॰ । अर्घ्यसाधारणादिकमिति सो॰ पु॰ पा॰ । पञ्चकमिति मू॰ पु॰ पा॰ ।

विह्वला कर्षणी लोला नित्या मदनमालिनी।
विनोदा कौतुका पुण्या पुराणा चतुरस्रगाः(१) ॥७॥
वागीशा वरदा विश्वा विभवा विघ्नकारिणी।
वीरा विघ्नहरा विद्येत्युक्ता यन्त्राष्टशक्तयः(२) ॥८॥
सुमुखी सुन्दरी सारा समरा च सरस्वती।
समया सर्वगा सिद्धेत्युक्ता अष्टास्रशक्तयः(३) ॥९॥
डाकिन्याद्याः षड़स्रेषु सर्वास्त्वग्रात्प्रदक्षिणम्।
मूलदेवीसमाकारवर्णायुधसमन्विताः ॥१०॥
शिवां वाणीं दूरसिद्धां त्वैविग्रहवतीमपि।
नादां मनोमयीं(४)षट्सु पत्रेषु परितोऽर्चयेत् ॥११॥
इच्छाज्ञानक्रियाशक्तीस्त्रिषु कोणेषु पूजयेत्।
मध्ये देवीं हेतिवृत्तां(५) पूजयेदष्टमीं शिवाम् ॥१२॥
तस्या ध्यानं शृणु प्राज्ञे! यन्मयं विश्वमीरितम्।
तथापि भक्तसन्त्राणहेतोः(६) कल्पमां परां तनुम् ॥१३॥

विह्वलेत्यादिभिः शिवामित्यन्तैः षड्भिः श्लोकैर्देव्याः परिवारशक्तीरुपदिशति। तत्र मदनमालिनी—मदना मालिनी चेति द्वे शक्ती। चतुरस्रगाः—चतुरस्रद्वारयुगस्य पार्श्वयोः प्रत्येकं द्वयं द्वयमेवं चतुष्टयं—कोणचतुष्टये चतुष्टयम्। उत्तरदक्षिणदिशोर्द्वयं एवं दश चतुरस्रगाः—चतुरस्रस्थिता इत्यर्थः॥७॥ यन्त्राष्ट(क)शक्तयः अष्टयन्त्रस्थशक्तयः ॥८॥९॥ सर्वाइत्युक्त्या अत्र डाकिन्याद्याश्च अग्रादारभ्य प्रादक्षिण्येनार्चयेत्। तच्छक्तयवस्थानन्तु प्रागवभिरुक्तं तिकोणादिषु—तेन डाकिनीराकिनी साकिनी-लाकिनी-डाकिनी इत्येवं पूजाक्रमः ॥१०॥ शिवामित्यादयो विद्याया द्वितीयाक्षरादिनामशक्तयः। त्वैविग्रहवती त्वैविग्रहेत्यर्थः ॥११॥ हेतिपूजनं तत्तन्नामभिः समाचर्यन्तैर्ब्राह्म्यादिनिरुक्त्यन्तं प्रादक्षिण्येन ॥१२॥

---

(१) नूपुराणाचरश्रागा इति सो० पु० पा०। (२) स्वद्राश्रशक्तय इति मू० पु० पा०।
(३) संशय इति सो० पु० पा०। (४) मनोन्मनीं इति मू० पु० पा।
(५) हृत्ते इति मू० पु० पा०। (६) भक्त्यानन्तार्थं इति सो० पु० पा०।

निदाघकालमध्याह्नदिवाकरसमप्रभाम् ।
नवरत्नकिरीटां च चीनया*मरुणाम्बराम् ॥१४॥
नानाभरणसम्भिन्नदेहकान्तिविराजिताम् ।
शुचिस्मितामष्टभुजां स्तूयमानां महर्षिभिः ॥१५॥
पाशं खेटं गदां रत्नचषकं वामबाहुभिः ।
दक्षिणैरङ्कुशं खड्गं कुठारं† कमलं तथा ॥१६॥
दधानामाधुकाभीष्टदानोद्यमसमन्विताम् ।
ध्यात्वैवं पूजयेद्देवीं दूतीं दुर्नीतिनाशिनीम् ॥१७॥
वृत्तद्वयं बहिस्त्र्यस्रं तद्वयं षड् दलाम्बुजम् ।
तथा षड्स्रमष्टास्रं तद्वदष्टदलाम्बुजम्(१) ॥१८॥
भुपुरे वह्निवासिन्या कृत्वा तन्मध्यगां शिवाम् ।
आवाह्याभ्यर्च्य ताः शक्तीः प्रागुक्तविधिना स्थिताः ॥१९॥
जप्त्वा हुत्वा नमस्कृत्य स्वात्मन्युद्वासयेत्तथा ।
साधनं चोक्तमार्गेण कुर्यान्नियमतन्द्रितः ॥२०॥
काम्यहोमविधिं देवि ! शृणु सङ्कल्पसिद्धिदम् ।
येनासौ वाञ्छितं क्षिप्रमवाप्नोति सुनिश्चितम् ॥२१॥

तस्या इत्यादिभिर्नाशिनीमित्यन्तैः पञ्चभिः श्लोकैर्देव्या नित्यपूजाविधानमुपदिशति। तत्र परां तनुं शृणु इति पूर्व्वत्रान्वयः। एतत्—सर्वदेवतासमानम्। भुजेषु—पाशाङ्कुशादिकं ऊर्ध्वादिवामदक्षिणक्रमेण कल्पयेत्। कह्लारं‡ असिधेनुः। दुर्नीतिनाशिनीं—सम्यक् विवेकप्रदानात् ॥१३॥१४॥१५॥१६॥१७॥

वृत्तद्वयमित्यादिभिरतन्द्रित इत्यन्तैस्त्रिभिः श्लोकैर्नित्यपूजाचक्रं तत्र पूजानिगमनं विद्यासाधनाति(२) देशं चोपदिशति। तत्र भूपुरे चतुरस्रद्वयं वह्निवासिनीमित्यासपर्याचक्रवत् चतुरस्रद्वयं कुर्यात् इत्यर्थः। अन्यचक्रनिर्माणं

---

(१) दष्टच्छदाम्बुजाम् इति मू० पु० पा०। * तीक्ष्णामिति मू० पु० पा०।
† कह्लारमिति मू० पु० पा०। ‡ कह्लारमिति व० पु० पा०।
(२) विद्यासाधनानिदेशं इति सो० पु० पा०।

वशयेद्वनितां होमाद्गुग्गुलैर्मधुमिश्रितैः ।
नालिकेरफलोपेतैर्गुडैर्लक्ष्मीमवाप्नुयात् ॥२२॥
तथाज्यसिक्तैः कह्लारैः चौरान्तैररुणोत्पलैः ।
त्रिमध्वक्तैश्चम्पकैश्च प्रसूनैर्बकुलोद्भवैः ॥२३॥
मधूकजैः प्रसूनैश्च हुतैः कन्यामवाप्नुयात् ।
पुन्नागजैर्हुतैर्वस्त्राण्याज्यैरिष्टमवाप्नुयात् ॥२४॥
माहिषैर्महिषानाज्यै राज्यैर्गव्यैश्च गास्तथा ।
अवाप्नोति हुतैः साज्यै(१) रत्नै रत्नं च साधकः ॥२५॥
शालिपिष्टमयीं कृत्वा पुत्तलीं सितसंयुताम् ।
हृद्येशन्यस्तनामार्णां पचेत्तैलाज्ययोर्निशि ॥२६॥
तामनश्नन्(२) दिवा रात्रौ विद्याजप्तां तु भक्षयेत् ।
सप्तरात्रप्रयोगेन नरो नारी नृपोऽथ वा ॥२७॥
दासवद्वशमायाति वित्तप्राणादिमर्पयेत् ।
हयारिपुष्पै रक्तैः सितैर्वा जुहुयात्तथा ॥२८॥
विसप्तरात्रान्महतीमवाप्नोति श्रियं नरः ।
छागमांसं त्रिमध्वक्तैर्होमात्स्वर्णमवाप्नुयात् ॥२९॥

सुगमम्॥१८॥१८॥ तथा-यथा ललितायाः प्रोक्तमार्गेण युगानुरूपमक्षरविलक्षादिकं प्राग्वत् ॥२०॥

काम्येत्यादिभिर्दिनैरित्यन्तैर्दशभिः श्लोकैर्द्रव्यविशेषहोमात् फलविशेषप्राप्तिमुपदिशति। तत्र अरुणोत्पलं प्राग्वद्रक्तकैरवम्। मधूकात्पूर्वाणि गुडादीनि पञ्चद्रव्याणि लक्ष्मीकराणि ॥२१॥२२॥२३॥ पुन्नागजैः—प्रसूनैरितिशेषः। चम्पकादीनां पुन्नागान्तानां चतुर्णां द्रव्याणां त्रिमधुश्लेषं कुर्यात् ॥२४॥ माहिषैरित्यादीनि आज्यैरित्यस्य विशेषणानि ॥२५॥ सितसंयुतां—शर्करासहिताम्। तैलाज्ययोर्मिश्रीभूतयोरितिशेषः ॥२६॥ अनश्नन्—अन्नमितिशेषः ॥२७॥ हयारिपुष्पैः—करवीरैः।

---

(१) हुतैराज्यैरत्नैरत्नंचेति मू० पु० पा०। (२) तामजश्रमिति सी० पु० पा०।

क्षीरान्नैः सस्यसम्पन्नां भुवमाप्नोति मण्डलात् ।
पद्माद्यैर्हवनाल्लक्ष्मीमवाप्नोति त्रिभिर्दिनैः ॥३०॥
अथ यन्त्राणि वक्ष्यामि नानाभीष्टप्रदानि तैः ।
शृणु तेषु विधानानि समाहितमनां शिवे ! ॥३१॥
दूतीनित्याक्षरेषु स्युरनावृत्तानि वै दश ।
तैः षोड़शस्वरयुतैः षष्ट्याशतमुदीरितैः ॥३२॥
चतुरस्रद्वयं कृत्वा तदन्तर्वृत्तयुग्मकम् ।
तदन्तरष्टकोणं च तदन्तर्वृत्तयुग्मकम् ॥३३॥
कृत्वा तत्र लिखेन्मध्ये विद्याद्यं नामसंयुतम् ।
वृत्तयोरन्तराशेषं बहिः कोणेषु चाष्टसु ॥३४॥
लिखेद्द्वे द्वेऽक्षरे तेषु बाह्यवृत्तद्वयान्तरा ।
कर्मानुरूपान् भूतार्णान् दशभूपुरमध्यतः ॥३५॥
मातृकां विलिखेद्दिक्षु द्वादश द्वादश क्रमात् ।
अन्त्यं चतुर्षु कोणेषु शेषाणां च विलेखने ॥३६॥

वा पक्षान्तरे ॥२८॥ त्रिसप्तरात्रान्—एकविंशतिदिनान् । क्षीरान्नैः छागमांसै-रित्यन्वयः । छागोमेषः ॥२९॥३०॥

अथ यन्त्राणीत्यादिभिर्वै इत्यन्तैः सप्तभिः श्लोकैः दशयन्त्राणि उपदिशति । तत्र एतदुक्तं भवति—इष्टप्रमाणक्रमेण वृत्तद्वयं निष्पाद्य तद्बहिरष्टकोणं प्राग्वद्वि-धाय तत्कोणाग्रस्पृष्टास्पृष्टिकया वृत्तद्वयं विधाय तद्बहिरन्तर्बहिर्विभागेन द्व्यङ्गु-लान्तरालं समचतुरस्रद्वयं निष्पाद्य सर्वमध्ये विद्यायां ह्रल्लेखां सनामाक्षरामा-लिख्य श(धि)विज्ञातविद्याशेषाक्षरषट्कमन्तर्वृत्तवीथ्यामालिख्य स्वरविज्ञाताक्षरेषु षष्ट्यधिकशतसङ्ख्येषु आदितः षोड़शाक्षराणि बहिरष्टसु कोणेषु प्रतिकोणमग्रमा-रभ्य प्रादक्षिण्येन द्वयं द्वयं समालिख्य बाह्यवृत्तवीथ्यामपि कर्मानुरूपं भूताक्षराणि तथा समालिख्य बहिश्चतुरस्रवीथ्यां तथैव मातृकाक्षराणि प्रतिदिशं द्वादश द्वादश ईशाग्निनिर्ऋतिवाय्वादि समालिखेत् । तद्विलेखने तु तेषु मातृकाक्षरेषु स्वराणामन्त्ययोर्विन्दुविसर्जनीययोर्विन्दुचतुर्दशस्तु स्वराक्षरेषु संयोज्य विसर्जनीयं

स्वरैर्बिन्दुं समायोज्य योजयेद्वाञ्जने* परम् ।
एवं यन्त्राणि जायन्ते दशसिद्धा(१)स्पदानि वै ॥३७॥
प्रथमं गैरिकैः कृत्वा तत्रावाह्य शिवां यजेत् ।
सप्तम्यां त्रिषु(२) सन्ध्यासु सितापूपसमन्वितम् ॥३८॥
कृत्वा निवेद्य पयसः प्रातर्मध्यन्दिने तथा ।
दधिभक्तन्तु† सायन्तु क्षीरं मोचाफलं तथा ॥३९॥
एवं मण्डलमर्द्धं वा कुर्यात् पूजां समाहितः ।
वाञ्छितं प्राप्नुयाद्देव्याः प्रसादेनाल्पयत्नतः ॥४०॥
द्वितीयं दरदैः कृत्वा तत्रावाह्याथ तद्दिने ।
सुपक्वं छागमांसेन क्षौद्रमन्नं निवेदयेत् ॥४१॥
तावद्भजे(३)न्महीपालं वशे कर्तुमयत्नतः ।
तथैव वनितां हृद्यां वशयेद्यावदायुषः ॥४२॥
तृतीयमपि सिन्दूरैर्विधायावाह्य तत्र ताम्(४) ।
तावद्दिनं तथाऽभ्यर्च्य वशयेद्द्विविधान् रिपून् ॥४३॥

कादिलान्ताक्षरेषु चतुस्त्रिंशत्सु संयोज्य अन्त्यं षकारं चतुरस्रकोणे चतुष्काभ्यन्तरे अष्टकोणबहिर्वृत्तद्वयाद्बहिः सविसर्जनीयमालिखेत्। एतत् प्रथमं यन्त्रम्। द्वितीयादीनि यन्त्राणि अस्यैव यन्त्रस्याष्टकोणेषु द्वितीयाक्षरादिषो शकं प्राग्वदालिखेत्। अन्यानि दश सुसमा(ना)नीति ॥३१॥३२॥३३॥३४॥३५॥॥३६॥३७॥

प्रथममित्यादिभिः समीरिता इत्यत्यन्तैरध्यर्धैस्त्रयोविंशति(भिः) श्लोकैर्दशविधयन्त्रप्रयोगांस्तत्फलानि चोपदिशति। तत्र—प्रथमे यन्त्रे । यजेत - नित्यक्रमतः। सिता—शर्करा ॥३८॥ पायसादीनि त्रीणि निवेद्यद्रव्याणि यथाक्रमं सन्ध्यात्रये निवेदयत् इत्यर्थः ३९॥ एवमर्द्धं—मण्डलार्द्धम् ॥४०॥ दरदैः—जातिलिङ्गैः। तद्दिने—सप्तम्याम् ॥४१॥ तावत्—प्रागुक्तमण्डलादि। भजेत्—नित्यक्रमतः। अत्र-

---

(१) सिद्धास्फुटानि इति मू० पु० पा० ।
(२) त्रिषु इति मू० पु० पा० ।
(३) द्भवेन्मही इति मू० पु० पा ।
(४) तमिति मू० पु० पा० ।
* द्वाञ्जने इति मू० पु० पा० ।
† भक्तञ्चमांसन्तु इति मू० पु० पा० ।

चतुर्थं कुङ्कुमैः कृत्वा तत्र मध्येऽर्चयेत्तथा ।
सप्ताहाद्दापदः सर्वाः प्रयान्त्यस्याः प्रसादतः ॥४४॥
पञ्चमं चन्दनैः कृत्वा तन्मध्ये पूजयेच्छिवाम् ।
केवलं पायसं मोचां सितां घृतसमन्विताम् ॥४५॥
निवेदयंस्त्रिसन्ध्यासु मासाद्रोगानशेषतः ।
जित्वा सुखी चिरं जीवेच्छेषमायुर्निरामयः ॥४६॥
अभिषिञ्चेच्च तत्रैव कुम्भं संस्थाप्य तैर्यजन् (जयम्) ।
कृत्वा तस्मै दक्षिणां च दद्या(द्द्रव्यं)द्भूरि स्वशक्तितः ॥४७॥
प्राणप्रदाय तस्मै तु दद्यात्सर्वस्वमेव वा ।
येनासौ तोषमायाति तावद्वित्तं समर्पयेत् ॥४८॥
षष्ठं कर्पूरसंयुक्तं पटीरैरालिखेत्ततः ।
मस्तृणे वा शिलापट्टे पीठे वा सौधभूतले ॥४९॥
अन्नाज्यं पायसापूपव्यञ्जनानि निवेदयेत् ।
पूजयेत्त्रिषु सन्ध्यासु जपन्विद्यां तथा वशी ॥५०॥
त्रिसप्तरात्रमात्रेण ज्वराद्गीमाभिचारजात् ।
मुच्यन्ते प्राणिनोऽचिन्त्याः शक्तयो मन्त्रयन्त्रयोः ॥५१॥
सप्तमं ताम्रपट्टे तु कृत्वाऽऽवाह्याभिपूज्य वा(१) ।
स्थापयेन्मन्दिरे तस्मिँल्लक्ष्मीरास्तेऽतिसुस्थिरा ॥५२॥
अष्टमं राजते कृत्वा बिभृयात् सर्वसम्पदे ।
नवमं हैमगं कृत्वा भूषादौ धारयेच्छिवे* ! ॥५३॥

प्रकरणे सर्वा(त्रा)र्चनं नित्यक्रमतः । तथैव—पूर्ववत् । द्वितीययन्त्रे पूजनात् ॥४२॥ तावद्दिनं—प्राग्वत् । तथा – द्वितीययन्त्रपूजानिवेद्यद्रव्यसहितम् । द्विविधान्—सहजकृत्रिमान् । तत्र सहजः—स्वकुलोत्पन्नः, कृत्रिमस्त्वापराधकृत् ॥४३॥ तथा—

---

(१) कृत्वाऽऽवाह्यानि पूजयेत् इति मू० पु० पा० ।

* च्छिये इति मू० पु० पा०

दशमे सर्वकार्य्याणि साधयेदर्चयन् शिवाम् ।
यद्यद्धि वाञ्छितं कार्य्यं तत्तन्मध्यगतं तथा ॥५४॥
कृत्वा तां पूजयेत्तत्र तत्कार्यं हृदये स्मरन् ।
तद्दिनैस्तदवाप्नोति नात्र कार्या विचारणा ॥५५॥
दशैव तानि यन्त्राणि भूर्जे कृत्वाऽभिपूज्य च ।
सिक्थनिर्मितपात्रस्थक्षौद्रमध्ये निवेश्य तत् ॥५६॥
त्रिसन्ध्य(१)मर्चयेद्रक्तगन्धपुष्पैः समाहितः ।
साध्यस्याभिमुखो विद्यां जपन्नित्यमनुस्मरन्(रेत्) ॥५७॥
पाशेन कण्ठमाबध्य यान्ति(पाति) तं निजपादयोः ।
न्यस्ताञ्जलिकरं शीर्षे दासोऽहमितिवादिनम् ॥५८॥
त्रिसप्तरात्राद्वश्याः स्युर्नरनारीनृपादयः ।
तदेव क्षोणं कृत्वा च(२) सन्ध्यासु त्रिषु नित्यशः ॥५९॥
कामार्ता वनिताः काम(३)ज्वरतप्ताशयात् शनैः ।
कुलं लज्जां विवेकं च परित्यजास्य किङ्कराः ॥६०॥
भवेयुरिति यन्त्राणां प्रयोगास्ते समीरिताः ।
प्राणप्रतिष्ठाविद्यां ते वक्ष्येऽहं शृणु पार्वति ! ॥६१॥

प्रागुक्तनिवेद्यद्रव्यसहितम्॥४४॥ पायसादि प्रतिसन्ध्यमेकैकम् ॥४५॥४६॥ तैः—यन्त्रविलिखितविद्याक्षरैः । तस्मै—अभिषेक्त्रे ॥४७॥ असौ—अभिषेक्ता ॥४८॥४९॥ अन्नादि प्रतिसन्ध्यं सर्वम् । जपन्—शतं सहस्रं वा ॥५०॥५१॥५२॥५३॥ तन्मध्यगतं—दशमयन्त्रमध्यगतम् । तथा—प्राग्वत् ॥५४॥ तां—दूतीनित्याम् । तद्दिनैः—प्राग्वन्मण्डलादिभिः ॥५५॥ दशैव तानि—प्रत्येकमितिशेषः । अभिपूज्य—प्राणप्रतिष्ठापुरःसरं तत्तल्लिखिताक्षरैः । सिक्थं—मधूच्छिष्टम् । तत्—यन्त्रमितिशेषः ॥५६॥ इत्यमिति वक्ष्यमाण प्रकारतः ॥५७॥५८॥ तदेव—यन्त्राधिष्ठितं क्षौद्रम् ॥५९॥ अस्य—प्रयोक्तुः ॥६०॥ भवेयुरिति पूर्वत्रान्वयः ।

---

(१) त्रिसन्धिम इति मू० पु० पा० । (२) तद्दैवक्षोष्ठं कुर्याश्च इति मू० पु० पा । (३) तीव्रज्वरेति मू० पु० पा० ।

वातोनभोधरायुक्तं स्पर्शौ व्याप्तेन संयुतः ।
जवौ दाहमरुद्युक्तो व्योमापि मरुता युतम् ॥६२॥
अग्निर्हंसस्य पूर्वार्णौ(१) पश्चादादित्रयं तथा ।
ज्यावह्नियुक्तार्थौ ऽम्बु स्यात् षष्ठसप्तमकौ पुनः ॥६३॥
ह्रच्छिख्यग्नियुतं माया रयगादित्रयं पुनः ।
हृद्दाहाम्बुचरैः खेन गोत्रादाहाग्निभिः परम् ॥६४॥
व्याप्तं मरुत्समोपेतं व्योमाग्निगमनन्तरम् ।
पुनराद्यत्रयं चाम्बुमरुद्व्युनभसा युतम्(२) ॥६५॥
शून्यं मायान्वितं पश्चाच्चतुर्थं पञ्चमं तथा ।
अग्निर्हंसो मरुद्युक्तो व्याप्तं च मरुता युतम् ॥६७॥
खं स्याद्द्रयधरायुक्तं हृदम्बुमरुदन्वितम् ।
हंसश्च मरुता युक्तश्चत्वारिंशल्लिपिर्मनुः ॥६८॥

प्राणेत्यादिना श्लोकोत्तरार्द्धेन सर्वतन्त्रसाधारणां प्राणप्रतिष्ठा विद्यां प्रस्तौति ॥६१॥

वात इत्यादिभिर्मनुरित्यन्तैः षड्भिः श्लोकैश्चत्वारिंशदक्षरां प्राणप्रतिष्ठाविद्यामुपदिशति। तत्र वातः—अकारः। नभोधरायुक्तं—मु इति। स्पर्शौव्याप्तेन संयुतः - ष्य इति। जवौ दाहमरुद्युक्तः—प्रा इति। व्योमापि मरुतायुतम्—ण इति॥६२॥ अग्निः—ईकारः। हंसो—हः। पूर्वार्णौ इत्यस्य पूर्ववर्णौ प्राणा इति। आदित्रयं—अमुष्य इति। ज्या वह्नियुक्ता—जी इति। अम्बु—वकारः। षष्ठ सप्तमकौ इ ह इति॥६३॥अथ ह्रच्छिख्यग्नियुतं—स्थि इति। माया—विसर्जनीयः। र य गा तकारोपरिस्थिता त—इति। आदित्रयं—प्राग्वत् अमुष्य इति अक्षरत्रयम्। हृत्—सकारः। दाहाम्बुचरैः खेन—वै इति। इत्येकं(व) त्रयोविंशमक्षरम्। गोत्रादाहाग्निभिः परं(द्रि)त्रि इत्येतत् चतुर्विंशमक्षरम्। त्रि(न्द्रिय) इत्यत्र आदौ विन्दुः सम्प्रदायप्राप्तः॥६४॥ व्याप्तं मरुत्समोपेतं—या इति। व्योमाग्निगमनन्तरं-णि इति षड्विंशमक्षरम्। आद्यत्रयं—अमुष्य इत्यक्षरत्रयम्। अम्बु-

---

(१) पूर्वार्णौ इति मू० पु० पा०।

(२) तासायुतमिति मू० पु० पा०

यादिसप्ताक्षरैः कुर्यात् षडङ्गानि द्वियोगतः।
त्वगादिषु च तान्येव न्यसेच्छक्तिपुटस्थितम्(१) ॥६९॥
ध्यायेद्देवीं प्राणशक्तिमरुणामरुणाम्बराम्।
अरुणाकल्पमुकुटामरुणाधरपल्लवाम् ॥७०॥
अरुणायतनेत्राब्जयुग्मचारुस्मिताननाम्।
प्रसूनपिण्डं पाशं च दधानां पाणियुग्मतः ॥७१॥
स्वसमानाभिरभितो वेष्टितां दशशक्तिभिः।
अनन्तशक्तियुक्ताभिः पूजयेत्पद्ममध्यतः ॥७२॥

मरुत्—अम्बुसहितोमरुदित्यर्थः वा इति। युनभसायुतंङ्म इति। एकत्रिंशमक्षरमितिशेषः (जम)इति ॥६५॥ शून्यं मायान्वितं—माया विसर्जनीयः नः इति। चतुर्थं प्रा इति। पञ्चमं—णाइति। अग्निः—ईकारः। हंसोमरुद्युतः—हा इति। व्याप्तं च मरुतायुतं—या इति॥६७॥खं स्याद्द्वयधरायुक्तं मु इति। हृदम्बुमरुदन्वितं- स्वाइति। हंसश्च मरुतायुक्तः - हा इति। एवं चत्वारिंशदक्षरः प्राणप्रतिष्ठामन्त्रः। एषं सर्वतन्त्रेषु सर्वयन्त्रपुत्तलिकाभिषेककुम्भदेवतावेशादीनां प्राणप्रतिष्ठामन्त्रः ॥६८॥

यादीत्यादिना श्लोकेन प्राणप्रतिष्ठाविद्याया षडङ्गादिन्यासमुपदिशति। तत्र द्वियोगतः—अक्षरद्वययोगतः। तद्यथा—(य)पराभ्यां हृदयं,रलाभ्यां शिरः,लवाभ्यां शिखा, वसाभ्यां कवचं,शषाभ्यां नेत्रं,षसाभ्यामस्त्रं, एवं षडङ्गानि जातिभिः सहितं कुर्यादित्यर्थः। त्वगादिषु—त्वगसृङ्मांसमेदोऽस्थिमज्जाशुक्रेषु सप्तसु धातुषु। तान्येव—प्रागुक्तानि यादि(सा)शान्तानि सप्ताक्षराणि। शक्तिपुटस्थितं—एतत्क्रियाविशेषणम्। सप्तसु प्रत्यक्षरं हृल्लेखापुटितं यथा स्यात्तथा तत्तन्नामयुक्तेषु ब्रह्मोद्वयमूलापरमङ्गलकत्वाद्वयहृदादिपाणिपादयुगाख्येषु स्थानेषु हृदय एव वा न्यसेदिति सम्प्रदायार्थः ॥६९॥

ध्यायेदित्यादिभिर्मध्यत इत्यन्तैस्त्रिभिः श्लोकैः प्राणशक्तिध्यानमुपदिशति। तत्र प्रसूनपिण्डं—दक्षिणे देव्याः प्राणात्मकत्वात्। (२)ततः प्राणनं प्रसूनपिण्डम्। दशशक्तिभिः—प्राणादिभिः। अनन्तशक्तियुक्ताभिः प्रत्येकमितिशेषः॥७०॥७१॥७२॥

---

(१) शक्तिपुटोत्थितमिति मू० पु० पा०।
(२) ततृप्राणनमिति टी० पु० पा०।

प्राणापानसमानाश्च व्यानोदाना च शक्तय: ।
नागा कूर्मा सकृकरा देवदत्ताधनञ्जया ॥७३॥
चतुरस्रद्वयं कृत्वा तदन्तर्वृत्तयुग्मकम् ।
तदन्तर्दशपत्राब्जं तदन्तस्तद्‌द्वयं तथा ॥७४॥
कृत्वा मध्ये समावाह्य कृतार्घ्य: पूजयेच्च ता: ।
लक्षं जपेत्पयोभक्षस्तद्दशांशं हुनेत्तथा ॥७५॥
तिलै: शुक्लै: सर्षपैश्च सितैर्मधुरसंयुतै: ।
तर्पयेत्सौरभाद्येन जलेनेत्थं सुसाधयेत् ॥७६॥
तन्त्रेऽस्मिन् यास्तु पुत्तल्यो यन्त्राण्युक्तानि सर्वत: ।
अनया विद्यया साध्य प्राणांस्तत्र नियोजयेत् ॥७७॥
यन्त्र मस्या: शृणु प्राज्ञे ! सद्य: प्रत्ययकारकम् ।
येन पुत्तलिका जीवस्पन्दयुक्ता मनोर्बलात् ॥७८॥
प्राक्प्रत्यक्दक्षिणोदक्च सूत्राण्यष्टौ निपातयेत् ।
कोष्ठान्येकोनपञ्चाशज्जायन्ते तेषु विन्यसेत् ॥७९॥
प्रागुत्तरं समारभ्य परितोपि प्रवेशत: ॥
शिष्टेषु मध्यनवसु लिखेदङ्गादित: क्रमात् ॥८०॥

प्राणेत्यादिना श्लोकेन प्राणशक्तिदेव्या: परिवारशक्तीरुपदिशति । तत्र प्रधानाप्राणशक्तिरेषां समष्टिरूपा ॥७३॥

चतुरस्रद्वयमित्यादिभि: साधयेदित्यन्तैस्त्रिभि: श्लोकैस्तत्पूजामण्डलं तत्पूजां तन्मन्त्रसाधनप्रकारं चोपदिशति । तत्र तद्‌द्वयम् —वृत्तद्वयम् । अन्यच्चक्रनिर्माणं सुगमम् ॥७४॥ कृतार्घ्य:—प्राग्वत् ॥७५॥ सितै:—गौरै: ॥७६॥

तन्त्रेऽस्मिन् नित्यादिना श्लोकेन सर्वत्र पुत्तल्यादिप्राणप्रतिष्ठाविधानमुपदिशति । तत्र तत्र– तेषु । अन्यत् सुगमम् ॥७७॥

यन्त्रमित्यादिभिर्भवेन्दित्यन्तैरध्यर्द्धैश्चतुर्भि: श्लोकै: तद्यन्त्रविधानं तत्प्रयोगं चोपदिशति । तत्रजोवस्पन्दयुक्ता—साध्यजीवागमत: । विन्यसेत् –प्राणप्रतिष्ठा-विद्याक्षराणोतिशेष: ॥७८॥७९॥ प्रागुत्तरं –ऐशान्याम् । परित:—प्राद-

ततः शिष्टद्वये साध्यनामालिख्याथ साधकम् ।
सञ्जप्य विद्यां हस्तेन सजीवेन स्पृशन् शतम् ॥८१॥
तेन पुत्तलिकाः कुर्यात्सिद्धये नान्यथा भवेत् ।
साध्यजीवाद्यानयनं शृणु वक्ष्यामि तेऽद्भुतम् ॥८२॥
मन्त्रवीर्यं स्मृतिं(१) कुर्वन् तया तद्देहगर्भतः ।
ज्ञानकर्मेन्द्रियाण्यर्थान् मनोजीवं तनुं तथा ॥८३॥
तस्मात्साध्यशरीरान्तात्पुत्तल्या(२) नामभिस्तथा ।
रक्तरज्ज्वा शक्तिमय्या(ध्या) तान्यानीयार्पयेद्धिया ॥८४॥
विद्यायास्त्र्यक्षरान्तेषु साध्यनामानि योजयेत् ।
एवं नियोजितां विद्यां सहस्रं प्रजपेत्स्पृशन् ॥८५॥
जीवहस्तेन(म) तच्चित्ते निशामध्येषु साधकः ।
एवं संस्थापितप्राणा पुत्तली स्पन्दतेऽब्दतः(३) ॥८६॥

च्छिष्टेन । प्रविशतः—अमु(नु)क्तक्रमम् । अङ्गोदितानि—यकारादिसप्ताक्षराणि । यन्त्रनिर्माणे अन्यत् सुगमम् ॥८०॥ स्पृशन्- यन्त्रमितिशेषः ॥८१॥ तेन—द्रव्येण । एतदुक्तं भवति—यैर्द्रव्यैः सप्तपुत्तलिकाकरणमुक्तं तानि द्रव्याणि यन्त्रे निधाय वा तेषु द्रव्येषु यन्त्रं निधाय वा तै र्द्रव्यैः पुत्तलिकां कुर्यादिति ।

साध्येत्यादिभिरब्दत इत्यन्तैरर्द्धाधिकैश्चतुर्भिः श्लोकैः पुत्तल्यादिषु साध्यजीवाद्यानयनमुपदिशति । तत्र मन्त्रवीर्यस्य पञ्चत्रिंशत्पटले वक्ष्यमाणत्वादिह नोच्यते॥८२॥ तया—स्मृत्या सार्द्धमितिशेषः । तद्देहगर्भतः—साध्यदेहाभ्यन्तरात् । अर्थान्—इन्द्रियार्थान् दश । जीवं आत्मानम् । तनुं – त्वगसृङ् मांसमेदोऽस्थिमज्जाशुक्रौजःसंज्ञानष्टधातून् । सविन्दूनि यादीन्यष्टाक्षराणि सर्वादौ संयोज्य तदनु तत्तद्धातूनां नामोच्चारणानन्तरं आकृष्य प्रतिष्ठापयाम्युक्त्या यथोपदेशमानयेदित्यर्थः ॥८३॥८४॥ त्र्यक्षरान्तेषु, एतदुक्तं भवति—प्राणप्रतिष्ठाविद्याया अमुष्य इति त्र्यक्षरान्तेषु साध्यनामानि योजयेदिति ॥८५॥ जीवहस्तेन—सश्वासप्रवाहपार्श्वस्थहस्तेन

---

(१) मन्त्रवीर्यास्मृतिं इति सो० पु० पा० । (३) तदा इति मू० पु० पा० ।
(२) शरीरान्ता पुत्तल्योतमभिश्चयेति मू० पु० पा० ।

साध्यस्य जन्मनक्षत्राण्याकर्णय वदामि ते ।
तज्जन्मलग्नसञ्जातनवां(ष्ट)शर्क्षप्रधानकम् ॥८७॥
अन्यानि च नवर्क्षाणि नवग्रहसमन्वयात् ।
तेषु तेषु प्रयोगेषु वक्ष्याम्यपरहोमके ॥८८॥
रिपोर्नखश्च केशश्च चरणोत्थं रजस्तथा ।
अन्यानि चाङ्गरोमाणि पुत्तल्यां योजयेन्मृतौ ॥८९॥
वश्यादिषु च सर्वत्र पुत्तल्यां प्रोक्तया तया ।
एवं सर्वं समाख्यातं प्राणाकर्षणकर्म ते ॥९०॥
अनया विद्यया कृत्वा प्राणाकर्षणमुक्तया ।
ततोनिर्दिष्टपुत्तल्यां तत्र तत्रोक्तमाचरेत् ॥९१॥
सर्वत्र मारणे प्रोक्ते साध्यर्क्षग्रहसंस्थितिम् ।
उक्तानां तु न वर्क्षाणां तथैवाष्टकवर्गकम् ॥९२॥

तच्चित्ते—पुत्तलीचित्ते एवमित्येतदुक्तं भवति – प्रागुक्ते यन्त्रमध्ये पुत्तलीं संस्थाप्य साध्यजीवाद्यानयनं कुर्यादिति ॥८६॥

साध्यस्येत्यादिना होमके इत्यन्तेन श्लोकद्वयेन साध्यप्राणिनां जन्मनक्षत्राणि दशविधान्युपदिशति । तत्र तज्जन्मलग्नसञ्जातनवांशर्क्षं प्रधानकम् । एतदुक्तंभवति— यस्य जन्मसमयलग्ननवांशे तन्नवांशविशिष्टमंशकं तन्नवांशविशिष्टनक्षत्रं च तस्य प्रधानमिति ॥८७॥ अन्यानि च नवर्क्षाणि अन्योन्यसमानि गौणानीत्यर्थः । नव-ग्रहसमन्वयात् । नक्षत्राणामिति शेषः । सच राश्यन्वयः होमके—होमपटले ॥८८॥

रिपोरित्यादिभिराचरेदित्यन्तैः त्रिभिः श्लोकैः पुत्तलीनिर्माणे गुणविधानोप-देशं उक्तनिगमनं च करोति । तत्र मृतौ मारणप्रयोगे॥८९॥ वश्यादिष्वित्यत्र आदि-शब्देन आकर्षणविद्वेषणादि । तया – साध्यनखकेशादिरहितया तत्र तत्र प्रोक्तद्रव्य-निर्मितया । तत्र—प्रयोग इति शेषः ॥९१॥

सर्वत्रेत्यादिना चणादित्यन्तेन श्लोकद्वयेन अभिचारप्रयोगे अभिचार्यस्य ग्रहानुकूल्यवीक्षणं तदनपेक्षणे प्रत्यवायं चोपदिशति । तत्र साध्यर्क्षग्रहसंस्थितिं— साध्यस्य प्रधाननक्षत्रराश्योर्ग्रहाणां बलाबलं च । तन्नवर्क्षाणां – तत्साध्यस्य नवग्रह-दशाप्राप्तजन्मनक्षत्राणां नवानां अष्टवर्गकं आदित्यादि सप्तग्रहाणां जन्मलग्नस्य

दशास्थितिं च संवीक्ष्य कुर्यान्मारणमात्मवान्।
अनवेक्ष्य कृतं कर्म स्वात्मानं हन्ति तत्क्षणात् ॥९३॥
ब्राह्मणं धार्मिकं भूपं वनितामास्तिकं नरम्।
वदान्यं सदयं नित्यमभिचारे न योजयेत् ॥९४॥
योजयेद्यदि वैरेण प्रत्यगेनं निहन्ति तत्।
अभिचारस्य विषयानाकर्णय वदामि ते ॥९५॥
पापिष्ठान्नास्तिकांश्चौरान् देवब्राह्मणनिन्दकान्।
प्रजानां घातकान् सर्वक्लेशकर्मसु संस्थितान् ॥९६॥
क्षेत्रवित्तधनस्त्रीणामाहर्तारं कुलान्तकम्।
निन्दकं समयानां च पिशुनं राजघातकम् ॥९७॥
विषाग्निक्षुरशस्त्राद्यैर्हिंसकं प्राणिनां सदा।
नियोजयेन्मारणेषु कर्मस्वेतैर्न पातकी ॥९८॥
कृत्वाऽऽशु मारणं कर्म तदन्ते स्वधनार्हतः।
पादतोवा गुरुं विप्रानाराध्य स्वेन नित्यया ॥९९॥
अभिषिंच्य ततोविद्यां जपेल्लक्षं हविष्यभुक्।
जन्मत्रये(१)प्यब्दमात्रमभिषेकं समाचरेत् ॥१००॥

च। अन्योन्यानुग्रहज्ञापकं ज्योतिःशास्त्रोक्तमुपायमष्टवर्गकमिति कथयति ॥९२॥
दशास्थितिं – कालचक्रमहादशादिस्थितिम्। ग्रहाणामानुकूल्यप्रातिकूल्यादेश्चणं मारणे कर्मण्येव, नान्यत्र ॥९३॥

ब्राह्मणमित्यादिना तदित्यन्तेनार्द्धाद्येन श्लोकेनानभिचार्यान् तदभिचारणे-प्रत्यवायं चोपदिशति। तत्र धार्मिकमिति भूपमित्यस्य विशेषणम्। अभिचारे— मारणे, अन्यत् सुगमम् ॥९४॥

अभिचारेत्यादिभिः पातकीत्यन्तैरर्द्धाद्यैस्त्रिभिः श्लोकैरभिचार्यानुपदिशति। तत्र एतैः—मारणकर्मभिः। पातकी—साधक इतिशेषः ॥९५॥९६॥९७॥९८॥

---

(१) जन्मत्रयेप्य इति मू० पु० पा०।

सदूर्वाहोममब्दन्तु तत्पापैरेष मुच्यते ।
एतत्ते कथितं सर्वं दूतीनित्याविधानकम् ॥१०१॥
पादतत्त्वमयी व्याप्तिरिति सम्यक् समीरिता ।
अस्या निष्फालनाच्चित्ते तत्तत्त्वं स्वात्मसात्कृतम् ॥१०२॥
इति श्रीषोड़शनित्यातन्त्रेषु श्रीकादिमते त्रयोदशंपटलम् ।

ज्ञात्वेत्यादिभिर्विधानत इत्यन्तैस्त्रिभिः श्लोकैरभिचारकरणप्रायश्चित्तमुपदिशति। तत्र आशु इति पदच्छेदः। हविष्यभुक्—हविष्यं नाम निर्लवणपक्वव्रीहितण्डुलान्नम्॥८८॥१००॥तत्पापैः—अभिचारकरणपापैः। एष - साधकः॥१०१॥१०२॥

इति श्रीषोड़शनित्यातन्त्रेषु श्रीकादिमताख्यस्य तन्त्रस्य परिपूर्णस्य तन्त्रस्य प्रपञ्चसारसिंहराजप्रकाशाभिधानेन श्रीसुभगानन्दनाथेन विरचितायां मनोरमाख्यायां व्याख्यायां शिवदूतीनित्याविद्याविधानप्रकाशनपरं त्रयोदशपटलं परिपूर्णं परामृष्टम् ॥ १२ ॥

ग्रन्थसङ्ख्या—

यन्त्राण्येकादश व्याख्याग्रन्थाः प्रोक्ताः शतात्परम् ।
सार्द्धसप्तदशैव स्युः पटलेऽस्मिंस्त्रयोदशे ॥०॥

अथ चतुर्दशपटलम् ।

अथ षोड़शनित्यासु नवमी या समीरिता ।
प्रोक्तैव त्वरिता विद्या प्रागेव द्वादशाक्षरा ॥१॥
तद्विधानं शृणु प्राज्ञे ! होम यन्त्रादिभिः(२) सह ।
येन(३) मन्त्री मन्मथाभो विक्षोभयति भूतलम् ॥२॥
विद्याचतुर्थवर्णादिसप्तभिस्त्वक्षरैस्तथा ।
कुर्यादङ्गानि युग्मार्णैः षट्क्रमेण कराङ्गयोः ॥३॥
शिरोललाटकण्ठेषु हृन्नाभ्याधारकै तथा ।
ऊर्वोर्जान्वोर्जङ्घयोश्च पादयोश्च क्रमेण वै ॥४॥
द्वितीयोपान्त्यमध्यस्थैर्मन्त्रार्णैरितरैर्न्यसेत् ।
ताराद्यैः शृणु तद्ध्यानं तच्छक्तीस्तत्प्रपूजनम् ॥५॥
श्यामवर्णां शुभाकारां नवयौवनशोभिनीम् ।
द्वि*द्विक्रमादष्टनागैः कल्पिताभरणोज्ज्वलाम् ॥६॥

अथ चतुर्दशपटलम् ।

पूर्वस्मिंस्त्रयोदशे पटले अष्टम्या दूतीनित्याया विधानमुपदिश्यानन्तरं नवम्यास्त्वरितानित्याविद्याया विधानमुपदिशति—अथ षोड़शेत्यादि पार्श्वतोऽइत्यन्तेन श्लोकशतरूपेण चतुर्दशेन पटलेन। तत्र अथ षोड़शेत्यादिना भूतलमित्यन्तेन श्लोकद्वयेन पटलार्थानुद्दिशति। तत्र प्रागेव—तृतीयपटले ॥१॥ विक्षोभयति—स्वात्मना प्रसिद्धिं करोति ॥२॥

विद्येत्यादिभिः पूजनमित्यन्तैस्त्रिभिः श्लोकैर्न्यासादिकमुपदिशति। तत्र तथा—यथा प्राणप्रतिष्ठाविद्यायां शृङ्खलाबन्धेन षडङ्गयोजनं ऊरुजानुजङ्घापादयोरेकैकम् ॥३॥४॥ द्वितीयोपान्त्यमध्यस्थैः द्वितीया-हृल्लेखा, अन्त्यस्य समीपमुपान्त्यं तयोर्मध्यस्थैर्मन्त्रार्णैरितरैरपि ताराद्यैः। एतदुक्तं भवति—प्रथमं हृल्लेखा, तदनु-

---

(१) समामिति मू० पु० पा० ।
(२) मन्त्रैरिति मू० पु० पा० ।
* द्विचिक्र इति वं० पु० पा०

ताटङ्कमङ्गदं तद्वद्रशनानूपुरान्वितैः ।
विप्रक्षत्रियविट्शूद्रजातिभिर्भीमविग्रहैः ॥७॥
पल्लवांशुकसंवीतां शिखिपुच्छकृतैः शुभैः ।
वलयैर्भूषितभुजां माणिक्यमुकुटोज्ज्वलाम् ॥८॥
बर्हिबर्हकृतापीड़ां तच्छत्रां तत्पताकिनीम् ।
गुञ्जागुणलसद्वक्षःकुचकुङ्कुममण्डनाम् ॥९॥
(१)त्रिनेत्रां चारुवदनां मन्दस्मितमुखाम्बुजाम् ।
पाशाङ्कुशवराभीतिलसद्भुजचतुष्टयाम् ॥१०॥
ध्यात्वैवं तोतलां देवीं पूजयेच्छक्तिभिर्वृताम् ।
तदग्रस्थां(२) च स्फाट्कारीं शरचापकरोज्ज्वलाम् ॥११॥
प्रसादे फलदाने च साधकानां त्वरान्विताम् ।
यतः सा त्वरितेत्युक्ता मायानित्या नवम्यसौ ॥१२॥

प्रणवस्तत उपान्त्यं छक्ले खामित्येवं क्रमेणान्या मन्त्रवर्णान्(३) वर्मादि फडन्तान् दशसङ्ख्यान् प्रोक्तेषु दशसु स्थानेषु न्यसेदिति ॥५॥

श्यामवर्णामित्यादिभिर्वृतामित्यन्तैरन्वर्थैः पञ्चभिःश्लोकैर्देव्या नित्यसपर्याध्यानमुपदिशति। तत्र द्विद्विक्रमादित्यादिना विग्रहैरित्यन्तेनार्द्धाधेनैकेन श्लोकेनैतदुक्तं भवति—द्विद्विक्रमात् ब्राह्मणक्षत्रियवैश्यशूद्रजातिभिरष्टभिर्भुजगेन्द्रैः ॥६॥ क्रमात् कल्पितताटङ्काङ्गदरशनानूपुरयुगलामिति। अत्र चातुर्वर्ण्योत्पत्तिक्रमेणाभरणकल्पनमिति बोद्धव्यम् ॥७॥ पल्लवांशुकसंवीतां—किसलयशाखापरिधानाम्। बर्हिबर्हकृतापीड़ां—आपोड़ा—चूड़ा। तच्छत्रां—बर्हिबर्हच्छत्राम्। तत्पताकिनीं तद्वत्। आयुधकल्पनं वामोर्ध्वादिदक्षिणाधरहस्तान्तं वामदक्षिणक्रमेण ॥१०॥ तोतलां—त्वरिताम्। देव्यास्तु त्वरितातोतलातूर्णेतिनामानि ॥

तदग्रस्थेत्यादिभिर्मध्यमेत्यन्तैरर्थाद्यैः पञ्चभिः श्लोकैर्देव्याः परिवारशक्त्यादिकमुपदिशति। तत्र—शरचापकरोज्ज्वलां—धनुर्बाणोज्ज्वलकरयुगलाम् ॥११॥

---

(१) द्वि इति सो० पु० पा०।
(२) स्फातुफट्कारी इति मू० पु० पा०।
(३) वर्माादि इति टी० पु० पा०।

कृष्णवर्णो गदापाणिर्वर्वरोर्द्ध्वशिरोरुहः ।
किङ्करस्त्वग्रतस्तस्याः पूज्यः सर्वार्थसिद्धये ॥१३॥
तद्वारपार्श्वयोः पूज्ये जयाविजयसंज्ञिके ।
शक्ती तत्सदृशी स्वर्णवेत्रवेत्रत्कराम्बुजे ॥१४॥
हुङ्कारी खेचरी चण्डा छेदिनी क्षेपणी ततः ।
स्त्रीहुङ्कार्यौ क्षेमकरी लोकपालसमा इमाः ॥१५॥
पूज्याः पद्माष्टपत्रेषु स्थिता मन्त्रार्णशक्तयः ।
याभिर्नित्यार्चिताभिः स्यान्नरो नारीषु मन्मथः ॥१६॥
शृणु पूजाविधिं तस्यास्त्वरितायाः महेश्वरि ! ।
प्राग्वदर्घ्यं विधायेशामष्टसिंहाङ्घ्रिके शुभे ॥१७॥
आसने हेमरचिते विदध्यात् भूपुरद्वयम् ।
पश्चिमद्वारसंयुक्तं तदन्तर्वृत्तयुग्मकम् ॥१८॥
तदन्तरष्टपत्राब्जं विधायात्र परां शिवाम् ।
प्राग्वदावाह्य परितः शक्तिभिर्वेष्टितां तथा ॥१९॥

प्रसादे—आभिमुख्ये । अनेन श्लोकेन देव्या नामनिर्वाहः॥१२॥ गदापाणिः—अस्यापि पाणिद्वयम् । वर्वरः—कुटिलः । किङ्करः—देव्याः प्रेष्यभूतो भूतविशेषः ॥१३॥ तत्सदृशी—देवतासमानवर्णे । स्वर्णवेत्रवेत्रत्कराम्बुजे—अनयोरपि बाहुद्वयम् ॥१४॥ स्त्रीहुङ्कार्यौ—स्त्रीकारी हुङ्कारी इति च द्वेशक्ती । लोकपालसमाः । वर्णायुधवाहनैरिति शेषः॥१५॥ मन्त्रार्णशक्तयः—त्वरितामन्त्राक्षरशक्तयः । याभिः—अक्षरशक्तिभिः । स्यात्—साधक इतिशेषः । मन्मथः—सर्वाः स्त्रियः कामवत् स्वात्मदर्शनेन क्षोभयतीत्यर्थः ॥१६॥

शृणिवत्यादिभिः समापयेदित्यन्तैः षड्भिः श्लोकैर्देव्या नित्यसपर्याक्रममुपदिशति । तत्र प्राग्वत्—षडङ्गमूलाभ्याम् । ईशां—सर्वाधिष्ठात्रीम् । अष्टसिंहाङ्घ्रिके—अष्टसिंहपादसहिते ॥१७॥ विदध्यादित्यादिना विधायेत्यन्तेन पादाद्येन श्लोकोत्तरार्द्धेन देव्या नित्यसपर्याचक्रमुपदिशति । तत्र एतदुक्तं भवति—पश्चिमद्वारोपेतं चतुरस्रद्वयं विधाय तदन्तर्वृत्तद्वयोपेतमष्टदलं पद्मं सकर्णिकं विदध्यादिति ॥१८॥ अत्र—चक्रे ।

मुद्रादर्शनपूर्वं तु पूजयेत्तां यथोदितम् ।
अग्रपत्राग्रके वृत्तमध्ये वाऽर्च्यौ पुरोदितौ(१) ॥२०॥
किङ्करस्य बलिं दद्याद्देव्यग्रे प्रागुदीरितैः ।
स्वसमानगणाकीर्णमण्डलस्थस्य भक्तितः ॥२१॥
एवं पूजां विधायाग्रे जपेद्विद्यां सहस्रकम् ।
शतं वा कृतहोमस्तु पूजां प्राग्वत्समापयेत् ॥२२॥
ततः साधितविद्यस्तु प्रयोगानाचरेन्नरः ।
(२)बैल्वैर्दशांशं जुहुयात्पत्राद्यैः साधने जपे ॥२३॥
एवं संसिद्धमन्त्रैस्तु मन्त्रितैश्चुलुकोदकैः ।
फणिदंष्ट्रामृतानान्तु मुखे सन्ताड्य जीवयेत् ॥२४॥
तत्कर्णयोर्जपेद्विद्यां यष्ट्या(३) वा जपसिद्धये ।
सन्ताड्य शीर्षे सहसा मृतमुत्थापयेदिति ॥२५॥
काम्यहोमविधिं देवि ! शृणु वक्ष्ये यथाविधि ।
कृत्वा योनिं कुण्डमध्ये तत्राग्नौ विधिवद्धुनेत् ॥२६॥

एतदुक्तं भवति—आवाह्य कर्णिकामध्ये इतिशेषः ॥१८॥ मुद्रादर्शनपूर्वं—स्थापनादिमुद्राचतुष्टयपूर्वम् । एतत्सर्वसाधारणम् । यथोदितम्—अग्रादि प्रादक्षिण्येन । अग्रपत्राग्रके अग्रएवाग्रके अष्टदलानां देव्यग्रदलाग्रे वृत्तमध्ये—पद्मबाह्यस्थवृत्तद्वयवीथ्याम् । पुरोदितौ—फट्कारीकिङ्करौ तौ यथाक्रममग्रदलाग्रे वृत्तमध्ये वीथ्योरर्चयेदित्यर्थः ॥२०॥ बलिं—अन्त्यमितिशेषः । देव्यग्रे—प्राग्वत्त्वरितासन्निधौ । सर्वत्र बलिदानं तत्तन्मूलेदेवतासन्निधौ । प्रागुदीरितैः—अन्नाद्यैः तन्मन्त्रेणेतिशेषः । (प्रागुदीरित)मण्डलं वृत्तमध्यम् ॥२१॥ प्राग्वत्- ललितासपर्यासमाप्तिवत् ॥२२॥ तत इत्यादिभिरितीत्यन्तैस्त्रिभिः श्लोकैर्विद्यासाधनं सिद्धविद्यस्य विषहरणविधानं चोपदिशति । तत्र पत्राद्यैः—आद्यशब्देन पुष्पमूलकाण्डफलान्यभिधीयन्ते । जपे—युगानुरूपमक्षरलक्षसङ्ख्याके दशांशं जुहुयादित्यन्वयः ॥२३॥ मन्त्रितैः ।

---

(१) पुरोहितौ इति सो० पु० पा० ।
(२) बिल्वैः इति मू० पु० पा० ।
(३) जप्ता इति सो० पु० पा० ।

तिलसर्षपगोधूमशालिधान्ययवैर्हुनेत्।
त्रिमध्वक्तैरेकशो वा समेतैर्वा समृद्धये ॥२७॥
बकुलैश्चम्पकैरब्जैः कह्लारैररुणोत्पलैः।
कैरवैर्मल्लिकाकुन्दमधुकैरिन्दिराप्तये ॥२८॥
अशोकैः पाटलैर्बिल्वैर्जातीविचकिलैः सितैः।
नवैर्नीलोत्पलैरश्वरिपुजैः(१) कर्णिकारजैः ॥२९॥
होमाल्लक्ष्मीं च सौभाग्यमायुर्वित्तं यशोनिधिम्।
यद्यद्धि वाञ्छितं सर्वमवाप्नोति सुनिश्चितम् ॥३०॥
दूर्वागुडूचीमश्वत्थं वटमारग्वधं तथा।
सितार्कं प्लक्षजं हुत्वा रोगान्मुक्तो नरोऽचिरात् ॥३१॥
इक्षुजम्बूनारिकेलमोचागुडसितैर्हुतैः।
अचलां लभते लक्ष्मीं भोक्ता च भवति ध्रुवम् ॥३२॥
एतैरुदीरितैराज्यमधुक्षीरप्लुतैर्हुतैः।
एकैकैर्वनिता वश्या यावज्जीवं धनादिभिः ॥३३॥

शतवारमितिशेषः। तत्कर्णयोः—दष्टस्य कर्णयोः। जपन्—जीवयेदितिशेषः॥२४॥ वा पक्षान्तरे। जपसिद्धया—करागस्पृष्टिकया विद्यासहस्रवारजपसिद्धया। मृतं—फणिदंशतः उत्थापयेत्। एष तृतीयः पक्षः ॥२५॥

काम्य होमइत्यादिभिः प्रियेइत्यन्तैः पञ्चभिः श्लोकैर्नानाविधद्रव्यहोमान्नाना-विधफलावाप्तिमुपदिशति। तत्र योनिं कुण्डमध्ये—कुण्डपटलवक्ष्यमाणप्रकारेण कुण्डं कृत्वा तन्मध्ये योनिं कुर्यादित्यर्थः। एतत्सर्वहोमसाधारणम्। तत्र—योन्याम्। अग्नौ—स्थापिते इति शेषः। विधिवत्—प्राग्वदग्निमुखादिकं कृत्वे-त्यर्थः ॥२६॥ एकशः—एकैकैः ॥२७॥ अरुणोत्पलं—प्राग्वत्। कैरवैः—सितैरिति-शेषः ॥२८॥ विचकिलानि—गुरुमुखादवगन्तव्यानि। स्मितैः—विकसितैः। अश्वरिपुजैः—करवीरपुष्पैः ॥२९॥३०॥ गुडूचीं—प्राग्वदमृतालताम्। सितैः—

---

(१) रक्तैरिपुजैरिति मू० पु० पा०।

तैस्तैराज्यप्लुतः भूपा वश्याः स्युर्हवनात्प्रिये ! ।
चोराक्तैस्तैर्हुतैर्मर्त्या वशे तिष्ठन्त्यशेषतः ॥३४॥
सर्षपाज्यैर्हुनेन्मृत्युकाष्ठाग्नौ वैरिमृत्यवे ।
तदक्तैर्वैरियोन्युत्थमांसैरपि च तत्कृते ॥३५॥
अत्रेन्धनाग्नौ योन्युत्थक्षतजोत्पाचितं चरुम् ।
आरुष्करघृतोपेतं फणिशीर्षस्रुचा हुनेत् ॥३६॥
कृष्णांशुकशिरोवेष्टा खड्गपाणिश्च रोषवान् ।
निशामध्ये हुनेत्सद्यो निहन्तुं वैरिणं हठात् ॥३७॥
मृत्युकाष्ठानले तस्य फलैः पत्रैश्च होमतः ।
सप्तरात्रादरातेस्तु गजाश्वा रोगमाप्नुयुः ॥३८॥
चतुरङ्गुलजैर्होमाच्चतुरङ्गं बलं रिपोः ।
सप्ताहाद्रोगदुःखार्तं भवत्येव न संशयः ॥३९॥
एवमस्यास्तु विद्याया वैभवं कोनु वर्णयेत् ।
तथापि तद्दिशा किञ्चिद्वर्ण्यते तच्छृणु प्रिये ! ॥४०॥

शर्कराभिः॥३१॥३२॥ एतैरुदोरितैः—तिलादिभिरिति शेषः। आज्यमधुक्षीरप्लुतैः—त्रिमधुसिक्तैः। त्रिमधुसिक्तत्वं सर्वसाधारणमेव। एकैकैरितिसर्वप्रयोगसाधारणमेव। धनादिभिरित्यत्रादिशब्दः- प्राणविषयः॥३३॥ तैस्तैराज्यप्लुतैः—केवलघृताभ्यक्तैस्तिलादिभिः सर्वैः षट्त्रिंशद्द्रव्यैरुक्तक्रमेण होमं कुर्यादित्यर्थः। क्षीराक्तैस्तैरुक्तक्रमेण होमं कुर्य्यादिति यावत्। एतदुक्तं भवति—तिलादिभिः सितान्तैः षट्त्रिंशद्द्रव्यैस्तत्तत्प्रयोगेषु प्रोक्तक्रमेण त्रिमध्वक्तैर्जुहुयादिति प्रथमपक्षः। केवलघृताभ्यक्तैस्तैर्जुहुयादिति द्वितीयः पक्षः। केवलक्षीराक्तैर्जुहुयादिति तृतीयः पक्षः इति। मृत्युः—कारस्करः। तदक्तैः—सर्षपाज्यसिक्तैः! वैरियोन्युत्थमांसैः—शत्रुनक्षत्रयोनिमांसैः। तत्कृते—वैरिमृत्यवे॥३५॥ योन्युत्थक्षतजोत्पाचितं—साध्यनक्षत्रयोनिरुधिरपाचितम्। फणिशीर्षस्रुचा—स्रुग्भूतेन छिन्नेन

---

(२) पणिशीर्षस्रु वा इति सो० फणिशीर्षं स्रुवा इति मू० पु० पा।

अथ यन्त्राणि वक्ष्यामि समस्ताभीष्टसिद्धये ।
तानि सर्वाणि देवेशि ! कुरु चित्ते क्रमेण वै ॥४१॥
प्राक्प्रत्यक्दक्षिणोदक्च सूत्राणि द्वादशार्पयेत् ।
तदग्राण्यभितः कुर्यात्त्रिशिखान्यस्य मध्यगे ॥४२॥
कोष्ठे तारस्य मध्यस्थं नाम कृत्वा शिवादिषु ।
प्रादक्षिण्यप्रवेशेन द्वादशावृत्ति मायया ॥४३॥
विद्यामालिख्य सञ्जप्य बिभृयात् सर्वसिद्धये ।
श्रियै कीर्त्यै च वश्याय सौभाग्यायाखिलाप्तये ॥४४॥
विषग्रहगदोन्मादशान्त्यै युद्धे जयाप्तये ।
नरनारीनृपादीनां वश्याय बिभृयाच्च तत् ॥४५॥
प्राक्प्रत्यक् दक्षिणोदकच नव सूत्राणि(१) पातयेत् ।
जायन्ते(२) च चतुःषष्टिकोष्ठानि परमेश्वरि ! ।

भुजङ्गमफणेनेत्यर्थः । निहन्तुं वैरिणं—वैरिनिधनाय दुनेदिति पूर्वत्रान्वयः॥३७॥ तस्य फलैः— मृत्युफलैः । पत्रैः— मृत्युपत्रैरित्यर्थः ॥३८॥ चतुरङ्गुलजैः—आरग्वधप्रसूनैः ॥३८॥ तत्—वैभवम् । दिशा—एकदेशेन । तत्-वैभवं शृणुत्वित्यन्वयः ॥४०॥

अथ यन्त्राणीत्यादिभिस्तदित्यन्तैः पञ्चभिः श्लोकैरेकविंशत्यधिकशतकोष्ठानुग्रहयन्त्रं तद्विनियोगं तत्फलानि चोपदिशति । तत्र त्रिशिखानि—प्रत्यग्रं त्रिशूलानि । मध्यगे—कोष्ठे सर्व्वमध्यस्थे कोष्ठे ॥४१॥४२॥ मायया—ह्रींलेखया सार्द्धमितिशेषः ॥४३॥ तत्—यन्त्रमितिशेषः । एतदुक्तं भवति—प्राक्प्रत्यगग्राणि दक्षिणोदगग्राणि च समान्तरालानि द्वादशद्वादशसूत्राण्यास्फाल्याभितोऽष्टाचत्वारिंशत्सङ्ख्यानि तदग्राणि प्रत्येकं त्रिशूलीकृत्य एकविंशत्यधिकशतसङ्ख्येषु कोष्ठेषु सर्वमध्यस्थकोष्ठमध्ये प्रणवं नामगर्भं समालिख्य शिवादिप्रादक्षिण्यप्रवेशेनामुक्तक्रमं मूलविद्यायाः प्रणवादीनि प्रथमह्रल्लेखाविधुरं दशाक्षराणि द्वितीयह्रल्लेखोदरे द्वादशकृत्वः समालिख्य प्रोक्तक्रमेण बिभृयादिति ॥४४॥४५॥

---

(१) नवसूत्रनिपातनात् इति मू० पु० पा० ।   (२) ऽत्र इति मू० पु० पा० ।

तेषु सर्वनिऋत्यादि लिखेल्लक्ष्मीमनुक्रमात् ।
बहिस्तूर्णाक्षरैरन्ते वषड्युक्तैस्तु (पूजयेत्) वेष्टयेत् ॥४७॥
अनुग्रहं महाचक्रं विद्यां शृणु महेश्वरि ! ।
सर्वतोभद्रविन्यासानुष्टुभं सर्वसिद्धिदम् ॥४८॥
दाहवह्नियुतं चाद्यं वियद्वृन्मरुता ततः ।
नभश्च मरुतोपेतं व्याप्तं तेन समन्वितम् ॥४९॥
एतान्येव विलोमानि प्रथमं चरणं भवेत् ।
द्वितीयाद्यं द्वितीयं स्याद्ध्रुवा शून्यं द्वितीयकम् ॥५०॥
तृतीयं तच्चतुर्थं स्याज्ज्ञा (तु)च साभ्रचरा ततः ।
प्रतिलोमं तथैतेषां द्वितीयं चरणं भवेत् ॥५१॥

प्रागित्यादिना वेष्टयेदित्यन्तेन श्लोकद्वयेन चतुःषष्टिकोष्ठानुग्रहयन्त्रमुपदिशति । तत्र एतदुक्तंभवति—प्राक्प्रत्यगग्राणि दक्षिणोदगग्राणि च समान्तरालानि नव नव सूत्राण्यास्फाल्य चतुःषष्टिकोष्ठानि कृत्वा तत्र शिवनिऋतिकोष्ठारम्भपङ्क्तिशोदक्षिणोत्तरावसानं चतुश्चतुःपङ्क्तिकं वक्ष्यमाणं(i) सर्वतोभद्ररूपं(i) श्रीविद्यानुष्टुभमालिख्य तद्बहिः प्रागादिषु चतसृषु दिक्षु ईशादीशान्तं चतुरावृत्ति तद्बाह्यरेखास्पृष्टां त्वरिताविद्यामन्तर्गतवष(फ)ट्कारैः त्वरिताक्षरैर्वेष्टयेदिति ॥४६॥४७॥

अनुग्रहमित्यादिभिः सङ्ख्येत्यन्तैः सप्तभिः श्लोकैः प्रस्तावपूर्व्वकसर्व्वतोभद्राकारानुष्टुप् श्रीविद्योद्धारं तद्वैभवं चोपदिशति । तत्र सर्व्वतोभद्रविन्यासानुष्टुभं—सर्व्वतोभद्रप्रतिपादकत्वं तु चतसृषु पङ्क्तिषु प्रतिलोमानुलोमतोऽष्टकृत्वोवाचनसिद्धेः ॥४८॥ दाहवह्नियुतं चाद्यं वियत्—दाहवह्निभ्यां समेतं वियदक्षरं श्रीविद्याया आद्यमक्षरमित्यर्थः - श्री इति । हृन्मरुता ततः—सा इति द्वितीयम् । नभश्च मरुतोपेतं—मा इति तृतीयम् । व्याप्तं तेन समन्वितम्—तेन—मरुता पा—इति चतुर्थम् ॥४९॥ एतान्येव—उक्तक्रमस्थितानि चत्वार्यक्षराण्येव । विलोमानि—उक्तक्रमविपर्यासतः । चरणं—पादः । एतदुक्तं भवति—उक्तक्रमस्थितानि चत्वार्यक्षराणि उक्तक्रमविपर्यासतोविलोमानि तान्येव यमोसाश्री

---

(१) बहिस्तूनाम्नतैरेते: इति मू० पु० पा० ।

तृतीयतुर्यौ परत इला वन्ह्या(१) ततस्त्विला ।
मरुद्युता प्राग्वदेतत्प्रतिलोमं तृतीयकम् ॥५२॥
चतुर्थं द्वादशं विंशं तत्पूर्वं ते विलोमगाः ।
एतच्चतुर्थं चरणं श्रीविद्यायां महेश्वरि ! ॥५३॥
सर्वतोभद्ररूपैषा विद्या सर्वार्थसाधिका ।
यत्र स्थिताऽसौ चक्रस्था न तत्राशुभसङ्कथा ॥५४॥

इत्येवमष्टाक्षराणि श्रीविद्यानुष्टभः प्रथमः पादः इति। द्वितीयाद्यं—द्वितीयं स्यात्—प्रोक्तप्रथमपादस्य द्वितीयाक्षरं द्वितीयपादस्य आद्यमक्षरमित्यर्थः। सा इति द्वितीयपादस्य आद्यमक्षरम्। भुवाशून्यं द्वितीयकं—(को)नो इति द्वितीयमक्षरम् ॥५०॥ तृतीयं तच्चतुर्थं स्यात्—प्रथमपादस्य पा इति चतुर्थमक्षरं द्वितीयपादस्य तृतीयमक्षरं भवेदित्यर्थः। ज्या च साभ्रचरा ततः—ज्या—जकारः। अभ्रं-अकारः। चर—एकारः—ये इति चतुर्थमक्षरं भवेत्। एतेषामुक्तक्रमस्थितानां चतुर्णामक्षराणां चरणं प्राग्वत्। एतदुक्तं भवति—प्रोक्तक्रमस्थितानां चतुर्णामक्षराणां प्रागवत् येयानोसा इति व्युत्क्रमं पठेत्। तस्या अनुष्टुभोद्वितीयः पादोभवेदिति ॥५१॥ तृतीयतुर्यौ परतः—प्रथमपादस्य तृतीयचतुर्थाक्षरे साया इति तृतीयपादस्य प्रथमद्वितीयाक्षरे स्यातामित्यर्थः। इला वन्ह्या—वह्निना। रलोत्वं स्वातन्त्र्यात्। ली इति तृतीयमक्षरम्। इला मरुद्युता—ला इति चतुर्थमक्षरम्। एतत्प्रतिलोमं—प्रोक्तक्रमस्थितस्याक्षरचतुष्टयस्य प्रतिलोमं लालीयामा इति तृतीयः पादोभवेदित्यर्थः। तृतीयकं चरणमितिशेषः। पादइत्यर्थः॥५२॥ चतुर्थं द्वादशं विंशं तत्पूर्व्वं—अस्या विद्याया चतुर्थं पा इत्यक्षरं द्वादशं ये इत्यक्षरं, विंशं ला इत्यक्षरं, तत्पूर्व्वं एकोनविंशं ली इत्यक्षरमेवं चत्वार्यक्षराणि प्रोक्तक्रमेण भवेयुः। ते विलोमगाः—उक्तक्रमस्थिता एते चत्वारोवर्णा विलोमतः पठिताः। एतत्—वर्णाष्टकम्। चरणं—प्राग्वत्। एतदुक्तं भवति—उक्तक्रमस्थिताश्चत्वारोवर्णास्तत्क्रमविलोमपठिताश्च चयो ये ला लीला येया इत्येव वर्णाष्टकं तस्याः श्रीविद्यानुष्टभश्चतुर्थः पादोभवेदिति ॥५३॥ सर्व्वतोभद्ररूपैषा—एतदुक्तं भवति—पूर्वोक्तचतुःषष्टिकोष्ठेषु ऊर्ध्वादिषु प्रथमद्वितीयतृतीयचतुर्थपङ्क्तिषु सर्वादि दक्षान्तं चतुरः पादान् समालिख्य तानेव पादान्

(१) वाय्वास्वत इति मू० पु० पा० ।

दशसूत्रनिपातेन कृत्वैकाशीति(सं)कं पदम् ।
तन्मध्यकोष्ठे (दावस्थं कृत्वा)मध्यस्थे दावे नामास्य वीथिषु ॥५५॥
लिखेद्वर्णचतुर्थं तत् (एकं तु) शृणु भद्रे ! यथाविधि ।
ज्याधराख्यैर्मायया द्वत्ततोऽम्बु स्पर्शगा इला ॥५६॥
ततः श्रियो लिखेद्विद्यां शिवरत्नोदिगादिकाम् ।
प्राग्वत्तूर्णामृतार्णैस्तैर्वेष्टयेद्वृद्धियोजितैः ॥५७॥
ततोऽम्बु खयुतं तेन मा(ला)याकलितरूपिणा ।
वृत्तद्वयेन निष्पाद्य कुम्भं पद्माधरोत्तरम् ॥५८॥
कृत्वा स्वर्णादिसूत्रेषु सम्पूज्याभ्यर्च्य तत् पुनः ।
स्थापयेज्जपसंसिद्धं तेषु पूर्वोदितेषु वै ॥५९॥

अधस्थपङ्क्तिषु चतसृषु सर्व्वाधस्तात् प्रथमपादो यथा भवति तथा तद्वत् प्रतिलोमेन समालिख्य पश्येद्वाद्यपङ्क्तिषु चतसृषु प्रतिलोमानुलोमतः प्रथमपादो दृश्यते। सर्व्वत्र द्वितीयपङ्क्तिषु चतसृषु तथाविधो द्वितीयपादश्च दृश्यते। तथा तृतीयासु चतसृषु पङ्क्तिषु तृतीयपादश्च दृश्यते। तद्वच्चतुर्थीषु पङ्क्तिषु चतुर्थपादश्च दृश्यत इति। असौ श्रीविद्येतिशेषः ॥५४॥

दशेत्यादिभिः सम्पदेत्यन्तैः सप्तभिः श्लोकैरेकाशीतिपदोपेतामृतकुम्भाख्यं यन्त्रं तद्विनियोगं तत्फलानि चोपदिशति। तत्र दावः—ठकारः ॥५५॥ तत्—शृणिवत्यन्वयः। ज्याधराख्यैः—जूँ इति। मायया द्वत्—विसर्जयीयेन सहितः सकारः स इति। अम्बु—वकारः। स्पर्शगा इला—षल(ट) इति। एतानि चत्वार्यक्षराणि सर्व्वमध्यस्थकोष्ठपार्श्वस्थचतुःपङ्क्तिस्थकोष्ठचतुष्टयेष्वभ्यन्तरात् निर्गमनगत्या क्रमेण विलिखेदिति सम्प्रदायार्थः। अत्र केवलसम्प्रदायिनश्चतसृषु पङ्क्तिषु चत्वार्यक्षराणि पङ्क्तिक्रमेण एकैकमक्षरं चतुर्षु चतुर्षु विलिखेदिति कथयन्ति। तत्राभिमतमस्मदाराध्यपादानाम् ॥५६॥ तूर्णामृतार्णैः—तूर्णामृताक्षरैः तूर्णामृताक्षराणि नाम फट्वियुक्तानि वषट्युक्तानि त्वरिताविद्याक्षराणि ॥५७॥ अम्बु खयुतं—वं इति। तेन—केवलं वं इत्यक्षरेण। मालाकलितरूपिणा—अन्योन्यानुषक्तलिखितविग्रहेण सार्द्धं इति शेषः। पद्माधरोत्तरं—अधरोत्तरतः ऊर्ध्वाधोमुखाभ्यां पद्माभ्यामुपेतं कुम्भमित्यर्थः ॥५८॥ सम्पूज्य—

तत्र लक्ष्मीरतिस्फीता नीरोगाश्च प्रजास्तथा।
गजाश्वा पशवस्त्वन्ये प्राणिनः सुखिनोऽनिशम् ॥६०॥
भूतप्रेतपिशाचादि पीड़ासु विभ्रयादिदम्।
अलक्ष्मीशान्तये वश्यसिद्धये सर्वसम्पदे ॥६१॥
निग्रहं शृणु देवेशि! शत्रवो यस्य शक्तितः।
स्वल्पेनैव तु कालेन भवन्त्येव परासवः ॥६२॥
प्राग्वदेकाशीतिपदं कृत्वा तन्मध्यकोष्ठवी।
दाहगर्भे नाम कृत्वा तथा दिग्वीथिषु क्रमात् ॥६३॥

देवतामितिशेषः। अभग्रार्थ—यन्त्रमितिशेषः। पूर्वोदितेषु—एकादशराश्युदयकालेषु तत्तद्राशिस्थानेषु चेतिशेषः ॥५८॥ एतदुक्तं भवति– प्राक्प्रत्यक् दक्षिणोदक्च समान्तरालमास्फालितैर्दशभिः सूत्रैरेकाशीतिपदानि विधाय तत्र सर्व्वमध्यकोष्ठे उपरि विन्दुयुक्तठकारोदरे नामालिख्य तत्कोष्ठपार्श्वस्थपङ्क्तिषु चतसृषु क्रमेणाग्रादिप्रादक्षिण्येन जूं इत्यक्षरं सः इत्यक्षरं वकारं षट् इति चतुर्षु कोष्ठेषु च अभ्यन्तरान्निर्गमनगत्या विलिख्य तत ईशादिकं निऋत्यादिकं च प्रागुक्तां श्रीविद्यानुष्टुभं मध्यवीथिचतुष्टयव(र्ग)र्जमालिख्य सर्वबाह्ये अभितः ईशादीशान्तं तूर्णामृताक्षराणि चतुरावृत्त्या प्राग्वत्समालिख्य सर्व्वमध्यकोष्ठमध्यमवष्टभ्य चतुष्कोणस्थतूर्णामृताक्षरमानेन भ्रमेण वृत्तं निष्पाद्य तद्बाह्येऽ(न)ङ्गुलमानेच तथावृत्तं निष्पाद्य उपरितनभागे च अधोभागेच मध्यतश्चतुरङ्गुलान्तरालं वृत्तद्वयं मार्जयित्वा तदग्रचतुष्टयात् मनाग्वक्रं समान्तरालमुपरि चतुरङ्गुलं कुम्भमुखाकारं यथा भवति तथा समुन्नमय्य तत्कुम्भमुखे तिर्यक्(च) रेखाद्वयं प्रसार्य तत्कुम्भवीथीमध्यं अन्योन्यस्पृष्टवकारमालया शृङ्खलारूपया अन्तर्मुखया समापूर्य सर्वत्रोपरि विन्दुं समालिख्य कुम्भाधस्तात् पद्मकर्णिकास्थं कुम्भं यथा भवति तथा समालिख्य कुम्भमुखे च अधोमुखमूर्द्धनालं च पद्मं समालिख्य प्रोक्तक्रमेण मनीषितेषु विनियोगात् प्रोक्तानि फलानि च स्युरिति ॥६०॥६१॥

निग्रहमित्यादिभिरसुरैरपीत्यन्तैरष्टादशभिः श्लोकैः एकाशीतिपदोपेतैः निग्रहयन्त्रं तत्र लेख्यानि कूटाक्षराणि सर्वतोभद्राकारां कालीविद्यां तथाविधं यममन्त्र

---

(५) स्वैरं प्रभवन्ति परासवः इति सो० पु० पा०।

लिखेद्बीजचतुष्कन्तु वह्निमारुतविग्रहम् ।
यैः सद्योवैरिणः स्वीयं विमुञ्चन्ति कलेवरम् ॥६४॥
रसोदाहक्ष्मास्वयुतो ग्रासोदाहक्ष्मया खगः ।
प्रभा दाहक्ष्मास्वयुत हंसोदाहादिसंयुतः ॥६६॥
ईश्वरचोदिगारभ्यात्पङ्क्तिशोविलिखेत्ततः ।
काल्या यमस्य क्रमतो विद्यांमन्त्रमसंक्रमम्(१) ॥६७॥
सर्वतोभद्ररूपा तु काल्यनुष्टुभमीश्वरि ! ।
शृणु वक्ष्यामि परतो यमानुष्टुभमीश्वरि ! ॥६८॥
प्राणोमरुत्समोपेत इला वन्ह्या समन्विता ।
नभो मरुद्युतं दाहश्चतुर्णां प्रतिलोमतः ॥६९॥
प्रथमं चरणं तस्य द्वितीयं शून्यमेव च ।
नभोभुवा ग्रास एतत् प्रतिलोमात् द्वितीयकम् ॥७०॥
तृतीयमेकादशमं ततो गोवा चरान्विता ।
रयस्तेषां विलोमं च तृतीयं चरणं मनोः ॥७१॥

तत्फलं चोपदिशति । तत्र यस्य– निग्रहप्रयोगस्य ॥६२॥ दाहगर्भे—उपरि बिन्दुयुक्तरेफोदरे ॥६३॥ वह्निमारुतविग्रहं—वह्निमारुतविग्रहत्वं नामाक्षरतोऽनुभावतश्च । यैः—कूटाक्षरैश्चतुर्भिः । कलेवरं—शरीरम्॥६४॥रसो दाहक्ष्मास्वयुतः भ्रूं इति । ग्रासो दाहक्ष्मयाखगः—क्ष्रूँ इति । प्रभा दाहक्ष्मास्वयुता—व्रूँ इति । हंसोदाहादि संयुतः—ह्रूँ इति ॥६६॥६७॥६८॥ प्राणोमरुत्समोपेतः—का इति । इलावन्ह्या समन्विता ली इति । नभोमरुद्युतं—माइति । दाहः—रेफः । चतुर्णां प्रतिलोमतः—प्रथमं चरणंस्यात् ॥६८॥ एतदुक्तं भवति—उक्तक्रमस्थितानां चतुर्णामक्षराणां प्रागवत् प्रतिलोमपठनात्कालीविद्यानुष्टुभः पादः स्यादिति । द्वितीयं-अस्या विद्यायाः प्रथमपादस्य द्वितीयमक्षरं द्वितोयपादस्य प्रथममक्षरमित्यर्थः ली इति । शून्यं—नकारोद्वितीयमक्षरम् । नभोभुवा—मो इति तृतीयमक्षरम् । ग्रासः—

---

(१) विद्यामन्त्रं च सङ्क्रममिति मू०पु० पा० ।

चतुर्थं द्वादशं विंशं रयोबाल(१)विलोमकम्।
चतुर्थं चरणं प्रोक्तं विद्यैषा सर्वनाशिनी ॥७२॥
व्याप्तं काली तृतीयं च मरुताम्बुसमन्वितम्।
नाद एषां विलोमं च प्रथमं चरणं यमे ॥७३॥
एतद्द्वितीयतुर्यौ च नभसा भूश्च नादकम्।
एतेषां प्रतिलोमं च द्वितीयं चरणो मनाः ॥७४॥

चकारः चतुर्थमक्षरम्। एतत्प्रातिलोम्याद्द्वितीयकम्—प्रोक्तक्रमस्थितानां चतुर्णामक्षराणां प्राग्वत्प्रातिलोम्यतो द्वितीयः पाद इत्यर्थः ॥७०॥ तृतीयं—प्रथमपादस्य तृतीयं मा इत्यक्षरं तृतीयपादस्य प्रथमाक्षरं भवति। एकादशमं—अस्या अनुष्टुभः एकादशंमो इति द्वितीयमक्षरम्। गोत्रा वरान्विता—दे इति तृतीयमक्षरम्। रयः—तकारः चतुर्थमक्षरम्। एषां विलोमश्च तृतीयं चरणं—प्रोक्तक्रमस्थितानां चतुर्णामक्षराणां प्रतिलोमपठनं तृतीयपाद इत्यर्थः। मनोः—विद्यायाः। मनुरितिमन्त्रविद्ययोः साधारणः शब्दः॥७१॥ चतुर्थं—अस्या विद्यायाः व इति चतुर्थमक्षरं चतुर्थपादस्य आद्यमक्षरं इत्यर्थः। द्वादशं—चकारो द्वितीयम्। विंशं—तकारः तृतीयमक्षरम्। रयः—तकारः। *अबा अम्बुवास्त्रोल्वं स्वातन्त्र्यात् त्व इति चतुर्थमक्षरम्। विलोमकं—प्रोक्तक्रमस्थितानामेषां चतुर्णामक्षराणां विलोमपठनात् चतुर्थपादो भवतीत्यर्थः। एषा—एवं प्रोक्ता। सर्वनाशिनी प्रयोगादितिशेषः। एवमेषा प्राग्वत् सर्वतोभद्राकारा काल्यनुष्टुबुक्ता ॥७२॥

व्याप्तमित्यादिभिः शिवे इत्यन्तैश्चतुर्भिः श्लोकैः सर्व्वतोभद्राकारां यमानुष्टुभमुपदिशति। तत्र व्याप्तं—यकारः प्रथममक्षरम्। कालीतृतीयं—काल्यनुष्टुभस्तृतीयमक्षरं मा इति अस्या द्वितीयमक्षरम्। मरुताम्बुसमन्वितं—वा इति तृतीयमक्षरम्। नादः—ठकारः चतुर्थमक्षरमित्यर्थः। एषां विलोमं—चतुर्णामक्षराणां प्राग्वद्विलोमपठनात्प्रथमः पादो भवति। यमे—यमयन्त्रे ॥७३॥ एतद्द्वितीयतुर्यौ च—एतस्य—यममन्त्रस्य द्वितीयचतुर्थाक्षरे द्वितीयपादस्य प्रथमद्वितीयाक्षरे माठ इति भवतः। नभसा भूः—सो इति तृतीयमक्षरम्। नादः ठकारश्चतुर्थमक्षरम्। एषां प्रतिलोमात् प्रोक्तक्रमस्थितानां चतुर्णामक्षराणां प्रतिलोमपठनात् प्राग्वत्

---

(१) वायो इति मू० पु० पा०।
* रयोंऽबाल इत टी० पु० पा०। रयोक्ता रयः तकारः चक्रः इति व० पु० पा०।

अभ्युक्तो मनु(१)श्चास्मिन्नेकादशकमेव च ।
रसः क्षमया वह्निदाहौ प्रतिलोमात् तृतीयकम् ॥७५॥
नादो नादो टाद्दवह्नीरयोर्वा तदनन्तरम् ।
प्रतिलोमं तु तेषां स्याच्चतुर्थं चरणं शिवे ! ॥७६॥
एवं मन्त्रद्वयं कोष्ठेष्वालिख्य बहिरप्यथो ।
वेष्टयेद्व्याप्तदाहाभ्यामुक्तक्रमसमन्वितम् ॥७७॥
मर्कटीदण्डिगरलैरालिप्तं स्थापितैरकम् ।
जप्तं विनिक्षिपेद्वृक्षविवरे चत्वरेऽथ वा ॥७८॥
वल्मीके मातृभवने शास्तुरायतनेऽथ वा ।
श्मशाने प्रोक्तसमये प्रोक्तक्रमसमन्वितम् ॥७९॥
यत्र देशादिगं यन्त्रं तत्रालक्ष्मीर्गदैः समम् ।
मारीतु सुस्थिरा साध्या सर्वैः देवासुरैरपि ॥८०॥

द्वितीयः पादइत्यर्थः॥७४॥ अभ्युक्तो मरुत्—वा इति तृतीयपादस्य प्रथममक्षरम् । अस्मिन्नेकादशं—अस्मिन्—यमयन्त्रे मोइत्येकादशमक्षरं तृतीयपादस्य द्वितीय-मक्षरम् । रसः क्षमयाभ्र इति तृतीयमक्षरम् । अग्निदाहौ-रि इति चतुर्थमक्षरं प्रतिलोमात् । एतदुक्तंभवति—प्रोक्तक्रमस्थितानामेषां चतुर्णां वर्णानां प्राग्वद्वि-लोमपठनात् तृतीयः पाद इति॥७५॥ नादोनादः—टद्वयं चतुर्थपादस्य प्रथमद्वितीया-क्षरे गग इति भवतः । दाहवह्नो—रो इति तृतीयमक्षरम् । योश्चत्व (यो'वद्यात्व) इति चतुर्थमक्षरम् । प्रतिलोमं च तेषां—प्राग्वत् प्रोक्तक्रमस्थितानां चतुर्णामक्षराणां प्रतिलोमपठनाच्चतुर्थः पादः स्यादित्यर्थः ॥७६॥ व्याप्तदाहाभ्यां—यकाररेफाभ्याम् । उक्तक्रमसमन्वितम् अनुष्ठितान्तरालम् ॥७७॥ दण्डी—ब्रह्मदण्डी । गरलयोजना-प्रकारमुत्तरत्र स्वयमेव वक्ष्यति । स्थापितैरकं—प्राग्वत् कृतप्राणप्रतिष्ठम् ॥७८॥७९॥ देशादिगमित्यत्रादिशब्दस्य ग्रामनगरखेटखर्वटादयो विषयः । मारो—जनपद-नाशकरो शक्तिः । नियहयन्त्रविरचनाक्रमस्तु प्रदर्श्यते । यथा—प्राक्प्रत्यग्दक्षिणो-दगग्रैः समान्तरालैर्दशभिः सूत्रैरेकाशीतिपदानि निष्पाद्य तत्र सर्वमध्येकोष्ठे उपरि-

---

(१) मरुश्चास्मिन्निति मू० पु० पा० ।

प्राग्वच्च नवभिः सूत्रैरष्टाष्टकपदं शिवे ! ।
कृत्वा तेष्वीशरक्षोदिगारभ्यात् कालिकामनुम्(१) ॥८०॥
विलिख्य यममन्त्रेण प्रोक्तबीजद्वयेन च ।
वेष्टयित्वा बहिश्चक्रं स्थापयेत् तदधोमुखम् ॥८१॥
एतच्च पूर्वचक्रोक्तफलकृत् परमेश्वरि ! ।
अनुक्तेष्वपि नामानि योजयेत्कोष्ठमध्यतः ॥८२॥
लवणोषणमेहाम्बु(२)गृहधूमाग्निसंयुत(तै)म् ।
श्मशानाङ्गारनिम्बोत्थनिर्यासो विषमीरितम् ॥८३॥

विन्दुसहिते रेफोदरे नामालिख्य प्राग्वत् तत्पार्श्वपङ्क्तिषु चतसृषु चतुर्षु कोष्ठेषु प्रागुक्तक्रमेण भ्रूँ घ्रूँ व्रूँ क्रूँ इत्यक्षरचतुष्टयं अभ्यन्तरान्निर्गमनगत्या अभितः समालिख्य अभिचार्यः पुरुषश्चेत्तदन्तः काल्यनुष्टुभं बहिर्यममन्त्रं, वनिता चेत् अन्तर्यममन्त्रं बहिः कालीविद्यां च समालिखेत् । लेखने तु ईशादिकं निर्ऋत्यादिकं च कालीमन्त्रं, अन्यदा तथा यममन्त्रं विलिख्य अन्यतरं बहिरीशादि-निर्ऋत्यन्तं निर्ऋत्यादीशान्तं च निरन्तरं द्विरालिख्य तद्बहिस्तन्निरन्तरं विन्दुयुक्तं यकारं रेफं च ईशादीशान्तं यथाक्रममन्तर्बहिर्विभागेन समालिख्य मनीषितेषु विनियुञ्ज्यात् । एतत् स्त्रीपक्षे च । स्त्री चेत् शास्तुरायतनाग्र एवाधस्तात्, पुरुषश्चेत् काल्याद्यायतनाग्र एवाधस्ताच्च खनेदिति ॥७९॥

प्राग्वत् इत्यादिभिः कोष्ठमध्यत इत्यन्तैस्त्रिभिः श्लोकैश्चतुःषष्टिकोष्ठोपेतं निग्रह-यन्त्रं तद्विनियोगफलादिविशेषश्चोपदिश्यति । तत्र यममन्त्रेण वेष्टनकथनं पुरुष-निग्रहविषयः । एतेन स्त्रीनिग्रहविषये अन्तर्यममन्त्रं भवति, बहिः कालीमन्त्र-वेष्टनं च बोद्धव्यमिति सम्प्रदायार्थः ॥८०॥ बीजद्वयेन—विन्दुसहितरेफयकाराभ्यां पूर्ववद्वेष्टयेत् ॥८१॥ अनुक्तेष्वपीत्युक्तिः स्त्रीविषया । अत्र कालीयममन्त्राभ्यां प्रसिद्धममोघनिग्रहमुक्त्वा तस्यापि प्रतिकारस्त्वरिताविद्यानुग्रहयन्त्रविधानेन भवति । एतदर्थमेव मन्त्राक्षराभ्यां निग्रहकथनम् । यन्त्रविरचनाक्रमो यथा-प्राग्वन्नवभिः सूत्रैश्चतुःषष्टिकोष्ठानि कृत्वा तेषु ईशादिकं निर्ऋत्यादिकञ्च अभिचार्यः पुरुषश्चेदन्तः कालिकामन्त्रं बहिर्यममन्त्रं स्त्री चेदन्तर्यममन्त्रं बहिः कालीविद्यां च प्राग्वत् समालिख्य पूर्वोक्ताभ्यां विन्दुसहिताभ्यां यकाररेफाभ्यां

---

(१) कालिकामुखम् इति मू० पु० पा० । (२) हेमाम्बु इति सी० हीमाम्बु इति मू० पु० पा० ।

विद्याद्यवर्णजठरे साध्यमालिख्य तद्बहिः ।
अष्टच्छेदेषु फट्वर्णमालिखेदष्टवर्णकम् ॥८४॥
कर्णिकास्थं ततोऽब्जं च वेष्टयेन्मायया ततः ।
बहिः कुम्भं विदध्याच्च प्रोक्ताक्षरविधानतः ॥८५॥
एवमन्यैश्च नवभिः विद्यावर्णैर्यथाक्रमम् ।
विदध्यान्नव यन्त्राणि दशानां च फलं शृणु ! ॥८६॥
सर्वरक्षां जयं वश्यं(१) नरनारीनृपादिनाम् ।
स्तम्भं लक्ष्मीयशोहेमवासांसि (च) समवाप्नुयात् ॥८७॥

प्रागुक्तक्रमेण वेष्टयित्वा प्रोक्तक्रमेण प्रोक्तेषु स्थानेषु अधोमुखं स्थापयेत्। तेन पूर्वोक्तान्येव फलानि स्युरिति ॥८२॥

लवणेत्यादिना श्लोकेन निग्रहयन्त्रालेखनार्थं विषस्वरूपमुपदिशति। तत्र—जषणं-जषः। मेहाम्बु—प्रस्रवः—अग्निः—चित्रकम्। अन्यदाराध्यमुखादवगन्तव्यम् ॥८३॥

विद्येत्यादिना यन्त्राणीत्यन्तेन त्रिपादाधिकेन श्लोकद्वयेन मूलविद्याक्षरेषु दशभिर्दशभिः अक्षरैर्दशयन्त्रविधानमुपदिशति। तत्र प्रोक्ताक्षरविधानतः—पूर्वोक्तसविन्दुकशृङ्खलारूपवकाराक्षरमालावेष्टनतः। एतदुक्तं भवति - अष्टदलं पद्मं विधाय तत्कर्णिकामध्ये विद्याप्रथमहृल्लेखां तदुदरे विद्याद्यभूतं प्रणवं तन्मध्ये नाम चालिख्य शेषाण्यष्टौ मन्त्राक्षराणि हृल्लेखाद्वय*फट्कारविधुराणि क्रमेण अग्रादिप्रादक्षिण्येनाष्टसु दलेषु समालिख्य तत्पद्मं द्वितीयहृल्लेखया उक्तक्रमेणाऽऽवेष्ट्य तद्बहिः प्राग्वत् सविन्दुकशृङ्खलितवकाराक्षरमालोपेतं उपर्यधश्च पद्मद्वयोपेतं कुम्भं कुर्यात्। एतत् प्रथमं यन्त्रम्। एवं अस्यैव यन्त्रस्य कर्णिकामध्ये हृल्लेखोदरे विद्याद्वितीयाक्षराणि क्रमेण एकमेकं नामगर्भं विन्यस्य तद(न)न्तरादितत्पूर्वान्तं प्राग्वदेभिरक्षरैः दलस्थैः पूर्वोक्तेन सार्द्धं नव यन्त्राणि हृल्लेखामध्ये सनामकं फट्कारमालिख्य प्रणवविधुरैस्तृतीयादिभिः शेषाक्षरैः प्राग्वत् दलस्थैः दशमं च एवं दशयन्त्राणि कुर्यात् इति ॥८४॥८५॥

दशानामित्यादिना आप्नुयादित्यन्तेन पादाधिकेन श्लोकेन दशानां यन्त्राणां क्रमेण असाधारणानि दशफलान्युपदिशति। तत्र अर्थः सुगमः ॥८६॥८७॥

---

(१) सर्वरक्षाभवेदित्थं इति सो० पु० पा०। * वषट्कार इति वं० पु० पा०।

अनावृत्तान्यक्षराणि अन्तेष्वेकादशाथ तैः।
स्वरभिन्नैर्भवेत्(१) सङ्ख्या षट्सप्तत्या शतं स्मृतम् ॥८८॥
तैर्यन्त्रकरणं तेषां फलानि च यथाक्रमम्।
शृणु वक्ष्यामि देवेशि! साधकाभीष्टसिद्धये ॥८९॥
वृत्तयोर्मध्यगं कृत्वा पद्मषोडशपत्रकम्।
तन्मध्ये कर्णिकामध्ये शक्तिं साध्यसमन्विताम् ॥९०॥
परेषु षोडशार्णानि वेष्टयेत्तच्च मायया।
वृत्तयोरन्तरा(२)बाह्ये कुम्भं प्रोक्तं समालिखेत् ॥९१॥
एवमेकादशोक्तानि यन्त्राणि प्रथितानि वै।
विनियोगानथैतेषां क्रमेण शृणु पार्वति! ॥९२॥
प्रथमं हयरक्षाकृत् द्वितीयं गजरक्षकम्।
तृतीयं नृपरक्षायां चतुर्थं दण्डरक्षकम् ॥९३॥
पञ्चमं कुरुते राजवेश्मरक्षां तु सर्वतः।

अनावृत्तानीत्यादिभि र्वै इत्यन्तैरर्धैश्चतुर्भिः श्लोकैः स्वरविकृतमूलविद्याक्षरैरेकादशयन्त्राण्युपदिशति। तत्र शक्तिं—ह्ल्लेखाम्॥८८॥८९॥९०॥ परेषु—दलेष्वित्यर्थः। तत्—पद्मम्। मायया—ह्ल्लेखया। वृत्तयोरन्तरा—पद्मबाह्यवृत्तद्वयवीथ्याम्। वृत्तयोरन्तरा मायया वेष्टयेदित्यन्वयः। बाह्ये—सर्वबाह्ये। प्रोक्तं—प्राग्वत्सविन्दुकश्रृङ्खलितवकारमालासहितम्। एतदुक्तं भवति—षोडशदलं पद्मं विधाय तत् बहिर्वृत्तद्वयं कृत्वा तद्बहिः प्राग्वत् सविन्दुकश्रृङ्खलितवकारमालासहितमुपर्यधश्च पद्मद्वयोपेतकुम्भं च विधाय तत्पद्मकर्णिकामध्ये नामगर्भां ह्ल्लेखामालिख्य षोडशदलेषु विद्यायाः स्वरविकृतेषु षट्सप्तत्यधिकशतसङ्ख्येष्वक्षरेषु आदितः षोडशाक्षराणि अग्रादिप्रादक्षिण्येनालिख्य पद्मबाह्यवृत्तयोरन्तरा ह्ल्लेखया समावेष्टयेत्। एतत् प्रथमं यन्त्रम्। एवमस्यैव यन्त्रस्य षोडशदलेषु अन्यानि च षोडशाक्षराणि समालिखेत्। एवं प्रोक्तेन सार्द्धमेकादशयन्त्राणि भवन्तीति ॥९१॥

---

(१) स्वरभिन्नैर्यया सङ्ख्यां स्वराषट्सप्ततिस्मृताम् इति सो पु० पा०।
(२) रन्तराबाह्ये इति सो पु० पा०।

षष्ठं सचिवरक्षाकृत् सप्तमं पुररक्षकम् ॥९४॥
अष्टमं गृहरक्षा स्यात् सर्वेषामपि सर्वदा ।
फणिचोरग्रहादिभ्यो भयेभ्यः शत्रुतस्तथा ॥९५॥
नवमं सर्वरोगार्त्तैः सर्वेषामपि सर्वदा ।
उत्तारकं स्याद्देवेशि ! प्राक्प्रोक्तविधिना युतम् ॥९६॥
दशमं भूर्जगं कृत्वा प्राग्वत्सिक्थोक्तलिङ्गकम्(१) ।
स्थापयेच्छीतले तोये घटादौ सविधेऽथ तम् ॥९७॥
पूजयेत्तानि च जपेत् स्पृशन् जीवकरेण त(म्)त् ।
घोराभिचारकृत्यादिजातो दाहज्वरः क्षणात् ॥९८॥
विमुच्य तं प्रयोक्तारं नाशयेत् तत्क्षणात् प्रिये ! ।
एवमेतानि यन्त्राणि नामतः सर्वकार्यकृत् ॥९९॥
सर्वासामपि नित्यानां प्रातरेव समृद्धये ।
पूजादौ च बलिं दद्यात् षोड़शार्णेन पार्वति ! ॥१००॥
पाणितत्त्वमयी व्याप्तिरिति सम्यक् समीरिता ॥
अस्या निष्कालनात्चित्ते तत्तत्त्वं स्वात्मसात् कृतम् ॥१०१॥

विनियोगेत्यादिभिः कार्यकृदित्यन्तैरर्द्धाधिः सप्तभिः श्लोकैस्तेषां यन्त्राणां विनियोगानुपदिशति। तत्र— दण्डरक्षकं-सेनारक्षाकरमित्यर्थः ॥८२॥८३॥८४॥८५॥ प्राक्प्रोक्तविधिना युतमिति—प्राणप्रतिष्ठाभिषेकोधारणमर्चनं चोच्यते ॥८६॥ दशमैकादशयोः प्रयोगस्य समानत्वात् पृथक् नाभिहितः। सविधे—रोगार्तस्येतिशेषः। तं—घटम् ॥८७॥ तानि—लिखितान्यक्षराणि ॥८८॥ तं—रोगार्तम्। प्रयोक्तारं—अभिचारकृत्यादीनामितिशेषः। नामतः सर्वकार्यकृत्—एतानि सर्वाणि यन्त्राणि मध्ये नामाक्षरविन्यासकौशलात् सर्वकार्य्यकराणीत्यर्थः ॥

सर्वासामपि इत्यादिना श्लोकेन सर्वासां नित्यानां प्रातः पूजासमारम्भे च बलिविधानमन्त्रमतिदिशति। तत्र—सर्वासामितिशेषः। षोड़शार्णेन—तृतीयपटलावसानोक्तेन मन्त्रेणेतिशेषः ॥९९॥१००॥

---

(१) लिङ्गके इति सी० पु० पा०।

इति श्रीषोड़शनित्यातन्त्रेषु श्रीकादिमते चतुर्दशं पटलम् ।

इति श्रीषोड़शनित्यातन्त्रेषु श्रीकादिमताख्यस्य तन्त्रस्य परिपूर्णस्य तन्त्रस्य प्रपञ्च-
सारसिंहराजप्रकाशाभिधानेन श्रीसुभगानन्दनाथेन विरचितायां
मनोरमाख्यायां व्याख्यायां शिवदूतीनित्याविद्याविधान-
प्रकाशनपरं चतुर्दशपटलं परिपूर्णं
परामृष्टम् ॥ १२ ॥

ग्रन्थसङ्ख्या—

षड् विंशतिश्च यन्त्राणि व्याख्याग्रन्थाः शतद्वयात् ।
सार्द्धपादा विंशतिश्च पटलेऽस्मिँश्चतुर्दशे ॥

अथ पञ्चदशपटलम् ।

अथ षोड़शनित्यासु दशमी या समीरिता ।
विद्योक्ता कुलसुन्दर्यास्तस्याः पूजाविधिं शृणु ॥१॥
तद्ध्यानमथ तन्न्यासं तच्छक्तीस्तत्समर्चनम् ।
तत्साधनं तथा रूपभेदान् यागांश्च वाक्प्रदान् ॥२॥
लोहितां लोहिताकारशक्तिवृन्दनिषेविताम् ।
लोहितांशुकभूषास्रग्लेपनां षण्मुखाम्बुजाम् ॥३॥
प्रतिवक्त्रं त्रिनयनां तथा चारुस्मितान्विताम् ।
अनर्घ्यरत्नघटितमाणिक्यमुकुटोज्ज्वलाम् ॥४॥
ताटङ्कहारकेयूररसनानूपुरोज्ज्वलाम् ।
रक्तस्तवकसम्भिन्नलसद्वक्षस्थलां शुभाम् ॥५॥
कारुण्यानन्दपरमामरुणाम्बुजविष्टराम् ।
भुजैर्द्वादशभिर्युक्तां सर्वेषां सर्ववाङ्मयीम् ॥६॥
प्रवालाक्षस्रजं पद्मं कुण्डिकां रत्ननिर्मिताम् ।
वसुपूर्णां(१) तच्चषकं (२)लुङ्गीव्याख्यानमुद्रिकाम् ॥७॥

पञ्चदशपटलम् ।

पूर्वस्मिँश्चतुर्दशे पटले नवम्यास्त्वरितानित्याया विधानमुपदिश्यानन्तरं दशम्याः कुलसुन्दरीनित्याविद्याया विधानमुपदिशति । अथ षोड़शेत्यादि विगाहत इत्यन्तेन श्लोकशतरूपेण पञ्चदशेन पटलेन । तत्र अथ षोड़शेत्यादि प्रदानित्यन्तेन श्लोकद्वयेन पटलार्थानुद्दिशति । तत्र उक्ता—तृतीयपटल इति शेषः । तद्ध्यानं—नित्यसपर्यार्थमिति शेषः । तत्साधनं—विद्यासाधनम् । तयोः—विद्यादेवतयोः ॥१॥२॥

लोहितामित्यादिभिरपेक्षया इत्यन्तैर्नवभिः श्लोकैर्नित्यपूजाध्यानं काम्यध्यान-

---

(१) रत्नपूर्णं इति मू० पु० पा० ।   (२) सलुङ्ग्याख्यान इति सो० पु० पा० ।

दधानां दक्षिणै र्वामैः पुस्तकं चारुणोत्पलम्।
हैमीं च लेखनीं रत्नमालां कम्बुवरं(१) भुजैः ॥८॥
अभितः स्तूयमानां च देवगन्धर्वकिन्नरैः।
यक्षराक्षसदेवर्षिसिद्धविद्याधरादिभिः ॥९॥
ध्यात्वैवमर्चयेन्नित्यं वाग्लक्ष्मीकान्तिसिद्धये।
सितां केवलवाक्सिद्ध्यै लक्ष्म्यै हेमप्रभामपि ॥१०॥
(२)धूमाभां वैरिविद्विष्ट्यै मृतये निग्रहाय च।
नीलां च मूकीकरणे (तां)(३) स्मरेत्त(त्त)दपेक्षया ॥११॥
त्रिभिस्तैरुदितैर्मूलवर्णैः कुर्यात् षडङ्गकम्।
आदिमध्यावसानेषु पूजाजपविधौ क्रमात् ॥१२॥
प्रत्येकं तैस्त्रिभिर्बीजैर्दीर्घस्वरसमन्वितैः।
कुर्यात्कराङ्गवक्त्राणां न्यासं प्रोक्तं यथाविधि ॥१३॥

भेदांश्चोपदिशति। तत्र षण्मुखाम्बुजां—ऊर्ध्वप्राग्दक्षिणोदक्पश्चिमापरत इत्युपरिष्टात् वक्त्रन्यासे स्वयमेव वक्ष्यति ॥३॥४॥५॥सर्ववाङ्मयीम्—सर्ववेदभाषाशब्दमयीम् ॥६॥ तक्षषकं—रत्नचषकम्। लुङ्गी—मातुलुङ्गी ॥७॥ दक्षिणैः भुजैरित्यन्वयः। अरुणोत्पलं - रक्तकैरवम्। अत्र उभयपार्श्वयोरूर्ध्वाद्यायुधकल्पनम् ॥८॥९॥१०॥ प्रति(वि)ग्रहाय व्याध्यादिक्लेशाय। तत्तदपेक्षया—तत्तत्प्रयोगानुगुण्येन ॥११॥

त्रिभिरित्यादिभिर्वर्णकैरित्यन्तैः पञ्चभिः श्लोकैः न्यासक्रममुपदिशति। तत्र आदिमध्यावसानेषु जपपूजाविधौ जपस्य सङ्कल्पितसङ्ख्याया अर्द्धांशावसानम्। तत्र न्यासं कृत्वाऽन्यार्द्धांशं जपेत्। जपमध्ये न्यासः। अस्याः कुलसुन्दर्या एव सपर्यामध्यमावाहनात्पूर्वं जपमध्यन्यासकालवर्जं अन्ये न्यासकालाः सर्वसाधारणाः। क्रमात्—यथाक्रमम् ॥१२॥ दीर्घस्वरसमन्वितैः—प्रथमे कूटे दीर्घस्वरयोजनं नाम तस्य स्वराक्षरत्वात् आँ ईँ ऊँ ऐँ औँ अः इति केवलदीर्घस्वरषट्कोच्चारणम्। एवं सर्वत्र स्वराक्षरेषु दीर्घस्वरयोजनम्। अन्ययोः प्राग्वत्। कराङ्गवक्त्राणां—करा-

---

(१) नवं भुजम् इति सी पु० पा०। (२) भूमाभां इति सो पु० पा०।
(३) तामिति मू० नास्ति।

ऊर्द्ध्वप्राग्दक्षिणोदक्च(१)पश्चिमापरनामभिः ।
शुचिनत्यन्तर(२)स्थैस्तैस्तदात्मसु यथाक्रमम् ॥१४॥
आधाररन्ध्रहृत्स्वेतद्द्वितीयं लोचनत्रये ।
तृतीयं श्रोत्रचिबुके चतुर्थं घ्राणतालुषु ॥१५॥
पञ्चमं चांसनाभीषु ततः पाणिपदद्वये ।
मूलमध्याग्रतोन्यस्येन्नवधा मूलवर्णकैः ॥१६॥

ङ्गयोः प्राग्वत् । वक्त्राणान्तु वक्ष्यमाणप्रकारेण॥१३॥ शुचिनत्यन्तरस्थैः—ऐँकारनमः-शब्दमध्यगतैः । तैः —वक्त्रनामभिः । तदात्मसु—तत्तत्त्वलास्थानाकारेषु । पूर्वोक्त-तत्तत्षडङ्गबीजानां क्रमात् एकैकमेकैकन्यूने * ऐँऊर्ध्ववक्त्रायनमः इति ऊर्ध्वावक्त्रे न्यसेत् । एवमितरेषु । पूर्वदक्षिणोत्तरपश्चिमापरवक्त्रेषु पञ्चसु तथा-विधैस्तत्तन्नाममन्त्रैरुद्दिष्टक्रमेण न्यसेदिति सम्प्रदायार्थः । पूजासमये चावा-हनानन्तरं देवतायास्तत्तद्वक्त्रेषु प्रथमकूटाक्षरषट्के तत्तन्मन्त्रैः पूजयेत् । एतदुक्तं भवति - विद्यायाः कुलसुन्दर्यास्त्रीणि बीजान्येकैकमुक्तक्रमेण दीर्घस्वरषट्कयो-जनात् षोढाषोढा कृत्वा सम्भूय अष्टादशसङ्ख्येष्वक्षरेषु प्रथमकूटाक्षरषट्कोन(ण)-पूजाजपविधिस्तत्प्रारम्भे प्रोक्तक्रमेण कराङ्गवक्त्रत्रयन्यासं कुर्यात् । तन्मध्ये द्वितीयकूटाक्षरषट्कोनं(णं) प्रोक्तक्रमेण कराङ्गवक्त्रत्रयन्यासं कुर्यात् । अवसाने तृतीयकूटाक्षरषट्कोनप्रोक्तक्रमात्न्यासत्रयं कुर्यादिति ॥१४॥

आधारेत्यादिना श्लोकेन मूलविद्याक्षरैस्त्रिभिर्नवावरणं† न्यासक्रममुपदिशति । तत्र एकं—एकवारमितिशेषः । एवं द्वितीयमित्यादीन्यपि वारवाचीनि ॥१५॥ पाणिपादद्वये—पादद्वये पादद्वयेच एवं चतुष्टयेपि । एकैकस्मिन्मूलमध्याग्रेषु त्रिषु स्थानेषु षष्ठवारं सप्तमं वारमष्टवारं नवमवारं च एवं पूर्वोक्तैः सह नवधा न्यसेदि-त्यर्थः । एतदुक्तं भवति—अत्र आधारादिषु नवसु त्रिकोणाकारेषु त्रिकेषु उद्दिष्टक्रमेण तत्तत्स्थानेषु त्रिभिर्विद्याक्षरैर्नववारं न्यासं कुर्यादिति । पूजाजपविधा-नारम्भमध्यावसानेषु व्यापकान्तमिवैतान् प्रोक्तान् न्यासान् कुर्यादितिसम्प्र-दायः ॥१६॥

---

(१) दक्षिणोत्तरपश्चिमेति ख़ो पु० पा०

(२) शुचिनः स्वन्तरस्थैः स्तदात्मसु इति मू० पु० पा० ।

* एकैकानने इति इति वं० पु० पा० ।

† नववारं इति वं पु० पा० ।

भाषा सरस्वती वाणी संस्कृता प्राकृता परा ।
खड्गरूपा वित्तरूपा रम्याप्यानन्दकौतुके(१) ॥१७॥
एता एकादश प्रोक्ता नवयोनिषु पूजयेत् ।
बहिरष्टच्छदाम्भोजे ब्राह्मयाद्याश्च समर्चयेत् ॥१८॥
चतुरस्रे लोकपालान् शक्तिरूपांस्तथाऽर्चयेत् ।
इन्द्राग्नियमरक्षोभिर्वरुणानिलसोमकान् ॥१९॥
ईशानं तद्विधिं प्रागाद्यष्टदिक्ष्वधरोत्तरम् ।
शक्त्यन्तैर्नामभिः प्राग्वत् पूजयेत् सर्वसिद्धये ॥२०॥
चतुरस्रद्वयं कृत्वा प्राक्प्रत्यग्द्वारसंयुतम् ।
तन्मध्ये वृत्तयुग्मस्थं कुर्यादष्टच्छदाम्बुजम् ॥२१॥
चतुस्त्रिपञ्चचत्वारिभागतोनवयोनिकम् ।
कृत्वाऽत्र तां समावाह्य प्रागवत्सम्यगथार्चयेत् ॥२२॥

भाषेत्यादिभिः सिद्धये इत्यन्तैश्चतुर्भिः श्लोकैर्देव्याः परिवारशक्तीरुद्दिशति—तत्र आनन्दकौतुके—आनन्दा कौतुका इति च द्वे शक्ती ॥१७॥ नवयोनिषु—मध्ययोन्यान्तु त्रिषु कोणेषु प्रथमां दशमीमेकादशीं च पूजयेत् ॥१८॥ तथा—वक्ष्यमाणप्रकारेण ॥१९॥ शक्त्यन्तैर्नामभिः—इन्द्रशक्तीत्यादिप्रागवत्* समाचर्यन्ते: ॥२०॥

चतुरस्रद्वयमित्यादिभिर्वै इत्यन्तैरद्धर्द्वैश्चतुर्भिः श्लोकैर्नित्यपूजाचक्रं पूजाक्रमं चोपदिशति । तत्र चतुस्त्रिपञ्चचत्वारिभागतः—वृत्तव्यासस्येतिशेषः । चत्वारीति स्वातन्त्र्योक्तिः । एतदुक्तं भवति—वृत्तव्यासे प्राक्प्रत्यग्रूपं ब्रह्मसूत्रं कृत्वा तत् षोड़शधा विभज्य प्रागादिचतुस्त्रिपञ्चांशेषु चिह्नानि विधाय तेषु चिह्नेषु त्रिषु तिर्यक् सूत्रत्रयं वृत्तावसानकं निष्पाद्य तेषु मध्यमसूत्रस्य दक्षिणोत्तरवृत्तसन्धिद्वयमारभ्य ब्रह्मसूत्रस्य पश्चिमवृत्तसन्ध्यवधि सूत्रद्वयमास्फाल्य पश्चिमसूत्रस्य दक्षिणोत्तरवृत्तसन्धिद्वयमारभ्य ब्रह्मसूत्रस्य पूर्वस्ववृत्तसन्ध्यवधि सूत्रद्वयमास्फाल्य ततः प्राक् सूत्रदक्षिणोत्तरवृत्तसन्धिद्वयमारभ्य पश्चिमसूत्रस्य ब्रह्मसूत्रसन्ध्यवधिसूत्र-

---

(१) कौतुकमिति सो० पु० पा० । (वाहुरूपा चित्ररूपारम्याथा इति मू० पु० पा० ।

* समाचर्यन्तम् इति टी० पु० पा० ।

एकादशस्वन्तशक्ती मध्ययोनेस्तु पार्श्वयोः ।
तथैव लोकपालान्तशक्ती द्वारद्वयेऽर्चयेत् ॥२३॥
विशेष एष सामान्यमन्यदर्चनमम्बिके ! ।
सप्ताचार्या बलिं दद्यात्पूजान्ते कुरुकुल्लया ॥२४॥
एवं नित्यार्चनं कुर्यान्नित्यहोमं घृतेन वै ।
प्रातः सलिलपानं च कुर्याद्विद्यात्मसिद्धये (१)॥२५॥
चन्दनोशीरकर्पूरकस्तूरीरोचनान्वितैः ।
काश्मीरकालागुरुभिर्मृगस्वेदमदैरपि ॥२६॥

द्वयमास्फाल्य प्रथमास्फालितं ब्रह्मसूत्रं सम्मार्जयेत् । एवं कृते वृत्तस्पृष्टाष्टास्रकं सुसमं नवयोनिचक्रं निष्पन्नं भवति । तद्बहिरष्टदलं पद्मं कृत्वा तद्बाह्ये प्राक्प्रत्यग्द्वारयुक्तं चतुरस्रद्वयं कृत्वा तत्र उक्तक्रमेण तां पूजयेदिति ॥२१॥२२॥ एकादशस्तु—भाषादिषु शक्तिष्वितिशेषः । अन्तशक्तिं* दशमीं आनन्दाख्यां शक्तिमेकादशीं कौतुकाख्यां शक्तिंच । मध्ययोनेस्तु पार्श्वयोः—मध्यस्थाया योन्या उत्तरदक्षिणयोः कोणयोरर्चयेत् । प्रथमाया भाषाख्यायाः शक्तेर्मध्ययोन्यग्रकोणस्थानां अष्टास्रपूजनन्तु मध्ययोनिशक्तित्रयार्चानन्तरम् । लोकपालान्तशक्ती—अनन्तब्रह्मशक्ती । द्वारद्वये—पूर्वपश्चिमयोरिति शेषः । एतदुक्तं भवति—पूर्वद्वारस्य† दक्षिणपार्श्वे इन्द्रशक्तिं उत्तरपार्श्वे अनन्तशक्तिं पश्चिमद्वारे दक्षिणपार्श्वे वरुणशक्तिं उत्तरपार्श्वे ब्रह्मशक्तिं अन्यास्तत्तद्दिक्षु समर्चयेदिति ॥१३॥ विशेष एषः—मध्ययोनेस्तु पार्श्वयोरित्याद्युक्तः । अत्र अष्टच्छदे पद्मे नवयोनिषु च अग्रादारभ्य प्रादक्षिण्येन पूजयेत् । चतुरस्रे तु उक्तक्रमेण पूर्वद्वारमारभ्य प्रादक्षिण्येनार्चयेदिति यावत् । सामान्यं पूर्वोक्तवदित्यर्थः ॥ ॥२४॥ एवं—उक्तप्रकारेण ।

प्रातरित्यादिना श्लोकोत्तरार्द्धेन ज्ञानसिद्ध्युपायमुपदिशति तत्र विद्यात्मसिद्धये—केवलया अनया कुलसुन्दरीविद्यया त्रिवारजप्तचुलुकसलिलपानेन सम्यक् ज्ञानसिद्ध्यात्मशुद्धिःस्यादिति यावत् ॥२५॥

चन्दनेत्यादिना सिद्धये इत्यन्तेनाध्यर्द्धेन श्लोकद्वयेन साधकस्य पूजारम्भे गुणविधानं देवीपूजागन्धद्रव्याणि चोपदिशति । तत्र मृगस्वेदमदैः—मृगस्वेदैः

---

(१) शुद्धये इति मो० पु० पा० ।
* अन्तशक्ती इति टी० पु० पा० ।
† पूर्वद्वारस्य इति टी० पु० पा० ।

आलिप्तगात्रो हृष्टान्तःकरणो मौनमास्थितः(१) ।
चित्रभूषाम्बरः स्रग्वी जपेद्विद्यां निशामुखे ॥२७॥
पूजयेच्च शिवामेतैर्गन्धैः सर्वार्थसिद्धये ।
सर्वाभिरपि नित्याभिः प्रातर्मातृकया समम् ॥२८॥
विजप्ताभिः पिबेत्तोयं तथा वाक्सिद्धये शिवे ! ।
अन्यैरपि च मन्त्रैस्तैर्विद्याभिस्तत्प्रसिद्ध्यति ॥२९॥
प्राग्वल्लक्षत्रयं जप्त्वा तद्दशांशं च तर्पयेत् ।
सुगन्धिसलिलैर्होमं तावत्तिमधुराप्लुतैः ॥३०॥
पालाशपुष्पैर्विकचैरदुष्टैरविखण्डितैः ।
सिद्धविद्या(?)पुनः कुर्यात्काम्यकर्माणि साधकः ॥३१॥
देव्या वर्णविभेदेन फलभेदाः समीरिताः ।
विद्यास्वरूपभेदाँस्तु शृणु वक्ष्ये यथाविधि ॥३२॥

मृगमदैश्च ॥२६॥ हृष्टान्तःकरणः—देवताहंभावनयेति शेषः । पूजयेच्च चकारेण । निशामुखे इत्याकृष्यते । एतैर्गन्धैः—चन्दनादिभिः दशविधैर्द्रव्यैः ॥२७॥

सर्वाभिरित्यादिना प्रसिद्ध्यतीत्यन्तेनार्द्धाद्येन चैकेन श्लोकेन सर्वनित्याभिरन्य-विद्याभिः सर्वमन्त्रैश्च वाक्सिद्धिप्रयोगमुपदिशति । तत्र सर्वाभिः—षोडश-भिरितिशेषः ॥२८॥ विद्याभिः—अन्याभिरिति शेषः । एतदुक्तं भवति—प्रातः-सन्ध्याविध्यवसाने चुलुकेनोदकमादाय तन्मध्ये वक्ष्यमाणं मातृकायन्त्रं विभाव्य मातृकामकारादिक्षकारान्तामेकपञ्चाशदक्षरां प्रत्यक्षरं बिन्दुमतीं त्रिवारं संजप्य पश्चात् स्वाभिमतां नित्यामन्यां विद्यां मन्त्रं वा त्रिवारं सञ्जप्य तत्सलिल-ममृतमयं भावयन् मूलाधारात् जिह्वाग्रान्तां सरस्वतींनाड़ीं दीपशिखाकारां ध्यात्वा तस्यां होमधिया आचामेत् । एवं प्रतिदिवसं प्रातर्विदधतश्चतुर्विधं पाण्डित्यं स्वात्मज्ञानञ्च नियतं भवतीत्युपस्कारः सम्प्रदायार्थः ॥२९॥

प्राग्वदित्यादिना साधक इत्यन्तेन श्लोकद्वयेन विद्यासाधनप्रकारमुपदिशति । तत्र प्राग्वत्—ललितावत् । तावत्—तद्दशांशम् ॥३०॥ अदुष्टैः—कृम्याद्यनुपहतैः । अविखण्डितैः—वृन्तस्थैः ॥३१॥

---

(१) मौनसंश्रुत इति मू० पु० पा० ।

त्रयीमयत्वं विद्याया स्तथा व्यञ्जनसङ्गमात् (१)।
वाच्यवाचकरूपस्य प्रपञ्चस्यामितात्मनः ॥३३॥
कारणत्त्वं (२) परात्मत्त्वममेयत्त्वं च वै क्रमात् ।
कथयामि शृणु प्राज्ञे! विधिविस्तरवैभवाः(३) ॥३४॥
अकारादिः सामवेदोऽप्यृग्वेदस्य तदादिकः ।
यजुर्वेद इकारादिस्तेषां संयोगतः शुचिः ॥३५॥
तन्निष्पत्तिं शृणु प्राज्ञे ! प्रोक्तं(४) पूर्वापरक्रमात् ।
विलिख्य योजयेत्पूर्वं शब्दशास्त्रानुसारतः ॥३६॥
गुणसन्ध्या*ऋग्यजुषां ततस्तेनापरं तथा ।
वृद्धिसन्ध्या†समायुज्यादित्युत्पन्नं शुचेर्वपुः ॥३७॥
तेन त्रयीमयीविद्याकार्यकारणयोगतः ।
आद्यक्षरप्रसूतानि सर्वाण्यन्यानि येन वै ॥३८॥

देव्या इत्यादिभि र्वैभवा इत्यन्तैस्त्रिभिः श्लोकैर्विद्याव्याप्तिवैभवादिकं प्रस्तौति । तत्र देव्या वर्णविभेदेन—सितां केवलवाक्सिद्ध्यै इत्यादिपूर्वोक्तेन देवीरूपवर्णभेदेन ॥३२॥ त्रयीमयत्वं—वेदमयत्वम् । विद्यायाः—कुलसुन्दर्या इति शेषः । वाच्यवाचकरूपस्य—शब्दात्मना अर्थात्मना च ॥३३॥ परात्मत्त्वं—परमोत्कृष्टत्त्वम् । अमेयत्त्वं—देशकालाकारैरनियन्त्रितत्त्वम् ॥३४॥

अकारादिरित्यादिभिर्वै इत्यन्तैश्चतुर्भिः श्लोकैर्विद्यायाः प्रथमकूटस्य वाग्मयस्य त्रयीमयत्वमुपदिशति। तत्र एतदुक्तं भवति--सामवेदस्यादिभूतमकारं तत्पार्श्वे ऋग्वेदस्यादिभूमकारम् । उभयोरप्युपरि यजुर्वेदस्यादिभूतमिकारं च विलिख्य पूर्वेणाकारेण (उ) इकारयोगात् गुणसन्ध्या एकारं उत्तरेणाकारेण तेनैव एकारेण चोक्तप्रकारेण वृद्धिसन्ध्या एकारं च निष्पाद्य एवं त्रयीप्रथमाक्षरनिष्पन्नत्वादैकारस्य त्रय्याः प्रथमाक्षरत एव उपरितनयोरक्षरसन्दर्भस्य बीजाङ्कुरवत् तेषां कारणत्वात् तन्मयत्वादैकारस्य च त्रयीमयत्वमुक्तमिति ॥३५॥३६॥३७॥३८॥

---

(१) संश्रयात् इति मू० पु० पा० ।
(२) कारणं परात्मत्त्वममें इति सो पु० पा० ।
(३) विचित्रा मन्त्रवैभवा इति मू० पु० पा० ।
(४) प्रोक्तामूर्द्धाधरःक्रमात् इति मू० पु० पा० ।
* गुणसञ्ज्ञा इति सो० पु० पा० ।
† वृद्धिसंज्ञा इति सो० पु० पा० ।

मध्यमार्णगतप्राणा व्यञ्जनादेस्तु मातृका ।
प्राग्वत्कारणकार्यत्वयोगाद्वाचकरूपकम् ॥३९॥
तदर्णकारसायोगा भूतादित्वेन वाच्यता ।
इति वाचकवाच्यत्वरूपाद्विश्वात्मतोदिता ॥४०॥
परारूपं तृतीयेन त्रिंश(तो)कोक्तं त्रिकात्मकम् ।
एवमेषा विश्वमयी विद्यारूपभिदाः शुभाः ॥४१॥
शुचिराद्या वाक्स्वरूपा द्वितीया वह्निरीरिता ।
विन्दुसर्गात्मनोरैक्यरूपा सात्वावयोर्वपुः* ॥४२॥

मध्यमित्यादिना उदिता इत्यन्तेन श्लोकद्वयेन विद्याया विशिष्टसन्दर्भरूपं त्रयीमयत्वमुक्त्वा अशेषशब्दानामशेषार्थानां चानयोन्यव्याप्तिरूपतां विद्यायाश्च ऐक्यमुपदिशति। तत्र एतदुक्तं भवति—विद्याया द्वितीयाक्षरगतककारलकारयोर्मध्ये व्यञ्जनात्ममातृकादिभूतत्वात्ककारस्य पञ्चभूतादिस्तृतीयखण्डस्य तस्यास्तत्रोक्तं व्यञ्जनस्य ज्ञेयरूपत्वं अचां ज्ञानरूपत्वं विसर्जनीयस्य ज्ञातृरूपत्वं एवं ज्ञातृज्ञानज्ञेयरूपत्रिकात्मकविश्वात्मकत्वमस्यास्तृतीयखण्डस्याप्युक्तभूतपृथिव्यक्षरात्मकत्वाल्लकारस्यचैवमादिग्रहणबलादशेषः शब्दःशेषः पञ्चभूतात्मकोवाच्यवाचकरूपः प्रपञ्चश्च एवमभिन्नरूपोऽनया विद्यया व्याप्त इति ॥३९॥४०॥

परारूपमित्यादिना श्लोकेन पूर्वं विद्यायाः प्रथमद्वितीयाक्षरव्याप्तिमुपदिश्य तृतीयाक्षरव्याप्त्यादिकमुपदिशति। तत्र—एतदुक्तं भवति—प्रागुपदिष्टत्रिंशिकाख्यागमप्रोक्तपराविद्यारूपत्वात् (अस्याविद्यायास्तृतीयखण्डस्य तस्यास्तत्रोक्तं व्यञ्जनस्य ज्ञेयरूपत्वं चोक्तज्ञानरूपत्वं विसर्जनीयस्य ज्ञातृरूपत्वं च, एवं ज्ञातृज्ञानज्ञेयरूपत्रिकात्मकविष्णवात्मकत्वमस्यास्तृतीयखण्डस्याप्युक्तमिति) एवमस्या विद्यायाःत्रिभिःखण्डैस्त्रिप्रकारतोऽशेषविश्वात्मता प्रतिपादिता। एवं रूपतोमियत्वं च सुप्रतिपादितत्वादुव्यक्तं † तेन अनया विद्यया नासाध्यमस्ति सत्सम्प्रदायतः साधकस्येत्यर्थः। रूपभिदा—अस्या विद्यायाः स्वरूपभेदान् शृणुइत्यर्थः ॥४१॥

शुचिरित्यादिभिरात्मिकाइत्यन्तैस्त्रिभिः श्लोकैः सकलत्रैपुरविद्याराशिकन्दभूतां सङ्केतविद्याख्यपरमरहस्यभूतां विद्यामुपदिशति—तत्र शुचिराद्या वाक्स्वरूपा

---

* ( ) एतदन्तर्गतोयन्यः सो० पु० नास्ति। † तस्यागमप्रोक्तं इति टी० पु० पा०।

तेन बीजेन विश्वात्मरूपा सा सम्यगीरिता ।
वनं तृतीयमाख्यातं मायया स्वेन वा युतम् ॥४३॥
एषा त्रैपुरकंदा स्यात्सङ्केतेति निगद्यते ।
ज्ञातृज्ञानज्ञेयदोषगुणतेजस्त्रयात्मिका ॥४४॥
अस्यास्तु मध्यमे बीजे रसाप्राणनियोजनात् ।
वाच्यवाचकरूपात्मा प्रपञ्चस्य हि कारणे ॥४५॥
तृतीये हृत्समायोगात् त्रिकविश्वात्मतोदिता ।
हंसहृद्योगतस्तेषु जङ्गमा स्थावरा त्मता ॥४६॥
एकद्व्यादिसमायोगाद्व्यञ्जनानां तथा त्रिषु ।
ज्ञातुं न शक्यते संख्या विद्यानां परमेश्वरि ! ॥४७॥

प्रथमा वाग्भवाख्या द्वादशस्वरविग्रहा। द्वितीया वह्निः---सकलमातृकाक्षरकारणभूतविन्दुविसर्जनीयैक्यरूपशिवशक्त्यात्मकश्चतुर्थस्वरः ॥४२॥ तेन बीजेन—तुर्यस्वरूपेण । विश्वात्मरूपा सा—प्रतिपादितशिवशक्तिरूपेण चतुर्थस्वरेण सा विद्या विश्वात्मरूपा प्रोक्तेत्यर्थः। वनं तृतीयम्—केवलश्चतुर्दशस्वरास्तृतीया विद्या। मायया स्वेन वा – विसर्जनीयेन विन्दुना वेत्यर्थः॥४३॥ त्रैपुरकन्देति सङ्केतेतिचास्या विद्यायाः संज्ञेति। तत्र कन्दवत्कन्दत्वम्। अस्या विद्यायास्त्रिषु खण्डेषु वक्ष्यमाणैकद्व्यादिव्यञ्जनयोगसम्भूतानामसङ्ख्यानां त्रैपुरविद्याराशीनां मूलभूतेत्यर्थः। ज्ञातृज्ञानज्ञेयदोषगुणतेजस्त्रयात्मिका। एतदुक्तं भवति—ज्ञातृज्ञानज्ञेयात्मत्वेन वातपित्तश्लेष्मरूपत्वेनाग्निसूर्यसोमात्मकत्वेन चाशेषं विश्वं सम्पूर्यावतिष्ठत इति ॥४४॥

अस्या इत्यादिना मात्मतादित्यन्तेन श्लोकद्वयेन अस्याविद्याया मध्यमे ककारलकारयोगादुपरमे सकारयोगाच्च प्रागुपदिष्टां सत्यामिं त्रिखण्डेषु हकारसकारयोगात् व्याप्तिवासनां चोपदिशति। तत्र अस्याः सङ्केतविद्यायाः कारणेति स्वातन्त्र्योक्तिः। कारणतेत्यर्थः॥४५॥ त्रिकविश्वात्मता—ज्ञातृज्ञानज्ञेयात्मरूपविश्वात्मता। तेषु—त्रिषु कूटेष्वितिशेषः। जङ्गमस्थावरात्मता। एतदुक्तं भवति। तेषु त्रिषु बीजेषु प्रत्येकं भकारसकारसंयोगात् अस्याश्च सङ्केतविद्याया जङ्गमस्थावरात्मत्ववासनोक्तेति ॥४६॥

एवं साऽनन्तविभवा तां निःशेषं वदेत्कथम्(१) ।
तथापि भक्तासन्त्राणहेतोः काञ्चन वच्मि ते ॥४८॥
आयुर्लक्ष्मीकीर्तिभोगसौन्दर्यारोग्यदायिका ।
ऐहिकामुष्मिकज्ञानमयी सकलसिद्धिदा ॥४९॥
विद्यायाः कुलसुन्दर्या हंसयोगात्त्रिषु क्रमात् ।
विजयाख्या महाविद्या विश्वसंत्राणतत्परा ॥५०॥
ह्रत्समायोगतस्तेषु जीवाख्या विश्वचिन्मयी ।
द्वयोर्नियोजनात्तेषु जायते (सा) आवयोर्वपुः ॥५१॥
ह्रदादिस्त्वन्मयी विद्या हंसादिर्मन्मयो मनुः ।
तेषु दाहसमायोगाद्विश्वाख्या विश्वविग्रहा ॥५२॥

एकद्व्येत्यादिना श्लोकेन तस्याः सङ्केतविद्याया एकद्व्यादिव्यञ्जनयोगादिना-ऽसङ्ख्यातरूपत्वमुपदिशति । तत्र एतदुक्तं भवति—तस्याः सङ्केतविद्याया स्त्रिषु खण्डेषु द्वितीयतृतीयविधुरं प्रथमे वा प्रथमतृतीयविधुरं द्वितीये वा प्रथमद्वितीय-विधुरं तृतीये वा तेष्वन्यतमविधुरमितरयोर्वा समस्तेषु वा कादिक्षान्ताक्षराणां पञ्चविंशत्सङ्ख्याकानां क्रमव्युत्क्रमापक्रम एकद्व्यादिसमायोगात् या विद्याः संभवन्ति तासां संख्यास्वरूपं ज्ञातुं वक्तुं वा न केनापि शक्यमिति ॥४७॥

एवमित्यादिना सिद्धिदा इत्यन्तेन श्लोकद्वयेन उक्तवक्ष्यमाणास्त्रैपुररत्नभूता-विद्यास्तवनमुखेन प्रस्तौति । तत्र सा—सङ्केतविद्या । तां—एकद्व्यादिसम्भूताम् । असङ्ख्याता विद्याः । काञ्चन—प्रधानभूताम् । ऐहिकामुष्मिकज्ञानमयी इत्युक्त्या असमीचीनतद्द्वयप्रतिपादकविद्याभ्योविशिषयति ॥४८॥

विद्याया इत्यादिभिः स्मृता इत्यन्तैः षड्भिश्लोकैरेकादशविद्यास्वरूपोपदेशं सम्भूयोक्तानां त्रैपुररत्नभूतानां विद्यानां सङ्ख्यानिगमनं च करोति । तत्र एतदुक्तं भवति—कुलसुन्दर्यास्त्रिषु खण्डेषूपरि प्रत्येकं हकारयोजनाद्विजयाख्या सर्वेषा-मैहिकामुष्मिकज्ञानप्रदानात् सर्वरक्षाकरोविद्या ॥५०॥ तेषु हकारमपास्य तत्र सका-रयोजनात् विश्वचैतन्यरूपिणो (वीजा) जीवाख्याविद्या ॥५१॥ तेषु तत्र हकारपूर्वं सकारयोजनात् मन्त्राख्योमन्त्रः सकारपूर्वहकारयोजनात् विद्याख्याविद्या तेषु त्रिषु

---

(१) तावच्छेषं मुखे कथमिति मू० पु० पा० ।

प्रत्येकं शक्तिपुटिता विद्या विश्वविमोहिनी ।
खेचराम्बुरसोपेतमायाभ्यां पुटिता तु सा ॥५३॥
त्रिपुरामृतसंज्ञा सा सर्वाप्ययन(१)विग्रहा ।
मायाद्या मोहिनी प्रोक्ता तन्मध्या क्षोभिणी मता ॥५४॥
तदन्ता क्लेदिनीत्याख्याता वातादिस्यान्महोदया ।
त्रयोदशेति कथितास्त्रिपुरा(रिनम)विधयः स्मृताः ॥५५॥
आसां क्रमविपर्यासजाताविद्याष्टसप्ततिः ।
तासां विधानं ते प्रोक्तमशेषं लक्षसागरे ॥५६॥
सम्पत्करोति काप्यस्ति विद्या साऽचिन्त्यवैभवा ।
तां वक्ष्ये शृणु देवेशि ! साधकाभीष्टसिद्धये ॥५७॥

कूटेषु प्रथमे हकारसकारयोरधस्तादन्त्ययोर्व्यञ्जनान्तरे च फयोजनात् विश्वमयी विश्वाख्याविद्या ॥५२॥ केवलक्रमे सुन्दर्यास्त्रिखण्डानि प्रत्येकं ह्स्लें खाभ्यां पुटयेत् । सा विश्वमोहिनी विद्या॥५३॥ पुनरपि तस्याएव ह्स्लें खा(क्लें कारा)भ्यां पुटनात् त्रिपुरामृताख्या विद्या ॥५४॥ तत्त्वज्ञानात् सर्वलाभात् (संयोग) संपोषणविग्रहा । तस्याः कुलसुन्दर्याः प्रथमकूटमपास्य तत्र ह्स्लें खायोजनात् मोहिनीनामविद्या । तथा-मध्यमखण्डमपास्य तत्र ह्स्लें खाया नियोजनात् क्षोभिणीनाम विद्या । तद्वत् चरमखण्डस्थाने ह्स्लें खानियोजनात् क्लेदिनीनाम विद्या । पुनस्तस्याः कुलसुन्दर्याः प्रथमखण्डमपास्य तत्र अकारयोजनात् महोदयाख्या विद्या । एवं त्रिपुराकन्दाख्या सङ्केतविद्या तदुवकुलसुन्दरीविद्याभ्यां समेता विजयादिकामहोदयान्ता कणादश-विद्याः सम्भूय त्रयोदशविद्याः त्रिपुरारत्नाख्याः समोरिता इति ॥५५॥

आसामित्यादिना श्लोकेन तासां त्रयोदशविद्यानां पञ्चत्रिंशत्पटलोक्तक्रमापक्रमव्युत्क्रमयोगान् प्रत्येकं षट्भेदतः सम्भूय अष्टसप्ततिसङ्ख्याता विद्यास्तासां प्रपञ्चितं विधानं लक्षसागराख्यागमे समुपदिष्टमिति चोपदिशति ॥५६॥

संपत्करोत्यादिभिः समुन्नयेदित्यन्तैनैकादशभिः श्लोकैस्तत्प्रस्तावपूर्वमन्वर्थ संज्ञसम्पत्करीविद्योपदेशं तद्ध्यानोपदेशं तद्विधानोपदेशं पूर्वोक्ताष्टसप्ततिविद्याना-मुपास्तिक्रमं च करोति । तत्र प्राणोरसामरुद्वह्निखयोगादाद्यमीरितं—ककार-

---

(१) प्यानय इति टी० पु० पा० ।

प्राणोरसामरुद्वह्निस्वयोग।दाद्यमीरित(।)म् ।
वातेन च चरस्वाभ्यां द्वितीयमपि पार्वति ! ॥५८॥
हंसहृद्वनमायाभिस्तृतीयं परमेश्वरि ! ।
एवं त्रिवर्णा सा विद्या विधानं चाथ कथ्यते ॥५९॥
ततीयबीजेनाङ्गानि दीर्घस्वरयुजा क्रमात् ।
कुर्यात्कराङ्गयोः प्रागवदित्थं ध्यायेच्च तां ततः ॥६०॥
दाड़िमीकेसरप्रख्यदेहवासोविभूषणाम् ।
चतुर्भुजां त्रिनयनां प्रसन्नस्मेरवक्त्रकाम् ॥६१॥
रत्नाभिषेकसम्पन्नामष्टपत्राब्जमध्यगे ।
त्रिकोणे स्वस्तिकासीनां करुणानन्दमन्दिराम् ॥६२॥
प्रवालाक्षस्रजं रत्नचषकं रत्नपूरितम् ।
पुस्तकं च वरं(दं) हस्तैर्दधानां सर्वमङ्गलाम् ॥६३॥
अकारादिसकारान्तषोड़शत्रयकल्पिते ।
कुलासने हलक्षार्णमध्ये तद्विद्ययाऽन्विते ॥६४॥

लकारआकारईकारविन्दुभिस्तस्याः प्रथमं कूटमुक्तमिति यावत्। अत्र आकार ईकारयोर्गुणसन्धिर्न भवति। वातेन च चरस्वाभ्यां द्वितीयम्- अकारएकारबिन्दुभिर्द्वितीयं कूटम्। अत्रापि वृद्धिसन्धिर्न भवति ॥५७॥५८॥ हंसहृद्वनमायाभिस्तृतीयम्—हकारसकारऔकारविसर्जनीयैस्तृतीयं कूटम्। परमेश्वरीति देवीसम्बुद्धिः ॥५८॥ कराङ्गयोः—कराङ्गन्यासयोः। विन्दुयुक्तेन दीर्घस्वरयुजा तृतीयबीजेन कुर्यादित्यर्थः। इत्थं—वक्ष्यमाणप्रकारेण ॥६०॥६१॥ स्वस्तिकासीनां—स्वस्तिकसंज्ञकेन आसनेन स्थिताम्। मन्दिरामिति स्वातन्त्र्योक्तिः—मन्दिरमित्यर्थः ॥६२॥ करेषु दक्षिणोर्ध्वादि वामाधरान्तं धार्याणि पार्श्वक्रमेण कल्पयेत् ॥६३॥ अकारादिसकारान्तषोड़शत्रयकल्पिते—अकारककारथकारोपक्रमविसर्जनीयतकारसकारावसानत्रिरेखा सर्वत्र त्रिकोणकल्प्तिः तन्मध्ये शिष्टहलाक्षिद्वयाच्चादिशब्दार्थप्रपञ्चविग्रहा परमा शक्तिः स्थितेति। शक्तिमन्त्रेषु परमोपह्वरः सम्प्रदायार्थः। कुलासनं नाम एवं विशिष्टं चक्रं त्रिकोणम्। तद्विद्ययाऽन्विते

समावाह्यार्घ्यसङ्कल्पपूर्वं तामर्चयेत्क्रमात् ।
मध्ये त्रिकोणकोणेषु रतिप्रीतिमनोभवान्(म) ॥६५॥
(१)अग्रादिसव्यगास्तद्वदष्टपत्रेषु मातरः ।
चतुरस्रे लोकपालान् प्राग्वच्छक्तीः समर्चयेत् ॥६६॥
विधानमष्टसप्तत्या(२) इति सम्यक्समीरितम् ।
बलिद्वयं च होमं च प्राग्वदन्यत् समुन्नयेत् ॥६७॥
चतुर्गुणचतुर्थांशस्वसमाननियोजिते ।
ब्राह्मीरसवचादुग्धे शृतं सर्पिस्त्रिभिर्दिनैः ॥६८॥

—तद्विद्यया सहिते । एतत्कुलासनविशेषणम् ॥६४॥ अर्घसङ्कल्पः प्राग्वत् ॥६५॥ सव्यगाः—वामावर्तक्रमेण । तद्वत्—अग्रादिवामावर्तक्रमेण । अष्टमातरः—ब्राह्मयाद्याः प्राग्वत् । शक्तीः—शक्तिरूपान् प्रागादिस्थितानित्यर्थः॥६६॥ अष्टसप्तत्या विद्यानामितिशेषः । अष्टसप्ततिविधानां विद्यानामेतदेव विधानमित्यर्थः । बलिद्वयं आद्यन्तयोरितिशेषः । होमं—नित्यहोमं प्राग्वत् । एतदुक्तं भवति—पूजादौ षोडशाक्षरेण मन्त्रेणावसाने कुरुकुल्लासप्ताक्षर्या च प्रोक्तक्रमेण बलिद्वयं दत्वा नित्यपूजाक्रमतो होमं कुर्यादिति । अन्यत्—आद्यन्तयोर्मन्त्राणां बीजद्वयसप्ताक्षरीयोजनादि । आसां नित्यसपर्याचक्रविरचनाक्रमो यथा—प्राक्प्रत्यक्द्वारोपेतं समचतुरस्रद्वयं विधाय तदन्तरष्टदलं पद्मं विधाय तत्कर्णिकायां यथामानं समत्रिरेखां योनिं विधाय तत्र प्रोक्तक्रमेण प्रोक्ताः शक्तीः पूजयेदिति ॥६७॥

चतुर्गुणेत्यादिना कविरित्यन्तेन श्लोकद्वयेन ब्राह्मीघृतोत्पादनविधिं तेन घृतेन मूकस्य वाक्सिद्धिप्रयोगं चोपदिशति—तत्र ब्राह्मीव चे* गुरुमुखादवगन्तव्ये । सर्पिः—घृतम् । एतदुक्तं भवति—सम्पादनीयघृतमानस्य चतुर्गुणं ब्राह्मीस्वरसमानं घृतमानचतुर्थांशं वचामानं घृतमानसमानं क्षीरं, एवमुक्तमानक्रमेण चत्वारि संयोज्य त्रिभिर्दिनैर्मृदग्निना सम्पाच्य चिक्कणघृतभाण्डे संशोध्यावतार्य शिशिरे तस्मिन्वक्ष्यमाणमातृकायन्त्रं रजतपट्टे विधाय कृतप्राणप्रतिष्ठं तद्यन्त्रमस्मिन् घृते निक्षिप्य कुशदूर्वादर्भेष्वन्यतमेन घृतं संस्पृशन् सबिन्दुकां मातृकामयुतवारं

(१) अग्रादिसर्वगा इति मू० पु० पा० । (२) विधानमीदृशं इति सो० पु० पा० ।

* ब्राह्मी च इति टी० पु० पा० ।

सयन्त्वं मातृकाविद्याजप्तं त्वयुतमादरात् ।
दिनशोऽविलिहेत्प्रातरब्दान्मूकोऽभवेत् कविः ॥६९॥
शिवोऽम्बिका कुमारश्च विधिर्विष्णुस्तथा रमा ।
कुबेरोरविचन्द्रारनागुरुसितसौरयः ॥७०॥
वारेशास्तेषु वारेषु तांस्तु तद्दिनविद्यया ।
नामसप्ताक्षरीयुक्त्या पूजयेत्तर्पयेद्धुनेत् ॥७१॥
वर्णौषधिसमुत्थेन भस्मना मन्त्रितेन तु ।
मातृकान्याससहितं स्पृशेद्रक्षाकृते मनुम्(३) ॥७२॥
विशेषतो महीपानामार्तानां च विधिं चरेत् ।
तेन ते सुखिनोभूयः सान्वया यावदायुषम् ॥७३॥

जपित्वा पश्चात् प्रोक्तविद्यास्वन्यतमां(च) तत्संख्यं जपित्वा सुरक्षितं निक्षिप्य क्वचित्सिसन्ध्यं मातृकया विद्यया च समर्चयेत् । प्रातः प्रातः मातृकाविद्याभ्यां त्रिवारमभिजप्तं निष्कत्रयमानं तद्घृतं लिहतः संवत्सरात् प्रोक्तफलसिद्धिरिति॥६८॥६९॥

शिव इत्यादि हुनेदित्यन्तेन श्लोकद्वयेन अर्कादिसप्तवाराणां प्रतिवारं देवताद्वयं तत्पूजादिकं तत्प्रयोजनं चोपदिशति। तत्र रमा—लक्ष्मीः। आरः—भौमः। सितसौरय इति स्वातन्त्र्यात् । सितसौरोत्यर्थः । सितः—शुक्रः ॥७०॥तेषु सप्तस्वर्कादिष्विति शेषः। तान् - वारेशान्। द्विविधान्। तत्तद्दिनजविद्यया-तत्तद्दिननित्याविद्यया। नामसप्ताक्षरीयुक्त्या—तत्तन्नाम तदन्ते च सप्ताक्षरीयुक्त्येत्यर्थः। हुनेत्—जुहुयात्। तेन वाञ्छितसिद्धिः स्यादिति शेषः। एतदुक्तं भवति—अर्कादिषु सप्तसु वारेषु प्रतिवारं प्रोक्तान् द्विविधान् वारेशान् प्रोक्तक्रमेण द्वौ द्वौ तत्तद्दिननित्याविद्यायुक्तेन सप्ताक्षर्यन्तेन तत्तन्नाममन्त्रेण तत्तन्मण्डले पूजातर्पणहोमादिना वाञ्छितसिद्धिरिति ॥७१॥

वर्णौषधीत्यादिना यावदायुषमित्यन्तेन श्लोकद्वयेन वक्ष्यमाणविद्यया मातृकावर्णौषधिभस्मना मातृकायन्त्रलेखनप्राणप्रतिष्ठापुरःसरं विद्यामातृकाभिजप्तेन विद्यया समेतया मातृकया वक्ष्यमाणमातृकाक्षरस्थानेषु क्रमेण सन्ध्ययोः स्पर्शतः सर्वापद्भ्यो रक्षा भवति सर्वेषामित्युपदिशति ॥७२॥७३॥

---

(३) कृतेन तु इति सी० पु० पा० ।

क्रूरेषु व्याधिषु प्राप्तेष्वभ्यर्च्यैवं तु मण्डले ।
नवकोष्ठे नव प्रोक्तान् राहुकेतुसमन्वितान् ॥७४॥
मध्येन्द्रयमपाशीन्दुवह्निरक्षोऽनिले(ख)परे ।
कोष्ठे तांस्तैर्यजेत्सद्योमुक्तरोगः सुखी भवेत् ॥७५॥
ग्रहार्त्तिषु रिपुक्लेशे दुर्भिक्षे त्रिविधे तथा ।
उत्पाते समरोद्योगे कुर्यादुक्तार्चनादिकम् ॥७६॥
सम्पूज्य तद्विदां सम्यग्दद्याद्गां स्वर्णमम्बरम् ।
तेन सर्वापदुन्मुक्तः सुखी जीवति भूतले ॥७७॥
ब्रूहि मे मातृकान्यासं तद्यन्त्रं परमेश्वर ! ।
कथयामि द्वयं तेऽद्य वक्ष्ये तत्पटलेऽखिलम् ॥७८॥
ह्रस्वदीर्घस्वरद्वन्द्वपुटितैः षण्ढवर्जितैः ।
कुर्यादङ्गानि षड्वर्गैः पञ्चपञ्चदशाक्षरैः ॥७९॥

क्रूरेष्वित्यादिभिर्भूतले इत्यन्तैश्चतुर्भिः श्लोकैर्नवग्रहपूजया विपत्तारणमुपदिशति । तत्र — एवं — अष्टाविंशपटलवक्ष्यमाणप्रकारतः । मण्डले नवकोष्ठगते — तत्तन्मण्डले इत्यर्थः ॥७४॥ मध्येत्यादिना ग्रहाणां वक्ष्यमाणं दिग्विभागं स्मारयति । शुभाशुभक्रमात् । तान् — नवग्रहान् । तैः — उक्तप्रकारैर्दिननित्यासप्ताक्षरीमध्यगतैर्नवभिर्नाममन्त्रैः ॥७५॥ त्रिविधे इत्यस्य उत्पाते इत्यत्रान्वयः ॥७६॥ तद्विदां — विद्याविदाम् । गां — धेनुम् । तेन — अर्चनादिना । एतदुक्तं भवति प्राक्प्रत्यक्दक्षिणोदगग्रैश्चतुर्भिः सूत्रैः समान्तरालं नवकोष्ठानि निष्पाद्य तेषूक्तक्रमेण नवग्रहाणां अष्टाविंशपटलवक्ष्यमाणानि मण्डलानि विधाय तत्र तत्तद्दिननित्यासप्ताक्षरीमध्यगतैस्तत्तन्नाममन्त्रैर्नवभिः पूजातर्पणहोमादिना तद्विद्याविदां सम्पूजनस्वर्णादिदानेन सर्वापद्भ्योविमुक्तः सुखी भवतीति ॥७७॥

ब्रूहीत्यादिभिर्न्यसेदित्यन्तैरष्टभिः श्लोकैर्मातृकाषडङ्गन्यासादिकं मातृकान्यासं चोपदिशति । तत्र तद्यन्त्रं — मातृकायन्त्रम् । द्वयं — न्यासं यन्त्रं च । अद्य-अस्मिन् पटले । तत्पटले — मातृकापटले । अखिलं — अन्यदितिशेषः ॥७८॥

ह्रस्वेत्यादिना द्वयमित्यन्तेन त्रिपादाधिकेन एकेन श्लोकेन एतदुक्तं भवति — स्वरेषु — ऋॠऌॡ इति चत्वारि षण्ढाक्षराणि । तद्वर्जितैरन्यैर्द्वादशभिः अइउए-

स्वरेषु मध्यतः प्रोक्तास्त्वारः षण्ढविग्रहाः।
कराङ्गयोर्विधायेत्थं आदिक्षान्ताक्षराणि वै ॥८०॥
भाले वक्त्रावृती नेत्रश्रोत्रनासाकपोलतः।
ओष्ठदन्तशिरोजिह्वास्वेकशोविन्यसेत्स्वरान् ॥८१॥
करयोः पादयोर्मूलमध्यसन्धिष्वथाग्रतः।
विन्यसेच्चतुरोवर्गान् पञ्चमं पार्श्वपृष्ठतः ॥८२॥
नाभौ हृदि च विन्यस्य व्यापकान् दशधातुषु।
त्वगसृङ्मांसमेदोऽस्थिमज्जाशुक्रान्तगामिषु ॥८३॥
प्राणशक्त्यात्मसु तथा न्यसेदेवं समाहितः।
हृदयस्पर्शिनां तेषां स्मरन् धातुषु विन्यसेत् ॥८४॥
अथवा हृदये स्कन्धयुगे च त्रिककक्षयोः।
(१)हृदयाधस्तथापादजठरे वदने न्यसेत् ॥८५॥

ओम् इति षड्भिर्ह्रस्वैः, आ ई ऊ ऐ औ अः इति दीर्घस्वरैः षड्भिश्च सविन्दुकैः कचटतपवर्गान् पञ्चपञ्चाक्षरान् यादिकं दशाक्षरं वर्गं च सविन्दुकान् तान् प्रोक्तक्रमेण पुटितान् कृत्वा तैः षड्भिः अन्ततो जातियुक्तैर्मन्त्रैः कराङ्गन्यासं कुर्यादिति ॥७९॥८०॥

आदिक्षान्तेत्यादिभिः न्यसेदित्यन्तैः पादाद्यैः पञ्चभिः श्लोकैर्देहे मातृकाक्षर-विन्यासक्रममुपदिशति। तत्र मूलमध्यसन्ध्योः। मूलसन्ध्योरितिदोःकूर्परयोः, मध्यसन्ध्योरितिमणिबन्धाङ्गुलि मूले चोच्येते, पादयोस्तु मूलमध्यशब्देन कटी जानुनी उच्येते। तत्र मध्यसन्धिद्वयमिति प्रपदाङ्गुलिसन्धो उच्येते। पञ्चमं वर्गमिति-शेषः ॥८१॥८२॥ व्यापकान्—वर्णानितिशेषः। यादिक्षान्तानां व्यापकत्वं तेषां धात्वादिस्वरूपत्वात् ॥८३॥ प्राणशक्त्यात्मसु—प्राणशक्त्यात्मानोपि धातुत्वेनेष्यन्ते। तेषां—धातूनाम्। द्वितीयार्थे षष्ठी धातूनित्यर्थः ॥८४॥ अथवा—पक्षान्तरे। त्रिके अपरगतं* हृदयाद्धस्तपादाग्रं हृदयादि हस्तयोरग्रावधि परामृशन् सकारं हृदयादिपादयुगाग्रावधि परामृशन् हकारं च न्यसेदित्यर्थः ॥८५॥

---

(१) हृदयाद्धस्तपादाग्रे जठरे सी० पु० पा०। * त्रिकोणपरगले इति टी० पु० पा०।

वृत्तद्वयावृतं चाष्टपत्रमब्जं(२) महीपरम् ।
विधाय विलिखेन्मध्ये हंसहृदनशक्तिजम् ॥८६॥
कूटं स्वरान् केशरेषु वर्गान् पत्रेषु चालिखेत् ।
पञ्चपञ्चाक्षरोपेतान्(३) दारुचाम्बुनि दिक्षु च ॥८७॥
स्वरेष्वपुनरुक्तानि पञ्चान्यानि तु पञ्च वै ।
सव्यञ्जनाव्यञ्जनत्वभेदतोऽभूद्द्विरन्वयः ॥८८॥
सवाताग्निधरात्वेन शक्तिस्तत्पञ्चकं भवेत् ।
अन्यान्येकादश शिवे ! सन्धिमात्रादि सम्भवा ॥८९॥

वृत्तद्वयेत्यादिभिर्वितन्वत इत्यन्तैः सप्तभिः श्लोकैर्मातृकायन्त्रनिर्माणं तद्विनियोगं तत्फलानि चोपदिशति । तत्र हंसहृदनशक्तिजं कूटं हकार-सकारऔकारविसर्जनीयैः संहतैरेकं कूटाक्षरम् ॥८६॥ स्वरान् केसरेषु—षोडश-स्वरान् केसरेषु प्रतिदलमूलं द्वन्द्वशोलिखेत् । वर्गान्—कादीन् पञ्चपञ्चा-क्षरोपेतान् वर्गानित्यन्वयः । सप्तेतिशेषः । दावाम्बु—ठकारवकारौ । दिक्षु ठकारं विदिक्षु वकारं चालिखेदिति केचन कथयन्ति । तदस्माकं नाभिमतम् । उभयमप्यष्टसु दिक्षु लेख्यमित्यस्मत्सम्प्रदायार्थः ॥८७॥ अपुनरुक्तपञ्चस्वराक्षराणि वक्ष्यमाणानि अष्टमे दले लिखेदित्यर्थः । अन्यानि तु पञ्च वै—अन्येषु सप्तसु दलेषु पञ्चपञ्चाक्षराणि लिखितानि । वै इति हेतौ । सव्यञ्जना-व्यञ्जनत्वभेदतः—स्वराणां स्थितिर्द्विविधा व्यञ्जनाश्लिष्टा एका स्वयं राजते इति स्वरशब्दनिर्वाहात् । स्वतन्त्रा चापरा । तेनाष्टदलकेसरयोर्द्विरन्वयः । एतदुक्तं भवति—स्वरेषु वक्ष्यमाणान्यपुनरुक्तानि पञ्चाक्षराणि अष्टमे दले विलिखे-दिति । तत्राष्टमे दले पञ्चाक्षरलेखनन्तु अन्येषु सप्तसु दलेषु पञ्चपञ्चाक्षराणां लिखितत्वात् । एवं व्यञ्जनसहितत्वेन व्यञ्जनरहितत्वेन च स्वराणां द्विधा स्थितत्वात् अत्र द्विरन्वयो भवति ॥८८॥ सवाताग्निधरात्वेन शक्तिः—अकार-इकार-उकार-विन्दुसहितो विसर्जनीयः । तत्पञ्चकं—अपुनरुक्तस्वराक्षरपञ्चकम् । एतदुक्तं भवति—अकार-इकार-उकार-विन्दु-विसर्जनीयाक्षराणि स्वरेष्वपुन-रुक्तानि । इतराणि तेषामेव सवर्णदीर्घादितः सम्भूतानि चत्वारि षण्ढाक्षराणि

---

(२) वृत्तं वृत्तद्वयावृतं चाष्टपत्र इति मू० पु० पा० । (३) वर्णान् वादीन्विदिक्षुचेति मू० पु० पा० ।

एतद्यन्त्रस्य मध्यस्थं नाम कृत्वा प्रयोजयेत्।
प्रातर्मूर्ध्नि स्मरेदिन्दुबिम्बस्थं सर्वसम्पदम् ॥९०॥
अभिषेकाद्धारणाच्च पूजनाल्लोहकल्पिते।
स्थापनाद्गृहदेशादौ यन्त्रं सर्वार्थसिद्धिदम् ॥९१॥
एतद्यन्त्रस्य मध्यस्था देवताः सकला अपि।
सन्निधिं फलदानं च साधकानां वितन्वते ॥९२॥

अकाररहितरेफलकारेण विभक्तरूपाणि। तेन तेषां पञ्चानामेव स्वरेषु प्राधान्यमन्यान्येकादशाक्षराणि सन्धिमात्रादिसम्भूतत्वात् पुनरुक्तानीति। यन्त्रविरचनाक्रमो यथा—स्वाभिमतमानेन भ्रमेण वृत्तं कृत्वा तद्बहिश्च एकाङ्गुलमानेन वृत्तं कृत्वा द्वितीयवृत्तव्यासार्द्धमानेन तद्बहिश्च वृत्तं कृत्वा तदन्तरष्टदलानि दिग्विभागेन कृत्वा तदन्तः केशरस्थानं च समान्तरालषोड़शरेखाभिः षोड़शधा कृत्वा तद्बहिरेकाङ्गुलमानेन चतुर्थं वृत्तं विधाय तस्य त्र्यङ्गुलात् बहिश्चतुरस्रमेकं रेखाग्राष्टशूलोपेतं कृत्वा कर्णिकायां हकारसकार—औकार—विसर्जनीयोपेतां शक्तिप्रसादाख्यामेकाक्षररूपां विद्यां हकारसकारान्तरालस्थनामवतीमालिख्य केशरस्थानेषु षोड़शस्वग्रादिप्रादक्षिण्येन षोड़शस्वरानालिख्य बहिरष्टदलेषु अग्रादिप्रादक्षिण्यक्रमेण कचटतपयशादीन् पञ्चाक्षरान् सप्तवर्गान् सप्तसु दलेषु समालिख्य अष्टमे अ इ उ अं अः इति पञ्चाक्षराणि समालिख्य चतुर्थवृत्तात् बहिरष्टसु दिक्षु प्राग्वत् ठकारवकारौ बहिरष्टौ समालिखेत्—सर्वाणि प्रोक्तान्यक्षराणि कर्णिकास्थाक्षरमन्तरेण सबिन्दून्यालिखेदिति ॥८९॥ एतद्—यन्त्रमितिशेषः ॥९०॥ लोहकल्पिते-यन्त्र इतिशेषः। पूजनादित्यस्यान्तेनान्वयः। स्थापनात्—यन्त्रस्येतिशेषः। आदिशब्दोग्रामादिविषयः ॥९१॥

एतद्यन्त्रस्येत्यादिना श्लोकेन सकलदेवताचक्रप्रतिष्ठासु हेमरजताभ्राणामन्यतमेन कृते पट्टे यन्त्रमुत्कीर्य मध्ये सन्निधेहीति नामाक्षरोपेतं सप्राणप्रतिष्ठं मासमात्रमभ्यर्चितं लक्षजप्तमातृकं प्रथमं तत्त्ववित् पूर्णात्मा सुपूजितम् संस्थाप्य तन्मध्ये सकलदेवतावेरं स्थापयेत्। एवं कृते तस्मिन् वेरे तासां देवतानां स्फुरणं समीचीनं भवति। स्थापयितुर्मनीषितफलं च सम्भवतीत्युपदिशति ॥९२॥

विद्यां तान्तु नरोमूर्खो जडोमूकोऽतिपातकी ।
नित्यशोजपपूजाद्यैः काले मत्समतां व्रजेत् ॥९३॥
जिह्वायामत्तराख्येतान्यसकृद्भावयेद्धिया ।
प्रविष्टोविद्वद्गोष्ठीषु(१) युज्यते वाग्मिभिर्जनैः ॥९४॥
मूर्द्धेन्दुबिम्बमध्यस्थं सुधावर्षविधायिनम् ।
विभावयन्निति मनुं जपेदेकाग्रमानसः ॥९५॥
मण्डलात्कवितासिद्धिः सर्वभाषामयी भवेत् ।
वादादिषु तु सर्वत्र देवतात्मा जयी भवेत् ॥९६॥
यन्त्राणि नित्यानित्यायाः समान्येकात्मयोगतः ।
प्रयोगजातमन्योन्यं विदध्यादैक्ययोगतः ॥९७॥
तेनात्मनोक्तानि शिवे ! सर्वसिद्धिकराणि वै ।
षोड़शस्वपि नित्यासु यन्त्रादन्यत्समोरितुम् ॥९८॥

विद्यानामित्यादिना भवेदित्यन्तैः चतुर्भिः श्लोकैः कुलसुन्दरीविद्यायाः प्रयोगविशेषैः फलविशेषानुपदिशति। तत्र तां—कुलसुन्दरीं विद्याम् । मूर्खः—अज्ञः । जड़ो –बालः । आद्यशब्दस्तर्पणहोमादिविषयः । मत्समतां – शिवसमताम् ॥९३॥ अक्षराख्येतानि—कुलसुन्दरीविद्याया इतिशेषः ॥९४॥ सुधावर्षविधायिनं—इन्दुमण्डलचोभतः । मनुं—कुलसुन्दरोविद्यां विभावयन्नित्यन्वयः । जपेन्मनुमित्यन्वयः ॥९५॥ आदिशब्दोव्यवहारद्यूतादिविषयः । देवतात्मा—देवताहम्भावनया । वादव्यवहारादिषु सर्वत्र देवताहम्भावनया तत्तत्करणाद्विजयो भवेदित्यर्थः ॥९६॥

यन्त्राणीत्यादिना श्लोकेन षोडशपटले नित्यानित्याप्रोक्तानि यन्त्राणि विद्ययोरैकरूप्यादस्याश्च तान्यपि यन्त्राणि साधारणानीत्यतिदिशति। तत्र – तद्यन्त्रातिदेशादत्रोक्तं यन्त्रद्वयं च नित्यानित्यासाधारणम् ॥९७॥

षोड़शस्वपीत्यादिना श्लोकेन नित्यानां सर्वासां विशेषसामान्यविधानं विभजते। तत्र –अन्यदिति जपतर्पणहोमार्चासेकभावनादिकम् । ऐक्ययोगतः—आसां षोड़शा-

---

(१) प्रविश्याविद्यागोष्ठीषु इति मू० पु० पा० ।

वृत्तयुग्मं षडस्रं च कृत्वा मध्याद्यमध्यतः ।
नामालिख्य बहिः षट्सु तत्त्रयं स्वेन मायया ॥९९॥
विलिख्य मातृकां वृत्ते कृत्वा तद्धारणान्मुखे ।
जिह्वायां भावनात् सर्वगोष्ठीष्वग्रं विगाहते ॥१००॥
वाचातत्त्वमयी व्याप्तिरिति सम्यक् समीरिता ।
अस्या निष्कालनाच्चित्ते तत्तत्त्वं स्वात्मसात्कृतम् ॥१०१॥

इति श्रीषोडशनित्यातन्त्रेषु श्रीकादिमते पञ्चदशं पटलं परिपूर्णं परामृष्टम् ॥१५॥

नामिकरूपपरमार्थयोगतः । एतदुक्तं भवति—सर्वासां षोडशानां नित्यानां तत्तत्पटलप्रोक्तानि यन्त्राणि विधुराणि प्रयोगजातान्यन्योन्यमासामैक(क्य)-रूप्यात् साधारणानीति ॥९८॥

वृत्तयुग्ममित्यादिना विगाहतेइत्यन्तेन विद्यागोष्ठीविजयप्रदं यन्त्रमुपदिशति । तत्र मध्याद्यमध्यतः—कुलसुन्दरीविद्याया मध्यमकूटस्य आद्यस्य ककाराक्षरस्य मध्ये इत्यर्थः । तत्त्रयं—विद्याकूटत्रयम् । मायया—विसर्जनीयेन॥९९॥ अग्रं विगाहते—अग्रेसरोभवति—गरिष्ठोभवतीत्यर्थः । यन्त्रविरचनाक्रमो यथा—इष्टमानेन भ्रमेण वृत्तं विधाय तन्मध्ये प्राग्वदभिमतमानेन(१) षट्कोणं विस्तीर्य(२) वृत्ताद्ब-हिरेकाङ्गुलमानेन च वृत्तं कृत्वा षट्कोणस्य मध्ये विद्याया मध्यमकूटाक्षरमालिख्य तस्यादिभूतस्य ककारस्योदरे नामाभिलिख्य तस्य षट्सु कोणेषु अधस्थेषु त्रिषु (३)मध्यादिप्रादक्षिण्येन विद्याक्षराणि त्रीणि(४) सविन्दूनि क्रमात् समालिख्य उपरिस्थेषु त्रिषु कोणेषु अमुक्तप्रादक्षिण्यक्रमात् विसर्जनीयोपेतानि तानि समालिख्य बहिर्वृत्तवीथ्यामग्रादिप्रादक्षिण्येन सविन्दुकान्यकारादिक्षकारान्ता-न्येकपञ्चाशदक्षराणि समालिख्य गुलिकीकृत्य प्रोक्तक्रमोपेतमास्ये तां कृत्वा (५) तच्च जिह्वायां विभावयन् प्रोक्तानि फलान्यवाप्नोति इति ॥१००॥

---

(१) दभिमताङ्गुलेनेति टी० पु० पा० । (२) विरच्येति टी० पु० पा० ।
(३) सव्यादिप्रा इति टी० पु० पा० । (४) यन्त्राणीति टी० पु० पा० ।
(५) धृत्वेति टी० पु० पा० ।

इति श्रीषोडशनित्यातन्त्रेषु श्रीकादिमताख्यस्य तन्त्रस्य परिपूर्णस्य तन्त्रस्य प्रपञ्च-
सारसिंहराजप्रकाशाभिधानेन श्रीसुभगानन्दनाथेन विरचितायां
मनोरमाख्यायां व्याख्यायां शिवदूतीनित्याविद्याविधान-
प्रकाशनपरं पञ्चदशपटलं परिपूर्णं
परामृष्टम् ॥ १५ ॥

ग्रन्थसङ्ख्या—

अत्र यन्त्रद्वयं प्रोक्तं व्याख्याग्रन्थाः शतत्रयात् ।
सत्रिपादोनविंशाः स्युः पटले दशपञ्चके ॥

अथ षोड़शं पटलम् ।

अथ षोड़शनित्यासु या प्रोक्तैकादशी तु ताम् ।
नित्यानित्यां शृणु प्राज्ञे! यदायत्तमिदं जगत् ॥१॥
विद्योद्धारः (१) कृतः पूर्वं तद्विधानमिहोच्यते ।
यासौ समस्तजीवानां देह(२)स्थितिविधायिनी ॥२॥
न्यासं ध्यानं ततः शक्तीस्ताभिः पूजां च साधनम् ।
यन्त्राणि वज्ररूपाणि षड़ाधारेषु संस्थितिम् ॥३॥
निग्रहानुग्रहौ षड् भिः कालव्याप्तिरिति क्रमात् ।
दीर्घस्वरसमेताभ्यां हंसहृद्भ्यां षड़ङ्गकम् ॥४॥

अथ षोड़शपटलम् ।

पूर्वस्मिन् पञ्चदशे पटले दशम्याः कुलसुन्दरीनित्याविद्याया विधानमुपदिश्यानन्तरमेकादश्या नित्यानित्याया विधानमुपदिशति । अथ षोडशेत्यादिना सर्वत इत्यन्तेन श्लोकात्मकरूपेण षोडशेन पटलेन । अत्र षोडशेत्यादिभिः क्रमादित्यन्तैरध्यर्द्धैस्त्रिभिः श्लोकैः पटलार्थानुद्दिशति । तत्र यदायत्तं—नित्यानित्याधीनम् । जगत्—जङ्गमम् । देहस्थितिकरत्वात् ॥१॥ पूर्वं—तृतीये पटले । तद्विधानं—विद्याविधानम् । समस्तजीवानां—समस्तप्राणिनाम् । देहस्थितिविधायिनी—षडाधारादिस्थितत्वात् ॥२॥ संस्थितिम्—देवतानामिति शेषः । एतदुक्तं भवति—षड़ाधारेषु डाकिन्यादीनां षण्णां देवतानामवस्थितिं तदधिष्ठातृरूपत्वेन नित्यानित्यायाः स्थितिं च वक्ष्यामीति ॥३॥ षड् भिः—आधारदेवताभिर्डाकिन्यादिभिः । (३) फलावाप्तिम्—कालेन देवताया ऐक्यव्याप्तिं च ॥

दीर्घस्वरेत्यादिना युतमित्यन्तेनार्द्धाधिकेन श्लोकेन न्यासक्रममुपदिशति । तत्र-दीर्घस्वरसमेताभ्यां—प्राग्वत् हंसहृद्भ्यां हकारसकाराभ्यां ह्सां ह्सीं इत्यादिभिर्जातियुक्तैर्मन्त्रैः प्राग्वत् षड़ङ्गानि विन्यसेदित्यर्थः॥४॥ विद्याक्षराणि—कूटप्रोक्तानि

---

(१) नित्योद्धार इति मू० पु० पा० । (२) देवस्थिति इति मू० पु० पा० ।
(३) कालव्याप्तिम् इति टी० पु० पा० । फलावाप्तिकालेन इति मं० पु० पा०

भ्रूमध्ये कण्ठहृन्नाभिगुह्याधारेषु च क्रमात् ।
विद्याक्षराणि क्रमशोन्यसेद्बिन्दुयुतानि तु वै ॥५॥
व्यापकं च समस्तेन विधाय विधिना युतम् ।
ध्यायेत् समस्तसम्पत्तिहेतोः सर्वात्मिकां शिवाम् ॥६॥
उद्यद्भास्करबिम्बाभ्यां माणिक्यमुकुटोज्ज्वलाम् ।
पद्मरागकृताकल्पामरुणांशुकधारिणीम् ॥७॥
चारुस्मितलसद्वक्त्रषट्सरोजविराजिताम् ।
प्रतिवक्त्रं त्रिनयनां भुजैर्द्वादशभिर्युताम् ॥८॥
(१)पाशेक्षुगुणपुण्ड्रेक्षुचापखेटत्रिशूलकान् ।
वहन्तीं वरदां वामैरङ्कुशं पुस्तकं तथा ॥९॥
पुष्पेक्षु मण्डलाग्रञ्च नृकपालाभये तथा ।
दधानां दक्षिणैर्हस्तैर्ध्यायेद्देवीमनन्यथा ॥१०॥
अनन्ताः शक्तयोदेव्यास्तास्वा(२)कर्णय वदामि ते ।
ललिताशक्तिद्वन्द्वोऽयं(३) बीजद्वयमथोक्रमात् ॥११॥

हकारादि डकारान्तानि संकेतविद्याविधुराणि षड़क्षराणि । विन्दुयुतानि—प्रत्येकं विन्दुयुक्तानि । एतदुक्तं भवति—विद्याया हकारादिडकारान्तानि प्रत्येकं विन्दुयुक्तानि प्रोक्तेषु षट्सु स्थानेषु क्रमादेकैकशोन्यसेदिति ॥५॥ व्यापकं—प्राग्वत् । समस्तेन—त्रिभिः कूटैः सङ्केतविद्योपेतैः ॥

ध्यायेदित्यादिभिरनन्यधीरित्यन्तैरर्द्धाद्यैश्चतुर्भिः श्लोकैर्देव्या नित्यसपर्याध्यानमुपदिशति । तत्र सर्वात्मिकां—सर्वचैतन्यरूपत्वात् । चैतन्यरूपत्वन्तु धातुरूपदेहात्मिकानां डाकिन्यादोनामधिष्ठातृरूपस्वात्मरूपत्वात् ॥६॥७॥ वक्त्रषट्(क)सरोजविराजितां—षड्वक्त्रपद्मविराजितामित्यर्थः॥८॥ भुजेष्वायुधान्यूर्द्ध्वादि कल्पयेत् । खेटं—चर्मफलकम्॥९॥ मण्डलाग्रं खड्गविशेषः । नृकपालं—शिरःकपालम्॥१०॥

अनन्ता इत्यादिभिरानता इत्यन्तैः पञ्चभिः श्लोकैर्देव्या आवरणशक्तीरुपदिशति । अत्र अनन्ता इत्यत्र शक्तीनामक्षरविग्रहत्वान्न वक्तुं शक्यते । देव्या अनन्तशक्ति-

---

(१) पाशाङ्कुशपुण्ड्र इति मू० पु० पा० ।
(२) तास्त्वाकर्णय काश्चन इति मू० पु० पा० । (३) शक्तिद्वन्द्वाद्या इति मू० पु० पा० ।

पूर्णमण्डलवर्णाः स्युस्ते शक्तीति च संयुताः ।
सप्ताद्यर्या(१) युता संज्ञा विद्याः स्युर्द्वादशाक्षराः ॥१२॥
षट्सप्तत्या ऽपिच शतं यजेत्ताभिर्वृतां शिवाम् ।
षट्कोणकोणेष्वासीनां डाकिन्याद्यास्तथाऽर्चयेत्(२) ॥१३॥
रक्षोनिलेन्द्रवह्नीशवरुणेषु क्रमाच्च ताः ।
डाकिनीं शाकिनीं पश्चाल्लाकिनीं काकिनीमपि ॥१४॥
साकिनीं हाकिनीं मूले देवीसदृशविग्रहाः ।
हेतोस्तामभितः शक्तिरूपास्तन्मुकुटानताः ॥१५॥
कृतन्यासार्घसङ्कल्पः पूजयेदीरितक्रमात् ।
कुर्याच्च नित्यहोमन्तु जपेद्विद्यां यथोदितम् ॥१६॥

परिवारत्वन्तु स्वात्मस्वरूपत्वात् । काश्चन आकर्ण्य—वक्ष्यमाणशक्तीरितिशेषः ॥११॥ पूर्णमण्डलवर्णाः—अकारादयः क्षः इत्यन्ताः प्रोक्तसङ्ख्याः । अकारादि क्षकारान्तानां षट्त्रिंशद्वर्णानां प्रत्येकं षोडशस्वरयोजनेन षट् सप्तत्यधिकपञ्चशतसंख्याः एषां पूर्णमण्डलस्वं पञ्चविंशपटले वक्ष्यमाणत्वादिह नोच्यते । संज्ञाविद्या—नामरूपाविद्याः द्वादशाक्षराः—ह्रीं श्रीं अं शक्तिपादुकां पूजयामीत्यादिकाः ह्रीं श्रीं क्षः शक्तिपादुकां पूजयामि इत्यन्ताः एवंरूपेण द्वादशाक्षराः इत्यर्थः । तासां शक्तीनां वर्गक्रमेण षोडशदलानि षट्त्रिंशत्पद्मानि षट्कोणाद्बहिः कृत्वा तेषु दलेषु ताः शक्तीः पूजयेदिति सम्प्रदायः । अथवा वर्गद्वयक्रमेण द्वात्रिंशद्दलानि अष्टदलपद्मानि कृत्वा तेषु ताः समर्चयेदिति स्वपारम्पर्यार्थः । डाकिन्यादीनां षट्कोणेष्वत्रोक्तानि स्थानानि पूर्वमेव व्याख्यातानि ॥१२॥१३॥१४॥ मूलदेवीसदृशविग्रहाः नित्यानित्यासमानरूपाः । तन्मुकुटाः—तत्तदायुधोपेतमुकुटाः । नताः—(कृताञ्जलयः प्रह्वा) कुचभरनम्राः तत्तद्भजस्थानस्थिताः । सर्वसाधारणमेतत् ॥१५॥

कृतेत्यादिभिर्गता इत्यन्तैः पञ्चभिः श्लोकैः चक्रविशेषैःशक्तिविशेषैश्च त्रिविधं पूजाक्रममुपदिशति । तत्र अर्घसङ्कल्पः—प्रागवत् । ईरितक्रमात्—प्रोक्तक्रमात् । यथोदितं—प्रागवत् ॥ १६ ॥ शताद्यैकदलान्वितं—एकपञ्चाशद्दलान्वितमित्यर्थः ।

---

(१) सप्ताद्यर्यन्तकाः संज्ञा इति मू० पु० पा० । (२) डाकिन्यादीन्वतस्तथा इति मू० पु० पा० ।

(१)षट्कोणाद्बहिरज्वन्तशताब्जैकदलान्वितम् ।
कृत्वा तेष्वपि ताभिस्तु वृतां पूजासु मध्यमाः(२) ॥१७॥
द्विचतुःषट्दशदलैर्द्वादशाष्टद्वयच्छदैः ।
पद्मैरावृत्तषट्कोणे (३)यजेल्लघ्वीस्मृतार्चनात् ॥१८॥
चतुरस्रद्वयं बाह्ये चतुर्द्वारसमन्वितम् ।
विधाय तेषु शाखासु शक्तीनां विंशतिं यजेत् ॥१९॥
ब्राह्म्यादिलोकपालाख्याः षोडशद्वारसंस्थिताः ।
अनन्तब्राह्मनियतिकालरूपा विगर्हिताः ॥२०॥

ताभिः—अकारादिक्षकारान्तैकपञ्चाशदक्षराणां शक्तिभिः ॥१७॥ अष्टद्वयच्छदैः—षोड़शदलैः ॥१८॥ शक्तीनां विंशतिम् – ब्राह्म्यादिलोकपालान्तानामष्टादशशक्तीनां नियतिकालशक्तिद्वयेन विंशतित्वम् । एतदुक्तं भवति—इष्टमानेन भ्रमेण वृत्तं कृत्वा तद्बहिः—षट्कोणोपेतं वृत्तं कृत्वा तद्बहिः सम्प्रदायात् षोड़शदलानि षड्विंशत्पद्मानि कृत्वा तद्बहिस्त्र्यङ्गुलान्तरालं चतुरस्रद्वयं कृत्वा ततश्चतस्रषु दिक्षु द्वाराणि सशाखानि कृत्वा तत्र सर्वमध्ये देवीं बहिः षट्कोणेषु प्रोक्तक्रमेण डाकिन्यादिषट्कं तद्बहिः पूर्णमण्डलाक्षरशक्तीर्वर्गक्रमेणाक्षरक्रमेण च षट्त्रिंशत्पद्मेषु तत्तत्षोडशदलेषु च प्रोक्तक्रमेणाभ्यन्तरान्निर्गमनगत्या पूजयेत् । तद्बहिश्चतुरस्रे चतस्रषु दिक्षु पश्चिमद्वारदक्षपार्श्वादि तद्वामपार्श्वान्तं प्रादक्षिण्यक्रमेण चतुर्द्वारपार्श्वाष्टकस्थानेषु ब्राह्म्याद्यष्टशक्तीः प्रादक्षिण्यक्रमेणार्चयेत् । ततस्तत्र पूर्वद्वारोत्तरशाखादि उक्तद्वारदक्षिणशाखावसानं प्रादक्षिण्यक्रमेणाष्टसु शाखासु इन्द्रादीशान्तं लोकपालशक्तीरष्टावर्चयेत् । तदनु तत्रानन्तब्रह्मनियतिकालशक्तीराग्नेयादिषु ईशान्तेषु चतुर्षु दिक्कोणेषु प्रादक्षिण्यक्रमेणार्चयेदिति च सम्प्रदायार्थः । अथवा प्रोक्तषट्कोणाद्बहिः प्राग्वत् सम्प्रदायात् द्वात्रिंशद्द्वात्रिंशद्दलान्यष्टादशपद्मानि कृत्वा तत्र वर्गद्वयक्रमेण पूर्णमण्डलवर्णशक्तीः समभ्यर्च्य चतुरस्रे प्राग्वदर्चयेदेष पक्षस्योत्तमः । मध्यमस्तु प्रागुक्तषट्कोणाद्बहिरेकपञ्चाशद्दलं पद्मं कृत्वा तद्दलेष्वकारादिक्षकारान्तकपञ्चाशदक्षरशक्तीरन्यत् प्राग्वत् समर्चयेदिति । लघुप्रक्रियायां षट्कोणाद्बहिः षोड़शदलं तद्बहिर्द्वादशदलं तद्बहिर्दशदलं

---

(१) षट्कोणविरचैवित्तं इति मू०पु०पा० । (२)मध्यमम् इति मू० पु० पा । (३) यजेत् लघ्वी इति मू०पु०पा०

विदध्यात्साधनं प्राग्वद्वर्णलक्षं पयोव्रतः ।
त्रिस्वादुसिक्तैररुणैरम्बुजैर्हवनं तथा ॥२१॥
जपतर्पणहोमार्चासिकसिद्धमनुर्नरः ।
कुर्यादुक्तान् प्रयोगांश्च नचेत्तद्घातुदेवताः ॥२२॥
प्राणांस्तस्य ग्रसन्त्येव कुपितास्तत्क्षणं शिवे ! ।
अनया विद्यया लोके यन्न साध्यं न तत् क्वचित् ॥२३॥
विद्याक्षराणि सप्त स्युस्तैः प्राग्वत्स्वरसंयुतैः ।
शतं द्वादशसंयुक्तं तैर्यन्त्राणि वदामि ते ॥२४॥
वृत्तद्वयान्तः षट्कोणं तदन्तर्वृत्तयुग्मकम् ।
विधाय मध्ये मायास्थमेकमक्षरमाख्यया ॥२५॥
बहिः षडालिखेत्षट्सु वृत्तयोर्भूतमातृका ।
कृत्वा नवभिरेवं स्युः क्रमाद्यन्त्राणि षोडश ॥२६॥

तद्बहिः षट्दलं तद्बहिश्चतुर्दलं च पद्मं कृत्वाऽन्यत् प्राग्वद्विलिख्य तेषु पद्मेषु तत्तद्दलेषु लकारशक्तिरहिता अकारादिक्षकारान्तपञ्चाशदक्षरशक्तीः षडाधारोक्त पूजाक्रमेण प्राग्वदर्चयेत् इत्येवं त्रयः पद्मा इति ॥१८॥२०॥

विदध्यादित्यादिभिः क्वचिदित्यन्तैस्त्रिभिः श्लोकैर्विद्यासाधनविधिमसिद्धस्य प्रयोगकरणे प्रत्यवायं विद्याया अनुभावं चोपदिशति। तत्र प्राग्वत्—ललिता विद्यावत्। पयोव्रतः—क्षीराहारी। तथा—जपदशांशतः ॥२१॥ नचेत्तद्घातुदेवताः इत्यत्र तच्छब्दः सर्वेषां षड्धात्वधीशत्वात् ॥२२॥ तस्य प्रयोक्तुः ॥२३॥

विद्येत्यादिना श्लोकेन विद्याक्षराणां स्वरसंयोगेन यन्त्रार्थं विस्तारमुपदिशति। तत्र सप्त—अनाहत्तानि तानि प्रथमकूटाक्षराणि ॥२४॥

वृत्तद्वयेत्यादिना षोडशेत्यन्तेन श्लोकद्वयेन स्वरविकृतविद्याक्षरैः षोडशयन्त्राण्युपदिशति। तत्र मायास्थं—ह्रीं खास्थम्। एतदुक्तं भवति—अभिमतमानेन भ्रमेण वृत्तद्वयमेकाङ्गुलान्तरालमन्तर्बहिर्विभागेन कृत्वा तद्बहिः षट्कोणं तद्बहिस्तथाविधं वृत्तद्वयं कृत्वा सर्वमध्ये प्रोक्तेषु स्वरविकृतेषु द्वादशाधिकशतसङ्ख्येषु विद्याक्षरेषु आद्यं नामगर्भं ह्रीं खोदरे समालिख्य द्वितीयादिषु षडक्षराणि षट्सु कोणेषु अग्न्यादि प्रादक्षिण्येनालिख्यान्तर्वृत्तवीथ्यां कर्मानुरूपाणि

प्रथमेन धृतेन स्यादौदरव्याधिसंहृतिः ।
द्वितीयेन शिरोरोगा नश्यन्ति परमेश्वरि ! ॥२७॥
तृतीयेनाक्षिरुक्शान्तिः श्रोत्रजानां परेण तु ।
पञ्चमेन भुजारोगाः प्रयान्त्यूर्ध्वेन पादजाः ॥२८॥
सप्तमेनान्तराधिस्था धृतेन निधनाश्रयाः ।
धृतेनाष्टमयन्त्रेण ज्ञानेन्द्रियगता गदाः ॥२९॥
परेण कर्मेन्द्रियगा दशमेनानिलोद्भवाः ।
एकादशेन पित्तोत्था द्वादशेन कफोद्भवाः ॥३०॥
त्रयोदशेन दोषाणां सन्निपातसमुद्भवाः ।
प्रयान्ति विलयं सद्यो यन्त्राणां शक्तिवैभवात् ॥३१॥
चतुर्दशेन यन्त्रेण भूतप्रेतपिशाचकाः ।
प्रयान्ति भीताः क्षणतः सर्वेऽन्येपि ग्रहाः शिवे ! ॥३२॥

भूताक्षराण्यालिख्य बाह्यवृत्तवीथ्यामग्न्यादिप्रादक्षिण्येन मातृकां सबिन्दुकामालिखेत् । एतत् प्रथमं यन्त्रम् । एवं षट्कोणमध्यस्थैः कोणस्थैश्च एवं सप्तभिः पूर्वपूर्वलिखितोपरितनैः स्वरविकृतविद्याक्षरैरन्यानि पञ्चदश यन्त्राणि भवन्तीत्येवं पूर्वोक्तेन सह षोडश यन्त्राणि भवन्ति ॥२४॥२६॥

प्रथमेत्यादिभिरन्यथा इत्यन्तैर्नवभिः श्लोकैः षोडशानां यन्त्राणां समस्तरोगशान्तिषु विनियोगात् सर्वत्राभिषेकक्रमादिकं चोपदिशति । तत्र औदरव्याधिः गुल्मादिः । परमेश्वरीति देवीसम्बुद्धिः ॥२७॥ श्रोत्रजानां—रोगाणामितिशेषः । परेण— चतुर्थेन यन्त्रेणेतिशेषः । ऊर्ध्वेन—षष्ठेन यन्त्रेणेतिशेषः । प्राग्वत्—पादजा रोगा इति शेषः ॥२८॥ अन्तराधिस्था—अन्तराधिरिति कटेरूर्ध्वं कराधस्थात् करद्वयाधस्ताद्देहप्रदेशः तत्स्था रोगा इति शेषः । निधनाश्रयाः—मरणाश्रयभूताः अन्तराधिस्था इत्यत्रास्यान्वयः । ज्ञानेन्द्रियगताः—श्रोत्रत्वक्चक्षुर्जिह्वाघ्राणसम्भूताः । गदा - रोगाः ॥२९॥ परेण—नवमेन यन्त्रेणेतिशेषः । कर्मेन्द्रियगाः—वाक्पाणिपादपायूपस्थसम्भूताः । अनिलोद्भवाः— वातरोगसम्भवाः गदा इति शेषः । कफोद्भवाः—श्लेष्मदोषसमुद्भवाः । अस्मिन् प्रकरणे अनुक्तेषु विशेष्येषु रोगा इत्ये-

तत्परेण महारोगा धृतेनाष्टौ न बाधकाः ।
षोडशेन धृतेन स्यादायुरारोग्यमीश्वरि ! ॥३३॥
यन्त्राणि षोडशैतानि धारयेद्व्याधिशान्तये ।
सर्वेषां प्राणिनां सम्यगनुक्तेषु गदेष्वपि ॥३४॥
सर्वत्र यन्त्रधारणं साभिषेकं सदक्षिणम् ।
सवन्दनं सविश्वासं फलत्येवान्यथाऽन्यथा ॥३५॥
*कुर्विहीना तु सा विद्या पञ्चकूटाभिधा शिवे !
वाक्सिद्धिमन्यत्सकलं कुरुते न भिदा तयोः ॥३६॥
(१)तद्विद्याकूटभेदाः स्युर्विंशत्या शतसप्तकम् ।
तैर्वञ्जयन्त्रनिर्माणं फलानि च शृणु प्रिये ! ॥३७॥

तद्विशेषणम् ॥३०॥ त्रयोदशेन—यन्त्रेणेति शेषः । दोषाणां सन्निपातसमुद्भवा—वातादीनां त्रयाणां दोषाः सन्निपातात्समुद्भूताः । वैभवात्—अतिशयादित्यर्थः ॥३१॥ यन्त्रेणेत्येतदस्मिन् प्रकरणे यन्त्रानुक्तौ सर्वत्रान्वेति । ग्रहा—भूताद्याः । शिवे इति देवीसम्बुद्धिः ॥३२॥ तत्परेण—पञ्चदशेन । महारोगा—वातादयः । षोडशेन धृतेन—धृतेन षोडशेन यन्त्रेणेत्यर्थः । अत्र प्रकरणे सर्वसाधारणार्चनसेकस्थापनादिविनि युञ्ज्यादितिसम्प्रदायार्थः ॥३३॥ व्याधिशान्तये—सर्वव्याधिशान्तये । एतदुक्तं भवति—एतानि सर्वाणि षोडश यन्त्राणि अनुक्तेष्वन्येषु रोगेषु तत्तद्व्याधिशान्तये धारणादीनि कुर्यादिति । एतेन सर्वाणि यन्त्राणि प्रत्येकं सर्वरोगहराणि भवन्तीत्यर्थः ॥३४॥ सर्वत्र—अस्मिंस्तन्त्रे इतिशेषः । अन्यथाऽन्यथा—प्रोक्तान्यथाकरणे न फलत्ये(व) । एतदुक्तं भवति—सर्वसाधारणं यन्त्रधारणं यन्त्रेणाभिषेकं कृत्वाऽभिषेक्तुर्यावत्सन्तोषं वित्तानि च दत्त्वा तं समभिवन्द्यैतत्फलत्येवेति विश्वस्य यन्त्रधारणं कुर्यात् । एवं कृते फलत्येव अन्यथा न फलत्येव ॥३५॥

कुर्विहीनेत्यादिना श्लोकेन पञ्चकूटविद्याविधानं तस्याश्चैतद्विद्यात्मकत्वं चोपदिशति । तत्र कुर्विहीना—(ङ)उकारविहीना । न भिदा तयोः—षट्कूटपञ्चकूटविद्ययोः ॥३६॥

तद्विद्येत्यादिना श्लोकेन नित्यानित्याविद्याक्षराणां सन्दर्भभेदसञ्जातस्वरूप—

---

(१) तद्विद्याक्षरभेदा इति मू० पु० पा० । * कुचिहीना इति मू० पु० पा० ।

प्राक्प्रत्यगुदग्दक्षिणोदक्च सूत्राण्यष्टादश क्षिपेत् ।
तैस्तु कोष्ठानि जायन्ते नवाशीतिशतद्वयम् ॥३८॥
प्राग्वत्तत्कोणकोष्ठानि षटत्रिंशन्मार्जयेत्क्रमात् ।
मध्ये वज्रं यथा भूयात्तथा कुर्यात् समन्ततः ॥३९॥
सपञ्चचत्वारिंशत्कं शतं कोष्ठैस्तु वज्रकम् ।
त्र्यस्त्राणि चत्वार्यग्राणि चतुःकोष्ठैस्तु पूर्ववत् ॥४०॥
विधाय तस्य मध्याधःकोष्ठमारभ्य संलिखेत् ।
प्रादक्षिण्यप्रवेशेन कूट(ाँस्ताना)न्तस्याद्यखण्डजान् ॥४१॥
मध्येऽवशिष्टनवके वामदक्षत्रयद्वये ।
प्रतिलोमानुलोमात्मविद्याद्वयमथालिखेत्(१) ॥४२॥
शिष्टेषु त्रिषु कोष्ठेषु साधकाख्यां तदूर्ध्वगे ।
कर्ममध्येऽधरे साध्यमालिखेदपि सर्वतः ॥४३॥

संख्यापूर्वं वज्ररूपयन्त्रनिर्माणादिकं प्रस्तौति। तत्र तद्विद्याभेदाः—षट्कूटविद्यायाः पञ्चत्रिंशत्पटलवक्ष्यमाणक्रमेण अक्षराणां क्रमपौर्वापर्या(याता)त् स्वरूपभेदाः। तेषां सङ्केतविद्याखण्डत्रयपौर्वापर्यात् तत्प्रकारजनित सविंशति(२)शतत्रयाधिकचतुःसहस्रेषु सङ्केतविद्याखण्डजैर्भेदैरेव षड्यन्त्रनिर्माणमवोक्तम्। तैः—कूटभेदैः। प्रिये इति देवीसम्बुद्धिः ॥३७॥

प्रागित्यादिभिः शिवे इत्यन्तैरष्टभिः श्लोकैः प्रस्तुतविद्याकूटाक्षरभेदैः कोष्ठवज्राकाराणि षट्यन्त्राण्युपदिशति—तत्र षट्त्रिंशत् प्रतिकोणमितिशेषः ॥३८॥३९॥ त्र्यस्त्राणि चत्वार्यग्राणि—वज्रयन्त्रस्य चत्वार्यग्राणि त्रिकोणानि कुर्यादित्यर्थः। चतुःकोष्ठैस्तु पूर्ववत्—प्रतिदिशं चतुर्भिश्चतुर्भिः कोष्ठैरित्यर्थः॥४०॥ तस्य—यन्त्रस्य। मध्याधःकोष्ठं—अधस्थत्र्यस्त्रोपरिस्थपङ्क्तिस्थकोष्ठपञ्चकमध्यस्थकोष्ठम्। आद्यखण्डजान्—षट्स्वितिशेषः। तान् कूटान्विंशत्यधिकशतसङ्ख्याकान्। यस्मां तेषां क्रमेण विद्याक्षरषट्कोपक्रमत्वात् खण्डत्वम् ॥४१॥ मध्येऽवशिष्टनवके वामदक्षत्रयद्वये—मध्यस्थेषु नवसु कोष्ठेषु ऊर्ध्वाधःक्रमस्थितेषु त्रिपङ्क्तिकेषु कोष्ठेष्वित्यर्थः।

---

(१) याखिलात् इति सो० पु० पा०। (२) संविदसतिसत इति सं० पु० पा०

चतुस्त्रिकोणमध्यस्थं* द्विरेखाभिर्नवीकृतम् ।
मध्यावद्विलिखेत्तेषु वज्रयन्त्रमितीरितम् ॥४४॥
एवमन्यैः पञ्चभिश्च खण्डैः पञ्च प्रकल्पयेत् ।
इति षट्वज्रयन्त्राणि प्रोक्तानि क्रमशः शिवे ! ॥४५॥
लोहत्रयकृते(१) पट्टे शिलायां वा चतुर्षु वा ।

प्रतिलोमानुलोमात्मविद्याद्वयं—नित्यानित्याविद्यायास्त्रीणि खण्डानि कुर्यादित्यर्थः। ॥४२॥ प्रतिलोमानुलोमक्रमेण लिखेदित्यर्थः॥४३॥ द्विरेखाभि(र्न)वीकृतं—प्रतिकोणं समान्तरालं मध्यतस्त्रिरेखा(त्रता)मात्रानुगुण्येन द्विद्विक्रमेण षड्भीरेखाभि र्नव-त्रिकोणानि कुर्यादित्यर्थः। मध्यवद्विलिखेत्तेषु—तेषु त्र्यस्रोदरस्थत्रिकोणनवकेष्वपि वामदक्षिणपार्श्वस्थत्रिकोणत्रये प्राग्वद्विद्यां मध्यत्रिकोणत्रये साधकादिनामाक्षराणि च लिखेदित्यर्थः॥४४॥ पञ्चभिश्च खण्डैः—नित्याविद्यायाः प्रागुक्तरूपैः प्रत्येकं विंश-त्यधिकशतकूटाक्षरात्मभिरितिशेषः। एतदुक्तं भवति - प्राक्प्रत्यक्दक्षिणोदगग्राणि अष्टादशसूत्राणि समान्तरालानि कृत्वा तैः सञ्जातेषु नवाशीत्यधिकद्विशतसङ्ख्येषु कोष्ठेषु चतुर्षु कोणेषु प्रतिकोणं (षट्त्रिंशत्) षट्त्रिंशत्कोष्ठानि त्यक्त्वा प्राग्वन्मध्ये वज्राकारानुगुण्येन मार्जयेत्। पश्चादवशिष्टेषु वज्ररूपेषु पञ्चचत्वारिंशदधिकशत-सङ्ख्येषु कोष्ठेषु चतसृषु दिक्षु प्रतिदिशं चत्वारि चत्वारि कोष्ठानि मार्जयित्वा तत्र प्रागुक्तक्रमेण प्रतिदिशमेकैकक्रमेण चत्वारि त्रिकोणानि समत्रिरेखाणि विधाय तत्र त्रिकोणरेखात्रयं विभागीकृत्य तेषु मध्ये मध्ये चिह्नद्वयं (चिह्नद्वयं) विधाय चिह्नाच्चिह्नं सूत्रद्वयानुगुण्येन द्वयं द्वयमितिक्रमेण षड्रेखाः समालिखेत्। एवं कृते ऊर्ध्वाधःक्रमेण त्रिकोणत्रयं तत्पार्श्वयोरूर्ध्वयो(रूपं) स्त्रिकोणद्वयं (त्रिकोणद्वयं) तत्पार्श्वयोरेकैकमेकं त्रिकोणं इत्येवं नवकोणानि सम्भवन्ति। तत्राधःस्थत्रिकोणो-परिस्थपङ्क्तिकोष्ठपञ्चकमध्यस्थकोष्ठमारभ्य बाह्यवीथिकोष्ठेषु यावदुपक्रान्तकोष्ठं तत्सङ्ख्यानि कूटाक्षराणि प्रथमखण्डकूटाक्षरेष्वालिख्यामुक्तक्रममन्तः प्रविश्य द्वितीयपङ्क्तौ च प्राग्वदालिख्य एवमन्तर्यावद्विंशत्यधिकशतसङ्ख्यावसानविद्या-प्रथमकूटाक्षराणि विलिख्य मध्यतोऽवशिष्टेषु नवसु कोष्ठेषु मध्यगतेषु त्रिषु कोष्ठे-ष्वूर्ध्वाद्यधरान्तं क्रमेण साधककर्मसाध्याक्षराणि विलिख्य तेषां वामभागस्थपङ्क्ति-गतकोष्ठत्रये अधरकोष्ठादूर्ध्वकोष्ठान्तदक्षिणभागपङ्क्तिस्थकोष्ठत्रये ऊर्ध्वकोष्ठा-

---

(१) लोहत्रयफले इति मू० पु० पा०। * मध्यर्वर्ति मू० पु० पा०।

पट्टे वा फलकायां वा षट्कं षट्सु प्रकल्पयेत् ॥४६॥
फलकापट्टयोः पूजां कुर्यान्नित्यश एव तु ।
इतराणि तु संस्थाप्य यजेत्तत्रैव तां शिवाम् ॥४७॥
तत्स्थापनप्रदेशे तु विदध्यान्मण्डपं शुभम् ।
नवहस्तायामततं पताकातोरणान्वितम् ॥४८॥
फलपुष्पवितानाढ्यैः रूपैतं परिकल्पयेत् ।
उत्सेधायामविस्तारहस्तां वेदीं च मध्यतः ॥४९॥
एकं चेत् षट्कमथ चेत्कुर्याद्द्वे द्व्यादिकं तथा ।
(१)ईशप्राग्वह्निरक्षां(२) तु वायुदिक्षु यथाक्रमम् ॥५०॥
प्रथमं राक्षसि त्वन्यान्यन्येषूक्तक्रमेण वै ।
निवेद्य गन्धपुष्पाद्यैर्नृत्यगीतादिभिस्तथा ॥५१॥
समाराध्यैवमेवन्तु त्रिदिनं प्रोक्तशक्तिभिः ।
हुत्वा जपित्वा जीवोच्चे भानूच्चे वा स्थिरोदये ॥५२॥

अधःस्थकोष्ठान्तं च विद्यात्रिखण्डं समालिख्य बहिश्चतुर्दिक्षु लिखितत्रिकोणोदरस्थत्रिकोणनवकेष्वपि विद्यानामाक्षराणि मध्यवत् समालिखेत्। एतत् प्रथमं वज्रयन्त्रम्। एवमन्यान्यपि पञ्चवज्रयन्त्राणि विद्यायाः पञ्चभिः खण्डैः कुर्यात्। एवं पूर्वोक्तेन सार्द्धं षड्वज्रयन्त्राणि सम्भवन्तीति ॥४५॥

लोहत्रयेत्यादिभिरपि वा इत्यन्तैस्त्रयोदशभिः श्लोकैस्तेषां वज्रयन्त्राणां सामर्थ्यापादनार्थं मण्डपवेदिकानिर्माणं तत्र तेषां स्थापनं तत्र देवतामूर्तिसप्तकप्रतिष्ठां तदाराधनप्रकारं तत्फलानि फलकापटयोस्तद्यन्त्राणि विलिख्य तदाराधनस्य फलं चोपदिशति। तत्र शिलायां—दृषदि। षट्कं षट्सु एकद्व्यादिषु षट्स्वधिकरणेषु एकद्व्यादिकानि षट्सु प्रत्येकं वा यथाक्रममेकैकं सर्वाणि वा सर्वत्र वा षड्यन्त्राणि वज्ररूपाणि कल्पयेदित्यर्थः ॥४६॥ पूजां—यन्त्रस्येति शेषः। इतराणि—लोहत्रयशिलालिखितानि च षड्यन्त्राणि। तत्रैव—संस्थापितेषु वज्रेषु। तां—नित्यानित्याम् ॥४७॥ तत्स्थापनप्रदेशे—वज्रयन्त्रषट्कस्थापनप्रदेशे। ततं—

---

(१) ईशेति सो० पु० पा०। (२) रक्षोम्भ इति मू० पु० पा०।

स्ववाम(भा)गे भूम्युदये संस्थाप्य परमेश्वरि ! ।
देव्यात्मा तच्छिलाभिस्तु दृढमाबध्य तत्र वै ॥५३॥
देवीं षड्भिन्नं तां ताभिर्डाकिन्यादिभिरम्बिके ! ।
मूर्तिसप्तकमुत्पाद्य प्रतिष्ठाप्य समर्चयेत् ॥५४॥
नित्यशस्तत्पुरोविद्याभजनं चापि कारयेत् ।
यत्र तत्र गदालक्ष्मीरिपुग्रहपिशाचकाः ॥५५॥
दुर्भिक्षक्षुद्रकर्मोत्थपीड़ाकृत्याः परेरिताः ।
न कदाचित्सम्भवन्ति विद्यायन्त्रानुभावतः ॥५६॥
मङ्गलान्येव जायन्ते सर्वेषां सर्वतः सदा ।
धार्मिकाश्चैव राजानः पूर्णसप्ताङ्गसंयुताः ॥५७॥
फलकापटयोः क्लृप्तपूजातोनिजमन्दिरे ।
वाञ्छितं समवाप्नोति मण्डलान्मासतोऽपि वा ॥५८॥

विस्तारः॥४८॥ मध्यतः—मण्डपस्येति शेषः॥४९॥ एकं—यन्त्रमितिशेषः । षट्कं यन्त्राणामिति शेषः ॥५०॥ उक्तक्रमेण—डाकिन्यादीनां प्रागुत्तरयोवायुशक्रवह्नीश-वरुणदिक्षु स्थापनादित्यर्थः ॥५१॥ प्रोक्तशक्तिभिः—डाकिन्यादीनां परिवारभूता-भिर्वक्ष्यमाणाभिः । जीवोच्चे—बृहस्पतेरुभयोच्चे नित्योच्चे वा । भानूच्चेपि—तद्वत् स्थिरोदये—स्थिरराश्युदये ॥५२॥ भूम्युदये—श्वासपटलवक्ष्यमाणपृथिव्युदये । तत्—यन्त्रमिति शेषः । तत्र—वेदिकासु ॥५३॥ आदिशब्दोराकिन्यादिविषयः । मूर्तिसप्तकं—(डा)राकिन्यादीनां षण्णां देव्याश्चेति शेषः ॥५४॥ तत्पुरः—तासां सन्निधौ । विद्याभजनं—मूलविद्याभजनं कारयेदित्यर्थः ॥५५॥ क्षुद्रकर्मोत्थपीड़ाः विद्वेषणादिप्रयोगजाः क्लेशाः । विद्यायन्त्रानुभावतः—उभयोः सामर्थ्यात् ॥ ॥५६॥५७॥ क्लृप्तपूजातः—कृतयन्त्रषटकपूजनात् । मण्डलात्—प्राग्वत् । एतदुक्तं भवति—प्रोक्तानि षट्वज्ररूपाणि यन्त्राणि देवीनित्यपूजाचक्रं (यन्त्रं) च लोहत्रये शिलायां वा उक्तक्रमेण समुत्कीर्य तेषां स्थापनार्थं प्रोक्तायामविस्तारं पताकाद्यलङ्कृतं मण्डपं परिकल्प्य स्थापनीयं यन्त्रमेकं चेत् तन्मध्यतः प्रोक्तो-त्सेधायामविस्तारामेकां वेदिकां कृत्वा स्थापनीयानि यन्त्राणि षट् चेत् षट् वेदिकाः

आसां देहस्थितिं वक्ष्ये शृणु सर्वार्थदायिनीम् ।
सुषुम्नामध्यसंस्थेषु षड़ाधाराम्बुजेषु ताः ॥५९॥
तिष्ठन्ति प्राणिनां देव्यः सिद्ध्यन्ति ज्ञानपूजिताः ।
बहिश्च मण्डले पूजानुग्रहानिग्रहात्मिका(म्) ॥६०॥
*विशुद्धाख्ये कण्ठदेशे षोड़शस्वरपत्रके ।
धूम्रवर्णाम्बुजे देवीं डाकिनीं तत्समाकृतिम् ॥६१॥
शक्तिभिः स्वरूपाभिरावृतां तत्र पूजयेत् ।
तया सर्वज्ञतासिद्धिर्भवत्येव न संशयः ॥६२॥

प्रोक्तदिक्षु परिकल्प्य तन्मध्ये चैकां वेदिकामुत्पाद्य तत्र प्रोक्तक्रमेण षट् यन्त्राणि निवेश्य मध्ये वेदिकायां देवीनित्यपूजाचक्रं निवेश्य गन्धपुष्पधूपाद्यैस्तेषु यन्त्रेषु डाकिन्यादिभिर्वक्ष्यमाणाभिस्तत्परिवारशक्तिभिर्देवीं च दिनत्रयं समाराध्य प्रतिदिनं सहस्रवारं जपित्वा तद्दशांशं हुत्वा बृहस्पत्युच्चे द्विविधे तरणेरुच्चे तथा-विधेभानूच्चे वा स्थिरराश्युदये वा स्ववामनासापुटपृथिवीस्थानश्वासोदये वा तानि यन्त्राणि तासु वेदिकासु प्रोक्तक्रमेण संस्थाप्य शिलाभिर्दृढ़माबध्य तासु वेदिकासु प्रतिवेदिकं डाकिन्यादीनां षण्णां देव्याश्च मूर्तिसप्तकमुत्पाद्य प्रतिष्ठाप्य समभ्यर्च्य तासां सन्निधौ मूलविद्याभजनं चापि कारयेत् । एवं यत्र क्रियते तत्र-प्रोक्तान्यमङ्गलानि न सम्भवन्ति । प्रोक्तानि मङ्गलानि भवन्त्येव । एतानि सर्वाणि वा एकमेकं वा फलकायां पटे वा कृत्वा निजमन्दिरे क्वचित्स्थाने स्थापयित्वा पूजनात् प्रोक्तकालात् समस्तं वाञ्छितं प्राप्नोति ॥५८॥

आसामित्यादिभिरास्पदमित्यन्तैस्त्रयोदशभिः श्लोकैः षडाधारस्थानानि तन्ना-मानि तत्तद्गताम्बुजानि तत्तदम्बुजस्थान्यक्षराणि तत्तदम्बुजगतानि दैवतानि तत्त द्वर्णं तत्तदनुग्रहार्थं पूजाक्रमं तत्तन्निग्रहार्थं पूजाक्रमादिकं चोपदिशति । तत्र आसां—डाकिन्यादीनाम् । देहस्थितिं—सर्वप्राणिनां देहेषु स्थितिम् । ताः—देव्यः इत्यत्रान्वयः डाकिन्यादय इति शेषः ॥५९॥ ज्ञानपूजिताः—आसां देहाधिष्ठातृरूपत्वं परमार्थं गुरुमुखाज्ज्ञात्वा पूजिता इत्यर्थः । बहिश्च मण्डले--वक्ष्यमाणरूपे । पूजां वक्ष्ये इत्यत्रान्वयः ॥६०॥ तत्समाकृतिं—मूलदेव्या-समाकृतिम् । आसां वर्णस्तु तत्तदाधाराम्बुजसमानः । विग्रहस्तु मूलदेवतास-

* विशुद्धाख्ये इति मू० पु० पा० ।

अनाहताख्ये हृद्देशे सिन्दूरारुणपङ्कजे।
राकिनीं द्वादशदले कादिठान्ताक्षरात्मभिः ॥६३॥
शक्तिभिः पूजयेन्नित्यं कीर्त्यायुःश्रीधनाप्तये।
मणिपूरकसंज्ञे च नाभिस्थे दशपत्रके ॥६४॥
इन्द्रनीलनिभे डादि दशवर्णात्मशक्तिके।
लाकिनीं पूजयेद्देवि जयश्रीसम्भृद्धये ॥६५॥
ध्वजमूले समस्तापत्तारणायेष्टसिद्धये।
वादिषड्वर्णशक्तीभिरावृतां डाकिनीं यजेत् ॥६६॥
स्वाधिष्ठानाह्वये पद्मे बालार्कत्विषि षड्दले।
आधाराख्ये चतुष्पत्रे सुवर्णाभे सरोरुहे ॥६७॥
वादिशान्तार्णशक्तीभिरावृतां शाकिनीं यजेत्।
पायुध्वजान्तरा त्र्यस्रमध्ये तेजः समन्विताम् ॥६८॥
आज्ञाखेऽब्जे भ्रुवोर्मध्ये द्विदले शु(भ)द्वविग्रहे।
सेवितां हक्षशक्तिभ्यां हाकिनीं पूजयेत्तथा ॥६९॥
त्रिकालज्ञोनरः सर्व(तो)चिन्तालोकनकारिणीम्।
विश्वसृष्टिस्थितिध्वंसशक्तिदामप्ययत्नतः ॥७०॥
उक्तक्रमविपर्यासान्निग्रहोन्तर्बहिस्तथा।
पूजनं सर्वदुःखार्तिनाशनं सम्पदास्पदम् ॥७१॥

मानः ॥६१॥ तया—पूजया ॥६२॥६३॥६४॥६५॥६६॥ ध्वजमूले—मेहनमूले ॥६७॥ पायुध्वजान्तरा—गुदरन्ध्रमेहनान्तरालप्रदेशे। त्र्यस्रमध्ये तेजः समन्वितां—कुण्डलिनीतेजोरूपाम् ॥६८॥ तथा—समुच्चये ॥६९॥ चिन्तालोकनकारिणीं हाकिनीमित्यत्रान्वयः। साधकस्य चित्तेषु भूतभविष्यवर्तमानकार्यज्ञानसामर्थ्यप्रदायिनीमित्यर्थः ॥७०॥ अन्तर्बहिः—षडाधारेषु वक्ष्यमाणरूपे बाह्यगतयन्त्रे च। तथा—पूजनं अन्तर्बहिश्च उक्तवक्ष्यमाणक्रमानुलोमपूजनमित्यर्थः। एतदुक्तं भवति—प्रोक्तेषु कण्ठादिषु भ्रूमध्यान्तेषु षट्स्वाधारेषु प्रोक्तरूपाणां पद्मानां मध्ये डाकि-

भूमौ विधाय षट्कोणसप्तकं प्रोक्तदिक्क्रमात् ।
मध्ये च तत्र तां नित्यानित्या गन्धादिनाऽर्चयेत् ॥७२॥
अभितस्तत्षडस्रेषु तत्षट्कं तत्क्रमाद्यजेत् ।
बाह्येष्वपि च ताः प्राग्वत्प्रोक्तवर्णाः समर्चयेत् ॥७३॥
तासां षण्णामपि तथा षट्सु कोणेषु शक्तयः ।
षट्त्रिंशत्ताः समादेव्याः सर्वरूपायुधादिभिः ॥७४॥
प्राग्वत्स्वरेषु पञ्च स्युरपू(र्वा) कादिमान्तकाः ।
परेषु यवलक्षार्णरहिता स्तैस्तथाऽर्चयेत् ॥७५॥

न्यादिहाकिन्यन्ताः षट्देवता मूलदेवतासमानविग्रहास्तत्तदाधाराम्बुजप्रोक्तवर्णसमानरूपवर्णाः स्वस्वसमानाकारवर्णाभिरक्षरशक्तिभिः प्रत्येकमाधाराम्बुज प्रोक्तदलसङ्ख्याभिरावृताः प्रोक्तक्रमेणानुग्रहाख्यां सृष्टिक्रमपूजां कुर्यात् । तत्र बीजहृदयादीनि स्वस्वनामानि सम्प्रदायसिद्धानि तत्पूजाविद्याः तत्तन्नामविद्या पूजान्ते मूलविद्यया च पूजयेत् । तत्तदावरणशक्तीनामक्षरात्मिकादीनां नित्यानित्यपूजोक्तद्वादशाक्षरविद्यया आसामवसानभूतहाकिन्याद्युपक्रमभूतडाकिन्यन्ताः पूजानिग्रहाख्या संहारक्रमपूजा एवमन्तर्बहिश्चानुग्रहपूजां च कुर्यादिति ॥७१॥

भूमावित्यादिभिरर्चयेदित्यन्तैः चतुर्भिः श्लोकैर्बाह्यानुग्रहं चक्रं तत्र पूजनीयशक्तिध्यानं तत्पूजाक्रमं चोपदिशति । तत्र प्रोक्तदिक्क्रमात्—निर्ऋतिवायुशक्रवह्नीशवरुणमध्यदिक्क्रमात् । मध्ये च तत्र—तस्मिन् चक्रे सर्वमध्यस्थ(कोण)षट्के मध्ये । गन्धादिभिरित्यत्रादिशब्देन षोडशोपचारा उच्यन्ते ॥७२॥ तत्षडस्रेषु—मध्ये षट्कोणेषु । तत्षट्कं तत्क्रमात्—डाकिन्यादिशक्तिषट्कं निर्ऋत्यादि प्रोक्तक्रमदिक्षु । बाह्येष्वपि च अपिचेति समुच्चये । बहिःषट्कोणषट्के । ताः—डाकिन्याद्याः । प्राग्वत् निर्ऋत्यादिक्रमेण —प्रोक्तवर्णाः । स्वस्वाधारप्रोक्तवर्णाः॥७३॥ तथा निर्ऋत्यादिक्रमेण । समादेव्याः तत्तन्मध्यदेव्या तत्तन्मध्यदेवतासमानरूपवर्णरूपायुधा इत्यर्थः॥७४॥ प्राग्वत्स्वरेषु पञ्चस्युः—कुलसुन्दरीपटलप्रोक्तमातृकायन्त्रस्याष्टमदलाक्षराणि तानि अइउऋ अं अः इति पञ्च अपूर्वाः । अपुनरुक्ताः पञ्चाशद्वर्णा इति शेषः । परेषु यवलक्षार्णरहिताः—यादिक्षान्तेषु दशसु वर्णेषु पुनरुक्तयवलक्षवर्ण चतुष्टय रहिताः तेषां चतुर्णां पुनरुक्तत्वं यणादेशसन्धिसम्भवेत्वात् यकारवकारयोः । अन्ययोस्तु रलयोरभेदत्वात् ककारषकाररूपत्वात् च क्षकारस्य । तैः—षट्त्रिंश-

ङ्गिरक्षरैः । तथा—प्रागुक्तहादशाक्षररूपैः । तत्राकारादिककारान्ताः षट्शक्तीः प्रथमे चक्रे पूजयेत् । एवमन्येष्वपि यथाक्रमं (षट्) षट् शक्तीः पूजयेत् । एतदुक्तं भवति—अन्योन्यानुगुणरेखाभिः सम्बद्धानि सप्त षट् कोणानि मध्यरक्षोवायुशक्रवह्नीशवरुणादिग्गतानि वरुणवायूशशक्रवह्निनिर्ऋतिस्पृष्टाग्रकाणि विधाय तेषु मध्यषट् कोणमध्ये प्रागुक्तारुणविग्रहां नित्यानित्यामावाह्य षोडशोपचारैरभ्यर्च्य तत्(त्रि) कोणषटके(तु)डाकिन्यादिहाकिन्यन्ताः षट् शक्तीस्तन्मध्यस्थनित्यानित्यासमानायुधविग्रहास्तत्तदाधारवर्णपद्मपर्णाश्च ध्यात्वा षोडशभिरुपचारैः क्रमादभ्यर्च्य ता एव डाकिन्यादिवह्निनिर्ऋत्यादिदिग्गतषट्कोणषट् कमध्ये षु प्रोक्तक्रमेणावाह्य पश्चिमाभिमुखा आधारवद्ध्यात्वा समभ्यर्च्य तासामभितः षट् कोणेष्वपि तत्तदावरणशक्तीः षट् त्रिंशतं तत्तदभिमुखाः निर्ऋत्यादिप्रोक्तक्रमेण तत्तद्द्वादशाक्षरविद्याभिः षड् भिः षट् षट् क्रमेण वक्ष्यमाणतत्तन्निवेद्यविशेषोपचारसहितमर्चयेत् । एवमियमनुग्रहपूजा सर्वसम्पदवाप्तिकरीति । अस्य चक्रस्यायं विरचनाक्रमस्त्रयोदशभिः श्लोकैः सार्द्धैः व्याख्यायते ।

चतुर्विंशाङ्गुलायामभ्रमात् वृत्तं विधाय तु ।
तत्र मध्ये ब्रह्मसूत्रं कृत्वा तस्यार्द्धमानतः ॥१॥
तत्पार्श्वयोश्चिह्नयुगं वृत्ते कृत्वा तथाऽन्यतः ।
विधाय चिह्नयुगलं चिह्नाच्चिह्नं द्वयोरपि ॥२॥
कृत्वा सूत्रद्वयं तिर्यक् पश्चिमाग्रयुगान्तयोः ।
ब्रह्मसूत्रस्थपूर्वाग्रावधि सूत्रद्वयं भवेत् ॥३॥
प्राक् सूत्राग्रद्वयात्तद्वत्कुर्यात्सूत्रद्वयं ततः ।
पश्चिमब्रह्मसूत्रान्तमित्थं षट् कोणकं भवेत् ॥४॥
ततस्तद्वह्निकोणादिवायुकोणान्तगं ततः ।
(तथेशानि)तद्दिगादि च रक्षोन्तं ब्रह्मसूत्रद्वयं भवेत् ॥५॥
प्रत्येकं ब्रह्मसूत्राणि त्रिधा कृत्वा तु चिह्नकम् ।
कृत्वाभितोऽथ वृत्तानि तत्तदर्द्धांशतोभ्रमात् ॥६॥
तेष्वेकं ब्रह्मसूत्रेषु चतुर्विंशतिभागकम् ।
कृत्वा तद्दशमांशेषु षट् सूत्राणि निपातयेत् ॥७॥
दिक्कोणवृत्तपर्यन्तं वायुवृत्तेषु षट्स्वपि ।
वृत्तस्पृक्सूत्रयुग्मारं मध्ये मध्ये निपातयेत् ॥८॥
सूत्राणि षट् ततस्तेषु वृत्तं कोणेषु मध्यतः ।
कृत्वा त्रिर्ब्रह्मसूत्राणि मार्जयेच्चक्रमुत्तमम् ॥९॥

एषामपि च चक्राणां शक्तीनां च विलोमतः ।
पूजा निग्रहसंज्ञा स्यात् सा शत्रूणां विपत्तये ॥७६॥
षट्सु चक्रेषु षट्कुम्भान्विधायारिमहीरुहः ।
क्वाथतोयाभिसम्पूर्णान् कृष्णाम्बरसमन्वितान् ॥७७॥
अर्द्धरात्रे यजेत्तास्तु तद्योनिबलिदानतः ।
क्षिप्रं त्वगादिभिस्ते स्युः पूर्णाः शत्रोः कलेवराः ॥७८॥
निवेद्यं योनिरक्तेन सम्पन्नं चरुणा रिपोः ।
होमं च कुर्यात्तेनैव फणिशीर्षस्तु चारुषा ॥७९॥
ध्यायेद्देवीश्च कुपिता दष्टौष्ठा बाहुभिर्निजैः ।
प्रहरन्तीः पिशाचेभ्योविकिरन्तीश्च तत्तनुम् ॥८०॥
जयागुलुच्छविलसत्कर्णा भीमार्तनिस्वनाः ।
ध्यात्वैवं निग्रहं कुर्याद्रिपूणां मारणाय वै ॥८१॥

रक्षोमारुतशक्राग्निशिववारिगतानि च ।
धूम्रसिन्दूरनीलोद्यद्भानुहेमेन्दु(भांसि)भानि च ॥१०॥
मध्यकोष्ठं विधायेत्थं डाकिन्यादीः समर्चयेत्
उद्यदर्यमबिम्बाभे नित्यानित्यां च मध्यमे ॥११॥
एतच्चक्रविनिर्माणमजानन्मान्त्रिकोनरः ।
निग्रहानुग्रहविधौ यतमानो विनश्यति ॥१२॥
रोगार्तौ द्वन्द्वयुद्धे च शत्रूणां च निपातने ।
तथा मनोषितप्राप्तौ सिद्धिरस्यार्चनाद्भवेत् ॥१३॥

अतः परं व्याख्येयानि ॥७५॥

एषामित्यादिभिर्मरणाय वै इत्यन्तैः षड्भिः श्लोकैरेष्वेव चक्रेषु निग्रहाख्यपूजाचक्रमुपदिशति । तत्र चक्राणां समानां षट्कोणरूपाणामिति शेषः । शक्तीनां—तत्रतत्रोक्तषट्शक्तीनाम् । विलोमतः—चक्रशक्त्योरनुग्रहोक्त पूजाक्रमविलोमतः ॥७६॥ अरिमहीरुहः क्वाथतोयाभिसम्पूर्णान्—शत्रुनक्षत्र—वृक्षस्य कषायक्वथितजलपूर्णान् ॥७७॥ तद्योनिबलिदानतः—शत्रुनक्षत्रयोनो-

चक्रं च निग्रहे प्रोक्तं वज्ररूपं भयङ्करम् ।
कांस्ये सीसेपि वा कृत्वा स्थापयेद्वैरिभूमिषु ॥८२॥
प्राक्प्रत्यक्दक्षिणोदक् च दशसूत्रनिपातनात् ।
एकाशीतिपदानि स्युस्तेषु कोणचतुष्टये ॥८३॥
प्रत्येकं दश कोष्ठानि मार्जयेच्छिष्टवज्रकैः ।
चतुर्दिक्षु त्रिकोणानि चतुःकोष्ठैः प्रकल्पयेत् ॥८४॥

च्छित्वा बलिदानतः । ते—कुम्भाः । कलेवराः—शरीराणि(१) ॥७८॥ योनिरक्तेन—शत्रुनक्षत्रयोनिरुधिरेण । तेनैव—चरुणा । फणिशीर्षस्रुचा—भुजङ्गमस्य फणं छित्वा स्रुग्गतेन तेन फणेनेत्यर्थः ॥७९॥ तत्तनुं—शत्रुदेहम् ॥८०॥ गुलुच्छः—कलिका । एतदुक्तं भवति—प्रोक्तेषु सप्तसु षट्कोणचक्रेषु तत्तच्छक्तीः सावरणा(हे)-भीमरूपा स्तिष्ठन्तीरावाह्य तत्तदभिमुखा ध्यात्वा तत्तच्चक्रस्थानस्थिता एवानुग्रहपूजाक्रम(प्रति)विलोमक्रमतः सचक्राद्वृतिशक्तीनां वक्ष्यमाणबलिं निवेद्य होमसहितं पूजयेत् । तेष्वेव सप्तसु षट्कोणचक्रेषु मध्यचक्रवर्जं षण्णां मध्येषु षट्कुम्भान्निधाय तेषु कुम्भेषु शत्रुनक्षत्रवृक्षकषायक्वथितजलान्यभिपूर्य प्रोक्तभीमरूपाः सर्वेषां त्वगादिधात्वीशाः प्राग्वत्तदभिमुखास्तिष्ठन्तीः(२) शत्रोस्तत्तत्त्वगादिधातूनाकृष्य तत्तत्कुम्भेषु सम्पूर्य तद्देहं स्वायुधैः शकलीकृत्य पिशाचेभ्योविकिरन्तीस्तैर्भक्ष्यमाणं तत्तद्देहं भावयन् तदिन्द्रियमनःप्राणान् स्वचेतसा प्राणप्रतिष्ठाप्रोक्तप्रक्रियया मध्यदेवतायां नियोजयन्ननुग्रहपूजोक्तक्रमंप्रतिलोमतः पूजयन् शत्रुनक्षत्रयोनिबलिं छिन्दन् तदुक्तेन सम्पादितचरुणा निवेद्यं च कुर्वंस्तेन होमं फणिफणास्रुचा कुर्वन्नेवं पूजयन् प्रोक्तं फलमवाप्नोति इति । आसां षण्णां डाकिन्यादीनां त्वगादीनां च नित्यानित्याविद्यासम्बन्धाधारादिषु ३) तत्तन्निग्रहानुग्रहपूजनेषु रहस्यार्थश्च स्वगुरुमुखादेवावगन्तव्यः ॥८१॥

चक्रमित्यादिभिर्मर्दनमित्यन्तैरर्धैः षड्भिः श्लोकैर्निग्रहकोष्ठवज्रचक्रनिर्माणं तत्प्रयोगविशेषं तत्फलं चोपदिशति । तत्र चतुःकोष्ठैः—प्रतिदिशमेकैकं कोष्ठं मार्जयित्वा तत्र त्रिकोणानि कुर्यादित्यर्थः ॥८२॥८३॥८४॥ मध्याधः

---

(१) कलेवरात् शरीरात् इति टी पु० पा० । कलेवरान् शरीराणि इति सो० पु० पा० ।
(२) स्तिष्ठन्तीति वङ्ग पु० पा० (३) धार आदिषु इति टी पु० पा० ।

तेषु मध्यस्थकोष्ठे च साध्यं कर्म समालिखेत् ।
शिष्टेषु मध्याधःकोष्ठमारभ्य प्रतिलोमजान् ॥८५॥
विद्याकूटांस्तु षट्त्रिंशदालिखेदप्रदक्षिणम् ।
साध्ययोन्यसृजा पिष्टतद्वृक्षक्षोदलेपितान् ॥८६॥
स्थापयेत्प्रोक्तसमये रिपुक्षेत्रगृहादिषु ।
श्मशाने चण्डिकागेहे कुलोत्सादकरं भवेत् ॥८७॥
इति निग्रहमाख्यातं समस्तरिपुमर्दनम् ।
अनुग्रहं शृणु प्राज्ञे ! पूजाचक्रविधानतः ॥८८॥
देवीस्ताः प्रोक्तरूपास्तु ध्यात्वा चक्रेषु पूजयेत् ।
नवेद्यमासां सम्प्रोक्तं यदासां प्रीतिदायकम् ॥८९॥

कोष्ठमारभ्य सर्वमध्यकोष्ठस्याधः स्थितं कोष्ठमारभ्याप्रादक्षिण्येनामुक्तक्रमं निर्गमनगत्या लिखेदित्यर्थः । प्रतिलोमजान्—पञ्च(त्रिं)विंशपटलवक्ष्यमाणक्रमभेदेषु प्रतिलोमतः क्रमरूपान्॥८५॥ साध्ययोन्यसृजा-- शत्रुनक्षत्रयोनिरक्तेन । पिष्टः—आघृष्टः । तद्वृक्षक्षोदः—शत्रुनक्षत्रवृक्षक्षोदः—पङ्कः ॥८६॥ प्रोक्तसमये अरातेर्वैनाशिकनक्षत्रे अष्टमराश्युदये । आदिशब्दो देशादिविषयः । तत्र तत्रापि अष्टमराशिस्थाने॥८७॥ इति उक्तप्रकारेण । अरिमर्दनं—शत्रुनाशकरमिति यावत् । एतदुक्तं भवति—प्रागवदेकाशीतिकोष्ठानि कृत्वा तेषु कोष्ठेषु प्रतिकोणं दशदशकोष्ठानि मध्यवज्राकारेण मार्जयित्वा चतुर्दिक्षु प्रतिदिशमेकमेकं कोष्ठं मार्जयित्वा तत्र तत्र त्रिकोणानि विधाय तेषु त्रिकोणेषु मध्ये च साध्यमालिख्य सर्वमध्यकोष्ठाधःपङ्क्तिमध्यकोष्ठमारभ्याप्रादक्षिण्येनामुक्तक्रमं निर्गमनगत्या पञ्चविंशे पटले वक्ष्यमाणक्रमभिन्नविद्याकूटान् प्रतिलोमजान् षट्सङ्केतविद्याजनितषट्प्रकारसम्बन्धान् एवं क्रमेण षट्त्रिंशत्कूटानालिख्य साध्यनक्षत्रयोन्यसृग्घृष्टतन्नक्षत्रवृक्षपङ्केनालिख्य प्रोक्तसमयेषु प्रोक्तस्थानेषु स्थापयित्वा प्रोक्तं फलमाप्नुयादिति ॥८७॥

अनुग्रहमित्यादिभिर्लघुविग्रह इत्यन्तै रर्द्धैः षड्भिः श्लोकैः प्रागुक्तानुग्रहचक्रपूजनं तत्तद्देवतानां निवेद्यविशेषांस्तासामङ्गनासु समर्चनमनुग्रहकोष्ठवज्र-

पायसान्नं गुडान्नं च मुद्गभिन्नान्नकं तथा ।
हरिद्रान्नं तिलान्नं च शुद्धान्नं षटकमेव च ॥९०॥
चक्रेषु सप्तसु तथा तद्वर्णाश्चारुविग्रहाः ।
युवतीः सप्त संस्थाप्य प्राग्वदभ्यर्च्य ताः क्रमात् ॥९१॥
भूषणाम्बरगन्धा(१)स्रग्भोजनाद्यैस्तु तोषयेत् ।
तासु तुष्टासु तुष्टाः स्युः शक्तयस्ताः समास्तदा ॥९२॥
प्रागुक्तवज्रे साध्याख्यं तथालिख्यानुलोमजान ।
कूटानुक्तसमारम्भान् प्रादक्षिण्येन सल्लिखेत् ॥९३॥
प्रोक्तेषु प्रोक्तरूपेण स्थापयेत् प्रोक्तभूमिषु ।
प्रोक्तान्येव फलानि स्युर्योगोऽयं लघुविग्रहः ॥९४॥

यन्त्रं तत्र पूजाक्रमं तत्फलानि चोपदिशति । तत्र पूजाचक्रविधानतः— पूजाविधानतः चक्रविधानतश्च । तत्र पूजाविधानं डाकिन्यादीनां युवतीनां च । चक्रविधानं तु वज्रयन्त्रादि ॥८८॥ ताः— डाकिन्यादीः । प्रोक्तरूपा इत्यनेनाधार(च)क्रमोक्त वर्णाः मूलदेवीसमानबाहुमुखाश्चेतिचोच्यते । सपुत्रदेव्या रक्तत्वमेव षट्कं मध्यस्थाया देव्या इति शेषः॥८८॥८०॥तद्वर्णाः— आधारप्रोक्तदेवतामूलदेवतासदृशवर्णाः प्राग्वदभ्यर्च्य— मध्यादिप्रागन्तम् । ताः— शक्तीः ॥८१॥ भोजनं— तत्तद्देवताप्रोक्तम् । आदिशब्देन यावच्छक्तिदक्षिणारूपं वित्तं चोच्यते । तासु— युवतिषु । ताः— डाकिन्यादीः । एतदुक्तं भवति— प्रागुक्तेषु सप्तसु चक्रेषु प्रोक्तक्रमेण प्रोक्ताः शक्तीः समावाह्य सम्पूज्य तत्तन्निवेद्यं तत्तद्देवतायै निवेद्य तन्निवेद्यषट्कं समुदितमध्यदेवतायै निवेदयेत् । तेष्वेव सप्तसु चक्रेषु तत्तद्देवतासमानवर्णाः सप्तयुवतीश्च संस्थाप्य तासु ताः शक्तीः प्रोक्तक्रमेण समावाह्याभ्यर्च्य तत्तन्निवेद्यपुरःसरं भूषादिभिस्तासां युवतीनां तोषणात्तत्तच्छक्तयः परितुष्टाः समस्तवाञ्छितं दद्युरिति ॥८२॥ प्रागुक्तवज्रे— निग्रहप्रोक्ते एकाशीतिकोष्ठे प्रोद्धृते वज्रयन्त्रे । अनुलोमजान् पञ्चत्रिंशत्पटलोक्तक्रमभिन्नविद्यानुलोमरूपान् षट्त्रिंशद्विद्याकूटान् । उक्तसमारम्भान्— सर्वमध्यकोष्ठाधःपङ्क्तिमध्यकोष्ठसमारम्भान् ॥८३ प्रोक्तेषु— स्वर्णादि-

---

(१) गन्धर्वभोजनेति मू० पु० पा० ।

(१) वज्रचक्रे इति टी० पु० पा० ।

आदिक्षान्ताक्षरैः प्राग्वद्रूपिणीशक्तिसंयुतैः ।
बीजद्वयाद्यैः सप्ताक्षर्यन्तैः पञ्चदशाक्षरैः ॥९५॥
पञ्चाशच्छक्तयः पूज्याः पञ्चाशत्क्षेत्रपालकैः ।
द्विनेषु घटिकायोगात् पञ्चाशन्मिथुनान्यपि ॥९६॥
तेषां बीजद्वयं वर्णाद्रूपक्षेत्रेशसंयुताः ।
सप्ताक्षर्या च संयुक्ता मन्त्राः पञ्चदशाक्षराः ॥९७॥
चतुःषष्टिपदे मध्ये चतुष्के दिनविद्यया ।
मनीषितं समालिख्य (रभ्रा) तेषु तन्मिथुनानि वै ॥९८॥
घटिकाक्रमयोगेन छन्मायामध्यमर्चयेत् ।
एवं मण्डलमासार्द्धात् प्राप्नोत्येवाभिवाञ्छितम् ॥९९॥

धिष्ण्यकरणेषु मैत्रादिषु नक्षत्रेषु एकादशराश्युदये एकादशराशिस्थानेषु चेत्यर्थः । प्रोक्तभूमिषु– गृहमण्डपादिषु । प्रोक्तान्येव फलानि स्युः—आयुःकीर्तिविजयादि-लाभरूपाणि । योगः—प्रयोगः । लघुविग्रहः– अनया सरूपः । एतदुक्तं भवति—प्रागुक्तरूपे वज्रयन्त्रे मध्यकोष्ठाधःपङ्क्तिमध्यमारभ्य प्रादक्षिण्येनामुक्तक्रमं निर्गमनगत्या पञ्चत्रिंशत्पटलवक्ष्यमाणक्रमभिन्नविद्यानुलोमरूपान् षट्सङ्केत-विद्याजनितषट्प्रकारसंयुक्तानेवं षट्त्रिंशत्सङ्ख्यान् कूटानालिख्य प्राग्वन्मध्ये चतु-र्दिग्गतत्रिकोणेषु च साध्याख्यामालिख्य प्रोक्तक्रमेण प्रोक्तेषु कालेषु प्रोक्तेषु अधिकरणेषूत्कीर्य प्रोक्तभूमिषु प्रोक्तेषु स्थानेषु स्थापनात् प्रोक्तफलावाप्तिः स्यात् एवमेष प्रयोगेष्वपियत्नसाध्य २) इति ॥८४॥

आदिक्षान्तेत्यादिभिः सर्वत इत्यन्तैः षड्भिः श्लोकैः कालघटिकारूपपञ्चाशत् मिथुनानां तन्मण्डले समर्चनादभीष्टफलावाप्तिमुपदिशति । तत्र—एतदुक्तं भवति– समान्तरालं प्राक्प्रत्यक् दक्षिणोदक्च नव सूत्राण्यास्फाल्य तत्र चतुःषष्टि-पदे चक्रे मध्यत ऊर्ध्वाधोद्विद्विक्रमेण चतुःकोष्ठान्येकीकृत्य तत्रैव पञ्चविंशपटल-वक्ष्यमाणप्रक्रियया तत्तद्दिननित्याविद्याक्षराणि त्रीणि मनोषितप्रार्थनमध्यमा-लिख्य तदनन्तरे बाह्याधःपंक्तिस्थमध्यद्वयदक्षिणकोष्ठमारभ्य प्रादक्षिण्यक्रमेणा-मुक्तक्रमं निर्गमनगत्या चक्रवामपश्चात्तराधःकोष्ठावधि तेषु पञ्चत्रिंशत्पटलवक्ष्यमाणो-

(२) एवमेषु प्रयोगे यत्नसाध्यमिति पु० पा० ।

नित्यशस्ताः समावाह्य तस्मिन् चक्रे समर्चनात्।
समस्तवाञ्छितप्राप्तिः सदा भवति सर्वदा ॥१००॥
प्राणतत्त्वमयी व्याप्तिरिति सम्यक्समीरिता।
अस्या निष्फालनाच्चित्ते तत्तत्त्वं स्वात्मसात्कृतम् ॥१०१॥
इति श्री षोड़शनित्यातन्त्रे कादिमते षोड़शपटलम् ॥१६॥

दयादक्षरादीनि मातृकाप्रोक्तपञ्चाशदक्षराण्यपगतक्षकारमपगतविसर्जनीयं वा मकारोपेतहृल्लेखागर्भस्थितमालिख्य शिष्टेषु दशसु कोष्ठेषु पुनरप्युदयादीनि दशाक्षराणि समालिख्य तेषु लिखितक्रमेण उदयादिषु षष्टिघटिकासु तत्तन्मिथुनानि षोड़शभिरुपचारैरभ्यर्च्य तत्तत्फलमवाप्नुयात्। तन्मन्त्रास्तु बीजद्वयानन्तरं (रूपक्षेत्रान्तरं) अं रूपिणीशक्तिपादुकां पूजयामीत्यादयः तच्छक्तिविद्याः पञ्चाशत्। पुनरपि बीजद्वयानन्तरं अरूपक्षेत्रेशपादुकां पूजयामीत्यादयस्तत्क्षेत्रपालमन्त्राश्च पञ्चाशत् एवं प्रत्येकं पञ्चाशदक्षरैः पञ्चाशत्पद्(दशाक्षरात्मभिर्विद्या)र्मन्त्रैश्च ता निमिथुनानि पूजयेदिति। अस्य चक्रस्य प्रागुक्तारम्भात् अप्रादक्षिण्यक्रमेण लेखनार्चनात् निग्रहोभवतीति सम्प्रदायार्थः ॥९५॥९६॥९७॥९८॥९९॥१००॥१०१॥

इति श्रीषोड़शनित्यातन्त्रेषु श्रीकादिमताख्यस्य तन्त्रस्य परिपूर्णस्य तन्त्रस्य प्रपञ्च-
सारसिंहराजप्रकाशाभिधानेन श्रीसुभगानन्दनाथेन विरचितायां
मनोरमाख्यायां व्याख्यायां शिवदूतीनित्याविद्याविधान-
प्रकाशनपरं पञ्चदशपटलं परिपूर्णं
परामृष्टम् ॥ १५ ॥

ग्रन्थसङ्ख्या—

षट्त्रिंशतिश्च यन्त्राणि व्याख्याग्रन्थाः शतद्वयात्।
पञ्चाशीतिः सार्द्धपादाः षोड़शे पटले स्मृताः ॥०॥

अथ सप्तदशपटलम् ।

अथ षोड़शनित्यासु द्वादशी या समीरिता ।
तस्या नीलपताकाया विधानं सर्वसिद्धिदम् ॥१॥
न्यासक्रमविधानं च ध्यानं शक्तीः प्रपूजनम् ।
साधनं सिद्धविद्यस्य विजयं कामरूपताम् ॥२॥
पादुकामञ्जनं खड्गं वेतालांश्च पिशाचकान् ।
यक्षिणीश्चेटकान्मायां यन्त्राणि च वदामि ते ॥३॥
प्रयोगानानुपूर्व्येण सन्दिष्टानामशेषतः ।
दशभिः सिद्धिभिर्मर्त्योभवेद्विद्याधरोऽपरः ॥४॥
मूलविद्याक्षरैरङ्गान्याचरेत् षड़ितिक्रमात् ।
(१)द्विचतुष्टयषड्वर्णैः क्रमेण षड़ितीरितैः ॥५॥

सप्तदशपटलम् ।

पूर्वस्मिन् षोड़शे पटले एकादश्या नित्यानित्याविद्याया विधानमुपदिश्यानन्तरं द्वादश्या नीलपताकानित्याविद्याया विधानमुपदिशति । तत्र अथ षोड़शीत्यादिभिः परइत्यन्तैश्चतुर्भिः श्लोकैः पटलार्थानुद्दिशति । तत्र विद्या तृतीये पटले प्रोक्तत्वादिह न कथिता । विधानं वदामीत्यन्वयः ॥१॥ न्यासक्रममित्यादिविधानरूपाणि । शक्तीः—आवरणशक्तीः । साधनं विद्याया इति शेषः । सिद्धविद्यस्य—पुरुषस्येति शेषः । विजयादीनां सिद्धीनां दशानामुपरिष्टात्स्वयमेव वक्ष्यमाणत्वादिह स्वरूपाणि नोच्यन्ते ॥२॥ यन्त्राणि—तासां साधनार्थानि यन्त्राणि ॥३॥ सन्दिष्टानां—सिद्ध्यादीनाम् ॥४॥

मूलविद्येत्यादिभिर्यथाविधीत्यन्तैस्त्रिभिः श्लोकैः न्यासप्रकारमुपदिशति । तत्र द्विचतुष्टयषट्वर्णैः क्रमेण मूलविद्यायाः प्रथमद्वितीयाभ्यामक्षराभ्यां हृदयं, तदनन्तरैश्चतुर्भिः शिरः, तदुपरितनैः षड्भिःशिखा तदनन्तरेणैकेन कवचं, तदुपरि

---

(१) विधानं द्वयषड् इति मू० पु० पा० ।

श्रोत्राक्षिनासायुगले वाचि कण्ठे हृदि क्रमात्।
नाभावाधारके पादसन्धिषु त्रिषु च क्रमात् ॥६॥
मन्त्राक्षराणि क्रमशोन्यसेत्सप्तदशापि वा।
व्यापकं च समस्तेन विदध्याच्च यथाविधि ॥७॥
इन्द्रनीलनिभां भास्वन्मणिमौलिविराजिताम्।
पञ्चवक्त्रां त्रिनयनामरुणांशुकधारिणीम् ॥८॥
दशहस्तां लसन्मुक्ताप्रायाभरणमण्डिताम्।
रत्नस्तबकसम्भिन्नदेहां चारुस्मिताननाम् ॥९॥
पाशं पताकां चर्माणि शार्ङ्गचापं वरं करैः।
दधानां वामपार्श्वस्थैः सर्वाभरणभूषितैः ॥१०॥
अङ्कुशं च ततः शक्तिं खड्गं बाणं तथाऽभयम्।
दधानां दक्षिणैर्हस्तैरासीनां पद्मविष्टरे ॥११॥

स्थेनैकेन नेत्रं तदनन्तरेणैकेनास्त्रं अवशिष्टयोर्मन्त्रार्णयोः पूर्वमेव हृदयमन्त्रे विनियोगात् पुनरुक्त्या नोपादानम्। क्रमेण षड्तिोरितिः—इत्येवंभेदक्रमेण इति ईरितैः जात्यन्तैर्वर्णैः—षडङ्गानि करयोरङ्गेषु च न्यसेदित्यर्थः। षड्तिोतिद्विरुपादानस्य सङ्क्षेपविकासार्थत्वान्न पुनरुक्तिदोषः ॥५॥

श्रोत्रेत्यादिना यथाविधीत्यन्तेन श्लोकद्वयेन मन्त्राक्षरन्यासक्रमं सव्यापकं न्यासक्रममुपदिशति। तत्र वाक्कण्ठहृदयनाभ्याधारेषु पञ्चस्वेकैकं, अन्येषु षट्सु श्रोत्राक्षिनासिकापादद्वयसन्धित्रयेषु द्वयं द्वयं, तत्र एकपादन्यासत्रयानन्तरमन्यपादन्यासत्रयम्—एवं मूलविद्याक्षराणि सप्तदशोद्दिष्टस्थानक्रमं न्यसेदित्यर्थः। व्यापकं च समस्तेन विदध्याच्च यथाविधि—समस्तेन मूलमन्त्रेण प्राग्वद्व्यापकन्यासं च कुर्यादिति यावत् ॥६॥७॥

इन्द्रनीलनिभामित्यादिभिः क्रमे इत्यन्तैः पञ्चभिः श्लोकैर्देव्याः सपरिवाराया नित्यसपर्याध्यानमुपदिशति। तत्र मौलि—मुकुटः। पञ्चवक्त्रां—तदवस्थानप्रकारस्तु ऊर्ध्वं चतुर्दिक्षु चेत्यर्थः। ऊर्ध्वस्थं मुखं साधकाभिमुखमिति सम्प्रदायः। त्रिनयनां—प्रतिवक्त्रमित्यर्थः ॥८॥ दशहस्तां—सम्भूयेतिशेषः ॥९॥ शार्ङ्गचापमित्येकं

स्वाकारवर्णवेषास्यपाण्यायुधविभूषणैः ।
शक्तिवृन्दैर्वृतां ध्यायेद्देवीं नित्यार्चनक्रमे ॥१२॥
त्रिषट्कोणयुतं पद्ममष्टपत्रं ततो बहिः ।
अष्टास्रं भूपुरद्वन्द्वाद्वृत्ते तत्पुरयुग्मकम् ॥१३॥
चतुर्द्वारयुतं दिक्षु शाखाभिश्च समन्वितम् ।
कृत्वा तामावृतां शक्तिगणैस्तत्रार्चयेच्छिवाम् ॥१४॥
इच्छाज्ञानक्रियाशक्तीस्त्रिषु कोणेषु पूजयेत् ।
अग्रात्प्रदक्षिणेनैव यजेदावृत्तिपञ्चकम् ॥१५॥

शृङ्गमयत्वाच्चापस्य । तेषामुभयतःक्रममूर्द्धादि कल्पयेत् ॥१०॥ पद्मविष्टरे—वक्ष्यमाणरूपे ॥११॥ आस्यं—मुखम् ॥१२॥

त्रिषडित्यादिना शिवामित्यन्तेन श्लोकद्वयेन नित्यसपर्यामण्डलविधानं तद्-पूजाप्रस्तावं च करोति। तत्र त्रिषट्कोणयुतं—त्रिकोणेन षट्कोणेन च युतम्। ततो बहिः—अष्टदलपद्माद्बहिः। भूपुरद्वन्द्वात्—दिग्विदिग्भूतकोणात्। वृत्ते इति द्विवचनम्। तत्पुरयुग्मकं—भूपुरद्वयमित्यर्थः। कृत्वेति पूर्वत्रान्वयः॥१३॥ तत्र—मण्डले। एतदुक्तं भवति—अभीष्टमानेन वक्ष्यमाणमार्गेण समचतुरस्रद्वयमन्त-र्बहिर्विभागेन कृत्वा चत्वारि तत्कोणान्यन्तःचतुरस्ररेखाग्रैर्बाह्यचतुरस्रस्पर्शेन चतु-ष्कोणानि कृत्वा चतसृषु दिक्षु मध्यतोमध्यतः शाखाद्वयोपेतानि चत्वारि द्वाराणि निर्माय (१)तदनन्तरमन्तस्थचतुरस्रस्पृष्टास्पृष्टं वृत्तं तदन्तर(२)प्येकाङ्गुलान्तराले वृत्तं विधाय तद्वृत्तमध्ये समान्तरालं सूत्रचतुष्टयं दिग्विदिग्गताष्टाग्रकं वृत्तरेखान्तं कृत्वा तेष्वेकान्तरितं सूत्राग्रात् सूत्राग्रमष्टसूत्रास्फालनादष्टकोणानि विधाय सूत्रचतुष्टयं मार्जयित्वा तदन्तरष्टास्ररेखाष्टकमध्ये स्पृष्टास्पृष्टं वृत्तद्वयं प्राग्वन्निष्पाद्य (तदन्तश्चतुरङ्गुलमानेन वृत्तद्वयं प्राग्वन्निष्पाद्य) तत्राष्टदलानि यथामानं कृत्वा तन्मध्यकर्णिकायां प्राग्वत् षट्कोणं तन्मध्ये वृत्तद्वयं तदन्तर्वृत्त(३)स्य समानांशा-कृष्ट्या गुरूक्तयुक्त्या स्वाभिमुखं समन्विरेखं कोणं च कृत्वा तत्र सपरिवारां देवीं वक्ष्यमाणक्रमेणार्चयेदिति ॥१४॥

---

(१) तदन्तर्वृत्तमन्तस्थेति टी० पु० पा० । (२) तदनन्तरमिति सो० पु० पा० ।
(३) व्यासमानार्द्धं कृत्यानुरूपकृत्या इति टी पु० पा० ।

डाकिन्यादीर्यजेत्षट्सु कोणेषु परितः क्रमात् ।
ब्राह्म्याद्यादीरष्टपत्रेष तत्कोणेष बहिस्तथा ॥१६॥
प्रागुक्तास्ता यजेच्छक्तीः नित्यानित्यादिषूदिताः ।
बलिद्वयं च कुर्वीत पूजां प्राग्वत्समापयेत् ॥१७॥
सर्वत्र नित्यहोमं(च) तु कुर्यादन्नाज्यतोऽपि वा ।
तिलतण्डुलकैर्वापि प्रोक्तं द्रव्यानुदीरणे ॥१८॥
विद्याक्षराणां सर्वेषां स्वरव्यञ्जनविन्दुकान् ।
पृथक्कृ(त्या) त्वाऽथगणिते त्रिपञ्चाशद्भवन्ति हि ॥१९॥
तेन तल्लक्षसङ्ख्यान्तु जपेद्विद्यां पयोव्रतः ।
तद्दशांशं हुनेदग्नौ सर्वत्राक्षरलक्षकी ॥२०॥
प्राङ्मुखोनित्यपूजासु साधनेषु च साधकः ।
नित्यानामपि सर्वासां वासनायामुदीरितम् ॥२१॥

इच्छेत्यादिभिः समापयेदित्यन्तैस्त्रिभिः श्लोकैर्देव्याः पञ्चावरणार्चनक्रममुपदिशति। तत्र—परितः क्रमादित्युक्त्या डाकिन्यादोनां प्राग्वत्स्थितानामेवाग्यादिप्रादक्षिण्येन पूजनमित्यर्थः। तत्पूजाक्रमः प्रागेव त्रयोदशपटले दशमेश्लोके व्याख्यातोऽस्माभिः। तत्कोणेषु—अष्टकोणेषु। बहिः—चतुरस्रे ॥१५॥१६॥ नित्यानित्यादिषूदिता इति प्रागुक्तातिदेशपरत्वान्न पुनरुक्तिदोषः। तत्रादिशब्देन दूतीनित्योच्यते, तेन तत्पटलोक्ताः सुमुखाद्या अष्टकोणशक्तयः प्रोच्यन्ते. ताः शक्तीश्चतुरस्रे तत्रोक्तारम्भक्रमेण पूजयेदित्यर्थः। अनेनात्र ब्राह्म्यादीनां द्विरर्चनमायातम्। षोड़शाक्षरकुलकुलासप्ताक्षरोभ्यां यथाक्रममाद्यन्तयोरिति शेषः। प्राग्वत्—आधारत्रये, तेज(स)स्लयभावनादिसहितमित्यर्थः ॥१७॥

सर्वत्रेत्यादिना श्लोकेन द्रव्यानुक्तौ सर्वदेवतासाधारणानि नित्यहोमद्रव्याण्युपदिशति। तत्र प्रोक्त - उक्तप्रकारतः। द्रव्यमिति शेषः ॥१८॥

विद्येत्यादिभिरुदीरितमित्यन्तैस्त्रिभिः श्लोकैर्विद्यासाधनादिकमुपदिशति। तत्र पृथक्कृत्य—प्रत्येकं वियुज्य। हिःहेतौ ॥१९॥ तत्र प्रथमादिचतुष्टयषष्ठाष्टमषोड़शसप्तदशाक्षराणि चतुर्भेदानि पञ्चमसप्तमनवमैकादश(द्वादश)चतुर्दशाक्षराणि द्विभे-

ततः सिद्धमनुर्मन्त्री कुर्यात् सिद्धिषु कौतुकम् ।
तद्विधानं शृणु प्राज्ञे ! वक्ष्ये विद्याविभेदतः ॥२२॥
दशानामपि सिद्धीनां विद्यास्तासां भिदागताम ।
सङ्ख्यांच(१) ताश्च सम्प्रोक्ताः क्रमेणासां फलानि च ॥२३॥
विद्यादिकूटे त्वाद्ये तु योजयेद्दशसु क्रमात् ।
ताभ्यामेव विलोमाभ्यां(२) पुटयेदुपगोगितान् ॥२४॥
मन्त्रवर्णान् दशानां च तत्तत्सङ्ख्याश्च ताः शृणु ।
परस्तात्तत्प्रभेदानां मन्त्रान्वक्ष्ये यथाविधि ॥२५॥

दानि । दशमत्रयोदशपञ्चदशाक्षराणि त्रिभेदानि विद्याक्षराणि सप्तदशेत्यर्थः । तन्नक्षसङ्क्रमिति विशेषविधानात् सर्वयुगेष्वपि त्रिपञ्चाशन्नक्षमित्यर्थः । पयोव्रतः—क्षीराहारी । तद्दशांशं—अक्षरलक्षदशमांशमितियावत् ॥२०॥ वासनायां—वासनापटले । उदीरितं—प्राङ्मुखत्वकारणम् ॥२१॥

तत इत्यादिना फलानि चेत्यन्तेन श्लोकद्वयेन सिद्धविद्यस्य दशसिद्धिसाधनयोग्यतोपदेशपुरःसरं मूलविद्याक्षरबीजरूपादयो दशसिद्धिविद्याः प्रत्येकं सिद्धिविद्यावान्तरभिदां सङ्ख्यां सिद्धसिद्धिस्वरूपाणि तत्फलानि च वक्ष्यामीति प्रस्तौति । तत्र सिद्धिषु—विजयादिषु दशसु । कौतुकं—आदरम् । तद्विधानं—दशसिद्धिविधानम् । विद्याविभेदतः—मूलविद्यायाः स्वरूपभूतानामक्षराणाम् । भिदातः—भित्वाभित्वा वक्ष्यमाणप्रकारयोजनत इत्यर्थः॥२२॥ तासां—सिद्धीनां विद्यानां च । भिदागतां—उपरिष्टात्स्वयमेव स्फुटं वक्ष्यमाणाम् । ताः—सिद्धीः । आसां—सिद्धीनाम् । एतदुक्तं भवति—मूलविद्यायाः स्वरूपयोजनाभेदप्रकारजनितविद्याविशेषान् सिद्धीनां दशानां तद्विद्यानां प्रत्येकमवान्तरभिदासङ्ख्यास्ताः सिद्धीस्तत्फलानि सर्वाणि पटलशेषे वक्ष्यमाणानि प्रस्तौति (इति) ॥२३॥

विद्यादीत्यादिना यथाविधीत्यन्तेन श्लोकद्वयेन वक्ष्यमाणानां सर्वेषां सिद्धिविद्याविशेषाणां स्वरूपयोजनासाधारणकूटाक्षर(३)पटलादिकमुपदिशति । तत्र विद्यादिकूटे—मूलविद्याया आदिभूतं संयुक्ताक्षरद्वयम् । आद्ये—अत्रापिद्विवचनम् ।

---

(१) सङ्ख्यावाताश्चेति मू० पु० पा० ।
(२) विलोमां तां पुटयेच्छ भिरौ इति मू० पु० पा० ।
(३) पुटनादिकमिति टी० पु० पा० ।

चतुर्विधः स्याद्विजयो द्वन्द्वे सचतुरङ्गके ।
कूटयुद्धे दुर्गजे च तेषां मन्त्राश्चतुर्विधाः ॥२६॥
कामरूपत्वमुदितं स्वेच्छयाऽभीष्टविग्रहम् ।
विधातुमात्मनः शक्तिं स एको मन्त्र ईरितः ॥२७॥
पादुकायुगलं विद्यावैभवाप्तं तु पादयोः ।
कृत्वा स्मरेद्वाञ्छितन्तु देशं तत्र तदा स्थितिः ॥२८॥
तन्मन्त्रः स्यादेकविधस्तथैवाञ्जनमीरितम् ।
येनाक्ताक्षोनिधिं पश्येद्देवाद्यांश्चान्तरिक्षगान् ॥२९॥
खड्गस्य तादृशः प्रोक्तः करस्थे नाहिताः क्षणात् ।
पलायिता वा पदयोः (१)प्रणमेयुर्वशङ्गताः ॥३०॥
वेतालाः स्युरसङ्ख्याताः सिद्धान्ते चै(क)व विद्यया ।
निधाय साधनं स्कन्धे चरेयुर्वाञ्छयाऽस्य ते ॥३१॥

सिद्धिमन्त्राणामाद्यमक्षरद्वयं योजयेदित्यर्थः । दशसु—सिद्धिषु विद्यानामिति शेषः । ताभ्यां—संयुक्ताक्षराभ्याम् । पुटयेत्—सिद्धिमन्त्रान्ते योजयेदित्यर्थः । उपरोरितान्—उपरिष्टाद्वक्ष्यमाणान् ॥२४॥ दशानां चेति काकाक्षिवत्पूर्वापरयोरन्वेति । तत्तत् सङ्ख्याः—सिद्धितद्विद्यावान्तरा(२)भिधानसङ्ख्याः । ताः—सिद्धीः । परस्तात्—सिद्धिसङ्ख्यासिद्धिस्वरूपोपदेशानन्तरम् । तत्प्रभेदानां—प्रत्येकं सिद्ध्यवान्तरभेदानाम् । मन्त्रान्—तत्सङ्ख्यादिभिः ॥२५॥

चतुर्विधइत्यादिभिः प्रसादने इत्यन्तैः पञ्चदशभिः श्लोकैर्दशानां सिद्धीनां स्वरूपं तद्भिदासङ्ख्यास्तद्विद्याभेदसङ्ख्याश्चोपदिशति । तत्र चतुरित्यादिना श्लोकेन विजयसिद्धिस्वरूपादिकमुपदिशति । तत्र द्वन्द्वे—युद्ध इति शेषः । तन्नामवैरिणोः प्रधानयोः ससैन्यं अन्योन्यं युद्धे(म्) । सचतुरङ्गके—शेषं प्रागवत् । दुर्गजे—दुर्गसंजाते—शेषं प्रागवत् । तेषां—विजयानां चतुर्विधानाम् ॥२६॥

कामित्यादिना श्लोकेन कामरूपत्वसिद्धिरूपादिकमुपदिशति—तत्र शक्तिः—सामर्थ्यम् । सः—कामरूपप्रदः ॥२७॥

---

(१) प्रणामं पूर्वमङ्गता इति मू० पु० पा०　　(२) न्तरभिदा इति टीपु० पा० ।

विकृताङ्गमुखाः केचित्केचित्तिर्यङ्मुखाङ्गकाः ।
केचिद्भीषणनादाढ्याः वेताला बहुविग्रहाः ॥३२॥
सर्वेऽपि वशगा वाक्यादस्य शत्रून् ग्रसन्ति च ।
किङ्कराः प्रोक्तकरणाद्भवेयुर्यावदायुषम् ॥३३॥
पिशाचास्तादृशाः प्रोक्ता कार्श्यवैरूप्यविग्रहाः ।
क्रुद्धाः क्षुद्राशयाः प्रोक्तकारिणः स्युरसङ्ख्यकाः ॥३४॥
तेषामेका भवेद्विद्या तया ते किङ्कराः सदा ।
तैरेव प्रहरेच्छत्रुमज्ञातमनिशं रणे ॥३५॥
षट्त्रिंशद्रूपसयुक्ता यक्षिण्यो वाञ्छितप्रदाः ।
सरूपा द्विभुजाश्चित्रवसनाभरणान्विताः ॥३६॥

पादुकेत्यादिना मन्त्रविगान् इत्यन्तेन श्लोकद्वयेन पादुकासिद्धिस्वरूपादिकमुपदिशति । तत्र विद्यावैभवाहं—पादुकासिद्धिविद्याप्रसादीकृतम् । पादयोः—स्वस्येतिशेषः । तत्र—देशे ॥२८॥ तन्मन्त्रः—पादुकामन्त्रः । तेनैव—यथा पादुकालाभः तन्मन्त्रसङ्ख्या वा । येन अञ्जनेन ॥२९॥

खड्गश्च तादृशेत्यादिना श्लोकेन खड्गसिद्धिस्वरूपादिकमुपदिशति । तत्र तादृशः—(लाभ)मन्त्रविद्याभ्यां करस्थेन खड्गेनेति शेषः । अहिताः—रिपवः ॥३०॥

वेताला इत्यादिभिरायुषमित्यन्तैस्त्रिभिः श्लोकैर्वेतालादिसिद्धिस्वरूपादिकमुपदिशति । तत्र अस्य—साधकस्य । ते-वेतालाः ॥३१॥ तिर्यङ्मुखाङ्गकाः—मृगमुखा मृगशरीराश्च । बहुविग्रहाः—प्रोक्तविग्रहान्तरेणापि ॥३२॥ सर्वे—वेताला अस्येति पूर्वापरयोरन्वेति ॥३३॥

पिशाचा इत्यादिना रणे इत्यन्तेन श्लोकद्वयेन पिशाचसिद्धिस्वरूपादिकमुपदिशति । तत्र तादृशा—नानाविधा इत्यर्थः । क्षुद्राशयाः—अल्पसत्त्वाः ॥३४॥ तेषां—साधने इतिशेषः । तया—विद्यया । ते—पिशाचाः । तैः—पिशाचैः । अज्ञातं—अप्रत्यक्षम् ॥३५॥

षट्त्रिंशदित्यादिभिः सम्मता इत्यन्तैस्त्रिभिः श्लोकैर्यक्षिणीसिद्धिरूपादिकमुपदिशति । तत्र—षट्त्रिंशद्रूपसंयुक्ताः—षट्त्रिंशत्सङ्ख्याता इत्यर्थः ॥ ३६ ॥

असहाया यौवनाढ्याः स्रगालेपनसौरभैः ।
समेत्य सर्वाभीष्टानि दद्युस्ताः साधकाय वै ॥३७॥
तासां विद्याश्च षट्त्रिंशद्वक्ष्ये ताश्च शृणु प्रिये ! ॥
याभिः सिद्धाभिरनिशं साधकाः सर्वसम्मताः ॥३८॥
चेटकाः स्युश्चतुःषष्टिस्तेषां मन्त्राश्च तत्समाः ।
तेऽपि नानाविधाकाराः सिद्धास्ते दद्युरीप्सितम् ॥३९॥
मायासङ्ख्याश्चित्ररूपाश्चित्राण्यस्येच्छयाऽनिशम् ।
वसून्युपहरेयुस्ता विद्यैका तत्प्रसा(ध)दने ॥४०॥
विद्याया नवमार्णादिवर्णैःषड्भिरुदीरितैः ।
दशविद्याः प्रजायन्ते शृणु वक्ष्ये च ताः क्रमात् ॥४१॥

असहायाः—परिवाररहिताः । ताः—यक्षिण्यः ॥३७॥ तासां—यक्षिणीनाम् । ताः—विद्याः । याभिः—विद्याभिः ॥३८॥

चेटकेत्यादिना श्लोकेन चेटकसिद्धिरूपादिकमुपदिशति । तत्र तेषां—चेटकानाम् । तत्समाः—चतुःषष्टिसङ्ख्या इत्यर्थः । ते—चेटकाः । ते—प्राग्वत् । ईप्सितं साधकस्येति शेषः ॥३९॥

मायेत्यादिना श्लोकेन मायासिद्धिरूपादिकमुपदिशति । तत्र मायाऽसंख्या इति स्वातन्त्र्योक्तिः । माया :—शक्तयः असङ्ख्या इत्यर्थः । चित्राणि—वस्तूनीति सम्बन्धः । अस्य—साधकस्य । ताः—मायाः । तत्प्रसादने—मायाप्रसादने । प्रसादनं—प्राप्तिः । एतदुक्तं भवति—विजयानां यक्षिणीनां चेटकानां विद्या यथाक्रमं चतस्रः षट्त्रिंशच्चतुःषष्टिः । अन्यासां सप्तानां प्रत्येकमेकैकरूपतो विद्याः सप्त, सम्भूय दशानां सिद्धीनां विद्यासङ्ख्याः एकादशाधिकं शतमिति ॥४०॥

विद्याया इत्यादिभिः व्याकुलक्रमादित्यन्तैरेकत्रिंशत्श्लोकैः सिद्धीनां प्रागुक्तैकादशाधिकशतसंख्यामन्त्रस्वरूपाण्युपदिशति । तत्र विद्यायाः—मूलविद्यायाः । उदीरितैः—वर्णप्रमाणैः । दशविद्या इति सिद्धग्रपेक्षयोक्तिः । ताः—विद्याः ॥४१॥

नित्येत्यादिना श्लोकेन विजयसिद्धिविद्यां चतुर्विधामुपदिशति—तत्र नित्य इति

नित्येति विजयं देहीत्युक्त्वा सम्पुटयेत्ततः ।
विद्या सा विजयप्राप्त्यां चतुर्ष्वे(१)कादशाक्षरा: ॥४२॥
मदेति कामरूपं मे देहीतिपुटयेत्तथा ।
त्रयोदशाक्षरी विद्या कामरूपप्रदेरिता ॥४३॥
नित्यदेपादुकां देहीत्युक्त्वा कुर्याच्च सम्पुटम् ।
द्वादशार्णा भवेद्विद्या सिद्धा दद्याच्च पादुके ॥४४॥
तथा नित्यप्रदेत्युक्त्वा देह्यञ्जनमितीरयेत् ।
पूजयेत्तद्द्वयेनाच्च द्वादशार्णा समीरिता ॥४५॥
द्रवीत्येदेहिषड्गारमित्युक्त्वा पुटयेत्तथा ।
द्वादशार्णा भवेत्सिद्धा सत्या दद्यात्सुशोभनम् ॥४६॥

मन्त्रयोजना। विजयप्राप्त्यां—चतुर्षु द्वन्द्वयुद्धादिषु विजयप्राप्त्यामित्यन्वय:। विजयसिद्धिविद्याया एकादशाक्षर्याश्चातुर्विध्यं द्वन्द्वयुद्धादिप्रोक्तानामविशेषयोजनत:। यथा द्वन्द्वयुद्धे चतुरङ्गयुद्धे कूटयुद्धे दुर्गयुद्धे इति तानि विजयशब्दात्पूर्वं योजनीयानि। तेन पञ्चदशाक्षरास्तिस्र:। एका सप्तदशाक्षरीति। अतिरहस्यत्वा-द्विद्या आञ्जस्येन न लिख्यन्ते ॥४२॥

मदेत्यादिना श्लोकेन कामरूपसिद्धिविद्यामुपदिशति। तत्र मद इति मन्त्रयोजना उक्तेतिशेष:। अस्मिन् प्रकरणे उक्तेत्याद्यनुक्तावुक्तेति शेष:। तथा—कूटद्वयेनेत्यर्थ:। अन्यत्सुगमम् ॥४३॥

नित्येत्यादिना श्लोकेन पादुकासिद्धिविद्यामुपदिशति। तत्र नित्य इति मन्त्रयोजना। विद्येति पूर्वापरयोरन्वेति। पादुके इति द्विवचनम् ॥४४॥

तथेत्यादिना श्लोकेनाञ्जनसिद्धिविद्यामुपदिशति। तत्र तथा—यथा पादुका-विद्यायोजनम्। नित्यमद इति मन्त्रयोजना। तद्द्वयेन—कूटद्वयेन। द्वाद-शार्णा विद्येति शेष: ॥४५॥

द्रवनित्येत्यादिना श्लोकेन खड्गसिद्धिविद्यामुपदिशति। तत्र द्रवनित्ये इति मन्त्रयोजना। तथा—प्रागवत्। द्वयेन—द्वादशार्णा विद्येति शेष:। सिद्धा—प्रागवच्छेष: ॥४६॥

---

(१) चतुर्दैका इति सी० पु० पा०।

नित्यद्रवेति वेतालान् देहीति पुटयेत्तथा ।
त्रयोदशाक्षरां विद्यां सिद्धां तान् दर्शयेत्तथा ॥४७॥
पिशाचान्मे प्रयच्छेति पूर्वं नित्यमदद्रवे ।
पुटयेत्पूर्ववद्वाभ्यां विद्या सप्तदशाक्षरा ॥४८॥
षटत्रिंशदुक्ता यक्षिण्यस्ताः सर्वा वाञ्छितप्रदाः ।
तासां नामानि विद्याश्च शृणु वक्ष्ये यथाविधि ॥४९॥
विचित्रा विभ्रमा हंसी भीषणी जनरञ्जिका ।
विशाला मदना रुद्रा(१) कालकण्ठी महाभया ॥५०॥
माहेन्द्री (२)शङ्खिनी चान्द्री मङ्गला वटवासिनी ।
मेखला सकला लक्ष्मीर्मालिनी विश्वनायिका ॥५१॥
सुलोचना सशोभा च कामदा सविलासिनी ।
कामेश्वरी नन्दिनी च स्वर्णरेखा(३) मनोरमा ॥५२॥
प्रमोदा रागिणी सिद्धा पद्मिनी सरतिप्रिया ।
कल्याणदा कलादक्षा ततश्च सुरसुन्दरी ॥५३॥

नित्येत्यादिना श्लोकेन वेतालसिद्धिविद्यामुपदिशति । तत्र नित्यद्रव इति मन्त्रयोजना । तथा—प्राग्वत् द्वयेन । तान्—वेतालानितिशेषः ॥४७॥

पिशाचानित्यादिना श्लोकेन पिशाचसिद्धिविद्यामुपदिशति । तत्र पूर्वं पिशाचशब्दान्नित्यमदद्रव इति मन्त्रयोजना । द्वाभ्यां—बीजाभ्यामितिशेषः ॥४८॥

षट्त्रिंशदित्यादिभिः सुन्दरीत्यन्तैः पञ्चभिः श्लोकैर्नामविद्याप्रस्तावपूर्वं यक्षिणीनामान्युपदिशति । तत्र तासां—यक्षिणीनाम् ॥४९॥

विचित्रेत्यादिना श्लोकेन द्वादश नामान्युपदिशति । तत्र महाभया इति दशमी॥५०॥

माहेन्द्रीत्यादिना श्लोकेन दश नामान्युपदिशति ॥५१॥

सुलोचनेत्यादिना श्लोकेनाष्ट नामान्युपदिशति । तत्र सुलोचनेति चतुरक्षरं नाम । सशोभेत्यत्र सकारः सहार्थः । सविलासिनी इत्यत्रापि सकारस्तद्वत्॥५२॥

---

(१) गह्वरातुष्टा इति मू० पु० पा० । (२) शशिनी इति मू० पु० पा०
(३) स्वर्णविशामयाग्रहा इति मू० पु० पा० ।

इति षट्‌त्रिंशदाख्याता यक्षिण्योऽभीष्टदायकाः ।
तासां विद्याः क्रमेणैव(१) तद्बीजद्वयसम्पुटैः ॥५४॥
नित्यद्रवमदेत्यन्तैः षड्‌वर्णैः स्वोक्तनामभिः ।
विद्याः षट्‌त्रिंशदाख्यातास्ताः सिद्धा दद्युरीप्सितम् ॥५५॥
तासां विद्यार्णसङ्ख्यास्तु शृणु वक्ष्ये यथाक्रमम् ।
पञ्चमी पञ्चदशमी विंशतिश्च तथाऽन्तिमा ॥५६॥
चतस्रः(२) पञ्चदशकास्तृतीया साऽष्टमी तथा ।
त्रयोदशी चाष्टदशी द्वाविंशा द्वादशाक्षरा ॥५७॥
सैकविंशच्च तद्वत्स्युश्चतुर्दशसमन्विताः ।
नवमी दशमी(३) चैकविंशा तद्वदनन्तरम् ॥५८॥

प्रमोदेत्यादिना श्लोकेनाष्ट नामान्युपदिशति । तत्र सरतिप्रियेत्यत्रापि सकारः प्राग्वत् । कलादक्षेत्येका । अन्यानि नामानि सुगमानि ॥५३॥

इतीत्यादिना ईप्सितमित्यन्तेन श्लोकद्वयेन प्रोक्तनिगमनं यक्षिणीसिद्धिविद्यां चोपदिशति। तत्र तासाम्—यक्षिणीनाम्। क्रमेण—वक्ष्यमाणेन। तद्बीजद्वयसम्पुटैः मूलविद्याद्यन्तबीजद्वयपुटितैः॥५४॥ षड्‌वर्णैश्च स्वनामभिरित्यत्रोत्तरश्लोकेनान्वयः। नित्यद्रवमद* इति मन्त्रयोजना। एतानि(४) मूलविद्याद्यन्त इत्युक्त्या स्वस्वरूपोपदेशानि बीजद्वयपुटेन सहितानि षडक्षराणि यक्षिणीविद्यासर्वसाधारणानि। उक्तनामभिः—विचित्राद्यैः षट्‌त्रिंशद्भिर्विद्याषडक्षरान्तैर्योजितैस्तन्नामभिरेव मन्त्रभेदः ॥५५॥

तासामित्यादिभिः परा इत्यन्तैश्चतुर्भिः श्लोकैर्विद्यानां प्रत्येकमक्षरसङ्ख्यामुपदिशति। तत्र तासां—यक्षिणीनाम्। अन्तिमा—षट्‌त्रिंशा ॥ ५६ ॥ चतस्रः—विद्या इति शेषः। पञ्चदशकाः—पञ्चदशाक्षरा इत्यर्थः ॥५७॥ सैकविंशच्चेत्यस्य (द्वादश)द्वादशाक्षरा इत्यत्रान्वयः। एवं सम्भूय द्वादशाक्षराविद्याः षट्। तद्वत्स्युश्चतुर्दशसमन्विताः—यद्वत् द्वादशाक्षराः तद्-

---

(१) क्रमेण स्युः इति मू० पु० पा० ।
(२) चतुरस्र सो० पु० पा० ।
(३) सैकविंशा इति मू० पु० पा० ।
(४) मूलविद्याव्यत्यस्तस्वरूपोपेतानि इति टी० पु० पा० ।
* नित्यमद्ररमवद्दमि इति वं० पु० पा० ।

चतुर्विंशा पञ्चविंशा सप्तविंशा तदूर्ध्वगा ।
त्रयस्त्रिंशा(धि)दिकास्तिसस्त्रयोदशयुताः पराः ॥५९॥
चेटकानां चतुःषष्टिं तन्मात्राणां च वदामि ते ।
शृणु* शुद्धास्तु ते नित्यं साधयेयुः समीहितम् ॥६०॥
विभ्रमो वाहको(१) वीरो विकर्षः क्रोकरः कविः ।
सिंहनादो महानादः सुग्रीवोमर्कटः शटः(२) ॥६१॥
विडालाक्षो विडालास्यः कुमारः †खचरोभवः ।
मयूरो मल्लोभीमो द्वीपिवक्त्रः षडाननः ॥६२॥
मातङ्गश्च निशाचारी विषग्राही‡ वृकोदरः ।
सैरिभास्यो गजमुखः पशुवक्त्रो(३)गजाननः ॥६३॥
क्षोभकोमणिभद्रश्च क्रीडकः सिंहवक्त्रकः ।
श्येनास्यः कङ्कवदनः काकास्यो हयवक्त्रकः ॥६४॥

चतुर्दशाक्षरा इत्यर्थः ॥५८॥ तदूर्ध्वगा इति । अष्टविंशेत्यर्थः । त्रयस्त्रिंशादिकास्तिस्रः—त्रयस्त्रिंशादिकाः पञ्चत्रिंशान्तास्तिस्र इत्यर्थः । सम्भूय चतुर्दशाक्षरविद्या दश । त्रयोदशयुताः पराः—अन्याः षोडशविद्यास्त्रयोदशाक्षराः, ताश्च प्रथमद्वितीयचतुर्थषष्ठसप्तमैकादशद्वादशचतुर्दशषोडशसप्तदशैकोनविंशतित्रयोविंशषड्विंशैकोनत्रिंश(त्रिंश)द्वात्रिंशाः । तत्र तासां नामानि—विद्याषडक्षरान्ते सम्बुद्धिरूपाणि योजयित्वा तदन्ते बीजद्वयं प्राग्वद्योजनीयमिति सम्प्रदायार्थः ॥५९॥

चेटकानामित्यादिभिः कीर्तिता इत्यन्तैरष्टभिः श्लोकैस्तन्मन्त्रप्रस्तावपूर्वं चेटकानां नामान्युपदिशति । तत्र ते—तवेत्यर्थः । ते—चेटकाः ॥६०॥

विभ्रमेत्यादिना श्लोकेन एकादश नामान्युपदिशति ॥६१॥

विडालाक्ष इत्यादिना श्लोकेन दश नामान्युपदिशति ॥

मातङ्ग इत्यादिना श्लोकेनाष्ट नामान्युपदिशति ॥६३॥

---

(१) विवर्गोवाहगो वीरः कर्षटकोरजकोरविरिति मू० पु० पा० । (२) सदा इति मू० पु० पा० ।
(३) वक्त्रोमृगाननः इति मू० पु० पा । * श्रृणु सिद्धासुतेतिव्यमिति मू० पु० पा० ।
† खेकर इति मू० पु० पा० । ‡ विषानन इति मू० पु० पा० ।

महोदरः स्थूलशिरा विकृतास्यो वराननः ।
चपलः कुक्कुटास्यश्च मायावी मदनालसः ॥६५॥
मनोहरो दीर्घजङ्घः (१)स्थूलदन्तो दशाननः ।
सुमुखः पीड़ितः क्रुद्धो वराहास्यः सटामुखः ॥६६॥
कपटः कौतुकी कालः किङ्करः कितवः खलः ।
भक्षकोभयदः सिद्धः(२) सर्वगश्चेति कीर्तिताः ॥६७॥
बीजद्वयपुटान्तस्थैर्मदनित्य(ा)द्रवेयुतैः ।
नामभिस्तैर्द्वितीयान्तैर्देहीतिपदसंयुतैः ॥६८॥
एवं मन्त्राश्चतुःषष्टिः क्रमादुक्ता महेश्वरि ! ।
तेषां सङ्ख्यामपि तथा शृणु वक्ष्ये यथाविधि ॥६९॥
चतुर्दशाक्षरास्तेषु नव मन्त्राः समीरिताः ।
तथा पञ्चदशार्णाः स्युः षड्विंशतिरितीरिताः ॥७०॥

क्षोभक इत्यादिना श्लोकेनाष्ट नामान्युपदिशति । तत्र सिंहवक्त्रक इति पञ्चाक्षरं नाम । हयवक्त्रक इति पञ्चाक्षरं नाम ॥६४॥

महोदरेत्यादिना श्लोकेनाष्ट नामान्युपदिशति ॥६५॥

मनोहरेत्यादिना श्लोकेन नव नामान्युपदिशति ॥६६॥

कपट इत्यादिना श्लोकेन दश नामान्युपदिशति । तत्र भयद इति पदच्छेदः । अन्यत्सुगमम् ॥६७॥

बीजेत्यादिना महेश्वरीत्यन्तेनार्धाद्येनैकेन श्लोकेन चेटकानां मन्त्रानुपदिशति । तत्रमदनित्यद्रवे इति मन्त्रयोजना । नामभिः—विभ्रमादिभिः चतुःषष्टिभिः । द्वितीयान्तैः—द्वितीयाविभक्त्यन्तैः । सम्पुटितानि एतानि मूलविद्याया उपक्रमरूपाणि । षडक्षराणि सर्वमन्त्रसाधारणानीति नामभिरेव मन्त्रभेदः । मन्त्रयोजनक्रमो यथा—बीजद्वयं मूलविद्यायाः षडक्षराणि इति द्वितीयान्तं तत्तन्नाम, तदन्ते देहीतिपदं तदन्ते बीजद्वयं विलोममिति ॥६८॥ एवं—उक्तप्रकारतः ॥

तेषामित्यादिना क्रमादित्यन्तेनार्द्धाद्येन चेटकनाममन्त्राक्षरसङ्ख्यामुपदिशति ।

---

(१) तृणदन्तो इति मू० पु० पा० । (२) ग्राह्य इति मू० पु० पा० ।

षोड़शार्णास्तु मनवः पञ्चविंशतिरीरिताः।
तथा (१)सप्तदशार्णाश्च चत्वारोव्याकुलक्रमात् ॥७१॥
विद्याक्षरैरनावृत्तान्यक्षराणि चतुर्दश।
सस्वरैस्तैर्भवेत्सङ्ख्या चतुर्विंशच्छतद्वयम् ॥७२॥
तैर्यन्त्राणि च सप्त स्युस्तेषु प्रोक्ताः क्रमाद्यजेत्।
देवताः सप्तवारेषु भास्करादिषु भक्तितः ॥७३॥

तत्र तेषां—मन्त्राणाम् ॥६९॥ चतुर्दशाक्षरास्तेषु नवमन्त्राः समीरिताः—तेषु मन्त्रेषु नव मन्त्राश्चतुर्दशाक्षरा इत्यन्वयः। ते च तृतीयषष्ठैकादशषोड़शैकोनविंशद्विपञ्चाश-सप्तपञ्चाशषष्टित्रिषष्टितमाः। पञ्चदशार्णाः स्युः षड्विंशतिः—ते च प्रथम-द्वितीयचतुर्थपञ्चमनवमदशमचतुर्दशपञ्चदशसप्तदशाष्टादशद्वाविंशत्रिंशद्द्वात्रिंशचतु-स्त्रिंशषट्त्रिंशद्द्विचत्वारिंशच्चतुश्चत्वारिंशत्पञ्चाशदेकपञ्चाशत्पञ्चपञ्चाशत्षट्पञ्चा-दष्टपञ्चाशदेकोनषष्टिद्विषष्टिचतुःषष्टितमाः॥७०॥षोड़शार्णास्तुमनवः पञ्चविंशतिः—ते च सप्तमाष्टमद्वादशत्रयोदशविंशैकविंशत्रयोविंशाद्येकोनत्रिंशान्त्सप्तकैकत्रिंशाष्ट-त्रिंशैकोनचत्वारिंशच्चत्वारिंशैकचत्वारिंशत्त्रिचत्वारिंशत्षट्चत्वारिंशत्सप्तचत्वा-रिंशदष्टचत्वारिंशैकोनपञ्चाशत्त्रिपञ्चाशच्चतुःपञ्चाशत्तमाः। सप्तदशार्णाश्चत्वारः—ते च त्रयस्त्रिंशत्पञ्चत्रिंशत्सप्तत्रिंशच्चत्वारिंशत्तमाः। व्याकुलक्रमात्—उत्क्रमतः। अन्यत् सुगमम्। अत्र मायासिद्धिविषयस्य मन्त्रस्य चेटकान्तर्गतत्वादनुक्तमिति-मुख्यागमः। तेन सर्वगशब्दस्थाने माया इतिशब्दसमादेशात्—तन्मन्त्रश्चतु-र्दशाक्षरः। एवमेकादशाधिकशतसङ्ख्यामन्त्रमूलमन्त्रा स्वरूपभेदसम्भिन्नाः समीचीनं दर्शिताः ॥७१॥

विद्याक्षरैरित्यादिभिः नरमित्यन्तैश्चतुर्विंशत्या श्लोकैः प्रागुक्तानामेकादशा-धिकशतसङ्ख्यानां सिद्धिमन्त्राणां साधनार्थं सप्तवाराणां स्वरविहीनमूलविद्याक्षरैः सप्त यन्त्राणि तत्तत्साधनस्थानानि तत्तत्प्रत्ययप्रकारांस्तत्फलानि चोपदिशति। तत्र सस्वरैः—प्रागवत्षोड़शस्वरप्रसादितैः। चतुर्विंशच्छतद्वयं—चतुर्विंशत्यधिकद्वि-शतमित्यर्थः ॥७२॥ तैः—अक्षरैः। तेषु—यन्त्रेषु। प्रोक्ताः—प्रागुक्तदशविधसिद्धि-प्रोक्ताः। सप्तवारेषु भास्करादिषु—रविवारादिषु सप्तवारेषु प्रतिवारं प्रोक्ताः(२) सिद्धिदेवताः सकलाः सप्तसु यन्त्रेषु एकस्मिन्नेकस्मिन् प्रत्येकं तत्तत्साधनादिषु

---

(१) तथा सप्तदशा इति मू० पु० पा०। (२) सिधिदेवता इति टी० पु० पा०

वाराख्यां सप्तमीयुक्तामिष्टं देहीति चालिखेत् ।
यन्त्रस्य मध्ये मायास्थं तत्र(१) सिद्धीश्च पूजयेत् ॥७४॥
वृत्तयोर्नवयोनिं तु कृत्वा बाह्येऽष्टकोणकम् ।
बहिः कलाब्जभूपद्मयुगं कुर्याद्यथाविधि ॥७५॥
विलिख्य तेषु क्रमशो वर्णान् द्वाविंशदालिखेत् ।
दलेषु कोणेषु(२) तथा वृत्तमध्यत्रये पुनः ॥७६॥
मातृकामकथाद्यां वै विलिखेदान्तरक्रमात् ।
तस्य कोणान्तरालेषु हलच्चार्णान् क्रमाल्लिखेत् ॥७७॥
अग्रात्प्रदक्षिणं त्वेवं सप्त यन्त्राणि तैर्भवेत् ।
सिद्धीनां यक्षिणीनां च चेटकानां तथैकशः ॥७८॥
चेटकानां विशेषोऽयं मध्ये ऽष्टच्छदमम्बुजम् ।
तेषामुक्तक्रमेणैव साधनानि (३)फलानि वै ॥७९॥

यजेदित्यर्थः॥७३॥सप्तमीयुक्तां—सप्तमीविभक्त्यन्ताम् । मायास्थं—ह्रींखागर्भस्थम् । इष्टं देहीति चालिखेदिति पूर्वत्रान्वयः । तत्र—मायोदरे । सिद्धीः—सर्वसिद्धिदेवताः ॥७४॥ बाह्ये—वृत्तद्वयतः । बहिः—अष्टकोणात् । कलाब्जं—षोड़शदलं पद्मम् । यथाविधि—यथामानं विलिख्येति पूर्वत्रान्वयः॥७५॥ तेषु—दलेषु । कोणेष्वित्युत्तरत्रान्वयः । वृत्तमध्यत्रये—नवयोनिबाह्यगताष्टकोणबाह्यगतषोड़शदलबाह्य गतवृत्तद्वयमध्यवीथीत्रये इत्यर्थः ॥७६॥ अकथाद्यां—अकारादिविसर्जनीयान्तान् षोड़श ककारादितकारान्तान् षोड़शथकारादि सकारान्तान् षोड़श वर्णानित्यर्थः । तस्य—तद्बाह्यलिखितस्य पुरयुग्मस्य । कोणान्तरालेषु हलच्चार्णान्—क्रमात् भूपद्मयुगस्य कोणान्तरालेषु चतुर्षु उक्तमक्षरत्रयं विलिखेदित्यर्थः ॥७७॥ अग्रात्प्रदक्षिणं—सर्वाक्षराणीति शेषः । सप्त यन्त्राणि—स्युरितिशेषः । तैः यन्त्रैः । एकशः—एकैकस्य साधनादिकमिति शेषः । भवेदित्यत्रास्य शेषस्यान्वयः ॥७८॥ मध्येऽष्टच्छदमम्बुजं—नवयोनिस्थानेऽष्टदलपद्ममित्यर्थः ॥७९॥ तेनापि सकर्णिकानि

---

(१) तत्रसर्वं स इति मू० पु० पा० ।
(२) यथा लिखेद्वृत्तत्रये इति मू० पु० पा० ।
(३) फलावलिः इति मू० पु० पा० ।

प्रयोगान् शृणु देवेशि! यैः सिद्धैर्मत्समोभुवि।
पूज्यते सर्वलोकैश्च सर्वतः सर्वदापि च ॥८०॥
अरण्यवटमूले च पर्वताग्रे गुहासु च।
उद्यानमध्ये कान्तारे मातृपादपमूलतः ॥८१॥
सिन्धुतीरवने चैता यक्षिणीः साधयेत्त्रिशः।
एकैकस्मिन् वर्णलक्षं जपेदुक्तविधानतः ॥८२॥

नवस्थानानि भवन्ति। तेषां—विजयादिचेटकान्तानाम्। यैः—प्रयोगैः। मत्समः—परमेश्वर इत्यर्थः। एतैर्नवभिः श्लोकैरेतदुक्तं भवति—अभीष्टमानभूमिणान्तर्बहिर्विभागैनैकाङ्गुलान्तरालवीथिकं वृत्तद्वयं विधाय तन्मध्ये प्रागुक्तमानविधानतो नवयोनिं कृत्वा तद्बहिर्दिग्विदिग्गतकोणचतुरस्रद्वयेनाष्टकोणं विधाय तद्बहिरेकाङ्गुलान्तरालवीथिकं वृत्तद्वयं कृत्वा तद्बहिः षोडशदलानि सबाह्यगतवृत्तद्वयं विधाय तद्बहिश्चतुरस्रद्वयमन्तर्बहिर्विभागेन कृत्वा सर्वमध्यस्थयोन्यामसुष्मिन्वारे इमां सिद्धिं देहीति हृल्लेखायां स्वसंज्ञायां मायांशे वाराख्यां रेफांशे तदन्तराले सिद्धिं देहीति समालिख्य तद्बहिरग्रादिप्रादक्षिण्येनाष्टसु कोणेषु स्वरविकृतमूलविद्याक्षरेषु चतुर्विंशत्यधिकशतसङ्ख्येषु आदितोऽष्टकं तद्बहिः (अष्टास्वष्टकं तद्बहि) षोड़शपत्रेषु षोड़शं(कं)च एवं द्वात्रिंशदक्षराण्यालिख्य वृत्तान्तरा वीथीत्रये अन्तर्नवयोनिबाह्यगतवृत्तद्वयवीथ्यां अकारादिविसर्जनीयान्तान् षोडशस्वरानालिख्य मध्यस्थायामष्टकोणबाह्यगतवृत्तद्वयवीथ्यां अकारादिविसर्जनीयान्तान् षोड़शस्वरानालिख्य मध्यस्थायामष्टकोणबाह्यगतवृत्तद्वयवीथ्यां ककारादितकारान्तानि षोड्शाक्षराण्यालिख्य षोड्शदलबाह्यगतवृत्तद्वयवीथ्यां थकारादिसकारान्तानि षोडशाक्षराणि तद्बहिश्चतुरस्रकोणान्तरालेषु चतुर्षु हलक्ष इत्यक्षरत्रयं प्रति(त्रि)कोणान्तराले समालिखेत्। एतत् प्रथमं यन्त्रम्। अन्येषु षट्सु यन्त्रेषु पूर्वपूर्वलिखिताक्षरद्वात्रिंशकोपरितनमुपरितनं द्वात्रिंशत्कं च विलिखेत्। एवं सप्त यन्त्राणि कृत्वा सर्व्वत्रार्कादिकेषु सप्तसु वारेषु प्रोक्तक्रमेण विनियुञ्ज्यादिति ॥८०॥ मातृपादपमूलतः—मातृपादपाश्चाष्टौ च पूर्वं प्रधाननित्याकाम्यकथने कथिताः तेनाष्टौ स्थानान्यायतनानि ॥८१॥ सिन्धुतीरवने—नदीतीरस्थवने इत्यर्थः। एवं सम्भूय द्वादश स्थानानि सम्भवन्ति। त्रिशः एकैकस्मिन्—द्वादशसु स्थानेषु एकस्मिन्नेकस्मिंस्तिस्रस्तिस्रो यक्षिणीः

तद्दशांशं तर्पणं च होमं कुर्यात् प्रसूनकैः ।
कदम्बबन्धूकजयाह्वयमारैश्च लोहितैः ॥८३॥
ततः प्रीताः समागत्य प्रत्यक्षा वाञ्छितप्रदाः ।
सुवर्णानि च वासांसि भूषणानि फलानि च ॥८४॥
आस्वाद्यानि च पेयानि भोज्यानि विविधानि च ।
आलेपनानि माल्यानि दद्युराजीवितावधि ॥८५॥
आयाते सर्वदा ग्राह्यं प्रत्यक्षादेहि वाञ्छितम् ।
इत्युक्त्वा नित्यशस्तास्तु पूजयेच्चजपेत्तथा ॥८६॥
अष्टोत्तरसहस्रं तु तां तां विद्यामनन्यधीः ।
एवं ताः सर्वयक्षिण्यः फलं दद्युर्यथेप्सितम् ॥८७॥
चेटकानान्तु सर्वेषां तेषूक्तेषु क्रमेण वै ।
एकस्मिन् पञ्च पञ्च स्युः सिद्धाः सिन्धुतटे नव ॥८८॥
तेषां च वर्णलक्षन्तु जपमुक्तविधानतः ।
मौनं दिनेषु सततं कुर्यात् सिद्धै न चालयेत् ॥८९॥
मध्यरात्रे सदा होमं तर्पणं च समीरितम् ।
जपेद्दिवानिशं प्रोक्तं सर्वेषामपि साधने ॥९०॥

साधयेदित्यर्थः । वर्णलक्षं—तत्तद्विद्यायाः ॥८२॥ तत्तच्छब्देन जपसंख्योच्यते । हयमारैश्च लोहितैः—रक्तकरवीरपुष्पै रित्यर्थः ॥८३॥

तत इत्यादीप्सितम् इत्यन्तश्लोकचतुष्टयोक्तयक्षिणीप्रत्यक्षीकरणतद्देयार्थ नित्यतदुपासनादिग्रन्थार्थः सुगमः ॥८४॥८५॥८६॥८७॥

तेषु—स्थानेषु । एकस्मिन् पञ्च पञ्च—एकस्मिन्नेकस्मिंस्थाने पञ्च पञ्च चेटकाः । सिन्धुतटे नव—द्वादशे स्थाने नव चेटकाः । पूर्वं यक्षिणीप्रोक्तद्वादश स्थानेषु एकादशेष्वेकैकस्मिन् स्थाने पञ्च पञ्च द्वादश सिन्धुतटे वन स्थाने नवचेटकान् एवं चतुःषष्टिष्वेकमेकं चेटकं प्रोक्तक्रमात् साधयेदित्यर्थः । एतानि स्थानान्यन्यसर्वसिद्धाष्टकसाधनसाधारणानीति सम्प्रदायः ॥८८॥ वर्णलक्षं—मन्त्रस्य । दिनेषु—

चेटकास्ते समागत्य मध्यरात्रेऽतिभीषणाः ।
क्षोभयुरमुं क्षोमं नचेदित्यथ तत्पुरः ॥९१॥
प्रत्यक्षाः किं तवेष्टं तत् करोमिति वदेन्निशि ।
प्रत्येकं ते तथेत्युक्त्वा न मां मुञ्चत इत्यपि ॥९२॥
नित्यशस्तान् जपार्चाभिरुपासीताचरेत्पुनः(१) ।
(स्मृ)सते तमेत्य सन्दिष्टं साधयेयुः समीहितम् ॥९३॥
शत्रूणां समरे भङ्गं प्रहारमहिते जने ।
कुर्वन्ति प्रार्थितार्थानां प्रदानं च दिवाऽनिशम् ॥९४॥
आनयेयुश्च वनिता वाञ्छितांस्तत्क्षणात् ध्रुवम् ।
निश्चलीकुर्वते मत्तं दन्तिनं वा हयं नरम् ॥९५॥
नित्याषोड़शकं सिद्धे देवर्षिपितृराक्षसैः ।
पिशाचैरुरगैः सिद्धैः किन्नरैरप्सरोगणैः ॥९६॥
मरुद्भिर्वसुभिः सप्तर्षिभिर्यक्षदानवैः ।
रुद्रैरेकादशविधैः साध्यैश्च नवभिर्ग्रहैः ॥९६॥

साधन(ा)दिनेषु, एतत् सर्वसाधारणम् ॥८८॥ दिवानिशं—सर्वदेत्यर्थः । सर्वेषां—प्रोक्तानामन्येषां विजयादिमायान्तानामष्टानामन्येषां च ॥९०॥ अमुं—साधकम् । तत्पुरः—साधकपुरः॥९१॥ प्रत्येकं—एक एकश्चेटक इत्यर्थः । अस्य वदेदित्यत्रा-न्वयः । ते—चेटकाः । तथेत्यादिना श्लोकशेषः साधकप्रार्थनावचनम् ॥९२॥ नित्यशः—तत्तच्चेटकसिद्ध्यनन्तरमुक्तक्रमात् । (स्मृ)ते—चेटकाः । समीहितं—साधकस्येति शेषः ॥९३॥ शत्रूणामित्यादि समीहितसाधनाप्रकारः । एतदुक्तं भवति चेटकेषु स्वाभिमतं स्वाभिमतमेकमेकं चेटकं प्रोक्तक्रमात्साधयेदिति । तत्र बहुवचनानि सर्वचेटकसाधारणत्वात् साधनादेरिति सम्प्रदायः । एवं मायासिद्धिविधानादिकं विजयादीनां सप्तानां विधानादिकमप्येवम् ॥९४॥९५॥

नित्येत्यादिभिर्भवेदित्यन्तैः पञ्चभिः श्लोकैः षोड़शनित्यासिद्धिलक्षणानुप्र-

---

(१) चरेत्तत इति मू० पु० पा० ।

द्वादशार्कैर्लोकपालैस्तथाऽन्यैरपि दैवतैः ।
राजभिर्वनिताभिश्च नरैरन्यैर्मृगैस्तथा ॥९८॥
पूज्यते सर्वदा सिद्धसमीहितसुखास्पदः ।
हृष्टाशयो वदान्यश्च दयावान् सुमुखः क्षमी ॥९९॥
पूर्णाशयः सदानन्दोनिरपेक्षफलान्वितः ।
धनी भोक्ताऽपरद्वेषी प्रेमभूरावयोर्भवेत् ॥१००॥
जिह्वातत्त्वमयी व्याप्तिरिति सम्यक् समीरिता ।
अस्या निष्फालनाच्चित्ते तत्तत्त्वं स्वात्मसात्कृतम् ॥१०१॥

इति षोडशनित्यातन्त्रेषु श्रीकादिमते सप्तदशं पटलं परिपूर्णं परामृष्टम् ॥१७॥

दिशति । तत्र अन्यैः—दक्षप्राजापत्यादिभिः ॥९६॥९७॥९८॥ सिद्धसमीहितसुखास्पदः—सिद्धसमीहितश्च सुखास्पदश्चेत्यर्थः॥९९॥ पूर्णाशयः ज्ञातव्यनिरपेक्षत्वात् । निरपेक्ष इति वित्तादिविषयः । अपरद्वेषी इति पदच्छेदः । परद्वेषकरणपराङ्मुख इत्यर्थः । आवयोः– शिवशक्त्योः ॥१००॥

इति श्रीषोडशनित्यातन्त्रेषु श्रीकादिमताख्यस्य तन्त्रस्य परिपूर्णस्य तन्त्रस्य प्रपञ्चसारसिंहराजप्रकाशाभिधानेन श्रीसुभगानन्दनाथेन विरचितायां मनोरमाख्यायां व्याख्यायां शिवदूतीनित्याविद्याविधानप्रकाशनपरं सप्तदशपटलं परिपूर्णं परामृष्टम् ॥१७॥

ग्रन्थसङ्ख्या—

यन्त्राणि सप्त प्रोक्तानि व्याख्यानं ग्रन्थसङ्ख्यया ।
पटलेऽस्मिन् सप्तदशे सषोडशशतद्वयम् ॥

अथाष्टादशपटलम् ।

अथ षोड़शनित्यासु सम्प्रोक्ता या त्रयोदशी ।
तद्विधानं शृणु प्राज्ञे ! विद्या प्रागुदिता तव ॥१॥
तदङ्गान्यक्षरन्यासं(१) ध्यानार्चे ऽस्यास्तु शक्तिभिः ।
तद्यन्त्रविनियोगांश्च वक्ष्येऽहं विजयप्रदान् ॥२॥
विद्याया व्यञ्जनैर्दीर्घस्वरयुक्तैश्चतुष्टयम् ।
शेषाभ्यां च द्वयं कुर्यात् षड़ङ्गानि कराङ्गयोः ॥३॥
ज्ञानेन्द्रियेषु श्रोत्रादिष्वथ चित्ते च विन्यसेत् ।
अक्षराणि क्रमाद्बिन्दुयुतान्यन्यत्तु पूर्ववत् ॥४॥

अथाष्टादशपटलम् ।

पूर्वस्मिन् सप्तदशे पटले द्वादश्या नीलपताकानित्याविद्याया विधानमुपदिश्यानन्तरं त्रयोदश्या विजयानित्याविद्याया विधानमुपदिशति । अथ षोड़शेत्यादिना समीरिता इत्यन्तेन श्लोकशतरूपेणाष्टादशेन पटलेन । तत्र अथ षोड़शेत्यादिना प्रदानित्यन्तेन श्लोकद्वयेन पटलार्थानुद्दिशति । तत्र त्रयोदशी—विजयानित्येत्यर्थः । प्राक्—तृतीयपटले ॥१॥ ध्यानार्चे इति द्वितीयाद्विवचनम् । ध्यानं चार्चा चेत्यर्थः । तद्यन्त्रविनियोगान्—तद्यन्त्राणि तद्विनियोगांश्चेत्यर्थः ॥२॥

विद्याया इत्यादिना पूर्ववदित्यन्तेन श्लोकद्वयेन मूलविद्याक्षरैः कराङ्गज्ञानेन्द्रियषट्कन्यासविधानादिकमुपदिशति । तत्र—विद्याया व्यञ्जनैर्दीर्घस्वरयुक्तैश्चतुष्टयम् । शेषाभ्यां च द्वयं कुर्यात् षड़ङ्गानि कराङ्गयोरित्यन्तेन श्लोकेनैतदुक्तं भवति—भाँ मीँ रूँ यैँ इत्यन्तर्मूलविद्याया दीर्घस्वरयुक्तव्यञ्जनाक्षरैः सबिन्दुकैः सजातिकैर्हृदयशिरःशिखाकवचानि न्यस्य विद्यायाः शेषस्वराक्षरद्वयेन, औकारजकाररूपेण सबिन्दुना शेषजातियुजा नेत्रास्त्रे(?) च, एवं षड़ङ्गानि करन्यासपूर्वं विदध्यादिति ॥३॥ ज्ञानेन्द्रियादिषु श्रोत्रादिषु—श्रोत्रत्वक्चक्षुर्जिह्वाघ्राणेषु । तत्र त्वचि विन्यासो व्यापकवत् । अन्यत्—व्यापकम् । पूर्ववत्—समस्तया विद्यया

---

(१) ध्यानं वेश्मासु इति मू० पु० पा० ।

पञ्चवक्त्रां दशभुजां प्रतिवक्त्रं त्रिलोचनाम् ।
भास्वन्मुकुटविन्यस्तचन्द्ररेखाविराजिताम् ॥५॥
सर्वाभरणसंयुक्तां पीताम्बरसमुज्ज्वलाम् ।
उद्यद्भास्वत्बिम्बतुल्यदेहकान्तिं शुचिस्मिताम् ॥६॥
शङ्खं पाशं खेटचापौ कह्लारं वामबाहुभिः ।
चक्रं तथाऽङ्कुशं खड्गं सायकं मातुलुङ्गकम् ॥७॥
दधानां दक्षिणैर्हस्तैः प्रयोगे भीमदर्शनाम् ।
उपासनेऽतिसौम्यां च सिंहोपरि कृतासनाम् ॥८॥
व्याघ्रारूढाभिरभितः शक्तिभिः परिवारिताम् ।
समरे पूजनेऽन्येषु प्रयोगेषु सुखासनाम् ॥९॥
शक्तयश्चापि पूजायां सुखासनसमन्विताः ।
सर्वादिव्या समाकारमुखपाण्यायुधान्यपि ॥१०॥

प्रागुक्तविधानेनेत्यर्थः । एतदुक्तं भवति—श्रोत्रादिषु पञ्चसु ज्ञानेन्द्रियेषु मनसि च सम्भूय षट्सु स्थानेषु श्रोत्रादिषु त्रिषु द्वन्द्वस्थानेषु प्रतिद्वन्द्वमेकमेकमन्ययोरेकमेकं इत्येवं सविन्दुकानि भँ मँ रँ यँ श्रौँ ॐ इत्येतानि मूलविद्यायाः षडक्षराणि क्रमेण विन्यस्य समस्तरूपया विद्यया व्यापकं च न्यसेदिति ॥४॥

पञ्चवक्त्रामित्यादिभिरपीत्यन्तैः षड्भिः श्लोकैर्देव्याः सपरिवाराया नित्यसपर्याध्यानं प्रयोगध्यानं चोपदिशति । तत्र पञ्चवक्त्रावस्थानं नीलपताकायाः प्रोक्तप्रकारेण । दशभुजामिति च तद्वत् । भुजेष्वायुधानि वामोर्ध्वादि दक्षिणोर्ध्वादिव (च) बोद्धव्यानि ॥५॥६॥७॥ प्रयोगे समरादिविजयप्रयोग इत्यर्थः । उपासने – नित्यभजने । सिंहोपरि कृतासनां—सिंहारूढाम् ॥८॥ समरे पूजने—समरविजयार्थे पूजन इत्यर्थः । सिंहाधिरूढां भयङ्कराम्—व्याघ्रारूढाभिः स्वसमानाभिः शक्तिभिः परिवारिताम्—युद्धविजयार्थं ध्यात्वा पूजयेदित्यर्थः । अन्येषु—वश्यादिषु ॥९॥ पूजायां—नित्यायाम् । अपीतिभिन्नक्रमः । सर्वा अपीत्यर्थः शक्तय इति शेषः । एतदुक्तं भवति—वश्यादिषु प्रयोगेषु नित्योपासनपूजायां च सुखासीनां सपरिवारां देवीं ध्यायेदिति ॥१०॥

चतुरस्रद्वयं कृत्वा चतुर्द्वारोपशोभितम्।
दलाष्टकसमोपेतं तत्र प्राग्वत् समर्चयेत् ॥११॥
तदन्तर्वृत्तयुग्मान्तरष्टकोणं विधाय तु(तत्)।
तदन्तश्च तथा पद्मं षोडशच्छदसंयुतम् ॥१२॥
तथैवाष्टच्छदं पद्मं विधायावाह्य तत्र ताम्।
तत्तच्छक्त्या वृतां सम्यगुपचारैस्तथाऽर्चयेत् ॥१३॥
अन्नाज्याभ्यां नित्यहोमं कुर्याद्वा तिलतण्डुलैः।
बलिद्वयं च कुर्वीत पूजां चाऽपि समापयेत् ॥१४॥
ललितारहिताः पञ्चदशनित्या(१)स्तिथीश्वराः।
चन्द्रखण्डलसन्मौलियुता सा तन्मयी मता ॥१५॥
मायासप्ताचरीमध्यगतैर्नामभिरर्चयेत्।
तदावरणगाः शक्तीस्तत्समाकारशक्तिकाः ॥१६॥

चतुरस्रद्वयमित्यादिभिः 'सुखी' इत्यन्तैः पञ्चदशभिः श्लोकैः देव्या नित्यसपर्यामण्डलविरचनाक्रमं तत्र चतुरावरणं नित्यसपर्याक्रमविधानमन्यासां पञ्चदशनित्यानां चन्द्रकलाधारणवासनां ललितायास्तद्धारणवासनां आवरणशक्तिनामानि चोपदिशति। तत्र प्राग्वत्--चतुरस्रे नित्या(नित्या)र्चनवदित्यर्थः ॥११॥ तदन्तः—चतुरस्रान्तः ॥१२॥ तत्र—चक्रे तथा--वक्ष्यमाणप्रकारेण। नित्यसपर्यामण्डलविरचनाक्रमो यथा—अन्तर्बहिर्विभागेन यथामानं चतुरस्रद्वयं प्रत्येकं शाखाद्वयोपेतं चतुर्द्वारं विधाय तदन्तर्वृत्तद्वयमन्तश्चतुरस्ररेखास्पृष्टास्पृष्टं विधाय तदन्तरष्टकोणं प्राग्वत् कृत्वा तदन्तः षोडशदलं पद्मं कृत्वा तदन्तरष्टदलं विरच्य (?) तत्कर्णिकायां सपरिवारां देवीमावाह्याभ्यर्चयेदिति ॥१३॥ वा—विकल्पे। बलिद्वयं प्राग्वत् ॥१४॥ तेजस्त्रयभावनादिना। सा तन्मयी- सा ललिता अक्षयचन्द्रकलारूपिणी इत्यर्थः। अनेन श्लोकेनैतदुक्तं भवति—क्षयवृद्ध्युपेतचन्द्रकलापञ्चदशकरूपाः पञ्चदशतिथयोऽन्यत्र व्यवच्छिन्नाः सर्वाः प्रत्येकं सर्वकलाकारणत्वानुस्यूतरूपया षोडश्या कलया

---

(१) नित्यात्मिकाश्वराः इति मू० पु० पा।

अग्रात् प्रदक्षिणेनैव ताः सर्वास्तेषु पूजयेत् ।
तासां क्रमेण नामानि शृणु वक्ष्ये यथाविधि ॥१७॥
नित्यानित्यावदुदितमर्चनं चतुरस्रके ।
अन्तःस्थिताष्टकोणेषु पूजयेदुक्तविग्रहाः ॥१८॥
जयां च विजयां दुर्गां भद्रां भद्रकरीमपि ।
क्षेमां क्षेमंकरीनित्यामष्टकोणेषु भक्तितः ॥१९॥
तदन्तः षोड़शदलेष्वर्चयेत्षोड़शाभितः ।
शक्तीस्ता(स्ता) गन्धपुष्पा(दि)युतोभक्तिसमन्वितः ॥२०॥
विदारिकां विश्वमयीं विश्वां विश्वविभञ्जिकाम् ।
वीरां विक्षोभिणीं विद्यां विनोदाञ्चितविग्रहाम् ॥२१॥
वीतशोकां विषग्रीवां विपुलां विजयप्रदाम् ।
विभवां विविधां विप्रां प्रोक्ताकारसमन्विताः ॥२२॥
तदन्तरष्टपत्रेषु शक्तीरष्टाभितो यजेत् ।
प्रोक्तक्रमेण गन्धाद्यैर्भक्तिनिष्ठाशयो वशी ॥२३॥

ऽक्षयया सहिताः किल भवन्ति। तेन ललितारहितानां पञ्चदशानां नित्यानां पञ्चदशतिथिरूपत्वात्तासामप्यक्षयषोड़शचन्द्रकलाधारणं भवति। ललिता तु सर्वतिथिमयत्वादनवच्छिन्ना सदकलाकारणरूपाऽक्षया षोड़शो कला भवति। तेन तस्याश्चन्द्रकलाराहित्यमिति ॥१५॥ मायासमाक्षरीमध्यगतैः—ह्स्रे खाद्यैः सप्तार्णैरित्यर्थः। नामभिः—मन्त्रैरिति शेषः ॥१६॥ ताः—शक्तीः। तेषु—चतुरस्रादिस्थानेषु। तासां—आवरणशक्तीनाम् ॥१७॥ अन्तःस्थिताष्टकोणेषु—चतुरस्रादिकस्येति शेषः। उक्तविग्रहाः—जयामित्याद्यनन्तरश्लोकवक्ष्यमाणाः ॥१८॥ अष्टकोणेष्वित्यस्य द्विरुपादानं सङ्क्षेपविस्ताररूपत्वाददोषः। भक्तितः—पूजयेदिति शेषः ॥१९॥ तदन्तः—अष्टकोणान्तः। ताः ताः—अनन्तरं विदारिकामित्यादिश्लोकद्वयवक्ष्यमाणाः ॥२०॥ विदारिकां—विदारिणीमित्यर्थः। विश्वविभञ्जिकां—विश्वविभञ्जिनीमित्यर्थः ॥२१॥ विविधामिति। पञ्चदशानामप्रोक्ताकारसमन्विताः—मूलदेवतासमाना इत्यर्थः। अर्चयेदित्यन्वयः ॥२२॥ तदन्तः—

मनोहरां मङ्गलां च मदोत्सिक्तां मनस्विनीम्।
मानिनीं मधुरां मायां मोहिनीमुक्तविग्रहाम् ॥२४॥
एवं पूजाजपध्यानहोमोपासनतो वशी।
भजते नित्यशोदेवीं योऽसौ स्यात्सर्वतः सुखी ॥२५॥
पूर्वोक्तक्रमतोविद्यावर्णलक्षं जपेद्वशी।
होमं रक्ताम्बुजैः कृत्वा सिद्धमन्त्रोदयान्वितः ॥२६॥
प्रयोगानाचरेन्मन्त्री होमयन्त्रविधानतः।
जपेन तर्पणेनापि पूजनेन यथाविधि ॥२७॥
कमलैः कैरवैरक्तैः सितैः सौगन्धिकोत्पलैः।
सुगन्धिशेफालिकया त्रिमध्वक्तैर्यथाविधि ॥२८॥
होमात् सप्तसु वारेषु कुर्य्यात्प्रोक्तैस्तु सप्तभिः।
प्रोक्तवारेशयोश्चापि तन्मण्डलत एव वै ॥२९॥

षोडशदलान्तः। शक्तीः—मनोहरामित्याद्यनन्तरश्लोकवक्ष्यमाणाः ॥२३॥ उक्तविग्रहाः प्राग्वत्। अस्या आवरणार्चनक्रमोबाह्यादावाभ्यन्तरप्रवेशतः ॥२४॥ एवं—प्रोक्तरूपतः ॥२५॥

पूर्वेत्यादिना यथाविधीत्यन्तेन श्लोकद्वयेन पुरश्चरणविधानं कृतपुरश्चरणस्यैव प्रयोगविधानयोग्यतां चोपदिशति। तत्र पूर्वोक्तक्रमतः—नीलपताकाप्रोक्तक्रमतः। तेन मूलविद्यायां स्वरव्यञ्जनविन्दून् वर्णान् पृथक्कृत्य गणयित्वा तदक्षरलक्षसंख्यं जप्यादित्युक्तं भवति। तदक्षरसङ्ख्यातु सप्त। अवशिष्टमन्यत्सुगमम् ॥२६॥२७॥

कमलैरित्यादिभिर्निश्चितमित्यन्तैरर्द्धाधिकैस्त्रिभिः सप्तसु वारेषु प्रोक्तसप्तपुष्पपूजाहोमविधानक्रमतः प्रोक्तां विजयसिद्धिमुपदिशति। तत्र रक्तैः सितैरित्यस्य कमलैः कैरवैरित्युभयत्रान्वयः। तेन रक्तैः कमलैः सितैः कमलैः रक्तैः कैरवैः सितैः कैरवैश्चेत्युक्तं भवति। त्रिमध्वक्तत्वमेतेषां होमविधावेव ॥२८॥ होमादितिल्यब्लोपे पञ्चमी। होमं कृत्वेत्यर्थः। सप्तसु वारेषु—रविवारादिषु। प्रोक्तैस्तु सप्तभिः—पुष्पैरिति शेषः। प्रोक्तवारेशयोः—कुलसुन्दरीपटले इति शेषः। तन्मण्डलतः—तान्यपि तत्रैवोक्तानि यदष्टादिंशतिपटलेऽवेक्षणीयानि। एतदुक्तं

विजयं समवाप्नोति समरे द्वन्द्वयुद्धके ।
(१)मल्लयुद्धे च वादे च द्वये द्यूतद्वयेऽपि च ॥३०॥
व्यवहारेषु सर्वत्र जयमाप्नोति निश्चितम् ।
चतुरङ्गुलजैः पुष्पैर्होमात्संस्तम्भयेदरीन् ॥३१॥
तथैव कर्णिकारोत्थैः पुन्नागोत्थैर्नमेरुजैः ।
चम्पकैः केतकैराजवृक्षजैर्मागधोद्भवैः ॥३२॥
प्राग्वद्वारेषु जुहुयात्क्रमात्पुष्पैस्तु सप्तभिः ।
प्रोक्तेषु स्तम्भनं शत्रोर्भङ्गो वा भवति ध्रुवम् ॥३३॥
शत्रोर्नक्षत्रवृक्षाग्नौ तत्समिद्भिस्तु होमतः ।
सर्पिषाज्याप्लुताभिस्ते प्रणमन्त्येव पादयोः ॥३४॥
मृत्युकाष्ठानले मृत्युपत्रपुष्पफलैरपि ।
समिद्भिर्जुहुयात्सम्यग्वारेशार्चनपूर्वकम् ॥३५॥

भवति—प्रोक्तैरक्तकमलसितकमलरक्तकैरवसितकैरवसौगन्धिकोत्पलसुगन्धिशेफालिकाख्यैः सप्तभिः (कर्णिकाराद्यैः) पुष्पैरुद्दिष्टक्रमतो रविवारादिषु सप्तसु तद्वारेशद्वयस्य तन्मण्डलेऽर्चनतो मूलविद्यया तैर्होमतश्चोक्तफलसिद्धिरिति ॥२८॥ समरे इति वक्ष्यमाणसप्तकविषयः। द्वन्द्वयुद्धके—प्राग्वत्। द्यूतद्वये—सजीवनिर्जीवरूपे ॥३०॥ सर्वत्र—अन्येषु विवादेष्वपि ॥

चतुरङ्गुलजैरित्यादिना ध्रुवमित्यन्तेनार्द्धाधिकेन श्लोकद्वयेन सर्वदा आरग्वधैः सप्तसु वारेषु सप्तभिः पुष्पैश्च होमविधानाच्छत्रुस्तम्भनादिकमुपदिशति। तत्र चतुरङ्गुलजैरारग्वधोत्थैः॥३१॥नमेरुजैः- सुरपर्णीपुष्पैः। राजवृक्षजैःआरग्वधपुष्पैः॥३२॥ प्राग्वत्—वारेशार्चनपूर्वम्। वारेषु सप्तसु रविवारादिषु। सप्तभिः—कर्णिकाद्यैः। अत्रारग्वधस्य द्विरुपादानं सर्वदा च तत्प्राग्वारेषु च होमविधानार्थम्। प्रोक्तेषु—द्वन्द्वयुद्धादिषु। एतदुक्तं भवति—प्रोक्तैः पुष्पैः सप्तभिः प्राग्वत्सप्तवारेषु तत्तद्वारेशार्चनपूर्वकमारग्वधैः सर्वदा च होमात्प्रोक्तफलसिद्धिरिति ॥३३॥

शत्रोरित्यादिभिः संशय इत्यन्तैरेकविंशत्या श्लोकैस्तिथिवारादिषु द्रव्यविशेषैः

---

(१) मल्लयुद्धे शस्त्रयुद्धेवादे इति सी० पु० पा०।

(१)अरातेश्चतुरङ्गन्तु बलं रोगार्दितं भवेत् ।
तेनास्य विजयोभूयान्निधनेनापि वा पुनः ॥३६॥
अर्कवारेऽर्कजैरिध्मैः समिद्धेऽग्नौ तदुद्भवैः ।
पत्रैः पुष्पैः फलैः काण्डैः मूलैश्चापि हुनेत्क्रमात् ॥३७॥
सवर्णारुणवत्साया घृतसिक्तैस्तु मण्डलात् ।
अरातिदिङ्मुखोभूत्वा कुण्डे त्र्यस्रे विधानतः ॥३८॥
पलायते वा रोगार्तः प्रणमेद्वा भयान्वितः ।
वैरी बलसमग्रोपि शौर्यमानान्वितोऽपि च ॥३९॥
पलाशेध्मानले तस्य पञ्चाङ्गै(२)स्तद्घृताप्लुतैः ।
होमेन सोमवारे(३) च भवेत्प्राग्वन्न संशयः ॥४०॥
खदिरेध्मानले तस्य पञ्चाङ्गैस्तद्घृताप्लुतैः ।
वारे भौमस्य हवनात्तदाप्नोति सुनिश्चितम् ॥४१॥
अपामार्गेध्मजे वह्नौ तत्समिद्भिर्हुनेत्तथा ।
बुधवारेषु शुभ्राया: सवंत्साया घृतान्वितम् ॥४२॥

होमविशेषविधानाद्विजयप्राप्तिप्रकारानुपदिशति । तत्र तत्समिद्भिः—नक्षत्रवृक्ष-समिद्भिः । तं—शत्रवः ॥३४॥ समिद्भिः—मृत्योरितिशेषः ॥३५॥ निधनेन—शत्रु-बलस्येतिशेषः ॥३६॥ तदुद्भवैः—अर्कसंभवैः । क्रमात्—उद्दिष्टक्रमैः पत्राद्यै-र्मूलान्तैः पञ्चभिरङ्गैरित्यर्थः ॥ ३७ ॥ सवर्णारुणवत्सायाः—अरुणवर्णवत्सायाः अरुणवर्णायाः गोरित्यर्थः । घृतसिक्तैः—पूर्वोक्तपञ्चाङ्गैरित्यर्थः । मण्डलात्—प्राग्वत् एकोनपञ्चाशद्दिनैरित्यर्थः । त्र्यस्रे—त्रिकोणकुण्डे इत्यर्थः ॥३८॥३९॥ तस्य—पलाशस्य । पञ्चाङ्गैः—पत्रपुष्पफलकाण्डमूलैः । पुनश्च तद्घृताप्लुतैः—सवर्णवत्सारुणगोघृताप्लुतैः । प्राग्वदिति भिन्नक्रमः । प्राग्वद्भवेदिति—विजयो भवेदित्यर्थः ॥४०॥ तस्य—खदिरस्य । पञ्चाङ्गानि प्राग्वत् । तद्घृताप्लुतैः—प्राग्वत् । तत्—विजयफलम् ॥४१॥ तत्समिद्भिः—अपामार्गस्य समिद्भिः ॥४२॥ पूर्वोक्तफलसं

---

(१) आगत चतुरङ्गं तु इति मू० पु० पा० ।　　(२) ङ्गैसघृतप्लुतैरिति मू० पु० पा० ।
(३) वारेषु इति मू० पु० पा० ।

पूर्वोक्तफलसंसिद्धिर्भवत्येव च तद्दिनैः ।
तच्चवारेषु(?) ते जन्म पूर्वमेव हि(१) तत्क्रिया ॥४३॥
सर्वत्र प्रोक्तहोमार्चाजपमन्त्रादिकर्मसु ।
तत्तन्नित्यार्चनं तत्तद्वारेशद्वयपूजनम् ॥४४॥
विधाय पश्चात् कर्माणि तानि कुर्यात् समाहितः ।
शीघ्रं तत्फलसंसिद्ध्यै भवत्येवान्यथाऽन्यथा ॥४५॥
पिप्पलाग्नौ गुरौ वारे तदुत्थैस्तद्घृतप्लुतैः ।
हुनेत्तथा तत्फलाप्तिस्तद्दिनैः स्यादसंशयम् ॥४६॥
उदुम्बराग्नौ भृगुजे वारे होमं तदुद्भवैः ।
तत्सिक्तैर्विदधीतेत्थं तद्दिनैस्तच्च सिद्ध्यति ॥४७॥
शमीवह्नौ तदुत्थैस्तु जुहुयात्कृष्णगोघृतैः ।
तद्दिनात्तत्फलानि स्युरिति वारेषु सप्तसु ॥४८॥
विजयोऽभिहितः सम्यक् हवनात्तिथिऋक्षयोः ।
विजयं शृणु देवेशि ! कथयामि क्रमेण ते ॥४९॥

सिद्धिः—विजयसिद्धिरित्यर्थः । तद्दिनैः—मण्डलादित्यर्थः । तत्क्रिया - भवेदिति शेषः॥४३॥सर्वत्र—तन्त्रे इत्यर्थः । तत्तन्नित्यार्चनमिति—तत्तद्दिवसप्राप्ततत्तत्तिथिप्राप्तनित्यां (२)चार्चयेदित्यभिधत्ते ॥४४॥ अन्यथा—नित्यद्वयार्चाकरणे । अन्यथा —निष्फलानि । एतदुक्तं भवति—सर्वत्र तन्त्रेषु सर्वप्रयोगेषु तत्तत्प्रयोगदिनप्राप्तां तत्तत्तिथिप्राप्तां नित्यां तद्वारेशद्वयं च पूजयित्वा पश्चात् प्रयोगान् कुर्यादिति ॥४५॥ पिप्पलाग्नौ—अश्वत्थेन्धनवह्नौ । तदुत्थैः—अश्वत्थसमिद्भिरित्यर्थः । तद्घृतप्लुतैः —सवर्णवत्सशुभ्रगोघृताप्लुतैः । तत्फलाप्तिः—जयाप्तिः । तद्दिनैः—प्राग्वन्मण्डलात् ॥४६॥ उदुम्बराग्नौ—प्राग्वदुदुम्बरेन्धनवह्नौ । तदुद्भवैः—उदुम्बरसमिद्भिरित्यर्थः । तत्सिक्तैः—पूर्वोक्तशुभ्रगोघृतसिक्तैः । तद्दिनैः—प्राग्वत् । तत्—जयफलमिति शेषः ॥ ४७ ॥ शमीवह्नौ प्राग्वत् शमीन्धनेऽग्नौ । तदुत्थैः—शमीसमिद्भिरित्यर्थः । जुहुयात्—मन्दवार इतिशेषः । कृष्णगोघृतैः—सवर्णवत्स-

---

(१) हितक्रिया इति मू॰ पु॰ पा॰। (२) नित्यांचर्चितमिति वङ्ग पु॰ पा॰।

प्रतिपत्तिथिमारभ्य पञ्चम्यन्तक्रमेण वै।
शालीचणकमुद्गैश्च यवमाषैश्च होमतः ॥५०॥
महिषाज्यप्लुतैस्ताभिस्तिथिभिः समवाप्नुयात्।
षष्ठ्यादि च दशम्यन्तमजाभवघृतैस्तथा ॥५१॥
प्रागुक्तैर्निस्तुषैर्होमात्प्रागुक्तफलमाप्नुयात्।
तदूर्ध्वं पञ्चदश्यन्ते समस्तैश्च(१) तिलद्वयैः ॥५२॥
सितान्नैः पायसैः सिक्तैराविकैस्तु घृतैस्तथा।
हवनात्तदवाप्नोति यदासौ फलमीरितम् ॥५३॥
एवं नक्षत्रवृक्षोत्थवह्नौ तैस्तैर्मधुप्लुतैः।
हवनादपि तत्प्राप्तिर्भवत्येव न संशयः ॥५४॥

कृष्णगोघृतैः। तद्दिनात्—प्राग्वन्मण्डलात्। तत्फलानि—जयफलानि। इति—प्रोक्तरूपतः ॥४८॥ विजयोऽभिहित इति पूर्वत्रान्वयः। हवनादिति पूर्वापरयोरन्वेति। पूर्वस्तु-इति-एवमुक्तप्रकारतः सप्तवारेषु च जयोऽभिहित इत्यर्थः। अपरस्तु तिथिऋक्षयोर्हवनाद्वक्ष्यमाणं विजयं शृण्वित्यर्थः ॥४८॥५०॥ताभिः तिथिभिः—प्रतिपदादिभिः पञ्चम्यन्ताभिः पञ्चभिः। समवाप्नुयात्—विजयमितिशेषः। तथा-षष्ठ्यादिभिर्दशम्यन्ताभिः पञ्चतिथिभिः ॥५१॥ प्रागुक्तैः- शाल्यादिभिः पञ्चभिः। निस्तुषैः—विगतत्वगादिभिः। प्रागुक्तं फलं—विजयफलम्। तदूर्ध्वं पञ्चदश्यन्ते—एकादश्यादिपञ्चदश्यन्ते तिथिपञ्चके इत्यर्थः। समस्तैः—शाल्यादिभिः पञ्चभिः एकादश्याम्। तिलद्वयैः—कृष्णसितरूपैः द्वादश्यां कृष्णरूपैः, त्रयोदश्यां सितरूपैश्च तिलैर्जुहुयादित्यर्थः॥५२॥ सितान्नैः - केवलान्नैः। तैश्चतुर्दश्याम्। पायसैः पञ्चदश्याम्। सिक्तैः—शाल्यादिभिः समस्तपञ्चकादिभिः। तथा—ताभिस्तिथिभिः। फलमीरितं - विजयफलमित्यर्थः ॥ ५३ ॥ नक्षत्रवृक्षोत्थवह्नौ—विषवृक्षादितत्तन्नक्षत्रवृक्षेन्धनेद्धे वह्नौ। तैस्तैः—तत्तन्नक्षत्रवृक्षाङ्गैस्तत्तत्समिद्भिरित्यर्थः। मधु—क्षौद्रम्। हवनात्—नित्यशः। तत्प्राप्तिः—विजयप्राप्तिः। एतदुक्तं भवति - अश्विन्यादिषु सप्तविंशतिसङ्ख्येषु नक्षत्रेषु एकस्मिन् क्रमात् तत्तन्नक्षत्रोक्तवृक्षेन्धनेद्धे वह्नौ तत्तद्वृक्षसमिद्भिः मधुसिक्तैर्होमात् तत्तत्फलावाप्तिरिति ॥५४॥

---

(१) बलिद्वयैरिति म पु० पा०।

विद्यायां प्राग्वदर्णानि पञ्च युञ्ज्यात्स्वरैस्तथा ।
अशीत्यर्णवतीं विद्यां तैर्यन्त्राणि शृणु प्रिये ! ॥५५॥
प्राक्प्रत्यक्दक्षिणोदक् च दशसूत्रनिपातनात् ।
एकाशीतिपदानि स्युस्तेषु तानि लिखेत्क्रमात् ॥५६॥
मध्यकोष्ठेऽभिधां कृत्वा प्रागुक्तविधिना युतम् ।
शूलीकृत्य च रेखाग्राण्यत्रावाह्याभिपूज्य ताम् ॥५७॥
उपासीत पुरोविद्यां जपं नित्यं समर्चयेत् ।
विद्याक्रमं तत्र यन्त्रे यजेत्तत्फलमाप्नुयात् ॥५८॥

विद्यायामित्यादिभिराप्नुयादित्यन्तैश्चतुर्भिः श्लोकैः स्वरविकृतमूलविद्यापञ्चकजनिताशीत्यक्षरनिर्मितकोष्ठयन्त्रपूजनेन विजयप्राप्तिमुपदिशति। तत्र प्राग्वत्—अपुनरुक्तानीत्यर्थः। पञ्च—तानि भकारमकाररेफयकारौकाराक्षराणि वक्ष्यमाणानि। जकारविन्द्वोरनुपादानं स्वरत्वपौनरुक्त्यात्। स्वरैः—षोड़शभिः। तथा—प्रागुक्तक्रमादित्यर्थः। स तु प्रत्यक्षरं षोड़शस्वरयोजनारूपः। तैः—अक्षरैः। यन्त्राणि—वक्ष्यमाणानि ॥५५॥ दशसूत्रनिपातनात्—समान्तरालमिति शेषः। तेषु—कोष्ठेषु। तानि—विद्याक्षराण्यशीतिसङ्ख्यानीति शेषः। क्रमात्—अग्रात्प्रादक्षिण्यप्रवेशगत्येत्यर्थः। ॥ ५६ ॥ मध्यकोष्ठे—एकाशीतितमे। अभिधां—साधकसाध्यकर्मणाम्। प्रागुक्तविधिना—उत्तराधरान्तरालैर्ष्वित्यर्थः। रेखाग्राणि—चत्वारिंशत्सङ्ख्यानि। अत्र—यन्त्रे। तां—विजयानित्याम् ॥ ५७ ॥ उपासीत—पूजाजपादिना। नित्यं—स्वनित्यक्रमम्। विद्याक्रमं—विद्याक्रमंप्रयोगार्थम्। अस्मिन्—यन्त्रे स्वनित्यक्रमं प्रयोगार्थं विद्याक्रमं च पूजयेदित्यर्थः। यजेत्—प्रोक्तप्रकारेण। तत्फलं—विजयफलम्। अयमत्र यन्त्रविरचनाक्रमो यथा—प्राक् प्रत्यक् दक्षिणोदक् च समान्तरालं दशसूत्राण्यास्फाल्य तेन सञ्जातेषु एकाशीतिसङ्ख्येषु कोष्ठेषु सर्वाधःस्थपङ्क्तिमध्यस्थकोष्ठमारभ्य प्रादक्षिण्यप्रवेशगत्या स्वरविकृतमूलविद्याक्षराण्यशीतिसङ्ख्यान्यालिख्य शिष्टे एकस्मिन्मध्यकोष्ठे प्रागुक्तलेखनक्रमतः साधकादित्रयाभिधामालिख्य यन्त्रस्य विंशतिरेखानां चत्वारिंशदग्राणि बहिः किञ्चिद्वर्धितान्यस्य प्रत्येकं त्रिशूलीकृत्य तस्मिन्यन्त्रे विजयानित्यां तामावाह्य पूर्वोक्तनित्यसपर्यामण्डलमपास्य ततः स्वनित्यक्रमं नित्यमर्चयेत्। तस्मिन् प्रयोगार्थं विद्याक्रमस्याप्यर्चयेत्। तेन विजयफलसिद्धिरिति ॥५८॥

प्राक्प्रत्यक्दक्षिणोदक् च चतुःसूत्रनिपातनात् ।
नवानि सम्भवन्त्यत्र कोष्ठानि परमेश्वरि ॥५९॥
तेषु प्रत्येकमब्जानि चाष्टपत्राणि संलिखेत् ।
तेषु मध्यस्थपद्मस्य कर्णिकायां समालिखेत् ॥६०॥
नामगर्भान्तु तां विद्यां तद्बहिश्चाष्टपत्रके ।
तेष्वादितोऽष्टौ संलिख्य विन्दुना तद्बहिस्तथा ॥६१॥
कर्णिकायां तु नाम्नैकं बहिरष्टौ तथाऽष्टसु ।
एवमष्टसु संलिख्य वेष्टयेन्मातृकाक्षरैः ॥६२॥
विलोमैरनुलोमैश्च मायाविन्दुसमन्वितैः ।
चतुरस्रत्रये बाह्ये(१) यन्त्रस्याग्रे समालिखेत् ॥६३॥
एवं कृत्वा हस्तयुग्ममाने कुम्भं निधाय ताम् ।
विद्याक्षरौषधिक्वाथजलैरापूर्य पूर्ववत् ॥६४॥

प्रागित्यादिभिः पुष्कलामित्यन्तैरक्षर्धैः पञ्चदशभिः श्लोकैर्नवकोष्ठस्थपद्मयन्त्रमभिषेकार्चनादिना विजयादिफलावाप्तिमुपदिशति। तत्र चतुःसूत्रनिपातनात्—समान्तरालमितिशेषः। अत्र- सूत्रपातप्रदेशे ॥५९॥ तेषु—नवसु कोष्ठेषु तेषु-पद्मेषु नवसु॥६०॥नामगर्भां—*भकारोदरे(साधनात् समान्तरालमिति शेषः)साधकस्य रेफांशे साध्यस्य तदन्तराले कर्मणश्चालेखनतः। तां विद्याम् विज्ञाताम्। तद्बहिः-कर्णिकाद्बहिः। तेष—सर्वस्वरविकृतविद्याक्षरेषु अशीतिषु। अष्टौ—वर्णान्। विन्दुना सहेतिशेषः। तद्बहिः मध्यपद्मात् बहिः स्थितेषु पद्मेषु ॥६१॥ एकं—पूर्व (पूर्व) लिखिताष्टकादुपरितनं उपरितनम्। बहिः—कर्णिकायाः। अष्टौ—कर्णिकायां लिखिताक्षरःल्लिखिताक्षरादुपरितनमष्टकम्। अष्टसु—दलेषु। एवं—उक्तरूपतः। अष्टसु—मध्यस्थपद्मवर्जितेषु सर्वाधःस्थपङ्क्तिमध्यकोष्ठस्थानेषु पद्मेष्वित्यर्थः ॥६२॥ माया—विसर्जनीयः। चतुरस्रत्रये- चतुरस्रत्रयान्तरालवीथीद्वये इत्यर्थः। तत्-मातृकास्थानम्। बाह्ये—चतुरस्रत्रयात्। अग्रे यन्त्रस्यास्य बाह्ये इत्यत्रान्वयः॥६३॥ हस्तयुग्ममाने—नवकोष्ठे इति शेषः। नवकोष्ठं हस्तद्वयमानं कुर्यादित्यर्थः।

---

(१) लघावज्रे इति सो० पु० पा०। लजम्बके इति मू० पु० पा०। * तकारो इति वं० पु० पा०।

अभ्यर्च्य विद्यामयुतं जपित्वा तैर्विधानतः ।
अभिषिञ्चेत्ततः क्लेशैर्विमुक्तो जायते सुखी ॥६५॥
विजयः सर्वतोभूयात् तत् प्रोक्तेष्वपि सप्तसु ।
नवग्रहार्तौ रिपुभिः सर्वतः क्लेशसम्भवे ॥६६॥
समरस्योद्यमे कीर्तिसम्पद्भ्योरथवाऽऽप्तये ।
पुत्राप्तौ वाञ्छितप्राप्तौ त्रिषु जन्मसु(१) कारयेत् ॥६७॥
एतद्यन्त्रं गैरिकेन पीठे संलिख्य तत्र ताम् ।
देवीमावाह्य सम्पूज्य जपेद्विद्यां तथाऽयुतम् ॥६८॥

तं—कुम्भं प्रतिकर्णिकमिति शेषः । पूर्ववत्—फलपल्लवादिभिः ॥६४॥ अभ्यर्च्य—नित्यक्रमादितः विद्यां—अविकृताम् । अयुतसंख्योक्तिरेकाक्षरत्वात् (तैः—जलैः) ततः—अभिषेकतः ॥६५॥ प्रोक्तेषु सप्तसु—अन्यस्मिन् पटले पूर्वत्र त्रिंशत्तमश्लोकप्रोक्तेषु द्वन्द्वयुद्धादिषु सप्तसु च ॥६६॥ कीर्तिसम्पद्भ्योरित्येतत् वाञ्छितद्वयम् । त्रिषु जन्मसु प्राग्वत् । कारयेत् अभिषेकमिति शेषः । एभिर्नवभिः श्लोकैरेतदुक्तं भवति । प्राक् प्रत्यक् दक्षिणोदक्च हस्तद्वयमिते प्रदेशे समान्तरालं चतुःसूत्रनिपातनान्नवकोष्ठानि कृत्वा तेषु नव पद्मानि अष्टदलोपेतानि कृत्वा तेषु मध्यकोष्ठस्थपद्मकर्णिकामध्ये विद्यामविकृतां प्राग्वन्नामगर्भामालिख्य स्वरविकृतमूलविद्याक्षरेष्वशीतिष्वादितोष्टकं अष्टसु दलेषु अग्रादिप्रादक्षिण्यात् प्रतिदलमेकमेकं सबिन्दुकमालिखेत् । तद्बहिः सर्वाधःस्थपङ्क्तिमध्यकोष्ठस्थादिष्वष्टसु प्रादक्षिण्यात् पूर्वपूर्वलिखिताष्टकादुपरितनोपरितनात्मकमक्षरं साध्यकर्णिकायां तदुपरितनोपरितनकोष्ठाक्षराष्टकमष्टदलेष्वष्टदलेष्वग्रात्प्रदक्षिणादालिख्य एवमशीतिभिरक्षरैर्नवपद्मोदरं नवकोष्ठयन्त्रं कृत्वा तद्बहिः चतुरस्रद्वयमेकाङ्गुलान्तरालं कृत्वा तदन्तरालवीथीद्वयेऽन्तर्वीथ्यां मातृकां विलोमां सविसर्जनीयां आलिख्य तद्बहिर्वीथ्यां तामेव सबिन्दुकामनुलोमामालिख्य सर्वयन्त्रबाह्येऽग्रे लक्षमित्यक्षरद्वयं चालिख्य तेषु नवसु कोष्ठस्थपद्मनवकर्णिकामध्ये प्रतिपद्ममेकमेकं कुम्भं निधाय विद्यावर्णौषधिक्वाथजलैरापूर्य प्राग्वत् संपूज्य नित्यक्रमतः फलपल्लवादिकं निधाय तत्र देवीमावाह्य नित्यक्रमतोऽभ्यर्च्य सञ्जप्य त्रिषु जन्मस्वभिषेकात् प्रोक्तफलसिद्धिरिति ॥६७॥

(१) सप्तसु इति मू० पु० पा० ।

एवं त्रिसप्तत्रिः सप्तरात्राद्विश्वं वशं नयेत् ।
राजानं वनितां मर्त्यानन्यांश्च प्राणिनोऽखिलान् ॥६९॥
हरिद्रायाः पटे कृत्वा कलशे वा शरावयोः ।
निधाय भित्तिमध्ये वा शयनस्थानके निजे ॥७०॥
अभ्यर्च्य विद्यया जापं कुर्यात्सन्ध्यासु नित्यशः ।
सहस्रं प्रोक्तकालेन स्तम्भयेदखिलं दृढ़म् ॥७१॥
शत्रोरुद्योगरोषाभ्यामनिष्टकरणं तथा ।
व्यवहारं रणोद्योगं वादे वाचं मतिं रुषाम् ॥७२॥
एतत्प्रागुक्तसुरभिद्रव्यैरालिख्य तत्र ताम् ।
सन्ध्यासु पूजयेन्नित्यं सहस्रं प्रजपेत्तथा ॥७३॥
प्रोक्तकालप्रयोगेण श्रियं प्राप्नोति पुष्कलाम् ।
अथान्यद्वज्ररूपं तु यंत्रं वक्ष्येऽतिवैभवम् ॥७४॥
प्राग्वद्विसप्तसूत्राणां पातेनोत्पादयेत्तथा ।
कोष्ठानि नवषष्ट्या च युतं शतमितिस्फुटम् ॥७५॥

एतत्—नवपद्मोदरनवकोष्ठरूपम् तत्र—यन्त्रे तथा—सम्पूज्य नित्यक्रमतः । तथा – यथाऽभिषेके ॥६८॥ त्रिसप्तत्रिःसप्तरात्रात् । एतदुक्तं भवति त्रिरात्रात् सप्तरात्रादेकविंशतिरात्राद्वेति । विश्वं—वक्ष्यमाणराजादिसङ्ग्रहोक्तिः । अखिलान् उक्तशेषान् तिर्यगादीनपि प्राणिनः॥६९॥कृत्वा—नवकोष्ठयन्त्रमिति शेषः । शरावयोः-ऊर्ध्वाधःस्थयोरन्योन्याभिमुखाश्लिष्टमुखयोः । वा —विकल्पे । शयनस्थानके—स्थापयित्वेति शेषः ॥७०॥ सहस्रं—प्रतिसन्ध्यम् । प्रोक्तकालेन—त्रिरात्रादिना । अखिलं-वक्ष्यमाणम् ॥ ७१ ॥ वादे - तर्के । वाचं—प्रतिवादिनः ॥७२॥ एतत्—यन्त्रम् । प्रागुक्तसुरभिद्रव्यैः—अष्टमपटलोक्तैश्चन्दनागुरुकस्तुरीकुङ्कुमैः । तत्र – यन्त्रे । तां—विजयानित्याम् । प्रयोगदिनेषु—सहस्रं प्रतिसन्ध्यम् ॥ ७३ ॥ प्रोक्तकालात् प्राग्वत्पुष्कलां राज्यश्रीसमाम् ।

अथान्यदित्यादिभिः समीरिताइत्यन्तैरर्द्धाद्यैः षड्विंशत्या श्लोकैः स्वरविकृतमूलविद्याचरैरेकाशीतिकोष्ठवज्रयन्त्रनिर्माणं तत्प्रयोगांस्तत्फलानि चोपदिशति । तत्र अतिवैभवं—अन्येभ्यः ॥७४॥ प्राग्वत्—प्राक्प्रत्यक्-

तच्चतुष्कोणकोष्ठानि मार्जयेत्सैकविंशतिम् ।
मध्ये च सम्भवत्येवाशीतिकोष्ठैर्यथाविधि ॥७६॥
तच्चतुर्दिक्षु विलिखेत्त्रिकोणान्येककोष्ठतः ।
सर्वमध्यस्थकोष्ठे च चतुर्दिक्ष्वग्रतस्तथा ॥७७॥
विद्यां नामोदरां कृत्वा प्राग्वद्वर्णांस्तु संलिखेत् ।
एतदग्रचतुष्कस्य स्पर्शात्त्रिचतुरस्रकम ॥७८॥
विधाय तत्र विलिखेन्मातृकां प्राग्विधानतः ।
एकेन वज्रयन्त्रेण विजया विजयप्रदा ॥७९॥
एतत् प्रोक्तेषु संलिख्य स्थापयेत्प्रोक्तरूपतः ।
विजयं समवाप्नोति प्रोक्तेष्वपि च सप्तसु ॥८०॥

दक्षिणोदक् च। द्विसप्तसूत्राणां—चतुर्दशसूत्राणाम् ॥७५॥ सैकविंशतिं—प्रतिकोणमिति शेषः। मध्ये—वज्रं प्रागुक्तरूपतः ॥ ७६ ॥ एककोष्ठतः—प्रतिदिशमिति ॥७७॥ विद्यां—अविकृताम् । नामोदराम्—प्राग्वत् सर्वाधःस्थपङ्क्तिस्थकोष्ठत्रयमध्यकोष्ठादिप्रादक्षिण्यप्रवेशगत्यामुक्तक्रमादित्यर्थः। वर्णान्—स्वरविकृतानशीतिसङ्ख्यान्। एतदग्रचतुष्कस्य स्पर्शात्—यन्त्राग्रभूतचतुर्दिग्गतत्रिकोणचतुष्काग्रस्पर्शादित्यर्थः। त्रिचतुरस्रकं—अन्तर्बहिर्विभागाच्चतुरस्रत्रयमित्यर्थः ॥७८॥ तत्र—तदन्तरालवीथीद्वये। प्राग्विधानतः—सविसर्जनीयां विलोमां सबिन्दुकामनुलोमां चेत्यर्थः। एकेन—अन्यनिरपेक्षेण। यन्त्रविरचनाक्रमो यथा—प्राक् प्रत्यक् दक्षिणोदक् च चतुर्दशभिश्चतुर्दशभिः सूत्रैरास्फालितैः समान्तरालं नवषष्ट्यधिकं शतं कोष्ठानि प्रागुक्तेन क्रमेण निष्पाद्य तेषु कोणेषु चतुष्टयेऽपि मध्ये वज्राकारं यथा भवति तथा प्रतिकोणमेकविंशतिकोष्ठानि मार्जयित्वा शिष्टेषु पञ्चाशीतिकोष्ठेषु चतुर्दिक्षु प्रतिदिशमेकैककोष्ठमार्जनतस्त्रिकोणचतुष्टयं कृत्वा शिष्टेष्वेकाशीतिकोष्ठेषु सर्वमध्यस्थकोष्ठदिग्गतत्र्यस्रे चतुष्टये चाविकृतां प्राग्वन्नामसम्पुटां मूलविद्यां लिखित्वा ततः शिष्टेष्वेकाशीतिकोष्ठेषु सर्वाधःस्थपङ्क्तिकोष्ठत्रयमध्यकोष्ठादिप्रादक्षिण्यप्रवेशगत्या मुक्तक्रमं स्वरविकृतमूलविद्याक्षराशीतिक्रमात्समालिख्य-दिग्गतत्र्यस्रचतुष्काग्रस्पर्शादन्तर्बहिर्विभागाच्चतुरस्रत्रयं विधाय तदन्तरालवीथीद्वये

विलिख्याश्वत्थफलकातले यन्त्रं कुचन्दनैः ।
जपाराधनसंसिद्धं स्थापयेच्छून्यवेश्मसु ॥८१॥
देशे वा तत्र दिनशो वर्द्धते श्रीरचञ्चला ।
पिशाचा राक्षसाः कृत्या वेतालाः स्युर्न तत्र वै ॥८२॥
पलाशफलकायान्तु विलिख्यैतद्यथाविधि ।
स्थापयेद्यत्रकुत्रापि तत्क्षेत्रं ब्राह्मणास्पदम् ॥८३॥
पूर्वोक्तस्थापनाद्राजधानी भवति सुस्थिरा ।
वटे विलिख्य खननात् पत्तनं भवति ध्रुवम् ॥८४॥
उदुम्बरे विधायेत्थं स्थापनादचिरेण वै ।
आहितानाश्रयं स्थानं भवत्येव न संशयः ॥८५॥
वज्रस्य दिक्त्रिकोणान्तरालात् कुर्यात् त्रिशूलकम् ।
दाहव्याप्ते खसंयुक्ते लिखेत् तच्छृङ्गमध्ययोः ॥८६॥
तत्र संस्थाप्य गदिनं विद्याजप्तविभूतिना ।
भालस्थेनाभिजप्तेन तमाविश्य गदो वदेत् ॥ ८७ ॥

प्राग्वन्मातृकां विलोमां सविसर्ज्जनीयां तामेवानुलोमां सविन्दुकामन्तर्वाह्यगत्या विलिख्य अनेन यन्त्रेणान्यनिरपेक्षेण विनियोगतो विजयादिसर्व्वफलप्राप्तिरिति ॥७८॥ प्रोक्तेषु—अष्टमपटलोक्तलोहत्रयादिषु । प्रोक्तेष्वपि च सप्तसु—अस्मिन् पटले त्रिंशत्तमेन श्लोकेन प्रोक्तद्वन्द्वयुद्धादिषु सप्तस्वित्यर्थः ॥ ८० ॥ यन्त्रं—वज्राकारम् । कुचन्दनैः—प्राग्वत् । देशे—शून्य इति शेषः । तत्र—गृहदेशयोः ॥ ८२ ॥ एतद्वज्ररूपं यन्त्रम् । यत्र कुत्रापि—क्षेत्र इति शेषः । पूर्व्वोक्तस्थापनात् राजधानी—स्थापितभूः । पत्तनं—स्थापितदेशः ॥ ८४ ॥ स्थानं—यन्त्राधिष्ठितम् ॥८५॥ वज्रस्य दिक्त्रिकोणान्तरालात्—चतुर्दिग्गतत्रिकोणमध्यावकाशादित्यर्थः । दाहव्याप्ते—रेफयकारौ । खमिति विन्दुः । तत्शृङ्गमध्ययोः—त्रिकोणान्तरालगतत्रिशूलमध्यरेखापार्श्वदेशशृङ्गयोः । एतदुक्तं भवति—प्रागुक्तवज्रदिग्गतत्रिकोणगतमध्यावकाशे त्रिशूलं कृत्वा तच्छृङ्गयोः रेफयकारौ वह्निमारुतात्मकौ सविन्दुकौ विलिख्य तत्र वक्ष्यमाणं प्रयोगं कुर्य्यादिति ॥ ८६ ॥ तत्र—त्रिशूलोपेते वज्रे । तं—

स्वावेशकारणं कर्मस्थापयापक्रम यथा ।
ग्रहभूतपिशाचाद्याः अस्याविश्यापयान्ति वै ॥८८॥
तदैवदासवत्तस्य वशे भवति तद्बलात् ।
यन्त्रमेतद्विलिख्यास्मिन्नभ्यर्च्य स्थापयेत् क्वचित् ॥८९॥
राज्ञो गेहे तस्य राजक्षमा मुञ्चति नावयम् ।
स्थाने गजानां वाहानां नव कृत्वा नवस्वपि ॥९०॥
स्थानेषु स्थापितान्येतान्यर्चयेद्दिनशस्तथा ।
दिक्षु मध्ये च तत्रैव रोगाः कृत्याः परेरिताः ॥९१॥
वीक्षितुं तं तु ते नैव शक्ताः स्युस्तत्प्रभावतः ।
चन्द्रचन्दनकाश्मीरैरालिख्याभिनवे पटे ॥९२॥
अभ्यर्च्य विद्याजप्तं तं पटमास्तीर्य शाययेत् ।
दाहज्वरार्तमचिरान्मुच्यते तज्ज्वरेण सः ॥९३॥
अन्येष्वपि गदेष्वेवं कारयेत्तद्विमुक्तये ।
समरेषु महीपानां यन्त्रमेतदुदीरितम् ॥९४॥
निशाने पटहेऽन्येषु वाद्येषु च समालिखेत् ।
दरदेनाथ तन्मध्ये तामावाह्य समर्चयेत् ॥९५॥
विजयां विजयावाप्त्यै युगपत्ताडयन् व्रजेत् ।
प्रत्यर्थिसेना तच्छब्दश्रवणेन पलायते ॥९६॥
दिशो दश भयोद्विग्नो नाभियाति कदाचन ।
सजीवद्यूतकालेषु यन्त्रमेतद्विनिर्मितम् ॥९७॥

गदिनम् ॥ ८७ ॥ यथा—गदः ॥ ८८ ॥ यन्त्रं—त्रिशूलरहितम् ॥ ८९ ॥ क्षमा—भूमिः ॥ ९० ॥ नव—स्थानापेक्षया । नवसु—स्थानेषु ॥ ९१ ॥ तत्प्रभावतः । चन्द्रचन्दनकाश्मीरैः—सम्मिलितैः ॥ ९२ ॥ दाहज्वरार्त्तमिति शाययेदित्यत्रा-न्वयः । स—गदी ॥ ९३ ॥ तद्विमुक्तये—रोगविमुक्तये । एतत्—वक्ष्य-रूपम् ॥ ९४ ॥ ९५ ॥ ताड़यन्—निस्सारयन् । तच्छब्द इति निस्सारण

गुलकीकृत्य तत्कण्ठे बद्ध्वा पश्चात्तु योजयेत ।
एतद्दर्शनमात्रेण पलायन्ते दिशो दश ॥९८॥
निर्जीवेषु च तद्यन्त्रं जयमाप्नोति सर्वतः ।
नासाध्यं विद्यते तेन वज्रयन्त्रेण पार्वति ! ॥९९॥
ध्यायेद्वक्त्रे रिपोर्यन्त्रं विद्यां वा लोहिताकृतिम् ।
तदैव दासवत्तस्य वशो भवति तद्बलात् ॥१००॥
इति ते विजयानित्यावैभवाः स्युः समीरिताः ।
नैवतत्त्वमयी व्याप्तिरिति सम्यक समीरिता ॥
अस्या निष्कालनाच्चित्ते तत्तत्त्व स्वात्मसात्कृतम् ॥१०१॥

इति षोड़शनित्यातन्त्रेषु श्रीकादिमतेऽष्टादशं
पटलं परिपूर्णं परामृष्टम् ॥१८॥

शब्दः ॥ ८६ ॥ ८७ ॥ तत्कण्ठे—कुक्कुटादिकण्ठे ॥ ८८ ॥ जयमाप्नोति—दधन्नन इति शेषः ॥ ८८ ॥ विद्यां मूलविद्यां वाविकल्पेन। लोहिताकृतिमिति यन्त्रस्यापि विशेषणं तदा लोहिताकृतीत्यन्वेति। तस्य—धातुः। भवति रिपुरिति शेषः। तद्बलात्—ध्यानबलात्। उक्तप्रकारतः ॥ १०० ॥

इति श्रीषोड़शनित्यातन्त्रेषु श्रीकादिमताख्यस्य तन्त्रस्य परिपूर्णस्य तन्त्रस्य प्रपञ्चसारसिंहराजप्रकाशाभिधानेन श्रीसुभगानन्दनाथेन विरचितायां मनोरमाख्यायां व्याख्यायां शिवदूतीनित्याविद्याविधान-प्रकाशनपरमष्टादशपटलं परिपूर्णं परमामृष्टम् ॥ १८ ॥

ग्रन्थसङ्ख्या—

यन्त्राणि द्वादश व्याख्याग्रन्थास्त्वष्टादशं शतम् ।
सार्द्धपादत्रिपादोर्द्ध्वद्वानवत्यायुतं स्मृताः ॥

ऊनविंशपटलम् ।

अथ षोड़शनित्यासु या प्रोक्ता तु चतुर्द्दशी ।
एकाक्षरा सा कथिता विद्या सा सर्वमङ्गला ॥१॥
न्यासक्रमं ध्यानविधिं शक्तीरावरणस्थिताः ।
पूजाक्रमं साधनञ्च विनियोगादिकान् क्रमात् ॥२॥
मूलविद्याक्षरैर्दीर्घस्वरभिन्नैः षड़ङ्गकम् ।
तानि तत्स्वरभिन्नानि न्यसेत् खेषु मनोऽवधि ॥३॥
सुवर्णवर्णरुचिरां मुक्तामाणिक्यभूषणाम् ।
माणिक्यमुकुटां नेत्रद्वयप्रेङ्खद्दयाभराम् ॥४॥

पूर्व्वस्मिन्नष्टादशे पटले त्रयोदश्या विजयानित्याया विधानमुपदिश्यानन्तरं चतुर्द्दश्याः सर्व्वमङ्गलानित्याया विधानमुपदिशति अथ षोड़शेत्यादिना षपि चेत्यन्तेन श्लोकशतरूपेण एकोनविंशेन पटलेन। तत्र अथ षोड़शेत्यादिना क्रमादित्यन्तेन श्लोकद्वयेन पटलार्थानुपदिशति। तत्र कथिता तृतीये पटले। विनियोगादिकान् यन्त्रादीनामिति शेषः ॥ २ ॥

मूलविद्येत्यादिना श्लोकेन न्यासजातक्रममुपदिशति। तत्र मूलविद्याक्षरैर्मूलविद्यायाः सकारवकारविन्दुभिः पिण्डीभूतैरित्यर्थः। अत्र बहुवचनं अवान्तरत्रयापेक्षया दीर्घस्वरभिन्नैः प्राग्वत्। एतदुक्तं भवति खां इत्यादि क्रमेण मूलविद्यया दीर्घस्वरयुजा सजातिकयाक्षरन्यासपूर्व्वकमङ्गन्यासं कुर्य्यादिति। तानि दीर्घस्वरयुक्तषड़्विधविद्यास्वरूपाणि खेषु श्रोत्रादिषु ज्ञानेन्द्रियेषु पञ्चसु। मनोऽवधि मनःप्रष्ठेष्वित्यर्थः। तत्र श्रोत्रादिषु चतुर्षु द्वन्द्वस्थानेष्वपि प्रतिद्वन्द्वमेकमेकमक्षरं न्यसेदित्यर्थः। तत्र त्वचि न्यासः प्राग्वत्। सर्व्वन्यासजातस्यानन्तरं व्यापकं प्राग्वन्न्यसेदिति सम्प्रदायः ॥ ३ ॥

सुवर्णेत्यादिभिः स्थिता इत्यन्तैः पञ्चभिः श्लोकैर्देव्याः सपरिवाराया नित्यसपर्य्यामण्डलनिर्म्माणगर्भं नित्यपूजाध्यानादिकमुपदिशति। तत्र नेत्रद्वयप्रेङ्खद्दया-

द्विभुजां स्वासनां पद्मे त्वष्टषोडशतद्द्वयैः।
पत्रैरुपेते सचतुर्द्वारभूसद्मयुग्मगे ॥५॥
मातुलुङ्गफलं दक्षे दधानां करपङ्कजे।
वामेन निजभक्तानां प्रयच्छन्तीं धनादिकम् ॥६॥
स्वसमानाभिरभितः शक्तिभिः परिवारिताम्।
षट्सप्ततिभिरन्याभिरक्षरोत्थाभिरन्विताम् ॥७॥
प्रयोगेष्वन्यदा नित्यसपर्य्यासूक्तशक्तिकाम्।
ताः शक्तीः शृणु देवेशि या नित्यावरणे स्थिताः ॥८॥
भद्रां भवानीं भव्याञ्च विशालाक्षीं सुविस्मिताम्।
करुणां कमलां कल्पां पूजयेदष्टपत्रगाः ॥९॥

भरां रक्तारुणकारुण्यभरसूर्य्याग्नितांशुनेत्रद्वयां इत्यर्थः। स्वासनां पद्मे वक्ष्यमाणरूपे मण्डले सुखस्थितां इत्यर्थः। अष्टषोडशतद्द्वयैः पत्रैः तद्द्वयैरिति षोड़शद्वयैरिति यावत्। द्वात्रिंशत्पत्रैरित्यर्थः। एतदुक्तं भवति आन्तरक्रमादष्टपत्रैः षोड़शपत्रैः द्वात्रिंशत्पत्रैरुपेत इति। सचतुर्द्वारभूसद्मयुग्मगे चतुर्दिक्षु चतुर्द्वारयुतचतुरस्र-द्वयमध्यगे इत्यर्थः। तन्नित्यसपर्य्यामण्डलनिर्म्माणक्रमो यथा। यथामानमन्तर्बहि-र्विभागरूपं चतुर्दिग्गतचतुर्द्वारोपेतं समचतुरस्रद्वयं कृत्वा तन्मध्ये द्वात्रिंशद्दलं पद्मं तदन्तः षोड़शदलं पद्मं तदन्तरष्टदलं च पद्मं कृत्वा तत्कर्णिकायां देवीमष्टपत्रादिषु परिवारशक्तीश्चावाह्य पूजयेदित्यर्थः। वामेन करपङ्कजेनेति शेषः। शक्तिभिः नित्यावरणशक्तिभिः। षट्सप्ततिभिः अष्टत्रिंशन्मिथुनरूपाभिः। अन्याभि-रित्यक्षरोत्थशक्तिविशेषणम्। अक्षरोत्थाभिः वक्ष्यमाणाभिरमृताद्याभिः सोम-सूर्य्याग्निरूपाक्षरशक्तिभिः अन्विताम्। प्रयोगेष्विति सम्बन्धः। अन्यदा नित्यसपर्य्या-स्विति सम्बन्धः। उक्तशक्तिकां वक्ष्यमाणभद्रादिशक्तिकां स्मरेदिति प्रकरणशेषः। शक्तीः नित्यपूजावरणशक्तीः। एतदुक्तम् भवति नित्यसपर्य्यायां भद्रादिशक्ति सहितामेव प्रयोगादिषु ताभिश्च वक्ष्यमाणाभिरमृतादिभिर्मातृकाक्षरोत्थाभिः सोमसूर्य्याग्निकलाख्याभिरष्टत्रिंशन्मिथुनरूपतः षट्सप्ततिभिः शक्तिभिश्चान्वितां प्रोक्तरूपतो ध्यात्वा पूजयेदिति ॥ ८ ॥

भद्रामित्यादिभिः सहस्रकमित्यन्तैर्नवभिः श्लोकैः नित्यसपर्य्यावरणपञ्चकशक्ति-

कलाञ्च पूरिणीं नित्याममृतां जीवितां दयाम् ।
अशोकाममलां पूर्णां पुण्यां भाग्यामथोद्यताम् ॥१०
विवेकां विभवां विश्वां विततांश्चाष्टयुग्मके ।
पूजयेदभितः शक्तीः प्रादक्षिण्यक्रमेण वै ॥११॥
कामिनीं खेचरीं सर्वां पुराणां परमेश्वरीम् ।
गौरीं शिवाममेयाञ्च विमलां विजयां पराम् ॥१२॥
पवित्रां पद्मिनीं दिव्यां विश्वेशीं शिववल्लभाम् ।
अशेषरूपामानन्दामम्बुजाक्षीमनिन्दिताम् ॥१३॥
वरदां वाक्प्रदां वाणीं विविधां वेदविग्रहाम् ।
विद्यां वागीश्वरीं सत्यां संयताञ्च सरस्वतीम् ॥१४॥
निर्म्मलां दानरूपाञ्च पूजयेत् षोडशद्वये ।
प्राग्वदिन्द्रादिभिः सर्व्वाः क्रमादन्वर्थसंज्ञकाः ॥१५॥

नामानि पूजासमापनादिकञ्चोपदिशति । तत्र भद्रामित्यादिना श्लोकेनाष्टपत्रपूज्यशक्त्यष्टकनामान्युपदिशति । कलामित्यादिना श्लोकेन षोड़शदलपूज्यशक्तिषु द्वादशशक्तिनामान्युपदिशति ॥ विवेकामित्यादिना श्लोकेनावशिष्टशक्तिचतुष्टयनामानि सर्वाः शक्तीरग्रादिप्रादक्षिण्यात् पूजयेदिति चोपदिशति । तत्राष्टयुग्मके षोड़शदलेषु । कामिनीमित्यादिना श्लोकेन द्वात्रिंशद्दलपूज्यशक्तिष्वेकादशशक्तिनामान्युपदिशति । पवित्रामित्यादिना श्लोकेनावशिष्टासु एकविंशतिशक्तिषु नवशक्तिनामान्युपदिशति । वरदामित्यादिना श्लोकेनावशिष्टासु द्वादशशक्तिषु दशशक्तिनामान्युपदिशति । तत्र वागीश्वरीमिति सप्तविंशतिशक्तिनाम । निर्म्मलामित्यादिना श्लोकेनावशिष्टशक्तिद्वयं तत्पूजादिकञ्चोपदिशति । तत्र षोड़शद्वये द्वात्रिंशद्दलेष्वित्यर्थः । प्राग्वत् प्रदक्षिणादग्न्यादिलोकपालाख्या इन्द्रादीशान्ता अष्टौ शक्तीः स्त्रीरूपाः द्वारेषु पार्श्वद्वयसहितेषु पश्चिमादिचतस्रः पश्चिमादिचतुर्दिग्गतद्वारेषु चतुर्षु प्रतिद्वारं चतस्रः चतस्रश्च पूजयेदित्यर्थः । चतस्र इति शब्दस्यार्थद्वयवशाद्विरन्वयो भवति तेनान्यदा चतस्र इत्यनन्तब्रह्मनियतिकालशक्ताय उच्यन्ते । प्रोक्तविग्रहाः सम्भूय विंशतिशक्तीश्च पूजयेदित्यर्थः । नित्यानित्यापटलोक्तारम्भ-

ब्राह्म्याद्या लोकपालाख्याः शक्तीर्द्वारेषु पूजयेत्।
पश्चिमादिचतुर्द्दिक्षु चतस्रः प्रोक्तविग्रहाः ॥१६॥
वलिद्वयञ्च होमञ्च कुर्य्यात् प्राग्वत् समापनम्।
जपन्तु नित्यशः कुर्य्यादग्रे तस्याः सहस्रकम् ॥१७॥
प्राग्वत्तां साधयेद्विद्यां द्वाविंशल्लक्षमानतः।
होमं दशांशतः कुर्य्यादन्नाज्याभ्यां घृतेन वा ॥१८॥
एवं संसिद्धविद्यस्तु कुर्य्यात् प्रोक्तानशेषतः।
प्रयोगानन्यथा तस्य नैष्फल्यमयशो मृतिम् ॥१९॥
विदध्यात्तेन तां प्रोक्तक्रमेणाराध्य भक्तितः।
संसाध्य पश्चात् कुर्व्वीत मङ्गलान्मङ्गलोदितान् ॥२०॥

श्चतुरस्रदिग्गतद्वारपार्श्वस्थानगा इत्यर्थः। एतदुक्तं भवति ब्राह्म्याद्यष्टमातृरिन्द्राद्या ईशान्ता अष्टलोकपालशक्तीः एवं सम्भूय षोडशशक्तीश्चतुरस्रद्वारचतुष्टये प्रतिद्वारं चतस्र इति क्रमेण पूजने तु ब्राह्म्याद्यष्टौ पश्चिमद्वारदक्षपार्श्वादितद्वामपार्श्वान्तं अष्टसु पार्श्वेषु पूजयित्वा ततश्चतुरस्रपूर्व्वद्वारोत्तरपार्श्वादुत्तर[1]पूर्व्वपार्श्वावसानम् इन्द्रादिलोकपालशक्तीरष्टौ समभ्यर्च्य ततोऽनन्तब्रह्मनिर्ऋतिकालशक्तीश्चतुरस्राग्नेयादीशान्तेषु कोणेष्वर्चयेत्। एवं त्रिरावर्त्तनात् पूजने कृते प्रतिदिशं पश्चिमादिचतुर्दिग्गतद्वारेषु चतस्रश्चतस्रः कोणादिषु एकैका चैवं विंशतिशक्तयस्तिष्ठन्तीति। वलिद्वयं प्राग्वत् समापनम्। प्राग्वत्तेजस्त्रयभावनादिना। तस्या देव्याः ॥ १७ ॥

प्राग्वदित्यादिभिरुदितानित्यन्तैस्त्रिभिः श्लोकैः पुरश्चरणविधानं कृतपुरश्चरणस्य प्रयोगविधानयोग्यतां अन्यथाकरणे प्रत्यवायादिकमुपदिशति। तत्र प्राग्वत् कालसन्ध्यात्रयपूजनादिभिः। वा विकल्पे अन्यथा प्रोक्तसाधनादीनामकरणे तस्य साधकस्य नैष्फल्यादिकं विदध्याद्विद्येति शेषः। तेन कारणेन तां मूलविद्याम् आराध्य नित्योपासनादिभिः संसाध्य पुरश्चर्य्य पश्चात् साधनादेः मङ्गलान् प्रयोगानिति शेषः। मङ्गलोदितान् सर्व्वमङ्गलोक्तान्। एतत्सर्व्वमङ्गलापटलोक्तान्मङ्गलान् प्रयोगानित्यर्थः ॥ २० ॥

१। इतर इति वा।

प्रयोगार्थां वर्णशक्तीर्वक्ष्ये देवीः शृणु प्रिये ।
सोमसूर्य्याग्निरूपाश्च तास्त्वष्टत्रिंशदेव ताः ॥२१॥
अमृता मानदा पूषा तुष्टिः पुष्टी रतिर्धृतिः ।
शशिनी चन्द्रिका कान्तिर्ज्योत्स्ना श्रीः प्रीतिरङ्गदा ॥२२॥
पूर्णा पूर्णामृता कामदायिन्यः सस्वराः कलाः ।
एताः षोड़श चन्द्रस्य कलाः कल्पद्रुमोपमाः ॥२३॥
तपिनी तापिनी धूम्रा मरीचिर्ज्वालिनी रुचिः ।
सुषुम्ना भोगदा विश्वा बोधनी धारणी क्षमा ॥ २४ ॥
एताः स्युः शक्तयः प्रोक्ताः क्रमाद्द्वादशभानुगाः ।
भकारादि डकारान्तवर्णोच्चारो विलोमतः ॥२५॥

प्रयोगेत्यादिभिर्भवेदित्यन्तैस्त्रयोदशभिः श्लोकैरष्टत्रिंशत्कलारूपमिथुनीभूताः प्राक् प्रस्तुता मातृकाक्षरशक्तीः प्रयोगार्थमुपदिशति। तत्र प्रयोगार्थाः । पूर्व्वप्रयोगेष्वित्यन्तं स्मारयति। वर्णशक्तीः मातृकायाः ताः पूर्वोक्तरूपसंख्या मिथुनरूपतः सोमसूर्य्याग्निरूपाः मातृकाया वक्ष्यमाणक्रमाः अक्षरविभागतः तद्रूपास्ता मिथुनीभूताः शक्तीः॥ अमृतेत्यादिना श्लोकेन षोड़शसु सोमकलासु चतुर्दशशक्तीरुपदिशति। तत्र पूषेति टावन्ता। पुष्टीरतिः पुष्टिः रतिः इति पदच्छेदः॥ पूर्णेत्यादिना श्लोकेन शिष्टकलाद्वयनामनी तासामिकैकस्याः षोड़शस्वराणामेकैकस्य क्रमाद्योजनादिकमुपदिशति। तत्र कामदायिन्यः इष्टप्रदाः। अत्र बहुवचनं षोड़शत्वापेक्षया। सस्वराः स्वराणां षोड़शानामेकैकस्य क्रमेणादौ योजनात्॥ तपिनीत्यादिना श्लोकेन सूर्य्यकलाद्वादशनामान्युपदिशति। क्रमादुद्दिष्टांद्विलोमतः भादिडान्तानि द्वादशाक्षराणि विलोमरूपाणि तासां मूलोक्तक्रमाणां आदौ प्राग्वद्योजयेदित्यर्थः॥ धात्रेत्यादिना श्लोकेन द्वादशार्कनामसु दशनामान्युपदिशति। तत्र समनन्तरः नवमस्य दशम इत्यर्थः। त्वष्टेत्यादिना श्लोकेन शिष्टनामद्वयं तदक्षराणि चोपदिशति। तत्र कादिठान्तार्णतनवः अनुलोमतः ककारादिठकारान्ताक्षरद्वादशकं तन्नामादौ योजयेदित्यर्थः। तत्र तन्मन्त्रयोजनाक्रमः पूर्वोक्ततपिन्यादिशक्तितदक्षरसहितः। यथाक्रमं कं भं धातृतपिनीभ्यां नमः इत्यादयः ठं डं विष्णु

धातार्य्यमा च मित्रश्च वरुणः शोभगस्तथा ।
विवस्वानिन्द्रपूषार्काः पर्जन्यः समनन्तरः ॥२६॥
त्वष्टा विष्णुरिति प्रोक्ता द्वादशार्काः क्रमेण वै ।
कादिठान्तार्णतनवः सर्वगाः सर्व्वसिद्धिदाः ॥२७॥
धूम्रार्चिरुष्मा ज्वलिनी ज्वालिनी विस्फुलिङ्गिनी ।
सुश्रीः सुरूपा कपिला हव्यकव्यवहे अपि ॥२८॥
यादिचान्ताक्षरमयाः शक्तयो दश कीर्त्तिताः ।
तेषां दशानां नामानि वासनोक्तानि ते शिवे ॥२९॥
कादिचान्ताक्षराणान्तु द्वाविंशन्मिथुनानि वै ।
प्रोक्तक्रमेण संपूज्य विधिं युञ्ज्यात्तु सर्वतः ॥३०॥
स्वराणान्तु स्वतन्त्रत्वात् स्वतन्त्राः शक्तयस्तथा ।
तासां नाथास्तत्सदृशनामरूपाः समीरिताः ॥३१॥

चमाभ्यां नमः इत्यन्ता द्वादशमन्त्रा एवं द्वादशमिथुनरूपेणार्ककलादेवताश्चतुर्विंशतिः ॥ धूम्रे त्यादिना श्लोकेन वह्निकलादशकनामान्युपदिशति । तत्र हव्यकव्यवहे हव्यवहा कव्यवहा च । यादिचान्ताक्षरमयाः यकारादिचकारान्ताक्षरदशकपूर्वा इत्यर्थः । तेषां दशानां वह्नीनां वासनोक्तानि पञ्चत्रिंशे वासनापटले अग्निर्वह्निरित्यादिनोक्तानि । एतदुक्तं भवति यकारादि-चकारान्ताक्षरदशकं क्रमेण वह्निकलानामेकैकस्या आदावेकमेकं वह्निनामानि च तद्वत् योजयेदिति । तन्मन्त्रा यथा यं अग्निधूम्रार्चिर्भ्यां नमः इत्यादयः चं ग्रासकव्यवहाभ्यां नमः इत्यन्ता दशमन्त्राः एवं वह्निकलादेवतामिथुनदशकरूपत्वात् विंशतिः द्वाविंशन्मिथुनानि सौराणि द्वादश आग्नेयानि दश एवं सम्भूय कादिचान्ताक्षराणां द्वाविंशन्मिथुनानीत्यर्थः । प्रोक्तक्रमेण तत्र क्रमोऽस्माभिर्दर्शितः । स्वतन्त्रत्वात् स्वयं राजन्ते इति निर्वचनात् स्वतन्त्राः स्वरमयत्वात् तत्सदृशनामरूपाः शक्तिनामानि पुमन्तानि योजयेदित्यर्थः । एतदुक्तं भवति स्वराणां स्वतन्त्रत्वात्तदधिष्ठात्र्यस्तु शक्तयः सोमकलाः पूर्वोक्ता अमृताद्याः षोडश-स्वतन्त्राः तेन तत्पतयस्तत्सदृशरूपनामानः तस्माच्छक्तिनामानि पुमन्तानि योजयेदित्यर्थः । एतदुक्तं भवति स्वरादिकानि

मिथुनान्येवमुक्तानि त्रिंशदष्टक्रमेण वै ।
तानि संपूज्य तत्तेजस्त्रयात्मनि जले शिवे ॥३२॥
प्रोक्तानि देवतारूपाण्यावाह्याभ्यर्च्य तैर्जलैः ।
अभिषिक्तास्तु तत्तेजस्त्रयं देव्यात्मता भवेत् ॥३३॥
वाताद्यैर्ग्रासमायान्तैः षट्सप्ततियुतैः शतैः ।
पञ्चभिर्योजयेन्नित्यां विद्यां तां सर्वमङ्गलाम् ॥३४॥
ततस्तस्या बलस्थाने स्वरान् षोड़श योजयेत् ।
ततः सहस्रैर्नवभिर्द्विशतेन च षोड़श ॥३५॥

तानि स्वरान्तान्येव योजनीयानि। तन्मन्त्रा यथा अं अमृतामृताभ्यां नम इत्यादयः अः पूर्णामृतपूर्णामृताभ्यां नम इत्यन्ताः षोडश। एतानि सोमकलामिथुनानि सर्वमिथुनानामादौ पूज्यानि। अत्र सूर्य्यकलाशक्तिमिथुनानां प्रत्येकं वर्णद्वयात्मकत्वं तन्मिथुनं भेदविवक्षयोपपन्नम्। अन्येषां मिथुनानामेकाक्षरात्मकत्वं मिथुनैक्यविवक्षया चोपपन्नम्। त्रिंशदष्टौ अष्टत्रिंशदित्यर्थः। एतदुक्तं भवति सोमकलाशक्तिमिथुनषोडशकेन सूर्य्यकलामिथुनद्वादशकेन वह्निकलादशकेन चैवमष्टत्रिंशन्मिथुनैः षट्सप्ततिः कला मातृकाक्षराः सन्ति। तान्युक्तक्रमेण विनियुञ्ज्यादिति तत्तेजस्त्रयात्मनि प्रोक्तमिथुनार्च्चनतः। शिवे इति सम्बुद्धिः। प्रोक्तानि सर्व्वतन्त्रेषूक्तानि स्वाभिमतानीत्यर्थः। अभ्यर्च्य तत्क्रमतः तत्तेजस्त्रयं देव्यात्मता सर्व्वदेवतानां सोमसूर्य्याग्निमयमातृकाक्षररूपत्वात् तत्तद्देवतात्मतेत्यर्थः। अभिषेचयेति शेषः॥ ३३॥

वातेत्यादिभिर्वदामि ते इत्यन्तैस्त्रिभिः श्लोकैः मूलविद्यायाः स्वरूपबाहुल्योपदेशं तद्विनियोगप्रस्तावञ्च करोति। तत्र वाताद्यैर्ग्रासमायान्तैरकाराद्यैः क्षकारान्तैः मातृकाविसराक्षरैः प्रोक्तसंख्यैरित्यर्थः। शतैः पञ्चभिः पञ्चशतैरित्यर्थः। एतदुक्तं भवति अकारादीनां षोड़शानां स्वराणां ककारादिक्षकारान्तानां पञ्चत्रिंशताञ्च प्रत्येकं षोडशस्वरयोजनतः षोडशानां षोडशानाञ्चैवं सम्भूय षट्सप्तत्यधिकपञ्चशतसंख्यानां मातृकाविसराक्षराणां मूलविद्याया आदौ क्रमशः प्रत्येकं योजनतः षट्सप्तत्यधिकपञ्चशतसंख्यानि विद्यारूपाणि भवन्ति इति। तस्या बलस्थाने मूलविद्यायाश्चतुर्दशस्वरस्थाने स्वरान् षोडश योजयेत्। षोडशस्वरान् क्रमशः

रूपाणि नित्याविद्याया जायन्ते परमेश्वरि ।
तैर्यन्त्राणि प्रयोगांस्तु फलानि च वदामि ते ॥३६॥
वृत्तद्वयं विधायास्य वहिः षट्कोणमालिखेत् ।
तद्वहिश्चाष्टपत्राब्जं तद्वहिस्तत्त्रयं तथा ॥३७॥
कृत्वा तेषु न्यसेद्विद्याकूटान्युक्तक्रमेण तु ।
तेष्वाद्यं मध्यतः साध्यसमेतं विलिखेद्वहिः ॥३८॥
वहिः कोणेषु चत्वारि प्रत्येकं विलिखेत्ततः ।
अष्टच्छदेषु प्रत्येकं पञ्च पञ्च समालिखेत् ॥३९॥
वहिर्वृत्तान्तरयुगे मातृकां माययान्विताम् ।
विलोमामनुलोमाञ्च स्वेन सम्यक् समालिखेत् ॥४०॥

प्रत्येकं योजयेत् । नित्याविद्यायाः सर्व्वमङ्गलानित्याविद्यायाः । एतदुक्तं भवति पूर्वोक्तैर्विद्यादियोजितैः षट्सप्तत्यधिकपञ्चशतसंख्यैर्मातृकाविसराक्षरैस्तत्संख्य-रूपभेदाया अन्त्ये प्रत्येकं क्रमात् षोडशस्वरयोजनतः सषोडशद्विशताधिकनव-सहस्रसंख्याविद्यातत्त्वरूपाणि भवन्तीति । तैः प्रोक्तसंख्यैर्विद्यारूपैः प्रयोगान् यन्त्रैरिति शेषः ॥ ३६ ॥

वृत्तद्वयमित्यादिभिः क्रमादित्यन्तैः षड्भिः श्लोकैः प्रोक्तसंख्याविद्यारूपैरेकैका वृत्तितश्चतुश्चत्वारिंशदधिकशतयन्त्राण्युपदिशति । तत्र अस्य वृत्तद्वयस्य । तद्वहिः षट्कोणाद्वहिः । तद्वहिः अष्टपत्राब्जाद्वहिः । तत्त्रयं वृत्तत्रयं कृत्वेति सर्व्वत्रान्वयः । तेषु स्थानेषु विद्याकूटान् मूलविद्यायाः प्रोक्तसङ्केतरूपानित्यर्थः । उक्तक्रमेण वक्ष्य-माणक्रमेण । तेष्वाद्यं प्रोक्तसंख्येषु कूटेष्वाद्यं मध्यतः सर्वमध्यतः साध्यसमेतं सकार-स्याधस्ताद्दकारमालिख्य तयोर्मध्यान्तरालप्रदेशे च साधकादित्रयं लिखेदित्यर्थः । वहिर्मध्यात् चत्वारि चत्वारि प्रतिकोणं तानि च मध्यलिखिताक्षरादीनि सम्भूय षट्-कोणलेखनीयाक्षराणि चतुर्विंशतिः । वहिः षट्कोणात् प्रत्येकं पञ्च पञ्च प्रतिदलं पञ्च पञ्चाक्षराणि लिखेदित्यर्थः । सम्भूयाष्टपत्रलेखनीयाक्षराणि चत्वारिंशत् । एवं सम्भूय चास्मिन् यन्त्रे लेखनीयाक्षराणि चतुःषष्टिः । वहिः अष्टपत्रात् । वृत्ता-न्तरयुगे अष्टपत्रवाह्यगतवृत्तत्रयान्तरालवीथीद्वये । मायया विसर्जनीयेन । स्वेन विन्दुना । अन्तःषडन्तरालेषु अन्तर्गतषट्कोणषडन्तरालेषु पर्य्यायदिनसम्भवे

अन्तःषड़न्तरालेषु पर्य्यायदिनसम्भवे।
नित्ये लिखेदग्रतस्तु प्रादक्षिण्येन सर्वतः ॥४१॥
एवं यन्त्राणि जायन्ते तैः कूटैरक्षभेदतः।
शतञ्च चत्वारिंशच्च चत्वारि च ततः क्रमात् ॥४२॥
एवमन्यानि कूटानि प्रोक्तानि विलिखेत् क्रमात्।
मध्ये नामसमेतानि तदन्यान्यभितो लिखेत् ॥४३॥

नित्ये प्रत्येकमक्षरत्रयात्मकतया षड़क्षररूपे विद्ये। सर्वतः यन्त्रस्य सर्वस्थानेषु। एवमुक्तयोगत इत्यत्रान्वयः। उक्तयोगत इत्येतदुक्तं भवति पूर्वपूर्वलिखिताक्षरचतुःषष्टिकादुपरितनमुपरितनं चतुःषष्टिकं वहिर्वहिरेवं क्रमेणोक्तसंख्यविद्याक्षरैरेकावृत्तितः प्रोक्तसंख्यानि यन्त्राणि जायन्त इति। यन्त्रविरचनाक्रमो यथा—प्रागुक्तमानतः षट्कोणं वृत्तद्वयगर्भं कृत्वा तद्वहिः अष्टदलं पद्मं कृत्वा तद्वाह्य-वृत्तद्वयाद्वहिर्वृत्तद्वयं विधाय सर्वमध्ये सषोडशशद्विशताधिकनवसहस्रसंख्येषु मातृकाविसरस्वरसंयोगादुत्पन्नयोगसञ्जातेषु विद्यारूपेष्वाद्यं प्रागवत् सनामकमालिख्य तद्वहिः षट्कोणेषु प्रतिकोणं मध्यलिखिताक्षरादीनि चत्वारि चत्वार्य्यक्षराणि सम्भूय चतुर्विंशत्यक्षराण्यालिख्य तद्वहिरष्टपत्रेषु प्रतिपत्रं षट्कोणाभिलिखितचतुर्विंशतिकादुपरितनानि पञ्चपञ्चाक्षराणि सम्भूय तत्र चत्वारिंशदक्षराण्यालिख्यैवं सम्भूय चतुःषष्टिसङ्ख्यान्यक्षराण्यालिख्य तद्वहिर्वृत्तत्रयान्तरालवीथीद्वये मातृकां विलोमां सविसर्जनीयामन्तर्वीथ्यामालिख्य तद्वाह्यवीथ्यामनुलोमां सविन्दुकामालिखेत्। एतत् प्रथमं यन्त्रम्। एवं पूर्वोक्तयन्त्रलिखितचतुःषष्टिकादुपरितनमुपरितनं चतुःषष्टिकम् एवं क्रमेणोक्तसङ्ख्यानां विद्याक्षराणामेकावृत्तितो वहिर्वहिर्लेखनतश्चतुश्चत्वारिंशदधिक शतसंख्यानि यन्त्राणि जायन्त इति ॥ ४२ ॥

एवमित्यादिभिर्वदेदित्यन्तैश्चतुर्भिः श्लोकैः पूर्वोक्तानां चतुश्चत्वारिंशदधिकशतसंख्यानां यन्त्राणामेवाक्षरन्यासस्थानभेदेन जातानां यन्त्राणां संख्यामन्यनित्यापञ्चदशकस्याप्येवं क्रमेण यन्त्राणि सम्भवन्तीति चोपदिशति। तत्र एवमुक्तप्रकारेण अन्यानि कूटानि प्रोक्तानि पूर्वेषां पूर्वोक्तसंख्यानां यन्त्राणां मध्यलिखितकूटाक्षरा-

त्रयोदशमितैर्लक्षैः सप्तविंशतिसंख्यकैः ।
सहस्रैश्च शतेनापि चतुर्भिस्तानि संख्यया ॥४४॥
यन्त्राणि देवि जायन्ते तैश्चासौ सर्व्वमङ्गला ।
एवमासान्तु नित्यानां यन्त्राणि स्युः पृथक् पृथक् ॥४५॥

दुपरितनमुपरितनं कूटाक्षरमुपरितनानां प्रोक्तसंख्यानां यन्त्राणां मध्ये मध्ये लिखेदित्यर्थः । तदन्यानि तत्तत्प्रथमप्रथमयन्त्रेषु मध्यमध्यलिखिताक्षरादीनि चतुःषष्टिसंख्यानि । सप्तविंशतिसंख्यकैः सहस्रैः सप्तविंशतिसहस्रैरित्यर्थः । तैर्यन्त्रैः । एतदुक्तं भवति यथा पूर्वोक्तानां चतुश्चत्वारिंशदधिकशतानां यन्त्राणां प्रथमस्य यन्त्रस्य मध्ये सषोडशद्विशताधिकनवसहस्रसंख्यानां विद्यारूपकूटाक्षराणां प्रथमं मध्ये विलिख्य तद्बहिः स्थानेषु प्रोक्तेषु लिखितैर्मध्यलिखितप्रथमाक्षरादिकैश्चतुःषष्टिकूटैः प्रथमं यन्त्रम् । द्वितीयं पञ्चषष्टितमकूटादिकैर्बहिर्लिखितैश्चतुःषष्टिकैः एवं क्रमेण सर्वप्रथमकूटे कर्णिकास्थ एवोक्तसंख्यानि यन्त्राणि लिखितानि । तथा द्वितीयं कूटं तत्प्रथमस्य यन्त्रस्य मध्ये विलिख्य बहिस्तदादिकैश्चतुःषष्टिकैश्चतुःषष्टिकैर्लिखितैश्चतुश्चत्वारिंशदधिकशतसंख्यानि यन्त्राणि जायन्ते । एवं तेषां तेषां तथा तथा एकैककूटमध्यस्थ एव लेखनात् प्रोक्तसंख्यानि यन्त्राण्येवमेव । मध्यतः प्रोक्तसंख्यानां सर्वेषां कूटानां क्रमात् यावत्तत्तत्क्रमेण कूटसंख्यावृत्तिलेखनतः । सषोडशद्विशताधिकनवसहस्रसंख्ययन्त्राणां चतुश्चत्वारिंशदधिकशतकं सम्भूय त्रयोदशलक्षं चतुरुत्तरशताधिकसप्तविंशतिसहस्रोत्तरं यन्त्राणि भवन्तीति । तत्र पूर्वपूर्वचतुश्चत्वारिंशदधिकशतयन्त्रप्रथमप्रथमयन्त्रमध्यमध्यलिखितकूटात् पूर्व्वपूर्व्वकूटाक्षराणि तत्तच्चरमचरमयन्त्रस्य चरमचरमाक्षराणि भवन्ति इति ॥ एवमासान्तु नित्यानां यन्त्राणि स्युः पृथक् पृथक् । एतदुक्तं भवति षोडशानां नित्यानां प्रत्येकं हृल्लेखावतीनां दशानां तस्यां हृल्लेखायामेवं सर्व्वमङ्गलावदाद्यन्तयोर्मातृकाविसरस्वरषोडशकयोजनतः सर्व्वमङ्गलोक्तसंख्यानि तस्या रूपाणि भवन्ति । तैस्तद्वत् तत्संख्यानि यन्त्राणि च विधेयानि । हृल्लेखाविहीनानां यन्त्राणां पञ्चानां सर्व्वमङ्गलावदाद्यक्षराणामाद्यन्तयोर्मातृकाविसरस्वरयोजनतस्तत्संख्यानि रूपाणि तैस्तत्संख्यानि च यन्त्राणि भवन्ति । ततस्तैस्तैस्तास्ताः सिद्धयश्च भवन्तीति । तत्र भेरुण्डाकुलसुन्दरीनित्ययोराद्या-

तस्मादाभिरसाध्यानि न कदाचिच्च कुत्रचित्।
विद्यन्ते तेषु यत्किञ्चिदच्ये कः शेषतो वदेत् ॥४६॥
नाथात्मकानि येन सुरस्तेन तानि नवक्रमैः।
भित्त्वा षोड़शधा देवि विदध्याद्विनियोगकम् ॥४७॥
विशालामध्यविन्यासं विधाय नवकोष्ठकम्।
प्रागादिमध्यसंयुक्तं नाथान् देवीश्च तत्क्रमात् ॥४८॥४९॥
* * * * *
यद्यद्विवाञ्छितं कर्म्म तत्तेषु विनियोजयेत्।
पीठे वा भूतले वापि पूजयेत् प्रोक्तवासरम् ॥५०॥

चरस्य हलमात्राभावात् मातृकाविसरमादिं कृत्वा तस्य विद्याचरस्य स्थाने प्रत्येकं षोडशस्वरयोगेन तत्तत्संख्यां सम्पादयेदित्युपदेशः। एवमत्राति-रहस्यमपि नाथाज्ञया सर्वं विविच्य समीचीनमुक्तमस्माभिः। आभिः पञ्चदश-नित्याभिः असाध्यानि कार्य्याणि कदाचित् काले कुत्रचित् स्थाने च तेषु कार्य्येषु यत्किञ्चिदेकदेशतः। अतः कः शेषतो वदेत् साकल्येन तत्साध्यानि कार्य्याणि अहमपि वक्तुं न शक्नोमीत्यर्थः॥ ४६ ॥

नाथात्मकानीत्यादिभिर्जपादिनेत्यन्तैस्त्रयोदशभिः श्लोकैः प्रोक्तयन्त्राणां विनि-योगप्रकारानुपदिशति। तत्र नाथात्मकानि येन नवसंख्यया आहरणे यन्त्राणां निःशेषत्वात् तानि यन्त्राणि नवक्रमैर्भित्त्वा नवकं नवकं विभज्येत्यर्थः। षोडशधा भित्त्वेति मिलित्वेति सम्बन्धः। पूर्व्वविभक्तं नवकं षोड़शकं षोड़शकं विभज्य विनियोगं कुर्य्यात्। तेन षोड़शभिः षोड़शभिर्नवकैर्विनियोगं कुर्य्यादित्युक्तं भवति। विशालामध्यविन्यासं प्रतिकोष्ठं यन्त्रविनिर्माणयोग्यमध्यविकाशं विधाय नवकोष्ठ-कम्। यथा प्राक्प्रत्यग्दक्षिणोदक् च चतुर्भिः सूत्रैः समान्तरालमास्फालितैर्नव-कोष्ठानि कुर्य्यादिति। प्रागादिमध्यपर्य्यन्तं प्रादक्षिण्यक्रमात् लिखेत्। नवानि नवसु प्राग्दिग्गतपङ्क्तिस्थकोष्ठत्रयमध्यकोष्ठमारभ्य मध्यमध्यस्थकोष्ठान्तं प्रादक्षिण्ये-ना(मु)युक्तक्रमं नवयन्त्राणि लिखेदित्यर्थः। तेषु नवसु यन्त्रेषु तत्रक्षराणि प्रथमेषु नवसु क्रमेणाश्विन्यादीनि नव नक्षत्राणि द्वितीयनवके मघादीनि नव नक्षत्राणि तृतीयनवके मूलादीनि नव नक्षत्राणि एवं यावत् फलावास्युपरितनेषु नवकेष्वपि

ततः प्राप्ते वाञ्छितार्थे स्वात्मन्युद्वास्य देवताः ।
चक्रं प्रक्षाल्य तत्तोयं केदारादिषु निक्षिपेत् ॥५१॥
एवमन्यानि यन्त्राणि प्रोक्तानि क्रमतः शिवे ।
विनियुञ्ज्यादभीष्टेषु कार्य्येषु क्रमतः शिवे ॥५२॥
परसंख्यासमेतानि तेषु तेष्वप्ययं विधिः ।
सर्वतः सौम्यकर्म्माणि सिध्यन्त्येवानया ध्रुवम् ॥५३॥
वश्येषु ज्ञानसंप्राप्तौ सर्वप्रत्यूहशान्तिषु ।
लक्ष्मीप्राप्तौ तथारोग्यसिद्धौ रोगार्त्तिशान्तिषु ॥५४॥
विजयाय समस्तापत्तारणायाभिसिद्धये ॥
पुत्राप्तौ सर्वरक्षायै पूजयेत्तेषु तत्क्रमात् ॥५५॥
गजाश्वगोखरोष्ट्राणां महिषाणां विवृद्धये ।
तेषां रोगादिपीड़ासु तच्छान्त्यै च यथाक्रमात् ॥५६॥

सर्व्वत्र कार्य्येषु नक्षत्राणि नव क्रमेण पुनःपुनर्लिखेत् । सप्तम्या विभक्त्या सप्तमीविभक्त्यन्तं नक्षत्रलेखनमिति यावत् । नाथानेकस्मिन्नेकमेकं देवीरिति यन्त्र बाहुल्यापेक्षया बहुवचनम् । नाथान्देवीः पूजयेदित्युत्तर श्लोकेनान्वयः । तत्क्रमात् प्रागादिक्रमात् प्रोक्तवासरं मण्डलानि तानि देवताः प्रागवद्बहुवचनम् । केदारादिषु केदारमिति क्षेत्रमुच्यते । आदिशब्दः उद्यानगिष्कुटादिविषयः । एवमित्यादिभिरुक्तार्थः । सौम्यकर्म्माणि वक्ष्यमाणवश्यादीनि । अनया प्रोक्तप्रक्रिययेत्यर्थः । परसंख्येत्यादिना एतदुक्तं भवति । सर्व्वमङ्गलामेतामन्तरेणान्यासां पञ्चदशानां नित्यानां प्रोक्तक्रमतो निर्मितानां परसंख्यापूर्वोक्तसंख्यासमेतानां यन्त्राणामप्युक्तक्रमतोऽयमेव विनियोगक्रम इति । तथा लक्ष्मीप्राप्त्यै तेषु यन्त्रेषु तत्क्रमात् प्रागुक्तक्रमतः पीडासु सतीषु तच्छान्त्यै पीड़ाशान्त्यै यथाक्रमं नवनवक्रमतः तेषु तेषु यन्त्रेषु वश्यादिषूक्तेषु अन्येष्वपि चेत्यर्थः । नवप्राकारयुक्तानि षोडशषोड़शनवकानीत्यर्थः । प्रथमादिषु तिथिषु पूजयेदित्युत्तरत्रान्वयः । प्रथमे नवके

निर्म्माय नव यन्त्राणि तत्र तत्राच्चयेच्छिवाम् ।
तेषु तेषूक्तकार्य्येषु तत्तत् सम्प्राप्तिहेतवे ॥५७॥
नवप्राकारयुक्तानि षोडश प्रथमादिषु ।
तिथिषु प्रोक्तरूपाणि तत्र तां सर्वमङ्गलाम् ॥५८॥
पूजयेद्वाञ्छितावाप्त्यै प्रथमे सर्वदापयेत् ।
एवमेषा महासिद्धिकरी पूजाजपादिना ॥५६॥

एषा सर्व्वमङ्गला षोडशयन्त्रनवकविन्यासार्थं मण्डलं सम्प्रदायप्राप्तं लिख्यते । यथा प्राक्प्रत्यग्दक्षिणोदक्पञ्चपञ्च सूत्राणि खेष्टमानात् समान्तरालानि कृत्वा तेषु षोड़शसु कोष्ठेषु प्रत्येकं मध्ये मध्ये तिर्य्यगूर्द्धञ्च समान्तरालरेखाद्वयविन्यासेन नवनव कोष्ठानि कृत्वा तेषु षोड़शस्वीशानादिमध्यान्तं प्रवेशगत्या तदन्तर्गतेषु(नवसु नवसु कोष्ठेषु प्रागादिप्रादक्षिण्यप्रवेशगत्या मध्यान्तञ्चैवं क्रमात्तेषु सर्वत्र यन्त्राणि कल्पयेदिति । सम्भूयैतदुक्तं भवति प्रोक्तसंख्यानां यन्त्राणां नवधाहरणनिःशेषतया नव नव यन्त्राणि पूर्वोक्तनवकोष्ठमण्डले प्रागादिप्रादक्षिण्यान्मध्यपर्य्यन्तं विलिख्य तद्यन्त्रमध्ये सप्तमीविभक्त्यन्तान्यश्विन्यादीनि मघादीनि मूलादीनि च नवनव-नक्षत्राणि तत्तत्साध्यसहितान्यालिख्यैवंक्रमेण पुनःपुनर्विलिख्योपरितननवकेष्वपि तत्तन्नक्षत्रे तद्यन्त्रार्च्चनादिकं यावत् फलावाप्ति कुर्य्यात् । किञ्च प्रागुक्तयन्त्रनव नवषोड़शकं प्रागुक्तनवकोष्ठगर्भे षोड़शकोष्ठे मण्डले प्रागुक्तक्रमेण विलिख्य प्रति-पदादिपञ्चदश्यन्तं पञ्चदशसु तिथिषु प्रतितिथि एकस्मिन्नेकस्मिन्नवके द्वितीयनवका-दिषु पञ्चदशसु नवकेष्वभ्यर्च्य सर्वासु तिथिषु पूर्व्वमीशदिग्गतप्रथमनवकेष्वर्च्चयेत् । एवं यावत् फलाप्ति तदुपरितनान्यपि नवकषोड़शकान्यालिख्य तिथिषु पूजनात् सर्व्वफलावाप्तिकरी सर्व्वमङ्गलेति । अत्र परसंख्यावान्तरसंख्याचतुश्चत्वारिंश-दधिकशतरूपा नव संख्याभरणतश्च निःशेषा भवति परसंख्यापि तथैव । तेन नाथात्मकत्वं षोड़शनित्यात्मकत्वं चैषामिति सम्प्रदायः ॥ ५८ ॥

लघुमन्त्रक्रियास्त्वासां पूजां सर्वार्थसिद्धिदाम् ।
पूर्णामनतिविस्तारं मङ्गलां ब्रूहि मे शिव ॥६०॥
देवर्षिसिद्धगन्धर्वयक्षदेवाङ्गनाश्रयाम् ।
पूजां वक्ष्यामि ते देवि ! गुह्यां शृणु मनोहरे ॥६१॥
विद्यया कुलसुन्दर्य्या कराङ्गन्यासपूर्वकम् ।
अर्चितया विधायाथ पीठे चक्रं विधाय तत् ॥६२॥
चन्दनागुरुकर्पूररोचनादरदादिषु ।
एकेन तत्र ताः सम्यगुक्तरूपमथार्चयेत् ॥६३॥
रत्नादिषूक्तेष्वालिख्य प्रतिष्ठाप्यात्र पूजयेत् ।
वृत्तस्यायामविस्तारद्वये त्वेकतुरीयतः ॥६४॥

लघुमन्त्रेत्यादिभिः पूजयेदित्यन्तैरध्यर्द्धैश्चतुर्भिः श्लोकैस्तत्प्रश्नोत्तररूपप्रस्तावपूर्वं वक्ष्यमाणायां लघुमन्त्रक्रियायां पूजायां षोडशनित्यासाधारणायां कराङ्गन्यासमर्घविधानं यन्त्रलेखनद्रव्याधिष्ठानादिकञ्चोपदिशति। तत्र लघुमन्त्रक्रियायां लघुमन्त्रां लघुक्रियाञ्चेत्यर्थः। आसां षोडशनित्यानां पूर्णां लघुत्वपरिहाराय मङ्गलां मङ्गलकरीं गुह्यां दिव्यत्वात्। तया कुलसुन्दर्य्या चक्रं वक्ष्यमाणद्वादशकोणरूपं। तदिति चक्रविशेषणम्। एकेन द्रव्येण विधायेति पूर्व्वत्रान्वयः। तत्र चक्रे ताः नित्याः उक्तरूपं वक्ष्यमाणरूपं यथा रत्नादिषूक्तेषु प्रधाननित्याकाम्योक्तेषु प्रतिष्ठाप्य चक्रमिति शेषः। अत्र चक्रे ॥ ६३ ॥

वृत्तस्येत्यादिना समाप्तकामित्यन्तेनार्द्धाधिकेन श्लोकद्वयेन द्वादशास्रचक्रनिर्माणक्रममुपदिशति। अत्र आयामविस्तारद्वये त्वेकतुरीयतः आयामविस्तारयोरन्यतमस्य चतुर्थांशमानत इत्यर्थः। तेषु चिह्नेषु सूत्राणि द्वादशेति शेषः। त्रयं चिह्नानां द्वादशकोणचक्रमिति शेषः। तेषां मर्मसु सूत्राणां द्वादशानां रेखाद्वयसङ्गतिस्थानेषु मध्ये सर्व्वमध्ये योनिं स्वाभिमुखं त्रिकोणम्। एतदुक्तं भवति अभीष्टमानेन भ्रमेण वृत्तं निष्पाद्य तस्य व्यासार्द्धं चतुर्विंशतिधा विभज्य तेष्वंशेषु

वृत्तं विधाय चिह्नानि तेषु सूत्राणि पातयेत्।
त्र्यमन्तरतो मुक्त्वा तेन द्वादशकोणकम् ॥६५॥
तेषां मर्मसु मध्ये च विदध्याद्वृत्तयुग्मकम्।
मध्यवृत्तस्य मध्ये तु योनिं कुर्यात् समासकाम् ॥६६॥
प्राग्वत्तिस्रोऽर्चयेन्नित्यास्तत्कोणेषु प्रदक्षिणम्।
अन्या अन्येषु कोणेषु पूजयेद्द्वादश क्रमात् ॥६७॥
अग्रात् प्रदक्षिणं पश्चाद्बलिं दद्याद्यथाविधि।
सप्ताक्षर्या केवलया केवलां ललितां यजेत् ॥६८॥

वृत्तात् सप्तमांशादल्पस्तदन्तः। षष्ठांशादल्पस्य वृत्तद्वयं कृत्वा सर्ववाह्यवृत्तस्य मध्यव्यासस्यायामविस्तारयोरन्यतमस्य चतुरंशीकृतस्य चतुर्थांशतः सर्ववाह्यवृत्ते-ऽभितो द्वादशचिह्नानि विधाय तेषु चिह्नेषु त्रिचिह्नान्तरितं चिह्नाचिह्नमित्येवं क्रमेण द्वादशसूत्राण्यास्फाल्य सर्वमध्यवृत्तमध्ये प्राग्वत् समत्रिरेखां स्वाभि-मुखां योनिं कुर्यात्। एवं कृते तन्मध्ये द्वादशकमध्ययोनिवृत्तोपेतं सर्वमध्य-वृत्तान्तर्गतयोनिकं प्रोक्तरूपं द्वादशास्रं चक्रं भवतीति ॥ ६६ ॥

प्राग्वदित्यादिना यजेदित्यन्तेन श्लोकद्वयेन तच्चक्रे प्रोक्तशेषां लघुपूजामुप-दिशति। तत्र प्राग्वन्मध्यस्थाया उपरितनाः तत्कोणेषु सर्वमध्यस्थत्रिकोणत्रये प्रदक्षिणम् अग्रादि। अन्याः तिसृभ्यो नित्याभ्यः। अन्येषु वाह्यस्थेषु कोणेषु द्वादशसु द्वादश नित्या इति शेषः। क्रमात् यथाक्रमं अग्रात् प्रदक्षिणमिति पूर्वत्र सम्बन्धः। बलिं दद्यात् पूजान्त एव यथाविधि अन्नादिद्रव्यैर्मुद्रया च सप्ताक्षर्या केवलया कुरुकुल्लयेति शेषः। अस्य पदस्य बलिं दद्यात् इत्यत्रान्वयः। पूजान्तरा। केवलां ललितां ललितानित्यायाः तृतीयखण्डस्यापि ललितेति नाम तामित्यर्थः। एतत्प्रधाननित्यायामङ्गित्वपूजने अन्यासां पञ्चदशानामङ्गित्वपूजने तत्तद्विद्यां जपेदित्यर्थः। ललिताविद्यायास्तृतीयखण्डात्मकत्वमन्यस्य खण्डद्वयस्य तृतीयपटले स्वयमेवोपदिष्टवान्। एवमुक्तं भवति प्रागुक्ते द्वादशास्रे चक्रे मध्ययोनिमध्ये ललितां विद्यातृतीयखण्डेनाभ्यर्च्य तद्योनिकोणत्रये अग्रादिप्रादक्षिण्यात् तिस्रः

नित्यानां ललिताद्यानां षोडशानाञ्च नामभिः ।
नित्यासप्ताक्षरीभिः स्युर्विद्याः पूजासु सर्वदा ॥६९॥
ताभिः षोडषविद्याभिर्नित्यास्ताः षोडशार्चयेत् ।
तद्विद्याक्षरसंख्यान्तु शृणु वक्ष्ये यथाक्रमम् ॥७०॥
प्रथमायाश्च सप्तम्या विद्या स्यात् षोडशाक्षरी ।
द्वितीयायाश्चतुर्थ्याः स्युश्चतुर्दशभिरक्षरैः ॥७१॥
तृतीयायाश्च षष्ठ्याश्च दशम्या दशपञ्चकम् ।
द्वादश्याश्च चतुर्दश्याः पञ्चदश्याः क्रमेण वै ॥७२॥

कामेश्वरीवज्रेश्वरीभगमालिनीः समाराध्य तत्तद्विद्याभिरन्या द्वादशनित्या नित्य क्लिन्नादीः द्वादशकोणेष्वग्रादिप्रादक्षिण्येन तत्तद्विद्याभिरर्चयेत्। कुरुकुल्लासप्ताक्षर्य्या वलिमन्ते दत्त्वा केवलतृतीयखण्डं जपेत्। अन्यासां पञ्चदशानां अङ्गाङ्गित्वपूजनेषु तदुपरितनास्तिस्रस्तद्विद्याभिः प्राग्वदभ्यर्च्य तदुपरितना द्वादशनित्या यथाक्रमं द्वादशकोणेषु तत्तद्विद्याभिरर्च्चयित्वा सर्वासां कुरुकुल्ला सप्ताक्षर्य्या वलिं दत्त्वा तत्तद्विद्यां जपेत्। तत्र पूजने अन्तर्द्वादशे अन्तः द्वादशकोणे मध्यस्थां पूजयेदिति ॥ ६८ ॥

नित्यानामित्यादिभिरुदिता इत्यन्तैः पञ्चभिः श्लोकैर्नित्यानां षोड्शानां नामरूपा विद्याः प्रत्येकं तदक्षरसंख्यास्ताभिर्नामरूपविद्याभिश्च तस्मिन् द्वादशारे चक्रे पूजाविधानञ्चोपदिशति। तत्र नामतस्तृतीयपटलप्रोक्तत्रिपुरसुन्दरीत्यादिनामभिः। नित्या सप्ताक्षराणि स्युः। नित्या इत्यक्षरद्वयं प्रागुक्तसप्ताक्षरीति स्युरित्यनयोः पूर्वापरयोरन्वयः। तेन इति प्रोक्तप्रकारविद्याः स्युरित्यर्थः। सर्व्वदा नित्यं ताभिर्नामरूपाभिरित्यर्थः। विद्यात्रयस्यापि दशपञ्चकमित्यत्रान्वयः। पञ्चम्या इत्यादि पदत्रयं विद्यापदविशेषणं प्राग्वत् त्रयोदशाक्षराणि। एकादश्या इत्यादित्रयं प्राग्वत् द्वादशोदिता वर्णा इति शेषः। एतदुक्तं भवति षोडशानां नित्यानां तृतीयपटले षोडशविद्योपदेशे यस्याः त्रिपुरसुन्दरीत्यादिरूपं यन्नाम प्रोक्तं तस्यान्ते नित्यासप्ताक्षरीति सर्वासां नवाक्षरयोजनमादौ सम्प्रदायात् सर्वासाम् प्रत्येकं

पञ्चम्याश्च नवम्याश्च त्रयोदश्यास्त्रयोदशी।
एकादश्यास्तु साष्टम्याः षोडश्या द्वादशोदिता: ॥७३॥
अस्मिन्नेवार्चयेच्चक्रे चतुर्विंशतिभिस्तथा।
सविंशतिशता विद्या जपेत्तास्ताश्च सिद्धये ॥७४॥
अन्या विंशत् सप्तशतं तैर्यन्त्रैर्न च पूजनम्।
आसां पूजाजपाद्येषु यन्त्रेषु च समीरितम् ॥७५॥
एतल्लघुप्रकारन्ते यन्त्रं सर्व्वार्थदायकम्।
तेन तन्त्रोक्तमखिलं साधयेद्वज्ररूपिणा ॥७६॥

क्रमेण प्रणवद्वन्द्वरेखायोजनञ्च कुर्य्यात्। तासां तत्रोदितनामाक्षरसंख्यामनुष्टुप् वाक्यरूपेणैव व्याख्यायतेऽस्माभिः। यथा :--सामस्तोमवनासङ्गभूतागीतावताचलैः। इत्यमर्णैः षोड्शभिः संख्या नामार्णगाः क्रमात्॥ इति। एवं प्रोक्तसंख्याक्षरनाम विद्या षोड्शमीच्छते पूर्व्वविद्या स्वस्वनामरूपाभिः प्रोक्तद्वादशारचक्रे पूर्वोक्तक्रमेण षोड्शनित्याः समर्च्चयेदिति॥ ७३॥

अस्मिन्नित्यादिना समीरितमित्यन्तेन श्लोकद्वयेनोपरिष्टाद्वक्ष्यमाणार्णाभिः प्रधमाङ्गिनित्याया ललिताया विद्यायास्तत्खण्डाक्षराणां षण्णां चतुरक्षरभेदजनिताभिश्चतुर्विंशतिभेदजनिताभिश्चतुर्विंशतिभिदाङ्गिविद्याभिस्तत्पञ्चाक्षरप्रभेदस्थाभिर्विंशत्यधिक-शतसंख्याभिर्विद्याभिस्तत्-षड़क्षरजनिताभिर्विंशत्यधिक-सप्तशतसंख्याभिर्विद्याभिश्चास्मिन्नेव द्वादशारे प्रोक्ते चक्रे तस्या ललितायाः समाराधनमुपदिशति। तत्र तास्ता याभिर्विद्याभिरर्च्चितैस्तैर्विद्यास्वरूपभेदैः। यन्त्रेषु तत्तत्पटलवक्ष्यमाणेषु। आसां प्रोक्तसंख्याविद्यानाम्। पूजाजपाद्येषु आद्यशब्दस्तर्पणहोमादिविषयः। समीरितं विधानमिति शेषः। आसां विद्यानां उक्तसंख्यानां पूजनादिषु यन्त्रेषु च विधानमुक्तमित्यर्थः। अत्र यन्त्रेष्विति द्विरुपादानं संक्षेपविवरणरूपम्। एतदुक्तं भवति प्रधाननित्याया ललितायास्तद्द्वादशारचक्रमध्ये पूजाविधौ तद्विद्यातार्तीयखण्डाक्षरप्रभेदजनिताभिः प्रोक्तसंख्याभिर्विद्याभिश्चार्चयेत्। आभिर्यन्त्रपटलवक्ष्यमाणयन्त्रेष्वपि पूजादिकं कुर्य्यात्॥ ७५॥

एतदित्यादिभिः कोणत इत्यन्तैरष्टभिः श्लोकैः षोड्शनित्यानामविद्याभिः

तद्वज्रं द्विविधं प्रोक्तं कोष्ठकोणात्मभेदतः ।
कोणात्मवज्रनिर्म्माणप्रयोगाः परतः शिवे ॥७७॥
तयोस्तु कोष्ठरूपन्तु वज्रं वच्म्ये यथाविधि ।
यत्साधकार्थितावाप्तौ सुराङ्घ्रिपसमो भवेत् ॥७८॥
प्राक्प्रत्यग्दक्षिणोदक्क चतुर्विंशतिसूत्रतः ।
नवविंशतिभिः पञ्चशतं कोष्ठानि तेन वै ॥७९॥
कोणेषु मार्जयेत् षड्भिः षष्टिकोष्ठानि पूर्ववत् ।
शिष्टेषु वकोष्ठानि पञ्चषष्ट्या शतद्वयम् ॥८०॥

ललिताचतुर्विंशतिभेदैश्च कोष्ठरूपवज्रयन्त्रनिर्माणक्रममुपदिशति । तत्र एतद् वक्ष्यमाणं ते वक्ष्यामीति शेषः । तेन यन्त्रेण तन्त्रोक्तमखिलं साधयेत् । षोडशनित्याविद्याक्षरमयत्वात् । परतः यन्त्रपटले । तयोः कोष्ठकोणात्मकयोः यद्यन्त्रं सुराङ्घ्रिपसम इति स्वातन्त्र्यं सममित्यर्थः । तेषु कोष्ठेषु नवविंशत्यधिकपञ्चशतसंख्येषु कोणेषु कोणदिक्षु । षड्भिः सहितानीति शेषः षट्षष्टिकोष्ठानीत्यर्थः । पूर्ववत् मध्ये वज्ररूपं यथा भवेत्तथेत्यर्थः । तेषु पञ्चषष्ट्यधिकद्विशतसंख्येषु कोष्ठेषु च चतुष्टयैः प्रतिदिशं अधोमध्यवाह्यारम्भात् सर्वाधःस्थपङ्क्तिस्थ-कोष्ठपञ्चकमध्यकोष्ठरूपवाह्यकोष्ठादारभ्य चित्रादिललितान्तिकं नामविद्याक्षराणि सम्भूय पञ्चविंशत्यधिकद्विशतसंख्यानीत्यर्थः । अवशिष्टेषु चतुर्विंशतिकोष्ठेष्वित्यर्थः । ललितार्णचतुर्भेदजनितामित्यस्य चतुर्विंशतिमित्यत्रान्वयः । नामशक्तियुक् तत्चतुर्विंशतिगतहृल्लेखोदरे प्राग्वन्नाम लिखेदित्यर्थः । ललितां तार्त्तीयां साध्यगर्भां प्राग्वत् हृल्लेखागतसाध्यां । मध्यकोणतः मध्ये च त्रिकोणेष्वित्यर्थः । तेन प्रतिलोमतश्चतुर्विंशतिरूपां विद्यां लिखेदित्यर्थः । एवं कृते अनुलोमरूपाश्चतुर्विंशतितया लिखिता मध्ये भवन्तीति यावत् । तामेव त्रिकोणचतुष्टयेषु च लिखेदित्यर्थः । एतदुक्तं भवति प्राक्प्रत्यग्दक्षिणोदक्समान्तरालानि चतुर्विंशतिसूत्राण्यास्फाल्य नवविंशत्यधिकपञ्चशतकोष्ठानि सम्पाद्य तेषु चतसृषु कोणदिक्षु प्रतिकोणदिशं षट्षष्टिषट्षष्टिसंख्यानि च एवं सम्भूय चतुःषष्ट्यधिकद्विशतसंख्यानि कोष्ठानि मध्ये वज्ररूपेण मार्जयित्वा मध्ये वज्र

तेषु प्राग्वत्त्रिकोणानि चतुर्दिक्षु चतुष्टयैः ।
कोष्ठैर्विधायाधो मध्ये वाद्यारभ्यात् प्रदक्षिणम् ॥८१॥
प्रवेशगत्या विलिखेच्चित्रादिललितान्तकम् ।
मध्येऽवशिष्टे खण्डानां चतुर्व्विंशतिमालिखेत् ॥८२॥
ललितायाश्चतुर्भेदजनितां नामशक्तियुक् ।
ललितां साध्यगर्भान्तु विलिखेन्मध्यकोणतः ॥८३ ॥
एवं यन्त्रं समालिख्य शिलालोहत्रयादिषु ।
संस्थाप्य कुत्रचित् स्थाने पूजयेद्वाञ्छितात्मये ॥८४॥
यस्मिन् देशे वज्रयन्त्रं स्थापितं योजनावधि ।
मङ्गलान्येव जायन्ते नामङ्गलकथा भवेत् ॥८५॥

रूपावशिष्टेषु पञ्चषष्ट्यधिकद्विशतेषु कोष्ठेषु प्राग्वच्चतुर्दिक्षु कोष्ठचतुष्टयमेवं सम्भूय षोड़शकोष्ठानि मार्जयित्वा तत्र समत्रिरेखं त्रिकोणचतुष्टयं कृत्वा शिष्टे ष्वेकोनपञ्चाशदधिकद्विशतसङ्ख्यकोष्ठेषु सर्व्वाधःस्थपङ्क्तिकोष्ठपञ्चकमध्यकोष्ट मारभ्य प्रादक्षिण्यप्रवेशगत्या मुक्तक्रमं चित्रादिललितान्तानि षोड़शनित्यानामरूप-विद्याक्षराणि पञ्चविंशत्यधिकद्विशतसङ्ख्यानि यावत्सङ्ख्यापरिसमाप्त्या विलिख्य शान्तरावशिष्टेषु चतुर्विंशतिकोष्ठेषु पूर्व्वलिखितानन्तरकोष्ठाद्यमुपात्त प्रदक्षिणप्रवेश-गत्या ललिताचतुरक्षरभेदजनितं तत्तत् ह्लक्ले खोदरस्थसाधकादित्रयसहितं विद्या-चतुर्विंशतिकमनुलोमरूपा तत्प्रथमभूता ललिता मध्ये यथा भवेत्तथा विलोमतः समालिख्य सर्व्वमध्यगतानुलोमरूपललिता ह्लक्ले खोदरे प्राग्वत् नामत्रयं लिखित्वा तामेव चतुर्दिग्गतत्रिकोणचतुष्टयेऽपि साध्यगर्भां समालिखेत् इति ॥ ८३ ॥

एवमित्यादिना भवेदित्यन्तेन श्लोकद्वयेन पूर्व्वोक्तयन्त्रप्रयोगफलान्युपदिशति । तत्र लोहत्रयादिषु आदिशब्दो रत्नादिविषयः । संस्थाप्य निधाय प्राणप्रतिष्ठादि-पुरःसरं अमङ्गलकथा अमङ्गलमिति शब्दस्तस्मिन्निति शेषः ॥ ८५ ॥

पूजाचक्रे च तासान्तु नामानि प्रतिकोणके ।
विलिख्य मध्ये ललितां साध्यगर्भां समालिखेत् ॥८६॥
वह्निर्वृत्ते मातृकाश्च तच्चक्रं स्थापयेद्भुवि ।
तेनापि पूर्व्ववत् प्रोक्तं देशे न स्यादभव्यकम् ॥८७॥
तस्मिन् सर्वञ्च संलिख्य तां विद्यां सर्वमङ्गलाम् ।
मध्ये साध्याक्षरोपेतां स्थापयेत्तत्फलाप्तये ॥८८॥
प्रागुक्तवज्रयन्त्रे वा द्वादशारेऽपि वा शिवे ।
संस्थाप्य कुम्भं तद्वर्णभूरुहक्वाथपूरितम् ॥ ८९ ॥
विद्याया विधिवज्जप्तैरभिषिञ्चेज्जलैः शुभैः ।
जन्मर्क्षेषु विशेषेण समस्तलयशान्तये ॥ ९० ॥
पूर्वसम्पत्समृद्ध्यै च ग्रहरोगादिशान्तये ।

पूजाचक्रेत्यादिना अभव्यकमित्यन्तेन श्लोकद्वयेन पूर्वोक्तद्वादशकोणचक्रे षोडश-श्लोकैः प्रागुक्तपूजाक्रमेण प्रोक्तस्थानेषु प्रतिस्थानमेकैकनाममन्त्रलेखनं तद्वह्नि-र्वृत्तवीथ्यां मातृकालेखनगतस्वस्वविनियोगमुपदिशति । तत्र एतदुक्तं भवति द्वादशारे चक्रे सर्व्वमध्ये ललितां प्राग्वत् ससाध्यामभिलिख्यान्येषु स्थानेषु पञ्चदशनित्यानां नामविद्याः पूजाक्रमतो लिखित्वा सर्व्ववाह्यवृत्तवीथ्यां मातृका-मनुलोमां सविन्दुकामालिख्य पूर्वोक्तदेशे स्थापनात् पूर्वोक्तफलसिद्धिरिति ॥ ८७ ॥

तस्मिन्नित्यादिना श्लोकेन प्रागुक्तद्वादशकोणे चक्रे सर्व्वस्थानेषु सर्व्वमङ्गला-विद्यालेखनतो विनियोगात् पूर्वोक्तफलसिद्धिरित्युपदिशति । तत्र मध्यसाध्याक्षरो-पेतां नान्यत्रेति यावत् ॥ ८८ ॥

प्रागुक्तेत्यादिना शान्तये इत्यन्तेनाध्यर्द्धेन श्लोकद्वयेन प्रागुक्तवज्रयन्त्रद्वादश-कोणचक्रयोरभिषेकविधानतो वा भव्यानि फलान्युपदिशति । तत्र तद्वर्णभूरुहं तदङ्गिविद्यावर्णप्रोक्तौषधिर्द्वादशकोणे वज्रे वा ललिताया एव विद्याया अङ्गिरूप-तया जन्मर्क्षेषु निजजन्मसु पूर्व्वसम्पत्समृद्ध्यै पूर्वोक्तफलसमृद्धये ॥ ९१ ॥

तथान्यदपि देवेशि प्रयोगं सर्वपावनम् ॥ ८१ ॥
दारिद्र्यवनदावाग्निं पापाब्धिवडवानलम्।
सङ्कोचध्वान्तमार्त्तण्डं सन्तोषाब्धिविधूदयम् ॥ ८२ ॥
प्रागुक्ताक्षरसम्भिन्नां विद्यां नित्यां समाहितः।
मौनी जपेत् प्रसूनैश्च पूजयेत् सौरभान्वितैः ॥ ८३ ॥
तर्पयेत् सलिलैः सिन्धुगामिनीसम्भवैः शिवैः।
सौरभाद्यैस्तिलैः शुभ्रैस्तण्डुलैर्विधिवद्धुनेत् ॥८४॥
संस्थाप्य कुम्भं प्रोक्ताम्बुपूर्णं संजप्य भक्तितः।
समस्तं तत्क्रमादेकवारं तैरभिषेकतः ॥८५॥
घोराभिचारकृत्यादिदुःखेभ्यो मुच्यते क्षणात्।
भूतप्रेतपिशाचाप * * ॥८६॥
कुमारा गुह्यका वीरा डाकिन्याद्याश्च दारुणाः।
विमुच्य तत्क्षणाद्भीताः प्रयान्ति चान्यतः क्षणात् ॥८७॥

तथान्यदपीत्यादिभिः क्षणादित्यन्तैरर्द्धाद्यैः षड्भिः श्लोकैः सर्व्वमङ्गलामित्याद्याद्यन्तयोर्मातृकाविसर्गषोड़शस्वरयोजनतो जनितानां प्रोक्तसंख्यानां विद्यानां जपादिना फलमुपदिशति। तत्र प्रयोगं वक्ष्यामीति शेषः। दारिद्र्यवनदावाग्निं दारिद्र्यं नामातुष्टिः। पापो नामाविमृश्यकारिता। सङ्कोच इति दुर्वासना। सन्तोषः स्वरूपानुभवः। प्रागुक्ताक्षरसम्भिन्नां मातृकाविसर्गषोड़शस्वरैराद्यन्तयोः सम्भिन्नामिति। विद्यां सर्व्वमङ्गलां च करोति भिन्नक्रमः। पूजयेच्च सर्व्वमङ्गलां नित्यां सौरभाद्यैः सलिलैरिति पूर्वत्रान्वयः। शुभ्रैरिति तिलतण्डुलयोर्विशेषणम्। संस्थाप्य द्वादशगुणितादिष्वन्यतम इत्यर्थः। प्रोक्ताम्बुपूर्णं मूलविद्याक्षरौषधिक्वाथाम्बुभिः। समुद्रगावहत्सलिलसरिदम्बुभिर्वा पूर्णं समस्तं तत्प्रोक्तसंख्यारूपमेकवारं एकावृत्तितः संजप्येत्यत्रान्वयः। तैर्जलैर्घोराभिचारकृत्यादिदुःखेभ्यः। आदिशब्दो ग्रहादिविषयः। तम् अभिषिक्तम् ॥ ८७ ॥

समुद्रगासरित्तोये ताः समावर्त्तयेत् स्थितः ।
कण्ठमात्रे मज्जनात्तु१ प्राग्जन्माद्यैर्विमुच्यते ॥९८॥
तथैव घृतहोमेन तर्पणैः शुद्धवारिभिः ।
एवं सकलकल्याणसंप्रोक्ता सर्वमङ्गला ॥९९॥
नामानुरूपं भजतां कृपया फलमानतः ।
चिप्रप्रसादतो नित्यं हर्षोत्पादनतोऽपि च ॥१००॥
प्राणतत्त्वमयी व्याप्तिरिति सम्यक् समीरिता ।
अस्या निफालना चित्ते तत्तत्त्वस्यात्मसात् कृतम् ॥१०१॥
इति षोडशनित्यातन्त्रे कादिमते एकोनविंशति पटलं
परिपूर्णं परामृष्टम् ।

समुद्रगेत्यादिभिरपिचेत्यन्तैस्त्रिभिः श्लोकैः सर्व्वमङ्गलायाः प्रोक्तसङ्ख्याविद्या-जपादितः पापनाशादिकं फलमुपदिशति । तत्र प्राग्जन्माद्यैश्चिरतनं दुर्वासनाभिः । तथैव प्राग्जन्माद्यैर्मुच्यत इत्यर्थः । एवमुक्तप्रकारतः । सकलकल्याणा सकलैर्मङ्गलरूपा इत्यर्थः । कृपयेति पूर्वोत्तरत्रान्वयः । फलदानत इत्यादिना सिद्धानां पदानां नामानुरूपेत्यत्रान्वयः । हर्षोत्पादनतः स्वरूपानुभवतः ॥ १०० ॥

इति षोडशनित्यातन्त्रेषु श्रीकादिमताख्यस्य परिपूर्णस्य तन्त्रस्य प्रपञ्चसार-सिंह-राजप्रकाशाभिधानेन सुभगानन्दनाथेन विरचितायां मनोरमाख्यायां व्याख्यायां सर्व्वमङ्गलानित्याविद्याविधानप्रकाशनपर-मेकोनविंशपटलं परिपूर्णं परामृष्टम् ॥१९ ॥

ग्रन्थसंख्या—ऊनविंशे तु पटले व्याख्याग्रन्थशतत्रयम् ।
अभ्यर्द्धाष्टादश श्लोकाः संख्याताः सम्यगीक्षणात् ॥
अत्र यन्त्राणि लक्षाणि त्रयोदश तथा पुनः ।
षडुत्तरशतेनापि सहस्रमुनिविंशकम् ॥

---

१ मज्जनात्तु इति पाठो दृश्यते ।

विंशपटलम् ।

अथ षोड़शनित्यासु पञ्चदश्युदिता तु या ।
तद्विधानं शृणु प्राज्ञे ज्वालामालिन्युदाहृता ॥ १ ॥
न्यासं ध्यानं तथा शक्तीः पूजामपि च साधनम् ।
यन्त्राणि विनियोगांश्च फलानि च शृणु क्रमात् ॥ २ ॥
एकद्वयचतुःपञ्च चतुष्टयदशाक्षरैः ।
कुर्य्यादङ्गानि मूलार्णैरादितः षट् कराङ्गयोः ॥ ३ ।
ज्वलज्ज्वलनसङ्काशां माणिक्यमुकुटोज्ज्वलाम् ।
षड्वक्त्रां द्वादशभुजां सर्वाभरणभूषिताम् ॥ ४ ॥

(२६ ल २७ स १ शङ्गीश्नो:) पूर्व्वस्मिन्नेकोनविंशे पटले चतुर्दश्याः सर्व्वमङ्गलानित्याविद्याया विधानमुपदिश्यानन्तरं पञ्चदश्या ज्वालामालिनीनित्याया विधानमुपदिदिति। अथ षोड़शनित्येत्यादिना वैभवादितीत्यन्तेन श्लोकशतरूपेण विंशेन पटलेन। तत्र अथ षोड़शेत्यादिना क्रमादित्यन्तेन श्लोकद्वयेन पटलार्थानुद्दिशति। तत्र ज्वालामालिन्युदाहृता तृतीये पटले ज्वालामालिनीविद्योपदिष्टेत्यर्थः। शक्तीः आवरणगाः। विनियागान् तेषां यन्त्राणामिति शेषः। क्रमात् प्रोक्तक्रमादित्यर्थः ॥ २ ॥

एकेत्यादिना श्लोकेन कराङ्गन्यासमुपदिशति। तत्र आदितः मूलविद्यायाः। एतदुक्तं भवति मूलविद्याया आदिभूतेन प्रणवाक्षरेण हृदयं तदुपरिगतेनाक्षरद्वयेन शिरस्तदुपरिगताक्षरचतुष्केण शिखां तदुपरिगताक्षरपञ्चकेन कवचं तदुपरिगताक्षरचतुष्टयेन नेत्राणि तदुपरिगताक्षरदशकेनास्त्रं एवंक्रमेण भिन्नैः सजातिभिः मूलविद्याक्षरैष्वादितः सम्भूय षड्विंशत्यक्षररूपैः षड्भिर्मन्त्रैः षड़ङ्गानि करन्यासपूर्वं न्यसेदिति ॥ ३ ॥

ज्वलदित्यादिभिरन्वितामित्यन्तैः त्रिभिः श्लोकैर्देव्याः सपरिवाराया नित्यसपर्य्याध्यानमुपदिशति। अत्र षड़्वक्त्रां अर्द्धपरचतुर्दिगन्तानि एतानि। द्वादश-

पाशाङ्कुशौ खड्गखेटौ चापबाणौ गदाधरौ ।
शूलवज्री वराभीती दधानां करपङ्कजैः ॥ ५ ॥
स्वसमानाभिरभितः शक्तिभिः परिवारिताम् ।
चारुस्मितलसद्वक्त्रसरोजां वीक्षणान्विताम् ॥ ६ ॥
ध्यात्वैवमुपचारैस्तैरर्चयेत्तान्तु नित्यशः ।
चतुरस्रद्वयं कृत्वा चतुर्द्वारसमन्वितम् ॥ ७ ॥
सशाखमष्टपत्राब्जं मन्तरष्टास्रकं ततः ।
षट्कोणं मध्यतस्त्र्यस्रं विधायात्र शिवां यजेत् ॥ ८ ॥
इच्छाज्ञानक्रियाशक्तीरर्चयेत्त्र्यस्रगाः क्रमात् ।
डाकिन्याद्याश्च षट्कोणे अष्टास्रे घस्मरादिकाः ॥ ९ ॥
घस्मरा विश्वकवला लोलाक्षी लोलजिह्विका ।
सर्वभक्षा सहस्राक्षी निःसङ्गा संहृतिप्रिया ॥ १० ॥

भुजां प्रतिवक्त्रं दक्षिणक्रमात्। अत्रायुधक्रमस्तु वामोर्ध्वादिदक्षिणाधरान्तं एकैकव्यत्यासे सति निबोद्धव्यः। वीक्षणान्वितां प्रतिवक्त्रमिति शेषः। ध्यायेदिति शेषः ॥ ६ ॥

ध्यात्वैवेत्यादिना यजेदित्यन्तेन श्लोकद्वयेन निगमनपुरःसरं नित्यसपर्याचक्रनिर्म्माणमुपदिशति। तत्र एवमुक्तप्रकारतः। तैः षोडशभिः। तां मूलदेवतां। सशाखं चतुर्षु द्वारेषु शाखाद्वयसहितमित्यर्थः। अन्तः यन्त्रान्तः ततः अष्टास्रः अन्तरिति शेषः। मध्यतः सर्व्वमध्ये इत्यर्थः। एतदुक्तं भवति प्राग्वदन्तर्वहिर्विभागेन चतुरस्रद्वयं सशाखाद्वयद्वारचतुष्टयोपेतं विधाय तदन्तः सवृत्तद्वयमष्टपत्रं पद्मं तदन्तरपि सवृत्तद्वयमष्टास्रं प्राग्वदन्तरपि सवृत्तद्वयं प्राग्वत् षडस्रं तदन्तरपि सवृत्तद्वयं समत्रिरेखं त्र्यस्रञ्च यथामानं कृत्वा तत्रार्च्चयेत् ॥ ८ ॥

इच्छेत्यादिभिः समीरितमित्यन्तैः पञ्चभिः श्लोकैः नित्यसपर्य्यायां पञ्चावरणशक्तिं तत्पूजाञ्चोपदिशति। तत्र क्रमात् अग्रादिप्रादक्षिण्येन षट्कोणे षट्कोणकोणेषु नित्यानित्यापटलोक्तवक्निर्ऋत्यादिदिगतकोणक्रमेण घस्मरादिकाः अनन्तरश्लोके

वहिरष्टच्छदेष्वेताः पूजयेच्च प्रदक्षिणम् ।
अचिन्त्यामप्रमेयाञ्च पूर्णरूपां दुरासदाम् ॥ ११ ॥
सर्वगां सिद्धिरूपाञ्च पावनामेकरूपिणीम् ।
वहिर्द्वारेषु कोणेषु पूजयेत् प्रागुदीरिताः ॥ १२ ॥
प्राग्वत् कृतार्च्चं चक्रे तामुक्तं प्रोक्तक्रमाद् यजेत् ।
वलिहोमावसानान्तमिति सम्यक् समीरितम् ॥ १३ ॥
अष्टलक्षं हविष्याशी जपेद्विद्यां जितेन्द्रियः ।
तद्दशांशं तर्पणञ्च होमं कुर्य्याच्च गोघृतैः ॥१४॥
एवं संसिद्धमन्त्रस्तु कुर्य्याद् यन्त्राण्यनुक्रमात् ।

वक्ष्यमाणवक्ष्यरित्यादिना श्लोकेनाष्टास्रेषु पूज्या अष्टशक्तीरुपदिशति। तत्र अग्न्यादिप्रादक्षिण्येन पूजनम्। वहिरष्टास्राद् वहिरष्टच्छदेष्वेता वक्ष्यमाणा अचिन्त्याद्याः। प्रदक्षिणम् अग्न्यादि। एतत् डाकिन्यादिवर्जं सर्वसाधारणम्। अचिन्त्यादिना एकरूपिणीमित्यन्तेनार्द्धद्वयेनाष्टपत्रेषु पूज्याः शक्तीरुपदिशति। वहिर्द्वारेषु चतुरस्रद्वारेषु। प्रागुदीरिताः एतदुक्तं भवति नित्यानित्याया विधानपटले प्रोक्ताब्राह्म्यादीरष्टाविन्द्रादीशान्ता लोकपालशक्तीरष्टावनन्तब्रह्मनियतिकालशक्तीश्चतस्रश्चतुरस्रे तत्तोक्तारम्भक्रमेण पूजयेदिति। प्राग्वत् अङ्गमूलाभ्याम्। चक्रे प्रागुक्ते। तां देवीं प्रोक्तक्रमात् अभ्यन्तराद्वाह्यनिर्गमनगत्या अग्न्यादिप्रादक्षिण्यक्रमतः वलिहोमावसानान्तम्। एतदुक्तं भवति आदौ षोड़शाक्षरेणान्ते कुलकुल्लासमाचर्य्या वलिं दत्त्वा प्रोक्तक्रमतो होमञ्च कुर्य्यादित्यर्थः। समीरितं पूजनमिति शेषः ॥ १३ ॥

अष्टलक्षमित्यादिना श्लोकेन विद्यायाः पुरश्चरणक्रममुपदिशति। तत्र हविष्याशी प्राग्वत्। जितेन्द्रियः स्त्रीसेवनालापादिराहित्यात्। ततो जपसंख्यायास्तर्पणञ्च चकारेण दशांशमित्याकृष्यते। गोघृतैः अजादिघृतनिवृत्त्यर्थं गोग्रहणम् ॥ १४ ॥

एवमित्यादिभिर्ध्रुवमित्यन्तैः सप्तभिः श्लोकैर्दशयन्त्रनिर्माणोपदेशं तद्विनि-

पूजाचक्रे वह्निभूतं चतुरस्रे त्वखण्डिते ॥ १५ ॥
विधाय तत्र विलिखेदक्षराणि यथाविधि ।
सर्वमध्ये तारगर्भे शक्तिमाख्यासमन्विताम् ॥ १६ ॥
यन्त्रस्य त्रिषु कोणेषु षट्सु षट्कमथाष्टसु ।
अष्टकं वह्निरप्येवं वाह्ये दिक्षु नव क्रमात् ॥ १७ ॥
एवं मूलाक्षरैः कृत्वा यन्त्रं तेनैव साधयेत् ।
समस्तं वाञ्छितं पूजाधारणं स्थापनैः शिवे ॥ १८ ॥
अकारादिक्षकारान्तवर्णेषु स्वरयोगिषु ।
चतुष्टयं प्रोक्तयन्त्रे वर्णांस्तत्स्थानतो लिखेत् ॥ १९ ॥

योगादिप्रस्तावञ्च करोति। तत्र यन्त्राणि वक्ष्यमाणानि। चतुरस्रे त्वखण्डिते विधाय चतुर्द्वारस्यान्तरेखाखण्डनमन्तरेण चतुरस्रद्वयं विधायेत्यर्थः। तत्र यन्त्रे अक्षराणि ज्वालामालिनीविद्यायाः। यथाविधि वक्ष्यमाणविधिना। सर्वमध्ये त्रिकोणमध्ये। तारगर्भे विद्यादिभूतप्रणवमध्ये। शक्तिं मूलविद्यापञ्चचत्वारिंश-दक्षररूपां हृल्लेखात्रयं विद्याद्वितीयाक्षरादि। त्रिषु कोणेषु त्रिकोणस्येत्यर्थः। षट्सु कोणेष्विति शेषः। षट्कं पूर्वोक्तत्रयादुपरितनम्। अष्टसु कोणेष्वित्यन्वयः। अष्टकं प्रागुक्तषट्कादुपरितनं वह्निरप्येवम्। अष्टपत्रेषु प्रागुक्ताष्टकादुपरितन-मष्टकं लिखेदिति यावत्। वाह्ये दिक्षु नवक्रमात् चतुरस्रे प्रतिदिशं नवनवक्रमेण चतुर्दिक्षु सम्भूय षट्त्रिंशदक्षराणि प्रागुक्तषट्चत्वारिंशत्तमाक्षरहृल्लेखाविधुराणि लिखेदित्यर्थः। मूलाक्षरैस्त्रिषष्टिसंख्यैः। तेन यन्त्रेण। अकारादीत्यादिना सम-न्वितमित्यन्तेनाध्यर्धेन श्लोकेन एतदुक्तं भवति अकारादिक्षकारान्तैः षट्त्रिंशत्-संख्यैरक्षरैः प्रत्येकं षोडशस्वरयोगतः षट्सप्तत्यधिकपञ्चशतसंख्यैर्मातृकाक्षराक्षरैः चतुर्वर्गाक्षरचतुःषष्टिक्रमतः प्रागुक्तयन्त्रे विद्याक्षरसमेतं तत्तत्स्थानलिखितै-स्त्रिषष्टिभिः सर्वमध्यलिखितचतुःषष्टितमलेखनतश्च नव यन्त्राणि प्रागुक्तैः केवल-मूलविद्याक्षरैरेकं यन्त्रं सम्भूय दशयन्त्राणि संजातानीति। तेषां यन्त्राणां। विनि-योगात् यन्त्राणामित्यन्वयः। फलावाप्तिं विनियोगात्। यैर्विनियोगैः।

शिष्टमेवं लिखेन्मध्ये साध्याक्षरसमन्वितम् ।
एवं यन्त्राणि जायन्ते दश तेषामनुक्रमात् ॥ २० ॥
विनियोगात् फलावाप्तिं प्रवक्ष्यामि शृणु प्रिये ।
यैरिष्टमखिलं प्राप्नोत्ययत्नात् साधको ध्रुवम् ॥ २१ ॥

दशयन्त्रविरचनाक्रमो यथा अन्तर्बहिर्विभागेन अवस्थितं चतुरस्रत्रयं यथामानं कृत्वा तदन्तरष्टदलपद्मं सवृत्तं कृत्वा तदन्तर्वृत्ताद्दिग्विदिक्स्पृष्टास्पृष्टकोणमष्टकोणं प्रागवत् कृत्वा तदन्तः सवृत्तं प्रागवत् षट्कोणं कृत्वा तदन्तः सवृत्तं त्रिकोणं समत्रिरेखं कृत्वा तत्र सर्व्वमध्यत्रिकोणमध्ये मूलविद्याया आद्याक्षरं प्रणवमालिख्य तदुदरे विद्यायाः षट्चत्वारिंशत्तमाक्षररूपां हृल्लेखां नामगर्भामालिख्य त्रिकोणस्य त्रिकोणेष्वग्न्यादिप्रादक्षिण्येन विद्याद्वितीयाक्षरादीनि त्रीण्यक्षराण्यालिख्य तद्बहिः षट्कोणस्य कोणेषु षट्स्वग्न्यादिप्रादक्षिण्येन पूर्वलिखितोपरितनानि षडक्षराणि समालिख्य तद्बहिरष्टकोणस्याष्टकोणेषु प्रागवत् क्रमेण षट्कोणलिखिताक्षरादुपरितनान्यष्टाक्षराण्यालिख्य तद्बहिरष्टदलपद्मस्याष्टसु पत्रेषु अग्न्यादिप्रादक्षिण्येन पूर्वलिखिताक्षरादुपरितनान्यष्टाक्षराण्यालिख्य सर्वबाह्यगतचतुरस्रत्रयान्तरवीथ्यां पूर्वलिखिताक्षरादुपरितनान्यक्षराणि मध्यलिखितहृल्लेखावर्जं पश्चिमादिप्रागन्तम् प्रतिदिशं नव नव क्रमेण चतसृषु दिक्षु षट्त्रिंशदक्षराण्यालिख्य एवं मूलविद्यायास्त्रिषष्टिसंख्यान्यक्षराण्यालिख्य तेन यन्त्रेण सर्ववाञ्छितानि साधयेत् । एतत् प्रथमं यन्त्रम् । प्रागुक्तयन्त्रस्थमूलविद्याक्षरैः सार्द्धं षट्सप्तत्यधिकपञ्चशतसंख्यमातृकाक्षरेष्वादितश्चतुर्वर्गाक्षराणि चतुःषष्टिसंख्यानि विद्याक्षरस्थानेषु त्रिषष्टिसंख्येषु त्र्यादिषष्टिसंख्यानि मध्ये पुनरपि शिष्टमेकमक्षरं लिखेत् । एवं कृते मध्ये द्वे अक्षरे हृल्लेखेति । एतद्द्वितीयं यन्त्रम् । एवमन्यान्यपि मातृकाविस्तराक्षराणि पूर्वलिखितचतुर्वर्गाक्षरचतुःषष्टिकोपरितनोपरितनचतुर्वर्गाक्षरचतुःषष्टिकालेखनतो यावत्परिसमाप्ति पूर्वोक्ताभ्यां यन्त्राभ्यां सह दश यन्त्राणि सम्भवन्ति तैरिष्टेषु विनियोगान् कुर्य्यादिति ॥ २१ ॥

द्वितीयादीनि यन्त्राणि मातृकार्णयुतानि वै ।
क्रमान्नवग्रहाणां स्युस्तत्तद्वारेषु तद्दिशि ॥ २२ ॥
तेषु देव्यर्चनात् प्रीतास्त्वनिष्टं ते न कुर्वते ।
राहुकेतू स्थितौ यत्र तद्राश्यधिपवारके ॥ २३ ॥
षड्ष्टास्रान्तरालेषु ग्रहनाम द्वितीयया ।
विभक्त्या भाजने सम्यक् प्रीणयामीति संलिखेत् ॥२४॥
आद्ये तु यन्त्रे संलिख्य प्रोक्तक्रममथार्चयेत् ।
सर्वेष्वपि च वारेषु सर्वेषां प्रीतिसिद्धये ॥ २५ ॥
अनिष्टशान्त्यै नियतमर्चयेत्तान् ग्रहान् प्रिये ।
एवं यन्त्रेषु दशसु पूजिता नित्यया सह ॥ २६ ॥

द्वितीयेत्याद्यैर्विधानत इत्यन्तैरेकोनषष्ट्या श्लोकैः प्रोक्तानां दशानां यन्त्राणां प्रयोगविशेषानुपदिशति । तत्र द्वितीयादीत्यादिभिर्वितन्वत इत्यन्तैः षड्भिः श्लोकैः ज्वालामालिनीनित्यया सह नवग्रहाणां तत्तद्वारेषु पूजनाद्दशसु यन्त्रेषु प्रयोगानुपदिशति । तत्र द्वितीयादीनि केवलविद्याक्षररचितप्रथमयन्त्रविधुराणि नव यन्त्राणीत्यर्थः । मातृकार्णयुतानि प्रागुक्तमातृकाविसराक्षरोपेतानि । तद्दिशि अष्टविंशत्पटलवक्ष्यमाणक्रमान्मध्ये रविः प्रागादिप्रादक्षिण्येन महादिक्षु चन्द्रादिशुभग्रहान् वक्रादीशान्तासु चतसृषु विदिक्षु क्रूरग्रहानित्यर्थः । तेषु नवसु यन्त्रेषु मध्यगतहृल्लेखोपरिस्थानेष्विति शेषः । देव्यर्चनात् ज्वालामालिनीपूजनात् । ते नवग्रहाः । राह्वित्यादिना श्लोकोत्तरार्द्धेनैतदुक्तं भवति । यस्मिन् यस्मिन् राशौ राहुकेतू तिष्ठतः तत्तद्राश्यधिपवार एव तयोर्वारः तेन तस्मिंस्तस्मिन् वारे तत्तद्वाराधिपपूजनानन्तरं तत्तत्प्राप्ते यन्त्रे तयोः पूजां कुर्य्यादिति । षडष्टास्रान्तरालेषु च ग्रहनाम प्रत्यन्तरालमिति शेषः । भाजने समालिखेदित्यन्वयः । एतदुक्तं भवति षट्कोणान्तरालेषु अष्टकोणान्तरालेषु च प्रत्यन्तरालं तत्तद्वाराधिपत्वप्राप्तग्रहनाम द्वितीयान्तं सम्यक् प्रीणयामीति वाक्यान्तं विलिखेदिति ॥२४॥

आद्ये मातृकाविसराक्षररहिते । प्रोक्तक्रमं प्रागुक्ततत्तद्ग्रहप्राप्तदिग्विलेखनं मध्ये देवीपूजनादिकं । सर्वेषां नवानां ग्रहाणाम् । तान् ग्रहान् तत्तन्नामालेखनस्था-

प्रीताः क्रूरा अपि क्रूरस्थानस्था अपि सर्वदा ।
सौम्याः सौम्यगतानान्तु फलान्येव वितन्वते ॥ २७ ॥
दशस्वपि च यन्त्रेषु दरदैर्गैरिकैस्तु वा ।
लिखितेष्वर्चितेष्वेवं कुमारं कन्यकान्तु वा ॥ २८ ॥
सुशुभावयवाम्मुग्धां स्नातां धौताम्बरां शुभाम् ।
तथाविधं कुमारं वा संस्थाप्याभ्यर्च्य विद्यया ॥ २९ ॥
स्पृष्ट्वा शीर्षं जपेद्विद्यां शतवारं तथार्च्चयेत् ।
प्रसूनैररुणैः शुभ्रैः सौरभाद्यैरथापि वा ॥ ३० ॥
दद्याद् गुग्गुलधूपञ्च यावत् कार्य्यावसानकम् ।
ततो देव्या समाविष्टे तस्मिन् संपूज्य यत्नतः ॥ ३१ ॥

नेषु नित्यया ज्वालामालिन्या । क्रूरा आदित्याङ्गारकशनिराहुकेतवः पञ्च क्रूरः क्रूरस्थानस्थाः जन्मद्वादशाष्टमादिस्थाः । एतन्नवग्रहसाधारणम् । सौम्याः प्रागुक्तपञ्चग्रहेतराश्चत्वारः सौम्यगतानां तेषामिति शेषः । सौम्यस्थानानि एकादशादीनि । एतदुक्तं भवति प्रोक्ततत्तद्दिग्गतेषु द्वितीयादिषु नवसु यन्त्रेषु तत्तद्वारेषु प्रोक्तस्थानेषु तत्तद्वाराधिपग्रहनाम प्रोक्तक्रमेणालिख्य सर्व्वमध्ये देवीमभ्यर्च्चय नामालेखनस्थानेषु तत्तद्ग्रहान् संपूज्य नित्यावरणशक्तीस्तत्तत्स्थानेषु पूजयेत् । प्रथमं यन्त्रं सर्वेषु वारेषु तत्तद्दिग्गतं कृत्वा तत्तद्ग्रहनाम पूर्वोक्तस्थानेषु प्राग्वदालिख्य तत्र प्रतिवारमेकैकग्रहार्च्चनात् सर्वमध्ये देव्यर्च्चनाच्च प्रोक्तफलसिद्धिरिति ॥२७॥

दशस्वित्यादिभिः सुखीत्यन्तैः सप्तभिः श्लोकैः प्रोक्तदशयन्त्रेः स्वस्थावेशप्रकारादिकमुपदिशति । तत्र दशस्वपि च एकस्मिन्नेकस्मिन्निति शेषः । अर्च्चितेषु तत्तल्लिखितविद्याक्षरादिकैः । वा विकल्पे । मुग्धाम् स्खलितेन्द्रियां । तथाविधं सुशुभावयवस्खलितेन्द्रियत्वादियुक्तं । विद्यया ज्वालामालिन्याः शतवारमभ्यर्च्येत्यर्थः । स्पृष्टशीर्षं आवेश्य तथार्चयेत् शतवारं पूर्वोक्तार्चनाप्रकार एव । अथापिवेति विकल्पार्थः । यावत् कार्य्यावसानकं देवतायाः समावेशावधि तस्मिन् देवता समाविष्टाधिकरणद्वये तां देवतामुपचारैः सम्पूज्येति पूर्वत्रान्वयः । प्रागुक्तैः षोडशभिः । विद्यया मूलविद्यया उपचारमन्त्रभूतया प्रजपन् विद्यामिति शेषः ।

ततस्तामुपचारैस्तैः प्रागुक्तैर्विद्यया वशी ।
पूजयेत्तां ततः पृच्छेदभीष्टं कथयेच्च सा ॥ ३२ ॥
भूतं भवद्भविष्यच्च यदन्यन्मनसि स्थितम् ।
जन्मान्तराण्यतीतानि सर्वं संपूजिता वदेत् ॥ ३३ ॥
ततस्तां प्राग्वदभ्यर्च्य स्वात्मन्युद्वास्य तां जपेत् ।
सहस्रवारं स्थिरधीः पूर्णात्मा विचरेत् सुखी ॥ ३४ ॥
तथा षट्कोणकोणेषु मध्ये चालिख्य दाहकम् ।
तत्र संस्थाप्य गदिनम् अभ्यर्च्योदीरितक्रमात् ॥३५॥
आविश्य रोगिणं रोगं पृच्छेत्तत्कारणं शमम् ।
प्रोक्त्वा तत् सकलं तस्य निदेशादपयाति च ॥ ३६ ॥

तां देवतां । सा देवता । अन्यदवाञ्छितं सा देवता । तां देवतां प्राग्वत् षोडशोपचारैः सम्पूज्येति शेषः । तां विद्यां पूर्णात्मा देवतासैक्येन । एतदुक्तं भवति प्रोक्तेषु दशसु यन्त्रेषु अन्यतमस्मिन् प्राग्वत् सम्पूजिते मध्ये प्रोक्तरूपं कुमारं कन्यकां वा संस्थाप्य मूलविद्ययाभ्यर्च्य शतवारं प्रोक्तैः पुष्पैर्गन्धादिभिश्च तच्छिरः स्पृशन् मूलविद्यां शतवारं जपित्वा पुनरपि प्राग्वदभ्यर्च्य गुग्गुलधूपं देवतासमावेशावधि दत्त्वा देवतासमाविष्टे तस्मिन्नधिकरणद्वये अन्यतमस्मिंस्तां देवतां षोडशभिरुपचारैर्मूलविद्ययाभ्यर्च्य तां विद्यां जपेत् तां देवतामात्मनोऽभीष्टं भूतं भवद्भविष्यच्च पृच्छेत् तया सर्वस्मिन् प्रश्नजाते कथिते सति प्रागवदुपचारैरभ्यर्च्य प्राग्वत् स्वात्मन्युद्वास्य पूर्णाशयः सुखी विचरेदिति ॥ ३४ ॥

तथेत्यादिना अपयाति चेत्यन्तेन श्लोकद्वयेन रोगावेशार्थं षट्कोणयन्त्रनिर्माणं तत्प्रयोगादिकमुपदिशति । तत्र दाहकं विद्यागतं सप्तकलः प्रोक्तार्णमात्रं रेफम् । तत्र षट्कोणमध्ये गदिनं रोगिणं उदीरितक्रमात् विद्यायन्त्रलिखिताक्षरसप्तकाभ्यां रोगमावेश्येत्यन्वयः । तत्कारणं रोगकारणं तत्शमनोपायं कारणं । तस्य मन्त्रिणः । अपयाति रोग इति शेषः । एतदुक्तं भवति अभीष्टमानभूमिष्ठ हस्तं लिप्याद्य तत्र प्रागुक्तक्रमात् षट्कोणं कृत्वा तन्मध्ये षट्सु कोणेषु च सूत्रविद्यागतं रेफसप्तकमालिख्य तैर्विद्यया च तद्यन्त्रमभ्यर्च्य तत्र मध्ये रोगिणं

प्रथमं स्त्रीकपालस्थं मध्यस्थं तापयेन्निशि।
जपन् विद्यां स्मरन् साध्यां सद्य आकृष्यतेऽथ सा ॥ ३७ ॥
भीतिलज्जाभिमानादिरहिता वेपिताङ्गका।
निरस्तेतरसद्भावा मन्मथार्त्ताभियाति सा ॥ ३८ ॥
तत् यन्त्रं पुंकपालस्थं तापयेत् प्रजपेत्तथा।
राजानो राजपुत्रा वा तथान्ये चापि योषितः ॥३९॥
विवेकविधुरा मूढास्त्यक्तजातिकुलक्रमाः।
वशगा दासवद्भूमौ तिष्ठन्त्यामरणाद् ध्रुवम् ॥४०॥
सर्वासामपि नित्यानामुपदेशेऽथ तं गुरुः।
तत्तच्चक्रस्य मध्यस्थं वेष्टविद्याजपान्वितम् ॥४१॥

संस्थाप्य शतवारं मूलविद्ययाभ्यर्च्य तामेव तच्छिरः स्पृष्टिकया शतवारं जपित्वा रोगिणं तं रोगमावेश्य तदावेशकारणं पृष्ट्वा तेन तस्मिन् वारणे कथिते जपेदिति सम्प्रदायोपदेशेन स रोगोऽपयातीति ॥ ३६ ॥

प्रथममित्यादिभिर्ध्रुवमित्यन्तैश्चतुर्भिः श्लोकैः प्रथमयन्त्रेणाकर्षणवशीकरणादिक मुपदिशति। तत्र प्रथमं यन्त्रं स्त्रीकपालस्य मध्यस्थं प्रागुक्तैर्द्रव्यैः स्त्रीकपालमध्ये प्रथमं यन्त्रं लिखित्वेत्यर्थः। तापयेत् अङ्गारे प्राणप्रतिष्ठाविद्याशतवारजपपुरः-सरमङ्गारे तापयेत् इति सम्प्रदायः। विद्यां जपन् तापनकाले स्मरन् साध्यां तदपि तत्काल एव। साध्या निरस्तेतरसद्भावा अनन्यचित्ता अभियाति स्वयमेवाभि-सरतीत्यर्थः। सा साध्या। तत् प्रथमं पुंकपालस्थं प्रागवत्तापयेत्। प्रागवत् प्राणप्रतिष्ठादिसहितं प्रजपेद्विद्यां। तथा यथा स्त्रीकपालस्थं। तेनैतदुक्तं भवति पुंकपाललिखितं तद्यन्त्रं कृतप्राणप्रतिष्ठादिकं निशि अङ्गारे विद्यां जपन् साध्यं स्मरन् तापयन् वक्ष्यमाणान् वशयतीति। दासवद्भूत्वा अस्य साधकस्य राजादयः साध्यवर्गाः ॥ ४० ॥

सर्व्वासामित्यादिभिस्तत इत्यन्तैस्त्रिभिः श्लोकैर्वक्ष्यमाणरूपस्य वेधद्वयस्य साधा-रणरूपं यामलवेधमुपदिशति। तत्र सर्वासां षोडशानां नित्यानामुपदेशे विद्या-देवतयोरैक्यरूप्यात्। तं शिष्यं तत्तच्चक्रस्य तत्तन्नित्यसपर्य्याचक्रस्य वा षट्कोण-

वह्निज्वालापरीताङ्गं भावयन्निन्द्रियाण्यपि ।
मनःषष्ठानि चाकर्षेन्मनसा प्राग्वदात्मनि ॥४२॥
एवं कृते चणादेवं विसंज्ञो निपतेद् भुवि ।
ततस्तमुत्थाप्य मुखे चिप्त्वार्घ्याम्बु वदेत्ततः ॥४३॥
एष वेधस्त्रिधा प्रोक्तः सद्यः प्रत्ययकारकः ।
शाक्तशाम्भवभेदाभ्यां द्वयोरैक्यात्मयामलात् ॥ ४४॥
शिष्यस्य मूलाधारादिस्थानेषु ब्रह्मरन्ध्रकी ।
स्मर टाद्यार्णकान् सप्त त्युक्त्वा प्राग्वदुदीक्षणात् ॥४५॥

दशयन्त्रेष्वन्यतमस्य वेत्यर्थः। अत्र नित्यसपर्याचक्रस्योपादानं गुरोर्भावनासिद्धित्व शिष्यविषयम्। विद्याजपान्वितम् तत्तन्नित्यानां। वह्निज्वालापरीताङ्गं भावयेत् नित्यसपर्याचक्रगतस्त्वेत्तं केवलाग्निज्वालावृत्तरूपं शिष्यं प्रोक्तयन्त्रदशकान्यतमगतस्वेत्तसद्गतरेफसप्तकरूपवह्निज्वालावृत्तरूपं च भावयन् इत्यर्थः। इन्द्रियाणि ज्ञानरूपाणि श्रोत्रादीनि पञ्चमतः षष्ठानि मनो येषां षष्ठस्तानीति। मनसा भावनया प्रागवत् प्राणप्रतिष्ठोक्तप्रक्रियया स्वात्मन्याकृष्य ततो विसंज्ञं भुवि निपातितं तन्मुखेऽर्घ्यजलं चिप्त्वा समुत्थाप्य ततः प्रागुक्तप्रक्रिययाधारत्रये विद्यान्तेजस्त्रयरूपिणीं स्वान्तादावाह्य संस्थाप्य तज्जीवकर्णे विद्यां वदेदिति ॥ ४३ ॥

एष इत्यादिभिः सम इत्यन्तैः सप्तभिः श्लोकैः त्रिविधे वेधे द्विवेधरूपादिकमुपदिशति। तत्र एषः पूर्वोक्तसामान्यरूपो यामलवेधः। त्रिधा प्रोक्तरूपेण स्वात्मना वक्ष्यमाणाभ्यां च प्रत्ययकारकः गुरुदेवतात्मैक्यविश्वासकारकः। द्वयोः शाक्तशाम्भवयोः। ऐक्यात्मयामलात् प्रोक्तरूपयोर्द्वयोः शाक्तशाम्भवयोरैक्यात्मरूपाद् यामलादित्यर्थः। मूलाधारादिस्थानेषु षट्स्विति शेषः। ब्रह्मरन्ध्रके एवं सम्भूय सप्तसु स्थानेष्वित्यर्थः। स्मर टाद्यार्णकान् सप्तेत्युक्त्वेति शिष्यस्य स्वभावनीयगुरूपदेशतः। टाद्यार्णकान् मूलविद्यागतरेफसप्तकं प्रागवदग्निज्वालावृताङ्गत्वादितः। एतत् सर्व्ववेधसाधारणं विदध्यादुक्तरूपतः। सिद्धविद्यया उपदेष्टव्यया। एतदुक्तं भवति प्रागुक्तयन्त्रमध्यगतं शिष्यं गुरुर्मूलाधारादिब्रह्मरन्ध्रान्तस्थानसप्तके विद्यागतरेफसप्तकं स्मरेत्युक्त्वा प्राग्वदुपदेष्टव्यविद्यया वीक्ष्य भावनादिना भुवि

विदध्याच्छाक्तवेधन्तु देशिकः सिद्धविद्यया।
शाम्भवन्तु शृणु प्राज्ञे वेधमद्भुतविग्रहम् ॥४६॥
तूष्णीं संस्थापितं शिष्यं तत्तच्चक्रे तदात्मना।
स्वयं प्रविश्य तद्देहमेकीभूत्वा पुनः स्वके ॥४७॥
समागत्यात्मरूपेण तदात्मानं विभाव्य वै।
कृतन्यासजपार्च्चस्तु तत्तनुं वह्निना दहेत् ॥४८॥
स्यादेष शाम्भवो वेधः प्रोक्तः प्रागेव यामले।
इति वेधत्रयं प्रोक्तं स्वद्भावसिद्धिसूचकम् ॥४९॥
यामले तु विशेषोऽयं सिद्धः पश्चाद् गुरोः श्रुतम्।
ज्ञानमन्यच्च सकलं संक्रमेत्तेन तत् समः ॥५०॥

निपातितं प्रागवदुत्थाप्य तत्तद्विद्यां वदेत्। एष शाक्तवेध इति। तत्र शाम्भवमित्यादिभिः सम इत्यन्तैः शिष्टैरर्द्धैश्चतुर्भिः श्लोकैरपुनरावृत्तिकरं शाम्भववेधं यामलवेधफलञ्चोपदिशति। तत्र शाम्भवं वक्ष्यमाणरूपमद्भुतविग्रहं सद्यः अपुनरावृत्तिकरत्वात्। तूष्णीं संस्थापितं प्रागुक्तशाक्तवेधभावनादिराहित्येन। तत्तच्चक्रे नित्यसपर्य्याचक्रादिषु। तदात्मना शिष्यात्मरूपेण। स्वयं गुरुः प्रविश्य सर्वात्मभावनया तद्देहं शिष्यदेहं प्रविश्येत्यन्वयः। एकीभूत्वा शिष्यात्मादिभिः पुनः स्वात्मादिभिः शिष्यात्मादीनामेकीकरणस्थैर्य्यानन्तरं स्वके देहे गुरुरिति शेषः समागत्य स्वके इत्यत्रान्वयः। आत्मरूपेण स्वात्मरूपेण स्वात्मविलापनेनेत्यर्थः। तदात्मानं शिष्यात्मानं कृतन्यासजपार्च्चः स्वात्मनंस्तत्तनुं शिष्यतनुम् मृतामित्यर्थः। वह्निना दहेन्मृतत्वादग्निसात् कुर्य्यादित्यर्थः। शाम्भवो वेधः प्रोक्तरूपः। एतदुक्तं भवति तत्तच्चक्रादिषु सद्गुरुः प्रागुक्तभावनाविरहितं तूष्णीं शिष्यं स्थापयित्वा तदात्मरूपेण तद्देहं सर्वात्मभावनया प्रविश्य तदात्मादिभिरेकीभूत्वा पुनः स्वशरीरमागत्य स्वात्मनि शिष्यात्मानं निःशेषं विलीनं विभाव्य कृतन्यासादिकः शिष्यशरीरं मृतं श्मशानं नीत्वाग्निसात् कुर्य्यादित्यर्थः। एष शाम्भवो वेधः केवलमोक्षेच्छोरिति। प्रोक्तः प्रागेव विसंज्ञो निपतेदित्यादिना। वेधत्रयं वेधस्तु स्वात्मना सच्चिदानन्दस्फुरणरूपपरिपूर्णपराहन्तात्मना शिष्यात्मनः सङ्कुचितरूपस्य एकीकरणतः पूर्वोक्त-

रक्तचन्दनपङ्केन लिखित्वा प्रथमं शिवे ।
लोहैर्विरचिते पट्टे फलकायां शिलातले ॥५१॥
भूमौ वा सुसमे शुद्धे लोष्टाङ्गारविवर्जिते ।
देवीमावाह्य तत्रैव पूजयेच्छक्तिभिर्युताम् ॥५२॥
दिनं दिनत्रयं सप्तवासरं सप्तमेव वा ।
मासं मण्डलमित्येवं क्रमादिष्टमवाप्नुयात् ॥५३॥
वश्यमाकर्षणं स्तम्भं नियहं लाभमीप्सितम् ।
अन्यच्च सकलमिष्टमवाप्नोत्यर्च्चनाद्भुतम् ॥५४॥
तदा प्रोक्तान् गदान् सर्वान् जयेदन्यानि चाखिलान् ।
साधयेत् प्रथमेनैव यन्त्रेण यत्नतः शिवे ॥५५॥

पराहन्तास्वस्वात्मीयकरणम् । एवमेतानि त्रीणि शाम्भवादीनि नामानि तत्तत् सिद्धान्तसिद्धानि । भावनासिद्धिसूचकं १ गुरोः इति शेषः । यामलेत्यादिना एतदुक्तं भवति यामलरूपे वेधे शिष्यात्मनः समाकृष्य चात्मन्येकीकृत्य प्रतिष्ठापनतो विद्धे पुनश्च तत्तद्देहे तस्मिन् गुरुगतं ज्ञानादिकं सकलं संक्रमेत् । तेन गुरुसमः शिष्य इत्येव विशेषो भवति इतराभ्यामस्येति ॥ ५० ॥

रक्तचन्दनमित्यादिभिः साधयेदित्यन्तैः त्रयोविंशत्या श्लोकैर्दशभिर्यन्त्रैः वश्यादि-प्रयोगाननुपदिशति । तत्र रक्तचन्दनेत्यादिभिः शिवे इत्यन्तैः पञ्चभिः श्लोकैः तेषु प्रथमयन्त्रेण साध्यान्युपदिशति । तत्र प्रथमं यन्त्रमिति शेषः । लोहैर्विरचिते पट्टे तत्रापि कुचन्दनमेव द्रव्यं फलकाशिलातलयोरपि तदेव । वा विकल्पे । तत्र यन्त्र-मध्ये । शक्तिभिः नित्यपूजावरणोक्तादिभिः । दिनम् एकमिति शेषः । मण्डलं प्राग्वत् इष्टं वक्ष्यमाणवश्यादिकं । ईप्सितं लाभमित्यन्वयः । अन्यत् प्रोक्तेभ्यः अर्चनाद्भुतमित्युक्तक्रमतः । प्रोक्तान् षष्ठपटले काम्यप्रकरणप्रोक्तान् वक्ष्यमाणान् प्रमेहादींश्च । अन्यानि चाखिलान् अखिलान् अन्यानीति सामानाधिकरण्यमागमत्वा-दवाप्नोति शेषः । शिवे इति देवीसम्बुद्धिः ॥ ५५ ॥

---

१ । त्वदभावस्थितिसूचकमिति पाठः मूलश्लोके तद्विवेच्यम् ।

द्वितीयं दरदे कृत्वा प्रोक्तेषूच्चं गते रवौ।
पूजयेत् प्रोक्तकालेन फलान्युक्तान्यवाप्नुयात् ॥५६॥
विलिख्य राजते पट्टे जपित्वा दिनशः स्पृशन्।
सहस्रवारं तन्नित्याविद्यां तद्वासिताम्बुभिः ॥५७॥
स्नानं पानं पाकजातं कुर्य्यादुक्तदिनं ततः।
प्रमेहैस्त्रिविधैर्घोरमूत्रकृच्छ्रैः सुदारुणैः ॥५८॥
अश्मरीमूत्रपाल्या १ दिरोगैर्मुक्तः सुखी भवेत्।
जीवेच्च सुचिरं भूमौ नीरोगः स्वस्थमानसः ॥५९॥
तृतीयं गैरिकैः कृत्वा वैरिनक्षत्रवृक्षजे।
तले भूमौ ततः खात्वा तत्राग्निं ज्वालयेत् सदा ॥६०॥
प्रोक्तैस्तैर्वासरैर्वैरी दाहज्वरगदादिभिः।
तच्चोत्क्षिप्य सलिले न प्रक्षिपेच्चेद्विनश्यति ॥६१॥

द्वितीयमित्यादिभिर्मानस इत्यन्तैश्चतुर्भिः श्लोकैर्द्वितीययन्त्रसाध्यान्युपदिशति। तत्र द्वितीयं यन्त्रं। प्रोक्तेषु प्रथमयन्त्रप्रोक्तलोहादिषु तेष्वपि दरदमेव द्रव्यम्। उच्चं गते उच्चराशिभूतमेषस्थे आदित्ये चैत्रमास इत्यर्थः। तत्रापि उच्चकाले पूजयेद्देवीं नित्यपूजाक्रमत इति शेषः। प्रोक्तकालेन दिनादितः। उक्तानि वश्यादीनि। विलिख्य द्वितीयं यन्त्रं तत्रापि इदमेव द्रव्यं स्पृशन् यन्त्रं। नित्याविद्यां ज्वालामालिनीविद्यां। तद्वासिताम्बुभिः यन्त्रोषितजलैः। पाकजातं अन्नादि। उक्तदिनम्—अत्यन्तसंयोगे द्वितीया प्रागवहिनानि। त्रिविधैर्दोषत्रयानुबन्धात्। मूत्रपालीति तत्राकारमेहवारिको रोगविशेषः। स्वस्थमानसः आधिराहित्यात् ॥५९॥

तृतीयमित्यादिना विनश्यतीत्यन्तेन श्लोकद्वयेन तृतीययन्त्रप्रयोगेण वैरिनिग्रहमुपदिशति। तत्र तृतीयं यन्त्रं। तले फलकायामित्यर्थः। तत्र यन्त्रखननप्रदेशे। प्रोक्तैर्दिनादिभिः। तत् यन्त्रं। सलिले न जलाशये विनश्यति तदा दाहज्वरेण रिपुरित्यर्थः ॥ ६१ ॥

१। मूत्रघाता।

चतुर्थं रोचनापङ्कैरालिख्योक्तप्रपूजनात् ।
प्राप्नोति विजयं प्रोक्तेष्वखिलेषु सुनिश्चितम् ॥६२॥
वादेषु द्विविधे द्यूते युद्धेष्वन्येषु सर्वतः ।
सर्वदा जयिनः सर्वे भवन्त्येतस्य वैभवात् ॥६३॥
पञ्चमं कुङ्कुमैः कृत्वा तत्र तत्पूजनाद्दिनैः ।
वशे भवन्ति मनुजा दन्तिनो वाजिनः स्त्रियः ॥६४॥
षष्ठं हरिद्रयालिख्य कर्पटे नामसंयुतम् ।
मन्दोच्चे स्थापयेत् क्वापि सुबद्धन्त्विष्टकापुटे ॥६५॥
शत्रोर्जिह्वां गतिं शेषं दिव्यं राज्ञां समुद्यमम् ।
वादेच्छां सकलस्यान्यदनिष्टं स्तम्भयेद् ध्रुवम् ॥६६॥
सप्तमं चन्दनैरिन्दुमिलितैरालिखेत्तथा ।
तत्रार्चयेन्नित्यशस्तां सन्ध्यासु भवने निजे ॥६७॥

चतुर्थमित्यादिना वैभवादित्यन्तेन श्लोकद्वयेन चतुर्थयन्त्रप्रयोगेण द्यूतादिषु जयमुपदिशति। तत्र चतुर्थं यन्त्रं। उक्तप्रपूजनादित्युक्तिरधिकरणसपरिवार-देवतादिवससंख्याविषया। तत्राधिकरणादीनि प्रथमयन्त्रप्रोक्तानीति सम्प्रदायः। प्रोक्तेषु वक्ष्यमाणेषु वादादिषु युद्धेषु पणबन्धेषु। एतस्य पूजितस्य यन्त्रस्य ॥६३॥

पञ्चमित्यादिना श्लोकेन पञ्चमयन्त्रप्रयोगेण मर्त्त्यादिवश्यमुपदिशति। तत्र तत्र यन्त्रे अधिकरणादीनि प्राग्वत्। तत् पूजनान्नित्यक्रमतः। दिनैः प्राग्वत् ॥ ६४ ॥

षष्ठमित्यादिना ध्रुवमित्यन्तेन श्लोकद्वयेन षष्ठयन्त्रप्रयोगेण शत्रुस्तम्भनमुपदिशति। तत्र षष्ठं यन्त्रं नामसंयुतम् एतत् सर्व्वयन्त्रसाधारणं। मन्दोच्चे शनौ तुलाराशिस्थिते तत्रापि तदुच्चकाल इति सम्प्रदायः। सुबद्धं त्विष्टकापुटे इष्टकामध्ये यन्त्रसन्निवेशानुरूपं रन्ध्रं तदिष्टकोत्सेधार्द्धखातमानं कृत्वा इष्टकान्तरेण सम्यग् वेष्टितया सुबद्धया दृढतरमावद्धमित्यर्थः। दिव्यं समुद्यमम् ॥ ६६ ॥

सप्तममित्यादिना शान्ताय इत्यन्तेन श्लोकद्वयेन सप्तमयन्त्रप्रयोगेण लक्ष्मीप्राप्ति-

तद्दिनैरिन्दिरा तस्य सर्वलोकातिशायिनी ।
भवत्येव महेशानि विचित्रा यन्त्रशक्तयः ॥६८॥
अष्टमन्त्वगुरुक्षोदैरालिखेत् फलकापुटे ।
पीठे वा तत्र तां देवीं गुरावुच्चं गते दिने ॥६९॥
तदुच्चकाले सुरभिप्रसूनैरर्चयेत्तथा ।
वासांसि च विचित्राणि भूषणान्यप्यवाप्नुयात् ॥७०॥
मृगखेदैस्तु नवममालिख्याभ्यर्च्य तत्र ताम् ।
तदालिप्तो व्रजेद् यत्र कुत्रापि जनसंसदि ॥७१॥
सर्वे तं गुरुवद् दृष्ट्वा वश्याः स्युर्वनिता यदि ।
तदिष्टसाधिका यावज्जीवमस्यानुभावतः ॥७२॥
विलिखेद्दशमं प्रोक्तद्रव्यैः सर्वैस्तथैकशः ।
यद्दृश्यत्तैरीरितं सर्वं कार्य्यमेतत् सुसाधयेत् ॥७३॥

मुपदिशति । तत्र सप्तमं यन्त्रं । तथा प्रागुक्ताधिकरणपूजाक्रमत इत्यर्थः । तत्र यन्त्रे तां देवीं तद्दिनैः प्रागुक्तादिनादिभिः । महेशानीति देवीसम्बुद्धिः ॥ ६८ ॥

अष्टममित्यादिना अवाप्नुयादित्यन्तेन श्लोकद्वयेनाष्टमयन्त्रप्रयोगेण वासोभूषणावाप्तिमुपदिशति । तत्र अष्टमं यन्त्रम् । अगुरुक्षोदैः अगुरुपङ्कैः । तत्र यन्त्रे गुरावुच्चं गते बृहस्पतौ कर्कटस्थे । तदुच्चकाले तद्राशौ नभोमध्यं गते । एवमर्कादीनामप्युक्तः कालः । तथा नित्यक्रमतः ॥ ७० ॥

मृगखेदैरित्यादिनानुभावत इत्यन्तेन श्लोकद्वयेन नवमयन्त्रप्रयोगेण लोकस्त्रीवश्यसिद्धिमुपदिशति । तत्र नवमं यन्त्रमालिख्य प्रागुक्ताधिकरणेषु अभ्यर्च्य नित्यक्रमतः तां ज्वालामालिनीं । तदालिप्तो व्रजेत् पूजान्ते तद्यन्त्रं मार्ज्जयित्वा तन्मृगखेदालिप्तः । सर्वे तत्रस्था जनाः । तं साधकं वनिता यदि साध्या । अस्य प्रयोगस्य ॥ ७२ ॥

विलिखेदित्यादिना श्लोकेन दशमयन्त्रेण प्रागुक्तनवमयन्त्रवाच्यफलान्यनेन प्राप्तुं प्रयोगादिकमुपदिशति । तत्र प्रोक्तद्रव्यैः सर्वैः एकमयन्त्रप्रोक्तकुचन्दनादिभि-

प्रोक्तेषु दशसु प्रोक्तद्रव्यैरालिख्य तेषु तु ।
संस्थाप्य कुम्भं विधिना जपित्वोग्रे ग्रहे तदा ॥७४॥
अभिषिञ्चेत्तद्ग्रहस्य दोषस्थानगतं फलम् ।
न भवेच्च भवेदेवं वश्यो यन्त्रेष्वशेषतः ॥७५॥
तथा तदुच्चे तत्पूजां होममन्त्राज्यपायसैः ।
निवेद्यञ्च प्रणम्यार्च्यं दद्याच्छिवत्वमवाप्नुयात् ॥७६॥
तत्तद्ग्रहार्त्तिषु क्षिप्रं ते ग्रहास्तत्प्रभावतः ।
एकादशस्थफलदा नित्यशो यजनादपि ॥७७॥
सुवर्णे रजते वा तद्यन्त्रेष्वन्यतमं शिवे ।
विलिख्याभ्यर्च्य तद्विद्याविदे दद्यात् सुपूजितम् ॥७८॥

नवमयन्त्रप्रोक्तमृगरूदान्तैर्नवभिर्द्रव्यैः समेतैरित्यर्थः । एकशः विकल्पार्थः एकैकेन वा । तैर्नवभिर्यन्त्रैः । सर्वमध्ये नामाक्षरविन्यासभेदतः । एतद्दशमं यन्त्रम् ॥ ७३ ॥

प्रोक्तेष्वित्यादिना अशेषत इत्यन्तेन श्लोकद्वयेन प्रोक्तेषु दशसु यन्त्रेषु अभिषेकविधानाद् ग्रहदोषशान्तिमुपदिशति । तत्र दशसु यन्त्रेष्विति शेषः । विधिना अष्टत्रिंशत्कलामिथुनार्चनादिपुरःसरं । जपित्वा विद्यां । उग्रे प्रतिकूले । तद्ग्रहस्य अशेषतः एवं सर्वयन्त्रेष्वित्यर्थः । एतदुक्तं भवति प्रोक्तेषु दशसु यन्त्रेषु प्रागुक्तक्रमात् तत्तद्ग्रहे प्राप्ते यन्त्रे तत्तद्ग्रहप्रातिकूल्यप्रोक्तक्रमाभिषेकात्तत्तद्ग्रहप्रातिकूल्यशान्तिरिति ॥ ७५ ॥

तथेत्यादिना अपीत्यन्तेन श्लोकद्वयेन प्रोक्तेषु यन्त्रेषु प्रागुक्तक्रमतो नवग्रहाणां प्रातिकूल्यशान्तिकरं पूजनमुपदिशति । तत्र तदुच्चे प्रतिकूलग्रहोच्चे । तत्पूजां प्रतिकूलग्रहपूजां । निवेद्यं चकारेण पायसैरित्याकृष्यते । ते प्रतिकूलाः नित्यशो यजनादपि कालयजनमन्तरेणापि । एतदुक्तं भवति प्रोक्तेषु दशसु यन्त्रेषु तत्तद्ग्रहस्य प्रागुक्तक्रमप्राप्ते यन्त्रे तत्तत्केवलप्रतिकूलग्रहोच्चकाले तत्कालमन्तरेण नित्यशस्तद्ग्रहपूजनेन देवीपूजामन्तरेण तत्तन्नाममन्त्रैः अन्नाज्यपायसैर्होमेन च तन्निवेद्येनार्घ्यपुरःसरेण च तत्तद्ग्रहाः प्रीताः सद्यः अनुकूला भवन्तीति ॥ ७७ ॥

सुवर्णेत्यादिभिर्विधानत इत्यन्तैस्त्रिभिः श्लोकैर्दशमाङ्कितसुवर्णपट्टादिदानेन तत्

षोड़श द्वादश नव षट् विनिष्कप्रकल्पितम् ।
नित्यार्चकस्य नित्यानामेकां पूजयितुं तु वा ॥७९॥
दद्यात् गन्धादिनार्च्चैतं प्रणम्य गुरुविग्रहम् ।
पश्चिमामुखमासीनं तस्मै प्रोक्तविधानतः ॥८०॥
विद्याजप्ताम्बुपानेन वर्द्धते कुक्षिगोऽनलः ।
भुक्ते च जठरस्पर्शजपादपि सुनिश्चितम् ॥८१॥
मेषादिराशिगे भानौ मासेषु द्वादशस्वपि ।
प्रोक्तेषु दशयन्त्रेषु प्रत्येकस्य त्रिवासरम् ॥८२॥
पूजयेद्देवीमब्देन धनधान्यगृहादिभिः ।
समृद्धो जीवति चिरमरोगः सुमना भुवि ॥८३॥

फलावाप्तिमुपदिशति। तत्र तद्यन्त्रेषु दशस्विति शेषः। अन्यतमं तत्तद्गुरुप्राप्तं अभ्यर्च्य विद्याविदे तद्विद्यादिदे ज्वालामालिनीविद्याविदे। सुपूजितं यन्त्रं षोड़श-द्वादशोत्तरहीनमानमशक्तविषयम्। एकां पूजयितुः षोड़शनित्यासु वा विकल्पे। दद्यादिति द्विरुक्तिः प्रस्तारविस्तारार्थत्वाददोषः। पश्चिमामुखं गुरुरूपत्वात्। तस्मै विद्याविदे गुरुरूपाय। एतदुक्तं भवति प्रोक्तयन्त्रेषु तत्तद्गुरुप्राप्तं यन्त्रं प्रोक्तकाले सुवर्णादिपट्टे विकीर्य्य तद्यन्त्राङ्कितं सुवर्णपट्टं विद्यया पूजितं ज्वाला-मालिनीनित्याविद्याविदं वा षोड़शनित्याविदं वा एतास्वन्यतमनित्याविदं वा पश्चिमाभिमुखं भूमौ विलिखिते तद्यन्त्रे संस्थ।प्य गन्धादिभिस्तद्विद्याभिस्तद्गुरु-रूपं ध्यात्वाभ्यर्च्य तस्मै दद्यादिति ॥ ८० ॥

विद्येत्यादिना श्लोकेन जठराग्निवृद्ध्युपायमुपदिशति। तत्र विद्या जप्ताम्बु-पानेन ज्वालामालिन्याः। तत्र जपसंख्या अष्टोत्तरशतम् ॥ ८१ ॥

मेषादीत्यादिना भुवीत्यन्तेन श्लोकद्वयेन प्रोक्तेषु दशसु यन्त्रेषु एकस्मिन्नेकस्मिन् यन्त्रे त्रिवासरं क्रमात् द्वादशसु मासेषु भास्करादिदेवतार्च्चनादवाप्यानि फला-न्युपदिशति। तत्र मेषादिराशिगे भानावित्युक्त्या चैत्रमासमारभ्येति प्रत्येकं त्रित्रिवासम् एकस्मिन् एकस्मिन् यन्त्रे त्रिदिनमित्यर्थः। एवं प्रतिमासमेकावृत्ति-र्भवति। पूजयेत् भास्करसहितां देवीं। तत्र भास्करार्च्चनस्थानं प्रागवदिति ॥८३॥

यद्राशौ यो ग्रहस्तिष्ठत्येको द्वौ बहवोऽथवा ।
तद्दिनेषु तदुच्चेषु कालेषु च तदर्चनात् ॥८४॥
तत्तद्ग्रहाः सुसंप्रीताः पालयन्त्यनिशञ्च तम् ।
तथा तर्पणहोमाभ्यां जपदानादिनापि वा ॥८५॥
नवस्वपि च यन्त्रेषु नवग्रहमयत्नतः ।
तत्तत् चोभं विलिख्यान्तः पूजयेद्वैरिमर्दने ॥८६॥
रिपुनामयुतान्युक्तान्यालिख्य रविचन्द्रयोः ।
उपरागे समे भूमौ दिनशो जयमाप्नुयुः ॥८७॥
विद्याच्चरौषधानान्तु प्रत्येकं कर्षमर्पितम् ।
भाण्डे नवे पञ्चगव्ये खारिमाणे पचेच्च तत् ॥८८॥

यद्राशावित्यादिना अपि वेत्यन्तेन श्लोकद्वयेन तेषु यन्त्रेषु सर्वग्रहसमाराधनात् फलमुपदिशति । तत्र अथवा विकल्पे दिनेषु तत्तद्राशितत्तद्ग्रहावस्थानदिनेषु तत्तद्वारेष्वित्यर्थः । तदुच्चेषु कालेषु प्रागुक्तेषु । तदर्चनात् तत्तद्यन्त्रेषु तत्तद्ग्रहैः समं देवतार्चनात् । अस्मिन् प्रकरणे सर्वग्रहार्चनेषु मूलदेवताया सार्द्धं पूजनम् । तम् उपासकं जपदानादिना पूर्वोक्तक्रमतः । दानं सुवर्णपट्टस्य यन्त्राङ्कितस्य ॥८५॥

नवस्वित्यादिना आप्नुयुरित्यन्तेन श्लोकद्वयेन प्रोक्तेषु द्वितीयादिनवयन्त्रेषु प्राग्वद्ग्रहपूजया शत्रुमर्द्दनमुपदिशति । तत्र तत्तत् चोभं विलिख्यान्तः साध्यस्य शत्रोः प्रतिकूलं गृहं कर्णिकास्थाने देवदत्तम् आदित्यः चोभयत्वित्यादि । वैरिमर्दनप्रयोगे उपरागे ग्रहणे रविचन्द्रयोरित्यन्वयः । आप्नुयुः शत्रवः ॥८७॥

विद्येत्यादिभिर्विभज्जकमित्यन्तैः पञ्चभिः श्लोकैः सर्व्वविद्याच्चरौषधभस्म-साधनतद्विनियोगादिकमुपदिशति । तत्र कर्षं निष्कत्रयम् एतन्मानमपुनरुक्तानां विद्याच्चरौषधानां पुनरुक्तानान्तु प्रागुक्तदावसंख्यागुणिताः । भाण्डे नवे तत् औषधं विद्यया संस्कृते तन्मूलविद्यया संस्कृते तदुदरोत्थिते भाण्डोदरोत्थिते वह्नौ हुत्वा सहस्रवारादहोनं । तत्र भस्मनि । तत्र भस्मगते यन्त्रे । देवीं तां तथा नित्या-क्रमतः अर्चयेत् । तद्भस्म सर्वाभिः षोड़शनित्याभिः । तदृष्टहे भस्माधिष्ठिते । श्रीखण्डाद्यैः चन्दनकुङ्कुमाद्यैः । एतदुक्तं भवति नवे भाण्डे खारिमाणं पञ्चगव्यं सर्वं समांशं तत्तदुपास्यमन्त्रविद्यादिभिर्निक्षिप्य तत्र सर्व्वमन्त्रविद्या पुनरुक्ता-च्चरौषधानि तत्तद्विद्याजपसहितं प्रीतमानसो निक्षिप्य तत्तद्विद्या संस्कृते वह्नौ

विद्यया संस्कृते वह्नौ ततस्तदुदरोत्थिते ।
घृतेन विद्यया हुत्वा तद्भस्मादाय तत्र वै ॥८९॥
यन्त्राणि दश निष्पाद्य तत्र देवीं यजेत्तथा ।
ततस्तद्भस्म संगृह्य निदध्याद्दिनशोऽर्चयेत् ॥९०॥
तद्भस्म सर्वरक्षाकृत् सर्वाभिरपि साधयेत् ।
गदचोरग्रहारिष्टक्लेशा न स्युश्च तद्गृहे ॥९१॥
नित्यशो धारणं देहे श्रीकण्ठाद्यैर्विलेपनम् ।
भक्षणं सर्वकृत्यादि दुरितार्त्तिविभञ्जकम् ॥९२॥
वह्न्यक्षरेषु दशसु व्यञ्जनैः सप्तभिः पृथक् ।
स्वरत्रयं क्रमाद् युञ्ज्यात्तेन तान्येकविंशतिः ॥९३॥
त्रिकोणद्वयमालिख्य वाह्याभ्यन्तरयोगतः ।
तदन्तर्वृत्तमध्यस्थं षडस्रञ्च विधाय तु ॥९४॥

दृढ़पिहितभाण्डमुखं पाच्य ततस्तद्भाण्डोदरप्रोक्ते वह्नौ तत्तद्विद्यया सहस्रवारादहीनं हुत्वा पश्चात्तद्भस्मादाय तदनु भस्स्पृष्टभूतलमाकाश एव गोमयं गृहीत्वा तेन तद्भस्म विलोड्य पिण्डीकृत्य संशोष्य सकरीषं दग्ध्वा पश्चात्तदौषधसहितं पिण्डभस्मादाय पटलोदिते तस्मिंस्तस्या दशयन्त्राणि निष्पाद्य अन्यासां तत्तन्नित्यसपर्य्यायन्त्राणि निष्पाद्य तत्र तत्तद्देवतामावाह्य नित्यक्रमतोऽभ्यर्च्य सहस्रवारं जप्त्वा तद्भस्म समुद्गके निधाय प्रतिदिनं तत्तद्विद्यया पुष्पाञ्जलिं विधाय प्रोक्तविधानतः प्रोक्तफलसिद्धिरिति ॥८२॥

वह्न्यक्षरेष्वित्यादिभिरितीत्यन्तैरष्टभिः श्लोकैः पञ्चभूतप्रोक्ताग्नेयाक्षरदशकस्वान्योन्यमेलितजनितसंख्याक्षरैरेकविंशतियन्त्राणि तैर्जठराग्निवृद्धिप्रयोगादिकमुपदिशति । तत्र वह्न्यक्षरेषु पञ्चभूताक्षराणां मध्ये इत्यर्थः । तानि ईकारादिक्षकारान्तानि दश । सप्तभिः आदिगतस्वरत्रयरहितैः खकारादिवर्गद्वितीयरेफक्षाक्षरैः । पृथक् प्रति व्यञ्जनं । स्वरत्रयं इ ई ऐ इति तदादिभूतमक्षरत्रयं । तानि स्वरत्रयसहितानि व्यञ्जनानि तद्रूपाणि यथा खिँ खीँ खैँ इत्यादीनि क्षिँ क्षीँ क्षैँ इत्यन्तानि । तदन्तः त्रिकोणद्वयान्तः । नाम्ना सह इति शेषः साध्यादीना-

नाम्नाद्यं विलिखेन्मध्ये षट्कोणेषु च षट् क्रमात्।
विलिखेदग्रमारभ्य प्रादक्षिण्येन पार्वति ॥६५॥
त्रिकोणान्तरतो लिख्य चतुर्दश तथा क्रमात्।
शिष्टे साध्याक्षरन्त्वग्रे लिखेत् पञ्चदशस्वपि ॥६६॥
क्रमेण मध्ये त्वन्येषां निवेशादेकविंशति।
भवन्ति यन्त्राणि तथा तैः कृत्यग्निः प्रवर्त्तते ॥६७॥
त्रिकोणाकारके पट्टे ताम्रे तानि विलिख्य वै।
स्पृशन् विद्यां जपेत्तच्च तद्वर्णकृतसम्पुटम् ॥६८॥

मिति। आद्यं खिँ इत्यक्षरं स्वरत्रययुक्तेषु एकविंशतिसंख्येषु आग्नेयव्यञ्जनाक्षरेषु आद्यं। क्रमात् एकस्मिन्नेकस्मिन्नेकैकक्रमात्। पार्व्वतीति सम्बुद्धिः। चतुर्दश तथा क्रमात् स्वस्य वामपार्श्वे अधरादि ऊर्द्धान्तस्थेकैकं पञ्चकं दक्षिणपार्श्वे ऊर्द्धाद्यधरान्तं पञ्चकमग्रे दक्षिणादिवामान्तञ्चतुष्टयं तदन्ते पञ्चदशमस्थाने साधकादित्रयं वा (च) लिखेत्। पञ्चदशस्वपि विंशतियन्त्रेषु पञ्चदशस्थानेष्वित्यर्थः। अन्येषां द्वितीयादीनामक्षराणां। तैरेकविंशतिभिः। त्रिकोणाकारके पट्टे कृत्यग्निवर्द्धनप्रयोगार्थमेकविंशतियोग्याधिकरणरूपे इत्यर्थः। तानि यन्त्राणि। तद्वर्णकृतसम्पुटं प्रागुक्तैकविंशत्यक्षराणि विद्याया आद्यन्तयोरनुलोमरूपेण योजयित्वा जपेदित्यर्थः। तद्यन्त्रपट्टं जपपूजितं उक्तरूपया विद्यया। पाकः प्राग्वदन्नादिभिर्भवति प्रदीप्तिमित्यत्रान्वयः। प्राग्जन्माघक्षयेण पूर्वजन्मपापनाशात् अभिषेकादिकृतात्। जायते प्रदीप्तिर्जायते इति निगमनरूपं। नित्यानामित्युक्त्या एष प्रयोगः सर्व्वसाधारण इत्यर्थः। इति प्रोक्ता इति शेषः। एकविंशतियन्त्रविरचनाप्रयोगक्रमो यथा पञ्चभूताक्षरेषु वक्ष्याक्षराणि अन्योन्यसम्मेलनजनितैकविंशतिसंख्यानि। प्रोक्तरूपाण्यक्षराणि त्रिकोणाकारके ताम्रपट्टे वाह्याभ्यन्तरयोगात् समत्रिरेखं त्रिकोणद्वयं प्रागग्रमालिख्य तदन्तर्वृत्तमन्तर्गतत्रिकोणरेखात्रयस्पृष्टास्पृष्टं विधाय तदन्तः प्रागुक्तमानेन षट्कोणं विधाय तत्र लिखेत् यथा सर्वमध्ये आद्याक्षरं नामगर्भं समालिख्य तद्वहिः षट्सु कोणेषु अग्रादिप्रादक्षिण्येन षडक्षराण्यालिख्य तद्वहिस्त्रिकोण-

सतोयभाण्डे दिनशो निक्षिपेज्जपपूजितम् ।
तत्तोयेनान्नपाकाभिषिक्तो भवति ध्रुवम् ॥९९॥
प्रदीप्तिर्जठराग्नेस्तु प्रागजन्माघक्षयेन वै ।
जायते परमेशानि नित्यानां वैभवादिति ॥१००॥
श्रीवत्सतत्त्वमयी व्याप्तिरिति सम्यक् समीरिता ।
यस्या निष्फालनाच्चित्ते तत्तत्त्वं स्वात्मसात् कृतम् ॥१०१॥

इति षोडशनित्यातन्त्रे श्रीकादिमते
विंशतिपटलम् ।

द्वयान्तरालवीथ्यां स्वस्य वामपार्श्वाधोभागमारभ्य तदूर्ध्वभागान्तपञ्चकं दक्षिणपार्श्वोर्ध्वभागादितदधोभागान्तपञ्चकं अग्रे दक्षिणपार्श्वादि वामपार्श्वान्तं चतुष्टयं तत्र तदग्रे पञ्चदशमस्थाने साध्याक्षरम्। एवं साध्याक्षरान्तानि शिष्टानि चतुर्दशाक्षराण्यालिख्य एवं सम्भूयैकविंशत्यक्षराणि लिखेत्। एतत् प्रथमं यन्त्रम्। अस्मिन्नेव यन्त्रे सर्वमध्ये द्वितीयादीनां विंशाक्षराणां निवेशादितरेषां मध्ये मध्यलिखिताक्षरोपरितनादीनां तत्तत्पूर्वपूर्वाक्षरान्तानां विंशत्यक्षराणां बहिः प्रागुक्तक्रमनिवेशनाच्च पूर्वोक्तेन यन्त्रेण सार्धमेकविंशतियन्त्राणि सम्भवन्ति। एष्वन्यतमं यन्त्रं विद्यया तद्वर्णपुटितया सप्राणप्रतिष्ठं लक्षवारजपपूजितं दिनशः शतवाराद्धीनं विद्यया तद्वर्णपुटितयाभिजप्तपूजितं तोयभाण्डे निक्षिप्य तैर्जलैः कृताः पानपाकाभिषेकाः अस्य चिरन्तनपापानि नाशयित्वा जठराग्निवृद्धिकराणि भवन्तीति ॥१००॥

इति श्रीषोडशनित्यातन्त्रेषु श्रीकादिमताख्यस्य परिपूर्णस्य तन्त्रस्य प्रपञ्चसारसिंहराजप्रकाशाभिधानेन सुभगानन्दनाथेन विरचितायां मनोरमाख्यायां व्याख्यायां ज्वालामालिनी-नित्याविद्याविधानप्रकाशनपरं
विंशतितमं पटलं परिपूर्णपराम्पृष्टम् ॥२०॥

ग्रन्थसंख्याः—यन्त्राणि विंशे पटले द्वात्रिंशद्व्याक्रिया कृता ।
अध्यर्धपादरहितं त्रिशतं ग्रन्थसंख्यया ॥

एकविंशपटलम् ।

अथ षोड़शनित्यासु या चित्रा षोड़शी शिवे ।
प्रोक्ता तत्कल्पमधुना शृणु सर्वार्थसिद्धिदम् ॥ १ ॥
विद्या प्रागेव कथिता तदङ्गन्याससंयुतम् ।
ध्यानं शक्तीः पूजनञ्च साधनं तत्फलानि च ॥ २ ॥
होमतर्पणयन्त्रार्चाभावनाः कथयामि ते ।
उपायैः पञ्चभिस्तैस्तैः साधयेदखिलेप्सितम् ॥ ३ ॥
विद्याद्यवायुना कुर्य्याद्दीर्घस्वरयुजा क्रमात् ।
षड़ङ्गानि यथापूर्वं मातृकां विद्यया न्यसेत् ॥ ४ ॥

पूर्वस्मिन् विंशे पटले पञ्चदश्या ज्वालामालिनीनित्याविद्याया विधानमुपदिश्यानन्तरं षोड़श्याश्चित्रानित्याविद्याया विधानमुपदिशति अथ षोड़शेत्यादिना षण्मशीरित्यन्तेन श्लोकशतरूपेणैकविंशेन पटलेन। तत्र अथ षोड़शेत्यादिभिरीप्सितमित्यन्तैस्त्रिभिः श्लोकैः पटलार्थानुपदिशति। तत्र शिवे इति सम्बुद्धिः। तत्कल्पं तद्विधानं। प्रागेव तृतीयपटले। शक्तीः आवरणस्थाः। साधनं पुरश्चरणं। तत्फलानि सिद्धविद्यस्य फलानि। एतैर्होमादिभिः ॥ ३ ॥

विद्येत्यादिना श्लोकेन षड़ङ्गन्यासोपदेशं मातृकान्यासातिदेशञ्च करोति। तत्र विद्याद्यवायुना विद्यादिभूतचकारेण। दीर्घस्वरयुजा प्राग्वत्। चां चीं इत्यादिरूपेण। यथापूर्व्वम् एतत् काकाक्षिवत् अर्थवशात् पूर्वापरयोरन्वेति तेन पूर्वत्रान्वये जाति सहितं न्यसेदित्यर्थः परत्रान्वये तत्तत् स्थानेषु प्रागुक्तेषु न्यसेच्चेत्यर्थः। विद्यया प्रागुक्तन्यासक्रमातिदेशेनैकैकेनाक्षरेणान्ते युतामिति शेषः। न्यसेत् कुलसुन्दरीपटलोक्तक्रमादित्यर्थः ॥ ४ ॥

उद्यदादित्यबिम्बाभां नवरत्नविभूषिताम्।
नवरत्नकिरीटाञ्च चित्रपट्टांशुकोज्ज्वलाम्॥ ५॥
चतुर्भुजां त्रिनयनां शुचिस्मितलसन्मुखीम्।
सर्वानन्दमयीं नित्यां समस्तेप्सितदायिनीम्॥ ६॥
चतुर्भुजां भुजैः पाशमङ्कुशं वरदाभये।
दधानां मङ्गलापद्मकर्णिकानवयोनिगाम्॥ ७॥
तच्छक्तिभिस्तु तच्चक्रे तथैवार्च्चनमीरितम्।
नवयोनावष्टवर्गयुता ब्राह्म्यादिका यजेत्॥ ८॥

उद्यदित्यादिभिर्नवयोनिगामित्यन्तैस्त्रिभिः श्लोकैः सविशेषनित्यसपर्य्यामङ्गला तिदेशगर्भं देव्या नित्यसपर्य्याध्यानमुपदिशति। तत्र चित्रपट्टांशुकोज्ज्वलां चित्रपट्टांशुकपरीधानामित्यर्थः। सर्वानन्दमयीं आनन्दरूपविग्रहवतीं। चतुर्भुजामिति पुनरुक्तिरायुधधारणप्रस्तावार्थत्वादभ्युपगन्तव्या। अत्रायुधक्रम जर्द्धादिवामदक्षिणक्रमेण। मङ्गलापद्मकर्णिकानवयोनिगां सर्व्वमङ्गलानित्यानित्यपूजाचक्रादस्याधिक्यं कर्णिकामध्यगतनवयोन्येव। एतदुक्तं भवति तत्रोक्तं चतुर्द्वारसहितं चतुरस्रद्वयं तदन्तः द्वात्रिंशद्दलं पद्मं तदन्त षोड़शदलं पद्मं तदन्तरष्टदलं पद्मं तत्कर्णिकायां नवयोनिं प्रोक्तमानेन कुर्य्यादिति॥ ७॥

तच्छक्तिभिरित्यादिना यजेदित्यन्तेन श्लोकद्वयेन देव्या नित्यसपर्य्याक्रमं षड़ावरणमुपदिशति। तत्र तच्छक्तिभिः सर्व्वमङ्गलावरणचतुष्टयशक्तिभिः। तथैव[1] अभ्यन्तरात् बाह्यनिर्गमनक्रमेणाष्टवर्गयुताः अकचटतपयशादिवर्गाष्टकपूर्वाः। तेन ब्राह्म्यादीनां द्विरर्चनमायातं। परितः मध्यत्रिकोणाद्बहिरित्यर्थः। तद्भुजान्तिके दक्षिणाधरभुजादि वामाधरभुजान्तं प्रादक्षिण्येनेत्यर्थः। एतदुक्तं भवति पूर्वोक्तसर्व्वमध्यकर्णिकागतनवयोनिमध्यविशिष्टे सर्व्वमङ्गलानित्यपूजाचक्रे सर्व्वमध्ये चित्रानित्यामावाह्योपचारैरभ्यर्च्य तत्पृष्ठभागे प्रागुक्तान्तराले नवनाथपंक्तिं प्राग्वत्त्रिक्रमतोऽभ्यर्च्य सर्व्वमध्ययोनि कोणेषु तदिच्छाज्ञानक्रियाशक्तीस्तद्बहिर्दिव्यास्तत्तद्भुजान्तिके दक्षिणाधरादि वामाधरान्तं प्रादक्षिण्यात्तदायुधान्यभ्यर्च्य तद्बहिरष्टसु कोणेषु अथादिप्रादक्षिण्येन वर्गोपेता ब्राह्म्यादीर-

[1] तथैवं।

इच्छाज्ञानक्रियाशक्तीरर्च्चयेन्मध्यकोणतः ।
इतोऽस्य परितो १ देव्याः पूजयेत्तद्वदन्तिके ॥९॥
सर्वासामपि नित्यानां नाथान् देव्यास्तु पश्चिमे ।
पूजयेत्तत्तदाकारांस्तत्तन्मन्त्रैर्यथाविधि ॥ १० ॥
गुरुमण्डलपूजादि साधारणमुदीरितम् ।
सर्वासामपि नित्यानां यदाद्यास्यन्दजा इमाः ॥ ११ ॥
साधनञ्च तथा प्रोक्तं तदङ्गहवनन्तथा ।
एवं संसाधिता विद्या विनियोगाय कल्पते ॥ १२ ॥

अर्च्च तद्बहिस्तद्वदष्टपत्रेषु सर्व्वमङ्गलापटलोक्ता भद्राद्यष्टशक्तीरभ्यर्च्च तद्बहिस्तद्वत् षोडशपत्रेषु तत्रोक्ताः कलाद्याः २ षोडशशक्तीरभ्यर्च्च तद्बहिस्तद्द्वात्रिंशद्दलेषु ३ तत्रोक्ताः कामिन्यादिद्वात्रिंशच्छक्तीः समभ्यर्च्च तद्बहिश्चतुरस्रे प्राग्वत्तत्रोक्ताः पश्चिमद्वाराद्ब्राह्म्यादीः पूर्व्वद्वारादिन्द्रादिका आग्नेयाद ४ नन्तादिकाश्च पूजयेदिति । तत्र वलिद्वयं पूजासमाप्त्यादि प्राग्वत् ॥ ८ ॥

सर्व्वासामित्यादिना इमा इत्यन्तेन श्लोकद्वयेन सर्वासां नित्यानां साधारणं नवनाथार्च्चनोपदेशं तत्तन्मण्डलादिषु प्रतिपर्व्व तदर्चनातिदेशं च करोति । तत्र तत्तदाकारान्मध्यमध्यदेवीसदृशरूपादिकान् । तत्तन्मन्त्रैः [ऽत्रि] द्वितीयपटलोक्तैः । यथाविधि त्रिविक्रमपंक्तितः । आद्यास्यन्दजाः आद्यायाः ललितायाः स्वेच्छोल्लासरूपत्वात् । आसां सर्व्वगुरुमण्डल सपर्य्यादिकं तत् समानमेवेत्यर्थः ॥ ११ ॥

साधनमित्यादिना श्लोकेन पुरश्चरणमुपदिशति । तत्र तथा यथा ललितायाः । तदङ्गहवनं साधनाङ्गो होमः । तथा प्राग्वत्तेनाक्षरविलक्षं कृतयुगे द्वादशलक्षं जपं दशांशमन्नाज्यादिभिर्होमञ्च कुर्य्यादित्यर्थः ॥ १२ ॥

१ । पुरत इति वा पाठः । २ । कलायाः ।
३ । तद्द्वात्रिंशद्दलेषु । ४ । आग्नेयाद्यनन्ता ।

काम्यहोमविधिं वक्ष्ये शृणु सर्वार्थदायकम्।
येनातिमन्दभाग्योऽपि श्रीमान् भोक्ता सुखी भवेत्॥ १३॥
मधुरत्रयसंसिक्तैररुणैरम्बुजैः श्रियम्।
प्राप्नोति मण्डलाद्धोमात् सितैस्तैश्च महायशाः॥ १४॥
क्षौद्राक्तैरुत्पलैरक्तैर्हवनात् प्रोक्तकालतः।
सुवर्णं समवाप्नोति निधिं १ वा च सुधान्तु वा॥ १५॥
क्षीराक्तैः कैरवैर्होमात् प्रोक्तकालमवाप्नुयात्।
धान्यानि विविधान्याशु सुभगः स भवेन्नरः॥ १६॥
आज्याक्तैरुत्पलैर्होमाद्वाञ्छितं समवाप्नुयात्।
तद्वत्तैरपि कल्हारैर्हवनाद्राजवल्लभः॥ १७।
पलाशपुष्पैस्त्रिस्वादुयुक्तैस्तत्कालहोमतः।
चतुर्विधन्तु पाण्डित्यं भवत्येव न संशयः॥ १८॥
लाजैस्त्रिमधुरोपेतैस्तत्कालहवनेन वै।
कन्यकां लभते यत्नात् समस्तगुणसंयुताम्॥ १९॥
नालिकेलफलक्षोदं ससितं सगुडन्तु वा।
क्षौद्राक्तं जुहुयात्तद्वदयत्नाद्धनदोपमः॥ २०॥

काम्यहोममित्यादिभिश्चेतन इत्यन्तैः सप्तदशभिः श्लोकैर्नाना होमद्रव्यैस्त्रिंशत्संख्यान् मङ्गलरूपान् होमविधीनुपदिशति। तत्र येन विधिना। तैरम्बुजैरुत्पलैः। रक्तैरक्तकुमुदैरित्यर्थः। कैरवैः सितैरिति शेषः। उत्पलैर्नीलोत्पलैः। तद्वत्तैराज्याक्तैश्चतुर्विधं प्राग्वद्वादित्वकवित्ववक्तृत्वशास्त्रत्वतः। लभते यत्नादयत्नादिति पदच्छेदः। ससितं खण्डशर्करामिलितं। वा विकल्पे। तद्वदिति च विकल्पार्थे तथैव धनदोपम इत्यर्थः। तद्वत् प्राग्वदाज्यतिलतण्डुलसर्वाक्षपुष्पवन्धूकपुष्पहोमाद्धनदोपमो भवतीत्यर्थः। सितरक्तैः पुष्पैः। गुड़ुचाः प्राग्व-

---

१। विधिं।

तथैवान्नाज्यहोमेन सतण्डुलतिलैरपि ।
प्रसूनैररुणैस्तद्वत्तथा बन्धूकसम्भवैः ॥ २१ ॥
सितैः प्रसूनैर्वाक्सिद्धिं हवनात् समवाप्नुयात् ।
सितरक्तैस्तु मिलितैरायुरारोग्यमाप्नुयात् ॥ २२ ॥
दूर्वात्रिकैस्त्रिमध्वक्तैर्हवनात्तु जयेद् गदान् ।
तथा गुडूच्या होमेन पायसेन तिलैन वा ॥ २३ ॥
श्रीखण्डपङ्ककर्पूरमिलितैः शतपत्रकैः ।
हवनाच्छ्रियमाप्नोति सा तदन्वयगा भवेत् ॥ २४ ॥
कुङ्कुमं हिमतोयेन पिष्ट्वा कर्पूरसंयुतम् ।
तत्पङ्कमर्दितैर्होमात् कह्लारैर्विकचैः शुभैः ॥ २५ ॥
राजकल्पः श्रिया भूयाज्जीवेद्वर्षशतं भुवि ।
निःसपत्नो निरातङ्को निर्द्वन्द्वो निर्मलाशयः ॥ २६ ॥
इक्षुकाण्डस्य सकलैर्हवनाद्वस्त्रमाप्नुयात् ।
तथैव करवीरोत्थैः प्रसूनैररुणैः सितैः ॥ २७ ॥
क्षौद्राक्तैः पाटलीपुष्पैर्हवनाद्वशयेद्वधूः ।
तथैव चम्पकैर्होमाद्रूपाजीवा वशं नयेत् ॥ २८ ॥
सरूपवत्सासितगोः क्षीराक्तसितहोमतः ।
लभतेऽनुपमां लक्ष्मीमपि पापिष्ठचेतनः ॥ २९ ॥

दमृतालतया चकारेण गदाञ्जयेदित्याकृष्यते । श्रीखण्डं चन्दनं । शतपत्रकैः तन्नाम गुरुमुखादवगन्तव्यं । सा लक्ष्मीः तदन्वयगा शाश्वतीं श्रियमवाप्नोतीत्यर्थः । शुभैः घुणक्षतादिरहितैः अखण्डितैः । निर्द्वन्द्वः निरुपमः । तथैव वस्त्रमाप्नुयादित्यर्थः । रूपाजीवाः वेश्याः । सितहोमतः शर्कराहोमतः । पापिष्ठचेतनः अविवेकी तस्य लक्ष्मी दुष्प्रापत्वात् ॥ २९ ॥

सौवीराक्तैस्तु कार्पासवीजैस्तत्कालहोमतः ।
अर्द्धेन्दुकुण्डे नियतं विद्विष्टा रिपवोऽम्बिके ॥ ३० ॥
अरिष्टपत्रै(१)स्तद्वीजैस्तत्तैलाक्तैस्तथा हुतैः ।
मृत्युवीजैर्निम्बतैलसिक्तैर्होमात्तु दन्तिनः ॥ ३१ ॥
रागाक्तैस्तुरगास्तद्वत्तत्पञ्चाङ्गैर्हुतैर्ध्रुवम् ।
अक्षवीजैस्तु तैलाक्तैर्होमः सर्वविनाशवान् ॥ ३२ ॥
करञ्जवीजैस्तत्सिक्तैर्होमाद्वैरिविनाशनः ।
तथैवाश्वतरुद्भूतपञ्चाङ्गहवनादपि ॥ ३३ ॥
निम्बतैलाप्लुतैरक्षद्रुमवीजैस्तु होमतः ।
तद्दिने स्यादपस्मारो वैरी भवति निश्चितम् ॥ ३४ ॥
अरातेर्जन्मनक्षत्रवृक्षैश्च न गतैस्तले (२) ।
तद्योनिपिष्टितैस्तैश्च हवनं मृतुरक्तद्रिपोः ॥ ३५ ॥
यक्षाक्षवीजैः सर्षपतैलाक्तैर्हवनात्तथा ।
जायन्ते वैरिणः कुष्ठरोगा देहविलापकाः ॥ ३६ ॥
मरीचैः सर्षपैर्होमात्तैलाक्तैर्मध्यरात्रके ।
दाहज्वरेण ग्रस्तः स्यादरातिस्तद्दिनैर्ध्रुवम् ॥ ३७ ॥

सौवीरेत्यादिभिर्ध्रुवमित्यन्तैरष्टभिः श्लोकैर्नवसंख्यं निग्रहहोममुपदिशति । तत्र अर्द्धेन्दुकुण्डे वक्ष्यमाणे । तद्वीजैः अरिष्टवीजैः । तत्तैलाक्तैर्निम्बतैलाक्तैः । तथा विद्विष्टा भवन्तीत्यर्थः । तद्वद् यद्वत् दन्तिनः । तत्पञ्चाङ्गैः मृत्युपञ्चाङ्गैः । तदक्तैर्निम्बतैलाक्तैः । सर्व्वविनाशवान् सर्व्वजन्तुविनाशकरः । तत्सिक्तैर्निम्बतैलाक्तैः तद्दिनैर्मण्डलादिभिः । तद्योनिपिष्टितैः शत्रुनक्षत्रयोनिमांसैः । तैश्च नक्षत्रवृक्षैः यक्षाक्षवीजानि गुरुमुखादवगन्तव्यानि । तैलाक्तैस्तिलसम्भवतैलाक्तैः ॥३७॥

(१) अरिष्टयन्त्रै । (२) नगतैतलै ।

एवं निग्रहहोमेषु स्वरचायै तथान्वहम् ।
स्निग्धैः सम्प्राप्तसद्दियैर्जपहोमादि कारयेत् ॥ ३८ ॥
मृत्युञ्जयेन वा तद्वत् प्रयोगस्ताभिरेव च ।
विद्याभिरन्यथा सिद्धं मन्त्रमप्याशु नाशयेत् ॥ ३९ ॥
प्रागुक्तानान्तु कुर्व्वीत निग्रहं स्वस्य रोषतः ।
वित्ताशया वा न कदाप्याचरेद्भूतिकामुकः ॥ ४० ॥
नित्यक्लिन्नाविधौ प्रोक्तैस्तर्पणैस्तानि साधयेत् ।
अनया विद्यया कर्म्माण्यशेषाणि महेश्वरि ॥ ४१ ॥
अथ यन्त्राणि वक्ष्यामि नानाभीष्टप्रदानि वै ।
यैः सर्व्वे सर्व्वदा सर्व्वं समीहितमवाप्नुयुः ॥ ४२ ॥
स्वरयुक्तलिपिव्रातगर्भां विद्यां समालिखेत् ।
सर्व्वोक्तेषु विधिवत् स्थानेषु परमेश्वरि ॥ ४३ ॥

एवमित्यादिना नाशयेदित्यन्तेन श्लोकद्वयेनाभिचारकर्त्तुः स्वरचाविधानक्रममुपदिशति । तत्र स्निग्धैः आत्मसमसुखदुःखैः । मृत्युञ्जयेन चतुस्त्रिंशत्पटलवक्ष्यमाणेन । वा विकल्पे । अन्यथा स्वरचाविधानवैपरीत्येन ॥ ३८ ॥

प्रागुक्तेत्यादिना श्लोकेनाभिचारेण गुणविधानमुपदिशति । तत्र प्रागुक्तानां त्रयोदशपटले नवतितमादिश्लोकत्रयोक्तानामेवेत्यर्थः । आचरेन्निग्रहम् अभिचार्य्याणां तत्रोक्तानामित्यर्थः ॥ ४० ॥

नित्यक्लिन्नेत्यादिना श्लोकेन तर्पणान्युपदिशति । तत्र तानि तत्रोक्तानि ॥४१॥

अथ यन्त्राणीत्यादिभिर्विचक्षण इत्यन्तैरर्द्धाधिकैः षड्भिः श्लोकैर्विद्याया आद्ये मातृकाविसराक्षरयोजनात् सञ्जातेषु षट्सप्तत्यधिकपञ्चशतसंख्येषु रूपेष्वादितः षोड़शाधिकचतुःशतसंख्यैस्तैः वर्गक्रमतः षड्विंशतिविधानि यन्त्राण्युपदिशति । तत्र सर्व्वे साधकाः । स्वरयुक्तलिपिव्रातगर्भां अकारादिक्षकारान्तानि षट्सप्तत्यधिक-पञ्चशतान्यक्षराणि विद्याया आदौ एकमेकं योजयेत् । तेन तत्संख्यानि विद्यारूपाणि सम्भवन्तीत्यर्थः । उक्तेषु वक्ष्यमाणेषु । परमेश्वरीति देवीसम्बुद्धिः । तद्द्वयं हस्तद्वयं । तद्वह्निः षट्कोणाद्वह्निः । तत्त्र्यं हस्तत्रयं ।

त्रिकोणं वृत्तयुग्मञ्च षट्कोणं तद्वयन्तथा ।
तद्बहिः षड्‌दलं पद्मं तत्तत्त्रयञ्च संलिखेत् ॥ ४४ ॥
आद्यकूटं लिखेत् साध्यं गर्भे मध्ये विधानतः ।
त्रिकोणेषु च षट्कोणे षट्पत्रेषु समालिखेत् ॥ ४५ ॥
कूटान्यन्यानि चोक्तानि तत्र पञ्चदशान्यपि ।
अन्तर्वृत्तान्तरद्वन्द्वे भूतार्णांश्च क्रियोचितान् ॥ ४६ ॥

त्रिकोणेषु यन्त्रस्य सर्वमध्यत्रिकोणत्रये इत्यर्थः। अन्यानि द्वितीयादीनि। तत्र पञ्चदशसु स्थानेष्वित्यर्थः। अन्तर्वृत्तान्तरद्वन्द्वे कोणवाह्यवृत्तद्वयवीथ्यां षट्कोणवाह्यवृत्तवीथ्याञ्चेत्यर्थः। क्रियोचितान् स्तम्भनवश्यादिक्रियोचितान् पार्थिववर्णादीन्। तत्र लेखनक्रमः प्रतिवीथिकं दशदशक्रमात्। ससाध्यकर्म्मवर्णं च अन्ते सहितमिति शेषः। मायाविन्दुयुक्तां क्रमोत्क्रमात्। एतदुक्तं भवति प्रत्यक्षरं विसर्जनीययुक्तां प्रतिलोमां मातृकां सर्व्ववाह्यवृत्तान्तरवीथीद्वये अन्तर्वृत्तवीथ्याम् अभितः समालिख्य प्रत्यक्षरं विन्दुयुक्तामनुलोमामेव वहिर्वीथ्या मभितः समालिखेदिति। एवं षड्विंशतिविधं। क्रमोत्क्रमात् वर्गक्रमतः। षड्विंशतियन्त्रविरचनाक्रमो यथा। इष्टप्रमाणभ्रमात् वृत्तं सम्पाद्य तदनन्तरेकैकाङ्गुलमानेन वृत्तद्वयं कृत्वा तदन्तरं चतुरङ्गुलमानेन वृत्तं कृत्वा तत्र षड्‌दलानि कृत्वा तदन्तरे एकाङ्गुलमानेन वृत्तं सम्पाद्य तद्वृत्तव्यासार्द्धमानतः प्राग्वत् षट्कोणं कृत्वा तदन्तरस्तत्सन्धिस्पृष्टास्पृष्टवृत्तं विधाय तदन्तरेकाङ्गुलमानेन वृत्तं निष्पाद्य तद्वृत्तरेखास्पृष्टत्र्यस्रं समरेखं त्रिकोणं विधाय तत्र सर्व्वमध्ये मूलविद्याया आदौ मातृकाविसरसंयोगसञ्जातेषु षट्सप्तत्यधिकपञ्चशतसंख्येषु कूटरूपेष्वाद्यं कूटं ससाध्यनामकमालिख्य त्रिकोणस्य त्रिकोणेषु अग्न्यादिप्रादक्षिण्येन द्वितीयादीनि त्रीणि कूटाक्षराण्यालिख्य तद्बहिः षट्सु कोणेषु अग्न्यादिप्रादक्षिण्येन पञ्चमादीनि षट्कूटाक्षराण्यालिख्य तद्बहिः षट्सु यन्त्रेषु एकादशाक्षरादीनि षट्कूटाक्षराणि संलिख्य एवं षोड़शाक्षराण्येकवर्गजाति समालिख्य त्रिकोणवाह्यवृत्तद्वयान्तरवीथ्यां षट्कोणवाह्यवृत्तद्वयान्तरवीथ्याञ्च कर्म्मोचितानि भूताक्षराण्यग्न्यादिप्रादक्षिण्येन दशदशालिख्य पद्मवाह्यवृत्तत्रयान्तरवीथीद्वये विन्दुविसर्जनीययुक्तामनुलोमप्रतिलोममातृकाञ्चान्ते साध्यादिसहितां वाह्यवीथ्यारभ्यतः प्राग्वद्विलिख्य प्रथमं यन्त्रं सम्पाद्यानन्तरमस्मिन्नेव

ससाध्यकर्म्मवर्णांश्च वह्निर्वृत्तान्तरद्वये ।
मातृकां विलिखेन्मायाविन्दुयुक्तां क्रमोत्क्रमात् ॥ ४७ ॥
एवं षड्विंशतिविधं यन्त्रं कुर्य्याद्विचक्षणः ।
परस्तात्तु शतेनापि षष्ट्या कूटैर्लिखेत् पविम् ॥ ४८ ॥
प्राक्प्रत्यग्दक्षिणोदक्च सूत्राण्यष्टादश क्षिपेत् ।
तैस्तु कोष्ठानि जायन्ते नवाशीतिशतद्वयम् ॥ ४९ ॥
तत्र कोणेषु कोष्ठानि द्वाविंशन्मार्जयेत्तथा ।
ततो वज्रं भवेन्मध्ये त्वेकषष्ट्या शतात्मकम् ॥ ५० ॥
तस्य दिक्षु त्रिकोणानि विदध्यादेककोष्ठतः ।
मध्यकोष्ठे लिखेद्विद्यां साध्याख्याकर्म्मसंयुताम् ॥ ५१ ॥
त्रिकोणेषु तु तत् कूटान्यालिखेत् साध्यवन्ति च ।
प्राग्वदारभ्य विलिखेत् प्रादक्षिण्यप्रवेशतः ॥ ५२ ॥

यन्त्रे वर्गक्रमतः प्रत्येकं यावत् षड्विंशतिसवर्गषोड़शाक्षरलेखनतः पूर्व्वोक्तेन यन्त्रेण सार्द्धं षड्विंशतिसंख्यानि यन्त्राणि सम्भवन्तीति ॥ ४७ ॥

परस्तादित्यादिभिः शुभमित्यन्तैः सार्द्धैः पञ्चभिः श्लोकैः मूलविद्यायाः प्रागुक्तषड्विंशतियन्त्रविनियुक्तशिष्टैः कूटरूपैः षष्ट्यधिकशतसंख्यैः कोष्ठवज्र-यन्त्रनिर्म्माणं तदनुभावञ्चोपदिशति। तत्र परस्तात् विनियुक्तकूटरूपेभ्यः। पवि-र्वज्रं। तैः सूत्रैः। द्वात्रिंशत् प्रतिकोणमिति शेषः। तथा यथा विषमवज्राकारं मध्येऽवशिष्टं भवेत्। तद्वैषम्यमेतद्यन्त्ररचनाव्याख्याने व्याख्यास्यामः। शतात्मकं शतकोष्ठात्मकमित्यर्थः। एककोष्ठतः प्रतिदिशं। विद्यां शुद्धरूपां मूलविद्यां। तत्र साध्याक्षरलेखनं ककारोदरे प्राग्वत्। कूटानीति सप्तविंशति-मवर्गप्रथमाक्षरादि प्रोक्तेषु (१) उक्तसंख्येषु आदितश्चत्वार्य्यक्षराण्यग्रकोणात् प्रादक्षिण्याच्चतुर्षु कोणेष्वालिखेदित्यर्थः। प्राग्वदारभ्य अग्रत्रिकोणोर्द्ध्वपंक्ति-कोष्ठपञ्चके मध्यकोष्ठमारभ्य त्रिकोणत्रिकोणचतुष्कलिखिताक्षरचतुष्टयो-परितनानीत्यर्थः। एतत् प्रोक्तरूपं (२)। एतत्कोष्ठवज्रयन्त्रविरचनाक्रमो यथा। प्राक्प्रत्यग्दक्षिणोदक्समान्तरालमास्फालितैरष्टादशभिः सूत्रैरेकोननवत्य

१। श्लोकेषु। २। मोक्षरूपं।

एतद्वश्यं महद्यन्त्रं समस्तापन्निवारणम् ।
समस्ताभीष्टदं सर्व्वं विजयश्रीप्रदं शुभम् ॥ ५३ ॥

धिकद्विशतसंख्यानि कोष्ठानि निष्पाद्य तत्र परितः सर्व्ववाह्यपङ्क्तिं मार्जयित्वा ततश्चतसृषु दिक्षु सर्वमध्यपंक्तिपर्य्यन्तपंक्तिद्वयवाह्यरेखाद्वयाग्राणि त्रिकोणाकाराणि कृत्वा ततस्तदन्तश्चतुर्षु कोणेषु प्रतिकोणं दृश्यमानवाह्यवीथ्यां नव नवकोष्ठानि मार्जयित्वा ततस्तदन्तश्चतुर्षु कोणेषु प्रतिकोणं दृश्यमानवाह्यवीथ्यां पञ्च पञ्च कोष्ठानि मार्जयित्वा ततस्तदन्तश्चतुर्षु कोणेषु प्रतिकोणं दृश्यमानवाह्यवीथ्यां त्रीणि त्रीणि कोष्ठानि मार्जयित्वा सम्भूयैवं प्रतिकोणे द्वात्रिंशत् द्वात्रिंशत् कोष्ठानि सम्भूयास्मिन् यन्त्रे त्रिकोणवश्यमष्टविंशत्यधिकशतकोष्ठानि मार्जयेत्। एवं कृते चतसृषु दिक्षु प्रतिदिशं त्रिकोणचतुष्टयान्तरालस्थानान्तरालस्थपंक्त्या पञ्च पञ्चकोष्ठानि तदन्तरालस्थानान्तरालस्थपंक्तिद्वये प्रतिदिशं सप्त सप्त कोष्ठानि तदन्तरालस्थपंक्तौ प्रतिदिशं तत् कोष्ठसप्तकादधिकं चतुर्षु कोणेषु चत्वारि कोष्ठानि प्रतिकोणमेकैकक्रमेण पृथक् निर्गतानि भवन्ति। ततस्तदन्तरः षसमचतुरस्रस्थानि (१) एकोनपञ्चाशत् कोष्ठानि चैवं सम्भूय सर्व्ववाह्यगतत्रिकोणचतुष्टयेन सार्द्धमेकषष्ट्यधिकशतसंख्यानि विषमेऽस्मिन् वश्ये यन्त्रे सम्भवन्ति। अस्य वश्यस्य मूले पूर्व्वोक्तं तथाशब्दाभिप्रेतं वैषम्यं तु (२) चतसृषु दिक्षु वाह्यतो द्वितीयतृतीयपंक्त्योः समसंख्यकोष्ठत्वं। तत्र सर्वमध्यकोष्ठे शुद्धां विद्यां प्रागुत् ककारोदरगतसाध्यादित्रयाख्यावतीमालिख्य सर्व्ववाह्यदिग्गतकोणचतुष्टये अग्न्यादिप्रादक्षिण्येन प्रागुक्तसंख्येषु मूलविद्यास्वरूपेषु पूर्वोक्तवर्गक्रमजनितषड्विंशतियन्त्रलिखितषड्विंशतिवर्गात्मषोड़शाधिकचतुःशताक्षरेभ्योऽवशिष्टेषु दशवर्गात्मसु षष्ट्यधिकशतसंख्येष्वादित (३) श्चत्वारि कूटरूपाक्षराणि प्राग्वत् साध्यगर्भाणि समालिख्य तदुपरिगतपञ्चकूटादीनि षट्पञ्चाशदधिकशतसंख्यानि कूटाक्षराणि शिष्टेषु तत्संख्येषु कोष्ठेषु अग्नित्रिकोणोर्द्ध्वस्थपंक्तिगत (४) कोष्ठपञ्चकमध्यकोष्ठमारभ्य प्रादक्षिण्य-प्रवेशगत्या (५) युक्तक्रमं विद्यागर्भं सर्वमध्यकोष्टवर्जमालिखेदिति। एतद्विषमं महद्वश्ययन्त्रं प्रोक्तफलसिद्धिप्रदमिति ॥ ५३ ॥

१। षषमसमचतुरस्रस्थानि।
२। वैषम्ये तु। ३। श्चादित।
४। गते। ५। मुक्तक्रमं।

सप्तविंशतिचक्राणि यन्त्राण्येवं महेश्वरि ।
सप्तविंशति नक्षत्रसमान्येतानि चेदपि ॥५४॥

* * * * ॥५५॥

फलानि तेषां क्रमशो वदाम्युक्तक्रमेण वै ।
विनियोगक्रमञ्चैव सुस्फुटं परमेश्वरि ॥ ५६ ॥
प्रथमेनार्च्चितेन स्याद्रोगा नश्यन्त्यशेषतः ।
स्ववेश्मनि विधायैतत् पीठे भूमितलेऽपि वा ॥ ५७ ॥
प्रोक्तद्रव्याणि संपिष्य तत्पङ्केनाथ सुस्फुटम् ।
त्रिरात्रं सप्तरात्रं वा सप्तविंशतिरात्रकम् ॥ ५८ ॥
सम्पूज्य तत्र कुम्भन्तु विद्यौषधिजलान्वितम् ।
निधायाभ्यर्च्य गदिनमभिषिञ्चेत्ततः सुखी ॥ ५९ ॥
एवमन्यानि यन्त्राणि प्रोक्तेषु विनियोजयेत् ।
तेषां विलेखनद्रव्याण्याकर्णय वदामि ते ॥ ६० ॥
कुचन्दनं चन्दनञ्च सिन्दूरं सेन्दुरोचनम् ।
काश्मीरमगुरुं कुष्ठं एलाकक्कोलजातिभिः ॥ ६१ ॥
स्वर्णद्रवैर्द्वादशभिर्हिमाम्बु परिपेषितैः ।
जलैर्नक्षत्रवृक्षोत्थैः शुभैर्वा सूक्ष्मपेषितैः ॥ ६२ ॥
द्वितीयं विजयं प्राप्नुयाद्विदध्यात् प्रोक्तरूपतः ।
वादे विवादे समरे द्यूतेषु च जयी भवेत् ॥ ६३ ॥

सप्तविंशतीत्यादिभिराप्नुयादित्यन्तैः षोड़शभिः श्लोकैः सम्भूय सप्तविंशतियन्त्रैः सप्तविंशतिनक्षत्रेषु तदात्मना समर्च्चनादिकं वारेषु च तथार्च्चनं ततस्तिथिसमर्चनादिक्रमं चोपदिशति । तत्र सप्तविंशतियन्त्राणि अनन्तर पूर्वोक्तेन सह सप्तविंशति यन्त्राणीत्यर्थः । तेन कारणेन तान्येव सप्तविंशतिनक्षत्राण्येव विभक्त्या सार्द्धमिति शेषः । तान्येवेत्यत्र एवास्यान्वयः । साध्यं प्रागुक्तानि यन्त्राणि । तत्तद्दिनेषु तत्तद्यन्त्रप्राप्तेषु अश्विन्यादिनक्षत्रेषु । तेषां यन्त्राणाम् । परमेश्वरीति सम्बुद्धिः । स्यात्

तृतीयाद्येषु नवसु ग्रहान्नव समर्च्चयेत् ।
देव्यात्मरूपोत्तेनास्य तैर्ब्बाधा न भवेद् ध्रुवम् ॥ ६४ ॥
स्तम्भयेद्द्वादशेनाशु प्रोक्तक्रमविधानतः ।
संग्राममगमनं वर्षामुद्योगं वाचमाग्रहम् ॥ ६५ ॥
त्रयोदशाद्यैर्वेञ्चान्तैर्यन्त्रैस्तिथिमयैरपि ।
तत्तत्तिथिषु तैः प्राग्वद्वाञ्छितानाप्नुयाद् ध्रुवम् ॥ ६६ ॥
तेषु तेषु तु यन्त्रेषु तत्तत्तिथिदिनाधिपान् ।
वारेशानपि संपूज्य तत्तत् फलमवाप्नुयात् ॥ ६७ ॥
कार्य्योद्योगेषु जातेषु वाञ्छितेष्वितरेष्वपि ।
वारर्च्चतिथिसंप्रोक्तयन्त्रे तां तैश्च दैवतैः ॥ ६८ ॥
आवृत्तामर्च्चयेदग्निरक्षोवाय्वीशदिग्गतैः ।
रोगशान्तिं समुद्योगफलाभीष्टान्यवाप्नुयात् ॥६९॥

अव्ययमिदमाख्यातप्रक्षेपकमवधारणार्थं । वा विकल्पे । प्रोक्तद्रव्याणि वक्ष्यमाणानि कुचन्दनादीनि । वा विकल्पे । तत्र यन्त्रे निधाय प्रोक्तदिवसपूजानन्तरं । सुखी गदीति शेषः । प्रोक्तेषु क्रमान्नक्षत्रेषु कार्य्येषु च वक्ष्यमाणेषु प्रोक्तेषु सेन्दुं सकर्पूरं । द्वादशभिः कुचन्दनादिनक्षत्रवृक्षोत्थैर्जलैः । शुभैः शुद्धरूपैः । वा विकल्पे सूक्ष्मपेषितैर्द्रव्यैरिति शेषः । द्वितीयं यन्त्रमिति शेषः । प्रोक्तरूपतः तत्तन्नक्षत्रादिषु तत्तद्दिनपूजनाभिषेकतः । तृतीयाद्येषु तृतीययन्त्राद्येषु नवसु यन्त्रेषु एकादशान्तेष्विति शेषः । देव्यात्मरूपात् देवीमयविग्रहात् तेन कारणेन । अस्य साधकस्य । तैर्ग्रहैः । एतद्ग्रहार्च्चनं तत्तद्वारेषु कर्त्तव्यमिति सम्प्रदायः । राहु-केत्वोर्वारौ प्राग्वत् । द्वादशेन प्रोक्तनवकात् परेण यन्त्रेणेति शेषः । प्रोक्तक्रमविधानतः तत्प्राशनचक्रतद्दिनार्च्चनादितः । त्रयोदशाद्यैः पूर्वोक्तात् परैः तिथिमयैः पञ्चदशसंख्याविशिष्टत्वात् । प्राग्वत् समर्चितैरिति शेषः । तिथि-दिनाधिपान् वक्ष्यमाणरूपान् । वारेशान् कुलसुन्दरीपटलोक्तान् द्विविधान् । तां देवीं । तैर्दैवतैः तिथ्यादीनामग्निरक्षोवाय्वीशदिग्गतैः तिथिनक्षत्रवारेशद्वय-पूज्यरूपैः प्रोक्तक्रमदिग्गतैः दैवतैरित्यत्रान्वयः । रोगशान्तिं प्रागुक्तां समस्ताम् । समुद्योगफलानि प्रारब्धकार्य्यफलानि ॥ ६९ ॥

वाराणामधिपाः प्रोक्तास्तिथिनक्षत्रदेवताः ।
ऋक्षवृक्षांस्तथा योनी र्निगदे (१) परमेश्वरि ॥ ७० ॥
वह्निर्दस्रावुमा विघ्नो भुजङ्गः षण्मुखो रविः ।
मातरश्च तथा दुर्गा दिशो धनदकेशवौ ॥ ७१ ॥
यमो हरः शशी चेति तिथीशाः परिकीर्त्तिताः ।
नक्षत्रदेवताश्चापि शृणु वक्ष्ये यथाविधि ॥ ७२ ॥
अश्विनी च यमो वह्निर्धाता चन्द्रः शिवोऽदितिः ।
गुरुः सर्पाश्च पितरः अर्य्यमा भग एव च ॥ ७३ ॥
दिनकृच्च तथा त्वष्टा मारुतेन्द्राग्निमित्रकाः ।
इन्द्रो निरृतितोयाख्यौ विश्वेदेवा हरिस्तथा ॥ ७४ ॥
वसवो वरुणः पश्चादज एकपदस्तथा ।
अहिर्ब्ध्नस्तथा पूषा प्रोक्ता नक्षत्रदेवताः ॥ ७५ ॥

वाराणामित्यादिभिर्गजा इत्यन्तैरेकादशभिः श्लोकैः प्रागुक्तवारदेवतास्मरणपुरःसरं तिथिनक्षत्रवृक्षनक्षत्रदेवतानक्षत्रयोनीश्चोपदिशति । तत्र प्रोक्ता कुलसुन्दरीपटले । तथा योनीर्नक्षत्रयोनीरित्यर्थः । वह्नीत्यादिना श्लोकेन तिथिदेवतासु पञ्चदशसु द्वादशदेवता उपदिशति । यम इत्यादिना श्लोकेनावशिष्टास्तिस्रस्तिथिदेवताः समुपदिश्य नक्षत्रदेवताप्रस्तावञ्च करोति । अश्विनावित्यादिना श्लोकेन सप्तविंशतिनक्षत्रदेवतासु तत्संख्यातासु द्वादशनामान्युपदिशति । तत्र शिवोऽदितिः शिवः अदितिरिति पदच्छेदः । दिनकृदित्यादिना श्लोकेन शिष्टासुपञ्च दशसंख्यासु तासु दशदेवतानामान्युपदिशति । तत्र इन्द्राग्नी इत्येकस्य नक्षत्रस्य देवते । वसव इत्यादिना श्लोकेन प्रोक्तावशिष्टदेवतापञ्चकनामोपदेशं प्रोक्तनिगमनञ्च करोति । कारस्कर इत्यादिना श्लोकेन सप्तविंशतिनक्षत्रवृक्षेषु तत्संख्येषु दशवृक्षनामान्युपदिशति । आमलकोदुम्बर इति दिव्यत्वात् सन्धिः आमलक उदुम्बर इत्यर्थः । पलाशेत्यादिना शिष्टेषु सप्तदशसंख्येषु तेषु एकादशवृक्षनामान्युपदिशति ।

योनिमिटमी ।

कारस्करश्चामलकोदुम्बरो जम्बुकस्तथा ।
खदिरः कृष्णवंशौ च पिप्पलो नागरोहिणौ ॥ ७६ ॥
पलाशप्लक्षकाम्बष्ठविल्वार्जुनविकङ्कताः ।
वकुलः सरलः सर्जो वञ्जुलः पनसस्तथा ॥ ७७ ॥
अर्कः शमी कदम्बश्च चूतो निम्ब स्तथाऽन्तिमे ।
मधूकश्चेति संप्रोक्ता वृक्षा भानां क्रमादमी ॥ ७८ ॥
अश्वगजमजसर्पसर्पिणीश्वविड़ालिकाः ।
अजामार्जारमूषाश्च मूषिका वृषमाहिषी ॥ ७९ ॥
व्याघ्रश्च महिषो व्याघ्री मृगी मृगशुनी कपिः ।
गोकर्णो (१) वानरी सिंही तुरगा सिंहगोगजाः ॥ ८० ॥
यदा रोगादि दुःखार्त्तिर्भवेत्तदर्द्धकैर्दिनैः ।
सूक्रत्तैः संख्ययाहोभिः शान्तिः स्याद्दिगुणेन वा ॥ ८१ ॥

अर्केत्यादिना श्लोकेन प्रोक्तावशिष्टषड्वृक्षनामोपदेशं प्रोक्तनिगमनञ्च करोति। अत्र अन्तिमे मधूक इत्यन्वयः। रेवत्यां मधूक इत्यर्थः। भानां नक्षत्राणाम्। अश्वमित्यादिना श्लोकेन सप्तविंशतिनक्षत्रयोनिषु तत् संख्यासु त्रयोदशयोनिनामानि उपदिशति। तत्र श्वविड़ालिका श्वा च विड़ालिका चेत्यर्थः। वृष महिषी वृषश्च महिषी चेत्यर्थः। व्याघ्र इत्यादिना श्लोकेन शिष्टयोनिनामान्युपदिशति। तत्र महिषव्याघ्री महिषश्च व्याघ्री चेत्यर्थः। मृगशनी मृगशन्याविति उत्तरार्द्ध-पदम्। अत्र तिथिदेवतादिनक्षत्रयोन्यन्तानां सर्वेषां नामानि गुरुमुखादवगन्तव्यानि ॥ ८० ॥

यदेत्यादिना श्लोकेन ज्वरादिरोगारम्भे समयज्ञानेन रोगशान्तिसमय-ज्ञानोपायमुपदिशति। तत्र एतदुक्तं भवति यदा ज्वरादिरोगारम्भस्तदा यस्मिन्नक्षत्रे यावत्संख्याघटिकागतास्तत्संख्यैरहोभिर्वा तदर्द्धसंख्यैरहोभिर्वा रोगमुक्तिं जानीयादिति। अत्र सौम्येषु नक्षत्रेषु रोगारम्भश्चेत् प्रोक्तक्रमतो रोगशान्तिः। क्रूरेषु नक्षत्रेषु चेद् रोगिणो देहत्याग इति सम्प्रदायः॥ ८१ ॥

---

(१) गोखण्डी ।

आधारे पञ्च यन्त्राणि स्वाधिष्ठाने चतुष्टयम्।
प्रोक्तेषु भावयेत्तानि तावन्ति मणिपूरके ॥ ८२ ॥
अनाहते ततः पञ्च यन्त्राणि परिभावयेत्।
विशुद्धाख्ये च चत्वारि पञ्चाज्ञायामिति क्रमात् ॥८३॥
तत्तत्तिथिदिनेष्वेवं भावयेत् षोडशीं शिवाम्।
तत्तच्चक्रगताः सर्वा भावयेत् सर्वसम्पदे ॥८४॥
आधारादिषु चक्राणि भावयेदुक्तयोगतः।
नतु सर्वत्र सर्वाणि भावयेन्न कदाचन ॥८५॥
भावनायामशक्तानां तत्तद्यन्त्राद्बहिस्तथा।
प्रोक्तान्याधारपद्मानि कृत्वा तत्रार्चयेच्छिवाम् ॥८६॥
एवं दिनेषु वारेषु नक्षत्रेषु त्रिषु क्रमात्।
संपूज्य देवीमिष्टानि प्राप्नुयात् प्रोक्तवासरैः ॥८७॥

आधारेत्यादिभिः कदाचनेत्यन्तैश्चतुर्भिश्लोकैः प्रोक्तानां सप्तविंशतिसंख्यानां यन्त्राणां मूलाधारादिषु षट्स्वाधारेषु उक्तविभेदक्रमप्राप्तं यन्त्रं विभावयतः फलावाप्तिमुपदिशति। तत्र प्रोक्तेषु सप्तविंशतिसंख्येषु। तावन्ति चत्वारि इत्यर्थः। इति क्रमात् प्रथमयन्त्रादिक्रमतः। तत्तत्तिथिदिनेषु यन्त्रप्राप्तेषु। एतदुक्तं भवति प्रथमादीनां यन्त्राणां प्रोक्तसंख्याविभिन्नानां तत्तद्यन्त्रप्राप्ततिथिदिनेषु मूलाधारादिषु प्रतिदिनमेकैकस्य भावनमिति। षोड़शीं चित्रानित्यां शिवां ध्यायतः। नतु सर्वत्र सर्वाणि सर्वाधारेषु सर्वाणि यन्त्राणि स्वेच्छया प्रोक्तसंख्याविभागेन भावनीयानि। उक्त प्रथमादिविभेदक्रमतः प्रोक्तेषु प्रोक्तान्येव भावनीयानि ॥ ८५ ॥

भावनायामित्यादिना वासरैरित्यन्तेन श्लोकद्वयेनाधारेषु भावनायामशक्तानां बहिस्तत्तदाधारपद्मानि प्रागवत् कृत्वा तत्तन्मध्ये तत्तत्प्राप्तं यन्त्रमालिख्य तत्तत्तिथिवारनक्षत्रेषु देवीं समाराध्य प्रोक्तवासरैः प्रागुक्त सप्तविंशत्या दिनैः। (१) प्रोक्तानि फलान्यवाप्नुयादित्युपदिशति ॥ ८७ ॥

---

(१) प्रागुक्त त्रिसप्तत्यदिनैः।

वलिञ्च दद्यात्तेष्वेव वासरेषु यथाविधि ।
पञ्चाशन्मिथुनानाञ्च प्रोक्तचक्रेऽर्द्धरात्रके ॥८८॥
मध्याह्ने सन्ध्ययोश्चापि चक्रस्थानामपीश्वरि ।
मिथुनोक्तक्रमे शक्तिमन्त्रवच्चक्रगामिनाम् ॥८९॥
कूटानां मन्त्ररूपाणि प्रोक्तानि स्फुटमीश्वरि ।
तैस्तेषां तेषु कालेषु वलिं दद्यात्तथेरितैः ॥९०॥
देव्यास्त्वनुग्रहप्रोक्तनिवेद्यैः शिक्थकं महत् ।
विधाय तस्य मध्ये तु कृत्वा दीपं घृताप्लुतम् ॥९१॥
विधाय तत्तन्मन्त्रैस्तु विदध्यात्तान्यनुक्रमात् ।
प्रत्येकं देवतानां वा मिथुनानामथापि वा ॥९२॥
दद्यादपूपपनसमोचाघृतगुड़ान्वितम् ।
कुल्माषपायसान्नेन व्यञ्जनं छागमांसयुक् ॥९३॥
इत्थं कार्य्यस्य गुरुतालाघवापेक्षया दिनैः ।
साधयेत् सप्तभिः पञ्चान्मासान्मण्डलतोऽपि वा ॥९४॥
मिथुनानां वलिं दद्यात् प्रतिमासं गृहेऽर्चयेत् ।
प्रत्यब्दं वा गृहे मन्त्री जीवेदाद्यामहोदयः ॥९५॥

वलिमित्यादिभिर्नरा इत्यन्तैर्नवभिः श्लोकैर्देव्याः प्रागुक्तपञ्चाशन्मिथुनानाञ्च वलिदानप्रकारं तत्फलानि चोपदिशति । तत्र तेष्वेव वासरेषु प्रोक्तयन्त्रप्रयोगवासरेषु । अन्यदपि मङ्गलार्थं अमङ्गलप्रतिघातार्थञ्च नित्यमस्य पञ्चाशन्मिथुनवलिप्रदानं कुर्य्यादिति सम्प्रदायः । पञ्चाशन्मिथुनानां षोड़शपटलोक्तानां प्रोक्तचक्रे तत्रैवोक्ते । एतदुक्तं भवति षोड़शपटले अष्टनवतितमश्लोकोक्तचतुःषष्टिपदे चक्रे मध्यतश्चतुष्कोष्ठान्येकोकृत्य तत्र दिननित्यां साध्यगर्भामालिख्य वह्निरग्रादिप्रादक्षिण्यनिर्गमन घटिकाक्रमतो मि नानामर्चनवलिप्रदानादि कुर्य्यादिति । सन्ध्ययोः प्रातःसायन्तन्योः । चक्रस्थानां कूटविद्याशक्तीनां मूल (१) शक्तिसहितानां वलिं दद्यादित्यत्रान्वयः । ईश्वरीति देवीसम्बुद्धिः । शक्तिमन्त्रवत् मिथुनोक्त-

---

(१) भूत

एवं कालात्ममिथुनवलिदानेन पूजनात् ।
स्मरणात् कीर्त्तनात् सर्ववाञ्छितानाप्नुयुर्नराः ॥९६॥
मिथुनानां वलिद्रव्याण्याकर्णय महेश्वरि ।
यैस्तुष्टिं प्राप्य तान्याशु प्रयच्छन्त्यभिवाञ्छितम् ॥९७॥
दशानां पायसं दद्याद्दशानान्तु गुडोदनम् ।
पञ्चानां मुद्गभिन्नान्नं पञ्चानां दधिभक्तकम् ॥९८॥
दद्यादपूपं पञ्चानां पञ्चानां क्षीरशर्करे ।
पञ्चानां नारिकेलस्य फलक्षोदं गुडान्वितम् ॥९९॥
पञ्चानां सितभक्ताभ्यां मोचाफलमुदीरितम् ।
मिथुनार्चारतो नित्यं योऽसौ स्यान्मान्त्रिकाग्रणीः ॥१००॥

शक्तिमन्त्रवत् । चक्रगामिनां कूटानामित्यत्रान्वयः । एतदुक्तं भवति—पूर्वं पञ्चाशन्मिथुनशक्तिविद्यावदत्रोक्तयन्त्रगतविद्याकूटशक्तीनामपि प्रोक्ताभिः प्रत्येकं पञ्चदशाक्षराभिः कूटसञ्ज्ञिताभिर्विद्याभिः पूजनं वलिदानञ्च कुर्य्यादिति । ताः विद्या यथा प्रथमं वीजद्वयपूर्वं तत्तत्कूटमुच्चार्य्य ततो रूपिणीशक्तीत्युक्त्वा ततः समाचरीं वदेत् तेन पञ्चदशाक्षर्य्यः षट्सप्तत्यधिकपञ्चशतविद्याः सम्भवन्ति । तैर्मन्त्रैस्तेषु कालेषु प्रागुक्तसन्ध्यात्रयादिषु । ईरिते वक्ष्यमाणैर्देव्याश्चित्रानित्यायाः अनुग्रहप्रोक्तनैवेद्यैः षोडशे पटले नवतितमश्लोकोक्तपायसान्नगुडान्नभिन्नान्नहरिद्रान्नतिलान्नकेवलशुद्धान्नैरित्यर्थः । शिक्थकं पिण्डमित्यर्थः । प्रत्येकमित्यादिनैतदुक्तं भवति प्रधानदेवताया एव षड्भिः समेतैर्वा तस्यास्तत्परिवाराणामपि वा तस्यास्तत्परिवाराणां मिथुनानामपि युग्मस्य एकमेकं वा पृथक् पृथगिति वा वलिदाने पञ्चत्रयचतुष्टयमुक्तं भवतीति । अपूपादिद्रव्यनवकं पूर्वोक्तनिवेद्यद्रव्यसहितं भवति । तन्नामानि गुरुमुखादवगन्तव्याणि । अपि वा विकल्पे । वा विकल्पार्थः । स्मरणान्मिथुनानां कालरूपित्वानुसन्धानात् ॥९६॥

मिथुनानामित्यादिभिरग्रणीरित्यन्तैश्चतुर्भिः श्लोकैर्मिथुनवलिद्रव्याणि नित्यंदेयानि तद्दर्शनफलं चोपदिशति । तत्र वलिद्रव्याणि नित्यदेयानि प्रयोगदेयानि

अहङ्कारमयी व्याप्तिरिति सम्यक् समीरिता।
अस्या निष्फालनाच्चित्ते तत्तत्त्वं स्वात्मसात् कृतम् ॥१०१॥

इति नित्यातन्त्रे श्रीकादिमते एकविंशति-
पटलं परिपूर्णम्।

च। दधिभक्तकं दधिमिश्रमन्नमित्यर्थः। सितभक्ताभ्यां मोचाफलं शर्करा-मिलितान्नकदलीफलानीत्यर्थः। एतान्येव नित्यबलिप्रदाने च मिथुनानां द्रव्याणि। असौ अर्चकः ॥१००॥

इति षोडशनित्यातन्त्रे श्रीकादिमताख्यस्य परिपूर्णस्य तन्त्रस्य प्रपञ्चसारसिंह-
राजप्रकाशाभिधानेन सुभगानन्दनाथेन विरचितायां मनोरमाख्यायां
व्याख्यायां चित्रानित्याविद्याविधानप्रकाशनपरमेकविंशतितमं
पटलम् परिपूर्णं परामृष्टम् ॥ २१ ॥

ग्रन्थसंख्या—सप्तविंशतियन्त्राणि व्याख्याग्रन्थाः शतद्वयम्।
पादाधिकाद्युत्तराः सुरः पटले त्वेकविंशके ॥

द्वाविंशपटलम् ।

अथ षोड़शनित्यानां या प्रोक्ता बलिदेवता ।
सा विद्या कुरुकुल्लायाः पञ्चविंशाक्षरोदिता ॥ १ ॥
सैव त्रिखण्डा तत्रैव प्रोक्ता विद्या तु संख्यया ।
सप्तभिः प्रथमा प्रोक्ता त्रयोदशयुता पुरा ॥ २ ॥
तृतीया सा पञ्चविंशदक्षरा सकलेष्टदा ।
एवं सा त्रिभिरप्येतैर्विद्यारूपैरभीष्टदा ॥ ३ ॥
इक्षुसुराघृतदुग्धाब्धिमध्यगे नवरत्नके ।
द्वीपे तां ललितां नित्यविनोदानन्दितां यजेत् ॥ ४ ॥

पूर्वस्मिन्नेकविंशे पटले षोड़श्याश्चित्रानित्याया विधानमुपदिश्यानन्तरं सर्वासां नित्यानां बलिदेवतायाः स्वस्मात् स्वस्मात् अपृथग्भूतायाः कुरुकुल्लाया विधानमुपदिशति अथ षोड़शनित्येत्यादिना तदित्यन्तेन श्लोकशतरूपेण द्वाविंशेन पटलेन। तत्र अथ षोड़शेत्यादिभिरभीष्टदा इत्यन्तैस्त्रिभिः श्लोकैः कुरुकुल्लाविद्यायास्तृतीयपटलोक्तस्वरूपं त्रैविध्यं तेषां त्रयाणां खण्डानां (१) प्रत्येकं तत्रोक्तामक्षरसंख्यां तैर्देवताया वाञ्छादायित्वञ्चोपदिशति। तत्र पञ्चविंशाक्षरोदिता तृतीये पटले इति शेषः। तत्र पञ्चविंशाक्षरा प्रथमद्वितीयखण्डप्रकृतिरूपा तृतीयखण्डभूता मूलविद्येत्यर्थः। सैव पञ्चविंशाक्षरैव। त्रिखण्डा त्रिरूपभेदा। तत्रैव तृतीयपटल एव। तृतीया सा सा खण्डद्वयमूलभूता विद्या तृतीयखण्ड इत्यर्थः। सा कुरुकुल्ला ॥ ३ ॥

इक्ष्वित्यादिना तीरपालिकामित्यन्तेन अध्यर्द्ध श्लोकेन सर्वाङ्गिनित्याया ललितायाश्चतुर्थादिपटलत्रयप्रोक्तपूजाक्रमस्मारणेन अत्र अस्याः कुरुकुल्लायाः तदङ्गत्वमभिप्रैति। तत्र नित्यविनोदानन्दितां सङ्गीतादिभिः। तत्तीरेत्यादिना श्लोकपूर्वार्द्धेन प्रसङ्गतस्तस्या ललिताया अङ्गभूतामुपरितनपटलवक्ष्यमाणविधानमस्याः कुरुकुल्लायाः पूर्वमेवाभ्यर्चनीयत्वात् पञ्चमीं वाराहीं यजेदिति प्रस्तौति। तत्र तत्तीरे इक्षुसागरतीरे तस्य चतुर्णां प्रथमत्वात्। "इक्षुसागरवेलायां वाराहीमर्चयेत् ततः" इत्यागमान्तरोक्तत्वाच्च। तत्र तस्याः समवस्थानं दक्षिणपश्चिमकोणदिक् प्रदेशे ललिताभिमुखमिति सम्प्रदायः ॥ ४ ॥

---

(१) षोडशानां।

तत्तीरे पूजयेद्देवीं पञ्चमीं तीरपालिकाम् ।
तत्सागरेषु परितो रत्नपोतचरीं यजेत् ॥ ५ ॥
तदाज्ञया रत्नपोतं तन्नाम्नैव समर्चयेत् ।
वलिचक्रञ्च तेनैव तन्मध्ये च समर्चयेत् ॥ ६ ॥
पूर्वपश्चिमदिग्द्वारसंयुतं चतुरस्रकम् ।
कृत्वा तदन्तः पद्मञ्च साष्टपत्रं सकर्णिकम् ॥ ७ ॥
कर्णिकायां चारु कृत्वा नवयोनिं समर्चयेत् ।
षडङ्गं वालया कृत्वा तेनार्घ्यमपि साधयेत् ॥ ८ ॥९॥

तत्सागरेष्वित्यादिना समर्चयेदित्यन्तेनार्द्धाधिकेन श्लोकेनास्याः कुरुकुल्लायाः पूजाप्रस्तावपूर्वकं तत्र रत्नपोतवलिचक्रार्चनमुपदिशति। तत्र तत्सागरेषु पञ्चम्यधिष्ठित तत्तीरसागरादिषु । रत्नपोतचरीं कुरुकुल्लां । तत्र तदाज्ञया तीरपालिकायाः पञ्चम्याः समनुज्ञया सागरेषु तस्याः कुरुकुल्लायाः पूजनं समवस्थानमिक्षुसागरे उत्तरपश्चिमकोणे । रत्नपोतचरीमितुग्रतया साधकाभिमुखमिति सम्प्रदायः। तत्तु दक्षिणपश्चिमकोणे पञ्चम्याः समवस्थानात् । रत्नपोतं रत्ननिर्म्मितप्रवहणरूपं अद्यतनप्रवहणस्वरूपवदिति सम्प्रदायः। तन्नाम्नैव रत्नपोतनाम्नैव नमोऽन्तेन वक्ष्यमाणविसर्जनीयहृल्लेखापूर्वेण । यथा ऐंः रत्नपोताय नमः इति समर्चयेत् । वलिचक्रञ्च वक्ष्यमाणरूपं । तेनैव नाम्नैव प्राग्वन्नमोऽन्तेन विसर्जनीयशक्त्याद्येन । यथा क्लीः वलिचक्राय नमः इति समर्चयेत् । तन्मध्ये रत्नपोतमध्ये ॥ ६ ॥

पूर्वेत्यादिना समर्चयेदित्यन्तेनाध्यर्द्धेन श्लोकेन देव्याः कुरुकुल्लायाः नित्यसपर्य्याचक्रमुपदिशति। तत्र पूर्व्वपश्चिमदिग्द्वारसंयुतमित्यत्र शाखानिर्म्माणानुक्तावपि उत्तरत्र दक्षशाखादौतुग्रतया प्रतिद्वारं शाखाद्वयोपेतत्वं चतुरस्रस्योक्तमिति सम्प्रदायः। चारु यथामानं। एतदुक्तं भवति प्राक्पश्चिमतः सशाखाद्वयद्वारयुग्मं समचतुरस्रद्वयं कोणेषु दिक्षु च देवतास्थानचिह्नितं विधाय तन्मध्यस्थलद्वयोपेतमष्टदलं पद्मं कृत्वा तस्य कर्णिकायां नवयोनिचक्रं प्रागुक्तचतुस्त्रिपञ्च चतुरंशैः विधाय तन्नाममन्त्रेण तदर्चयेदिति ॥ ८ ॥

षडङ्गमित्यादिना श्लोकोत्तरार्द्धेन षडङ्गन्यासमर्घ्यसाधनञ्चोपदिशति। तत्र वालया कुलसुन्दरीविद्यया सजातिकयेति शेषः। तेन षडङ्गेन मूलविद्यया पञ्चविंशत्यक्षरया त्रिवारादद्योनमभ्यर्चयेच्च ॥ ९ ॥

त्रिखण्डमुद्रया मूलमन्त्रेणाद्येन चावहेत् ।
ध्यात्वेत्थं परिवारैस्तां देवीं गन्धादिभिः क्रमात् ॥ १० ॥
विकीर्णकुन्तलां नग्नां रक्तामानन्दविग्रहाम् ।
दधानां चिन्तयेद्बाणं चापपाशशृणीः करैः ॥ ११ ॥
तत् समानायुधाकारवर्णा देव्यस्तु वाह्यगाः ।
ऋतुस्नाताः स्फुरद्योन्यः सदानन्दारुणेक्षणाः ॥ १२ ॥
हृल्लेखया स्थापनादीनुपचारान् समाचरेत् ।
ततस्तदाज्ञया रोहे भ्रामिणीं द्राविणीं यजेत् ॥ १३ ॥
पश्चिमद्वारमारभ्य दक्षशाखादि पूजयेत् ।
सूर्य्यसोमं तिथिवारं योगर्क्षकरणान्यपि ॥ १४ ॥

त्रिखण्डेत्यादिभिरीक्षणा इत्यन्तैस्त्रिभिः श्लोकैरावाहनमुद्रामन्त्रपुरःसरं देव्याः सपरिवाराया नित्यसपर्य्याध्यानमुपदिशति । तत्र आद्येन समाक्षररूपेण मन्त्रेणेति शेषः । इत्थं वक्ष्यमाणरूपतः । गन्धादिभिर्यजेदिति शेषः । नग्नां दिगम्बरां देव्या दिगम्बरत्वकथनं सच्चि (च्चि) दानन्दमयत्वात् । अनावृतत्वमित्यपस्कारः सम्प्रदायार्थः । आनन्दविग्रहां सच्चिदानन्दरूपत्वात् । आयुधक्रमस्तु स्वदक्षिणाधरादित उत्तरान्तं अप्रादक्षिण्यात् । ऋतुस्नाताः स्फुरद्योन्यः एतद्देव्या अपि साधारणं तस्याः ऋतुस्नातत्वस्फुरद्योनित्वकथनं प्रागुक्तसच्चिदानन्दमयत्वनित्योल्लासातिशयत्वमिति सम्प्रदायः । अस्या ललिताङ्गत्वपूजनेऽप्येतदेव ध्यानं नतु तत्समानमिति च सम्प्रदायः ॥ १२ ॥

हृल्लेखेत्यादिभिः पूजयेदित्यन्तैरध्यर्द्धैः षड्भिः श्लोकैर्देव्या उपचारपूर्वं सावरणचतुष्टयनित्यसपर्य्याक्रममुपदिशति । तत्र हृल्लेखया सविसर्जनीययेति सम्प्रदायः । तया तत्तन्मन्त्रादिगतया अत्र सर्व्वशक्तीर्यजेदिति । स्थापनादीन् आदिशब्दः सन्निरोधादिविषयः । उपचारान् अर्घपाद्यादीन् । तदाज्ञया देव्याज्ञया । भ्रामिणीं द्राविणीं यजेत् । तयोरवस्थानन्तु रत्नपोतपूर्व्वपश्चिमकोण्योः । दक्षशाखादि देव्याः पश्चिमाभिमुखाया दक्षिणपार्श्वशाखादिप्रादक्षिण्याच्च । यक्षिणीस्त्वित्यत्र वहुवचनान्तं तासां षट्त्रिंशत् संख्याविशिष्टत्वात् । तन्मन्त्रो यथा । क्लीः यक्षिणीरूपिणीशक्तिपादुकाः पूजयामि इति । अन्यासां तत्तन्नामान्ते पादुकां

यक्षिणीश्च तथा तारां पूर्वद्वारस्य शाखयोः ।
व्योमवाय्वग्नितोयक्ष्मारूपिणीशक्तिसंयुतम् ॥ १४ ॥
शब्दस्पर्शञ्च रूपञ्च रसगन्धञ्च पूर्ववत् ।
प्राणान् बुद्धिं तथाशक्तिमष्टपत्रेषु पूजयेत् ॥ १५ ॥
तदन्तरष्टकोणेषु वाग्देव्यष्टकमर्चयेत् ।
ततो बाणान् धनुःपाशमङ्कुशञ्चाभितो यजेत् ॥ १६ ॥
मध्यत्रिकोणकोणेषु सेच्छाज्ञानक्रियात्मिकाः ।
शक्तीर्यष्ट्वाथ तन्मध्ये सम्बिदासनमर्चयेत् ॥ १७ ॥
ततस्तां पञ्चविंशार्णमूलमन्त्रेण पूजयेत् ।
ततस्तदाज्ञया पोतपरीतं द्वीपमागतः ॥ १८ ॥
पश्चिमं पुष्परागञ्च संप्राप्यावतरेत् क्रमात् ।
परीयमाणे दिक्ष्वेतानर्चयेत्तत्र तत्र वै ॥ १९ ॥
इक्षुक्षीराज्यतदुग्धाब्धीन् पश्चिमादि विलोमतः ।
नमोऽन्तैर्नामभिः पूर्व्वं पूजयेद्गन्धपुष्पकैः ॥ २० ॥

पूजयामीति क्लीं व्योमरूपिणीशब्दशक्तिपादुकां पूजयामीत्यादयः शब्दादीनां मन्त्रा बोद्धव्या इति। पूर्व्ववत् अग्रादिप्रादक्षिण्येन तथा रूपिणीशक्त्यादिसहितम् अर्चयेत्। अग्रादिप्रादक्षिण्येन अभितः प्राग्वन्मध्यत्रिकोणाद्बहिरभितस्तत्तद्भुजान्तिकेष्वप्रादक्षिण्येन यद्वा प्राग्वत् क्रमात्तन्मध्ये त्रिकोणमध्ये। सम्बिदासनमिति देवताया भर्त्तृभूतं सम्बिदात्मकं पुरुषमिति सम्प्रदायः। तत्र देवतास्थानप्रकारस्त्वावरणशक्तीनामवस्थानप्रकारस्य गुरुमुखादेवावगन्तव्यः। तन्मन्त्रो यथा क्लीं सम्बिदासनाय नमः इति। पञ्चविंशार्णमूलमन्त्रेण खण्डत्रयप्रकृतिभूतेन तृतीयेनेत्यर्थः ॥ १८ ॥

तत इत्यादिना पुष्पकैरित्यन्तेनार्द्धाधिकेन श्लोकद्वयेन देव्याः प्रधानदेवतारूपललिताङ्गत्वेन स्थितिमिक्ष्वादिसागरपूजाञ्चोपदिशति। तत्र तदाज्ञया कुरुकुल्लाज्ञया परीतं भवेदिति शेषः। पश्चिमं पुष्परागमिति ललितादेव्या नित्यपूजापटलोक्तनवरत्नद्वीपाग्रखण्डस्य पुष्परागमयत्वात् तत् स्मारयति। परीयमाणे परितो

नवरत्नमयं द्वीपमित्यादि प्रागुदीरितम् ।
एवं समर्चितं देव्या ललितायाः प्रियङ्करम् ॥ २१ ॥
एवं देवी पूजयितुः शीघ्रं बहु मनीषितम् ।
प्रसीदति यतस्तस्मात् पूजयेदेवमीश्वरि ॥ २२ ॥
देवीनां कुरुकुल्लान्तु तोयादुपरि पूजयेत् ।
पञ्चविंशार्णमूलेन पूजान्ते परमेश्वरि ॥ २३ ॥
देव्या बलिः समाख्यातस्ताराशक्तेस्तु विद्यया ।
तां शृणु त्वं प्रिये वच्मि ताराविद्यां दशाक्षरीम् ॥ २४ ॥
भूः स्वेन मरुता युक्तो रयो दाहस्वरान्वितः ।
रयो धरान्वितः पश्चाद्रययुग्मं मरुत्युतम् ॥ २५ ॥
एतत्तृतीयं षष्ठं स्याच्चतुर्थं सप्तमं भवेत् ।
षष्ठं तदष्टमं विद्यात् हृदम्बुमरुदन्वितम् ॥ २६ ॥

भ्राम्यमाणे तत्र तत्र प्रदेशे इति शेषः । पश्चिमादि विलोमतः प्रोक्तक्रमेण इक्षुसागरादीन् नमोऽन्तैर्नामभिः पूर्वं पूर्वमिति बीजद्वयं स्मारयति बीजद्वयं नामभिरादौ संयोज्य तैरित्यर्थः । तन्मन्त्रा यथा क्लीं श्रीं इक्षुसागराय नमः इत्यादयः ॥ २० ॥

नवरत्नमयमित्यादिना ईश्वरीत्यन्तेन श्लोकद्वयेन ललिताया देव्याः समाराधन विशेषे फलविशेषमुपदिशति । तत्र प्रागुदीरितं ललितानित्यपूजनोपदेशे प्रोक्तरूपतः । एवं प्राग्वत् । प्रसीदति प्रयच्छति देवी इति शेषः । ईश्वरीति देवीसम्बुद्धिः ॥ २२ ॥

देवीनामित्यादिना श्लोकेन कुरुकुल्लाया देव्याः स्वतन्त्रपूजाक्रममुपदिशति ॥२३॥

देव्या इत्यादिभिः परमेश्वरीत्यन्तैश्चतुर्भिः श्लोकैर्देव्याः कुरुकुल्लायाः स्वतन्त्रनित्यपूजायां बलिं तद्विद्यां दशाक्षरीं तथा बलिदानञ्चोपदिशति । तत्र देव्याः कुरुकुल्लायाः भूः स्वेन युक्तेति शेषः ॐ इति । मरुता युक्तो रयः ता इति । दाहस्वरान्वितः रे इति । रयो धरान्वितः तु इति । रययुग्मं मरुद्-युतं ता इति । एतत्तृतीयं षष्ठं स्यात् । एतस्या एव विद्यायाः रे इति तृतीय-

हंसश्च मरुता युक्तः प्रोक्ता विद्या दशाक्षरी ।
अनयास्या वलिं दद्याद्विद्यया परमेश्वरि ॥ २७ ॥
ध्यानं देव्याः शृणु प्राज्ञे समस्तापन्निकृन्तनम् ।
अस्यास्तोयेषु सर्व्वत्र वाधो न भवति स्मृतेः ॥ २८ ॥
श्यामवर्णां त्रिनयनां द्विभुजां वरपङ्कजे ।
दधानां वहुवर्णाभिर्व्वहुरूपाभिरावृताम् ॥ २९ ॥
शक्तिभिः स्मेरवदनां रत्नमौक्तिकभूषणाम् ।
रत्नपादुकयोः न्यस्तपदाम्बुजयुगां स्मरेत् ॥ ३० ॥
होमं कुर्य्यान्नित्यशस्तु घृताक्तै रक्तपुष्पकैः ।
सुगन्धिभिः सितैः पुष्पै रन्नाज्याभ्यां घृतेन वा ३१ ॥
प्राग्वद्व्रतयुतो विद्यां पञ्चविंशति लक्षकम् ।
जपित्वा पूजयेत् सन्ध्यास्वथ तर्पणहोमकम् ॥ ३२ ॥

मक्षरमेवास्याः षष्ठमक्षरं स्यादित्यर्थः। चतुर्थं सप्तमं। अस्या एव विद्यायाश्चतुर्थं तुकाराक्षरमेवास्याः सप्तममक्षरं भवेदित्यर्थः। षष्ठं तदष्टमं। अस्या एव विद्यायाः षष्टं रेफं रे इत्यक्षरमेवस्या अष्टममक्षरं विद्यात् जानीयादित्यर्थः। हृदम्बुमरुदन्वितं स्वा इति नवममक्षरं। हंसश्च मरुता युक्तः हा इति दशममक्षरं भवति। अनया प्रोक्तया दशाक्षर्य्या अस्याः कुरुकुल्लायाः वलिम् अतएव विद्यया। ताराशक्तेः सर्व्वपूजादौ षोड़शार्णेन वलिरिति सम्प्रदायः। परमेश्वरीति देवीसम्बुद्धिः ॥ २७ ॥

ध्यानमित्यादिभिः स्मरेदित्यन्तैस्त्रिभिः श्लोकैर्वलिदेवतायाः ताराशक्तेर्वलिसमयध्यानमुपदिशति। तत्र अस्यास्ताराशक्तेः यस्मात् कारणात् स्मृतेः वक्ष्यमाणध्यानादित्यर्थः। वरपङ्कजे वामदक्षिणाभ्यां। शक्तिभिः आवृतामिति पूर्व्वेणान्वयः। न्यस्तपादाम्बुजयुगां वलिग्रहणार्थमभिमुखमायान्तीमित्यर्थः ॥ ३० ॥

होममित्यादिना श्लोकेन देव्याः कुरुकुल्लाया नित्यहोमद्रव्याण्युपदिशति। तत्र वा विकल्पे ॥ ३१ ॥

प्राग्वदित्यादिना क्रियामित्यन्तेनार्द्धेनैकेन श्लोकेन पञ्चविंशत्यर्णाया मूल-

कुर्य्यान्नित्योदितेष्वन्यतमेन हवनक्रियाम् ।
एवं संसिद्धविद्यस्तु नित्यार्च्चानिरतस्तथा ॥ ३३ ॥
प्रयोगानाचरेद्भक्त्या काम्यान् प्रोक्तक्रमेण वै ।
होमेन पूजया यन्त्रभावनेन च तान् शृणु ॥ ३४ ॥
घृताक्तैः सर्षपैर्होमाद्वशयेद्वनिताजनम् ।
सर्षपस्नेहसंसिक्तैर्मरिचैरानयेच्च ताः ॥ ३५ ॥
तैलाक्तैस्तु तिलैर्होमान्मध्यरात्रे यथाविधि ।
नारीनरनृपानन्यान् वशयेद् यावदायुषम् ॥ ३६ ॥
अजाघृताक्तैर्बन्धूककुसुमैर्मध्यरात्रकी ।
हवनाद्वनिताः सर्व्वा मोहयेत् प्रेसकौतुकैः ॥ ३७ ॥
चौराक्तैर्मल्लिकापुष्पैर्हवनाद्ब्राह्मणान्नृपान् ।
वशयेच्छतपत्रैश्च तथा विचकिलैः शुभैः ॥ ३८ ॥
सवत्ससितगोदुग्धसमेतैर्नारिकेलजैः ।
फलखोदैः सितयुतैर्हवनात् स्वर्गमाप्नुयात् ॥ ३९ ॥
नारिकेलफलखोदैर्गुड़चौद्रघृताहुतैः ।
प्रागुक्तकालतो वित्तनिचयं समवाप्नुयात् ॥ ४० ॥
कदलीफलहोमेन स्याद्राद्योऽम्बुजहोमतः ।
कह्लारहोमतोऽभीष्टं लभते कुमुदद्वयैः ॥ ४१ ॥

विद्यायाः पुरश्चरणमुपदिशति । तत्र व्रतं संकल्पः । विद्यां पञ्चविंशत्यक्षरां नित्योदितेष्वन्यतमेन नित्यहोमोक्तेषु रक्तपुष्पादिष्वन्यतमेन ॥ ३२ ॥

एवमित्यादिना शृण्वित्यन्तेनार्द्धाधिकेनैकेन श्लोकेन कृतपुरश्चरणस्यैव प्रयोगयोग्यतां प्रयोगप्रकारांश्चोपदिशति । तत्र नित्यार्च्चानिरतः पुरश्चरणानन्तरमपि । तान् प्रयोगान् ॥ ३४ ॥

घृतेत्यादिभिः कुमुदद्वयैरित्यन्तैः सप्तभिः श्लोकैः चतुर्द्दशभिर्द्रव्यैर्होमात् नानाफलप्राप्तिमुपदिशति । तत्र ता वनिताः । तैलाक्तैस्तिलस्नेहाक्तैः । अन्यान्

उत्पलैः पूजयेद्देवि समस्तापद्विमुक्तये।
पद्मैः सितैर्लोहितैश्च पूजयेदिन्दिराप्तये ॥ ४२ ॥
कुमुदाभ्यां यजेद्वित्तलाभकामनया तथा।
जपाव॰ कुसुमैस्तथा दाड़िमजैरपि ॥ ४३ ॥
सौगन्धिकैर्विचकिलैः कुटजैः शतपत्रकैः।
पुन्नागजैः पाटलैश्च चम्पकोत्थैर्यजेच्छिवे ॥ ४४ ॥
सप्तभिः सप्तवारेषु भास्करादिषु पूजयेत्।
प्रोक्तकालेषु वित्ताढ्यो धराधान्यांशुकादिमान् ॥ ४५ ॥
चन्दनैरर्च्चयेन्नित्यं समस्तमपि वाञ्छितम्।
लभते प्रोक्तकालेन तथा कालागुरुद्रवैः ॥ ४६ ॥
कुङ्कुमैर्नित्यशः पूजां कुर्य्यात् सौभाग्यसिद्धये।
कर्पूरैरायुषः सिद्धै वश्यस्त्रीधनसिद्धये ॥ ४७ ॥
मृगस्वेदमदाभ्याञ्च पूजयेन्मासमात्रकम्।
कन्दर्पसमसौभाग्यो वनितासु नरो भवेत् ॥ ४८ ॥
एलालवङ्गकक्कोलजातिभिर्नित्यशो यजेत्।
अब्दमात्रं ततो लोके विश्रुतः स्यात् स वैभवैः ॥ ४९ ॥
कर्पूरशकलैः पूजा सर्व्वाभीष्टप्रदा भवेत्।
पूजितैस्तैस्तु जगधैः स्यान्नरो यात्यखिलप्रियः ॥ ५० ॥

सामन्तादीनपि। प्रेमकौतुकैः प्रणयोत्कण्ठाभिः। ब्राह्मणान् विप्रान्। वशयेदित्यन्वयः। तथा विकल्पं। सितयुतः शर्करासंमिलितः। प्रागुक्तकालतः मण्डलादितः। आद्यः अम्बुजकह्लारयोरपि विषयः। कुमुदद्वयैः रक्तसितैः ॥ ४१ ॥

उत्पलैरित्यादिभिः प्रिय इत्यन्तैर्नवभिः श्लोकैर्नानाद्रव्यैः पूजनैर्नानाफलप्राप्तिमुपदिशति। तत्र सितैः पद्मैरित्यन्वयः। लोहितैस्तद्वत् कुमुदाभ्यां प्राग्वज्जपादिभिरपि श्रीलाभाय। सौगन्धिकैः कह्लारैः सप्तभिः सौगन्धिकादिभिः। तथा समस्ताभीष्टलाभ इत्यर्थः। वश्यस्त्रीधनसिद्धये कर्पूरैरित्य-

वृत्तत्रयं तथाष्टारमब्जं तन्मध्यतस्तथा।
नवयोनिं विधायात्र मध्ये मायां ससाध्यकाम् ॥ ५१ ॥
आलिख्याष्टसु कोणेषु मन्त्रार्णाष्टकमालिखेत्।
बहिर्दलेष्वपि तथा लिखेद्द्विद्विक्रमेण वै ॥ ५२ ॥
वह्निर्मातृकया मायास्वगया प्रतिलोमया।
क्रमेण चाभिसंवेष्ट्य तेन यन्त्रेण साधयेत् ॥ ५३ ॥
समस्तवाञ्छितं पूजाधारणस्थापनादिभिः।
यन्त्रं रोचनयालिख्य भूर्जे वा क्षौमखण्डके ॥५४ ॥

न्वयः। मृगखेदमदाभ्यां मृगखेदेन मृगमदेन चेत्यर्थः। ततः यजनतः। तैः कर्पूरादिभिः। जग्धैर्भक्षितैः ॥ ५० ॥

वृत्तत्रयमित्यादिभिः स्थापनादिभिरित्यन्तैरध्यर्द्धैस्त्रिभिः श्लोकैः पञ्चविंशत्यक्षरया तृतीयया मूलविद्यया यन्त्रनिर्माणोपदेशं तद्विनियोगप्रकारप्रस्तावं च करोति। तत्र तन्मध्यतः अष्टदलाब्जमध्यतः। तथा कुलसुन्दरीपटलोक्तप्रक्रियया। अत्र मध्ये सर्वमध्ययोनिमध्ये। मायां प्राग्वत् हृल्लेखां सविसर्जनीयां पञ्चविंशत्यक्षरविद्यायामेकादशाक्षरभूतां। अष्टसु कोणेषु मध्यकोणविधुरेषु मन्त्रार्णाष्टकं प्रथमद्वितीयखण्डप्रकृतिभूतपञ्चविंशत्यक्षरमूलविद्याक्षरपञ्चविंशकेषु आदितोऽक्षराष्टकमित्यर्थः। आलिखेत् अग्रात् प्रादक्षिण्यमिति सम्प्रदायः। वह्निः नवयोनेः। तथा प्रागुक्तक्रमसूचकः। द्विद्विक्रमेण प्रतिदलञ्च योनिलिखित विद्याक्षरनवकादुपरितनानि षोड़शाक्षराणीति शेषः। वह्निः अष्टपत्रपद्माद्बहिर्गतवृत्तत्रयान्तरालवीथीद्वये। मायया स्वगया विसर्जनीययुक्तया विन्दुयुक्तया च। क्रमेण अनुलोमेन च। स्थापनादिभिरित्यत्रादिशब्दोऽभिषेकादिविषयः। यन्त्रविरचनाक्रमो यथा—अभीष्टमानभ्रमतोऽन्तर्वहिर्विभागेन वृत्तत्रयं समध्यसूत्रं निष्पाद्य तत्राष्टदलं पद्मं विधाय तत्कर्णिकायां प्राग्वत् नवयोनिचक्रं विधाय तत्र सर्वमध्यस्थयोनिमध्ये प्रथमद्वितीयखण्डप्रकृतिभूतपञ्चविंशाक्षरतृतीयमूल विद्यायामेकादशाक्षरभूतां सविसर्जनीयां हृल्लेखां साधकादित्रययुक्तामालिख्य वाह्यकोणेष्वष्टस्वग्रादिप्रादक्षिण्यात्तन्मूलविद्याक्षरैरष्वादितोऽष्टौ संलिख्य तद्बहिरष्टदलेषु प्रागुक्तक्रमात् सर्वमध्यलिखितहृल्लेखाविधुर शिष्टाक्षरषोड़शकं प्रतिदलं द्विद्व्यक्षरं क्रमात् समालिख्य तद्वाह्यगतवृत्तत्रयान्तरालवीथीद्वये

गुलिकीकृत्य सिक्थस्य मध्यगं तद्विधाय तु ।
तापयेद्रात्रिषु दिनैः प्रागुक्तैः स्त्रियमानयेत् ॥ ५५ ॥
दरदेन विलिख्यैतत् पटे वा फलकोदरे ।
तत्र देवीं समावाह्य पूजयेत्तैर्दिनैर्भवेत् ॥ ५६ ॥
वशे त्रिभुवनं सर्व्वं नरनारीनृपादिकम् ।
गजवाजितरक्षादितिर्य्यग्जातीरपि ध्रुवम् ॥ ५७ ॥
तद्यन्त्रं सिन्धुतीरे वा नदीतीरेऽथवा लिखेत् ।
गौरक्षीरेण समावाह्य देवीं तत्रैव पूजयेत् ॥ ५८ ॥
समस्तरोगदुःखार्त्तिशान्तिः स्यादुदितैर्दिनैः ।
लाभाश्च पूजनात्तत्र पशुदासीधनादिनाम् ॥ ५९ ॥
तद्यन्त्रं चन्दनैः कृत्वा पीठे तद्दिनपूजनात् ।
पुत्रपौत्रकलत्राद्याधनधान्यादिमान् भवेत् ॥ ६० ॥
तद्यन्त्रं हेमरूप्ये वा भूर्जे वालिख्य धारणात् ।
समस्तरोगदुःखार्त्तिरहितो वर्द्धते सुखी ॥ ६१ ॥

अन्तर्वीथ्यां मातृकया विसर्जनीययुक्तया प्रतिलोमया प्रागवत् संवेष्ट्य तद्बाह्यवीथ्या-मनुलोमया अनया विन्दुयुक्तया च तथा प्रागवत् संवेष्ट्य वक्ष्यमाणपूजादि-क्रमेण विनियोगात् सर्वफलसिद्धिरिति ॥ ५४ ॥

यन्त्रमित्यादिभिः सुखी इत्यन्तैरर्द्धैः सप्तभिः श्लोकैस्तस्य यन्त्रस्य प्रयोगपञ्चकमुपदिशति । तत्र यन्त्रं प्रोक्तं । आलिख्येति पदच्छेदो वा विकल्पे । सिक्थस्य मधूच्छिष्टस्य । गुलिकीकृत्य यन्त्रं । प्रागुक्तैर्मण्डलादिभिः । दरदेन प्रागवत् । एतद् यन्त्रं । वा विकल्पार्थः । तत्र यन्त्रमध्ये पूजयेन्नित्यक्रमतः । तैः प्रागवत् वशे भवेदिति पूर्वेण सम्बन्धः । तरक्षः व्याघ्रः तिर्य्यग्जातीश्चतुष्पदी जातीः वशयेदिति शेषः । सिन्धुतीरे समुद्रतीरे । वा विकल्पार्थः । अथवेति च तद्वत् आलिखेत् । तत्र तत्र सुसमे भूतले इति शेषः । तत्र यन्त्रे पूजयेत् प्रागवत् । उदितैः प्रागवत् तत्र पूजनादित्यन्वयः । तत्रेति सिन्धुतीरादिविषयः ।

प्राक्प्रत्यगुदक्चिणोदक्क सूत्रषट्कनिपातनात् ।
कोष्ठेषु पञ्चविंशत्सु त्रीणि कोणेषु मार्जयेत् ॥ ६२ ॥
कोष्ठैर्व्वज्रं ततः शेषैस्त्रयोदशभिरीरितम् ।
तन्मध्ये शक्तिमायास्थामालिख्याख्यां ततोऽभितः ॥ ६३ ॥
लिखेद्विद्यां ततस्तस्मिन् पूजयेदर्द्धरात्रके ।
वाञ्छितां वनितां मानकुललज्जातिलङ्घिनीम् ॥ ६४ ॥
दृणराजदले कृत्वा यन्त्रं सर्षपरिङ्गुभिः ।
पट्टशुण्ठीमागधिकामरिचार्कपयोयुतम् ॥ ६५ ॥
निशासु सिक्थगं दीपवह्नौ सन्तापयेज्जयम् ।
विद्यां त्रयोदशार्णान्तु तद्दिग्वक्त्रो दिनैः स्त्रियम ॥ ६६ ॥

धनादीनां लाभाश्चेति चान्वयः । आज्ञाचरा वलालंघनीयवचनतः । वाद्वयं विकल्पार्थः ॥ ६१ ॥

प्राक्प्रत्यगित्यादिभिः सन्निभा इत्यन्तैर्दशभिः श्लोकैस्त्रयोदशाक्षरया द्वितीयया मूलविद्यया कोष्ठवज्रयन्त्रनिर्म्माणं तेन यन्त्रेण प्रयोगचतुष्टयञ्चोपदिशति । तत्र त्रीणि प्रतिकोणमिति शेषः । शेषैः कोष्ठैस्त्रयोदशभिरित्यत्रान्वयः । तन्मध्ये यन्त्रस्य सर्वमध्यकोष्ठे । शक्तिमायास्थां शक्तिरिति विसर्जनीय हृल्लेखाया ईकारस्यापि नाम अत्र सम्प्रदायात् प्रकरणाच्च विसर्जनीयस्य नाम मायेति च पूर्वोक्तानां नाम अत्र प्राग्वत् हृल्लेखाया मायेति नाम तेन विद्याया-मेकादशाक्षरभूतविसर्जनीयहृल्लेखास्थं यथा भवति तथा इत्यर्थः । आख्यां साधकादीनां । ततः मध्यकोष्ठतः वहिरिति शेषः । विद्यां सशक्तिहृल्लेखाविधुरां द्वादशाक्षरां । तस्मिन् यन्त्रे पूजयेद्देवीमिति शेषः । यन्त्रविरचनाक्रमो यथा— प्राक्प्रत्यगुदक्चिणोदक्क समान्तरालानि षटसूत्राण्यास्फाल्य पञ्चविंशतिकोष्ठानि निष्पाद्य तेषु कोष्ठेषु प्रतिकोणं प्रतिकोणं चतुर्षु कोणेषु त्रीणि त्रीणि कोष्ठानि सम्भूय द्वादशकोष्ठानि मध्ये वज्रकपं यथा भवेत्तथा मार्ज-यित्वा शिष्टकोष्ठत्रयोदशके सर्वमध्यकोष्ठमध्ये त्रयोदशाक्षरद्वितीयमूलविद्या-क्षरत्रयोदशके एकादशाक्षरभूतां सविसर्जनीयां हृल्लेखां प्राग्वत्

आकर्षयेन्नवागच्छेत्तत्र कामज्वराकुलैः ।
अवस्थाभिश्च दशभिर्मृतिमेति सुनिश्चितम् ॥ ६७ ॥
भूर्जे तालदले वा तदालिख्य स्पष्टविग्रहम् ।
मधूच्छिष्टप्रतिकृतौ ऋजु तं तापयेत्तथा ॥ ६८ ॥
नरनारीनृपश्चान्यं प्राणिनां स्त्रं हविह्वलाम् ।
करोति यावद्देहान्तं ते प्रतीपा लपन्ति च ॥ ६९ ॥
कज्जलैर्यन्त्रमालिख्य भूर्जे चौमे सिते(ऽ)थवा ।
जपित्वा धारयेत् सर्वरोगदुःखार्त्तिनाशनम् ॥ ७० ॥
गैरिकैश्चन्दनोपेतैरालिख्य विमलाम्बरे ।
तदा स्त्रियः शयानस्य वैरिण्यो दाससन्निभाः ॥ ७१ ॥
वृत्तद्वयान्तराकृत्वा षट्कोणं तस्य मध्यतः ।
भूः स्वगर्भगतं नाम विलिख्यास्त्रिषु षट्स्वपि ॥ ७२ ॥

साधकादित्रयाख्यायुक्तामालिख्य तदधःपंक्तिकोष्ठमध्यत्रिकमध्यकोष्ठमारभ्य युक्तक्रमं स्वप्रादक्षिण्यनिर्गमनगत्या शिष्टकोष्ठद्वादशके मध्यकोष्ठलिखितसविसर्जनीयक्षकारस्वाविधुरं द्वितीयमूलविद्याक्षरद्वादशकमालिख्य तत्र पूजादिभिर्वक्ष्यमाणैः प्रयोगैर्वक्ष्यमाणफलसिद्धिरिति । तृणराजदले तालपत्र इत्यर्थः । यन्त्रं प्रोक्तं । पटुलवणं मागधिका पिप्पली सिक्थगं प्राग्वत् । दीपवह्नौ दीपरूपाग्नौ । तद्दिग्वक्त्रः साध्याशाभिमुखः । दिनैर्मण्डलादिभिः । नचागच्छेत् साध्यापदिति शेषः । तत्र यन्त्रे स्थिता अवस्थाभिश्च दशभिः नयनप्रीत्यादिभिर्मरणादिभिः । मृतिमिति दशमावस्थास्वरूपं । वा विकल्पे । तद् यन्त्रं । मधूच्छिष्टैः प्रतिकृतैः साध्यायाः । तन्निर्माणमेकत्रिंशे पटले वक्ष्यमाणांशकानुगुणतः । तथा विद्याजपसहितं दीपाग्नौ प्रोक्तदिनादित्यर्थः । अन्यशब्दः सामन्तादिविषयः । ते प्राणिनः । प्रतीपाः प्रतिकूलाः । कज्जलैर्मसीभिः । सितं चौमविशेषणमेतत् । अथवेति विकल्पार्थः । जपित्वा प्राणप्रतिष्ठादिसहितं मूलविद्याम् । आलिख्य यन्त्रमिति शेषः । धारयेत् तद्यन्त्रसहिताम्बरमितिशेष. ॥ ७१ ॥

वृत्तद्वयेत्यादिभिर्वह्निरित्यन्तैर्दशभिः श्लोकैः सप्ताक्षरया प्रथमया मूलविद्यया यन्त्रनिर्माणक्रमं तेन यन्त्रेण प्रयोगकल्पोपदिशति । तत्र तस्य षट्कोणस्य

षड़क्षराणि विलिखेत् सप्ताक्षर्य्याः क्रमेण वै ।
यन्त्रमेतत्तालपत्रे भूर्जे क्षौमेऽर्कपत्रके ॥ ७३ ॥
प्रजप्य विद्यामयुतं वल्मीके निक्षिपेच्च तत् ।
तत्र स्थिता ये भुजगाः पलायन्तेऽथ तद्दिने ॥ ७४ ॥
तदूर्म्मिकादौ संलिख्य संजप्याभ्यर्च्य कुत्रचित् ।
विधाय नित्यशः पूजासमेते रक्षतो गृहे ॥ ७५ ॥
भूतप्रेतपिशाचापस्मारवेतालराक्षसाः ।
यक्षगन्धर्वभुजगवृश्चिकाद्या न तत्र वै ॥ ७६ ॥
तन्निक्षिप्ता कुम्भसलिले जपित्वा विद्ययानया ।
सहस्रवारं सलिलैरासेकः क्ष्वेड़नाशनः ॥ ७७ ॥
तत्पीतं जठरे प्राप्तमशेषं नाशयेद्विषम् ।
देहगं परमेशानि त्रिविधं भीषणात्मकम् ॥ ७८ ॥

भूः स्वगर्भगतं भूरिति ओकारः स्वमिति विन्दुः प्रथममूलविद्यादिवर्णभूतसविन्दुकत्रयोदशस्वरगर्भगतमित्यर्थः। नाम प्राग्वत्। षड़क्षराणि मध्यलिखित प्रथमाक्षरमूलप्रणवविधुराणि सप्ताक्षर्य्या मूलविद्यायाः क्रमेण अग्रादिप्रादक्षिण्यरूपेण एतस्मिन्खल्वेति शेषः। अथवेत्यध्याहार्य्यं। विद्यां सप्ताक्षरीं। तद्यन्त्रं। तद्दिने निक्षेपदिने। यन्त्रस्यायं विरचनाक्रमः—यथा अभीष्टमानभ्रमणेनान्तर्वहिर्विभागतो वृत्तद्वयं विधाय तत्रान्तर्वृत्तमध्ये प्राग्वत् षट्कोणं विधाय तत् षट्कोणमध्ये प्रथमभूतसप्ताक्षरमूलविद्याद्यक्षरभूतं प्रणवं प्राग्वत् साध्यगर्भमालिख्य वहिःपटसु कोणेषु अग्रादिप्रादक्षिण्येन मध्यलिखितप्रणवविधुराणि मूलविद्यायाः सप्ताक्षर्य्याः (? षड़क्षर्य्याः) षड़क्षराण्यालिखेत्। एवमेतद्यन्त्रं भूर्जादिष्वन्यतमे लिखित्वा सप्राणप्रतिष्ठं सप्ताक्षरीविद्यामयुतं जपित्वा तस्य यन्त्रस्य वल्मीकनिक्षेपणात्तत्रस्थाः सर्पाः तद्दिन एवोच्चाटिता भवन्तीति। तद्यन्त्रं ऊर्म्मिकादौ ऊर्म्मिकेत्यङ्गुलीयकम् आदौ शब्दो वलयाङ्गदाद्याभरणविषयः। रक्षतः पुरुषस्य। वृश्चिकाद्याः आद्यशब्दो लूतामूषकादिविषयः। तत्र स्थापितगृहविशेषणम्। तत् ऊर्म्मिकादिलिखितं यन्त्रम्। अनया प्रथमया सप्तवर्णया आसेकः अभिषेकः। क्ष्वेड़नाशनः सर्व्वविषापहरः। तद्यन्त्राधिवासिताभिरद्भिः सेकः

तद्विलिख्य नखाग्रेण नारिकेलदले स्मरन् ।
तद्रूपं फणिनं विद्याजपपूर्व्वं नखादिना ॥ ७९ ॥
पीड़नात् पाटनाद्रोगी पीड़ितः पाटितो भवेत् ।
एवं सर्व्वं त्रिप्रकारं गरलं नाशयेदिदम् ॥ ८० ॥
वालुकासु समालिख्य यन्त्रमभ्यर्च्च्य देवताम् ।
तत्र तैर्वेष्टयेत् सप्त भोगिनं न व्रजेद्बहिः ॥ ८१ ॥
अनावृत्तानि विद्यायामक्षराणि त्रयोदश ।
तैः षोड़शस्वरोपेतैः संख्याष्टौ च शतद्वयम् ॥ ८२ ॥

देहगमिति विषविशेषणं त्रिविधं प्रागवत्तत्स्थावरजङ्गमकृत्रिमात्मकम् । एतदुक्तं भवति यन्त्राभिवासिताभिजप्तं जलं पीतं जठरगतविषं देहगतं त्रिविधञ्च नाशयेदिति । तद् यन्त्रं । तद्रूपं यन्त्रं लिखितनालिकेरपत्ररूपं स्मरन्नित्यत्रान्वयः । पीड़ितं पाटितमिति दिव्यत्वादङ्गीकरणीयं यन्त्रपीड़नात् पाटनात् पीड़ितः पाटितश्चेत्यर्थं । एवमुक्तरूपतः । त्रिप्रकारं । प्रागवत् इदं यन्त्र वालुकासु सिकतासु । यन्त्रं प्रोक्तम् तत्र यन्त्रे । तैः ताभिरित्यर्थः । वालुकाविशेषणत्वात् । अत्रापि दिव्यत्वादचिन्त्यं व्रजेत् । प्रबुद्धोपि भोगी वह्निः वालुकावेष्टनात् ॥ ८१ ॥

अनावृत्तानीत्यादिना महेश्वरीत्यन्तेन श्लोकद्वयेन पञ्चविंशाक्षरायां खण्डद्वयप्रकृतिभूतायां तृतीयायां मूलविद्यायां प्रागवदपुनरुक्तैस्त्रयोदशभिरक्षरैः स्वरप्रसारणादष्टोत्तरद्विशतसंख्यैस्तैर्यन्त्राष्टकमुपदिशति । तत्र विद्यायां सर्व्वप्रकृतिभूतायां पञ्चविंशाक्षरायां मूलविद्यायां त्रयोदश तानि तु ककार उकार रेफ लकार यकार ओकार हकार सकार वकार जकार नकार शकाराक्षराणि । अत्रामस्तृतस्वरग्रहणेऽपि प्रागुक्तप्रयोजकातिलङ्घनेन संयुक्तस्यापि स्वरस्य ग्रहणे त्रयोदशेतुग्रक्तिप्रावल्यात् तयोरक्षरयोरनावृत्तत्वमस्त्येव । तैः अनावृत्ताक्षरैः । तानि अष्टोत्तरद्विशतसंख्यान्यक्षराणि । पूर्व्वाद्ययन्त्रे पूर्व्वोक्तेषु यन्त्रेष्वाद्ययन्त्रे । अस्मिन्नेव पटले पूर्व्वत्र वृत्तत्रयमित्याद्येकपञ्चाशत्तमाद्येन श्लोकत्रयेण प्रोक्ते । मध्यतः सर्व्वमध्यतो द्वयं । अक्षरयोः । वह्निर्मध्ययोनितः । प्रागवद्विलिखेदिति सम्बन्धः । तैः अष्टोत्तरद्विशतसंख्यैरक्षरैः । अष्टौ सम्भूय । महेश्वरीति

तानि पूर्व्वाद्ययन्त्रे तु विलिखेन्मध्यतो द्वयम ।
वह्निः प्राग्वत्ततस्तैः स्यात् यन्त्राण्यष्टौ महेश्वरि ॥ ८३ ॥
तेष्वाद्यं सर्व्ववारेषु विनियुञ्ज्यादुदीरिते ।
द्वितीयादीनि यन्त्राणि सप्त भान्वादिवासरे ॥ ८४ ॥
विनियुञ्ज्यात् प्रोक्तकर्म्मस्वाख्यालेखनपूर्व्वकम् ।
वाराख्यां सप्तमीयुक्तामालिखेत् साधयेति तत् ॥ ८५ ॥
वश्याकर्षणशान्त्याप्त्यै विदध्यादाद्ययन्त्रतः ।
प्रोक्तक्रमेण विधिना शान्तिमर्चनतस्तथा ॥ ८६ ॥
सप्तमं पूजितं क्वापि स्थापितं पोतगर्भके ।
तन्नाशयन्ति तत्पोतमब्धौ सर्व्वं तथा शिवे ॥ ८७ ॥

सम्बुद्धिः । एतदुक्तं भवति पूर्वोक्तेषु यन्त्रेषु आद्ये वाह्यादभ्यन्तरप्रवेशक्रमाद्वृत्तत्रयाष्टपत्राम्बुजनवयोनिरूपे यन्त्रे सर्वमध्ये स्वरविकृतपञ्चविंशाक्षरे मूलविद्यानाद्यन्ताक्षरत्रयोदशकमंजाताष्टोत्तरद्विशतसंख्येष्वक्षरेष्वादितोऽक्षरद्वयं प्रत्यक्षरं साध्यादुपेतमालिख्य तद्वाह्यगतकोणेष्वष्टसु सर्वमध्यलिखिताक्षरद्वयादुपरितनान्यष्टाक्षराण्यग्रात्प्रादक्षिण्येनालिख्य तद्वहिरष्टपत्रेषु प्रतिपत्रं द्वयंद्वयमितिक्रमेण नवयोनित्रिलिखिताक्षरदशकादुपरितनानि षोड़शाक्षराणि प्राग्वदालिख्य एवं संभूय षड़्विंशत्यक्षराणि क्रमाद्विलिख्य वाह्यवृत्तत्रयान्तरालवीथिद्वये प्राग्वत् मातृकावेष्टनं कुर्य्यात् । एतत् प्रथमं यन्त्रं । एवमस्मिन्नेव यन्त्रे पूर्वलिखिताक्षरषड़्विंशतिकादुपरितनमुपरितनमक्षरषड़्विंशतिकं क्रमेणालिख्य पूर्वोक्तेन यन्त्रेण सहाष्टौ यन्त्राणि सम्पादयेदिति ॥ ८३ ॥

तेष्वादिभिजन्मिनामित्यन्तैः षड़्भिः श्लोकैस्तद्यन्त्राष्टकविनियोगादिकमुपदिशति । तत्र तेषु अष्टसु यन्त्रेषु । आद्यं यन्त्रमिति शेषः । उदीरिते वश्याकर्षणेत्यादिषड़शीतितमश्लोकेन वक्ष्यमाणे । सप्त इति पदच्छेदः । भान्वादिवारके आदिशब्दः सोमाङ्गारकवुधवृहस्पतिशुक्रशनैश्चरविषयः तेषां वारे इत्यर्थः । प्रोक्तकर्मसु वक्ष्यमाणकर्मसु । आख्यालेखनपूर्वकं प्राग्वत् साध्यादिनामालिखनपूर्वकमित्यर्थः । वाराख्यां साध्याधः साधयेति । तदिति लेखनीयवाक्यरूपं । एतदुक्तं भवति सर्वमध्यगताक्षरद्वयमध्ये प्रत्येकस्मिन् वारे एतत्

तथा वारेषु तैरुक्तान्यालिख्याभ्यर्च्य येच्छिवाम्।
वाञ्छितेषु समस्तेषु तैर्दिनैस्तान्यवाप्नुयात् ॥ ८८ ॥
रोगशान्तिं जयं लाभं नानाभीष्टार्थविग्रहम्।
शत्रुभङ्गं व..ं नारीन्नृपमर्त्यादिजन्मिनाम् ॥ ८९ ।
प्राक्प्रत्यग्दक्षिणोदक्कसूत्राण्यास्फालयेत् क्रमात्।
द्वाविंशतिं ततश्चैकचत्वारिंशच्चतुःशतम् ॥ ९० ॥
तेषु कोणेषु परितो मार्जयेत् पूर्ववत् क्रमात्।
पञ्चपञ्चाशदन्यानि कोष्ठवज्रं महेश्वरि ॥ ९१ ॥
शतद्वयं चैकविंशं तेषु दिक्षु विकोणकम्।
मध्येऽवशिष्टनवकमध्ये नामोदरां लिखेत् ॥ ९२ ॥

साधयेति भूर्जराद्यधरादूर्ध्वान्तमालिखेदिति। आद्ययन्त्रतः अष्टस्विति शेषः। प्रोक्तक्रमेणेति विधिनेत्यस्य विशेषणम्। स विधिस्तु प्राणप्रतिष्ठापुरःसरं आधारस्थापनादिः। अर्चनतः तत्र देवीपूजनतः। तथेति समुच्चये पूजितम्। तत्तत्प्राप्तवारेषु नाशयन्तीति यन्त्रसप्तकसंख्यापेक्षया बहुवचनम्। शिवे इति देवीसम्बोधः। तेष्विति वारविशेषणम्। उक्तानि यन्त्राणीति शेषः। तैः प्राग्वन्मण्डलादिभिः। तानि रोगशान्त्यादीनि वक्ष्यमाणानि। मर्त्त्यादिजन्मिनामित्यादिशब्दः अमात्यसामन्तादि सकलप्राणिजातविषयः ॥ ८८ ॥

प्राक्प्रत्यगित्यादिभिः शिवे इत्यन्तैः षड्भिः श्लोकैः प्रागुक्तैः स्वरप्रसारितैरष्टोत्तरद्विशतसंख्यैर्मूलविद्याक्षरैर्विकृतमूलविद्याक्षरपञ्चविंशतिकैश्चैकविंशत्यधिकद्विशतकोष्ठरूपवज्रयन्त्रनिर्माणं तद्विनियोगांश्चोपदिशति। तत्र क्रमाद्द्वाविंशतिं प्राक्प्रत्यग्द्वाविंशतिं दक्षिणोदग्द्वाविंशतिमिति एवं क्रमादित्यर्थः। तत आस्फालनतः। तेषु एकचत्वारिंशदधिकचतुःशतसंख्येषु कोष्ठेषु। कोणेषु चतुर्षु। पूर्ववन्मध्ये वज्राकारं यथा भवति। क्रमात् पञ्चपञ्चाशत् प्रतिकोणं पञ्चपञ्चाशत् कोष्ठानि इत्येवं क्रमादिति यावत्। संभूय चतुर्षु कोणेषु विंशत्यधिकद्विशतसंख्येषु कोष्ठेष्वित्यर्थः। चतुःकोष्ठैः प्रतिदिशमेकैककोष्ठमार्जनत इत्यर्थः। अन्यानि मार्ज्जनावशिष्टानीति शेषः। तेषु एकविंशत्यधिकद्विशतसंख्येषु कोष्ठेष्वित्यर्थः। चतुः कोष्ठेषु प्रतिदिशं एकैककोष्ठमार्जनत इत्यर्थः। प्राङ्मध्यतः प्राग्दिगन्त पङ्क्तिकोष्ठेषु मध्यकोष्ठमारभ्येत्यर्थः। तानि अष्टोत्तर-

मायां तदभितो मन्त्रवर्णांस्त्रिस्त्रिःक्रमेण वै ।
त्रिकोणेषु च साध्यानि लिखेद्वज्रमितीरितम् ॥ ९३ ॥
तद्वज्रयन्त्रे तु पटे क्षौमे वा सुसिते शुभे ।
विलिख्याभ्यर्च्य तद्यन्त्रं पोते रक्षति वार्धौ ॥ ९४ ॥
प्रागुक्तानि समस्तानि साधयेद्वज्ररूपिणा ।
यन्त्रेणानेन कालेन प्रोक्तेन सततं शिवे ॥ ९५ ॥

द्विशतसंख्यानि स्वरविकृतमूलविद्याक्षराणि लिखेत् । यावदक्षरपर्य्यवसानतः । मध्ये यन्त्रस्येति शेषः । नवकमध्ये नवकमध्यकोष्ठ इत्यर्थः । नामोदरां साधकादिनामगर्भां । मायां पञ्चविंशार्णमूलविद्याया एकादशाक्षरभूतां । तदभितः तदन्तर्गतमध्यकोष्ठानन्तरप्राक्पङ्क्तिमध्यकोष्ठमारभ्य प्रादक्षिण्यनिर्गमनगत्या त्रिःत्रिःक्रमेण मध्यकोष्ठवर्जं प्रतिकोष्ठमिति शेषः । त्रिकोणेषु चेत्यत्र चकाराच्चतुर्षु त्रिकोणेष्वपि साध्याक्षराणि मायास्थानि लिखेदिति । तद्यन्त्रं वज्रयन्त्रमिति शेषः । यन्त्रविरचनाक्रमो यथा – प्राक्प्रत्यगुदक्षिणोदक्समान्तरालानि द्वाविंशति द्वाविंशति सूत्राण्यास्फाल्य तैरेकचत्वारिंशदधिकचतुःशतसंख्यानि कोष्ठानि निष्पाद्य तेषु चतुर्षु कोणेषु प्रतिकोणं पञ्चपञ्चाशत्कोष्ठानि सम्भूय विंशत्यधिक द्विशतसंख्यानि कोष्ठानि प्रागवन्मध्ये वज्राकारं यथा भवति तथा तथा मार्जयित्वा ततश्चतुर्षु दिक्षु प्रतिदिशमेकैक कोष्ठमार्जनतश्चत्वारि त्रिकोणानि कृत्वा शिष्टेषु सप्तदशाधिक द्विशतसंख्येषु कोष्ठेषु सर्वप्राचीनपङ्क्तिस्थकोष्ठत्रये मध्यकोष्ठमारभ्य प्रादक्षिण्यप्रवेशगत्या युक्तक्रममष्टोत्तरशतद्विशतसंख्यानि स्वरविकृतमूलविद्याक्षराणि यावदक्षरपर्य्यवसानमालिख्य ततो मध्यतः शिष्टेषु नवसु कोष्ठेषु सर्वमध्यस्थकोष्ठमध्ये पञ्चविंशार्णमूलविद्याया एकादशाक्षरभूतहृल्लेखां साध्यगर्भामालिख्य शिष्टेष्वष्टसु कोष्ठेषु मध्यकोष्ठानन्तर प्राचीनपंक्तिमध्यकोष्ठमारभ्यायुक्तक्रमं प्रादक्षिण्यनिर्गमनगत्या प्रतिकोष्ठं पञ्चविंशाक्षरमूलविद्याक्षराणि हृल्लेखाविधुराणि त्रीणि त्रीण्यालिख्य चतुर्दिग्गत त्रिकोणचतुष्केष्वपि मध्यकोष्ठवत् ससाध्यां हृल्लेखामालिख्य तेन यन्त्रेण वक्ष्यमाणान् विनियोगान् कुर्य्यादिति । वा विकल्पे । सुसिते इति क्षौमविशेषणम् । रक्षति यन्त्रमित्यत्रान्वयः । तेन कर्त्तृभूतं यन्त्रमिति । प्रागुक्तानि अत्र प्रोक्तानि कार्य्याणि । प्रोक्तेन प्रागवन्मण्डलादिना । शिवे इति देवीसम्बुद्धिः ॥ ९५ ॥

तां देवीं पाशसम्बद्धं साध्यमङ्कुशताड़नात् ।
आकर्षन्तीं स्वपादान्ते साञ्जलिं प्रणतिं मुहुः ॥ ९६ ॥
रक्ष रक्षेति भाषन्तं स्मरन् विद्यां जपन्निशि ।
साध्यो नरोथ नारी च वशमेति सुनिश्चितम ॥९७॥
अथवा साञ्जलिं साध्यं प्राग्वद्वादिनमङ्कुशे ।
प्रातर्केशसमाकृष्टं जपेत् प्राग्वद्वशो भवेत् ॥९८॥
मन्त्राक्षराणां तेजोभिः परीतं वा तथाविधाम् ।
स्वयमेवानयेत्तान्तु स्मरन् जापैर्व्वशं नयेत् ॥ ९९ ॥
एवं सा कुरुकुल्ला ते प्रोक्ता सर्व्वार्थसाधिका
ललिताविग्रहा येन वशिन्यादियुता ततः ॥१००॥
बुद्धितत्त्वमयी व्याप्तिरिति सम्यक् समीरिता ।
अस्या निफालनाच्चित्ते तत्तत्त्वं स्वात्मसात् कृतम् ॥१०१॥

इति षोड़शनित्यातन्त्रे श्रीकादिमते द्वाविंशत पटलः ॥२२॥

तामित्यादिभिस्तत इत्यन्तैश्चतुर्भिः श्लोकैर्मन्त्रदेवताभावनाकर्षणवशीकरणं त्वैविध्यं तस्याः कुरुकुल्लाया देव्या वशिन्यादिशक्त्यष्टकपरिवृतत्ववासनं चोपदिशति। तत्र तामित्यस्योत्तरश्लोके (वातत्) स्मरन्नित्यनेनान्वयः। साध्यमित्यस्य यदस्यास्य श्लोकस्योत्तरार्द्धगताकर्षन्तीमित्यनेनान्वयः। विद्यां पञ्चविंशार्णां। अथवेति पक्षव्यावृत्तौ। प्राग्वद्वादिनं रक्षरक्षेति प्राग्वत्। आकर्षन्तीं देवीं स्मरन् विद्यां जपेदित्यर्थः। भवेत् प्रागुक्तः साध्यवर्गः। मन्त्राक्षराणां पञ्चविंशार्णमूलविद्याक्षराणां। तथाविधां रक्षरक्षेति भाषणादियुक्तां। स्वयमेव आकर्षणादृते। एतदुक्तं भवति साध्य मन्त्राक्षरतेजोभिः परीतं तेजःसहनाशक्तत्वात् प्राग्वद्भाषमाणादियुक्तः स्वयमेव देवताकर्षणादिव तामन्तः स्मरन् विद्यां जपन् वशयतोति। एवं प्रोक्तरूपतः। ते इति देवीं निर्दिशति। येन ललिताविग्रहवत्त्वकारणेन। ततः कारणात् ॥१००॥

इति षोड़शनित्यातन्त्रेषु श्रीकादिमताख्यस्य परिपूर्णस्य तन्त्रस्य ऽपञ्च-सार-सिंह-राजप्रकाशाभिधानेन श्रीसुभगानन्दनाथेन विरचितायां मनोरमाख्यायां व्याख्यायां षोड़शनित्यावलिदेवतारूपककुरुकुल्लाविद्याविधानप्रकाशनपरं द्वाविंशत् पटलम् परिपूर्णं परामृष्टम् ।

ग्रन्थसंख्या । द्वादशाक्तानि यन्त्राणि द्वाविंशे व्यक्रियागताः ।
ग्रन्थाः स्युः सार्द्धपादैकचत्वारिंशच्छतद्वयाम् ॥

त्रयोविंशपटलम् ।

अथ षोड़शनित्यानामङ्गभूता तु पञ्चमी ।
तद्विधा कथिता पूर्वं तदङ्गानि च पूजनम् ॥ १ ॥
साधनं सिद्धमन्त्रस्य प्रयोगध्यानपूजनैः ।
होमैर्यन्त्रैश्च वच्यामि समस्ताभीष्टसिद्धये ॥ २ ॥
अङ्गानि कृत्वा मन्त्रार्णैः सप्तभिः षड़्युगेन च ।
दशभिः सप्तभिः सप्तसंख्यैर्जातिभिरन्वितम्॥ ३ ॥
त्रिकोणवृत्तषट्कोणवृत्तद्वयसमन्वितम् ।
विधाय चक्रं तत्रैव स्वनाम्नावाह्य पूजयेत् ॥ ४ ॥

पूर्वस्मिन् द्वाविंशे पटले षोड़शनित्यानां वलिदेवतायाः कुरुकुल्लाया विधानमुपदिश्यानन्तरं षोड़शनित्याङ्गभूतायाः पञ्चम्याख्याया वाराह्या विधान मुपदिशति। अथ षाड़शेत्याद्यनयेत्यन्तश्लोकशतरूपेण त्रयोविंशेन पटलेन। तत्र अथ षोड़शेत्यादिना सिद्धये इत्यन्तेण श्लोकद्वयेन पटलार्थानुपदिशति। तत्र पूर्वं तृतीये पटले। साधनं विद्याया इति शेषः ॥२॥

अङ्गानीत्यादिना श्लोकेन षड़ङ्गन्यासमन्त्रानुपदिशति। अत्र अङ्गानि षट् कृत्वा इत्यस्योत्तरश्लोकोत्तरार्द्धान्तर्गतपूजयेदित्यनेनान्वयः। मन्त्रार्णैर्वच्यमाण-संख्याक्रमभिन्नैर्मूलविद्यायामादितः सभूय त्रिचत्वारिंशताक्षरैः। षड़् युगेन षड़्भिरक्षरैः शिरोमन्त्रः षड़्भिरक्षरैः शिखामन्त्रश्चेत्यर्थः। जातिभिः हृदयाय नमः इत्यादिभिः षड़्भिः। अन्वित क्रियाविशेषणमेतत् ॥ ३ ॥

त्रिकोणत्यादिभिरितत्यन्तैः षड़्भिः श्लोकैर्देव्या नित्यपूजाचक्रं सावरण-द्वयपूजाविधानं नित्यभजनक्रमं तत्फलञ्चापदिशति। तत्र समन्वितं चक्र-मित्यस्य विशेषणं। नित्यपूजाचक्रविरचनाक्रमोयथा अभीष्टमान (प्रमाण भ्रमादन्तर्बहिर्विभागेनेकाङ्गुलान्तरालं वृत्तद्वयं विधाय तदन्तर्वृत्तमध्ये प्रागुक्त-मानतः षट्कोणं विधाय तन्मध्यतः सन्धिरेखास्पृष्टास्पृष्टं वृत्तं विधाय

दशोत्तरशतार्च्याभ्यां वाराहीविद्यया प्रिये।
सर्वमध्ये समभ्यर्च्य वामदक्षाग्रकोणतः ॥ ५ ॥
क्रोधिनीं स्तम्भिनीं चण्डोच्चण्डाञ्चैव स्वनामभिः।
आद्यबीजान्त्यसप्राणैरुपेतामथ पूजयेत् ॥ ६ ॥
षट्सु कोणेषु स्वाग्रादिब्राह्म्याद्या वामतोऽर्चयेत्।
वृत्ते चैव महालक्ष्मीं पञ्चमीं मध्यतस्तथा ॥ ७ ॥
वलिन्तु षोड़शार्णेन कृत्वाभ्यर्च्योपचारकैः।
तदग्रे तां जपेद्विद्यां सहस्रमथवा शतम् ॥ ८ ॥
होमञ्च कुर्य्याद्दिनशः सुशुद्धैस्तिलतण्डुलैः।
घृतेन वा ततो विद्या सिद्धा स्याद्दष्टतस्ततः ॥ ९ ॥

तन्मध्ये प्राग्वत् समत्रिरेखं त्रिकोणं यथोपदेशं विधाय तत्र देवीमावाह्य वक्ष्यमाणक्रमेण पूजयेदिति। स्वनाम्नावाह्य सविन्दुकहस्रेखाद्येन नाम्ना। द्वितीयान्तेन क्रियायुक्तेन। तन्मन्त्रो यथा—ह्रीं वाराहीमावाहयामीति पूजयेत्। वक्ष्यमाणक्रमतः दशोत्तरशतार्च्याभ्यां तृतीयपटलोक्तया। प्रिये इति देवीसम्बुद्धिः। सर्व्वमध्ये चक्रस्य सर्वमध्यत्रिकोणमध्य इत्यर्थः। वामदक्षाग्रकोणतः देव्याः। चण्डोच्चण्डामित्यत्रत्रा स्वस्वनामभिः अस्याः परिवारशक्तीर्नमोऽन्तैर्नाममन्त्रैश्चतुर्थ्यन्तैः पूजयेदिति सम्प्रदायः। आद्यबीजान्त्यसप्राणैरित्यनेनैतदुक्तं भवतीति। क्रोधिनीं स्तम्भिनीञ्च तत्तन्नामाद्याक्षरे सविन्दुके क्रों इति स्तं इति चोच्चार्य्य ततस्तन्नामभ्यां चतुर्थ्यन्ताभ्यां नमोन्ताभ्यामर्चयित्वा ततश्चण्डोच्चण्डान्तु मातृकान्त्याक्षरभूतक्षकारस्य ओंकारप्रकरणप्राप्तविन्दुश्च तैः संयुतं क्षों इत्युच्चार्य्य तदनन्तरं पारम्पर्य्यप्रोक्त क्रोमिति चोच्चार्य्य ततश्चण्डोच्चण्डायै नम इत्यत्रत्राचर्येदिति। अत्र 'क्रोधिन्यादिशक्तित्रयस्य हस्रेखावैधुर्य्यं स्वस्वबीजाद्यत्वादिति सम्प्रदायः। वामतः अप्रादक्षिण्येन अर्चयेत्। हस्रेखादैरनमोन्तैर्नामभिः। अत्रासां शक्तीनां सप्तानां हस्रेखादत्वं स्वस्वबीजाद्यराहित्यादिति च सम्प्रदायः। वृत्ते सर्ववाह्यगतवृत्तद्वयवीथ्यां। तदग्रे देव्या अग्रे। अभिमुखं चामरतालवृन्तसङ्गीतादिव्यापृताभिरनन्ताभिः शक्तिभिर्वृत्तद्वयवीथ्यां परितः स्थिताभिर्महालक्ष्म्यादिभिरिति सम्प्र-

जितेन्द्रियो हविष्याशी मौनी सन्ध्यासु पूजयन्।
विद्यां जपेल्लक्षसंख्यां तद्दशांशेन तर्पणम्॥ १०॥
अर्चनं हवनं कृत्वा सिद्धमन्त्रो दयान्वितः।
गुरुभक्तः सुसन्तुष्टः शान्तचित्तः क्षमान्वितः॥ ११॥
प्रयोगानाचरेद्भक्त्या यैरिष्टमखिलं क्षणात्।
सिध्यत्यय ततो देव्याः प्रसादाद्वैभवादपि॥ १२॥
ध्यायेच्च देवीं कोलास्यां तप्तकाञ्चनसन्निभाम्।
आकण्ठं वनितारूपां ज्वलत्पिङ्गशिरोरुहाम्॥ १३॥

दायः। पञ्चमीं वाराहीं मूलदेवतां। मध्यतः प्राग्वत्। तथा मूलविद्यया त्रिवारादहीनमिति शेषः। अर्चयेदिति पूर्वत्रान्वयः। एतदुक्तं भवति चक्रमध्ये देवीमावाह्य तदनन्तरं सविन्दुकया ह्लक्षं खया विधुरैर्नमोन्तैर्नामभिरभ्यर्च्य (१) तद्बहिः षट्सु कोणेषु ब्राह्म्यादयाश्चामुण्डान्ताः षट्शक्तीश्च सर्वा बाह्यवृत्तद्वयवीथ्यां देव्यग्रमभिमुखमासीनां प्रोक्तराज्यचिह्नपरिवारां महालक्ष्मीं चैवं सम्भूय सप्तशक्तीस्तन्नाममन्त्रैः ह्लक्षं खाद्यैर्नमोन्तैरर्चयित्वा पुनरपि मध्ये देवीं तद्विद्यया त्रिवारादहीनमर्चयेत् इति। वलिन्तु षोड़शार्णेन षाड़शाक्षरेण वलिमन्त्रेण पूजारम्भावसानसमये वलिं प्राग्वत् कुर्य्यादित्यर्थः। सर्वत्र वलिद्वयप्रदानं मूलदेवताग्रभागे इति सम्प्रदायः। उपचारकैः षोड़शभिः। आवाहनाद्यनन्तरं पूजान्ते च अत्राघ्र्यस्थापनमनुक्तमपि पूर्वमेव साधारणोक्तत्वात्। षड़ङ्ग मूलाभ्यां प्राग्वत् स्थापयेदिति मुख्यागमः। तां दशोत्तरशताक्षरीं। अथवा विकल्पार्थः। वा पक्षान्तरे इति प्रोक्तनित्यभजनतः॥ ९॥

जितेन्द्रिय इत्यादिभिर्वैभवादपीत्यन्तैस्त्रिभिः श्लोकैर्मूलदेवतायाः पुरश्चरणं कृतपुरश्चरणस्य प्रयोगार्हत्वञ्चोपदिशति। तत्र जपेल्लक्षसंख्यं केवलमर्चनं हवनं जपदशांशंतर्पणं हवनं च कुर्य्यादिति सर्वमन्त्रसामान्यं। सिद्धमन्त्रः प्रोक्तरूपतः दयान्वित इत्यादिसिद्धमन्त्रलक्षणं। वैभवात् देव्या वैश्वरूप्यात्। अपिः समुच्चये॥ १२॥

ध्यायेदित्यादिभिर्विश्रुत इत्यन्तैश्चतुस्त्रिंशता श्लोकैः देव्याः सपरिवारायाः स्वतन्त्रनित्यपूजासु ध्यानं आवाहनञ्चोपदिशति। तत्र ध्यायेदित्यादिभिः शिवे

१। "स्थापनादीनुपचारान् विधाय मूलविद्यया एकवारमभ्यर्च्य" इत्यधिकः पाठः।

विनेत्रामष्टहस्ताञ्च चक्रशङ्खमथाम्बुजम्।
पाशञ्च मुशलं शीरमभयं वरदं तथा ॥ १४ ॥
दधानां गरुड़स्कन्धे सुखासीनां विचिन्तयेत्।
नित्यपूजासु तच्छक्तीस्तत्समानाः स्मरेच्छिवे ॥ १५ ॥
प्रयोगेषु स्मरेद्देवीं सिंहस्थां व्याघ्रगामपि।
गजारूढ़ां हयारूढ़ां तार्च्यारूढ़ाञ्च शक्तिभिः ॥ १६ ॥
श्यामामप्यरुणां पीतामसितां धूम्रविग्रहाम्।
तत्प्रयोगेषु च तथा ध्यायेत्तत्तदवाप्तये ॥ १७ ॥
अरुणामरुणाकल्पामरुणाभिश्च शक्तिभिः।
आवृतां पञ्चमीं ध्यायन् जपेद्वश्याप्तयेऽनिशम् ॥ १८ ॥

इत्यन्तैस्त्रिभिः श्लोकैर्देव्याः स्वतन्त्रनित्यपूजासु क्वचित्प्रयोगेषु च ध्यानावाहनविशेषादिकमुपदिशति। तत्र ध्यायेच्च देवीमित्यत्र चकारेण देव्याः सपरिवारायाः ललिताङ्गपूजायां तत्समानायुधाकारात्मकध्यानमन्तरेण च स्वतन्त्रनित्यपूजादिषु वक्ष्यमाणक्रमेण ध्यायेदिति सम्प्रदायार्थः। कोलास्यां वराहमुखीं आकण्ठवनितारूपामित्यन्तेन कण्ठादधोरूपविग्रहस्य वराहात्मकत्वं प्रमादेनापि न चिन्तनीयमिति परिहरतीति यावत्। ज्वलत्पिङ्गशिरोरुहां ज्वलदिव उर्द्धाग्रपिङ्गलकेशां ॥ १३ ॥ अत्रायुधक्रमस्तु अष्टभुजेषूर्द्धादिदक्षिणवामक्रमेण। दधानां भुजैरिति शेषः। सीरं हलं विचिन्तयेदिति नित्यपूजासु। वक्ष्यमाणगरुड़ेतरवाहनध्यान परिवारार्थत्वान्न पुनरुक्तिदोषः। तच्छक्तीः परिवारशक्तीः स्मरेदिति नित्यपूजास्विति पूर्वेणान्वयः ॥ १५ "

प्रयोगेष्वित्यादिना अवाप्तये इत्यन्तेन श्लोकद्वयेन सर्वप्रयोगेषु सामान्येन वाहनवर्णादिकमुपदिशति। तत्र शक्तिभिः परिवारशक्तिभिः। सहेति शेषः। वक्ष्यमाणक्रमेण ॥ १७ ॥

अरुणामित्यादिना श्लोकेन तस्या एव ध्यानमुपदिशति। तत्र अरुणाकल्पां पद्मरागादिभिः कृताकल्पाम् ॥ १८ ॥

पीतां पीताम्बरां पीतभूषणस्रग्विलेपनाम् ।
पीतशक्त्यावृतां ध्यायेत् स्तम्भनेषु तु सर्वदा ॥ १९ ॥
श्यामाञ्च दुर्गमे मार्गे सिंहस्थां भीमविग्रहाम् ।
शक्तिभिः स्वसमानाभिरनन्ताभिः समायुताम् ॥ २० ॥
चिन्तयन् प्रजपन् विद्यां यजेत्तच्छक्तिमध्यतः ।
स्वात्मानं भावयन्मन्त्री व्रजेदक्लिष्टवैभवः ॥ २१ ॥
सिंहर्क्षद्वीपिशरभशृङ्गिकुक्कुरशूकरैः ।
गवयैर्भुजगैर्भीमैर्दन्तिभिर्मदमन्थरैः ॥ २२ ॥
चौरैः क्रूरप्रहरणैः क्रूरैरन्यैर्भयावहैः ।
भूतप्रेतपिशाचाद्यैराकुलेऽरण्यसङ्कटे ॥ २३ ॥
अलब्धमार्गे विपिने गिरिशृङ्गे तथाविधे ।
स्मरेद्देवीमुक्तरूपां निरातङ्को व्रजेत् सुखी ॥ २४ ॥
समरेष्वपि भीमेषु पतत्सु रथदन्तिभिः ।
सङ्कटेषु दुरन्तेषु स्मृत्वेत्थं विजयी भवेत् ॥ २५ ॥

पीतामित्यादिना श्लोकेन स्तम्भनप्रयोगमुपदिशति। तत्र पीतशक्त्यावृतां पीतवर्णाभिः शक्तिभिरावृताम् ॥ १९ ॥

श्यामामित्यादिभिः सुखी इत्यन्तैः पञ्चभिः श्लोकैर्दुर्गममार्गरक्षाविधानमुपदिशति। तत्र अनन्ताभिः प्रत्येकमसंख्याताभिः क्रोधिन्यादिभिस्तत्वरणस्थाभिः। अक्लिष्टवैभवः अध्वश्रान्त्यादिभिरप्यक्लिष्टपरिच्छदादियुतः। भीमैरिति सिंहादीनां सर्वेषां विशेषणम्। अन्यैः शाखामृगादिभिः। आकुले निविड़े। अरण्यसङ्कटे अरण्यैः पिहितमार्गे। अलब्धमार्गे इतः पूर्वममानुषगोचरतयेति शेषः। तथाविधे इति पूर्वत्र गिरिशृङ्गे इत्यनेनान्वयः। उक्तरूपां श्यामामित्यादिना श्लोकेनेति शेषः। निरातङ्कः नितरां क्लेशरहितः। व्रजेदिति प्रोक्तोपसंहारार्थत्वात्त्र पुनरुक्तिदोषः ॥ २४ ॥

समरेष्वित्यादिभिर्मदोद्धतैरित्यन्तैः पञ्चभिः श्लोकैः समरविजयध्यानमुपदिशति। तत्र दुरन्तेषु मरणनिरोधनप्रलापनाम जल्पविशेषः (?)। इत्थं

नखरं छुरिकां खड्गं वाणं शूलं गदां सृणिम् ।
चक्रञ्च दक्षिणैर्बिभ्रद्बाहुभिर्भीमविग्रहाम् ॥ २६ ॥
तर्जनीं खेटकं चर्म्म चापं डमरुकं हलम् ।
पाशं शङ्खञ्च दधतीमन्यैर्नीलां स्वशक्तिभिः ॥ २७ ॥
गजाधिरूढ़ां द्विरदैः शक्त्यारूढ़ैः समावृताम् ।
वैरिसेनां समन्ताच्च निपात्य परिघैर्भुवि ॥ २८ ॥
तदुपर्य्यभितः प्रेङ्खत् कदलीकेतुसङ्कुलम् ।
चरन्तीं शक्तिवृन्दैश्च भीमारावैर्म्मदोद्धतैः ॥ २९ ॥
भानुमण्डलमध्यस्थां शूलप्रोतारिविग्रहाम् ।
तद्देहनिर्य्यद्रक्ताक्तशूलां देवीं विचिन्तयेत् ॥ ३० ॥
कण्ठमात्रे जले स्थित्वा जपेद्विद्यामनन्यधीः ।
सप्तरात्रप्रयोगेण वैरिणं मारयेज् ज्वरात् ॥ ३१ ॥

वक्ष्यमाणप्रकारेण। छुरिकं असिधेनुं भीमविग्रहामिति देवीविशेषणम्। अन्यैः दामैः अष्टभिर्व्वाहुभिरिति शेषः। तत्र आयुधानां नामान्याराध्यमुखादवगन्तव्यानि। अत्र आयुधक्रमस्तु उभयपार्श्वयोरप्यधरादूर्द्धान्तमित्यवगन्तव्यम्। नीलां वर्णेनेति शेषः। स्वशक्तिभिः तद्वर्णाभिः शक्तिभिः सहितामिति यावत्। परिघैः देव्याः परिवारशक्तीनाञ्च दक्षिणपार्श्वोर्द्धादित्नतीयभुजस्थैः। तदुपरि सेनोपरि कदलीकेतुसङ्कुलं कदलीनिभगजपताकासङ्कुलं देशमिति शेषः ॥ २८ ॥

भानुमण्डलेत्यादिना ज्वरादित्यन्तेन श्लोकद्वयेण ज्वरेण रिपुमारणप्रयोगमुपदिशति। तत्र भानुमण्डलेत्यादिनैतदुक्तं भवति। पूर्वोक्तषोड़शभुजविधृतायुधां नीलाभां देवीं भानुमण्डलमध्ये निजदक्षिणोर्द्धादिचतुर्थजस्थशूलप्रोतारिविग्रहां तद्देहान्निःसरद्रक्ताक्ततच्छूलां विचिन्तयन्निति। अनन्यधीः एकाग्रचित्तः ॥ ३१ ॥

देव्याः सपरिवारायाः हेतिभिः शकलीकृतम् ।
रिपुदेहं स्मरेत् फेरुकङ्कक्रव्यादकुक्कुरैः ॥ ३२ ॥
भक्ष्यमाणं जपेद्वियां त्रिदिनं सलिले स्थितः ।
प्राग्वत्तावद्दिनैर्वारिहतं मृ(स्मृ)त्वा समुत्तरेत् ॥ ३३ ॥
द्विभुजां धूम्रवर्णाभां साध्यजिह्वाहृदम्बुजे ।
उत्पाटयन्तीं संचिन्त्य जपन् शत्रून् यमं नयेत् ॥ ३४ ॥
तथाविधां पीतवर्णां स्मृत्वा संजप्य वैरिणः ।
क्रोधं संशमयेद्वादे विवादे समरेऽपि च ॥ ३५ ॥
तार्क्ष्यारूढाश्च तां तार्क्ष्यगणस्थाभिश्च शक्तिभिः ।
वृतां तार्क्ष्यगणोद्दामपक्षमारुतमूर्च्छिताम् ॥ ३६ ॥

देव्या इत्यादिना समुत्तरेदित्यन्तेन श्लोकद्वयेन रिपुमारणप्रयोगविशेषमुपदिशति। तत्र देव्याः षोडशकरायुधनीलवर्णादिविशिष्टविग्रहाया इति शेषः। फेरुः क्रोष्टा क्रव्यादाः पिशाचाद्याः कुक्कुरः सारमेयः भक्ष्यमाणं पूर्वोक्तैः फेरुप्रमुखैः। प्राग्वत् कण्ठमात्रे जले तावद्दिनैः सप्तदिनैः त्रिदिनैर्वा। तत्र कण्ठमात्रजलापेक्षया पश्चान्तरेदिति। वारिहतं जले मृतं रिपुमिति शेषः ॥ ३३ ॥

द्विभुजामित्यादिना श्लोकेन रिपुमारणप्रयोगध्यानमुपदिशति। तत्र साध्यजिह्वाहृदम्बुजे द्वितीयाद्विवचनमेतत्। यमं मृत्युं। एतदुक्तं भवति साध्यं रिपुमुत्तानशायिनं भूमौ निपात्य तदुदरकण्ठयोः पादद्वयं विन्यस्य एकेन करेण तस्य हृदयाम्बुजमितरेण तस्य जिह्वाञ्चोत्पाटयन्तीं धूम्रवर्णां देवीं संचिन्त्य जपन् शत्रुं मारयेदिति सम्प्रदायार्थः ॥ ३४ ॥

तथाविधामित्यादिना श्लोकेन क्रोधस्तम्भनध्यानमुपदिशति। तत्र तथाविधां साध्यजिह्वाहृदम्बुजोत्पाटनादिना अत्र देवीं चतुर्भुजां साध्यं ऊर्द्ध्ववामभुजस्थहलेनाकृष्य तद्दक्षिणभुजस्थमुशलेन प्रहृत्य प्राग्वदुत्पाटयन्तीं ध्यायेदिति सम्प्रदायार्थः ॥ ३५ ॥

तार्क्ष्यारूढामित्यादिना क्षणादित्यन्तेमार्द्धाधिकेन श्लोकेन रिपुसेनाविद्रावणमुपदिशति। तत्र तां देवीं। तार्क्ष्यगणोद्दामपक्षमारुतमूर्च्छितामित्यस्य उत्तरत्र सेनामित्यनेनान्वयः। क्षणात् स्मृतिमात्रेण ॥ ३६ ॥

स्मृत्वा जयेद्रिपोःसेनां दूरतो द्रावयेत् क्षणात् ।
तथैवाष्टभुजैः खड्गान् दधानां शक्तिभिर्वृताम् ॥ ३७ ॥
तथैवारातिपृतनां समरे नाशयेत् क्षणात् ।
विकीर्य्य केशानरुणवारवाणधरो हयैः ॥ ३८ ॥
तरक्षकेशरिकपिकोलर्क्षगरुडस्थितैः ।
शक्तिवृन्दैस्त्रिशूलाग्रप्रोतपत्त्यश्ववारणैः ॥ ३९ ॥
क्रीड़ाविनोदां माणिक्यमण्डपे सिंहविष्टरे ।
ध्यायन्नरातेः पृतना नाशयेत् स्वैर्बलैर्नृपः ॥ ४० ॥
पीतप्रसूनैः पीताभामर्च्चयेत् स्तम्भनाय वै ।
प्रागुक्तैर्म्मण्डलाद्यैस्तु वासरैः परमेश्वरि ॥ ४१ ॥
अरातीनां गतिं सेनां मतिं जिह्वां समुद्यमम् ।
दुष्टमन्यच्च सकलं स्तम्भयेत् साधकः क्षणात् ॥ ४२ ॥

तथैवेत्यादिना क्षणादित्यन्तेनार्द्धद्वयेनारातिसेनाविनाशध्यानमुपदिशति । तत्र तथैव गरुड़स्कन्धाधिरूढ़ां । शक्तिभिस्ताक्षर्य्याधिरूढ़ाभिरिति शेषः । तथैव जपादिना । क्षणात् प्रागवत् ॥ ३७ ॥

विकीर्य्येत्यादिना नृप इत्यन्तेनार्द्धाद्येन श्लोकद्वयेनारिसेनाविनाशनध्यानमुपदिशति । तत्र अरुणवारवाणधरः अरुणकञ्चुकधरः । इत्यस्य उत्तरत्र नृप इत्यनेनान्वयः । हयैः सहित इति शेषः । त्रिशूलाग्रप्रोतपत्त्यश्ववारणैरिति शक्तिवृन्दविशेषणम् । सिंहविष्टरे स्थितां देवीमिति शेषः । एतदुक्तं भवति तरक्षादिषड्वाहनारूढ़ैः शक्तिवृन्दैः स्वस्वकरस्थशूलाग्रप्रोते रिपुसेनापत्त्यश्ववारणैर्दर्शितक्रीड़ाविनोदां माणिक्यमण्डपान्तः सिंहासनस्थां देवीं ध्यायन्नरुणकञ्चुकधरः स्वकेशान् विकीर्य्य हयवृन्दसहितो हयारूढ़ो नृपः शत्रुसेनां स्वबलैर्नाशयेदिति ॥ ४० ॥

पीतेत्यादिना क्षणादित्यन्तेन श्लोकद्वयेन पूजासु पुष्पादिविशेषेण स्तम्भनीयपञ्चाङ्गादिकं चोपदिशति । तत्र पीताभां देवीमिति शेषः । स्तम्भनाय अभिमतानामिति शेषः । अरातीनामित्यस्य गत्यादिभिः पञ्चभिः प्रत्येकमन्वयः । क्षणात् प्रागवत् ॥ ४२ ॥

अरुणामरुणैः पुष्पैरर्चयेन्मध्यरात्रतः।
निहन्तुकामः सर्वांस्तु रिपुं कुर्य्याद्वशे ध्रुवम् ॥ ४३ ॥
विषनाड्यां दग्धयोगे मृतियोगे सनाशके।
यमकण्टककाले वा कृष्णापुष्पैस्तथाविधाम् ॥ ४४ ॥
पूजयंस्तद्दिनैः शत्रून् जीवितेशपुरं नयेत्।
श्यामाञ्च सौरभाद्यैस्तैः पुष्पैरभ्यर्च्य वासरैः ॥ ४५ ॥
उदितैरिन्दिराढ्यः स्यादरोगः सुमना वशी।
सुखं जीवति भूमौ स शतवर्षाणि विश्रुतः ॥ ४६ ॥

अरुणामित्यादिना श्लोकेन रिपुवश्यार्थं पुष्पविशेषात् पूजाविशेषमुपदिशति। तत्र अरुणां अरुणवर्णां देवीं ध्यात्वेति शेषः। अरुणैः अरुणवर्णैः मध्यरात्रतः मध्यरात्रे ॥ ४३ ॥

विषनाड्यामित्यादिना नयेदित्यन्तेनार्द्धाद्येन श्लोकेन कालविशेषेषु पूजाविशेषेण रिपुमारणप्रयोगमुपदिशति। तत्र सनाशके नाशयोगसहिते यमकण्टककाले रव्यादिसप्तवारेषु क्रमेण पञ्चमचतुर्थतृतीयद्वितीयप्रथमसप्तमषष्ठसंख्याङ्कसहितकाले। विषनाड्यश्च यथा—अश्विनीनक्षत्रस्य पञ्चाशत्घटिकानन्तरं चतस्रो नाड्यः विषनाड़िकाः। एवमग्रेऽपि। तथाचोक्तं—

अश्वादीनां क्रमाज्ज्ञेयाश्चतस्रो विषनाड़िकाः।
खाद्बाणा ५० ज्जिनात् २४ विन्दुगुणा ३०त् खाब्धे ४० रिन्द्रात् १८ कुपक्षतः २१।
खाग्ने ३० र्नखात् १० पदा ३२ दष्टादशा १८त् खाग्ने ३० र्नखा १० त्ततः।
कुदस्राः २१ विंशतेः २० खेन्दो १० रिन्द्रात् १४ खेन्दो १० श्चतुर्दशात् १४।
षट्पञ्चतो ५६ जिना २४ द्विंशात् २० दिशः १० पङ्क्तेः १०स्मृतेः१८न्नृपात् १२।
जिना २४ त्तथा च खाग्ने श्च ३० ता नाड्यः परतः स्थिताः ॥ इति ॥
कृष्णैः कृष्णवर्णैः। तथाविधां कृष्णवर्णां। तद्दिनैः प्रागुक्तमण्डलाद्यैः ॥ ४५ ॥

श्यामामित्यादिना विश्रुत इत्यन्तेनार्द्धाद्येन श्लोकेन पूजापुष्पादिविशेषेण लक्ष्मीप्राप्तिप्रयोगादिकमुपदिशति। तत्र श्यामां श्यामवर्णां। तैः श्यामवर्णैरुदितैर्वासरैरिति पूर्वत्रान्वयः ॥ ४६ ॥

होमं कुर्य्यात्तथा रात्रौ चतुरस्रेऽथ कुण्डके।
हरिद्रामिलितैरन्नैस्तिलैर्म्माषैः सतण्डुलैः ॥ ४७ ॥
पीतैः पुष्पैस्तथा पीतैः फलैस्तालदलैरपि।
सकलीकृत्य लिखितसाध्यवर्णसमन्वितैः ॥ ४८ ॥
निशाघृतसमोपेतैः स्तम्भयेत् प्रागुदीरितान्
निशाचूर्णघृताक्तैस्तु होमः स्तम्भयते तथा ॥ ४९ ॥
अर्द्धरात्रेऽरिनक्षत्रेद्भववह्नौ तद्योनिदेहजैः।
मांसैस्तद्देहसम्भूतस्नेहाक्तैर्हवनाद्दिनैः ॥ ५० ॥
मारयेद्वैरिणं रोगशस्त्रशृङ्गफणीजलैः।
दहनैर्व्वारिचौरन्यैः प्रमादैः कण्टकादिभिः ॥ ५१ ॥
निर्घाततरुकुड्यादिपतनाद्विषभक्षणात्।
शत्रुभिर्व्वा प्रयोगामी न भवन्त्येव भङ्गुराः ॥ ५२ ॥

होममित्यादिभिः भूतल इत्यन्तैश्चतुर्द्दशभिः श्लोकैर्होमद्रव्यादिकविशेषैः फलविशेषादिकमुपदिशति। तत्र होममित्यादिभिस्तथेत्यन्तैस्त्रिभिः श्लोकैः स्तम्भनहोमद्रव्यविशेषानुपदिशति। तत्र तथा रात्रौ मध्यरात्रे इत्यर्थः। चतुरस्रे कुण्डपटलवक्ष्यमाणलक्षणे। हरिद्रामिलितैः हरिद्राचूर्णसहितैः एतदन्नादिचतुर्णां द्रव्याणां विशेषणम्। सकलीकरणं साध्यादिनामविलेखनादिकं तालपत्राणामेव निशाघृतसमोपेतैर्हरिद्राचूर्णघृतसमोपेतैः तालदलैरिति पूर्वेणान्वयः। ईरितान् अरातिगत्यादिपञ्चकं। निशाचूर्णैः घृताक्तैर्घृतपरिप्लुतैः। तथा मण्डलादिभिः ॥ ४९ ॥

अर्द्धरात्र इत्यादिभिः भङ्गुरा इत्यन्तैस्त्रिभिः श्लोकैर्मारणप्रयोगहोमविशेषं तेन तत्र साधारणमारणप्रकारविशेषांश्चोपदिशति। तत्र अरिनक्षत्रोद्भववह्नौ शत्रुनक्षत्रवृक्षसमुद्भूतकाष्ठप्रदीप्तवह्नौ। तद्योनिदेहजैः शत्रुनक्षत्रयोनिदेहसमुद्भूतैः। तद्देहसम्भूतस्नेहाक्तैः साध्ययोनिसमुद्भूत स्नेहाप्लुतैः। दिनैः प्राग्वन्मण्डलादिभिः। अन्यैर्व्याघ्रादिभिः। प्रमादैरनवधानैः। कण्टकादिभिरित्यत्रादिशब्दः शल्यादिविषयः। निर्घातः अशनिः। प्रयोगामी प्रयोगाः अमीति दिव्यत्वात् पदच्छेदः। भङ्गुराः निष्फलाः ॥ ५२ ॥

धूम्रां काङ्कसमारूढां नखराद्यायुधैर्युताम् ।
ध्यायन् रिपोरष्टमे तु राशौ छागघृताप्लुतैः ॥ ५३ ॥
मरीचैः सर्षपैर्होमैस्तद्दिनैर्मारयेद्रिपून् ।
तीव्रदाहज्वरग्रस्तं विसंज्ञं विकृताङ्गकम् ॥ ५४ ॥
बालार्काभां स्मरन्नाद्यहेतिभिः संयुतां शिवाम्
सरूपवत्सारुणगोघृताक्तैररुणैः शुभैः ॥ ५५ ॥
प्रसूनैः किंशुकोद्भूतैस्तथा बन्धूकसम्भवैः ।
जपाप्रसूनैः पालाशैः करवीरसमुद्भवैः ॥ ५६ ॥
कह्लारैरुत्पलै रक्तैः कमलैः पाटलोद्भवैः ।
अशोकजैः कुसुम्भोत्थैरन्यैः पुष्पैश्च लोहितैः ॥ ५७ ॥
हवनान्नृपतुल्यः स्यादैश्वर्य्येणान्नया धनैः ।
अन्यैरपि च तत्सन्नपरैरङ्गैः सुनिश्चितम् ॥ ५८ ॥

धूम्रामित्यादिना विकृताङ्गकमित्यन्तेन श्लोकद्वयेन मारणहोमविशेषमुपदिशति। तत्र धूम्रां धूम्रवर्णां। नखराद्यायुधैर्युतां पूर्वं वज्रखरमित्यादिषट्त्रिंशत्श्लोकप्रोक्तषोड़शभुजस्थैरिति शेषः। छागः अजविशेषः। मरीचैः सर्षपैः। एतद्द्वयं घृताप्लुतैरित्यस्य विशेष्यं। तद्दिनैः प्रागवत् विकृताङ्गकं अस्वाधीनाङ्गम् ॥ ५४॥

बालार्काभामित्यादिभिः सुनिश्चितमित्यन्तैश्चतुर्भिः श्लोकैरैश्वर्य्यप्राप्तिकरणहोममुपदिशति। तत्र आद्यहेतिभिः संयुतां स्वतन्त्रनित्यपूजोक्तायुधाष्टकसंयुतां शिवां पञ्चमीं। सरूपवत्सारुणगोघृताक्तैः निजसदृशवत्सारुणवर्णगोघृताप्लुतैः। शुभैः मुकुलपतितम्लानशीर्षजन्तुदूषितघ्राताङ्गस्पृष्टरहितैः प्रसूनैः इत्येतत् पूर्वं त्वारुणैरित्यस्य विशेष्यं कर्त्तव्यं। करवीरसमुद्भूतैः अरुणैरिति शेषः। रक्तैरित्येतदुत्पलकमलपाटलानां विशेषणम्। अङ्गैः छत्रचामरादिभिः परिष्कृतैः ॥ ५८ ॥

अरुणां नखराद्यैस्तु युतां ध्यायन् समाहितः।
मध्यरात्रे हुनेत् साध्यदिङ्मुखो मरिचैस्तथा ॥ ५९ ॥
प्रोक्तैर्द्दिनैर्नृपो नारीनरलोकोऽपि वा वशी।
भवेत् कीर्त्तीन्दिरायुक्तश्चिरं जीवति भूतले ॥ ६० ॥
विलिख्य भूपुरं मध्ये निजसाध्यं समालिखेत्।
भौमाक्षराणि तद्बाह्ये दशाग्रादभितो लिखेत् ॥ ६१ ॥
वह्निरष्टदलं पद्मं कृत्वा तत्र लिखेत् क्रमात्।
मन्त्राक्षराणि ऋतुशस्तद्बहिर्वृत्तयुग्मकम् ॥ ६२ ॥
तत्रापि पार्थिवानर्णान् वह्निः षट्कोणमालिखेत्।
तत्कोणेष्वन्तरालेषु मन्त्रार्णान् भूदशान्वितान् ॥ ६३ ॥

अरुणामित्यादिना भूतल इत्यन्तेन श्लोकद्वयेन वश्यादिकहोमविधानमुपदिशति। तत्र नखराद्यैः पूर्वत्रास्मिन् पटले षट्त्रिंशच्छ्लोकोक्तनखराद्यायुधषोड़शकेन। समाहितः अनन्यचित्तः। प्रोक्तैर्दिनैः प्रागवममण्डलादिभिः अपिवा अपिचेत्यर्थः ॥ ६० ॥

विलिख्येत्यादिभिरानयेदित्यन्तैश्चत्वारिंशता श्लोकैरेतद्विद्याक्षरजनितानि स्तम्भनादिकराणि अष्ट यन्त्राणि विद्यावैभवञ्चोपदिशति। तत्र विलिख्येत्यादिभिर्वाहिनीमित्यन्तैः पञ्चभिः श्लोकैर्लोकपालस्य शत्रुसेनायाश्च स्तम्भनकरं यन्त्रमुपदिशति। तत्र मध्ये भूपुरस्य। तद्बाह्ये भूपुरबाह्ये। भौमाक्षराणि पञ्चमप्रष्ठत्रयोदशस्वरपुरःसरकादिवर्गतृतीयाक्षराणि सविन्दूनि दशसंख्यानि। अभितः प्रादक्षिण्येन [वह्निः भौमाक्षरवेष्टनात् तत्र तेषु दलेषु क्रमात् अग्न्यादिप्रादक्षिण्यक्रमात्। ऋतुशः षट्षड़क्षराणि प्रतिदलमिति शेषः। तद्बहिः पद्माद्बहिः। तत्र वृत्तवीथ्यां। पार्थिवानर्णान् प्रागवत्। वह्निर्वृत्तयुग्मात्। तत्कोणेषु षट्कोणेषु अन्तरालेषु कोणान्तरालेषु षट्सु। मन्त्रार्णान् भूदशान्वितान् अष्टदललिखितशिष्टान् प्रागुक्त भूतदशार्णसहितान् मूलविद्यावर्णान्। प्रागवत् प्रतिस्थानं षट्षट्क्रमेण। अभितः अग्न्यादिप्रदक्षिणं वह्निः षट्कोणात्। तत्र वीथ्यां। न्यस्य विलिख्य। वह्निः वृत्तद्वयात्। कृत्वेति पूर्वत्रान्वयः मूलविद्यया सहेति शेषः।

विलिखेत् प्रागवदभितो वहिर्वृत्तद्वयं लिखेत् ।
विलोममातृकां तत्र न्यस्य भूमिपुरं वहिः ॥ ६४ ॥
कृत्वानुलोममालिख्य मातृकां मूलविद्यया ।
पूजयन्नखिलं लोकं स्तम्भयेदरिवाहिनीम् ॥ ६५ ॥

पूजयन् नित्योक्तक्रमतो देवीमिति शेषः । अरिवाहिनीं शत्रुसेनां । चकारोऽत्राध्याहार्थ्यः । अयं यन्त्रविलेखनक्रमः । अभीष्टमानेन प्रोक्तलक्षणं भूपुरं विलिख्य तद्वहिस्तत्कोणाग्रस्पृष्टास्पृष्टिकया वृत्तं कृत्वा तद्वहिरेकाङ्गुल षड़ङ्गुलमानान्तरालं वृत्तद्वयं कृत्वा तत्र वाह्यविषाणवीथ्यामष्टदलं पद्मं विधाय वाह्यवृत्ताद्वहिः वृत्तमेकाङ्गुलमानेन वृत्तं कृत्वा तद्वहिस्तद्वृत्तमध्यविष्कम्भार्द्धमानेन वृत्तं कृत्वा तदन्तराले प्राग्वत् षट्कोणं विधाय षट्कोणाग्रवृत्ताद्वहिरेकाङ्गुलमानेन वृत्तं कृत्वा तद्वहिरेकाङ्गुलमानेन चतुरस्रं कृत्वा सर्वमध्यस्थभूपुरमध्ये साध्यसाधककर्माण्यूर्ध्वाधोन्तरालक्रमेण लिखित्वा तद्वहिर्भूपुरवाह्यवृत्तद्वयवीथ्यामग्रादिप्रादक्षिण्येन] भौमानि उं ऊं ओं गं जं डं दं वं लं ळं इति दशाक्षराणि समालिख्य तद्वहिः पद्मदलेष्वष्टावग्रादिप्रादक्षिण्येन मूलविद्याक्षरेषु दशोत्तरशतसंख्येषु प्रतिदलं षट्षट्क्रमेणाष्टचत्वारिंशदक्षराण्यालिख्य तद्वहिर्वृत्तवीथ्यां प्राग्वत् क्रमेण भौमाक्षरदशकमालिख्य तद्वहिः षट्कोणेषु प्राग्वदग्रादिप्रादक्षिण्येन पूर्वमष्टदललिखितमूलविद्याक्षरशिष्टेषु अक्षरेषु द्विषष्टिसंख्येषु षट्त्रिंशदक्षराणि प्रतिकोणं षट् षट्क्रमेणालिख्य तत् षट्कोणान्तरालेषु षट्सु च प्रत्यन्तरालं प्राग्वत् क्रमेणाग्रकोणोत्तरपार्श्वादिदक्षिणपार्श्वान्तं षट्कोणलिखितविद्याक्षरशिष्टाक्षरषड्विंशतिकं भौमाक्षरदशकञ्च सम्भूय षट्त्रिंशदक्षराणि षट्षट्क्रमेणालिख्य तद्वहिर्वृत्तवीथ्यां अग्रादिप्रादक्षिण्येन विलोमां मातृकां सविसर्जनीयामालिख्य तद्वहिर्वृत्तभूपुरान्तरालवीथ्यामीशादीशान्तं प्रादक्षिण्येन मातृकाक्षराण्येकपञ्चाशत् सविन्दूनि मूलविद्याक्षरदशोत्तरशतकं च सम्भूयैकषष्ट्युत्तरशताक्षराणि प्रतिदिशं चत्वारिंशत् चत्वारिंशदक्षराणि उत्तरस्यां दिश्येकचत्वारिंश दक्षराणि चालिख्य तत्र देवीमावाह्य स्वतन्त्रनित्यपूजाक्रमेण पूजयन् प्रोक्तं फलं प्राप्नोतीति ॥ ६५ ॥

नवास्रं वृत्तयुग्मञ्च वस्वस्रं तद्द्वयं वहिः ।
चतुरस्रञ्च संलिख्य मन्त्रार्णान् षट् षड़ालिखेत् ॥ ६६ ॥
अष्टान्तरालेष्वेकैकं वाह्यवृत्ते तु मातृकाम् ।
चतुरस्रे च विलिखेत् प्रतिलोमानुलोमकम् ॥ ६७ ॥
साध्याख्यां सर्वतो लिख्य (१) यजेदष्टभुजां शिवाम् ।
स्तम्भः स्यात् पूर्व्वमुक्तानां विधानात् परमेश्वरि ॥ ६८ ॥

नवास्रमित्यादिभिः परमेश्वरीत्यन्तैस्त्रिभिः श्लोकैः सर्वस्तम्भनकरं यन्त्रमुपदिशति। तत्र नवास्रं नवयोनिं। वस्वस्रं प्राग्वदष्टकोणं। तद्द्वयं वृत्तद्वयं। षट् षट् नवकोणेषु अष्टकोणेषु च प्रतिकोणमित्यर्थः। अष्टान्तरालेषु अष्टकोणान्तरालेषु एकैकं मूलविद्याक्षराणि कोणलिखितशिष्टान्यष्टौ प्रत्यन्तरालमेकमेकमित्यर्थः। वाह्यवृत्ते अष्टकोणवाह्यवृत्तद्वयान्तरालवीथ्यां। तुः समुच्चये। प्रतिलोमानुलोमकं वृत्तवीथ्यां प्रतिलोमं चतुरस्रेऽनुलोमञ्च। सर्व्वतः अक्षरलेखस्थानेषु। पूर्वमुक्तानामरातिगत्यादीनाम्। परमेश्वरीति सम्बुद्धिः। अयं यन्त्रलेखनक्रमः अभीष्टमानेन वृत्तं कृत्वा तन्मध्ये प्राग्वन्नवयोनिं कृत्वा तद्वहिरेकाङ्गुलान्तराले वृत्तद्वयं कृत्वा तद्वहिर्भूपुरद्वयरूपदिग्विदिग्गत कोणमष्टकोणं कृत्वा तद्वहिस्तत्कोणाष्टकस्पृष्टास्पृष्टिकया वृत्तं विधाय तद्वहिरेकाङ्गुलान्तराले चतुरस्रं कृत्वा सर्वमध्यस्थयोनिमारभ्य निर्गमनगत्याग्रादि प्रादक्षिण्यक्रमेण नवसु कोणेषु प्रतिकोणं षट् षट् क्रमात् मूलविद्याक्षरेषु प्रोक्तसंख्येष्वादितः पञ्चाशदक्षराण्यालिख्य तद्वहिरष्टकोणेष्वष्टसु प्राग्वत् अग्रादिप्रादक्षिण्येन पूर्वलिखितमूलविद्याशिष्टाक्षरेषु षट्पञ्चाशत्सु प्रतिकोणं षट् षट्क्रमेणाष्टचत्वारिंशदक्षराण्यालिख्य तदष्टकोणान्तरालेषु अष्टस्वग्रकोणोत्तरपार्श्वमारभ्य तद्दक्षिणपार्श्वान्तशिष्टविद्याक्षरात्मकं प्रत्यन्तरालमेकं विलिख्य तद्वाह्यवृत्तद्वयान्तरालवीथ्यां प्राग्वदग्रादिप्रादक्षिण्येन विलोमां सविसर्जनीयां मातृकां विलिख्य तद्वहिर्वृत्तचतुरस्रान्तराले प्राग्वदीशादीशान्तं प्रादक्षिण्यात् प्रतिदिशं त्रयोदशत्रयोदशक्रमेणोत्तरस्यां दिशि द्वादशक्रमेण च सम्भूय मातृकाक्षराण्येकपञ्चाशत् सविन्दूनि समालिख्य सर्व्वत्राक्षरलेखनस्थानेषु सप्तविंशतिषु साधकादीनां नामत्रयं विलिख्य तत्र नित्यपूजाक्रमेणाष्टभुजां देवीमावाह्य पूजयन्नरातिगत्यादिकं स्तम्भयतीति ॥ ६८ ॥

१। "ध्यायेद्" इति वा।

वृत्तं त्र्यस्रं पुनर्वृत्तं षडस्रं वृत्तयुग्मकम् ।
अष्टास्रं तद्बहिर्वृत्ते इति कृत्वात्र विन्यसेत् ॥ ६९ ॥
एकं मध्ये बहिः कोणेष्वन्तरालेषु च क्रमात् ।
त्रयं त्रयं समालिख्य बहिः शिष्टन्तु पार्थिवैः ॥ ७० ॥
विलिख्य मध्ये नामापि जपित्वाभ्यर्च्य साधकः ।
स्थापयेत् क्वापि तत्रैव नित्यशश्च बलिं क्षिपेत् ॥ ७१ ॥

वृत्तमित्यादिभिः क्षिपेदित्यन्तैस्त्रिभिः श्लोकैः स्तम्भनयन्त्रान्तरमुपदिशति । तत्र अत्र यन्त्रे एकं मध्ये सर्वमध्ये मूलविद्याप्रथमाक्षरं त्रिकोणाकारं लिखेदिति सम्प्रदायः । मध्ये सर्वमध्यस्थप्रथमाक्षररूपत्रिकोणमध्ये । क्वापि भित्त्यादिषु । तत्रैव स्थापितप्रदेशे । अयं यन्त्रविरचनाक्रमः—अभीष्टमानेन भ्रमेण वृत्तं कृत्वा तद्बहिस्तद्वृत्तविष्कम्भार्धमानं वृत्तं कृत्वा तदन्तराले प्राग्वत् षट्कोणं कृत्वा तद्बहिरेकाङ्गुलमानेन वृत्तं कृत्वा तद्बहिः प्राग्वत् अष्टास्रं कृत्वा तद्बहिस्तत्कोणाग्रस्पृष्टास्पृष्टिकया वृत्तं कृत्वा तद्बहिरेकाङ्गुल माने च वृत्तं कृत्वा तत्र सर्वमध्यस्थवृत्तमध्ये मूलविद्याक्षरप्रथमाक्षरं त्रिकोण-रूपं च ससाधकादित्रयमुपरि सविन्दुकं समालिख्य तद्बहिस्त्रिकोणकोणेषु त्रिषु मूलविद्याया द्वितीयाक्षरादिदशमाक्षरान्तं प्रतिकोणं त्रयं त्रयमग्रादिप्रादक्षिण्येन नवाक्षराण्यालिख्य तत्कोणान्तरालेषु त्रिषु एकादशाक्षरादीनि एकोनविंशा-क्षरान्तानि प्राग्वत् त्रित्रिक्रमेणाग्रकोणोत्तरपार्श्वादितद्दक्षिणपार्श्वान्तं नवाक्षरा-ण्यालिख्य तद्बहिः षट्कोणकोणेष्वग्रादिप्रादक्षिण्येन विद्याविंशतितमाक्षरादीनि सप्त विंशाक्षरान्तानि प्रतिकोणं त्रित्रिक्रमेणाष्टदशाक्षराण्यालिख्य तत्कोणान्त-रालेषु च प्राग्वदष्टत्रिंशाक्षरादीनि पञ्चपञ्चाशत्तमाक्षरान्तान्यष्टादशाक्षराण्या-लिख्य तद्बहिरष्टास्रकोणाष्टके षट्पञ्चाशत्तमाक्षरादीन्येकोनाशीतितमाक्षरा-न्तानि चतुर्विंशत्यक्षराणि प्राग्वत्त्रित्रिक्रमेणालिख्य तदन्तरालाष्टके चाशीति-तमाक्षरादीनि त्र्यधिकशततमाक्षरान्तानि चतुर्विंशत्यक्षरान्तानि प्राग्वदारम्भ-क्रमादालिख्य चतुरधिकशततमाक्षरादीनि शिष्टमूलविद्यासप्ताक्षराणि तदन्ते भौमदशाक्षराणि च सम्भूय सप्तदशाक्षराणि अष्टकोणबाह्यवृत्तद्वयान्तरालवीथ्यां प्राग्वदभितो विलिख्य तत्र देवीमावाह्य प्राग्वत् संपूज्य तद्यन्त्रं शरा-वादिसंपुटितं कृत्वा भित्त्यादिषु संस्थाप्य तत्र प्रतिदिनमभ्यर्च्य तत्र बलिं दत्त्वा पूर्वोक्तफलं प्राप्नोतीति ॥ ७१ ॥

कृत्वा षड़ष्टकोणानि षट्कोणानि पृथक् पृथक्।
क्रमात्त्रिकोणवृत्तान्तरालान् षट्कोणसंयुतान् ॥ ७२ ॥
वाह्यात् क्रमेण मध्यान्तं नक्षत्रतिथिवारयुक्।
विलिखेल्लिपिशः सर्व्वां मातृकां शक्तिसंयुताम् ॥ ७३ ॥
साध्यं सप्तसु मध्येषु विलिखेच्च प्रदक्षिणम्।
मायामध्यगतं देवि धारयेत् सर्व्वसिद्धये ॥ ७४ ॥
भूतप्रेतपिशाचादिशान्त्यै सर्व्वार्त्तिशान्तये।
गजवाजिखरोष्ट्रादिरोगशान्त्यै च धारयेत् ॥ ७५ ॥

कृत्वेत्यादिभिर्द्धारयेदित्यन्तैश्चतुर्भिः श्लोकैः सर्व्वरोगशान्तिकरं यन्त्रमुपदिशति। तत्र षड़ष्टकोणानि षट्कोणानि अष्टकोणानीति पदच्छेदः। अन्तः षट्कोणानि वहिः अष्टकोणानि चेत्यर्थः। पृथक् पृथक् क्रमात् त्रिकोणवृत्तान्तरालान् षट्कोणयुतान् पूर्वलिखितषट्कोणाष्टकोणयोः षट्कोणसंयुतान् त्रिकोणवृत्तान्तरालप्रदेशान् पृथक् पृथक् प्रत्येकं षट्कोणानि कुर्य्यादिति ग्रन्थयोजनाक्रमः। वाह्यात् क्रमेण मध्यान्तं वाह्याष्टकोणकोणादिसर्वमध्यगतषट्कोणं कोणमध्यान्तं। नक्षत्रतिथिवारयुक् साध्याक्षरलेखनस्थानेष्विति शेषः। लिपिश इत्यस्य शक्तियुतामित्यत्रान्वयः। मातृकां विसर्जनीयरहितां पञ्चाशदक्षरवतीं प्रत्यक्षरं विसर्जनीययोगात्तद्राहित्यं। शक्तिसंयुतामित्यस्याक्षरद्वयमाराध्यमुखादवगतं लिख्यते—यथा विसर्जनीयसहितां मूलविद्याक्षरसंहिताञ्चेति। सप्तसु मध्येषु षट्कोणसप्तकस्य सप्तसु मध्येष्वित्यर्थः। विलिखेच्च चकारेण पूर्वोक्तयन्त्रवद्विद्याशिष्टाक्षरदशकं भौमाक्षरदशकञ्च वाह्यवृत्तवीथ्यां विलिखेदित्येकोऽर्थः। समाकृष्यत इति सम्प्रदायार्थः। प्रदक्षिणं सर्वाणि उक्ताक्षराणि मायामध्यगतं हृल्लेखया क्रोड़ीकृतम्। भूतप्रेतपिशाचादिशान्त्यै आदिशब्देनापस्मारादयः। तैः कृतपीड़ाशान्त्यै गजवाजिखरोष्ट्रादि इत्यत्रादिशब्देन गोमहिषाजादयश्चतुष्पदा उच्यन्ते। अयमत्र विलेखनक्रमः—अभीष्टमानेन भ्रमेण वृत्तं कृत्वा तत्र-नित्यानित्यापटले प्रोक्तानुग्रहचक्रक्रमेण षट्कोणसप्तकमालिख्य तद्वहिः प्राग्वदष्टकोणं कृत्वा तद्वहिरष्टकोणाग्रस्पृष्टास्पृष्टिकया वृत्तं कृत्वा तद्वहिरेकाङ्गल-

प्राक्प्रत्यग्दक्षिणोदक्करेखाष्टादश संलिखेत्।
रेखाग्रे सर्व्वतः शूलास्तन्मध्याग्रे च पार्श्वयोः ॥ ७६ ॥
स्तम्भयेति समालिख्य मध्यकोष्ठेऽरिनाम च।
परितो विलिखेन्मन्त्रवर्णान् भौमसमन्वितान् ॥ ७७ ॥
भूर्जे वा कर्पटे लोहे शिलायां वा समालिखेत्।
गृहपट्टनयोर्लोहहृद्दृशदोरिष्टसिद्धिदम् ॥ ७८ ॥

मानेन वृत्तं कृत्वा तत्र वाह्याष्टकोणेष्वग्निकोणादि प्रादक्षिण्येन सविसर्ज-नीयाम्मातृकावर्णानादितोऽष्टौ समालिख्य तेष्वेव कोणेषु मूलविद्याया आदितः षोड़शाक्षरेषु प्रतिकोणमेकमेकं चैवमष्टाक्षराण्यादितः समालिख्य तत्कोणान्त-रालेषु अष्टसु मातृकाया विद्यायाश्च नवमाक्षरादीनि षोड़शाक्षरान्तमष्टाक्षराणि प्रागवत् क्रमादालिख्य तदन्तः षट्कोणमारभ्य प्रादक्षिण्येन प्रतिषट्कोणं षट्सु षट्सु कोणेषु तदन्तरालेषु च षट्सु षट्सु च संभूय चतुरशीतिसंख्येषु स्थानेषु मातृकाया विद्यायाश्च सप्तदशाक्षरादीनि पञ्चाशत्तमाक्षरान्तानि चतु-स्त्रिंशदक्षराणि चतुस्त्रिंशत्स्थानेष्वालिख्य शिष्टेषु पञ्चाशत्स्थानेषु पुनरप्य-कारादीनि विसर्जनीयरहितानि क्षकारान्तानि प्रत्यक्षरं त्रिसर्जनीययुक्तानि मातृकाक्षराणि पञ्चाशत् संख्यानि मूलविद्यैकपञ्चाशत्तमाक्षरादिभिः शततमा-क्षरान्तैः पञ्चाशद्भिरक्षरैः सह प्रागवत् क्रमेण समालिख्य विद्याशिष्टाक्षरदशकं भौमार्णदशकञ्च प्रागवत् सर्ववाह्यसप्तवीथ्यामालिख्य षट्कोणसप्तकमध्यसप्तके तत्तत्प्रयोगदिवसप्राप्तनक्षत्रतिथिवारान् सप्तम्यन्तानालिख्य तत्तदुपरि साधकादि-त्रयं प्रागवदालिख्य तत्सर्वं यन्त्रं हृल्लेखाया उपरिगतचतुर्थस्वरेण क्रोड़ीकृत्य तत्र देवीमावाह्याभ्यर्च्य प्रोक्तक्रमसन्धारणात् प्रोक्तफलसिद्धिरिति ॥ ७५ ॥

प्राक्प्रत्यगित्यादिभिर्द्वयोरित्यन्तैः पञ्चभिः श्लोकैः स्तम्भनकरं कोष्ठयन्त्र-मुपदिशति। तत्र तन्मध्याग्रे च पार्श्वयोः तत्तच्छूलं मध्यरेखाग्रे तत्तच्छूल-मध्यरेखापार्श्वयोश्च स्तम्भय इति त्र्यक्षराणि यथाक्रमं त्रिशूलमध्यरेखाग्रे तद्दक्षिणवामपार्श्वयोश्च मध्यकोष्ठे सर्वमध्यस्थकोष्ठमध्ये सर्वमध्ये कोष्ठाधः पङ्क्तिमध्यकोष्ठमारभ्य निर्गमनगत्येत्यर्थः। भौमसमन्वितान् भौमवर्णसम-न्वितान् मन्त्रवर्णान् गृहपत्तनयोर्निर्माणस्तम्भने तद्गतामङ्गलस्तम्भने वा इति शेषः। लोहदृशदोः पूर्वोक्ताधिकरणचतुष्टयस्य मध्ये तालेन हरितालेन शुभं मनोहरं क्रमतः शरावादिसंपुटनाक्रमतः यावत् फलावाप्तिस्तावत् कुर्व्वीत

गोरक्षीणाथ शिलायां तालेन विलिखेच्छुभम् ।
स्थापयेद्भित्तिमध्ये च भूमौ च क्रमतः शिवे ॥ ७९ ॥
नित्यशः पूजयेत् पुष्पैः सुगन्धैः प्रजपेत्तथा ।
यावत्फलाप्ति कुर्वीत नियतं सन्ध्ययोर्द्वयोः ॥ ८० ॥
प्राक्प्रत्यग्दक्षिणोदक् कुर्य्यात् सूत्राणि षोडश ।
तैस्तु कोष्ठानि जायन्ते पञ्चविंशैः शतद्वयम् ॥ ८१ ॥
तेषु कोणेषु परितो मार्जयेत् प्राग्वदीश्वरि ।
अष्टाविंशति कोष्ठानि ततः शिष्टेषु दिक्ष्वपि ॥ ८२ ॥
प्राग्वदेकैकतः कुर्य्यात्त्रिकोणानि यथाविधि ।
मध्ये त्रिषु तु कोष्ठेषु साध्यसाधककर्म्म च ॥ ८३ ॥
उपर्य्यधो मध्यतश्च शेषेषु प्राग्वदालिखेत् ।
मन्त्रार्णानग्रमारभ्य विलिखेदभितः शिवे ॥ ८४ ॥

जपार्च्चनादिकमित्यर्थः । नियतं प्रतिदिवसं । यन्त्रविरचनाक्रमो यथा— प्राक्प्रत्यग्दक्षिणोदक् द्वादश द्वादश रेखाः समालिख्यैकविंशत्यधिकशतसंख्यानि कोष्ठानि निष्पाद्य तत्तद्रेखाग्राष्टचत्वारिंशत्कोष्ठ परितः प्रत्येकं त्रिशूलं कृत्वा तत्र सर्व्वमध्यस्थकोष्ठमध्ये साधकादित्रयं प्राग्वदालिख्य तत्कोष्ठाधःपङ्क्तिस्थमध्यकोष्ठमारभ्य प्रादक्षिण्यनिर्गमनगत्या यावदक्षरसमाप्ति मूलविद्याक्षराणि विलिख्य शिष्टकोष्ठदशके भौमाक्षरदशकमालिख्य बाह्यगतत्रिशूलेषु मध्यगतत्रिशूलेषु मध्यगतरेखाग्रतद्दक्षवामपार्श्वयोश्च स्तम्भय स्तम्भयेति त्र्यक्षरं प्रतित्रिशूलमालिखेत्तदयन्त्रं भूर्जाद्यधिकरणचतुष्टयाद्यन्यतमस्थं प्रोक्तद्रव्येण विलिखत्र प्राणप्रतिष्ठादिकं कृत्वा तत्र देवीमावाह्याभ्यर्च्य प्राग्वच्छुरावादिपुटितं कृत्वा प्रोक्तस्थानयोः संस्थाप्य तत्र सन्ध्याद्वयेपि प्रतिदिवसं गन्धसुपुष्पैरिष्टसिद्ध्यवधि पूजयन्नभीष्टं फलमाप्नोतीति ॥ ८० ॥

प्राक्प्रत्यगित्यादिभिर्ध्रुवमित्यन्तैरष्टभिः श्लोकैः समस्ताभीष्टफलप्रदं महावज्रयन्त्रमुपदिशति । तत्र तैः सूत्रैः । तेषु कोष्ठेषु अष्टाविंशतिकोष्ठानि प्रतिकोणमिति शेषः । शिष्टेषु त्रयोदशाधिकशतसंख्येषु । एकैकतः एकैककोष्ठात् ।

एतदुच्चं महायन्त्रं समस्ताभीष्टसाधकम् ।
यत्रैतत् स्थापितं लोहशिलादिलिखितं शिवे ॥ ८५ ॥
तत्र चोरग्रहव्याधिरिपुसर्पसमुद्भवाः ।
भूतप्रेतपिशाचादिकोपजाश्चाप्युपप्लवाः ॥ ८६ ॥
न भवन्ति कदाप्यत्र सम्भवन्ति च सम्पदः ।
वास्तुमर्म्मादिदुःखादि शमयेद् गेहगञ्च तत् ॥ ८७ ॥
यस्मिन् गृहे स्थापितन्तु यन्त्रं तद्गेहवर्त्तिनाम् ।
कृत्याभिचारक्षुद्रादि पीड़ा न भवति ध्रुवम् ॥ ८८ ॥

साध्यसाधककर्म च साध्यसाधककर्म्माणीत्यर्थः । अग्रमारभ्य विलिखेदित्यनेनान्वयः । उपर्य्यधो मध्यत इति पूर्वत्र साध्यसाधककर्म चेत्यनेनान्वयः । तन्नेत्रनप्रकारास्तूपरिकोष्ठे साधकमधः कोष्ठे साध्यं मध्यकोष्ठे कर्म्म चेति । शेषेषु दशोत्तरशतसंख्येषु । प्राग्वत् प्रादक्षिण्यप्रवेशगत्या दशोत्तरशताक्षरान् मन्त्रार्णान् लिखेदित्यनेनान्वयः । शिलादीत्यत्रादिशब्देन भूर्जपत्रपटतालान्युच्यन्ते । पिशाचादीत्यत्रादिशब्दोऽपस्मारादिविषयः । उपप्लवाः उपद्रवाः न भवन्तीति पूर्व्वत्रान्वयः । मर्म्मादीत्यादिशब्दो द्वारभित्तिभागादिविषयः । गेहगञ्च तत् गृहस्थापितं तद्यन्त्रमित्यर्थः । क्षुद्रादीत्यादिशब्दः पिशाचादिविषयः । अयमत्र विलेखनक्रमः—प्राक्प्रत्यग्दक्षिणोदक्क षोड़शसूत्रास्फालनेन पञ्चविंशत्यधिकशतद्वयकोष्ठानि निष्पाद्य तेषु कोष्ठेषु चतुर्षु कोणेषु प्रतिकोणमष्टाविंशत्यष्टाविंशतिकोष्ठानि सम्भूय द्वादशाधिकशतसंख्यानि कोष्ठानि प्राग्वन्मध्ये वज्राकारं यथा भवति तथा मार्जयित्वा तथा शिष्टेषु त्रयोदशाधिकशतसंख्येषु कोष्ठेषु चतस्रषु दिक्षु प्रतिदिशमेकैकं कोष्ठं सम्भूय चत्वारि कोष्ठानि मार्जयित्वा तत्र त्रिकोणानि प्राग्वत् समत्रिरेखानि कृत्वा तत्र सर्वमध्यकोष्ठे कर्म्म तदुपरितनकोष्ठे साधकं तदधःस्थितकोष्ठे साध्यञ्चालिख्य शिष्टेषु चतुर्दिग्गतत्रिकोणचतुष्टयसहितेषु दशोत्तरशतसंख्येषु कोष्ठेषु अग्रत्रिकोणादिप्रादक्षिण्यप्रवेशगत्या ततसंख्यानि मूलविद्याक्षराणि विलिख्य एतद् यन्त्रं प्रोक्ताधिकरणान्यतमगतं कृत्वा प्रोक्तेषु देशेषु प्राणप्रतिष्ठादिपुरःसरमभ्यर्च्य स्थापनात् प्रोक्तफलसिद्धिरिति ॥ ८८ ॥

वायुग्निनैर्ऋतेशञ्च कुर्य्याद्द्वादशसूत्रकम् ।
तैर्व्वज्ररूपकोष्ठानि एकविंशशतम्भवेत् ॥ ८९ ॥
तेषु मध्ये समालिख्य साध्यनाम ततो वहिः ।
अग्रादभित एवान्यान्यक्षराणि समालिखेत् ॥ ९० ॥
निर्गमेन महीवर्णपूर्व्वाणि क्रमतः शिवे ।
स्थापितं लोहशिलादिलिखितं पूजितन्तु वा ॥ ९१ ॥
रोगभूतग्रहोन्मादपिशाचापस्मृतिद्विषः ।
अन्यानि क्लेशकारीणि यानि तानि विनाशयेत् ॥ ९२ ॥

वाय्वित्यादिभिर्भूतलइत्यन्तैः सप्तभिः श्लोकैर्व्वज्राभिधं यन्त्रं तद्विनियोगादिकञ्चोपदिशति। तत्र तैः सूत्रैस्तेषु वज्ररूपकोष्ठेषु। मध्ये सर्वमध्यस्थवज्रकोष्ठे। साध्यनाम साधककर्म्माणि अग्रान्मध्यकोष्ठाधःस्थकोष्ठारभ्य तः। अभितः प्रादक्षिण्येन। अन्यानि कोष्ठानि। अक्षराणि मूलविद्याक्षराणि अन्येषु कोष्ठेषु अक्षराणि लिखेदित्यर्थः। महीवर्णपूर्वाणि पूर्वं भौमाक्षराणि विलिख्य शेषेषु कोष्ठेषु विद्याक्षराणि लिखेदित्यर्थः। शिवे इति सम्बुद्धिः। शिलादौत्यत्रादिशब्दो भूर्जपत्रपटादिविषयः। अन्यानि शत्रुस्थापितकृत्याकालभस्मादीनि प्रोक्तेषु रोगादिषु आर्त्तिषु पीड़ासु प्रोक्तरोगादिसञ्ज्ञातासु पीड़ास्वित्यर्थः। तद्यन्त्रं वज्रवज्रं मध्ये सर्वमध्यस्थकोष्ठमध्ये तुविशेषः। क्षीरद्रुक्वाथपूरितं अश्वत्थोडुम्बरप्लक्षवटानां चतुर्णां क्षीरवृक्षाणां त्वग्भिः सह क्वाथितैः प्रशमितोष्णैः खारिमाणैस्तोयैः पूरितम्। निधाय इत्यस्य पूर्वत्रान्वयः। देवीं पञ्चमीं। सलिले कुम्भस्थे इति शेषः। आत्मवान् अधिगतः। तैर्जलैर्यन्त्रविद्यादिशक्तिसंक्रमतः कलितानुभावैः। अयमत्र विलेखन क्रमः—इष्टमानभ्रमेण वृत्तं निष्पाद्य तत्र प्राक्प्रत्यगदक्षिणोत्तरञ्च तद्वृत्तावधि ब्रह्मसूत्रद्वयमास्फाल्य प्राक्प्रत्यग्ब्रह्मसूत्रस्य प्रागग्राद्दक्षिणोत्तरब्रह्मसूत्रदक्षिणाग्रान्तं तदग्रात् प्राक्पश्चिम ब्रह्मसूत्रपश्चिमाग्रान्तं तदग्राद्दक्षिणोत्तरब्रह्मसूत्रोत्तराग्रान्तं तदग्रात् प्राक्पश्चिमब्रह्मसूत्रप्रागग्रान्तं ज्यारूपं सूत्रचतुष्टयमास्फाल्य ब्रह्मसूत्रद्वयस्य वृत्तस्य च मार्जनाद्दिग्गतकोणचतुष्टयं समचतुरस्रं विधाय वायुदिक्स्थरेखादिवह्निदिक्स्थरेखान्तं नैर्ऋतदिक्स्थरेखादि ईशदिक्स्थरेखान्तं च समान्तरालदशसूत्रास्फालनेन वज्रवज्राकारमेकविंशत्यधिकशतसंख्यवज्ररूपकोष्ठसहितं यन्त्रं विधाय तत्र

प्रोक्तोष्वाप्तिं ष्वपि तथा तद्वज्रं गौरकैर्भुवि।
विलिख्य मध्ये कुम्भन्तु क्षीरद्रुक्वाथपूरितम् ॥ ९३ ॥
निधाय देवीं सलिले समावाह्याभिपूज्य च।
स्पृशञ्जलं जपेद्विद्यां सहस्रत्रयमात्मवान् ॥ ९४ ॥
तैर्जलैरभिषिञ्चेत्तं गदिनं प्राङ्मुखं ततः।
तैः क्लेशैर्मुक्तदेहस्तु सुखी जीवति भूतले ॥ ९५ ॥
विद्याप्राप्त्यभिषेकन्तु वज्रेऽस्मिन् कोष्ठवज्रके।
सैकविंशशते वापि कुम्भं संस्थाप्य सेचयेत् ॥ ९६ ॥
वेदाङ्गुलपरिभ्रान्त्या वृत्तं कृत्वा ततो बहिः।
द्व्यङ्गुले द्व्यङ्गुले कुर्य्यादेकादश ततः क्रमात् ॥ ९७ ॥
तेषु द्व्यङ्गुलमानेषु तिर्य्यक् सूत्राणि पातयेत्।
एकादश ततस्तेषु प्राङ्मध्यात्तु प्रदक्षिणम् ॥ ९८ ॥
भूदशांशैस्तु तां विद्यामालिखेन्निर्गमक्रमात्।
रेखाग्राणि च शूलानि कृत्वा साध्यञ्च मध्यतः ॥ ९९ ॥

सर्वं मध्यस्थकोष्ठमध्ये साधकसाध्यकर्माणि प्राग्वदालिख्य तदधःस्थवज्रकोष्ठमारभ्य प्रादक्षिण्यनिर्गमनगत्या भौमाक्षरदशकं वज्रकोष्ठदशके विलिख्य शेषेषु दशोत्तरशतसंख्यवज्ररूपकोष्ठेषु तत्संख्यानि मूलविद्याक्षराणि विलिख्यैतद्यन्त्रं प्रोक्ताधिकरणेष्वन्यतमगतं कृत्वा स्थापनेन पूजनेन च तद्यन्त्रे प्रोक्तक्रमाभिषेकेन वा प्रोक्तफलसिद्धं भवतीति ॥ ८५ ॥

विद्येत्यादिना श्लोकेन प्रोक्तेषु सप्तसु यन्त्रेषु यन्त्रत्रयं विद्याप्राप्त्यभिषेके अप्यतिदिशति। अत्र च तुर्विशेषे। वज्रेऽस्मिन् अनन्तरपूर्वोक्तवज्रवज्राभिध सप्तमे यन्त्रे। कोष्ठवज्रके कोष्ठवज्ररूपे षष्ठे यन्त्रे। सैकविंशशते सैकविंशशतसंख्यकोष्ठरूपे पञ्चमे यन्त्रे। वा विकल्पे तेषु त्रिषु अन्यतमंयन्त्रे इत्यर्थः ॥ ८६ ॥

वेदाङ्गुलेत्यादिभिरनयेत्यन्तैश्चतुर्भिः श्लोकैरखिलसिद्धिकरं यन्त्रं विद्यावैभवस्योपदिशति। तत्र वेदाङ्गुलपरिभ्रान्त्या प्रतिदिशं चतुरङ्गुलमानपरिभ्रान्त्या। ततस्तद्वृत्तात्। द्व्यङ्गुले द्व्यङ्गुले द्व्यङ्गुलमाने द्व्यङ्गुलमाने एकादश-

तद्यन्त्रं प्राग्वदखिलविनियोगेषु योजितम् ।
नासाध्यमस्ति भुवने विद्यया सिद्धयाऽनया ॥ १०० ॥
मनस्तत्त्वमयी व्याप्तिरिति सम्यक् समीरिता ।
अस्या निष्कालनाच्चित्ते तत्तत्त्वं स्वात्मसात्कृतम् ॥

इतिश्रीषोड़शनित्यातन्त्रेषु श्रीकादिमते
त्रयोविंशपटलं परिपूर्णम् ॥

वृत्तानीति शेषः। तेषु वृत्तेषु तत् द्व्यङ्गुलमानेषु स्वैकादशांशसहितेष्विति शेषः। एतन्मानमन्तर्वृत्तस्यैवोक्तम्। तिर्य्यक् सूत्राणि सर्व्वमध्यवृत्तात् सर्ववाह्यवृत्तान्तग-रूपाणीत्यर्थः। तेषु कोष्ठेषु। प्राङ्मध्यात् सर्वमध्यवृत्तान्तर्भूतप्रदेशरूपकर्णि-काया वहिस्तदनन्तरवीथ्यां प्राङ्मध्यकोष्ठोत्तरकोष्ठे च साधकसाध्यकर्माणि लिखेदिति सम्प्रदायार्थः। प्राग्वत् प्राणप्रतिष्ठापुरःसरमर्च्चनधारणस्थापना-दिभिः। अखिलविनियोगेषु प्रोक्तेष्विति शेषः। अयमत्र लिखनक्रमः—प्रतिदिशं चतुरङ्गुलमानभ्रमेण वृत्तं निष्पाद्य तद्वहिर्द्व्यङ्गुलद्व्यङ्गुलमानेन प्राग्वदेकादशवृत्तानि निष्पाद्य तत्र सर्वमध्यवृत्ते तत्सर्ववाह्यवृत्ते च तत्त द्विष्कम्भमानं त्रिगुणीकृत्य तत्तन्मानमेकादशधा विभज्य तत्तद्देशेष्वेकादश चिह्नानि पश्चिमादिविधाय तत् सर्वमध्यवृत्तस्थचिह्नैकादशकमारभ्य तत् सर्ववाह्यवृत्तस्थचिह्नैकादशचिह्नमध्ये एकादश सूत्राण्यास्फाल्य तत्सर्ववाह्य-वृत्तस्थैकादशरेखाग्रं किञ्चित् प्रसार्य्य प्रत्येकं शूलाकारं कृत्वा एवं मध्य-कर्णिकाया वहिरेकविंशत्युत्तरशतकोष्ठसहितं वृत्ताकारं वहिः शूलोपेतं यन्त्रं निष्पाद्य तत्र तत्कर्णिकायां साधकादीनि प्राग्वदालिख्य तदनन्तरवाह्य-वृत्तवीथ्यां प्राङ्मध्यकोष्ठमाराभ्य उक्तक्रमात् प्रादक्षिण्यनिर्गमनगत्या दशोत्तर शतसंख्येषु कोष्ठेषु विद्याक्षराणि तत्संख्यानि विलिख्य शिष्टकोष्ठैकादशके भीमाक्षरदशकमालिख्य शिष्टे चैकस्मिन् प्राग्वत् साधकादित्रयमालिखेत्ततप्रोक्ता-धिकरणेष्वन्यतमगतं कृत्वा प्राग्वत् प्रोक्तप्रयोगेषु प्राणप्रतिष्ठापुरःसरमर्च्चना दिभिः प्रोक्तफलसिद्धिर्भवेदिति ॥ १०० ॥

इति षोड़शनित्यातन्त्रेषु श्रीकादिमताख्यस्य परिपूर्णस्य तन्त्रस्य प्रपञ्च-सार-सिंह राजप्रकाशाभिधानेन श्रीसुभगानन्दनाथेन विरचितायां मनोरमाख्यायां व्याख्यायां षोड़शनित्याङ्गभूतपञ्चमीविद्याविधानप्रकाशनपरं त्रयोविंशं पटलम् परिपूर्णं परामृष्टम् ॥ २३ ॥

ग्रन्थसंख्या। त्रयोविंशे तु पटले यन्त्राणि मुनिसंख्यया।
व्याख्याग्रन्था नवशतमेकाशीतिस्तथार्द्धकम् ॥

चतुर्विंशपटलम् ।

अथ षोड़शनित्यानां ध्यानानि विविधानि ते ।
कथयामि शृणु प्राज्ञे वाञ्छितार्थसुरद्रुमान् ॥ १ ॥
एकैकमङ्गाङ्गित्वेन तासां तच्छक्तिभिस्तथा ।
प्रयोगेषु समस्तेषु वाह्याभ्यन्तरतः क्रमात् ॥ २ ॥
श्रियै कीर्त्त्यै जयावाप्त्यै वश्याकर्षणसिद्धये ।
ध्यायेद्देवीः समस्ताश्च लोहिताकारमण्डनाः ॥ ३ ॥
विद्याप्तौ शान्तिके मुक्ताविन्दुकर्पूरसन्निभाः ।
विद्वेषोच्चाटनिधननिग्रहेष्वसिताः स्मरेत् ॥ ४ ॥
धूम्रा वा चिन्तयेत् सर्व्वाः प्रोक्तद्वेषादिसिद्धये ।
सर्व्वत्र स्वसमाकारवर्णशक्तिभिरावृताः ॥ ५ ॥

पूर्वस्मिंस्त्रयोविंशे पटले षोड़शनित्यानामङ्गभूताया वाराह्या विधानमुपदिश्यानन्तरं षोड़शनित्यानां विविधानि ध्यानानि तासां प्रत्येकमङ्गाङ्गित्वक्रमतः प्रयोगादिकञ्चोपदिशति—अथ षोड़शेत्यादिना सिद्धिकृदित्यन्तेन श्लोकशतरूपेण चतुर्विंशेन पटलेन। तत्र अथ षोड़शेत्यादिना क्रमात् इत्यन्तेन श्लोकद्वयेन पटलार्थानुपदिशति। तत्र सुरद्रुमान् सुरद्रुमसदृशानि अभिमतार्थप्रदानादिष्वमोघतयेति यावत्। एकैकं एकैकक्रमेण तासां नित्यानां तच्छक्तिभिः तत्तत्परिवारशक्तिभिः सहेति शेषः। वाह्याभ्यन्तरतः स्थूलसूक्ष्मभेदतः। ध्यानानीति पूर्वत्रान्वयः ॥ २ ॥

श्रियै इत्यादिना श्लोकेन श्रीकीर्त्तिजयवश्याकर्षणेषु सामान्यध्यानमुपदिशति। तत्र वश्याकर्षणसिद्धये च वश्यसिद्धये आकर्षणसिद्धये च। समस्ताः षोड़शनित्याः सपरिवारा लोहिताकारमण्डना इत्यत्र मण्डनशब्दो वसनभूषणमाल्यानुलेपनादिविषयः ॥ ३ ॥

विद्याप्ताविल्यादिना श्लोकपूर्वार्द्धेन विद्याप्राप्तिकरं शान्तिकरं मुक्तिसिद्धिकरं सामान्यध्यानमुपदिशति। तत्र इन्दुकर्पूरसन्निभाः इन्दुसन्निभाः कर्पूरसन्निभाश्च कान्तिवर्णाभ्यामिति शेषः ॥ विद्वेषेत्यादिना वृता इत्यन्तेनार्द्धाधेन श्लोकेन

क्षित्यादिभूतैः सत्त्वादिगुणैरेकैकसंहतैः।
एकद्व्यादिसमारब्धैर्व्वर्णाकारैस्तु शक्तयः॥ ६॥
असंख्याता भवन्त्यासां कार्त्स्न्याद्ध्यानन्तु को वदेत्।
को वा शृणोति साकल्यात् ततः किञ्चिद्वदामि ते॥ ७॥
भौमाकाराः पीतवर्णाः सर्वाः स्तम्भनकारिकाः।
आप्याः सत्त्वगुणाः सर्व्वाः सिताकाराः समीरिताः॥ ८॥
ताः सर्व्वा ज्ञानशान्तिश्रीकीर्त्तिसौभाग्यमुक्तिदाः।
आग्नेया राजसाः सर्व्वा लोहिताकारसंयुताः॥ ९॥

विद्वेषोच्चाटननिधननिग्रहेषु सामान्यध्यानमुपदिशति। तत्र असिताः आकार-वसनमाल्यभूषणानुलेपनादिभिरिति शेषः। धूम्राः प्रागवदाकारादिभिरिति शेषः। वा विकल्पे। सर्व्वा नित्याः। सर्वत्र प्रोक्तेषु ध्यानभेदेषु॥ ५॥

क्षित्यादीत्यादिना वदामि ते इत्यन्तेन श्लोकद्वयेन परिच्छिन्नरूपायाः परायाः शक्तेः परिच्छिन्नाकारतया विविधवर्णाद्युपलब्धिकारणं तत्तदुपलब्धशक्तीनाम-संख्यातत्वादिकञ्चोपदिशति। तत्र क्षित्यादिभूतैः पृथिव्यप्तेजोवाय्वाकाशैः। सत्त्वादिगुणैः सत्त्वरजस्तमोभिः एकैकसंहतैः पृथक् पृथक् सम्बद्धैः परस्पर-मिति शेषः। एकद्व्यादिसमारब्धैः भूतानां पृथक् पृथक् सम्बद्धगुणाना-मेकद्व्यादिसमसमांशविषमविषमांशपरिकल्पितैर्वर्णाकारैः संजाता इति शेषः॥ आसां शक्तीनां कार्त्स्न्येन ध्यानन्तु को वदेत् कोवा शृणोति साकल्यात् वक्तॄणां श्रोतॄणाञ्चानित्यत्वादिति यावत् ततस्तस्मात् किञ्चिदितुरक्तिस्तेषु शक्तिभेदेषु मन्त्रेषु वक्ष्यमाणरूपस्यैकदेशत्वात्। एतदुक्तं भवति सत्त्वादिगुणैः पृथक् पृथक् नित्यसम्बन्धानां क्षित्यादिभूतानामेकद्व्यादिसमविषमांशपरिकल्पनाभेद-भिन्नवर्णाकाराणां शक्तीनामसंख्यातत्वात्तासामाकारमिदमनुभावञ्च वक्तुं श्रोतुं वाऽशक्यत्वात्तेषु शक्तिभेदेषु विश्वपरित्राणार्थं शक्तितः किञ्चिद्वदामीति॥ ७॥

भौमाकारा इत्यादिभिः स्मृता इत्यन्तैरर्द्धाधिकैस्त्रिभिः श्लोकैरेकैकगुण-युक्तानां पञ्चभूतशक्तीनां क्रमेण ध्यानं तत्प्रयोगांश्चोपदिशति। तत्र भौमाकारा भूमिस्वरूपाः। पीतवर्णाः विग्रहवसनभूषणानुलेपनमाल्यादिभिरितिशेषः। सर्वाः परिवारा नित्याः स्तम्भनकारकाः। भूमेरचलात्मकत्वात्। आप्या जला-त्मिकाः शक्तयः। सत्त्वगुणाः सत्त्वगुणयुक्ताः। सर्वाः प्रागवत् सिताकाराः प्राग-

वश्याकर्षणशान्तिश्रीसौभाग्यविजयप्रदाः।
वायुरूपा धूम्रवर्णा सर्वा द्वेषादिकारकाः॥ १०॥
नाभसा नीलवर्णास्ता मारणोत्सादयोः स्मृताः।
आसां मुखभुजादेहविधानं शृणु पार्वति॥ ११॥
एकवक्त्राश्चतुर्वक्त्रा नववक्त्रास्तथा पराः।
षोडशास्याः पञ्चविंशद्वदना अपि काश्चन॥ १२॥
षट्त्रिंशद्वदना क्वापि चत्वारिंशन्नवाननाः।
चतुःषष्टिमुखास्तद्वदेकाशीतिशताननाः॥ १३॥

वह्निगृहादिभिः। ताः सर्वा जलरूपाः शक्तयः। जलशक्तीनां स्नानादिप्रदत्वं सुष्ठ्वा-त्मकत्वात्। लोहिताकारसंयुताः प्रागवह्निगृहादिभिः। आग्नेयानां शक्तीनां वश्यादिप्रदत्वं ग्रासाद्यात्मकत्वात्। वायुरूपाः शक्तय इति शेषः। धूम्रवर्णाः प्राग्वह्निगृहवसनादिभिः। द्वेषादिकारका इत्यत्रादिशब्द उच्चाटनादिविषयः वायोरुच्चाटनादिकारकत्वं चलनात्मकत्वात्। नाभसा आकाशात्मिकाः शक्तयः। नीलवर्णाः प्रागद्विगृहादिभिः। ताः सपरिवारा नित्या मारणोत्सादनयोः उत्सादो नाम मृतवत् अकिञ्चित्करत्वं तयोः कर्मणोरिति शेषः। स्मृता ध्याताः। आकाशात्मकशक्तीनां निधनसिद्धिकरत्वमाकाशस्याविग्रहत्वात् वायु-नभसोराजसगुणात्मकत्वमस्तीति सम्प्रदायः॥ १०॥

आसामित्यादिनोत्तरार्द्धेनैकद्व्यादिसमविषमांशयोगसंजातानां तासां शक्तीनां मुखभुजदेहस्वरूपभेदविधानं प्रस्तौति। तत्र पार्वतीतिसम्बुद्धिः॥ ११॥

एकवक्त्रा इत्यादिना शताननना इत्यन्तेन श्लोकद्वयेन गुणानां भूतानामेकद्व्यादि समसमांशगुणयोगात्तासां वक्त्रसंख्याभेदध्यानमुपदिशति। तत्र एकवक्त्रा एक-वदनयुक्ताः। चतुर्वक्त्राः प्राग्वत्। अपरा अन्याः शक्तय इति शेषः। षोडशास्याः षोडशमुखाः काश्चन प्राग्वत् शक्तयः। क्वापि प्रयोगविशेषे चत्वारिंशन्न-वाननाः एकोनपञ्चाशदाननाः। एकाशीतिशताननाः एकाशीत्याननाः शता-ननाश्च भूतानामेकद्व्यादिदशान्तानामंशानां गुणानामेकद्व्यादिदशान्तैरंशैः समसंख्यांशक्रमेण संगुणनादेवं संजातसंख्यवक्त्राः शक्तयो दशविधा दर्शिता भवन्ति। तासां मुखक्रमस्तु कण्ठपीठोपरि एकवक्त्रं चतुर्वक्त्रपक्षे तु

वहुना किं मुखभुजसंख्यासाधनवाञ्छया ।
तथापि दर्शितं किञ्चिद्वक्त्रे भुजद्वयं द्वयम् ॥ १४ ॥
नामरूपातिगा येन तेन साऽनन्तविग्रहा ।
वसन्ति नानारूपाश्च भवेयुस्तव वाञ्छया ॥ १५ ॥
आद्याया ललितायास्तु अन्याः पञ्चदशाङ्गगाः ।
ललिताङ्गित्वरूपेण सर्वासामात्मविग्रहाः ॥ १६ ॥
तेन तासान्तु सर्वासां स्वान्तान्ताः परिचारिकाः ।
तत्तद्वर्णायुधाकारवाहनैश्च सुसंयुताः ॥ १७ ॥
तथाविधैः स्वस्वशक्तिवृन्दैश्च वेष्टिता अपि ।
इति तासां ध्यानभेदाः स्थूलाः प्रोक्ता महेश्वरि ॥ १८ ॥

प्रथमवक्त्रोपरि तिर्य्यग्रूपेण वक्त्रत्रयं तेन सह चतुर्वक्त्रम् । नववक्त्रपक्षे तु तदुपरि च तिर्य्यक्पङ्क्तिरूपेण पञ्चवक्त्रं तैः सह नववक्त्रम् । एवमुत्तरत्रापि उपरि उपरि सप्तनवैकादशत्रयोदशपञ्चदशसप्तदशैकोनविंशतिसंख्यान्तं वक्त्रं परिकल्पनात् प्रोक्तसंख्यवक्त्रा भवन्ति इति च सम्प्रदायार्थः ॥ १३ ॥

वहुनेत्यादिना वाञ्छयेत्यन्तेन श्लोकद्वयेन नामरूपातिगाया ललितायाः प्रोक्तक्रमेणोत्तरत्रापि भूतांशानां गुणांशानां समसंख्यगुणनादेकद्व्यादिदशदशांशगुणनाच्च संजातानां शक्तीनामसंख्यातत्वात्तासां मुखभुजादिभेदपरिकल्पितविग्रहादेः साधकाभिमतानुगुणत्वमुपदिशति । तत्र वहुना विग्रहविशेषपरः शतेन च । वक्त्रे वक्त्रे भुजद्वयं प्रोक्तानां मुखसंख्यानामेकैकस्य मुखस्य द्विद्विभुजक्रमेण यावत्संख्यं कल्पयेदिति यावत् । नामरूपातिगा नाम्नां रूपाणाञ्चापरिच्छिन्नत्वात् परायाः शक्तेर्वहुलाच्चेति शेषः । आसां नित्यानाम् ॥ १५ ॥

आद्याया इत्यादिभिर्महेश्वरीत्यन्तैस्त्रिभिः श्लोकैः षोडशनित्यानामङ्गाङ्गित्वक्रमादिकमुपदिशति । तत्र अङ्गगा मध्यनित्याङ्गगाः । आत्मविग्रहाः तत्तन्नित्याविग्रहाः । स्वान्तान्ताः तत्तन्नित्यान्ताः शेषनित्यान्ताः । तत्तद्वर्णायुधाकारवाहनैः मध्यस्थमध्यस्थनित्यावर्णायुधाकारवाहनैः । तथाविधैः तत्तद्वर्णायुधाकारवाहनैः । महेश्वरीति सम्बुद्धिः । एतदुक्तं भवति षोडशनित्यानामङ्गाङ्गित्वध्यानेष्वङ्गिरूपेण मध्ये स्थिताया ललितायाः कामेश्वर्य्यादिपञ्चदशनित्याः परिवारत्वेन

सूक्ष्मरूपाणि च तथा कथयामि तवानघे ।
येन ते साधकाः सर्व्वं वाञ्छितं प्राप्नुयुः क्षणात् ॥ १९ ॥
प्रोक्तेष्वाधारपद्मेषु लोहितात्मैक्यविग्रहाम् ।
विभाव्य तेजोनिचये तत्र सिद्धिञ्च चिन्तयेत् ॥ २० ॥
तेन सर्व्वमभीष्टन्तु समवाप्नोत्ययत्नतः ।
पूजातर्पणहोमादिरहितं भावनेन वै ॥ २१ ॥
परन्तु ध्यानमुदितमखण्डात्मविमर्शतः ।
निर्व्वातदीपसङ्काशमात्मनात्मसमीक्षणात् ॥ २२ ॥

वह्निर्ललितासदृशविग्रहायुधवाहनादियुताः । कामेश्वरीनित्याया अङ्गित्वे तु कामेश्वरीविग्रहादियुता ललितैवमित्येतदात्मकत्वे नाङ्गिरूपेण स्थिता । तदनन्तरं भगमालिन्यादिचित्रान्ताश्चतुर्दशनित्याश्च तदन्ते कामेश्वरी च सम्भूय पञ्चदश नित्याः परिवारत्वेन वह्निः स्थिताः । एवं भगमालिन्यादीनामङ्गित्वेपि तत्तन्नित्याविग्रहा ललितैव मध्याङ्गित्वेन तद्बहिस्तदनन्तरनित्यास्तत्तन्नित्यान्ताः पञ्चदश नित्यास्तत्तदाकाराः परिवारत्वेन स्थिताश्च ध्येया भवन्तीति ॥ १८ ॥

सूक्ष्मरूपेत्यादिभिर्भावनेन वै इत्यन्तैस्त्रिभिः श्लोकैः प्रस्तावादिपुरःसरं सूक्ष्मरूपध्यानं तेन प्रयोगादिकञ्चोपदिशति । तत्र सूक्ष्मरूपाणि तासां ध्यानानि इति शेषः । अनघे इति सम्बुद्धिः । येन सूक्ष्मध्यानानुसन्धानेन । प्रोक्तेषु नित्यानित्यापटले इति शेषः । लोहितात्मैक्यविग्रहां लोहिताकारत्वेन स्वैक्यविग्रहवत्तां । तत्र तेजोनिचये । सिद्धिं अभिमतामिति शेषः । तेन भावनेनेत्यनेनान्वयः । एतदुक्तं भवति प्रोक्तेष्वाधारपद्मेषु लोहिताकारं स्वस्मादपृथग्भूतं तेजोनिचयं विभाव्य तत्तेजोमध्ये साध्यसाधककर्मणां स्वरूपेण भावनया समीहितफलं प्राप्नोतीति ॥ २१ ॥

परमित्यादिना श्लोकेन परध्यानमुपदिशति । तत्र अखण्डात्मविमर्शतः कटकमुकुटाद्यखिलभूषणादिविशेषेष्वपृथक्त्वेन तत्तदाकारतया स्थितकनकसत्तामात्रवदिदमाकारतया प्रतीतेषु सकलपदार्थेष्वपृथक्त्वेन तत्तदाकारतया स्थित परशक्तिविमर्शतः । निर्वातदीपसङ्काशं देशकालाद्यपरिच्छिन्नतया निश्चलपूर्णप्रकाशरूपमुपलब्धमिति शेषः । आत्मनात्मसमीक्षणात् अनन्यप्रकाशरूप-

स्थूलेन साधयेत्तत्तदिष्टञ्चैव शुभाशुभम् ।
प्रोक्तक्रमेण देवेशि सततं साध्यसाधकौ ॥ २३ ॥
सिद्धस्तु सूक्ष्मरूपेण ध्यानेन सकलेप्सितम् ।
साधयेत् पररूपन्तु साध्यं साधनसिद्धये ॥ २४ ॥
ब्रूहि देव महेशान स्थूलसूक्ष्मस्वरूपयोः ।
ध्यानयोः कर्म्मणा सिद्धिं विविधां फलयोगतः ॥ २५ ॥
तासां तत्तत्करेषूक्तान्यायुधान्यप्यशेषतः ।
शृणु वक्ष्ये महेशानि क्रमेण तव साम्प्रतम् ॥ २६ ॥
वामदक्षिणयोः स्यातां द्विभुजे तु वराभये ।
पाशाङ्कुशौ चतुर्ब्बाहौ षड्भुजे चापसायकौ ॥ २७ ॥

त्वादात्मन इत्यर्थः। एतदुक्तं भवति अखण्डात्मविमर्शतः आत्मनात्मसमीक्षणा दुपलब्धं निर्वातदीपसङ्काशस्वरूपं परध्यानमिति ॥ २२ ॥

स्थूलेत्यादिना सिद्धये इत्यन्तेन श्लोकद्वयेन प्रोक्तत्रिविधध्यानेषु साध्यादीनां प्रयोगादिषु ध्यानविभागक्रममुपदिशति। तत्र स्थूलेन ध्यानेनेति शेषः। साधयेत् साधयेतामित्यर्थः। तुर्विशेषे। पररूपं विमर्शात्मकमिति यावत्। तुर्विशेषे। साध्यं प्राप्यं उपपेयंरूपं विश्रान्तिभूमिरित्यर्थः। अपृथक्त्वभावनयेति शेषः। अपरिच्छिन्नायां परायां शक्तौ स्वस्मादपृथक्त्वेन सिद्धायामप्यपरप्राप्याभावादात्मलाभान्न परं विद्यत इति वचनाच्च तदेव प्राप्यमिति यावत् ॥ २४ ॥

ब्रूहीत्यादिना श्लोकेन स्थूलसूक्ष्मध्यानयोः कर्म्मणा सिद्धिक्रमं देवी पृच्छति। तत्र फलयोगतः समीहितफलं प्राप्नोति ॥ २५ ॥

तासामित्यादिना श्लोकेन वक्ष्यमाणायुधविशेषान् पृष्टार्थकथनञ्च प्रस्तौति। तत्र अपिशब्देन त्वत्पृष्टविविधकर्म्मसिद्धीश्च वक्ष्ये इत्युपात्तमिति सम्प्रदायः। महेशानीति सम्बुद्धिः। क्रमेण द्विसंख्यचतुःसंख्यभुजादिक्रमेण ॥ २६ ॥

वामेत्यादिना वाञ्छयेत्यन्तेन श्लोकद्वयेनायुधसामान्यपरिभाषाक्रमादिकमुपदिशति। तत्र वामदक्षिणयोः करयोरिति शेषः। द्विभुजे द्विभुजध्याने। वराभये वराभयसंज्ञे मुद्रे एतत् प्रथमाद्विवचनं। पाशाङ्कुशौ चतुर्बाहौ चतुर्भुजध्याने। ऊर्द्ध्वभुजवामदक्षिणे पाशाङ्कुशौ इतरयोः प्रागवत् वराभयमुद्रे चेत्यर्थः।

चर्म्मखड्गौ चाष्टभुजे गदाशूलौ दशोदिते।
मुखपाण्यायुधानान्तु रूपसंख्यादिवाञ्छया ॥ २८ ॥
यस्मिन् कर्म्मणि तां देवि यथा स्मरति साधकः।
तथा तस्याग्रतो भूत्वा पालयति तमादरात् ॥ २९ ॥
सर्व्वत्र स्मेरवदननयनाः शुभकर्म्मसु।
दंष्ट्रोग्रा भीमनयनवदनाः क्रूरकर्म्मसु ॥ ३० ॥
शुभेषु कर्म्मस्वासीना स्थिता वाहनगा अपि।
शुभेतरेषु ताः सर्व्वाः प्रयोगेषु तु सर्व्वदा ॥ ३१ ॥
वलयैरङ्गदै रत्नमयैरप्यङ्गुलीयकैः।
विराजमानास्ताः सर्व्वा दिव्यांशुकधरा अपि ॥ ३२ ॥

षड्भुजे चापसायकौ षड्भुजध्याने प्रागवत् ऊर्द्ध्वभुजयोः पाशाङ्कुशौ तदधःस्थयोः प्रागवद्वराभयमुद्रे च। चर्म्मखड्गौ अष्टभुजे अष्टभुजध्याने प्रागवदूर्द्ध्वभुजयोः पाशाङ्कुशौ तदधःस्थयोः प्रागवच्चापसायकौ तदधस्थयोर्वामदक्षिणक्रमेण चर्म्मखड्गौ तदधःस्थयोः प्रागवद्वराभयमुद्रे। गदाशूलौ दशोदिते दशभुजध्याने प्रागवदूर्द्ध्वभुजयोः पाशाङ्कुशौ तदधस्थयोश्चापसायकौ तदधस्थयोश्चर्मखड्गौ तदधःस्थयोर्वामदक्षिणक्रमेण गदाशूलौ तदधःस्थयोः प्रागवद्वराभयमुद्रे च। रूपसंख्यादीत्यत्रादिशब्दः प्रोक्तविषयसंख्येतरविषयः ॥ २८ ॥

यस्मिन्नित्यादिना श्लोकेनाभिमतकर्म्मणि तासामभिमतसिद्धिप्रदत्वमुपदिशति। तत्र तस्य साधकस्य। भूत्वा इत्यस्य तथा इत्यनेनान्वयः। आविर्भूयेत्यर्थः ॥ २९ ॥

सर्वत्रेत्यादिभिर्महेश्वरीत्यन्तैरध्यर्द्धैश्चतुर्भिः श्लोकैः शुभाशुभकर्मसु सामान्यध्यानमुपदिशति। तत्र सर्वत्र इत्येतत्तन्त्रसामान्यं। सर्वत्रेत्याद्यर्द्धेन शुभकर्मसु ध्यानं। दंष्ट्रोग्रा इत्युत्तरार्द्धेनाशुभकर्म्मसु ध्यानम् ॥ ३० ॥

शुभेष्वित्यादिना श्लोकेन श्लोकपूर्वार्द्धस्याद्यपादेन शुभकर्म्मसु ध्यानं। स्थिता इत्यादिना श्लोकावशिष्टपादत्रयेण तदितरध्यानम्। अपि अपिवेत्यर्थः। रत्नमयैरित्येतद्वलयादित्रयाणां विशेषणम्। दिव्यांशुकधरा इत्यत्र दिव्यत्वं तत्त्ववेदिभिः कैश्चिद्दृशा दृष्टत्वात्। सर्वाः सपरिवारा नित्याः। अत्र भूषणानां

हारग्रैवेयरत्नादिमुद्रिका नूपुरादिभिः ।
नवरत्नमयैः सर्व्वास्तवकैश्चोपशोभिताः ॥ ३३ ॥
एवं सामान्यमुदितं ध्यानं तासां महेश्वरि ।
विशेषं शृणु वक्ष्यामि तत्तत्कर्म्मसु सिद्धिदम् ॥ ३४ ॥
गजवाजिरथारूढ़ा(१) विमानस्थाश्च सिंहगाः ।
व्याघ्रताक्ष्यसमारूढ़ा ध्येया रक्षासु सर्व्वदा ॥ ३५ ॥
समरेषु जयावाप्त्यै नृपराष्ट्रादिरक्षणे ।
पिशाचचोरव्यालादिदुर्गमेऽरण्यवर्त्मनि ॥ ३६ ॥
ध्यायेत्ता देवताः सर्व्वाः सर्व्वशक्तिभिरावृताः ।
एकैकशः समस्ता वा सुखी भवति निश्चितम् ॥ ३७ ॥
ऋक्षवानरभल्लूकखरसैरिभवाहनाः ।
उच्चाटनेषु सर्व्वास्ता भीमा ध्येयाः सुदारुणाः ॥ ३८ ॥

नामान्याराध्यपादादवगन्तव्यानि । एतानि भूषणानि सर्वप्रयोगसाधारणानि । महेश्वरीति देवीसम्बुद्धिः ॥ ३३ ॥

विशेषमित्यादिभिः समीरिता इत्यन्तैरर्द्धैः सप्तभिः श्लोकैर्विशेषध्यानप्रस्तावपूर्वं प्रयोगविशेषेषु सामान्यवाहनभेदध्यानादिकमुपदिशति । तत्र विशेषमित्याद्यर्द्धेन विशेषध्यानं प्रस्तौति । तत्र विशेषं सामान्येन प्रोक्तरूपादिति शेषः ॥ ३४ ॥

गजेत्यादिभिर्निश्चितमित्यन्तैस्त्रिभिः श्लोकै रक्षादिषु वाहनविशेषध्यानादिकमुपदिशति । तत्र रक्षासु आत्मरक्षास्विति शेषः । राष्ट्रादीत्यत्रादिशब्दः पुरग्रामनगरपत्तनखर्वटगृहादिविषयः । व्यालादीत्यत्रादिशब्दः सिंहतरक्ष्वादिविषयः । एकैकशः समस्ता वा नित्यासु षोड़शस्वभीष्टां नित्यां स्वपरिवारादिसहितां सर्वाः स्वस्वपरिवारसहिता वा । निश्चितमित्यन्तेनामोघफलत्वमुच्यते ॥ ३७ ॥

ऋक्षेत्यादिना श्लोकेनोच्चाटने वाहनभेदध्यानमुपदिशति । तत्र भीमा विग्रहादिभिरिति शेषः । सुदारुणाः कर्म्मणीति शेषः ॥ ३८ ॥

---

१ । समारूढा ।

काङ्ग्ध्ये नवकक्रौञ्चकाककौशिकवाहनाः।
विद्वेषणेषु सर्वास्ता घोरप्रहरणाकुलाः॥ ३९॥
खड्गगोमायुशललीगवयाहरिणाप्लवगाः।
चिन्तयेत् सकलाः सर्व्वं चुद्रकर्म्मसु साधकः॥ ४०॥
पिशाचवेतालगता ध्येयाः सर्व्वत्र मारणे।
इति वाहनभेदेन फलभेदाः समीरिताः॥ ४१॥
सर्वास्तार्च्यगता वह्निवायुहस्तद्वयान्विताः।
द्विनेत्रास्त्वेकवदना दंष्ट्रोग्रा भीमविग्रहाः॥ ४२॥
दहन्त्यो वैरिनिवहं ध्येयाः स्वाकारशक्तिभिः।
भीमरावाभिरभितो वेष्टिता रणमूर्द्धनि॥ ४३॥
विजयी भवति चिप्रं वैरिसेनाविनाशतः।
पलायनोत्सगहनात् पादयोः पतनेन वा॥ ४४॥

काङ्गेत्यादिना श्लोकेन विद्वेषणेषु वाहनभेदध्यानमुपदिशति। तत्र कौशिकः दिवाभीतः। घोरप्रहरणाकुला घोरायुधनिविड़ाः॥ ३९॥

खड्गेत्यादिना श्लोकेन वश्याकर्षणादिकर्म्मसु वाहनविशेषमुपदिशति॥ चुद्र-कर्मसु वश्याकर्षणादिषु॥ ४०॥

पिशाचेत्यादिना श्लोकेन मारणकर्मसु वाहनभेदध्यानादिकमुपदिशति। तत्र वाहनभेदेन ध्यानेनेति शेषः॥ ४१॥

सर्वा इत्यादिभिः षोड़श इत्यन्तैः पञ्चविंशतिभिः श्लोकैर्वाहनवक्त्रायुधादि-भेदेन समरविजयादिध्यानादिकमुपदिशति। तत्र सर्वा नित्याः सपरिवाराः। वह्निवायुहस्तद्वयान्विता इत्यत्र दक्षिणवामहस्तयोर्वह्निवायुक्रमेणेति यावत्। दहन्त्यः स्वस्वकरस्थस्वापायुधसंधुक्षितेन वह्निनेति यावत्। भीमरावाभि-र्भीमरावं कुर्वन्तीभिः। वेष्टिता इत्येवं तत्पूर्वत्र सर्वा इत्यनेनान्वयः। वा विकल्पे। वैरिसेनाया विनाशपलायनसंग्राहनपादपतनेष्वन्यतमेनेति यावत्। छिन्दन्त्यः मर्द्दयन्त्यः। उक्तक्रमेणारिसेनाविनाशादिचतुर्ष्वन्यतमप्रकारेण। तद्द्विगुणभुजा अष्टादशभुजाः। वा विकल्पे। वामैर्भुजैर्नवभिरिति शेषः। तर-

चतुर्मुखा अष्टभुजा छिन्दन्त्यः महतीं चमूम् ।
विभाव्य वा जयं युद्धे प्राप्नोतुक्तक्रमेण वै ॥४५॥
नवाननास्तद्द्विगुणभुजा वा भीमविग्रहाः ।
वामैः कोदण्डनिवहमन्यैः खड्गञ्च बिभ्रतीः ॥ ४६ ॥
ध्यात्वारिसेनां सकलां शरभिन्नकलेवराम् ।
वमद्रुधिरधाराञ्च विजयं प्रोक्तमाप्नुयात् ॥ ४७ ॥
अथवा नवभिः खेटमन्यैः खड्गञ्च बिभ्रती ।
चतुरङ्गरिपोः सेनां छिन्दतीस्तरवारिभिः ॥ ४८ ॥
चिन्तयित्वा जयं युद्धे भीमाकारे सुदुर्जये ।
पत्त्यश्वभरथाटोपवाद्यनिःश्वनसङ्कुले ॥ ४९ ॥
प्राप्नोत्ययत्नतः क्षिप्रं प्रागुक्तक्रमयोगतः ।
अथवा नवभिर्हस्तैर्गदा वामैस्तथेतरैः ॥ ५० ॥
नखरान् पाणिभिर्भीमा दधतीः समरे स्मरन् ।
तद्भिन्नचतुरङ्गांश्च सेनां विजयमाप्नुयात् ॥ ५१ ॥
तथा शूलकुठारौघैः पातयन्तीर्द्विषां बलम् ।
विजयी भवति प्रोक्तक्रमाद्दारे रणाङ्गणे ॥ ५२ ॥
तथैव चर्मच्छूरिकानिवहैर्निघ्नतीर्बलम् ।
ध्यात्वा वा विजयी भूयात् समरे रोमहर्षणे ॥ ५३ ॥

वारिभिः स्वस्वदक्षिणकरस्थैः खड्गैः चिन्तयन्नित्यस्य पूर्वत्र छिन्दन्त्य इत्यनेनान्वयः। आटोपः संरम्भः। प्राप्नोतीत्यस्य पूर्वत्र विजयमित्यनेनान्वयः। प्रागुक्तक्रमयोगतः वैरिविनाशादिष्वन्यतमेन। अथवा प्राग्वत् पक्षान्तरे तथा प्राग्वद्रिपुविनाशादिना। इतरैर्दक्षिणैः पाणिभिरित्यस्य पूर्वत्रेतरैरित्यनेनान्वयः। भीमा विग्रहादिभिः। तद्भिन्नचतुरङ्गान्तासां शत्रूणां दक्षिणक नवहस्तस्थनखरैर्भिन्न चतुरङ्गां। विजयमाप्नुयादित्यस्य पूर्वत्र तथा इत्यनेनान्वयः। तथा प्राग्वद्वामदक्षिणभुजनिवहक्रमेण। शूलकुठारौघैः शूलौघैः कुठारौघैश्च। प्रोक्त-

निद्रातिमिरहस्ता वा मोहयन्ती द्विषां बलम् ।
ध्यात्वा विजयमाप्नोति नियतं समरे नृपः ॥ ५४ ॥
पिशाचसर्पहस्ता वा तैः सेना मृद्नतीः स्मरन् ।
विजयं समरे शश्वदश्नुते शङ्करोपमः ॥ ५५ ॥
पाशकर्त्तरिकाभिर्वा निघ्नतीः पृतनां रणे ।
स्मृत्वा विजयमाप्नोति नृपः प्रोक्तक्रमात् ध्रुवम् ॥ ५६ ॥
अङ्कुशक्रकचाभ्याञ्च दारयन्तीश्चमूः क्षणात् ।
चिन्तयन् समरे भीमे विजयी स्यात् सुनिश्चितम् ॥ ५७ ॥
हलैश्च मुशलैर्नित्यं प्रहरन्तीर्द्विषां बलम् ।
स्मरन् प्रविजयं युद्धे प्राप्नोति ध्यानवैभवात् ॥ ५८ ॥
तथा षोड़शवक्त्रास्ता द्वात्रिंशैर्व्वाहुभिर्युताः ।
प्राग्वत् प्रमथितारातिपृतनाश्चिन्तयन् जपेत् ॥ ५९ ॥
पञ्चविंशतिवक्त्रा वा पञ्चाशद्भुजसंयुताः ।
तथैकादशभिर्भेदैरायुधैर्निघ्नतीर्व्वलम् ॥ ६० ॥

क्रमात् सेनाविनाशाद्यन्यतमप्रकारेण । तथैव वामदक्षिणभुजक्रमेण चर्म्मच्छुरिकानिवहैः चर्म्मनिवहैः च्छुरिकानिवहैश्च । वलं रिपूनामिति शेषः । वा विकल्पे । रोमहर्षणे वीराणामिति शेषः । निद्रातिमिरहस्ता वामदक्षिणक्रमेनेत्यर्थः । पिशाचसर्पहस्ता वामदक्षिणहस्तक्रमेणेति शेषः । अश्नुते प्राप्नोति । पाशकर्त्तरिकाभिः वामदक्षिणहस्तनिवहस्थाभिः । प्रोक्तक्रमात् प्रागुक्तवैरिसेनाविनाशाद्यन्यतमेन । अङ्कुशक्रकचाभ्यां वामदक्षिणहस्तनिवहस्थाभ्यामिति शेषः । हलैः वामभुजनिवहस्थैरिति शेषः । मुशलैः दक्षिणभुजनिवहस्थैरिति शेषः । तथा प्रागुक्तवह्निवाय्वादिषु हलमुशलान्तेष्वेकादशविधायुधद्वन्द्वयुक्तहस्तक्रमेण दधाना इति यावत् । ताः शक्तीः । प्रागुक्तवैरिसेनाविनाशादिष्वन्यतमेन । एकादशभिर्भेदैः वह्निवाय्वादिभिरिति शेषः । वलं रिपूणामिति शेषः । विचिन्त्य इत्यस्य पूर्वत्र

विचिन्त्य जयमाप्नोति समरे सर्वदा नृपः ।
तथा स्मरणसंयुक्तैः पूजयेत्तास्तदाऽऽग्रहे ॥ ६१ ॥
षट्त्रिंशद्वदना देवीर्द्विसप्ततिकराः स्मरेत् ।
तथैव दशरूपैस्तैर्वारैः प्रहरणैर्युताः ॥ ६२ ॥
एकोनपञ्चाशद्वक्त्रा हस्तैस्तद्विगुणैर्युताः ।
प्रहरन्तीस्तथारातीन् स्मृत्वा जयमवाप्नुयात् ॥ ६३ ॥
चतुःषष्टिमुखा देवीः करैस्तद्विगुणैर्युताः ।
प्रहरन्तीः स्मरेद् युद्धे जयी भवति निश्चितम् ॥ ६४ ॥
एकाशीतिमुखा देवीस्तद्द्वैगुण्यभुजैर्युताः ।
तथाविधैः प्रहरणैः स्मरन् युद्धे जयी भवेत् ॥ ६५ ॥
शतवक्त्रास्तद्विगुणकरास्तद्धेतिभिर्युताः ।
स्मृत्वा विजयमाप्नोति समरे ताश्च षोडश ॥ ६६ ॥
एवं वक्त्रकरैर्युक्तास्त्वनेकैरिष्टरूपतः ।
तथा तैर्हेतिनिवहैर्व्याकुलक्रमहस्तकैः ॥ ६७ ॥
असंख्याता भवेयुस्ताः साधकाभीष्टसिद्धिदाः ।
एवमुद्दामसमरसंकटादिषु चिन्तयन् ॥ ६८ ॥

निघ्नतीरित्यनेनान्वयः। तथा स्मरणसंयुक्तैः पूजयेत्ताः प्रोक्तरूपरूपध्यानसंयुक्तैः साधकैस्तद्विग्रहादिभिरुपलक्षितानां तासां नित्यानां पूजां कारयेदित्यर्थः। तदा समरकाले। तथा प्रागवद्वैरिसेनाविनाशादिष्वन्यतमेन। तद्विगुणैरष्टनवतिसंख्यैः। तद्विगुणैरष्टाविंशत्युत्तरशतसंख्यैः। तद्द्वैगुण्यभुजैर्युताः द्विषष्ट्युत्तरशतसंख्यैर्भुजैर्युताः। तथाविधैः दहनादिभिः। तद्विगुणकराः शतद्वयसंख्यभुजाः। तद्धेतिभिः पूर्व्वोक्तैकादशविधद्वन्द्वहेतिभिः ॥६६॥

एवमित्यादिभिर्निश्चितमित्यन्तैश्चतुर्भिः श्लोकैः प्रोक्तसंख्यामन्तरेणापि वाञ्छितसंख्यवक्त्रभुजादिविशेषसहितेन व्याकुलक्रमायुधादिध्यानेन समरविजयप्रयोगं तत्र साधकविशेषांश्चोपदिशति। तत्र एवं प्रोक्तक्रमेण। व्याकुलक्रम-

देवीस्तास्तरति क्षिप्रमापदो मनुजोऽथवा ।
देवो वा राक्षसो यक्षः किन्नरो वा भुजङ्गमः ॥ ६९ ॥
पिशाचो वा गुह्यको वा सिद्धो वा दानवोऽथवा ।
न कदाचित् स्मरन्नित्यं भङ्गमाप्नोति निश्चितम् ॥ ७० ॥
चोरादिसङ्कटेऽरण्ये गिरिदुर्गमवर्त्मनि ।
द्विविधैर्वैरिभिर्जातैः कृच्छ्रे राजभयेऽथवा ॥ ७१ ॥
क्षुद्रपीड़ासु भूतापस्माररात्तससङ्कटे ।
पिशाचडाकिनीवृन्दब्रह्मराक्षसपीड़ने ॥ ७२ ॥
अन्येष्वपि च कृच्छ्रेषु विस्तरेषु महत्स्वपि ।
स्मरन्नित्थं जयेत् सर्वा विपदो ध्यानवैभवात् ॥ ७३ ॥
एकवक्त्राश्च द्विभुजाः साधकाभीष्टधारिकाः ।
सपादुकाः समागत्य सर्वाभरणभूषिताः ॥ ७४ ॥
स्वसमानाभिरभितः शक्तिभिः परिवारिताः ।
गायन्तीभिश्च नृत्येषु वनमालाभिरन्विताः ॥ ७५ ॥
ध्यायन्नभिमतं सर्वमाप्नुयात् षोड़शापि ताः ।
नासाध्यमस्ति भुवने ध्यानादासां महेश्वरि ॥ ७६ ॥

हस्तकैः वासनापटलप्रोक्तप्रकारेणेति शेषः । उद्दाममरसंकटादिष्वित्यत्रादिशब्दो वादयुद्धसङ्कटादिविषयः । देवीः इत्येतत् पूर्वत्र चिन्तयन्नित्यनेनान्वयः । इत्थमभीष्टमुखकरायुधादिरूपतः । भङ्गं पराजयम् ॥ ७० ॥

चोरादीत्यादिभिर्महेश्वरीत्यन्तैः षड्भिः श्लोकैर्नित्यानां ध्यानविशेषेण सर्वापत्तारणप्रयोगमुपदिशति । तत्र चोरादिसङ्कटे इत्यत्रादिशब्दो व्याघ्रादिविषयः । द्विविधैः सहजप्राकृताद्यैः । क्षुद्रपीड़ासु शत्रुभिः प्रयुक्तकालभङ्ग्यादिसमुद्भवपीड़ासु । अन्येषु आध्यात्मिकादितापत्रयात्मकेषु । इत्थं वक्ष्यमाणध्यानप्रकारेण । द्विभुजाभीष्टधारिकाः द्विभुजाभ्यां साधकाभीष्टं दधानाः । स्वसमानाभिः द्विनयनादिविग्रहविशेषैरिति शेषः । ताः नित्याः । आसां नित्यानां । महेश्वरीति सम्बुद्धिः ॥ ७६ ॥

अलङ्कृतहयारूढ़ाः शक्तिभिश्च तथावृताः ।
स्मेराननाश्च गायन्तीः स्मृत्वा विश्वं वशं नयेत् ॥ ७७ ॥
तथाविधा गजारूढ़ास्तथा शक्तिभिरावृताः ।
सङ्गीतासक्तमहिलावृन्दसंकुलमध्यगाः ॥ ७८ ॥
स्मृत्वा लक्ष्मीमवाप्नोति राजमान्यामतिस्थिराम् ।
नानाभोगसमोपेतां प्रख्यातनिजवैभवाम् ॥ ७९ ।
तथाविधरथारूढ़ास्तथाशक्तिभिरावृताः ।
तथा सङ्गीतसंसक्तशक्तिवृन्दसमन्विताः ॥ ८० ॥
स्मरन् भुवमवाप्नोति राजा वै वैरिमण्डलम् ।
एवं तत्त्रिविधध्यानात् सौभाग्यमतुलं यशः ॥ ८१ ॥

अलङ्कृतेत्यादिना श्लोकेन विश्ववशीकरणध्यानमुपदिशति। तत्र शक्तिभिश्च तथावृताः अलङ्कृतहयारूढ़ाभिः शक्तिभिः परिवृताः ॥ ७७ ॥

तथेत्यादिना वैभवामित्यन्तेन श्लोकद्वयेन लक्ष्मीप्राप्तिप्रयोगध्यानमुपदिशति। तत्र तथाविधाः प्रागुक्तद्विनेत्रादिविग्रहविशिष्टाः। गजारूढ़ा अलङ्कृतगजारूढ़ाः तथा शक्तिभिरावृताः अलङ्कृतगजारूढ़ाभिः स्वस्वसमानविग्रहाभिः शक्तिभिरावृताः। सङ्गीतासक्तमहिलावृन्दं नाम संगीतासक्तयोगिनीवृन्दम्। अतिस्थिरां राजचौराद्यप्रधृष्यां। नानाभोगसमोपेतां नानाभोग्यैर्द्रव्यविशेषैस्तत्तद्भोगशक्त्यादिभिश्च समोपेतां। प्रख्यातनिजवैभवां आकार(१)गुणविद्यादर्पपौरुषादिभिरिति शेषः ॥ ७९ ॥

तथाविधेत्यादिना यश इत्यन्तेन श्लोकद्वयेन भूमिप्राप्त्यादिकप्रयोगध्यानमुपदिशति। तत्र तथाविधरथारूढ़ाः प्राग्वदलङ्कृतरथारूढ़ा इत्यर्थः। तथा शक्तिभिरावृताः अलङ्कृतरथारूढ़शक्तिभिरावृताः। तथा सङ्गीतसंसक्तशक्तिवृन्दसमन्विताः अलङ्कृतरथारूढ़ा संगीतादिरतशक्तिवृन्दसमन्विताः। भुवं अभीष्टामिति शेषः। वैरिमण्डलं शत्रुराज्यं। एवं तत्त्रिविधध्यानात् प्रोक्तक्रमालङ्कृतहयगजरथारूढ़ध्यानात्। अतुलं निरुपमम् ॥ ८१ ॥

१। अपार ; आचार।

कदलीकाननेऽरण्ये निर्जने तास्तथा स्मरन् ।
पादुकासक्तचरणा आगच्छन्ति स्वशक्तिभिः ॥ ८२ ॥
मण्डलं मासमर्द्धं वा जपन् विद्यां ततो विशेत् ।
निधिं संप्राप्य भुवने भोगी स्यात् यावदायुषम् ॥ ८३ ॥
पूगारामे तथा स्मृत्वा निधिमाप्नोत्ययत्नतः ।
एवं चम्पकपुन्नागनमेरुवकुलेष्वपि ॥ ८४ ॥
तथा पर्वतकुञ्जेषु ताः स्मृत्वा वित्तमाप्नुयात् ।
राजतो धनितोऽन्यस्मात् येनासौ स्यात् सुखी चिरम् ॥ ८५ ॥
समुद्रतीरेऽरण्येषु तथा नित्यं स्मरन् धिया ।
प्राप्नोत्यनर्घरत्नानि वह्नि ध्यानप्रभवात् ॥ ८६ ॥
समुद्रगासरिन्मध्यतरुवाटीषु तास्तथा ।
स्मरन् कनकमाप्नोति वर्णोत्कृष्टमसंख्यकम् ॥ ८७ ॥

कदलीत्यादिना आयुषमित्यन्तेन श्लोकद्वयेन निधिप्राप्तिप्रयोगध्यानमुपदिशति । तत्र ता नित्याः । तथा पूर्वोक्तद्विनेत्रादिविग्रहविशिष्टशक्तिभिः सहेति शेषः । मण्डलं प्राग्वदेकपञ्चाशद्दिनानि (१)। अर्द्धं मण्डलमासयोः। वा विकल्पे यावत् सिद्धीत्यर्थः । विद्यां नित्याविद्यास्वभीष्टामित्यर्थः । यावदायुषं यावज्जीवम् ॥ ८३ ॥

पूगेत्यादिना श्लोकेन प्रोक्तध्यानेन निधिप्राप्तग्रामस्थानपञ्चकविशेषानुपदिशति । तत्र तथा अनन्तरपूर्व्वोक्तप्रकारेण ॥ ८४ ॥

तथेत्यादिना श्लोकेन पूर्वोक्तध्यानेन वित्तप्राप्तिप्रयोगादिविशेषमुपदिशति । तत्र तथा प्रोक्तप्रकारेण । पर्वतकुञ्जेषु पर्वतगुहासु । ता नित्याः । राजतः राजसकाशात् । येनासौ स्यात् सुखी चिरं यावता धनेन साधकः चिरं सुखी स्यात्तावद्धनमित्यर्थः ॥ ८५ ॥

समुद्रेत्यादिना श्लोकेन पूर्व्वोक्तध्यानेनानर्घ्यरत्नप्राप्तिप्रयोगमुपदिशति । तत्र तथा पूर्वोक्तध्यानप्रकारेण ॥ ८६ ॥

समुद्रेत्यादिना श्लोकेन पूर्वोक्तध्यानेनासंख्यातोत्तमकनकप्राप्तिप्रयोगमुपदिशति । तत्र तथा प्रागवत् ध्यानप्रकारेण ॥ ८७ ॥

---

१ । एकोनपञ्चाशद्दिनानीत्यपि पाठो दृश्यते ।

निर्जने विपिने स्मृत्वा प्राप्नोति महिलाः शुभाः ।
रूपयौवनशीलाढ्याः प्रेमनिघ्नास्त्वनन्यगाः ॥ ८८ ॥
उक्तेषु तेषु स्थानेषु हयारूढ़ाः स्मरन्नरः ।
नृपतिं कुरुते वश्यं मनोवाक्कायकर्म्मभिः ॥८९ ॥
तेषूक्तेषु गजारूढ़ाः स्मृत्वा नारीर्नरान्नृपान् ।
वशीकरोति भुवने प्राणिनश्चा विशेषतः ॥ ९० ॥
तथा तेषु रथारूढ़ाः स्मृत्वा देवीस्तथोदिताः ।
वाञ्छितं समवाप्नोति मुक्तः स्यान्निगड़ादितः ॥ ९१ ॥
शतवक्त्रास्तद्द्विगुणभुजास्तेष्वायुधान्यपि ।
वाञ्छितानि लिखित्वा ताः पटेषु नवसु स्फुटम् ॥ ९२ ॥
पटांस्तान्मध्यपर्य्यन्तद्वये संस्थापयेत्तथा ।
रथदन्तिहयानान्तु तिरस्करणिकायुतान् ॥ ९३ ॥
प्रतिसैन्याभिमुख्ये तु तांस्तु सम्यक् प्रदर्शयेत् ।
वस्त्रालिखितनिशानभेरीपणवमर्द्दलान् ॥ ९४ ॥

निर्जनेत्यादिना श्लोकेन पूर्वोक्तध्यानेन महिलाप्राप्तिप्रयोगध्यानमुपदिशति । तत्र स्मृत्वा प्रोक्तप्रकारेणेति शेषः । प्रेमनिघ्नाः प्रेमपरवशाः ॥ ८८ ॥

उक्तेष्वित्यादिभिरादित इत्यन्तैस्त्रिभिः श्लोकैर्नृपादिवशीकरणसहितं निगड़ादिमोचनध्यानमुपदिशति । तत्र उक्तेषु तेषु स्थानेषु अनन्तरपूर्वोक्तेषु कदलीकाननादिषु निर्जनविपिनान्तेषु तेषु दशसु स्थानेषु । तेषु उक्तेषु प्रागवत् स्थानेषु । प्राणिनश्चा विशेषतः सुरनरमृगपक्षिसरीसृपाद्यविशेषेण सर्वान् प्राणिनश्च । तेषु प्रागवत् स्थानेषु । निगड़ादित इत्यत्रादिशब्दो राजादिभिः कृतबन्धनविशेषादि-विषयः ॥ ८१ ॥

शतेत्यादिभिरनघे इत्यन्तैः पञ्चभिः श्लोकैः समरविजयप्रयोगविशेषमुपदिशति । तत्र वाञ्छितानि स्वपरिचिन्तितानि । ता नित्याः । नवसु नवसंख्येषु । स्फुटं सुव्यक्तं मध्यपर्य्यन्तद्वये संस्थापयेत् । तथा रथदन्तिहयानान्तु । तेषु नवसु पटेष्वश्वरथादीनां त्रयाणां मध्ये तत्तद्वामदक्षपार्श्व-

आहत्य वादयन् शृङ्गशङ्खकाहलकादिकम् ।
वज्रादभिमुखं वैरी धावत्याशु पराजितः ॥ ९५ ॥
तत्सेनासंमुखा पश्चान्न जातु भवति ध्रुवम् ।
इति ध्यानान्यशेषेण कथितानि तवानघे ॥ ९६ ॥
सूक्ष्मध्यानेन सिद्धानां साधकानां फलोदयः ।
अतस्तच्छृणु वक्ष्यामि सर्वाभीष्टाभिकारकाः ॥ ९७ ॥
दाडिमीकेसरप्रख्यतेजोरूपां स्मरन् धिया ।
तन्मध्ये साध्यरूपञ्च निजवाञ्छानुरूपकम् ॥ ९८ ॥
समस्तमिष्टमाप्नोति शुभानप्यशुभानपि ।
तथा सुषुम्नान्तस्तच्च चिन्तयेद्वा गमागमम् ॥ ९९ ॥
तेनाखिलं निजेष्टन्तु प्राप्नोति ध्यानवैभवात् ।
साधकस्य तथा सिद्धस्तयोरेवाशुसिद्धिकृत् ॥ १०० ॥

पर्यन्तद्वये च त्रीन् त्रीन् संस्थापयेत्। तिरस्करणिकायुतान् तिरस्करणीभिः सहेति शेषः। तिरस्करणिका नाम प्रावरणपटी प्रतिसैन्याभिमुख्ये। तान् नव पटानिति शेषः। वज्रालिखितनिशानभेरीपणवमर्द्दलान् विजयानित्यापट-लोक्तसमरेष्वित्यादिचतुर्नवतितमादिश्लोकत्रयप्रोक्तप्रकारवज्रयन्त्रेणालिखित निशान-भेरी पणवमर्द्दलनिवहान्। काहलकादिकमित्यत्रादिशब्दो भेर्य्यादिविषयः। तत् सेना वैरिसेना। अनघे इति सम्बुद्धिः ॥ ९६ ॥

सूक्ष्मेत्यादिभिः सिद्धिकृदित्यन्तैश्चतुर्भिः श्लोकैः प्रस्तावपुरःसरं सूक्ष्मध्यानं तेन प्रयोगादिकमुपदिशति। तत्र तत् सूक्ष्मध्यानम् आधारेष्विति शेषः। तन्मध्ये नित्यानिवहात्मकतेजोमध्ये। निजवाञ्छानुरूपकं स्वसमीहितकर्म्मानु-गुणम्। तथा तत्तेजोरूपतया। सुषुम्नान्तः सुषुम्नानाडीमध्ये। तत्निजवाञ्छानु-रूपं स्वसाध्यम्। वा विकल्पे। गमागमं मूलाधारादिब्रह्मरन्ध्रान्तं ब्रह्मरन्ध्रादि-मूलाधारान्तं मुहुर्म्मुहुरारोहावरोहक्रमेणेत्यर्थः। तेन प्रोक्तोभयप्रकारेण। तयोरेव इत्यत्र एवकारेण साध्यस्य सूक्ष्मरूपध्यानप्रयोगेष्वनधिकार-त्वमुच्यते ॥ १०० ॥

प्रकृत्यात्ममयी व्याप्तिरिति सम्यक् समीरिता ।
अस्या निष्फालनाच्चित्ते तत्तत्त्वं स्वात्मसात्कृतम् ॥

इति षोड़शनित्यातन्त्रे श्रीकादिमते चतुर्व्विंशति
पटलं परिपूर्णं परामृष्टम् ।

इति षोड़शनित्यातन्त्रेषु श्रीकादिमताख्यस्य परिपूर्णस्य तन्त्रस्य प्रपञ्चसारसिंह-
राजप्रकाशाभिधानेन श्रीसुभगानन्दनाथेन विरचितायां मनोरमाख्यायां
व्याख्यायां षोड़शनित्याध्यानप्रपञ्चप्रकाशनपरं चतुर्व्विंशं
पटलम् परिपूर्णं परामृष्टम् ॥ २४ ॥

ग्रन्थसंख्या । पटलेऽस्मिंश्चतुर्विंशे यन्त्राणि न भवन्ति च ।
व्याख्याग्रन्थाः षोड़श स्युरधिकास्ते शतद्वयात् ॥

पञ्चविंशपटलम् ।

अथ षोड़शनित्यानां षट्विंशत्तत्त्वविग्रहैः ।
वर्णैस्तज्जनितैर्मन्त्रैर्यन्त्रैः कालात्मतां क्रमात् ॥ १ ॥
कथयामि प्रयोगांश्च नानाभीष्टाप्तिकारणान् ।
यजज्ञानोपास्तिभेदाभ्यां मन्त्राः सिध्यन्ति वर्णिनः ॥ २ ॥
स्वराः षोड़श नित्याः स्युः कादिक्षान्ताः स्वरान्विताः ।
तेषु तत्त्वानि षड्विंशद्वर्गा नाथनवात्मिकाः ॥ ३ ॥

पूर्वस्मिन् चतुर्विंशे पटले षोड़शनित्यानां प्रयोगेषु ध्यानादिकमुपदिश्यानन्तरं षोड़शनित्यानां षट्विंशत्तत्त्वस्वरूपैर्वर्णात्मशरीरविभूतवर्णैस्तत्तद्योगभूतभेदोत्पन्नैर्मन्त्रैर्यन्त्रैश्च कालात्मकत्वं तैः प्रयोगादिकञ्चोपदिशत्यथषोड़शेत्यादिना शिव इत्यन्तेन श्लोकशतरूपेण पञ्चविंशेन पटलेन। तत्र अथेत्यादिना वर्णिन इत्यन्तेन श्लोकद्वयेन पटलार्थांस्तदनुभावञ्चोपदिशति। तत्र षोड़शनित्यानां षोड़शस्वराणां षट्त्रिंशत्तत्त्वविग्रहैः षट्त्रिंशद्व्यञ्जनाक्षरैः व्याप्तेति शेषः। वर्णैर्वक्ष्यमाणसंख्यैः संजातैरिति शेषः। तज्जनितैः तेषां संयोगभेदजातैः। कालात्मतां कालस्वरूपतां। यजज्ञानोपास्तिभेदाभ्यां आभ्यन्तरानुसन्धानभेदेन वाह्यपूजाभिषेकहोमादिभेदेन च वर्णिनः वर्णवत्तामात्राः। शासनापटलवक्ष्यमाणाः सत्त्वादिविहीनाः ॥ २ ॥

स्वरा इत्यादिना श्लोकेन षोड़शस्वराणां षोड़शनित्याभिः षट्त्रिंशद्व्यञ्जनानां षट्त्रिंशत्तत्त्वैः मातृकानववर्गाणां नवनाथैश्च तादात्म्यमुपदिशति। तत्र स्वरान्विताः अकाराक्षरसंयुताः। ककारादिक्षकारान्तानां पञ्चत्रिंशदक्षराणां स्वरेण सह (१) षट्त्रिंशत्तत्त्वात्मकत्वेनोभयात्मकत्वात्तदात्मकस्य प्रथमस्वरस्यापि स्वरव्यञ्जनात्मकत्वेनोभयात्मकत्वमस्तीतुरपस्कारसंप्रदायाच्च (१) स्वरसंज्ञया प्रथमस्वर एवात्र विवक्षित इति यावत्। तुरवधारणे। एतदुक्तं भवति—ये षोड़श स्वरास्त एव षोड़श नित्याः स्युः। ये षट्त्रिंशद्व्यञ्जनवर्णा स्त एव षट् त्रिंशत्तत्त्वानि स्युः। ये मातृकाया नवात्मका वर्गास्त एव नवात्मका नाथाः स्युरिति ॥ ३ ॥

१। षट्त्रिंशत्तत्त्वात्मतोपदेशात् प्रथमातिक्रमे कारणाभावादितिन्यायेन च महानित्यायाः शिवशक्त्यात्मकत्वेनोभयात्मकत्वात् तदात्मकस्य प्रथमस्वरस्यापि स्वरव्यञ्जनात्मकत्वेनोभयात्मकत्वमस्ती तूपस्कार सम्प्रदायाच्च ।

अष्टावष्टौ स्वरे वर्गः परतः पञ्च पञ्च वै ।
मातृणान्तु स्वरैरेको वर्गः पूर्ववदुत्तरम् ॥ ४ ॥
नित्यानां तत्त्वसंयोगि वर्णसंख्याः समीरिताः ।
षट्सप्तत्या पञ्चशतं तत्संख्याब्दैस्तु पूर्णता ॥ ५ ॥
तत्संख्यानाञ्च यन्त्राणां तावदब्दैस्तु पूर्णता ।
पूर्णकालसमावृत्तिर्युगकल्पादिनामभाक् ॥ ६ ॥
त्रिसहस्रसमावृत्त्या प्रोक्तः कृतयुगावधिः ।
तस्य तुर्य्यांशतुर्य्यांशहान्या त्रेतादिसम्भवः ॥ ७ ॥

अष्टावित्यादिना श्लोकपूर्वार्द्धेन मातृकाया नववर्गस्वरूपमुपदिशति। तत्र अष्टावष्टौ स्वरे वर्गः। अष्टभिरष्टभिरक्षरैः स्वरैश्चैकैको वर्गो भवति। मातृणामित्युत्तरार्द्धेन वशिन्यादीनां मातृणामष्टवर्गव्याप्तिं मातृकाक्षराणां अष्टवर्गस्वरूपञ्चोपदिशति। तत्र मातृणां वशिन्यादीनां। तुरवधारणे। स्वरैः षोड़शभिरिति शेषः। पूर्ववदुत्तरं कादिक्षान्ताक्षरेषु पञ्चत्रिंशत्संख्येषु व्यञ्जनेषु वर्गप्रोक्तरूपेण पञ्चभिः पञ्चभिरेकैको वर्गो भवति ॥ ४ ॥

नित्यानामित्यादिना नामभागित्यन्तेन श्लोकद्वयेन स्वराणां व्यञ्जनानाञ्च प्रत्येकयोगजातां वर्णसंख्यां तद्वर्णानां तत्संख्यानां मातृकाचक्राणाञ्च तत्संख्याब्दैर्व्याप्तिं तत्संख्यानामब्दानामावृत्तेरवान्तरयुगकल्पादिसंज्ञाञ्चोपदिशति। तत्र नित्यानां तत्त्वसंयोगि प्रत्येकं षोड़शस्वराणां प्रत्येकमकारादिक्षकारान्तैः षट्त्रिंशद्व्यञ्जनाक्षरैः संयोगि पूर्णता तेषामुक्तसंख्यानां वर्णानामिति शेषः। यन्त्राणामस्मिन् पटले वृत्तमित्यादिना समीरिता इत्यन्तेनार्द्धाधिकश्लोकद्वयेन प्रोक्तानां तत्संख्यानां चक्राणामित्यर्थः। एतदुक्तं भवति कृतादियुगेषु प्रतियुगमारभ्य षट्सप्तत्यधिकपञ्चशत-(५७६) संख्यानां वर्णानां तत्संख्यानां मातृकाचक्राणाञ्च तत्तदात्मकत्वेन तत्संख्यैस्तत्संख्यैरब्दैः पूर्णता भवतीति। युगकल्पादिनामभाक् युगकल्पादिसंज्ञा भवति ॥ ६ ॥

त्रिसहस्रेत्यादिना श्लोकेन प्रोक्तमण्डलाब्दसमावृत्तिभिः कृतादिचतुर्युगानामब्दानां संख्यामुपदिशति। तत्र तस्य कृतयुगस्य। एतदुक्तं भवति पूर्णकालाब्दानां षट्सप्तत्यधिकपञ्चशतानां सहस्रत्रयावृत्तिजनितसंख्याष्टाविंशतिसहस्रा-

मायाधराग्निवातखैः कृताद्यर्णाः समीरिताः ।
तान् दिनाक्षरसंयुक्तान्मध्ययोनौ समालिखेत् ॥ ८ ॥
दिनार्णेषु स्वरा न्यासे विन्दुरूपा अनुक्रमात् ।
वामोर्द्धदक्षपार्श्वेषु पञ्च पञ्च समीरिताः ॥ ९ ॥
तत्तद्युगार्णास्तत्स्थाने स्वरूपेण व्यवस्थिताः ।
व्यञ्जनेषु तु सर्व्वत्र सुश्लिष्टाः स्वेन संयुताः ॥ १० ॥

धिकसप्तदशलक्षवर्षैः (१७२८०००) कृतयुगो भवति। कृतयुगस्य तुर्य्यांश-हान्या द्वात्रिंशत्सहस्राधिकचतुर्लक्षविहीनैस्तत्कृतयुगाब्दैः षण्णवतिसहस्रोत्तर-द्वादशलक्षमितैर्वर्षैः (१२९६०००) त्रेता युगो भवति। पुनः कृतयुगतुर्य्यांश-प्रोक्तवर्षविहीनैस्त्रेतायुगवर्षैश्चतुःषष्टिसहस्रोत्तराष्टलक्षमितैर्वर्षैः (८६४०००) द्वापर-युगो भवति। पुनश्च तत् कृतयुगवर्षतुर्य्यांशविहीनैस्तद्द्वापरवर्षैस्तदर्द्धमितैर्वर्षैः द्वात्रिंशत्सहस्राधिकचतुर्लक्षमितैर्व्वर्षैः (४३२०००) कलियुगो भवति। तेषां सम्भूय विंशति सहस्राधिकत्रिचत्वारिंशल्लक्षवर्षैः (४३२००००) रेकश्चतुर्युगो भवतीति॥७॥

मायेत्यादिभिः संयुता इत्यन्तैस्त्रिभिः श्लोकैः कृतादियुगविग्रहवर्णान् तद्वर्णानां अस्मिन् पटले वक्ष्यमाणघटिकाचक्रेषु वक्ष्यमाणघटिकावर्णैः सह लेखनक्रमादिकञ्चोपदिशति। तत्र मायाधराग्निवातखैः माया विसर्जनीयः, धरा उकारः, अग्निरिकारः, वातः अकारः, खं विन्दुः। एतदुक्तं भवति अः उं इं अं इति चतुर्वर्णाः क्रमात् कृतादिचतुर्युगविग्रहा भवन्तीति। तान् युगार्णान् दिनाक्षर-संयुक्तान् घटिकानां दिवसावयवत्वात्। वक्ष्यमाणघटिकाक्षरसंयुक्तानित्यर्थः। मध्ययोनौ वक्ष्यमाणघटिकायन्त्राणामिति शेषः। दिनार्णेषु प्राग्वत् घटिकार्णेषु। स्वराः विसर्जनीयरहितवक्ष्यमाणघटिकात्मकपञ्चदश स्वराः। विन्दुरूपाः विन्द्वाकारलिखितरूपाः। वामोर्द्धदक्षपार्श्वेषु प्राग्वद्वक्ष्यमाणघटिकायन्त्राणां मध्ययोनौ देवताया इति शेषः। तत्स्थाने सर्व्वमध्ययोनिमध्ये प्राग्वत्। एतदुक्तं भवति वक्ष्यमाणघटिकाक्षरयन्त्रेषु घटिकाक्षरत्वेन कदाचित् स्वररूपाक्षरे लेखनीये सति तद्यन्त्राणां मध्ययोनौ देवताया वामपृष्ठदक्षपार्श्वेषु पञ्च पञ्च चाङ्गीकृतेषु तान् वर्णान् वामपार्श्वस्थांशमारभ्य अकारादीनां पञ्चदशस्वराणां स्थानं परिकल्प्य घटिकाक्षरत्वेन तत्कालायातस्वरस्थांशे एकविन्दुं तदात्मकत्वेन विलिख्य

सर्वत्र यन्त्रविन्यासप्रतिष्ठार्चाद्यनुग्रहे ।
निग्रहे वास्तुविन्यासे गर्भन्यासेष्टसिद्धिकृत् ॥ ११ ॥
आरभ्य भानोरुदयमेकशो घटिकाक्रमात् ।
एकैकं मातृकावर्णपञ्चाशत्परिवृत्तितः ॥ १२ ॥

तदा तत्कालायातयुगाक्षरं मध्ये देवतास्थाने स्वरूपेण लिखेत्। व्यञ्जनेषु घटिकाक्षरत्वेन लेखनीयेष्विति शेषः। सर्व्वत्र अस्मिन् पटले घटिकाक्षरयुगाक्षरयोर्विलेखने स्वरूपेण लिखेत्। व्यञ्जनेषु सुश्लिष्टाः सुश्लिष्टसम्बद्धाः तत्तत्प्राप्तसन्धिकार्य्यवर्गाः अविभक्तरूपा इति यावत्। एतदुक्तं भवति अस्मिन् पटले सर्व्वत्र घटिकाक्षरयुगाक्षरयोर्विलेखने घटिकाक्षरं स्वररूपञ्चेत् प्रोक्तरूपप्रकारेण वामादिपार्श्वेषु स्वररूपघटिकाक्षरं स्वांशे विन्दुरूपं लिखित्वा मध्ययोनिमध्ये युगार्णं स्वरूपेण लिखेत्। व्यञ्जनं चेत्तन्मध्ययोनिमध्ये तेन घटिकाक्षररूपेण व्यञ्जनेन युगार्णं प्रागवत् सुश्लिष्टसम्बद्धं कृतयुगे सविसर्जनीयमितरेषु सविन्दुकं लिखेदिति ॥ १० ॥

सर्व्वत्रेत्यादिना श्लोकेन घटिकाचक्राणां विनियोगं तत् फलानि च उपदिशति। तत्र गर्भन्यासेष्टसिद्धिकृत् गर्भन्यासे इष्टसिद्धिकृदिति पदच्छेदः। आगमानां सन्धिर्दिव्यत्वादस्माभिर्न विचारणीयः ॥ ११ ॥

आरभ्येत्यादिना प्रवर्त्तत इत्यन्तेन श्लोकद्वयेन मातृकावर्णचक्रस्य घटिकात्मकत्वेन ज्योतिश्चक्रेण व्याप्तिक्रममुपदिशति। तत्र भानोरुदयं लङ्कायामिति शेषः। पञ्चाशत्परिवृत्तितः अकारादिक्षकारान्तानामन्त्यस्वरवर्जितानां वर्णानां पञ्चाशत् परिवृत्तितः। तस्याः परिवृत्तिरूपिण्या मातृकायाः। एतदुक्तं भवति प्रतियुगं युगप्रथमदिवसे लङ्कार्कोदयमारभ्यैकैकघटिकाक्रमेण मातृकाया अकारादिक्षकारान्तानि विसर्जनीयस्वररहितानि पञ्चाशदक्षराणि पञ्चाशद्भिः घटिकाभिरुद्यन्ति। अ ए च त य इति पञ्चमातृका घटिकापारायणी ज्ञेयाः। पुनरपि प्रथमदिवसशिष्टघटिकाभिर्दशभिरकारादिलृकारान्तानि दशाक्षराणि समुद्यन्ति। द्वितीयदिवसे प्राग्वदर्कोदयादेकादशाक्षरमेकारमारभ्य शिष्टचत्वारिंशदक्षराणि चत्वारिंशद्घटिकाभिः समुद्यन्ति। पुनर्द्वितीयदिवसे शेषघटिकाभिर्विंशतिभिरकारादि ङकारान्तानि विंशत्यक्षराणि समुद्यन्ति। पुनस्तृतीयदिवसे तदनन्तरं

दिवसैः पञ्चभिस्तस्याः षड़ावृत्त्या उदीरिताः।
एवं युगादिमारभ्य कालात्मार्णैः प्रवर्त्तते ॥ १३ ॥
योनौ त्रिकोणमालिख्य तस्मिन् योनिं समालिखेत्।
तेषु पर्य्यायनित्यार्णवर्णानालिख्य वाह्यतः ॥ १४ ॥
युगार्णं घटिकार्णेन मध्ये विन्यस्य तत्र वै।
नित्याः षोढ़श देवेशि पूजयेन्नित्यमर्च्चकः ॥ १५ ॥

चकारादि त्रिंशदक्षराणि अकारादि ण कारान्तानि त्रिंशदक्षराणि च समुद्यन्ति। चतुर्थे दिवसे तदनन्तरं तकारादिविंशत्यक्षराणि अकारादिमकारान्तानि चत्वारिंशदक्षराणि च समुद्यन्ति। पञ्चमे दिवसे तदनन्तरं यकारादिदशाक्षराणि अकारादिक्षकारान्तानि पञ्चाशदक्षराणि च समुद्यन्ति। एवं क्रमात् पञ्चभिः पञ्चभिर्दिवसैः मातृकायाः प्रोक्तपरिवृत्तिक्रमरूपिण्याः षट्षड़ावृत्तयः सम्भवन्तीति ॥ १३ ॥

योनावित्यादिभिरयोग्यतेत्यन्तैस्त्रिभिः श्लोकैर्घटिकाचक्रविरचनाक्रमं तत्र युगपर्य्यायदिवसघटिकाभेदतो विद्यालेखनक्रमं तच्चक्रे षोड़शनित्याचनस्यावश्य-कर्त्तव्यतां तदकरणे साधकस्यायोग्यताञ्चोपदिशति। तत्र योनौ स्वाभिमुखाग्र-त्रिकोणमध्ये। त्रिकोणं स्वानभिमुखाग्रत्रिकोणं। तस्मिन् तन्मध्ये। योनिं प्राग्वत्। तेषु वाह्यावरणमध्यमावरणयोर्योनित्रिकोणरूपयोस्त्रिषु कोणेषु। पर्य्यायनित्यार्णवर्णान् अनन्तरवक्ष्यमाणसंख्यासु विद्यासु गतपर्य्यायसंख्याप्राप्त-विद्यार्णत्रयं दिनप्राप्तविद्यार्णत्रयञ्च। वाह्यतः वाह्यावरणमारभ्येति शेषः। मध्ये मध्यस्थयोनिमध्ये। नित्यं प्रतिदिवसम्। उत्तमा नित्यनित्यमित्युक्त्या प्रतिदिवस-मर्च्चनस्यावश्यकर्त्तव्यतामुपदिशति। पर्वपर्वणि उक्तेषु पर्वसु प्रतिपर्वेति यावत्। मासमात्रेण तेषु पर्वसु प्रतिमासमन्यतमस्मिन् पर्वणि। अत्र मध्यमाधमपक्षयो-र्विधानं राष्ट्रक्षोभदुर्भिक्षव्याध्यादिकृच्छ्रेष्वेव अयोग्यता द्वितीये पटले सहस्रमित्या दिना सप्ततितमश्लोकोत्तरार्द्धेनोक्तप्रायश्चित्तमकृत्वा नित्यभजनादिषु साधकस्येति शेषः। अयमत्र घटिकाचक्रविरचनाक्रमः। इष्टमानभ्रमेण वृत्तं निष्पाद्य तत्र प्राक्प्रत्यग्ब्रह्मसूत्रमास्फाल्य तदर्द्धमानेन प्राग्ब्रह्मसूत्राग्रवृत्तसन्धिमवष्टभ्य तद्वृत्तपार्श्वयोश्चिह्नयुगं कृत्वा तच्चिह्नद्वयगताग्रयुगं तिर्य्यक्सूत्रमास्फाल्य तद-

उत्तमा नित्यनित्यं हि मध्यमा पर्वपर्वणि।
अधमा मासमात्रेण मासादूर्द्धमयोग्यता ॥ १६ ॥
पूर्णमण्डलवर्णाः स्युः प्रथमे त्वादितः क्रमात्।
षट्त्रिंशत्तत्त्ववर्णास्तद्द्वितीया मरुता क्रमात् ॥ १७ ॥
तृतीया सर्वतो वह्निरेवं विद्यास्तु वाक्चराः।
त्रिपुराः सर्व्वसिद्धानामाकराः कथिताः क्रमात् ॥ १८ ॥

ग्रद्वयादारभ्य ब्रह्मसूत्रपश्चिमाग्रावधि सूत्रद्वयं विन्यस्य योनिं निष्पाद्य तद्योनिवामदक्षिणपार्श्वरेखामध्यगताग्रद्वयां तिर्य्यग्रेखां कृत्वा तदग्रद्वयात्तद्योनेः तिर्य्यग्रेखामध्यान्तसूत्रद्वयविन्यासात्त्रिकोणं निष्पाद्य तत्त्रिकोणपार्श्वद्वयमध्यगताग्रद्वयं तिर्य्यक् सूत्रं कृत्वा तदग्रद्वयादारभ्य तत्त्रिकोणतिर्य्यग्रेखामध्यान्तं सूत्रद्वयास्फालनेन मध्ययोनिं कृत्वा ब्रह्मसूत्रवृत्तञ्च मार्जयित्वा एवं घटिकाकालात्मकं चक्रं निष्पाद्य तत्र वाह्ययोनेरग्राद्यप्रादक्षिण्येन कोणत्रयेषु पूर्वोक्तविद्यागतपर्य्यायात्तत्तद्विद्याक्षरत्रयं विलिख्य तदन्तर्गतत्रिकोणकोणेषु पूर्वाग्राद्यप्रादक्षिण्येन नित्याविद्याक्षरत्रयं विलिख्य तदन्तर्गतयोनिमध्ये तत्तद्घटिकार्णेन प्रागुक्तप्रकारेण सहितं युगार्णं विलिख्य तत्र कालात्मके चक्रे नानाज्ञानं मनोमतस्थं तद्विद्धि इत्येकादशाक्षरवाक्यजनितसंख्या (८४६७५०५०००) भेदाभिन्ने प्रोक्तकाले षोड़श नित्याः समर्च्चयेदिति ॥ १६ ॥

पूर्णमण्डलेत्यादिना क्रमादित्यन्तेन श्लोकद्वयेन पूर्णमण्डलवर्णेष्वक्षरयोगविशेषप्रक्रियावशेन जातास्त्र्यक्षरास्त्रिपुराविद्यास्तासामनुभावञ्चोपदिशति। तत्र पूर्णमण्डलवर्णाः अ आ इत्यादीनि चं चः इत्यन्तानि षट्सप्तत्यधिक पञ्चशतसंख्यान्यक्षराणि। प्रथमे प्रथमान्यक्षराणि विद्यानामिति शेषः। वाग्भवत्वेन भवतीत्यर्थः। आदितः क्रमात् अकारादिक्रमतः षट्त्रिंशत्तत्त्ववर्णाः प्रागुक्ता अकारादयः क्षान्तवर्णाः। तद्द्वितीया वर्णाः कामराजात्मकाः मरुता आकारेण कृतसन्धिका इति शेषः। तृतीया लिपिरिति शेषः। तासां विद्यानां तृतीया लिपिः सर्व्वतः वक्ष्यमाणसंख्यास्वासु विद्यासु वह्निः वह्निसंज्ञालिपिः इकारः तासां विद्यानां शक्तिवीजत्वेन स्थिता इत्यर्थः। एवं उक्तप्रकारेण त्रिपुराः संज्ञया स्वरूपेणेति शेषः। एतदुक्तं भवति अस्मिन् पटले

एताः पुस्तकमारोप्य पीठे संस्थाप्य पूजयेत् ।
यत्र तत्र गदालक्ष्मीग्रहदुर्भिक्षशात्रवाः ॥ १९ ॥
भूतापमृत्युकृत्याद्या न भवन्ति पुरादिके ।
अभीप्सितानि सिध्यन्ति तस्य योऽर्चति नित्यशः ॥ २० ॥
षट्त्रिंशत्तत् सप्तशतं सहस्राणि च विंशतिः ।
तासां संख्या समाख्याता तदावृत्तिस्तदाप्तिकृत् ॥ २१ ॥

षट्त्रिंशदित्याद्येकविंशतितमेन श्लोकेन वक्ष्यमाणसंख्यानां प्रत्येकशः त्र्यक्षरात्मकानां त्रिपुराविद्यानामुद्धारे प्रथमाक्षरत्वेन प्रोक्तेषु पूर्णमण्डलवर्णेषु यथाक्रममेकमेकं प्रथममुच्चार्य्यानन्तरं तद्द्वितीयाक्षरत्वेन क्रमात् प्रागुक्तानि षट्त्रिंशत्तत्त्वात्मकान्यक्षराण्याकारेण कृतसन्धिकानि समुच्चार्य्यानन्तरं तत्तृतीयाक्षरत्वेन सर्व्वत्र ईकारमुच्चारयेत्। तेन पूर्णमण्डलवर्णेषु एकमेकमक्षरं षट्त्रिंशत् षट्त्रिंशद्विद्यानामाद्यमाद्यमक्षरं भवति। तेन वक्ष्यमाणसंख्या विद्याः सम्भवन्तीति ॥ १८ ॥

एता इत्यादिना नित्यश इत्यन्तेन श्लोकद्वयेन तासां त्रिपुराविद्यानां विनियोगं फलानि चोपदिशति। तत्र एता विद्याः। आरोप्य विलिख्य। पीठे पूजयेदित्यत्रान्वयः। संस्थाप्य प्रतिष्ठां कृत्वा। शात्रवाः शत्रव इत्यर्थः। कृत्याद्या इत्यत्राद्यशब्दः हत्यादिविषयः। पुरादिके इत्यत्रादिशब्दो ग्रामपत्तननगरखेटखर्व्वटगृहादिविषयः। तस्य अर्च्चकस्य ॥ २० ॥

षट्त्रिंशदित्यादिना श्लोकेनोक्तविद्यानां संख्यां तदनुसन्धातुः फलं तेन तन्त्रेण पर्य्यायनित्यादिकं चोपदिशति। तत्र तदावृत्तिस्तासां विद्यानां वक्ष्यमाणक्रमेण परिवृत्तिः। तदाप्तिकृत् देव्यात्मत्वं करोति इति यावत्। अत्राद्युपस्कारः सम्प्रदायार्थो नाथाज्ञया लिख्यते। आसां विद्यानां देव्यात्मकत्वात्तच्छब्देन विद्योच्यते। तस्माद्दिननित्यात्मकत्वेन तासामावृत्तिः तासां दिननित्यानामेकैकस्या एव विद्यायाः पर्य्यायात्मकत्वेन प्राप्तिं करोतीति यावत्। किञ्च तासां विद्यानां पर्य्यायात्मकत्वेनावृत्तिश्च। तासामेकैकस्या एव विद्यायाः पर्य्यायात्मकत्वेन च प्राप्तिं करोति। घटिकाचक्रादिषु पर्य्यायविद्यालेखनस्थानेष्वेव पर्य्याये पर्य्यायात्मिकां विद्यां तत्तत् पर्य्यायविद्यया सह विलिखेत्। युगान्तेषु यदा दिननित्यात्वेन विद्याद्वयं भवति तदा तद्द्वयं तत् स्थानेष्वेव लिखेत् ॥ २१ ॥

स्तम्भनाद्येषु तद्वर्णास्तद्रूपा हेतिवाहनैः ।
एतद्ग्रथितजापेन मन्त्राः सिध्यन्ति वर्णिनः ॥ २२ ॥
नाथावृत्तिर्मन्त्रराशौ द्विसहस्रं शतद्वयम् ।
चत्वारि चेति विज्ञेयास्तत्त्वावृत्तिरुदीरिता: ॥ २३ ॥
पूर्णमण्डलसंख्यैव नित्यावृत्तिः सहस्रतः ।
द्विशतं षण्णवत्यश्च निःशेषं समुदीरिता: ॥ २४ ॥
कृतादीनां युगानान्तु दिनेष्वेकैकशः क्रमात् ।
ता विद्यास्तत्त्वरूपिण्यः शेषास्त्वन्ते द्विशः स्मृताः ॥ २५ ॥

स्तम्भनाद्येष्वित्यादिभिः समुदीरिता इत्यन्तैस्त्रिभिः श्लोकैस्तासां प्रोक्तसंख्यानां विद्यानां विनियोगप्रकारं नवनाथव्याप्तिक्रमं षट्त्रिंशत्तत्त्वव्याप्तिक्रमं षोड़शनित्याव्याप्तिक्रमञ्चोपदिशति । तत्र स्तम्भनाद्येषु आद्यशब्दश्चतुर्विंशत्पटलोक्तषट्कर्म्मादिविषयः । तद्वर्णास्तत्तद्विद्यावर्णाश्चतुर्विंशतिपटलोक्तपीतादिवर्णाश्च । तद्रूपाः पञ्चत्रिंशत् पटलवक्ष्यमाणषड़्भेदरूपाः । एतैः प्रथमभेदरूपैर्मन्त्रैर्ग्रथितजापेन एकान्तरितजापेन मन्त्राः सर्वे इति शेषः । वर्णिनः प्राग्वत् । एतदुक्तं भवति नित्याविद्यासु मनीषितां विद्यामाभिर्विद्याभिरेकैकविद्यान्तरितं जपेत् । एष जपप्रकारः उक्तप्रकारेण सर्वाक्षराणां नित्यात्मकत्वात् सर्व्वमन्त्राणां अक्षरात्मकत्वाच्च सर्व्वमन्त्रसाधारण इति । अस्य रहस्यार्थस्त्वाराध्यमुखादवगन्तव्यः । नाथावृत्तिः नवसंख्यावृत्तिः । तत्त्वावृत्तिः षट्त्रिंशत् संख्यावृत्तिः । पूर्णमण्डलसंख्या षट्सप्तत्यधिकानि पञ्चशतानि । नित्यावृत्तिः षोड़शषोड़शसंख्यावृत्तिः निःशेषं समस्तव्याप्तिः ॥ २४ ॥

कृतादीनामित्यादिना सिद्धये इत्यन्तेन श्लोकद्वयेन कृतादिषु चतुर्युगेष्वहर्गनानामुक्तविद्याव्याप्तिक्रमं प्रयोगेषु तत्तद्दिनपूजावश्यकर्त्तव्यतां तत्फलानि चोपदिशति । तत्र एकैकशः एकैका विद्याः । तत्त्वरूपिण्यः प्रत्येकं तत्त्वाक्षराः । प्रत्येकमक्षरत्रयात्मकतया ज्ञातृज्ञानज्ञेयात्मकत्वाच्चाशेषविद्यानामिति शेषः । अन्ते युगानामिति शेषः । द्विशः प्रतिदिनं द्वे द्वे विद्ये । एतदुक्तं भवति कृतादिषु चतुर्युगेषु परिवृत्तितः प्रोक्तसंख्या विद्या एकैकस्य दिवसस्य यथाक्रममेकैका विद्या भवति । तत्तद्युगान्तेषु केषुचिद्दिनेषु प्रतिदिनं द्वे द्वे विद्ये भवतः ।

प्रयोगेषु तु सर्व्वत्र तत्तद्दिनप्रपूजनम् ।
विशेषतो विधातव्यं जयारोग्यादिसिद्धये ॥ २६ ॥

तत् सर्व्वमालिख्यते । यथा कृतयुगे प्रोक्तक्रमेण सप्तत्रिंशदधिकचतुःशतोत्तरत्रिंशत्सहस्र (३०४३७) संख्येषु पर्य्यायेषु गतेषु अनन्तरपर्य्याये चतुःषष्ट्युत्तरद्विशताधिकनवसहस्रसंख्यासु (८२६४) दिननित्याविद्यासु गतासु अनन्तरं ताटाई इतिरूपिणीं विद्यामारभ्य तत्पर्य्यायशेषमनन्तरपर्य्यायञ्च प्रतिदिनं विद्या द्वयं द्वयं भवति। सम्भूय कृतयुगे पर्य्याया एकोनचत्वारिंशदधिकचतुःशतोत्तरत्रिंशत् सहस्रसंख्या (३०४३९) भवन्ति। त्रेतायुगे च प्रोक्तक्रमेणाष्टाविंशत्यधिकाष्टशतोत्तरद्वाविंशतिसहस्रसंख्येषु (२२८२८) पर्य्यायेषु गतेषु अनन्तरपर्य्याये अष्टचत्वारिंशदधिकनवशतोत्तरषट्सहस्रसंख्यासु (६९४८) दिननित्याविद्यासु गतासु अनन्तरं ठाथाई इतिरूपिणीं विद्यामारभ्य तत्पर्य्यायशेषं अनन्तरपर्य्यायशेषञ्च प्रतिदिनं विद्याद्वयं द्वयं भवति। सम्भूय त्रेतायुगपर्य्याया एकोनत्रिंशदधिकाष्टशतोत्तरद्वाविंशतिसहस्रसंख्या (२२८२९) भवन्ति। द्वापरयुगे च प्रोक्तक्रमेणाष्टदशोत्तरशतद्वयाधिकपञ्चदशसहस्रसंख्येषु (१५२१८) पर्य्यायेषु गतेषु अनन्तरपर्य्याये द्वाविंशदधिकषट्शतोत्तरचतुःसहस्रसंख्यासु (४६२२) दिननित्याविद्यासु गतासु अनन्तरं जडाई इति रूपिणीं विद्यामारभ्य तत्पर्य्यायशेषमनन्तरपर्य्यायञ्च प्रतिदिनं द्वे द्वे विद्ये भवतः। सम्भूय द्वापरपर्य्याया विंशत्यधिकशतद्वयोत्तरपञ्चदशसहस्रसंख्या (१५२२०) भवन्ति। कलियुगे च प्रोक्तक्रमेण नवाधिकषट्शतोत्तर सप्तसहस्रसंख्येषु (७६०९) पर्य्यायेषु गतेषु अनन्तरपर्य्याये षोड़शाधिकशतत्रयोत्तरसहस्रद्वयसंख्यासु (२३१६) दिननित्याविद्यासु गतासु अनन्तरं घढाई इति रूपिणीं दिननित्याविद्यामारभ्य तत् पर्य्यायशेषमनन्तरपर्य्यायञ्च प्रतिदिनं द्वे द्वे विद्ये भवतः। सम्भूय कलियुगे पर्य्याया दशोत्तरषट्शताधिकसप्तसहस्रसंख्या (७६१०) भवन्ति। सम्भूय चतुर्युगपर्य्यायाः साष्टनवतिषट्सप्ततिसहस्रसंख्या (७६०९८) भवन्तीति। युगानामन्ते प्रतिदिनं दिननित्याविद्याद्वयभजनवासना पूज्यपादमुखादवगन्तव्या। युगदिनसंख्यापि ज्योतिःशास्त्रे सिद्धान्तशिरोमणौ द्रष्टव्या। "पञ्चाङ्गरामास्तिथयः खवह्नी सार्द्धद्विदस्नार्कदिनाख्यमब्दे:"। अस्यार्थः एकस्मिन् सौरवत्सरे पञ्चषष्ट्यधिकशतत्रयं दिनानि (३६५) पञ्चशद्दण्डाः (१५) त्रिंशत्पलाः (३०) सार्द्धद्वा-

विंशतिविंपलाः (२२।३०) भवन्तीति । तत्र द्वात्रिंशत्सहस्राधिकचतुर्लक्षवर्षसंख्ये (४३२०००) कलियुगे दिनसंख्यापञ्चषष्ट्यधिकशतत्रयदिनसम्बन्धीनि अशीति-सहस्राधिकषट्सप्ततिलक्षोत्तरपञ्चदशकोटिसंख्यानि (१५७६८००००) दिनानि भवन्ति कलियुगे पञ्चदशदण्डसम्बन्ध्यशीतिसहस्राधिकचतुःषष्टिलक्षदण्ड-सम्बन्धीनि अष्टसहस्राधिकलक्षसंख्यानि (१०८०००) दिनानि भवन्ति कलियुग एव त्रिंशत्पलसम्बन्धिषष्टिसहस्राधिकोनविंशल्लक्षोत्तरकोटिसंख्यपलसम्बन्धीनि षट्शताधिकसहस्रत्रयसंख्यानि (३६००) दिनानि भवन्ति कलियुगे सार्द्ध-द्वाविंशतिविपलसम्बन्धि विंशतिसहस्राधिकसप्तनवतिलक्षसंख्य (९७२००००) विपलसम्बन्धीनि पञ्चचत्वारिंश (४५) दिनानि भवन्ति अत्र कलियुगे दिन-सम्बन्धीनि दिनानि (१५७६८००००) दण्डसम्बन्धीनि दिनानि (१०८०००) पल-सम्बन्धीनि दिनानि (३६००) विपलसम्बन्धीनि दिनानि पञ्चचत्वारिंश (४५) एवं सम्भूय पञ्चचत्वारिंशदधिकषट्शतोत्तरैकनवतिसहस्राधिकसप्तसप्ततिलक्षोत्तर-पञ्चदशकोटि संख्यानि (१५७७९१६४५) कलियुगदिनानि भवन्ति । ततः षट्त्रिंश-दधिकसप्त शतोत्तरविंशतिसहस्र संख्यानां (२०७३६) मन्वाणां नवाधिकषट्शतो-त्तरसप्तसहस्रावृत्तिभिः (७६०९) चतुर्विंशत्यधिकशतद्वयोत्तराशीतिसहस्राधिक-सप्तसप्ततिलक्षोत्तरपञ्चदशकोटिसंख्यानि (१५७७८०२२४) दिनानि भवन्ति तदनन्तरं दशमावृत्तौ अवशिष्टेषु एकविंशत्यधिकचतुःशतोत्तरैकादशसहस्रसंख्येषु (११४२१) दिनेषु षडुत्तरैकविंशतिशतसंख्येषु (२१०६) दिनेषु एकैका विद्या भवति । पञ्चदशाधिकशतत्रयोत्तरनवसहस्रसंख्येषु (९३१५) दिनेषु द्वे द्वे विद्ये भवतः । तेन दशमपर्य्यायपूर्त्तिरिति । द्वापरादि द्वैगुण्यादिना ज्ञेयमिति । अङ्कतो यथा ३१५५५८३२९० द्वापरदिनानि ४७३३७४९३५ त्रेतायुगदिनानि ६३११६६५८० सत्ययुगदिनानि । अत्रैते संग्रहश्लोकाः:—

पञ्चा (५)ङ्ग (६)रामा(३)स्तिथयः(१५)खा(०)ग्नि(३) सार्द्धाक्षि(२)चक्षुषी (२) ।
दिनादिविंपलान्तस्य कालः सौरे तु वत्सरे ॥
वाण (५) वेदो (४) ग्नि (६) रात्रीश (१) ग्रह (९) भूधर (७) भूधरे (७) ।
वाण (५) श्चन्द्रः (१) कलियुगे दिनसंख्याः समीरिताः ॥
पर्य्याया स्तत्र विज्ञेयाः ख (०) चन्द्र (१) रस (६) भूधराः (७) ।
नव (९) शून्या(०) ङ्ग (६) पाताल (७) पर्य्यायदिवसाः पुनः ॥
वेद(४) द्वि(२)नेत्र(२)खा(०) ष्टा (८)श्व(७)मुनी(७)षु (५) शशि(१)संख्यया ।
शिष्टेषु चन्द्र (१) नेत्रा (२) ब्धि (४) भू (१) भू (१) संख्या दिनेषु च ॥

धातुचेवेशयोः पूजां कुर्य्यात्तत्तदवाप्तये ।
तत्प्रकारः प्रयोगानां पटले साधु वच्यते ॥ २७ ॥
तेषु पञ्चाशदर्णानां पञ्चाशन्मिथुनानि वै ।
घटिकाक्रमयोगेन भजन्ते परिवर्त्तनम् ॥ २८ ॥
अथ यन्त्राणि वच्यन्ते प्रोक्तसंख्यान्यनुक्रमात् ।
इत्तं षट्‌विंशदस्रञ्च तद्दष्टादशास्रकम् ॥ २९ ॥

पर्य्याये त्वङ्ग (६) शून्ये (०) न्दु (१) नेत्र (२) संख्ये दिने गते ।
एकैकस्मिन् दिने द्वे द्वे विद्रे ज्ञेये क्रमादिति ॥
वर्षं दिनादिकं बुद्धा युगवासरकादिकम् ।
द्वापरादिषु तत्सर्व्वं द्विगुणत्रिगुणादिकम् ॥ इति ।

प्रयोगेषु प्रयोगदिनेषु तत्तद्दिनेषु तत्तद्दिनप्रपूजनं यस्मिन् यस्मिन् दिवसे प्रयोगाः क्रियन्ते तत्तद्दिनपतीनां पूजनं । तेन तद्दिनपतयः दिननित्या च तिथिनित्या च तिथ्यधिपो वासरेशो नचत्रेशश्च षड्‌विधाः । तेषां दिननित्यासमर्च्चनमस्मिन् पटले वच्यति । तत्तत्तिथिनित्यार्चनं तत्तत्पटले प्रोक्तं । तिथीशनचत्रेशयोर्नामार्चने चित्रानित्यापटले प्रोक्ते वारेशद्वयनामार्च्चने कुलसुन्दरीपटले विशेषतः प्रोक्ते । तदकरणे नैष्फल्यं कर्त्तृपीड़ाप्रसङ्गात् । एतदुक्तं भवति प्रयोगदिवसेषु प्रोक्तषड्‌विधदिनपतीनां प्रोक्तक्रमात् पूजनमवश्यं विधातव्यमिति ॥ २६ ॥

धात्वित्यादिना परिवर्त्तनमित्यन्तेन श्लोकद्वयेनोत्तरत्र प्रयोगपटले वच्यमाणप्रकारेण धातुचेत्रेशयोरर्चनमपि प्रयोगदिवसेषु अवश्यकर्त्तव्यतया मातृकाव्याप्ती प्रस्तौति । तत्र धात्वीशाः डाकिन्यादयः । प्रोक्ताः चेत्रेशाः । परिवर्त्तनं मण्डलीकरणम् ॥ २८ ॥

अथ यन्त्राणीत्यादिभिरन्यवदित्यन्तैर्नवभिः श्लोकैः षट्‌सप्तत्यधिकपञ्चशतपूर्णमण्डलासरैस्तावत्संख्यातानामब्दानां प्रत्यब्दमेकैकशस्तावत्संख्यातानि चक्राण्युपदिशति । तत्र प्रोक्तसंख्यानि षट्‌सप्तत्यधिकपञ्चशतसंख्यानीत्यर्थः ।

द्वादशास्रं नवास्रं वा स्वरे चास्रं नवास्रकम् ।
चतुरस्रमथ त्र्यस्रमिति भेदा नव क्रमात् ॥ ३० ॥
एतानि वर्णविन्यासभेदात् प्रत्येकमष्टधा ।
तेन द्वासप्ततिर्भेदास्तेषु नित्यार्णभेदतः ॥ ३१ ॥
प्रत्येकमष्टधेत्येवमुक्तसंख्याः समीरिताः ।
एतेष्वाद्यस्य वृत्तस्य विन्यासेनान्यदुन्नयेत् ॥ ३२ ॥
षडङ्गुलपरिभ्रान्त्या वृत्तमेकन्तु वर्त्तयेत् ।
एवं पुनः पुनः कुर्य्यादेकैकाङ्गुलतो वहिः ॥ ३३ ॥
यदा सप्तदशाभुवंस्तदा तद्विभजेदरैः ।
षट्‌विंशद्भिस्ततस्तेषु न्यसेद्वर्णान् तथादितः ॥ ३४ ॥

वृत्तमित्यादिना श्लोकोत्तरार्द्धेन चक्रत्रयं द्वादशास्रमित्यर्द्धेन चक्रचतुष्टयं तत्र स्वरे षोड़शारे चक्र इत्यर्थः। चतुरस्रमित्यादिना श्लोकोत्तरार्द्धाद्यपादेन चक्रद्वयं। एतानि प्रोक्तानि नव चक्राणि। वर्णविन्यासभेदात् अस्मित् पठले अनुलोमेत्यादिना पञ्चत्रिंशेन श्लोकेन वक्ष्यमाणतत्त्वार्णविन्यासभेदेन। तेषु द्वासप्ततिभेदेषु। नित्यार्णभेदतः षोड़शस्वरविन्यासभेदेन। उक्तसंख्याः षट्सप्तत्यधिकपञ्चशतसंख्याः। एतदुक्तं भवति प्रोक्तानां वृत्तादीनां त्र्यस्रान्तानां नवानां चक्राणां च वक्ष्यमाणप्रकारेण तत्त्वाक्षरनित्याक्षरविन्यासभेदात् प्रत्येकं चतुःषष्टिरूपत्वात् सम्भूय प्रोक्तसंख्या भवन्तीति। एतेषु नवसु चक्रेषु। वृत्तस्य वृत्तरूपस्य चक्रस्य। अन्यत् वृत्तेतरं चक्रं। उन्नयेत् प्रस्तारविन्यासतन्त्रानादिकं कुण्डपटले वक्ष्यमाणप्रकारेणोह्ययित्वा लिखेदित्यर्थः। षड़ङ्गुलपरिभ्रान्त्या प्रतिदिशमिति शेषः। वर्त्तयेत् भ्रमयेत् यदा सप्तदशाभुवन् वृत्तानीति शेषः। तच्चक्रान्तेषु पूर्णमण्डलसंख्येषु कोष्ठेषु। अर्णान् पूर्णमण्डलवर्णान्। आदितः अ आ इत्यादिक्रमतः चं च इत्यन्तः। चक्रविरचनाक्रमो यथा—समे तले हंसपदं विधाय तत्सन्दंशस्थानमध्यभेदेन प्राक्प्रत्यग्‌ब्रह्मसूत्रं कृत्वा तदवष्टम्भेन षड़ङ्गुलप्रमाणसूत्रभ्रमेण वृत्तं निष्पाद्य तद्बहिरेकैकाङ्गुलान्तरालं षोड़शवृत्तानि सम्भय सप्तदशवृत्तानि विधाय एकोनत्रिंशत्पटले वक्ष्यमाणक्रमेण

अनुलोमविलोमौ च वाह्याभ्यन्तरसंपुटे।
वाह्याभ्यन्त:परावृत्तौ तथा व्याकीर्णमित्यपि ॥ ३५ ॥

परित: षट्त्रिंशदरान् समान्तरालान्विधायात्र ब्रह्मसूत्रं मार्जयित्वा तद्वीथीगतेषु कोष्ठेषु पूर्णमण्डलसंख्येषु वक्ष्यमाणक्रमेण तत्संख्यान् वर्णान् विन्यस्य वृत्तरूपेऽस्मिन्नेव चक्रे चतु:षष्टिचक्राणि सम्पादयेत्। षट्त्रिंशदस्त्रादिसर्व्वचक्रेषु प्राग्वत् सर्व्वमङ्गलापटलोक्तप्रकारेण तत्तदुक्तारसंख्यचिह्नानि परितो वृत्तेषु विधाय विह्नाच्चिह्नं ज्यारूपेण सूत्राण्यास्फाल्य तद्वृत्तखण्डमार्जनात्तत्तदस्त्रात्मकं चक्रं भवति। अष्टास्त्रं चक्रं सप्तत्रिंशद्भिर्वृत्तै: प्राग्वत् षोड़शारैश्च कुर्य्यात् ॥ ३४ ॥

अनुलोमेत्यादिना श्लोकेन तेषु नवसु चक्रेषु वर्णविन्यासभेदक्रममुपदिशति। तत्र अनुलोमविलोमौ च चकार: समुच्चयार्थ:। तेनैव स्वराणां विन्यासभेदा आकथ्यन्ते। वाह्याभ्यन्तरसंपुटौ वाह्याभ्यन्तरार्द्धयो: स्थानभेदादन्योन्यसंपुटद्वयं वाह्याभ्यन्तरपरावृत्तौ प्राग्वदर्द्धद्वयस्य मध्यकोष्ठद्वयादुभयत: प्रतिलोमानुलोमेन द्विधा लेखनं। तथा वाह्याभ्यन्तरस्थानभेदत:। एतदुक्तं भवति प्रोक्तेषु नवसु चक्रेषु वाह्यात् कर्णिकावधि प्रत्येकं षोड़शकोष्ठात्मिका वीथय: षट्त्रिंशत्संख्या: परित: सम्भवन्ति। तास्व वीथयोऽनुलोमानुलोमात्मकेषु प्रतिचक्रमष्टस्वष्टसु भेदेष्वग्रादि प्रादक्षिण्येन तत्तत्तत्त्वाक्षराणां विलेखनवीथयो भवन्ति। तासु वीथीष्वग्रवीथीस्थकोष्ठषोड़शके वाह्यादाभ्यन्तरप्रवेशगत्या षोड़शस्वरान् विलिख्य प्रदक्षिणक्रमयोगात्तदनन्तरवीथीगतकोष्ठषोड़शके ककारस्य षोड़शस्वरभिन्नरूपाणि प्राग्वद्विलिखेरेवं प्रदक्षिणक्रमेण वीथीषु खादिक्षान्तानामक्षराणां षोड़शस्वरयोजनेन भिन्नानि रूपाणि प्रतिवीथिकं षोड़शसु कोष्ठेषु प्राग्वद्विलिखेत्। अयमनुलोमानुलोमक्रम:। एतच्चक्रं पूर्णमण्डलाख्ययुगेषु प्रथमवत्सरात्मकं। अस्मिन् एव चक्रे षट्त्रिंशत्तत्त्वाक्षराणां प्रत्यक्षरं षोड़शस्वरभिन्नानि रूपाणि पूर्णानि। तत्तदनुलोमक्रमवीथिस्थितादेरेवाभ्यन्तरकोष्ठारम्भतो वाह्यकोष्ठान्तं विलेखनादनुलोमविलोमाख्यं तद्युगद्वितीयसम्वत्सरात्मकं चक्रम्। अस्मिन्नेव चक्रे तासु वीथीष्वेव षट्त्रिंशत् तत्त्वाक्षराणां प्रत्यक्षरं स्वरभिन्नेषु रूपेषु वाह्यकोष्ठादिषु क्रमादष्टसु कोष्ठेषु प्रवेशगत्याष्टौ रूपाण्यनुलोमतो लिखित्वा तत: सर्वाभ्यन्तरकोष्ठादिनिर्गमनगत्या शेषेष्वष्टसु च कोष्ठेषु शेषरूपाष्टकानि क्रमाद्वि-

कर्णिकायां मरुद्वह्निनाम्ना संलिख्य सर्व्वतः।
योजयेद्वाह्यकोष्ठस्थैः प्रागुक्तविधिना क्रमात्॥ ३६॥

लिखेत्। एतच्चक्रमनुलोमवाह्यसंपुटाख्यं प्रोक्तयुगहतीयसम्वत्सरात्मकं चक्रं भवति। अस्मिन्नेव चक्रे तासु वीथीष्वेव तत्त्वाचराणां प्राग्वत् षोड़शसु रूपेषु आदितः क्रमादष्टौ रूपाणि सर्वाभ्यन्तरकोष्ठादिष्वष्टसु कोष्ठेषु निर्गमनगत्या च शेषरूपाष्टकं क्रमाद्वाह्यकोष्ठारम्भतः प्रवेशगत्या च लिखेत्। एतदनुलोमाभ्यन्तरसंपुटाख्यं तद्युगचतुर्थवत्सरात्मकं चक्रम्। अस्मिन्नेव चक्रे तास्वेव वीथीसु प्रागुक्ताचराणां प्राग्वत् षोड़शसु रूपेषु आदितः क्रमादष्टौ रूपाणि अष्टमकोष्ठादिसर्व्ववाह्यकोष्ठान्तम् अष्टसु कोष्ठेषु निर्गमनगत्या च नवमकोष्ठादिसर्वाभ्यन्तरकोष्ठान्तमष्टसु कोष्ठेषु शेषरूपाष्टकं क्रमात् प्रवेशगत्या च विलिखेत्। एतदनुलोमवाह्यपरावृत्ताख्यं प्रोक्तयुगपञ्चमसंवत्सरात्मकं चक्रं भवति। अस्मिन्नेव चक्रे तास्वेव वीथीषु तत्त्वाचराणां तेषु षोड़शस्वररूपेषु आदितः क्रमादष्टौ रूपाणि नवमकोष्ठारम्भतः सर्वाभ्यन्तरकोष्ठान्तमष्टसु कोष्ठेषु प्रवेशगत्या चाष्टमकोष्ठादिसर्ववाह्यकोष्ठान्तं शिष्टेष्वष्टसु कोष्ठेषु निर्गमनगत्या शेषरूपाष्टकानि विलिखेत्। एतदनुलोमाभ्यन्तरपरावृत्ताख्यं तद्युगषष्ठसम्वत्सरात्मकं चक्रम्। अस्मिन्नेव चक्रे प्राग्वत्तत्त्वाचराणां षोड़शरूपाणि प्रतिवीथिकं षोड़शसु कोष्ठेषु प्रथमे षोड़शे द्वितीये पञ्चदशे हतीये चतुर्दशे चतुर्थे त्रयोदशे पञ्चमे द्वादशे षष्ठे एकादशे सप्तमे दशमे ऽष्टमे नवमे च कोष्ठे आदितः क्रमाद्विलिखेत्। एतदनुलोमवाह्यव्याकीर्णाख्यं प्रोक्तयुगसप्तमसंवत्सरात्मकं चक्रं भवति। अस्मिन्नेव चक्रे तास्वेव वीथीषु प्रोक्ततत्त्वाचराणां प्रोक्तानि रूपाणि प्रतिवीथि षोड़शसु कोष्ठेषु षोड़शे प्रथमे पञ्चदशे द्वितीये चतुर्द्दशे हतीये त्रयोदशे चतुर्थे द्वादशे पञ्चमे एकादशे षष्ठे दशमे सप्तमे नवमे अष्टमे च कोष्ठे आदितः क्रमाद्विलिखेत्। एतदनुलोमाभ्यन्तरव्याकीर्णाख्यं तद्युगाष्टमसम्वत्सरात्मकं चक्रं भवति। अस्मिन्नेव षट्त्रिंशदरसप्तदशवृत्तात्मके चक्रे प्रतिवीथिकं षोड़शकोष्ठात्मिकासु षट्त्रिंशतसु वीथिषु अग्रवीथ्यां चकारस्य षोड़शस्वरभिन्नानि रूपाणि वाह्यकोष्ठारम्भादाभ्यन्तरप्रवेशगत्या क्रमाद्विलिख्य प्रादक्षिण्यक्रमायाततदनन्तरवीथ्यादिषु पञ्चत्रिंशतसु वीथिषु ल्वादीनां शेषतत्त्वाचराणां षोड़शस्वरभिन्नानि रूपाणि प्राग्वद्विलिखेत्। एतद्विलोमानुलोमाख्यं

तद्युगनवमसम्वत्सरात्मकं चक्रं भवति। अस्मिन्नेव चक्रे प्रागुक्तप्रक्रियाभिस्तत्त्वाक्षराणां स्वरभिन्नानां रूपाणां क्रमाद्विलेखनतो विलोमविलोमाख्यं विलोमबाह्यसंपुटाख्यं विलोमाभ्यन्तरसंपुटाख्यं विलोमबाह्यपरावृत्ताख्यं विलोमाभ्यन्तरपरावृत्ताख्यं विलोमबाह्यव्याकीर्णाख्यं विलोमाभ्यन्तरव्याकीर्णाख्यं तद्युगदशमसम्वत्सरादिषोडशसम्वत्सरात्मकं यथाक्रममेकैकवत्सरात्मकं चक्रं भवति। भूयोऽपि तस्मिन्नेव प्रागुक्तरूपे चक्रे अग्रवीथ्यां ककारस्य षोडशरूपाणि बाह्यतोऽभ्यन्तरप्रवेशगत्या विलिख्य प्रदक्षिणक्रमायाततदनन्तरवीथ्यादिषु सप्तदशसु वीथीषु ककारादिथकारान्तानां सप्तदशाक्षराणां प्रत्यक्षरं षोडशस्वरभिन्नानि रूपाणि प्राग्वद्विलिख्य तत्तत्क्रमायाततदनन्तरैकोनविंशवीथ्यादिषु शिष्टास्वष्टादशसु वीथिषु चकारादिदकारान्तानामष्टादशाक्षराणां प्राग्वत् स्वरभिन्नानि रूपाणि प्राग्वद्विलिखेत्। एतद्बाह्यसंपुटानुलोमाख्यं तद्युगसप्तदशवत्सरात्मकं चक्रं भवति। अस्मिन्नेव चक्रे तेषां तत्त्वाक्षराणां प्राग्वत् षोडशस्वरसहितानां रूपाणां प्रागुक्तप्रक्रियाभिर्विलेखनतो बाह्यसंपुटविलोमाख्यम् बाह्यसंपुटबाह्यसंपुटाख्यम् बाह्यसंपुटाभ्यन्तरसंपुटाख्यम् बाह्यसंपुटबाह्यपरावृत्ताख्यम् बाह्यसंपुटाभ्यन्तरपरावृत्ताख्यम् बाह्यसंपुटबाह्यव्याकीर्णाख्यम् बाह्यसंपुटाभ्यन्तरव्याकीर्णाख्यञ्च तद्युगाष्टादशवत्सरादिचतुर्विंशवत्सरान्तमेकैकवत्सरात्मकं चक्रं भवति। अस्मिन्नेव चक्रे प्रोक्तरूपेऽग्रवीथ्यां दकारस्य प्राग्वत् षोडशरूपाणि प्राग्वद्बाह्यादभ्यन्तरप्रवेशगत्या विलिख्य प्रदक्षिणक्रमायाततदनन्तरवीथ्यादिषु सप्तदशसु वीथिषु धकारादीनां चकारान्तानां सप्तदशाक्षराणां प्रत्यक्षरं षोडशस्वरभिन्नानि रूपाणि प्राग्वद्विलिख्य तत्तत्क्रमायाततदनन्तरैकोनविंशवीथ्यादिषु अष्टादशसु वीथिषु थकारादीनामकारान्तानामष्टादशाक्षराणां प्राग्वत् स्वरभिन्नानि रूपाणि प्रोक्तक्रमात् विलिखेत्। एतदाभ्यन्तरसंपुटानुलोमाख्यम् तद्युगपञ्चविंशवत्सरात्मकं चक्रं भवति। अस्मिन्नेव चक्रे तत्त्वाक्षराणां प्राग्वत् षोडशस्वरभिन्नानां रूपाणां प्रागुक्तप्रक्रियाभिर्विलेखनादाभ्यन्तरसंपुटविलोमाख्यम् आभ्यन्तरसंपुटबाह्यसंपुटाख्यम् आभ्यन्तरसंपुटाभ्यन्तरसंपुटाख्यमाभ्यन्तरसंपुटबाह्यपरावृत्ताख्यमाभ्यन्तरसंपुटाभ्यन्तर-परावृत्ताख्यमाभ्यन्तर-संपुटबाह्य-व्याकीर्णाख्यमाभ्यन्तरसंपुटाभ्यन्तरव्याकीर्णाख्यम् च तद्युगषड्विंशवत्सरादिद्वात्रिंशवत्सरान्तमेकैकवत्सरात्मकं चक्रं भवति। भूयोऽपि तस्मिन्नेव प्रोक्तरूपे चक्रेऽग्रवीथ्यां थकारस्य प्रागवत् षोडशरूपाणि बाह्यादभ्यन्तरप्रवेशगत्या विलिख्य

अन्येषामरविन्यासः षट्‌त्रिंशत् समुदीरितः।
अष्टास्रे षोड़शाराः स्युः षट्‌त्रिंशद्वृत्तमन्यवत् ॥ ३७ ॥

प्रदक्षिणक्रमायाततदनन्तरवीथ्यादिषु सप्तदशसु वीथीषु तकारादीनामकारान्तानां सप्तदशाक्षराणां प्रागवत् षोड़शरूपाणि प्रागवद्विलिख्य तत्क्रमायाततदनन्तरैकोनविंशवीथ्यादिषु अष्टादशसु वीथिषु दकारादीनां चकारान्तानां प्रागवत् षोड़शरूपाणि विलिखेत्। एतद्बाह्यपरावृत्तानुलोमाख्यं तद्युगलत्रयस्त्रिंशद्वृत्सरात्मकं चक्रं भवति। अस्मिन्नेव चक्रे तेषां तत्त्वाक्षराणां प्रागवत् षोड़शरूपाणां प्रागुक्तप्रक्रियाभिर्विलेखनतो बाह्यपरावृत्तविलोमाख्यं बाह्यपरावृत्तबाह्यसंपुटाख्यं बाह्यपरावृत्ताभ्यन्तरसंपुटाख्यं बाह्यपरावृत्तबाह्यपरावृत्ताख्यं बाह्यपरावृत्ताभ्यन्तरपरावृत्ताख्य बाह्यपरावृत्तबाह्यव्याकीर्णाख्यं बाह्यपरावृत्ताभ्यन्तरव्याकीर्णाख्यम् च तद्युगचतुस्त्रिंशवत्‌रादिचत्वारिंश (४०) -वत्सरान्तं यथाक्रममेकैकवत्सरात्मकं चक्रं भवति। पुनश्च तस्मिन्नेव चक्रेऽग्रवीथ्यां चकारस्य प्रागवत् षोड़शरूपाणि बाह्यादाभ्यन्तरप्रवेशगत्या विलिख्य प्रदक्षिणक्रमायाततदनन्तरवीथ्यादिषु सप्तदशसु वीथिषु लृकारादीनां दकारान्तनां सप्तदशानामक्षराणां प्रागवत् षोड़शरूपाणि प्रागवद्विलिख्य तत्क्रमायात तदनन्तरैकोनविंशवीथ्यादिषु अष्टादशसु वीथिषु अकारादीनां थकारान्तानामष्टादशाक्षराणां प्रागवत् षोड़शरूपाणि विलिखेत्। एतदाभ्यन्तरपरावृत्तानुलोमाख्यमेकचत्वारिंशद्वत्सरात्मकं चक्रं भवति। अस्मिन्नेव चक्रे तेषां तत्त्वाक्षराणां प्रागवत् षोड़शरूपाणां प्रागुक्तप्रक्रियाभिर्विलेखनादाभ्यन्तरपरावृत्तविलोमाख्यं माभ्यन्तरपरावृत्तबाह्यसंपुटाख्यमाभ्यन्तरपरावृत्ताख्यमाभ्यन्तरसंपुटाख्यमाभ्यन्तरपरावृत्तबाह्यपरावृत्ताख्यम् आभ्यन्तर-परावृत्तबाह्यव्याकीर्णाख्यमाभ्यन्तरपरावृत्ताभ्यन्तर-व्याकीर्णाख्यं च तद्युगद्विचत्वारिंशवत्सराद्यष्टचत्वारिंशवत्सरान्तमेकैकवत्सरात्मकं चक्रं भवति। पुनरपि तस्मिन्नेव चक्रेऽग्रवीथ्यां प्रागवत् थकारस्य षोड़शरूपाणि बाह्यादभ्यन्तरप्रवेशगत्या विलिख्य प्रदक्षिणक्रमायाततदनन्तरवीथ्यादिषु पञ्चविंशत्सु यथाक्रमं अकलख इगसघ षङ शच वछ लज रझ यञ मट भठ बड फढ पण नत धथ दइत्येषां अक्षराणां पञ्चविंशानां प्रत्यक्षरं प्रागवत् स्वरभिन्नानि रूपाणि प्रागवद्विलिखेत्। एतद्बाह्यव्याकीर्णानुलोमाख्यं तद्युगैकोनपञ्चाशद्वत्सरात्मकं चक्रं भवति। अस्मि-

न्नेव चक्रे तेषां तत्त्वाक्षराणां षोडशस्वरभिन्नानां रूपाणां प्रागुक्तप्रक्रियाभि र्विलेखनतो बाह्यव्याकीर्णविलोमाख्यं बाह्यव्याकीर्णबाह्यसंपुटाख्यं बाह्यव्याकीर्णा-भ्यन्तरसंपुटाख्यं बाह्यव्याकीर्णबाह्यपरावृत्ताख्यं बाह्यव्याकीर्णाभ्यन्तरपरावृत्ताख्यं बाह्यव्याकीर्णबाह्यव्याकीर्णाख्यं बाह्यव्याकीर्णाभ्यन्तरव्याकीर्णाख्यं च तद्युग-पञ्चाशद्वत्सरादिषट्पञ्चाशद्वत्सरान्तं यथाक्रममेकैकवत्सरात्मकं चक्रं भवति। पुनरपि तस्मिन्नेव चक्रेऽग्रवीथ्यां बाह्यादभ्यन्तरप्रवेशगत्या त्तकारस्य षोडश-रूपाणि विलिख्य प्रदक्षिणक्रमायाततदनन्तरवीथ्यादिषु पञ्चत्रिंशत्सु वीथिषु यथाक्रमं मल्लकहखसगघगडझमवमत्तभटवलफडटपनणधतछवठ? इत्येषाम क्षराणां पञ्चत्रिंशतां प्रत्यक्षरं षोडशरूपाणि प्राग्वद्विलिखेत्। एतदाभ्यन्तर-व्याकीर्णानुलोमाख्यं तद्युगसप्तपञ्चाशद्वत्सरात्मकं चक्रं भवति। अस्मिन्नेव चक्रे तेषां तत्त्वाक्षराणां प्राग्वत् षोडशस्वरभिन्नानां रूपाणां प्रागुक्त-प्रक्रियाभिर्विलेखनादाभ्यन्तरविलोमाख्यम् आभ्यन्तरव्याकीर्णबाह्यसंपुटाख्यम् आभ्यन्तरव्याकीर्णाभ्यन्तरसंपुटाख्यम् आभ्यन्तरव्याकीर्णबाह्यपरावृत्ताख्यम् आभ्यन्तरव्याकीर्णाभ्यन्तरपरावृत्ताख्यम् आभ्यन्तरव्याकीर्णबाह्यव्याकीर्णाख्यम् आभ्यन्तरव्याकीर्णाभ्यन्तरव्याकीर्णाख्यं च तद्युगाष्टपञ्चाशद्वत्सरादि-चतुःषष्टितमवत्सरान्तं यथाक्रममेकैकवत्सरात्मकं चक्रं भवति। एवं सम्भूय तस्मिन्नेव वृत्तात्मके चक्रे तद्युगप्रथमचतुःषष्टिवत्सरात्मकानि चतुःषष्टि-चक्राणि भवन्ति। एवं षट्त्रिंशदस्रादीनां व्यस्रान्तानां अष्टानां चक्राणां प्रोक्तप्रकारलेखनभेदैः प्रतिचक्रं यथाक्रमं तद्युगचतुःषष्टिवत्सरात्मका-न्येवं सम्भूय पूर्णमण्डलाख्यतद्युगवत्सरात्मकानि षट्सप्तत्यधिकपञ्चशतसंख्यानि चक्राणि भवन्ति। तत्राष्टास्रचक्रे तु षोडशसु वीथिषु प्रतिवीथिकं षट्त्रिंशत् कोष्ठात्मिकासु अग्रवीथ्यां बाह्यादाभ्यन्तरप्रवेशगत्या अकखादीनां चान्तानां षट्-त्रिंशत्तत्त्वात्मकानामक्षराणां प्रत्यक्षरं षोडशस्वररूपेष्वाद्यस्वरभिन्नानि रूपाणि विलिख्य प्रदक्षिणक्रमायाततदनन्तरवीथ्यादिषु पञ्चदशसु वीथिषु शेषपञ्चदशस्वर-भिन्नानि तेषां रूपाणि षट्त्रिंशत्संख्यानि प्रागुक्तक्रमप्रवेशगत्या विलिखेत्। एतदष्टास्रे चक्रे प्रथमं चक्रं भवति। एवं व्यञ्जनाक्षरस्वराक्षर-विलेखनस्थानविनिमयेन पूर्वोक्तप्रकारभेदैरेवावशिष्टानि त्रिषष्टिचक्राणि परि-कल्पयेदिति। कर्णिकायां प्रोक्तानां पूर्णमण्डलचक्राणामिति शेषः। मरुदङ्को आकारईकारावक्षतसन्धिकाविति शेषः। नाम्ना सहितं साधकसाध्यकर्मणा-मिति शेषः। तल्लिखनन्तु ईकारस्योदरे प्राग्वत्त्रिपंक्तिकं लिखेदिति सम्प्र-

एतत् पटे समालिख्य वहिरष्टच्छदाम्बुजम् ।
कृत्वा दलेषु क्रमशो वाग्देव्यष्टकमालिखेत् ॥ ३८ ॥
प्रोक्तरूपं ततस्तस्य प्रतिष्ठा सम्यगीरिता ।
विधाय पूजयेन्नित्यं पुस्तपूजोक्तसिद्धये ॥ ३९ ॥
उभयं यः प्रकुरुते तस्य वंशे स्थिरा रमा ।
न कदाचिच्छ्रियो हानिर्भविष्यति च तत्कुले ॥ ४० ॥

दायार्थः । सर्वतः सर्वचक्रसर्ववीथिषु योजयेत् । मवङ्क्ती इत्यन्वयः । वाह्य-कोष्ठस्थैः षट्त्रिंशत्तत्त्वाक्षरैरिति शेषः । प्रागुक्तविधिना क्रमात् प्रोक्तचतुःषष्टिभेदविधिना अग्रादिप्रादक्षिण्यक्रमात् । एतदुक्तं भवति प्रोक्तेषु चक्रेषु कर्णिकामध्ये साधकादिसहितम् भा ई इत्यक्षरद्वयम् ज्ञातसन्धिकं विलिख्य तत्तच्चक्राग्रवीथिवाह्यकोष्ठस्थाक्षरादिभिः सर्ववीथिवाह्यकोष्ठस्थैरक्षरैः प्रागुक्तचतुःषष्टिभेदभिन्नैः कर्णिकागताक्षरद्वयं क्रमाद्योजयेदिति । अष्टास्रे तु अग्रवीथिकोष्ठानि वाह्यानि कल्पयेदित्यानुअविकोऽर्थः । अन्यवत् यथा अन्य चक्रेषु चतुःषष्टिभेदभिन्नाः पारायणमन्त्रयोजनक्रमस्तथेत्यर्थः । अस्मिन् श्लोके अन्यत् सर्वं पूर्वमेवास्माभिर्व्याख्यातम् ॥ ३७ ॥

एतदित्यादिभिः कुल इत्यन्तैस्त्रिभिः श्लोकैस्तेषां प्रोक्तानां चक्राणां साधारणं शेषरूपं तद्विनियोगांस्तत्फलानि चोपदिशति । तत्र एतदिति प्रति चक्र-विषयं । वहिस्तच्चक्राणां प्रत्येकं प्रोक्तरूपाद्वहिरित्यर्थः । अष्टच्छदाम्बुजं अष्टपत्रमम्बुजमिति यावत् । अम्बुजमित्युक्त्या तदम्बुजस्य कर्णिकामध्ये प्रोक्त-चक्राणां विनिर्माणात्तच्चक्रवाह्ये कर्णिकार्थमेकवृत्तं विलिख्य तद्वहिरष्टपत्राणि विलिखेदित्यर्थः । क्रमशः अग्रादिप्रादक्षिण्यक्रमतः । वाग्देव्यष्टकं वशिन्या-दीनां मन्त्राष्टकं प्रोक्तरूपं विलिखेदिति पूर्वत्रान्वयः । ललितार्चनायामिति शेषः । वीजद्वयतत्तद्वर्गवीजनाम सप्ताक्षरीयुक्तमित्यर्थः । तस्य इति प्राग्वत् प्रतिचक्रविषयः । ईरितं द्वितीयपटल इति शेषः । एतदुक्तं भवति प्रतिष्ठायां द्वितीये पटले प्रोक्तरूपे प्रोक्तचक्रेषु सर्वमध्ये कर्णिकामध्ये देवतामावाह्य गन्धादिभिरभ्यर्च्य देवताप्रष्ठभागे श्रीनाथपङ्क्तीः प्रोक्तप्रक्रियया पञ्चदश नित्याश्च समभ्यर्च्य परितो द्वैतीय वहिर्वशिन्यादीः समभ्यर्च्य षट्त्रिंशदधिक

वर्णौषधिक्वाथजलैरापूर्य्य कलशं महत् ।
तत्र देवीं समावाह्य संपूज्य विधिवन्निशि ॥ ४१ ॥
नित्यानां तत्त्वविद्याश्च जपित्वाऽन्येद्युरासने ।
संपूज्य शिष्यं संस्थाप्य शक्त्या तमभिषिचयेत् ॥ ४२ ॥
एवं जन्मानुजन्मादि पौर्णमासीषु साधकः ।
कुर्य्यात् कर्षसुवर्णस्य मुद्रिकां गाश्च दक्षिणाम् ॥ ४३ ॥
एवं निरन्तरं वर्षं योऽभिषिक्तः स साधकः ।
पार्थिवस्तस्य वन्द्यो वा भविष्यति न संशयः ॥ ४४ ॥
वर्षद्वयाभिषेकेन तस्य वंशे स्थिरा रमा ।
वर्षत्रयाभिषेकेण सिद्धिर्वैद्याधरी भवेत् ॥ ४५ ॥

सप्तशतोत्तरविंशतिसहस्रसंख्यान् (२०७३६) मन्त्रांस्तच्चक्रोद्धृतक्रमादर्चयेदिति। नित्यं प्रतिदिवसं एतदनुलोमादिमङ्गलप्रदचक्रविषयम्। इतरेषां चक्राणां तत्तत्कार्य्यकाले प्रतिष्ठार्चनादि कृत्वा तत्कार्य्यपरिसमाप्तौ देवतां सपरिवारां मुद्राश्च पटगतं तच्चक्रं मार्जयित्वा प्रोक्तप्रायश्चित्तादि कुर्य्यात्। पुस्तकपूजोक्तसिद्धये पूर्वोक्तपुस्तकलेखनपूजाफलसिद्धये। उभयं मातृकाचक्रार्चनं पुस्तकार्चनञ्च ॥ ४० ॥

वर्णौषधीत्यादिभिराप्नुयादित्यन्तैरष्टभिः श्लोकैस्ताभिर्विद्यादिभिरभिषेकप्रकारं तत्फलावाप्तिश्चोपदिशति। तत्र वर्णौषधिक्वाथजलैः पञ्चत्रिंशे पटले वक्ष्यमाणाक्षरौषधिक्वथितजलैः। महत् खारीमानतोयपूरणीयम्। तत्र जले विधिवत् पूर्वोक्तचक्रविधानप्रक्रियया। निशि पूर्व्वेद्युरिति शेषः। नित्यानां तत्त्वविद्याः स्वराणां षट्त्रिंशत्तत्त्वाक्षरयोगजातविद्याः। आसने संस्थाप्येत्युत्तरत्रान्वयः। शक्त्या देवतात्वेन वृतया योषिता सहेति शेषः। तं शिष्यं। जन्मानुजन्मादि पौर्णमासीषु आदिशब्दो विषुवायनयुगादिविशेषदिवसविषयः। पौर्णमासीशब्दः शेषपर्वविषयः। कर्षः निष्कत्रयं। मुद्रिकां अङ्गुलीयकं। दक्षिणां अभिषेक्तुरिति शेषः। एवं प्रोक्तप्रकारेण। निरन्तरं उक्तकालानतिलङ्घनेन। वर्षं अत्यन्तसंयोगे

चतुर्व्वर्षाभिषेकेण खेचरीमेलनं भवेत् ।
पञ्चवर्षाभिषेकेण पञ्चत्वं नाधिगच्छति ॥ ४६ ॥
षड़्वर्षमभिषेकेण लोकपालसमो भवेत् ।
सप्तवर्षाभिषेकेण दिवाकरसमो भवेत् ॥ ४७ ॥
अष्टवर्षाभिषेकेण चन्द्रमःसदृशो भवेत् ।
नववर्षाभिषेकेण देवीसारूप्यमाप्नुयात् ॥ ४८ ॥
जयाय विद्याः षट्त्रिंशदेकपञ्चाशदेव वा ।
आवृत्तीर्जपहोमार्चातर्पणैः साधु साधयेत् ॥ ४९ ॥
तेन जित्वा रिपून् सर्व्वानेधते तपनो यथा ।
तथोत्पातेषु सर्व्वेषु तथा रोगाद्युपद्रवे ॥ ५० ॥

द्वितीया । तस्य वन्द्यः पार्थिवस्य वन्द्यः । एतद्ब्राह्मणजातिविषयं । तस्य अभिषेचकस्य खेचरीमेलनं आकाशचरयोगिनीसंलापादि पञ्चत्वं स्वस्वरूपापरिज्ञानं । षड़्वर्षं प्राग्वद्द्वितीया । लोकपालसमः तत्तद्गुणवैभवेन । दिवाकरसमः प्रतापादितः । चन्द्रमःसदृशः आह्लादकरत्वादिना । देवीसारूप्यं पराहन्तात्मताम् ॥ ४८ ॥ ॐ ॥

जयायेत्यादिभिः सम्प्रदायत इत्यन्तैः पञ्चभिः श्लोकैश्चतुर्विधोपास्तिभेदेन फलावाप्तिं प्रपञ्चस्य तत्तच्चक्ररूपत्वं तज्ज्ञानसिद्धौ सर्वाणि फलानीष्टानि सिध्यन्तीति चोपदिशति । तत्र विद्याः प्रोक्तसंख्याः कालनित्याः । षट्त्रिंशत् एकपञ्चाशदिति तासामावृत्तिविशेषणं । वा विकल्पे । साधु अनन्यगतचित्तं यथा तेन साधनेन सर्वान् सहजप्राकृतकृत्रिमान् एधते दीप्यते यथा इवेत्यर्थः । अस्मिन् प्रकरणे तथाशब्दः पूर्वोक्तप्रकारजपादिविषयः । सर्वेषु भौमान्तरीक्षदिव्येषु । रोगादीत्यत्रादिशब्दो भूतवेतालप्रेतपिशाचापस्मारादिविषयः । कृत्यानिवारणे परोत्थापितकृत्याप्रतिनिवर्त्तने । कृत्यासमुत्पत्तौ स्वात्मरक्षार्थमिति शेषः । इत्थमिति प्रोक्तविषयः । एतत्प्रकारमास्थाय ग्रहचारादि प्रवर्त्तते आदिशब्दो राश्यादिविषयः । एतदुक्तं भवति ज्योतिश्चक्रं प्रत्येकतत्तद्द्रेक्काणात्मकद्वादशराशिमयं भवति तेन तत्तच्चक्राणि च प्रत्येकमारत्रयात्मकद्वादशराशिमयानि भवन्ति । तस्माद् यथा द्वादशराश्यात्मके ज्योतिश्चक्रे ग्रहचारादि काले काले प्रवर्त्तते तथा

तथा वाञ्छितसिद्ध्यर्थं तथा कृत्यानिवारणे ।
तथा कृत्यासमुत्पत्तावित्थं सर्व्वार्थसिद्धिदम् ॥ ५१ ॥
एतच्चक्रारमास्थाय ग्रहर्क्षादि प्रवर्त्तते ।
एतच्चक्रारविन्यासरूपा भूमिश्च दृश्यते ॥ ५२ ॥
तस्मादेतन्मयं सर्व्वमेतस्य भजनेन च ।
सर्व्वे मनोरथाः सिद्धा भजनं सम्प्रदायतः ॥ ५३ ॥
कालप्राप्तक्रमं पूर्व्वमावर्त्त्यान्यक्रमं भजेत् ।
कृष्णपक्षेषु शुक्लेषु केवलोक्तक्रमं भजेत् ॥ ५४ ॥
जपतर्पणहोमार्च्चास्थापनेष्वप्ययं क्रमः ।
अमुं ज्ञात्वा विधातव्यमन्यथानर्थमावहेत् । ॥ ५५ ॥

एतेषां ज्योतिश्चक्रमयत्वादेतेषु चक्रेष्वेकस्मिन्नेकस्मिन्नेव प्रत्यरं ग्रहनक्षत्रादीनि मातृकाक्षरमयानि तत्तद्युगवर्षभेदक्रमेण प्रवर्त्तत इति भूमिः । भूचक्रस्य द्वादशराश्यात्मकत्वात् प्राक् प्रतिपादितक्रमतस्तदपि तत्तच्चक्रात्मकं भवतीति यावत् । एतन्मयं मातृकाचक्रमयं सर्वं दृश्यं । एतस्य प्रोक्तचक्रान्यतमस्य भजनेनेति पूर्व्वमेवोक्तं । भजनं सम्प्रदायतः कर्त्तव्यमिति पुनरुक्तिदोषो न भवतीत्यर्थः ॥ ५३ ॥

कालप्राप्तेत्यादिना आवहेदित्यन्तेन श्लोकद्वयेन तासां विद्यानां चन्द्रक्षयवृद्धिकालभेदेन भजनविशेषं तदवश्यकर्त्तव्यतां तदकरणे प्रत्यवायञ्चोपदिशति । तत्र कालप्राप्तक्रमं प्रागुक्तसम्वत्सरचक्रदर्शितानुलोमानुलोमादिप्रकारभेदेषु तत्तत्सम्वत्सरप्राप्तप्रकारभेदक्रमं । अन्यक्रमं तत्तत्कर्मोक्तं केवलोक्तं क्रमं । तत्तत्कालप्राप्तक्रमवर्जतत्तत्कर्मानुगुणक्रमं । एतदुक्तं भवति कृष्णपक्षे काम्यकर्म्मारम्भे नित्योपासनारम्भे च तत्तत्संवत्सरात्मकचक्रप्रदर्शितक्रमं पूर्व्वमावर्त्त्य पश्चात्तत्तत्कर्म्मोक्तक्रमं भजेत् । शुक्लपक्षे तु तत्तत्कर्म्मप्राप्तक्रममेव भजेदिति । अयं कृष्णपक्षशुक्लपक्षभेदः प्रदर्शितः । अमुं पक्षभेदप्रदर्शितं क्रमं । विधातव्यं नित्यकर्म्म काम्यकर्म्म वेति शेषः । अन्यथा तत्प्रकाराकरणे ॥ ५५ ॥

कृत्योत्पत्तौ शत्रुभङ्गे निग्रहे प्रतिलोमकम् ।
कालेन प्राप्तमन्यच्च सर्वत्र समुदीरितम् ॥ ५६ ॥
वशीकरणरक्षासु सम्पुटद्वितयं क्रमात् ।
रोगशत्रुजये प्रोक्ते परावृत्तक्रमेण वै ॥ ५७ ॥
गोभूहिरण्यवाहादिलाभेषु च समीरितः ।
उच्चाटनेषु व्याकीर्णं तेषु शान्त्यै क्रमं यजेत् ॥ ५८ ॥
एतद्विधाननिष्णातं प्रणमन्ति सुरासुराः ।
तस्मिन्नरिकृताः पीडाः कृत्याद्या नैव सम्मुखाः ॥ ५९ ॥
प्रत्युतैव परावृत्ताः कर्त्तारं नाशयन्ति वै ।
यत्रासौ निवसत्येष तत्तच्चैवं तत्तपोवनम् ॥ ६० ॥

कृत्योत्पत्तावित्यादिभिर्यजेदित्यन्तैस्त्रिभिः श्लोकैः प्रतिलोमानुलोमजेषु कृत्योत्पत्तिशत्रुभङ्गादिरूपाणि फलानि तद्विधानप्रायश्चित्तञ्चोपदिशति । तत्र कालेन प्राप्तं प्रतिलोमाद्यमङ्गलयोग्यानि अनुलोमादिमङ्गलयोग्यानि च सर्व्वत्र सर्व्वकर्म्मसु वक्ष्यमाणेषु। एतदुक्तं भवति कृत्योत्पत्त्याद्यमङ्गलप्रद प्रतिलोमादिकक्रमभजनतो मङ्गलेषु कर्म्मसु क्रियमाणेषु तत्तत् कालप्राप्तक्रम इत्यवश्यकर्त्तव्यतया भजनात्तत्तदमङ्गलप्रदो न भवति । एवमनुलोमादिकमङ्गल फलप्रदक्रमभजनतः अमङ्गलकर्म्मसु क्रियमाणेषु कालप्राप्तक्रमभजनावश्यकर्त्तव्यतया भजनात्तत्तदमङ्गलफलविनाशको न भवति। संपुटद्वितयं स्वरव्यञ्जनयोर्बाह्याभ्यन्तरभेदतः। परावृत्तौ प्रागवद्भेदतः चकारः प्रागुक्तपरावृत्तक्रमद्वयसमुच्चयार्थः। समीरितः परावृत्तक्रमद्वितयक्रम इति शेषः। व्याकीर्णः प्रागवद्भेदतः। तेषु प्रोक्तेष्वमङ्गलेषु परप्रयुक्तेष्वपि क्रमं अनुलोमात्मकं नित्यभजनक्रमं एतेष्वनुलोमादिष्वष्टसु भेदेषु स्वरव्यञ्जनयोरेकप्रकारं अनुलोमानुलोमादिको भेदः। तत्तत्कर्म्मसु शीघ्रफलप्रदो निश्चितममोघश्च भवति। एतस्मिन् पटले उत्तरत्र सर्वव्याकीर्णत्यादिना व्याकीर्णव्याकीर्णचक्रस्यामोघत्वप्रतिपादनात् सम्प्रदायाच्च ॥ ५८ ॥

एतदित्यादिना तपोवनमित्यन्तेन श्लोकद्वयेन एतासु विद्यासु निष्णातस्य

श्मशाने पर्वते शून्ये विपिने क्षुद्रपीड़ने।
प्रतिष्ठिते यन्त्रराजे तत् स्याज्जनपदं महत् ॥ ६१ ॥
सर्वव्याकीर्णचक्रेण स्थापितेनामरावती।
उच्चाटिता पुनर्द्देवि मयापि च न रक्ष्यते ॥ ६२ ॥
शिलायां ताम्रपट्टे वा राजते हैमनिर्म्मिते।
विलिख्य भूमौ निखनेद् ग्रामराष्ट्रपुरादिषु ॥ ६३ ॥
कृत्वा देवालयं तत्र चक्रं संस्थाप्य तस्य वै।
कर्णिकामध्यगे वेरं कुर्य्यात् सान्निध्यसिद्धये ॥ ६४ ॥

वैभवमुपदिशति। तत्र निष्णातं साधकं। तस्मिन् साधके। कर्त्तारं प्रयोक्तारं। असौ साधकः। एष इत्यस्य असावित्यत्रान्वयः। चैत्रं पुष्यचैत्रम् ॥ ६० ॥

श्मशाने इत्यादिना श्लोकेन श्मशानादिशून्यभूमिषु ग्रामनगरपत्तनादिकरणोपायमुपदिशति। तत्र क्षुद्रपीड़ने कालभस्मादिक्षुद्रोपद्रवभूयिष्ठे देशे यन्त्रराजे अनुलोमानुलोमाख्ये चक्रे, तस्य सर्व्वयन्त्रकारणत्वादयन्त्रराजत्वं। तदिति जनपदविशेषणम्। स देशो जनपदं भवतीत्यर्थः ॥ ६१ ॥

सर्वव्याकीर्णेत्यादिना श्लोकेनोच्चाटनचक्रवैभवमुपदिशति। तत्र सर्वव्याकीर्णचक्रेण स्वरव्यञ्जनाभ्यां वाह्याभ्यन्तरभेदजातानि चत्वारि चक्राणि सर्व्वशब्दविषयाणि। उच्चाटिता उन्मूलयितसकलदेवजातिः। मया ईश्वरेण अपिशब्देन किंपुनरल्पसामर्थ्यैरित्यर्थः ॥ ६२ ॥

शिलायामित्यादिभिः सिद्धिदायकमित्यन्तैः पञ्चभिः श्लोकैर्ग्रामादिषु रक्षार्थं तच्चक्रस्थापनविधानं तच्चक्रस्थापनेन सर्व्वदेवतासान्निध्यसिद्ध्यादिकञ्चोपदिशति। तत्र वा वकल्पे। विलिख्य अमुलोमानुलोमाख्यचक्रमिति शेषः। निखनेत् अस्मिन् पटले ग्रामादीत्यादिपञ्चषष्टितमश्लोकादिभिस्त्रिभिः श्लोकैर्वक्ष्यमाणप्रकारेण रक्षार्थमिति शेषः। पुरादिष्वित्यत्रादिशब्दो नगरखर्वटपत्तनादिविषयः। तत्र देवालये। चक्रं अनुलोमानुलोमात्मकं मातृकाचक्रमित्यर्थः। संस्थाप्य देवतास्थापनस्थाने एकस्मिन्नेव वक्ष्यमाणप्रकारेण तस्य चक्रस्य कर्णिकामध्यगे स्थान इति शेषः। वेरं अभीष्टदेवतायाः कुर्य्यात् प्रतिष्ठापयेदित्यर्थः। सान्निध्य-

ग्रामादिरक्षणे तत्र मध्ये चाष्टसु दिक्ष्वपि ।
खात्वावटं पुनस्तेषु पाषाणैर्घटितं दृढम् ॥ ६५ ॥
समावाह्याभिपूज्याथ स्थापयेन्मूलविद्यया ।
पाषाणेन तदाच्छाद्य पीठं कृत्वोपरि स्थिरम् ॥ ६६ ॥
नित्यशः पूजयेद् गन्धपुष्पधूपादिभिः समम् ।
त्रिसन्ध्यमेवं कुर्व्वीत नान्यथा सिद्धिदायकम् ॥ ६७ ॥

सिद्धये देवताया इति शेषः। एतदुक्तं भवति प्रोक्तेषु वास्तुष्वभीष्टदेशे अभीष्टदेवतालयं कृत्वा तत्र देवतास्थापनस्थानमध्ये एकमवटं खात्वा तं वक्ष्यमाणप्रकारेण शिलाभिरावध्य तत्र प्रोक्तमनुलोमानुलोमात्मकचक्रं शिलादिषूक्तेष्वधिकरणेषूत्कीर्य्य प्राग्वत् कृतप्राणप्रतिष्ठादिकं संस्थाप्याभ्यर्च्य तत्पाषाणेनाच्छाद्य तत्र कर्णिकामध्यस्थानोपरि तत्तद्देवतावेरप्रतिष्ठापनात् तस्मिन् वेरे तत्तद्देवतासान्निध्यसिद्धिरिति। ग्रामादिरक्षणे पूर्व्वप्रस्तुते आदिशब्दः प्राग्वत्। तत्र तस्मिन् (तस्मिन्) मध्ये सर्व्वमध्ये अवटं गर्त्तम्। मध्ये च प्रतिदिशश्चेति शेषः। तेषु अवटेषु घटितं तत्तदन्तस्थले इति शेषः। समावाह्य प्रोक्तचक्रकर्णिकामध्ये अभीष्टनित्यामिति शेषः। अभिपूज्य तन्नित्यार्चनक्रमेण तच्चक्रगतविद्याक्रमेण चेत्यर्थः। अन्तः शिलाघटितावटानामिति शेषः। स्थापयेत् प्रतिष्ठितं चक्रं मूलविद्यया अभीष्टनित्यायाः तत् अवटगतं चक्रं पीठं शिलादिभिर्घटितं धिष्ण्याकारं। उपरि आच्छादिततलोपरि। स्थिरं शिलादिभिर्घटितत्वात्। पूजयेत्तस्मिन् धिष्ण्ये चक्रसमावाहितां नित्यां। एवं उक्तप्रकारं गन्धादिभिः। अन्यथा प्रोक्तप्रक्रियाव्यतिरेकेण। एतदुक्तं भवति ग्रामपुरनगरखेटखर्वटपत्तनादिवास्तुरक्षणे तस्मिंस्तस्मिन् वास्तुप्रदेशे सर्व्वमध्येऽष्टसु दिक्ष्वपि एवं नवसु स्थानेषु नवावटान् खात्वा तेषामन्तःस्थलानि पाषाणैरावध्य प्रोक्ताधिकरणेष्वन्यतमे रूपे अधिकरणनवके उभयानुलोमात्मकं उभयसम्पुटं वा चक्रनवकमुत्कीर्य्य कृतप्राणप्रतिष्ठादिके तस्मिन् अभीष्टां नित्यामावाह्य तत्तन्नित्याक्रमेणाभ्यर्च्य तत्तत् चक्रभेदादिभिः कालनित्याभिश्चाभ्यर्च्य एवं दिनत्रयादहीनं सम्पूज्य तत्तच्चक्रनवकमेकमेकमेकस्मिन्नेकस्मिन्नवटे संस्थाप्यावटोपरि तच्छिलाभिराच्छाद्य तत्तलोपरि शिलादिभिर्दृढतराणि पीठरूपाणि नव

तत्कालोक्तानि कुण्डानि नव होमेषु सर्वतः।
होतॄणां दक्षिणा वस्त्रभूषादासगोधनैः ॥ ६८ ॥
यद्यद्यन्निजेप्सितं तत्तद्दुष्करं सुकरन्तु वा।
जपतर्पणहोमैर्व्वा सेकैः संसाधयेत् स्थिरः ॥ ६९ ॥
नैताभिः सदृशी कापि विद्या लोकेषु विद्यते।
तस्मात्तदाभिरुपायैः साधयेत् सर्व्वमीप्सितम् ॥ ७० ॥
पञ्चाशद्वारमावर्त्त्य विद्याभक्तिसमन्वितः।
मुच्यते निगडैः कृच्छ्रैर्वैरिरोधैः सुदारुणैः ॥ ७१ ॥
शतवारं समावर्त्त्य विद्याविविधवैभवाः।
लभन्ते तनयान् वन्ध्या अपि सर्व्वगुणान्वितान् ॥ ७२ ॥

धिष्ण्यानि ज्ञात्वा तत्र तत्र धिष्ण्ये प्रतिदिनं प्रोक्तक्रमात्त्रिसन्ध्यार्चनात् प्रोक्तग्रामादिरक्षासिद्धिः। एतत्समं चक्रान्तरं न विद्यत इति ॥ ६७ ॥

तत्कालेत्यादिना होमेन प्रागुक्ते चक्रे व्याप्तिक्रमप्राप्तकालदर्शितनवविधकुण्डेषु होमविधानं होतृदक्षिणाञ्चोपदिशति। तत्र तत्कालोक्तानि कुण्डानि नव। तत्तत्संवत्सरोक्तानि वृत्तादीनि नव चक्राणि कुण्डाकाराणि कुर्य्यादित्यर्थः। सर्व्वतः नित्यनैमित्तिककाम्यकर्म्मसु। गोधनैर्गोभिर्धनैश्च। एतदुक्तं भवति पूर्णमण्डलसंख्येषु युगवत्सरेषु चतुःषष्टिवत्सरेषु प्रोक्तवृत्तादिषट्त्रिंशदस्रादिचक्रनवकाकाराणि नवकुण्डानि कुण्डपटलवक्ष्यमाणक्रमात् द्वितीयवृत्तादिवृत्तान्तरान्तरत्यासवर्ज्जं कल्पयित्वा तत्तत्सम्वत्सरप्राप्ते कुण्डे सर्व्वकर्म्मसु होमं कारयित्वा होतृणामुक्तानि द्रव्याणि दक्षिणां दद्यादिति ॥ ६८ ॥

यद्यदित्यादिना ईप्सितमित्यन्तेन श्लोकद्वयेन ताभिस्ताभिर्विद्याभिः पञ्चविधोपासनेन समीहितसिद्धिं विद्यावैभवादिकञ्चोपदिशति। तत्र तत्तत् समीहितं दुष्करं अति महता यत्नेन साध्यमपि। तुरवधारणे। वा समुच्चये। स्थिरः फलत्येवेति निश्चितबुद्धिः। एताभिर्विद्याभिः। आभिः विद्याभिः। उपायैस्तैः प्रोक्तपञ्चविधसाधनैः ॥ ७१ ॥

पञ्चाशदित्यादिभिरवाप्नुयादित्यन्तैरध्यर्द्धैः सप्तभिः श्लोकैस्तासां विद्यानां

अध्यर्द्धशतवारन्तु विद्या आवर्त्त्य भक्तितः ।
गुणरूपादिसम्पन्नां भार्य्यां विन्दन्त्ययत्नतः ॥ ७३ ॥
तावदावर्त्त्य कन्या वा पतिं सर्व्वगुणान्वितम् ।
लभन्ते पुत्रपौत्राद्यैरेधन्ते सम्पदन्विताः ॥ ७४ ॥
द्विशतं ताः समावर्त्त्य दारिद्र्यान्मुच्यते ध्रुवम् ।
त्रिशतैर्भूमिशस्याढ्यश्चतुर्भिस्तु शतैर्धनी ॥ ७५ ॥
पञ्चभिस्तु शतैर्भूपो भवेत् षड्भिः शतैर्नृपः ।
सप्तभिस्तु शतैरस्य न मुञ्चत्यन्वयं रमा ॥ ७६ ॥
अष्टभिस्तु शतैरासां नृपाः सर्व्वेऽस्य किङ्कराः ।
नवभिस्तु शतैरेष कन्दर्पो वनिताजने ॥ ७७ ॥
एवं नवशतं जप्त्वा सर्व्वान् कामानवाप्नुयात् ।
आसान्तु विद्यानित्यानामङ्गानि शृणु सुन्दरि ॥ ७८ ॥

पञ्चाशद्वारादिनवशतवारान्तमावृत्त्याधिक्येन फलाधिक्यमुपदिशति । तत्र विद्या इति पदच्छेदः । लाच्छैर्व्यंसनैः । विद्याः प्राग्वद्विविधवैभवाः फलवैविध्यात् । अध्यर्द्ध शतवारं पञ्चाशदुत्तरशतवारमित्यर्थः । गुणरूपादीत्यत्रादिशब्देनाभिजनादि प्रोच्यते । विन्दन्ति लभन्ते साधका इति शेषः । तावत् पञ्चाशदुत्तरं शतवारं । कन्या इति प्रथमाबहुवचनम् । वा समुच्चये । एधन्ते वर्द्धन्ते । सम्पदन्विता इत्येतत् कन्या इत्यस्य विशेषणं । ताः विद्याः । दारिद्र्यादकिञ्चनत्वादसन्तोषादित्यर्थः । त्रिशतैर्वारैः । चतुर्भिस्तु शतैश्चतुर्भिःशतैरित्यन्वयः । तुः समुच्चये प्रागवत् शेषः । पञ्चभिस्तु शतैः प्राग्वदन्वयशेषावित्यर्थः । भूपः भूमीशः 'षट्शतैः प्राग्वत् शेषः । नृपः दासदासीभृत्यादिभिराढ्यः । तुः प्राग्वत् शेषश्च । अस्य साधकस्य । तुः प्राग्वत् शेषश्च । आसां विद्यानां । नृपाः प्रागुक्ताः । अस्य साधकस्य । एष साधकः । एवमित्यादिनैतदुक्तम्भवति नवशतवारावृत्त्यास्मिन् प्रकरणे उक्तान्यन्यानि दुर्लभान्यभीष्टानि सिध्यन्तीति ॥ ७८ ॥

द्विरुक्त्या तैः षडङ्गानि कुर्य्यादर्णैः कराङ्गयोः।
विन्यस्य मातृकायुक्तां जपेद्विद्यान्तमेकशः॥ ७९॥
रक्ता रक्ताम्बरा रक्तभूषणस्त्रग्विलेपनाः।
पाशाङ्कुशेक्षुकोदण्डप्रसूनविशिखाः स्मरेत्॥ ८०॥
तदा वृत्तानां पद्मानां शक्तीस्तत्सदृशाः स्मरेत्।
चतुरस्रद्वयं कृत्वा द्वारद्वयविभूषितम्॥ ८१॥

आसामित्यादिना एकश इत्यन्तेनार्द्धाद्येनैकेन श्लोकेन प्रोक्तानां तासां सर्व्वासाञ्च विद्यानां प्रत्येकं भजने त्रिविधन्यासादिकमुपदिशति। तत्र सुन्दरीति देवीसम्बुद्धिः। द्विरुक्त्या द्विवारोच्चारणेन। तैः अर्णैः इत्यस्य विशेषणम्। मातृकायुक्तां कुलसुन्दरीपटलोक्तक्रमेण सषडङ्गमातृकां न्यसेदित्यर्थः। एकशः एकामेकां विद्यामित्यर्थः। एतदुक्तं भवति प्रोक्तानामासां कालनित्याविद्यानामन्यतमविद्याभजने कुलसुन्दरीपटलोक्तप्रकारेण पूर्वं सषडङ्गां मातृकां विन्यस्यानन्तरं तत्तद्विद्याक्षरत्रयेष्वाद्येनाक्षरेण हृदयं द्वितीयेनाक्षरेण शिरः। तृतीयेन शिखा। पुनरपि तत्तद्विद्याद्येनाक्षरेण कवचं। द्वितीयेनाक्षरेण नेत्रं। तृतीयेनास्त्रञ्च एतद्विद्याक्षरत्रयद्विरावृत्त्या जातियुक्तषडङ्गानि करन्यासपुरःसरं विन्यस्य तथा व्यापकं कृत्वा तां विद्यां जपेदिति। तन्मन्त्रा यथा—ऐं हृदयाय नमः। आं शिरसे स्वाहा। ईं शिखाय वषट्। ऐं कवचाय हुँ। आं नेत्रत्रयाय वौषट्। ईं अस्त्राय फट्। इति एवमन्यास्वपि विद्यासु योजयेत्। आसां विद्यानां समुदायभजने प्राग्वत् मातृकां निजषडङ्गपुरःसरं विन्यस्य जपेदिति सम्प्रदायः। षोड़शनित्याविद्यास्वन्यतमविद्यया सह भजने तत्तन्नित्याविद्योक्तन्यासजातपुरःसरं जपेदिति च सम्प्रदायः॥ ७९॥

रक्ता इत्यादिना स्मरेदित्यन्तेनाध्यर्द्धेन श्लोकेन तासां सर्व्वासां विद्यादेवतानां सावरणशक्तीनां ध्यानमुपदिशति। तत्र आयुधक्रमस्तूर्द्धादिवामदक्षिणक्रमेण बोद्धव्यः। षोड़शनित्यात्मकललिताध्यानसमानरूपादिध्यानादासां तादात्म्यं सम्पादयतीति सम्प्रदायः। तत्सदृशा मूलदेवतासदृशाः वर्णादिभिरिति शेषः॥ ८०॥

अष्टपत्राम्बुजं मध्ये नवयोनौ च तां यजेत्।
अङ्गावृत्तिं मध्ययोनावन्तरे त्वायुधावृतिम् ॥ ८२ ॥
पृष्ठतो गुरुपंक्तिञ्च कोणेष्वष्टसु च क्रमात्।
वहिर्दलेष्वपि तथा यजेद्वर्णौर्विलोमतः ॥ ८३ ॥
रूपिणीशक्तिसहितैर्म्मायया सप्ताक्षरीयुतैः।
ब्राह्म्यादिशक्तीस्तद्वाह्ये चतुरस्रद्वये यजेत् ॥ ८४ ॥

चतुरस्रद्वयमित्यादिभिः स्मरन् धियेत्यन्तैरर्द्धाद्यैश्चतुर्भिः श्लोकैस्तासां देवतानां नित्यपूजाचक्रस्य सर्व्वसाधारणरेखारूपविन्यासरूपमनन्तरवक्ष्यमाणविशेषविभिन्ने तस्मिन् तस्मिन्नित्यपूजाचक्रे तत्तद्देवतापूजाक्रमविधानञ्चोपदिशति। तत्र चतुरस्रद्वयमन्तर्वहिर्विभागेन द्वारद्वयविभूषितम् पूर्व्वपश्चिमयोर्द्दिशोरिति शेषः। मध्ये अन्तर्गतचतुरस्रस्येति शेषः। नवयोनौ च चकारेण पूर्व्वगते मध्ये इतिशब्दमाकर्षयति। तेन तदष्टदलाम्बुजमध्यकर्णिकायां लिखितनवयोनौ। ताः तद्देवताः। मध्ययोनौ नवयोनिचक्रमध्यत्रिकोणमध्ये प्रागुक्तवाह्यादिक्रमेण। अन्तरे प्राग्वन्मध्ययोनेर्वहिरभितः। पृष्ठतः मध्यदेवतायाः। चकारः समुच्चये क्रमाद्वक्ष्यमाणाक्षरलेखनक्रमात्। तथा वक्ष्यमाणप्रकारेण। विलोमतः अग्राद्यप्रादक्षिण्येन। रूपिणीशक्तिसहितैः रूपिणीशक्ति इति पञ्चाक्षरसहितैः माया ह्रल्लेखा सप्ताक्षरी प्राग्वत्। एतदुक्तं भवति ह्रल्लेखां प्रथममुच्चार्य्य ततस्तद्विद्यामध्याक्षरस्य षोड़शस्वरभिन्नेषु रूपेष्वेकमेकं यथाक्रममुच्चार्य्य तदनु रूपिणीशक्ति इति पञ्चाक्षराण्युच्चार्य्य ततः सप्ताक्षरीं योजयेत्। सर्वे मन्त्राश्चतुर्द्दशाक्षरात्मका भवन्तीति। मन्त्रा यथा—ह्रीं अरूपिणीशक्तिपादुकां पूजयामि ह्रीं आरूपिणीशक्तिपादुकां पूजयामीत्यादय इति। तथा प्राग्वत्। तन्मन्त्रा यथा—ह्रीं ब्रह्माणीपादुकां पूजयामीत्यादय इति। अत्र पूजाचक्रे सर्व्वसाधारणे रेखारूपविन्यासप्रकारो यथा—अन्तर्वहिर्विभागेन प्राग्वत् चतुरस्रद्वयमुत्पाद्य तन्मध्येऽष्टपत्रमम्बुजं कर्णिकायां नवयोनिं कुलसुन्दरीपटलोक्तप्रकारेण कृत्वा तत्रास्मिन् पटले अनन्तरश्लोकादिभिर्वक्ष्यमाणक्रमाद्वर्णान् विलिख्य तत्र ताः प्रत्येकं प्रोक्तक्रमादभ्यर्च्चयेदिति। वलिप्रदानञ्च करोतु पूजान्त इति शेषः। चकारेणास्मिंस्तन्त्रे सर्व्वसाधारणेन षोड़शाक्षरेण पूजादौ वलिं प्रदद्यादित्य-

आसां बलिप्रदानञ्च करोतु कुरुकुल्लया ।
सम्प्राच्यर्य्या केवलया प्रोक्तरूपां स्मरन् धिया ॥ ८५ ॥
विलिख्य नाम्ना विद्यान्तु मध्ये वाह्येऽष्टयुग्मके ।
तन्मध्यार्णं स्वरैर्भिन्नं लिखित्वास्त्रिषु मायया ॥ ८६ ॥
हंसिलाग्रासमालिख्य निरृत्यादिविलोमतः ।
वाताद्यर्णं हृदन्तं स्याद्द्वादश द्वादश क्रमात् ॥ ८७ ॥

सुमर्थं समुच्चयति । कुरुकुल्लया सम्प्राच्यर्य्या आद्यया विद्यया । केवलया द्वितीय-तृतीयवैधुर्य्येण । प्रोक्तरूपां तत्पटलध्यानोक्तरूपां । अत्रासां कालनित्यानां षोड़शनित्यासाधारणबलिद्वयविधानात् ताभिस्तादात्म्यं दर्शयतीत्याराध्यपाद-मुखादवगतोऽर्थः ॥ ८५ ॥

विलिख्येत्यादिभिः समुद्वसेदित्यन्तैस्त्रिभिः श्लोकैस्तासां विद्यानां पूर्वोक्त-साधारणरेखारूपे पूजाचक्रे पूर्व्वप्रस्तुतविशेषभूतेन विद्याक्षरन्यासेन रूपभेदं तत्तद्विनियोगं पूजापरिसमाप्तिञ्चोपदिशति । तत्र नाम्ना विद्यान्तु साध्यादि-त्रिकस्य सहेति शेषः । नित्यपूजाचक्रे विद्यां कालनित्यास्वन्यतमां । विद्यालेखन-मेव नित्यपूजाचक्रे कर्त्तव्यमित्युक्तं भवति । मध्ये नवयोनिमध्यगतयोन्यां वाह्ये । अष्टयुग्मके सर्व्वमध्ययोन्या वहिर्भूताष्टकोणेषु तद्वहिर्भूताष्टदलेषु च । तन्मध्यार्णं तत्तन्मध्ययोनिगतविद्यामध्यमाक्षरं । स्वरैर्भिन्नं प्रागवत् षोड़शस्वरविकृतं लिखित्वा अग्राद्यप्रादक्षिण्येन । अस्त्रिषु वृत्तचतुरस्रान्तरालगतास्त्रिषु मायया हंसेन ग्रासं हकारं लकारं चकारं ह्लक्षाञ्च । निरृत्यादिविलोमत इत्येतत् पूर्वापरयोः काकाक्षिन्यायेनान्वेति । तत्र पूर्व्वत्रान्वये निरृतिवह्नीशवायुकोणे यथाक्रमं हकारादि प्रोक्तं चतुष्टयं विलिखेदिति । परत्रान्वये वक्ष्यमाणान्यक्षराणि वक्ष्यमाणप्रकारेण चतुरस्रवीथ्यां निरृत्यादितदन्तर्विलोमतो लिखेदिति । वाताद्यर्णं हृदन्तं स्यात् । वातादि अकारादि अर्णं अर्णा इत्यर्थः । हृदन्तं सकारान्तं स्यात् स्युरित्यर्थः । मातृकायां पूर्व्वलिखितहंसाद्यक्षरत्रयशिष्टा-नीति शेषः । तत्रार्णमिति नपुंसकोक्तिर्वचनव्यत्यासश्च दिव्यत्वात् । द्वादशद्वादशक्रमात् अकारादिसकारान्तान् वर्णान् अष्टचत्वारिंशतं चतुरस्र-वीथ्यां प्रतिवीथिकं द्वादश द्वादश वर्णान् विलिखेदित्यर्थः । तैर्द्वितीयपटलोक्ते-

साधयेदीप्सितं सर्व्वं षट्कर्म्मात्मकमीश्वरि।
स्तुत्वा द्वादशभिः श्लोकैस्तैः स्वान्ते ताः समुद्वसेत् ॥ ८८ ॥
एतासां चक्रमध्यस्थो जपेद्विद्यां यदा वशी।
तदैव देवताचक्रसाम्यमस्य भविष्यति ॥ ८९ ॥
महाचक्रस्य मध्यस्थं कृत्वा श्रीचक्रमुज्ज्वलम्।
तत्रैव देवीमावाह्य पूजयेत् सर्वसिद्धये ॥ ९० ॥

गणेशेत्यादिभिः। स्वान्ते हृदये। ताः मूलदेवताः परिवारदेवताश्च। एतदुक्तं भवति पूर्वोक्तसर्व्वसाधारणे रेखारूपे नित्यपूजाचक्रे नवयोनिमध्यस्थयोनिमध्ये कालनित्याविद्यास्वन्यतमामिव नित्यपूजासु विलिख्य काम्यकर्म्मसु चैतां साध्यादित्रिकनामसंयुतां विलिख्य तद्विद्यामध्यमाक्षरस्य षोड़शस्वरविकृतानि रूपाणि तत्रनवयोनिचक्राष्टकोणेष्वष्टदलेषु चाग्नाद्यप्रादक्षिण्येन यथाक्रमं विलिख्य तद्बहिश्चतुरस्रद्वयान्तरालवीथ्यां परितो निर्ऋत्यादितदन्तःप्रादक्षिण्येन अकारादिसकारान्तान्यष्टचत्वारिंशदक्षराणि प्रतिदिशं द्वादशद्वादशक्रममालिख्य तदन्तः पञ्चवाह्यप्राकारचतुरस्रान्तरालानि निर्ऋत्यादीशान्तं हकारादिशेष वर्णत्रयं विलिख्य वायुकोणे क्षकारं चालिख्य पूर्वोक्तप्रकारेणावाह्य ध्यात्वा अभ्यर्च्य द्वादशश्लोक्या स्तुत्वा सपरिवारां तां स्वान्ते समुद्वसेत्। एवं काम्यकर्मस्वप्युपासनेन तत्तत्फलसिद्धिः। तत्र विशेषो विद्यया सह मध्ये नामत्रयलेखनं तेन चक्रो सुनेत्रेति पञ्चाक्षरवाक्यजनितसंख्यानि चक्राणि भवन्तीति ॥ ८८ ॥

एतासामित्यादिना श्लोकेन प्रोक्तसंख्येषु कालनित्याचक्रेषु भजनविशेषेण फलविशेषमुपदिशति। तत्र विद्यां षोड़शनित्यानां कालनित्यानाञ्च। अस्य साधकस्य। एतदुक्तं भवति षोड़शनित्याविद्याभजने तत्तद्दिनप्राप्तनित्याभजने च तत्तद्दिनप्राप्तकालनित्याचक्रस्थो जपेत्। कालनित्याविद्यास्वन्यतमभजने तच्चक्रमध्यस्थ एव नित्यशः २०७३६ जपेत्। कालनित्याविद्यासमुदायभजने षोड़शनित्याभजने च तत्तत्सम्वत्सरकालप्राप्तान्यतमचक्रेऽनुलोमानुलोमेषु चक्रेषु सर्व्वकालचक्राकारणे वृत्ताकारानुलोमानुलोमचक्रे वा स्थित्वा जपेत्। तेन प्रोक्तफलसिद्धिरिति ॥ ८९ ॥

एवं कृत्वा प्रतिष्ठाप्य विधानेनार्चयेद्यतः ।
तत्राज्ञासिद्धयो लोके प्रकाशन्ते महाद्भुताः ॥ ९१ ।
तथा च कृत्वा तन्मध्ये लोहितां लोहिताम्बराम् ।
सुन्दरीं युवतीं तत्र संस्थाप्याभ्यर्चयेत् क्रमैः ॥ ९२ ॥
प्रत्यब्दमेवं कुर्वीत मीनस्थे भास्करे विधौ ।
पूर्णे तु दिवसे तेन देवी तुष्टेष्टदा भवेत् ॥ ९३ ॥

महाचक्रस्येत्यादिभिर्भवेदित्यन्तैश्चतुर्भिः श्लोकैः प्रागुक्तेषु महाचक्रमध्ये ललितार्चाचक्रं तत्र तत्पूजां तत्फलं तत्रैव कालविशेषे पूजाविशेषेण फलविशेषञ्चोपदिशति। तत्र महाचक्रस्य प्रागुक्तपूर्णमण्डलयुगवत्सरात्मकानाञ्चक्राणां प्रथमरूपस्य वृत्ताकारानुलोमानुलोमात्मकस्य तत्तत्संवसरप्राप्तस्य वा। श्रीचक्रं ललितार्चाचक्रम् त्रयस्त्रिंशे पटले वक्ष्यमाणं। उज्ज्वलं सुव्यक्ताकारं तेन महाचक्रस्य कर्णिकाव्यासविकाशमुपपन्नमिति सम्प्रदायः। तत्र महाचक्रस्य मध्यस्थश्रीचक्रमध्ये। एतदुक्तं भवति प्रागुक्तचक्रेषु तत्तत्सम्वत्सरप्राप्तं वा केवलानुलोमानुलोमात्मकवृत्ताकारं चक्रं वा ललिताचक्रनिर्म्माणयोग्यकर्णिकाविकाशं कृत्वा तत्कर्णिकायां वक्ष्यमाणलक्षणोपेतं ललितार्चनश्रीचक्रं विधाय तत्र देव्यर्चनात् सर्वाभीष्टसिद्धिरिति। एवम् उक्तरूपमध्यस्थश्रीचक्रं महाचक्रमित्यर्थः। कृत्वा रत्नत्रिलोहद्दृषत्स्वन्यतमेऽधिकरणे विधानेन द्वितीयपटलोक्तप्रक्रियया। अभ्यर्चयेत् सपरिवारां देवीमिति शेषः। यतः यत्र देशे इत्यर्थः। तत्र देशे आज्ञासिद्धयः चराचरस्य जगतो निदेशवर्त्तित्वं। तथा च कृत्वा पूर्ववत् महाचक्रस्य मध्यस्थं श्रीचक्रं कृत्वेत्यर्थः। तन्मध्ये महाचक्रस्थ श्रीचक्रमध्ययोनिमध्ये। क्रमैः ललितानित्यार्चनक्रमैः। मीनस्थे भास्करे सौरे फाल्गुने मासि विधौ पूर्णे पौर्णमास्यामित्यर्थः। तुरवधारणे। तेन पूजनेन। देवी ललिता। एतदुक्तं भवति प्रोक्ते सौरफाल्गुनमासे पूर्णायां सिन्दूरादिविरचित प्रोक्तमहाचक्रमध्यस्थश्रीचक्रमध्ययोनिमध्ये प्रोक्तवर्णाम्बरविभूषणां सुन्दरीं युवतीं निवेश्य तस्यां परदेवतामावाह्य नित्यार्चनक्रमेण प्रतिवत्सरमर्चयेत् ततो ललिता देवी तुष्टाभीष्टप्रदा भवेदिति ॥ ९३ ॥

नखरं छुरिकां खड्‌गं चापशूलगदाशरान् ।
अन्यद्वा शस्त्रमखिलं महाचक्रस्य मध्यगम् ॥ ९४ ॥
कृत्वाभिपूज्य विद्याभिः साध्ययोनिवलिं पुरः ।
दत्त्वा तैः समरे शत्रून् हत्वा विजयमाप्नुयात् ॥ ९५ ॥
दिनतो वारतः पक्षान्मासात् षट्‌त्रिंशता दिनैः ।
जपन्तो वारमेकन्तु विद्या नित्यात्मिकास्तु ताः ॥ ९६ ॥

नखरमित्यादिना आप्नुयादित्यन्तेन श्लोकद्वयेन तन्महाचक्रमध्येष्वायुधपूजनात् समरविजयमुपदिशति। तत्र नखरं असि धेनुं अन्यत् कुन्तप्राशलगुड़ादि। महाचक्रस्य श्रीचन्द्रविरचितेषु प्रोक्तसम्बत्सरात्मकेषु चक्रेषु तत्तत्सम्बत्सरप्राप्तस्य परावृत्तपरावृत्तात्मकचतुष्टयस्य। कृत्वा मध्यगमिति पूर्व्वश्लोकान्त्यपादेनान्वयः। विद्याभिः तच्चक्रक्रमप्राप्ताभिः कालनित्याभिरिति शेषः। साध्ययोनिं पूर्व्वत्र साध्यनक्षत्रप्रोक्तयोनिं। पुरः अग्रे समावाहितदेवतायाः। दत्त्वा प्राग्वत् छिनत्तीति शेषः। तैः देवतात्मभिः चक्रगास्त्रैः। एतदुक्तं भवति प्रोक्तेषु सम्बत्सरमातृकाचक्रेषु तत्तत्सम्बत्सरप्राप्ते वा जयप्रोक्तपरावृत्तपरावृत्तात्मकषट्‌त्रिंशच्चक्रेष्वन्यतमे केवलानुलोमानुलोमात्मकवृत्तरूपचक्रे वा। नखरादीनि सर्व्वाणि शस्त्राणि निविश्य तेष्वभीष्टां नित्यामावाह्य तां सपरिवारां तत्तत्क्रमैरभ्यर्च्य तत्तच्चक्रप्राप्तक्रमरूपाः कालनित्याश्चाभ्यर्च्य साध्यशत्रुनक्षत्रप्रोक्तयोनिं प्रोक्तलक्षणां प्रोक्तप्रकारेण तच्छस्त्ररूपदेवताग्रे छिन्दन् प्रोक्तवलिमन्त्रेण वलिं निवेद्यैवं साध्यशत्रुवलगुरुलघुतापेक्षया सप्तदिनादर्व्वाचीनं कृत्वा तैस्तैर्देवतात्मभिः युद्धे सर्व्वशत्रून् हत्वा विजयं प्राप्नोतीति। ९५ ॥

दिनत इत्यादिभिः कल्पत इत्यन्तैस्त्रिभिः श्लोकैः प्रागुक्तविद्यागणशेराद्वृत्तिकालविशेषेण फलविशेषं ललितायाः विद्याया आभिः सर्व्वविद्याभिः सत्सम्प्रदायवस्त्वादिकञ्चोपदिशति। तत्र दिनतः वारमेकमित्यत्रान्वयः। प्रागुक्तविद्याः प्रतिदिनमेकवारं जपेदित्यर्थः। एवं वारपक्षमासषट्‌त्रिंशद्दिवसैः प्रत्येकमेकैकं वारमित्यर्थः। वारेष्वावृत्तौ प्रथमं भास्करवारे वशिनीकामेश्वरीवर्गीत्था विद्याः। अन्येषु षट्सु प्रतिवारं मोदिन्यादिमातृकावर्गषट्कोत्थविद्याश्च

आयुरारोग्यमैश्वर्य्यं विजयं वाञ्छितं क्रमात्।
लभन्ते ललिता याभिः सम्प्रदायवती भवेत्॥ ९७॥
अन्यथासम्प्रदायत्वाज्जपहोमार्च्चनादिकम्।
कृतं जन्मान्तरे सम्यक् सम्प्रदायाय कल्पते॥ ९८॥
जपतर्पणहोमार्चाक्रमे विद्या भजेदिमाः।
तेनाक्षराणां सिद्धत्वान्मन्त्राः सिध्यन्त्यशेषतः॥ ९९॥

यथाक्रमं जपेत्। पक्षे त्वेकवारावृत्तौ पूर्णात्रयरूपासु पञ्चमीदशमीपञ्चदशीषु तिथिषु पंक्तिचतुष्टयचतुष्टयोत्थाः अन्यासु पंक्तिद्वयपंक्तिद्वयोत्था विद्या जपेदिति। पक्षद्वयरूपे मासे एकवारावृत्तौ पूर्वोक्तरूपासु पूर्णासु षट्सु द्वि द्वि पङ्क्त्युत्था विद्याः। अन्यासु चतुर्विंशतितिथिषु एकैकपङ्क्त्युत्थाश्च विद्या जपेदिति सम्प्रदायः। नित्यात्मिकाः अनुलोमानुलोमात्मिकाः। आयुरादि फलपञ्चकं पूर्वोक्तजपप्रकारपञ्चके एकैकस्य प्रकारस्य विषयः। क्रमात् कालाद्रीत्याविलम्बनक्रमात्। लभन्ते इत्यस्य पूर्वार्द्धेनान्वयः। ललिता आद्या नित्या याभिः कालनित्याविद्याभिः। सम्प्रदायवती युगपर्य्यायदिनघटिकारूप-पारम्पर्य्यभजनेनाविच्छिन्नत्वात्। आसां विद्यानां नवनाथरूपव्याप्त्या तत्तत्-पारम्पर्य्यभजनादविच्छिन्नरूपतया एतत् सर्वं सर्व्वनित्याविद्योपलक्षणम्। अन्यथा-सम्प्रदायत्वात् असम्प्रदायत्वादिति पदच्छेदः। अन्यथा आभिर्विधुरभजने असम्प्रदायत्वात् युगादिरूपव्याप्तरूपभजनासम्भवान्नाथव्याप्तरूपपारम्पर्य्य-भजनासम्भवाच्च। कृतम् असम्प्रदायेनेति शेषः। जन्मान्तरे कालान्तरे पुत्रपौत्रादिषु वा। एतदुक्तं भवति आभिर्विद्याभिः ललिताद्यानां षोड़शनित्या-विद्यानां पूर्वोक्तव्याप्तिरूपज्ञानेनोपास्यमानतया अविच्छिन्नत्वात् सत्सम्प्रदाया भवन्ति। प्रोक्तरूपभजनवैधुर्य्ये भजनस्य विच्छिन्नत्वादेतत् क्रमविधुरमक्षर-क्रमरहितं कृतभजनस्य साधकस्य कालान्तरे पुत्रपौत्रादिषु वा सत्सम्प्रदाया भवन्तीति॥ ९८॥

जप इत्यादिना शिव इत्यन्तेन श्लोकद्वयेन तद्विद्याराशेरुपासनतः सकलमन्त्र सिद्धिमुपासितुर्वैभवं फलञ्चोपदिशति। तत्र तेन भजनेन कालनित्याविद्या-

तासामुपासितुर्लोके नास्ति साधनदुष्करम् ।
नृपाणामङ्गनानाञ्च वल्लभो जायते शिवः ॥ १०० ॥
पुरुषात्ममयी व्याप्तिरिति सम्यक् समीरिता ।
यस्या निष्फालनाच्चित्ते तत्तत्त्व स्वात्मसात् कृतम् ॥

इति षोडशनित्यातन्त्रे श्रीकादिमते मातृकाव्याप्तिर्नाम पञ्चविंशतिपटलम् ॥ २५ ॥

मिति शेषः । सिद्धत्वात् तादात्म्येन सिध्यन्ति भजनवैधुर्य्येणापि । अशेषतः सर्वे । आसां कालनित्याविद्यानां । उपासितुः साधकस्य । असाध्यं अशक्यं । दुष्करं कर्त्तुमशक्यं । शिवः परिपूर्णाहन्तात्मा ॥ १०० ॥

इति षोडशनित्यातन्त्रेषु श्रीकादिमताख्यस्य परिपूर्णस्य तन्त्रस्य प्रपञ्चसार-सिंहराजप्रकाशाभिधानेन सुभगानन्दनाथेन विरचितायां मनोरमाख्यायां व्याख्यायां षोडशनित्यामातृकाकाल-व्याप्तिप्रकाशनपरं पञ्चविंशपटलं परिपूर्णं परामृष्टम् ॥ २५ ॥

यन्त्रसंख्या—यन्त्राणि रम्यगमशार्थनामसूक्तिविधिस्थितेः ।
८४६७५०७१३१२ ।
रुद्रार्णवाक्यसंख्यानि विना श्रीचक्रयोगतः ॥
व्याख्याग्रन्थाः पञ्चशतनवत्या समयुक्तया ।
सार्द्धमेवं समुद्दिष्टाः पटले पञ्चविंशके ॥

षड्विंशपटलम् ।

अथ षोड़शनित्यानां विद्याव्याप्तिस्वरूपतः ।
मन्त्राणां वैभवं वक्ष्ये शृणु देवि यथाविधि ॥ १ ॥
नादोत्पत्तिञ्च तद्रूपं स्थानाप्त्या तस्य वर्णताम् ।
ततः पदानि वाक्यानि मन्त्ररूपाणि कानिचित् ॥ २ ॥
तत्संख्यां विद्यया स्वात्मसंस्कारस्य क्रमं तथा ।
अमृतेश्वरिदेव्यास्तु वर्णैस्तैर्म्मिथुनैरपि ॥ ३ ॥

पूर्व्वस्मिन् पञ्चविंशे पटले षोड़शनित्यानां मातृकाकालव्याप्तिमुपदिश्यान-न्तरं षोड़शनित्यानां व्याप्तिवैभवप्रकाशिकां मन्त्रव्याप्तिं तत्क्रयामृतेश्वरीविद्यादिकं चोपदिशत्यथ षोड़शेत्यादिना सचराचरमित्यन्तेन श्लोकशतरूपेण षड्विंशेन पटलेन । तत्र अथ षोड़शेत्यादिभिरशेषत इत्यन्तैश्चतुर्भिः श्लोकैः पटलार्थानुपदिशति । तत्र षोड़शनित्यानामित्यस्य द्विरन्वयो भवति । यथा विद्याव्याप्तिस्वरूपतः इत्यत्र वैभवमित्यत्र च । विद्याव्याप्तिस्वरूपतः मन्त्राणां सर्व्वमन्त्राणां आभिर्विद्याभिर्व्याप्तिस्वरूपत इत्यर्थः । वैभवं षोड़शनित्यानाम् । एतदुक्तं भवति षोड़शनित्यानां विद्याभिः सर्व्वमन्त्राणां व्याप्तिस्वरूपतः तासां नित्यानां व्याप्तिस्वरूपतो वैभवं वक्ष्ये इति । तत्र मन्त्रवैभवं नादोत्पत्तिं अत्रैव पटले वक्ष्यमाणां । तद्रूपं नादस्य पश्यन्त्यादिरूपं स्थानाप्त्या कण्ठादिस्थानयोगेन । तस्य नादस्य । ततः वर्णैरित्यर्थः । वाक्यानि पदैरिति शेषः । मन्त्ररूपाणि मन्त्राणां रूपाणि तानि तु वर्णैः पदैश्च वाक्यैश्च भवन्ति । कानिचित् तेषु वर्णजानि मन्त्ररूपाणि षट्सप्तत्युत्तरपञ्चशतकोटिः कानिचिदित्युक्तिर्वर्णादिजातानां मन्त्राणामसंख्यातत्वात् प्रोक्तसंख्याया एकदेशत्वात् । तत्संख्यमन्त्राणां तत्सम-कोटिसंख्याविद्यया स्वात्मसंस्कारस्य क्रमं स्वाभिलषितया विद्यया अभिषेकादिभि रात्मसंस्कारस्य क्रमममृतेश्वरिदेव्या अमृतेश्वरीदेव्या इत्यर्थः । क्रममित्यत्रा-न्वयः । वर्णैस्तैरमृतवर्णैः । मिथुनैः नित्यानित्यापटलप्रोक्तैः सार्द्धमिति

व्याप्तिं प्रयोगांस्तैः सम्यगभीष्टप्राप्तिहेतवे ।
समुद्दिष्टक्रमेणैव सर्व्वमेतदशेषतः ॥ ४ ॥
स्वात्मेच्छाशक्तिघातेन प्राणवायुस्वरूपतः ।
मूलाधारे समुत्पन्नः पराख्यो नादसम्भवः ॥ ५ ॥
स एव चोर्द्ध्वतां नीतः स्वाधिष्ठाने विजृम्भितः ।
पश्यन्त्याख्यामवाप्नोति तथैवोर्द्ध्वं शनैः शनैः ॥ ६ ॥

शेषः । व्याप्तिं नित्यानां । तैः प्रणवादिसर्व्वमन्त्रैः ५७६००००००० संख्यातैर्मन्त्रैः प्रयोगानित्यन्वयः ॥ ४ ॥

स्वात्मेत्यादिना श्लोकेन नादोत्पत्तिमुपदिशति । तत्र स्वात्मेच्छाशक्तिघातेन आत्मनः पररूपस्य स्वेच्छाशक्त्या कालमय्या घातेन प्रेरणेन । प्राणवायुस्वरूपतः प्राणाख्यस्य षट्त्रिंशत्पटलवक्ष्यमाणवायोरेकाकारतः । मूलाधारे नित्यानित्यापटले प्रोक्तरूपे प्राणिनामिति शेषः । नादसम्भवः नादस्योत्पत्तिः प्रथमावस्थेत्यर्थः । नादरूपमाराध्यपादमुखादवगन्तव्यम् । एतदुक्तं भवति सर्व्वप्राणिनां नित्यानित्यापटलप्रोक्तरूपे मूलाधारे परायाश्चिन्मात्रायाः शक्तेः स्वेच्छारूपया कालशक्त्या प्रेरितप्राणवायुस्वरूपा परासंज्ञा नादविन्दुप्रथमावस्था सञ्जायत इति ॥ ५ ॥

सएवेत्यादिभिः चकावधीत्यन्तैश्चतुर्भिःश्लोकैः प्रोक्तसंज्ञस्य नादस्य पश्यन्त्यादिवैखर्य्यन्तावशिष्टावस्थात्रयकथनपूर्व्वकमकारादिचकारान्तानामेकपञ्चाशद्वर्णानामुत्पत्तिस्थानान्युपदिशति । तत्र स परावस्थो नादः । तया इच्छाशक्त्या । स्वाधिष्ठाने मेढ्रमूले । तथैव यथा स्वेच्छाशक्त्या ऊर्द्ध्वं नीतो नादः स्वाधिष्ठाने जृम्भितः पश्यन्त्याख्यो भवति । अनाहते हृदयदेशे । वुद्धितत्त्वसमेतः तस्मिन् स्थाने वुद्धेरुपलब्धिः । तथा यथा अनाहते । तया प्राग्वच्छक्त्या । विशुद्धौ कण्ठदेशतः विशुद्धिसंज्ञे कण्ठदेशे इत्यर्थः । ततः वैखर्य्यवस्थानन्तरं । जिह्वामूलाग्रपृष्ठस्थः जिह्वामूलस्थो जिह्वाग्रस्थो जिह्वापृष्ठस्थश्चेत्यर्थः । जिह्वापृष्ठस्थस्तु लकाराक्षरो भवति । क्रमात् प्रोक्तात् कण्ठताल्वोश्च स्थित इति शेषः । कण्ठोष्ठात् स्वबलोपि पञ्चमो कण्ठौष्ठमात्रस्थित इत्यर्थः । दन्तौष्ठद्वयतः दन्तौष्ठद्वये स्थित इत्यर्थः ।

अनाहते वह्नितत्त्वसमेतो मध्यमाभिधः।
तथा तयोर्हृन्नुन्नः स विशुद्धौ कण्ठदेशतः ॥ ७ ॥
वैखर्याख्यस्ततः शीर्षकण्ठताल्वोष्ठदन्ततः।
जिह्वामूलाग्रपृष्ठस्थस्तथा नासाग्रतः क्रमात् ॥ ८ ॥
कण्ठताल्वोष्ठकण्ठौष्ठाद्दन्तौष्ठद्वयतस्तथा।
समुत्पन्नान्यक्षराणि क्रमादादिक्षकावधि ॥ ९ ॥
आदिक्षान्तरतेत्येषामक्षरत्वमुदीरितम्।
तेषु स्वराः स्वतन्त्राः स्युस्तैर्व्यज्याद्व्यञ्जनं भवेत् ॥ १० ॥

एतदुक्तं भवति प्रोक्तस्थानेषु पराद्यवस्थाचतुष्टयात्मको नादः स्वेच्छावशाच्छीर्षादि प्रोक्तस्थानयुक्तोऽकारादिक्षकारावध्येकपञ्चाशदक्षरात्मा भवतीति ॥ ९ ॥

आदिक्षान्तेत्यादिभिस्तद्दिशा इत्यन्तैरर्धैः षड्भिः श्लोकैरक्षरशब्दनिर्वचनपुरःसरं मातृकायाः स्वरव्यञ्जनात्मनावस्थानं तयोरन्योन्यसंश्लेषजनितरूपविशेषांस्तैः शब्दप्रपञ्चस्यानन्तत्वादिकञ्चोपदिशति। तत्र आदिक्षान्तरता प्रागुक्तपरारूपा मातृका। एषामक्षराणां। तेषु अक्षरेषु। स्वतन्त्रा व्यञ्जनवैधुर्येऽप्यक्षरस्वरूपनिष्पत्तेः। तैः स्वरैः। व्यज्यात् अक्षरत्वपूर्त्तेः प्रकाश्यमानत्वात्। तद्रूपाणि मातृकापटलोक्तपूर्णमण्डलाक्षररूपाणि। तुरवधारणे। संख्यया उत्तरत्रान्वयः। तैः उक्तसंख्यैरक्षरैस्तैः पदैः मन्त्राश्च वर्णपदवाक्यैरिति शेषः। वेदभाषान्यभेदतः अन्यशब्द आर्षादिविषयः अस्य वाचका इत्यत्रान्वयः। व्याकरणादीनां नियमादियुताः। अत्र प्रथमादिशब्दो निरुक्तादिविषयः। द्वितीयादिशब्दो व्याकरणाद्यनियतसंज्ञाशब्दकूटमन्त्रादिविषयः। तेषामक्षराणामेकयुग्मतः त्रिभिः एकेन जाता भेदाः पूर्णमण्डलसंख्या एव ५१ द्वाभ्यां जाता भेदा एतानेव पूर्णमण्डलसंख्यया संगुणय्य तस्थौ साका वाला इति २२१७७६ षड्क्षरवाक्यजनितसंख्या भवतीति। त्रिभिरक्षरैर्जाता भेदा एतानेव पूर्णमण्डलसंख्यया संगुणय्य तस्थौ धीरो नित्याकलङ्क इति १९११०२९७६ मन्त्राक्षरवाक्यजनितसंख्या भवन्तीति। एवमुत्तरत्रापि तत्तद्भेदान् पूर्णमण्डलसंख्यया संगुणय्य एवं पूर्णमण्डलसंख्यावधि संगुणनादनन्ता भेदा भवन्ति। तद्रूपाणां

षोड़शानां स्वराणाञ्च षट्‌त्रिंशद्व्यञ्जनैः क्रमात्।
संयोगेनैव जायन्ते तद्रूपाणि तु संख्यया ॥ ११ ॥
षट्‌सप्ततियुतं पञ्चशतं तैः स्युः पदानि वै।
तैर्व्वाक्यानि च मन्त्राश्च वेदभाषान्यभेदतः ॥ १२ ॥
वाचका विश्वरूपस्य प्रपञ्चस्यात्मनस्तथा।
शब्दव्याकरणादीनां नियमादियुतास्तथा ॥ १३ ॥
तेषामन्योन्यसम्भेदजातानामेकयुग्मतः।
त्रिभिरित्यादिरूपाणां संख्या कर्त्तुं न शक्यते ॥ १४ ॥
अनन्तत्वादचिन्त्यत्वात्तद्रूपाणां न कीर्त्तनम्।
एवं शब्दस्य माहात्म्यं वक्तुं कस्यापि नास्ति हि ॥ १५ ॥
शक्तिस्तथापि ते किञ्चिद्वदामि शृणु तद्दिशा।
ललिताचक्रनवके प्रत्येकं शक्तयः प्रिये ॥ १६ ॥
चतुःषष्टिमिताः कोट्यस्ताः सम्भूय पुरोदिताः।
कोट्यः स्युस्तत्क्रमात्तासां विद्या वक्ष्यामि ताः क्रमात् ॥१७॥

प्रागुक्तप्रकारयोगवर्णयोगजनितसिद्धयोगिनीमन्त्रशब्दादिरूपाणां। शक्तिः सामर्थ्यं अस्य पूर्व्वश्लोकेनान्वयः। दिशा उपायेन ॥ १५ ॥

ललितेत्यादिना क्रमादित्यन्तेनार्द्धाधेन श्लोकेन ललिताचक्रस्य देवताछन्द-संख्यां तासां तत्संख्या विद्या उपदेष्टुं प्रस्तौति। तत्र ललिताचक्रनवके वक्ष्यमाणरूपस्य श्रीचक्रस्य त्रैलोक्यमोहनचक्रादिसर्वानन्दमयचक्रान्तचतुरस्रादि सर्व्वमध्यान्तचक्रनवके। प्रत्येकं प्रतिचक्रं। शक्तयः गुप्तसंज्ञाः। ता गुप्तसंज्ञाः शक्तयः पुरोदिताः कोट्यः स्युः षट्‌सप्ततिकोट्यधिकपञ्चशतकोट्यः (५७६००००००)। तत्क्रमाच्चक्रनवकक्रमात्। तासां उक्तकोटिसंख्यानां शक्तीनां। क्रमात् यथा-क्रमम् ॥ १७ ॥

षट्सप्तत्या पञ्चशतं प्रथमान्यक्षराणि वै ।
द्वितीयानि च तान्येव क्रमेण स्युरथादितः ॥ १८ ॥
तृतीयानि च तान्येव योजयेदादितः क्रमात् ।
क्षान्तैः षट्त्रिंशद्वर्णैस्तैः समायैरुक्तसंख्यकाः ॥ १९ ॥

षट्सप्तत्येत्यादिभिस्त्रिचतुरर्णका इत्यन्तैस्त्रिभिः श्लोकैस्त्रिचतुरक्षरा विद्या उपदिश्य ताश्चैकाकाराभिर्विद्याभिर्विना षट्सप्ततिकोट्यधिकपञ्चशतकोटिसंख्याता विद्या उपदिशति । तत्र षट्सप्तत्या पञ्चशतं प्रथमान्यक्षराणि वै । एतदुक्तं भवति श्र श्रा इत्यादि चं चः इत्यन्तानि षट्सप्तत्यधिकपञ्चशतान्यक्षराणि वक्ष्यमाणक्रमाज्जनितसंख्याविद्यानां प्रत्येकमाद्यक्षराणि भवन्तीति । द्वितीयानि च तान्येव क्रमेण स्युरथादितः । एतदुक्तं भवति तान्येव षट्सप्तत्यधिकपञ्चशत संख्यान्यक्षराणि वक्ष्यमाणसंख्यानां गुप्तयोगिनीविद्यानां प्रत्येकं द्वितीयाक्षराणि भवन्तीति । तृतीयानि च तान्येव तान्येव प्रोक्तसंख्यान्यक्षराणि प्रत्येकं वक्ष्यमाणसंख्यानां तासां विद्यानां तृतीयाक्षराणि भवन्तीति । योजयेदादितः क्रमात् क्षान्तैः षट्त्रिंशद्वर्णैः । एतदुक्तं भवति अकारादिक्षकारान्तैः षट्त्रिंशताक्षरैः प्रोक्तसंख्यानि द्वितीयाक्षराणि तेषामादितो योजयेदिति । तैः समायैरुक्तसंख्यका विद्या भवन्ति । एतदुक्तं भवति प्रोक्तप्रकारोद्धृतैस्तैर्विद्यारूपैरन्ते विसर्जनीयसहितैः प्रोक्तकोटिसंख्या एकाकारवर्णा विद्या भवन्तीति । शिष्टाः स्युरेकाकारास्तु तैः । एतदुक्तं भवति प्रोक्तप्रकारप्रोद्धृतासु विद्यासु शिष्टा विद्यास्तैरक्षरैरेकाकारा भवन्तीति । विना ताभिरेकाकाराभिर्विनेत्यर्थः । तत्कोटिसंख्याकाः प्रोक्तकोटिसंख्यास्त्रिचतुरर्णकाः चतुरक्षररूपास्त्रैपुरा भवन्तीत्यर्थः । तासु मध्यस्थाभ्यां मध्यस्थाभ्यामक्षराभ्यां एकमेकं कूटं परिकल्पयेत् । आसां प्रागुक्तगुप्तयोगिनीविद्यानां अत्र मन्त्रप्रोद्धारप्रकारः । अकारादीनां पूर्णमण्डलाक्षराणामिव प्रथमद्वितीयतृतीयाक्षरात्मनावस्थितत्वात्तेषु प्रथमाक्षरत्वेन स्थितानामक्षराणामेकैकस्य कोटिकोटिसंख्याविद्यानामाद्यक्षरत्वं भवति । तत्तत्कोटिषु तृतीयाक्षरत्वेनावस्थितानामक्षराणां प्रत्येकं विसर्जनीययोजनात्तेषु सविसर्जनीयानि तानि षट्त्रिंशदक्षराणि सर्वासां विद्यानां विसर्जनीयान्तत्वविधानात् चतुर्णां विसर्गान्तानि षट्त्रिंशदक्षराणि विसर्गान्तानि षट्त्रिंश-

विद्या भवन्ति शिष्टाः स्युरेकाकारास्तु तैर्विना।
ताभिस्तत्कोटिसंख्याका विद्यास्त्रिचतुरर्णकाः ॥ २० ॥

दक्षराणि च षण्डाक्षराणां विसर्जनीयोजनात् रेफे लकारान्तर्भूतत्वात् पुनरुक्ततया तानि चत्वारि च सम्भूय षट्सप्ततिसंख्यान्यक्षराण्येकत्वावशिष्टानि पञ्चशतान्यक्षराणि एकैकं विंशतिविंशतिसहस्रसंख्यातानां विद्याक्षराणां तृतीयाक्षराणि भवन्ति। तेषु द्वितीयाक्षरत्वेन स्थितानां तेषामक्षराणामन्ते एकैकस्य षट्त्रिंशत्तत्त्वाक्षरसंयोजनविधानात् षट्त्रिंशदधिकसप्तशतोत्तरविंशतिसहस्रसंख्यानि भेदरूपाणि भवन्ति। तेषूक्तसंख्येषु रूपेषु तत्त्वाक्षरयोगे कर्त्तव्ये तेषां स्वरयोगेन विनातिसिद्धरूपमन्त्रकरणरूपान्तरासम्भवात् तत्तत्स्वरयोग इति। तानि षट्सप्तत्यधिकपञ्चशतरूपाणि पुनः प्रतिवर्गषण्डाक्षरेषु पूर्व्वद्वये रेफयोगेन अपरद्वये लकारयोगेनापि समानरूपत्वात् तच्चतुष्टयाक्षरजनितानि चतुश्चत्वारिंशदधिकशतरूपाणि। किञ्च चकारवर्गस्य चकारेण योगकर्त्तव्यतया तानि षोड़शरूपाणि च सम्भूय प्रतिविंशति सहस्राणि रूपाणि भवन्ति। * षट्त्रिंशदधिकसप्तशतसंख्यानि रूपाणि परित्यज्य शिष्टानि विंशतिसहस्राणि रूपाणि भवन्ति। तानि विंशतिसहस्ररूपाणि तृतीयाक्षरत्वेन स्थितैः प्रागुक्तप्रकारपञ्चशतसंख्यैरक्षरैः संगुणनात् कोटिसंख्यानि विद्यारूपाणि प्रथमाक्षरत्वेन स्थितैः षट्सप्तत्युत्तरपञ्चशतैरक्षरैः संगुणनात् पूर्णमण्डलकोटिसंख्यानि भिन्नाकाराणि चतुरक्षररूपत्रैपुरात्मकानि विद्यारूपाणि भवन्तीति। अत्र एकाकारत्वेन त्यक्ताख्यानां विद्यानां संख्या तद्गुणितप्रकारश्च लिख्यते। यथा मध्यस्थाक्षरजनितभेदेषु रूपेषु पूर्वोक्तप्रकारेणैकाकारत्वेन परित्यक्तरूपाणि षट्त्रिंशदधिकसप्तशतानि तृतीयाक्षरत्वेन प्रोक्तपूर्णमण्डलसंख्याक्षरसंगुणनात् तुङ्गधीगुरुर्वः इति ४२३८३६ षड़क्षरवाक्यजनितसंख्यानि रूपाणि। मध्यस्थानि भिन्नाकाराणि विंशतिसहस्राणि रूपाणि तृतीयाक्षरैश्चैकाकारेण परित्यक्तैः षट्सप्तत्यक्षरसंख्यैः संगुणनात् नानाज्ञानाश्रमोयम् इति १५२०००० सप्ताक्षरवाक्यजनितसंख्यानि रूपाणि च सम्भूय तुङ्गधीगर्भधन्य इति १९४२९३६ सप्ताक्षरवाक्यजनितसंख्यानि रूपाणि भवन्ति। तेषां रूपाणां प्रथमाक्षरत्वेन स्थितपूर्णमण्डलसंख्या-

---

* तानि विंशतिविंशतिसहस्ररूपाणि तृतीयाक्षरत्वेन स्थितैः प्रागुक्तप्रकारपञ्चशतसहस्रमित्यधिकः।

तासामपि तु सर्व्वासां ध्यानार्च्चायन्त्रपूजनैः ।
पुरुषार्थास्तु सिध्यन्ति तदुक्तं मातृकायुधैः ॥ २१ ॥
संस्कारान् शृणु देवेशि गुरुणा शिष्यरक्षणे ।
समानत्वेऽपि देहादेर्व्यापारे गुरुशिष्ययोः ॥ २२ ॥
पूज्यपूजकभावत्वकारणैः प्रत्ययं तथा ।
प्रत्यक्षं यैस्तु दृष्टान्तैराशु ते दर्शयाम्यहम् ॥ २३ ॥

ष्नरसंगुणनात् चण्डिकापूर्व्वेत्र तस्थौ धीरो नित्याकलङ्क इति वाक्यजनितसंख्यां तत्त्वाक्षरैः संगुणय्य तुङ्गः पथ्यः साधुः सदोच्चे इति ६८७८७०७१२६ दशाक्षरवाक्यजनितसंख्यास्तु विद्यास्तु एकाकारविद्यात्यागात् प्रोक्तासंख्या भवन्तीति। चण्डिका सनाथार्द्धकायोयमिति १११८७०७१२६ दशाक्षर-वाक्यजनित संख्यानि रूपाणि एकाकारत्वेन त्यक्तव्यानि भवन्तीति। अत्र भेद-विद्यास्वरूपं किञ्चित् प्रदर्श्यतेऽस्माभिः। यथा—स्वरतत्त्व योगपरित्यागात् प्रथम-विद्यापञ्चत्रिंशत्कस्य ममकमः ममखमः इत्यादीनि ममक्षमः इत्यन्तानि तद्द्वितीयपञ्चत्रिंशतिकविद्यारूपाणि ममाकमः ममाखमः ममागमः इत्यादीनि ममाक्षमः इत्यन्तानि भवन्तीति ॥ २० ॥

तासामपीत्यादिना श्लोकेनासामुक्तसंख्याविशिष्टानां विद्यानां तद्देवतानां च ध्यानं सावरणं पूजनं प्रत्येकं यन्त्रादिप्रयोगांश्च प्रागुक्तानेवातिदिशति। तत्र तासां विद्यानाञ्च तद्देवतानाञ्च ध्यानार्च्चायन्त्रपूजनैः ध्यानेनार्च्चया यन्त्रैश्च तत्पूजनेन च। तत्र यन्त्राणि तत्तद्विद्यायां तत्त्वाक्षरैः स्वरभिन्नैः। तत्र ध्यानादि मातृकापटले। एतदुक्तं भवति प्रोक्तसंख्यानां विद्यानामेकैकस्या विद्याया भजने आसां चतुरक्षरविद्यानां मध्याक्षरमध्याक्षरद्वयमेकाक्षररूपं परिकल्प्य प्राग्वत् द्विरुक्त्या षडङ्गानि च विन्यस्य तत्तत् पूजायन्त्रनिर्म्माणे मातृका-पटले कालनित्याप्रोक्तानि चतुरस्रत्रयाष्टपत्राम्भुजनवयोनिरूपाणि चक्राणि विधाय तत्तन्नवयोनिमध्ययोनिमध्ये तत्तद्विद्यां प्राग्वत् ससाध्यां विन्यस्यतद्बहिः कोणाष्टके तद्बहिर्दलाष्टके मध्याक्षरोपेततत्त्वाक्षरस्य स्वरभिन्नानि प्राग्वद्विन्यस्य शेषं प्राग्वत् कृत्वा तन्मध्ये प्राग्वदावाह्य प्राग्वत् ध्यात्वा प्राग्वत् समभ्यर्च्च्य प्राग्वत् बलिद्वयं दत्त्वा प्रागुक्तान् प्रयोगांश्च कृत्वा प्रागुक्तानि फलान्याप्नोतीति ॥ २१ ॥

संस्कारो मन्त्रयन्त्रार्च्चाभिषेकाद्यैस्तनोर्यदि।
सा जरारोगमरणक्लेशैर्न स्पृश्यतेऽन्यथा॥ २४॥
प्राणस्य वै तदारभ्य नित्यता स्यात्तु देहिनाम्।
आत्मनश्चेदरूपस्य संस्कारो नैव युज्यते॥ २५॥
इन्द्रियाणां यदि भवेत्तदा प्राणसमानता।
बुद्धेश्चेदात्मना साम्यात् कस्य स्याद् गुरुवीक्षणम्॥ २६॥
इत्यादिसंशयैः खिन्नचित्तानां क्षीणपाप्मनाम्।
सेवीक्षणोपदेशैस्तु गुरुणा क्रियते तु यत्॥ २७॥

संस्कारानित्यादिभिर्वीक्षणमित्यन्तैः पञ्चभिः श्लोकैः देशिकेन शिष्यस्य क्रियमाणं मन्त्रसंस्कारं तत्तत् कर्म्मादि प्रस्तावपुरःसरमाक्षिपति। तत्र संस्कारान् अभिषेककटाक्षोपदेशान् अस्मिन् पटले वर्णान्तरवक्ष्यमाणान्। गुरुणा शिष्यस्य रक्षणे शिष्यानुग्रहे गुरुणा क्रियमाणान्। संस्कारानित्यत्रान्वयः। देहादेर्व्यापारे आदिशब्दः प्राणेन्द्रियबुद्ध्यादिविषयः। व्यापारः षडूर्म्मिरूपक्षुधा-पिपासाशोकमोहजरामरणानि द्विद्विक्रमेण प्राणबुद्धिदेहधर्म्मादिरूपे तस्मिन् पूज्यपूजकभावत्वकारणैः दृष्टान्तैरित्यत्रान्वयः। प्रत्ययं विश्वासं। एतदुक्तं भवति गुरुशिष्ययोर्देहेन्द्रियप्राणबुद्ध्यादिधर्म्मस्य समानत्वेऽपि गुरोः प्रणामादिभिः पूज्यत्वे शिष्यस्य तैः पूजकत्वे चोपपत्तिकारणभूतैः निदर्शनैः प्रत्यक्षं प्रत्यय-मुत्पत्तिनिश्चयं दर्शयामि इत्युपदिशतीति। संस्कारः वस्तुनः कस्यचित् स्वाभाविकासद्गुणापनयनेन क्रियाविशेषेण सद्गुणविशेषाधिक्यकरणः। तेन शिष्यसंस्कारो दुर्वासनापनयनेन परमार्थज्ञानप्रतिष्ठा। मन्त्रयन्त्रार्च्चाभिषेकाद्यैः। आद्यशब्दः कटाक्षोपदेशादिविषयः। तनोः शरीरस्य शिष्यस्येति शेषः। सा शिष्यतनुः। अन्यथा स्पृश्यत एवेत्यर्थः। प्राणस्य शिष्यस्येति शेषः। चेत् संस्कार इत्याकृष्यते। नित्यता स्यात्तु देहिनां कृतसंस्काराणामिति शेषः। आत्मनः जीवरूपस्य। प्राणसमानता नित्यता आत्मना साम्यात् अरूपत्वसाम्यात्। कस्य शोक्तव्यतिरेकेण॥ २६॥

इतीत्यादिभिर्भवेदित्यन्तैर्नवभिः श्लोकैः स्वयमाक्षिप्तं अर्थं सनिदर्शनं समा-

तदहं सुस्फुटं सम्यग्वच्मे गुह्यतरं परम् ।
यदवाप्य त्यजत्याशु संशयाख्यं महामलम् ॥ २८ ॥
देहेन्द्रियमनःप्राणसाक्षिणस्त्वात्मनः प्रिये ।
संस्कारः क्रियते सम्यग् गुरुणा तत्त्ववेदिना ॥ २९ ॥
सेकेन देहे यत्किञ्चिदशुभं तन्निरस्यते ।
वीक्षणादात्मनो बुद्धेरयथार्थनिकृन्तनम् ॥ ३० ॥
उपदेशेन या तस्य चिरारूढ़ा तु वासना ।
दुस्तरां तां धिया स्वात्मविमर्शेन विनाशयेत् ॥ ३१ ॥

धत्ते । तत्र इत्यादिसंशयैः आदिशब्दस्त्रैगुण्यादिजपपूजादिफलभोक्तृत्वविषयः । क्षीणपाप्मनां प्रोक्तप्रकारेण संशयेन देहेन्द्रियबुद्ध्यात्मादिविवेकस्य परमार्थलाभपर्य्यन्तत्वात् । तेषां वच्मे इत्यन्वयः । यद्विशेषापादनः । यदवाप्य यद्विशेषापादनं ज्ञात्वा महामलं स्वात्मविनाशकत्वात् । देहेन्द्रियमनःप्राणसाक्षिणः आत्मनः देहेन्द्रियमनःप्राणेषूपाधिरूपेषु उपलभ्यमानस्यानादिवासनया तदौपाधिकानां गुणानां स्वगुणेन जाग्रत्स्वप्नसुषुप्त्यवस्थासु सुखदुःखरूपाणां अनुसन्धानावस्थायां जीवाख्यस्य चितः संस्कारो वक्ष्यमाणरूपः । तत्त्ववेदिना तत्त्वयोरुपाध्यात्मनोः परमार्थविदा सेकेन प्रोक्तविधानेनाभिषेकेण देहे उपाधिभूते । अशुभं रोगादिपीड़ा । वीक्षणात् ज्वालामालिनीपटलवेधोक्तक्रमात् गुरोरिति शेषः । आत्मनो बुद्धेः स्वबुद्धेरित्यर्थः । अयथार्थनिकृन्तनं अतस्मिंस्तद्बुद्धिविनाशनं । उपदेशेन श्रीविद्यादीनां विद्यानां तदर्थानाञ्च वासनापटलवक्ष्यमाणेन त्रैगुण्यानामिति शेषः । तस्य शिष्यस्य । चिरारूढ़ा जन्मतः प्रभृति मनोलग्ना । वासना परिचयः । दुस्तरां तां दुस्त्यजां वासनामित्यर्थः । धिया बुद्ध्या स्वात्मविमर्शेन गुरूपदिष्टेन रूपेण पराहन्तारूपपरामर्शेन । एवं कृते प्रोक्तरूपसंस्कारकरणे । बुद्धिवृत्तेः संसाराज्ञानरूपिता विनाशः संसारज्ञानस्वभावाया बुद्धिवृत्तेर्मायादापोहेन संसारज्ञानाभावरूपो विनाशो भवतीत्यर्थः । स्वरूपालम्भः स्वरूपस्याग्राह्यत्वात् प्रवृत्तिहान्या तन्मयता विश्रान्तिः । उभे उभावित्यर्थः । भवत उभे इति पूर्व्वेणान्वयः । एतदुक्तं

एवं कृते बुद्धिवृत्तेः संसाराज्ञानरूपिता ।
विनाशो नित्यशुद्धात्मस्वरूपालम्भ इत्युभे ॥ ३२ ॥
भवतस्तत्र दृष्टान्तं प्रत्यक्षं पश्य पार्वति ।
शस्यानां वीजरूपस्य वह्निस्पर्शात् प्ररोहिता ॥ ३३ ॥
न भवत्येव तत्रास्य शक्तिरेव तु दह्यते ।
तथास्याज्ञानजन्मादि कारणं यत्तथैव तत् ॥ ३४ ॥

भवति देहेन्द्रियमनःप्राणसंघातात्मकोपाधिषूपलब्धया जलचन्द्रवत्तत्तदौपाधिकान्यगुणानस्वगुणत्वेनानुभवविमोहितस्य जीवात्मनश्चिद्रूपस्य तत्त्वविदा गुरुणा गुणसंस्कारकरणं नाम प्रोक्तरूपेणाभिषेकेण प्राक्तनजन्मादिप्राप्तौपाधिकाशुभनिराकरणं तत्कटाक्षेण बुद्धेः स्वभावप्रवृत्तिरूपान्यथाज्ञाननाशमुपदेशेन पुनः पुनरुपदिष्टप्रकारस्वात्मविमर्शेन च सुचिरारूढदुर्वासनाविनाशनञ्च भवेत्। एवं कृते स्वभावतो वहिर्विषयप्रवृत्ताया बुद्धिवृत्तेस्तद्विषयवृत्त्यभावरूपो विनाशः। तेनास्याः प्रत्यङ्मुखप्रवृत्तौ स्वरूपस्य विषयभूतत्वात्तस्मिन्नेव तादात्म्येन विश्रान्तिरूपो विनाशश्च इत्युभौ भवत इति। तत्र प्रतिपादितरूपतो गुरुकृतसंस्कारादिभिर्बुद्धेर्दुर्वासनाविनाशे स्वानुभवसिद्धौ च तत्र प्ररोहणाभावे अस्य वीजरूपस्य शक्तिः प्ररोहणशक्तिः न वीजरूपमित्यर्थः। तथास्याज्ञानजन्मादि अत्रादिशब्दो जरामरणादिविषयः। अन्यथाज्ञानसंसिद्धजन्मजरामरणादि। यथा वह्निस्पर्शात् शस्यानां वीजरूपस्याप्ररोहिता तथा शिष्यस्याज्ञानजन्मादि न भवतीत्यर्थः। कारणं यत्तथैवतत् यथा वह्निस्पर्शाद्वीजरूपे पूर्व्वस्थितेऽपि तत्प्ररोहस्य कारणभूता शक्तिर्दह्यते तथा अज्ञानजन्मादीनां दुर्वासनारूपं कारणं यत्तदपि दह्यत इत्यर्थः। किञ्च संस्कारादिना स्वात्मप्रकाशकारणं निदर्शनान्तरात् दृश्यत इत्यर्थः। तत्प्ररोहः कार्पासवीजप्ररोहः। पुष्पादि आदिशब्दः फलमूलादिविषयः। तथा लाक्षारागारुणवर्णं भवतीत्यर्थः। एतदुक्तं भवति यथा शस्यानां वीजस्य वह्निस्पर्शमात्रेण तत्प्ररोहकारणभूतशक्तिविनाशात् कार्य्यरूपः प्ररोहश्च न भवति तथा तस्य शिष्यस्य संसारादिप्रवृत्तिजन्मभूतस्य मनसो गुरुकृतसंस्कारात्तस्य मनसः संसृतिप्रवृत्तिवीजकारणभूतदुर्वासनानाशात्तत्कार्य्यभूतसंसृत्यादिप्रवृत्तिरपि च न भवति। यथा च कार्पास

किञ्च कार्पासवीजानि लाक्षया रञ्जितानि तु ।
दृश्यते तत्प्ररोहस्य पुष्पादि च तथा भवेत् ॥ ३५ ॥
रहस्यं परमं सर्व्वसिद्धिचिन्तामणिस्थिरम् ।
सुसाध्यं सद्गुरुप्राप्तमघानां सङ्गवर्ज्जितम् ॥ ३६ ॥
पुरश्चरणहोमार्च्चातर्पणस्तुतियन्त्रकैः ।
रहितं ते वदाम्यद्य मन्त्रविद्यास्त्वनन्तकाः ॥ ३७ ॥
ताः शृणु त्वं महेशानि सर्व्वाभीष्टाप्तयेऽनिशम् ।
साधकानाञ्च सिद्धानां नेतरेषां कथञ्चन ॥ ३८ ॥
वेदभाषेतरात्मत्वविभेदानामशेषतः ।
सद्वासनां साध्वसाधुचिन्ताविरहितं सदा ॥ ३९ ॥

वीजस्य लाक्षया कृतसंस्कारस्य प्ररोहपुष्पादि तत् लाक्षारागरूषवत् दृश्यते तथा तस्य शिष्यस्य मनसो गुरुकृतसंस्कारादिना संस्कृतस्य प्रवृत्तिर्गुरूक्तिरूप स्वानुभूतिस्वरूपिणी भवतीति ॥ ३५ ॥

रहस्यमित्यादिभिः सदा इत्यन्तैरष्टाभिः श्लोकैः सकलाक्षरपदवाक्यादीनां मन्त्रस्वरूपत्वमुपदिशति । अत्र परममित्यादीनां रहितमित्यन्तानां षष्ठां द्वितीयान्तानां पदानां रहस्यमित्येतद्विशेष्यं वदामीत्यत्रान्वयः । मन्त्रविद्यास्त्वनन्तकाः मन्त्राश्च विद्याश्च प्रागुक्तप्रकारेणैकद्व्यादियोगादनन्ता विदन्त्वे इत्यर्थः । ता मन्त्रविद्याः । साधकानाञ्च सिद्धानां इत्यस्याभीष्टाप्तये इत्यत्रान्वयः । नेतरेषां न साध्यानामित्यर्थः । कथञ्चन केनापि प्रकारेण तेषां तत्त्वज्ञाना भवात् । इतरात्मकत्वमार्थात्मकत्वं । सद्वासनां साध्वसाधुचिन्ताविरहितं सदा शब्दानां साधुत्वासाधुत्वयोः सांकल्पिकत्वात् । त्वदात्मकं शक्तिरूपमित्यर्थः । समुदयं नादस्य प्रागुक्तपरापश्यन्त्यादिस्वरूपाणां । विश्रान्तिः पूर्व्वोक्तानामेव । मदात्मकं शिवरूपम् । उभयात्मकम् उदयविश्रान्तिरूपशिवशक्त्यात्मकम् । आत्मस्वरूपं प्रागुक्तमहमितिरूपं । तैरन्तरैः सहेति शेषः । कालेन क्रमेण अन्यत्वदुःखार्त्तिवासनानाशतः भेदात्मकदुःखोत्पन्नार्त्तिवासनाविलयनात् पराहन्तामयं परिपूर्णाहन्तात्मकम् । सर्वस्वरूपस्वात्मविग्रहं सर्वपदार्थस्वरूपाणि

त्वदात्मकं समुदयं विश्रान्तिश्च मदात्मकम्।
उभयात्मकमात्मस्वरूपं नादस्य तस्य तैः ॥ ४० ॥
कालेनान्यत्वदुःखार्त्तिवासनानाशतो ध्रुवम्।
पराहन्तामयं सर्वस्वरूपस्वात्मविग्रहम् ॥ ४१ ॥
सदात्मकं स्फुरत्ताख्यमशेषोपाधिवर्जितम्।
प्रकाशरूपमात्मत्वे वस्तु तद्भासते परम् ॥ ४२ ॥
यत एवमतो लोके नास्त्यमन्त्रं यदचरम्।
वति मन्दि न्वीधेह्वि दासतः वं सथावस ॥ ४३ ॥
षडष्टद्वादशार्णानां वैष्णवानामशेषतः।
मन्त्राणां परतत्त्वार्थवाचकत्वादभेदता ॥ ४४ ॥

निजं रूपं विग्रहं यस्य तत्। इदंरूपाणि सकलवस्तूनि रहस्यनादरूपस्य तादात्म्येन सह भवन्तीत्यर्थः। सदात्मकं सद्भावरूपं स्फुरत्ताख्यं स्फुरणाख्यं चिदाख्यमित्यर्थः। अशेषोपाधिवर्जितं औपाधिकसर्वविकाररहितं प्रकाशरूपं पदार्थानां प्रत्येकं तादात्म्यत्वेनेति शेषः। आत्मत्वे स्वरूपत्वे वस्तु यदिति शेषः। तद्भासते परं तत् परं भवतीत्यर्थः। यतएवं एवं भवतीति यस्मादित्यर्थः। अतः अस्मात् अमन्त्रम् मन्त्रान्यभूतं यत् अचरं। एतदुक्तं भवति अचरपदवाक्यादिरूपाणां सर्वेषां मन्त्राणां उदयविश्रान्तिरूपशक्तिशिवपरमार्थरूपत्वादचराणामुदयविश्रान्तिपरत्वादुभयात्मकस्य चिद्रूपपरमार्थस्य स्वात्मनस्तैर्मन्त्रैरपृथग्भावेन भावनावैशद्येन क्रमेण प्रोक्तरूपपराहन्तात्मकपरवस्तुस्वरूपत्वात् सर्व्वे वर्णा मन्त्रा भवन्तीति ॥ ४३ ॥

षड़ित्यादिभिराप्नुयुरित्यन्तैः पञ्चभिः श्लोकैर्वैष्णवशैववैदिकमन्त्रैः प्रधानभूतैरेकादशभिर्ललिताविद्यया व्याप्तिमुपदिशति। तत्र षड़ष्टद्वादशार्णानां षड़चरस्याष्टाचरस्य द्वादशाचरस्य च वैष्णवानाम् उक्तत्रयाणां मन्त्राणामित्यन्वयः। अशेषतः पदपदार्थरूपेणापि। परतत्त्वार्थवाचकत्वात् परस्वरूपवाचकत्वात्। अभेदता व्याप्तिः ललिताविद्यया अभेदतेत्यत्रान्वयः। एतदुक्तं भवति षड़चरमन्त्रेण ॐ नमो विष्णवे इतिरूपेण स्ववाच्यदेवतारूपस्य व्याप्त्यर्थं विष्णुस्वरूप-

ललिताविद्यया तद्वत् प्रासादस्य त्रयात्मनः ।
तथैव च परायाश्च गायत्र्याश्चोक्तरूपतः ॥ ४५ ॥
व्याहृतीनां महावाक्यपरमात्माजपात्मनाम् ।
प्रणवस्य च तद्रूपयोगात् स्यात्तत्तदात्मता ॥ ४६ ॥

प्रतिपादनात्। अष्टाक्षरेण व्याप्तिं स्ववाच्यदेवतारूपस्य नारायणस्य नरसमुदायवाचकनारशब्दप्रतिपादितसकलविश्वस्यायतनत्वात् स्थानत्वात् अस्या देवताया नारवाच्यविश्वान्तर्यामित्वेन स्थितत्वप्रतिपादनाच्च। द्वादशाक्षरमन्त्रेण स्ववाच्यदेवतारूपस्य भगवतो वासुदेवस्य सर्व्वशक्तिकारणत्ववाचकभगवच्छब्देन सर्व्वपदार्थेषु तादात्म्यनिवासवाचकवासुदेवशब्देन विभुत्वप्रतिपादनात् एवञ्च परस्वरूपवाचकत्वादेतेषां परस्वरूपपरमार्थया ललिताविद्यया व्याप्तिरिति। तद्वत् परतत्त्वार्थवाचकत्वात् प्रासादस्य शैवतन्त्रमूलभूतस्य मन्त्रस्य त्रयात्मनः त्रयात्मकत्वादित्यर्थः। त्रयात्मकत्वं नाम ज्ञातृज्ञानज्ञेयात्मकत्वं। तस्य मन्त्रस्य ज्ञातृरूपो विन्दुः ज्ञानरूपश्चतुर्द्दशस्वरः ज्ञेयरूपो हकारः। एतदुक्तं भवति प्रासादमन्त्रेण स्ववाच्यदेवताया ज्ञातृज्ञानज्ञेयरूपाविकल्पपरमार्थस्वरूपत्वकथनात्तस्य ललिताविद्यया व्याप्तिर्भवतीति। तथैव पररूपवाचकत्वादित्यर्थः। परायाः कुलसुन्दरीविद्यातार्त्तीयबीजरूपायाः तस्याः परमार्थवाचकत्वं पूर्व्वोक्तत्रैविध्यात्। एतदुक्तं भवति श्रीपराविद्यया प्रोक्तरूपया स्ववाच्यदेवताया ज्ञातृज्ञानज्ञेयात्मभिः विसर्ज्जनीयचतुर्दशस्वरसकारैरपृथग्भूतानुत्तरपरमार्थस्वरूपकथनेन ललिताविद्यया व्याप्तिरिति। गायत्र्याः सावित्र्याः उक्तरूपवत्। वैष्णवमन्त्रत्रये अशेषत इति शब्देन प्रोक्तपदपदार्थरूपेणापीत्यर्थः। एतदुक्तं भवति अनया गायत्र्या स्ववाच्यदेवतायाः सकलप्रपञ्चसवितृत्वं स्फुरत्तामात्रप्रवृत्तिरूपत्वं समस्तभेदज्ञानापोहनक्षमशक्तित्वं विश्वात्मत्वं चोच्यत इति। व्याहृतीनां गायत्र्याः पादत्रयस्य कारणभूतानां तिसृणां। एतदुक्तं भवति ताभिः स्ववाच्यदेवतायाः सच्चात्मत्वं सकलप्रपञ्चकारणत्वं तत्कारणाभेदश्चोच्यत इति। महावाक्यपरमात्माजपात्मनां महावाक्यस्य परमात्ममन्त्रस्याजपामन्त्रस्य च। एतदुक्तं भवति महावाक्येन स्ववाच्यदेवतायाः सद्रूपपरमार्थत्वपृथग्ब्रह्मभावरूपपरमार्थस्वरूपमजपामन्त्रे परमात्ममन्त्रेण स्ववाच्यदेवतायाः सकलप्रपञ्च-

विन्दुभ्यां तां तथा मायामुभयोरैक्यविग्रहम्।
हंसरूपां प्राणशक्तिं तद्वैलोम्यसमुद्भवम्॥ ४७॥
प्रणवञ्च विजानाति योऽसौ नित्याविदीरितः।
इतरे भक्तिमन्तश्चेत् कालात्तज्ज्ञानमाप्नुयुः॥ ४८॥
अभक्तिभजनं लोके नित्यानां क्लेशदायकम्।
भक्तिभेदे च कथय ययाप्नोत्यखिलं ध्रुवम्॥ ४९॥
देवतामन्त्रयन्त्राणां ध्यानादीनामशेषतः।
यदन्वयात् फलावाप्तिर्यद्वियोगे श्रमो वृथा॥ ५०॥

कारणभूतेन चिद्रूपेण परमात्मना तत्तत्कार्यभूतप्रपञ्चात्मिकायाः स्वेच्छाशक्तेरपृथगभूतरूपपरमार्थस्वरूपमजपामन्त्रेण स्ववाच्यदेवतायाः प्रोक्तरूपस्वेच्छाशक्तुग्रज्ञासरूपप्रपञ्चात्मना पररूपस्य भासनं परमार्थरूपं चोच्यत इति। प्रणवस्य अनन्तरश्लोकवक्ष्यमाणरूपस्य। तद्रूपयोगात् पररूपतादात्म्यार्थसम्बन्धात् तत्तादात्मता ललिताविद्यया इति शेषः। एतदुक्तं भवति वैष्णवशैववैदिकेषु मन्त्रेषु मूलभूतानामेतेषामेकादशानां मन्त्राणां सकलकारणभूतस्य चिन्मात्रस्वरूपस्य स्वेच्छाशक्तुग्रज्ञासविजृम्भितेन प्रपञ्चेन तादात्म्येन तादात्म्यप्रतिपादनात् ललितायाश्च तदर्थप्रतिपादकं भवतीत्यर्थः। तद्वैलोम्यसमुद्भवं प्रणवं तदात्मकयोर्विन्दुविसर्जनीयसुक्तयोर्हंकारसकारयोर्वैलोम्यजातसन्धिसमुद्भवं प्रणवं। एतदुक्तं भवति शिवशक्तिसामरस्यविग्रहपरमार्थायाः श्रीमहात्रिपुरसुन्दरीनित्यायाः परमार्थस्वरूपकामकलायां शिवरूपस्य विन्दोः शक्तिरूपस्य विसर्जनीयस्य चानुलोम्ययोगे परमार्थजपात्मिकां प्राणशक्तिं तद्वैलोम्ययोगात् प्रणवञ्च विजानानस्तत्त्वतो नित्याविद्भवतीति। इतरे एतत्सामरस्यविज्ञानरहिताः। भक्तिमन्तः नित्यासु। कालात् क्रमेण। तज्ज्ञानं सामरस्यज्ञानम्। एतदुक्तं भवति एतत्सामरस्यरूपज्ञानमन्तरेणापि तासां नित्यानां केवलं सुदृढ़या भक्त्या भजनेन क्रमेण तद्भक्तिभंजनं तत्सामरस्यरूपपरमार्थज्ञानं ददातीति॥ ४८॥

अभक्तीत्यादिभिर्दुःखिनः इत्यन्तैः पञ्चभिः श्लोकैः भक्तिप्रशंसां भक्तिस्वरूपमभक्तिभजनप्रत्यवायञ्चोपदिशति। तत्र अभक्तिभजनं नित्यानामित्यत्रान्वयः।

तां भक्तिं तव वक्ष्यामि रहस्यामङ्गुताद्भुताम् ।
सम्यक् फलमयीं सिद्धिमलभ्यामल्पपुण्यतः ॥ ५१ ॥
उक्तलक्षणसम्पन्ने गुरौ तत्प्रोक्तयोस्तथा ।
विद्यानुष्ठानयोः स्थैर्य्यं धियः संशयनाशतः ॥ ५२ ॥
तारकत्वाप्रमत्तत्त्वे भक्तिरुक्ताखिलार्थदा ।
यया विहीना नियतमिहामुत्र च दुःखिनः ॥ ५३ ॥
सर्व्वक्लेशापदम्भोधिपोतरूपां महाद्युतिम् ।
आधिव्याधिमहादावप्रावृषम्ब्रामृतेश्वरीम् ॥ ५४ ॥
शृणु वक्ष्ये समस्तानां प्राणिनां जीवविग्रहाम् ।
षड्विधां जपहोमार्च्चातर्पणध्यानयन्त्रकैः ॥ ५५ ॥
दावाम्बुखैर्भवेदाद्या त्वन्या हृद्धंसमायया ।
ज्याकं दाद्दवनस्वैः स्यात्तृतीया सामृतेश्वरी ॥ ५६ ॥

क्लेशदायकं साधकस्येति शेषः। यया भक्त्या। अखिलमिष्टफलं यदन्वयात् भक्तियोगेन। यद्वियोगे भक्तिराहित्ये। श्रमः अभ्यासः। पूर्वोक्तदेवतामन्त्रादीनां सम्यक् फलमयीं सिद्धिं सर्व्वफलसिद्धिकारणत्वात्। उक्तलक्षणसम्पन्ने प्रथम पटलोक्तसुन्दरः सुमुख इत्यादि लक्षणसम्पूर्णे। तत्प्रोक्तयोः सद्गुरुप्रोक्तयोः धियः संशयनाशत इत्येतत् काकाक्षिवत् पूर्व्वापरयोरन्वेति। अखिलार्थदा स्वरूपसिद्धिदा। यया विहीना जना इति शेषः ॥ ५३ ॥

सर्व्वक्लेशेत्यादिना यन्त्रकैरित्यन्तेन श्लोकद्वयेनामृतेश्वरीविद्यास्तवनपुरःसरं प्रस्तौति। तत्र सर्व्वक्लेशापदम्भोधिपोतरूपां सर्व्वक्लेशापदां भौतिकदिव्यादीनां पीड़ानां समुद्ररूपाणां पोतरूपां तारिकामित्यर्थः। महाद्युतिं निरतिशय वैभवाम् अमृतेश्वरीं विद्यामिति शेषः। जीवानां प्राणिनां प्राणविग्रहां अमृत-मयत्वात्। जपहोमार्च्चातर्पणध्यानयन्त्रकैः सहेति शेषः ॥ ५५ ॥

दावेत्यादिना श्लोकेनामृतेश्वरीविद्यामुपदिशति। तत्र दावाम्बुखैर्भवेदाद्या ठकारवकारविन्दुभिरादद्या विदेत्यर्थः। अन्या द्वितीया विद्येति शेषः।

वासनोक्तप्रकारेण षड् विधा सा समीरिता ।
अङ्गानि तासामाद्याया दीर्घस्वरनियोजनात् ॥ ५७ ॥
कृत्वा कराङ्गयोः पश्चात्तत्त्रयं षोडशस्वरैः ।
संयोज्यामृतसंस्थानान्न्यसेदन्यत्तु तद्गतम् ॥ ५८ ॥

हृहंसमायया सकारहकारहल्लेखाभिर्द्वितीया विद्येत्यर्थः । ज्याकं दाहवनखैः स्यात्तृतीया जकारहकारेफश्रोकारविन्दुभिस्तृतीया विद्येत्यर्थः। एतेषां वीजानां त्रयाणामेकैकस्य विद्यात्वं त्रियते । साम्रतेश्वरी पूर्वप्रस्तुताम्रतेश्वरी विद्या इत्यमुक्तेत्यर्थः ॥ ५६ ॥

वासनेत्यादिभिः चीणकल्मष इत्यन्तैः षड्भिः श्लोकैरस्याः षड्विधरूपभेदांस्तदङ्गानि शरीरे अमृतकलाः शरीरेषु तन्न्यासविधानक्रमञ्चोपदिशति। तत्र वासनोक्तप्रकारेण वासनापटलवच्यमाणसर्व्वविद्यारूपभेदोक्तप्रकारेण षड्विधा सा साम्रतेश्वरी विद्या षड्रूपभेदा भवन्तीत्यर्थः। तद्रूपाणि यथा तत्र प्रथमं रूपं प्रोद्धारक्रमं द्वितीयं रूपन्तु प्रथमतृतीयद्वितीय-कूटयोजनक्रमेण भवति। तृतीयरूपन्तु द्वितीयतृतीयप्रथमकूटयोजनक्रमेण भवति। चतुर्थरूपन्तु द्वितीयप्रथमतृतीयकूटयोजनक्रमेण भवति। पञ्चमरूपन्तु तृतीयप्रथमद्वितीयकूटयोजनक्रमेण भवति। षष्ठरूपन्तु तृतीयद्वितीय-प्रथमकूटयोजनक्रमेण भवति। प्रथमरूपस्य प्रतिलोमरूपं भवतीति। तासां षण्णां विद्यानां आद्यायाः तत्तद्भेदेषु प्रथमप्रथमकूटरूपायाः दीर्घस्वरयोजनं प्राग्वत् कराङ्गयोः प्राग्वत्। एतदुक्तं भवति अमृतेश्वरीविद्यारूपभेदेषु षट्सु प्रथमद्वितीयरूपयोर्द्वयोः प्रथमकूटस्यैवाद्यत्वात् तस्मिन् दीर्घस्वरयोजनात् ह्रां ह्रीं इत्यादिभिर्जातियुक्तै रूपैस्तद्रूपभेदद्वयभजने कराङ्गन्यासादिकं कुर्य्यात्। तेषु तृतीयचतुर्थयोर्द्वितीयकूटस्यैवाद्यत्वात् तस्मिन् दीर्घस्वरयोजनात् स्ह्रां स्ह्रीं इत्यादिभिर्जातियुक्तै रूपैस्तद्रूपभेदद्वयभजने षडङ्गन्यासादिकं कुर्य्यात्। तेषु पञ्चमषष्ठयोस्तृतीयकूटस्यैवाद्यत्वात् तस्मिन् दीर्घस्वरयोजनात् ज्फ्रां ज्फ्रीं इत्यादिभिर्जातियुक्तै रूपैस्तद्रूपभेदद्वयभजने षडङ्गन्यासादिकं कुर्य्यादिति। तत्त्रयं कूटत्रयं षोडषस्वरैः संयोज्य प्रतिकूटमिति शेषः। अमृतसंस्थानात् अनन्तरवच्यमाणक्रमादमृतकलास्थितस्थानसारभ्ये

अङ्गुष्ठपृष्ठतत्सन्धिलिङ्गनाभिषु हृत्स्तने ।
गलनासाक्षिकर्णभ्रूशङ्खमूर्द्धसु वै क्रमात् ॥ ५९ ॥
दक्षवामसमारम्भात् पुंस्त्रियोरप्ययं क्रमः ।
शुक्ले पूर्णान्तमितरे मूर्द्धादिप्रतिलोमतः ॥ ६० ॥
भागद्वयस्य व्यत्यासाद्दर्शान्तेऽङ्गुष्ठगा क्रमात् ।
नित्यशो मृतगस्थानसमारम्भावसानकम् ॥ ६१ ॥

त्यर्थः । अन्यत् विसर्जनीयस्वरसंयुक्तस्वरूपं तद्गतं न्यासस्थानारम्भभूता-मृतस्थाने न्यसेदित्यर्थः । एतदुक्तं भवति अमृतेश्वरीविद्यायाः प्रथमद्वितीय-तृतीयकूटानां प्रतिकूटं षोड़शस्वरयोजनादेकैकस्य कूटस्य षोड़शरूपाणि भवन्ति । तानि षोड़शरूपाणि वक्ष्यमाणक्रमामृतस्थानमारभ्य वक्ष्यमाणामृतकला-गत्या पञ्चदशरूपाणि विन्यस्य षोड़शं रूपं पुनरप्यमृतस्थाने न्यसेदिति । पृष्ठे प्रपदे । तत्सन्धिः गुल्फजानुसन्ध्योः शङ्खे भालपार्श्वास्थिनि । दक्षवामसमारम्भात् पुंस्त्रियोरप्ययं क्रमः । शुक्ले पूर्णान्तं । एतदुक्तं भवति शुक्लपक्षे पूर्वदक्षिण पादाङ्गुष्ठमारभ्य मूर्द्धान्तं तत्तत्पार्श्वस्थेषु पञ्चदशसु प्रोक्तेषु स्थानेषु तत्प्रथमादि -पूर्णान्तं पञ्चदशसु तिथिषु प्रतितिथि यथाक्रममारोहक्रमादमृतकलायाः स्थिति र्भवतीति । स्त्रियास्तु वामपादाङ्गुष्ठमारभ्य मूर्द्धान्तं तत्पार्श्वस्थेषु प्रोक्तेषु पञ्च-दशसु स्थानेषु तत्प्रथमादिपूर्णान्तं पञ्चदशसु तिथिषु प्रतितिथि यथाक्रम मारोहक्रमादमृतकलायाः स्थितिर्भवतीति । एवं पुंस्त्रियोः शुक्लपक्षे समारम्भ-पार्श्वक्रमव्यत्यासेऽपि स्थानक्रमव्यत्यासो न भवतीति । इतरे कृष्णपक्षे मूर्द्धादि अङ्गुष्ठान्तं प्रतिलोमतः अवरोहणक्रमेणेत्यर्थः । भागद्वयस्य व्यत्यासात् पुं-स्त्रियोरिति शेषः । अङ्गुष्ठगा अमृतकलेति शेषः । एतदुक्तं भवति कृष्णपक्षे पुंसो वामपार्श्वमूर्द्धादिवामाङ्गुष्ठान्तं प्रोक्तेषु पञ्चदशसु स्थानेषु पूर्णान्तप्रतिपद-मारभ्य दर्शान्तं पञ्चदशसु तिथिषु प्रतितिथि यथाक्रममवरोहक्रमेणामृतकला-स्थितिर्भवतीति । स्त्रियास्तु दक्षिणपार्श्वमूर्द्धादि दक्षिणाङ्गुष्ठान्तं प्रोक्तेषु पञ्चदशसु स्थानेषु पूर्णान्तप्रतिपदमारभ्य दर्शान्तं पञ्चदशसु तिथिषु प्रतितिथि यथाक्रम-मवरोहक्रमेणामृतकलायाः स्थितिर्भवतीति । नित्यश इत्यादिना कल्मष इत्यन्ते-नार्द्धाद्येनैकेन श्लोकेनैतदुक्तं भवति । अमृतेश्वरीविद्याभेदेषु षट्सु स्वभजनीयस्वे-

न्यसेत्ताः षड् विधाः प्रोक्तक्रमान्ते न तु नित्यशः।
न्यासेनामृतरूपी स्यात् साधकः क्षीणकल्मषः॥ ६२॥
ध्यानं तासां प्रवक्ष्यामि शृणु प्रोक्तक्रमेण वै।
यासां स्मरणमात्रेण क्लेशा नश्यन्त्यशेषतः॥ ६३॥
शुद्धस्फटिकसङ्काशां मौलिबद्धेन्दुनिर्गतैः।
अमृतैरार्द्रदेहास्तास्त्वमलाभरणान्विताः॥ ६४॥
कुमुदं पुण्डरीकञ्च राकेन्दुममृतं करैः।
दधानाः स्मेरवदना मुक्ताभरणभूषिताः॥ ६५॥

कैकस्य भेदस्यैव कूटत्रयवतः प्रतिकूटञ्च षोड़शस्वरयोजनात् जातानि षोड़श षोड़शरूपाणि एवं सम्भूयाष्टचत्वारिंशद्रूपाणि प्रोक्तक्रमेणामृतकलास्थितिस्थान मारभ्य पञ्चदशसु स्थानेषु पञ्चदश रूपाणि पुनरप्यारम्भस्थाने षोड़शरूपमेवं षोड़शषोड़शविभागेन त्रिशस्त्रिशः न्यसेत्। तेन साधकः प्रोक्तरूपी भवतीति॥ ६२॥

ध्यानमित्यादिभिः परिवारिता इत्यन्तैश्चतुर्भिः श्लोकैरमृतेश्वरीध्यानं तत्-पूजां तदावरणशक्तिनिवहञ्चोपदिशति। तत्र तासां अमृतेश्वरीमूर्त्तिविद्याभेद-षट्कानां। यासां मूर्त्तीनां। क्लेशाः तापत्रयरूपाः। शुद्धस्फटिकसङ्काशां मूर्त्तिमिति शेषः। दधाना इत्युपरितनश्लोकोत्तरार्द्धस्य प्रथमपादेनान्वयः। मूर्त्तेरेक-वचनत्वं तासां षस्रां ऐक्यपरमार्थत्वात्। अन्विता इति बहुवचनं भेदरूपाङ्गी-कारेण। अत्रायुधानि ऊर्द्ध्वादिदक्षिणवामदक्षिणवामक्रमेण। स्मेरवदनाः प्राग्वत् मूर्त्तिविशेषणं प्राग्वद्दधाना इत्यत्रान्वयः। मुक्ताभरणभूषिताः मौक्तिक-मयैराभरणैरलङ्कृताः। दलमध्यगाः ताभिः षष्टिशतार्णात्मशक्तिभिः पूर्वोक्तामृता-क्षरषष्ट्युत्तरशतिकाभिः शक्तिभिरित्यर्थः। एतदुक्तं भवति अभीष्टमानक्रमेण वृत्तं निष्पाद्य वहिरेकाङ्गुलमानेन वृत्तं कृत्वा तद्वहिः पञ्चाङ्गुलमानेन वृत्तं विधाय तद्वहिः पुनरप्येकाङ्गुलमानेन वृत्तं विधाय एवमन्तर्वहिर्विभागेन प्रोक्तचतुष्टयेन सार्द्धं विंशतिवृत्तानि विधाय तासु पञ्चाङ्गुलान्तरालासु दशसु वीथिषु एकस्या-मेकस्यां वीथ्यां षोड़श षोड़श दलानि कृत्वा तत्र सर्व्वमध्यकर्णिकायां प्रधान-

षोड़शच्छदयुक्तानां पद्मानां दलमध्यगाः ।
ताभिः षष्टिशतार्णात्मशक्तिभिः परिवारिताः ॥ ६६ ॥
तत्तद्विद्याक्षरोपेतं तदर्णं रूपिणीपदम् ।
शक्तीतिद्व्यक्षरं प्रोक्तसम्प्राचर्य्या च संयुतम् ॥ ६७ ॥
चतुर्दशाक्षरी विद्या कृत्वैवं ताभिरर्चयेत् ।
बाह्यात् प्रवेशगत्यैव प्रादक्षिण्यात् सुगन्धिभिः ॥ ६८ ॥
सितैः प्रसूनैः श्रीखण्डकर्पूरद्रवलोलितैः ।
पूजयेद्बहिरासान्तु विदध्याद्बलियुग्मकम् ॥ ६९ ॥
निवेद्य पायसं दुग्धकदलीफलशर्कराः ।
होमश्च तैस्तर्पणान्तु जलैः कर्पूरवासितैः ॥ ७० ॥

देवताममृतेश्वरीं बहिर्दलेषु भगमालिनीपटलोक्तषष्ट्युत्तरशतामृताक्षरात्मिकाभिः शक्तिभिः परिवारितां पूजयेत् । एतदन्यासां पद्मानामपि साधारणम् ॥ ६६ ॥

तत्तद्विद्येत्यादिभिर्वासितैरित्यन्तैश्चतुर्भिः श्लोकैरावरणशक्तीनां पूजाविद्याः देव्याः पूजाद्रव्याणि बलिहोमतर्पणानि चोपदिशति । तत्र तत्तद्विद्याक्षरोपेतं पूर्वोक्तसंख्यानां प्रत्येकमाद्याक्षरत्वेन योजनीयमित्यर्थः । तदर्णं प्रोक्तसंख्येष्वमृतार्णेषु एकैकं प्रोक्तसम्प्राचर्य्या द्वितीयपटल इतिशेषः । चतुर्दशाक्षरी प्रतिविद्यमिति शेषः । कृत्वैवं एवं प्रोद्धृत्येत्यर्थः । ताभिर्विद्याभिः । प्रादक्षिण्यात् अग्रादारभ्येति शेषः । एतदुक्तं भवति अमृतेश्वरीविद्यारूपभेदषट्कभजनीयस्य रूपस्य प्रथमकूटं पूर्व्वमुच्चार्य्यानन्तरममृताक्षरेषु बिन्दुयुक्ताशीतिषु चैवं सम्भूय षष्ट्युत्तरशतेषु प्रोक्तक्रमेणैकैकमक्षरमुच्चार्य्यानन्तरं रूपिणीशक्तिपादुकां पूजयामीति द्वादशाक्षराण्युच्चार्य्य एवं सम्भूय प्रतिविद्यं चतुर्दशाक्षरात्मिकाभि र्विद्याभि र्बाह्याभ्यन्तरप्रवेशगत्याग्रादिप्रादक्षिण्येनार्चयेदिति । सुगन्धिभिः प्रसूनैरित्यत्रान्वयः । श्रीखण्डं चन्दनं । बहिर्नित्यपूजामण्डलतः । आसां षड्विधानाममृतेश्वरीणां । तुना आसामपि ललितात्मकत्वमुच्यते । बलियुग्मकं आद्यन्तयोर्यथाक्रमं षोड़शाक्षरमन्त्रेण कुरुकुल्लासम्प्राचर्य्या च । तैः पायसादिभिश्चतुर्भिः ॥७०॥

दशलक्षं जपेद्विद्यां पयोभक्ष्यः समाहितः।
एवं जपादिसंसिद्धविद्यो मन्त्री यदा जलम्॥ ७१॥
समुद्रजं स्पृशन् हस्ततलेन प्रजपेच्च ताः।
एकैकशः शतादेवं तत्तोयं दुग्धसन्निभम्॥ ७२॥
तेष्वेव तत्तद्विद्यार्णसमेतान् षष्टिसंयुतान्।
शतार्णानालिखेन्मध्ये तदाद्यं मध्यतो लिखेत्॥ ७३॥

दशलक्षमित्यादिना सन्निभमित्यन्तेन श्लोकद्वयेन विद्यासाधनविधानं सिद्धविद्यस्य लक्षणञ्चोपदिशति। तत्र दशलक्षं प्रतिविद्यमिति शेषः। अत्र तर्पणहोमौ प्रतिविद्यं तद्दशांशाविति सम्प्रदायः। एवमुक्तप्रकारेण जपादीत्यत्रादिशब्दस्तर्पणहोमपूजादिविषयः। समुद्रजं जलमिति पूर्व्वश्लोकोक्तपदेनान्वयः। ताः षड्विधा विद्याः। एकैकशः शतात् षड्विद्यासु तासु स्वसिद्धां स्वसिद्धामेकैकां विद्यां शतवारं जपेदित्यर्थः। एवमुक्तप्रकारजापेन तत्तोयं समुद्रजलं दुग्धसन्निभम् रसादिभिः॥ ७२॥

तेष्वित्यादिना अनन्तका इत्यन्तेन श्लोकद्वयेन पद्मयन्त्रविधानं तस्यानन्तसंख्यात्मकत्वञ्चोपदिशति। तत्र तेषु नित्यसपर्य्यामण्डलत्वेन प्रोक्तेष्वन्तर्वहिर्विभागस्थितेषु प्रत्येकं षोड़शदलरूपेषु दशसु पद्मेषु। तत्तद्विद्यार्णसमेतान् षड्विधामृतेश्वरीविद्यासु स्वाभिमतविद्यायामेकैककूटसमेतान्। षष्टिसंयुतान् शतार्णान् पूर्वोक्तामृतार्णानित्यर्थः। मध्ये कर्णिकाया इति शेषः। तदाद्यं मध्यतो लिखेत् साध्याक्षरसमोपेतं स्वमध्यतः साध्याक्षरसमोपेतं तत्तद्दाद्यलिखितेष्वाद्यस्वरूपं लिखेदित्यर्थः। तेषां उक्तसंख्यानामक्षरस्वरूपाणां। अन्योन्यमभेदालेखनात् वासनापटलवक्ष्यमाणभेदक्रमालेखनात्। अनन्तकाः अनन्तानीत्यर्थः यन्त्राणीति शेषः। अयमत्र यन्त्ररचनाक्रमः। प्रागुक्तक्रमादन्तर्वहिर्विभागस्थितानि प्रत्येकं षोड़शदलानि पद्मानि कृत्वा तेषु षष्ट्युत्तरशतसंख्येषु दलेषु वाह्यात् प्रवेशगत्या अग्रादग्रादिप्रादक्षिण्येनामृतेश्वरीविद्यासु षड्विधास्वाद्यविद्याप्रथमकूटसहितानमृतार्णान् षष्ट्युत्तरशतसंख्याकान् विलिख्य तन्मध्यकर्णिकायाञ्च तेषां वाह्यदललिखिताक्षररूपेष्वाद्यदललिखिताक्षरस्वरूपं विद्याक्षरप्रथमकूटमध्यमध्यगसाध्याक्षरोपेतं लिखेत्। एतत् प्रथमं यन्त्रं। अस्मिन्नेव यन्त्रे प्रोक्तेषु दशसु

साध्याक्षरसमोपेतं यन्त्रं स्यादिष्टसिद्धिकृत् ।
तेषामन्योन्यसम्भेदालिखनात् स्युरनन्तकाः ॥ ७४ ॥
प्राक्प्रत्यगुदक्षिणोदक्क कृत्वा विंशतिसूत्रकम् ।
कोष्ठान्युत्पाद्य सुसमान्येकषष्ठ्या शतत्रयम् ॥ ७५ ॥
तत्कोणतो मार्जयीत चत्वारिंशत् सपञ्चकम् ।
शेषं वज्रं भवेत् कोष्ठैरेकाशीतिशतेन वै ॥ ७६ ॥
तत्र दिक्षु यथा पूर्वं चतुर्भिः स्यात्त्रिकोणकम् ।
तेषु तास्ता लिखेद्विद्यां षट्साध्याख्यासमायुताम् ॥ ७७ ॥

पञ्चेषु प्रतिपन्नममृताक्षरेषु दशसु वासनापटलवक्ष्यमाणभेदक्रमात् । षोडशस्वर-योजनभेदेन जाता यन्त्रसंख्या चतुर्दशाक्षरवाक्येनोच्यते ज्ञानानन्दोदधौ धीद-साररात् धनरात् २०८२२३८८८८०००० इत्येतेषु एकमेकं यन्त्रं वासनापटल-वक्ष्यमाणभेदक्रमादेतद्दशपञ्चान्तर्वहिर्विभागस्थितदशामृतव्यञ्जनार्णभेदेन ज्ञानदो हरस्मृग ३६२८८०० इति सप्ताक्षरवाक्यजनितसंख्य भवति । सम्भूय एककूटजनितयन्त्रसंख्या विंशत्यक्षरवाक्येनोच्यते अनन्तज्ञानभावः सोमशम्भुधी-र्धन्यस्थिहरो धर्म्मस्य ७५६८२१८८४५५७४४०००० इत्येवमन्यकूटद्वयस्यापि प्रति--कूटमेतत्संख्यानि यन्त्राणि भवन्तीति । तस्मादेकैककूटोद्भवानां यन्त्राणामेव परार्द्धसंख्याधिकत्वादनन्तत्वं । अन्यासामेतत्कूटयन्त्रयोर्वैपर्य्यजनितानां पञ्चानां विद्यानां कूटान्तराभावादेतान्येव यन्त्राणि भवन्ति । तेन चासां परमार्थतो न भेदो विद्यत इति ॥ ७४ ॥

प्राक्प्रत्यगित्यादिभिः सम्पद इत्यन्तैरष्टभिः श्लोकैः कोष्ठवज्रयन्त्रषट्कं तद्वि-नियोगांश्चोपदिशति । तत्र सुसमानि प्रत्येकं परस्परं समचतुरस्राणि । तत्-कोणतः तस्य प्रोक्तसंख्यकोष्ठस्य यन्त्रस्य चतसृषु कोणदिक्षु । चत्वारिंशत् सपञ्चकं पञ्चचत्वारिंशत् कोष्ठानीति शेषः । चतुर्भिः प्रतिदिशमिति शेषः । तेषु चतुर्षु कोणेषु । तास्ताः स्वसिद्धाः । साध्याख्यासमायुताम् साधकसाध्यकर्म्माख्यायुता-मित्यर्थः । प्राङ्मध्यमारभ्यात् सर्व्वप्राचीनपंक्तिस्थ कोष्ठपञ्चकमध्यमकोष्ठारम्भा-दित्यर्थः । कोणमध्यस्थपञ्चकेत्युक्त्या कोष्ठाष्टकरूपे सप्तमावरणे चतुर्दिग्गत-

प्राग्वत् प्राङ्मध्यमारभ्यात् प्रादक्षिण्यप्रवेशतः ।
विलिखेदमृतार्णांस्तु क्रमात् षष्टिशतं प्रिये ॥ ७८ ॥
शेषेषु कोणमध्यस्थपञ्चकेऽभिहितक्रमात् ।
वाह्यादिमध्यमान्तन्तु लिखेदन्यास्तु पञ्च वै ॥ ७९ ॥
साध्याक्षरयुतान्येव षड्भिः षड्वज्रकाणि तु ।
यन्त्राणि तेषां सर्वत्र गदादिपरिरक्षणम् ॥ ८० ॥
उत्पातशान्तिमन्यानि मङ्गलानि च कारयेत् ।
यस्मिन् देशे त्विदं यन्त्रषट्कं त्वेवं सुपूजितम् ॥ ८१ ॥

कोणे लिखेत् । वाह्यादिवह्निकोणस्थकोष्ठादि अन्यास्तु पञ्चत्रिकोणलिखितस्व-सिद्धविद्याव्यतिरिक्ताः । साध्याक्षरयुतानि तत्तद्विद्याकूटाक्षराणि षड्भिर्विद्याभिः । तेषां यन्त्राणां गदादिपरिरक्षणं फलमिति शेषः । अन्यानि मङ्गलानि आयुः-श्रीपुत्रधनलाभादीनि । तत्र देशे । मारी यावज्जलमेकव्याधिना नाशकरो शान्तिः । अयमत्र यन्त्रविलेखनक्रमः प्राक्प्रत्यगुदक्षिणोदक्समान्तरालानि विंशतिसूत्राण्यास्फाल्य तेनैकषष्ट्यधिकत्रिशतकोष्ठान्युत्पाद्य तेषु चतुर्षु कोणेषु प्रतिकोणं पञ्चचत्वारिंशत्पञ्चचत्वारिंशत् कोष्ठानि सम्भूयाशीत्यधिकशतकोष्ठानि प्राग्वद्वज्राकारं मार्जयित्वा शिष्टेष्वेकाशीत्यधिकशतकोष्ठेषु चतसृषु दिक्षु प्रतिदिशं प्राग्वत् कोष्ठचतुष्टयं सम्भूय षोडश कोष्ठानि मार्जयित्वा तत्र तत्र प्राग्वत्त्रिकोणानि कृत्वा तेषु त्रिकोणेष्वमृतेश्वरीविद्यासु षट्सु प्रथमं स्वाभिमतविद्यां साध्यादिसंयुक्तकूटत्रयगर्भामालिख्य शिष्टकोष्ठपञ्चषष्ट्याधिकशतैः प्राग्वत् सर्वप्राचीनपंक्तिस्थकोष्ठपञ्चकमध्यकोष्ठमारभ्य प्रादक्षिण्यप्रवेशगत्या प्राग्वदमृतार्णषष्ट्यधिकशतके षट्पञ्चाशदधिकशताक्षराणि यावत् षष्ठावरणान्तं विलिख्य शिष्टाक्षरचतुष्टयं सप्तमावरणकोष्ठाष्टके प्रागादि चतुर्दिग्गत कोष्ठचतुष्टये कोणकोष्ठचतुष्टयवर्जं विलिख्य वर्जिततत्कोणगतकोष्ठचतुष्टये मध्यकोष्ठे च सम्भूय पञ्चकोष्ठेषु वह्निकोष्ठादारभ्य मध्यकोष्ठान्तं प्रादक्षिण्येन दिगन्तत्रि-कोणलिखितामृतेश्वरीविद्याशिष्टविद्यापञ्चकं प्राग्वत् ससाध्यं समालिखेत् । एतत् प्रथमं यन्त्रम् । एवं अमृतेश्वरीद्वितीयादिविद्यापञ्चके स्वाभिमतां विद्यां प्रत्येकं

तत्र चौरग्रहव्याधिमारीदुर्भिक्षशत्रवः ।
सदा न सम्भवन्त्येव भवन्त्येव च सम्पदः । ८२ ॥
प्राक्प्रत्यग्दक्षिणोदक्क कृत्वा द्वादशसूत्रकम् ।
सैकविंशच्छतं कोष्ठान्यभितो मार्जयेत् क्रमात् ॥ ८३ ॥
दशपञ्चसमोपेतं शिष्टे वज्रैकषष्टिके ।
मध्ये तद्दिनजां विद्यां आलिख्याख्यासमन्विताम् ॥ ८४ ॥
तद्दिक्ष्वेकैकतः कृत्वा त्रिकोणानि यथाविधि ।
प्राग्वदग्रत्रिकोणात्तु विलिखेदुदयाच्चरात् ॥ ८५ ॥

वह्निस्त्रिकोणेषु प्राग्वद्विलिख्य तदनन्तरादि तदन्यपञ्चकस्य तदन्यपञ्चकस्य प्राङ्मध्यकोष्ठपञ्चकविलेखनात् पञ्चयन्त्राणि सम्भूय पूर्वोक्तेन सह षड्यन्त्राणि निष्पाद्य तैः प्रोक्तान् विनियोगान् कुत्वा प्रोक्तानि फलान्यवाप्नुयादिति ॥ ८२ ॥

प्राक्प्रत्यगित्यादिभिः संयुत इत्यन्तैरष्टभिः श्लोकैरेकषष्टिकोष्ठात्मकवज्रयन्त्रनिर्माणं तत्र मिथुनपूजनं तत्सामान्ये फलं द्रव्यविशेषपूजनात् फल-विशेषावाप्तिं कालविशेष पूजनात् फलविशेषं चोपदिशति । तत्र अभितः प्राग्वत् कोणचतुष्टये प्रतिकोणमित्यर्थः । दशपञ्चसमोपेतं क्रियाविशेषणमेतत् । पञ्चदशकोष्ठाणि मार्जयेदित्यर्थः । वज्रैकषष्टिके वज्ररूपयन्त्रकोष्ठैकषष्टिके इत्यर्थः । मध्ये सर्व्वमध्यकोष्ठे । तद्दिनजां विद्यां पञ्चदशपटले प्रोक्तासु कालनित्याविद्यासु तत्तद्दिननित्यात्वेन प्राप्तां विद्याम् । आख्यासमन्वितां प्राग्वत् साधकादित्रयगर्भाम् । एकैकतः कोष्ठत इत्यर्थः । प्रतिदिशमिति शेषः । यथाविधि समत्रिरेखमित्यर्थः । प्रागवत् द्वाशखोदरे । अग्रत्रिकोणात् पश्चिमादग्रतः त्रिकोणमारभ्येत्यर्थः । उदयाच्चरात् पञ्चविंशपटलोक्तक्रमात्तत्तद्दिनेष्वर्कोदय-घटिकाप्राप्ताच्चरमारभ्येत्यर्थः । क्रमतः दिवसपञ्चकषड़ावृत्ति क्रमतः । मिथुनानि नित्यानित्यापटलोक्तानि । अत्र यन्त्रे । घटिकाक्रमयोगेन तत्तद्घटिकासु प्रतिघटिकं तत्तद्घटिकाप्राप्तमिथुनक्रमादित्यर्थः । तथा नित्यानित्यापटलोक्तादिभिरित्यर्थः । अन्यजासु भूतप्रेतग्रहादुद्यथास्वित्यर्थः । सप्तमी बहुवचनान्यन्यानि

षष्ट्यक्षराणि क्रमतो मिथुनान्यत्र पूजयेत् ।
घटिकाक्रमयोगेन गन्धपुष्पादिभिस्तथा ॥ ८६ ॥

तीव्रार्त्तिषु रुगोत्थासु गदोत्थास्वन्यजासु च ।
शीघ्रं शमं प्रयान्त्येव क्लेशास्तत्र प्रपूजनात् ॥ ८७ ॥

सम्पदे चार्च्चयेदेवमरुणैर्गन्धपुष्पकैः ।
सितैर्व्वा सौरभोपेतैर्मण्डलाच्छ्रियमाप्नुयात् ॥ ८८ ॥

पूर्णास्वेवं समाराध्य मिथुनानि यथाविधि ।
समस्तवाञ्छितं वर्षादवाप्नोत्येव निश्चितम् ॥ ८९ ॥

एवं त्रिजन्मस्वर्च्चातो जीवेद्वर्षशतं सुखी ।
नीरोगो निर्गताधिश्च निवृत्तिनीतिसंयुतः ॥ ९० ॥

क्रूरेषु चाभिचारेषु पूजयेन्मिथुनानि वै ।
मध्ये साध्यसमोपेते वज्रयन्त्रे दिवानिशम् ॥ ९१ ॥

पदानि त्रीणि तीव्रार्त्तिषु पदविशेषणानि। तत्र यन्त्रे । मण्डलात् प्रागुक्तैः । पूर्णासु त्रिविधासु त्रिजन्मसु प्रागुक्तत्। एतदुक्तं भवति प्राक्प्रत्यगुदक्षिणोदक् च समान्तरालानि द्वादशसूत्राण्यास्फाल्य एकविंशत्यधिकशतकोष्ठानि निष्पाद्य तेषु चतुर्षु कोणेषु प्रतिकोणं पञ्चदश पञ्चदश कोष्ठानि सम्भूय षष्टिकोष्ठानि प्रागुक्तवज्राकारं मार्जयित्वा शिष्टेष्वेकषष्टिकोष्ठेषु चतसृषु दिक्षु प्रतिदिशमेकमेकं कोष्ठं मार्जयित्वा तत्र तत्र समत्रिरेखानि त्रिकोणानि विधाय तत्र पश्चिमदिग्गतत्रिकोणमारभ्य त्रिकोणसहितबाह्यावरणविंशतिकोष्ठेषु द्वितीयावरणषोडशकोष्ठेषु तृतीयावरणद्वादशकोष्ठेषु चतुर्थावरणाष्टकोष्ठेषु पञ्चमावरणचतुष्कोष्ठेषु एवं सम्भूय षष्टिकोष्ठेषु घटिकाक्रमात्तत्तद्दिनोदयप्राप्तघटिकाक्षरात् प्रवृत्तषष्टिघटिकाक्षराणि हल्लेखोदरे प्रादक्षिण्यप्रवेशगत्या विलिख्य सर्व्वमध्यकोष्ठे हल्लेखोदरे तत्तद्दिननित्याविद्यां साधकादिनामगर्भामालिख्य तत्तद्दिनादिप्रतिघटिकं तत्तद्घटिकाप्राप्तमिथुनानि नित्यानित्यापटलोक्तमन्त्रादिभिः प्रोक्तकालेषु प्रोक्तकालावधिपूजनात् प्रोक्तफलसिद्धिरिति ॥ ८० ॥

मान्त्रिकैर्यामतो वारकल्पितैः स्वगृहे नृपः ।
नित्याभक्तैः समीचीनैः स्निग्धैः संप्राप्तदक्षिणैः ॥ ९२ ॥
सुदक्षिणैर्दिनैः कैश्चित् प्रयोक्तारं निहन्ति सः ।
तथा विलोहाश्मतले कृत्वा वज्रं सुविस्तृतम् ॥ ९३ ॥
सर्वतो विलिखेच्छक्तीस्तत्पुटे तानि संलिखेत् ।
मध्ये साध्यं समालिख्य तत् खनेद्भवनादिषु ॥ ९४ ॥
तत्रानिशं सम्पदः स्युर्गोष्ठिताश्च निराकुलाः ।
निःसपत्ना निरुपमा नीतियुक्ता निरन्तराः ॥ ९५ ॥
पूर्णाभिषेके यासक्रे पूज्याः प्रोक्तास्तु शक्तयः ।
तासां विद्यां शृणु प्राज्ञे याभिः स्यात् सिद्धविग्रहः ॥९६॥

क्रूरध्विन्यादिभिर्निरन्तरा इत्यन्तैः पञ्चभिः श्लोकैः तेनैवाभिचारप्रतीकारविधानं तत्स्थापनेन गृहरक्षादिविधानञ्चोपदिशति । तत्र पूजयेत् प्रागुक्तनैवेद्यमन्त्रक्रमादिभिरिति शेषः । वज्रयन्त्रे पूर्व्वप्रोक्ते । यामतो वारकल्पितैः अहोरात्रस्य यामाष्टके एकैकयामरूपैकैकवारैर्वृत्तैरष्टभिरित्यर्थः । सुदक्षिणैः नित्यातन्त्रप्रोक्तप्रयोगनिपुणैः । दिनैः कैश्चित् कार्य्यगौरवलाघवापेक्षया एकद्व्यादिमण्डलादिभिः । प्रयोक्तारं अभिचारकर्त्तारं । सः अभिचारः । वज्रं मिथुनवज्रयन्त्रं । सर्व्वतः तस्य यन्त्रस्यैकषष्टिपदेषु । शक्तीं ह्स्ख्रें खां । तत्पुटे ह्स्ख्रें खारेफांशे । तानि घटिकाक्षराणि । मध्ये घटिकाक्षरमध्ये । तद्यन्त्रं प्रागवत् प्राणप्रतिष्ठा पूजादिसहितं खनेत् मातृकापटले प्रोक्तक्रमतः । तत्र प्रदेशे । निरन्तराः मन्तव्यमानाः ॥ ८५ ॥

पूर्णाभिषेकेत्यादिभिश्चराचरमित्यन्तैः पञ्चभिः श्लोकैः द्वितीयपटलप्रोक्तपूर्णाभिषेकचक्रे पूज्यदेवतानां सचत्वारिंशच्चतुःशताधिकसहस्रसंख्यानां तासां प्रत्येकं षोड़शाक्षरमन्त्रस्वरूपञ्चोपदिशति । तत्र चक्रे द्वितीयपटल प्रोक्तेऽपि । तासां शक्तीनां । याभिः शक्तिविद्याभिः । सिद्धविग्रहः देव्यात्मा भवति ।

खरोत्थाभिः सहोत्थाभिर्नित्याविद्याभिरेव तु ।
समीरिता विषोढ़ाभिः खरवर्जमशेषतः ॥ ९७ ॥
सहस्रेण समायुक्तश्चत्वारिंशच्चतुःशतम् ।
ललिताशक्तिपूजोक्तबीजद्वयसमन्वितम् ॥ ९८ ॥
रूपशक्तीति सहितं समाचर्य्यन्तमर्चयेत् ।
प्रत्येकं षोड़शार्णाभिर्विद्याभिस्ताभिरम्बिके ॥ ९९ ॥
एवं ते गदितं सर्वं विद्याया व्याप्तिवैभवम् ।
यन्मयं विश्वमखिलं दृश्यते सचराचरम् ॥ १०० ॥

खरोत्थाभिः पञ्चविंशपटलोक्तकालनित्याविद्यासु वशिनीवर्गजनितनित्याविद्याभिः षट्सप्तत्यधिकपञ्चशतसंख्याभिः। सहोत्थाभिः तासु सकारहकारजनितनित्याभिस्तत्संख्याभिः नित्याविद्याभिरिति विशेष्यं। समीरिताः विद्याः विषोढ़ाभिः खरवर्जं वशिनीवर्गवर्जं सकारहकारयोः षण्डाक्षरचतुष्टय चतुष्टयजनितचतुश्चत्वारिंशदधिकशतसंख्यनित्याविद्यारहिताभिरित्यर्थः। चत्वारिंशच्चतुःशतं चत्वारिंशदधिकचतुःशतं। एतदुक्तं भवति पञ्चविंशपटलोक्त २०७३६ कालनित्याविद्यावशिनीवर्गजनितषट्सप्तत्यधिक पञ्चशतसंख्या विद्यास्तासु सकारोत्थासु प्रोक्तसंख्यासु विद्यासु षण्डाक्षरजनितचतुश्चत्वारिंशदधिकशतसंख्या विद्यारहिताः शिष्टद्वात्रिंशदुत्तरचतुःशतसंख्या विद्यास्तत्संख्यविषण्डहकाराक्षरविद्याश्च [चतुःशतोत्तरसहस्र संख्यानित्याविद्याः] तच्छ्रीचक्राङ्गत्वेनोक्तानां विद्यानामसाधारणत्वरूपा भवन्तीति। बीजद्वयसमन्वितं मायाश्रीबीजसमन्वितं सर्व्वादाविति शेषः। रूपशक्तीति सहितं रूपशक्ति इति चतुरक्षरोपेतं। पूर्व्वोक्तासाधारणरूपत्वाक्षर कालनित्याविद्यानामन्त इत्यर्थः। समाचर्य्यन्तं सर्व्वचरमे द्वितीयपटलोक्तसमाचरीविद्यासहितमित्यर्थः। एतत् सर्व्वमसाधारणत्वाक्षरनित्याविद्यारूपस्य विशेषणं। ताभिः पूर्व्वसंप्रस्तुताभिः। ता विद्या यथा--ह्रीं श्रीं अ आ इरूपशक्तिपादुकां पूजयामीत्यादि ह्रीं श्रीं हः ल ई रूपशक्तिपादुकां पूजयामीत्यन्ताः। ताः प्रोक्तसंख्याः शक्तयो ललिताश्रीचक्रस्थशक्तीनामणिमादिमहात्रिपुरसुन्दर्य्यन्तानां षण्णवतिसंख्यानां प्रत्येकं पञ्चदशापञ्चदशसंख्याविभागेनावरणशक्तयो भवन्तीति।

नियमात्ममयी व्याप्तिरिति सम्यक् समीरिता ।
अस्या निष्फालनाच्चित्ते तत्तत्त्वं स्वात्मसात् कृतम् ॥

इति षोड़शनित्यातन्त्रेषु श्रीकादिमते मन्त्रवैभवं नाम
षड् विंशं पटलं परिपूर्णं परामृष्टम् ॥२६॥ ॐ ॥

तेन तासामणिमादीनामपि प्रत्येकं मूलदेवतावत् षोड़शनित्यात्मकत्वं । तस्मात्ताः सम्भूय षट् त्रिंशदधिकपञ्चशतोत्तरसहस्रसंख्याः प्रकटयोगिन्यो भवन्तीति यावत् । विदशायाः ललिताविद्यायाः यन्मयं विद्यामयम् ॥ १०० ॥

इति षोड़शनित्यातन्त्रेषु श्रीकादिमताख्यस्य परिपूर्णस्य तन्त्रस्य प्रपञ्चसार-
सिंहराजप्रकाशाभिधानेन सुभगानन्दनाथेन विरचितायां
मनोरमाख्यायां व्याख्यायां षोड़शनित्याव्याप्तिवैभव-
प्रकाशक मन्त्रस्य व्याप्तिप्रकाशनपरं षड् विंशपटलं परिपूर्णं
परामृष्टम् ॥ २६ ॥ ॐतत्सत् ॥

यन्त्रसंख्या--२२७७७३८५८८३६७२३२००.००० ।

ज्ञानेन निम्ना श्रीगौरीसिताङ्गा दुग्धशब्दगा ।
स्वात्मसुरश्रीरित्येकविंशार्णयन्त्रसंख्यकाः ॥

ग्रन्थसंख्याः—षड्विंशे पटले प्रोक्ता व्याख्याग्रन्थास्चतुःशतात् ।
परमष्टयुतं त्रिंशदधिकं संख्यया स्फुटम् ॥

सप्तविंशपटलम्।

अथ षोड़शनित्यानां कालेन प्राणतोच्यते।
मातृकाभूतनाथाद्यैः श्रीचक्रेण च शक्तिभिः ॥ १ ॥
लवादीनान्तु कालस्य दुर्लक्ष्यत्वात्तदीरितम्।
एकश्वासं समारभ्य तत्संख्याभिः क्रमेण वै ॥ २ ॥
अहोरात्रस्य तद्व्याप्तिमुक्त्वा तेनान्यदूहयेत्।
विशेषांस्वान्तराद्बाह्यात्तत्तत्सिद्ध्युपपादकान् ॥ ३ ॥

पूर्व्वस्मिन् षड्विंशे पटले षोड़शनित्यानां व्याप्तिवैभवप्रकाशनपरं मन्त्रव्याप्तिं तन्मयामृतेश्वरीविद्यादिकञ्चोपदिश्यानन्तरं षोड़शनित्यानां मातृकाभूतनाथाद्यैः श्रीचक्रेण शक्तिभिश्च कालेन प्राणात्मतादिकमुपदिशत्यथषोड़शेत्यादिभिर्भवेदित्यन्तेन श्लोकशतरूपेण सप्तविंशेन पटलेन। तत्र अथ षोड़शेत्यादिभिरुपपादकानित्यन्तैस्त्रिभिः श्लोकैः पटलार्थमुपदिशति। तत्र कालेन प्राणता प्राणात्मककालत्वयेण तदात्मता। मातृकाभूतनाथाद्यैः आदिचान्तेविसर्जनीयरहितैः पञ्चाशद्भिर्मातृकाक्षरैः पञ्चभिर्भूतैः नवभिर्नाथैः आद्यशब्देन षट्त्रिंशत्तत्वादिभिश्च। श्रीचक्रेण नवचक्रात्मकेन शक्तिभिः तत्रस्थपञ्चनवतिभिरेकनवतिभिश्च। लवादीनान्तु कालस्य लवादित्रुट्यन्तानां मात्रायादुर्लक्ष्यत्वात् ज्ञातुमशक्यत्वात्तदीरितं स्वरूपमिति शेषः। तत्संख्याभिः श्वाससंख्याभिः घटिकाहोरात्रादिरूपसंजाताभिः। क्रमेण वक्ष्यमाणक्रमेण अहोरात्रस्येत्यस्य तत्संख्याभिरिति पूर्व्वत्रान्वयः। तद्व्याप्तिं श्वासात्मकत्वं उक्त्वा तेनान्यदूहयेदिति। भिन्न कर्त्तृत्वं स्वातन्त्र्यात्। अन्यश्वासवर्षादिकालरूपं विशेषात् गतिवृत्तौ श्वासानामिति शेषः। आन्तरात् भूतोदयाद्यात्मकात् वाह्यात् दक्षवामपार्श्वाद्युद्देशात् तत्तत्सिद्ध्युपपादकान् शुभाशुभसिद्धिकरान्। एतदुक्तं भवति षोड़शनित्यानां तदात्मकानां मातृकादीनां स्वरूपेण श्वासात्मकेन कालरूपेण सवाह्याभ्यन्तर-

मूलाधारोद्भवो वायुः प्राणाद्याख्यां समश्नुते ।
स तु पञ्चविधो भूतभेदादुद्भवदेशतः ॥ ४ ॥
नासायाः पुटयोः पार्श्वतुङ्गमध्याधरन्ध्रगाः ।
प्राणाग्नीलाम्बुखात्मानः पवनाः स्युर्यथाक्रमम् ॥ ५ ॥
गुरुकेतू भृगुकुजौ बुधार्कौ चन्द्रसूर्य्यजौ ।
क्रमाच्चतुर्षु भूतेषु व्योम सर्व्वात्मकं भवेत् ॥ ६ ॥
उभयस्थो भवेद्राहुश्चन्द्रसूर्य्यौ पुटक्रमात् ।
वामदक्षौ तयोस्तस्य प्रवेशो निर्गमस्तथा ॥ ७ ॥
जीवश्चन्द्रो रविः शून्यो भागः स्त्रीपुरुषौ तथा ।
पृथिवी सलिलं चन्द्रो रविरन्यत्त्रयं भवेत् ॥ ८ ॥

व्याप्तिद्वयं तेषां श्वासानां शुभाशुभफलप्रदानाद्वक्ष्यमाणात् बाह्याभ्यन्तरान् विशेषान् वक्ष्यतीत्युक्तं भवतीति ॥ ३ ॥

मूलाधारेत्यादिना यथाक्रममित्यन्तेन श्लोकद्वयेन श्वासानामुदयं तद्वृत्तिभेदात्तत्तत्संज्ञाप्राप्तिं तस्य भूतात्मकत्वेनोदयविशेषक्रमञ्चोपदिशति। तत्र मूलाधारोद्भवः नित्यानित्यापटलोक्तरूपमूलाधारप्रदेशसमुद्भवः। प्राणाद्याख्यां आदिशब्दस्त्वपानव्यानादीतरभेदविषयः। स प्रोक्तरूपो वायुरुद्भवदेशतः उपलब्धिस्थानेष्वनन्तरवक्ष्यमाणनासापुटद्वयगतेषु। पुटयोः रन्ध्रयोः। पार्श्वतुङ्गमध्याधोरन्ध्रगाः तिर्य्यगूर्द्ध्वदण्डाधरमध्यगतप्रवाहाः। विसर्गलोपः स्वातन्त्र्यात् ॥ ५ ॥

गुर्वित्यादिभिरीरितावित्यन्तैः सप्तभिः श्लोकैः श्वासानामुदयविशेषैः दृष्टस्थान पञ्चकालविशेषैश्चैकादशविधचन्द्रसूर्य्यात्मकत्वं राह्वात्मकत्वसहितमुपदिशति। तत्र गुरुकेत्वित्यादिना श्लोकेनैतदुक्तं भवति। उभयोरपि नासापुटयोः प्राणाग्नीलाम्बुरूपेषु चतुर्षु भूतोदयेषु वामदक्षिणपुटक्रमेण प्रवाहे प्रोक्तक्रमग्रहद्वन्द्वात्मकत्वं व्योमोदये राहुविधुग्रहाष्टकात्मकत्वं च भवतीति। उभयस्थः उभयपुटस्थः श्वासानामेवमेवं प्रकारप्रवाहकारणं गुरुमुखादवगन्तव्यम्। वामदक्षावित्यस्य पुटाविति पूर्व्वेणान्वयः। तयोः पुटयोरेकैकस्मिन्नपि। तथा चन्द्रसूर्य्यौ जीव

गृहेषु चन्द्रो गुर्व्विन्दुगुरुणा भास्करः परे ।
मातृकाश्च तथा विद्या स्वरव्यञ्जनभेदतः ॥ ६ ॥
अधः पृष्ठश्च चन्द्रः स्यादूर्द्धाग्रे दिनकृद्भवेत् ।
शरीरेऽपि घटेरूर्द्धं चन्द्राधो रविरीरितः ॥ १० ॥
अस्तीति वाक्यं चन्द्रः स्यान्नास्तीत्युक्तो रविः स्मृतः ।
शुक्लकृष्णौ तथा पक्षाविति चन्द्रा दशान्तराः ॥ ११ ॥
एवं सूर्य्या दश प्रोक्ता बाह्याभ्याञ्च यशस्विनि ।
एकादशविधौ चन्द्रभास्करौ सम्यगीरितौ ॥ १२ ॥
तयोश्चन्द्राः प्रीतिकरा भास्कराः क्लेशकारिणः ।
राहुः शून्यश्च सर्व्वत्र नाशाय भवति क्षणात् ॥ १३ ॥
सूर्य्येषु शस्तः सर्व्वत्र मृधभोजनमैथुनैः ।
संग्रहश्चान्यदखिलं चन्द्रे सिध्यत्ययत्नतः ॥ १४ ॥

भाग इत्युत्तरत्रान्वयः। तथा चन्द्रसूर्य्यावित्यर्थः। अन्यत्त्रयं अग्नोरव्योमात्मकं परे कुजसौरिकेत्वर्काः। तथा चन्द्रसूर्य्यौ ऊर्द्धाग्रे प्रथमाद्विवचनमेतत्। तथा चन्द्रसूर्य्यौ आन्तराः पक्षात्मकत्वविधुराः। एवमुक्तप्रकारेण। दशेत्यस्य आन्तरा इति पूर्व्वत्रान्वयः। वाह्याभ्यां शुक्लकृष्णरूपाभ्यां चन्द्रसूर्य्याभ्यां। चकारः समाहारे ॥ १२ ॥

तयोरित्यादिना श्लोकेन प्रोक्तचन्द्रसूर्य्यराहुशून्यानां सामान्यं फलमुपदिशति। तत्र भास्कराः शून्यरूपविधुराः ॥ १३ ॥

सूर्य्येष्वित्यादिभिः परमेश्वरीत्यन्तैश्चतुर्भिः श्लोकैः चन्द्रसूर्य्यराहुशून्येषु कर्त्तव्यानि कर्म्माणि प्रश्नप्रकारविशेषे फलविशेषादिकञ्चोपदिशति। तत्र सूर्य्येषु एकादशविधेषु। मृधभोजनमैथुनैः युद्धभोजनमैथुनैः सहेति शेषः। संग्रह इत्यस्य शस्त इति पूर्व्वत्रान्वयः। अन्यदखिलं शिष्टमङ्गलरूपकर्म्मजातं। चन्द्रे एकादशविधे। तथ्यं इष्टं वानिष्टं वा निश्चित्य भवतीत्युक्तं अस्तीति निश्चित्य नास्तीति निश्चित्य

जीवे तु कथितं तथ्यं मेध्यदर्शश्च १ सिध्यति ।
निश्चित्य भवतीत्युक्तमन्यथा चेत्तदन्यथा ॥ १५ ॥
अनिश्चिते विधौ कन्या गर्भप्रश्नेऽन्यतः पुमान् ।
शून्ये गर्भविपत्तिः स्यादित्याद्यूह्य वदेद्दृढम् ॥ १६ ॥
शून्ये नभसि राहौ च शुभान्येवाशुभान्यपि ।
शुभानि तत्र सर्वाणि नश्यन्ति परमेश्वरि ॥ १७ ॥
वामे वहति वायौ तु वदेद्देशिकशिष्ययोः ।
तत्स्थाने स्थापयित्वा तं तत्कर्णे कथयेन्मनुम् ॥ १८ ॥
अथवा जीवगस्थाने तत्कर्णे मन्त्रमादिशेत् ।
अन्यथा शून्यराहोस्तु नाशाय गुरुशिष्ययोः ॥ १९ ॥

चोक्तं कार्य्यं भवतीति यावत्। अन्यथा चेत्तदन्यथा शून्ये कथितं चेच्छून्यं भवति। अनिश्चये निश्चयरहिते गर्भप्रश्न इत्यस्य विशेषणं गर्भप्रश्न इति पदच्छेदः। अन्यतः सूर्य्ये शून्यव्यतिरिक्ते शून्ये शून्यरूपसूर्य्ये इत्यादीत्यत्रादिशब्दः निश्चितकार्य्यप्रश्न विषयः। एतदुक्तं भवति अनिश्चिते कार्य्यप्रश्ने चन्द्रश्चेद्यदयदभिमतं तद्भवति। सूर्य्यश्चेद्यदनभिमतं तच्च भवतीति। तत्र शून्यनभोराहुषु नश्यन्ति अशुभानि भवन्तीत्यर्थः ॥ १७ ॥

वामे इत्यादिना शिष्ययोरित्यन्तेन श्लोकद्वयेन गुरुणा शिष्यस्य मन्त्रोपदेश-कालविशेषं तदकरणे प्रत्यवायश्चोपदिशति। तत्र देशिकशिष्ययोरित्यस्य वामे इति पूर्व्वेणान्वयः। तत्स्थाने वामभागे। तं शिष्यं तत्कर्णे वामकर्णे। अथवा पक्षान्तरे जीवगस्थाने वामदक्षिणभेदतः। तत्कर्णे जीवकर्णे। अन्यथा उक्त प्रकारद्वयवैपरीत्येन। एतद्वामभागजीवस्थापनं नित्याविद्याविधुरसमस्तमन्त्रोपदेशे नित्यानान्तु सवाराहोकुरुकुल्लानां तत्तत्पूजाचक्रे स्वपुरस्थापनमस्माभिः पूर्व्वोक्तमेव। अत्र श्वासानां भूतादिस्वरूपोदयावगमनोपायान्तरमाराध्यमुखा-दवगन्तव्यम् ॥ १८ ॥

---

(१) मेध्यंदर्शश्च ः

षष्ट्या युतैस्तु विंशतैर्निश्वासैर्नाड़िका मता ।
तासां षष्ट्या दिनं पूर्णं तद्दिनं स्यात् पुनः पुनः ॥ २० ॥
एकस्मिंस्तु दिने श्वासाः सहस्राण्येकविंशतिः ।
षट्शतञ्च ततस्तेषां स्वरूपं शृणु सुन्दरि ॥ २१ ॥
आरभ्यार्कोदयं प्रातः सप्तत्या द्विशतं क्रमात् ।
प्राणाग्नौलाम्बुखानि स्युर्नवत्यानान्न संक्रमः ॥ २२ ॥
तत्राप्येवमतोनान्नाप्येवञ्च दशमक्रमात् ।
दिनमेवं व्रजेदादौ दर्शप्रतिपदं प्रति ॥ २३ ॥

षष्टेत्यादिना सुन्दरीत्यन्तेन श्लोकद्वयेन घटिकादिनरूपेण श्वासानां संख्याविशेषैः कालात्मकत्वोपदेशं तत्श्वासरूपप्रस्तावञ्च करोति। तत्र तासां नाड़िकानां। तद्दिनं नाड़िकाषष्ट्यात्मकं। पुनः पुनः परिवृत्तितः। तेषां श्वासानां। सुन्दरीति देवीसम्बुद्धिः ॥ २१ ॥

आरभ्येत्यादिभिर्भवन्ति द्वीत्यन्तैस्त्रिभिः श्लोकैः श्वासानां पुटयोः पूर्व्वपक्षप्रतिपदादिभूतेषूदयकालं पुटान्तरसंक्रमणकालक्रमं प्रोक्तनिगमनविपर्य्यासे फलञ्चोपदिशति। तत्र सप्तत्या द्विशतं प्रतिभूतं श्वासा इति। नवत्या श्वासैरन्यत्र पुटान्तरे संक्रमः पुटात् पुटसंक्रान्तकालः तदुभयपुटप्रवाहितया स राहुर्भवतीति यावत्। तत्रापि संक्रान्तपुटान्तरेऽपि। एवं प्रोक्तकालावधि। अतोऽन्यत्र संक्रान्तपुटान्तरसंक्रम इति पूर्व्वोक्तकालावधि। एवं प्रोक्तप्रकारपरिवृत्त्या पञ्चदशपरिवृत्तयः। आदौ युगानामिति शेषः। दर्शप्रतिपदं प्रति प्रतिदर्शं प्रतिप्रतिपदमित्यन्वयः प्रतिशुक्लप्रतिपदमित्यर्थः। सर्व्वेषां जीवानां। एतदुक्तं भवति युगादिषु शुक्लप्रतिपदि सूर्य्योदयमारभ्य एकस्मिन् पुटे पञ्चाशदधिकत्रयोदशशत ॥ १३५० ॥ श्वासैः पञ्चानां भूतानामुदयः। ततो नवत्या श्वासैः नाड्यन्तरे संक्रमः। एवञ्च चत्वारिंशदधिकचतुर्द्दशशत ॥ १४४० ॥ श्वासै रेकावृत्तिः। एवं पञ्चदशावृत्तिषु षट्शताधिकान्येकविंशतिसहस्राणि श्वासा भवन्तीति पर्य्यवसितोऽर्थः। युगादिषु शुक्लप्रतिपदि प्रातरर्कोदयं प्रारभ्य पुटयोर्व्वामदक्षिण-

२४

एवं क्रमेण सर्व्वेषां प्राणोदय उदीरितः।
एतत्क्रमविपर्य्यासादभव्यानि भवन्ति हि ॥ २४ ॥
बलाधिकाश्चरा वामे बलिनो दक्षिणे स्थिराः।
उभयतोभयात्मानः शुभाशुभपरीक्षणे ॥ २५ ॥
सार्द्धद्वाविंशतिश्वासक्रमाद्द्वादशराशयः।
तत्र सार्द्धचतुष्केण भूतानि स्युरिति क्रमात् ॥ २६ ॥
घटिकार्णेषु सर्वत्र वाय्वाद्यकान्तरोदये।
तत्तदर्णभवाः श्वासाः षष्ट्या त्रिशतमीरितम् ॥ २७ ॥

क्रमेण पञ्चभूतेषु प्रतिभूतं प्रोक्तकालावधि श्वासानां प्रवाहसंक्रमौ। प्रवाहसंक्रमादेवं पञ्चदशपरिवृत्तितो दिनमेकं भवति। अनन्तरदिने दक्षिणपुटमारभ्यैवं क्रमाद्भवति। एवं क्रमेण दर्शान्तं प्रतिदिनं पुटव्यत्यासारम्भक्रमेण सर्वेषां प्राणो-दयो भवत्येतत् क्रमविपर्य्यासे तु महान्त्यमङ्गलानि च भवन्तीति ॥ २४ ॥

बलाधिका इत्यादिना श्लोकेन श्वासानां वामदक्षिणोभयप्रवाहकाले चरादीनां वस्तूनां बलाधिक्यमुपदिशति। तत्र वामे वायौ प्रवहति दक्षिणे इत्यत्र प्राग्वत्। उभयत्रेति च प्राग्वत् शुभाशुभपरीक्षणे। चरस्थिरोभयात्मकानां कर्म्मणामिति शेषः ॥ २५ ॥

सार्द्धेत्यादिना श्लोकेन भूतानां राशीनाञ्च श्वासक्रमादन्योन्यंव्याप्याकारत्व-मुपदिशति। तत्र सार्द्धद्वाविंशतिश्वासक्रमाद्द्वादशराशयः प्रतिराश्युक्तसंख्य-(२२) श्वासक्रमात् सम्भूय राशिद्वादशकं (२७०) प्रागुक्तसंख्यश्वासात्मकं एकैकं भूतं भवतीत्यर्थः। तत्र राशिषु एकस्मिन्नेकस्मिन्निति शेषः। सार्द्धचतु-ष्केण श्वासानामिति शेषः। एतदुक्तं भवति प्रत्येकं प्रोक्तसंख्यश्वासात्मकेषु द्वादशसु राशिष्वेकस्मिन्नेकस्मिन् राशौ प्रतिभूतं प्रोक्तसंख्यश्वासात्मकानि च भूत्वा भूतानि समुद्यन्तीति ॥ २६ ॥

घटिकेत्यादिना अक्षरैरित्यन्तेन श्लोकद्वयेन प्रतिदिनमुदयघटिकाक्षराणि तद्-घटिकाक्षराणां श्वासात्मकत्वं तेषु श्वासेषु भूताक्षरोदयक्रमञ्चोपदिशति। तत्र

तेषु तद्भूतवर्णानां दशानामादितो दश।
सम्प्रावृत्त्या ततः शेषाः प्राणाग्नीलाम्बुखाक्षरैः॥ २८॥
संख्याभिर्व्वासनाव्याप्तिं श्वासानां शृणु सुन्दरि।
यया विहितया मन्त्री सदा दर्शनवान् (१) भवेत्॥ २९॥

सर्व्वत्र सर्वेषु दिनेषु वाय्वादि एकान्तरा उदये इति पदच्छेदः। एतदुक्तं भवति सर्वेषु युगदिनेषु घटिकार्णेषु विषये एकैकान्तरितं। अतएव य इति वायव्याक्षरपञ्चकं दिवसपञ्चकक्रमादुदयघटिकाक्षरत्वं प्रतिपद्यत इति। तत्तद्वर्णभवाः तत्तद्घटिकार्णात्मकाः। एतदुक्तं भवति पूर्वोक्तप्रकारा घटिकात्मकाः श्वासास्तत्तद्घटिकात्मका वर्णरूपाश्च भवन्तीति। तेषु श्वासेषु प्रोक्तषष्ट्युत्तरत्रिशतसंख्येषु तद्भूतवर्णानां घटिकाक्षरेषु प्रत्यक्षरं तत्तत्प्रागभूतवर्णानां दशश्वासा इति शेषः। शेषाः पञ्चाशदधिकशतत्रयसंख्याः। एतदुक्तं भवति पूर्वोक्तोदयाक्षरादि षष्ट्यात्मकाक्षरात्मिकासु घटिकासु प्रतिघटिकं षष्ट्युत्तरत्रिशतसंख्येषु श्वासेष्वादितो दशश्वासास्तत्तद्घटिकाप्रागाक्षरप्रागभूताक्षरवर्णानां दशानां तदादितत्पूर्व्वान्तानां स्वरूपेण समुद्यन्ति। शेषास्तु पञ्चाशदुत्तरत्रिशतसंख्याः श्वासा एवं दशदशक्रमेण तदनन्तरभूतादितद्भूतान्तानां पञ्चानां प्रतिभूतं दशदशाक्षररूपाणां स्वरूपेण सम्प्रावृत्त्योद्यन्ति। एवंभूते सति प्रतिघटिकं तत्तदक्षरप्रागभूताक्षराणां दशानामष्टावावृत्तयः शेषभूतचतुष्टयाक्षराणां सम्प्रावृत्तयश्चैवं क्रमेणैकैकघटिकाक्रमेण पञ्चभूतात्मकवर्णात्मिका भवतीति॥ २८॥

संख्याभिरित्यादिभिरीश्वरीत्यन्तैश्चतुर्भिः श्लोकैः प्रस्तावादिपुरःसरमहोरात्रादि श्वासानां प्रोक्तसंख्यानां कालनित्यादिश्रीचक्रस्थप्रथमान्तानामेकादशविधानामप्यवान्तरव्याप्तिं समव्याप्तिं तदनुसन्धानवैभवञ्चोपदिशति। तत्र संख्याभिः श्वासानामित्युत्तरत्रान्वयः। वासनाव्याप्तिं वासनाश्च व्याप्तिं च वासनात्मिकाव्याप्तिमित्यर्थः। वक्ष्यमाणानामेकादशविधानामिति शेषः। सुन्दरीति देवीसम्बुद्धिः। यया व्याप्त्या नित्यातद्व्याप्तिविद्यानां पञ्चविंशपटलप्रोक्तसंख्यानां पूर्व्वमहोरात्र-श्वाससंख्यानां मध्ये एकशः प्रतिविद्यमेकैकश्वास इत्यर्थः। ततः पूर्वोक्तश्वास-

---

(१) भजनवान्।

नित्याविद्याप्तितत्त्वानां संख्याः स्युः पूर्वमेकशः ।
ततो दिनार्णाः सन्ध्याः स्युस्ततश्च घटिकार्णकाः ॥ ३० ॥
राशयो द्वादश ततो ग्रहा भूतानि पञ्च वै ।
मातृकाश्चापि पञ्चाशच्छ्रीचक्रस्थाश्च शक्तयः ॥ ३१ ॥

संख्यायाः परमित्यर्थः । दिनार्णाः पूर्णमण्डलार्णाः । सन्ध्याः सन्ध्यात्रयप्रातिकषष्टिसंख्याः । पूर्णमण्डलश्वाससंख्यायाः परमिति शेषः । ततस्तत्संख्यायाः परं । घटिकार्णकाः षष्टिसंख्या इति शेषः । द्वादशराशयो घटिकार्णसंख्यायाः परमिति शेषः । ततः राशिसंख्यातः । ग्रहाः नव भूतानि पञ्चसंख्यातः । मातृका भूतसंख्यातः परमिति शेषः । पञ्चाशद्विसर्जनीयविधुरा वर्णा इति शेषः । शक्तयः मातृकासंख्यातः परमिति शेषः । सैका नवतयः आयुधाष्टकस्य मिथुनचतुष्टयत्वेन गृह्यमाणत्वान्मध्यदेवताविधुरत्वाच्च । देवी ललिता सर्वात्मना श्वाससमष्टिरूपेण । एतदुक्तं भवति अहोरात्रात्मकानां षट्शतोत्तरैकविंशतिसहस्रसंख्यानामादितः कालनित्यारूपाः षट्त्रिंशदधिकसप्तशतोत्तरविंशतिसहस्रसंख्याः श्वासा भवन्ति । तच्छिष्टेषु चतुःषष्ट्यधिकाष्टशतसंख्येषु श्वासेषु षट्सप्तत्यधिकपञ्चशतसंख्यश्वासाः पूर्णमण्डलवर्णरूपा भवन्ति । तच्छिष्टेष्वष्टाशीत्यधिकद्विशतसंख्येषु श्वासेषु सन्ध्यात्रयरूपनाथतत्त्वनित्यात्मकरूपा एकषष्टिश्वासा भवन्ति । तच्छिष्टसप्तविंशत्यधिकद्विशतश्वासेषु षष्टिश्वासा अहोरात्रषष्टिकाक्षररूपा भवन्ति । तच्छिष्टेषु सप्तषष्ट्यधिकशतश्वासेषु द्वादश श्वासा द्वादश राश्यात्मका भवन्ति । तच्छिष्टेषु पञ्चपञ्चाशदुत्तरशतश्वासेषु नवश्वासा नवग्रहात्मका भवन्ति । तच्छिष्टेषु षट्चत्वारिंशदधिकशतश्वासेषु पञ्चश्वासाः पञ्चभूतात्मका भवन्ति । तच्छिष्टेष्वेकचत्वारिंशदुत्तरशतश्वासेषु पञ्चाशच्छ्वासाः विसर्जनीयरहिता मातृकाक्षरात्मका भवन्ति । तच्छिष्टा एकनवतिसंख्य श्वासाः प्रोक्तक्रमसंख्यश्रीचक्रस्य शक्तिरूपा भवन्ति । एवं क्रमेणाहोरात्रात्मकश्वासाः समष्टिरूपा (१) परिच्छिन्नविग्रहविश्वरूपा ललितात्मका भवन्ति । अत्र पूज्यपादमुखादवगतोऽर्थस्तदाज्ञया लिख्यते यथा—अहोरात्रोक्तसंख्याः श्वासाः पञ्चाशदक्षरात्मिकाया मातृकाया द्वात्रिंशदधिकचतुःशतावृत्त्या तदात्मका भवन्ति । ते

---

(१) समष्टिरूपा ।

सैका नवतयः प्रोक्ता देवी सर्व्वात्मना स्थिता ।
एवं विद्यां वासनां यो भावयेत् परमेश्वरि ॥ ३२ ॥
नाड़ीचक्रस्य मर्म्माणि देहान्तर्म्मरुतां क्रियाम् ।
योगाभ्यासं तदङ्गैश्च स्वेच्छोत्क्रान्तिविधानकम् ॥ ३३ ॥
परकायप्रवेशञ्च योगसिद्धस्य लक्षणम् ।
आसन्नमृत्युचिह्नानि कथयामि यथाक्रमम् ॥ ३४ ॥
प्राक्प्रोक्तमूलाधारस्य मध्यगा त्रासमध्यतः ।
सुषुम्ना पृष्ठवंशाख्यवीणादण्डस्य मध्यगा ॥ ३५ ॥
मूलादिब्रह्मरन्ध्रान्ता नासाग्राद्द्वादशाङ्गुले
तदग्रात् पायुगा प्रोक्तालम्बुषाख्या तु नाड़िका ॥ ३६ ॥

पुनरपि विंशत्युत्तरशतत्रयाधिकचतुःसहस्रपरिवृत्तितः पञ्चभूतात्मका भवन्ति । पुनरपि ते नवनाथश्रीचक्रग्रहाणां चतुःशतोत्तरद्विसहस्रावृत्त्या तत्तदात्मका भवन्ति । ते पुनरपि षट्त्रिंशत्तत्त्वानां षट्शतावृत्त्या तदात्मका भवन्ति । ते पुनरपि षोड़शनित्यात्मकस्वराणां पञ्चाशदुत्तरशतत्रयाधिकसहस्रसंख्यावृत्त्या तदात्मका भवन्ति । ते पुनरपि षष्टिघटिकाक्षराणां षष्ठ्युत्तरत्रिशतावृत्त्या तदात्मका भवन्ति। ते पुनरपि द्वादशराशीनां अष्टशतोत्तरसहस्रावृत्त्या तदात्मका भवन्ति। ते पुनरपि श्रीचक्रस्थानां षण्णवतिशक्तीनां पञ्चविंशत्युत्तरशतद्वयावृत्त्या तदात्मका भवन्तीति । अत्रान्यद्रहस्यं पूज्यपादमुखादवगन्तव्यम् ॥ ३२ ॥

नाड़ीत्यादिना यथाक्रममित्यन्तेन श्लोकद्वयेन पटलशेषार्थानुपदिशति । तत्र मर्माणि स्थानानीति शेषः । स्वेच्छोत्क्रान्तिर्नाम स्वेच्छया प्राणपरित्यागः । परकायप्रवेशं मृतशरीरे स्वजीवप्रवेशनं तस्मात् स्वशरीरे तत्प्रवेशनं वा ॥ ३४ ॥

प्रागित्यादिभिः परेत्यन्तैर्दशभिः श्लोकैर्नाड़ीचक्रस्वरूपं तत्र कुण्डलिनी-स्थितिश्चोपदिशति । तत्र प्राक्प्रोक्तमूलाधारस्य नित्यानित्यापटलप्रोक्तस्य । मध्यगा मणौ सूत्रवन्मध्यरन्ध्रस्यूतेत्यर्थः । ब्रह्मरन्ध्रान्ता ब्रह्मरन्ध्रावसाना सुषुम्नेति पूर्व्व-

वस्त्राग्रादुत्थिता नाडी कुहूर्नाम ध्वजान्तिका ।
तद्वामदक्षपार्श्वाभ्यां सविश्वोदरवारणे ॥ ३७ ॥
जठरान्ता सर्वगा च प्रोक्ते तद्वदनन्तरे ।
हस्तिजिह्वायशस्विन्यौ तत्तदङ्गुष्ठगे पदोः ॥ ३८ ॥
तथैवेडापिङ्गले च नासारन्ध्रद्वयान्तगे ।
गान्धारी च तथा पूषा नेत्रद्वयगते क्रमात् ॥ ३९ ॥
तथा कर्णगते शङ्खपयस्विन्यौ क्रमेण वै ।
सरस्वती तु या नाडी सा तु जिह्वाग्रगामिनी ॥ ४० ॥
एवं चतुर्दश प्रोक्ता नाड्यो देहे प्रधानकाः ।
तासां सन्धिषु तत्सन्धिष्वेवं नाड्यः स्थितास्तनौ ॥ ४१ ॥

वान्वयः । नासाग्रात् द्वादशाङ्गुले नासाग्रमारभ्य द्वादशाङ्गुलमानावधिके स्थाने ब्रह्मरन्ध्रमित्यर्थः । तदग्रात् सुषुम्नारम्भपुरोभागस्थानमारभ्य पायुगा गुदरन्ध्रावसाना । वस्त्राग्रात् मूलाधाररूपवस्त्राग्रकोणात् ध्वजान्तिका मेहनपर्य्यवसाना । तद्वामदक्षपार्श्वाभ्यां कुहूसंज्ञिकाया नाड्या इति शेषः । जठरान्ता विश्वोदरा जठरमध्यान्ता सर्व्वगा अधश्चोर्द्ध्वप्रसृता सर्व्वगा वारणा । प्रोक्ते इत्यस्य विश्वोदरवारणेति पूर्व्ववान्वयः । तद्वदनन्तरे तदनन्तरवामदक्षस्थिते । तत्तदङ्गुष्ठगे पदोः वामदक्षयोः पादयोस्तत्तदङ्गुष्ठावसानके भवत इत्यर्थः । तथैव तदनन्तर वामदक्षपार्श्वारम्भतः नासारन्ध्रद्वयान्तगे । एतदुक्तं भवति मूलाधारवस्त्रमध्यस्थसुषुम्नाया वामपार्श्वमारभ्य प्रोत्थितवक्राकारा ध्वजमूले सुषुम्नाश्लेषतो दक्षिणभागं गत्वा पुनस्तत्रापि वक्रगत्या नाभिप्रदेशे पुनरपि सुषुम्नाश्लेषतो वामभागवक्रगत्या हृदये भूयोऽपि सुषुम्नाश्लेषदक्षिणभागाष्टकाश्रयवक्रगत्या कण्ठदेशे पुनरपि सुषुम्नाश्लेषतो वामांशजत्रुमध्योर्द्ध्ववक्रगत्या ब्रह्मरन्ध्रप्रदेशे पुनरपि सुषुम्नाग्राश्लेषतो दक्षिणवक्रगत्याधोमुखा सुषुम्ना भ्रूमध्यप्रदेशे सुषुम्नाश्लेषतो वामनासारन्ध्रपर्य्यवशायिनी इड़ासंज्ञा नाड़ी भवति । पिङ्गला तु प्राग्वद्दक्षिणभागारब्धा दक्षिणवामदक्षिणवामविनिमयक्रमवक्रगत्या सुषुम्नोर्द्ध्वश्लेषपर्व्व-

तासां प्रधाननाड़ीनां संख्या सार्द्धत्रिलक्षकम्।
अप्रधानाः शिरा देहे त्वसंख्या याभिरेव वै ॥ ४२ ॥
वेष्टितैर्व्याप्तैर्नरैः सर्वैः स्वकीयैरक्षया निशम्।
नाड्यः सुषिरा रक्तमरुत्पूर्णाश्च सर्व्वगाः ॥ ४३ ॥
सुषुम्नामध्यगा वज्रा नाड़ी तन्मध्यगा परा।
चित्राभिधाना तन्मध्ये स्थिता सा कुण्डली परा ॥ ४४ ॥

मर्म्मध्यगा दक्षिणनासिकान्ता च भवतीति। तथा अनन्तरवामदक्षिणारम्भतः नेत्रद्वयगते तत्तन्नेत्रद्वयपर्य्यवसिते तथा तदनन्तरवामारम्भतः कर्णगते तत्तत् कर्णपर्य्यवसिते। सरस्वती पूर्वोक्तनाड़ीद्वयावशिष्टमध्यस्था नासारम्भतः जिह्वाग्रगामिनी जिह्वाग्रपर्य्यवसिता॥ तासां चतुर्द्दशानां तत्सन्धिषु प्रधाननाड़ीनां सन्धिषु। तासां प्रधानचतुर्द्दशनाड़ीसम्ख्यारम्भानां (१) तत्सम्ख्याख्यानाञ्च सार्द्धत्रिलक्षकं पञ्चाशत्सहस्राधिकत्रिलक्षमित्यर्थः। याभिः प्रधानाभिः अप्रधानाभिश्च। नाड्यो नाड़िकाः प्रोक्तास्ताः सर्व्वाः सुषिराः रन्ध्रवत्यः। सुषुम्नामध्यगा सुषुम्नामध्यरन्ध्रान्तरालगता। तन्मध्यगा वज्रानाड़ीरन्ध्रान्तरालगता। तन्मध्ये स्थिता चित्रानाड्यन्तःस्थिता सा त्रिंशे पटले चतुःषष्टितमश्लोकादिभिः षड्भिः श्लोकैर्वक्ष्यमाणरूपा। भूमौ त्रिकोणमालिख्य तद्वहिस्त्र्यङ्गुले च त्रिकोणं लिखित्वा तयोर्मध्ये तिर्य्यक् द्वादशरेखा विलिख्य सर्व्वमध्ये सुषुम्नाया आद्यक्षरं तस्याधोभागे अलम्बुषाया आद्यक्षरं तत्पूर्व्वभागे तयोर्मध्यकोष्ठे कुह्वा आद्यक्षरं एवं प्रादक्षिण्येन कोष्ठान्तरालेषु च नाड़ीनामाद्यक्षराणि वायुपो पूषशं संज्ञां इहयि वापपि पूयसाशङ्गं पूर्वोक्तैः सह चतुर्दशाक्षराणि लिखित्वा प्रदर्शयेदिति सम्प्रदायः। अत्र संग्रहश्लोकास्त्रयो लिख्यन्ते।

सुषुम्नालम्बुषामध्ये कुहू्र्वारणसंज्ञिका।
पयस्विनी पिङ्गला तु सुषुम्ना सुयशस्विनी॥
सरस्वती शङ्खिनी च गान्धारीड़ा द्विपास्यगा।
विश्वोदरेति नाड्यः स्युरयं तासां स्थितिक्रमः॥
रन्ध्रपायुध्वजाशू षपन्नासानेत्रकर्णगाः।
जिह्वाकर्णाक्षिनासाङ्घ्रि जठरान्ताः प्रदक्षिणात्॥ इति ॥ ४४ ॥

---

(१) नाड़ीसंख्यारम्भाणां इति, नाडी सम्यवस्थानाम् इति च पाठान्तरम्॥

मर्म्माण्यङ्गुष्ठगुल्फाङ्घ्रिपृष्ठजङ्घाख्यजानुषु ।
ऊरुसीवनिकामुष्कमेढ्रनाभिषु पार्श्वयोः ॥ ४५ ॥
हृदयस्तनकण्ठांसकृकाटीकर्णमूर्द्धसु ।
शङ्खयोः फालगुनासादिमध्यान्तास्यकपोलतः ॥ ४६ ॥
अष्टत्रिंशदिति प्रोक्तान्येषु वायोस्तु धारणात् ।
परकायप्रवेशश्च स्वेच्छोत्क्रान्तिश्च सिध्यति ॥ ४७ ॥
दशानामपि वायूनां देहस्थानां क्रियाः शृणु ।
ऊर्द्ध्वाधोगमनासक्तौ प्राणापानौ सदा तनौ ॥ ४८ ॥
नाग उद्गारकृत् प्रोक्तः क्षुत्कृत् कृकरकस्तथा ।
देवदत्तो जृम्भणकृत् रवकृच्च धनञ्जयः ॥ ४९ ॥
कूर्म्म उन्मेषकृत् प्रोक्त उदानोऽपि तथा हिक्कृत् ।
समानवायुः कायाग्निं सम्धुक्षयति पाचितुम् ॥ ५० ॥
व्यानाख्यो रसमादाय व्यापयेदखिलां तनुम् ।
एषां दशानामंशास्तु मरुतां स्युरनन्तकाः ॥ ५१ ॥

मर्माणीत्यादिभिः सिध्यतीत्यन्तैस्त्रिभिः श्लोकैरष्टत्रिंशत्मर्मस्थानानि तेषु वायुधारणफलं चोपदिशति। तत्र सीवनिका मुष्कपायुरन्ध्रयोर्मध्यगता नाड़ी कृकाटी कर्णोपरिभागस्थोन्नतास्थिपार्श्वप्रदेशः। शङ्खयोः भालपार्श्वोन्नतास्थ्नोः। कपोलतः कपोलेषु अष्टत्रिंशत् एतेष्वष्टत्रिंशन्मर्मसु द्वन्द्वस्थानानि षड्विंशति। शेषस्थानानि द्वादश सम्भूयाष्टत्रिंशन्मर्माणि। एषु मर्मसु ॥ ४७॥

दशानामित्यादिभिः कल्पते इत्यन्तैः पञ्चभिः श्लोकैस्तत्प्रस्तावपुरःसरं देहस्थानां दशानां वायूनां नामानि तत्क्रियास्तदनुभावश्चोपदिशति। तत्र ऊर्द्ध्वाधोगमनासक्तौ परस्परं शृङ्खलावत् बद्धस्वरूपाविककाले ईर्षयेति शेषः। प्राणापानौ प्राणापानाख्यौ। नाग इति वायुनाम कृकर इति च देवदत्तो धनञ्जयश्चेति। कूर्म्म इति वायुनाम। उदान इति हिक्कृत् उन्मेषनिमेषकृत्। समान-

तेषां प्रसाराद्देहस्य समीचीना स्थितिर्भवेत् ।
वैलोम्ये विकृताङ्गत्वाल्लोकैर्नाशाय कल्प्यते ॥ ५२ ॥
जीवात्माभेदरूपेण मनसा परमात्मनः ।
योगो योगस्तु विज्ञेयस्तस्याङ्गानि तथाष्ट वै ॥ ५३ ॥
यमोथ नियमः पश्चादासनं तदनन्तरम् ।
प्राणायामस्तथा प्रत्याहारस्तदनु धारणम् ॥ ५४ ॥
ध्यानं समाधिरित्युक्तान्यष्टाङ्गानि यथाक्रमात् ।
कथयामि शृणु प्राज्ञे यैर्मर्त्त्यो मत्समो भवेत् ॥ ५५ ॥
तत्प्रत्यूहाः षडाख्याताः कामक्रोधौ ततस्तथा ।
लोभमोहौ मानमदौ वह्निवत् सर्वनाशकाः ॥ ५६ ॥

वायुः समानाख्योवायुः । कायाग्निं जठराग्निं यद्वक्ष्यधःस्थं इत्यर्थः । पाचितुं भुक्ताहारं । व्यानाख्यः वायुरिति शेषः । रसं भुक्ताहारस्येति शेषः । अंशाः सम्भवाः । प्रसारात् यथावत् संचारानुकूल्येन । वैलोम्ये अयथातथा सञ्चारप्रातिकूल्ये: विकृताङ्गत्वात् अहितादिभिः ॥ ५२ ॥

जीवात्मेत्यादिना श्लोकेन योगनिर्वचनोपदेशं तदङ्गप्रस्तावञ्च करोति । तत्र जीवात्माभेदरूपेण एतदेकं पदं मनसा सहेति शेषः । परमात्मनः सन्मात्रस्फुरत्तारूपस्य चित इत्यर्थः । योगः तादात्म्यसम्बन्धः । तस्य योगस्य । एतदुक्तं भवति भेदरूपवत् प्रतीयमानानां जीवमनःपरमात्मनां इदन्ताविलयनरूपमैक्यं योग इति ॥ ५३ ॥

यमेत्यादिना भवेदित्यन्तेन श्लोकद्वयेन योगस्याष्टाङ्गनामानि तत्स्वरूपप्रस्तावं तदनुभावञ्चोपदिशति । तत्र तथा समुच्चये । अष्टाङ्गानीत्यस्य काकाक्षिवदुक्तानीति पूर्व्वत्र कथयामीत्युत्तरत्रान्वयः । कथयामि स्वरूपत इति शेषः । यैः अष्टाङ्गस्वरूपैः । मत्समः मन्मयः शिवरूपः ॥ ५५ ॥

तत्प्रत्यूहेत्यादिना यमइत्यन्तेनाध्यर्द्धेन श्लोकेन प्रत्यूहान् यमस्वरूपञ्चोपदिशति । तत्र तत्प्रत्यूहाः योगप्रत्यूहाः । सर्व्वनाशकाः स्वरूपलाभप्रत्यूहरूपत्वात् । आत्मापरोक्षप्रत्यूहकर्मणस्तु यमो यमः । स्वरूपापरोक्षप्रत्यूहभूतानां प्रोक्तानां कामादीनां षण्णां उद्योगेभ्य उपरमणं यमः यमाख्यमङ्गम् ॥ ५६ ॥

आत्मापरोक्षप्रत्यूहकर्म्मणस्तु यमो यमः ।
तथैकादशरूपः स्यान्नियमः परिकीर्त्तितः ॥ ५७ ॥
अहिंसा सत्यमास्तिक्यमार्जवं समता धृतिः ।
क्षमा दया त्रिधाशौचं सन्तोषो गुरुसेवनम् ॥ ५८ ॥
पद्मस्वस्तिकवीराख्यभद्राण्युक्तानि वै क्रमात् ।
आसनानि मनःस्थैर्य्यकरणे साधकानि वै ॥ ५९ ॥
ऊर्वोरुपरि विन्यस्य व्यत्यासात् पादयोस्तले ।
वाह्यपार्श्वद्वयस्पर्शात्तत् पद्मासनमीरितम् ॥ ६० ॥
तथा तयोरधोभागतदन्तः पार्श्वसङ्गमात् ।
स्वस्तिकाकारतः प्रोक्तं तद्भद्रासनमीश्वरि ॥ ६१ ॥

तथैकादशेत्यादिना सेवनमित्यन्तेनार्द्धाधेन एकश्लोकेनैकादशविधनियमस्वरूपमुपदिशति । तत्र तथा यथा यमः तथा नियमः नियमाख्यमङ्गं । समता लाभहान्योः । त्रिधा शौचं मनोवाक्कायरूपतः । सन्तोषः पूर्णता ॥५८॥

पद्मेत्यादिभिः स्मृतमित्यन्तैश्चतुर्भिः श्लोकैर्नामपुरःसरमष्टविधान्यासनस्वरूपाण्युपदिशति । तत्र मनस्थैर्य्यकरणे योगाभ्यास इति शेषः । साधकानि उपकारकानि । ऊर्वोरुपरोत्यादिना श्लोकेनैतदुक्तं भवति वामपादतलकनिष्ठासम्बन्धिपार्श्वस्य दक्षिणोरुमध्योपरि दक्षिणपादतलकनिष्ठासम्बन्धिपार्श्वस्य वाम-जङ्घोपर्य्याक्रमणेन वामोरुमध्योपरि चैवं व्यत्यासक्रमात् विन्यासेन वामजङ्घाया दक्षिणजङ्घोपर्य्याक्रमणेन च पूर्व्ववद्विन्यासाद्द्विविधं पद्मासनं भवतीति । तथा द्विविधव्यत्यासक्रमात् । तयोरूर्व्वोः तदन्तःपार्श्वसङ्गमात् । एतदुक्तं भवति वामपादतलाङ्गुष्ठसम्बन्धिदक्षिणोरोरधोभागस्य दक्षिणपादतलाङ्गुष्ठसम्बन्धिपार्श्वोपरि वामोरोरधोभागस्य च प्राग्वत् व्यत्यासविन्यासात् पुनः पूर्व्ववत् जङ्घाद्वयोपर्य्यन्योन्याक्रमणविन्यासात् च पादतलद्वयाङ्गुष्ठसम्बन्धिपार्श्वान्योन्याक्रमेण विन्यासाच्च द्विविधं स्वस्तिकासनं भवतीति । तलान्त इत्यादिना श्लोकेनैतदुक्तं भवति एकं पादमूर्व्वोरन्यतमस्याधोभागे स्वतलाङ्गुष्ठसम्बन्धिपार्श्वेन सङ्गतं कुर्य्यात् । पुनश्च वामदक्षिणव्यत्यासेनैव कुर्य्यात् । तेनैतद्द्विविधं भद्रासनं

तलान्तः पार्श्वगं कुर्य्यादेकमन्यन्तु बाह्यगम् ।
ऊर्वोरधस्तथोर्द्ध्वे च द्विधा भद्रासनं स्मृतम् ॥ ६२ ॥
व्यत्यस्ततलयोरूर्द्धसंस्पर्शादुच्चजङ्घयोः ।
पादयोर्जानुदेशे वै वीराख्यं योगपट्टतः ॥ ६३ ॥
प्राणायामस्त्रिधा प्रोक्त उत्तमाधममध्यमाः ।
लाघवो भूतलत्याग उत्तमे चित्तनिर्वृतिः ॥ ६४ ॥
सर्व्वाङ्गे स्वेदसंवृद्धिरधमे मध्यमे तथा ।
सर्व्वाङ्गकम्पनं प्रोक्तमभ्यासात् कालसंयुतात् ॥ ६५ ॥
तेष्युत्तमगुणा भूयुरभ्यासात् कालयोगतः ।
तस्मात् समभ्यसेत् प्रातः सायञ्च नियमेन वै ॥ ६६ ॥
वामेन नासारन्ध्रेण पूरयेदमृतात्मना ।
स्मरन्नम्बु मरुत् पश्चाद्दक्षिणेनापसारयेत् ॥ ६७ ॥

भवतीति। सम्भूयाष्टावासनानि। अत्र द्विधेत्युक्त्या सर्वासनद्वैविध्यमिति सम्प्रदायः ॥ ६२ ॥

व्यत्यस्तेत्यादिना श्लोकेनैतदुक्तं भवति जङ्घोर्द्धसंस्पर्शादूर्द्धभूतं जङ्घयोर्व्यत्यस्ततलकनिष्ठासम्बन्धिपार्श्वाक्रान्तभूतलयोः पादयोर्जानुदेशे स्वान्तराधिमध्ये च योगपट्टबन्धनाज्जान्वोरुपरि प्रसारितबाहुदण्डप्रकोष्ठविन्यासात् पुनःप्राग्वज्जङ्घाद्वयबाह्याभ्यन्तरस्पर्शविन्यासभेदाच्च द्विविधं वीरासनं भवतीति ॥ ६३ ॥

प्राणायामेत्यादिभिस्तुरीयत इत्यन्तैः पञ्चभिः श्लोकैः प्राणायामभेदांस्तद्ध्यानं तस्य स्वरूपञ्चोपदिशति। तत्र लाघवः देहस्येति शेषः। भूतलत्यागः तुलाघटयोरेकैकस्यां पूर्वतः स्वसमानप्रमाणानि वस्तूनि निक्षिप्यान्यस्यां स्थित्वा प्राणायामेण स्वघटोन्नतिरिति सम्प्रदायार्थः। उत्तमे प्राणायामे इति शेषः। अधमे प्राणायामे मध्यमे प्राणायामे इति शेषः। अभ्यासात् कालसंयुतात् चिरकालकृतादभ्यासादित्यर्थः। उत्तममध्यमाधमाः भूयुरिति

एवं सुसाधिते पश्चाद्द्वात्रिंशन्मात्रयाहरेत्।
धारयेत्तच्चतुःषष्ट्या रेचयेत्तत्तुरीयतः॥ ६८॥
कम्पश्च पुलकानन्दौ वैमल्यस्थैर्य्यलाघवाः।
तद्वत् कान्तिप्रकाशौ च योगसिद्धस्य लक्षणम्॥ ६९॥
मूलाधारे मनः कृत्वा वायुनापूर्य्य मूलतः।
नाड़ीचक्रान्तरं नीत्वा सर्व्वाङ्गानि च चारयेत्॥ ७०॥
एवं संसाधिते वायावष्टविंशत्सु मर्म्मसु।
धारयन् वारयेदिच्छावशेनाङ्गानि सर्वतः॥ ७१॥
तथाधारगतं कृत्वा मनः पवनसंयुतम्।
रसाम्बुदाहव्याप्तस्वैः सहंसैर्व्यापयेत्तनुम्॥ ७२॥

दिव्यत्वात् भूयासुरित्यर्थः। समभ्यसेत् प्राणायामान्। अम्बु वकारं मरुद्दिव्यत्वान्मरुतमित्यर्थः। अस्यार्थद्वयं विद्यते एकदा यकाराक्षरं स्मरन्निति पूर्व्वेणान्वयः। अन्यदा श्वासं अपसारयेदित्युत्तरेणान्वयः। रेचयेदित्यर्थः। मात्रा नाम स्वाङ्गुलीस्फोटाष्टककालः। चतुःषष्ट्या मात्राभिरिति शेषः। तुरीयतः षोड़शमात्राभिः॥ ६८॥

कम्प इत्यादिना श्लोकेन योगसिद्धलक्षणमुपदिशति। वैमल्यस्थैर्य्यलाघवाः वैमल्यं मनोविषयं स्थैर्य्यलाघवे देहविषये। प्रकाश इति स्वतेजसो वह्निः प्रकाशनं वीजादिवत्॥ ६९॥

मूलाधारेत्यादिना श्लोकेन प्रत्याहारस्वरूपमुपदिशति। तत्र मूलतः मूलाधारात्॥ ७०॥

एवमित्यादिना श्लोकेन धारणस्वरूपमुपदिशति। तत्र चारयेत् वायुमिति शेषः। इच्छावशेन स्वाभिमताङ्गधारणवशेन॥ ७१॥

तथेत्यादिभिर्व्रजेदित्यन्तैर्नवभिः श्लोकैर्धारणासिद्धिफलानि समाधिस्वरूपसहितान्युपदिशति। तत्र तथेत्यादिना भुवीत्यन्तेन श्लोकद्वयेन समाधिना त्रिकालज्ञानादिसिद्ध्युपायमुपदिशति। तथा प्राग्वत्। रसाम्बुदाहव्याप्तस्वैः सहंसैः लकारवकाररेफयकारहकारैः प्रत्यक्षरं विन्दुसहितैः सहेति शेषः।

एवं तैरचरैर्देहे वायुना तन्मयीकृते ।
त्रिकालज्ञो विशुद्धात्मा सुखी जीवेच्चिरं भुवि ॥ ७३ ॥
स्वेच्छाचारी व्योमगश्च व्रजेद्देवैश्च सङ्गमम् ।
स्वेच्छया देहमध्यस्थः कुड्मगृहगतो यथा ॥ ७४ ॥
एवं संसिद्धयोगस्तु स्वेच्छया देहमात्मनः ।
प्राणानाकृष्य मध्यस्थसुषुम्नारन्ध्रतस्तथा ॥ ७५ ॥
ब्रह्मरन्ध्राद्विनिर्गत्य भूयात् सर्व्वात्मनात्मवान् ।
अथवोत्तरसंप्रोक्तचूर्णास्वादनतो वशी ॥ ७६ ॥
विरक्तचित्तः स्वं देहं तेनोपायेन सन्त्यजेत् ।
स्वेच्छोत्क्रान्तिरिति प्रोक्ता योगयुक्तात्मनां प्रिये ॥ ७७ ॥

व्यापयेत् पवनमिति शेषः । तन्मयीकृते ध्यातृध्यानध्येयविभेदसमाधिना तत्तद्भूतमयीकृते । एतदुक्तं भवति प्रागुक्तमूलाधारे मनः संयोज्य तत्र वायुं सन्धार्य्य प्रोक्तैर्भूताचरैः पञ्चभिः सह तं पवनं सर्व्वदेहव्यापनेन स्वदेहे तत्तद्भूतमयीकृते प्रोक्तफलसिद्धिरिति ॥ ७३ ॥

स्वेच्छेत्यादिना श्लोकेनाकाशगमनादिसिद्ध्युपायमुपदिशति । तत्र स्वेच्छाचारी अव्याहतगतिर्गृहगतो यथा गृहगतपुरुषवत् शरीरव्यासङ्गरहितः ॥७४॥

एवमित्यादिभिः प्रिये इत्यन्तैस्त्रिभिः श्लोकैः स्वेच्छोत्क्रान्त्युपायद्वयमुपदिशति । तत्र देहं संत्यजेदिति शेषः । प्राणान् श्वासान् मध्यस्थसुषुम्नारन्ध्रतः नाड़ीचक्रस्येति शेषः । तथा प्रागुक्तं । सर्वात्मनात्मवान् देहपरिच्छेदं संत्यज्यापरिच्छिन्नबहुरूपवान् । अथवा पक्षान्तरे । उत्तरसंप्रोक्तचूर्णास्वादनतः उत्तरत्र चतुस्त्रिंशपटले उग्रेत्याद्यात्मवानित्यन्तश्लोकत्रयप्रोक्तचूर्णास्वादनतः तेन चूर्णास्वादनरूपेण । एतदुक्तं भवति पूर्वावस्थानचारितान् प्राणान् मनसा सुषुम्नारन्ध्रमार्गेण निःशेषमाकृष्य ब्रह्मरन्ध्रात् विनिर्गमय्य वक्ष्यमाणचूर्णास्वादनसंजातानुसन्धानेन वानवच्छिन्नस्वरूपो भवतीति ॥ ७७ ॥

परकायप्रवेशन्तु वक्ष्ये देवि महाद्भुतम् ।
कलौ दुःशाटकं प्रायो मर्त्त्यैः सिद्धिरपीश्वरि ॥ ७८ ॥
अक्लेशतः परित्यज्य प्राणान् स्वकतनुं तथा ।
परिपूर्णाङ्गसंयुक्तामग्रतो वीक्ष्य योगतः ॥ ७९ ॥
प्रविशेत्ततनुं प्राणप्रतिष्ठोक्तविधानतः ।
स्वां तनुं गोपयेत् स्वीयैस्ततस्तांश्च तथा व्रजेत् ॥ ८० ॥
सिद्धस्य लक्षणान्यष्टौ योगाभ्यासेन सर्वदा ।
शृणु तानि महादेवि यैरन्यैर्ज्ञायते गुणैः ॥ ८१ ॥
द्वन्द्वहानिः सुखावाप्तिरारोग्यं वश्यवृत्तिता ।
जितेन्द्रियत्वमक्रोधः कृपया जनगोपिता ॥ ८२ ॥
आसन्नमृत्योश्चिह्नानि कथयामि शृणु प्रिये ।
यैः साध्यसाधकौ ज्ञात्वा देहत्यागमतन्द्रितौ ॥ ८३ ॥
देवतास्वात्मभजनपरौ स्यातां ततस्तु तौ ।
सुगतिं प्राप्य सिद्धौ तु भवतो जातमात्रतः ॥ ८४ ॥

परकायेत्यादिभिर्व्रजेदित्यन्तैस्त्रिभिः श्लोकैः प्रस्तावपुरःसरं परकायप्रवेशनं तस्माद्भूयोऽपि स्वकायप्रवेशश्चोपदिशति । तत्र दुःशाटकं दुष्करं परकायप्रवेशमिति पूर्व्वत्रान्वयः । अक्लेशतः क्रूरव्याध्यादिभिः कृतक्लेशाभावेन । योगतः प्रविशेदित्युत्तरत्रान्वयः । प्राणप्रतिष्ठोक्तविधानतः दूतीनित्यापटले इति शेषः । स्वीयैः स्निग्धैः पुरुषैरिति शेषः । ततः तस्मात् प्रतिष्ठान्यशरीरात्तां स्वतनुं । तथा प्राग्वत् प्राणप्रतिष्ठाविधिना ॥ ८० ॥

सिद्धस्येत्यादिना शोचितेत्यन्तेन श्लोकद्वयेन प्रस्तावसंख्यापुरःसरं योगसिद्धलक्षणान्युपदिशति । तत्र तानि लक्षणानि । गुणैः लक्षणैरित्यर्थः । द्वन्द्वहानिः शीतोष्णसुखदुःखादिविकारहानिः । सुखावाप्तिः स्वरूपानुसन्धानेन ॥८२॥

आसन्नेत्यादिभिर्भवेदित्यन्तैरष्टादशभिः श्लोकैः प्रस्तावज्ञानफलपुरःसरमासन्नमृत्युचिह्नान्युपदिशति । तत्र आसन्नमृत्योः पुरुषस्य । यैः चिह्नैः । तौ साध्य-

अकारणं निजां पूर्वां विमुच्य प्रकृतिं नरः ।
समाश्रयेत्ततस्त्वब्दान्मृतिस्तस्य सुनिश्चितम् ॥ ८५ ॥
अरुन्धतीं ध्रुवं व्योम्नि नेक्षते च तदर्द्धतः ।
दृशौ नासान्तिकाक्रान्त्या चन्द्रके योऽङ्गयोर्न चेत् ॥ ८६ ॥
विलोकयति तस्यार्द्धान्मृतिमेति सुनिश्चितम् ।
गुल्फाधः स्फुरणं नाड्योः पादयोश्चेन्न जायते ॥ ८७ ॥
तस्याशु नाशो गदितो भानौ रुण्डं च पश्यतः ।
निरुद्धकर्णरन्ध्रस्य न चेत् कुण्डलिनीध्वनिः ॥ ८८ ॥
धूमो वा दृश्यते मूर्द्धि गृहच्चैत्यादितोऽपि वा ।
मूर्द्धि गा विहगा लीनाः परासुं तं न को वदेत् ॥ ८९ ॥
पश्चात्कृतार्को गण्डूषे न पश्येच्छक्रचापकम् ।
सद्यः परासुमात्मानं जानीयात् सर्वथा नरः ॥ ९० ॥
स्वमस्तककरः पश्येत् प्रकोष्ठं स्थूलमात्मनः ।
आगुल्फोरन्तराष्टभा पश्यन्नातो विनश्यति । ९१ ॥

साधकौ । सुगतिमित्यस्य जातमात्रत इत्यस्य चार्थौ गुरुमुखादवगन्तव्यः । पूर्वां सौम्यां क्रूरां वा समाश्रयेत् पूर्व्वविपरीतामिति शेषः । ततः समाश्रयतः । ध्रुवं नक्षत्ररूपं । तदर्द्धतः षण्मासतः । नासान्तिकाक्रान्त्या नासान्तिकयोरङ्गुलिद्वयाक्रान्त्या । चन्द्रके मयूरविम्बमध्यस्थचन्द्रकरूपे ज्योतिषी । न चेदित्यस्य विलोकयति इत्युत्तरत्रान्वयः विलोकयतीत्यस्य चन्द्रके इति पूर्व्वत्रान्वयः । तस्यार्द्धात् मासत्रयात् । तस्य गुल्फाधोनाड़ीद्वयस्फुरणहीनस्य । रुण्डं कवन्धं । चकारो भिन्नक्रमः । पश्यतश्चेति पद्मान्तरे । गृहचैत्रादिषु आदिशब्दः पुरपत्तनादिविषयः । अपि धूमो दृश्यत इत्याकृष्यते । वा विकल्पे । तं पुरुषं । पश्चात्कृतार्कः पृष्ठीकृतार्कः गण्डूषे पूरितविनिर्गमितमुखजले । चापकं शक्रचापसदृशं ज्योतिः । प्रकोष्ठं कूर्परं । कूर्परमणिवन्धयोर्मध्यप्रदेशं । तौ

श्लेष्मशुक्रमलानि सुर्निमग्नानि जले यदा ।
तस्मिन् पक्षे प्रयात्येव यमं सन्त्यज्य जीवितम् ॥ ९२ ॥
हाटकां प्रतिमां पश्यन् ध्रुवं याति यमालयम् ।
भास्करं भगणैः पश्यन्नपि याति यमालयम् ॥ ९३ ॥
जलादिषु तनुच्छायां विकृतां वीक्ष्य मासतः ।
प्रयाति निधनं छिद्रं पश्यन् भानोश्च मण्डले ॥ ९४ ॥
स्नातानुलिप्तगात्रस्य पुरः शुष्यति चेदुरः ।
स पश्चाद्याति निधनं सर्वैरपि सुरक्षितः ॥ ९५ ॥
गुरुमातृगणान् विप्रान् चन्द्रसूर्य्यौ च देवताः ।
आस्तिकान् सततं निन्दन्नकारणत एव च ॥ ९६ ॥
श्वासश्वैरस्य दलने परित्यागे स्वरोषतः ।
गुरुमन्त्रपरित्यागेऽप्यचिराज्जायते मृतिः ॥ ९७ ॥
गुरुं विद्यां च जनकं जननीं सर्वदेवताः ।
सदाधिक्षेपशापाभ्यां न्यक्कुर्वन्नाशु नश्यति ॥ ९८ ॥
पुस्तकं निजगेहं वा विष्टरं शयनन्तु वा ।
निष्कारणे निराकुर्वन्नाशु नश्यति मानवः ॥ ९९ ॥

जनौ । तस्मिन् पक्षे अर्द्धमासादर्वाक् । भगणैः सहेति शेषः । विकृतां कुत्सिताकारां निरोजस्कां । भानौ छिद्रं रन्ध्रं । सर्वैरपि ब्रह्मादिभिः । अकारणत इत्यस्य श्वासश्वैरस्य दलने इत्युत्तरत्रान्वयः । परित्यागे श्वासश्वैरस्य । अधिक्षेपशापाभ्यां

हृद्गेहचक्रवालानां वैवर्ण्ये मासतो मृतिः ।
ध्याते स्वदेववैरूप्ये मासतो निधनं भवेत् ॥ १०० ॥
कालतत्त्वमयी व्याप्तिरिति सम्यक् समीरिता ।
अस्या निफालनाच्चित्ते तत्तत्त्वं स्वात्मसात् कृतम् ॥

इति षोडशनित्यातन्त्रे श्रीकादिमते श्वासरूपं
नाम सप्तविंशं पटलम् ॥ २७ ॥

निन्दाप्रियवचनाभ्यां । निराकुर्वन् परित्यजन् । वैवर्ण्यं रूक्षता । स्वदेववैरूप्यं वर्णविग्रहप्रसादादिभिरिति शेषः ॥ १०० ॥

इति षोडशनित्यातन्त्रेषु श्रीकादिमताख्यस्य परिपूर्णस्य तन्त्रस्य
प्रपञ्चसारसिंहराजप्रकाशाभिधानेन श्रीसुभगानन्दनाथेन
विरचितायां मनोरमाख्यायां व्याख्यायां षोडश-
नित्यानां कालात्मकप्राणव्याप्त्यादिविधान-
प्रकाशनपरं सप्तविंशं पटलम् परिपूर्णं
परामृष्टम् ॥२७॥ ॐ तत्सत् ॥

ग्रन्थसंख्या—सप्तविंशे यन्त्रमिकं व्याख्याग्रन्थास्य संख्यया ।
पादार्द्धं पञ्चपञ्चाशदधिकं द्विशतं स्मृताः ॥

अष्टविंशपटलम् ।

अथ षोड़शनित्यानां लोकात्मत्वं वदामि ते ।
यन्मयं विश्वमखिलं वर्त्तते सचराचरम् ॥ १ ॥
कालमातृकयोर्व्याप्तिः प्रागेवोक्ता मया तव ।
वाच्यवाचकयोगेन मातृकालोकयोरपि ॥ २ ॥
व्याप्तिमद्य प्रवक्ष्यामि सम्यक् ते काललोकयोः ।
यदायत्तमिदं विश्वं नित्यास्तत्कालविग्रहाः ॥ ३ ॥
कालस्य षोड़शाकारो रूपो दृश्यत एव हि ।
वृद्धिक्षयाभ्यां चन्द्रस्य आद्यया कलया तथा ॥ ४ ॥

पूर्व्वस्मिन् सप्तविंशे पटले षोड़शनित्यानां कालेन प्राणात्मकतादिकमुपदिश्या-नन्तरं षोड़शनित्यानां लोकात्मकत्वमुपदिशति अथ षोड़शेत्यादिना विग्रहेत्यन्तेन श्लोकशतरूपेणाष्टाविंशेन पटलेन। तत्र अथ षोड़शेत्यादिना श्लोकेन षोड़श-नित्यादीनां लोकात्मत्वकथनप्रस्तावपुरःसरं सचराचरस्य विश्वस्य तन्मयत्वेन वर्त्तनमुपदिशति। तत्र लोकात्मत्वं लोकतादात्म्यं। यन्मयं नित्यात्मकलोकमयं। वर्त्तते प्रतीयते ॥ १ ॥

कालेत्यादिना श्लोकेन पञ्चविंशपटलप्रोक्तकालमातृकयोः षड़्विंशपटल-प्रोक्तमातृकालोकयोश्च व्याप्तिं स्मारयति। तत्र प्रागेव पञ्चविंशे पटले। वाच्य-वाचकयोगेन मातृकालोकयोरपि शब्दरूपमातृकातदर्थरूपलोकयोरपृथग्भावेन मातृकालोकयोर्व्याप्तिरपि षड़्विंशे पटले मया तवोक्तेत्यर्थः ॥ २ ॥

व्याप्तिमित्यादिना श्लोकेन काललोकयोर्व्याप्तिकथनादिप्रस्तावपुरःसरं नित्यानां कालविग्रहत्वमुपदिशति। तत्र अद्य अस्मिम् पटले यदायत्तमिदं विश्वं तादात्म्येन विश्वस्य कालपराधीनत्वात्। नित्यास्तत्कालविग्रहाः सकल-विश्वकारणभूतः काल एव नित्यानां विग्रह इत्यर्थः ॥ ३ ॥

कालस्येत्यादिना श्लोकेन महानित्याया अपरिच्छिन्नकालात्मकत्वमन्यासां तद-

लोकरूपं तत्प्रमाणं कालचक्रञ्च तादृशम्।
तयोरन्योन्यनित्यात्वव्याप्तिं तद्वत् स्थितिं तयोः ॥ ५ ॥
नित्यालोकस्थितिं मानं तासां कवचविग्रहम्।
ग्रहाणां मातृकारूपं शृणु प्रोक्तं क्रमेण वै ॥ ६ ॥
हेमरूपो भुवो मध्ये मेरुस्तिष्ठति पर्व्वतः।
तस्याभितो महीपार्श्वे पञ्चाशच्छतयोजनाः ॥ ७ ॥

वयवभूतकालात्मकत्वञ्चोपदिशति। तत्र कालस्य षट्त्रिंशे पटले वक्ष्यमाणरूपस्य। दृश्यत एव हि अपरमार्थोपि प्रकाशत इत्यर्थः। वृद्धिक्षयाभ्यां पञ्चदशानां कलाना-मिति शेषः। तथा समुच्चये। एतदुक्तं भवति षोड़शकलामयस्य चन्द्रविम्बस्याक्षर कलारूपापरिच्छिन्नकालात्मिकायां महानित्यायामितरकलापञ्चदशकरूपावान्तर कालात्मिकानां च नित्यानां शुक्लप्रतिपदादि पौर्णमास्यन्तं कृष्णप्रतिपदादि दर्शान्तञ्च प्रतितिथ्येकैकक्रमेणोदयविश्रान्तिप्रतीतिर्भवतीति ॥ ४ ॥

लोकेत्यादिना क्रमेण वै इत्यन्तेन श्लोकद्वयेन पटलशेषार्थानुपदिशति। तत्र लोकरूपं द्वीपाब्धिक्रमतः। तत्प्रमाणं द्वीपाब्ध्यादीनां। तादृशं मानोपेतमित्यर्थः। तयोरन्योन्यनित्यात्वव्याप्तिं लोकस्य नित्यात्वव्याप्तिं कालस्य नित्यात्वव्याप्तिञ्च। तद्वत् स्थितिं तयोः लोकस्य कालचक्रस्य च षोड़शषोड़शाकारतयान्योन्यव्याप्तिं। नित्यालोकस्य स्थितिं वक्ष्यमाणनित्यालोकस्थितिं। मानं नित्यालोकस्येति शेषः। तासां कवचविग्रहं नित्यानां कवचात्मना स्थितिं साधकानामिति शेषः। ग्रहाणां सूर्य्यादीनां नवानामिति शेषः। मातृकारूपं मातृकात्मत्वम् ॥ ६ ॥

हेमेत्यादिना आवृतेत्यन्तेनाचरतयोत्तरेण श्लोकद्वयेन लोकरूपं तस्मानञ्चो-पदिशति। तत्र तस्य मेरोः। पञ्चाशच्छतयोजनाः पञ्चसहस्रयोजनानि। एतदुक्तं भवति वृत्ताकाररूपिण्या भूमेर्मध्ये हेमरूपो मेरुः पद्मस्य कर्णिकेव तिष्ठति। तस्य मेरोः परितो भूमिः प्रतिपार्श्वं पञ्चसहस्रपञ्चसहस्रयोजनात्मिका स्थिता भवति। तस्या विष्कम्भयोजना सर्व्वत्र दशसहस्रदशसहस्रयोजना भवतीति। सिन्धुभिः समुद्रैः। द्वीपैस्तत्तत्समुद्रान्तरालभूप्रदेशैर्वक्ष्यमाणनामभिः। तत्-संख्यैर्द्विगुणोत्तरैः मेरुपार्श्वमहीमानात् प्रत्येकमुत्तरोत्तरं द्विगुणमानैः। एत-

लवणेक्षुसुरासर्पिर्दधिक्षीरजलात्मभिः ।
सिन्धुभिः सप्तभिर्द्वीपैस्तत्संख्यैर्द्विगुणोत्तरैः ॥ ८ ॥
आवृता बाह्यसलिलजलधेर्बाह्यपार्श्वयोः ।
मध्ये विस्तारमानात्तु बहिरावृत्य तत् पुनः ॥ ९ ॥
कालचक्रं पराशक्तिमारुतेन सदैव तु ।
नूनं परिभ्रमत्येव पश्चिमाद्योपसव्यतः ॥ १० ॥

वृत्तं भवति। महामेरोः परितः प्रतिपार्श्वं पञ्चसहस्रपञ्चसहस्रयोजनमिताया भूमेर्बहिरपि परितः प्रतिपार्श्वं दशसहस्रदशसहस्रयोजनात्मको लवणसमुद्रः। तद्बहिः प्राग्वत् विंशतिसहस्रविंशतिसहस्रयोजनात्मकः प्लक्षद्वीपः। तद्बहिः प्राग्वच्चत्वारिंशत्सहस्रचत्वारिंशत्सहस्रयोनात्मक इक्षुरससमुद्रः। तद्बहिरपि प्राग्वदशीतिसहस्राशीतिसहस्रयोजनात्मकः शाल्मलीद्वीपः। तद्बहिः प्राग्वत् षष्टिसहस्रोत्तरशतसहस्रयोजनात्मकः सुरासमुद्रः। तद्बहिः प्राग्वद्विंशति-सहस्रोत्तरशतत्रयसहस्रयोजनात्मकः कुशद्वीपः। तद्बहिः प्राग्वच्चत्वारिंशत् सहस्राधिक षट्शतसहस्रयोजनात्मको घृतसमुद्रः। तद्बहिः प्राग्वन्नूननिदारभ्येति सप्ताक्षरवाक्यजनितसंख्ययोजनात्मकः क्रौञ्चद्वीपः। तद्बहिः प्राग्वन्न्मिनानीतः शौरिरिति (१२८००००) सप्ताक्षरवाक्यजनितसंख्ययोजनात्मको दधिसमुद्रः। तद्बहिः प्राग्वत् ज्ञानीणूनं क्रियात्मादिति सप्ताक्षरवाक्यजनितसंख्ययोजनात्मकः शाकद्वीपः। तद्बहिरपि प्राग्वज्ज्ञानाज्ञानभरोनित्यमित्यष्टाक्षरवाक्यजनित-संख्ययोजनात्मकः क्षीरसमुद्रः। तद्बहिः प्राग्वत् नूनंज्ञानदोविश्वर इत्यष्टाक्षर-वाक्यजनितसंख्ययोजनात्मकः पुष्करद्वीपः। तद्बहिरपि प्राग्वत् ज्ञानिना मोता धुन भूरित्यष्टाक्षरवाक्यजनितसंख्ययोजनात्मकः सलिलसमुद्र इति। आवृते-त्यस्य महीति पूर्व्वेणान्वयः ॥ ८ ॥

बाह्यसलिलमित्यादिना विशद्भेरित्यन्तेन सपञ्चाक्षरत्रिपादाद्येन श्लोकद्वयेन बाह्यसलिलाम्बुधिकालचक्रयोर्मध्यस्थदेशभागं कालचक्रपरिवृत्तिकारणं तत् परि-भ्रमणप्रकारं तत्कक्षाभेदान् तन्मानं राशिस्वरूपञ्चोपदिशति। तत्र बाह्यसलिल-जलधेः सर्वबाह्यसलिलसमुद्रात् मध्यविस्तारमानाद्बहिरावृत्य तत्पुनः पुनरपि

तच्च तन्मानवीथिभिर्युतमष्टभिरद्भुतैः ।
तेजोमयैर्द्वादशारैर्युतं मेषादिविग्रहैः ॥ ११ ॥
तेषु वीथिषु पूर्व्वाशामुखाः सप्तग्रहाः स्थिताः ।
राशियुक्तेन कालेन प्रोक्तेनोपर्य्यधस्तथा १ ॥ १२ ॥

तत्सप्तद्वीपसप्तसमुद्रसमवायमध्यविष्कम्भमानात् (१६३८३७००) द्वीपाद्यात्मक भूरूपं कालचक्रं कालात्मकं चक्रं तस्य कालात्मकत्वं तत्परिभ्रमणस्य विश्वविकारकारणत्वात् । पराशक्तिमारुतेन महानित्याया इच्छाशक्तिरूपेण मारुतेनानुप्रेरितं । एवकारेण कारणान्तरं न भवतीत्यर्थः । पश्चिमाधोपसव्यतः पश्चिमाभिमुखमूर्द्धाधः-क्रमात् प्रादक्षिण्येन । तत् कालचक्रं । तन्मानवीथिभिरुत्तरोत्तरं प्रतिपार्श्वं तत्तद्द्विगुणद्विगुणमानवीथिभिः । अद्भुतैः सर्वाश्चर्य्यमयत्वात् केनापि अकृतत्वाच्च । तेजोमयैः ज्योतीरूपैः । द्वादशारैः भूमध्यादिपरव्योमान्त मूर्द्धोर्द्ध्वविकाशरूपैः समान्तरालैरिति शेषः । मेषादिविग्रहैः मेषादिमीनान्तराशिस्वरूपैः । एतदुक्तं भवति सर्ववाह्यसलिलजलधिवाह्यपार्श्वद्वयमध्यविष्कम्भमानं तद्बाह्यगतं तत्सर्वं क्रोडीकृत्य पराशक्तिरूपमारुतप्रेरितं पूर्वोक्तवाह्यसलिलजलधिवाह्यपार्श्ववह्निर्मानात् प्रतिपार्श्वं प्राग्वद्द्विगुणोत्तरमानवीथ्यष्टकं तदन्तरालाष्टकोपेतं ज्योतीरूपमेषादिराशिद्वादशारयुक्तं कालचक्रं पश्चिमाभिमुखमूर्द्धाधः प्रादक्षिण्यक्रमात् परिभ्रमतीति ॥ ११ ॥

तेष्वित्यादिना स्थितिरित्यन्तेनार्द्धाधिकेनैकेन श्लोकेन तत्कालचक्रवीथिषु सप्तग्रहावस्थानं तेषां स्वोक्तकालेन तच्चक्रगतराशिषु चारेण लोकस्थितिञ्चोपदिशति । तत्र तेषु वीथिषु तासु वीथिषु तेषु राशिष्वित्यर्थः । स्थिताः चन्द्रबुधशुक्रार्कभौमगुरुमन्दानां अधरोत्तरवीथिस्थितिक्रमालङ्घनेन । राशिषु तद्वीथिगतेषु । प्रोक्तेन ज्योतिःशास्त्रे । तथा पूर्वाशामुखा एव । प्रयान्ति चरन्ति । तेषां ग्रहाणां स्थितिः जननसत्ताविपरिणामवृद्ध्यपचयनाशात्मिका । एतदुक्तं भवति प्रोक्तकालचक्रगतवीथ्यष्टकं प्रोक्तक्रमालङ्घनस्थित्या स्थिताः पूर्वाभिमुखास्तत्तद्ग्रहास्तत्तद्गतराशिषु स्वोक्त चारेण लोकानामुत्पत्त्यादिरूपां स्थितिं कुर्व्वन्तीति ॥ १२॥

१। राशियुक्तेन कालेन स्वोक्तेन परिधिस्तथा-इति वा।

प्रयान्ति तेषां चारेण लोकानां भवति स्थितिः।
मध्यस्थमेरौ ललिता सदैवास्ते महाद्युतिः॥ १३॥
तस्याभितो जलान्तस्थाः शेषास्ताः सुरश्चतुर्दश।
तद्बहिः परमे व्योम्नि त्वेता चित्रा तु संस्थिता॥ १४॥
कृतादिवर्षादारभ्य प्रतिवर्षमिति स्थिता।
द्वितीयादिषु वर्षेषु क्रमात्ताः परिवृत्तिभिः॥ १५॥
षोड़शाब्दे परे व्योम्नि ललिता सलिलाम्बुधौ।
चित्रा च भवतीत्थं हि भजन्ते परिवर्त्तनम्॥ १६॥

मध्यस्थेत्यादिभिः रूपतः इत्यन्तैरर्द्धाधिकैस्त्रिभिः श्लोकैः षोड़शनित्यानां मेरुद्वीपादिपरमव्योमान्तषोड़शविधेषु देशेषु कृतयुगादिवर्षादारभ्य प्रतियुगं चतुर्युगवर्षेषु परिवृत्तिक्रममुपदिशति। तत्र सदैवास्ते सर्व्वदा सकलात्मकेन प्रधानरूपेण तिष्ठतीत्यर्थः। महाद्युतिः देशकालादिभिरनवच्छिन्नप्रकाशरूपत्वात्। तस्य मेरोः। अभितः सर्व्वतः। जलान्तस्था मेरोरनन्तरजम्बुद्वीपाद्यादिसर्ववाह्यस्थजलसमुद्रपर्य्यन्तं चतुर्द्दशस्थानस्थिताः। शेषाः कामेश्वर्य्यादयश्चतुर्द्दश ज्वालामालिन्यन्ताः। तद्बहिः सर्ववाह्यसलिलजलधेर्बहिः। अत्र षोड़शा प्रतिवर्षं प्रतिकृतयुगादिवर्षं। ता नित्या ललिता भवतीत्युत्तरत्रान्वयः। चकारः समुच्चये। इत्थं उक्तप्रकारेण। एवमित्यस्य प्रोक्तरूपत इत्यत्रान्वयः। अन्येषु त्रेतादिषु। एतदुक्तं भवति मेरुजम्बूद्वीपलवणसमुद्रप्लक्षद्वीपेक्षुरससागरशाल्मलीद्वीपसुरासमुद्र कुशद्वीपघृतसागर क्रौञ्चद्वीपदधिसमुद्र शाकद्वीपक्षीरसागरपुष्करद्वीपसलिलसमुद्र परव्योमसंज्ञकेषु षोड़शसु स्थानेषु कृतयुगादिचतुर्युगप्रथमवर्षेषु ललितादिचित्रान्ताः षोड़शनित्यास्तदात्मकत्वेन स्थित्वा तत्तद्युगद्वितीयद्वितीयवर्षेषु जम्बूद्वीपादिमेरुपर्य्यन्तेषु षोड़शसु षोड़शसु स्थानेषु ललितादिचित्रान्ताः षोड़श नित्यास्तिष्ठन्ति। एवं तत्तद्युगतृतीयादितृतीयादि षोड़शषोड़शवर्षान्तेषु चतुर्द्दशसु चतुर्द्दशसु वर्षेषु लवणसमुद्रादि परमव्योमान्तेषु विशिष्टेषु चतुर्द्दशसु वर्षेषु क्रमात् प्रतिवर्षं ललिता तिष्ठति। ललितास्थितस्थानान्तरालमारभ्य तत्तत्पूर्व्वपूर्व्वस्थानान्तमन्याः कामेश्वर्य्यादि चित्रान्ताः पञ्चदशनित्यास्तिष्ठन्ति। एवं वर्षषोड़शकवर्षषोड़शकैनैकामेकां परिवृत्तिं भजन्तीति॥ १६॥

एवं युगेषु चान्येषु वर्त्तते प्रोक्तरूपतः।
कालेष्वपि च मध्यादि परव्योमान्तमीश्वरि॥ १७॥
परिवृत्तिं भजन्ते ता मध्यस्था स्वांशतश्चरेत्।
अन्याः सर्व्वास्तत्र तत्र चरन्ति स्वयमेव वै॥ १८॥
तथा कालक्रमात्तास्तु भजन्ते परिवर्त्तनम्।
कालतो देशतश्चक्रादैक्यं संजायते यदा॥ १९॥
तदा भवन्ति भूपाला धार्म्मिकाः कालवर्षतः।
प्रजाश्च सुखिनो भूयुररोगाः कालमृत्यवः॥ २०॥

कालेष्वित्यादिभिः समुदीरितमित्यन्तैरर्द्धाधैः पञ्चभिः श्लोकैः षोडशनित्यानां कालचक्रमयत्वप्रकारं कालदेशैकाधिपत्यफलं कालचक्रस्य वाह्यवीथिरूपपरव्योमस्थितिं प्रोक्तनिगमनञ्चोपदिशति। तत्र कालेषु कालचक्रस्य चन्द्रस्य कक्षा भूम्योरन्तरान्तरालदेशादिताराकक्षान्तेषु षोडशसु स्थानेषु मध्यादि चन्द्रकक्षान्तर्भूतमध्यव्योमादि। ताः षोडशनित्याः। मध्यस्था ललिता। स्वांशतः स्वसमानमूर्त्त्यन्तरेण। अन्याः पञ्चदशनित्याः। तत्र तत्र देशे देशे काले काले च। तथा कालक्रमात् पूर्वोक्तयुगादि वर्षादि षोडशषोडशवर्षपरिवृत्तिक्रमेण तुर्विशेषे। कालतः परिवृत्तिकालक्रमात्। देशतः देशस्य चक्रात् कालचक्रेण। भूयुः प्रागवत्। कालमृत्यवः हिताय मृत्यव इत्यर्थः। वाह्यस्थवीथ्यां शनैश्चरकक्षावहिर्भूतवीथ्यां। तारकाः नक्षत्राणि। तद्वहिः नक्षत्रकक्षावहिः। स्थितिः कालचक्रस्येति पूर्व्वेणान्वयः। तत्र कालचक्रे। तदन्तिका तदवधिका परव्योमाङ्कभूता। अपिचेत्यनेन पूर्व्वश्लोकात् स्थितिरित्येतदाकृष्यते। तत्क्रमात् पूर्वोक्तपूर्वोक्तयुगवर्षषोडशक्रमात्। तन्मयं नित्यामयं। एतदुक्तं भवति कृतादिचतुर्युग प्रथम प्रथमवर्षादिवर्षषोडशषोडशकक्रमाल्ललितादथश्चित्रान्ताः षोडशनित्याः क्रमेण कालचक्रे चन्द्रकक्षाभूम्यन्तरालप्रदेश चन्द्रकक्षा तदन्तरालवुधकक्षा तदन्तरालशुक्रकक्षा तदन्तरालरविकक्षा तदन्तरालभौमकक्षा तदन्तराल गुरुकक्षा तदान्तराल शनिकक्षा तदन्तरालनक्षत्र कक्षाविभागेन षोडशसु स्थानेषु देशपरिवृत्तिपरितः परिवृत्तिक्रमतः परिवर्त्तन्ते। तेन क्रमेण या या नित्या चन्द्रकक्षास्थिता सा सा नित्यैव तत्काल-

कालचक्रस्य बाह्यस्थवीथ्यां तिष्ठन्ति तारकाः ।
तद्वहिः परमव्योम स्थितिस्तत्र तदन्तिका ॥ २१ ॥
तासामपि च नित्यानां षोडशानाञ्च तत् क्रमात् ।
एवं देशे च काले च तन्मयं समुदीरितम् ॥ २२ ॥
देशवर्षतिथीनाञ्च सम्पातादैक्यमागताम् ।
पूजयेत् सविशेषं तां प्रजपेच्चाखिलाप्तये ॥ २३ ॥
तेषु विद्योपदेशात्तु तस्यास्तत् सन्निधिर्भवेत् ।
महाशक्तिश्च जायेत त्रयाणामैक्यवैभवात् ॥ २४ ॥
कालप्राप्तां यजेत् स्वाब्दजन्मवासरर्क्षे तु तां ।
देशप्राप्तान्तु तन्मासपूर्णायां पूजयेच्छिवे ॥ २५ ॥
प्रत्यब्दमेवं कुर्व्वाणं न मुञ्चति रमा यशः ।
कदाचिदपि दीर्घायुररोगो ज्ञानवान् सुखी ॥ २६ ॥

चक्रस्याधिपा भवति। तस्मादेवं देशकालपरिवृत्तिभेदतो जम्बुद्वीपादीनां परव्योमान्तानामष्टानां स्थानानां एकैकवर्षक्रमेण वर्षाष्टकेनैकनित्याधिपत्वं सिध्यति। यथा जम्बुद्वीपस्य कामेश्वरीकुलसुन्दर्य्यौ क्रमात् प्रथमनवमयोर्वर्षयोः प्लक्षद्वीपस्य द्वितीयदशमवर्षयोर्भगमालिनीनित्यानित्ये शाल्मलीद्वीपस्य तृतीयैकादशयोर्वर्षयोर्नित्यक्लिन्नानीलपताके कुशद्वीपस्य चतुर्थद्वादशयोर्वर्षयोर्भेरुण्डाविजये क्रौञ्चद्वीपस्य पञ्चमत्रयोदशयोर्वर्षयोर्वह्निवासिनीसर्व्वमङ्गले शाकद्वीपस्य षष्ठचतुर्द्दशयोर्वर्षयोर्वज्रेश्वरीज्वालामालिन्यौ पुष्करद्वीपस्य सप्तमपञ्चदशयोर्वर्षयोर्दूतीचित्रे परव्योमाष्टमषोड़शयोर्वर्षयोस्त्वरितालल्लिते एवं देशकालौ नित्यात्मकौ भवत इत्युक्तमिति ॥ २२ ॥

देशेत्यादिभिः पूजनादित्यन्तैः पञ्चभिः श्लोकैः देशकालतिथिप्राप्तनित्यापूजनं तत्कालविशेषं तत्फलञ्चोपदिशति। तत्र देशवर्षतिथीनां देशकालचक्रतिथीनां त्रयाणां वा द्वयोर्वा तां तिथिनित्याविद्यां। तेषु देशवर्षतिथिषु। तस्याः तद्देशाद्यधिपायाः। महाशक्तिः साधकस्येति शेषः। त्रयाणां देशादीनाम् ॥२४॥ कालप्राप्तां कालचक्राधिपां। तन्मासपूर्णायां स्वजन्ममासपूर्णायां। एवं कुर्व्वाणम्

राजभिर्म्मनुजैस्त्रीभिरन्यैः प्राणिभिरप्यसौ ।
मान्यते सर्वमन्त्राश्च सिद्धाः सुरस्तव पूजनात् ॥ २७ ॥
जम्बूः प्लक्षः शाल्मली च कुशक्रौञ्चौ यथाक्रमम् ।
शाकश्च पुष्करश्चेति सप्तद्वीपेषु भूरुहाः ॥ २८ ॥
तेषां नामभिरेव सुरास्तत्तन्नामानि तन्मुखात् ।
तत्तन्नामभिरभ्यर्च्य तद्वीपं तत्र पूजयेत् ॥ २९ ॥
तां तां नित्यां तत्र तत्र काले काले तु साधकः ।
एवं पूजयितुर्लोके न समोऽस्ति न चाधिकः ॥ ३० ॥
मध्ये भूमिं तामभितः कालचक्रं ततो वहिः ।
महाव्योम च निःसीमं तत्रैतद्वयसंस्थितिः ॥ ३१ ॥

पूजाजपहोमादिकं अन्यैः तिर्य्यगादिभिः । असौ साधकः । तत्र देशादिसम्पातकाले । एतदुक्तं भवति सप्तद्वीपेषु तत्तद्वीपेश्वरीनित्यां द्वीपपूजापूर्वकं स्वजन्ममासपूर्णायां कालचक्रेश्वरीनित्यां स्वाब्दजन्मदिवसे उभे अपि प्रतिपच्चतत्तत्प्राप्ततिथीश्च पूजयन् प्रोक्तफलसिद्धिभागिति ॥ २७ ॥

जम्बित्यादिभिरधिक इत्यन्तैस्त्रिभिः श्लोकैः सप्तद्वीपगतभूरुहसमकनामभिः प्राप्तानि तत्तद्वीपनामानि तत्तत्पूजनं तत्र तत्राधिगतनित्यापूजनं तत्फलञ्चोपदिशति । तत्र भूरुहाः पादपाः । तेषां पादपानां । तत्तन्नामानि द्वीपनामानि । तन्मुखात् तत्तद्भूरुहप्रावोख्यद्वारा तत्तन्नामभिः मेरुद्वीपादिपरमव्योमान्तनामभिः प्रणवादिभिश्चतुर्थीनमोऽन्तैः । यथा ॐ मेरवे नमः इत्यादि । तत्र मेरुप्रमुखेषु षोड़शसु स्थानेषु यत्र स्थितस्तत्र तत्र काले काले पुनः स्थितं तत्र पूर्व्वं पूजयित्वा तद्वर्षे तस्मिंस्तस्मिन् वर्षे । एतदुक्तं भवति षोड़शसु नित्यासु स्वभजनीया नित्या षोड़शसु स्थानेषु यत्र स्थिता तत्र पूर्वं पूजयित्वा तत्तद्वर्षे तत्तत्स्थानगतां भावयन् तत्तन्निरयार्च्चनक्रमात् पूजयन् प्रोक्तरूपप्रभावो भवेदिति ॥ ३० ॥

मध्ये इत्यादिभिर्विंयत इत्यन्तैस्त्रिभिः श्लोकैर्भूमिकालचक्रमहाव्योमस्थितिक्रमं कालचक्रे ग्रहाणां स्थितिं तत्कारणञ्चोपदिशति । तत्र मध्ये महाव्योम्नः

२७

सुस्थिराया भुवो मध्ये चक्रस्य भ्रमतोऽनिशम् ।
ग्रहाणां तत्र संवासप्रचारनियतात्मनाम् ॥ ३२ ॥
कारणं परमेशानि तवेच्छैव तु केवलम् ।
न त्वन्यदवलम्बाय तयोः कुत्रापि विद्यते ॥ ३३ ॥
तयोर्बहिः परे व्योम्नि क्वचिदब्धिचतुष्टयम् ।
प्रागुक्तरूपां तत्तीरे कोलवक्त्रान्तु पश्चिमे ॥ ३४ ॥
सलिले कुरुकुल्लाञ्च पोतारूढां शुचिस्मिताम् ।
तन्मध्ये नवरत्नानि महाद्वीपश्च तत्र वै ॥ ३५ ॥
कल्पकोद्यानमृतुभिः षड्भिः सेवितविग्रहम् ।
तन्मध्येऽसंख्यरूपाभिर्वृतां सङ्गीतशक्तिभिः ॥ ३६ ॥
गीतवादित्रनृत्यादिसंसक्ताभिरनारतम् ।
विनोद्यमानां विलसन्मदमन्थरवीक्षणाम् ॥ ३७ ॥
रत्नमण्डपमध्यस्थरत्नसिंहासनोपरि ।
शुचिस्मितां शक्तिवृन्दगीताकर्षणनन्दिताम् ॥ ३८ ॥

भूमिं तां स्थितामिति शेषः । ततः कालचक्रतः । निःसीमं निः सीमेत्यर्थः । तत्र महाव्योम्नि । एतद्द्वयसंस्थितिः भूमिकालयोरवस्थानं । मध्ये महाव्योम्नः । तत्र कालचक्रे संवासप्रचारनियतात्मनां स्वस्ववीथिसंवासतत्तद्गतराशिषु प्रचारनियमवतां । तवेच्छा परायाः शक्तेराज्ञा । तयोर्भूमिकालचक्रयोः । एतदुक्तं भवति महाव्योममध्यस्थभूमिकालचक्रतद्गतभूतग्रहाणां यथाक्रमं सुस्थिरावस्था भ्रमणे सन्ततैकाकारप्रमाणं प्रोक्तसंवासप्रचारकारणात् तदवलम्बनञ्च केवलं परायाः शक्तेरिच्छेति ॥ ३२ ॥

तयोरित्यादिभिः सुनिश्चितमित्यन्तैः नवभिः श्लोकैः नित्यालोकावस्थानं तत्र देव्याः सपरिवारायाः स्थितिं तत्तत्पूजयितुः फलञ्चोपदिशति । तत्र तयोः मही‌कालचक्रयोः क्वचित् प्रदेशे अब्धिचतुष्टयं इक्षुसागरादि । प्रागुक्तरूपां अङ्गपूजोक्त ललितासदृशविग्रहां । कोलवक्त्रां वाराहीं चतुर्विंशेषे पोतीस्वरूपेणेत्यर्थः ।

सहजासवसम्भोगैः संजातानन्दविग्रहाम् ।
दयामदारुणापाङ्गविलोकितसुसाधकाम् ॥ ३९ ॥
परितो भूषणैश्चित्रैः स्वर्णचामरकादिभिः ।
विराजमानान्दिरदानश्वानपि तथाविधान् । ४० ॥
शक्तिभिर्दर्शितानग्रे पश्यन्तीमभितोत्सवाम् ।
स्वसमानाभिरभितो नित्याभिः सेवितान्तथा ॥ ४१ ॥
याति तासां पूजयिता तत्समाकारतां शनैः ।
तद्विनोदस्तत्समीपनिवासो स्यात् सुनिश्चितम् ॥ ४२ ॥
कोटियोजनविस्तीर्णसमायामं महाद्भुतम् ।
नवरत्नमयं द्वीपं तन्मानाब्धिभिरावृतम् ॥ ४३ ॥
तत्तृतीयांशमानस्य सहस्रादित्यतेजसम् ।
रत्नद्वीपस्य मध्यस्थतृतीयांशे तु मण्डपे ॥ ४४ ॥
कोट्यादित्यद्युतिप्रान्तेष्वभितोऽसंख्यशक्तिभिः ।
तथा समन्वितां ध्यायन्नरो भवति मत्समः ॥ ४५ ॥

पञ्चमीं श्रीचक्रस्थब्राह्म्यादिमातृष्टकं अत्र पञ्चमीग्रहणं ललिताविग्रहसाम्यार्थं । सलिले इक्षुसागरस्य तन्मध्ये चतुरब्धिमध्ये । तन्मध्ये कल्पकोद्यानमध्यस्थ-सर्व्वमध्यगपद्मरागखण्डमध्यस्थरत्नमण्डपमध्ये इति यावत् । असंख्यरूपाभिरिति पदच्छेदः । मदमन्थरवीक्षणां अनन्तरतृतीयश्लोकवक्ष्यमाणानन्दत्रयेण सङ्गीतानन्देन च उपरि स्थितामित्यर्थः । सुसाधकां सत्सम्प्रदायिसाधकां । तथा-विधान् भूषितान् । तथा समुच्चये । अत्र प्रकरणे द्वितीयैकवचनान्तानां पदानां ललितामिति विशेष्यमध्याहार्य्यम् तां ध्यात्वेत्यर्थः । तासां सपरिवारनित्यानां तद्विनोदः सङ्गीतादिविशेषविनोदः ॥ ४२ ॥

कोटीत्यादिभिस्त इत्यन्तैर्नवभिः श्लोकैर्नित्यालोकादिमानं तत्र देवीपूजनात् फलं परमव्योमस्वरूपनित्यावैभवविदामनुभावञ्चोपदिशति । तत्र समायामं कोट्यायामं । तन्मानाब्धिभिः प्रत्येकं कोटियोजनविस्तीर्णैरब्धिभिस्तृतीयांशमानस्य योजनतृतीयांशसहितत्रयस्त्रिंशदधिकशतत्रयोत्तरत्रयस्त्रिंशत्सहस्रा-

एवं ध्यात्वार्च्चयेद्देवीं भक्त्या परमयोक्तया ।
नरो निरस्तसंसारमूलाज्ञानो जितेन्द्रियः ॥ ४६ ॥
निपुणश्च कलादक्षः सुखिभिः समवित्तवान् ।
अपापः पुण्यशीलश्च सत्यार्जवसमन्वितः ॥ ४७ ॥
देशिकः स्वकुलोत्तुङ्गः सर्व्वसम्भावितात्मवान् ।
जायते तस्य परितो योजनं पावनं भवेत् ॥ ४८ ॥
तदालोकनसंलापसंस्पर्शादिकृतां नृणाम् ।
पापकर्म्मक्षयात्तेन रहिताः स्युश्च तत्समाः ॥ ४९ ॥
कालचक्रस्य नित्याया लोकस्य च वहिःस्थितिः ॥
व्योमरूपमनाद्यन्तं यत्तच्चिन्मयमावयोः ॥ ५० ॥
यो वेत्त्येवमशेषन्तु नित्यावैभवमीरितम् ।
स जीवन्मुक्त एवेति प्रोक्तं तल्लक्षणञ्च ते ॥ ५१ ॥
समस्तापद्विमुक्त्यर्थं सर्वसम्पदवाप्तये ।
भूतप्रेतपिशाचादिपीड़ाशान्त्यै सुखाप्तये ॥ ५२ ॥

धिकत्रयस्त्रिंशल्लक्षयोजनमानविस्तारायामसहितस्य रत्नद्वीपस्य मध्यगस्य मध्यस्य रत्नद्वीपमध्यगतपद्मरागखण्डस्य तृतीयांशे योजननवांशसहितैकादशो· त्तरशताधिकैकादशसहस्रोत्तरैकादशलक्षयोजनमानविस्तारायामसहिते मण्डपे माणिक्यमण्डपे। प्रान्तेषु पार्श्वेषु मण्डपस्येति शेषः। तथा प्राग्वत्। मत्समः शिवभूतः। उक्तया षड़्विंशत्पटलोक्तया। अज्ञानं नाम दुर्वासना। आर्जवं नाम मनोवाक्कायकर्म्मणामेकाकारता। तस्य परितः साधकस्य निवासस्थानस्य परितः। स्युर्नरा इति शेषः। नित्यायाः सकलनित्यात्मिकाया महानित्यायाः। तद्व्योमरूपं चिन्मयं निर्विषयज्ञानमयं। आवयोः शक्तिशिवयोः। एवं उक्त-प्रकारेण। प्रोक्तं पञ्चत्रिंशत् पटले वक्ष्यत इत्यर्थः ॥ ५१ ॥

समस्तेत्यादिभिर्मत्सम इत्यन्तैः विंशत्या श्लोकैस्तदनुभावप्रस्ताव पुरःसरं

समस्तरोगनाशाय समरे विजयाय च ।
चोरसिंहद्वीपिगजगवयादिभयानके ॥ ५३ ॥
अरण्ये शैलगहने मार्गे दुर्भिक्षके तथा ।
सलिलादिमनःपीड़ास्वब्धौ पोतादिसङ्कटे ॥ ५४ ॥
प्रजप्य नित्याकवचं सकृत् सर्व्वं तरत्यसौ ।
सुखी जीवति निर्द्वन्द्वो निःसपत्नो जितेन्द्रियः ॥ ५५ ॥
शृणु तत् कवचं देवि वक्ष्ये तव तदात्मकम् ।
येनाहमपि युद्धेषु देवासुरजयी सदा ॥ ५६ ॥
सर्वतः सर्वदात्मानं ललिता पातु सर्वगा ।
कामेशी पुरतः पातु भगमाला त्वनन्तरम् ॥ ५७ ॥
दिशं पातु तथा दक्षपार्श्वं मे पातु सर्वदा ।
नित्यक्लिन्ना च भेरुण्डा दिशं पातु सदा मम ॥ ५८ ॥
तथैव पश्चिमं भागं रक्षेत् सा वह्निवासिनी ।
महावज्रेश्वरी रक्षेदनन्तरदिशं सदा ॥ ५९ ॥
वामपार्श्वं सदा पातु दूती मे त्वरिता ततः ।
पालयेत्तु दिशं चान्यां रक्षेन्मां कुलसुन्दरी ॥ ६० ॥

नित्याकवचं तत्फलञ्चोपदिशति । तत्र पिशाचादीत्यत्रादिशब्देनापस्मारादय उच्यन्ते । सुखाप्तये स्वरूपलाभात् । गवयादीत्यत्रादिशब्दः शरभादिविषयः । भयानको भयङ्करः । अस्य मार्ग इत्युत्तरत्रान्वयः । दुर्भिक्षके मर्य्यादाप्राप्ताच्यपकर्षे । तथा समुच्चये । पोतादीत्यत्रादिशब्दो नावादिविषयः । असौ जपिता । निर्द्वन्द्वः शीतोष्णादिद्वन्द्वपीड़ादिरहितः अथवा निरुपमः । तदात्मकं त्वदात्मकमित्यर्थः । येन कवचेन अहमपि शिवोऽपि । सर्व्वतः वक्ष्यमाणसकलस्थानेषु । सर्व्वगा विश्वमयत्वात् । पुरतः पूर्व्वस्यां दिशि । तुः समुच्चये । अनन्तरं आग्नेयीं दिशमित्युत्तरत्रान्वयः । तथा समुच्चये । नित्यक्लिन्ना दक्षिणपार्श्वं मे पात्विति पूर्व्वत्रा-

नित्या मामूर्द्ध्वतः पातु साधो मे पातु सर्व्वदा ।
नित्या नीलपताकाख्या विजया सर्व्वतश्च माम् ॥ ६१ ॥
करोतु मे मङ्गलानि सर्व्वदा सर्व्वमङ्गला ।
देहेन्द्रियमनःप्राणान् ज्वालामालिनिविग्रहा ॥ ६२ ॥
पालयेदनिशं चित्रा चित्तं मे पातु सर्व्वदा ।
कामात् क्रोधात्तथा लोभान्मोहान्मानान्मदादपि ॥ ६३ ॥
पापान्मत्सरतः शोकात् संशयात् सर्व्वतः सदा ।
स्तैमित्याच्च समुद्योगादशुभेषु तु कर्म्मसु ॥ ६४ ॥
असत्यक्रूरचिन्तातो हिंसातश्चौर्य्यतस्तथा ।
रक्षन्तु मां सर्व्वदा ताः कुर्वन्त्विच्छां शुभेषु च ॥ ६५ ॥
नित्याः षोडश मां पान्तु गजारूढ़ाः स्वशक्तिभिः ।
तथा हयसमारूढ़ाः पान्तु मां सर्वतः सदा ॥ ६६ ॥
सिंहारूढ़ा स्तथा पान्तु मान्तरक्षगता अपि ।
रथारूढ़ाश्च मां पान्तु सर्वतः सर्वदा रणे ॥ ६७ ॥

न्वयः । अथ अनन्तरं नैऋतिमित्यर्थः । तथा समुच्चये । सा प्रागुक्तवैभवा । अनन्तरदिशं वायवीं दिशं । वामपार्श्वं उत्तरां दिशं त्वरितेत्यस्य पालयेदित्युत्तरत्रान्वयः । तुः समुच्चये । अन्यां ऐशानीं मामित्यूर्द्ध्वाधरान्तरालस्थदिगुपलक्षणार्थं । नित्यानाम दशमी नित्या नित्येत्यर्थः । सेति नीलपताकाख्येत्युत्तरत्रान्वयः । नित्यानीलपताकाख्या नीलपताकानित्येत्यर्थः । अस्य अधो मे पात्विति पूर्व्वत्रान्वयः । सर्व्वतः प्रोक्तैकादशदिक्षु चकारेण पूर्व्वत्र पात्वित्येतदाकृष्यते । ज्वालामालिनिविग्रहा ज्वालामालिनी नित्येत्यर्थः । पालयेदित्यस्य पूर्व्वत्रान्वयः । तथा समुच्चये । अपिशब्दः समुच्चये । पापात् अविवेकात् संशयात् अनध्यवसायरूपात् अज्ञानात् सर्व्वतः सर्व्वत्र । सदा असंशयरूपेण स्तैमित्यात् शुभकर्म्मस्विति शेषः । तुः समुच्चये अशुभेषु कर्म्मसु समुद्योगादिति सम्बन्धः । तथा समुच्चये । पूर्वोक्त·

ताक्ष्यारूढ़ाश्च मां पान्तु तथा व्योमगता स्तथा ।
भूगताः सर्वदा पान्तु माञ्च सर्वत्र सर्वदा ॥ ६८ ॥
भूतप्रेतपिशाचापस्मारकृत्यादिकान् गदान् ।
द्रावयन्तु स्वशक्तीनां भीषणैरायुधैर्मम ॥ ६९ ॥
गजाश्वद्वीपिपञ्चास्यतार्क्ष्यरूढ़ाखिलायुधाः ।
असंख्याः शक्तयो देव्याः पान्तु मां सर्वतः सदा ॥ ७० ॥
सायं प्रातर्जपन्नित्याकवचं सर्वरक्षकम् ।
कदाचिन्नाशुभं पश्येन्न शृणोति च मत्समः ॥ ७१ ॥
ग्रहाणां मातृकाविद्याविग्रहं विग्रहं यतः ।
तेन तेषान्तु पूजार्थं वक्ष्ये तद्धाममण्डलम् ॥ ७२ ॥
सुधास्वरैर्भवेदिन्दोर्मण्डलं भास्करस्य तु ।
सुधाव्यञ्जनरूपं स्यादितरे तन्मया यतः ॥ ७३ ॥

कामादिपञ्चम्यन्तपदषोड़शकस्य रक्षन्तु मामित्यत्रान्वयः । ताः नित्याः । स्वशक्तिभिः सहेति शेषः । तथा प्रागवत् स्वशक्तिभिः सहेत्यर्थः । तरक्षगताः व्याघ्ररूढ़ा अपि स्वशक्तिभिः सहेत्यर्थः । चकारात् स्वशक्तिभि! सहेत्यर्थः चकारात् स्वशक्तिभिः सहेत्यर्थः । तथा व्योमगताः स्वशक्तिभिः सहेत्यर्थः । तथा व्योमगताः स्वशक्तिभिः सह व्योमस्था इत्यर्थः । कृत्यादिकानित्यत्रादिशब्दो डाकिन्यादिविषयः । गदान् पीड़ातः । मत्समः शिवभूतः ॥ ७१ ॥

ग्रहाणामित्यादिभिः श्रेयस्करात्मकमित्यन्तैश्चतुर्भिः श्लोकैर्नवग्रहाणां मातृकात्मकत्वं तेषां तन्मयमण्डलसामान्यनिर्म्माणोपदेशं चन्द्रार्कात्मकत्वं इतरेषां ग्रहाणाञ्च चन्द्रार्कयोर्विशेषमण्डलप्रस्तावादिके च करोति । तत्र मातृकाविद्याविग्रहं अकारादिक्षकारान्तमातृकाख्यविद्यास्वरूपं विग्रहं ग्रहाणामित्यर्थः । विग्रहमिति दिव्यत्वात् विग्रह इत्यर्थः । तेन कारणेन तद्धाम -मण्डलं तेषामावासभूतं स्वरूपं सुधास्वरैः अमृतात्मकैः षोड़शस्वरैर्मण्डलं वक्ष्यमाणरूपं । तुर्विशेषे सुधाव्यञ्जनरूपं प्रागवत् सुधास्वरूपव्यञ्जनरूपमित्यर्थः ।

तेन तेषां मण्डलानि तैस्तैर्व्वर्णैर्व्वदामि ते ।
तेषां नवानां पूजासु तन्मयं नवमण्डलम् ॥ ७४ ॥
चन्द्रार्कयोः पृथक् पूजास्वभ्यर्च्य मण्डलं तयोः ।
क्रमेण शृणु देवेशि सर्वश्रेयस्करात्मकम् ॥ ७५ ॥
प्राक्प्रत्यग्दक्षिणोदक्कचतुःसूत्रनिपातनात् ।
त्रिहस्तमात्रे जनयेन्नव कोष्ठानि तेषु वै ॥ ७६ ॥
मध्ये प्रकोष्ठयोः कृत्वा वृत्तत्रयमतिस्फुटम् ।
तन्मध्ये तिर्य्यगूर्द्धस्थ सूत्रद्वयनिपातनात् ॥ ७७ ॥
विधाय नवधा मध्यमीशादि विलिखेत् क्रमात् ।
वाताद्यष्टस्वरान्मध्ये प्रणवं नभसा युतम् ॥ ७८ ॥

अस्य मण्डलमित्यस्येति पूर्व्वत्रान्वयः। इतरे भौमादयः। तन्मयाः चन्द्रादित्यमयाः। तेन हेतुना। तैस्तैश्चन्द्रसूर्य्यात्मकैः। नवानां पूजासु समुदायपूजासु तन्मयं मातृकात्मकं पृथक् पूजासु स्वतन्त्रपूजासु तयोश्चन्द्रार्कयोः ॥७५॥

प्रागित्यादिभिरनुग्रहमित्यन्तैश्चतुर्दशभिः श्लोकैर्नवग्रहाणां समुदायपूजासु मण्डलविशेषनिर्माणं तत्र तेषां पूजादिकञ्चोपदिशति। तत्र त्रिहस्तमात्रे आयामविस्ताराभ्यां। तेषु कोष्ठनवके मध्यप्रकोष्टसर्व्वमध्यकोष्ठे तद्बाह्यप्राग्दिग्गतान्तकोष्ठत्रयमध्यकोष्ठे च तन्मध्ये वृत्तत्रये सर्व्वमध्यवृत्तमध्ये ईशादि ईशादिनवकोष्ठाद्युत्तरकोष्ठान्तं। क्रमात् प्रादक्षिण्यक्रमाच्च वाताद्यष्टस्वरान् अकारादि ऋकारान्तानष्टौ स्वरान्मध्ये सर्व्वमध्यस्थकोष्ठमध्ये नभसा मकारेण वृत्तवीथ्योः वृत्तत्रयान्तरालवीथिद्वयस्थरोपितं नभः षोड़शस्वरप्रसारितमकाराक्षरं। तत्र मण्डले द्वादशोदितैः एकोनविंशपटले धाता इत्यादिनार्द्धाद्येन षड्विंशेन श्लोकेन द्वादशधा प्रोक्तैः। नमोन्तैरित्यनेन चतुर्थी विभक्त्यन्तत्वं तन्नाम्नां सूचितमेव। ते मन्त्रा यथा ॐ धात्रे नमः इत्यादि ॐ विष्णवे नमः इत्यन्ताः। सोमस्याद्यं सौमशब्दस्याद्यमक्षरं सो इत्येतत्। खसंयुक्तं विन्दुसंयुक्तं। तेन अस्य तन्नाम्ना इत्युत्तरत्रान्वयः। तेन चतुर्थीनमोन्तेन तन्नाम्ना तस्य प्रोक्तनाममन्त्रेण तत्र प्राचीनपंक्तिस्थकोष्ठत्रयमध्यकोष्ठगतवृत्तमध्यगतकोष्ठनवके। विलिखेत् प्राग्वदीशादि-

वृत्तवीथ्योः स्वरोपेतं नभसा मातृकां लिखेत् ।
तत्रार्कमर्च्चयेत्तस्य नामभिर्द्वादशोदितैः ॥ ७९ ॥
प्रणवाद्यैर्नमोन्तैश्च भानोः सर्व्वत्र सर्व्वदा ।
सोमस्याद्यं स्वसंयुक्तं कृत्वा तेन तथार्च्चयेत् ॥ ८० ॥
तन्नाम्ना तत्र विलिखेद्विन्द्वाढ्यञ्च स्वराष्टकम् ।
षोड़शस्वरयुक्तञ्च * मातृकाञ्च स्वयोगतः ॥ ८१ ॥
विलिखेद्वृत्तयोर्म्मध्ये मध्यकोष्ठेपि तं लिखेत् ।
दाहवक्निस्वसहितमर्च्चयेत्तत्र मण्डले ॥ ८२ ॥
सोममुक्तक्रमेणैव प्रोक्तकालेषु सर्व्वदा ।
निवेद्य शर्करादुग्धपायसैश्चोपचारकैः ॥ ८३ ॥
सप्तस्वन्येषु कोष्ठेषु कृत्वा वृत्तत्रयं तथा ।
तत्तद्वर्गादिवर्णांश्च स्वरैस्तां मातृकामपि ॥ ८४ ॥
विलिख्य मध्यञ्च तथा कृत्वा तेषु च तत्क्रमात् ।
तत्तद्वर्गाक्षराण्याख्यावाक्षरैरालिखेदपि ॥ ८५ ॥

विन्द्वाढ्यं ऋकारान्तं हकारं षोड़शस्वरयुक्तं षोड़शस्वरप्रसारितं । स्वयोगतः विन्दुयुतं । मध्यकोष्ठे सर्व्वमध्यस्थकोष्ठमध्ये । तं हकारं । दाहवक्निस्वसहितं रेफ ईकार विन्दुसहितं क्रीं इत्यक्षरं । प्रोक्तकालेषु ग्रहप्रातिकूल्यादिषु । उपचारैः पञ्चभिः षोड़शभिर्वा । अन्येषु आग्नेयादीशान्तेषु शिष्टेषु । तथा यथा मध्यप्राक्कोष्ठयोः । तत्तद्वर्गादिवर्णं भौमादिकोष्ठेषु तत्सप्तग्रहात्मकव्यञ्जनवर्गसप्तकस्य कचटतपयश इत्याद्यक्षरसप्तकं स्वरैः प्राग्वत् प्रत्येकं प्रसारितमिति शेषः । विलिख्य प्राग्वत् वृत्तवीथ्योर्मध्यं सर्व्ववृत्तमध्यस्तवृत्तमध्यं । तथा कृत्वा प्रागुक्तवत्तथा कृत्वेत्यर्थः । तेषु प्रतिमण्डलजनितकोष्ठनवके । तत्क्रमात् प्रागुक्तदीशाद्युत्तरान्तप्रादक्षिण्यक्रमात् । तत्तद्वर्गाक्षराण्याख्यावाक्षरैः तत्तद्वर्गाक्षरपञ्चकं अर्व्वाक्सुत्तरत्र समाश्रोतितमश्लोकवक्ष्यमाणचतुर्थीविभक्त्यन्तग्रहनामाक्षरत्रयमेवं सम्भूयाष्टावष्टावक्षराणीत्यर्थः । मध्ये तत्तत्कोष्ठनवकसर्व्वमध्यस्थकोष्ठमध्ये । वर्गाद्यक्षरं तत्तद्वर्गा-

---

* हकारञ्च ।

मध्ये प्रणवगर्भस्थवर्गाद्यक्षरमालिखेत् ।
एवं कृतेषु नवसु पूजयेच्च नवग्रहान् ॥ ८६ ॥
अग्न्यादीशान्तमभितो लिखेन्नामान्यनुक्रमात् ।
ताक्षराणि चतुर्थ्यन्तान्यर्चयेत्तैश्च तानिति ॥ ८७ ॥

दिभूतपूर्वान्ताक्षरसप्तकं । नवसु मण्डलेष्विति शेषः। अग्न्यादीशान्तमित्यस्य काकाक्षिवत् पूर्व्वपरयोरन्वयः। एकदा पूजयेदिति पूर्व्वत्र अन्यदा लिखेदित्युत्तरत्र। अनुक्रमात् वक्ष्यमाणक्रमात्। तैः प्रणवादिनमोन्तैर्नाममन्त्रैः। तान् ग्रहान्। इति उक्तप्रकारतः। एतैर्नाममन्त्रैः। एवं उक्तप्रकारात्। तेषु मण्डलेषु। तेषां ग्रहाणां। ते ग्रहाः। तदनुग्रहं पूजकानुग्रहं। एतदुक्तं भवति प्राक्प्रत्यग्दक्षिणोदक्प्रत्येकमेकहस्तमानान्तरालं सूत्रचतुष्टयमास्फाल्य नव कोष्ठानि निष्पाद्य तेषु कोष्ठेषु प्रत्येकं वृत्तं कोष्ठरेखाचतुष्टयस्पृष्टास्पृष्टं कृत्वा तदन्तरैकैकाङ्गुलमानेन वृत्तद्वयं निष्पाद्य सर्व्वमध्यस्थवृत्तमध्यकर्णिकायां समान्तरालं सूत्रद्वयं प्राक्प्रत्यग्दक्षिणोदगास्फालनेन नवकोष्ठानि कृत्वा तत्र सर्व्वमध्यस्थकोष्ठमध्यगतवृत्तत्रयकर्णिकास्थकोष्ठनवकमध्यकोष्ठे सां इत्यक्षरं साध्ययुतं विलिख्य शिष्टकोष्ठाष्टके ईशादुत्तरान्तं अं आं इं ईं उं ऊं ऋं ॠं इत्यष्टावक्षराण्यालिख्य वाह्यवृत्तवीथिद्वयान्तःवीथ्यां प्राग्वत् षोड़शस्वरप्रसारितविन्दुयुतानां मकारपंक्तिं प्रादक्षिण्यात् समालिख्य वाह्यवीथ्यां सविन्दुकां मातृकां प्राग्वत् लिखित्वा ततस्तत्प्राक्पंक्तिस्थकोष्ठवृत्तत्रयसर्वमध्यकर्णिकास्थकोष्ठनवकसर्वमध्यं कोष्ठे क्रौं इत्यक्षरं साध्यादियुतं विलिख्य शिष्टकोष्ठाष्टके प्राग्वदीशादुत्तरान्तं लृं ॡं एं ऐं ओं औं अं अः इत्यष्टाक्षराणि लिखित्वा तत्र वाह्यवृत्तवीथिद्वयेन्तर्वीथ्यां स्वरविकृतां विन्दुयुक्तां उकारपंक्तिं प्रादक्षिण्यक्रमाल्लिखित्वा तद्वाह्यवीथ्यां मातृकाञ्च विन्दुयुतां प्राग्वद्विलिख्य ततश्चाग्नेयादीशान्तकोष्ठसप्तकगतवृत्तत्रयमध्यकर्णिकास्थकोष्ठनवकमध्यकोष्ठे प्रणवं लिखित्वा तत्प्रणवमध्ये यथाक्रमं कं चं टं तं पं यं शं इति तत्तद्वर्गाक्षराण्येकमेकं लिखित्वा तद्बहिरीशकोष्ठाद्युत्तरकोष्ठान्तं कवर्ग चवर्ग टवर्ग तवर्ग पवर्ग यवर्ग शवर्ग सप्ताक्षरपञ्चकपञ्चकं भौमाय बुधाय सौरये गुरवे राहवे शुक्राय केतवे इत्येतानि प्रत्येकं अक्षराणि सप्तनामानि यथाक्रममेकैकं संयोज्य एवं सम्भूयाष्टावष्टाक्षराणि लिखित्वा तत्तद्वाह्यवृत्तवीथिद्वये प्रागवदन्तरन्तर्वीथ्यां तत्तद्वर्गाद्यक्षराणि स्वर-

भौमं बुधं तथा सौरिं गुरुं राहुञ्च शुक्रकम्।
केतुमेतैस्तु सर्वत्र मन्त्रानुक्तौ च पूजनम्॥ ८८॥
एवं नवग्रहाणान्तु मण्डलान्युदितानि वै।
तेष्वेव तेषामर्च्चातस्ते कुर्य्युस्तदनुग्रहम्॥ ८९॥
भास्करेन्द्वोश्च तद्वारद्वये दर्शे च पूर्णिके।
स्वोच्चयोः स्थितपूजाञ्च मण्डलं शृणु पार्वति॥ ९०॥
विलिख्य वृत्तयुगलं तन्मध्ये तिर्य्यगूर्द्ध्वतः।
रेखाभिरष्टभिर्म्मध्ये त्वेकाशीतिपदे लिखेत्॥ ९१॥
ईशकोष्ठादिपरितः प्रवेशेनामृतार्णकान्।
मायान्ताशीतिसंख्यातान्मध्ये दावगतञ्च तत्॥ ९२॥

विकृतानि यथाक्रममेकैकपंक्तिक्रमादालिख्य तत्तद्बाह्यवाह्यवीथ्यां प्राग्वन्मातृका लिखित्वा एवं नवमण्डलानि निष्पाद्य प्रोक्तक्रमाणां ग्रहाणां प्रोक्ततत्तत्प्रातिकूल्यादिषु प्रणवादिचतुर्थीनमोन्तैर्नाममन्त्रै रर्कस्योक्तद्वादशभिः चन्द्रस्य सों सोमाय नमः भौमादीनान्तु जं भौमाय नमः इत्यादिभिः जं केतवे नमः इत्यन्तैश्च प्रोक्तद्रव्यादिभिरर्चनात् प्रोक्तफलसिद्धिः। एवं क्रमेण शुभग्रहा महादिषु अशुभग्रहा विदिक्षु च भवन्तीति॥ ८८॥

भास्करेत्यादिभिरीश्वरीत्यन्तैर्नवभिः श्लोकैः पूजाकालं तत्प्रस्तावपुरःसरं चन्द्रार्कयोः पृथक् पूजामण्डलं तन्निर्माणद्रव्याणि तत्र पूजनञ्चोपदिशति। तत्र तद्वारद्वये यथाक्रमं रविवारे सोमवारे च। पूर्णिके पूर्णायामित्यर्थः। स्वोच्चयोः स्थितयोः आदित्ये मेषराशौ दशमभागस्थे मध्याह्नगते ऋषभराशौ तृतीयभागगते चन्द्रे नभोमध्यं गते। तन्मध्ये वृत्तयुगलान्तर्वृत्तमध्ये रेखाभिरष्टभिः संजायेत इति शेषः। अस्य एकाशीतिपदे इत्यत्रान्वयः। मध्ये तत्तत्कोष्ठमध्ये इत्यर्थः। अमृतार्णान् अष्टमे पटले ज्याकमित्यादि षट्त्रिंशश्लोकोत्तरार्द्धप्रोक्तान् जकार झकार ठकार वकार सकारान् षोड़शस्वरविकृतान्। मायान्ताशीतिसंख्यातान् विसर्जनीयान्तान् अशीतिसंख्यातान्। मध्ये सर्व्वमध्यस्थकोष्ठ-

वृत्तयोरन्तरा कृत्वा मातृकां ग्रथिताञ्च तैः ।
पञ्चभिश्च लिखेत्तत्र विम्बे सोमं समर्चयेत् ॥ ९३ ॥
कर्पूरचन्दनाभ्यान्तदालिखेदिन्दुविम्बकम् ।
रक्तचन्दनसिन्दूरगैरिकैरेकतो रवेः ॥ ९४ ॥
कृत्वा विम्बं तत्र तञ्च पूजयेत् प्रोक्तरूपतः ।
द्विवृत्तान्तस्तिर्य्यगूर्द्ध्वाः कृत्वा रेखाः समान्तरम् ॥ ९५ ॥
एकोनविंशं तन्मध्यष्वालिखेत् प्राग्वदीरितान् ।
प्राणादिकान्नभोऽन्तांस्तु खैरुपेतान् स्वरैर्युतान् ॥ ९६ ॥

मध्ये । दावगतं ठकारमध्यस्थं तत्पूर्व्वं चन्द्रमण्डलकोष्ठमध्यप्रोक्तक्रींकारं कृत्वेति भिन्नक्रमः ग्रथितं कृत्वेत्यर्थः । ग्रथितां एकान्तरितां । तैः विसर्जनीयान्तैरमृतार्णैः पञ्चभिः स्वरविकारविधुरैः एकतः अन्यतमेन रवेः कृत्वा विम्बं रवेरिति पूर्व्वत्रान्वयः । तत्र विम्बे तं रविं प्रोक्तरूपतः प्रोक्तमन्त्रोपचाराद्यैः । द्विवृत्तान्तः वृत्तद्वयं कृत्वा तदन्तरित्यर्थः । एकोनविंशं एकोनविंशतिरित्यर्थः । अस्य रेखा इति पूर्व्वत्रान्वयः । तन्मध्येषु तद्रेखाजनितकोष्ठचतुःशतकमध्येष्वित्यर्थः । प्राग्वत् ईशादिप्रादक्षिण्यप्रवेशगत्या । प्राणादिकान्नभोन्तान् ककारादिमकारान्तान् पञ्चविंशतिवर्णान् । खैर्विन्दुभिः स्वरैर्युतान् एकैकं षोड़शस्वरविकृतान् । तैः ककारादिमकारान्तैः स्वरविकारभिन्नैः । स्वरैर्भान्तयुतैः स्वरविकृतमकारसहितैः । वह्निदशार्णैः अग्निभूताक्षरदशकेन । लिपिं मातृकां विलिखेदित्यस्य लिपिमिति पूर्व्वत्र विशदाकारमित्युत्तरत्र च काकाक्षिवदन्वयः । तन्मध्ये मण्डलमध्ये । प्राग्वन्नाममन्त्रोपचारादिभिः । एतदुक्तं भवति त्रिहस्तायामविस्तारमानेन वृत्तं निष्पाद्य तद्वहिरेकाङ्गुलमाने च वृत्तं निष्पाद्य सर्वमध्यवृत्तमध्ये कर्णिकायां प्राक्प्रत्यग्दक्षिणोदक् च अष्टाभिरष्टाभिः रेखाभिः समान्तरालाभिरेकाशीतिकोष्ठानि निष्पाद्य तेषु कोष्ठेष्वीशदिग्गतकोष्ठादिप्रादक्षिण्यप्रवेशगत्या प्रोक्तान्यमृताक्षराणि स्वरविकृत्या अशीतिसंख्यानि मायान्तानि विलिख्य शिष्टसर्व्वमध्यकोष्ठमध्ये ठकारमालिख्य तदन्तरे प्रागवत् क्रीं इत्यक्षरं ममाध्यादिकञ्च विलिख्य तद्वहिर्वृत्तवीथ्यां स्वरविकारविधुरा-

वृत्तयोरन्तरा तैश्च पञ्चविंशतिवर्णकैः ।
स्वरैर्भान्तयुतैर्वह्निदशार्णैर्ग्रथितां लिपिम् ॥ ९७ ॥
विलिख्य विशदाकारं विहस्तायामविस्तरम् ।
तन्मध्ये भानुमावाह्य पूजयेत् प्राग्वदीश्वरि ॥ ९८ ॥
पीठे वा सुधया क्लिप्ते भूतले वा शिलातले ।
सुसमेनावृते कृत्वा विम्बान्युक्तानि पूजयेत् ॥ ९९ ॥
एवं सर्वत्र तन्त्रेस्मिन् ग्रहपूजा समीरिता ।
विशेषादेशरहिते तत्र तत्क्रमतोर्च्चयेत् ॥ १०० ॥

मृताक्षरपञ्चकग्रथितां मातृकां विन्यस्य एवमेतन्मण्डलं कर्पूरचन्दनाभ्यां विरच्य प्रोक्तकालेषु प्रोक्तनाममन्त्रेण प्रोक्तोपचाराद्यैः सोममर्च्चयेत्। ततः प्रागुक्तमानेन वृत्तद्वयं निष्पाद्य प्रागुक्तत्कर्णिकायां प्राक् प्रत्यक् दक्षिणोदक् च समान्तराला एकोनविंशत्येकोनविंशतिरेखाः समालिख्य चतुःशतकोष्ठानि निष्पाद्य तेषु कोष्ठेष्वीशादिप्रादक्षिण्यप्रवेशगत्या ककारादिमकारान्तानि पञ्चविंशतिमक्षराणि प्रत्येकं षोड़शस्वरविकृत्या षोड़शषोड़शसंख्यातानि सम्भूय चतुःशतसंख्यातानि सविन्दुकानि विलिख्य तद्वहिर्वृत्तवीथ्यां स्वरविकारविधुरककारादिमकारान्तैः पञ्चविंशत्यक्षरैः स्वरविकृतमकाररूपषोड़शकेन वह्निभूताक्षरदशकेन सम्भूयैकपञ्चाशदक्षरैः सविन्दुकैरेकान्तरा ग्रथितां मातृकां सविन्दुकां विलिख्य एवमेतन्मण्डलं प्रोक्तरक्तचन्दनादिना विलिख्य तत्र प्रोक्तकालेषु प्रोक्तनाममन्त्रैर्द्वादशभिः प्रोक्तोपचाराद्यैरर्कं चार्च्चयेत्। तेन प्रोक्तफलसिद्धिभागिति ॥ ९८ ॥

पीठे इत्यादिभिर्विग्रहा इत्यन्तैस्त्रिभिः श्लोकैस्तन्त्रसाधारणनवग्रहमण्डललेखनस्थानविशेषोपदेशं प्रोक्तपूजातिदेशं पटलार्थनिगमनं ग्रहाणां नित्यात्मकत्वोपदेशञ्च करोति। तत्र वा विकल्पे। अनावृते जनाद्यावरकरहिते। तत्र विशेषादेशरहिते तत्क्रमतः विशेषोपदेशक्रमतः विद्यायाः नित्यानामिति

एवं ते देवि विद्यायाः कालदेशात्मतोदिता ।
सर्व्वात्मना सर्वदा च सैवार्च्या सर्वविग्रहा ॥ १०१ ॥
रागतत्त्वमयी व्याप्तिरिति सम्यक् समीरिता ।
अस्या निफालनाच्चित्ते तत्तत्त्वं स्वात्मसात् कृतम् ॥

इति षोड़शनित्यातन्त्रेषु श्रीकादिमते
लोकतादात्म्यादिकथनं नाम
अष्टाविंशं पटलम् ॥
॥ २८ ॥

शेषः । सैव ललितैव अर्च्चनीया सर्व्वविग्रहा सर्व्वदेवताविग्रहा इति ॥ १०१ ॥ ॐ ॥

इति षोड़शनित्यातन्त्रेषु श्रीकादिमताख्यस्य परिपूर्णस्य तन्त्रस्य प्रपञ्चसार-
सिंहराजप्रकाशाभिधानेन सुभगानन्दनाथेन विरचितायां
मनोरमाख्यायां व्याख्यायां षोड़शनित्यानां लोककाल-
तादात्म्यादिप्रकाशनपरं अष्टाविंशपटलं परिपूर्णं
परामृष्टम् ॥ २८ ॥ ॐतत्सत् ॥

ग्रन्थसंख्या—अष्टाविंशे तु यन्त्राणि प्रोक्तान्येकादशात्र तु ।
सपादाशीतिरधिका व्याख्याग्रन्थाः शतद्वयात् ॥

एकोनत्रिंशपटलम् ।

अथ षोड़शनित्यानां होमाय विधिवच्छिवे ।
प्राच्यादिदिग्विभागञ्च मण्डपादेस्तु लक्षणम् ॥ १ ॥
कुण्डानां स्थाननिर्म्माणैर्नाभियोन्यादिलक्षणम् ।
मानानि तेषामग्नेस्तु ध्यानं जिह्वास्तदर्च्चनम् ॥ २ ॥
होमद्रव्याणि सामान्यविशेषाणि हुतक्रियाम् ।
उपक्रमोपसंहारौ फलानि च यथाक्रमम् ॥ ३ ॥
कथयामि शृणु प्राज्ञे यैर्मन्त्री सिद्धिमाप्नुयात् ।
यदि कुर्य्याद् यथादृष्टं विपन्नो निरयं व्रजेत् ॥ ४ ॥
भानोर्गत्या दिशो ज्ञात्वा कुर्य्यात् कर्म्माणि देशिकः ।
तद्गत्या दिक्परिज्ञानं शृणु वक्ष्ये यथाविधि ॥ ५ ॥

पूर्व्वस्मिन्नष्टाविंशे पटले षोड़शनित्यानां लोककालतादात्म्यादिकमुपदिश्यानन्तरं षोड़शनित्यानां नित्यहोमार्थं मण्डपकुण्डादिनिर्माणादिक्रममुपदिशति । अथ षोड़शनित्यानामित्यादिना वाञ्छितमित्यन्तेन श्लोकशतरूपेणैकोनत्रिंशेन पटलेन । तत्र अथ षोड़शेत्यादिभिर्व्रजेदित्यन्तैश्चतुर्भिः श्लोकैः पटलार्थोद्देशमुक्तान्यथा करणे प्रत्यवायोपदेशञ्च करोति । तत्र मण्डपादेरित्यत्रादिशब्दः कुण्डादिविषयः । योन्यादीत्यत्रादिशब्दो मेखलादिविषयः । तेषां मण्डपादीनां । तद्ध्यानं क्रूरसौम्यादिविभागात् तत्तद्ध्यानं । तदर्च्चनं अग्नेर्जिह्वानाञ्चार्च्चनं । उपक्रमोपसंहारौ पुरस्तात्तन्त्रे उपरिष्टात् तन्त्रे च यैः प्रोक्तमण्डपादिगुणविधानैः । यथादृष्टं प्रोक्तगुणविधानवर्ज्जं । निरयं नरकं देवताप्रातिकूल्यमित्यर्थः ॥ ४ ॥

भानोरित्यादिभिः कल्पयेदित्यन्तैः पञ्चभिः श्लोकैः शङ्कुच्छायया दिक्परिज्ञानक्रमं प्रस्तावसहितमुपदिशति । तत्र भानोर्गत्या आदित्यस्य दक्षिणोत्तरायणक्रमगतिभेदजातया छाययेति यावत् । कर्माणीति मण्डपकुण्डादीनीति शेषः । तद्गत्या भानुगत्या । सुसमे भूतले जलयन्त्रादिभिरिति शेषः । ज्ञात्वेति भिन्नक्रमः ।

सुसमे भूतले कृत्वा वृत्तं भ्रमणरूपतः ।
तन्मध्यं विन्दुमध्यन्तु शङ्कुं संस्थाप्य तस्य वै ॥ ६ ॥
अग्रच्छायान्वयवशाद्वृत्ते पूर्वापरद्वये ।
पूर्वापराह्लयोः कृत्वा चिह्ने तमभितस्तथा ॥ ७ ॥
स्वसमानपरिभ्रान्त्या कृत्वा वृत्तद्वयं पुनः ।
तयोः संश्लेषसञ्जातमध्यदक्षोत्तरस्थिते ॥ ८ ॥
सन्धिद्वये च प्राक्प्रत्यक्सूत्रमध्ये तु विन्यसेत् ।
सूत्रं दक्षोत्तरं तेषां अग्रैः प्रागादि कल्पयेत् ॥ ९ ॥

वृत्तं कृत्वेति यावत् । तन्मध्यं विन्दुमध्यं इत्येतत् क्रियाविशेषणं । वृत्तमध्यस्य मध्यं विन्दुमध्यं शङ्कुमध्यं यथा तथेत्यर्थः । तुरवधारणे । तस्य शङ्कोर्वृत्ते इत्येतत् पूर्वापरयोरन्वेति । पूर्वापरद्वये पूर्वापराख्यिकयोर्द्वयोर्दिशोः कृत्वा प्राग्वच्चिह्ने कृत्वेत्यन्वयः । तदभितः तच्चिह्नद्वयमभितः । तथा तद्द्वयमवष्टभ्य स्वसमान परिभ्रान्त्या तच्चिह्नद्वयान्तरालमानस्य स्वेष्टसार्धमानेनान्योन्यतुल्येन परिभ्रान्त्या कृत्वा वृत्तद्वयं वृत्तद्वयं कृत्वेत्यर्थः । तयोः पूर्वापरयोर्वृत्तयोः । संश्लेषसञ्जातमध्यदक्षोत्तरस्थिते इत्यस्य उत्तरत्र सन्धिद्वये इत्येतद्विशेष्यं । प्राक्प्रत्यक्सूत्रमध्ये प्राक्प्रत्यागात्मकसूत्रमध्ये । तुः समाहारे । दक्षोत्तरं दक्षिणोत्तरं तेषां मण्डपादीनां सूत्रैः अग्रैःसूत्राग्रैः । एतदुक्तं भवति जीमूतौघपरिवेष्टितभानौ दिवसे छदिरादिभिरनावृते देशे जलयन्त्रादिभिः सुसमीकृतस्य दर्पणोदरसङ्काशस्य भूतलस्य मध्ये विन्दुं कृत्वा तदवष्टम्भतः प्रतिदिशं द्वादशाङ्गुलमानं वृत्तं निष्पाद्य तत्र षडङ्गुलमानपरिणाहमूलमुत्तरोत्तरपरिणाहापचयेन सूचीमात्रीकृताग्रपरिणाहमृज्वाकृति शङ्कुं द्वादशाङ्गुलमानच्छायासहितं वृत्ताकारं शिल्पिवरेण निर्मितं तद्वृत्तमध्यस्य विन्दुमध्ये यथा शङ्कुमूलपरिणाहमध्यं भवति तथा संस्थाप्य तच्छङ्कुच्छायाग्रस्य पूर्वाह्णे तद्वृत्तरेखापश्चिमभागे यत्र सम्पातस्तत्र च ततोऽपराह्णे तच्छङ्कुच्छायाग्रस्य तद्वृत्तरेखापूर्वभागे यत्र सम्पातस्तत्र च चिह्नं विधाय तत्चिह्नद्वयप्रापि यत् सूत्रं तत् पूर्वापरं परिकल्पितचिह्नद्वयावष्टम्भेन तच्चिह्नान्तरालमानस्य स्वेष्टाधिकेनार्धमानेनान्योन्यसमेन किञ्चिदन्योन्यसंश्लिष्टं पूर्वापरं वृत्तद्वयं विधाय तद्वृत्तरेखादक्षिणोत्तरसन्धिद्वयप्रापि प्राक्पश्चिमसूत्रमध्यगत्या तिर्यग्रूपेण यत्सूत्रं तद्-

राज्ञां होमाभिषेकादिप्रयोगार्थन्तु मण्डपम् ।
विदध्यान्नवहस्तेन विस्तारायामसंयुतम् ॥ १० ॥
षोड़शस्तम्भसंयुक्तं चतुर्द्वारं सुतोरणम् ।
उदुम्बरवटाश्वत्थप्लक्षैश्छदनमालया ॥ ११ ॥
पिहिताशेषकोणञ्च तत्तु भागैकभागतः ।
विदध्यान्मध्यतो वेदीं करमात्रसमुन्नताम् ॥ १२ ॥
दर्पणोदरसङ्काशमध्यां तदभितस्तथा ।
प्रागादिदिक्षु कोणेषु वह्न्यादिषु च कल्पयेत् ॥ १३ ॥

क्षिणोत्तरं परिकल्प्य तत् प्राक् प्रत्यग् दक्षिणोत्तरसूत्रद्वयसम्पातात् वक्ष्यमाणपरिकल्पितसूत्राग्रैस्तैस्तेषां मण्डपकुण्डादीनां प्राक् प्रत्यग् दक्षिणोत्तरात्मकदिक् चतुष्टयं कल्पयेदिति ॥ ८ ॥

राज्ञामित्यादिभिर्लक्षणमित्यन्तैर्दशभिः श्लोकैः मण्डपनिर्माणक्रमं तत्र वेदीकुण्डनिर्माणस्थानानि चोपदिशति। तत्र नवहस्तेन विस्तारायामसंयुतं नवहस्तमानविस्तारेण नवहस्तमानायामेन संयुतं। षोड़शस्तम्भसंयुक्तं प्राक् प्रत्यग् दक्षिणोदक् च प्रत्येकं समान्तरालं प्रसारितसूत्रचतुष्टयषोड़शसन्धिष्विति शेषः। चतुर्द्वारं दिक्ष्विति शेषः। छदनमालया दर्भमालया। पिहिताशेषकोणं पिहिताशेषकोणभक्तिं। तत्तु भागैकभागतः मण्डपस्य त्रिभागैकभागतः। मध्यतः मण्डपमध्यस्थस्तम्भचतुष्टयमध्यतः। तदभितः वेदीमभितः। तथा एकत्रिंशे पटले वक्ष्यमाणमेषादिमीनान्तद्वादशराशिस्थानात्मकेषु। चः समुच्चये। कल्पयेदित्यस्य कुण्डानीत्यनेनोत्तरत्रान्वयः। चतुष्कं कुण्डानामिति शेषः। एतदुक्तं भवति प्राक्प्रत्यग्दक्षिणोदक् च नव नवहस्तमानविस्तारायामेन वाह्यकोणचतुष्टये चतुर्भिः प्रतिदिशं द्विद्विक्रमाद्दिक् चतुष्टयेऽष्टभिर्मध्यभक्तिमभितः कोणचतुष्टये चतुर्भिश्च सम्भूय षोड़शस्तम्भैः संयुतं निःशेषपिहितकोणचतुष्टयं प्रागादिषु मण्डपचतुर्द्वारेषु उदुम्बरवटाश्वत्थप्लक्षाख्यदुग्धतरुभिः क्रमात् कल्पितछदनमालयोपेतेन तोरणचतुष्टयेन युतं त्रिहस्तमानविस्तारायामात्मकभक्तिनवकोपेतं मण्डपं विधाय तन्मध्यचतुःस्तम्भमध्यस्थभक्तिमध्ये त्वेकहस्तमानोन्नतियुक्तां त्रिहस्तायाम-

कुण्डान्यष्टौ चतुष्कञ्च तेषां रूपञ्च नामकम्।
निर्म्माणं सकलं वच्ये यथाविधि तवानघे ॥ १४ ॥
तुलाकुलीरमेषाणां मकरस्य च देशत:।
विदध्याद्वृत्तकुण्डानि चरराशिचतुष्टये ॥ १५ ॥
वृषे सिंहे वृश्चिके च कुम्भे च स्थिरराशिषु।
विदध्याच्चतुरस्राणि तत: कुण्डान्यनुक्रमात् ॥ १६ ॥
मिथुने कन्यकायाञ्च चापे मीने क्रमेण वै।
उभयात्मसु कुर्वीत योनिकुण्डानि मङ्गले ॥ १७ ॥

विस्तारां दर्पणोदरसङ्काशां वेदीं विधाय तत् परितो वाह्यभक्त्यष्टके द्वादशराशिस्थानेषु प्रतिदिशं द्विद्विक्रमेण कुण्डाष्टकं प्रतिकोणमेकैकक्रमेण कुण्डचतुष्टयञ्च सम्भूय द्वादशकुण्डानि वच्यमाणक्रमेण नृपाणां होमाभिषेकादिमङ्गलप्रयोगार्थं विदध्यादिति। तेषां द्वादशानां कुण्डानां रूपं चतुरस्राद्यात्मकं। कुलीरशब्देन कर्कटराशिरुच्यते। च: समाहारे। देशत: देशे। वृत्तकुण्डानि वृत्ताकाराणि कुण्डानि। स्थिरराशिषु प्रोक्तवृषादिषु चतुर्षु। विदध्याच्चतुरस्राणि चतुरस्रचतुष्टयं विदध्यादित्यर्थ:। कुर्य्यात् कुण्डानि तानि चत्वारि चतुरस्राणि। अनुक्रमाद्वच्यमाणक्रमात् कुण्डानि कुर्य्यादित्यर्थ:। उभयात्मसु प्रोक्तमिथुनादिषु चतुर्षु राशिस्थानेषु योनिकुण्डानि योन्याकारवच्यमाणलक्षणकुण्डानि। मङ्गले प्रयोगे इति शेष:। अमङ्गलेषु प्रयोगेष्विति शेष:। चरेषु चरराशिस्थानेषु अर्द्धशशाङ्कं अर्द्धचन्द्राकाराणि। स्थिरेषु स्थिरराशिषु। अपि शब्देन पूर्व्वकुण्डानीत्येतदाकृष्यते। त्रिकोणानि त्रिकोणाकाराणि। परेषु उभयराशिषु। तुर्विशेषे। चतुष्टये कोणानामिति शेष:। अष्टकोणे अष्टास्रे। एतदुक्तं भवति प्रोक्तमण्डपवाह्यस्थभक्त्यष्टके प्रागादिचतुर्दिग्गतासु चतसृषु भक्तिषु एकस्यामेकस्यां द्विद्विराशिक्रमेण कोणदिग्गतासु भक्तिष्वेकैकक्रमेण सम्भूय प्राक्पंक्तिगतस्थानद्वये तूत्तरस्थानमारभ्य प्रादक्षिण्यक्रमेणैशानकोणभक्तिपर्य्यन्तं मेषादिद्वादशराशिस्थानानि परिकल्प्य तेषु स्थानेषु मङ्गलप्रयोगे मेषकर्कटतुलामकरराशिषु वृत्तकुण्डानि चत्वारि वृषसिंहवृश्चिककुम्भराशिषु चतुरस्रकुण्डानि चत्वारि मिथुन

अमङ्गलेषु कुर्वीत चरेष्वर्द्धशशाङ्ककम् ।
स्थिरेष्वपि त्रिकोणानि परेषु तु चतुष्टये ॥ १८ ॥
पञ्चास्रञ्च षडस्रञ्च चाष्टकोणे सकर्णिकम् ।
एवं नवानां कुण्डानां शृणु मानादिलक्षणम् १९ ॥
मध्यमाङ्गुलिमध्यस्थपर्वणः परिणाहतः ।
तृतीयांशो भवेदत्र तन्त्रे सर्वत्र चाङ्गुलिः ॥ २० ॥
तैश्चतुर्भिर्भवेन्मुष्टिर्वितस्तिस्तत्त्रिभिर्गुणैः ।
अरत्निस्तद्द्वयेन स्याद्धस्तस्तद्द्वयतः शिवे ॥ २१ ॥
तद्द्वयन्तु भवेद्व्यामः तन्मानं स्यान्नरोन्नतिः ।
षण्णवत्यङ्गुला सा स्यात्तन्मानैः कुण्डकल्पनम् ॥ २२ ॥

कन्याचापमीनराशिषु योन्याकाराणि चत्वारि कुण्डानि च पुनरमङ्गलप्रयोगे तस्मे-षादिचरराशिचतुष्टये अर्द्धचन्द्राकारकुण्डचतुष्टयं स्थिरराशिचतुष्टये त्रिकोणाकारकुण्डचतुष्टयं उभयराशिचतुष्टये क्रमात् पञ्चास्रषडस्रसप्तास्राष्टास्रात्म-कान्येकैक कुण्डानि च कृत्वा सम्भूय वृत्तचतुरस्रयोन्यर्द्धचन्द्रत्रिकोणपञ्चास्र-षडस्रसप्तास्राष्टास्राणां नवविधानां कुण्डानां मानादिलक्षणं शृणुवेति ॥१८॥

मध्यमेत्यादिभिः कल्पनमित्यन्तैस्त्रिभिः श्लोकैरङ्गुल्यादिमानक्रमं कुण्डमान-वासनाञ्चोपदिशति। तत्र मध्यमाङ्गुलीत्यादिना श्लोकेनैतदुक्तं भवति यजमान-दक्षिणहस्तस्य मध्यमाङ्गुलिमध्यपर्व्वप्रदेशपरिणाहमानं त्रिधा कृत्वा तेषां त्रयाणामंशानामेकोंऽशः सर्व्वत्रास्मिन् तन्त्रेऽङ्गुलिमानं भवेदिति। तैश्चतुर-ङ्गुलिमितांशैः मुष्टिरिति नाम वितस्तिः नाम तत्त्रिभिर्गुणैस्त्रिगुणितैर्मुष्टिमानां-शैर्द्वादशाङ्गुलमानैरित्यर्थः। अरत्निः संज्ञा तद्द्वयेन वितस्तिद्वयेन। अङ्गुलि-चतुर्विंशत्येति यावत्। हस्तः संज्ञा तद्द्वयतः अरत्निद्वयेन अष्टचत्वारिंशदङ्गुलि-भिरिति यावत्। शिवे इति देवीसम्बुद्धिः। तद्द्वयं हस्तद्वयं व्यामः नाम तन्मानं व्याममानं। नरोन्नतिः नराणां मानमित्यर्थः। सा नरोन्नतिस्तन्मानैः षण्णवत्यङ्गुल-मानैः अवयवैः प्रमाणैश्च। एतदुक्तं भवति सर्व्वेषां कुण्डानामायामविस्तारख्यातानां प्रत्येकं चतुर्विंशत्यङ्गुलविशिष्टत्वात् सम्भूय द्वासप्तत्यङ्गुलैश्च तैर्मेखलानामुत्-सेधविस्तारयोः प्रत्येकं द्वादशाङ्गुलविशिष्टत्वलाभात ताभ्यां सम्भूय षण्णवत्यङ्गुलात्मः

प्राक्प्रत्यक् सूत्रमास्फाल्य तन्मध्ये चिह्नकल्पनम् ।
कृत्वा तत्पूर्वतः पश्चाद्द्वादशाङ्गुलमानतः ॥ २३ ॥
परं प्रमृज्य तत्रापि विदध्याच्चिह्नयुग्मकम् ।
प्राक्प्रत्यक्चिह्नमानेन तयोरेवावलम्बतः ॥ २४ ॥
दक्षिणोत्तरतो हंसपदे कृत्वा ततस्तयोः ।
प्रसार्य्य सूत्रं तत्रापि मार्जयित्वोक्तमानतः ॥ २५ ॥
ततस्तदग्राण्यालम्ब्य मध्यचिह्नस्य मानतः ।
कुर्य्याद्धंसपदं कोष्ठान्यभितस्तेषु पातयेत् ॥ २६ ॥

त्वाच्च परिणाहतः पञ्चत्यङ्गुलात्मकत्वाच्च तत्संख्याङ्गुलमितपुरुषदेहोन्नति समानानि कुण्डानीति ॥ २२ ॥

प्रागित्यादिभिर्मानत इत्यन्तैः पञ्चभिः श्लोकैः समचतुरस्रकुण्डनिर्माणक्रमं तच्चतुरस्रे कुण्डेऽन्यतरकुण्डनिर्माणं प्रस्तावसहितमुपदिशति । तत्र तन्मध्यप्राक्-प्रत्यक्सूत्रमध्ये चिह्नकल्पनं कृत्वा चिह्नं कृत्वेत्यर्थः । तत्पूर्व्वतः पश्चिमाच्चिह्नात् पूर्व्वतः । पश्चाच्च द्वादशाङ्गुलमानतः प्रत्येकमिति शेषः । परं अधिकं तत्रापि उभयतः प्रोक्तद्वादशद्वादशाङ्गुलमानेपि । तयोः प्राक्प्रत्यक्चिह्नयोः अवलम्बतः अवष्टम्भतः भ्रमादित्यर्थः । तयोर्दक्षिणोत्तरहंसपदयोः तद्दक्षिणोत्तरतिर्य्यक्सूत्र-मानतः द्वादशाङ्गुलद्वादशाङ्गुलमानतः अधिकमिति शेषः । तदग्राणि प्राक्-प्रत्यग्दक्षिणोत्तरसूत्रचतुष्टयाग्राणि मध्यचिह्नस्य मानतः द्वादशाङ्गुलमानतः पातयेदित्यस्य चतुष्टयमित्यत्रान्वयः । एतदुक्तं भवति प्राक्कल्पितदिक्क्रमात् प्राक्प्रत्यगायतं सूत्रमास्फाल्य तन्मध्ये चिह्नं कृत्वा तच्चिह्नात् पूर्व्वतः पश्चिमतः च द्वादशाङ्गुलद्वादशाङ्गुलमाने चिह्ने कृत्वा तत्तदधिकांशं मार्जयित्वा तच्चिह्न-द्वयावष्टम्भेन तत्सूत्रं तुल्यमानभ्रमेण पूर्वापरतः किञ्चिदन्योन्यसंश्लिष्टवृत्तद्वयं विधाय तयोर्दक्षिणोत्तरहंसपदप्रापि प्राक्प्रत्यग्वृत्तसूत्रमध्यस्थहंसपदसम्भेदा द्दक्षिणोत्तरं सूत्रमास्फाल्य तत्रापि मध्यचिह्नाद्द्वादशाङ्गुलद्वादशाङ्गुलमाने दक्षिणो-त्तरतश्चिह्नद्वयं विधाय तत्तदधिकांशञ्च मार्जयित्वा तत्तत्सूत्राग्रचतुष्टयावलम्बनेन द्वादशद्वादशाङ्गुलमानेन चतुर्षु कोणेष्वपि हंसपदचतुष्टयं विधाय तत्तदग्रा-त्तत्तद्धंसपदप्रापि प्राक्प्रत्यक्सूत्रद्वयं दक्षिणोत्तरसूत्रद्वयञ्च सम्भूय सूत्रचतुष्टयमा-

चतुष्टयन्तु सूत्रं च चतुरस्रं भवेत् समम् ।
तस्मिन्नन्यानि कुण्डानि वदामि तव मानतः ॥ २७ ॥
तेषां प्रोक्तक्रमेणैव चरादिषु तु राशिषु ।
माननिर्म्माणयोर्वक्ष्ये विधानं सुस्फुटं शिवे ॥ २८ ॥
तन्मध्याष्टादशांशेन प्राक्सूत्राग्रं विकाशयेत् ।
तिर्य्यक्सूत्राद्वहिस्तेन मानेन भ्रमयेत्तथा ॥ २९ ॥
मध्यचिह्नावलम्बेन भवेत्तद्वृत्तकुण्डकम् ।
चतुरस्राभितः सा तु त्याज्या भूरन्यतस्तथा ॥ ३० ॥
लभ्यते सर्वकुण्डेषु तेन सर्वाणि सर्वतः ।
तत्समान्येव जायन्ते षण्णवत्यङ्गुलात्मना ॥ ३१ ॥
तन्मध्ये दशमांशं तु परित्यज्याधऊर्द्धतः ।
तेषां शशाङ्कमानेन तन्मध्याद्भ्रामयेत्तथा ॥ ३२ ॥

स्फाल्य समचतुरस्रं कुर्य्यादिति। तस्मिन् समचतुरस्रे अन्यानि वृत्तादीनि मानतः चतुरस्रकुण्डप्रोक्तषण्णवत्यङ्गुलमानान्न्यूनाधिकमानत इति यावत् ॥ २७ ॥

तेषामित्यादिभिरात्मना इत्यन्तैश्चतुर्भिः श्लोकैः सप्रस्तावं वृत्तकुण्डनिर्माण-क्रमादिकमुपदिशति। तत्र तेषां कुण्डानां सुस्फुटं गमकं। शिवे इति सम्बुद्धिः। तन्मध्याष्टादशांशेन चतुरस्रमध्यसूत्रमानस्याष्टादशांशेन। तिर्य्यक्-सूत्राद्वहिर्दक्षिणोत्तरायततिर्य्यक्सूत्रद्वये प्राक्सूत्राद्वहिः। तथा अभितः परितः कोणेषु चतुर्षु। सा भूः। अन्यतः अन्यस्मिन् दिक्चतुष्टये इत्यर्थः। तेन वक्ष्य-माणविधानेन। सर्वाणि कुण्डानि। तत्समानि चतुरस्रपरिणाहमानसमानि। एतदुक्तं भवति प्राग्वत् समचतुरस्रं कृत्वा तन्मध्यविष्कम्भमानमष्टादशधा विभज्य तेष्वेकांशमानात् प्राग्गतदक्षिणोत्तरायाततिर्य्यक्सूत्राद्वहिः प्राक्-प्रत्यगायतसूत्रं प्रागग्रं निःसार्य्य तन्मानेन चतुरस्रमध्यस्थहंसपदमध्यावलम्बनेन भ्रमाद्वृत्ताकारं कुण्डमानं कल्पयेत्। एवं कृते कोणचतुष्टये वृत्ताद्वहिर्गतं भूमिमानं दिक्चतुष्टये लभ्यते तस्मात् सर्व्वकुण्डानि वक्ष्यमाणविधानेन षण्णव-त्यङ्गुलपरिणाहतश्चतुरस्रचेत्रसमानि भवन्तीति ॥ ३१ ॥

अर्द्धचन्द्राकृतिर्येन भवेत् कुण्डं तदीरितम् ।
येन द्वयं चराणां स्याद्राशीनां क्रमतः शिवे ॥ ३३ ॥
तस्यैव षष्ठमंशन्तु पार्श्वयोस्तु विकाशयेत् ।
प्रत्येकं पश्चिमं सूत्रं तन्मानेनाथ सूत्रयोः ॥ ३४ ॥
विन्यासाद्‌ब्रह्मसूत्रान्तं तद्वयाग्रावलम्बनात् ।
कुण्डं त्रिकोणमुदितं चतुर्षु स्थिरराशिषु ॥ ३५ ॥

तन्मध्ये इत्यादिना शिवे इत्यन्तेन श्लोकद्वयेनार्द्धचन्द्राकारकुण्डनिर्माण विधानोपदेशं तस्य वृत्तकुण्डस्योक्तचरराश्यात्मकत्वनिगमनञ्च करोति। तत्र तन्मध्ये दशमांशं चतुरस्रब्रह्मसूत्रमानस्य दशमांशं। तुः समाहारे। अधऊर्द्ध्वतः प्राक्पश्चिमतः। तन्मध्यात् पश्चिमदिग्गततिर्य्यक्सूत्रादधोऽष्टांशमाने कल्पित-दक्षिणोत्तरायततिर्य्यक्सूत्रमध्यात्तथा तत्सूत्रदक्षिणोत्तराग्रावधीति यावत्। येन विधानेन इत्यनेन दक्षिणोत्तरतिर्य्यक्सूत्राग्रद्वयं चतुरस्राद्बहिस्त्रींस्त्रीनंशान् प्रसारयेदित्यर्थः। एतदुक्तं भवति चतुरस्रस्य मध्यविष्कम्भमानं दशधा विभज्य तेष्वेकैकांशं तत् प्राक्पश्चिमतः परित्यज्य चिह्नद्वयं कृत्वा तत्पश्चिमचिह्नाद्दक्षि-णोत्तरायततिर्य्यक्सूत्रं तच्चतुरस्राद्बहिरप्यंशत्रयत्रयाधिकमास्फाल्य तदग्रद्वया-वधि तत्कल्पितपश्चिमसूत्रब्रह्मसूत्रसन्धिमध्यावलम्बनेन कल्पिताग्रचिह्नावधष्टांश-मानेन भ्रमादर्द्धचन्द्राकृति कुण्डं भवेदिति। एतद्द्वयं वृत्ताकारकुण्डमर्द्धचन्द्रा कारकुण्डं च क्रमतः मङ्गलामङ्गलयोः। शिवे इति सम्बुद्धिः॥ ३३ ॥

तस्यैवेत्यादिना राशिष्वित्यन्तेन श्लोकद्वयेन त्रिकोणकुण्डनिर्माणक्रममुपदि-शति। तत्र तस्यैव चतुरस्रस्यैव। पार्श्वयोर्दक्षिणोत्तरयोः। तन्मानेन प्रसारित-सूत्रमानेन। तद्वयाग्रावलम्बनात् प्रसारितपश्चिमसूत्रद्वयाग्रावलम्बनात्। एतदुक्तं भवति प्राग्वच्चतुरस्रं कृत्वा तत् ब्रह्मसूत्रं प्रागग्रं वहिर्गत्वा प्रसार्य्य तच्चतुरस्रविष्कम्भमानं षोढा विभज्य तेष्वेकैकांशेन पश्चिमतिर्य्यक्सूत्राग्रद्वयं पार्श्वयोर्बहिः प्रसार्य्य तदग्रद्वयात् तत्सूत्रमानोपेतसूत्रद्वयस्य प्राक्प्रसारितब्रह्म-सूत्रस्य च यत्र सम्पातस्तदवध्यास्फाल्य त्र्यस्रं कुण्डं कल्पयेत्। एतदमङ्गलप्रयोगे स्थिरराशिषु चतुर्ष्वुदितमिति ॥ ३५ ॥

तन्मध्यपञ्चमांशेन विकाश्य ब्रह्मसूत्रकम् ।
पूर्वतः पश्चिमद्वन्द्वं कोष्ठयोर्मध्यदेशतः ॥ ३६ ॥
तत्कोणमानेन तथा भ्रामयेत् पश्चिमाग्रकान् ।
उत्तराग्रावधि तथा दक्षिणाग्रावधि प्रिये ॥ ३७ ॥
तन्मध्यतिर्य्यक्सूत्राग्रद्वयावष्टम्भतस्तथा ।
विकाशितब्रह्मसूत्रावधि सूत्रद्वयं भवेत् ॥ ३८ ॥
योनि कुण्डमिदं भद्रे स्याच्चतुर्ष्वभयात्मसु ।
राशिषु प्रोक्तकल्याणकर्म्मसूक्तार्थसिद्धिकृत् ॥ ३९ ॥
तन्मध्यसप्तमांशेन ब्रह्मसूत्रं विकाश्य तत् ।
मानेन परितो भ्रान्त्वा कृत्वा वृत्तं तथा ततः ॥ ४० ॥

तन्मध्येत्यादिभिः सिद्धिकृदित्यन्तैश्चतुर्भिः श्लोकैर्योनिकुण्डनिर्माणसन्धानं तदुक्तनिगमनं तत्फलञ्चोपदिशति। तत्र तन्मध्यपञ्चमांशेन चतुरस्रस्य मध्यमानपञ्चमांशेन तत्कोणमानेन तन्मध्यकोणयोरन्तरमानेन पश्चिमाग्रकान् उत्तराग्रावधि ब्रह्मसूत्रपश्चिमाग्रादिमध्यस्थ तिर्य्यक्सूत्रोत्तराग्रावधि तथा दक्षिणाग्रावधि ब्रह्मसूत्रपश्चिमाग्रादि मध्यस्थतिर्य्यक्सूत्रदक्षिणाग्रावधि। प्रिये इति देवीसम्बुद्धिः। तन्मध्यतिर्य्यक्सूत्राग्रद्वयावष्टम्भतः चतुरस्रमध्यस्थदक्षिणोत्तर सूत्राग्रद्वयावष्टम्भेन। भद्रे इति देवीसम्बुद्धिः। एतदुक्तं भवति चतुरस्रमध्यसूत्रमानपञ्चमांशेन ब्रह्मसूत्रस्य प्रागग्रं वह्निर्विकाश्य तत्कोष्ठचतुष्टयात्मकचतुरस्रपश्चिमभागस्थदक्षिणोत्तरकोष्ठयार्द्वयोः नैर्ऋत्यादीशान्तमाग्नेयादिवायव्यान्तं कोणसूत्रद्वयास्फालनेन लक्षिततत्सूत्रद्वयसम्पातविदितमध्यदेशावष्टम्भतस्तत्तत्कोणावधिमानेनान्तरकोष्ठे प्राक् ब्रह्मसूत्रपश्चिमाग्रादिदक्षिणोत्तरमध्यतिर्य्यक्सूत्रोत्तराग्रावधि तद्दक्षिणकोष्ठे तत्सूत्रपश्चिमाग्रादि तद्दक्षिणाग्रावधि च भ्रमात्तन्मध्यतिर्य्यक्सूत्राग्रद्वयमारभ्य प्राक्प्रसारितब्रह्मसूत्राग्रावधि सूत्रद्वयास्फालनेन च कल्पिततत्मङ्गलकर्मसूभयराश्यात्मकस्थानचतुष्टये प्रोक्तं योनिकुण्डमुक्तफलसिद्धिकरमिति ॥ ३९ ॥

तन्मध्येत्यादिना कुण्डकमित्यन्तेन श्लोकद्वयेन पद्मास्रकुण्डनिर्म्माणविधानमुपदिशति। तत्र तन्मध्यसप्तमांशेन चतुरस्रमध्यसूत्रमानस्य सप्तमांशेन तदिति ब्रह्मसूत्रमित्यस्य विशेषणम्। मानेन विकाशितमानेन कृत्वा वृत्तं कृत्वेत्यर्थः।

तत्त्र्यंशमानात्तद्वृत्ते कृत्वा चिह्नानि तत्र वै ।
पातयेत् पञ्चसूत्राणि तत् स्यात् पञ्चास्रकुण्डकम् ॥ ४१ ॥
तन्मध्यषोडशांशेन विकाश्य ब्रह्मसूत्रकम् ।
तेन मानेन च तथा कृत्वा वृत्तमतिस्फुटम् । ४२ ॥
तद्वृत्ते वृत्तमध्यस्य कुर्य्यादर्द्धेन चाङ्कनम् ।
तत्र षट्सूत्रपातेन भवेत् कुण्डं षडस्रकम् ॥ ४३ ॥
तन्मध्यदशमांशेन विकाश्य ब्रह्मसूत्रकम् ।
तेन मानेन सम्भ्रान्त्या कृत्वा वृत्तं तथा ततः ॥ ४४ ॥
तच्चतुःषष्टिभागेषु त्रयस्त्रिंशांशमानतः ।
वृत्ते विधाय चिह्नानि सप्तसूत्राणि पातयेत् ॥ ४५ ॥

तथा ततश्चतुरस्रमध्यस्थहंसपदमधरावलम्बनत इत्यर्थः । तत्त्र्यंशमानात् तच्चतुरस्रमधरसूत्रत्रिपादमानेन तत्र तेषु चिह्नेषु । एतदुक्तं भवति प्रागवच्चतुरस्रं कृत्वा तन्मधरमानस्य सप्तमांशेन ब्रह्मसूत्रप्रागग्रं वहिः विकाश्य तन्मानेन तच्चतुरस्रमधरस्थहंसपदावलम्बनतो भ्रमाद्वृत्तं निष्पाद्य तच्चतुरस्रमधरसूत्रं चतुर्द्धा कृत्वा तेष्वंशत्रयेणांशत्रयेण तद्वृत्ते ब्रह्मसूत्रप्रागग्रादिपरितः पञ्चचिह्नानि विधाय तत्तच्चिह्नाच्चिह्नं ज्यारूपाणि पञ्चसूत्राण्यास्फाल्य तत्तच्चापरूपवृत्तखण्डमार्जनात् पञ्चास्रं कुण्डं मङ्गलकर्म्मणि मिथुनराशिस्थानवह्निदिक् प्रोक्तं भवेदिति ॥४१॥

तन्मधेत्यादिना षडस्रकमित्यन्तेन श्लोकद्वयेन षडस्रकुण्डनिर्माणविधानमुपदिशति । तत्र तन्मधषोडशांशेन चतुरस्रब्रह्मसूत्रमानस्य षोडशांशेन विकाश्य चतुरस्राद्वहिरिति शेषः । तथा प्रागवत् । वृत्तमधस्य हंसपदमधरात् ब्रह्मसूत्रमानस्य । अङ्कनं चिह्नं । एतदुक्तं भवति प्रागवच्चतुरस्रं विधाय तन्मध्यमानं षोडशधा विभज्य तेष्वेकांशेन ब्रह्मसूत्राग्रं वहिर्विकाश्य तन्मानेन चतुरस्रमध्यस्थहंसपदमध्यावलम्बनेन भ्रमाद्वृत्तं निष्पाद्य तन्मध्यविष्कम्भमानार्द्धेन तन्मध्यतिर्य्यक्सूत्रदक्षिणाग्रादि परितो वृत्ते चिह्नषट्कं विधाय तत्तच्चिह्नाच्चिह्नज्यारूपं सूत्रषट्कमास्फाल्य तत्तच्चापरूपवृत्तखण्डमार्जनेनामङ्गले कर्मणि कन्याराशिस्थाननिर्ऋतिदिक् प्रोक्तं षडस्रकुण्डं भवेदिति ॥ ४३ ॥

तन्मध्ये त्यादिभिः शिवे इत्यन्तैस्त्रिभिः श्लोकैः सप्तास्रकुण्डनिर्माणविधानं तत्

तत् सप्तास्रं भवेत् कुण्डं चापगं वायुदिग्गतम् ।
समस्तवैरिनाशाय प्रोक्तं कुण्डमिदं शिवे ॥ ४६ ॥
तन्मध्यस्य चतुर्विंशमाने बाह्येपि पूर्ववत् ।
विधाय चतुरस्रन्तु पूर्वकोणार्द्धमानतः ॥ ४७ ॥
कोणादभित एवास्य कृत्वा चिह्नानि चाष्ट वै ।
तेषु चिह्नेषु कृत्वाष्ट सूत्राणि परितः शिवे ॥ ४८ ॥

फलञ्चोपदिशति । तत्र तन्मध्यदशमांशेन चतुरस्रमध्यसूत्रस्य दशमांशेन विकाश्य चतुरस्राद्बहिरिति शेषः । कृत्वा वृत्तं वृत्तं कृत्वेत्यर्थः । तथा प्राग्वत् । ततः अनन्तरमिति शेषः । तच्चतुःषष्टिभागेषु चतुरस्रमध्यसूत्रस्य चतुःषष्टिभागेषु त्रयस्त्रिंशांशमानतः त्रयस्त्रिंशदंशमानतः । चापगं चापराशिस्थानगतं । एतदुक्तं भवति प्राग्वत् समचतुरस्रं कृत्वा तन्मध्यमानं दशधा विभज्य तेष्वेकांशमानेन तद्बाह्यसूत्रं वहिः विकाश्य तन्मानेन तच्चतुरस्रमध्यस्थहंसपदमवष्टभ्य वृत्तं कृत्वा तच्चतुरस्रमध्यसूत्रमानं चतुःषष्टिभागीकृत्य तेषु त्रयस्त्रिंशदंशमानेन भ्रमसूत्रं प्रागग्रादारभ्य वृत्ते सप्तचिह्नानि कृत्वा तत्र चिह्नाच्चिह्नं ज्यारूपेण सप्तसूत्राण्यास्फाल्य तत्सञ्चापरूपवृत्तखण्डमार्जनादेतत् सप्तास्रं वायुदिग्गतचापराशिस्थाने प्रोक्तं वैरिनाशकरं कुण्डं भवेदिति ॥ ४६ ॥

तन्मध्येत्यादिभिः क्रमेण वै इत्यन्तैस्त्रिभिः श्लोकैः अष्टास्रकुण्डनिर्माणविधानं प्रोक्तकुण्डानां मेखलादिनिर्माणविधानकथनप्रस्तावसहितमुपदिशति । तत्र तन्मध्यस्य चतुरस्रमध्यसूत्रस्य । चतुर्विंशमाने चतुर्विंशांशमाने । बाह्ये चतुरस्रादिति शेषः । पूर्व्वकोणार्द्धमानतः पूर्वलिखितचतुरस्रकोणसूत्रस्यार्द्धमानेन । कोणादभितः कोणचतुष्टयादुभयोः पार्श्वयोः । कृत्वा चिह्नानि चिह्नानि कृत्वेत्यर्थः । शिवे इति सम्बुद्धिः । एतदुक्तं भवति पूर्व्ववच्चतुरस्रं विधाय तन्मध्यसूत्रमानं चतुर्विंशतिधा विभज्य तेष्वेकं कांशमानात्तद्बहिः प्रतिदिशं प्रसारितसूत्राग्रे पूर्व्ववच्चतुरस्रं प्रोक्तक्रमेण विधाय तत्कोणसूत्रस्यार्द्धमानेन बाह्यचतुरस्रे, कोणचतुष्टयव्यत्यासावष्टम्भादुभयतः प्रतिरेखं चिह्नद्वयं क्रमात् सम्भूयाष्टचिह्नानि कृत्वा तत्र चिह्नाच्चिह्नं प्राग्वत् सूत्रचतुष्कमास्फाल्य तद्बहिर्गतकोणमार्जनादीशदिक्स्थमीनराशिप्रोक्तमष्टास्रं कुण्डं कल्पयेदिति । एतेषां

कुर्य्यादष्टास्रकं कुण्डमेतेषां मेखलादिकम् ।
प्रवच्यामि शृणु प्राज्ञे समुद्दिष्टं क्रमेण वै ॥ ४९ ॥
वृत्तमध्यभुवो मानं त्रिगुणं विभजेत् क्रमात् ।
स्ववाञ्छितेन मानेन तदस्राणि भवन्ति हि ॥ ५० ॥
एवं यन्त्रादिषूक्तेषु षट्त्रिंशेषु विधिर्भवेत् ।
कुण्डेषु च तथा कोटिहोमादिषु समीरितम् ॥ ५१ ॥
प्रोक्तेष्वन्यतमे कुण्डे नवहस्तप्रमाणके ।
कारयेत् कोटिहोमन्तु पुरुषैरष्टभिस्तथा ॥ ५२ ॥
दिग्विदिक्स्थैः क्रमात् पञ्चवासरैः सर्वसिद्धये ।
तेषाञ्च दक्षिणां दद्यात् पूजाप्रणतिपूर्वकम् ॥ ५३ ॥

कुण्डानां । मेखलादिकमित्यत्रादिशब्दो योन्यादिविषयः । प्राज्ञे इति सम्बुद्धिः ॥ ४९ ॥

वृत्तेत्यादिना समीरितमित्यन्तेन श्लोकद्वयेनाष्टास्रयन्त्रकुण्डादिकल्पनोपायोपदेशं प्रोक्तनिगमनञ्च करोति । तत्र वृत्तमध्यभुवः वृत्तमध्यविष्कम्भस्य । त्रिगुणं त्रिगुणितं । स्ववाञ्छितेन स्ववाञ्छितास्रिमानेन । तदस्राणि अष्टास्रयन्त्रकुण्डानि । उक्तेषु पञ्चविंशे पटले । चकारः समुच्चये । कोटिहोमादिषु वक्ष्यमाणेषु अत्रादिशब्दो महासंख्यहोमादिविषयः । एतदुक्तं भवति प्रोक्तक्रमाद्वृत्तं कृत्वा तन्मध्यविष्कम्भमानं स्वाभीष्टास्रिसंख्यया विभज्य तेषु तत्तदंशमानेन वृत्ते परितश्चिह्नानि स्वेष्टास्रिसंख्यानि विधाय तत्तच्चिह्नाच्चिह्नं ज्यारूपाणि सूत्राणि स्वेष्टास्रिसंख्यान्यास्फाल्य तत्तच्चापरूपाणि वृत्तखण्डानि मार्जयित्वा एवं मातृकापटलोक्तषट्त्रिंशाद्यादियन्त्रेषु तत्तत्कुण्डेषु च कोट्यादिमहासंख्यहोमप्रोक्तकुण्डेषु च विधानं समीरितमिति ॥ ५१ ॥

प्रोक्तेष्वित्यादिभिरास्तिकैरित्यन्तैः षड्भिः श्लोकैः कोटिहोमकुण्डप्रमाणं होतृसंख्यां तद्धोमप्रकारं होतृदक्षिणां गुरुदक्षिणां तत्कोटिहोमकर्त्तव्यकालविशेषांस्तद्विध्यां होतृलक्षणञ्चोपदिशति । तत्र प्रोक्तेषु मङ्गलामङ्गलत्वभेदतः अन्यतमे तत्तदनुगुणे । नवहस्तप्रमाणके आयामेन विस्तारेण च । तथा वक्ष्य-

गोचर्म्मद्वयमात्रन्तु भुवं गां प्रस्नुतस्तनीम् ।
महिषीं सप्रजामश्वदासदासीविभूषणाम् ॥ ५४ ॥
वासांसि हैमनिष्काणां शतं तेषामथैकशः ।
ततो गुरोश्च तान्येव तैः समानमुदीरितम् ॥ ५५ ॥
दिव्योत्पातेषु रोगार्त्तौ घोरे च रिपुनिग्रहे ।
तथा दिग्विजयेऽन्यस्य परकृत्यादिसम्भवे ॥ ५६ ॥
कारयेत् कोटिहोमन्तु विद्यया नित्ययाद्यया ।
सुरूपैश्च सुशीलैश्च नित्याभक्तैस्तथास्तिकैः ॥ ५७ ॥
प्रोक्तानां सर्वकुण्डानां अरत्निखातमात्रकम् ।
कोटिहोमस्य कुण्डस्य खातमूर्द्धन्तु तस्य वै ॥ ५८ ॥

माणलक्षणैर्विद्याविद्भिः । क्रमात् त्रिंशत्पटलवक्ष्यमाणहोमविधानक्रमात् । एतदुक्तं भवति वक्ष्यमाणेत्यादिना समुक्तवप्रोक्तकुण्डेषु तत्तदनुगुणं कुण्डं नवहस्तप्रमाणं वक्ष्यमाणमेखलादियुतं कृत्वा प्रतिदिवसं दिवसपञ्चकं दिग्विदिक्स्थैरष्टभिरष्टभिः पुरुषैर्वक्ष्यमाणलक्षणसम्पन्नैर्वक्ष्यमाणविद्यया स्वाभिमतसिद्धिपर्य्यन्तं होमं कारयेदिति । तेषां होतॄणां । दद्यादित्यस्य भुवमित्यादिभिरष्टभिः पदैर्द्विंतीयान्तैः प्रत्येकमुत्तरत्रान्वयः । दद्यात् पञ्चसु पञ्चसु दिनेषु । गोचर्म्मद्वयमात्रं गोचर्म्ममात्राया भुवः प्रमाणं बृहस्पतिराह ।

सप्तहस्तप्रमाणेन त्रिंशद्दंशनिवर्त्तनम् ।
दश तान्येव गोचर्मेति ॥

तद्द्विगुणमेकशः एकैकहोत्रे । तान्येव वस्तूनि । तैर्होतृभिः । समानमुदीरितं प्रोक्तद्रव्यजातमिति । दिव्योत्पातेषु ग्रहनक्षत्रादिविकृतिषु । आद्यया ललितया । नित्याभक्तैः षोडशनित्याभक्तैः । आस्तिकैः नित्यनैमित्तिकादिकर्मभजनपरैः ॥ ५७ ॥

प्रोक्तेत्यादिना श्लोकेन कुण्डानां खातमानमुपदिशति । तत्र अरत्निः चतुर्विंशत्यङ्गुलमानं । तस्य कोटिहोमप्रोक्तनवहस्तमानकुण्डस्य ॥५८॥

सर्वेषां मेखलामानं वितस्त्यष्टतदर्द्धकैः ।
विस्तारोत्सेधयोः कुर्य्याद्योनिं होत्रासनाग्रतः ॥ ५९ ॥
महाकुण्डस्य तु पुनर्मेखला हस्तमानतः ।
तिसृणामपि विस्ताराः प्रत्येकं षोड़शाङ्गुलाः ॥ ६० ॥
तेषामुत्सेधसंख्याश्च षोड़श स्युः क्रमेण वै ।
योनिनिर्म्माणमधुना वासनाञ्च शृणु प्रिये ॥ ६१ ॥
वहिष्ठमेखलामध्यादारभ्य निजनालकम् ।
वितस्तिमात्रकां कोष्ठामश्वत्थदलसन्निभाम् ॥ ६२ ॥

सर्वेषामित्यादिना श्लोकेन सर्व्वकुण्डमेखलामानं योनिनिर्माणञ्चोपदिशति। तत्र वितस्त्यष्टतदर्द्धकैः द्वादशाङ्गुलचतुरङ्गुलमानैः एष मानक्रमो विस्तारस्य चाधारादि उत्सेधोर्द्ध्वादिश्च बोद्धव्यः। एतदुक्तं भवति महाकुण्डरहितानां सर्व्व-कुण्डानां परितस्त्र्यंकाङ्गुलमानाद्वहिरधो मेखलां द्वादशाङ्गुलद्वादशाङ्गुलमान-विस्तारेण चतुरङ्गुलमानोत्सेधेन च युतां कृत्वा तदुपरि वाह्ये परितश्चतुरङ्गुल-मानं मुक्त्वा तदन्तरष्टाङ्गुलमानविस्तारेण चतुरङ्गुलमानोत्सेधेन च युतां द्वितीय-मेखलां तदुपरि प्राग्वत् वाह्ये चतुरङ्गुलमानं मुक्त्वा तदन्तर्विस्तारोत्सेधाभ्यां चतुरङ्गुलमानमितां तृतीयां मेखलाञ्च कृत्वा तन्मेखलायां होतुरासनाग्र-पार्श्वमध्ये वक्ष्यमाणलक्षणां योनिं कुर्य्यादिति ॥ ५९ ॥

महेत्यादिना प्रिये इत्यन्तेन श्लोकद्वयेन महाकुण्डस्य मेखलामानं योनि-निर्माणविधानञ्च तद्वासनाकथनप्रस्तावसहितमुपदिशति। तत्र तुर्विशेषे। हस्त-मानतः अष्टचत्वारिंशदङ्गुलमानतः। तिसृणां मेखलानामिति शेषः। तेषां मेखलानां दिव्यत्वात् तासामित्यर्थः। षोड़शाङ्गुलानीति शेषः। एतदुक्तं भवति महाकुण्डस्य परितो विस्तारेणाष्टचत्वारिंशदङ्गुलमितामुत्सेधेन षोड़शाङ्गुलमान-मितामधोमेखलां तदुपरि वाह्यतः षोड़शाङ्गुलमानं मुक्त्वा तदन्तर्द्वात्रिंशदङ्गुलमान-विस्तारां षोड़शाङ्गुलोत्सेधां द्वितीयां मेखलां तदुपरि वाह्ये षोड़शाङ्गुलं मुक्त्वा तद-न्तर्विस्तारोत्सेधाभ्यां षोड़शाङ्गुलमानां तृतीयां मेखलां कुर्य्यादिति। योनिस्वरूप-तः निर्माणं तस्या वासनां योनिनिर्माणस्य। प्रिये इति देवीसम्बुद्धिः॥ ६१ ॥

वहिष्ठेत्यादिभिः समूहत इत्यन्तैरर्द्धाद्यैश्चतुर्भिः श्लोकैर्योनिस्वरूपं तन्निर्माण-

वितस्त्यायामसंयुक्तां तदर्द्धेन तु विस्तृताम्।
एकाङ्गुलोत्सेधयुतां मेखलोपरि सर्वतः ॥ ६३ ॥
मूलान्निम्नाग्रकां स्तोकं कुर्य्याद्योनिञ्च सर्वतः।
योनिः कारणभूतस्य तत्त्वस्य स्यात् पदं महत् ॥ ६४ ॥*
तेन तत्रैव द्रव्यानां विधानं तन्मयत्वतः।
फलानि पूर्णान्यचिराद्यत्नाद्वितरत्यसौ ॥ ६५ ॥

क्रमं तद्दासनां महाकुण्डस्य योनेरूहेन मानक्रमित्योपदिशति। तत्र वहिष्ठ-मेखलामध्यात् प्रथममेखलामध्यभूतभूप्रदेशाद्वितस्तिमात्रकां कोष्ठां द्वादशाङ्गुलोत्सेधकल्पितनालां अश्वत्थदलसन्निभां अश्वत्थपत्राकारां वितस्त्यायामसंयुक्तां द्वादशाङ्गुलायामसंयुक्तां तदर्द्धेन तु विस्तृतां षडङ्गुलविस्तारयुतां। सर्व्वतः सर्वेषु कुण्डेषु। स्तोकं किञ्चित्। सर्व्वतः सर्व्वस्य अस्य कारणभूतस्य इत्युत्तरत्रान्वयः। एतदुक्तं भवति सर्व्वकुण्डेषु होतुरासनप्रदेशे प्रथममेखलामध्यप्रदेशभूमौ द्व्यङ्गुलायामविस्तारमेकाङ्गुलोत्सेधं चतुरस्रं पीठं मृदा कृत्वा तदाद्युपरितनमेखलाग्रान्त-मध्यतनमेखलोपरिस्तरणार्थं कृतरन्ध्रान्तर्मेखलास्पर्शिवृत्ताकारं नालं कृत्वा तन्नाल-सम्बन्ध्युपरितनमेखलोपरि षडङ्गुलमानविस्तारमध्यां तत्प्रदेशादुभयपार्श्वक्रम सङ्कोचिताग्रद्वादशाङ्गुलमानायामामेकाङ्गुलोत्सेधामश्वत्थपत्राकारां मूलात् किञ्चित् क्रमान्निम्नाग्रां योनिं कुर्य्यादिति। वृत्तकुण्डव्यतिरिक्तकुण्डानां योनिं जानीयादेवेति सम्प्रदायः। कारणभूतस्य तत्त्वस्य विश्वकारणभूतस्य जातरूप-तत्त्वस्य पदं उदयविश्रान्तिस्थानं महत् पूर्णत्वात्। तत्र योन्यां असौ अपरि-च्छिन्नात्मिका योनिः। महाकुण्डस्य कोटिहोमप्रोक्तकुण्डस्य। मान योनेरिति शेषः। समूहतः सम्यगूहेन। ऊहो यथा वितस्तिमात्रमेखलस्य कुण्डस्य नालोत्सेधमानं वितस्तिः तद्योनेर्विस्तारमानमङ्गुलषट्कं आयाममानं वितस्तिः उत्सेधमानमेकाङ्गुलं तदा हस्तमात्रमानमेखलस्य महाकुण्डस्य तत्तन्मानानि कियन्तीति तत्प्रकरणात्तन्मानानि लिख्यन्ते। नालमानमष्टचत्वारिंशदङ्गुलमानं। योनेः विस्तारमरत्निः। आयाममानं हस्तः। उत्सेधमानमङ्गुलचतुष्टयञ्च। योनिकुण्डस्य तन्मेखलोपरि योनिकृतिं विनैव तत्फलसिद्धिकृदिति सम्प्रदायः ॥ ६६ ॥

* योनिः कारणभूतस्य तत्त्वं स्यात् परमं महत्।

महाकुण्डस्य चैवैतत् कुर्य्यान्मानं समूहतः।
नाभिं कुर्य्यात्तु सर्व्वत्र कुण्डमध्ये विधानतः॥ ६६॥
अष्टच्छदं सरोजन्तु विदध्याच्चारुविग्रहम्।
चतुर्भिरङ्गुलैः कुर्य्यात् कर्णिकां दलमेव च॥ ६७॥
विस्तारादपि चोत्सेधं षड्भिः षड्भिरुदीरितम्।
प्राग्वन्महति कुण्डे च कुर्य्यादूहेन तत्तथा॥ ६८॥
ध्यानमग्नेर्द्विधा प्रोक्तं सौम्यक्रौर्य्यविभागतः।
सौम्यं नित्यासमाकारं ध्यानमन्यच्छृणु प्रिये॥ ६९॥

नाभिमित्यादिना तथेत्यन्तेनार्द्धाधेन श्लोकद्वयेन सर्व्वकुण्डमध्ये नाभिनिर्माण-विधानं तल्लक्षणं महाकुण्डस्य प्रोक्तवदूहकल्पनञ्चोपदिशति। तत्र विधानतः वक्ष्यमाणप्रकारेण। चारुविग्रहं अन्यूनाधिकमानं। चतुर्भिः प्रतिदिशमिति शेषः। च: समुच्चये। षड्भिः षड्भिः अपि चेत्यनेन अङ्गुलैरिति पूर्वश्लोकादाकृष्यते। एतदुक्तं भवति प्रोक्तानां सर्वकुण्डानां कुण्डमध्यस्थहंसपदावलम्बनेन प्रतिदिशं दशाङ्गुलमानपरिभ्रामत्या वृत्तं निष्पाद्य तद्वृत्तान्तराले षडङ्गुलोत्सेधयुतं पीठं कृत्वा तन्मध्यस्थहंसपदावलम्बनेन प्रतिदिशं चतुरङ्गुलमानेन वृत्तं निष्पाद्य तद्बहिः षडङ्गुलमानेन च वृत्तं कृत्वा तदन्तर्वृत्तमध्यं कर्णिकां परिकल्प्य तद्बहिःस्थवृत्तान्तरालवीथ्यामष्टदलविधानेन च सम्भूय विंशत्यङ्गुलमध्यसंस्थं नाभिपद्मं कुर्य्यादिति। महति कुण्डे कोटिहोमप्रोक्ते कुण्डे ऊहेन यदा अरत्निमानविस्तारायामकुण्डे नाभिपद्मस्याधोदलविस्तारमञ्च षडङ्गुलात्मके कर्णिकामानं चतुरङ्गुलात्मकं तदा नवहस्तविस्तारायाममहाकुण्डे। नाभिपद्मस्य तत्तन्मानानि कियन्तीत्यूहेन तन्मानसंख्या लिख्यते। यथा उत्सेधमानानि अष्टोत्तरशताङ्गुलसंख्यानि दलमानानि प्रतिदिशमष्टोत्तरशताङ्गुलानि कर्णिकार्द्धविस्तारमानानि द्विसप्तत्यङ्गुलानि सम्भूय पद्मविष्कम्भमानाङ्गुलानि षष्ट्युत्तरत्रिशतसंख्यानि भवन्ति। तन्नाभिपद्मं तथा तन्मानेन॥ ६८॥

ध्यानमित्यादिना श्लोकेन सौम्यक्रौर्य्यविभागेन अग्नेर्ध्यानद्वयप्रस्तावपुरःसरं सौम्यध्यानमतिदिश्य क्रूरध्यानं प्रस्तौति। तत्र नित्यासमाकारं ध्यानं तत्तन्नित्याप्रोक्तस्थूलरूपध्यानं। प्रिये इति देवीसम्बुद्धिः॥ ६९॥

द्विशीर्षं सप्तहस्तञ्च त्रिपादसप्तजिह्वकम्।
त्रिधारूपमतिक्रूरैररुणैः षड्भिरीक्षणैः ॥ ७० ॥
सव्यैश्चतुर्भिर्हस्तैस्तु शक्त्यन्नस्रुक्स्रुवौ तथा।
इतरैस्तोमरं तालवृन्तं सर्पिःसुभाजनम् ॥ ७१ ॥
निहन्तुमनिशं व्यात्तवक्त्रं ध्यायेद्विभुजम्।
क्रूरेषु सर्व्वहोमेषु ध्यानवैभवमीरितम् ॥ ७२ ॥
वक्त्रैः शिरसि देहे वा श्रोत्रेष्वक्षिषु वा तथा।
जुहुयाच्चेत्तदा क्षिप्रं तद्देवस्तं विनाशयेत् ॥ ७३ ॥
ततस्तद्वक्त्रयोर्जिह्वासप्तकं सम्यगर्च्चयेत्।
जुहुयाच्च समाप्नोति वाञ्छितं सकलं क्षणात् ॥ ७४ ॥
हिरण्या कनका रक्ता कृष्णा जिह्वा यथार्थका।
दक्षवक्त्रगता सर्व्वसिद्धिदा तु समर्च्चनात् ॥ ७५ ॥

द्विशीर्षेत्यादिभिरीरितमित्यन्तैस्त्रिभिः श्लोकैरग्नेः क्रूरध्यानमुपदिशति। तत्र त्रिधारूपं सत्त्वादिगुणभेदेनेति शेषः। सव्यैर्दक्षिणैः। इतरैर्वामैर्हस्तैः सर्पिः सुभाजनं सर्पिःपूर्णहेमपात्रं। अत्रायुधक्रमस्तूर्द्ध्वभुजाद्याधरभुजान्तमित्यवगन्तव्यः। व्यात्तवक्त्रं विस्तृतवक्त्रम् ॥ ७२ ॥

वक्त्रैरित्यादिना श्लोकेनाग्नेर्जिह्वाव्यतिरिक्ताङ्गेषु होमे प्रत्यवायमुपदिशति। तत्र वा समुच्चये। तं साधकम् ॥ ७३ ॥

तत इत्यादिना श्लोकेन जिह्वासप्तकार्च्चनं तत्र होमं तत्फलञ्चोपदिशति। तत्र तद्वक्त्रयोः अग्नेर्वक्त्रयोर्जुहुयात्। चकारात् जिह्वासप्तके इत्यर्थः। क्षणात् प्रोक्तमण्डलादिकालालङ्घनेन ॥ ७४ ॥

हिरण्येत्यादिना श्लोकेनाग्नेः दक्षिणवक्त्रजिह्वाचतुष्टयनामानुपदिशति। तत्र यथार्थका रूपादिभिरिति यावत्। सर्व्वसिद्धिदा वाञ्छितफलदायिनो ॥ ७५ ॥

सुप्रभेत्यादिना श्लोकेन वामवक्त्रजिह्वात्रयनामानि तदन्यजिह्वायाः सर्व्व-

सुप्रभा चातिरिक्ता च बहुरूपा च वामगा ।
बहुरूपायां जिह्वायां होमः सर्व्वार्थसाधकः ॥ ७६ ॥
इतरासु हुनेत् क्रूरकर्म्मस्वभिमतेषु तु ।
यस्यां जुहोति तामाद्यां समभ्यर्च्याथ सप्तमः ॥ ७७ ॥
ततो हुनेच्च जिह्वायामुक्तायां तत्र कर्म्मणि ।
सामान्यतो नित्यहोमे द्रव्याणि शृणु सुन्दरि ॥ ७८ ॥
आज्यमन्नं पायसञ्च तिलतण्डुलमप्यथ ।
तद्द्वयं चेति संप्रोक्तान्युक्तान्येतानि नित्यके ॥ ७९ ॥
शुभैर्दर्भैः परिस्तीर्य्यं सर्व्वत्र शुभकर्मसु ।
अभिचारेषु वान्येषु क्रूरेष्वन्येष्वपि प्रिये ॥ ८० ॥
नक्षत्रवृक्षैस्तद्योनिरक्तोत्थचरुणा तथा ।
तन्मांसैस्तत्र तत्रोक्तैर्द्रव्यैः क्रूरेषु कर्मसु ॥ ८१ ॥

कर्म्मसु सिद्धिप्रदत्वञ्चोपदिशति । तत्र वामगा वामवक्त्रगता । सर्वार्थसाधकः सर्व्व-होमेषु तत्तत्सिद्धिदत्वात् । नित्यहोमं तस्यामेव कुर्य्यादिति सम्प्रदायः ॥ ७६ ॥

इतरास्वित्यादिना सुन्दरीत्यन्तेन श्लोकद्वयेन इतरजिह्वाषट्के क्रूरहोमस्य कर्त्तव्यतां तत्तत्कर्म्मणि तत्तज्जिह्वापुरःसरं तत्पूर्व्वजिह्वान्तं इतरजिह्वार्च्चनं तस्याः होमविधानं सामान्यतो नित्यहोमद्रव्यकथनप्रस्तावञ्च करोति । तत्र इतरासु बहु-रूपाख्यजिह्वाव्यतिरिक्तासु षट्सु । यस्यां जिह्वायां । ततः जिह्वार्च्चनानन्तरं । उक्तायां तत्तत्कर्मानुरूपायां । सुन्दरीति देवीसम्बुद्धिः ॥ ७८ ॥

आज्यमित्यादिना श्लोकेन नित्यहोमद्रव्याण्युपदिशति । तत्र प्रथमार्द्धेन पञ्चद्रव्याणि कथितानि । तद्द्वयं तिलसहिततण्डुलं । नित्यके नित्यहोमे ॥७९॥

शुभैरित्यादिना श्लोकेन शुभकर्म्मस्वभिचारादिषु च परिस्तरणीयभेदमुपदि-शति । तत्र सर्व्वत्र तन्त्रे । अन्येषूच्चाटनादिषु । प्रिये इति सम्बुद्धिः ॥८०॥

नक्षत्रेत्यादिना श्लोकेन क्रूरकर्म्मसु होमद्रव्याण्युपदिशति । तत्र सर्व्वत्र

प्रसूनान्येकमेकन्तु फलानि च तथा हुनेत्।
अन्नाज्यादि समस्तन्तु निष्कमात्रं हुनेत् क्रमात्॥ ८२॥

स्नातो विशुद्धवसनो धूपस्रग्गन्धवासितः।
प्रसन्नचित्तवदनः कुर्य्याद्धोमन्तु साधकः॥ ८३॥

प्राङ्मुखो विष्टरासीनः प्राणायामपुरःसरम्।
न्यस्तगात्रोऽर्घतोयेन प्रोक्षयेत् कुण्डमध्यकम्॥ ८४॥

द्रव्याण्यन्यानि तत्रस्थान्यशेषाणि विशुद्धये।
दर्भेण विलिखेत् कुण्डमध्ये रेखाचतुष्टयम्॥ ८५॥

नक्षत्रद्रुमैः एकविंशे पटले षट्सप्ततितमश्लोकादित्रिभिः श्लोकैरुक्तैः रिपोरिति शेषः। तद्योनिरक्तोत्थचरुणा एकविंशे पटले त्वेकोनाशीतितमाशीतितमश्लोकद्वयोक्तरिपुनक्षत्रयोनिरक्तपाचितचरुणा। तथा समुच्चये। तन्मांसैः रिपुनक्षत्रयोनिमांसैः। तत्र तत्र तत्तत्पटले॥ ८१॥

प्रसूनानीत्यादिना श्लोकेनैकैकाहुतिद्रव्यपरिमाणमुपदिशति। तत्र तथा एकमेकं। अन्नाज्यादीत्यत्रादिशब्दः पायसतिलतण्डुलादिविषयः। निष्कमात्रमित्यनेनाज्यादीनां प्रस्थमात्रेण षष्ठ्वत्याहुतीः कुर्य्यादिति यावत्॥८२॥

स्नात इत्यादिना श्लोकेन होतुस्तत्कालपरिकर्म्मोपदिशति। तत प्रसन्नचित्तवदन इत्येतन्नित्यनैमित्तिकमङ्गलहोमविषयः॥ ८३॥

प्राङ्मुख इत्यादिभिरुदीरित इत्यन्तैरध्यर्द्धदशभिः श्लोकैः सर्व्वमङ्गलहोमानां सामान्यपुरस्ताच्चोपरिष्टाच्च तत्तद्विधिं क्रूरहोमस्यापि तत्तत्साधारणताञ्चोपदिशति। तत्र न्यस्तगात्रः तत्तन्नित्याप्रोक्तन्यासमन्त्रै रिति शेषः। तत्रस्थानि तद्योनिस्थानि कुण्डपरिसरस्थानि च। तत्र नवकोष्ठे। प्रागादिषु कोष्ठेषु। सप्त इत्यस्य जिह्वा इत्येतद्विशेष्यं। मध्ये मध्यकोष्ठे। वह्निं तथा स्मरन् नित्यहोमोक्तप्रकारेण वह्निं तत्तन्नित्यारूपं स्मरन्। अस्य पदस्य अनन्तरश्लोके पूजयेदित्यनेनान्वयः। प्रोक्तैः वह्नेर्नाम्नेति शेषः। चः समुच्चये। द्यक्षरादिकं शक्तिवीजलक्ष्मीवीजद्वयादिकम्। अष्टानां अग्नेश्च सप्तजिह्वानां। तन्मन्त्रो यथा ह्रीं श्रीं अग्नये स्वाहा ह्रीं श्रीं

प्राक्प्रत्यग्दक्षिणोदक् च तत्र जिह्वाः समर्चयेत् ।
प्रागादिषु तु सप्तापि मध्ये वह्निं तथा स्मरन् ॥ ८६ ॥
पूजयेत् सर्पिषा होमं कुर्य्यात् सप्त क्रमेण वै ।
जिह्वानामभिरेकैकं वह्नेश्च ह्यक्षरादिकम् ॥ ८७ ॥
स्वाहान्तमन्त्रमुदितमष्टानां क्रमतः शिवे ।
वह्निं सभाजनं हस्ते गृहीत्वाङ्गारकञ्च तत् ॥ ८८ ॥
क्रव्यादेभ्यो नम इति प्रोक्त्वान्यत्तु सभाजनम् ।
विपरिभ्राम्य कुण्डन्तु तन्मध्ये विन्यसेत्ततः ॥ ८९ ॥
प्रज्वाल्य ललिताद्याभिर्विद्याभिः परिषेचनम् ।
कृत्वा दर्भैः परिस्तीर्य्य पलाशाश्वत्थपत्रकैः । ९० ॥

हिरण्यायै स्वाहा इत्यादयः। सभाजनं भाजनसहितं क्रव्यादेभ्यो नमः इति शेषः। अन्यत् त्यक्तशेषं मङ्गारं। तन्मध्ये कुण्डमध्ये। दर्भैः प्राक्पश्चिमयोरुत्तराग्रैः दक्षिणोत्तरयोः प्रागग्रैश्च मध्यस्थमेखलास्विति शेषः। पलाशाश्वत्थपत्रकैः पलाशाश्वत्थयोरन्यतरपत्रकैः। तथा घृताहुतीः पञ्चमे पटले एकोनषष्टितम-श्लोकोत्तरार्द्धेन तदनन्तरश्लोकार्द्धपादेन चोक्तक्रमेण तत्तत् जिह्वानां स्मरणपूर्वं प्रतिजिह्वं नवनवाहुतीः परिवारशक्तीनामेकैकाहुतीश्च। मूलतः तत्तन्नित्या-विद्यया। नाथनित्यात्मभूतज्ञैः नवनाथपञ्चदशनित्यादिननित्यात्माष्टाक्षरपञ्चभूता-त्मकैर्मन्त्रैरिति शेषः। स्वाग्नास्थानगतां स्वभ्रूमध्यान्तर्गतद्विदलपद्माधारमध्यस्थ-शक्तिरूपमहावह्निस्वरूपतादात्म्यं गतां। परिस्तरणपूर्व्वकं परिस्तरणं पूर्वादित उत्तरान्तेषु। भस्मना दग्धपरिस्तरणदर्भाणाम्। एतदुक्तं भवति विष्टरे प्राङ्-मुखस्थितः प्राणायामपुरःसरं न्यासं कृत्वा स्थापितार्घजलेन कुण्डं होमद्रव्यं संप्रोक्ष्य कुण्डमध्यस्थनाभिपद्मकर्णिकायां प्राक्प्रत्यग्दक्षिणोदक् च दर्भेण लिखितरेखाचतुष्टयेन नव कोष्ठानि निष्पाद्यार्घतोयेन संप्रोक्ष्य भाजननिहित मङ्गारं हस्ते गृहीत्वा क्रव्यादेभ्यो नमः इति मन्त्रेण तस्मादङ्गारसकलं दक्षिणस्यां

तथा घृताहुतीः कृत्वा नित्या षोड़श मूलतः ।
जुहुयादेकमेकन्तु नाथनित्यात्मभूतजैः ॥ ८१ ॥
ततश्च परिषिच्यात्मानं स्वात्मानं † विभाव्य ताम् ।
स्वाज्ञास्थानगतां बुद्धा परिस्तरणपूर्वकम् ॥ ८२ ॥
दग्ध्वाग्नौ भस्मना कृत्वा तिलकं न्यस्तगावकः ।
पूजां समाप्य विचरेत् सुखी तद्रूपवान्नरः ॥ ८३ ॥

दिश्यपास्य सभाजनमङ्गारं कुण्डमभितः त्रिःप्रदक्षिणं परिभ्राम्य तन्मध्यस्थकोष्ठे तं वह्निं संस्थाप्य प्रज्वाल्य ललितादितत्तन्नित्याविद्यासु स्वभजनीयविद्यया परिषिच्य तत्कुण्डमध्यमेखलायाः परित उदगग्रैः प्रागग्रैश्च दर्भैः कुशैर्वा परिस्तीर्य्य पलाशाश्वत्थयोरन्यतरस्य पत्रैर्देवीं परिकल्प्य मध्ये वह्निं तदभितः प्रागादिकुण्डकोष्ठेषु स्वाभिमतादिसप्तजिह्वा ध्यात्वा क्रीं श्रीं अग्नये नमः इति मध्ये वह्निं समभ्यर्च्य क्रीं श्रीं हिरण्यायै नमः इत्यादिभिः स्वाभिमतादिभिः सप्तजिह्वामन्त्रैः समभ्यर्च्य ललिताहोमे तत्तज्जिह्वास्मरणपूर्व्वं श्रीविद्यातृतीयखण्डदिननित्याभ्यां प्रतिजिह्वं नवनवाहुतीर्हुत्वा तदन्यनित्याहोमे तत्तज्जिह्वामन्त्रैः स्वाहान्तैस्तासु प्रत्येकं नवनवाहुतीर्हुत्वा नित्यनैमित्तिकमङ्गलहोमेषु वह्निं तत्तन्नित्याविग्रहं मङ्गलकर्मसु तत्र प्रोक्तविग्रहं तत्पूजाक्रमेणैकैकाहुतिं स्वभजनीयविद्यया नित्यनैमित्तिकयोः षोड़शाहुतीश्च घृतेन हुत्वा काम्ये तत्तत्कर्म्मप्रोक्तद्रव्यैस्तत्तत्संख्याहुतीश्च हुत्वा ललिताहोमे नाथमन्त्रैस्तिथिनित्यया तद्दिननित्ययात्माष्टाक्षरेण भूतमन्त्रैश्च तदितरनित्याहोमे नाथमन्त्रैरेव हुत्वा प्रागुवत् परिषिच्य वह्निं देवीं विभावयन् स्वाज्ञाधारस्थशक्तिरूपमहावह्निना तादात्म्यं विभाव्य परिस्तरणदर्भादिकं तदग्नौ दग्ध्वा तद्भस्मना तिलकं कृत्वा तत्तन्नित्याविद्यां हुतसंख्यामावर्त्त्य प्रागुवन्न्यासं कुर्य्यादिति । क्रूरकर्मसु अभिचारादिषु ॥ ८४ ॥

---

† स्वात्मानं ।

क्रूरकर्म्मसु होमेषु विधिरेष उदीरितः ।
तेषु तद्धोमकरणं समाप्ते नित्यशस्तथा ॥ ९४ ॥
साभ्यङ्गं विद्ययात्मानं कुर्य्यात् सम्पूजयेत्तथा ।
नित्यक्रमं ततो नित्यं तत्तद्दिवसविद्यया ॥ ९५ ॥
मिथुनानि च पश्चाच्च पूजयेत् प्रणमेदपि ।
मङ्गले पूर्वमुदिते पाहि मामित्युदीरयेत् ॥ ९६ ॥
एवं ते कथितं सर्वं कुण्डादिषु समीरितम् ।
होमं तं त्रिविधं प्रोक्तं स्थूलसूक्ष्मपरत्वतः ॥ ९७ ॥
स्थूलं परस्मोत्तरस्मिन् पटले सम्यगीरितम् ।
इतरस्य विधानि तु यानि ज्ञेयानि तानि तु ॥ ९८ ॥
प्रोक्तानि सकलानीत्थं होमाल्लक्ष्मीमवाप्नुयात् ।
विनाशयेदरातींश्च होमैः पापानि चात्मनः ॥ ९९ ॥

तेष्वित्यादिभिर्वाञ्छितमित्यन्तैरर्द्धाद्यैः षड्भिः श्लोकैः क्रूरहोमानन्तर तत्-शान्त्यर्थं होमः कर्त्तव्यः तदर्थं पूर्वोक्तदिननित्यामिथुनार्च्चनस्मरणसहितं सूक्ष्मपरहोमद्वयस्योत्तरपटले वक्ष्यमाणत्वप्रस्तावसंहितमुक्तनिगमनं तत्फल-ञ्चोपदिशति । तत्र नित्यशः प्रतिदिनं । तथा उक्तप्रकारेण । विद्यया तत्तन्नित्या-विद्यया । सम्पूजयेत् तत्तनित्यामिति शेषः । नित्यक्रमं तत्तन्नित्याया नित्य-पूजाक्रमं । ततस्तन्नित्यापूजानन्तरं । तत्तद्दिवसविद्यया पञ्चविंशपटलोक्त-तत्तद्दिनविद्यया सहेति शेषः । पूर्व्वमुदिते षोड़शपटले प्रोक्तचतुःषष्टि-कोष्ठात्मके । पाहि मामिति अक्षरात्मकमन्त्रमिति शेषः । सर्व्वं क्रूरहोमा-नन्तरं साधककर्त्तव्यं । कुण्डादिषु समीरितं कुण्डादिषु मेखलानाभि-योन्यादिनिर्माणविधानमीरितं । तुर्विशेषे । उत्तरस्मिन् द्वात्रिंशे पटले । इतरस्य स्थूलहोमस्य । तानीत्यस्योत्तरत्र प्रोक्तानीत्येतद्विशेष्यं । इत्थं होमात् प्रोक्त-

नासाध्यमस्ति होमेन नानवाप्यमपीश्वरि ।
तस्माद्धोमेन सकलं साधयेत् सर्ववाञ्छितम् ॥ १०० ॥
विद्यातत्त्वमयी व्याप्तिरिति सम्यक् समीरिता ।
अस्या निफालनाच्चित्ते तत्तत्त्वं स्वात्मसात् कृतम् ॥

इति षोड़शनित्यातन्त्रेषु श्रीकादिमते
कुण्डक्लृप्तिर्नाम एकोनत्रिंशं
पटलम् ॥ २९ ॥ॐ॥

प्रकारद्धोमात् । पापानि अमङ्गलानि । नासाध्यमित्येतदरातिविषयः । नान-वाप्यमित्येतदभिमतविषयः ॥ १०० ॥

इति षोड़शनित्यातन्त्रेषु श्रीकादिमताख्यस्य परिपूर्णस्य तन्त्रस्य प्रपञ्चसार-
सिंहराजप्रकाशाभिधानेन सुभगानन्दनाथेन विरचितायां
मनोरमाख्यायां व्याख्यायां षोड़शनित्यानां लोककाल-
तादात्म्यादिप्रकाशनपरमेकोनत्रिंशपटलं परिपूर्णं
परामृष्टम् ॥ २८ ॥ ॐतत्सत् ॥

ग्रन्थसंख्या—न सन्ति यन्त्राण्येकोनत्रिंशेऽस्मिन् पटले कृताः ।
अष्टार्धत्रिंशदधिका व्याख्याग्रन्थाः शतत्रयात् ॥

त्रिंशपटलम् ।

अथ षोड़शनित्यानां सामान्या वास्तुदेवता: ।
तासां चक्रं तत्र पूजाक्रमं सम्यग्वदामि ते ॥ १ ॥
तत्फलानि च तद्धोमविधानानि तथा वलिम् ।
सूक्ष्महोमविधानानि तत्फलानि परं तथा ॥ २ ॥
क्रमेण शृणु देवेशि प्रोक्तानि फलसिद्धये ।
यैर्विना भुवने मन्त्राः सर्वे स्युर्निष्फला ध्रुवम् ॥ ३ ॥
चतुरस्राकृतिः कश्चिदसुरः सर्वनाशकृत् ।
पुरा तस्य वधायैव सर्वे देवाः समुद्यमम् ॥ ४ ॥
कृत्वा निहन्तुमुद्युक्तास्तैरवध्योऽभवद्वरात् ।
आवयोस्तन्निरासाय मामेत्याकथयत्तदा ॥ ५ ॥

पूर्वस्मिन्नेकोनत्रिंशे पटले षोड़शनित्यानां होमार्थं मण्डपकुण्डादिनिर्माण-विधानमुपदिश्यानन्तरं षोड़शनित्यानां सामान्या वास्तुदेवता: तासां चक्रं तत्र तत्पूजनं तत्तत्फलानि तद्धोमविधानानि तद्बलिं सूक्ष्महोमविधानानि परहोम-विधिञ्चोपदिशति अथ षोड़शेत्यादिना अशेषत इत्यन्तेन श्लोकशतरूपेण त्रिंशेन पट-लेन। तत्राथ षोड़शेत्यादिभिर्ध्रुवमित्यन्तैस्त्रिभिः श्लोकैः पटलार्थांस्तज्ज्ञानानुष्ठान-वैधुर्य्येण सवमन्त्राणां नैष्फल्यं चोपदिशति। तत्र तासां वास्तुदेवतानां। तत्र चक्रे। ते तव। तत्फलानि वास्तुदेवतापूजाफलानि। तद्धोमविधानानि वास्तुदेवताहोम-विधानानि। तथा वलिं वास्तुदेवतावलिं। तत्फलानि सूक्ष्महोमफलानि। परं तथा परहोमात् फलानि क्रमेण उद्दिष्टानीति शेषः। देवेशीति सम्बुद्धिः। यैः प्रोक्तवक्ष्यमाणानुष्ठितैः। ध्रुवं निश्चितम् ॥ ३ ॥

चतुरस्राकृतिरित्यादिभिस्ते इत्यन्तैः सप्तभिः श्लोकैर्वास्तुदेवतोत्पत्तिकारणं तदुत्पत्तिं तत्संख्यां तत्पूजाकरणे प्रत्यवायं पूजाफलञ्च तच्चक्रादिविधान-कथनप्रस्तावसहितमुपदिशति। तत्र सर्व्वनाशकृत् सर्व्वप्राणिनां हिंसातत्परः।

कथयास्माकमधुना तद्वास्तुपुरुषस्य तु ।
दर्पशान्तिं नचेत्तेन विश्वमासीदुपद्रुतम् ॥ ६ ॥
इत्युक्ते तैर्मया प्रोक्तं निधनं तस्य दुःशकम् ।
खात्वा तमवनौ तस्य शरीरे स्थापयेत्तथा ॥ ७ ॥
नित्यशश्च त्रिपञ्चाशन्निःस्पन्दाक्रमणाय वै ।
नियोज्य तेषां ये पूजाविमुखास्तैः कृतानि तु ॥ ८ ॥
सुकृतानि समादद्यार्दुष्कृतानि च कुर्वते ।
तस्मात्तेषामर्च्चनन्तु प्रत्यहं कुर्वतां सदा ॥ ९ ॥
शुभान्येवाशु जायन्ते नैवाशुभकथापि च ।
तच्चक्रादिविधानन्तु शृणु सम्यग्वदामि ते ॥ १० ॥
प्राक्प्रत्यग्दक्षिणोदक् च कृत्वा वै दशसूत्रकम् ।
तैरेकाशीतिकोष्ठानि जातानि सुशः समानि च ॥ ११ ॥

तस्य असुरस्य । देवा ब्रह्मादयः । कृत्वेत्यस्य समुद्यममित्यनेन पूर्व्वेणान्वयः । तैर्देवैः आवयोः शक्तिशिवयोः । तन्निरासाय असुरवधाय । मां शिवं । अस्माकं देवानां । तुर्विशेषे । दर्पशान्तिं अवध्यत्वाभिमानोत्पन्नगर्वनिर्व्वापणं । नचेद्दर्पशान्तिं कथयसि । तेन वास्तुपुरुषासुरेण । उक्ते सतीति शेषः । तैर्देवैर्मया शिवेन । निधनं मरणं । तस्य वास्तुपुरुषस्य । दुःशकं दुष्करं । तं असुरं । तस्य असुरस्य । स्थापयेत् स्वार्थे णिच् बहुलत्वात्तिष्ठेदित्यर्थः । अस्य त्रिपञ्चाशदित्युत्तरत्रान्वयः । त्रिपञ्चाशद्देवानामिति शेषः । अयमत्रान्वयः तस्यासुरस्य निधनस्य दुःशकत्वात्तमवनौ खात्वा तच्छरीरे निःस्पन्दाक्रमणाय देवानां त्रिपञ्चाशत् तिष्ठेदिति मया देवान् प्रति नियोज्य प्रोक्तमिति । तेषां देवानां । तैः पूजाविमुखैः । कृतानीत्यस्योत्तरत्र-सुकृतानीत्येतद्विशेष्यं । तस्माद्धेतोस्तेषां देवानां । तच्चक्रादीत्यत्रादिशब्दस्तत्त-द्देवतास्थितितदर्च्चातच्चक्रप्रतिष्ठादिविषयः । ते तव ॥ १० ॥

प्रागित्यादिभिरीरितमित्यन्तैश्चतुर्भिः श्लोकैर्वास्तुदेवताचक्रनिर्माणविधानमुपदिशति । तत्र तैः आस्फालितैः सूत्रैः । समानि समान्तरालानि । तेषु कोष्ठेषु नवकोष्ठानीत्यन्वयः । एकं तु कुर्य्यात् एकीकुर्य्यादित्यर्थः । तद्बहिः एकीकृत-

तेषु मध्ये नवैकन्तु कुर्य्यात् कोष्ठानि तद्बहिः ।
एकीकुर्य्यात्त्रिकोष्ठानि दिक्षु प्रागादिषु क्रमात् ॥ १२ ॥
ततश्चतुर्षु कोणेषु तिर्य्यक्सूत्रचतुष्कतः ।
द्विधा कुर्य्यात् कोणकोष्ठान्यष्टौ तत्पार्श्वयोः पुनः ॥१३॥
एकीकुर्य्यात्तथा द्वे द्वे तद्वीथ्यां दिक्षु मध्यतः ।
एकमेकं भवेच्छिष्टं बहिर्द्वात्रिंशदीरितम् ॥ १४ ॥
सर्वमध्ये यजेत् सम्यग्ब्रह्माणं कमलासनम् ।
हेमाभञ्च चतुर्वक्त्रं वेदाध्ययनशीलिनम् ॥ १५ ॥

नवकोष्ठकाद्बहिः वीथ्यामिति शेषः । चतुर्षु कोणेषु एकीकृतकोष्ठनवकात् बाह्य-वीथिद्वयोरिति शेषः । तिर्य्यक्सूत्रचतुष्कतः कोष्ठानीत्यन्वयः । प्रतिकोणं कोष्ठ-द्वयस्यैकैकतिर्य्यक्सूत्रक्रमेण तत्पार्श्वयोः मध्यवीथिकोष्ठपार्श्वयोः । द्वे द्वे कोष्ठे इति शेषः । तद्वीथ्यां मध्यवीथ्यां । मध्यतः एकीकृतद्विद्विकोष्ठयोरिति शेषः । बहि-र्बाह्यवीथ्यां द्वात्रिंशत् कोष्ठानीति शेषः । एतदुक्तं भवति प्राक्प्रत्यग्दक्षिणोदक् च समान्तरालं दशदशसूत्रास्फालनेनैकाशीतिसंख्यकोष्ठानि निष्पाद्य तन्मध्ये कोष्ठ-नवकमेकीकृत्य तदन्तरबाह्यवीथ्यां परितः षोड़शसंख्यकोष्ठात्मिकायां प्रतिदिशं त्रीणि त्रीणि कोष्ठान्येकीकृत्य तद्वीथ्यां प्रतिकोणमेकैकक्रमेणावशिष्टकोष्ठचतुष्टयं तद्बाह्यवीथिगतचतुर्विंशतिकोष्ठेषु प्रतिकोणमेकैकक्रमेण कोष्ठचतुष्टयं चैवं क्रमात् प्रतिकोणं कोष्ठद्वयं तिर्य्यक्सूत्रेण द्विधा कृत्वा सम्भूय कोणचतुष्टयस्थार्द्ध-कोष्ठद्वयाष्टकमेकैकक्रमाद्देवताष्टकस्थानं परिकल्प्य पुनस्तद्विनीथवीथ्यां तत्तत् कोणोभयपार्श्वयोः कोष्ठद्वयं कोष्ठद्वयमेकीकृत्य पुनस्तद्वीथ्यां प्रतिदिशं मध्ये शिष्टमेकैकं कोष्ठं वक्ष्यमाणक्रमादक्षरन्यासार्थं परिकल्प्य पुनस्तद्बाह्यवीथ्यां द्वात्रिंशत् कोष्ठानि द्वात्रिंशद्देवतास्थानान्येवं सम्भूयाक्षरन्यासस्थानकोष्ठचतुष्टय-वर्जं त्रिपञ्चाशद्देवतास्थानानि भवन्तीति ॥ १४ ॥

सर्व्वमध्ये इत्यादिभिः समीरिता इत्यन्तैर्द्वादशभिः श्लोकैस्त्रिपञ्चाशद्वास्तु-देवतानामानि प्रोक्तचक्रे प्रोक्तस्थानेषु तासां स्थितिक्रमं तत्तन्नाममन्त्रांश्चोपदि-शति । तत्र सर्व्वमध्ये एकीकृतनवकोष्ठात्मकस्थाने । तद्बहिस्तदनन्तरवीथ्यामभि

प्रागादि तद्बहिश्चापि यजेदेतान् प्रदक्षिणम् ।
आर्य्यकञ्च विवस्वन्तं मित्रमन्यं महीधरम् ॥ १६ ॥
कोणार्द्धकोष्ठयोरेकमेकमष्टौ च तद्द्वये
वह्न्याद्यीशान्तमभितः पूजयेत् पूर्ववत् प्रिये ॥ १७ ॥
सावित्रः सविता शक्र इन्द्रजिद्रुद्रतज्जयौ ।
आयापवत्सकौ चेति प्रोक्तास्तेऽष्टौ तु नामतः ॥ १८ ॥
कोणार्द्धकोणपार्श्वस्थ ष्वग्न्याद्यीशान्तमर्च्चयेत् ।
अष्टौ क्रमेण ताराद्यैर्नमोन्तैर्नामभिस्तथा ॥ १९ ॥
अन्यानपि च चक्रेऽस्मिन् प्रोक्तान् सर्व्वांस्तथार्च्चयेत् ।
सर्व्वं गुहञ्चार्य्यमणं भञ्जकं पिलिपिच्छकम् *॥ २० ॥
चरकी च विदारी च पूतना च महेश्वरि ।
वहिरीशादि परितो यजेदष्टौ दिशं प्रति ॥ २१ ॥
ईशानश्चाथ पर्जन्यो जयन्तः शक्रभास्करौ ।
सत्यो हृषोन्तरिक्षश्च पूर्व्वाशाकोष्ठगाः क्रमात् ॥ २२ ॥

तस्त्वेकीकृतकोष्ठत्रयात्मककोष्ठत्रयात्मकेषु चतुर्षु स्थानेषु। एतानार्य्यकादीन्। अन्यं चतुर्थं। अष्टौ दैवतानीति शेषः। तद्द्वये वह्न्याद्यीशान्तमभितः तदर्द्धकोष्ठद्वये वह्निकोणगतार्द्धकोष्ठद्वयादीशकोणगतार्द्धकोष्ठद्वयान्तमित्यर्थः। पूर्व्ववत् प्रादक्षिण्येन। प्रिये इति सम्बुद्धिः। रुद्रतज्जयौ रुद्रो रुद्रजयश्च। ते देवाः। अष्टौ अनन्तरश्लोकवक्ष्यमाणसर्वादीन्। ताराद्यैः प्रणवाद्यैः। नमान्तैरित्यनेन तत्तन्नाम्नां चतुर्थीविभक्त्यन्तत्वं चोच्यते। तथा प्रादक्षिण्येन। अन्यान् प्रोक्तान् ब्रह्मादीन्। तथार्चयेत् प्रोक्तक्रमेण तत्तन्नाममन्त्रैरर्चयेत्। सर्वमित्यादिनोत्तरार्द्धेन पञ्च नामानि। चरकीत्यादिना पूर्व्वार्द्धेन नामत्रयं। महेश्वरीति सम्बुद्धिः। वहिः सर्ववाह्यवीथ्यां। अष्टौ देवान्। दिशं प्रति प्रतिदिशमित्यर्थः॥ ईशानेत्यादिना

* परिपृच्छकम ।

अग्निः पूषा च वितथो यमोऽथ गृहरक्षकः ।
गन्धर्व्वो भृङ्गराजश्च मृगो दक्षिणकोष्ठगः ॥ २३ ॥
निरृतिश्च तथा दौवारिकः सुग्रीवकस्तथा ।
वरुणः पुष्पदन्तश्चासुराख्यशोषरोगकाः ॥ २४ ॥
पश्चिमाशास्थकोष्ठेषुपूज्या एते यथाक्रमम् ।
वायुर्नागस्तथा मुख्यः सोमो भल्लातकस्तथा ॥ २५ ॥
अर्गलो दितिरप्येवमदितिश्च यथाक्रमम ।
कोष्ठेषूत्तरसंस्थेषु देवतास्ताः समीरिताः ॥ २६ ॥
द्वितीयवीथिमध्यस्थचतुष्कं कोणसूत्रतः ।
कृत्वा चतुर्द्धा तेष्वेव प्रागादिषु यथाक्रमात् ॥ २७ ॥

श्लोकेन नामाष्टकम् । अग्निरित्यादिना श्लोकेन नामाष्टकं । निरृतिरित्यादिना श्लोकेन नामाष्टकम् । एते नैरृत्यादयः । (वायुरित्यादिनोत्तरार्द्धेन नामपञ्चकम् । अर्गल इत्यादिना पूर्व्वार्द्धेन नामत्रयं । तत्र अर्गलः दितिरिति पदच्छेदः । ताः वाय्वादयः । एतदुक्तं भवति प्रोक्ते चक्रे एकीकृतनवकोष्ठमध्ये प्रोक्तरूपं ब्रह्माणं तद्बाह्यवीथ्यां प्रतिदिशमेकीकृतत्रित्रिकोष्ठात्मकस्थानचतुष्टये प्रागादितः प्रादक्षिण्यक्रमादार्य्यकादींश्चतुरस्तद्वीथितद्बाह्यवीथ्योः प्रतिकोणं तिर्य्यक्सूत्रास्फालनोत्पन्नार्द्धद्वयकोष्ठाष्टके वह्न्यादीशान्तं प्रादक्षिण्यक्रमात् सावित्रादीन् अष्टौ पुनस्तन्मध्यवीथीप्रतिकोणं शिष्टकोणपार्श्वद्वयेष्वेकीकृतकोष्ठद्वयद्वयोत्पन्नेषु अष्टसु स्थानेषु वह्न्यादीशान्तं प्रादक्षिण्येन सर्व्वादीनष्टौ पुनः सर्व्वबाह्यवीथ्यामीशानकोष्ठादिद्वात्रिंशत्कोष्ठेषु प्रादक्षिण्येनेशादीन् द्वात्रिंशद्देवांश्च तत्तन्नाममन्त्रैः प्रणवादिभिर्नमोऽन्तैः पूजयेदिति ॥२६॥

द्वितीयेत्यादिभिस्तानित्यन्तैस्त्रिभिः श्लोकैः प्रोक्तवास्तुचक्रमध्यवीथ्यां प्रतिदिशमेकैकक्रमादवशिष्टकोष्ठचतुष्टये युगादिवर्णन्यासक्रममुपदिशति । तत्र द्वितीयवीथिमध्यस्थचतुष्कं प्रतिदिशमेकैककोष्ठक्रमात् कोणसूत्रतः कोणसूत्राभ्यां तेष्वेव एकैककोष्ठस्थस्थानचतुष्कक्रमात प्राग्वत् प्रादक्षिण्यात् । प्राच्ये प्राक-

प्राच्ये युगार्णपर्य्यायनित्यार्णानालिखेत् क्रमात् ।
प्रागादिषु तथा दक्षे नित्यार्णानुदयार्णकम् ॥ २८ ॥
पश्चिमे भूमितोयाग्निवायुकर्म्मान्तिकान् लिखेत् ।
उत्तरे पूजयामीति विलिख्यात्र यजेच्च तान् ॥ २९ ॥
प्रत्येकं तैर्हुनेत् कुण्डे चतुरस्रेन्द्रदिङ्मुखः ।
व्रीहिमुद्गयवैः क्षौद्रघृतदुग्धाप्लुतैः क्रमात् ॥ ३० ॥
अष्टोत्तरशतं वाष्टोत्तरविंशतिमेव वा ।
प्रत्येकं तैर्हुनेद्द्रव्यैर्मन्त्रैस्तद्वच्च पायसैः ॥ ३१ ॥
बलिञ्च तेषां कुर्व्वीत पायसैर्व्यञ्जनान्वितैः ।
ससितैर्दुग्धकदलीफलापूपादिसंयुतम् ॥ ३२ ॥

कोष्ठस्थस्थानचतुष्टये । युगार्णपर्य्यायनित्यार्णान् तत्तत्कालीनं युगार्णं पर्य्यायनित्यार्णत्रयञ्च । क्रमात् प्राग्वत्प्रादक्षिण्येन । तथा प्रादक्षिण्येन । दक्षे दक्षिणपार्श्वस्थकोष्ठस्थस्थानचतुष्टये । नित्यार्णानुदयार्णकं उदयार्णं तत्तद्दिननित्यार्णत्रयञ्चेत्यर्थः । पश्चिमे पश्चिमकोणस्थस्थानचतुष्टये भूमीत्याद्यस्यापि स्वरूपग्रहणम् । कर्म्मान्तिकान् द्वितीयाविभक्त्यन्तान् । उत्तरे उत्तरकोष्ठस्थस्थानचतुष्टये । पूजयामीति चत्वार्थ्यक्षराणि । अत्र चक्रे । तान् प्रोक्तान् ब्रह्मादीन् ॥ २८ ॥

प्रत्येकमित्यादिना पायसैरित्यन्तेन श्लोकद्वयेन वास्तुदेवतानां होमार्थं कुण्डादिकं होमद्रव्याण्याहुतिसंख्याञ्चोपदिशति । तत्र तैः प्रोक्तनाममन्त्रैः स्वाहान्तैरित्यर्थः । हुनेत् जुहुयादित्यर्थः । चतुरस्रेन्द्रदिङ्मुखः अत्र सन्धिर्दिव्यत्वात् । इन्द्रदिङ्मुखः प्राङ्मुखः । क्रमात् एकैकक्रमात् । वा विकल्पे । तद्वत् प्रोक्तसंख्यालङ्घनेन । एतदुक्तं भवति चतुरस्रकुण्डे प्राङ्मुखः प्रोक्तप्रकारेण वह्निस्थापनादिपुरःसरं तत्र (?) कृत्वा क्षौद्रादित्रयाप्लुतैर्व्रीह्यादिभिस्त्रिभिः पायसैश्च ब्रह्मादीनां प्रत्येकमेकैकद्रव्येण प्रोक्तसंख्ययोरन्यतमसंख्या आज्याहुतीर्जुहुयादिति ॥ ३१ ॥

बलिमित्यादिना श्लोकेन तेषां बलिविधानं तद्द्रव्याणि चोपदिशति । तत्र तेषां ब्रह्मादीनां । दुग्धकदलीफलापूपादिसंयुतम् एतत् क्रियाविशेषणम् ।

एवं सिंहगते भानौ पूर्णायां प्रतिवत्सरम्।
स्वगेहे वास्तुपूजायां मण्डले सर्वतः क्रमात्॥ ३३॥
कुर्य्यात्तद्दिवसे विप्रान् नित्याभक्तान् यथावलम्।
त्रयादह्रीनान् विविधैर्म्मधुराद्यैस्तु भोजयेत्॥ ३४॥
भुक्तेभ्यो दक्षिणां दद्याद्यथाशक्ति समर्च्य तान्।
एवं विदधतो गेहे नाकल्याणं कदाचन॥ ३५॥
न वालमरणं व्याधिभूतप्रेतादिकानि च।
न सर्पपीड़ा नान्योन्यकलहान्यशुभानि च॥ ३६॥
पुत्रपौत्रधनारोग्यपशुदासीसमृद्धिभाक्।
अरोगी विजयी ख्यातश्चिरं जीवति तद्गृहे॥ ३७॥

अपूपादीत्यत्रादिशब्दो घृतादिविषयः। एतदुक्तं भवति उक्तेषु त्रिपञ्चाशत्स्थानेषु उक्तानि त्रिपञ्चाशद्दैवतान्यावाह्य गन्धपुष्पधूपदीपैरभ्यर्च्य पायसेन तन्त्रोक्तद्रव्यैर्वा प्रत्येकं वलिसिक्थानि निवेद्यानन्तरं अन्नानि पात्रान्तरे यथास्थानं निवेश्य रक्ताम्बरोष्णीषो खड़्गपाणिः खड़्गपाणिभिः पुरुषैरावृतस्त्वरे देवतायतननदी-तीरप्रख्यातवनस्पतिमूलानामन्यतमप्रदेशे स्थण्डिले यथास्थानं निक्षिप्य पश्चादनपेक्षरक्षिभिः सार्द्धं श्रीविद्याजापी गृहमेत्य न्यस्तगात्रो देवतात्मा भवेदिति॥ २२॥

एवमित्यादिभिर्भवेदित्यन्तैः सप्तभिः श्लोकैः प्रतिवर्षं स्वगेहे वास्तुदेवतार्चनकालं तत्तद्दिवसे नित्याचक्रोपास्तिक्रमात् तत्फलं राजादिगृहाद्येतदर्चनस्यावश्य-कर्त्तव्यतां तदकरणे प्रत्यवायस्योपदिशति। तत्र एवं प्रोक्तक्रमात्। स्वगेहे साधक-गेहे। मण्डले प्रोक्तगेहे (शक्तवक्रे?)। कुर्य्यादित्यस्य वास्तुपूजायामित्यनेन पूर्व्वत्रा-न्वयः। तद्दिवसे वास्तुदेवतोपास्तिदिवसे। नित्याभक्तान् षोड़शनित्याभक्तान्। त्रया-दह्रीनान् पुरुषत्रयादह्रीनान्। मधुराद्यैरित्यत्र आद्यशब्दस्त्वितररसपञ्चकविषयः। तान् भक्तान् भूतप्रेतादिकानित्यत्रादिशब्दः अपस्मारकृत्यादिविषयः। अशुभानि

राजवेश्मसु सर्वत्र तथा च महिषीगृहे ।
सचिवामात्यसेनानीभवनेषु पुरे तथा ॥ ३८ ॥
विदध्यात् प्रतिवर्षन्तु प्रोक्तसिद्धै तु देशिकः ।
न चेदुक्तान्यथारूपफलैः क्लेशोऽनिशं भवेत् ॥ ३९ ॥
त्रिलोहाश्मतलेष्वन्यतमे हस्तप्रमाणके ।
तत्तद्दैवतनामानि मायागर्भे समालिखेत् ॥ ४० ॥
तत्र तान् पूजयेत् सप्तपञ्चत्रिवेकवासरैः ।
स्थापयेद्वेश्मसु क्वापि नित्यशश्चापि तत्र वै ॥ ४१ ॥
स्मरेत्तान् देवताबुद्ध्या कुर्य्यात् पुष्पाञ्जलिं त्रिशः ।
तद्वेश्ममङ्गलं ग्रामपुरखर्वटकादिषु ॥ ४२ ॥
विदध्यादखिलं क्षुद्रक्लेशशान्त्यै समृद्धये ।

दारिद्र्यादीन्यमङ्गलानि । तद्गृहे अर्चितवास्तुदेवताभिः परिरचितगृहे । सर्व्वत्र राजनिवासस्थानेषु मण्डपादिषु । तथा च महिषीगृहे राजमहिषीणां गृहे विनिवासस्थानेषु । तथा सर्व्वदिग्विदिक्षु मध्ये चेत्यर्थः । तुरवधारणे । नचेत् प्रोक्तक्रमाद्वास्तुदेवतापूजा न कृता चेत् ॥ ३८ ॥

त्रिलोहेत्यादिभिः समृद्धये इत्यन्तैरर्ध्याधिकैस्त्रिभिः श्लोकैरधिकरणेषु वास्तुचक्रनिर्म्माणविधानादिकं गृहादिषु तत्प्रतिष्ठां तत्फलञ्चोपदिशति । तत्र त्रिलोहाश्मतलेषु हिरण्यरूप्यताम्राश्मतलेषु । हस्तप्रमाणके विस्तारायामाभ्यां । तत्तद्दैवतनामानि प्रोक्तानि द्वितीयान्तानीति शेषः । तेषां द्वितीयान्तत्वं पूजयामीत्यस्य तच्चक्रे लेख्यत्वेनोपदिष्टत्वात् भूम्यादिनामचतुष्टयविलेखने द्वितीयान्तत्वविधानाच्च । मायागर्भे ह्रीं खोदरे । तत्र चक्रे । तान् देवान् । क्वापि अनुपहतदेशे । तत्र स्थापितदेशे । त्रिशः त्रिवारादन्नीनं । खर्वटकादिष्वित्यत्रादिशब्दः पत्तनादिविषयः । विदध्यात् प्रोक्तप्रकारेण वास्तुदेवताचक्रं प्रतिष्ठादिकमिति शेषः ॥ ४२ ॥

ततः सूक्ष्मैः पराख्यैश्च होमैः सिद्धिं शृणु प्रिये ॥ ४३ ॥
स्वमूलाधारके वह्नौ कुण्डलिन्यास्यगामिनि ।
वाच्यवाचकरूपञ्च प्रपञ्चं जुहुयात्तथा ॥ ४४ ॥
येनावयोः समो देवि जायते हवनेन वै ।
तद्विधानं वद प्राज्ञ शम्भो सम्यङ्ममाधुना ॥ ४५ ॥
आधारे वह्निसंस्थानं कुण्डलिन्याः स्थितिं ततः ।
तद्रूपं तत्क्रियां सर्वं वद मे विशदं प्रभो ॥ ४६ ॥
शृणु वक्ष्ये विधानं ते सम्यग्विस्तरतोऽधुना ।
प्राणाग्निहोत्रविद्येति यत्तु्ष्यां श्रूयते परम् ॥ ४७ ॥

तत इत्यादिना वै इत्यन्तेनार्द्धाधिकेन श्लोकेन सूक्ष्मपरहोमैः सिद्धिकथनप्रस्ताव-पुरःसरं संक्षेपात् सूक्ष्महोमविधानं तद्वैभवञ्चोपदिशति । तत्र चः समाहारे । प्रिये इति सम्बुद्धिः । स्वमूलाधारके षोड़शपटलप्रोक्तरूपे । वाच्यवाचकरूपं वाच्य-वाचकात्मकं । तथा उच्यमानप्रकारेण । येन विधानेन । आवयोः शक्तिशिवयोः । एतदुक्तं भवति मूलाधारस्थकुण्डलिनीशक्तिमुखगामिवह्नौ वाच्यवाचकात्मकं प्रपञ्चं तथा जुहुयात येन हवनविधानेन आवयोः समः साधको जायते इति ॥ ४४ ॥

तद्विधानमित्यादिना प्रभो इत्यन्तेनार्द्धाधिकेन श्लोकेन तद्विधानं मूलाधारे वह्निसंस्थानं कुण्डलिन्याः स्थितिं तद्रूपं तत्क्रियाश्च देवी पृच्छति । तत्र तद्विधानं सूक्ष्महोमाङ्गविधानं । प्राज्ञ शम्भो इति पदद्वयमीश्वरसम्बुद्धिः । अधुना अस्मिन् पटले । तद्रूपं कुण्डलिनीरूपं तत्क्रियां कुण्डलिनीक्रियां । विशदं सुस्पष्टं । प्रभो इति देवसम्बुद्धिः ॥ ४६ ॥

शृण्वित्यादिभिः किञ्चनेत्यन्तैश्चतुर्भिः श्लोकैस्तद्विधानकथनप्रस्तावपुरःसरं तद्विद्यानां वेदषु प्रशस्तिं तद्वैभवादिकञ्चोपदिशन्नस्मिन् पटले प्रोक्ततद्वैभवशेषस्य

यज्ज्ञात्वा वनितागर्भं न प्रयाति नरो ध्रुवम् ।
यद्व्यायायासरहितमनन्यापेक्षनिर्वहम् ॥ ४८ ॥
यन्मनः क्लेशविश्रान्तेः स्थानं निःशेषकल्मषम् ।
सुखास्पदं स्वगं विश्वमयं चिद्वेद्यवेदनात् ॥ ४९ ॥
अत्रोक्तशेषमखिलं षड्विंशे पटले स्फुटम् ।
प्रदर्श्यते ततस्तत्र वर्णयामि च किञ्चन ॥ ५० ॥
नित्यानित्योदिते मूलाधारमध्येऽस्ति पावकः ।
सर्वेषां प्राणिनां तद्वद्धृदये च प्रभाकरः ॥ ५१ ॥
मूर्द्धनि ब्रह्मरन्ध्राधश्चन्द्रमाश्च व्यवस्थितः ।
तत्त्रयात्मकमेव स्यादाद्या नित्या त्रिखण्डकम् ॥ ५२ ॥

षट्त्रिंशपटले वक्ष्यमाणत्वं कथयति । तत्र विधानं सूक्ष्महोमाङ्गं । अधुना अस्मिन् पटले । यद्विधानं परं निरतिशयं । वनितागर्भं मातुरुदरं । यत् व्यायासरहितं चर्य्याव्यदक्षिणाद्यर्थव्ययकृच्छ्रचान्द्रायणाद्यायासानपेक्षत्वादनुसन्धानमात्रत्वाच्च । अनन्यापेक्षनिर्वहं ऋग्विशेषत्रिगुपद्रष्टाद्यनपेक्षत्वात् स्वभेदप्रतीतेः स्वात्मन्येव विलयनानुसन्धानमात्रत्वाच्च । यन्मनः क्लेशविश्रान्तेः स्थानं सङ्कल्पविकल्पविलयरूपत्वात् । निःशेषकल्मषं स्वव्यतिरिक्ताभावात् । सुखास्पदं स्वस्मिन्नेव मनसो निर्व्युत्थानविलापकत्वात् । स्वगं स्वस्मिन् अन्तर्हितत्वात् । विश्वमयं चिद्वेद्यवेदनात् ज्ञातृज्ञानज्ञेयात्मकत्वाद्विश्वमयं । अत्र अस्मिन् पटले । ततस्तस्मात् ॥ ५० ॥

नित्येत्यादिभिस्तैरित्यन्तैः पञ्चभिः श्लोकैः सूक्ष्मस्वरूपं तदनुसन्धानं तद्धोमप्रकारञ्चोपदिशति । तत्र नित्यानित्योदिते नित्यानित्यपटले प्रोक्ते तद्वत् तन्त्रोक्तवत् स्थिते हृदये अनाहतचक्रे ब्रह्मरन्ध्राधः शिरःकपाले* ब्रह्मरन्ध्रप्रदेशाधोभागे त्वधोमुखपद्ममध्ये । तत्त्रयात्मकं अग्निसूर्य्यसोमात्मकं । आद्यानित्यात्रिखण्डकं श्रीविद्याखण्डत्रयम् ॥ तेषामित्यादिना श्लोकेनैतदुक्तं भवति मूलाधारे वह्न्यात्मकं श्रीवि-

---

* शक्तिकपाले ।

तेषां त्रयाणामैक्यन्तु मनसा भावयेत्तथा ।
गमागमाभ्यां तेजोभिस्तेषामन्योन्यजैः शिवे ॥ ५३ ॥
तथा समिद्धं तत्तेजस्त्रयं बुद्धाथ तन्मयम् ।
चित्तविकल्पविधुरं भावयेदद्वुताञ्च यत् ॥ ५४ ॥
तेषां त्रयाणां वर्णानां प्रागुक्तानां क्रमेण वै ।
द्वाभ्यामन्यतमं कृत्वा पुटितं जुहुयाच्च तैः ॥ ५५ ॥
पुटितान् भानुहृद्वर्णैः स्वरांस्तारिण हुङ्कृतैः ।
कुण्डलीमुखमार्गाग्नौ जुहुयान्निश्चलाशयः ॥ ५६ ॥

त्रयाणां: प्रथमखण्डमूर्द्ध मुखप्रसृततेजस्कत्वात्तदादिब्रह्मरन्ध्रान्तं हृदये सूर्य्यात्मकं श्रीविद्याया मध्यमखण्डमुभयतः प्रसृततेजस्कत्वात्तदादिकं मूलाधारान्तं ब्रह्मरन्ध्रान्तगञ्च ब्रह्मरन्ध्राधःप्रदेशाधोमुखपद्मकर्णिकायां श्रीविद्यायाः तृतीयखण्डं चन्द्रात्मकममृतमयत्वेनाधोमुखप्रसृततेजस्कत्वात् तदादिकं मूलाधारान्तमेवं तेजस्त्रयात्मकं खण्डत्रयं गमागमानुसन्धानेनान्योन्यमेकीभूतं तन्मयमनसा सह स्वात्मानं च भावयेदिति। तथा प्राक्तप्रकारेण। तन्मयं कनकादिभिन्नमुकुरादिभेदवदिति शेषः। विकल्पविधुरं भेदरहितं। तेषां त्रयाणां अग्निसूर्य्यसोमानां व्यधिकरणे षष्ठी। वर्णानां प्रागुक्तानां पञ्चदशे पटले अकारादीत्यादिना चतुःषष्टितमेन श्लोकेनाभिप्रेतत्वेनाक्तानां। द्वाभ्यामग्निसूर्य्यसोमात्मकवर्गवर्णत्रयान्यतमाभ्यां अन्यतमं वर्णवर्गं तैः वक्ष्यमाणक्रमेण पुटितैः। एतदुक्तं भवति पञ्चदशपटलोक्तानां सूर्य्यसोमात्मककुलासनरेखात्रयात्मकत्रयाभिप्रेतानां वर्णानां मध्ये सोमात्मकषोडशस्वरवर्णः सूर्य्यात्मककाकारादितकारान्तषोडश वर्णवर्गश्चाग्न्यात्मकथकारादिसकारान्तषोडशवर्णवर्गं चान्यतमाभ्यां वर्गाभ्यां हितेजोमयाभ्यां तत्तदितरतेजोमयवर्गवण वक्ष्यमाणक्रमात्तैस्तैर्वर्णैः पुटिताभिः ज्ञातृज्ञानज्ञेयात्मिकाभिः षोडशभिः प्रोक्त निर्विकल्पे स्वतेजसि वक्ष्यमाणक्रमेण जुहुयादिति ॥ ५५ ॥

पुटितानित्यादिभिः समभित्यन्तैः पञ्चभिः श्लोकैः प्राणाग्निहोत्रमन्त्रादिकमुपदिशति। अत्र भानुहृद्वर्णाः कुलासन सूर्य्यात्मकरेखास्थककारादितकारान्ताः

वह्निभानुपुटान्तःस्थैश्चान्द्रैः स्तद्वद्धुनेत् क्रमात् ।
चन्द्रभानुपुटान्तःस्थैर्व्व्योम्नाग्नौ जुहुयात्तथा ॥ ५७ ॥
भानुचन्द्रपुटान्तःस्थैर्व्योम्नाग्नौ जुहुयात्तथा ।
चन्द्रवह्निपुटान्तःस्थैर्भान्वर्णैर्जुहुयादपि ॥ ५८ ॥
वह्निचन्द्रपुटान्तःस्थैरपि तद्वद्धुनेत्ततः ।
तथा तेषां प्रातिलोम्यात् षोड़शानां हुनेदपि ॥ ५९ ॥

षोड़श भानुवर्णाः । हृदिनि सकारः । तदासनं वह्निरेखास्थानामाम्नेया-क्षराणां प्रतिलोमक्रमात् सकारस्य प्रथमभावितया तद्वाचकरूपहृच्छब्देन तदादि-थकारान्ता वह्निरूपाः षोड़शवर्णा उच्यन्ते । तस्मात् ककारादितकारान्तैः षोड़शभिर्भानुवर्णैः सकारादिथकारान्तैर्व्युतक्रमात् षोड़शभिरग्निवर्णैश्च । स्वरान् तत्कुलासनं सोमात्मकरेखास्थानकारादींश्चन्द्रात्मकान् । तारेण प्रणवेन हुङ्कृतैरित्यत्र हुङ्कारस्यार्थो गुरुमुखादवगन्तव्यः । निश्चलाशयः अनन्यमनाः । तन्म न्त्रा यथा—कअसौ, खआषौ इत्यादयः तअःथौ इत्यन्ताः षोड़श । वह्नि-भानुपुटान्तःस्थैः थकारादिसकारान्तानामनुलोमानां ककारादितकारान्तानां प्रति-लोमानां वर्णानां पुटान्तःस्थैश्चान्द्रैः स्वरैः । तद्वत् प्रणवेन हुङ्कृतैरित्यर्थः । क्रमात् अकारादिविसर्जनीयान्तक्रमात् । तन्मन्त्रा यथा—थअतौ दआणौ इत्यादयः सअःकौ इत्यन्ताः षोड़श । चन्द्रभानुपुटान्तःस्थैः अकारादि विसर्जनीयान्तानां सौम्यषोड़शवर्णानां तकारादिककारान्तानां भानु-षोड़शवर्णानां पुटान्तःस्थैर्व्योम्नाग्नौः थकारादिसकारान्तैः । तथा तारेण हुङ्कृतैरिति यावत् । तन्मन्त्रा यथा अथतौं आदणौं इत्यादयः अःसकौं इत्यन्ताः षोड़श । भानुचन्द्रपुटान्तःस्थैः ककारादितका-रान्तानां भानुवर्णानां विसर्जनीयाद्यकारान्तानां चन्द्रवर्णानां पुटान्तःस्थैर्व्योम्नाग्नौः थकारादिसकारान्तैः । तथा प्राग्वत्तारेण हुङ्कृतैः । तन्मन्त्रा यथा—कअःथौं खअंदौं गऔधौं इत्यादयः तअसौं इत्यन्ताः षोड़श । चन्द्रवह्निपुटान्तःस्थैः स्वराणां अकारादिविसर्जनीयान्तानां सकारादिथकारान्तानां च पुटान्तःस्थैः । भान्वर्णैः ककारादितकारान्तैः । अग्र्या तारेण हुङ्कृतैः इत्यनुषज्यते । तन्मन्त्रा

एवं द्वादशधा होममक्षरैः स्यादुदीरितैः ।
कृत्वा तद्वाच्यमखिलमर्थरूपञ्च तैः समम् ॥ ६० ॥
तेजस्त्रयात्मरूपं स्यादावयोरपि तद्वपुः ।
अन्यानि चावयोरिच्छागृहीतानि वपूंषि वै ॥ ६१ ॥
तान्यन्यदेवतादेहसम्यगिच्छावशानि च ।
मुक्तिश्च तन्मयीभावस्थैर्य्यमेव समीरितम् ॥ ६२ ॥

यथा—अकसों आकषों इत्यादयः अःतथों इत्यन्ताः षोड़श। वह्निचन्द्र-पुटान्तःस्थैः थकारादिसकारान्तानां विसर्जनीयाद्यकारान्तानाञ्च पुटान्तःस्थैः। तद्वत्तारेण हुकृतैः। अप्या ककारादितकारान्तैः भान्वर्णैः। तन्मन्त्रा यथा—थकःॐ दखंॐ इत्यादयः सतॐ इत्यन्ताः षोड़श। एवमुक्तप्रकारेण षड्विधप्रकारप्रोक्तभेदानां मन्त्राणां तारेण चतुर-क्षरात्मकत्वे सत्यपि सम्प्रदायेन ते कृतसन्धिका एव लिखिताः। तेषां षड्विधभेदप्रकारप्रोक्तानां प्रातिलोमशात् षोड़शानां षाड़शमन्त्राणा-मिति शेषः। एवमनुलोमविलोमाभ्यां। होमं दिव्यत्वात् होमः स्यादित्यर्थः। अक्षरैस्तेजस्त्रयात्मभिरिति शेषः। उदीरितैः प्रोक्तेषु द्विन-वत्यु त्तरशतरूपेष्वभीष्टैः षोड़शभिर्मन्त्रैः। अखिलं ज्ञातृज्ञानज्ञेयात्मकं। तैः-र्ज्ञातृज्ञानज्ञेयात्मभिर्वाचकरूपैः त्रिभिस्त्रिभिरक्षरैः समं तदपृथग्रूपं। एतदुक्तं भवति एवं प्रोक्तेषु द्वादशसु भेदेष्वभीष्टभेदमन्त्ररूपैस्त्रितय ज्ञानमयैर्वाचकरूपैस्त्रिभिस्त्रिभिरक्षरैस्तत्तत्तेजस्त्रयात्मकं वाच्यमखिलमर्थ-रूपमपृथग्रूपं कृत्वा मूलाधारस्थनिर्विकल्परूपमात्ममहावह्नौ होमः स्यादिति ॥ ६० ॥

तेजस्त्रयेत्यादिना समीरितमित्यन्तेन श्लोकद्वयेन शक्तिशिवयोः याथात्म्य-स्वरूपस्य तेजस्त्रयात्मकत्वमितरं पाञ्चभौतिकविग्रहस्वेच्छागृहीतात्मकत्वं मुक्ति-स्वरूपञ्चोपदिशति। तत्र आवयोः शक्तिशिवयोः। तद्वपुः अनश्वरं वपुः। अन्यानि पाञ्चभौतिकानि। आवयोः प्राग्वत्। तन्मयीभावस्थैर्य्यं प्रोक्ततेजस्त्रय-तादात्म्यभावस्थैर्य्यम् ॥ ६२ ॥

तत्र कुण्डलिनीं ब्रूहि स्फुटं मे परमेश्वर ।
तां वदामि शृणु प्राज्ञे रहस्यं परमाद्भुतम् ॥ ६३ ॥
मूलाधारस्थवह्न्यात्मतेजोमध्ये व्यवस्थिता ।
जीवशक्तिः कुण्डलाख्या प्राणाकारेण तेन सा ॥ ६४ ॥
प्रसुप्तभुजगाकारा त्रिरावर्त्ता महाद्युतिः ।
मायाशीर्षा नदन्ती तामुच्चरन्त्यनिशं स्वगे ॥ ६५ ॥
सुषुम्नामध्यदेशे सा यदा कर्णद्वयस्य तु ।
पिधाय न शृणोत्यस्या ध्वनिं तस्य तदा मृतिः ॥ ६६ ॥
एवं सा जीवशक्तिस्तु यदा कुण्डलिनीस्थितिम् ।
विहाय ऋजुतां याति स्वेच्छादण्डाहता सती ॥ ६७ ॥
तदा विश्वप्रतीतिः स्यात् प्राणिनामन्यदा पुनः ।
निशान्धकारे भुवनस्थितिवत् स्वात्मनः स्थितिः ॥ ६८ ॥

तत्रेत्यादिना श्लोकपूर्वार्द्धेन कुण्डलिनीस्वरूपं देवी पृच्छति। तत्र स्फुटं सुस्पष्टं। तामित्यादिना श्लोकोत्तरार्द्धेन कुण्डलिनीस्वरूपकथनं प्रस्तौति। तत्र तां कुण्डलिनीं। रहस्यं देशिककटाक्षाद्दृते ज्ञातुमशक्यत्वात्। परमाद्भुतम् ज्ञानात्मकत्वात्तादात्म्यात्मकत्वाच्च ॥ ६३ ॥

मूलाधारेत्यादिभिः साधक इत्यन्तैः षड्भिः श्लोकैः कुण्डलिनीस्वरूपं तदनुभावञ्चोपदिशति। तत्र तेन प्राणाकारेण। सा कुण्डलिनी। महाद्युतिः विश्वप्रकाशकत्वात्। मायाशीर्षा विसर्जनीयशीर्षा। तां मायां उच्चरन्ती तदात्मना ऊर्द्ध्वोर्द्ध्वं सञ्चरन्ती। स्वगे इत्येतदुत्तरत्र सुषुम्नामध्यदेशे इत्यस्य विशेषणं। सा कुण्डलिनी। तदा अत्यासन्नतः। एवमुक्तरूपा। तुर्विशेषे। ऋजुतां याति मूलाधाराद्विनिर्गत्य तदुपरि श्रोत्रादीन्द्रियगामिनी। स्वेच्छादण्डाहता स्वेच्छाप्रेरणापरवशा। अन्यदा तस्यां प्रसुप्तभुजगाकारतया स्थितायां। निशान्धकारे भुवनस्थितिवत् अप्रकाशतया। एतदुक्तं भवति यदा स्वात्मस्फुरत्तारूपिणी बुद्ध्यात्मिका कुण्डलिनी शक्तिः मूलाधारात् प्रसुप्तभुजगाकारतां विहाय स्वेच्छाप्रेरिता

एवं तां वेत्ति यो देहे देशिकादेशदर्शिताम् ।
स वेत्ति ब्रह्म परमं मां त्वामपि च साधकः ॥ ६९ ॥
जीवन्मुक्तः स विज्ञेयः शुद्धात्मासक्तमानसः ।
अस्पृष्टपुण्यपापश्च शोकहर्षातिभूमिगः ॥ ७० ॥
रागद्वेषविनिर्मुक्तस्त्यक्तसर्व्वक्रियाफलः ।
निरुपाधिकसन्तुष्टः स्वेच्छाधीनेच्छया युतः ॥ ७१ ॥
स्वदेहमात्रयात्रश्च समश्च स्तुतिनिन्दयोः ।
समारिमित्रकल्याणगुणशीलदयान्वितः ॥ ७२ ॥
एवं स कथितो जीवन्मुक्तो लोकेषु साधकः ।
इतरः पूजने देव्या भजने च सकौतुकः ॥ ७३ ॥
कालेन सिद्धिभाग्भूयादितरो दुःखभाजनम् ।
जन्मभिर्व्बहुभिः क्लिष्टो* मूर्खो विद्याधनोज्झितैः ॥ ७४ ॥

उर्द्ध्वं गता व्याप्ता विलदेहात्तत्तदिन्द्रियद्वारा विनिर्गत्य विश्वं कवलीकरोति तदा विश्वप्रतीतिर्भवति । पुनः स्वेच्छया यदा मूलाधारे सा प्रसुप्तभुजगाकारमात्रस्वरूपतां याति तदा निशास्वन्धकारे भुवनस्थितिवत् तद्विश्वप्रतीतिः न स्यादिति । एवं प्रकाशकरीं । तां कुण्डलिनीं । देशिकादेशदर्शितां देशिकोपदेशदर्शितां । मामपि शिवं शक्तिश्च त्वाम् ॥ ६९ ॥

जीवन्मुक्त इत्यादिभिः साधक इत्यन्तै रध्यर्द्धैस्त्रिभिः श्लोकैर्जीवन्मुक्तलक्षणमुपदिशति । तत्र असक्तमानसः इति पदच्छेदः । शोकहर्षातिभूमिगः शोकहर्षयोरपि पारं गतः । निरुपाधिकसन्तुष्टः स्वभावसन्तोषयुक्तः । स्वेच्छाधीनेच्छया युतः अपरप्रेरितबुद्धिः । समारिमित्रः रागद्वेषाभावात् । जीवन्मुक्तः जीवन्नेव मुक्तः परमार्थतः स्वात्मनोन्याद्यभावादित्यर्थः ॥ ७२ ॥

इतर इत्यादिना योनिष्वित्यन्तेनार्द्धाद्यन्तेन श्लोकेनोक्तज्ञानरहितस्यापि देव्यर्चनात् कालेन तत्सिद्धिः भणितः तदर्चनादिरहितस्य प्रत्यवायश्चोप-

---

* क्ल्प्षा

मुर्देरुन्मत्तचित्तः सन्नधोधो याति योनिषु ।
नित्यासु भक्तिर्भुवने प्रक्षीणे पापकर्म्मणि ॥ ७५ ॥
जायते यद्बलाल्लोके भवेत् प्रागुक्तलक्षणः ।
नरो भवन्ति तां भक्तिं प्राप्य लोकेषु देवताः ॥ ७६ ॥
दृश्यन्ते भानुचन्द्रारबुधजीवसितासिताः ।
अन्ये च लोकपालाद्यास्तद्भक्तिप्राप्तसम्पदः ॥ ७७ ॥
बहुना किं परं देवि नित्याभिः सदृशानघ ।
न सन्ति देवता विद्यास्तस्मात्ता एव सर्व्वदा ॥ ७८ ॥
भावयाम्यहमद्यापि त्रिकाले विग्रहान्वितः ।

दिशति । तत्र इतरः प्रोक्तज्ञानरहितः । देव्याः सर्वकारणभूताया ललितायाः । कालेन भक्त्युपासनादिगौरवलाघववशात् कालदैर्घ्यविलम्बनेन । इतरः तद्भक्त्यादिरहितः । जन्मभिर्बहुभिः अपरमार्थज्ञानसर्वैर्विविधजन्मभिः । मूर्खः अविवेकी । विद्याधनोज्झवैरित्येतदुत्तरत्र मुर्देरित्यस्य विशेषणम् । उन्मत्तचित्तः कर्त्तव्याकर्त्तव्यज्ञानरहितः । अधोधो याति योनिषु नीचैर्नीचैर्विषयेषु परवशो भवतीत्यर्थः ॥ ७४ ॥

नित्यास्वित्यादिभिरन्वित इत्यन्तैरर्द्धाधिकैस्त्रिभिः श्लोकैः नित्यासु भक्तेर्दौर्लभ्यं तद्भक्तिवैभवं नित्यावैभवविग्रहान्वितेनेश्वरेण तदुपास्तिं चोपदिशति । तत्र प्रक्षीणे सद्गुरुकटाक्षादिभिः । पापकर्म्मणि अज्ञानदुर्वासनाद्युपहतकर्मणि । यद्बलाद्भक्तिबलात् । प्रागुक्तलक्षणः जीवन्मुक्तलक्षणः । नरः प्रागुक्तलक्षणो भवेदित्यन्वयः । तां भक्तिं अस्मिन् पटले वक्ष्यमाणरूपां । देवताः—इत्यस्य भवन्तीत्यनेनान्वयः । लोकपालाद्या इत्यत्राद्यशब्दस्त्रयस्त्रिंशत्कोटिदेवताविषयः । तद्भक्तिप्राप्तसम्पदः उक्तरूपभक्तिप्राप्तैश्वर्य्याः । बहुना भाषणेन । सदृशाः अनघे इति च पदच्छेदः । भावयामीत्यस्य ता एव इत्यनेन पूर्वत्रान्वयः । अहं शिवः । त्रिकाले सन्ध्यात्रये । विग्रहान्वितः न्यस्तविग्रहः । अनेन लब्धज्ञानानामपि सन्ध्यात्रयोपास्तेरवश्यकर्त्तव्यता कथितेति सम्प्रदायार्थः ॥७८ ॥

तद्वर्णव्याप्तचक्रस्था ग्रहाश्च तद्द्दर्शिताः ॥ ७९ ॥
विधिविष्णुशिवात्मत्वं तासामेव निजेच्छया ।
अन्याश्च देवता या यास्तास्तास्तन्मयविग्रहाः ॥ ८० ॥
पररूपन्तु वक्ष्यामि होमन्ते महदद्भुतम् ।
यत्सिद्धिः सिद्धरूपाणां प्रागुक्तानां भवेत् सदा ॥ ८१ ॥
अन्येषां न भवेद्भावः तथा सर्व्वाश्च यो महान् ।
प्रक्षीणाशेषपापानां भक्तिः स्यात्तज्जुसेविनाम् ॥ ८२ ॥

तद्वर्णेत्यादिना श्लोकोत्तरार्द्धेन पञ्चविंशपटलप्रोक्तमातृकाचक्रारस्थग्रहाणां दशां तत्स्थितिरूपञ्च स्मारयति। तत्र तद्वर्णव्याप्तचक्रस्थाः नित्यात्मकमातृकावर्णव्याप्तचक्रस्थाः ॥ ७९ ॥

विधीत्यादिना श्लोकेन त्रिमूर्त्तीनामन्यदेवतानाञ्च नित्यानां स्वेच्छाविग्रहात्मकत्वमुपदिशति तत्र विधिविष्णुशिवात्मत्वं ब्रह्मविष्णुरुद्रात्मकत्वं। तासां षोड़शनित्यानां। निजेच्छया स्वेच्छया। अन्याः अन्यतन्त्रेषूपदिष्टाः। तन्मयविग्रहाः चक्रान्तरस्थषोड़शनित्यामयविग्रहाः ॥ ८० ॥

पररूपमित्यादिना महानित्यन्तेनार्द्धाधिकेन श्लोकेन पररूपहोमकथनप्रस्तावपुरःसरं सिद्धसाध्यसाधकादित्रयेषु सिद्धानामेव तत्परहोमयोग्यतामितरेषामुभयेषां तदयोग्यताञ्चोपदिशति। तत्र तु विशेषे। महदद्भुतं समस्तभेदविलयनात्मकत्वात्। यत्सिद्धिः पररूपहोमभावसिद्धिः। सिद्धरूपाणां प्रागुक्तानां अस्मिन्नेव पटले प्रोक्तसूक्ष्महोमसिद्धानां। अन्येषां साधकसाध्यानां*। भावः पररूपहोमस्येति शेषः। तथा सिद्धवत् ॥ ८१ ॥

प्रक्षीणेत्यादिना श्लोकोत्तरार्द्धेन तत्परहोमभावसिद्धानां अनुभावं हृदीकृत्य नित्यासु भक्त्युपलब्धिकरणमुपदिशति। तत्र प्रक्षीणाशेषपापानां देशिककटाक्षादिभिर्दूरीकृतदुर्व्वासनानां। तज्जुसेविनां विदितपरमार्थनाथसेवादितत्पराणाम् ॥ ८२ ॥

---

* सिद्धसाधकसाध्यानां

नित्याविद्यासु भक्तानां लक्षणं शृणु सुन्दरि ।
आमुष्मिकासंशयत्वं सन्तोषो नित्यपूर्णता ॥ ८३ ॥
सुखिता त्यागिता ज्ञानं कृतज्ञत्वमलुब्धता ।
अकार्पण्यमदीनत्वं परचिन्तानिरुद्यमः ॥ ८४ ॥
दयालुता मनस्वित्वमवैषम्यं मनःस्थितौ ।
लाभहान्योः प्रीतिरोषाभावः कल्याणशीलता ॥ ८५ ॥
कल्याणाभिनिवेशित्वं सदा कल्याणकीर्त्तनम् ।
अकल्याणकथालापवैमुख्यं स्वेच्छया स्थितिः ॥ ८६ ॥
सदैश्वर्य्यञ्च भोक्तृत्वं नैष्ठिकत्वमजिह्मता ।
सर्व्वानुकूल्यं सङ्गीतप्रियत्वं वाञ्छिताश्रयः ॥ ८७ ॥

नित्येत्यादिभिरित्यन्तैः षड्भिः श्लोकैः सप्रस्तावपुरःसरं नित्याभक्तलक्षणोपदेशं प्रोक्तनिगमनञ्च करोति । तत्र नित्याविद्यासु षोडशनित्यानां विद्यासु । सुन्दरीति देवीसम्बुद्धिः । आमुष्मिकासंशयत्वं परमार्थपरिज्ञानात् । सन्तोषः अवाप्तव्यविषये काङ्क्षाद्यभावात् । नित्यपूर्णता देशकालाद्यनवच्छिन्नभावेन । सुखिता स्वात्मपरमानन्दानुभवरसेन । त्यागिता नैरपेक्ष्यं । ज्ञानं सदनुसन्धानं । कृतज्ञत्वं गुरुचरणनलिनयुगलभजनपरत्वं । अलुब्धता इतरानपेक्षा । अकार्पण्यं द्रव्यविषयमुद्दिश्य महाप्रयत्नराहित्यं । अदीनत्वं अक्षुद्रभावः । परचिन्तानिरुद्यमः भेदराहित्यात् । दयालुता सर्वप्राणिषु । मनस्वित्वं उदारभावः । अवैषम्यं मनःस्थितौ लाभहान्योः लाभहान्योः मनस्थितावावैषम्यमिति वान्वयः । प्रीतिः रोषाभावः सर्वप्राणिषु प्रीतिः कोपाभावश्च । कल्याणशीलता मङ्गलाचरणस्वभावता । कल्याणाभिनिवेशित्वं मङ्गलकर्म्मस्वभिनिवेशित्वं । कल्याणकीर्त्तनं मङ्गलस्वभावानां महतां नामानुभावकीर्त्तनं । अकल्याणकथालापवैमुख्यं अकल्याणेषु कर्म्मसु तदाचारवतां कथालापे च वैमुख्यं । स्वेच्छया स्थितिः अपराधीनतया स्थितिः । सदैश्वर्य्यं राजचोरदुर्जनारात्याद्यनुपहतमहिमत्वं । भोक्तृत्वं भोक्तृशक्तिमत्त्वं । नैष्ठिकत्वं सर्वदेवताविग्रहेष्वनुस्यूतनित्यात्मभावाव्यभिचारित्वं । अजिह्मता अकुटिलहृदयता । सर्वानुकूल्यं सुरनरतिर्य्य-

*राजयोषित् प्रभुप्राज्ञबहुमानममत्सरः ।
सर्वोत्तरत्ववाञ्छा च लक्षणानीरितानि ते ॥ ८८ ॥
यद्विकल्पस्वरूपन्तु मनस्तन्निर्व्विकल्पके ।
निधानं परहोमन्तु स्थूलसूक्ष्मश्च यन्मयम् ॥ ८९ ॥
उच्चावचविकल्पानां वस्तूनामग्निदाहतः ।
तन्मयत्वादैक्यरूपं स्थूलहोममुदीरितम् ॥ ९० ॥

गाद्यभेदेन सर्वविग्रहाणां नित्याविग्रहात्मकत्वप्रतिपत्तेः । सङ्गीतप्रियत्वं नादस्वरूपस्य नित्यात्मकत्वात् । वाञ्छितामयः स्वस्माद्भिन्नविषयाभावात् । राजयोषित्प्रभुप्राज्ञबहुमानं स्वस्याभिरामात्मकभावसिद्धेः । अमत्सरः स्वसमानाधिकराहित्यात् । सर्वोत्तरत्ववाञ्छा देवतातादात्म्यसिद्धिवाञ्छा ॥ ८८ ॥

यद्विकल्पेत्यादिना श्लोकेन परहोमस्वरूपं स्थूलसूक्ष्महोमयोरपि तन्मयत्वं चोपदिशति । तत्र विकल्पस्वरूपं सकलविश्वविकल्पकारणस्वरूपं । निर्व्विकल्पके परस्वरूपे । निधानं विलापनं । एतदुक्तं भवति संकल्पविकल्पकारणभूतस्य मनसो निर्विकल्परूपे स्वात्मनि विलापनं परहोम इति । यन्मयं परहोममयम् ॥ ८९ ॥

उच्चावचेत्यादिभिः समीरित इत्यन्तैश्चतुर्भिः श्लोकैः स्थूलसूक्ष्महोमयोः परहोमेन तादात्म्यवासनां तदनुसन्धानञ्चोपदिशति । उच्चावचविकल्पानां समित्पुष्पफलादिभेदभिन्नानां वस्तूनां तद्धोमद्रव्याणां । तन्मयत्वात् होममयत्वात् अग्निमयत्वात् । ऐक्यरूपं अपृथग्भावः । एतदुक्तं भवति समिदादिसकलवस्तूनां स्थूलहोमादग्निमयत्वेनैकरूपमुदीरितमिति । तथा एकीकुर्य्यादित्यर्थः । एतदुक्तं भवति सूक्ष्महोमात् स्वमूलाधारमध्यस्थकुण्डलिनीमुखसविसर्गमहावह्नौ सकलशब्दोदयविश्रान्तिपदे नानारूपवाचकैः शब्दैः तद्वाच्यानर्थान् वेद्यवेत्तृविदात्मनैकीकुर्य्यादिति । स्थितिरित्यादिनाद्यार्द्धेन सर्वभेदविलापनात् स्थितिरेव परहोमो भवतीति मतान्तरमुच्यते । स्वात्मरूपमहावह्निज्वालारूपिषु स्वात्मरूपापृथग्भूता महाशक्तिः स्वात्मरूपवह्निः तज्ज्वाला तदिच्छा स्वात्मरूपमहाशक्तौच्छे-

---

*शतयोषित् ।

सूक्ष्महोमं तथा शब्दैर्नानारूपैस्तु वाचकैः ।
वाच्यार्थानामशेषेण वेद्यवेत्तृविदात्मना ॥ ९१ ॥
स्थितिः परो भवेद्धोमः सर्व्वभेदविलापनात् ।
स्वात्मरूपमहावह्निज्वालारूपिषु सर्व्वदा ॥ ९२ ॥
निरिन्धनेद्धरूपेषु परमार्थात्मनि स्थिरे ।
निर्व्युत्थानविलापस्तु परहोमः समीरितः ॥ ९३ ॥
तेषु प्रोक्तेषु कुण्डेषु चतुरस्रे समाचरेत् ।
होमकर्म्म समस्तं तु शुभात्मकमुदीरितम् ॥ ९४ ॥
अशुभात्मकमुक्तन्तु कुर्य्यात्त्र्यस्रे समीरिते ।
अन्येष्वन्यानि कार्य्याणि प्रोक्तानि प्रोक्तरूपतः ॥ ९५ ॥
प्रागुदक्शिवदिग्वक्त्रः कुर्य्याद्धोमन्तु मङ्गलम् ।
दक्षिणास्योभिचारन्तु गदे वह्निमुखो द्विषाम् ॥ ९६ ॥

तत्रार्थः । सैव येषां रूपाणि ते स्वात्मरूपस्वस्ववह्निज्वालारूपिणः तेषु स्वात्मरूपमहावह्निज्वालारूपिषु निरिन्धनेद्धरूपेषु अनन्याधिष्ठितप्रकाशरूपेषु परमार्थात्मनि सत्तामात्रस्वरूपे स्थिरे अविकारिणि निर्व्युत्थानविलापः निरवशेषविलयनभावः । एतदुक्तं भवति स्वरूपमहाशक्त्योच्छारूपेषु निरधिष्ठानप्रकाशात्मकेषु सकलरूपेषु परमार्थतः स्फुरिततत्स्वरूपेऽविकारिणि सत्तामात्रे स्वात्मनि तेषां निःशेषविलयनभावः परहोमः समीरित इति ॥ ९३ ॥

तेष्वित्यादिना रूपत इत्यन्तेन श्लोकद्वयेनोक्तकुण्डेषु सामान्येन चतुरस्रहोमकुण्डेषु शुभकर्म्महोमविधानमुपदिशति । तत्र चतुरस्रे उक्तरूपे । त्र्यस्रे प्रोक्तरूपे । अन्येषु कुण्डेष्विति शेषः । प्रोक्तरूपतः प्रोक्तविधानेन ॥ ९५ ॥

प्रागित्यादिना क्रतुक्षम इत्यन्तेन श्लोकद्वयेन मङ्गलादिकर्म्मसु होतुर्दिग्विशेषाभिमुख्यमुपदिशति । तत्र प्रागुदक्शिवदिग्वक्त्रः प्रागभिमुख उदगभिमुखः शिवदिगभिमुखश्च । तुर्विशेषे । दक्षिणास्यः दक्षिणदिङ्मुखः । तुर्विशेषे । गदे गदार्थोपक्रमे । वह्निमुखः वह्निदिङ्मुखः । वायुमुखः वायुदिङ्मुखः ।

उच्चाटनं वायुमुखो विद्वेषं राक्षसान्मुखः ।
विदध्यात् पश्चिमास्यस्तु क्रूराण्यन्यानि कृत्स्नशः ॥ ९७ ॥
स्वदेशग्रामगेहादौ तानि कर्म्माणि तद्दिशि ।
विदध्यादपविर्य्योक्तमन्यथानर्थमावहेत् ॥ ९८ ॥
कुण्डादिकरणाशक्तौ स्थण्डिले होममाचरेत् ।
गोमयैः परिमृष्टे तु सुसमे भूतले शुभे ॥ ९९ ॥
वालुकाहस्तविस्तारायाममास्तीर्य्य तत्र वै ।
मध्ये विदध्याद्धोमन्तु प्रोक्तमेवमशेषतः ॥ १०० ॥
कालतत्त्वमयी व्याप्तिरिति सम्यक् समीरिता ।
अस्या निष्फालनाच्चित्ते तत्तत्त्वं स्वात्मसात् कृतम् ॥

इति षोडशनित्यातन्त्रेषु श्रीकादिमते
त्रिंशत्तमं पटलम् ॥ ३० ॥

राक्षसान्मुखः निर्ऋतिदिङ्मुखः । पश्चिमास्यः पश्चिमदिङ्मुखः । अन्यानि प्रोक्तेतराणि । एतदुक्तं भवति होतुराभिमुख्यदिग्भेदेऽपि तां तां दिशं प्राचीं परिकल्प्य कुण्डं निर्माय जुहुयादिति ॥ ९७ ॥

स्वदेशेत्यादिना श्लोकेन स्वदेशादौ प्रोक्तकर्म्मसु प्रोक्तदिङ्मुखतया अवश्यकर्त्तव्यतां तदकरणे प्रत्यवायञ्चोपदिशति । गेहादावित्यत्रादिशब्दः पुरादिविषयः । कर्म्माणि प्रोक्तानि । तद्दिशि प्रोक्तदिशि । अन्यथा विपरीतकरणे ॥ ९८ ॥

कुण्डादीत्यादिना शेषत इत्यन्तेन श्लोकद्वयेन कुण्डादिकरणाशक्तानां स्थण्डिले होमविधानपुरःसरं स्थण्डिलनिर्म्माणविधानमुक्तनिगमनसहितमुपदिशति । तत्र तुविशेषे । शुभे लोमास्थिलोष्टादिरहिते धूमाद्यनाकुले च । तत्र प्रोक्तप्रकारेण कृतकोष्ठनवके । मध्ये सर्वमध्यकोष्ठमध्ये ॥ १०० ॥

इति षोडशनित्यातन्त्रेषु श्रीकादिमताख्यस्य परिपूर्णस्य तन्त्रस्य प्रपञ्चसारसिंहराजप्रकाशाभिधानेन सुभगानन्दनाथेन विरचितायां मनोरमाख्यायां व्याख्यायां वास्तुदेवताचक्रतत्पूजादि सूक्ष्मपरहोमविधानप्रकाशनपरं त्रिंशत् पटलं परिपूर्णं

पञ्चमाष्टम ॥ २८ ॥ ॐतत्सत् ॥

एकत्रिंशपटलम् ।

सूक्ष्मं परं च होमं ते कथितं परमेश्वरि ।
इदानीं स्थूलहोमन्तु कथयाम्यरिमर्द्दनम् ॥ १ ॥
तत्तत्कर्म्मोदिते कुण्डे कुर्य्याद्धोममुदीरितैः ।
विधानैर्द्वेषनिधनरागनिग्रहचाटनम ॥ २ ॥
आयुर्दायं रिपोर्ज्ञात्वा लग्नोक्तर्क्षानुगुण्यतः ।
तदात्मिकग्रहाणाञ्च स्थितिमष्टकवर्गकम् ॥ ३ ॥
त्रयाणामानुगुण्ये न कुर्य्यात्तदभिचारकम् ।
अन्यथा क्रूरकर्म्माणि कुर्व्वाणं नाशयन्ति हि ॥ ४ ॥
तान्येव कर्म्माणि तथा तत्त्रयप्रातिकूल्यतः ।
कुर्य्यात्तद्दैवताभक्तिमास्तिक्यं वर्त्तनं गुरुम् ॥ ५ ॥

पूर्वस्मिन् त्रिंशे पटले षोड़शनित्यानां वासुदेवताचक्रं तत्पूजादिविधान-सहितं सूक्ष्मपरहोमविधानमुपदिश्यानन्तरं षोड़शनित्याभक्तिनिष्ठानां अरि-मर्द्दनकर्म्महोमादिविधानमुपदिशति । सूक्ष्ममित्यादिना विधानत इत्यन्तेन श्लोकशतरूपेणैकत्रिंशेन पटलेन । तत्र सूक्ष्ममित्यादिना चाटनमित्यन्तेन श्लोकद्वयेन प्रोक्तनिगमनसहितं प्रोक्तकुण्डेषु प्रोक्तविधानेनारिमर्द्दनविधानकथनं प्रस्तौति । तत्र ते तव । कथितं पूर्वस्मिन् पटले । द्वेषनिधनरोगनिग्रह चाटनमित्यत्र द्वेषशब्दो मारणविषयः निग्रहशब्दो युद्धादिषु पराजयादि-विषयः चाटनम् उच्चाटनम् ॥ २ ॥

आयुर्द्दायमित्यादिभिरात्मनाशनमित्यन्तैश्चतुर्भिः श्लोकैरभिचारकर्म्मकरण-काले ज्ञातव्यांश तदनवेक्षणे प्रत्यवायञ्चोपदिशति । तत्र लग्नोक्तर्क्षानुगुण्यतः त्रयोदशे पटले तज्जन्मेत्यादिना षड़शीतितमश्लोकोत्तरार्द्धाद्यार्द्धद्वयेन प्रोक्तनक्षत्र-नामानुगुण्यतः । तदात्मिकग्रहाणां तत्प्रयोगकाले गोचरग्रहाणां । चः समु-च्चये । अष्टकवर्गकं फलमिति शेषः । त्रयाणां प्रोक्तानामायुर्दायदशा-

तत्पार्श्ववर्त्तिमन्त्रज्ञानालोच्य रिपुनिग्रहम् ।
विदध्यादन्यथा शङ्का नैष्फल्यं ह्यात्मनाशनम् ॥ ६ ॥
रिपोरष्टमलग्ने च काले त्वष्टमराशिगे ।
स्थाने कुर्य्यादनिष्टानि तद्विनाशाय साधकः ॥ ७ ॥
प्राच्यां मेषवृषौ वह्नौ मिथुनं दक्षिणे तथा ।
कुलीरसिंहमथ तन्नैऋत्यां कन्यका स्थिता ॥ ८ ॥

गोचरफलाष्टकानां । आनुगुण्यं आनुकूल्योऽभिचार्य्यस्य रिपोः प्रातिकूल्ये इत्यर्थः । अन्यथा कुर्य्यात् यदि । तान्येव एवकारो भिन्नक्रमः । तस्य प्रातिकूल्यत एवेत्यर्थः । एतदुक्तं भवति रिपोरभिचारकाले ज्योतिःशास्त्रे होरास्कन्धोक्तप्रकारेण तस्य तात्कालिकमायुर्दायगोचराष्टकवर्गेषु ग्रहाणां स्थितिं विचार्य्य तस्य यानुकूल्ये त्वभिचारकर्म्म न कुर्य्यात् । तमनवेक्ष्य क्रूरकर्म्माणि कुर्वाणं तान्येव नाशयन्ति । तस्य यप्रातिकूल्य एव तद्रिपुनाशाय तानि क्रूरकर्माणि कुर्य्यादिति । तद्दैवताभक्तिं रिपोर्दैवताभक्तिम् । आस्तिक्यं रिपोर्देवब्राह्मणादिविषयनिष्ठां । वर्त्तनं आचारं आलोच्य तज्ज्ञैस्तेषां अनुभावादिकमित्यर्थः । अन्यथा प्रोक्तान्यथाकरणे । शङ्का विकल्पे । एतदुक्तं भवति रिपोरभिचारप्रयोगादिषु तस्य देवताभक्तिमास्तिक्यमाचारं गुरुं तत्पार्श्ववर्त्तिमन्त्रज्ञान् विज्ञाय तेषामनुभावादिकं तद्विद्भिरालोच्य तत्प्राबल्ये तस्याभिचारादिकं न कुर्य्यादन्यथाकरणे तत्फलस्य नैष्फल्यं तत्प्रयोक्तुर्नाशनं वा भवतीति ॥ ६ ॥

रिपोरित्यादिना श्लोकेनक्रूरप्रयोगारम्भकालं गृहादिषु तद्देशविशेषादिक चोपदिशति । तत्र अष्टमलग्ने जन्मनराशेश्चन्द्रलग्नराशेर्वेति शेषः । काले तदुदयकाले । अष्टमराशिगे स्थाने अनन्तरश्लोकद्वयवक्ष्यमाणराश्यात्मकेषु स्थानेषु द्वादशसु । तद्विनाशाय रिपुविनाशाय ॥ ७ ॥

प्राच्यामित्यादिना सुस्थितमित्यन्तेन श्लोकद्वयेन मण्डपगृहादिसकलवस्तूनां द्वादशराश्यात्मकतामुपदिशति । तत्र वह्नौ कोणे । दक्षिणे दक्षिणदिग्देशे । तन्नि-

तुलाकोटौ पश्चिमतो धनुर्वायौ तु संस्थितम् ।
नक्रकुम्भावुत्तरतो मीन ईशे तु संस्थितम् ॥ ६ ॥
एवं राशिक्रम ज्ञात्वा कुर्य्यात् कर्म्माणि देशतः ।
काले तु पञ्च पञ्च सुग्घटिकाः क्रमयोगतः ॥ १० ॥
चैत्रादिषु तु मासेषु द्वादशस्वपि भास्करः ।
मेषादिराशिगो याति तथान्यैर्ग्रहमण्डलैः ॥ ११ ॥
देहेषु प्राणिनां तद्वदष्टाङ्गुलिविभेदतः ।
मूर्द्धादिचरणान्तन्तु तान् द्वादशसु लक्षयेत् ॥ १२ ॥

ऋत्यां विदिशि । पश्चिमतः पश्चिमदिशि । वायौ कोणे । उत्तरतः उत्तरस्यां दिशि । ईशे कोणे । सुस्थितं कालचक्रस्थराशिचक्रवन्न भ्रमतीत्यर्थः ॥ ८ ॥

एवमित्यादिना श्लोकेन प्रोक्तनिगमनं चक्रगतद्वादशराशीनां प्रतिराश्युदयकालघटिकासंख्याञ्चोपदिशति । तत्र एवं उक्तक्रमात् । राशिक्रमं राशीनां स्थितिक्रमं । कर्म्माणि कुर्य्यादिति शेषः । देशतः देशात्मकत्वेन । काले तु कालचक्रे तु । पञ्चपञ्च स्युः एकैकराशेः । क्रमयोगतः अपक्रमचक्रस्थितिस्तु कालदेशयोर्वैषम्यात् । गणितशास्त्रोक्तक्रमयोगेन स्वस्वदेशे राशीनामुदयघटिकामानवशात् वक्ष्यमाणप्रकारेण सूर्य्याधिष्ठितराश्यादिक्रमयोगतः ॥ १० ॥

चैत्रादीत्यादिना श्लोकेन कालचक्रे ग्रहाणां गतिक्रमम पदिशति । तत्र चैत्रादिषु तत्र दिव्यत्वात् चैत्रादिशब्दः सौरमासविषयः । तु विशेषे । याति एकैकसौरमासस्यैकैकराशिभुक्तिक्रमेणेति शेषः । तथा तथाविधः अन्यैश्चन्द्रादिभिः । ग्रहमण्डलैः ज्योतिःशास्त्रे तत्तद्ग्रहपरिवृत्तिप्रोक्तकालविशेषैरित्यर्थः ॥ ११ ॥

देहेष्वित्यादिना श्लोकेन सकलप्राणिनां देहमात्र द्वादशराश्यात्मकत्वमुपदिशति । तत्र तद्वत् मेषादिमीनान्तक्रमेण । तान् राशीन् । द्वादशसु, स्थानेषु ॥ १२ ॥

त्रयाणामानुगुण्येन कुर्य्यात् कर्माणि नान्यथा ।
शुभाशुभानि सर्व्वाणि फलन्त्येवं कृते ध्रुवम् ॥ १३ ॥
तथाहनि विषस्थानान्यमृतस्थानकानि च ।
ज्ञात्वा विदध्यात् पुत्तल्याः प्रयोगं सर्वतस्तथा ॥ १४ ॥
सिते हृदि स्तनगले नासाक्षोणि तथा श्रुतौ ।
भ्रूशङ्खमूर्द्धमध्येषु तत्र भ्रूशङ्खमध्यतः ॥ १५ ॥
कर्णे नेत्रे नासिकायां वर्त्तते पुरुषस्य तु ।
सव्यकण्ठस्तनतटे हृदि नाभौ च गुह्यके ॥ १६ ॥
जानुसन्ध्यङ्घ्रिपार्श्वेषु तथाङ्गुष्ठे च दक्षिणे ।
अङ्घ्रौ सन्धौ जानुगुह्ये नाभौ चेति सितेतरे ॥ १७ ॥

त्रयाणामित्यादिना श्लोकेन प्रोक्तकालविग्रहराशिवशेन शुभाशुभकरणीयत्व-मुपदिशति। तत्र त्रयाणां देशकालविग्रहात्मकानां। आनुगुण्येन आनुकूल्येन। अन्यथा उक्तलङ्घनेन। एवं कृते कृतप्रकारालङ्घनेन शुभाशुभप्रयोगे कृते ॥ १३ ॥

तथेत्यादिना श्लोकेन पुत्तलीप्रयोगार्थं देहे विषामृतस्थानयोर्ज्ञातव्यत्व-मुपदिशति। तत्र तथेत्यस्यामृतस्थानकानीत्यनेनान्वयः। षड्विंशपटले प्रोक्तक्रमेण दक्षवामभागयोः प्रतिभागं पञ्चदशपञ्चदशस्थानभेदक्रमेण स्थितानीत्यर्थः। अहनि प्रयोगदिवसे। विषस्थानानि अनन्तरश्लोके वक्ष्यमाणानि। सर्वतः कर्म्मसु। तथा वक्ष्यमाणप्रकारेण ॥ १४ ॥

सितेत्यादिभिर्वर्त्तत इत्यन्तैरर्द्धाधिकैस्त्रिभिः श्लोकैः पुरुषाणां योषिताञ्च विषपरिवृत्तिक्रमस्थानान्युपदिशति। तत्र सित इत्यादिना श्लोकेन द्वादश स्थानानि उपदिशति। सिते शुक्लपक्षे। स्तनगले स्तने च गले च। भ्रूशङ्खमूर्द्धमध्येषु तत्र मूर्द्धो मध्ये। शङ्खभ्रूमध्यतः शङ्खमध्ये भ्रूमध्ये च॥ कर्णेत्यादिना श्लोकेन स्थानाष्टकं तत्र सव्यकण्ठे वामकण्ठे॥ जान्वित्यादिना श्लोकेन दश स्थानानि। तत्र अङ्घ्रिपार्श्वशब्देनाङ्घ्रिपृष्ठदेश उच्यते। अङ्गुष्ठे वामपादाङ्गुष्ठे। दक्षिणे दक्षिणपादाङ्गुष्ठे। अङ्घ्रौ

तिष्ठेद्विषकला पुंसि स्त्रियां वामादि वर्त्तते ।
विषनाड्यां विषस्थाने वेधयेत् कण्टकेन तु ॥ १८ ॥
सङ्कोचकाख्येन तदा तीव्रेणास्थिमयेन वै ।
वदरादिसमुत्थैर्व्वा तथायःसारसूचिभिः ॥ १९ ॥
पुत्तल्यां यत्र तद्विद्धं तदङ्गं शत्रुदेहजम् ।
व्याधिना पीड़ितं कालादविधेयं भवेद्ध्रुवम् ॥ २० ॥
तत्र तेनार्त्तिना क्लिष्टो जीवितेशपुरं व्रजेत् ।
पुत्तलीकरणं वच्मि शृणु निग्रहसिद्धये ॥ २१ ॥

अङ्‌घ्रिपृष्ठे । सन्धौ तदनन्तरसन्धौ । जानुगुल्फे जानौ गुल्फे । इति उक्त-प्रकारेण । सितेतर कृष्णपक्षे । वामादि वामभागे प्रोक्तहृदयस्थानादि । एतदुक्तं भवति शुक्लपक्षप्रथमादिषु कृष्णपक्षदर्शान्तासु त्रिंशत्तिथिषु पुंसां दक्षिणभागे हृदयस्थानादिमूर्द्धान्तेषु नवसु स्थानेषु पुनस्तद्वामपार्श्वे मूर्द्धादिपादाङ्गुष्ठान्तं पञ्चदशसु स्थानेषु पुनर्दक्षिणपादाङ्गुष्ठादिनाभ्यन्तं षट्सु स्थानेषु च सम्भूय त्रिंशत् स्थानेषु च । स्त्रीणां तत्तत्तिथिषु तत्तत्स्थानेषु दक्षिण-वामपार्श्वविनिमयक्रमेण च विषस्य परिवृत्तिर्भवतीति ॥ १७ ॥

विषनाड्यामित्यादिभिः सिद्धये इत्यन्तैरर्द्धाद्यैस्त्रिभिः श्लोकैः पुत्तलीप्रयोगे तद्वेधकालं तदङ्गं तत्साधनं तत्फलञ्च पुत्तलीकरणकथनप्रस्तावादि सहितं उपदिशति । तत्र विषनाड्यां सप्तविंशतिनक्षत्रेषु प्रतिनक्षत्रं विषात्मक-प्रोक्तनाड़ीचतुष्टयकाले । विषस्थाने अनन्तरपूर्वोक्ते पुत्तल्या इति शेषः । तु विशेषे । सङ्कोचकाख्येन सङ्कोच इति मत्स्यविशेषः । तीव्रेण अस्थिमयेन तद्देहजतीव्रसङ्कोचकास्थिमयेन । वदरादिसमुत्थैः कण्टकैरिति शेषः । वा विकल्पे । तथा वेधयेदित्यर्थः । यत्र अङ्गे तद्विद्धं कण्टकादिविद्धं तदङ्गं व्याधिना पीड़ितं इत्येतदुत्तरत्र शत्रुदेहजमित्यस्य विशेष्यं । कालात् प्रयोगस्य गौरवलाघवादिना कालदैर्घ्यविलम्बनात् । ध्रुवं निश्चितं । आर्त्तिना तदङ्ग-व्याध्युत्पन्नेनेति शेषः । पुत्तलीकरणं पुत्तलीनिर्म्माणविधानं ॥ २१ ॥

भौमशुक्रबुधाश्चन्द्रो भास्करः सौम्यभार्गवौ ।
मङ्गलो गुरुमन्दार्किगुरवोंशकराशिपाः ॥ २२ ॥
नक्षत्राणि चतुष्पादान्यंकमष्टोत्तरं शतम् ।
एतावत्यश्च पुत्तल्यस्त्वंशकक्रमयोगतः ॥ २३ ॥
प्रथमे नवके चन्द्रभास्करांशकयोः क्रमात् ।
षोडश द्वादश तथा मानमङ्गुलिसंख्यया ॥ २४ ॥
अन्यांशकेषु सर्व्वाश्च चतुर्द्दश समीरिताः ।
द्वितीये नवकेन्येषामध्यर्द्धाः स्युस्त्रयोदश ॥ २५ ॥
तृतीये नवकेन्येषां त्रयोदश समीरितम् ।
चन्द्रार्कयोरेकविधः प्रोक्तसंख्याक्रमस्तथा ॥ २६ ॥

भौमेत्यादिना श्लोकेन द्वादशराशीनामश्विन्यादिविंशतिनक्षत्रोद्भवद्वादश द्वादशांशकानां च क्रमेणाधिपतीनुपदिशति। तत्र अंशकराशिपाः अंशकानां मेषादिराशीनाञ्च पतयः ॥ २२ ॥

नक्षत्राणीत्यादिना श्लोकेन प्रतिनक्षत्रं चतुश्चतुरंशकक्रमेण सम्भूयाष्टोत्तरशतांशकानामष्टोत्तरशतपुत्तलीविशेषं प्रस्तौति। तत्र एतावत्यः अष्टोत्तरशतसंख्याः ॥ २३ ॥

प्रथमे इत्यादिभिस्तथेत्यन्तैस्त्रिभिः श्लोकैः पुत्तलीमानविशेषानुपदिशति। तत्र प्रथमे नवके अश्विन्याद्यश्लेषान्तेषु नवसु नक्षत्रेषु। अन्यांशकेषु इतरग्रहांशकेषु। सर्वाः पुत्तल्यः चतुर्द्दशाङ्गुलीमानेन मिता इत्यर्थः। द्वितीये नवके मघादिज्येष्ठान्तेषु नवसु नक्षत्रेषु। अन्येषां चन्द्रार्करहितग्रहांशकानां। अध्यर्द्धाः सार्द्धत्रयोदश पुत्तलीनामङ्गुलिसंख्या इति शेषः। तृतीये नवके मूलादिरेवत्यन्तनवसु नक्षत्रेषु। अन्येषां प्राग्वत् कुजादीनामंशकानां त्रयोदशाङ्गुलीमानानि समीरितमिवं इत्यर्थः। एकविधः सर्व्वत्रेति शेषः। प्रोक्तसंख्याक्रमस्तथा प्रथमनवके प्रोक्तसंख्यामानमेव द्वितीयतृतीयनवकयोरपीत्यर्थः ॥ २६ ॥

पुत्तलीकरणे द्रव्यं चक्रिहस्तमृदान्वितम् ।
चितामृद्भस्मलवणं शुण्ठीपिप्पलिकायुतम् ॥ २७ ॥
मरीचं गृहधूमञ्च लसुनं हिङ्गुसैन्धवम् ।
गैरिकञ्चेति कथितं पुत्तलीद्रव्यमीश्वरि ॥ २८ ॥
साध्यर्त्तवत्त्वैः पिष्टैश्च माषचूर्णैश्च सिक्थकैः ।
वैरिदेहजरोमाद्यैरुपेतैः पुत्तलीक्रिया ॥ २९ ॥
पुत्तलीदैर्घ्यमानन्तु कृत्वाष्टांशमथैकतः ।
शीर्षं त्रयात् कटेरूर्द्ध्वं त्रयात् पादद्वयं तथा ॥ ३० ॥
कटिप्रपदयोरेकमंशमे[व]कन्तु पुत्तलीम् ।
विधाय तन्त्रे सर्व्वं च प्रयोगानाचरेन्नरः ॥ ३१ ॥

पुत्तलीत्यादिभिः क्रिया इत्यन्तैस्त्रिभिः श्लोकैः पुत्तलीनिर्माणद्रव्याण्युपदिशति। तत्र चक्रिहस्तमृदान्वितं कुलालकरमृत्तिकासहितं। चितामृद्भस्मलवणं श्मशानमृद्भस्मसहितं लवणं। शुण्ठीपिप्पलिकायुतं शुण्ठीपिप्पल्योश्चूर्णैर्युतम्। मरीचं मरीचचूर्णं। गृहधूमं गृहधूमचूर्णं। लसुनं रसोनरसं। एतानि शुण्ठ्याद्यष्टद्रव्याणि सर्व्वपुत्तलिकासाधारणानि। साध्यर्त्तवत्त्वैः साध्यनक्षत्रप्रोक्तवृक्षैः। पिष्टैरित्येतन्माषचूर्णैरित्यस्य विशेषणं। सिक्थकैर्मधूच्छिष्टैः। वैरिदेहजरोमाद्यैरित्यत्राद्यशब्दो नखपादपार्श्वादिविषयः। उपेतैरित्येतद्द्वारव्यतिरिक्तेषु चक्रिहस्तमृत्सहितेषु त्रिष्वन्वेति ॥ २८ ॥

पुत्तलीत्यादिना नर इत्यन्तेन श्लोकद्वयेन पुत्तलीदैर्घ्यमानविभागीकरणवशात् तदवयवमानान्युपदिशति। तत्र पुत्तलीदैर्घ्यमानं तत्तदंशकवशेन प्रोक्तपुत्तलीदैर्घ्याङ्गुलमानं। एकतः एकांशेन। त्रयात् अंशत्रयेण। त्रयात् प्राग्वत्। कटिप्रपदयोरर्द्धांशेन कटिद्वयमर्द्धांशेन प्रपदद्वयञ्चेत्यर्थः। सर्व्वत्र पुत्तलीप्रयोगे। प्रयोगान् प्रोक्तान् ॥ ३१ ॥

पातालयोगे नीचाख्ये विषयोगे च मृत्युजे ।
नाशयोगे च दिनजमृत्यौ क्रकचयोगके ॥ ३२ ॥

पातालेत्यादिभिरवाप्नुयादित्यन्तैस्त्रिभिः श्लोकैः क्रूरकर्मप्रयोगारम्भकालादिकमुपदिशति । तत्र पातालेत्यादिना श्लोकेन षड्विधं क्रूरकालमुपदिशति । तत्र मृत्युजे मृत्युयोगे । दिनजमृत्यौ मेषादिराशिस्थनक्षत्रांशेषु तत्तद्राशेरष्टमांशके इति यावत् । चण्डीशेत्यादिना श्लोकेन दशविधक्रूरकर्मकालमुपदिशति । तत्र चण्डीशचण्डायुधके योगे । काणके काणनक्षत्रे काणके इत्यनेनान्धनक्षत्रे किं पुनरित्यर्थः । ज्योतिःशास्त्रोक्तानि तद्वचनानि विलिख्यन्ते । तत्र नीचाख्यः पातालयोगः ।

तौलिभे दशमांशस्थस्तौलगो याति यदोदयम् ।
तदा नीचाह्वयो योगः पातालो गर्हितः शुभे ॥

विषयोगाः । चतुर्थी सप्तमो चार्के चन्द्रे षष्ठ्यष्टमी तथा ।
इन्द्राह्विधर्मा भौमे तु (वि) चिक्राद्ये रवयोबुधे ॥
* षड्वत् स्वरयो जीवे विष्णुधर्मार्कणस्थिते † ।
एकादशी शुभेक्षि च ‡ मन्दे स्युस्तिथयो विषम् ॥
पञ्चद्विराकाः सप्ताद्य षड्ष्टतिथिभिर्विषम् ।
श्विचित्रा जयास्येन्द्रश्रोणान्त्यः सूर्य्यवारतः ॥
मृत्युयोगा यमर्क्षाणि मैत्रचित्रामघोत्तराः ।
चित्रात्रोषु § त्तराषाढ़ा श्रविष्ठा च पदक्रमात् ॥
चित्राप्यु $ त्तरफाल्गुन्यो मैत्रस्वात्यैन्द्रवैष्णवम् ।
पौष्णतिष्यादितिश्रोणा मृत्यवोर्कादिवारगाः ॥

नाशयोगाः । पित्रेन्द्राम्बैश R मूलर्क्षवारुणाजाप्यभैर्युताः ।
सूर्य्यादिवाराः क्रमशो नाशयोगाः समीरिताः ॥

दिनमृत्यवः । वसुहस्ते विशाखार्द्रे [बुध्या] ब्रह्माह्वो याम्यनैऋते ।
इन्द्वेष्वषु चतुर्थांशाः क्रमशो मृत्यवो [हि] क्षि चेत् ॥

---

* मडवक्षरयो । † दुपस्थिते । ‡ एकादशोश भेदौ च । § पितु । $ प्यु । R र्यस ।

चण्डीशचण्डायुधकौ महाशूले च काणकौ।
रक्तस्थूणो कण्टकाख्ये स्थूणो पञ्चार्कसंज्ञकौ॥ ३२॥

क्रकचायोगाः।

तिथेश्च वारस्य च यत्र संख्यया त्रयोदश स्यु मिलनं गते सति।
स्मृतः स योगः क्रकचाभिधानको विवर्जनीयः शुभकर्मसु ध्रुवम्॥

चण्डीशचण्डायुधं।

सूर्य्याधिष्ठितभाद्गुजङ्गपितृभत्वाष्ट्रेषु मैत्रे श्रुतौ।
पौष्णे च क्रमशो भानुगमया * शीतांशुना संयुतम् †॥

धिष्ण्ये तपतिथेपतत्यवितथं चण्डीशचण्डायुधं।
तस्मिन्नात्महिते च्छुभिनि जहितं कार्य्यं न कार्य्यं बुधैः॥

महाशूलम्। कृत्तिकाद्याः सप्त सप्त ताराः ¶ पूर्व्वादिषु क्रमात्।
भं शहादिमुखं तत्र महाशूलमशोभनम्॥

काणाख्यनक्षत्राणि।

त्यजेद्‌जैकपादादेस्त्रिसप्तवासरात् परे।
षड़ावानवकाणाः स्युर्दोषघ्नं वारभे विना॥

रक्तस्थूणं। $ धान्यस्त्रं चतुरो राशींस्त्यजेद्धिन्नां Rs ततःस्फुटाम्।
तं जिष्ठलब्धनक्षत्रं रक्तस्थूणमिति स्मृतम्॥

कण्टकस्थूणं। भौमेनार्केण संयुक्ता दशाद्यावति मूलकं।
मूलान्ता च त्रिभे स्यूणकण्ठकाख्ये इमे क्रमात्॥

धूमाद्यावतिधामूलकण्टकावतिधर्षकं।
तावन्ति कण्टकस्थूणतत्त्रयमप्यदोषदं॥

पञ्चार्कदोषाः। वालात् कोंगस्तु गोपाले सार्कशे सर्वसारथे।
त्वर्के च पञ्चधूमाद्या लग्ने एते युते स्त्यजेत्॥

---

* त्रिभाकृगणमया। † संयुते। ¶ भागाः। $ धन्यस्त्र। Rs कज।

कुर्य्यात् प्रयोगान् प्रत्यर्थिभङ्गाय निधनाय वा ।
निग्रहाय निरीक्ष्यैवं कुर्य्यात् सिद्धिमवाप्नुयात् ॥ ३४ ॥
वश्याकर्षणविद्वेषस्तम्भनोच्चाटमारणे ।
विदध्यात् पुत्तलीः सम्यक् चतस्रः प्रोक्तयोगतः ॥ ३५ ॥
पिष्टेन सिक्थेन तथा चक्रिहस्तमृदापि च ।
साध्यनक्षत्रवृक्षेणाप्युक्तलक्षणसंयुताः ॥ ३६ ॥
आसने पादयोः स्थाने कुण्डमध्ये च साधकः ।
पिष्टमृत्तरुजाः खात्वा स्थापयेत् सिक्थमम्बरे ॥ ३७ ॥
कुण्डमध्ये उपर्य्यूर्द्ध्वपदान्यक्षीर्षिकामपि ।
एवं साधारणं कृत्वा कुर्य्यात् कर्म्म समीरितम् ॥ ३८ ॥

एतदुक्तं भवति रिपोरायुर्दायगोचराष्टकवर्गग्रहेषु प्रतिकूलेषु पातालयोगादिभिः प्रोक्तदोषैर्दुष्टदिवसे तदष्टमराशौ विषनाड्यां वा प्रारब्धं क्रूरकर्म सद्यः फलतीति। वा समुच्चये। एवमुक्तप्रकारेण ॥ ३४ ॥

वश्येत्यादिभिः समीरितमित्यन्तैश्चतुर्भिः श्लोकैर्व्वश्यादिषु कर्म्मसु षट्सु पुत्तलीप्रयोगप्रक्रियामुपदिशति। तत्र सम्यक् सर्वावयवशोभनं। प्रोक्तयोगतः प्रोक्तमानेन रिपुदेहजरोमादियोगतः। अपिः समुच्चये। आसने होतुरासनस्थाने। पादयोः स्थाने होतुः पादविन्यासप्रदेशस्याधःस्थाने। पिष्टमृत्तरुजाः पिष्टजा मृजजाः तरुजाः पुत्तलीः। खात्वा होतुरासनादिस्थानत्रये क्रमात्। अपिः समुच्चये। एवं प्रोक्तप्रकारेण साधारणवश्यादिषु प्रोक्तकर्म्मस्विति शेषः। एतदुक्तं भवति प्रोक्तमानाद्यलङ्घनेन साधारणद्रव्याष्टकरिपुदेहजरोमादिभिः सह पिष्टमयीं सिक्थमयीं मृण्मयीं चैव तिस्रः। साध्यनक्षत्रवृक्षेणैकां प्रोक्तद्रव्याष्टकलेपितां च सम्भूय चतस्रः पुत्तलीः कृत्वा तासु क्रमात् पिष्टमयीं होतुरासनस्याधः स्थाने मृण्मयीं होतुः पादविन्यासप्रदेशस्याधः स्थाने तरुमयीं कुण्डमध्यस्थनाभिपद्मस्याधःस्थाने च स्थापयित्वा सिक्थमयीं कुण्डादुपरि तोरणतिर्य्यक्विष्कम्भदारुण्यूर्द्ध्वपादामवाक्शीर्षामम्बरे लम्बमानामर्क-

सर्पशीर्षस्रुचा होमं कुर्य्यादशुभकर्म्मसु ।
वैरियोन्यसृजा कृत्वा तया तु जुहुयात्तथा ॥ ३९ ॥
त्रिकोणकुण्डे यमदिङ्मुखो भूत्वार्द्धरात्रके ।
श्मशाने निर्जने देशे विदध्यादभिचारकम् ॥ ४० ॥
यत्राभिचारहोमन्तु करोति भुवि साधकः ।
तत्राभितो नृपो रक्षां कारयेदात्मसिद्धये ॥ ४१ ॥
न चेदरातिनृपतिश्चारैर्ज्ञात्वा निहन्त्यमुम् ।
स्वराष्ट्रसन्धौ कुर्व्वीत न कुर्व्वीत स्वमण्डले ॥ ४२ ॥
यदि कुर्य्यात् प्रमादेन मान्त्रिको ज्ञानमोहतः ।
तद्राष्ट्रं पीड़यन्त्येव शनकैर्व्वैरिभूभृतः ॥ ४३ ॥

तरुजसृवेण वक्ष्यैवं साधारणं कृत्वोक्तानि वश्यादीनि कर्म्माणि वक्ष्यमाण-विधानक्रमेण कुर्य्यादिति ॥ ३८ ॥

सर्प इत्यादिना श्लोकेन क्रूरकर्म्मसु स्रुचं चरुं चोपदिशति। तत्र सर्प-शीर्षस्रुचा सर्पशीर्षकल्पितस्रुचा। अशुभकर्म्मसु विद्वेषोच्चाटनमारणादिषु। वैरियोन्यसृजा वैरिनक्षत्रप्रोक्तयोनिरुधिरेण। तया इत्यस्य सर्पशीर्षस्रुचा इत्येतद्विशेष्यम् ॥ ३९ ॥

त्रिकोणेत्यादिभिर्भूभृत इत्यन्तैश्चतुर्भिः श्लोकैः अभिचारकर्म्मणि कुण्डं होतुरभिमुखीकरणीयां दिशं तद्देशविशेषं होतुर्नृपेण रक्षाविधानं तदकरणे प्रयोक्तुः प्रत्यवायं राष्ट्रसन्धिदेशेन तत्कर्मणः तत्करणीयत्वं तदकरणे राष्ट्रस्य प्रत्यवायश्चोपदिशति। तत्र यमदिङ्मुखः दक्षिणदिङ्मुखः। तत्र अभिचारभूमौ। आत्मसिद्धये प्रयोक्तुः प्राणादिसिद्धये। अरातिनृपतिः शत्रूराजा। अमुं प्रयोक्तारं। कुर्व्वीत अभिचारमिति शेषः। तद्राष्टं अभिचारप्रयोगस्थान राष्ट्रं। शनकैः कालक्रमेण ॥ ४३ ॥

अश्वद्रुमसमिद्धेऽग्नौ तत्फलैर्वा तथाहुतैः * ।
हैमीदलरसाक्तैस्तु होमाच्छत्रुं विनाशयेत् ॥ ४४ ॥
नक्तमालसमिद्धेऽग्नौ तत्फलैर्वा तथा हुतैः † ।
रिपुरुग्रोऽपि रोगार्त्तः प्रयाति यमसादनम् ॥ ४५ ॥
उन्मत्तकाष्ठैः प्रज्वाल्य वह्निं तद्बीजकैर्हुनेत् ।
तत्पत्राम्बुप्लुतैर्मासादरातिर्भ्रान्तिमाप्नुयात् ॥ ४६ ॥
आरग्वधसमिद्धेऽग्नौ तत्समिद्भिश्च तत्फलैः ।
वितस्तिमात्रैस्तैलाक्तैर्हवनाद्वैरिणो मृतिः ॥ ४७ ॥
अरुष्करसमिद्धेऽग्नौ तद्बीजैस्तद्घृताप्लुतैः ।
होमादरातेस्तीव्रार्त्तिज्वरेण स्यान्मृतिर्ध्रुवम् ॥ ४८ ॥

अश्वद्रुमेत्यादिना श्लोकेन शत्रोरुच्चाटकरणविधानहोममुपदिशति। तत्र अश्वद्रुमसमिद्धेऽग्नौ अश्वद्रुमभवकाष्ठसमिद्धे वह्नौ। तत्फलैः अश्वफलैः। हैमीदलरसाक्तैः हैमीदलजलाप्लुतैः ॥ ४४ ॥

नक्तेत्यादिना श्लोकेन शत्रोर्मारणप्रयोगहोममुपदिशति। तत्र नक्तमालसमिद्धेऽग्नौ करञ्जकाष्ठवह्नौ। तत्फलैः करञ्जफलैः ॥ ४५ ॥

उन्मत्तेत्यादिना श्लोकेन शत्रोरुच्चाटकरणविधानहोममुपदिशति। तत्र तद्बीजकैः उन्मत्तबीजैः। तत्पत्राम्बुप्लुतैः उन्मत्तपत्रोत्थरसप्लुतैः ॥ ४६ ॥

आरग्वधेत्यादिना श्लोकेन रिपुमारणप्रयोगमुपदिशति। तत्र तत्समिद्भिः आरग्वधसमिद्भिः। तत्फलैः आरग्वधफलैः। वितस्तिमात्रैः द्वादशाङ्गुलमात्रैः ॥ ४७ ॥

अरुष्करेत्यादिना श्लोकेन रिपोस्तीव्रज्वरेण मारणप्रयोगमुपदिशति। तत्र अरुष्करसमिद्धेऽग्नौ अरुष्करकाष्ठसमिद्धे वह्नौ। तद्बीजैः अरुष्करबीजैः। तद्घृताप्लुतैः अरुष्करतैलाप्लुतैः ॥ ४८ ॥

---

* करञ्जकैः। † समाहरेत्।

सौवीराक्तैस्तु कार्पासबीजैर्होमात्तु मन्त्रजात् ।
अरातीनामथान्योन्यकलहान्निधनं भवेत् ॥ ४९ ॥
सर्षपाज्यप्लुतैः शुण्ठीमागधीमरिचैर्हुनेत् ।
वैरिजन्मर्क्षवृक्षाग्नौ मण्डलान्तं मृतिज्वरात् ॥ ५० ॥
प्रागुक्तैः पुत्तलीं कृत्वा द्रव्यैरुक्तविधानतः ।
सर्षपारुष्करघृतसंसिक्तैर्जुहुयान्निशि ॥ ५१ ॥
प्राग्वच्छित्त्वा तदङ्गैस्तु क्रुद्धचित्तोऽरुणाम्बरः ।
रक्तस्रग्गन्धपुष्पादियुतः शत्रून् विनाशयेत् ॥ ५२ ॥
अरुष्करघृताभ्यक्तैस्तद्बीजैः सर्पशीर्षकैः ।
हवनाद्वैरिणो दाहज्वरप्राप्तिस्त्रिभिर्दिनैः ॥ ५३ ॥

सौवीरेत्यादिना श्लोकेनारातेः कलहान्मारणप्रयोगमुपदिशति । तत्र सौवीराक्तैः आरनालाप्लुतैः ॥ ४९ ॥

सर्षपेत्यादिना श्लोकेन रिपोर्ज्वरान्मारणप्रयोगहोममुपदिशति । तत्र सर्षपाज्यप्लुतैः सर्षपबीजोत्पन्नतैलाप्लुतैः । शुण्ठीमागधीमरिचैः त्रिकटुकेन । वैरिजन्मर्क्षवृक्षाग्नौ वैरिजन्मनक्षत्रोत्थवृक्षकाष्ठसमिदग्नौ । तन्मृतिः शत्रोर्मृतिः ॥५०॥

प्रागुक्तेत्यादिना विनाशयेदित्यन्तेन श्लोकद्वयेन पुत्तल्या होमविधानेन शत्रुविनाशनप्रयोगमुपदिशति । तत्र प्रागुक्तैरित्येतद्द्रव्यैरित्यस्य विशेषणम् । उक्तविधानतः उक्तमानादिकं । सर्षपारुष्करघृतसंसिक्तैः सर्षपारुष्करयोस्तैलाभ्यां संसिक्तैः । निशि मध्यरात्रे इत्यर्थः । प्राग्वच्छित्त्वा नवमपटले चत्वारिंशेकचत्वारिंशच्छ्लोकद्वयेन प्रोक्तप्रकारेण द्वादशधा छित्त्वा । तदङ्गैः छिन्नैः । क्रुद्धचित्तः क्रूरचित्तः शत्रुं प्रतीति शेषः । अरुणाम्बरः काषायवस्त्रधरः । रक्तस्रग्गन्धपुष्पादियुतः रक्तस्रग्रक्तगन्धरक्तपुष्परक्तासनादियुतः ॥ ५२ ॥

अरुष्करेत्यादिना श्लोकेन वैरिणो दाहज्वरप्राप्तिप्रयोगहोममुपदिशति । तत्र तद्बीजैः अरुष्करबीजैः । सर्पशीर्षकैः सर्पशिरःकल्पितस्रुग्भिः ॥ ५३ ॥

वैरिनक्षत्रयोन्युत्थमांसैस्तद्रक्तसंप्लुतैः।
हवनात्तत्तरूद्भूतसमिधां हवनादपि ॥ ५४ ॥
दिनैः कैश्चिद्रिपुः क्लृप्तो नाशमेति सुनिश्चितम्।
द्रुमकुड्यसर्पदंशान्मत्तद्विपादिघातनात् ॥ ५५ ॥
द्रुमकुड्यकनिर्घातसलिलानलपातनात्।
यक्षराक्षसगन्धर्वपिशाचब्रह्मराक्षसैः ॥ ५६ ॥
अन्यैर्वा कारणैः क्षिप्रं नाशमेति रिपुर्ध्रुवम्।
निम्बपत्रैश्च कार्पासबीजैस्तज्जैः करञ्जजैः ॥ ५७ ॥
हवनात् सर्षपस्नेहसिक्तैर्विद्वेषणं भवेत्।
नीचयोगे हुनेदग्नौ रिपुवृक्षसमेधिते ॥ ५८ ॥
तद्वृक्षखण्डैस्तैलाक्तैर्निशामध्ये रिपुर्दिनैः।
उच्चाटनं प्रयात्येव मन्त्रशक्त्याभिताड़ितः ॥ ५९ ॥
मृत्युपत्रैश्च तत्काण्डैस्तद्बीजैस्तत्कुचौ हुनेत्।
अरातेर्दन्तिनो वाहा रोगैर्नश्यन्ति निश्चितम् ॥ ६० ॥

वैरीत्यादिभिर्ध्रुवमित्यन्तैरर्धद्वैस्त्रिभिः श्लोकैर्द्रुमकुड्यनिपातादिव्याजेन रिपुविनाशप्रयोगहोममुपदिशति। तत्र तद्रक्तसंप्लुतैः वैरिनक्षत्रयोन्युद्भवरक्ताप्लुतैः। तत्तरूद्भूतसमिधामपि अपिचेत्यर्थः। निर्घातेन अशनिपातेन सलिले निमज्जनेन पावके पतनेन अन्यैः अपस्माराद्यैः। वा विकल्पे ॥ ५६ ॥

निम्बपत्रैरित्यादिनार्धद्वयेन विद्वेषणप्रयोगमुपदिशति। तत्र चः समुच्चये तज्जैर्निम्बजैः बीजैरिति शेषः। करञ्जजैः पत्रैः फलैश्चेति शेषः। सर्षपस्नेहसिक्तैः सर्षपोद्भवतैलाप्लुतैः ॥ ५७ ॥

नीचेत्यादिना ताड़ित इत्यन्तेनार्धद्वयेन श्लोकेनोच्चाटनप्रयोगहोममुपदिशति। तत्र नीचयोगे नीचसंज्ञे पातालयोगे। हुनेत् जुहुयादिति यावत्। तद्वृक्षखण्डैः रिपुनक्षत्रवृक्षखण्डैः। दिनैः प्रोक्तैर्मण्डलादिभिः ॥ ५८ ॥

मृत्युपत्रैरित्यादिना श्लोकेन शत्रुवाहनदन्तिनां रोगैर्विनाशप्रयोगहोममुप-

गैरिकैः पुत्तलीं कृत्वा रिपोरष्टमराशिके ।
प्रागुक्तकण्टकाद्यैस्तु यदङ्गं वेधयेच्छनैः ॥ ६१ ॥
विषनाड्यां विषस्थाने तथा च यमकण्टके ।
अर्द्धप्रहरके शीर्षं प्रहरेद्वा शनैः शनैः ॥ ६२ ॥
अरातेस्तत्तदङ्गैः स्यान्निधनं प्रहरादिना ।
ग्रन्थिभिर्वा कण्टकादिजतवह्निविदारणैः ॥ ६३ ॥
तन्नचवोक्तवृक्षोत्थपुत्तलीं स्थापितेरकाम् ।
गर्दभीमेहसलिले संस्थाप्य क्वाथयेच्छनैः ॥ ६४ ॥
रिपुर्दाहज्वरग्रस्तः स निर्याति यमालयम् ।
मधूच्छिष्टेन तां कृत्वा तापयेन्निशि तां शनैः ॥ ६५ ॥

दिशति तत्र मृत्युपतेः विषवृक्षपत्रैः। तत्काष्ठे विषवृक्षसमिद्भिः। तद्बीजैः विषवृक्षबीजैः। तच्छूर्णे विषवृक्षकाष्ठज्वलितवह्नौ। इनेज्यइत्यात् दन्तिनो गजाः वाहाः हयाः ॥ ६० ॥

गैरिकैरित्यादिभिर्दारुणैरित्यन्तैस्त्रिभिः श्लोकैः अभीष्टाङ्गोत्पन्नैरोगादिभिर्वैरिनिधनप्रयोगहोममुपदिशति। तत्र अष्टमराशिके अष्टमराश्युदयसमये। कण्टकाद्यैरित्यत्राद्यशब्दोऽस्थिसूच्यादिविषयः। शनैः शनैः क्रमशः। विषस्थाने तद्दिनविषयुताङ्गे। यमकण्टके यमकण्टकसंज्ञे काले। अर्द्धप्रहरके अर्द्धप्रहरसंज्ञे काले। यमकण्टकार्द्धप्रहरसंज्ञयोः कालविशेषयोः स्वरूपं ज्योतिःशास्त्रोक्तमार्गेण लिख्यते।

सरोगवा (गा) तथोर्द्धार्द्ध यामांश्च यमकण्टकान्।
वासरे मन्दगीतार्द्धयामान्वारक्रमाद्भजेदिति ॥

शीर्षे पुत्तल्या इति शेषः। वा विकल्पे। तत्तदङ्गैः प्रच्छन्नशीर्षेण च। प्रहरादिना इत्यत्रादिशब्दः छेदनादिविषयः। वा विकल्पे ॥ ६३ ॥

तन्नचवेत्यादिना यमालयमित्यन्तेनाध्यर्द्धेन श्लोकेन दाहज्वरेण रिपुमारणप्रयोगमुपदिशति। तत्र स्थापितेरकां स्थापितप्राणां। गर्दभीमेहसलिले गर्दभीमूत्रे। शनैः कैश्चिद्दिवसैः ॥ ६५ ॥

तेनोन्मादज्वरग्रस्तः प्रयाति निधनं शनैः ।
तां तत्कण्टकविद्धाङ्गीं खनेत् पितृगृहे निशि ॥ ६६ ॥
व्रणात् पिशाचाविष्टः स रिपुर्याति यमालयम् ।
प्रागुक्तैरेव तद्द्रव्यैरशेषैः पुत्तलीं तथा ॥ ६७ ॥
निर्म्माय कुण्डमध्ये तां चैवारातिमहीरुहैः ।
समिद्धेऽग्नौ तत्समिद्भिस्तैलाक्तैर्जुहुयान्निशि ॥ ६८ ॥
सन्निपातज्वरस्तस्य वक्त्र(क्र)जिह्वे(ह्व)ति मूढधीः ।
प्रलयं शनकैर्देहं त्यजन् याति यमालयम् ॥ ६९ ॥
तथाविधां तां प्रतिमां निखनेत् कृष्णपक्षके ।
नवम्यङ्गारदिवसे मातृगेहेऽग्रपीठके ॥ ७० ॥

मधूच्छिष्टेत्यादिना यमालयमित्यन्तेनार्द्धाद्यन्तेन श्लोकेनोन्मादज्वरेण रिपुमारणविधानमुपदिशति । तत्र तां पुत्तलीं । निशि अर्द्धरात्रे । तां पुत्तलीं । तेन तापनेन । तामित्यादिनार्द्धद्वयेन पुत्तलीखननप्रयोगाद्रिपुमारणविधानमुपदिशति । तत्र तां पुत्तलीं । तत्कण्टकविद्धाङ्गीं प्रोक्तकण्टकादिष्वन्यतमेन विद्धाङ्गीं । पितृगेहे श्मशाने । निशि मध्यरात्रे । चः समाहारे ॥ ६६ ॥

प्रागुक्तैरित्यादिना यमालयमित्यन्तेनाद्याद्येन श्लोकद्वयेन सन्निपातज्वरेण रिपुमारणहोमविधानमुपदिशति । तत्र प्रागुक्तैः अस्मिन् पटले समविंशादि श्लोकाभ्यां इति शेषः । तद्द्रव्यैः पुत्तलीविधानप्रोक्तद्रव्यैः । अशेषैर्द्वादशभिः । तथा प्रोक्तमानेन । तां शत्रुनक्षत्रवृक्षनिर्म्मितां पुत्तलीं । अरातिमहीरुहैः अरातिनक्षत्रवृक्षकाष्ठैः । तत्समिद्भिः रिपुनक्षत्रवृक्षसमिद्भिः । निशि मध्यरात्रे । याति यमालयं रिपुरिति शेषः ॥ ६८ ॥

तथाविधेत्यादिना लक्षितमित्यन्तेन श्लोकद्वयेन पुत्तलीखननविशेषेण रिपुविनाशप्रयोगमुपदिशति । तत्र तथाविधां प्रोक्तक्रमादिभिः प्रोक्तद्रव्यद्वादशभिर्निर्म्मितां । प्रतिमां पुत्तलीं । नवम्यङ्गारदिवसे नवमीसहिताङ्गारवारे । मातृगेहे चण्डिकायतने । अग्रपीठके अग्रपीठस्याधः स्थाने । निशि मध्यरात्रे ।

सप्ताहान्निधनं वैरी प्रयाति निशि ताड़ितः ।
भूताद्यैः शिरसि स्वीये निर्घातवदलक्षितम् ॥ ७१ ॥
सर्षपं माषचूर्णञ्च तिलं शालिजतण्डुलम् ।
पिष्ट्वा साध्यनक्षत्रवृक्षस्य शकलैरपि संयुतम् ॥ ७२ ॥
एरण्डबीजैर्मिलितं कृत्वा पुत्तलिकां ततः ।
तद्वक्षोऽन्तर्निधायारिनाम तालस्य पत्रगम् ॥ ७३ ॥
संजप्य तां स्पृशन् विद्यां तार्त्तीयप्रतिलोमजाम् ।
सहस्रवारं साध्यस्य वधर्क्षेऽष्टमराशिगे ॥ ७४ ॥
निबध्य तां पादयोस्तु भानुवृक्षोत्थतन्तुना ।
गृहीत्वा जीवहस्तेन तां जपेत् प्रयजेच्छुचौ ॥ ७५ ॥
हुत्वाग्नौ तैः सहस्रन्तु तामूर्द्ध्वाङ्घ्रिमवाङ्मुखीम् ।
तद्दिने तापतृष्णार्त्तिविह्वलेन ज्वरेण सः ॥ ७६ ॥

भूताद्यैरित्यत्राद्यशब्दः प्रेतादिविषयः । निर्घातवत् अशनिवत् । अलक्षितं एतत् क्रियाविशेषणम् ॥ ७१ ॥

सर्षपमित्यादिभिः शिवे इत्यन्तैः षड्भिः श्लोकैस्तापज्वरेण रिपुविनाशाय पुत्तलीप्रयोगविशेषमुपदिशति । तत्र सर्षपमित्यर्द्धेन द्रव्यचतुष्टयं । साध्यर्क्षस्य वृक्षस्य शकलैः खण्डैः । अपिः समुच्चये । कृत्वेति भिन्नक्रमः । पुत्तलिकां कृत्वेत्यर्थः । ततः पश्चात् प्रोक्तद्रव्यषट्केन तद्वक्षोऽन्तः पुत्तलीवक्षःप्रदेशान्तः निधायेति भिन्नक्रमः । अरिनाम विधायेत्यर्थः । पत्रगं इत्यस्यारिनाम इत्येतद्विशेष्यं । संजप्येत्यस्य विद्यामित्यनेनान्वयः । पुत्तलीं प्रतिष्ठितप्राणां । तार्त्तीयप्रतिलोमजां तार्त्तीयखण्डस्य प्रतिलोमभेदात्मिकासु चतसृषु विद्यास्वन्यतमां । साध्यस्य साध्यनक्षत्रस्य । वधर्क्षे सप्तमनक्षत्रे । निबध्य तां पुत्तलीं निबध्येत्यर्थः । तुर्विशेषे । भानुवृक्षजतन्तुना अर्कवृक्षोद्भवतन्तुना । जीवहस्तेन प्रवहत्श्वासपुटपार्श्वहस्तेन । तां प्रतिलोमजां विद्यां । शुचौ वह्नौ । तैः सर्ष-

ग्रस्तदेहो लुठन् भूमौ विसंज्ञः प्रलपन्मुहुः ।
प्रयाति निधनं तूर्णं प्रयोगबलतः शिवे ॥ ७७ ॥
साध्यर्क्षवृक्षसंभूतां पुत्तलीमर्कदुग्धतः ।
वज्रीक्षीरेण वा लिप्तां बद्धां प्राग्वदधोमुखीम् ॥ ७८ ॥
साध्यनामादिसंयुक्तां कुण्डादूर्ध्वं प्रलम्बयेत् ।
जुहुयात्तत्समिद्भिस्तु तत्क्षीराक्तैर्निशान्तरा ॥ ७९ ॥
ज्वरार्त्तः स्यादरातिस्तु त्रिभिरेव दिनैस्ततः ।
यद्यस्ति तस्य रक्षेच्छा तां तटाकोदरे खनेत् ॥ ८० ॥
जम्बालमध्ये तेनास्मात् सौख्यं तस्य शनैः शनैः ।
तथा यदि न कुर्व्वीत चिरं रोगात्मको भवेत् ॥ ८१ ॥
तथा तामनुभाण्डे तु निवेश्याङ्गारवासरे ।
चण्डिकायतने खात्वा तद्योनिं तत्पुरो बलिम् ॥ ८२ ॥

पादिभिर्द्रव्यैः । सहस्रं सहस्रवारं । तुरवधारणे । तां पुत्तलीं । तद्दिने प्रयोगदिवसे । स साध्यः । शिवे इति सम्बुद्धिः ॥ ७७ ॥

साध्यर्क्षेत्यादिभिः भवेदित्यन्तैश्चतुर्भिः श्लोकैः ज्वरोन्मादप्रयोगं तद्रक्षणविधानादिकञ्चोपदिशति । तत्र अर्कदुग्धतः अर्कवृक्षोत्पन्नदुग्धेन च । वज्रीक्षीरेण वज्रीलतोत्पन्नक्षीरेण । वा समुच्चये । बद्धां तोरणविष्कम्भदारुणि । प्राग्वत् अर्कतन्तुसूत्रेण । साध्यनामादिसंयुक्तां वक्षसि लिखितसाध्यकर्म्मनामयुतां । कुण्डादूर्ध्वं कुण्डादुपरि । तत्समिद्भिः साध्यनक्षत्रवृक्षसमुद्भूतसमिद्भिः । तुर्विशेषे । तत्क्षीराक्तैः अर्कवज्रीक्षीराभ्यक्तैः । निशान्तरा मध्यरात्रे । तुरवधारणे । ततः तेन प्रयोगेन । तस्य वैरिणः । तां प्रलम्बितां पुत्तलीं । तटाकोदरे तटाकजलोदरे । तेन खननेन । अस्मात् प्रयोगात् । तस्य ज्वरार्त्तस्य । तथा प्रोक्तप्रकारेण ॥ ८१ ॥

तथेत्यादिना उपसर्गैरित्यन्तेनाध्यर्द्धेन श्लोकेन तत्तत् पुत्तलीखननविशेषात् रिपुमारणप्रयोगविशेषमुपदिशति । तत्र तथा तां साध्यनक्षत्रवृक्षनिर्म्मितां

निहत्य दत्त्वारातिन्तु निहन्यादुपसर्गकैः ।
स्वगेहे वल्यधः खात्वा तदुपर्य्यग्निवर्द्धनात् ॥ ८३ ॥
अविच्छिन्नमरातेः स्याज्ज्वरादिगदसम्भवः ।
तां तथाकृतरूपान्तु रुरुजङ्घास्थिसंयुताम् ॥ ८४ ॥
निवध्य पूर्व्वसूत्रेण द्विषद्गेहे खनेन्निशि ।
राशौ तदष्टमे मासात् प्रयात्युद्वाट्यात्यतोन्यतः ॥ ८५ ॥
तथाविधं पुत्तलिकायुगं कृत्वोक्तमार्गतः ।
विड़ालमूषिकाचर्म्मनद्धं साध्याख्यया युतम् ॥ ८६ ॥
निखनेत्तीरयोर्नद्याः पितृगेहेथवा ततः ।
मातृगेहे नदीपूर्त्त्यां विद्वेषः स्याद्द्वयोस्तदा ॥ ८७ ॥

पुत्तलीं । चण्डिकायतने अग्रपीठाधःस्थाने इति शेषः । तद्योनिं साध्यनक्षत्र-योनिं । तत्पुरः चण्डिकाग्रपीठे । निहत्येत्यस्य तद्योनिमितिपूर्व्वेणान्वयः । दत्त्वे-त्यस्य वलिमित्यनेनान्वयः । तुर्विशेषे । उपसर्गकैः क्लेशैः ॥ ८२ ॥

स्वगेहे इत्यादिना सम्भव इत्यन्तेनार्द्धद्वयेन तत्पुत्तल्या ज्वरादिरोगोत्थापन-प्रयोगविशेषमुपदिशति । तत् खात्वा पुत्तलीं इति शेषः । तदुपरि पुत्तल्युपरि । अविच्छिन्नमित्यस्य काकाक्षिन्यायेनोभयत्रान्वयः । पूर्वत्राग्निवर्द्धनादित्यनेनोत्तरत्र ज्वरादिगदसम्भव इत्यनेन च ॥ ८३ ॥

तामित्यादिनान्यत इत्यन्तेनार्द्धत्रयेन श्लोकेन पुत्तलीविशेषरचनादुच्चाटन-प्रयोगमुपदिशति । तत्र तां साध्यनक्षत्रवृक्षसम्भूतां पुत्तलीं । तथाकृतरूपां प्रोक्त-मानादितः । तुर्विशेषे । रुरुजङ्घास्थिसंयुतां व्याघ्रजङ्घास्थिसंयुतां । पूर्वसूत्रेण अर्कवृक्षतन्तुकृतसूत्रेण । निशि मध्यरात्रे । राशौ तदष्टमे शत्रोरिति शेषः ॥८५॥

तथाविधमित्यादिना तदा इत्यन्तेन श्लोकद्वयेन विद्वेषणप्रयोगमुपदिशति । तत्र तथाविधं तत्तन्नक्षत्रवृक्षनिर्म्मितं । उक्तमार्गतः तत्तदंशकानुगुणमानेन । विड़ालमूषिकाचर्म्मनद्धं विड़ालमूषिकाचर्म्मभ्यां परिणद्धं । द्वयोः वाधकवाध्यात्म-कयोः क्रमादिति शेषः । साध्याख्यया युतं साध्यादिनामद्वययुतं । निखने-दित्यस्य पुत्तलिकायुगमित्यनेन पूर्वेणान्वयः । पितृगेहे श्मशाने । अथवा वि-कल्पे । मातृगेहे चण्डिकायतने । नदीपूर्त्त्यां सत्यामिति शेषः ॥ ८७ ॥

ता एव प्रागवदुत्थाय साध्याख्यादिसमन्विताः।
तद्विद्याजापसिद्धास्ताः खनेद्वैरिगृहे पुनः॥ ८८॥
मध्येष्टदिक्षु तु तथा तत्कुलोत्सादनं भवेत्।
एवं निकटवर्त्तिनां अभिचार उदीरितः॥ ८९॥
दूरस्थितानां द्विषतां कथं स्यादभिचारकम्।
वदामि ते शृणु प्राज्ञे सुदूरस्थस्य वैरिणः॥ ९०॥
विनाशने प्रयोगन्तु क्षिप्रमप्यभिचारकम्।
येनारिर्निकटः स्यात्तु प्रागेव निधनं व्रजेत्॥ ९१॥
तत्साध्यवृक्षैः पुत्तलिका विधायाष्टौ शतं क्रमात्।
ताः प्रागुदीरितक्षीरद्वयसिक्ताः ससंज्ञकाः॥ ९२॥
तत्तदंशकमानापघनास्ता मध्यरात्रतः।
एकामेकां हनेद्वैरिदिङ्मुखस्ता अशेषतः॥ ९३॥

ताइत्यादिना भवेदित्यन्तेनाध्यर्द्धेन श्लोकेन पुत्तलीखननविशेषात् रिपुकुलोत्सादनप्रयोगमुपदिशति। तत्र ताः पुत्तलीः नव नव संख्याताः। प्रागवत्तत्तद्वृक्षैः प्रोक्तमानतः। साध्याख्यादीत्यत्रादिशब्दः कर्म्मविषयः। तद्विद्याजापसिद्धास्ताः प्रतिलोमात्मकतार्त्तीयविद्याभिः मन्त्रिताः पुत्तलीः। तत्कुलोत्सादनं रिपुकुलोत्सादनम्॥ ८८॥

एवमित्यादिना श्लोकार्द्धेन प्रोक्तानां निकटवर्त्तिविषयप्रयोज्यत्वमुपदिशति। तत्र एवं प्रोक्तपुत्तलीखननादिविधानेन॥ ८९॥

दूरेत्यादिना व्रजेदित्यन्तेन श्लोकद्वयेन दूरस्थितानां रिपूणां अभिचारप्रयोगं देवी पृच्छति। तत्र कथं केन प्रकारेण। वदामीत्यादिनार्द्धाद्येन श्लोकेन दूरस्थितवैरिनिधनकथनादिप्रस्तावसहितं तत्सामर्थ्यमुपदिशति। तत्र वदामीत्यस्य प्रयोगमित्युत्तरत्रान्वयः। ते तव। प्राज्ञे इति सम्बुद्धिः। येन प्रयोगेन निकटस्थात् अरातीरितिशेषः॥ ९१॥

तत्साध्ये त्यादिना नाशभागित्यन्तेनाध्यर्द्धेन श्लोकद्वयेन दूरस्थारिनिधनप्रयोगहोममुपदिशति। तत्र तत्साध्यवृक्षैः दूरस्थशत्रुनक्षत्रवृक्षैः। अष्टौ शतं अष्टोत्तरशतं। ताः पुत्तल्यः। प्रागुदीरितक्षीरद्वयसिक्ताः अर्कवज्रीक्षीराभ्यां सिक्ताः।

तत्तदंशककाले वा सुदूरस्थोऽपि नाशभाक् ।
कथं वा मान्त्रिकवलो निहन्तुं शक्यतां व्रजेत् ॥ ९४ ॥
तच्छृणुष्व शिवे वच्मि प्रकारं तस्य निग्रहे ।
तैर्म्मान्त्रिकैस्तस्य पूर्व्वं विद्वेषे कारयेत्ततः ॥ ९५ ॥
तैर्द्विष्टे निधनं तस्मिन् सुशकं स्यादनाश्रयात् ।
भाग्याधिकं महारक्षाकरं मातृकसङ्गतम् ॥ ९६ ॥
राजानं राजपात्रं वा कथं हन्यात् प्रयोगतः ।
तन्मे कथय देवेश यद्युपायन्तु विद्यते ॥ ९७ ॥
वदामि ते शृणु प्राज्ञे त्वमोघं घोरविग्रहम् ।
अभिचारमरातीनामाशुनाशकरं परम् ॥ ९८ ॥

ससंज्ञकाः साध्यनामकर्म्मसमेताः । तत्तदंशकमानापघनाः अश्विनीप्रथमांशादि-रेवत्यंशान्ताः अष्टोत्तरशतांशकप्रोक्तमानत्रिनिर्मितदेहाः । ताः पुत्तलीः । वैरिदिङ्-मुखः शत्रुनिवासदेशदिङ्मुखः । तत्तदंशककाले तत्तत्पुत्तलीमानानुगुणांशक-काले । कथमित्यादिनार्द्धेन बलवत्तरमान्त्रिकाभिरक्षितवैरिणं निहन्तुमुपायं देवी पृच्छति । तत्र कथं वा केन प्रकारेण । मान्त्रिकवलो प्रबलमान्त्रिकाभि-रक्षितः रिपुरिति शेषः । निहन्तुं शक्यतां व्रजेत् वध्यतां व्रजेदित्यर्थः ॥ ९४ ॥

तदित्यादिना पूर्व्वार्द्धेन तद्वैरिनिधनोपायकथनं प्रस्तौति । तत्र शिवे इति देवीसम्बुद्धिः । तस्य अरातेः । तैरित्यादिना अनाश्रयादित्यन्तेनार्द्धद्वयेन वैरिनि-धनोपायमुपदिशति । तैः अरातिरक्षाविधानतत्परैः । तस्य अरातेः स्वप्रयोगारम्भ-कालादिति शेषः । कारयेत्तदरातिपार्श्ववर्त्तिभिरिति शेषः । तैः मान्त्रिकैः । द्विष्टे द्वेषं गते । तस्मिन् अरातौ । सुशकं सुकरं । अनाश्रयात् रक्षकाभावात् ॥ ९५ ॥

भाग्याधिकमित्यादिना विद्यत इत्यन्तेनार्द्धाद्येन श्लोकेन भाग्याधिक्यादियुतस्य राजादिकस्य निधनप्रयोगप्रकारं देवी पृच्छति । तत्र भाग्याधिकं प्रोक्तायु-र्दायादित्रिविधग्रहानुकूल्येन देवतोपास्त्यादिना चाधिकं । कथं केन प्रयोगतः प्रयोगे वा । देवेशेति ईश्वरसम्बुद्धिः । उपायं दिव्यत्वादुपायाः ॥ ९७ ॥

वदामीत्यादिना श्लोकेन पृष्टार्थकथनप्रस्तावपुरःसरं तमर्थं स्तौति । तत्र प्राज्ञे इति सम्बुद्धिः । परं प्रोक्तप्रकारादिति शेषः ॥ ९८ ॥

सिद्धमन्त्रानतिस्निग्धान् षोड़शातिस्थिराशयान् ।
तैरवच्छिन्नदर्पैन्तु होमयेद्यामदिक्-क्रमात् ॥ ९९ ॥
तेन तन्निधनं ब्रूयाद्रचितस्याप्ययत्नतः ।
अरातिनिग्रहं कुर्य्यादेवमुक्तविधानतः ॥ १०० ॥

मायातत्त्वमयी व्याप्तिरिति सम्यक् समीरिता ।
अस्या निष्फालनाच्चिते तत्तत्त्वं स्वात्मसात् कृतम् ॥

इति षोड़शनित्यातन्त्रेषु श्रीकादिमते
होमात् काम्यफलोदयं नाम
एकत्रिंशत् पटलम् ॥ ३१ ॥

सिद्धेत्यादिना विधानत इत्यन्तेन श्लोकद्वयेन महामान्त्रिकादिरचितशत्रोरभिचारप्रयोगमुक्तनिगमनोपेतमुपदिशति । तत्र सिद्धमन्त्रान् होतॄन् परिकल्प्येति शेषः । अतिस्थिराशयान् परप्रयुक्तोपायैरभेद्यहृदयान् । तैः सिद्धमन्त्रैः । यामदिक्क्रमात् यामद्विद्विक्रमात् प्रतियामं द्विद्विपुरुषक्रमात् इत्यर्थः । तेन प्रयोगेन । तन्निधनं भाग्याधिकराजादेर्निधनं । रचितस्यापि अस्य महामान्त्रिकादिभिरित्यर्थः । अयत्नतः इत्यस्य कुर्य्यादितुत्तरत्रान्वयः । एवं प्रकारेण ॥ १०० ॥

इति षोड़शनित्यातन्त्रेषु श्रीकादिमताख्यस्य परिपूर्णस्य तन्त्रस्य प्रपञ्चसारसिंहराजप्रकाशाभिधानेन सुभगानन्दनाथेन विरचितायां मनोरमाख्यायां व्याख्यायां अरिमर्द्दनप्रकाशनपरं एकत्रिंशत् पटलं परिपूर्णं परामृष्टम् ॥ ३१ ॥ ॐतत्सत् ॥

ग्रन्थसंख्या—२६८ ।

एकत्रिंशे तु पटले न स्याद्ग्रन्थसमुदीरितम् ।
व्याख्यानग्रन्थसंख्या तु साष्टषष्ट्या शतद्वयम् ॥

द्वात्रिंशपटलम् ।

अथ होमं प्रवक्ष्यामि ललिताविद्यया शिवे ।
येन मर्त्त्योऽपि भुवने प्रख्यातो देवतासमः ॥ १ ॥
तद्विधानं शृणु प्राज्ञे द्रव्यकालादिभेदतः ।
प्रोक्तेषु नवकुण्डेषु तत्तत्कर्म्मसु चोदिते ॥ २ ॥
जुहुयादुक्तमार्गेण तत्राग्निध्यानपूर्वकम् ।
शुक्लप्रतिपदारभ्यात् पूर्णान्ते पङ्कजैर्हुनेत् ॥ ३ ॥
कैरवैर्हवनात्तेषु दिनेषु श्रियमाप्नुयात् ।
मधुरत्रयसंसिक्तैः पुष्पैरव्यङ्गैः शुभैः ॥ ४ ॥
अखण्डितैरब्दमात्रं नरो नृपतिसन्निभः ॥
तेष्वेव दिवसेष्वब्जैः सितैस्तद्धवनाद्धृतैः ॥ ५ ॥
कह्लारैर्हवनात्तेषु दिनेषु धनधान्यवान् ।

पूर्व्वस्मिन्नेकत्रिंशे पटले शत्रुमर्द्दनहोमविधानादिकमुपदिश्यानन्तरं षोड़श-नित्याविद्यासिद्धानां सौम्यहोमविधानमुपदिशत्यथहोममित्यादिनोदीरितैरित्यन्तेन श्लोकशतरूपेण द्वात्रिंशेन पटलेन। तत्र अथेत्यादिना भेदत इत्यन्तेनाध्यर्द्धेन श्लोकेन पटलार्थकथनप्रकारं तद्वैभवञ्च प्रस्तौति। तत्र ललिताविद्यया श्रीविद्यया। शिवे इति देवीसम्बुद्धिः। येन होमेन। प्राज्ञे इति देवीसम्बुद्धिः। द्रव्य कालादिभेदत इत्यत्रादिशब्दः कुण्डादिविषयः ॥ १ ॥

प्रोक्तेष्वित्यादिना पूर्व्वकमित्यन्तेनार्द्धद्वयेन सामान्यहोमविधानमुपदिशति। तत्र प्रोक्तेषु एकोनत्रिंशे पटले। चोदिते कुण्डे इति शेषः। उक्तमार्गेण एकोन-त्रिंशपटलोक्तपरिषेचनपरिस्तरणादिविधानेन ॥ २ ॥

शुक्लेत्यादिभिर्जीवतोत्यन्तैरर्द्धाद्यैः सप्तभिः श्लोकैः शुक्लप्रतिपदादिपूर्णान्त-तिथिष्वैश्वर्य्यादिसिद्धिकरहोमं जलजपुष्पभेदैरुपदिशति। तत्र हुनेज्जुहुया दित्यर्थः। मधुरत्रयसंसिक्तैः क्षीरसर्पिर्म्मधुभिः दधिघृतमधुभिर्वा संसिक्तैः। शुभैः अमुकुलापतिताम्लानाशीर्णाजन्तुदूषितानाघ्रातानङ्गस्पृष्टानुषितैः। नृपतिसन्निभः

तेष्वेवोत्पलहोमेन श्रियमाप्नोति पुष्कलाम् ॥ ६ ॥
अरुणैरुत्पलैर्होमात् कन्यकां समवाप्नुयात्।
सौभाग्यं कीर्त्तिमारोग्यमवाप्नोत्यर्च्चनादपि ॥ ७ ॥
तैः षड्भिः कुङ्कुमक्षौद्रप्लुतैस्तद्दिनहोमतः।
अचलाञ्च श्रियं प्राप्य सुखी जीवति भूतले ॥ ८ ॥
तेश्चन्दनाक्तैर्हवनात्तद्दिनेषु यथाविधि।
पुत्रदासीदासयुतश्चिरं जीवति मानवः ॥ ९ ॥
तैरेवेन्दुद्रवाक्तैस्तु होमात् कन्दर्पसन्निभः।
वनिताजनसन्दोहविनोदी भुवि जीवति ॥ १० ॥
कृष्णप्रतिपदारम्भाद्दर्शान्तं जुहुयात् सितैः।
घृताक्तैरब्दमात्रेण निःसपत्नां लभेच्छ्रियम् ॥ ११ ॥
तेष्वेव दिवसेष्वग्नौ गुड़ैः क्षौद्राप्लुतैर्हुनेत्।
कान्तिलक्ष्मीजयारोग्ययुतो जीवति भूतले ॥ १२ ॥

सम्यग्भिरिति शेषः। तेषु शुक्लप्रथमादितिथिरूपेषु। अब्जैः पद्मैः। सितैः सितवर्णैः। तेषु प्राग्वद्दिवसेषु। अरुणैः उत्पलैः अरुणकुमुदैः। तेषु दिनेषु प्राग्वदर्चनादपीत्यनेन प्रोक्तपुष्पहोमप्रयोगेषु तत्तत्पुष्पैस्तत्र तत्रार्च्चनमप्युच्यते। तैः षड्भिः अरुणसितपङ्कजद्वयकह्लारेन्दीवरकैरवद्वयैः। तद्दिनहोमतः शुक्लप्रथमादितिथिरूपदिवसेषु होमतः। तैः प्रोक्तषड्भिरिति शेषः। तद्दिनेषु शुक्लप्रथमादितिथिरूपदिवसेषु। यथाविधि प्रोक्तपरिस्तरणपरिषेचनादिविधानेन। तैः प्राग्वत् षड्भिः। इन्दुद्रवाक्तैः कर्पूरद्रवाक्तैः। तुर्विशेषे ॥ १०॥

कृष्णेत्यादिभिः हुनेदित्यन्तैरध्यर्द्धैर्नवभिः श्लोकैः कृष्णपक्षप्रतिपदादिदर्शान्तपञ्चदशतिथिरूपदिवसेषु होमद्रव्यविशेषैर्लक्ष्मीप्राप्त्यादिसम्पत्करहोमविधानमुपदिशति। तत्र सितैः शर्करादिभिरिति यावत्। तेषु कृष्णपञ्चदशतिथिरूपदिवसेषु। हुनेत् जुहुयादिति यावत्। तद्दिनैः कृष्णतिथिपञ्चदशकरूपैःदिनैः।

द्राक्षाभिर्दुग्धसिक्ताभिस्तद्दिनैर्हवनान्नरः ।
क्षीराहारी चिरं भूमौ जीवत्यकलुषाशयः ॥ १३ ॥
खर्जूरीफलहोमेन त्रिमध्वक्तेन तद्दिनैः ।
आयुरारोग्यविजयसम्पन्नां श्रियमश्नुते ॥ १४ ॥
कदलीफलहोमेन तथा तद्दिवसेषु तु ।
पुण्यकीर्त्तिर्नृपैर्मान्यो जीवेद्वर्षशतं सुखी ॥ १५ ॥
नारिकेलफलक्षोदैः सितक्षौद्रसमन्वितैः ।
हवनात्तद्दिनैरिष्टमखिलं समवाप्नुयात् ॥ १६ ॥
तैरिक्षुवारिसंसिक्तैर्हवनात्तद्दिनेषु वै ।
वासांसि नानावर्णानि महार्हाणि लभेत सः ॥ १७ ॥
षड्भिश्च तैस्त्रिमधुक्तैर्हवनाच्छ्रियमाप्नुयात् ।
तैः सवत्ससितागव्यपयोक्तैर्हवनादपि ॥ १८ ॥
महिषीक्षीरसंसिक्तैर्होमादिष्टमवाप्नुयात् ।
अजाक्षीरयुतैस्तैश्च तथाविक्षीरसंप्लुतैः ॥ १९ ॥

अकलुषाशयः प्रसन्नहृदयः । तद्दिनैः प्राग्वद्दिनैः । तथा शब्देन त्रिमधुराप्लावनमुच्यते । तद्दिवसेषु प्राग्वत् । तुर्विशेषे । तद्दिनैः प्राग्वत् । तैर्नारिकेलफलक्षोदैः । तद्दिनेषु प्राग्वत् कृष्णपक्षतिथिरूपेषु । सः साधकः । षड्भिश्च तैः सितागुडद्राक्षाखर्जूरीफलकदलीनारिकेलफलक्षोदैः । तैः प्रोक्तैः षड्भिः । सवत्ससितागव्यपयोक्तैः समानवर्णवत्ससहितायाः सितवर्णायाः गोः क्षीराक्तैः । अपिः समुच्चये । तैः प्राग्वत् षड्भिर्द्रव्यैः । तथा प्राग्वत् । तैः षड्भिर्द्रव्यैः । अविक्षीरसंप्लुतैः इति पदच्छेदः । नारिकेलक्षोदक्षीराक्तैः नालिकेरफलक्षोदोत्पन्नक्षीराक्तैः । अपिशब्देनेष्टमाप्नुयादित्येतदत्राप्याकृष्यते । तैः प्राग्वत् षड्भिः ॥ १९ ॥

नारिकेलफलक्षोदक्षीराक्तैरपि तैर्हुनेत् ।
तथा द्वादशभिर्द्रव्यैरेकैकैः सङ्गतैस्तु वा ॥ २० ॥
नित्यशो हवनाद्दुग्धक्षौद्रसर्पिःसमन्वितैः ।
गोभूहिरण्यवासोभिः समृद्धो जीवति क्षितौ ॥ २१ ॥
रविवारे सितान्नैस्तु क्षीराक्तैर्जुहुयात्तथा ।
अब्दादन्नसमृद्धिः स्याद् घृताक्तैर्वा मधुप्लुतः ॥ २२ ॥
सोमवारे सितोपेतैर्नारिकेलफलैर्हुतैः ।
सम्पन्नशस्यां पृथिवीमवाप्नोति सुनिश्चितम् ॥ २३ ॥
अङ्गारवारे क्षौद्राक्तैरन्नैर्होमाच्छ्रियं लभेत् ।
तैरिष्टद्रव्यमिलितैर्हवनात्तां महीं लभेत् ॥ २४ ॥
बुधवारे घृताक्तैस्तु होमेन तिलतण्डुलैः ।
श्रियं सकलकल्याणनिलयां लभतेऽब्दतः ॥ २५ ॥
गुरुवारे दुग्धसिक्तपनसास्थिपरागकैः ।
जुहुयादब्दमात्रेण लभते गेहमुत्तमम् ॥ २६ ॥
सितवारे नारिकेलक्षोदैः सितसमन्वितैः ।
गुडान्वितैर्वा जुहुयाच्छ्रिया सुचिरमेधते ॥ २७ ॥

तथेत्यादिना क्षिताविन्त्यन्तेनार्द्धाद्येन श्लोकेन शुक्लपक्षप्रोक्तपुष्पषट्केन कृष्णपक्षप्रोक्तसितादिद्रव्यषट्केन च सम्भूय द्वादशभिर्द्रव्यैः समस्तरूपैश्च नित्यहोमात् गोभूमिहिरण्यवासःसिद्धिकरत्वमुपदिशति । तत्र तथा द्वादशभिः शुक्लकृष्णपक्षतिथिप्रोक्तद्वादशभिः । वा विकल्पे । नित्यशः प्रतिदिनम् ॥ २१ ॥

रविवार इत्यादिभिर्मनोहरामित्यन्तैः सप्तभिः श्लोकैः अर्कवारादिषु सप्तसु सम्पत्करणहोमद्रव्याण्युपदिशति । तत्र सितान्नैः सितोपेतान्नैः । तुर्विशेषे । क्षीराक्तैः गव्याद्युक्तक्षीरेषु चतुर्ष्वन्यतमाक्तैः । तथा प्रोक्तविधानेन । घृताक्तैः

शनिवारे तैलसिक्तैस्तिलैः शुद्धैस्तथेतरैः।
हवनाल्लभते लक्ष्मीमब्दादतिमनोहराम् ॥ २८ ॥
तैः समस्तैः समस्ताक्तैर्जुहुयात् सप्तसु क्रमात्।
तद्दिनैरिन्दिराग्र्यः स्याद्विद्याहवनवैभवात् ॥ २९ ॥
तद्दिनेषु च तद्विद्याभक्तांस्त्रीन् द्वौ सुभोजयेत्।
घृतक्षीरतिलक्षौद्रगुडापूपसमन्वितम् ॥ ३० ॥
अश्विन्यादिषु ऋक्षेषु नवस्वपि हुनेत् क्रमात्।
शालिभिस्तण्डुलैर्मुद्गैर्माषैर्गौरितरैस्तिलैः ॥ ३१ ॥
तथाविधैः सर्षपैश्च कोद्रवैरिन्दिराप्तये।
क्षौद्रसर्पिस्तिलैर्दुग्धक्षीरोन्देक्षुरसाप्लुतैः ॥ ३२ ॥

प्रोक्तगव्यादिष्वन्यतमघृताक्तैः। वा विकल्पे। सितोपेतैः शर्करोपेतैः। तैः अन्नैः। तां इष्टां। तिलतण्डुलैः तिलमिश्रतण्डुलैः। दुग्धसिक्तपनसास्थिपरागकैः क्षीरमिश्रितपनसबीजपरागैः ॥ २८ ॥

तैरित्यादिना श्लोकेन समस्तद्रव्यैः सप्तवारेषु हवनात् सम्पत्करत्वादिकमुपदिशति। तत्र तैः समस्तद्रव्यैरित्यर्थः। समस्ताक्तैः समस्ताप्लवनद्रव्याक्तैः। सप्तसु वारेष्विति शेषः। तद्दिनैः एतद्दिनादिमण्डलप्रोक्तदिनैः। विद्याहवनवैभवात् ललिताविद्यावैभवात् होमवैभवाच्च ॥ २९ ॥

तद्दिनेष्वित्यादिना श्लोकेन तत्तत्सम्पत्करप्रयोगहोमदिवसेषु कर्त्तव्यमुपदिशति। तत्र तद्दिनेषु तत्तत्प्रयोगदिनेषु। तद्विद्याभक्तान् ललिताविद्याभक्तान्। त्रीन् द्वौ त्रीन् वा द्वौ वा इत्यर्थः। सुभोजयेत् ॥ ३० ॥

अश्विन्यादीत्यादिना क्रमादित्यन्तेनाध्यर्द्धश्लोकद्वयेनाश्विन्यादिषु नवसु नक्षत्रेषु क्रमात् सम्पत्करहोमद्रव्यनवकं तदाप्लावनद्रव्यनवकसहितमुपदिशति। तत्र हुनेत् जुहुयात्। क्रमात् एकैकक्रमात्। शालीत्यादिना

महिष्यजाविकाक्षीरप्लुतैस्तैर्नवसु क्रमात्।
मघादिषु तथा होमं नवभिः स्यान्नवस्वपि ॥ ३३ ॥
चणकैश्चणकान्नैश्च मुद्गान्नैः कृशरैस्तथा।
माषान्नैश्च हरिद्रान्नैर्गुडान्नैः पायसैस्तथा ॥ ३४ ॥
दुग्धान्नैः शुद्धान्नैश्च विमध्वक्तैः कीर्त्तिलक्ष्मीजयाप्तये।
तथा मूलादिनवके बलिभिर्जुहुयात्तथा ॥ ३५ ॥
पृथुकैः शक्तुभिर्लाजैरिक्षुकाण्डैः पयःप्लुतैः।
शालीचणकमुद्गोत्थैर्माषपिष्टतिलोद्भवैः ॥ ३६ ॥

श्लोकोत्तरार्द्धेन द्रव्यषट्कमुक्तं। तत्र गौरेतरैस्तिलैः सितवर्णतिलैः कृष्णवर्णतिलैश्च। तथाविधैरित्याद्यर्द्धेन द्रव्यत्रितयं तत्फलञ्च। तत्र तथाविधैः सर्षपैः सितसर्षपैः कृष्णसर्षपैश्च। क्षौद्रेत्यादुत्तरार्द्धेन प्लवन-द्रव्यषट्कं। तत्र कैरोन्दशब्देन नालिकेरोदकमुच्यते। महिषीत्याद्युत्तरार्द्धेना-प्लावनद्रव्यत्रयं तत्क्रमश्च। तत्र महिष्यजाविकाक्षीराप्लुतैः महिषीक्षीराजाक्षीरा-विकाक्षीराप्लुतैः। तैर्द्रव्यैः प्रोक्तैः। नवसु प्रोक्तेषु अश्विन्यादिषु। क्रमात् एकैका-प्लुतैः एकैकद्रव्यक्रमात् ॥ ३२ ॥

मघेत्यादिनाप्तये इत्यन्तेनार्द्धत्रयेनार्द्धान्तेन च श्लोकेन मघादिषु नवसु क्रमेण सम्पत्करणहोमद्रव्याण्युपदिशति। तत्र तथा जुहुयात्। नवभिः अनन्तरवक्ष्यमाणैश्चणकादिभिः। अपिः समुच्चये। चणकैरित्यादिनाद्यर्द्धेन द्रव्यचतुष्टयं। माषान्नैः इत्याद्यर्द्धेन द्रव्यचतुष्टयमुक्तं। दुग्धान्नै [शुद्धान्नै] रित्याद्यर्द्धेन द्रव्यमेकं तदाप्लुतद्रव्यं तत्फलञ्च ॥ ३४ ॥

तथेत्यादिना ध्रुवमित्यन्तेनार्द्धाद्येन श्लोकद्वयेन मूलादिनवनक्षत्रेषु सम्पत्कर-होमद्रव्यनवकमुपदिशति। तथा एकैकक्रमात्। तथा प्रोक्तविधानेन। पृथुकै-रित्याद्यर्द्धेन द्रव्यचतुष्टयं तदाप्लवनद्रव्यञ्च। तत्र पयःप्लुतैः क्षीराप्लुतैः। शालीत्यादिनोत्तरार्द्धेन शिष्टदिवसपञ्चकहोमद्रव्यापूपपञ्चकस्य द्रव्यपञ्चकं। तत्र माषपिष्टतिलोद्भवैः एषां पिष्टोद्भवैश्च। एतानि शाल्यादीनुपात्तरत्नापूपै

अपूपैर्म्मधुराभ्यक्तैर्विजयं कीर्त्तिमिन्दिराम् ।
आरोग्यमायुः सौभाग्यं मान्यताञ्च लभेद्ध्रुवम् ॥ ३७ ॥
सिद्धयोगेषु यद्द्रव्यैर्जुहुयात्तत्समृद्धिमान् ।
तथामृताख्ययोगेषु जुहुयाद्रोगशान्तये ॥ ३८ ॥
गुडूचीतिलदूर्व्वाभिस्त्रिमध्वक्ताभिरादरात् ।
उच्चयोगेषु जुहुयादरुणैरुत्पलैः शुभैः ॥ ३९ ॥
उच्चैर्भवति सर्वेषां स्वकुलानां सुनिश्चितम् ।
पर्व्वताख्ये हुनेद्योगे यद्द्रव्यैस्तद्धि पर्वतम् ॥ ४० ॥
भवेदस्याचिरेणैव कालेन परमेश्वरि ।
अथान्यमद्भुतं होममाकर्ण्णय वदामि ते ॥ ४१ ॥
स्वक्षेत्रगे स्वोच्चगे वा जुहुयाद्ग्रहतृप्तये ।
पायसैर्घृतसंसिक्तैः सितमिश्रैस्तु विद्यया ॥ ४२ ॥

रित्यस्य विशेषणानि । विजयादिफलसप्तकं मूलादिनक्षत्रनवकप्रोक्तहोमसाधारणम् ॥ ३७ ॥

सिद्धेत्यादिभिस्ते इत्यन्तैश्चतुर्भिः श्लोकैः सिद्धादिशुभयोगेषु सम्पत्करहोमविधानमुक्तं होमं हुतहोमकथनप्रस्तावसहितं उपदिशति । तत्र सिद्धयोगेषु तिथिवारादिसंयोगोत्पन्नेषु । यद्द्रव्यैरवाप्तुमभिमतैर्द्रव्यैः । तत्समृद्धिमान् हुतद्रव्यसमृद्धिमान् । तथा समुच्चये । नक्षत्रवारादिसमायोगोत्पन्नेषु अमृताख्ययोगेषु । गुडूची अमृतालता । आदरात् भक्तितः । उच्चयोगे रव्यादिष्वन्यतमस्मिन् ग्रहे स्वातुङ्गभागं गते लग्नाद्दशमस्थिते । अरुणैरुत्पलैः अरुणैः कैरवैः । शुभैः प्रागवम्भुकुलाद्यष्टदोषरहितैः । उच्चैः अधिकः । पर्व्वताख्ये इत्यस्य योगे इत्येतद्विशेष्यम् । स्वातुङ्गभागस्थितार्कोदयराशौ वा यदा मेषतुलाकर्कटकेषु क्रमात् कुजशुक्रचन्द्राः स्थिताः तदा मकरराश्युदये वेति यावत् । हुनेत् जुहुयात् । यद्द्रव्यैरवाप्तुमभिमतैः । तद्द्रव्यं पर्वतं सम्पूर्णं । परमेश्वरीति सम्बुद्धिः ॥ ४१ ॥

स्वक्षेत्रेत्यादिना ततकुले इत्यन्तेन श्लोकद्वयेन ग्रहतृप्तिकरहोमकालं होम-

सर्वदा यो हुतविधिमेनं कुर्य्याद् यथाविधि ।
तत्तत्प्रोक्तेषु कालेषु ग्रहार्त्तिः स्यान्न तत्कुले ॥ ४३ ॥
मासेषु जन्मत्रितये होमं कुर्य्याद् यथाविधि ।
दूर्वामृतातिलैर्नित्यं यावज्जीवं सुखी भवेत् ॥ ४४ ॥
तद्दिनेषु जपेद्विद्यां सहस्रं दिननित्यया ।
न तस्य कुत्रचित् कश्चित् कदाचित् क्लेशसम्भवः ॥ ४५ ॥
तर्पणं कारयेच्चन्द्रवासितैर्मधुरैर्जलैः ।
सौरभ्याढ्यैः प्रसूनैश्च पूजयेद्वाथ तद्दिने ॥ ४६ ॥
अवन्ध्यजन्मत्रितयं स्यात् कदाचिन्न मान्त्रिकः ।
यदि स्यात्तस्य रोगादिपीड़ा भवति निश्चितम् ॥ ४७ ॥

द्रव्यञ्च उपदिशति । तत्र स्वच्चे त्वगे एकत्रिंशे पटले भौमित्यादिना श्लोकेन प्रोक्त-स्वस्वराशिगते अर्कादिष्वन्यतमस्मिन् ग्रहे इति शेषः । स्वोच्चगे मेषवृषमकरकन्या-कर्कटमीनतुलाराशयो रव्यादिसप्तग्रहाणां क्रमादुच्चराशयः । तेषु रव्यादिष्वन्य-तमे ग्रहे स्वस्वप्रोक्तोच्चराशौ यदा स्थितः तत्काले । वा विकल्पे । ग्रहत्रये तद्ग्रहत्रये । सितमिश्रैः शर्कमिश्रैः । तुर्विशेषे । विद्यया ज्वलिताविद्यया । तत्तत्प्रोक्तेषु स्वस्वप्रोक्तच्चेत्वोच्चराशिषु स्थिता यदा ग्रहास्तेषु । तत्कुले साधककुले ॥ ४३ ॥

मासेष्वित्यादिभिर्निश्चितमित्यन्तैश्चतुर्भिः श्लोकैः त्रिजन्मसु होमजपतर्पणपूजा विधानं तेष्वन्यतमस्यावश्यकर्त्तव्यतां तदकरणे प्रत्यवायञ्चोपदिशति । तत्र मासेषु द्वादशस्विति शेषः । दूर्वामृतातिलैः तेष्वन्यतमेन द्रव्येणेत्यर्थः । नित्यं प्रतिजन्मत्रयं । तद्दिनेषु त्रिजन्मदिनेषु । विद्यां सहस्रं सहस्रवारं दिननित्यया सहेति शेषः । तस्य जपितुः । कुत्रचिद्देशे । कश्चिदित्यस्य क्लेशसम्भव इत्येतद्विशेष्यं । चन्द्रवासितैः कर्पूरमिश्रैः । वा समुच्चये । तद्दिने जन्मत्रितये । अवन्ध्यजन्मत्रितयं होमतर्पणपूजनेष्वन्यतमेनेति शेषः । यदि स्याद्वन्ध्यजन्मत्रितयं । तस्य मान्त्रि-कस्य । रोगादीत्यत्रादिशब्दो भूतादिविषयः ॥ ४७ ॥

उच्चस्थे वा स्वराशौ वा स्थिते चन्द्र दिवाकरे ।
विद्यां जपेत् सहस्रं वा शतं वा पूजयेच्छिवाम् ॥ ४८ ॥
यस्तस्य रोगतो बाधा कदाचिन्न भवेद्ध्रुवम् ।
तस्मादुक्तेषु कालेषु तथा कुर्व्वन् सुखी भवेत् ॥ ४९ ॥
ग्रहरोगादिदारिद्र्यक्लेशयुक्तस्य मन्त्रिणः ।
मान्त्रिकत्वं भवेल्लोके शोकहासास्पदं भवेत् ॥ ५० ॥
पलाशपुष्पैश्च फलैः पत्रैः काण्डैश्च मूलकैः ।
हवनादब्दमात्रेण वाग्मी स्यात् कुण्ठवागपि ॥ ५१ ॥
अर्कपुष्पैस्त्रिमध्वक्तैर्होमादिष्टमवाप्नुयात् ।
मण्डलात्तस्य पत्रैश्च समिद्भिरपि मूलतः ॥ ५२ ॥
विल्वप्रसूनैस्तु फलैः पत्रैः काण्डैस्तथा हुनेत् ।
मूलैश्च लक्ष्मीसंसिद्ध्यै मा तदन्वयगा भवेत् ॥ ५३ ॥

उच्चस्थेत्यादिभिर्भवेदित्यन्तैस्त्रिभिः श्लोकैः सूर्य्यादिषु स्वचे तस्योच्चस्थेषूपास्ति-क्रमं तत्फलं तदकरणे प्रत्यवायञ्चोपदिशति। तत्र वाद्वयं समुच्चये। विद्यां ललिताविद्यां। सहस्रं सहस्रवारं। वाद्वयं विकल्पे। शतं शतवारं। शिवां प्रागुक्तनित्यां। यः मान्त्रिकस्तस्य मान्त्रिकस्य रोगतः रोगैः। तथा कुर्व्वन् प्रोक्तप्रकारभजनं कुर्व्वन्। शोकहासास्पदं स्वपचपरपच्चयोः ॥ ५० ॥

पलाशपुष्पेत्यादिना श्लोकेन वाग्मित्वप्रदहोमविधानमुपदिशति। तत्र फलैः पत्रैः काण्डैश्च मूलकैः पलाशोत्पन्नैरित्यर्थः। कुण्ठवागपि मूकोपीत्यर्थः ॥ ५१ ॥

अर्केत्यादिना श्लोकेन इष्टाप्तिहोमविधानमुपदिशति। तत्र अर्कपुष्पैः अर्कवृक्षपुष्पैः। इष्टमभिमतं। मण्डलात् प्रागुक्तैकोनपञ्चाशद्दिनैः। तस्य अर्कवृक्षस्य मूलतः मूलैः खण्डरूपैः ॥ ५२ ॥

विल्वेत्यादिना श्लोकेन लक्ष्मीप्राप्तिकरहोमविधानमुपदिशति। तत्र फलैरित्यादिना तृतीयाबहुवचनान्तानां चतुर्णां पदानां विल्वप्रसूनैरिति विशेष्यं। विल्वप्रसूनशब्देन विल्वस्येति षष्ठ्यन्तेन सम्बन्धः। तथा त्रिमध्वक्तैः। हुनेत जुहुयात्। मा लक्ष्मीः तदन्वयगा साधकस्य वंशगामिनी ॥ ५३ ॥

पद्माक्षैर्मधुराभ्यक्तैर्होमात्तावद्दिनैर्नरः ।
इन्दिरां लभते रम्यां सर्वलोकचमत्कृताम् ॥ ५४ ॥
चम्पकैर्मधुसंमिश्रैर्जुहुयात्तद्दिनावधि ।
आढ्यः स्यादप्रजः पुत्रानवाप्नोति गुणाधिकान् ॥ ५५ ॥
तैरेवाज्यप्लुतैर्होमान्मङ्गले तूच्चसंस्थिते ।
लभते सर्वशस्याढ्यां भुवं भोक्ता च जायते ॥ ५६ ॥
तैः क्षीराक्तैर्हुतैश्चन्द्रे स्वोच्चगे तद्दिनैर्भवेत् ।
शतगुः साधकस्तद्वत्त्रिमध्वक्तैर्लभेत्त्रयम् ॥ ५७ ॥
पाटलैः क्षौद्रसंसिक्तैर्होमात् कन्यामवाप्नुयात् ।
तगरोत्थैरपि तथा लाजैश्च कुटजैरपि ॥ ५८ ॥

पद्माक्षैरित्यादिना श्लोकेन लक्ष्मीप्राप्तिकरहोमविधानमुपदिशति। तत्र पद्माक्षैः पद्मफलान्तःस्थमणिभिः। मधुराभ्यक्तैः त्रिमधुराक्तैः। तावद्दिनैः मण्डलदिनैः ॥ ५४ ॥

चम्पकैरित्यादिना श्लोकेन लक्ष्मीपुत्रसिद्धिकरहोमविधानमुपदिशति। तत्र तद्दिनावधि मण्डलदिनावधि ॥ ५५

तैरेवेत्यादिना श्लोकेन शस्यशालिन्या भूमेः प्राप्तिकरहोममुपदिशति। तत्र तैः चम्पकैः। एवावधारणे। मङ्गले भौमे। तुर्विशेषे। उच्चसंस्थिते मकरराशिस्थिते। चः समाहारे ॥ ५६ ॥

तैरेवेत्यादिना श्लोकेन गोशतप्राप्तिकरलक्ष्मीपुत्रभूमीनां प्राप्तिकरहोमद्वयविधानमुपदिशति। तत्र तैः चम्पकैः। स्वोच्चगे वृषभराशिगते। तद्दिनैः मण्डलात्। शतगुः गवां शतयुक्तः। तद्वन्मण्डलात। त्रिमध्वक्तैः तैः चम्पकैरिति शेषः। लभेत् दिव्यत्वात् लभेतेत्यर्थः। त्रयं गोभूमिपुत्रवर्गाणाम् ॥ ५७ ॥

पाटलैरित्यादिना श्लोकेन कन्यासिद्धिकरहोमद्रव्याण्युपदिशति। तत्र तगरोत्थैः प्रागुक्तजलजपुष्पैर्नन्द्यावर्त्तपुष्पैर्वा। कुटजैर्गिरिमल्लिकापुष्पैः। अपिः समुच्चये ॥ ५८ ॥

तैः क्षौरमिश्रैर्हवनाच्चतुर्भिर्लभते धनम् ।
अम्बराणि विचित्राणि महार्हाणि च तद्दिनैः ॥ ५९ ॥
शतपत्रैस्तु मध्वक्तैर्होमाल्लक्ष्मीमवाप्नुयात् ।
केशरैश्च कदम्बैश्च कुण्डै[न्दै]र्विचकिलैरपि ॥ ६० ॥
मल्लिकामालतीजातिपुन्नागैश्च नमेरुभिः ।
जुहुयात् प्रथमारभ्य पञ्चम्यन्तं मधुप्लुतैः ॥ ६१ ॥
एकैकशः समस्तैश्च महालक्ष्मीमवाप्नुयात् ।
तथाज्याक्तैस्तु हवनाल्लभते भूषणैः श्रियम् ॥ ६२ ॥
प्रसूनैः कर्णिकारोत्थैः क्षौद्राक्तैर्हवनाद्दिनैः ।
उदितैरचलां लक्ष्मीं अवाप्नोति सुनिश्चितम् ॥ ६३ ॥
कह्लारै रक्तकुमुदैरुत्पलैः कमलद्वयैः ।
प्राग्वन्नन्दादिपूर्णान्तमेकैकैर्वापि पञ्चभिः ॥ ६४ ॥

तैरित्यादिना श्लोकेन धनवस्त्रप्राप्तिकरहोममुपदिशति । तत्र तैः पाटलतगरजलजकुटजैः । चः समाहारे । तद्दिनैः मण्डलात् ॥ ५९ ॥

शतपत्रैरित्यादिना श्लोकेन लक्ष्मीप्राप्तिकरहोमार्थं पुष्पपञ्चकमुपदिशति । तत्र केशरैर्बकुलैर्विचकिलैः विचकिलो मल्लिकाविशेषः । अप्या पूर्वत्र तद्दिनैरित्येतदाकृष्यते ॥ ६० ॥

मल्लिकेत्यादिभिः सुनिश्चितमित्यन्तैस्त्रिभिः श्लोकैः प्रथमादिपञ्चम्यन्ततिथिषु सम्पत्करहोमभेदानुपदिशति । तत्र मल्लिकेत्याद्यर्द्धेन पुष्पपञ्चकं । तत्र नमेरुभिः सुरपर्णीपुष्पैः । समस्तैस्ताश्चैकैकस्यां तिथौ तत्पुष्पपञ्चकसमुदायः । च शब्दो विकल्पार्थः । तैरेव प्रोक्तपञ्चविधपुष्पैरेव । तथा एकैकशः । समस्तैश्चेति यावत् । भूषणैः सहेति शेषः । दिनैः उदितैः प्रोक्तान्मण्डलात् । एष फलकालावधि प्रकरणसमानः ॥ ६३ ॥

कह्लारैरित्यादिना साधकोत्तम इत्यन्तेन श्लोकद्वयेन सामान्येन नन्दादिपूर्णान्ततिथिपञ्चके प्रागवदेकैकशः समस्तैश्च सम्पत्करपुष्पहोमविधानमुपदि-

हवनाल्लभते लक्ष्मीं सभूभूषणवाहनाम्।
विमध्वक्तैस्तथैकैकैः सर्व्वैर्व्वा साधकोत्तमः॥ ६५॥
केतकीकुसुमैः चौद्रप्लुतैर्होमात्तु तद्दिनैः।
वासांसि लभते चित्राण्यनर्घाणि बहून्यपि॥ ६६॥
सितैः प्रसूनैः चौराक्तैर्होमादाप्नोति तद्दिनैः।
सितानि वासांसि तथा मुक्तादामानि रूप्यकम्॥ ६७॥
हुनेत् कुरुवकैः चौद्रप्लुतैर्व्वाञ्छितसिद्धये।
तथा दमनकैः पत्रैर्हवनाच्छ्रियमश्नुते॥ ६८॥
यद्वर्णानि प्रसूनानि जुहुयाद्विद्यया प्रिये।
तद्वर्णान्येव वासांसि लभते साधको ध्रुवम्॥ ६९॥
मरीचैः सर्षपैस्तैलप्लुतैर्होमान्निशासु तैः।
लज्जामानकुलत्यागलोलामिष्टां समानयेत्॥ ७०॥

श्रति। तत्र कमलद्वयैः रक्तकमलैः सितकमलैश्च। प्रागवत् चौद्राक्तैः। नन्दादिपूर्णान्तं प्रतिपत्षष्ठेरकादश्यादि पञ्चमोदशमीपञ्चदशान्तं। वा विकल्पे। तथा कह्लाराद्यैः पञ्चभिः॥ ६५॥

केतकीत्यादिना श्लोकेनानर्घविचित्रवासःसिद्धिकरहोमविधानमुपदिशति। तत्र तुर्विशेषे। तद्दिनैः प्रागवन्मण्डलात्। लभते साधक इति शेषः। अनर्घाणि वरार्घाणि॥ ६६॥

सितैरित्यादिना श्लोकेन सितवासोमुक्तादामरूप्यसिद्धिकरहोमविधानमुपदिशति। तत्र तथा लभते इति यावत्॥ ६७॥

हुनेदित्यादिना श्लोकेन वाञ्छितकरं लक्ष्मीसिद्धिकरं च होमविधानमुपदिशति। तत्र हुनेत् जुहुयात्। तथा चौद्रप्लुतैरिति यावत्। पत्रैः तमालस्य॥ ६८॥

यद्वर्णानीत्यादिना श्लोकेनाभीष्टवर्णवासःसिद्धिकरहोमविधानमुपदिशति। तत्र विद्यया ललितया। प्रिये इति सम्बुद्धिः। तद्वर्णानि हुतप्रसूनवर्णानि॥ ६९॥

मरीचैरित्यादिभिः सितान्वितैरित्यन्तैश्चतुर्भिः श्लोकैः वनिताकर्षणवशी-

पाटलीकुन्दमन्दारशेफालिकुसुमोद्भवैः।
चम्पकाशोकपुन्नागनमेरुकुसुमैः शुभैः॥ ७१॥
हवनाद्वशयेत् सर्ववनिताः क्षौद्रसंप्लुतैः।
तैरेवाज्यप्लुतैर्होमाद्वशयेत् पुरुषानपि॥ ७२॥
तै राज्यलक्ष्मीं लभते घृताक्तैर्हवनान्निशि।
समस्तजीवभुवनं वशयेत्तैः सितान्वितैः॥ ७३॥
अन्नैर्घृताप्लुतैर्नित्यं हवनादन्नवान् भवेत्।
तथैव जुहुयान्नित्यमायुषे तिलतण्डुलैः॥ ७४॥
मध्यरात्रे तु लवणैः सुश्लिष्टपरिचूर्णितैः।
त्रिमध्वक्तैर्हुतैः सर्वान् वशयेदङ्गनाजनान्॥ ७५॥
तथा दध्यन्वितैर्लोणैर्होमाद्द्वेष्यं वशं नयेत्।
तथा पुण्ड्रेक्षुतोयाक्तैर्हुतैः सुरवशगा नृपाः॥ ७६॥
आज्यैस्तु केवलैर्होमाद्दिनैकत्वैर्धनी भवेत्।
नित्यशो घृतहोमेन श्रीमान् भोगी च जायते॥ ७७

करणपुरुषवशीकरणराज्यलक्ष्मीसिद्धिकरसमस्तप्राणिवशीकरणहोमविधानमुपदिशति। तत्र निशासु मध्यरात्रेषु। इष्टां दयितां वनितां। नमेरुकुसुमैरित्यत्र कुसुमशब्दः पूर्वार्द्धसमुद्भवैरित्यत्र वश्ययोगः। तैः पाटल्यादिभिरष्टभिः पुष्पैः। अपि शब्दः समुच्चये। तैः अष्टभिः पुष्पैः। निशि प्रागवदर्द्धरात्रे। तैः प्रागवत् पुष्पैः। सितान्वितैः शर्करायुक्तैः॥ ७३॥

अन्नैरित्यादिभिर्नृपा इत्यन्तैस्त्रिभिः श्लोकैः वश्यसिद्धिकरहोमविधानमुपदिशति। तत्र नित्यहवनात् प्रतिदिनहोमेन। तथैव घृताप्लुतैः। तिलतण्डुलैः तिलैस्तण्डुलैश्च। तुर्विशेषे। तथा मध्यरात्रे। तथा प्रागवत्॥ ७६॥

आज्यैरित्यादिना श्लोकेन केवलाज्यहोमस्य फलमुपदिशति। तत्र तुर्विशेषे। दिनैकत्वैर्मण्डलात्। चः समुच्चये॥ ७७॥

स्नातोनुलिप्तः स्रग्वी च सितगन्धस्रगम्बरः ।
संपूज्य देवीं हृष्टात्मा संस्कृते हव्यवाहने ॥ ७८ ॥
सवत्सायाः सितायाः गोः पयसि द्विगुणे पचेत् ।
प्रस्थमात्रं तण्डुलन्तु शालिजं सितमेव च ॥ ७९ ॥
सितदुग्धघृतोपेतं कृत्वा वै सिक्थकं महत् ।
गृहीत्वा पाणिना विद्यां जपित्वा शतवारकं ॥ ८० ॥
श्रियं मे देहि देवीति कृत्वा काष्ठोज्ज्वलानले ।
हुत्वा समाप्य पूजान्तु तथा भुक्त्वा तु तद्दिनं ॥ ८१ ॥*
निरन्तरं नित्यशश्च जुहुयाच्च तदन्वयम् ।
न कदाचिद्रमा मुञ्चत्यद्भुता मन्त्रशक्तयः ॥ ८२ ॥
पायसैर्जुहुयात् पूर्णास्विकंवारेषु साधकः ।
निवेदयेच्च पूजायामब्दाढ्यतमो भवेत् ॥ ८३ ॥

स्नात इत्यादिभिः शक्तय इत्यन्तैः पञ्चभिः श्लोकैः साधकतत्कालकर्त्तव्यसहितं लक्ष्मीप्राप्तिकरहोममुपदिशति । तत्र चः समुच्चये । सितगन्धस्रगम्बर इत्यत्र सितशब्दः प्रत्येकमन्वेति । देवीं ललितां । सितायाः सितवर्णायाः । द्विगुणे प्रस्थद्वयमात्रे । तुर्विशेषे । सितमिति तण्डुलविशेषणम् । वा विकल्पे । सितदुग्धघृतोपेतं शर्करादुग्धघृतोपेतं । सिक्थमित्यस्य काकाक्षिन्यायेनोभयत्रान्वयः । कृत्वेति पूर्वत्र गृहीत्वेत्युत्तरत्र च । विद्यां ललिताविद्यां । श्रियं मे देहि देवीति सप्ताक्षरीविद्यां हुत्वा । तत सिक्थकं तथा भुक्त्वा सवत्ससितगोक्षीरपाचितमन्नं सितदुग्धघृतसमेतं भुक्त्वा । तद्दिनं हुतदिनं । निरन्तरं प्रतिदिवसं । नित्यशः यावज्जीवं । तदन्वयं साधककुलं । रमा लक्ष्मीः । अद्भुताः अप्रमेयवैभवाः ॥ ८२ ॥

* इतः परमधिकं पद्यार्द्धं पुस्तकान्तरे दृश्यते—मौनी तु गमयेदब्दाच्छ्रियं प्राप्नोति पुष्कलाम् ।

सवत्सारुणवर्णाया गोः चीराननवनीतकम् ।
तद्दिनान्नन्तु कह्लारप्रसूने विचिपेत्ततः ॥ ८४ ॥
तदुद्धृत्य हुनेदग्नौ भौमवारे तदुच्चगे ।
काले तावद्दिनैर्लक्ष्मीं भूम्याद्यां लभते ध्रुवम् ॥ ८५ ॥
तथा धवलरूपाया नवनीतं सिताम्बुजे ।
निधायादाय मौनी तु हुनेदग्नौ भृगोर्दिने ॥ ८६ ॥
सप्तवारप्रयोगेन महतीमाप्नुयाच्छ्रियम् ।
नृपमान्यां सर्वहृद्यां नानाभोगान्वितां शुभाम् ॥ ८७ ॥
तथारुणासमुद्भूतं नवनीतं रवेर्दिने ।
निधाय विकचे पद्मे कर्णिकायां ततस्तु तत् ॥ ८८ ॥
जुहुयादष्टभिर्वारैराढ्यः स्यात् साधकः शिवे ।
कर्णिकारस्य पुष्पाणि तथा चम्पकजानि वै ॥ ८९ ॥

पायसैरित्यादिना श्लोकेन लक्ष्मीप्राप्तिकरं पूर्णास्वकं वारेषु च होममुपदिशति । तत्र निवेदयेत् पायसमिति शेषः । चः समुच्चये ॥ ८३ ॥

सवत्सेत्यादिभिर्गामिनोत्यन्तैरध्यर्द्धैः सप्तभिः श्लोकैः सम्पत्प्राप्तिकरं नवनीतसहितकह्लारादिपुष्पहोममुपदिशति । तत्र तद्दिनान्नं अनुषितं । तुर्विशेषे । कह्लारप्रसूने दीर्घिकास्थविकसितकह्लारप्रसूनोदरे । ततः दीर्घिकायाः । तन्निचिप्तनवनीतकह्लारप्रसूनं उद्धृत्य मौनिनेति शेषः । हुनेत् जुहुयात् । अग्नौ संस्कृते इति शेषः । तदुच्चगे काले मङ्गलाधिष्ठितराशेश्चतुर्थराश्युदयकाले । तावद्दिनैर्मण्डलात् । तथा धवलरूपायाः सवत्साया धवलवर्णाया गोः नवनीतं तद्दिनात्तमित्यर्थः । सिताम्बुजे प्रागवत् सितपद्मे । भृगोर्दिने तत्रापि तदुच्चकाले । सप्तवारप्रयोगेन भृगुवारसप्तकप्रयोगेन । तथारुणासमुद्भूतं सवत्सारुणगोसमुद्भूतं नवनीतं तद्दिनात्तमिति शेषः । ततः दीर्घिकायाः उद्धृत्येत्यर्थः । तुर्विशेषे । तत् पद्मं प्रागवन्मौनिनेत्यर्थः । अष्टभिर्वारैः रवेरिति शेषः । शिवे इति सम्बुद्धिः । तथा गुरुवारे नवनीताक्तानि नवनीतरूषितानि । उच्चे रवि-

जुहुयान्नवनीताक्तानुग्रचे सूच्चगते गुरौ ।
निरातङ्को महार्घांश्च राजचोरापहारकैः ॥ ९० ॥
प्राप्नोति महतीं लक्ष्मीं सा तदन्वयगामिनी ।
केवलं नवनीतेन सितोपेतेन होमतः ॥ ९१ ॥
कीर्त्तिलक्ष्मीधनारोग्यविजयैरायुराप्नुयात् ।
बन्धूकैः किंशुकैश्चूतैस्त्रिमध्वक्तैर्हुतक्रिया ॥ ९२ ॥
सौभाग्यलक्ष्मीविजयकान्तिप्रज्ञावहा भवेत् ।
दध्यन्नहोमादन्नाढ्यः साधकः स्यात्त्रिमासतः ॥ ९३ ॥
आर्द्रेषु तालपत्रस्य खण्डेषु निजवाञ्छितम् ।
विलिख्य नवनीतेन समेतं जुहुयान्निशि ॥ ९४ ॥
मण्डलान्मासतो वारात् प्राप्नोत्येव स्ववाञ्छितम् ।
तथा पलाशपर्णेषु विलिख्य दरदैर्हुनेत् ॥ ९५ ॥
कुङ्कुमैश्चूतपत्रेषु लिखित्वा वा हुनेन्निशि ।
चन्दनैः पानसे पत्रे विलिख्य जुहुयात्तथा ॥ ९६ ॥

मध्यस्थलग्नाद्दशमराशिस्थिते इत्यर्थः। सूच्चगते कर्कटराशिगते । तदन्वयगामिनी साधककुलगामिनी ॥ ९१ ॥

केवलमित्यादिनार्द्धद्वयेन केवलं सितोपेतनवनीतहोमफलमुपदिशति । तत्र केवलं पुष्परहितं । सितोपेतेन शर्करोपेतेन । कीर्त्तिलक्ष्मीधनारोग्यविजयैः सहेति शेषः ॥ ९२ ॥

बन्धूकैरित्यादिना मासत इत्यन्तेनार्द्धाधेन श्लोकेन किंशुकचूतपुष्पदध्यन्नहोमफलमुपदिशति । तत्र चूतैः सहकारपुष्पैः । दध्यन्नहोमात् दधिमिश्रितान्नहोमात् ॥ ९३ ॥

आर्द्रेष्वित्यादिभिरुदीरितैरित्यन्तैः सप्तभिः श्लोकैः निजवाञ्छितसिद्धिकरं तल्लिखितपत्रहोमविधानं तद्विद्याह्वनवैभवञ्चोपदिशति । तत्र निशि अर्द्धरात्रे ।

पद्मवोदै विलिख्येष्टं नागवल्लीदलैर्युतैः ।
हुतैरवाप्नोति निजं वाञ्छितं प्रोक्तकालतः ॥ ९७ ॥
कस्तूरीलिखितन्त्विष्टं पत्रे चम्पकभूरुहः ।
तैर्हुतैस्तदवाप्नोति तद्दिनैस्तद्विधानतः ॥ ९८ ॥
एलालवङ्गकङ्कोलजातीफलसमन्वितैः ।
सितैरालिख्य च स्वेष्टं पत्रे पद्मसमुद्भवे ॥ ९९ ॥
जुहुयात्तस्य संसिद्ध्यै बहुभिः किमिहोदितैः ।
नासाध्यमस्ति भुवने विद्याहोमैरुदीरितैः ॥ १०० ॥
शुद्धविद्यामयी व्याप्तिरिति सम्यक् समीरिता ।
यस्या निफालनाच्चित्ते तत्तत्त्वं स्वात्मसात् कृतम् ॥

इति षोड़शनित्यातन्त्रेषु श्रीकादिमते होमात् काम्यफलोदयो नाम द्वात्रिंशपटलम् ॥ ३२ ॥ ० ॥

इति यावत् । मण्डलाभ्यासतो वारात् कार्य्यगौरवलाघवानुगुण्यतः । तथा नवनीतसमेतं । विलिख्य निजवाञ्छितमिति शेषः । वा समुच्चये । निशि मध्यरात्रे । तुर्विशेषे । तैः नागवल्लीदलैः । प्रोक्तकालतः प्रागुक्तमण्डलादितः । चम्पकभूरुहः चम्पकवृक्षस्य । तैः चम्पकपत्रैः । तद्दिनैः प्रागवत् । तद्विधानतः प्रोक्तहोमविधानतः । सितैः शर्कराभिः । स्वेष्टं स्ववाञ्छितं । जुहुयात् तत् पद्मपत्रैरिति शेषः । तस्य स्वाभिमतस्य ॥ १०० ॥ ॐ ॥ ० ॥

इति षोड़शनित्यातन्त्रेषु श्रीकादिमताख्यस्य परिपूर्णस्य तन्त्रस्य प्रपञ्चसारसिंहराजप्रकाशाभिधानेन सुभगानन्दनाथेन विरचितायां मनोरमाख्यायां व्याख्यायां सोमहोमविधानप्रकाशनपरं द्वात्रिंशत् पटलं परिपूर्णं परामृष्टम् ॥ ३२ ॥ ॐतत्सत् ॥

ग्रन्थसंख्या—द्वात्रिंशे पटले प्रोक्ता व्याख्याग्रन्थाः शतात् परम् ।
एकाधिका सप्ततिस्तु न स्युर्य्यन्नापि चात्र वै ॥

त्रयस्त्रिंशपटलम् ।

अथ षोड़शनित्यानामाद्या या ललितोदिता ।
तस्या यन्त्राणि कथ्यन्ते तद्विद्याभेदसम्भवैः ॥ १ ॥
रूपैः षष्टिसमोपेतैर्नवशत्या यथाविधि ।
समस्तवाञ्छितावाप्तिकारणानि कृतात्मनाम् ॥ २ ॥
ललितानित्यपूजायां यन्त्रं विश्वात्मविग्रहम् ।
षोड़शानाञ्च तस्याश्च पूजाकमलचक्रकम् ॥ ३ ॥
अमृताख्यघटं यन्त्रं सिद्धवज्रमतः परम् ।
कोष्ठवज्रं वज्रलिङ्गं मेरु[सेतु]लिङ्गं यथाविधि ॥ ४ ॥

पूर्वस्मिन् द्वात्रिंशे पटले षोड़शनित्याविद्यासिद्धानां सौम्यहोमविधानमुपदिश्यानन्तरं तेषां वाञ्छितप्राप्तिकराणि ललिताविद्यायाः स्वरूपभेदसमुत्थानि कानिचिद्यन्त्राण्युपदिशत्यथषोड़शनित्यानामित्यादिना यन्त्रसिद्ध्यभिधागमे इत्यन्तश्लोकशतरूपेण त्रयस्त्रिंशेन पटलेन। तत्र अथ षोड़शेत्यादिभिः क्रमादित्यन्तैः पञ्चभिः श्लोकैः पटलार्थकथनप्रस्तावपुरःसरं तदर्थानुद्दिशति। तत्र आद्या सकलकारणभूता प्रधानेत्यर्थः। ललिता संज्ञेति शेषः। उदिता तृतीयपटले। तस्या ललितायाः। तद्विद्याभेदसम्भवैः तत्श्रीविद्यातार्त्तीयखण्डभेदसमुत्थैः। रूपैः षष्टिसमोपेतैर्नवशत्या। एतदुक्तं भवति श्रीविद्यायाः तार्त्तीयखण्डस्य चतुरक्षरभेदाः चतुर्विंशतिः। तत्पञ्चाक्षरविद्याभेदा विंशत्यधिकशतं। तत्षड़क्षरभेदा विंशत्यधिकसप्तशतं। अपुनरुक्ताक्षराणां षण्णां प्रत्येकं षोड़शस्वरयोगतो भेदाः षण्णवतिः सम्भूय षष्ट्युत्तरनवशतभेदाः तैरिति। एतेषां भेदनप्रकारं पञ्चत्रिंशे पटले वक्ष्यतीति। यथाविधि अनूनाधिकप्रमाणादिति। कृतात्मनां गुरुचरणकमलभजनभव्यचेतसां। यन्त्रं श्रीचक्रं। विश्वात्मविग्रहं पञ्चभूतत्रिधामकालात्मकत्वात्। षोड़शानां नित्यानां निर्द्धारणे षष्ठी। तस्या ललितायाः। चः समाहारे। पूजाकमलचक्रकं कमलरूपं पूजा-

महालिङ्गं योनियन्त्रं तथा तद्वज्रवज्रकम् ।
तदेव च महाकारं कोष्ठयन्त्राणि च क्रमात् ॥ ५ ॥
नवहस्तं त्रिहस्तं वा श्रीचक्रमभिषेचने ।
कुर्य्यात् स्थण्डिलपूजायां हस्तमात्रेऽतिसुन्दरम् ॥ ६ ॥
रत्नादिषु तु निर्म्माणे मानमिच्छावशाद्भवेत् ।
सदा सुविहिते पूजा शुभान्यस्मिंस्तथान्यथा ॥ ७ ॥
भ्रमेण वृत्तं निष्पाद्य सुसमे चतुरस्रके ।
प्रमृज्य तिर्य्यङ्मध्यस्थं सूत्रं तिर्य्यङ्निपातयेत् ॥ ८ ॥

चक्रम् । अमृताख्येत्यादिना श्लोकेन यन्त्रपञ्चकं । तत्र अमृताख्यघटं अमृतघटाख्यं । अतःपरं सिद्धवज्रयन्त्रविधानोपदेशात् परं । यथाविधि प्राग्वत् । महालिङ्गं महालिङ्गाभिधानं । योनियन्त्रं योनिसंज्ञं यन्त्रम् । तद्वज्रवज्रकं वज्रवज्रयन्त्रमित्यर्थः । तदेव च महाकारं महावज्रं महावज्राभिधानं यन्त्रमित्यर्थः । कोष्ठयन्त्राणि कोष्ठाकाराणि समविषमभद्राद्यात्मकान्यनन्तानि यन्त्राणि । क्रमात् उद्दिष्टक्रमात् ॥ ५ ॥

नवहस्तमित्यादिभिः सिद्धिदमित्यन्तैः षोड़शभिः श्लोकैः ललिताया अभिषेकनित्यपूजाश्रीचक्रनिर्माणसमुदायमात्रादिकमुपदिशति । तत्र नवहस्तेत्यादिना श्लोकेनाभिषेके स्थण्डिलपूजायां च श्रीचक्रस्य मानमुपदिशति । तत्र वा विकल्पसमुच्चये । हस्तमात्रे स्थण्डिले इत्यर्थः । एतदनुक्तश्रीनाथादि सकलार्चाचक्रसाधारणं । अतिसुन्दरं वक्ष्यमाणमानाद्यलङ्घितं कुर्य्यादित्यर्थः ॥ ६ ॥

रत्नेत्यादिना श्लोकेन रत्नाद्यधिकरणेषु विनिर्माणे श्रीचक्रस्य स्वेच्छामानत्वं तस्य समीचीनविनिर्माणे फलं तदकरणे प्रत्यवायञ्चोपदिशति । तत्र तुर्विशेषे । सुविहिते समीचीनविनिर्मिते श्रीचक्रे । अन्यस्मिन् उक्तलक्षणादिरहिते तथा पूजा अन्यथा अशुभा ॥ ७ ॥

भ्रमेणेत्यादिभिरुक्तममित्यन्तैः सप्तभिः श्लोकैः श्रीचक्रस्यकर्णिकान्तर्गतत्रि-

सूत्राणि नव तेषु द्वे वृत्तस्पृष्टोभयान्तके ।
विधाय तद्द्वयोरन्तान्मध्यसूत्रान्ततः क्रमात् ॥ ९ ॥
कृते सूत्रचतुष्के तु षट्कोणं स्यात्त्रिसप्तकम् ।
द्व्यष्टायतः समारम्भान्नवमं प्रथमान्तरा ॥ १० ॥
कुर्य्यात् सूत्रचतुष्कन्तु चतुर्मर्म्मानुगुण्यतः ।
नवमप्रथमाग्राभ्यां तिर्य्यक् सप्तमकावधि ॥ ११ ॥
कुर्य्यात् सूत्रचतुष्के तु मर्म्माष्टकविभेदनात् ।
ततश्चतुष्कषष्ठान्तद्वयारम्भात्तथाष्टगम् ॥ १२ ॥
द्वितीयगञ्च सूत्राणां चतुष्कं पातयेत्तथा ।
चतुर्म्मर्म्मानुगुण्येन ततः पञ्चमकान्तयोः ॥ १३ ॥

चत्वारिंशद्योन्यात्मकं स्थितिसंहारात्मकं प्रत्येकं पञ्चीकरणात्सद्वत्त्रिविधं मध्य चक्रद्वयमुपदिशति । तत्र चतुरस्रके एकोनत्रिंशपटलोक्तरूपे । तत्र वृत्तमध्ये तिर्य्यगुदक्षिणोत्तरं निपातयेदित्यस्य सूत्राणीत्यनेनोत्तरत्रान्वयः । नव नव-संख्यानि । तेषु तिर्य्यक्सूत्रेषु नवसु । द्वे पश्चिमादिद्वितीयसप्तमे सूत्रे । वृत्तस्पृष्टोभयान्तके वृत्तस्पृष्टोभयाग्रे । तद्द्वयोः वृत्तस्पृष्टसूत्रयोः । अन्तात् अग्रचतुष्कात् आर-भ्येति शेषः । मध्यसूत्रान्ततः प्राक्प्रत्यगायतब्रह्मसूत्रस्य प्रागग्रान्तं पश्चिमा-ग्रान्तञ्च । क्रमात् प्रोक्तव्यत्यासक्रमात् । सूत्रचतुष्के सम्भूयेत्यर्थः । तुरवधारणे । षट्कोणं स्यात् त्रिसप्तकं ब्रह्मसूत्रस्य प्राक्प्रत्यगग्रात् तृतीयसप्तमतिर्य्यक् सूत्रदक्षिणोत्तराग्रान्तं षट्कोणं स्यात् सम्भूयेत्यर्थः । तुरवधारणे । चतुर्म्मर्मानु-गुण्यतः पूर्व्वलिखित षट्कोणगतमर्मचतुष्टयभेदेन नवमप्रथमाग्राभ्यां पश्चिमादि-नवमतिर्य्यक्सूत्राग्रद्वयात् प्रथमतिर्य्यक्सूत्राग्रद्वयाच्च आरभ्येत्यर्थः । तुर्य्य-सप्तमकावधि तुर्य्यसप्तमसूत्रयोर्मध्यावधि । चतुर्थसूत्राग्रद्वयारम्भात् षट्सूत्राग्रद्व-यारम्भात् च । तथाष्टगं द्वितीयगञ्च । अष्टमरेखामध्यान्तं द्वितीयरेखा

तृतीयगं सूत्रयुगं कुर्य्यान्मर्म्मद्वयाश्रयम् ।
मार्जयेन्मध्यगं ब्रह्मसूत्रं स्याचक्रमुत्तमम् ॥ १४ ॥
वहिरष्टच्छदाम्भोजं तथा तद्विगुणच्छदम् ।
विधाय षड्भिर्वृत्तैश्च चतुरस्रे तथाष्टभिः ॥ १५ ॥
सूत्रैर्विधाय तत्रैव प्राक्प्रत्यग्द्वारसंयुतम् ।
दक्षिणोत्तरतो रेखात्रयात् स्थानद्वयात्तथा ॥ १६ ॥
कोणेषु तिर्य्यक् सूत्रैश्च चतुर्भिस्तान्यनुक्रमात् ।
द्विधा कुर्य्याच्च चत्वारि पदानि परमेश्वरि ॥ १७ ॥

मध्यान्तञ्च । तथा व्यत्यासक्रमात् । पञ्चमकान्तयोः पञ्चमतिर्य्यग्रेखाग्रयोः आरम्भात् तृतीयगं तृतीयसूत्रमध्यगं ॥ १४ ॥

वहिरित्यादिभिः परमेश्वरीत्यन्तैः त्रिभिः श्लोकैः तद्वाह्यस्थस्वष्टात्मकपद्मद्वय-चतुरस्रनिर्माणद्वयमुपदिशति । तत्र वहिः प्रोक्तचक्रवाह्यगततद्वृत्ताद्वहिः । अष्ट-च्छदाम्भोजमित्युक्त्या तत्कर्णिकोदरे प्रोक्तचक्रस्य विलेखनीयत्वात्तद्वहिरपि केशरार्थमेकं वृत्तं निष्पाद्य तद्वहिरष्टपत्राणीति यावत् । तथा तद्विगुणच्छदं षोड़श-पत्रं पद्मं । अष्टपत्रकमलाद्वहिःस्थवृत्तवाह्ये षोड़शपत्रकमलस्य केशरार्थमेकं वृत्तं निष्पाद्य षोड़शपत्राणि षड्भिर्वृत्तैः कर्णिकोदरे प्रोक्तमध्यचक्रद्वयनिर्माणार्थ-मेकं तद्वहिस्तत्संलग्नतया कर्णिकार्थमेकं तद्वहिरष्टपत्रपद्मकेशरार्थमेकं तत् पद्माद्वहिस्तत्पर्य्यन्तसाम्यार्थमेकं तद्वहिः षोड़शपत्रपद्मकेशरार्थमेकं परिवेषार्थ-मेकं च सम्भूय षड्भिर्वृत्तैरित्यर्थः । अष्टभिः सूत्रैः अष्टसूत्रैः पूर्वोक्तचतुरस्ररेखा-चतुष्टयेन सार्द्धमस्य सूत्रैरितुत्तरत्रान्वयः । तस्य चतुरस्रस्य । प्राक्प्रत्यग्द्वार-संयुतं प्राक्प्रत्यक्पार्श्वयोश्चतुरस्रविस्तारमानस्थानद्वयद्वारसंयुतमित्यर्थः । दक्षि-णोत्तरतः चतुरस्रस्य रेखात्रयात् चतुरस्रविस्तारमानेन मध्ये तत्प्राक्पश्चिम-तिर्य्यग्रूपरेखात्रयेणेत्यर्थः । तथा विधाय । कोणेषु तिर्य्यक्सूत्रैश्चतुर्भिः । तान्यनु-क्रमात् द्विधा कुर्य्याच्चत्वारि पदानि इत्यन्तेनैतदुक्तं भवति चतुरस्रकोणकोष्ठ-चतुष्टये प्रतिकोष्ठं सूत्रास्फालनेन द्विधा कुर्य्यादिति । परमेश्वरीति सम्बुद्धिः ॥ १७ ॥

ललितार्चाचक्रमिदं लभ्यं सद्गुरुतः क्रमात् ।
सुन्दरं सुसमं सर्वलक्षणैश्च समन्वितम् ॥ १८ ॥

ललितेत्यादिभिः सिद्धिदमित्यन्तैश्चतुर्भिः श्लोकैः ललिताचक्रस्य सद्गुरुप्रसादात् लभ्यत्वं तल्लक्षणादिकञ्चोपदिशति। तत्र इदं प्रोक्तं लभ्यं सद्गुरुतः क्रमात् अविच्छिन्नपारम्पर्य्यक्रमसंसिद्धक्रमागमसमयाचारनिरतात् कृतपूर्णाभिषेकात्तत्त्वविदो गुरोर्द्वितीयपटले उक्तलक्षणेत्यादिभिर्धनादिभिरित्यन्तैर्द्विपञ्चाशत्तमश्लोकादिषड्भिः श्लोकैः उक्तक्रमात्। लब्धविद्येन साधकेनेत्यर्थः। सुसमं अन्यूनाधिकप्रमाणं। सर्व्वलक्षणैः अनन्तरवक्ष्यमाणैः। अधोमुखैः त्रिकोणैः। नवभिः सम्भूय। एकसूत्रस्थैः ब्रह्मसूत्रस्थिताग्रैः। एतच्छ्रीचक्रं अतिसुन्दरं। अतएव वृत्तस्पृष्टषड़स्रं वाह्यगतचतुर्दशारराग्रेषु प्रोक्तप्रकारेण प्रथमलिखितषट्कोणाग्रषट्कं। तदस्पृष्टाष्टकं वृत्तास्पृष्टतदितरास्राष्टकं। तथा उक्तप्रकारेण। मर्मभिः अनन्तरवक्ष्यमाणलक्षणोपेतैः षड्रेखासन्धिस्थानमिति शेषः। द्वयसङ्गमात् रेखयोरिति शेषः। चतुर्विंशतियुतं सन्धिचतुर्विंशतियुतं। अयमत्र कुम्भस्थापनपक्षे त्रिहस्तमानचक्रस्य विरचनाक्रमः। सुसमे शुद्धे भूतले मध्ये हंसपदं विधाय तत्सदृशस्थानमारभ्य प्रतिपार्श्वं षट्त्रिंशदङ्गुलत्र्यङ्गुलदशाङ्गुलमानभ्रमेण वृत्तं निष्पाद्य तद्वहिस्तत्संलग्नं वृत्तं तद्वहिस्त्र्यङ्गुलदशाङ्गुलमानक्रमेण सम्भूय प्रथमनिष्पादितेन वृत्तेन सह वृत्तषट्कमलान्तरात् वाह्यतो विधाय तत्र प्राक्प्रत्यग्ब्रह्मसूत्रं दक्षिणोत्तरतिर्य्यङ्मध्यसूत्रञ्च सर्व्ववाह्यवृत्ताद्वहिः प्रतिदिशं दशदशाङ्गुलमानावध्यास्फाल्य तत्सूत्राग्रचतुष्टयस्य तत्सर्व्ववाह्यवृत्ते यत्र यत्र सम्पातस्तत्तत्स्पृष्टास्पृष्टिकया मानं तत्सूत्राग्रचतुष्टयस्पृष्टास्पृष्टिकया च चतुश्चत्वारिंशदधिकशताङ्गुलमानैरष्टभिः सूत्रैः परितोऽन्तर्वहिर्विभागेन समचतुरस्रद्वारद्वयं कोणकोष्ठसहितं कृत्वा चतुरस्रस्य पश्चिमप्राचीनवीथीद्वये मध्यसूत्राद्दक्षिणोत्तरयोः पञ्चपञ्चाङ्गुलमानेन त्वेकैकां तिर्य्यग्रेखां कृत्वा तयोर्मध्यस्थाङ्गुलदशकमानेन समचतुरस्रद्वारद्वयं विधाय तयोर्द्वारयोर्दक्षिणोत्तरतो दशदशाङ्गुलमाने तिर्य्यक्सूत्रमेकमेकमास्फाल्य तच्चतुरस्रदक्षिणोत्तरवीथ्योर्मध्यसूत्रात् प्राक्पश्चिमतो दश दशाङ्गुलमाने तिर्य्यक्सूत्रमेकैकं कृत्वा तच्चतुरस्रकोणकोष्ठचतुष्टये तिर्य्यग्रूपं कोणसूत्रमेकमेकं सम्भूय तच्चतुष्टयं वाह्याभ्यन्तरतो विधाय तदन्तर्दशाङ्गुलमानवृत्तवाह्यवीथ्यां दिग्विदिक्षु तदन्त-

अधोमुखैः पञ्चभिश्च चतुर्भिश्च तथोर्द्ध्वगैः।
नवभिस्त्वेकसूत्रस्थैः स्यादेतदतिसुन्दरम् ॥ १९ ॥
वृत्तस्पृष्टषड्स्रञ्च तदस्पृष्टाष्टकं तथा।
मर्म्मभिश्चाष्टदशभिर्युतं चक्रं सुलक्षणम् ॥ २० ॥

रालेषु च सम्भूय षोड़शदलान्यन्योन्यतुल्यमानानि सोपदलानि षोड़श निष्पाद्य तदन्तर्दशाङ्गुलमानवृत्तवीथ्यां दिग्विदिक्ष्वष्टदलानि प्रागवद्विधाय ततः सर्व्वमध्यस्थवृत्तमध्ये दक्षिणोत्तररेखां मार्जयित्वा द्विसप्तत्यङ्गुलमानात्मकं तत्सर्व्वमध्यमस्मिन् पटले चतुर्विंशश्लोकादिवक्ष्यमाणक्रमादष्टचत्वारिंशदंशं कृत्वा तद्ब्रह्मसूत्रे प्रागादिषट्षट्पञ्चांशमानि तिर्य्यक्सूत्रत्रयं कृत्वा पुनरपि पश्चिमादिषट् षट् षड्ंशमानि तिर्य्यक्सूत्रत्रयञ्च विधाय तत्प्रागादितृतीयसूत्रस्य सप्तमसूत्रस्य च मध्ये वक्ष्यमाणमर्मानुगुणतिर्य्यक्सूत्रत्रयस्य स्थानं कर्त्तव्यतया मनसा परिकल्प्य तैः सह नवसु तिर्य्यक्सूत्रेषु सर्व्वपश्चिमस्थं सूत्रं प्रथमं परिकल्प्य तत्(सं)क्रमात्तेषु तृतीयसप्तमरेखाद्वयं वृत्तस्पर्शि कृत्वा तत्तृतीयसूत्राग्रद्वयादिब्रह्मसूत्रप्रागग्रवृत्तसम्पातं सूत्रद्वयं तत्सप्तमसूत्राग्रद्वयादिब्रह्मसूत्रपश्चिमवृत्तसम्पातान्तं सूत्रद्वयञ्च सम्भूय सूत्रचतुष्टयमास्फाल्य षट्कोणं कृत्वा पुनस्तन्नवमरेखामध्यादिप्राग्विलिखितषट्कोणपश्चिममर्मानुगुणगतिवशेन यावद्वितीयरेखोभयपार्श्वगतं सूत्रद्वयं तत् प्रथमरेखामध्यादि षट्कोणप्राचीन मर्मद्वयानुगुणगतिवशेन यावदष्टमरेखाग्रद्वयान्तं सूत्रद्वयं सम्भूय सूत्रचतुष्टयं मर्म्मचतुष्टयानुगुणमास्फाल्य पुनर्ब्रह्मसूत्रप्रागादिप्रसारितरेखाद्वये त्वष्टमसूत्रोभयपार्श्वयोः सम्पातस्य नवमसूत्रमध्यात् प्रसारितरेखाद्वये सप्तमसूत्रोभयपार्श्वयोः सम्पातस्य चानुगुणान्नवमसूत्रोभयपार्श्वादिब्रह्मान्तञ्च सम्भूय मर्म्मचतुष्टयानुगुणं सूत्रद्वयमास्फालयेत्। तत्सूत्रद्वयस्य ब्रह्मसूत्रे यत्र सम्पातः तत्पश्चिमादिचतुर्थतिर्य्यक्सूत्रस्य स्थानं भवति। पुनस्तत्सप्तमसूत्रमध्यादिपश्चिमत उभयपार्श्वस्थमर्म्मद्वयानुगुण्येन यावत् प्रथमतिर्य्यक्सूत्रोभयपार्श्वं सम्भूय चतुर्मर्मानुगुण्येन सूत्रद्वयमास्फाल्य पुनरष्टमतिर्य्यक्सूत्रमध्यमारभ्य प्रथमसूत्रमध्यात् प्रसारितसूत्रमध्यद्वयावधि प्रस्तुततुर्य्यतिर्य्यग्रेखाद्वयान्तं सूत्रद्वयं विन्यसेत्। पुनरष्टमरेखामध्यादिपश्चिमतः प्रस्तुतसूत्रद्वयस्य तुर्य्यरेखामध्यादि प्राक्प्रसृत सूत्रद्वयस्य च सम्पातद्वया-

षड्रेखासन्धिमर्म्माख्यं सन्ध्याख्यद्वयसङ्गमात् ।
तच्चतुर्व्विंशतियुतं चक्रं सर्व्वार्थसिद्धिदम् ॥ २१ ॥
अन्यथा भिन्नमर्म्मादियुतं चक्रं समर्चयेत् ।
यस्तस्य वधं महाव्याधिं दारिद्र्यमयशो मृतिम् ॥ २२ ॥
तस्माल्लक्षणसंयुक्तमुक्तरूपं विधाय वै ।
चक्रं तत्रैव तां नित्यमर्चयन् मत्समो भवेत् ॥ २३ ॥
विधाय वृत्तयोर्म्मध्यं चत्वारिंशत् सहाष्टभिः ।
प्रागादितिर्य्यक्सूत्राणि षट्सु षट्सु च पञ्चसु ॥ २४॥

गुगुणं नवमसूत्रमध्यात् पश्चिमतः प्रसृतोभयरेखामध्यात् पश्चिमतः प्रसृतोभयरेखामध्यावधि तिर्य्यक् सूत्रं प्रसारयेत् । तत् षष्ठसूत्रं तदग्रद्वयादि द्वितीयरेखामध्यान्तं मर्म्मद्वयानुगुण्येन सूत्रद्वयमास्फालयेत् । मध्यात् सप्तमसूत्रमध्यादि प्रसृतसूत्रद्वयस्य चोभयाग्रपार्श्वयोर्यत्र सम्पातस्तत्सम्पातद्वयानुगुण्याष्टम सूत्रमध्यात् पश्चिमतः प्रसृतसूत्रद्वयावधि तिर्य्यक् रेखां कुर्य्यात् । सा पञ्चमरेखा तदग्रद्वयमारभ्य तृतीयरेखामध्यावधि सूत्रद्वयमास्फाल्य ब्रह्मसूत्रमार्जनात् वृत्तस्पृष्टषडस्रे तदस्पृष्टाष्टास्रमष्टादशमर्मोपेतं चतुर्विंशतिसन्धिपूतं श्रीचक्रं भवतीति । अत्र मानवासना मत्प्रोक्तवासनाविमर्शिन्यां द्रष्टव्या ॥ २१ ॥

अन्यथेत्यादिना श्लोकेन प्रोक्तप्रकारमन्तरेण यथादृष्टं चक्रं निर्माय तत्र पूजयतामनर्थविशेषानुपदिशति । तत्र अन्यथा प्रोक्तलक्षणव्यतिरेकेण । मर्मादीत्यत्रादिशब्दः सन्धिविषयः । यस्तस्य वधमित्यादिफलपञ्चकमर्च्चकाय प्रयच्छतीत्यर्थः ॥ २२ ॥

तस्मादित्यादिना श्लोकेन प्रोक्तप्रकारे चक्रे पूजयनां फलमुपदिशति । तत्र श्रीचक्रे । एवावधारणे । तां ललितां नित्यं प्रतिदिनं अर्च्चयन् पूजयन् मत्समः शिवसमो भवेदिति ॥ २३ ॥

विधायेत्यादिना सुन्दरमित्यन्तेन श्लोकद्वयेन ललितायाः श्रीचक्रनिर्माणे सर्व्वमध्यवृत्तान्तर्भूतचतुर्दशारादिचक्रस्य मानसङ्केतमुपदिशति । तत्र वृत्तयोर्मध्यं सर्व्वमध्यवृत्तप्राक्पश्चिमरेखयोर्मध्यब्रह्मसूत्रमिति यावत् । चत्वारिंशत् सहाष्टभिः अष्टचत्वारिंशदित्यर्थः । अस्य पदस्य विधायेत्यनेनान्वयः । प्रागादितिर्य्यक् सूत्राणि त्रीणीति शेषः । षट्सु षट्सु च पञ्चसु अंशेष्वंशेष्विति शेषः ।

पश्चिमात् षट्त्रयेऽप्येवं तन्मध्ये मर्म्मयुक्तितः ।
विदध्यात्त्रीणि सूत्राणि कुर्य्यात्तेनातिसुन्दरम् ॥ २५ ॥

पश्चिमात् पश्चिमब्रह्मसूत्राग्रस्य सर्व्वमध्यवृत्तस्य च सम्पातमानमारभ्येत्यर्थः । षट्त्रये षट्षड़ंशमानस्थानत्रये । अपिः समुच्चये । एवं त्रीणि सूत्राणि तन्मध्ये प्रागादिद्वितीयसूत्रस्य पश्चिमादिद्वितीयसूत्रस्य च मध्ये । मर्मयुक्तितः मर्मभेदयुक्तिवशात् तत्तत्सूत्रस्य ब्रह्मसूत्रस्य च सम्पातस्थाने । तेन विधानेन । एवं सर्व्वमध्यस्यचक्रस्यैव मानोपदेशात्तन्मध्यचक्रतुल्यमानं वाह्यमपि प्रतिपार्श्वं चतुर्विंशत्यंशं कृत्वा अष्टस्वंशेषु केशरदलपरिवेषचतुरस्रादीनां अवान्तरमानं कलशस्थापनानुगुणं यथाशोभनमिति सम्प्रदायः । विद्याप्राप्त्यादिसकलाभिषेकेष्वेककुम्भस्थापनपक्षे त्रिहस्तमानं चक्रं कर्त्तव्यं । विद्याप्राप्त्यभिषेके कलशानां नवकस्य चतुष्टयस्य वा स्थापनपक्षे पूर्णाभिषेके चत्वारिंशत्कलशस्थापनपक्षे नवहस्तप्रमाणं चक्रं परिकल्पनीयं । एककुम्भस्थापनपक्षे सर्व्ववृत्तमध्यान्तर्भूतानि नवनाथहेतिव्यतिरिक्तानि देवतास्थानानि केशरद्वयं परिवेषं दलानि उपदलानि द्वारद्वयव्यतिरिक्तचतुरस्रञ्च प्रोक्तरजसा रञ्जयेत् । पूर्णाभिषेके चत्वारिंशत्कलशस्थापनपक्षे सर्व्वमध्यस्याभिमुखत्रिकोणे प्रतिरेखं समान्तरालमेकमेकं चिह्नं विधाय त्रिभिः सूत्रैर्मध्ये त्र्येकं परितस्त्रिकञ्च सम्भूय त्र्यस्रचतुष्टयं कुर्य्यात् । विद्याप्राप्त्यभिषेके कलशचतुष्टयस्थापनपक्षेऽप्येवं कुर्य्यात् । पुनः पूर्णाभिषेके तु एकतिर्य्यग्रेखान्योन्याभिमुखं त्र्यस्रद्वयं चतुर्षु हेतिचतुष्टयस्थापनद्वयप्रदेशेषु त्रिकोणानि विधाय अष्टदलेषु चतुरस्रादिप्रापि वहिस्त्र्यस्रं विधाय तान्यपि रञ्जयेत् । महाशङ्खकलशस्थापनपक्षे प्रोक्तक्रमेण महाचक्रं कृत्वा प्राग्वत् सर्वमध्यहेतिचतुष्टयस्थानद्वारप्रदेशेषु त्रिकोणानि विधायाष्टदलेषु चतुरस्रगतदेवताष्टकस्थानेषु च वहिस्त्र्यं त्रिकोणानि विधाय सम्भूय चत्वारिंशत्त्रिकोणेषु प्रतिरेखं समान्तरालं चिह्नत्रयं कृत्वा चिह्नाच्चिह्नं नवसूत्रास्फालनेन प्रतिकोणं वाह्याभ्यन्तरान्तं षोड़श त्रिकोणानि कृत्वा तान्यपि रञ्जयेत् । तत्र सर्व्वमध्ययोन्यां लेखनप्रकारो द्वितीयपटले व्याख्यातोऽस्माभिः । अत्र नवकुम्भस्थापने नवयोनिषु चतुष्कुम्भस्थापने मध्ययोनिस्थत्रिकोणचतुष्टये सर्व्वत्र सर्व्वमध्यस्थापनीयकुम्भएव खारिमाणतोयपूरणीयः । इतराः कलशाः द्विद्विप्रस्थमानतोयपूरणीया इति सम्प्रदायः ॥ २५ ॥

त्र्यस्रं वृत्तं पञ्चदश च्छदानि च ततो बहिः ।
अष्टपत्राम्बुजं बाह्ये दशच्छदसरोरुहम् ॥ २६ ॥
पुनर्दशच्छदं पद्मं चतुर्द्दशदलं ततः ।
अष्टच्छदाब्जं द्विगुणच्छदमष्टादशच्छदम् ॥ २७ ॥
विधाय तस्य मध्ये तां समावाह्य यजेत्तथा ।
पश्चान्नाथान् पार्श्वयोश्च हेतोरन्यास्तथार्च्चयेत् ॥ २८ ॥

त्र्यस्रमित्यादिभिराप्नुयादित्यन्तैश्चतुर्भिः श्लोकैर्ललितायाः पञ्चरूपसकलशक्त्यावरणपरिपूर्णं पूजाचक्रं तत्र पूजाफलञ्चोपदिशति । तत्र त्र्यस्रं स्वाभिमुखमित्यर्थः । वृत्तत्र्यस्राद्बहिस्तत्कोणत्रयस्पृष्टाप्रुष्टिकयेति यावत् । पञ्चशदच्छदानि च ततो बहिः इत्यनेनैतदुक्तं भवति वृत्ताद्बहिः केशरार्थं वृत्तं त्र्यस्राद्बहिः तत्कोणं कृत्वा तत्र बाह्ये पञ्चदश च्छदानि लिखेदित्यर्थः । अष्टपत्राम्बुजमित्युक्त्या केशरार्थं वृत्तमालिख्य तद्बहिः अष्टपत्राणि विलिखेदित्यर्थः । बाह्ये अष्टपत्रपद्मबाह्ये पुनर्बहिश्चतुर्दशदलं पद्मं । तद्द्विगुणच्छदं षोड़शदलपद्मं अष्टादशच्छदं प्राग्वद्विशेष्यं । सर्वत्र चक्रेषु दलानामवान्तरमाणं कुण्डपटलोक्ताष्टास्रमानवत् तत् कल्पयेत् । तत्र पुराभागे ब्रह्मसूत्रं दलमध्यं यथा तथा कुर्य्यात् । विधायेत्यस्य त्र्यस्रमित्यादिभिर्द्वितीयान्तपदैरन्वयः । तस्य पद्मचक्रस्य । मध्ये सर्व्वमध्यत्रिकोणमध्ये । तां ललितां । तथा नित्यत्वेन कृतिकाद्युक्तक्रमेण पश्चात्तथा । अन्तस्त्रिकोणस्य प्राग्रेखावृत्तयोर्मध्ये पार्श्वयोः अन्तस्त्रिकोणपार्श्वरेखाद्वयमध्यत इत्यर्थः । अन्याः तिथिनित्या अणिमादयश्च । तथा युक्त्या । एतदुक्तं भवति सुसमे भूतले हंसपदं विधाय तत् सन्दंशस्थानमारभ्य प्रतिदिशमष्टादशाङ्गुलमानेन भ्रमेण वृत्तं निष्पाद्य तद्वृत्तमध्ये स्वाभिमुखां योनिं समरेखां निष्पाद्य तद्बहिर्द्व्यङ्गुलपञ्चाङ्गुलमानक्रमेण पूर्व्वनिष्पादितवृत्तेन सह सप्तदशवृत्तानि निष्पाद्य तत्रैकैकान्तरितासु पञ्चाङ्गुलवीथिष्वष्टस्वाभ्यन्तराद्बाह्यगत्या पञ्चदशदलाब्जेऽग्रादिप्रादक्षिण्येन तिथिनित्याः सबबाह्यस्याष्टदशदलेषु प्राक्प्रत्यग्दलद्वयं द्वारस्थानं परिकल्प्य एवं क्रमाद्दिग्विदिक्षुक्रमेण प्राग्वच्चतुरावृत्त्याणिमादींस्तदन्तःषोड़शदलेषु प्राग्वन्नित्याकलाः तदन्तरष्टदलेषु प्राग्वदनङ्गकुसुमादीं स्तदन्तश्चतुर्दशदलेषु प्राग्वत् सं-

एतस्मिन् पद्मचक्रस्य मध्ये तासां प्रपूजनात्।
महतीं श्रियमाप्नोति ज्ञानान्मांश्च समाप्नुयात् ॥ २९ ॥
पूर्व्वस्मिन् पूजयेद्देवीमुक्तक्रमसमन्वितम्।
श्रियं ज्ञानात्तथावाञ्च संयाति परमेश्वरि ॥ ३० ॥
घटद्वयं समालिख्य वाह्याभ्यन्तरभेदतः।
तन्मध्ये नवधा कृत्वा कोणेषु प्रथमं लिखेत् ॥ ३१ ॥
द्वितीयं दिक्षु संलिख्य मध्ये तार्त्तीयमालिखेत्।
घटयोरन्तरा कृत्वा तिर्य्यग्रेखाः समन्ततः ॥ ३२ ॥

क्षोभिण्यादीं स्तदन्तर्दशदलेषु प्रागवत् सर्व्वसिद्धिप्रदादींस्तदन्तर्दशदलेषु प्रागवत् सर्व्वज्ञादींस्तदन्तरष्टदलेषु प्रागवत् वाग्देवताः सर्व्वमध्यस्थवृत्ततन्मध्यत्र्यस्रपार्श्वरेखान्तराले प्रागवद्धेतोस्तदन्तरस्त्रत्रये प्रागवत् पोठेश्वरीं सर्व्वमध्ये प्रागवद्देवीं चैवं क्रमात् प्रोक्तक्रमेणार्च्चयेदिति। एतस्मिन् ऐहिके प्रपूजनात्। अस्य पदस्य श्रियमाप्नोतीत्यनेनान्वयः। तासां सपरिवारिकाया देव्याः। महतीं राजादिभिरनवहार्य्यां। ज्ञानात् परमार्थादितिशेषः। मां शिवम् ॥ २८ ॥

पूर्व्वस्मिन्नित्यादिना श्लोकेन पूर्व्वोक्तश्रीचक्रे समर्च्चनफलमुपदिशति। तत्र पूर्व्वस्मिन् प्रोक्ते श्रीचक्रे। उक्तक्रमसमन्वितं चतुर्द्दशपटलत्रयप्रोक्तार्च्चनक्रमसमन्वितं। श्रियं ऐहिके इत्यर्थः। ज्ञानात् षट्त्रिंशपटलवक्ष्यमाणात्। तथा अपृथग्रूपिणा। आवां शक्तिं शिवं च। चः समुच्चये। स साधकः। परमेश्वरीति देवी सम्बुद्धिः ॥ ३० ॥

घटद्वयमित्यादिभिरपमृत्युजिदित्यन्तैर्नवभिः श्लोकैरमृतघटाख्यं यन्त्रं तत्प्रयोगान् फलानि चोपदिशति। तत्र घटद्वयं वाह्याभ्यन्तरवृत्तद्वयं तन्मध्यं नवधा कृत्वा प्राक्प्रत्यगदक्षिणोत्तरद्विद्विरेखाभ्यामिति शेषः। कोणेषु कोणकोणकोष्ठेष्वित्यर्थः। प्रथमं श्रीविद्यायाः प्रथमखण्डं। द्वितीयखण्डं दिक्षु प्रागवत् कोष्ठेषु। मध्ये प्रागवत् कोष्ठे तार्त्तीयं खण्डं। घटयोर्वाह्याभ्यन्तरवृत्तयोः। तिर्य्यग्रेखाः सप्तेत्यर्थः। समन्ततः परितस्तेषु कोष्ठेषु विद्यातार्त्तीयाक्षरसप्तकं

तेषु प्रदक्षिणं विद्यातार्त्तीयाक्षरसप्तकम् ।
लिखेद्बिन्दुविसर्गाभ्यां मुखे पञ्चामृताम्बुजम् ॥ ३३ ॥
आद्यनालमयं द्वन्द्वपत्त्रकेशरकर्णिकम् ।
विधाय च घटाधस्ताद्दिदध्याद्विनियोगकम् ॥ ३४ ॥
मध्ये साध्याक्षरोपेतं कृत्वा तममृतं घटम् ।
विभृयादभिषिञ्चेच्च जन्मर्क्षेष्वायुराप्तये ॥ ३५ ॥
कुहूपरागसंक्रान्तिदोषेष्वखिलशान्तये ।
अभिषिञ्चेदशेषार्त्तिशान्त्यै सिद्ध्यै च सम्पदा ॥ ३६ ॥

श्रीविद्यातार्त्तीयखण्डस्य व्यस्तरूपाक्षरसप्तकं बिन्दुविसर्गाभ्यां अनुस्वारेण विसर्जनीयेन च सहेति शेषः । पञ्चामृताम्बुजं अष्टमे पटले ज्याकमित्यादिना सप्तत्रिंशश्लोकोत्तरार्द्धेन प्रोक्तामृताक्षरपञ्चकसहितमम्बुजं । आद्यनालमयं आद्यामृताक्षरसहितनालं । द्वन्द्वपत्त्रकेशरकर्णिकं अत्र द्वन्द्वशब्दः पत्त्रे समष्टितः इतरयोर्व्यष्टिरूपतश्च योज्यः । द्वितीयतृतीयाक्षरसहितं पत्त्रं चतुर्थामृताक्षरसहितकेशरं पञ्चमामृताक्षरसहितकर्णिकमित्यर्थः । चः समाहारे । तेनाम्बुजमित्याकृष्यते । घटाधस्तात् घटस्याधःस्थाने । मध्ये सर्व्वमध्यकोष्ठस्थतार्त्तीयखण्डोदरे साध्याक्षरोपेतं साधकसाध्यकर्मोपेतं कृत्वा तममृतघटं अमृतघटसंज्ञं तद्यन्त्रं कृत्वेत्यर्थः । अथमत्र विरचनाक्रमः । सुसमे भूतले अभीष्टमानभ्रमेण वृत्तं कृत्वा तद्बहिरेकाङ्गुलमाने च वृत्तं कृत्वा तदन्तर्मध्ये प्राक्प्रत्यग्दक्षिणोदक्समान्तरालं द्विद्विसूत्रास्फालनान्नव कोष्ठानि निष्पाद्य तेषु कोणकोष्ठचतुष्टये श्रीविद्याप्रथमखण्डं तद्दिक्कोष्ठचतुष्टये तद्द्वितीयखण्डं तत् सर्वमध्यकोष्ठे तार्त्तीयं खण्डं साधकसाध्यकर्मोपेतं चालिख्येत् । तत् प्राग्गत कोष्ठमध्ये चतुरङ्गुलमानेन प्राग्वद्वृत्तयोरन्तरालवीथ्योः समान्तरालं सप्तधा कृत्वा तेषु सप्तसु कोष्ठेषु श्रीविद्यातार्त्तीयखण्डस्य व्यस्तरूपाक्षरसप्तकं प्रागादिप्रादक्षिण्यक्रमात् विलिख्य तत् प्राग्गतकोष्ठमध्ये चतुरङ्गुलमानेन प्राग्गत् कुम्भमुखं कृत्वा तद्घटमुखेऽधोमुखं पङ्कजं घटस्याधः स्थाने तूर्ध्वमुखं पङ्कजं चालिख्य तदम्बुजयोः क्रमान्नाले जं जः इत्यक्षरद्वयं तयोः पत्त्रे जं जः जं ठः

अपमृत्युमहारोगचयापस्मारशान्तये ।
त्रिवर्षमभिषेकन्तु कुर्य्याज्जन्मत्रये तथा ॥ ३७ ॥
सर्व्वक्लेशविनिर्मुक्तः सुखी वर्षशतं भुवि ।
आरोग्यो विजयी विश्ववन्द्यो भवति मानवः ॥ ३८ ॥
सुवर्णे राजते ताम्रे कृत्वैतत् सिक्थलिङ्गगम् ।
विधाय स्थापयेत् चौद्रे यजेत् सर्व्वापमृत्युजित् ॥ ३९ ॥
तार्क्षीयविद्यापुटितं नामालिख्य तु साधकः ।
ऊर्म्मिकादौ वहेत् सर्व्वसम्पदे रिष्टशान्तये ॥ ४० ॥

इत्यक्षरचतुष्टयं तयोः केशरस्थाने वं वः इत्यक्षरद्वयं तयोः कर्णिकायां सं सः इत्यक्षरद्वयञ्चालिखेत्। एतदमृतघटात्मकं यन्त्रं भवतीति। जन्मर्चेषु त्रिष्विति शेषः। अखिलशान्तये इत्यत्राखिलशब्देन क्रूरदशागोचरेत्यादय उच्यन्ते। चः समाहारे। महारोगशब्देन वाताद्यष्टरोगा उच्यन्ते। त्रिवर्षमित्यत्यन्तसंयोगे द्वितीया। तुर्विशेषे। तथा द्वितीयपटलोक्ताभिषेकप्रकारेण। विजयी वादद्यूत युद्धादिष्विति शेषः। सुवर्णे रजते ताम्रे तेषु त्रिष्वन्यतमे पट्टे इत्यर्थः। सिक्थलिङ्गगं मधूच्छिष्टमयलिङ्गान्तर्भूतं। चौद्रे कलशान्तर्गते। एतदुक्तं भवति सुवर्ण-रजतताम्रेष्वन्यतमाधिकरणे तदमृतघटद्वयं यन्त्रं विधाय गुलिकीकृत्य प्राण-प्रतिष्ठादिकं कृत्वा तत् सिक्थमयलिङ्गान्तर्निधाय तल्लिङ्गं कलशमध्ये सं-स्थाप्य तत्कलशं चौद्रेणापूर्य्य तत्कलशमुखं शरावेण पिधाय तत् क्वचित् संस्थाप्य तदुपरि मृत्पीठं विधाय तत्र प्रोक्तविधानेन स्वाभिमतफलपर्य्यन्तं देवीं सपरिवारामभ्यर्च्य पुनः प्रोक्तफलसिद्धौ सत्यां उद्वास्य नमस्तेति तत् चौद्रा-दिकं विसर्जयेदिति ॥ ३८ ॥

तार्क्षीयेत्यादिना श्लोकेनोर्म्मिकादिषु सर्व्वरक्षाविधानमुपदिशति। तत्र तार्क्षीयविद्यापुटितं श्रीविद्याया इति शेषः। नाम साधकसाध्यकर्म्मणां। तुर्विशेषे। ऊर्मिकादावित्यत्रादिशब्दः केयूरादिविषयः। एतदुक्तं भवति। कनक-मये पट्टे श्रीविद्यातार्क्षीयखण्डमनुलोमप्रतिलोममन्योन्यं रेफांशेन रेफो मायांशेन मायांशश्च यथा पुटितो भवति तथा तथालिख्य तन्मायांशे साधकं

कृत्वाश्मनि तथा यन्त्रं तड़ागादिषु मध्यतः ।
स्थापयेत्तत्र ये स्नाता नराः स्युः सुखिनोऽनिशम् ॥ ४१ ॥
प्राकप्रत्यग्दक्षिणोदक्क सूत्रैरष्टभिराहृतैः ।
कोष्ठान्येकोनपञ्चाशत्तेषु कोणेषु मार्जयेत् ॥ ४२ ॥
चतुर्विंशतिकोष्ठानि शेषेषु विलिखेत् क्रमात् ।
दिक्ष्वेकतस्त्रिकोणानि प्रागारम्भात् प्रवेशतः ॥ ४३ ॥
तार्त्तीयस्य च भेदोत्थचतुर्व्विंशतिमालिखेत् ।
विलोमेनाथ मध्यस्थे तत् ससाध्यं समालिखेत् ॥ ४४ ॥
सिद्धवज्राभिधं यन्त्रं अशेषशुभदायकम् ।
विनाशनमनिष्टानां जयसौभाग्यदायकम् ॥ ४५ ॥

तद्रेफांशे साध्यं तयोरन्तराले प्राग्वत् कर्म चालिख्योर्मिकाभूषणान्तर्भूतं कृत्वा प्राणान् प्रतिष्ठाप्य समभ्यर्च्य तद्धारणात् प्रोक्तफलसिद्धिभागिति ॥ ४० ॥

कृत्वेत्यादिना श्लोकेनामृतघटाख्ययन्त्रस्य तड़ागादिषु स्थापनं तत्फलञ्चोपदिशति। तत्र तथा प्रोक्तप्रकारेण। तड़ागादिष्वित्यत्रादिशब्दो नदीकूपादिविषयः। मध्यतः मध्ये यत्राधिष्ठिततड़ागादिषु ॥ ४१ ॥

प्राक्प्रत्यगित्यादिभिस्त्वेतन इत्यन्तैर्नवभिः श्लोकैः सिद्धवज्रयन्त्रनिर्माणं तत्प्रयोगांस्तत्तत्फलानि च तत्स्तवनसहितमुपदिशति। तत्र तेषु कोष्ठेषु कोणेषु चतुर्ष्विति शेषः। मार्जयेदित्यस्य चतुर्विंशतिकोष्ठानीत्युत्तरत्रान्वयः। चतुर्विंशतिकोष्ठानि प्रतिकोणं कोष्ठषट्कं षट्कं सम्भूयेत्यर्थः। शेषेषु कोष्ठेषु निर्द्धारणे सप्तमी। विलिखेदित्यस्य त्रिकोणानीत्यनेनान्वयः। एकतः कोष्ठतः इतिशेषः। सम्भूय चतुर्भिः। प्रागारम्भात् प्राक्त्रिकोणारम्भात्। प्रवेशतः प्रवेशगत्येति यावत्। तार्त्तीयस्य श्रीविद्यात्तार्त्तीयखण्डस्य भेदोत्थचतुर्व्विंशतिं पञ्चत्रिंशपटलवक्ष्यमाणप्रकारेण। चतुरक्षरात्मिका भेदोत्थचतुर्विंशतिसंख्याता विद्याः। विलोमेन अप्रादक्षिण्यान्मध्यस्थे कोष्ठे। तत् श्रीविद्यातार्त्तीयखण्डं ससाध्यं साधकसाध्यकर्मोपेतं। सिद्धवज्राभिधं सिद्धवज्रसंज्ञं। अयमत्र विरचनाक्रमः। प्राक्प्रत्यग्

समरे विजयप्राप्त्यै विभ्रयात्तद्विवादजे ।
समस्ते धारयेत् क्लेशे विजयं सुखमाप्नुयात् ॥ ४६ ॥
प्रतिमासञ्च पूर्णायामभिषिञ्चेच्च तत्र वै ।
स्थापयित्वा घटं प्राग्वत् समस्ताभ्युदयाय वै ॥ ४७ ॥
पुत्राप्त्यै कन्याकावाप्त्यै वराप्त्यै कन्यका तथा ।
धराधनपशुप्राप्त्यै नरनारीनृपादिनाम् ॥ ४८ ॥
वन्ध्यायाविघ्नसंसिद्धै वाक्सिद्धै गेहसिद्धये ।
धारयेत् सिद्धवज्रन्तु समस्तेषु प्रसिद्धये ॥ ४९ ॥
ललिताविद्यया विद्यामन्यां यन्त्रेण वामुना ।
यन्त्रमन्यत् समं वेत्ति योऽसौ स्यान्मूढचेतनः ॥ ५० ॥
प्राक्प्रत्यग्दक्षिणोदक्क सूत्राण्यष्टादश क्षिपेत् ।
तैस्तत्र कोष्ठानि तथा नवाशीतिशतद्वयम् ॥ ५१ ॥

दक्षिणोदक्कसमान्तरालाष्टसूत्रास्फालनेनैकोनपञ्चाशत् कोष्ठानि निष्पाद्य तेषु प्रतिकोणं षट् षट् सम्भूय चतुर्षु कोणेषु चतुर्विंशति कोष्ठानि शिष्टमध्ये वज्राकारं यथा तथा मार्जयित्वा शिष्टेषु पञ्चविंशतिकोष्ठेषु प्रतिदिशमेकैककोष्ठेन सम्भूय चतुर्भिः चतसृषु दिक्षु चत्वारि त्रिकोणानि विधाय तेषु प्रागग्रादिप्रादक्षिण्यप्रवेशगत्या श्रीविद्यातार्त्तीयखण्डप्रथमभूतांश्चतुर्विंशतिभेदान् क्रमेणालिख्य शिष्टसर्वमध्यकोष्ठे तार्त्तीयखण्डं लिखित्वा तन्मायांशे साधकं तद्रेफांशे साध्यं तयोः सन्धौ कर्म चालिखेदेतत् सिद्धवज्राभिधं यन्त्रमिति । अनिष्टानां अमङ्गलानां । तत् सिद्धवज्राभिधं यन्त्रं । विवादजे इत्यस्य क्लेश इत्येतद्विशेष्यं । तत्र यन्त्रे प्राग्वत् द्वितीयपटलोक्तक्रमेण अभिषिञ्चेत् । नरनारीनृपादिनामित्यस्य वन्ध्याय इत्यनेनान्वयः । नृपादिनामिति स्वातन्त्र्योक्तिः । तुः समुच्चये । अमुना सिद्धवज्रयन्त्रेण समं वैभवात् । असौ एवं वेत्ता मूढचेतनः । अन्यथाज्ञानाविष्टहृदयः । अन्येषामधिकत्वेन वेदनात् किं पुनरित्यर्थः ॥ ५० ॥

प्राक्प्रत्यगित्यादिभिः प्रिये इत्यन्तैः षड्भिः श्लोकैः कोष्ठवज्रयन्त्रनिर्माण-

तेषु कोणेषु कोष्ठानि मार्जयेत् पूर्ववत् प्रिये ।
षट्त्रिंशच्छिष्टवज्रे तु चतुर्भिर्दिक्त्रिकोणकम् ॥ ५२ ॥
विधाय प्राग्वहिर्मध्यात् प्रादक्षिण्यप्रवेशतः ।
विलिखेत्तद्द्वितीयार्द्धं भेदात्तु विलिखेत्ततः ॥ ५३ ॥
त्रिकोणेषु च तार्त्तीयं ससाध्यं मध्यतस्तथा ।
नवसु विलिखेद्विद्याकूटत्रयमथ त्रिशः ॥ ५४ ॥

विधानमेतत्पटलोक्तयन्त्रफलकथनप्रस्तावसहितमुपदिशति । तत्र तैः सूत्रैः । तत्र यन्त्रे । तथा जायते । नवाशीतिशतद्वयं एकोननवत्यधिकं शतद्वयं । तेषु कोष्ठेषु निर्द्धारणे सप्तमी । कोष्ठानीत्यस्य षड्विंशदित्यनेनान्वयः । पूर्ववद्वज्राकारं यथा भवति तथेत्यर्थः । षट्त्रिंशत् प्रतिकोणं सम्भूय चतुश्चत्वारिंशदधिकशतसंख्यानीत्यर्थः । शिष्टवज्रे शिष्टपञ्चचत्वारिंशदधिकशतसंख्यकोष्ठात्मके वज्रे । तुर्विशेषे । चतुर्भिः कोष्ठैः प्रतिदिशमित्यर्थः । दिक्त्रिकोणकं प्रतिदिशमेकं त्रिकोणं । विधायेत्यस्य दिक्त्रिकोणकमिति पूर्वेणान्वयः । प्राग्वहिर्मध्यात् प्राच्यां दिशि वहिर्भूतपंक्तिमध्यस्थकोष्ठात् प्राक्त्रिकोणं तत्तद्भूतपंक्तिस्थकोष्ठपञ्चके मध्यकोष्ठात्तदारभ्येत्यर्थः । प्रादक्षिण्यप्रवेशतः प्रादक्षिण्यप्रवेशगत्या । तद्द्वितीयार्द्धं भेदात् श्रीविद्यातार्त्तीयखण्डस्य पञ्चत्रिंशपटलप्रोक्तपञ्चाक्षरोत्पन्नभेदात् विंशत्युत्तरशतसंख्यातान् । तुर्विशेषे । ततः अनन्तरं । चः समाहारे । तार्त्तीयखण्डमिति शेषः । ससाध्यं साधकसाध्यकर्म्मयुक्तं । मध्यतः तद्वज्रयन्त्रस्य । तथा अनन्तरश्लोकवक्ष्यमाणक्रमेण । नवसु शिष्टेषु कोष्ठेषु । त्रिशः त्रिरावृत्त्या । दक्षत्रये दक्षिणभागकोष्ठत्रये । मध्ये मध्यकोष्ठत्रये । तथा समुच्चये । वामत्रये द्वितीयं कूटं साध्ये तृतीयकं मध्यत्रये पूर्ववल्लेख्यतृतीयकूटं ससाध्यादिकं लिखेदितर्थः । तुर्विशेषे । अयं अत्र यन्त्रविरचनाक्रमः । प्राक्प्रत्यग्दक्षिणोदक्समान्तरालाष्टादशाष्टादशसूत्रास्फालनादेकोननवत्युत्तरशतद्वयकोष्ठानि निष्पाद्य तेषु-प्रतिकोणं षट्त्रिंशत् षट्त्रिंशतकोष्ठक्रमेण सम्भूय चतुश्चत्वारिंशदधिकशतकोष्ठानि शिष्टमध्ये वज्राकारं यथा तथा मार्जयित्वा पुनः शिष्टवज्राकारे पञ्चचत्वारिंशदधिकशतकोष्ठात्मके प्रतिदिशं वहिरेकत्रिक्रमेण सम्भूय कोष्ठचतुष्टयेन कोष्ठ-

दक्षत्रये त्वाद्यकूटं मध्ये तार्त्तीयकं तथा ।
वामत्रये द्वितीयञ्च लिखेत् साध्ये तृतीयकम् ॥ ५५ ॥
एतत्तु कोष्ठवज्राख्यं यन्त्रमिष्टार्थदायकम् ।
फलानि सर्वयन्त्राणां पटलेऽस्मिन् शृणु प्रिये ॥ ५६ ॥
तन्त्रेऽस्मिन्नन्यतन्त्रेषु यस्य यन्त्रस्य यत् फलम् ।
प्रोक्तं तदेषामेकैकं योजयेत् सर्वमेव च ॥ ५७ ॥
तेनात्र यन्त्रनिर्म्माणमानमेवोच्यते मया ।
फलानि वाञ्छयावाप्नोत्ययत्नान्नामयोजनैः ॥ ५८ ॥
अतः फलानि तन्त्राणामिह नोक्तानि कृत्स्नशः ।
सर्वञ्च सर्वदा सर्वसमीहितफलाप्तिकृत् ॥ ५९ ॥
प्राक्प्रत्यग्दक्षिणोदक्षषड्विंशत्या समाहतैः ।
सूत्रैः कोष्ठानि जायन्ते षट्शतं पञ्चविंशति ॥ ६० ॥

चतुष्टयेनैकैकं त्रिकोणं कृत्वा तच्छिष्टैकोनत्रिंशदुत्तरशतकोष्ठेषु प्राग्गतपंक्तिस्थकोष्ठपञ्चके मध्यकोष्ठमारभ्य श्रीविद्यातार्त्तीयखण्डस्य द्वितीयभेदात् विंशत्युत्तरशतरूपान् प्रादक्षिण्यप्रवेशगत्या विलिख्य शिष्टमध्यकोष्ठेषु नवसु दक्षिणपंक्तिस्थकोष्ठत्रये श्रीविद्याप्रथमखण्डं वामपंक्तिस्थकोष्ठत्रये मध्यखण्डं मध्यपंक्तिस्थकोष्ठत्रये दिग्गतत्रिकोणचतुष्टये तार्त्तीयखण्डञ्चालिख्य तार्त्तीयखण्डे प्रागवत् साधक साध्यकर्म्माणि विलिख्य एतत् कोष्ठवज्रयन्त्रमुक्तविनियोगादभिमतसिद्धिदमिति । प्रिये इति देवीसम्बुद्धिः ॥ ५६ ॥

तन्त्रे इत्यादिभिराप्तिकृदित्यन्तैस्त्रिभिः श्लोकैरेतत्पटलोक्तानां यन्त्राणां सर्वेषां फलान्यतिदेशतः स्वरूपतश्चोपदिशति । तत्र तन्त्रेऽस्मिन्नन्यतन्त्रेषु अस्मिन् तन्त्रे न्यतन्त्रेषु च । तत् फलं । एषां अस्मिन् पटले प्रोक्तानां यन्त्राणां एकैकस्य यन्त्रस्य सर्वं फलं । तेन हेतुना अत्र अस्मिन् पटले । नामयोजनैः साध्यसाधककर्म्मयोजनैः । अतः अस्मात् । इह पटले । सर्व्वं यन्त्रं ॥ ५८ ॥

प्राक्प्रत्यगित्यादिभिरुदितैः इत्यन्तैस्त्रयोदशभिः श्लोकैर्वज्रलिङ्गाभिधानयन्त्र-

तेषु कोष्ठेषु परितो मार्जयेदष्टसप्ततिम् ।
शिष्टे चतुर्भिस्त्र्यस्रञ्च विदध्याद्दिक्षु पूर्ववत् ॥ ६१ ॥
तेषु तार्त्तीयविद्यान्तु ससाध्यां प्राग्वदालिखेत् ।
शिष्टेषु सप्तनवति द्विशते मध्यतस्तथा ॥ ६२ ॥
सर्वमध्यस्थकोष्ठस्य पार्श्वयोरुभयोरपि ।
कोष्ठानि त्रीणि तिर्य्यक् च समीकृत्य तयोस्तथा ॥ ६३ ॥
उपर्य्यधश्च द्वे द्वे तु समीकुर्य्यात्ततस्तथा ।
तयोरधोर्द्ध्वं च तथा द्वे द्वे कुर्य्यादथैकधा ॥ ६४ ॥

निर्माणविधानमस्मिन् पटले प्रोक्तयन्त्राणामनुभावञ्चोपदिशति। तत्र षट्शतं पञ्चविंशति पञ्चविंशत्यधिकं षट्शतमिति यावत्। तेषु कोष्ठेषु अष्टसप्तति कोष्ठानि प्रतिकोणमित्यर्थः। शिष्टे त्रयोदशाधिकशतत्रयकोष्ठरूपे वज्रे। चतुर्भिः कोष्ठैः। पूर्ववत् एकत्रिक्रमेणेत्यर्थः। तेषु चतुर्षु अस्रेषु। तुः समुच्चये। ससाध्यां साधकसाध्यकर्मोपेतां। प्राग्वत्तथा मायावह्निमध्यांशेषु क्रमादिति यावत्। शिष्टेषु कोष्ठेषु। सर्वमध्यस्थकोष्ठस्य पश्चिमाद्येकादशात्मकतिर्य्यक्पंक्तिस्थ एकविंशतिकोष्ठेषु मध्यकोष्ठस्य। तिर्य्यग्दक्षिणोत्तरं। समीकृत्य एकीकृत्य। तयोः एकीकृतकोष्ठयोः। तथा प्राग्वत्तयोः। तथा यथाधिष्ठानपिण्डिके भवतः। द्वे द्वे कोष्ठे तिर्य्यगिति शेषः। एतदुक्तं भवति पश्चिमादि द्वादशदशमपंक्त्योस्तत्तन्मध्यकोष्ठस्योभयपार्श्वयोः एकैकं मुक्त्वा तदन्तरकोष्ठयो(र्द्वंपत्र)द्वत्तयोर्मार्जयेदिति। ततः अनन्तरं। तथा प्राग्वत्। तयोः एकीकृतकोष्ठद्वयोः। अधोर्द्ध्व दिव्यत्वादध ऊर्द्ध्वमिति यावत्। चः समाहारे। तथा उभयपार्श्वयोः। एतदुक्तं भवति नवमत्रयोदशपंक्त्योस्तत्तन्मध्यकोष्ठस्योभयपार्श्वयोः कोष्ठयोर्द्वयं द्वयं मुक्त्वा तदन्तरकोष्ठयोर्द्वयं द्वयं मार्जयेदिति। तदधश्चोपरि अनन्तरपूर्व्वमेकीकृतयोः कोष्ठयोरधश्चोपरि च। तथाष्टमचतुर्दशपञ्चदशपंक्तिषु तत्तन्मध्यकोष्ठयोरुभयपार्श्वयोः कोष्ठानां त्रयं केवलतिर्य्यग्रेखामार्जनेन। तुर्विशेषे। उपरितनकोष्ठद्वयमार्जनं केवलमूर्द्ध्वत एव तिर्य्यगित्यर्थः। एकैकस्य द्वयं द्वयं

तदधस्थोपरि तथा त्वेकैकञ्च द्वयं द्वयम् ।
एकीकृत्य पुनस्तोर्द्ध्वें द्वे द्वे तु मार्जयेत्तथा ॥ ६५ ॥
ततो माला तदुपरिपार्श्वयोश्च प्रमार्जयेत् ।
दशखण्डानि शिष्टैस्तु मध्ये लिङ्गो भवेत्तथा ॥ ६६ ॥
एवं लिङ्गः समाख्यातश्चत्वारिंशद्भिरेव वै ।
शिष्टानि कोष्ठवज्राणि द्विशतं दश पञ्च च ॥ ६७ ॥
लिङ्गस्य पार्श्वयोर्मृष्टान्येकविंशतियुग्मकम् ।
तस्य लिङ्गस्य मध्यस्थपङ्क्त्यां तार्त्तीयमालिखेत् ॥ ६८ ॥

यथाक्रमतः। एतदुक्तं भवति अष्टमचतुर्दशपञ्चदशपंक्तिषु तत्तन्मध्यकोष्ठस्योभयपार्श्वयोः कोष्ठानां त्रयं त्रयं मुक्त्वा तदनन्तरमेकमेकं कोष्ठं मार्जयेदिति। पुनस्तोर्द्ध्वें पूर्व्वमेकीकृतकोष्ठपंक्तिषूपरितनपंक्त्यामेकमेवेत्यर्थः। द्वे द्वे कोष्ठे अन्तःप्रथममार्जितकोष्ठस्य। तथा तिर्य्यगित्यर्थः। ततः अनन्तरं। उपरिपार्श्वयोः लिङ्गरूपकोष्ठनवकस्येत्यर्थः। दशखण्डानि रेखाभिः खण्डनात् खण्डशब्देन रेखा उच्यते तस्माद्दशभिः खण्डैः नवकोष्ठानि भवन्तीति। दशखण्डमार्जनात् नव कोष्ठान्येकीकृतानीत्यर्थः। शिष्टैर्नवभिः कोष्ठैः। तुर्विशेषे। मध्ये एकीकृतखण्डदशकस्य। तथा इत्यस्य मार्जयेदित्यनेन पूर्व्वेण सम्बन्धः यथा मध्ये शिष्टैर्लिङ्गं भवेत्। तथा नवकोष्ठानि मालावदेकीकुर्य्यादित्यर्थः। एवमुक्तरूपेण चत्वारिंशद्भिः अधिष्ठानमध्यपिण्डिकालिङ्गगतैः कोष्ठैरित्यर्थः। शिष्टानि लिङ्गान्येकीकृतानि च कोष्ठानि मुक्त्वेत्यर्थः। द्विशतं दश पञ्च च अत्र चकारस्य समाहारार्थत्वादेकसंख्याधिकं (स) द्योतयतीति सम्प्रदायः। तस्मात् षोड़शाधिकं शतद्वयमित्यर्थः। पार्श्वयोरुपरि चेत्यर्थः। मृष्टानि एकीकृतानि कोष्ठानि एकविंशतियुग्मकं एकेन विंशतियुग्मं एकचत्वारिंशदित्यर्थः। मध्यस्थपंक्त्यां दशकोष्ठात्मिकायां तार्त्तीयं कूटं। ऊर्द्धादि ऊर्द्धाधःक्रमात् स्थितायां अस्य पंक्त्यामित्यत्रान्वयः। सर्व्वमध्ये अधिष्ठानपिण्डिकयोर्मध्यस्थकोष्ठे। ससाधकसाधकसाध्यकर्म्मोपेतं प्राग्लिखिततार्त्तीयकूटमित्यर्थः। सर्वत्र यन्त्रमाले। लिङ्ग-

ऊर्द्धादि मायामध्यस्थं सर्वमध्ये ससाध्यकम् ।
सर्वत्र तार्त्तीया विद्या लेखनं समुदीरितम् ॥ ६९ ॥
लिङ्गरूपेषु नवसु पार्श्वषट्के तु पूर्ववत् ।
विद्याशेषं समालिख्य प्राग्वदारभ्भतस्तथा ॥ ७० ॥
विद्याद्वितीयभेदोत्थं तद्विंशशतमालिखेत् ।
द्विशस्तत्र यजेद्देवीमावाह्य परिवारकैः ॥ ७१ ॥

रूपेषु पिण्डिकोपरिष्टेषु नवसु कोष्ठेषु। इयं निर्द्धारणे सप्तमी। पार्श्वषट्के प्रतिपार्श्वं त्रित्रिक्रमेण। तुः समुच्चये। पूर्व्ववत् अनन्तरपूर्वोक्तवज्रयन्त्रवत्। विद्याशेषं श्रीविद्यायाः प्रथमकूटं द्वितीयकूटञ्च तद्दक्षिणकोष्ठत्रये वामकोष्ठत्रये च क्रमादिति यावत्। प्राग्वदारभ्भतः कोष्ठवज्रयन्त्रवत्। प्राक्त्र्यस्रान्तर्गत पंक्त्या मध्यकोष्ठमारभ्य तथा प्रादक्षिण्यप्रवेशगत्येति यावत्। तदिति वासनापटले वक्ष्यमाणं सूचयति। विंशशतं विंशत्युत्तरं शतमित्यर्थः। द्विशः पर्य्यायतः तत्र वज्रलिङ्गयन्त्रे। अयमत्र विरचनाक्रमः। प्राक्प्रत्यग्दक्षिणोदक्क समान्तरालं षड्विंशति षड्विंशति सूत्रास्फालनात् पञ्चविंशत्यधिकषट्शतकोष्ठानि निष्पाद्य तेषु प्रतिकोणमष्टसप्तत्यष्टसप्ततिकोष्ठं क्रमेण सम्भूय द्वादशाधिकशतत्रयकोष्ठानि शिष्टं वज्राकारं यथा तथा मार्जयित्वा पुनः शिष्टवज्राकारे त्रयोदशाधिकशतत्रयकोष्ठात्मके प्रतिदिशमेकत्रिकक्रमेण सम्भूय कोष्ठचतुष्टयेनैकैकं त्रिकोणं कृत्वा तेषु तार्त्तीयविद्यां प्राग्वत् साधकसाध्यकर्म्मोपेतां आलिख्य तच्छिष्टसप्तनवत्यधिकशतद्वयकोष्ठेषु पश्चिमादेकादशात्मकसर्व्वमध्यस्थपंक्त्यां तत्सर्व्वमध्यस्थकोष्ठस्य दक्षिणवामपार्श्वयोः तिर्य्यग्रूपेण कोष्ठत्रयं यन्त्रमूर्द्धाधोगतपश्चिमादिद्वादशपंक्तिरूपे तत्तन्मध्यकोष्ठस्योभयपार्श्वयोः कोष्ठद्वयं कोष्ठद्वयं मुक्त्वा तिर्य्यग्रूपेण प्राग्वत् द्वयं द्वयं पश्चिमाद्यष्टमचतुर्दशपञ्चदशपंक्तित्रये तत्तन्मध्यकोष्ठस्योभयपार्श्वयोः कोष्ठत्रयं त्रयं मुक्त्वा त्वेकमेकं कोष्ठं पुनश्चैकोक्तकोष्ठासु पंक्तिषूपरितनपञ्चदशपंक्त्यामेवोभयपार्श्वयोस्तिर्य्यग्रूपेण कोष्ठद्वयं कोष्ठद्वयं ततश्च मालाक्रमेण लिङ्गरूपकोष्ठनवकस्योभयपार्श्वयोरुपरि च दशरेखामार्जनेन नवकोष्ठान्यष्टादशपंक्तिस्थकोष्ठेषु मध्यस्थकोष्ठपञ्चकञ्च सम्भूयैकचत्वारिंशत् कोष्ठानि मध्य चत्वारिंशद्भिः कोष्ठैः साधिष्ठानं लिङ्गं वहिर्वज्रे शिष्टानि षोड़शा-

स्थापयेद्विनियोगेषु प्रोक्तेषु परमेश्वरि ।
नासाध्यमस्ति भुवने यन्त्रैरेतैर्मयोदितैः ॥ ७२ ॥
एकादिद्वयसंवृद्ध्या पार्श्वयोः कोष्ठवर्द्धनम् ।
एकोनविंशकोष्ठान्तं कृत्वा लिङ्गं तथोपरि ॥ ७३ ॥
कृत्वा प्राङ्मध्यतः प्राग्वच्चत्वारिंशद्भिरेव वै ।
तेषु मूलादिपरितो मध्यान्तं विन्यसेत् क्रमात् ॥ ७४ ॥

धिकशतद्वयकोष्ठानि च यथा तथा मार्जयित्वा तल्लिङ्गचत्वारिंशत् कोष्ठमध्य-गतोर्द्धाधःक्रमरूपपंक्तिस्थकोष्ठदशके श्रीविद्यातार्त्तीयखण्डमुक्तप्रकारेणालिख्य तस्य सर्व्वमध्यकोष्ठे लिखिततार्त्तीयविद्याहृल्लेखोदरे साधकं साध्यं कर्म्म च पिण्डिकोपरि नवकोष्ठात्मके दक्षिणपार्श्वस्थकोष्ठत्रये श्रीविद्यायाः प्रथमकूटं वामपार्श्वस्थकोष्ठत्रये द्वितीयकूटञ्च सम्भूय षोड़शसु कोष्ठेषु विलिख्य परि-शिष्टं लिङ्गगतकोष्ठचतुर्विंशत्या सहितेषु चत्वारिंशदधिकशतद्वयकोष्ठेषु प्राक्त्र्यस्रान्तर्गतपंक्त्या मध्यकोष्ठमारभ्य प्रादक्षिण्यप्रवेशगत्या तार्त्तीयविद्या द्वितीयभेदोत्थविंशत्यधिकशतत्रयद्विद्वारमालिखेदिति । परमेश्वरीति देवी-सम्बुद्धिः ॥ ७२ ॥

एकादीत्यादिभिस्तामित्यन्तैरष्टभिः श्लोकै मेरुलिङ्गनिर्म्माणविधानं तत् प्रयोगां-स्तत्फलानि चोपदिशति । तत्र एकादिद्वयसंवृद्ध्या एककोष्ठादि प्रतिपंक्तिकं कोष्ठद्वयकोष्ठद्वयवर्द्धनेन उपर्य्युपरि इति शेषः । एकोनविंशकोष्ठान्तं एकोन-विंशसंख्यकोष्ठपर्य्यन्तं एवं क्रमाभिवृद्ध्या दशमपंक्त्यामेकोनविंशतिकोष्ठानि भवन्ति तदवधीत्यर्थः । प्राग्वत् वज्रलिङ्गोक्तक्रमेण । मध्यतः सर्व्वमध्यपंक्तिमध्य-गतसप्तकोष्ठानुसारेणेत्यर्थः । चः समुच्चये । चत्वारिंशद्भिः कोष्ठैरित्यर्थः । एवाव-धारणे । तेषु कोष्ठेषु । मूलादि सर्वाधःस्थितप्रथमकोष्ठादि । परितः अधिष्ठानो-परितनपंक्तिपर्य्यन्तं प्रादक्षिण्येन । मध्यान्तं मूलादिसप्तःपंक्तिमध्यकोष्ठान्तं विन्यसेदित्यत्रोत्तरश्लोके विद्या इत्यनेन सम्बन्धः । तथा क्रमात् प्रवेशगत्या विंशशतं विंशत्यधिकशतं । प्रिये इति देवीसम्बुद्धिः । लिङ्गस्य मध्यकोष्ठान्तं लिङ्गमध्यकोष्ठपर्य्यन्तं तदधोगतकोष्ठेषु सर्वेषूक्तक्रमात् विन्यस्य तदन्ते तल्लिङ्ग-

विद्याद्वितीयभेदोत्था विद्या विंशशतं प्रिये ।
लिङ्गस्य मध्यकोष्ठान्तं शिष्टं कोणेषु संलिखेत् ॥ ७५ ॥
विधाय चतुरस्रन्तु सूत्रद्वयनिपातनात् ।
सर्वंबाह्ये तदावद्धं तस्योपरि समालिखेत् ॥ ७६ ॥
पंक्तिशः सप्तकोष्ठेषु पर्य्यायादींस्तथार्णकान् ।
नित्यापर्य्यायजनिते पार्श्वयोर्दक्षवामयोः ॥ ७७ ॥

मध्यस्थकोष्ठान्तमिति यावत् । शिष्टं विद्याचतुष्टयं कोणेषु वक्ष्यमाणचतुरस्रकोणेषु वायव्यादिनिर्ऋत्यन्तमिति शेषः । विधाय चतुरस्रं चतुरस्रं विधायेत्यर्थः । तुर्विशेषे । सूत्रद्वयनिपातनात् प्रतिदिशमन्तर्वहिर्विभागेनेत्यर्थः । सर्व्वबाह्ये उक्तरूपस्य बाह्ये । तदावद्धं प्रथमकोष्ठाधोरेखासम्बद्धं । तस्य चतुरस्रस्य उपरि उभयोर्मध्ये इति शेषः । समालिखेदित्यस्योत्तरत्र पर्य्यायादीनित्यनेन सम्बन्धः । सप्तकोष्ठेषु चतुरस्रप्राचीनवीथिस्थसप्तकोष्ठेषु । पर्य्यायादीनित्यत्रादिशब्दो युगघटिकार्णदिननित्यादिविषयः । अर्णकान् वर्णानित्यर्थः । नित्यपर्य्यायजनिते विद्ये । मध्ये सप्तकोष्ठेषु मध्यस्थे । तुः समुच्चये । प्रोक्तक्रमेण लिङ्गाग्रमध्यात् लिङ्गाग्रपंक्तिमध्यकोष्ठमारभ्येत्यर्थः । अभितः प्रादक्षिण्येन । पिण्डिकायां च तदधःस्थितकोष्ठानां प्रागेव विनियुक्तत्वात् । संलिखेदित्यस्योत्तरश्लोके विद्या इत्यनेन सम्बन्धः । तथा प्रवेशगत्या । कृत्वैवमेकलिङ्गमेकलिङ्गं कृत्वेत्यर्थः । तुर्विशेषे । अयमत्रविरचनाक्रमः प्रथममेकं चतुरस्रं कोष्ठं विधाय तदुपर्य्युभयपार्श्वयोः प्रतिपार्श्वमेकैकक्रमात् सम्भूय प्रतिपंक्तिकं कोष्ठद्वयाभिवृद्ध्या सर्व्वमूलादिदशमपंक्त्यामेकोनविंशति कोष्ठानि यथा तथा कृत्वा तत् दशमपंक्त्यामुभयत्र षट् षट् कोष्ठानि मुक्त्वा तन्मध्यस्थकोष्ठसप्तकानुसारेण तदुपरि प्राग्वच्चत्वारिंशद्भिः कोष्ठैः साधिष्ठानपिण्डिकं लिङ्गं तद्बहिस्तदग्रगतदक्षिणोत्तररेखया प्रथमकोष्ठाधःस्थदक्षिणोत्तररेखया च सम्बध्य द्वाविंशतिकोष्ठप्रमाणोपेतं दक्षिणोत्तरमेकैकं सूत्रं पुनरुभयपार्श्वयोर्दशमपंक्तेर्वहिरधार्द्धकोष्ठप्रमाणप्रदेशाद्बहिर्द्वाविंशतिकोष्ठप्रमाणोपेतं प्राक्प्रत्यगेकैकं सूत्रं तद्बहिः परितस्तत्तत्सूत्राग्रावधिकञ्च सम्भूयाष्टभिः सूत्रैः परितः समचतुरस्रद्वयं प्रतिकोणमेकैककोष्ठोपेतं यथा तथा विधाय तत्र प्राग्वद्द्वितीयभेदोत्थं विंशत्यधिकशतविद्यास्वरूपं

मध्ये युगोदयार्णौ तु लिखेत् प्रोक्तक्रमेण वै।
लिङ्गाग्रमध्यादभितः पिण्डिकायाश्च संलिखेत्॥ ७८॥
विद्याः प्रथमभेदोत्थाश्चतुर्विंशतिकास्तथा।
कृत्वैवं मेरुलिङ्गन्तु यन्त्रं तत्रैव तां लिखेत्॥ ७९॥
ममस्तवाञ्छितप्राप्त्यै जयारोग्यायुराप्तये।
पटादौ तत् समालिख्य पूजयेन्नित्यशश्च ताम्॥ ८०॥
प्राक्प्रत्यगदक्षिणोदक्सैकविंशतिसूत्रतः।
चतुःशतानि कोष्ठानि भवन्ति सुसमानि वै॥ ८१॥

मूलकोष्ठमारभ्याधिष्ठानोपरितनपंक्त्यवधि पञ्चदशोत्तरशतसंख्यकोष्ठेषु प्राद-क्षिण्यप्रवेशगत्या तन्मध्यकोष्ठान्तं प्रत्यावरणं षट्त्रिंशदष्टाविंशतिविंशति-चतुर्द्दशदशषड्कक्रमादावरणसप्तके च तदनन्तरमेकं लिङ्गाधिष्ठानपिण्डिका-न्तरालमध्यकोष्ठे च ततः परिशिष्टविद्याचतुष्टयं वहिश्चतुरस्रकोणचतुष्टये वायव्यादिनैऋत्यन्तमेकैकक्रमाच्चैवं सम्भूय विंशत्यधिकं शतं विद्या विन्यस्यानन्तरं तल्लिङ्गपिण्डिकाकोष्ठचतुर्विंशतके लिङ्गाग्रपंक्तिमध्यकोष्ठमारभ्य पिण्डिकाधःस्थ पंक्तिपर्य्यन्तं प्रादक्षिण्यप्रवेशगत्या त्वमुक्तक्रमं तार्त्तीयविद्याचतुरक्षरभेदांश्चतुर्विं-शतिमालिख्यानन्तरं वहिश्चतुरस्रस्य प्राचीनवीथीं समान्तरालां सप्तधा विभज्य तेषु सप्तसु कोष्ठेषु पंक्तिशो वामपार्श्वस्थकोष्ठत्रये क्रमात् पर्य्यायनित्याविद्याक्षर-त्रयं दक्षिणपार्श्वस्थकोष्ठत्रये दिननित्याविद्याक्षरत्रयं मध्यकोष्ठे युगार्णसहितं घटिकार्णञ्च विन्यसेदिति। तत्र यन्त्रे। एवावधारणे। तां ललितां सपरिवारां। पटादावित्यत्रादिशब्दः कनकरजतताम्राश्मादिविषयः। तद्यन्त्रं नित्यशः प्रत्यनु-दिनं। तां ललितां प्राग्वत्॥ ८०॥

प्राक्प्रत्यगित्यादिभिः इष्टदा इत्यन्तैः षड्भिः श्लोकैर्मेरुलिङ्गयन्त्रनिर्म्माण विधानादिकमुपदिशति। तत्र सुसमानि आयामविस्तारवैषम्याभावात्। तस्य कोष्ठसमुदायरूपस्य। एकपार्श्वाधोभागे अधः पंक्त्यामेकस्मिन् पार्श्वे। ततः तस्याः पंक्तेरित्यर्थः। चः समुच्चये। उपरि उपर्य्युपरीति यावत्। षट्सप्तत्येकमेका-दशावधि षट्सप्ताष्टनवदशैकादशसंख्यावधीति यावत्। मार्ज्जयेत् कोष्ठानीत्यर्थः

तस्यैकपार्श्वाधोभागे पञ्च कोष्ठानि मार्जयेत् ।
ततश्चोपरि षट्सप्तेत्येवमेकादशावधि ॥ ८२ ॥
मार्जयेदुपरिष्टाच्च तस्यैव प्रतिलोमकम् ।
तथा कुर्य्यात् पार्श्वयोश्च तेनाधिष्ठानपीण्डिके ॥ ८३ ॥
भवतश्चोपरिष्टात्तु पञ्चविंशतिकोष्ठकैः ।
लिङ्गमन्यानि पार्श्वस्थमार्जनाद्भवति प्रिये ॥ ८४ ॥
अधिष्ठाने पिण्डिकायां तद्द्वितीयविभेदजाः ।
लिङ्गे प्रथमभेदोत्थस्तन्मध्यस्थे स्ववाञ्छितम् ॥ ८५ ॥

उपरिष्टात् अष्टमादिषु षट्सु पंक्तिष्विति शेषः । चः समुच्चये । तस्य पञ्चषड़ादिक्रमस्य । एवावधारणे । प्रतिलोमकं दशादिपञ्चकान्तक्रमादित्यर्थः । तथा कुर्य्यात् यथाधिष्ठानपिण्डिके षष्ट्या षष्ट्या कोष्ठैस्तत्र लेख्यत्वेन वक्ष्यमाणविंशत्यधिकशतविद्याभेदसमसंख्यकोष्ठे भवतः । पार्श्वमन्यत्तेनाधिष्ठानपिण्डिके भवतः । येन क्रमेण मार्जनादधिष्ठानपिण्डिके भवतः । तेन क्रमेण तदन्यत् पार्श्वं मार्जयेदिति । चः समुच्चये उपरिष्टात्त्रयोदशपंक्तेरित्यर्थः । तुर्विशेषे । पञ्चविंशतिकोष्ठकैः लिङ्गं अस्योत्तरत्र भवतीत्यत्रान्वयः । अन्यानि लिङ्गरूपाणि तानि कोष्ठानि पार्श्वस्थमार्जनात् पार्श्वस्थकोष्ठमार्जनादवशिष्टानीत्यर्थः । प्रिये इति देवीसम्बुद्धिः । तद्द्वितीयविभेदजाः विद्या इत्यर्थः । लिङ्गे पञ्चविंशतिकोष्ठात्मके प्रथमभेदोत्था तार्त्तीयस्येति शेषः । तन्मध्यस्थे लिङ्गमध्यस्थे कोष्ठे । स्ववाञ्छितं प्राग्वत् साध्यादिकं । मध्ये अधिष्ठानपिण्डिकयोरन्तरालस्थकोष्ठत्रये । तद्दिनजां प्राग्वद्विद्याप्राप्तिदिनजां प्रयोगदिनजां वा । अनघे इति देवीसम्बुद्धिः । तत्र यन्त्रे । अयमत्र विरचनाक्रमः । प्राक्प्रत्यग्दक्षिणोदक्समान्तरालमेकविंशत्येकविंशतिसूत्रस्फालनाच्चतुःशतानि कोष्ठानि निष्पाद्य तदधःपंक्त्यामेकपार्श्वे पञ्चकोष्ठानि तस्मिन्नेव पार्श्वे द्वितीयादिसप्तमपंक्त्यवधि षट्सप्ताष्टनवदशैकादशकोष्ठाणि च मार्जयित्वा पुनस्तस्मिन्नेव पार्श्वे अष्टमादित्रयोदशान्तपंक्तिषट्के दशनवाष्टसप्तषट्पञ्चकोष्ठानि पुनस्तस्मिन्नेव पार्श्वे चतुर्दशाद्यष्टादशान्तपंक्तिपञ्चके दशदश कोष्ठानि तदुपरिगतमेकोनविंशविंशात्मकं पंक्तिद्वयं च

मध्ये तद्दिनजां विद्यामिति प्रोक्तं तवानघे।
महालिङ्गाभिधं यन्त्रं तत्र पूजाखिलेष्टदा ॥ ८६ ॥
समत्रिरेखां निष्पाद्य योनिं तस्यास्तु मध्यतः।
तत्तत्सूत्रवशात् कुर्य्याद्दश त्रिषु तथा समम् ॥ ८७ ॥
एवं कृतेत्र परितो लिखेत्ता विंशतां शतम्।
शिष्टमध्यत्रिकोणे तु लिखेद्वाञ्छितमात्मनः ॥ ८८ ॥

मार्जयेत्। अनन्तरमन्यस्मिन् पार्श्वेऽपि यथा षष्ट्या षष्ठ्या कोष्ठैः तदुपरिगतमेकोनविंशविंशात्मकपंक्तिद्वयं अधिष्ठानपिण्डिके भवतस्तथावशिष्टकोष्ठानि युक्त्या मार्जयेत्। एवं कृते षष्ठ्या षष्ट्या कोष्ठैरधिष्ठानपिण्डिके त्रिभिः कोष्ठैः तयोरन्तरालं पञ्चविंशतिभिः कोष्ठैर्लिङ्गमप्येवं क्रमान्महालिङ्गं निष्पाद्याधिष्ठानपिण्डिकयोः पश्चिमपंक्तिस्थमध्यकोष्ठादि प्रादक्षिण्यप्रवेशगत्या विद्याद्वितीयभेदांस्तल्लिङ्गगतपञ्चविंशतिकोष्ठेषु अग्रपंक्तिमध्यकोष्ठादिप्रादक्षिण्यप्रवेशगत्या विद्याप्रथमभेदांस्तन्मध्यकोष्ठे स्ववाञ्छितमधिष्ठानपिण्डिकयोरन्तरालकोष्ठत्रये पंक्त्या दिननित्याद्यालिखेदिति ॥ ८६ ॥

समत्रिरेखामित्यादिभिरनुभावत इत्यन्तैस्त्रिभिः श्लोकैर्योनिचक्रनिर्म्माणादिकमुपदिशति। तत्र योनिं स्वाभिमुखत्र्यस्रं। तस्या योन्याः। तुर्विशेषे। मध्यतः मध्ये। तत्तत्सूत्रवशात्तत्तद्रेखानुगुणतः कुर्य्यात्। दश सूत्राणि। त्रिषु सूत्रेषु। तथा यथैकविंशत्यधिकशतयोनयः सम्भवन्ति तथेत्यर्थः। समं समान्तरालम् अन्तरालसाम्यात्तत्र मर्मणामसम्भवात्। अत्र योनिचक्रे। परितः अग्रादिप्रादक्षिण्येन। ताः द्वितीयभेदजा विद्याः। तुः समुच्चये। अयमत्र विरचनाक्रमः स्वाभिमुखं समत्रिरेखात्मिकां योनिमुक्तवन्निष्पाद्य तद्रेखात्रयं दशभिर्दशभिश्चिह्नैः समान्तरालमेकादशधा विभज्य तद्रेखाचिह्नेषु चिह्नाच्चिह्नं तत्तत्सूत्रानुगुण्याद् यथा मर्मभेदं सम्भूय त्रिंशत्सूत्रास्फालनादेकविंशत्यधिकशतयोन्यात्मकं चक्रं विधाय तद्योनिष्वग्रादिप्रादक्षिण्यप्रवेशगत्या तार्त्तीयविद्याद्वितीयभेदान् शिष्टमध्ययोन्यां स्ववाञ्छितञ्च विन्यसेदिति। तत्र योनिचक्रे। तां ललितां विद्यां सपरिवारामित्यर्थः। प्रागव-

तत्र तामर्च्चयेत् प्राग्वत् स्थापयेच्च तथा तथा।
तत्र स्वेष्टमवाप्नोति योनिचक्रानुभावतः॥ ८९॥
समत्रिरेखं निष्पाद्य चास्रं योनिञ्च सङ्गतम्।
तत्र तिर्य्यक् चतुःसूत्रपातनादन्यतस्तथा॥ ९०॥
तिर्य्यक्सूत्रं मार्जयित्वा पूर्व्वशृङ्गात्तथाभितः।
प्रवेशगत्या विलिखेत्तास्वतुर्व्विंशतिं क्रमात्॥ ९१॥
विलिख्य शिष्टवज्रस्थं विलिखेन्निजवाञ्छितम्।
तत्र तां पूजयेद्देवीं पूर्णास्विष्टार्थसिद्धये॥ ९२॥

दुष्टविनियोगेषु। चः समुच्चये। तथा तथा यथा यथा प्रयुक्तं तथा तथेत्यर्थः॥८९॥

समत्रिरेखमित्यादिभिः सिद्धये इत्यन्तैस्त्रिभिः श्लोकैर्वज्रवज्रयन्त्रनिर्माणविधानादिक्रमुपदिशति। तत्र त्र्यस्रं जर्द्ध्वमुखत्रिकोणं। योनिं अधोमुखत्रिकोणं। चः समुच्चये। सङ्गतम् अन्योन्यमूर्द्ध्वाधःक्रमेण तिर्य्यग्रेखयैकयैवोभयं कुर्य्यादित्यर्थः। तत्र चक्रे। अन्यतः जर्द्ध्वगतत्र्यस्रवामरेखामारभ्याधोगतयोनिदक्षिणरेखावधि तद्दक्षिणरेखामारभ्येतरवामरेखावधि। तथा समान्तरालमिति यावत्। तिर्य्यक्सूत्रं त्र्यस्रयोन्योर्मध्यस्थं। पूर्व्वशृङ्गात् प्राग्वद् वज्रवजकोष्ठादारभ्येत्यर्थः। तथा प्रादक्षिण्येन। ताः प्रथमभेदविद्याः। शिष्टवज्रस्थं मध्यवज्रस्थमित्यर्थः। अयमत्र विरचनाक्रमः। मध्ये हंसपदं विधाय तत् सन्दंशस्थानावगाहि प्राक्प्रत्यग् ब्रह्मसूत्रं प्राग्वदभितो जनितमत्स्यद्वयावगाहि याम्योदक्सूत्रञ्च आस्फाल्य तत्सन्दंशस्थानमारभ्य याम्योदक्सूत्रोभयपार्श्वयोः समप्रमाणेन चिह्नद्वयं कृत्वा तच्चिह्नयोरन्तरे प्रमाणोपेतं सूत्रयोर्द्वयं द्वयं तच्चिह्नद्वयमारभ्य प्राक्पश्चिमयोर्ब्रह्मसूत्रावधि सम्भूय सूत्रचतुष्टयं यथा त्र्यस्रयोन्यात्मकचक्रं तथास्फाल्य तद्ब्रह्मसूत्रं तिर्य्यग्रेखां च मार्जयित्वा त्र्यस्रयोन्योर्वामदक्षिणरेखयोर्द्वयं द्वयं चतुर्भिश्चिह्नैः पञ्चधा पञ्चधा विभज्य तच्चिह्नक्रमवशात्त्र्यस्रवामरेखादि योनिदक्षिणरेखान्तं त्र्यस्रदक्षिणरेखादि योनिवामरेखान्तञ्च सम्भूयाष्टसूत्रास्फालनेन तन्मध्ये पञ्चविंशति वज्रकोष्ठानि विधाय तत्प्राक्शृङ्गमारभ्य प्रादक्षिण्यप्रवेशगत्या श्रीविद्यातार्त्तीयप्रथमभेदान् शिष्टमध्ये निजवाञ्छितञ्च विन्यसेदिति। तत्र वज्रवज्रयन्त्र। पूर्णासु पञ्चमीदशमीपञ्चदशीषु॥ ९२॥

तथा विधाय दशभिर्द्दशभिः सूत्रपातनैः।
द्वितीयभेदाः विलिखेत्तथा साध्यसमन्विताः॥ ९३ ॥
तत्रापि पूजनाद्यैस्तु सिद्ध्येयुः निजवाञ्छिताः।
एवमूह्यं तृतीयोत्थविद्याभिरपि कल्पयेत्॥ ९४ ॥
तेपि वाञ्छितसंसिद्धीः कुर्य्युरेव सुनिश्चितम्।
कोष्ठयन्त्रविभेदानि शृणु वक्ष्ये यथाविधि॥ ९५ ॥

तथेत्यादिना सुनिश्चितमित्यन्तेनार्द्धाद्येन श्लोकद्वयेन महावज्रवज्राभिधानं यन्त्रमेवमूह्यपरतोयं यन्त्रनिर्म्माणविधानादिकञ्चोपदिशति। तत्र तथा विधाय प्रागन्योन्यसङ्गतं त्र्यस्त्रयोनिं विधाय। द्वितीयभेदाः विद्याः। तथा शिष्टमध्ये। अयमत्र विरचनाक्रमः। प्रागवदन्योन्यसङ्गतं त्र्यस्त्रयोनिचक्रं विधाय तन्मध्ये प्रागव द्दशसूत्रास्फालनादेकविंशत्यधिकशतवज्रकोष्ठानि निष्पाद्य प्राक्त्र्यस्त्रमारभ्य प्रादक्षिण्यप्रवेशगत्या विद्याद्वितोयभेदान् शिष्टमध्ये स्ववाञ्छितञ्चालिखेदिति। तत्र महावज्रवज्रयन्त्रे। पूजनाद्यैरित्यत्रादिशब्दः स्थापनादिविषयः। एवमुक्तप्रकारेण। तृतीयोत्थविद्याभिः तार्त्तीयविद्यात्तृतीयभेदविद्याभिः। ऊहनप्रकारे त्वेकं यन्त्रमुदाहरणत्वेन लिख्यते। प्रागवत्त्र्यस्त्रं योनिचक्रं विधाय तन्मध्ये षड्विंशतिषड्विंशतिसूत्रास्फालनादेकोनत्रिंशदधिकसप्तशतं वज्रकोष्ठानि विधाय तत्र प्रागगतशृङ्गादिप्रादक्षिण्यप्रवेशगत्या वासनापटले वक्ष्यमाणतार्त्तीयविद्यात्तृतोयभेदान् विंशत्यधिकं सप्तशतं परिशिष्टेषु पुनर्नवसु कोष्ठेषु त्रित्रिकोष्ठक्रमेण श्रीविद्याकूटत्रयं मध्यस्थतार्त्तीयकूटे प्रागवत् स्वमनीषितं च विन्यसेदिति। एवं कोष्ठवज्रादिष्वपि ऊह्यकोष्ठानि परिकल्प्य विद्याभेदान् विषमान् न्यसेत्। ते ऊह्य परिकल्पिता यन्त्रभेदाः। एवावधारणे॥ ९४ ॥

कोष्ठत्यादिभिरागमे इत्यन्तैरर्द्धाद्यैः पञ्चभिः श्लोकैर्विषमसमकोष्ठचतुरस्रचक्रेषु पंक्तिस्थमनीषितसंख्यमङ्कानालिख्य तदनुरूपसंख्यविद्याकूटलेखनादनन्तानि यन्त्राण्यमोषां सर्वेषां तन्त्रान्तरोक्तत्वञ्चोपदिशति। तत्र यथाविधीत्यनेन कोष्ठेषु विवक्षितसंख्याकलेखनस्य तन्त्रान्तरोक्तत्वं द्योतयति। नवषोडशकोष्ठादि नवकोष्ठं षोडशकोष्ठं षोडशकोष्ठचक्रं चारभ्येति यावत्। सम्बधंश पूर्वोक्तपूर्वोक्तचक्रवाह्ये परितः। विषमं विषमसंख्यकोष्ठात्मकं चतुरस्रं। समं

नवषोड़शकोष्ठादि संवर्द्धा विषमं समम् ।
तेष्वङ्कानि समं कृत्वा पंक्तौ तेषु समालिखेत् ॥ ९६ ॥

समसंख्यकोष्ठात्मकं चतुरस्रं । तेषु चक्रेषु । समं समसंख्यं कृत्वा तन्त्रान्तरोक्त-क्रमादित्यर्थः । तेष्वित्येतत् पंक्ताविति पूर्व्वत्र समालिखदित्युत्तरत्र चान्वेति । तेन पंक्तौ स्थितेषु काष्ठेष्वित्येकं तेषु विद्याभेदान् समालिखेदित्यन्यः । तेषां कोष्ठानां । मध्यस्थकोष्ठतः विषमकोष्ठे चतुरस्रे सर्व्वमध्यस्थकोष्ठे समकोष्ठे चतुरस्रे मध्यस्थकोष्ठचतुष्टये च । सर्व्वमेभिरसाध्याभावात् । अयमत्र विरचना-क्रमः । प्राक्प्रत्यगुदक्चिणादक्चतुःपञ्चसूत्रास्फालनाच्च क्रमान्नवकोष्ठात्मकं षोड़श-कोष्ठात्मकं चक्रं विषमं समञ्च विधाय तत्तत्परितस्तयाश्च प्रतिदिशमेकैकपंक्ति-वर्द्धनक्रमात् सम्भूय पंक्तिचतुष्टयपंक्तिचतुष्टयवर्द्धनेन विषमसमसंख्यकोष्ठात्मक-समचतुरस्राणि चक्राणि स्वाभिमतानुगुणं चिह्नं निष्पाद्य तेषु प्रतिपंक्तिकं कोष्ठेषु वाञ्छितसंख्यादिवाञ्छितसंख्यादिक्रमेण यदङ्कादूर्द्धाधःपंक्तिक्रमात्तिर्य्यक्पंक्ति-क्रमाद्द्विविधपंक्तिकोणक्रमाच्च समसंख्यमालिख्य तत्तत्कोष्ठेषु तत्तदङ्कानुगुणं तात्तीयविद्याभेदेष्वेकमेकमालिख्य मध्ये निजवाञ्छितं चालिखेदिति । अत्राङ्कानां लेखनक्रमस्यातिरहस्योपि पारंपर्य्याविच्छित्त्यर्थं श्रीनाथपादाज्ञया यथासम्प्रदायं विलिख्यते । अत्र विषमभद्रालेखनक्रमे अध्यर्द्धश्लोके ।

विषमे विलिखेद्भद्रे भुजमध्यात् स्वदक्षिणात् ।
इष्टादिष्टोत्तरैरङ्कै (रेकै) र्द्धनजाद्युत्तरैस्तु वा ॥
कोष्ठानि पूरयेन् मन्त्रिगत्या पतति चेद्बहिः ।
प्रतिराशेरूर्द्धकोष्ठे लिखेदङ्कमनन्तरम् ॥
द्विधाप्यालिख्य कोष्टाङ्कः संस्थाप्य पूर्ववामतः । इति ।

अत्र विषमभद्रादिलक्षणमुत्तरत्र वक्ष्यति । विषमे भद्रे ऊर्द्धाधोरूप-तस्तिर्य्यग्रूपतश्च विषमे कोष्ठे पंक्तिकल्पिते समचतुरस्रचक्रे । भुजमध्यात् स्वदक्षिणात् स्वस्य सर्व्वदक्षिणपार्श्वस्थपंक्तिकाष्ठेषु सर्व्वमध्यस्थकोष्ठादारभ्या-ङ्कान् लिखेदिति । इष्टादिष्टोत्तरैः परिकल्पितयोरिष्टमादौ विलिख्य ततः प्रतिकोष्ठमुत्तराधिकै (भिधे)रेकैरङ्कैर्धनजाद्युत्तरैस्तु वा अभीष्टसंख्याध-नात्प्रचेराद्युत्तरैर्वा एकपंक्तिधनसमुदायेन आद्युत्तरानयनं वक्ष्यति । तदा-

विद्यात्तृतीयभेदोत्थांस्तत्तदङ्कानुगुण्यतः
मनोषितञ्च संलिख्य तेषां मध्यस्थकोष्ठतः ॥ ९७ ॥
विदध्याद्दाञ्छितं सर्व्वं तैर्यन्त्रैः कल्पितैस्तथा ।
वश्याकर्षणविद्वेषस्तम्भनोच्चाटनादिकम् ॥ ९८ ॥

दुग्रत्तैरङ्कैरित्यर्थः। काष्ठानि पूरयेदित्यस्य अङ्कैरित्यनेनान्वयः। मन्त्रिगत्या पूर्व्वलिखितपंक्तिकोष्ठानन्तरानन्तरदक्षिणपंक्त्यामूर्द्ध्वतः सचिवगतिकोष्ठेऽनन्तरमनन्तरमङ्कं लिखेदित्यर्थः। पतन्ति चेद्बहिः सर्व्वदक्षिणपंक्तिकोष्ठे सर्व्वोर्द्ध्व पंक्तिकोष्ठे चालिखिते सतीत्यर्थः। द्विधापीत्यादि मन्त्रिगत्या च। प्रतिराशिगत्या लब्धे स्थाने सति लेखनीयमनन्तरमङ्कपूर्व्वकं लिखितकोष्ठस्य वामकोष्ठे लिखेदित्यर्थः। एतदुक्तं भवति विषमभद्रे निजसर्व्वदक्षिणपंक्तिमध्यस्थकोष्ठे आद्यमङ्कं विन्यस्य तिर्य्यक्पंक्तौ सर्व्ववामकोष्ठस्योर्द्ध्वकोष्ठे द्वितीयमङ्कं सर्व्वाधःस्थपंक्तिमध्यकोष्ठे तृतीयं तद्वामे चतुर्थं पश्चात् सचिवगत्या चालिख्य उपरितनकोष्ठेष्वेकैकमस्मिन् लिखिते सति अनन्तरमङ्कं तत्प्रतिराशिर्दक्षिणकोष्ठे विलिख्य ततः सचिवगत्या विलिखेत्। एवमुभयतोप्यलब्धस्थाने स्वपूर्व्वलिखितकोष्ठस्य वामकोष्ठात् प्रागवद्विलेखनात् सर्व्वतः साम्यं भवतीति। विषमगर्भलेखने चाद्वीयं श्लोकचतुष्टयम्।

गर्भे तु विषमे वर्गचतुष्के वज्रतो लिखेत् ॥
वर्गपंक्तिं त्रिभिर्हृत्वा फले त्वेकं विनिक्षिपेत् ।
शेषश्चेत्तत्समं कोष्ठं व्यत्यस्येत् प्रतिपंक्तिकम् ॥
आद्यन्तवर्गयोरूर्द्धाधःपंक्तिषु यथाक्रमम् ।
अयं विशेषो व्यत्यस्ते विद्यात्तद्वर्गपंक्तितः ॥
त्रिभिर्हृतफलं कोष्ठं पूर्वं तत् कर्णयोः क्रमात् ।
व्यत्यस्य शेषकोष्ठानि कर्णादितरतस्तथा ॥
द्वितीयफलशेषो यस्तत्संख्यां पंक्तिमन्ययोः ।
व्यत्यस्येद्वर्गयोस्तिर्य्यक् समाङ्कं सर्व्वपंक्तयः ॥ इति ॥

अस्यार्थः। गर्भे तु विषमे विषमभद्रचतुष्टयसम्पाते विषमगर्भः तस्मिन्। वज्रतो लिखेत् अस्मिन् गर्भचतुष्टये अभीष्टमेकं प्रथमं संकल्प्य तत्कोणस्थं द्वितीयं तत्तत्पार्श्वस्थं तृतीयं तत्कोणस्थं चतुर्थं संकल्प्य प्रतिवर्गं विषमभद्रोक्तक्रमादङ्कान-

मुत्क्रमाद्दिलिखेदित्यर्थः । वर्गपंक्तिष्वपीत्यादि । एषु चतुष्कवर्गेषु एकपंक्ति-संख्यां त्रिभिर्हृत्वा लब्धं फलं क्वचित् संस्थाप्य भागहारशेषश्चेदेकमेतत् फले योज्यं तदाज्यं फलं सम्भवति । तत्र फलसंख्यानि काष्ठानि प्रथमचतुर्थवर्गयोरूर्द्ध्वाधः पंक्तिषु प्रतिपंक्ति तत्तत्पंक्तिकोष्ठक्रमानतिलङ्घनेन विन्यस्येदित्यर्थः । अयं विशेष इत्यादिनार्द्धाद्यनेकेन व्यत्यस्तकोष्ठविशेषः कथितः । यथा एकवर्ग-पंक्तिसंख्यां द्विगुणीकृत्य त्रिभिर्विभज्य तत्फलं द्वितीयसंज्ञं भवति । शेषसंख्या क्वचित् स्थातव्या तत्र द्वितीयफलमुभयकर्णकोष्ठेष्वेकानुत्क्रमेण प्रागेव व्यत्यस्य तत्तत्पंक्तिषु प्रथमफलोपान्तसंख्यावशिष्टसंख्या क्वचित् स्थातव्या । तया तावत् स्वकर्मकोष्ठव्यतिरिक्तकोष्ठेष्वङ्कान् प्राग्वत् क्रमात् व्यत्यस्येत् । तद्वितीयेत्यादि-पूर्व्वस्थापिता द्वितीयफलशेषसंख्या यावत् संख्यामभीष्टपंक्तिद्वयत्ततीयवर्गयोस्ति-र्य्यग्रूपासु पंक्तिषु पंक्तिकोष्ठक्रमानतिलङ्घनेन व्यत्यस्येदित्यर्थः । एवं कृते सर्व्वतः साम्यं भवतीत्यर्थः । विषमगर्भलङ्घने लघूपायश्लोकद्वयं ।

> यद्वान्त्यफलसंख्यातां पंक्तिमारभ्य पंक्तिशः ।
> स्वकामाग्रफलसंख्यातः तिर्य्यग् व्यत्यस्य तत्परम् ॥
> क्रमादुभयकोणान्तं कोणान्येवोभयोरतः ।
> आद्यन्तवर्गयोः प्राग्वद्व्यत्यस्येदन्यवर्गयोः ॥

अस्यार्थः । सर्व्वप्रथमचतुर्थवर्गयोस्तिर्य्यग्रूपपंक्तिषु ऊर्द्ध्वपंक्तिमधः-पंक्तिं वा समारभ्य गणयित्वा तास्वेव पंक्तिषु एकहीनाद्यफलसंख्यां पंक्तिं तिर्य्यग्रूपतयान्योन्यं पंक्तिशः प्राग्वद्व्यत्यस्यानन्तरमेकां पंक्तिमुभयकर्णकोष्ठा-वधि व्यत्यस्य तदवशिष्टपंक्तिषूभयकोष्ठस्थानङ्कानेव व्यत्यस्येत् । एवं कृते प्रथमचतुर्थवर्गयोरूर्द्ध्वाधःपंक्तिषु प्रतिपंक्ति प्रथमफलसंख्यकोष्ठान्येव व्यत्यस्तानि भवन्ति । द्वितीयतृतीयवर्गयोः पूर्व्वोक्तद्वितीयफलशेषसंख्यापंक्तिमपि तिर्य्यग्व्य-त्यस्येदित्यर्थः । समभद्रलेखने अर्द्धश्लोकः ।

> समे भद्रे वतानङ्कान् पूर्व्वमश्वस्य वर्त्मना ।
> यस्यैवैकान्तरेणाथ पुनस्तस्य च संलिखेत् ॥
> तत्तच्छिरस्था वान्त्यादितद्दत्तद्दगजाध्वना । इति ॥

अस्यार्थः । षोडशकोष्ठात्मके समभद्रे स्ववामभागाधःस्थकोष्ठे आदिम-मङ्कं विन्यस्य तस्मादश्वमार्गेण ऊर्द्ध्वादि द्वितीयतिर्य्यक्पंक्तौ वामतो द्वितीयकोष्ठे द्वितीयमङ्कं तत् पंक्तावेव सर्व्वदक्षिणकोष्ठे तृतीयं सर्व्वाधःस्थ पंक्तौ वामतस्तृ-

आयुरारोग्यविजयं विभूत्याद्यञ्च सिध्यति ।
स्थापनाद्धारणाच्चान्यैरुपायैः साधकोनिशम् ॥ ६६ ॥

तीयकोष्ठे चतुर्थञ्च विन्यस्य विलोमगत्या चतुर्थादिप्रथमान्ताङ्कोपरितनोपरिमन-कोष्ठेषु पञ्चमाद्यष्टमान्तानङ्कान् विन्यस्य तदष्टमादिप्रथमाङ्कोपर्य्युपलक्षित कोष्ठानां गजमार्गगत्या तेष्वष्टसु कोष्ठेषु नवमादिशिष्टाष्टकं विलिखेदिति ।

समगर्भविन्यासेऽर्द्धाद्यश्लोकः ।

समगर्भेपि वै कृत्वा वर्गान् षोड़शभिः पदैः ।
प्रतिवर्गे चतुःकोष्ठे पुर्व्वोक्तक्रमतो लिखेत् ॥
अन्त्यादि तत्तच्छिरसि गजमार्गेण चान्यतः ॥ इति ॥

अस्यार्थः । षोड़शभिः षोड़शभिः कोष्ठैरेकमेकं वर्गं प्रतिकल्प्य प्रतिवर्गं सम भद्रोक्तप्रक्रियया चतुरश्चतुरोनुक्रमात् प्रतिलोमक्रमात् क्रमेण विन्यस्य पश्चात्त-दन्त्याङ्कादिप्रथमाङ्कान्तां व्युत्क्रमात्तत्तत्गजमार्गल्लिखितकोष्ठेषु शिष्टाङ्कान् क्रमाद्विलिखेत् इति ।

कोष्ठाष्टकक्रमात् प्राग्वत् प्रतिवर्गं लिखेत्तु वा ।

इत्यर्द्धेन प्रक्रियान्तरेणैतदुक्तं भवति । समगर्भे तु भद्रप्रोक्तवत् प्रतिवर्गं मङ्का-नामष्टकं अष्टकं प्रथमं विन्यस्य अन्त्यवर्गे लिखिताल्यान्त्याङ्कादि प्रथमवर्गाल्लिखित-प्रथमाङ्कान्तं विलोमतस्तत्तत् गजमार्गेण शिष्टाङ्कान् विलिखेदिति ।

उद्दिष्टाङ्के पंक्तिकोष्ठहृते लब्धं पुनर्हरेत् ।
ह्येकसर्वपदार्द्धेन फलशेषौ च पादिकौ ॥

इत्यर्द्धाभ्यामेकैकपंक्तावुद्दिष्टधनस्य आद्युत्तरानयनप्रकारः कथितः । यथा उद्दिष्टाङ्कमेकपंक्तिकोष्ठसंख्यया विभज्य तत्तत्फलं सर्व्वपंक्तिकोष्ठे स्यात् । पंक्तिस्थौ संख्यन्त्वेकमपास्य तदर्द्धीकृत्य तत्संख्यया विभजेत् । तत्तत्फलमुत्तरं भवति भागहारशेषश्चादिर्भवतीति ।

ह्येकसर्वपदार्द्धश्च यमादिषु युतं पुनः ।
गुणयेत् पंक्तिकोष्ठे स्यात् पंक्तिकोष्ठेषु तत्फलम् ।

इत्यर्द्धाभ्यामिष्टादिष्टोत्तरं लिखितसर्वभद्रेष्वेकैकपंक्तिस्थसमुदयाङ्कानयनं कथितं । अस्यायमर्थः । तत्र भद्रं सर्वं पंक्तिकोष्ठसंख्यास्त्वेकमपास्य तदर्द्धीकृत्य तत्संख्यया संगुणय्य तस्मिन्नादि संयोज्य तदेकपंक्तिकोष्ठसंख्यया गुणयेत् । तत्फलमेक-पंक्तिस्थाङ्कः समुदायो भवतीति ।

इति देव्या यन्त्रभेदास्तवोक्ताः सर्व्वसिद्धिदाः ।
अशेषं देवि ते प्रोक्तं यन्त्रसिद्धाभिधागमे ॥ १०० ॥
ईश्वरात्ममयो व्याप्तिरिति सम्यक् समीरिता ।
अस्या निफालनाच्चित्ते तत्तत्त्वं स्वात्मसात् कृतम् ॥

इति षोड़शनित्यातन्त्रे श्रीकादिमते त्रयस्त्रिंशत् पटलम् ॥ ३३ ॥ ० ॥

त्र्यादिद्विद्व्युत्तरं भद्रं विषमं पंक्तिकोष्ठतः ।
चतुश्चतुष्टयं षट्कं भद्रं विषमगर्भकम् ॥
तद्वच्चतुष्कं पंक्तीनां भद्रं स्यात् समगर्भकम् ।

इत्यर्द्धाधेन श्लोकेन विषमभद्रादिलक्षणं कथितं । प्रतिबाहु त्रित्रिकोष्ठपंक्त्यादि-द्विद्विकोष्ठपंक्त्युत्तरचतुरस्रं विषमभद्रसंज्ञं भवति । प्रतिबाहु षट् षट्कोष्ठ-पंक्त्यादि चतुश्चतुःकोष्ठपंक्त्युत्तरं भद्रं विषमगर्भसंज्ञं तद्वच्चतुश्चतुःकोष्ठपंक्त्यादि-चतुश्चतुष्कोष्ठ पंक्त्युत्तरं भद्रं समगर्भसंज्ञं चेति । अथ मूलग्रन्थव्याख्या लिख्यते । उच्चाटनादिकं इत्यादिशब्दो निधनादिविषयः। विभूत्याद्यमित्यत्र आद्यशब्दो भूमग्रादि विषयः । अन्यैरभिषेकादिभिः । देवीति सम्बुद्धिः । प्राक्तं प्रागेवेति शेषः । यन्त्रसिद्धाभिधागमे यन्त्रसिद्धिसंज्ञे आगमे ॥ १०० ॥ ० ॥

इति षोड़शनित्यातन्त्रेषु श्रीकादिमताख्यस्य परिपूर्णस्य तन्त्रस्य प्रपञ्चसार सिंहराजप्रकाशाभिधानेन सुभगानन्दनाथेन विरचितायां मनोरमा-ख्यायां व्याख्यायां लिङ्गयन्त्रप्रकाशनपरं त्रयस्त्रिंशं पटलं परिपूर्णं परामृष्टम् ॥ ३३ ॥ ॐ तत्सत् ॥

ग्रन्थसंख्या—त्रयस्त्रिंशे तु पटले व्याख्याग्रन्था उदीरिताः ।
साध्यर्द्धपादादधिका नवतिश्च चतुःशतम् ॥
श्रीचक्राद्यानि यन्त्राणि प्रोक्तान्येकादश क्रमात् ।
उद्योतप्रद्मान्यनन्तानि तथा कोष्ठभवानि च ॥

चतुस्त्रिंशपटलम् ।

अथ षोड़शनित्यानां विद्याकौतुकिनामिह ।
चमत्कारकरीं विद्यां वच्यामि शृणु सुन्दरि ॥ १ ॥
सिद्धसारस्वतं मृत्युञ्जयं त्रिपुटगारुड़े ।
अश्वारूढ़ामन्नपूर्णां नवात्मानं नवात्मिकाम् ॥ २ ॥
ततश्च देवीद्वयं गौरीविद्याश्च लचदाम् ।
निष्कवयप्रदामिष्टदायिनीञ्च मतङ्गिनीम् ॥ ३ ॥
राज्यलक्ष्मीं महालक्ष्मीं सिद्धलक्ष्मीमनन्तरम् ।
गोपालभेदानौषधान् वदाम्युक्तक्रमेण वै ॥ ४ ॥
*शुचिः स्वेन ततो माया वियद्दाहस्ववह्नियुक् ।
हंसद्वत्तेजसां योगाद्युतिदाहचरस्वकैः ॥ ५ ॥

पूर्व्वस्मिंस्त्रयस्त्रिंशे पटले षोड़शनित्याविद्यासिद्धानि वाञ्छितप्राप्तिफलानि ललिताविद्यायाः स्वरूपभेदसमुत्थानि कानिचिद्‌यन्त्राण्युपदिश्यानन्तरं तेषां लोकचमत्कारकरान् प्रयोगान् विद्याभिरुपदिशत्यथ षोड़शनित्यानामित्यादिना आत्मवानित्यन्तश्लोकशतरूपेण चतुस्त्रिंशपटलेन। तत्र अथ षोड़शेत्यादिभिः क्रमेण वै इत्यन्तैश्चतुर्भिः श्लोकैः सप्रस्तावपटलार्थानुपदिशति। तत्र इह पटले सुन्दरीति सम्बुद्धिः। सिद्धसारस्वतमित्यादिना श्लोकेन विद्याष्टकमुपदिशति। तत्र त्रिपुटगारुड़े त्रिपुटाविद्यां गारुड़विद्याञ्च। ततश्चेत्यादिना श्लोकेन विद्याषट्कं। राज्यलक्ष्मीमित्यर्द्धेन विद्यात्रयं। गोपालभेदान् सप्तेत्यर्थः। सप्तधा इति तदुद्धारक्रमे वच्यमाणत्वात्। औषधानि सकलभुजङ्गमविषहराणि स्वेच्छोत्क्रान्तिकरणानि च ॥ ४ ॥

शुचिरित्यादिना विग्रहेत्यन्तेन श्लोकद्वयेन सिद्धसारस्वतविद्यास्वरूपमुपदिशति। तत्र शुचिः ऐकारः स्वेन विन्दुना सहेति शेषः। ततः अनन्तरम-

ऐं ह्रीं श्रीं ह्स्ख्फ्रें

पुनश्च हंसहृद्वंसद्वयदाहवनैरपि ।
समायैरुदिता विद्या पञ्चार्णामृतविग्रहा ॥ ६ ॥
पटलेऽस्मिन्ननुक्तानामङ्गानि निजविद्यया ।
मायया वा विदध्याच्च ध्यानं चाद्यानुदीरिते ॥ ७ ॥
पयोव्रतः पञ्चलक्षं जपित्वा कुलसुन्दरीम् ।
ध्यात्वा सिद्धमनुः पश्चाद्विदध्याद्विनियोगकम् ॥ ८ ॥
अनया मन्त्रितैरद्भिः शोधयित्वा तु कन्यकाम् ।
पाययित्वा च तां ब्रूयात् श्लोकयेति समाहितः ॥ ९ ॥

चरमिति शेषः । माया हृल्लेखा । वियद्दाहस्ववक्रियुक् रेफ ईकारविन्दुसहितः प्रकारः श्रीवीजमित्यर्थः । हंसहृत्तेजसां योगाद्युतिदाहचरस्वकैः हकारसकारखकाररेफकाररेफएकारविन्दुसप्तभिरनन्तरं वीजमित्यर्थः । पुनश्च अनन्तरमक्षरं हंसहृद्वंसद्वयदाहवनैरपि समायैः हकारसकारहकारद्वयरेफऔकारविसर्जनीयात्मभिः सप्तभिरक्षरैः पञ्चमं वीजमिति यावत् । अमृतविग्रहा सप्तविंशतिपटले प्रागुक्तामृतेश्वरीविद्यायाः प्रोक्तध्यानविग्रहा । प्रयोगविशेषे ध्यानविशेषः प्रोक्तश्च तत्रैवेत्यर्थः ॥ ६ ॥

पटलेत्यादिना श्लोकेनास्मिन् पटले प्रोक्तानां विद्यानामङ्गध्यानयोः परिभाषोच्यते । तत्र अनुक्तानां विद्यानामित्यर्थः । निजविद्यया स्वस्वविद्यया षोढाविभिन्नेनाद्यवीजेन गुरूक्तक्रमेणेत्यर्थः । मायया हृल्लेखया दीर्घस्वरषट्कभिन्नयेत्यर्थः । वा विकल्पे । आद्यामृतविग्रहा ध्यानमिति यावत् । चः समुच्चये । अनुदीरिते ध्याने इति शेषः । एतदुक्तं भवति अनुदीरिते ध्याने सति तत्तद्देवतानां ध्यानममृतेश्वरीध्यानमेवेति ॥ ७ ॥

पयोव्रत इत्यादिभिर्महाद्भुतमित्यन्तैस्त्रिभिः श्लोकैर्विद्यासाधनप्रकारं सिद्धविद्यासारस्वतविद्यया दिव्यप्रयोगञ्चोपदिशति । तत्र पयोव्रतः क्षीराहारी । कुलसुन्दरीं ध्यात्वा पञ्चदशे पटले प्रोक्तकुलसुन्दरीविग्रहं ध्यात्वेत्यर्थः । सिद्धमनुः सिद्धविद्यः । अनया सिद्धसारस्वतविद्यया । मन्त्रितैः दिव्यत्वान्मन्त्रिताभिरिति यावत् । तुर्विशेषे । कन्यकां अविक्षुब्धेन्द्रियामिति यावत् । चः समुच्चये । तां कन्यां ब्रूयात् ।

गङ्गाप्रवाहवत्तस्या भारती निःसरेन्मुखात् ।
आचष्टे च त्रिकालस्थानर्थान् पृष्टा महाद्भुतम् ॥ १० ॥
भूः स्वेन ज्याधराश्वेता हृन्मायया समन्वितम् ।
पालयेति द्विरुक्त्वा तत् प्रतिलोममुदीरयेत् ॥ ११ ॥
विद्या मृत्युञ्जयाख्यासौ दीर्घस्वरयुजा हृदा ।
विद्ययाङ्गानि नियतं स्वात्मानं चिन्तयेदिति ॥ १२ ॥
आद्यमध्यतृतीयार्णनालपद्मसुकर्णिके ।
समासीनं सुधार्द्राङ्गं मौलाविन्दुकलायुतम् ॥ १३ ॥

श्लोकयेति । अत्र भिन्नक्रमेणान्वयः । श्लोकयेति ब्रूयादिति । समाहितः अन्यवुद्धिव्यापारादिरहितः । तस्याः कन्यायाः । चः समुच्चये । त्रिकालस्थानर्थान् भूतभविष्यद्वर्त्तमानकालस्थान् । पृष्टा कन्येत्यर्थः । महाद्भुतं महाचमत्कारभूतं यथा ॥ १० ॥

भूस्वेनेत्यादिना श्लोकेन मृत्युञ्जयविद्यास्वरूपमुपदिशति । तत्र भूः ओकारः स्वेन विन्दुना सहितेति शेषः । ज्या जकारः धरा श्वेता उकारविन्दुभ्यां सहिता । हृत् सकारः मायया समन्वितं विसर्जनीयेन समन्वितं । पालयेति द्विरुच्चार्य्य पालय पालयेत्यर्थः । तत् उद्धृताक्षरत्रयं । प्रतिलोमं प्रतिक्रमात् । अत्र प्रयोगेषु तु प्रथमं प्रणवाद्यक्षरत्रयमुच्चार्य्यानन्तरं पालनीयस्याख्यां द्वितीयान्तामुच्चार्य्य ततः पालययुगं ततो व्युत्क्रमेणाद्यक्षरत्रयञ्चोच्चरेदिति सम्प्रदायार्थः ॥ ११ ॥

विद्येत्यादिभिरेधत इत्यन्तैस्त्रिभिः श्लोकैः मृत्युञ्जयविद्याध्यानस्वरूपमुपदिशति । तत्र दीर्घस्वरयुजा हृदा दीर्घस्वरषड्भिन्नेन सकारेण सविन्दुनेति सम्प्रदायः । स्वात्मानं निजविग्रहं चिन्तयेदिति वक्ष्यमाणप्रकारेण ॥ १२ ॥

आद्येत्यादिनार्द्धेनैतदुक्तं भवति आद्याक्षरनालं द्वितीयाक्षरदलं तृतीयाक्षरकर्णिकमूर्द्धाधोमुखं सितकमलद्वयं सङ्कल्प्य तयोरन्तराले सितकमले इति । सुधार्द्राङ्गं तत् पद्मद्वयाक्षरमौलिस्थचन्द्रकलानिःसृतसुधार्द्राङ्गं । सुसितं वर्णतः । हरिणी-

सुसितं हरिणाक्षस्रक्चिन्तापाशकरं हरम् ।
स्वैक्येन भावयेन्नित्यं जयदीर्घायुरेधते ॥ १४ ॥
तृतीयममृताख्याया द्वितीयं तदनन्तरम् ।
रसावह्निस्वसहितप्राणास्तैस्त्रिपुटोदिता ॥ १५ ॥
त्रिभिर्द्विरुक्तैरङ्गानि कृत्वा विद्यान्तु नित्यशः ।
जपेदक्षो मुखे स्वैक्यं भावयंस्त्रिसहस्रकम् ॥ १६ ॥
तेन विद्यां श्रियं कान्तिं कवितां गानकौशलम् ।
नरनारीनृपाणाञ्च वाक्षभं लभते नरः ॥ १७ ॥
अरुणामरुणाक्षस्थां प्रसन्नवदनाम्बुजाम् ।
पुष्पेष्वङ्कुशपद्मानि पद्मपाशेक्षुचापकान् ॥ १८ ॥
दधानां बाहुभिः षड्भिः माणिक्यमुकुटोज्ज्वलाम् ।
शृङ्गारभूषापिकवाक्चामरादर्शपीड़काः ॥ १९ ॥

त्वाद्यायुधचतुष्टयं वामोर्द्ध्वकरादि तदधःकरान्तमप्रादक्षिण्यक्रमेण । तत्र चिन्तेति व्याख्यानमुद्रा । स्वैक्येन स्वापृथक्त्वेन ॥ १४ ॥

तृतीयेत्यादिना श्लोकेन त्रिपुटाविद्यास्वरूपमुपदिशति । तत्र तृतीयममृताख्यायाः सिद्धसारस्वतविद्यातृतीयबीजं श्रीबीजमित्यर्थः । एतच्छ्रीत्रिपुटाविद्यायाः प्रथमं बीजमित्यर्थः । द्वितीयं तदनन्तरं सिद्धसारस्वतविद्याया द्वितीयं बीजं । रसावह्निस्वसहितप्राणाः लकार ईकारबिन्दुभिः सहितः ककारः । तेन कामबीजमुच्यते । तैस्त्रिभि र्बीजैः ॥ १५ ॥ श्रीं ह्रीं क्लीं

त्रिभिरित्यादिभिः स्मरेदित्यन्तैः पञ्चभिः श्लोकैस्त्रिपुटाविद्यायाः षडङ्गानि साधनक्रमं सिद्धविद्यस्य प्राप्यानि फलानि तद्ध्यानं तत्परिवारध्यानञ्चोपदिशति । तत्र त्रिभिर्बीजैर्द्विरुक्तैर्वारद्वयमुच्चारितैः । तुर्विशेषे । त्रिसहस्रकं वाराणामिति शेषः । तेन जपेन । चः समुच्चये । नरः साधकः । अत्रायुधक्रमस्तु दक्षिणाधोहस्तादिवामाधरहस्तान्तं प्रादक्षिण्येन बोद्धव्यः । षड्भिः सम्भूयेत्यर्थः । दधाना इत्यस्यानन्तरपूर्व्वश्लोकोत्तरार्द्धेन सम्बन्धः । तस्या देव्याः ।

दधानाः परितस्तस्या गायन्त्यश्चापि शक्तयः ।
परिवार्य्य स्थितास्ताभिर्वृतां तां स्वैक्यतः स्मरेत् ॥ २० ॥
भूः स्वेन हंसदाहाभ्यां मरुद्वह्निक्ष्मया युतौ ।
वैरिमोहीत्यक्षराणां चतुष्कं गरुड़ेति च ॥ २१ ॥
जवी सवह्निग्रासश्च हंसहिंसद्वयन्तथा ।
स्वाहान्तो गदितो मन्त्रस्तार्क्ष्यस्याखिलरक्षितुः ॥ २२ ॥
त्रयोविंशार्णको मन्त्र उपरागे सुसाधितः ।
फणिदष्टान् पिशाचाद्यैः क्लिष्टानन्यांश्च रोगिणः ॥ २३ ॥

स्थिताः नचा(स्वा)सीना इत्यर्थः । देव्या एवासीनत्वं । ताभिः शक्तिभिः । तां देवीं । स्वैक्यतः अपृथग्भावेन ॥ २० ॥

भूः स्वेत्यादिना सुसाधित इत्यन्तेनाध्यर्द्धेन श्लोकद्वयेन गारुड़मन्त्रस्वरूपं तत्साधनप्रकारश्चोपदिशति । तत्र भूः ओकारः स्वेन विन्दुना सहिता इति शेषः । एतत् काकाक्षिवत् पूर्व्वापरयोरन्वेति । हंसदाहाभ्यां हकाररेफाभ्यां अन्योन्यसुश्लिष्टाभ्यां । मरुद्वाह्निक्ष्मया क्ष्मया सहितौ मरुद्वह्नी मरुच्च वह्निश्च क्ष्मा चेत्यर्थः। ते वाकार ईकार लकाराः तेन मरुदादिवर्णाः पृथक् पृथगिति सम्प्रदायः। तेन क्ष्रां क्ष्रीं क्ष्रूं इत्यक्षरत्रयं निष्पन्नं । वैरिमोहीत्यक्षराणां चतुष्कं वैरिमोहीति अक्षराणां चतुष्टयस्य स्वरूपग्रहणं । गरुड़ेति च चकारेण गरुड़ इत्यक्षरत्रयस्य च स्वरूपग्रहणत्वं द्योत्यते । जवी पकारः सवह्निग्रासः वह्निना सहितो ग्रासः वह्निरितीकारस्य संज्ञाप्याग्नेयत्वसामग्रात् सम्प्रदायाच्च ईकारः । ग्रासः इति क्षकारः ईकारसहितः क्षकार इत्यर्थः । हंसहिंसद्वयं हंस इत्यक्षरद्वयं हिंस इत्यक्षरद्वयञ्च । तथा स्वरूपग्रहणं । त्रयोविंशार्णः त्रयोविंशतिवर्णात्मकः । उपरागे चन्द्रसूर्य्ययोरिति शेषः । सुसाधितः भवेदिति शेषः । जपतर्पणहोमार्च्चादिभिरित्यर्थः ॥ २२ ॥-*

फणीत्यादिना जपेदित्यन्तेनार्द्धाद्येन श्लोकद्वयेन गारुड़मन्त्रसिद्धस्य प्रयोगविशेषात् फलानि तद्ध्यानञ्चोपदिशति । तत्र पिशाचाद्यैरित्यत्राद्यशब्दो भूतप्रेतापस्मारकृत्यादिविषयः च: समुच्चये । त्रिविधैर्विषैः स्थिरकृत्रिमजङ्गमा-

*· ॐ क्षां क्षीं क्षूं वैरिमोहि गरुड़ प्रीं क्षीं हंस हिंस

विषार्त्तान् विविधैरुग्रैर्मूर्च्छितांश्च गतासुकान् ।
पालयेच्छतजप्तेन तोयेनाभ्युक्षणात् क्षणात् ॥ २४ ॥
कुर्वतस्ताण्डवं शम्भोरग्रे मेरुसमं विभुम् ।
अहितानि च खादन्तं स्मरंस्तार्क्ष्यमनुं जपेत् ॥ २५ ॥
पद्माक्षवीजतैलेनाप्याशु नस्येन नाशयेत् ।
गरलं भुजगानाञ्च समस्तानामयत्नतः ॥ २६ ॥
प्रणवं चरहंसाग्निजवौदाह्वो नभश्चरी ।
शून्याम्बु रसदाहोग्निहृदम्बुमरुदन्वितः ॥ २७ ॥
हंसश्च मरुता युक्तः प्रोक्ता विद्या दशाक्षरी ।
षडङ्गं मायया कृत्वा जपेदक्षरलक्षकम् ॥ २८ ॥

ख्यैर्विषविशेषैः । मूर्च्छितान् गतसंज्ञान् । गतासुकान् देहे कस्मिंश्चित् प्रदेशे विषवेगेन सङ्कुचितप्राणान् । शतजप्तेन शतवारमभिमन्त्रितेन । कुर्व्वतस्ताण्डवमित्यत्र भिन्नक्रमान्वयः । ताण्डवं कुर्व्वत इत्यर्थः । मेरुसमं विग्रहस्य महत्तया वर्णतया च । विभुं तत्त्वतः । अहितानि प्रागुक्तविषादीनि ॥ २५ ॥

पद्माक्षेत्यादिना श्लोकेन सकलभुजङ्गमविषनाशनमौषधं तत्प्रयोगश्चोपदिशति । तत्र पद्माक्षवीजेभ्यस्तैलं लब्धं तेन । उपायो गुरुमुखादवगन्तव्यः ॥२६॥

प्रणवमित्यादिना दशाक्षरीत्यन्तेनाध्यर्द्धेन श्लोकद्वयेनाश्वारूढाविद्यामुपदिशति । तत्र चरहंसाग्नी इति मध्यपदलोपो समासः । तेन चरयुतहंसाग्नी इत्यर्थः । चर एकारः हंसाग्नी इकारसहितो हकारः जवो यकारः दाह्वो रेफः नभश्चरी मकारसहितो एकारः । शून्याम्बु दिव्यत्वात् शून्याम्बुनो इति यावत् । अत्र वियच्छब्दस्य पर्य्यायत्वात् सम्प्रदायाच्च शून्यमिति शकारः वकारसहितः शकार इत्यर्थः । सदाहोग्निः इकारसहितो रेफ इति यावत् । हृदम्बुमरुदन्वितः हृत् सकारः अम्बु वकारः आकारसहितः स्वकारः । हंसः हकारो मरुता युक्तः आकारसहितः ॥ २७ ॥

षडङ्गेत्यादिभिर्विदारयेत्यन्तैरर्द्धाद्यैः षड्भिः श्लोकैरश्वारूढाविद्यया अङ्गानि

ततो यमुद्दिश्य जपं निशि कुर्य्यादयत्नतः ।
समानयेत् स्वगेहे तमानाशात् प्रोक्तकारिणम् ॥ २९ ॥
वश्यमाकर्षणं लक्ष्मीं सुवर्णं वाञ्छितानि च ।
प्राप्नोत्ययत्नादनया विद्यया सिद्धयानिशम् ॥ ३० ॥
लोहितां लोहिताश्वस्थां लोहिताम्बरभूषणाम् ।
चतुर्भुजां त्रिनयनां प्रसन्नवदनाम्बुजाम् ॥ ३१ ॥
भल्लां दक्षेण वामेन चर्म्मयष्टिं समुज्ज्वलाम् ।
अन्याभ्यां हेमपाशेन कण्ठे बद्धा स्वसाध्यकम् ॥ ३२ ॥
हेमवेत्राहतं बद्धा करयुग्मकृताञ्जलिम् ।
दासोहमिति भाषन्तं पतितं निजपादयोः ॥ ३३ ॥
स्मरन् विद्यां जपेन्मर्त्यो वशी कुर्य्यादयत्नतः ।
समस्तं जीवभुवनमश्वारूढ़ाख्यविद्यया ॥ ३४ ॥
प्रणवं नमसा युक्तं तथा भगवतीति च ।
माहेश्वरीति प्रोक्त्वान्नपूर्णे स्वाहेति तन्मनुः ॥ ३५ ॥

साधनप्रकारं सिद्धविद्यस्य प्रयोगान् तद्ध्यानं तत्फलविशेषांश्चोपदिशति । तत्र मायया प्राग्वत् हृल्लेखया । अक्षरलक्षं विद्यया अक्षरसंख्यालक्षं दश-लक्षमित्यर्थः । ततो विद्यायां सिद्धायामिति यावत् । तं साध्यं । आनाशात् यावच्छरीरं । प्रोक्तकारिणं दासवदित्यर्थः । अनया अश्वारूढ़ाख्यया विद्यया । लोहिताश्वस्थां लोहितवर्णाश्वस्थां । दक्षेण दक्षिणकरेणेत्यर्थः । वामेन प्राग्वत् । समुज्ज्वलां विविधवर्णां । अन्याभ्यां ऊर्द्धकराभ्यां । हेमपाशेन तयोर्वामकरस्थेने-त्यर्थः । हेमवेत्राहतं तयोर्दक्षिणकरस्थहेमवेत्राहतं । स्मरन् उक्तरूपां देवीं ॥३४॥

प्रणवमित्यादिना श्लोकेनान्नपूर्णाख्यां सप्तदशाक्षरविद्यामुपदिशति । तत्र नमसा नमः पदेन प्रणवादनन्तरं नम इत्यक्षरद्वयं । तथा समुच्चये । भगवतीति भगवति इति चतुरक्षराणि माहेश्वरीति माहेश्वरि इति चतुरक्षराणि अन्नपूर्णे स्वाहेति अन्नपूर्णे स्वाहा इति षड़क्षराणि तन्मनुः अन्नपूर्णाविद्या ॥ ३५ ॥

विधाय माययाङ्गानि जपेद्विद्यामहर्मुखे ।
सहस्रवारं नियतं न तस्य स्याद्दरिद्रता ॥ ३६ ॥
भुजङ्गत्रासकरणनृत्यासक्तावलोकिनीम् ।
स्मितवक्त्रां हेमपात्रात् पायसं दधतीं करे ॥ ३७ ॥
भवानीं सर्वदा विद्याजपवान्न कदाचन ।
बुभुक्षितो भवेदेव न कदाचिच्च कुत्रचित् ॥ ३८ ॥
तथा नृत्यस्थितं मां त्वां तदालोकनकौतुकाम् ।
आभ्यां भजेन्नित्यशो यो मन्त्राभ्यां याचते वरम् ॥ ३९ ॥
तस्यावयोः प्रसादेन सिध्यत्येवाशु चिन्तितम् ।
तिष्ठेच्चोपरि सर्वेषां सर्वथा सर्वतः सदा ॥ ४०
हंसक्षद्व्यासनभसां रसाम्बुव्याप्तदाहकैः ।
क्षमास्वयोगान्नामतश्च नवात्म नवभिश्च तैः ॥ ४१ ॥

विधायेत्यादिभिः कुत्रचिदित्यन्तैस्त्रिभिः श्लोकैरन्नपूर्णादेव्या अङ्गानि ध्यानं विद्यासाधनप्रकारं विद्यासिद्धस्य लभ्यानि फलानि चोपदिशति। तत्र मायया प्राग्वत् हृल्लेखया। विद्यां अन्नपूर्णाख्यां। अहर्मुखे प्रातःकाले। तस्य जपितुः। भुजङ्गत्रासकरणनृत्यासक्तावलोकिनीं ताण्डवविशेषासक्तपरमेश्वरावलोकनशीलां। हेमपात्रात् हेमपात्रादिति ल्यव्लोपे पञ्चमी। हेमपात्रमापूर्य्य स्थितां। विद्याजपवान् अन्नपूर्णायाः ॥ ३८ ॥

तथेत्यादिना सदेत्यन्तेन श्लोकद्वयेनानन्तरवक्ष्यमाणनवात्मविद्ययोर्ध्यानं तत्फलानि चोपदिशति। तत्र तथा नृत्यस्थितं भुजङ्गत्रासनृत्यपरं। तदालोकनेन कौतुकां नृत्यावलोकनकौतुकां। आभ्यां वक्ष्यमाणाभ्यां। वरमभीष्टं। तस्य याचितुः। एवावधारणे ॥ ४० ॥

हंसेत्यादिना सिद्धिदावित्यन्तेन श्लोकद्वयेन नवात्मकयोर्विद्यास्वरूपमुपदिशति। तत्र हंसक्षद्व्यासनभसां हकारसकारक्षकारमकाराणां। रसाम्बुव्याप्तदाहकैः लकारवकारयकाररेफैः सहितानामिति। तैरक्षरैः। तस्य नवात्मक-

तस्यैव क्ष्माक्षरं हित्वा वह्निं तत्र प्रयोजयेत् ।
नवात्मिका तु ते विद्या द्वावेतौ सर्वसिद्धिदौ ॥ ४२ ॥
प्रणवं त्रिपुटान्त्यार्णं नमसा चतुरक्षरी ।
देवीहृदयसंज्ञासौ विद्या सर्वार्थसिद्धिदा ॥ ४३ ॥
ध्यानमुक्तममुष्यास्तु सततं सर्वमङ्गलाम् ।
सितकुष्ठं स्वर्णपुष्पीमूलं तत्पत्रवारिणा ॥ ४४ ॥
पिष्ट्वा शुद्धः पायसाशी विद्याजापी जितेन्द्रियः ।
भूमौ शयीत तां रात्रिं विजने सुशुभे गृहे ॥ ४५ ॥
तन्निशाप्राक्कण्ठहृत्कस्तत्रालिखितमायकः ।
आज्ञास्थितं(ता) तथा सा तं वदेदस्याभिवाञ्छितम् ॥४६॥

मन्त्रस्य । एवावधारणे । क्ष्मा जकारः । वह्निं ईकारम् । तत्र जकाराक्षरस्थाने । नवात्मिका प्राग्वत् । तुर्विशेषे । ते विद्ये देव्यास्तव विद्ये ॥ ४२ ॥

प्रणवमित्यादिना श्लोकेन देवीहृदयविद्यास्वरूपमुपदिशति । तत्र प्रणवं प्रथममक्षरं त्रिपुटान्त्यार्णं त्रिपुटाविद्यायास्तृतीयाक्षरं कामबीजं । एतद्देवीहृदयविद्याया द्वितीयाक्षरमित्यर्थः । नमसा नम इत्यक्षरद्वयेन तृतीयचतुर्थाक्षरभूतेन चतुरक्षरी सम्भूयेति यावत् ॥ ४३ ॥

ध्यानमित्यादिभिर्विजयावहेत्यन्तैः चतुर्भिः श्लोकैः देवीहृदयध्यानं सकलमन्त्रविद्याभिस्तत्तद्देवतानां स्वप्रकथनफलावाप्त्यादिकञ्चोपदिशति । तत्र ध्यानमुक्तं अमुष्याः अस्या देवीहृदयविद्यायाः ध्यानं एवमुक्तमिति यावत् । तुर्विशेषे । सर्वमङ्गलां ध्यायेदित्यर्थः । अत्रौषधयोः संज्ञा गुरुमुखादवगन्तव्या । तत्पत्रवारिणा स्वर्णपुष्पीपत्रवारिणा । भूमौ दर्भसञ्चरे मृगत्वचि वेति सम्प्रदायः । सुशुभे निद्राविरोधकरकीटादिरहिते । तन्निशाप्राक्कण्ठहृत्कः प्रोक्तौषधद्वयलिप्ताप्राक्कण्ठहृत्कः तत्रात्रेति भ्रुवोर्मध्यं । तत्र आलिप्तस्थानत्रये लिखितमायकः

देवीहृदयविद्येयं स्त्रीणां सद्यःफलप्रदा।
सौभाग्यलक्ष्मीकीर्त्त्यायुरारोग्यविजयावहा ॥ ४७ ॥
प्रणवं रुद्रदयिते तथा योगेश्वरीति च।
स्वाहान्तिका तु विद्येयं कथिता द्वादशाक्षरी ॥ ४८ ॥
गौरीविद्येत्यसौ प्रोक्ता लक्षजप्ता सुसाधिता।
ध्यात्वा प्राग्वद्धयारूढ़ा देवी साधयतीप्सितम् ॥ ४९ ॥
निशामध्ये तु निशया निजवामोरुदेशतः।
साध्यनामसमोपेतामालिख्यैतान्तु तन्मनाः ॥ ५० ॥
ध्यायंस्तथा जपेद्विद्यां तदैवाकर्षयेत् प्रियाम्।
नानया सदृशी विद्या विद्यते वनितावशे ॥ ५१ ॥
राजवश्ये तथा लोकवश्ये स्त्रीवशकर्म्मणि।
न विद्याः सन्ति भुवने हयगौरीमनुद्वयात् ॥ ५२ ॥

लिखितहृल्लेखः। भ्रूमध्यस्थित भ्रूमध्यस्थितं। तथा समुच्चये। सा देवी। तं साधकं। अस्य साधकस्य सौभाग्यादिफलषट्कप्रोक्तफलम् ॥ ४७ ॥

प्रणवमित्यादिना श्लोकेन गौरीविद्यास्वरूपमुपदिशति। तत्र रुद्रदयिते इत्यक्षरपञ्चकं योगेश्वरीत्यक्षरचतुष्टयं स्वाहेत्यक्षरद्वयं द्वादशाक्षरी सम्भूयेति यावत् ॥ ४८ ॥

गौरीत्यादिभिर्द्वयादित्यन्तैश्चतुर्भिः श्लोकैः गौरीविद्यायाः साधनं ध्यानं सिद्धविद्यस्य प्रयोगविशेषान् फलभेदादिकञ्चोपदिशति। तत्र ध्यात्वेत्यादिनोत्तरार्द्धेन एतदुक्तं भवति प्रागुदीरिताश्वारूढ़ास्वरूपविद्यान्ता गौरीदेवी निजमनीषितं साधयतीति। तुर्विशेषे। निशया हरिद्रया। निजवामोरुदेशतः साधकस्य वामोरुदेशे। साध्यनामसमोपेतां साध्यसाधककर्म्मणा समोपेतां। एतां गौरीविद्यां। तन्मनाः साध्यमना इत्यर्थः। तथा यथासम्प्रदायभावनया। विद्यां गौर्य्या इति शेषः। तदैव अनया गौरीविद्यया। हयगौरीमनुद्वयात् अश्वारूढ़ाविद्या गौरीविद्याद्वयतः अधिकाश्च सदृशाश्चेति यावत् ॥ ५२ ॥

अग्निर्नादस्य तद्युक्तः ताविवाथ नभोधरौ ।
एतद्द्वितीयं तौ स्यातां काकण्ठेति ततः परम् ॥ ५३ ॥
मुण्डिस्वाहेति विद्येयमुक्ता पञ्चदशाक्षरा ।
कृताङ्गो मायया ध्यात्वा तां देवीं सर्वमङ्गलाम् ॥ ५४ ॥
जपेद्विद्यां मौनयुतः कदलीपूगमध्यतः ।
त्रिसन्ध्यार्चासमोपेतं सा प्रीता लक्षदा दिनैः ॥ ५५ ॥
प्रणवं नवकेशां च कनकवतिसंयुतम् ।
स्वाहान्तं द्वादशार्णेयं विद्या निष्कत्रयप्रदा ॥ ५६ ॥

अग्निरित्यादिना पञ्चदशाक्षरेत्यन्तेनाध्यर्द्धेन श्लोकेन लक्षसुवर्णप्रदाविद्यास्वरूपमुपदिशति। तत्र अग्निः हकारः। नादस्य तद्युक्त हकारेण (ठ)रकारो युक्तः। तौ प्रोक्तौ। एवावधारणे। अस्य मन्त्रस्य प्रथमद्वितीयवर्णाविव तृतीयचतुर्थवर्णौ भवत इत्यर्थः। नभोधरौ उकारसहितो मकार इति यावत्। एतद्द्वितीयं अस्य मन्त्रस्य द्वितीयमक्षरमेव षष्ठमक्षरमित्यर्थः। तौ स्यातां पञ्चमषष्ठवर्णाविव सप्तमाष्टमौ स्यातामिति यावत्। काकण्ठेति काकण्ठ इति त्रीण्यक्षराणि मुण्डिस्वाहेति मुण्डि स्वाहा इति चत्वार्य्यक्षराणि पञ्चदशाक्षरा। सम्भूयेति यावत् ॥ ५३ ॥

कृताङ्ग इत्यादिना दिनैरित्यन्तेनार्द्धाधेन श्लोकेनाङ्गानि ध्यानं साधनक्रमं सिद्धविद्यस्य फलसिद्धिश्चोपदिशति। तत्र मायया प्राग्वत् हृल्लेखया। तां देवीं लक्षप्रदाख्यां देवीं सर्व्वमङ्गलां सर्व्वमङ्गलासमानविग्रहां। कदलीपूगमध्यतः कदलीवनमध्ये पूगवनमध्ये वा। त्रिसन्ध्यार्चासमोपेतमिति क्रियाविशेषणम्। सा देवी लक्षदा लक्षस्वर्णप्रदा। दिनैः प्राग्वत् ॥ ५५ ॥

प्रणवमित्यादिना श्लोकेन निष्कत्रयप्रदाविद्यास्वरूपमुपदिशति। तत्र नवकेशां नवकेशामिति चत्वार्य्यक्षराणि। कनकवतिसंयुतं कनकवति इति पञ्चाक्षराणि स्वाहा इत्यक्षरद्वयं उच्चरेदिति शेषः। द्वादशार्णा सम्भूयेति यावत्। निष्कत्रयप्रदा प्राग्वन्नामतस्त्वार्थतश्च ॥ ५६ ॥

नित्यशो गिरिशृङ्गस्थवटमूले त्रिलक्षकम् ।
जपित्वा वर्णशो विद्यां फलमुक्तमवाप्नुयात् ॥ ५७ ॥
चरः प्राणो मरुद्युक्तो व्याप्तं प्राणो धरान्वितः ।
व्योमद्वयं मरुद्युक्तं रयश्च धरया युतः ॥ ५८ ॥
चरः प्राण इति प्रोक्ता विद्याभीष्टं वदेन्मिथः ।
जातिपुष्पैर्निशामध्ये पूजिता मङ्गलाकृतिः ॥ ५९ ॥
सिद्धसारस्वतस्यादौ त्र्यक्षराणि ततः परम् ।
मातङ्गिन्यै तथा स्वाहा पुनस्त्रीणीति तन्मनुः ॥ ६० ॥
द्वादशार्णैयमचिरात् सौभाग्यं कवितां श्रियम् ।
गानाभियोगं विश्वेषां मान्यताञ्च प्रयच्छति ॥ ६१ ॥

नित्यश इत्यादिना श्लोकेन निष्कत्रयप्रदाविद्यासाधनप्रकारं शिवश्चोपदिशति। तत्र त्रिलक्षकं जपित्वा वर्णश सम्भूय षट्त्रिंशल्लक्षवारं जपित्वेत्यर्थः। उक्तनिष्कत्रयमितं स्वर्णमित्यर्थः। अवाप्नुयादित्यस्य नित्यश इत्यनेन च सम्बन्धः ॥ ५७ ॥

चर इत्यादिना कृतिरित्यन्तेन श्लोकद्वयेनाभीष्टवादिनीविद्यास्वरूपं तत्फलं तत्साधनक्रमं तद्ध्यानञ्चोपदिशति। तत्र चर एकारः। प्राणो मरुद्युक्तः आकार सहितः ककारः। व्याप्तं यकारः। प्राणो धरान्वितः उकार सहितः ककारः। व्योमद्वयं मरुद्युक्तं सुश्लेषोच्चारित णकारद्वयं आकारयुक्तं। रयश्च धरया युतः उकारसहितः तकारः। चर एकारः। प्राणः ककारः। विद्या अष्टाक्षरेति यावत्। मङ्गलाकृतिः सर्व्वमङ्गलादेव्याः प्रोक्तविग्रहा ॥ ५८ ॥

सिद्धेत्यादिना श्लोकेन मातङ्गेश्वरीविद्यास्वरूपमुपदिशति। तत्र सिद्धसारस्वतस्यादौ त्र्यक्षराणि सिद्धसारस्वतमन्त्रस्याद्यानि त्र्यक्षराणि मातङ्गेश्वरीविद्याया अपि प्रथमभूतान्यक्षराणि त्रीणि तानि वाग्भवकामेश्वरीबीजानि। मातङ्गिन्यै इति चत्वार्य्यक्षराणि। स्वाहा इत्यक्षरद्वयं। त्रीणि प्रथमभूतानि वाग् भवादीनि प्रतिलोमानि। तन्मनुः मातङ्गेश्वरीविद्या ॥ ६० ॥

द्वादशेत्यादिभिः श्रितामित्यन्तैः पञ्चभिः श्लोकैः तद्विद्याक्षरसंख्यां तदङ्गानि

मायाकृताङ्गो नित्यशस्तां प्रजपेदुदये रवेः ।
सहस्रवारं तेनासौ सिद्धा सर्वं प्रयच्छति ॥ ६२ ॥
इन्द्रनीलनिभां रक्तवसनाभरणोज्ज्वलाम् ।
प्रलम्बवेणीसन्नद्धसौगन्धिकसमुज्ज्वलाम् ॥ ६३ ॥
तत्कृप्तमुण्डमालाश्च मुक्तास्तवकशोभिताम् ।
ऊर्म्मिकावीरकटकनूपुरैर्मण्डिताङ्घ्रिकाम् ॥ ६४ ॥
वादयन्तीं महावीणां स्वसमानाङ्गनाजनैः ।
स्तूयमानाश्च परितो ध्यायेद्देवीं शुचिस्मिताम् ॥ ६५ ॥
मातङ्गिन्या द्वितीयञ्च तृतीयं तदनन्तरम् ।
रमाचरस्वैरम्बु स्वाहातान्मी तदनन्तरम् ॥ ६६ ॥
राज्यदे राज्यलक्ष्मीति हन्मायाव्युत्क्रमात्त्रयम् ।
विद्यासौ राज्यलक्ष्म्यास्तु षोड़शार्णा समीरिता ॥ ६७ ॥

तद्विद्यासिद्धस्य फलानि विद्यासाधनप्रकारदेवताध्यानञ्चोपदिशति । तत्र इयं मातङ्गेश्वरीविद्या । मायाकृताङ्गः प्रागवत् हृल्लेखया न्यस्तषड़ङ्गः । तां विद्यां । तेन जपेन । असौ विद्या । सर्वं वाञ्छितमिति शेषः । अस्मिन् श्लोके प्रथमपादे त्वेकाक्षराधिक्यं दिव्यत्वात् । रक्तवसनाभरणोज्ज्वलां रक्तवसनरक्ताभरणमण्डितां । तत्कृप्तमुण्डमालां सौगन्धिकैः कृप्तशिरोमालां । स्वसमानाङ्गनाजनैः स्वसमानाकारवर्णभूषणादिभिः शक्तिभिः ॥ ६५ ॥

मातङ्गीत्यादिना समीरिता इत्यन्तेन श्लोकद्वयेन राज्यलक्ष्मीविद्यास्वरूपमुपदिशति । तत्र मातङ्गिन्या इत्यर्द्धेनैतदुक्तं भवति । मातङ्गिनीविद्याया द्वितीयतृतीयाक्षरद्वयं हृल्लेखाश्रीबीजरूपं राज्यलक्ष्मीविद्यायाः प्रथमद्वितीयाक्षरद्वयं भवतीति । रमाचरस्वैः लकार एकारबिन्दुभिरुपेतोऽम्बु वकारः तेन व्लें इति । वातान्मी थकारस्य इकारस्य पृथक् पृथगिति यावत् ॥ ६६ ॥

राज्यदे राज्यलक्ष्मीति सप्ताक्षराणि हन्मायाविसर्जनीयसहितः सकार इति यावत् । व्युत्क्रमात्त्रयं आद्याक्षरत्रयं प्रतिलोमक्रमेणेत्यर्थः । षोड़शार्णा षोड़शाक्षराणि सम्भूयेति यावत् ॥ ६७ ॥

ध्यात्वा तां विजयां विद्यां जपेन्नित्यञ्च पूजयेत् ।
राज्यं प्रयच्छति प्रीता साधकायाविलम्बितम् ॥ ६८ ॥
प्रणवं श्रीपुटां मायां कमले तदनन्तरम् ।
कमलातो लये पश्चात् प्रसीदद्वितयं पुनः ॥ ६९ ॥
आद्यत्रयं महालक्ष्म्यै नमः प्रोक्ता महेश्वरि ।
विद्या ते सप्तविंशार्णा समस्ताभीष्टदानिशम् ॥ ७० ॥
बीजत्रयैः षडङ्गानि द्विरुक्तैर्विहितानि वै
ध्यानञ्च विजयारूपं प्रजपाद्दिनशस्तथा ॥ ७१ ॥
कीर्त्तिलक्ष्मीधनारोग्यविजयाद्यखिलेष्टदा ।
तुलास्थे भास्करे पूजा पूर्णायां सकलेष्टदा ॥ ७२ ॥

ध्यात्वेत्यादिना श्लोकेन तद्ध्यानं तदुपासनक्रममुपासितुः फलावाप्तिञ्चोपदिशति । तत्र तां राज्यलक्ष्मीं विजयां विजयानित्यासमानविग्रहां ॥ ६८ ॥

प्रणवमित्यादिनाऽनिशमित्यन्तेन श्लोकद्वयेन महालक्ष्मीविद्यास्वरूपमुपदिशति । तत्र श्रीपुटां मायां श्रीबीजपुटितहृल्लेखां कमले इत्यक्षरत्रयं कमलातो लये कमला इत्यक्षरत्रयात् परं लये इत्यक्षरद्वयं । प्रसीदद्वितयं प्रसीद प्रसीद इति षडक्षराणि । आद्यत्रयं श्रीबीजपुटितहृल्लेखेति यावत् । महालक्ष्म्यै नमः इत्यक्षरषट्कं । महेश्वरीति देवीसम्बुद्धिः । सप्तविंशार्णा सम्भूय इति यावत् ॥ ७० ॥

बीजेत्यादिनेष्टदा इत्यन्तेन श्लोकद्वयेन तदङ्गानि तद्ध्यानं तदुपासनक्रमं तत्फलानि सर्व्वाभीष्टसिद्धिकरभजनकालञ्चोपदिशति । तत्र बीजेत्याद्यर्द्धेनैतदुक्तं भवति अस्या विद्याया द्वितीयाद्यक्षरत्रयस्य द्विरावृत्त्या षडङ्गानि विहितानि स्युरिति । ध्यानञ्च विजयारूपं विजयानित्याया ध्यानमस्या अपि ध्यानमिति यावत् । विजयादीत्यत्रादिशब्दो विविधमङ्गलत्रयगृहच्छेत्रादिविषयः । तुलास्थे तुलाराशिगते भास्करे । पूर्णायां पौर्णमास्याम् ॥ ७२ ॥

ज्यासकदाहवह्निस्थान्नभो हंसो मरुद्युतः ।
चण्डतेजश्च सङ्कर्षणवर्णाः स्युस्तदनन्तरम् ॥ ७३ ॥
व्योमाग्न्या कालीमन्थाने वर्णा हंसश्च मायया ।
सिद्धलक्ष्म्यादिविद्येयं प्रोक्ता सप्तदशाक्षरा ॥ ७४ ॥
आद्येन कृत्वा चाङ्गानि जपेद्विद्यान्तु नित्यशः ।
प्रातः सहस्रवारन्तु तर्पयेत्तद्दशांशकम् ॥ ७५ ॥
प्रसन्ना वर्षतो नित्यपूजायां साधकस्य सा ।
प्रयच्छति जयं युद्धे श्रियं सर्वातिशायिनीम् ॥ ७६ ॥
भूतप्रेतपिशाचापस्मारकृत्यादिवारणम् ।
करोति मार्गे कान्तारगिरिकृच्छ्रेभिरक्षति ॥ ७७ ॥
ध्यानन्तु तस्या देवेशि मङ्गले मङ्गलासमा ।
युद्धमार्गादिरक्षासु शृणु वक्ष्ये यथाविधि ॥ ७८ ॥

ज्यासकेत्यादिनाक्षरेत्यन्तेन श्लोकद्वयेन सिद्धलक्ष्मीविद्यास्वरूपादिकमुपदिशति । तत्र ज्यासकदाहवह्निस्थात् जकार रकारईकारात् विन्दुभिः प्रथमं वीजमुच्चार्य्येति यावत् । नभः मकारः । हंसो मरुद्युतः आकारसहितो हकारः । चण्डतेजः इत्यक्षरचतुष्टयं । सङ्कर्षणवर्णाः सङ्कर्षण इति वर्णचतुष्टयं । व्योमाग्न्या ढकारेण सहितो हकारः । कालीमन्थाने वर्णाः कालीमन्थाने इति पञ्चवर्णाः । हंसश्च मायया विसर्जनीयेन सहितो हकारः । सप्तदशाक्षरा सम्भूय इति यावत् ॥ ७४ ॥

आद्येनेत्यादिभिर्ध्रुवमित्यन्तैः षड्भिः श्लोकैस्तदङ्गानि तदुपासनक्रमं तत्तत्फलानि तस्या नित्योपास्यध्यानं प्रयोगध्यानादिकञ्चोपदिशति । तत्र आद्येन वीजेन प्राग्वत् स्वरभिन्नेन । तद्दशांशकं शतवारमित्यर्थः । सा सिद्धलक्ष्मीः । कृत्यादीत्यत्रादिशब्दो रोगग्रहभयादिविषयः । तस्याः सिद्धलक्ष्म्याः । देवेशीति देवीसम्बुद्धिः । मङ्गले प्रयोगे मङ्गलासमानविग्रहा । युद्धमार्गादीत्यादि-

शतशीर्षां त्रिनयनां प्रतिवक्त्रं भयानकाम्।
हस्तद्विशतसंयुक्तां स्वसमाकारशक्तिभिः॥ ७९॥
वृतामनन्तैर्हस्तेषु साधकाभीष्टहेतिकाम्।
ध्यात्वैवमर्चयेदिष्टमवाप्नोत्यखिलं ध्रुवम्॥ ८०॥
प्राक्प्रत्यग्दक्षिणोदक्क कृत्वा सूत्राष्टकं ततः।
मार्जयेद्वाह्यवीथीषु पञ्चपञ्च तथैकधा॥ ८१॥
तदन्तरपि कोणेषु त्रयमेकीकृते ततः।
मध्यादि विलिखेन्मन्त्रवर्णान् षोड़श नाम च॥ ८२॥

शब्दो गिरिकान्तारादिपार्श्वस्थलविषयः। शृणिवत्यस्य ध्यानमिति पूर्व्वेणान्वयः। भयानकां भीषणरूपाम्। अनन्तैः दिव्यत्वादनन्ताभिरिति यावत्। साधकाभीष्टहेतिकां तत्तत्प्रयोगानुगुणमिति यावत्॥ ८०॥

प्रागित्यादिभिर्नित्यश इत्यन्तैस्त्रिभिः श्लोकैर्नित्यार्चनाचक्रनिर्म्माणादिकमुपदिशति। तत्र कृत्वा सूत्राष्टकं समान्तरालमित्यर्थः। तथा यथा प्रतिकोणमेकमेकं कोष्ठमवशिष्येत तथेत्यर्थः। तदन्तः वीथ्यामिति शेषः। त्रयं कोष्ठत्रयं। एतदुक्तं भवति। द्वितीयवीथ्यां प्रतिदिशं मध्ये एकमेकं कोष्ठमवशिष्यते तथा मार्जयेदिति। मध्यादि एतत् क्रियाविशेषणं। सर्व्वमध्यकोष्ठे आद्यमक्षरं यथा तथेत्यर्थः। मन्त्रवर्णान् षोड़श अवशिष्टानिति यावत्। नाम साध्यादीनां प्रागवन्मध्यकोष्ठलिखितवीजोदरे इति यावत्। मध्ये इत्यनन्तरश्लोके वक्ष्यमाणत्वात्। प्रादक्षिण्यक्रमात् विलिखेदिति पूर्व्वेणान्वयः। तत्र चक्रे अयमत्र विरचनाक्रमः। प्राक्प्रत्यग्दक्षिणोदक्कसमान्तरालं सूत्राष्टकाष्टकास्फालनादेकोनपञ्चाशत् कोष्ठात्मकं समचतुरस्रं विधाय तत्तद्वाह्यवीथिगतकोष्ठेषु चतुर्विंशत्यां प्रतिदिशं मध्यस्थमध्यस्थकोष्ठपञ्चपञ्चकमेकीकृत्य तदन्तर्वीथीस्थकोष्ठषोड़शके प्रतिकोणमेकमेकं तत्तदुभयपार्श्वस्थकोष्ठाभ्यां सह त्रीणि त्रीणि कोष्ठान्येकीकृत्य शिष्टसमदशकोष्ठेषु सर्व्वमध्यस्थकोष्ठे साध्यादिसमेतं प्रथमं वीजं तद्वाह्यवीथीस्थेषु अष्टसु कोष्ठेष्वग्रादिप्रादक्षिण्येन तद्वाह्यवीथ्यादिकोष्ठचतुष्टये प्रागवत्

प्रादक्षिण्यक्रमान्मध्ये पूजयेत्तत्र तां सदा ।
समस्ताभीष्टसंसिद्ध्यै सिद्धलक्ष्मी तु नित्यशः ॥ ८३ ॥
कदाचिदाद्या ललिता पुंरूपा कृष्णविग्रहा ।
स्ववंशनादसमारम्भादकरोद्विवशं जगत् ॥ ८४ ॥
ततः स गोपीसंज्ञाभिरावृतोऽभूत् स्वशक्तिभिः ।
तदा तेन विनोदाय स्वं षोढाकल्पयद्वपुः ॥८५ ॥
तेषां षण्णाञ्च षण्मन्त्राः समस्ताभीष्टदायकाः ।
तैर्यन्त्रपूजाहवनजपतर्पणसेचनैः ॥ ८६ ॥
भवन्ति लक्ष्मीकान्तिश्रीविजयारोग्यसंयुताः ।
शृणु तान् षट्क्रमान्मन्त्रान् ध्यानार्चाविनियोगकैः ॥८७॥
स्थिरारसाव्याप्तवनस्वैरुक्तोऽभून्महामनुः ।
प्रणवद्वयमध्यस्थः सिद्धगोपालकाभिधः ॥ ८८ ॥

क्रमात्तद्बाह्यवीथ्यां कोणकोष्ठचतुष्टये वायव्यादिनिरृत्यन्तं च विद्यायाः सप्तदशार्णान् क्रमेण विलिखेदिति ॥ ८३ ॥

कदाचिदित्यादिभिर्विनियोगकैरित्यन्तैश्चतुर्भिः श्लोकैर्ललिताविद्याया गोपालस्वरूपत्वं तन्मूर्त्तिभेदांस्तदुपास्तिफलानि तन्मन्त्रोद्धारप्रस्तावादिसहितमुपदिशति । तत्र आद्या नित्यानाम ललिता । पुंरूपा कृष्णविग्रहा परमार्थलक्षणशः प्राग्वत् कृष्णः स्वशक्तिभिः नित्याभिरणिमादिभिश्च । तेन वपुषा । तेषां वपुषां । तैर्मन्त्रैर्लक्ष्मीकान्तियशोविजयारोग्यसंयुताः साधका इति यावत् । ध्यानार्चाविनियोगकैः सहेति यावत् । अस्मिन् श्लोके प्रथमपादे त्वक्षराधिक्यं दिव्यत्वात् ॥ ८७ ॥

स्थिरेत्यादिना श्लोकेन सिद्धगोपालमन्त्रस्वरूपमुपदिशति । तत्र स्थिरारसाव्याप्तवनस्वैः गकारलकारयकारऔकारविन्दुभिः कूटरूपैः । महामनुः संज्ञया वैभवेन च । प्रणवद्वयमध्यस्थः प्रणवपुटितः ॥ ८८ ॥

प्रोक्तैस्तैः पञ्चभिः काममन्त्रैरेकैकतः क्रमात् ।
पुटनान्नामतस्तस्माद्बाणैस्तैः पुटनाद्भवेत् ॥ ८९ ॥

सम्मोहनाख्यस्त्वेवञ्च सप्तधाभून्महामनुः ।
आद्यः पञ्चाङ्गको मन्त्रस्त्वितरे स्युः षडङ्गकाः ॥ ९० ॥

तत्तद्बीजादिकेन स्यात् षड़ङ्गानि यथाविधि ।
अष्टपत्राब्जमध्यस्थं पूजयेत् सप्तातिक्रमात् ॥ ९१ ॥

यन्त्राणि तानि तन्मन्त्रयुतमध्यान्यनुक्रमात् ।
वारेषु भास्कराद्येषु तेषां पूजा क्रमेण वै ॥ ९२ ॥

प्रोक्तैरित्यादिभिः क्रमादित्यन्तैस्त्रिभिः श्लोकैः षड़्विधगोपालमन्त्रस्वरूपं तदङ्गानि तदाराधनक्रमञ्चोपदिशति। तत्र प्रोक्तैः सप्तमे पटले सहंसेत्यादिना पञ्चत्रिंशादेरनाध्यर्द्धश्लोकद्वयेनेति यावत्। एकैकतः प्रत्येकमेकैकबीजेन। नामतः सप्तमे पटले प्रथम इत्यादिना त्रिंशादेरनाध्यर्द्धश्लोकेन प्रोक्तकामराजादिनामानि प्रोक्तकूटस्येति यावत्। बाणैः कामराजस्य पञ्चबाणमन्त्रैः। तैः पञ्चकामबीजैः। अत्र चकारः समाहार्य्यः। तुद्वयं समुच्चये। एवं उक्तक्रमात्। एतदुक्तं भवति प्रणवेन पुटितो महामनुः सिद्धगोपालसंज्ञः मन्त्रः। पञ्चसु कामबीजेष्वेकैकबीजपुटितेन महामनुना क्रमात् कामराजगोपालमन्मथगोपालकन्दर्पगोपालमकरकेतनगोपालमनोभवगोपालसंज्ञाः पञ्चमन्त्राश्च सम्भूय त्र्यग्चरात्मकाः षण्मन्त्राः प्रथममन्त्रेण सह सप्तगोपालमन्त्राः सन्तीति। आद्यस्तेषु सिद्धगोपालमन्त्र इत्यर्थः। पञ्चाङ्गकः नेत्रन्यासरहित इति यावत्। इतरे षण्मन्त्राः कामराजगोपालाद्याः। तत्तद्बीजादिकेन महामनुनेति शेषः। स्याद्बहुत्वात् स्युरिति यावत्। यथाविधीति दीर्घस्वरषट्कभिन्नक्रमेणेत्यर्थः। अष्टपत्राणां मध्यस्थां एषु सप्तस्वन्यतमां ॥ ९१ ॥

यन्त्राणीत्यादिभिरवाप्नुयादित्यन्तैः त्रिभिः श्लोकैस्तेषां यन्त्राणि कालस्वरूपेण वारेषु सप्तसु भजनक्रमं निवेद्यविशेषादिकञ्चोपदिशति। तत्र तानि सिद्धगोपालादिसंज्ञानि। तन्मन्त्रयुतमध्यानि निजनिजमन्त्रलिखितकर्णिकानि। वारेषु

सकलेष्टप्रदा नित्यं दुग्धक्षौद्रघृतान्नकैः।
पायसैर्नारिकेलैश्च ससितैः कदलीफलैः॥ ९३॥
क्रमाद्वारेषु नैवेद्यं दद्यादिष्टार्थसिद्धये।
इतीरितैः सप्तभिस्तैः सर्वमिष्टमवाप्नुयात्॥ ९४॥
अरुणं षड्भुजं वंशवादिनं पाशमङ्कुशम्।
पुण्ड्रेक्षुचापपुष्पेषून् दधानं शक्तिभिः स्मरेत्॥ ९५॥
सुवर्णपुष्पीमूलेन पिष्टेन निजवारिणा।
हृत्कण्ठाद्यालेपनतो देवतादर्शनं भवेत्॥ ९६॥
उग्रगन्धां च नीलीं च धातकीफलसंयुताम्।
आरग्वधं मुण्डिनीं च शाकोटं * जम्बुमूलकम्॥ ९७॥

सप्तसु। तेषां सिद्धगोपालादीनां। सकलेष्टप्रदेत्यस्य पूजा इत्यनेन पूर्व्वत्र सम्बन्धः। नित्यं प्रतिवारं। दुग्धक्षौद्रघृतान्नकैः दुग्धैः क्षौद्रैः घृतान्वितैः अन्नैश्च। ससितैः शर्करोपेतैः नारिकेलैः दुग्धाद्यैः॥ ९४॥

अरुणमित्यादिना श्लोकेन तेषां ध्यानमुपदिशति। तत्र अरुणं वर्णं। वंशवादिनं अधरकराभ्यां गृहीत्वा। अत्र पाशाद्यायुधचतुष्टयमूर्द्धादि वामदक्षिणवामदक्षिणक्रमेण। शक्तिभिर्गोपीवेषधराभिरिति यावत्॥ ९५॥

सुवर्णेत्यादिना श्लोकेन सकलदेवतानामपरोक्षोपायौषधयोगादिविधानमुपदिशति। तत्र सुवर्णपुष्पीरुक्तमौषधं प्रागवदवगन्तव्यं। निजवारिणा प्रागवत्। हृत्कण्ठाद्यालेपनतः प्रागवत्। अत्रैतत प्रयोगविधानं गुरुमुखादवगन्तव्यम्॥ ९६॥

उग्रगन्धामित्यादिभिरात्मवानित्यन्तैस्त्रिभिः श्लोकैर्देवतानामपरोक्षं खेच्छोत्क्रान्तिं वा(च)औषधप्रयोगैरुपदिशति। तत्र उग्रगन्धामित्यादिना श्लोकेनौषधानि सप्त कर्णिकारमित्यादिना श्लोकेनौषधानि दश। तदौषधनामान्याराध्यमुखादवगन्तव्यानि। समं सर्व्वाणि समभागानि इत्यर्थः। सितेन शर्करया। तन्निम-

* शंखोटमित्यपि पाठो दृश्यते।

कर्णिकारिं हंसपदीं वाराहीं मृगराजकम् ।
कोरण्टं पिप्पलं मूलं त्रिफलं चूर्णयेत् समम् ॥ ९८ ॥
सितेनाज्येन मधुना दग्ध्वा तल्लिप्ततत्त्रय: ।
भावयंस्तन्मयो भूयाद्दिवसै: कैश्चिदात्मवान् ॥ ९९ ॥
सदाशिवमयी व्याप्तिरिति सम्यक् समीरिता ।
अस्या निष्कालनाच्चित्ते तत्तत्त्वं स्वात्मसात् कृतम् ॥

इति षोड़शनित्यातन्त्रेषु श्रीकादिमते चतुस्त्रिंशत्
पटलम् परिपूर्णम्॥ ३४ ॥

तत्त्रय: तत् सप्तदशौषधलिप्ताज्यादित्रय: । तन्मय: देवतामय: । आत्मवान् भावनास्थैर्य्यात् ॥ ९८ ॥

अस्मिन् पटले सप्तविंशश्लोकात् परं एक: श्लोक: पतित: ॥

इति षोड़शनित्यातन्त्रेषु श्रीकादिमताख्यस्य परिपूर्णस्य तन्त्रस्य प्रपञ्चसार-
सिंहराजप्रकाशाभिधानेन सुभगानन्दनाथेन विरचितायां मनोरमा-
ख्यायां व्याख्यायां लिङ्गयन्त्रप्रकाशनपरं चतुस्त्रिंशं
पटलं परिपूर्णं परामृष्टम् ॥ ३४ ॥ ॐतत्सत् ॥

ग्रन्थसंख्या: २२६—चतुस्त्रिंशे तु पटले व्याख्याग्रन्था: शतद्वयम ।
षट्त्रिंशतायुतं प्रोक्तं यन्त्राण्यष्टौ च तत्र वै ॥

पञ्चत्रिंशपटलम् ।

अथ षोड़शनित्यानां स्वात्मत्वे वासनां शृणु ।
यया तन्मयतासिद्धिः प्रत्यक्षा भवति ध्रुवम् ॥ १ ॥
गुरुराद्या भवेच्छक्तिः सा विमर्शमयी मता ।
नवत्वं तस्य देहस्य रन्ध्रत्वेनावभासते ॥ २ ॥
वलिदेव्यः स्वमायाः स्युः पञ्चमी जनकात्मिका ।
कुरुकुल्ला भवेन्माता पुरुषार्थास्तु सागराः ॥ ३ ॥

पूर्व्वस्मिन् पञ्चत्रिंशे पटले षोड़शनित्याविद्यासिद्धानां लोकचमत्कारान् प्रयोगान् विद्याभिरुपदिश्यानन्तरं षोड़शनित्यादीनां तत्तत्परिवारशक्त्यादीनाञ्च स्वात्मत्वेन वासनादिकं विद्यास्वरूपभेदेन प्रस्तारप्रकारादिकञ्चोपदिशति अथ षोड़शेत्यादिना सिद्धय इत्यन्तेन श्लोकशतरूपेण पञ्चत्रिंशेन पटलेन। अथ षोड़शेत्यादिभिः प्रपञ्चतेत्यन्तैः त्रयोविंशत्या श्लोकैर्गुरुपूजादिकं मुद्रादर्शनान्तं नित्यास्वरूपपरिवारन्यासजपतर्पणहोमाभिषेकोपचारादीनां वासनामुपदिशति। तत्र षोड़शनित्यानां परिवारादिसहितानां। स्वात्मत्वे देहेन्द्रियमनःप्राणाद्याकारेण प्रतीयमानात्मस्वरूपत्वे। यया वासनया। तन्मयतासिद्धिः नित्यात्मतासिद्धिः। प्रत्यक्षा अपरोक्षानुभवविषया। आद्याविमर्शमन्तरेण किञ्चिदपि सुस्फुटं ज्ञातुमशक्यत्वात्। सा स्वसंवेद्यस्वरूपेत्यर्थः। विमर्शमयी विमर्शमात्रविग्रहा। एतदुक्तं भवति आद्याविमर्शविग्रहा शक्तिरेव गुरुरिति। तस्य गुरोः। रन्ध्रत्वेन नवरन्ध्रत्वेन। एतदुक्तं भवति यथा रन्ध्रैरुपादेयग्रहणमनुपादेयमोचनञ्च क्रियते तथाविमर्शपरमार्थस्य गुरोः कटाक्षे साधकानां अर्थप्रवृत्तिरनर्थादुपरतिश्च। अत्र श्रोत्रद्वयं वाक् च दिव्यं त्रयं दृग्द्वयमुपस्थं च सिद्धं उत्तरत्रयं मानुष्यमिति सम्प्रदायः। स्वमायाः अतस्मिंस्तद्बुद्धिं जनयित्वा उन्मार्गप्रवर्त्तिकाः शक्तयः। पञ्चमी ब्राह्म्यादिषु पञ्चमीत्वात् वाराहीत्यर्थः। जनकात्मिका साधकानां जनकवदभिभवस्य स्तम्भनकरी शक्तिरिति यावत्। कुरुकुल्ला माता

रत्नद्वीपो भवेद्देहो नवत्वं धातुरोमभिः ।
सङ्कल्पाः कल्पतरवः स्वाधारा ऋतवः स्मृताः ॥ ४ ॥
ग्रहर्क्षराशिचक्रेण कालात्मा पश्चिमामुखः ।
तेन पूर्व्वाभिमुख्यं स्यादन्यत्ते कथितं मिथः ॥ ५ ॥
ज्ञाता स्वात्मा भवेज्ज्ञानमर्घ्यं ज्ञेयं वहिःस्थितम् ।
श्रीचक्रं पूजनं तेषां एकीकरणमीरितम् ॥ ६ ॥

मातृरूपा शक्तिः साधकानां मातृवदभिमतप्रदा शक्तिरित्यर्थः। एतदुक्तं भवति स्वात्मत्वेन परिभावनायां जनकजनन्योरंशत्वेन देहेन्द्रियवुद्ध्यादिषु संक्रान्तौ धर्म्माधर्म्मौ वाराहीकुरुकुल्लात्मकौ भावयेदिति। पुरुषार्था धर्म्मादयः। तुरवधारणे। सागराः महत्त्वया निरवसानतया च। रत्नद्वीपो भवेद्देहः देहत्वं स्वात्मोपलब्धेः। नवत्वं नवखण्डात्मकत्वं द्वीपस्येति यावत्। धातुरोमभिः श्रोजःशुक्रमज्जास्थिमेदोमांसरोमत्वग्रुधिरैर्मध्यप्रागादिक्रमैः। सङ्कल्पाः कल्पतरवः। सङ्कल्पपुरःसरं कर्म्मणि प्रवृत्त्या फलसिद्धेः। स्वाधाराः षोड़शपटले विशुद्धाख्ये इत्यादिभिरेकषष्ट्यादिनवभिः श्लोकैर्डाकिन्यादीनां निवासस्थानत्वेन प्रोक्तमूलाधाराद्याज्ञापर्य्यन्तानि सुषुम्नान्तर्गतानि स्थानानीति यावत्। ऋतवः वसन्ताद्याः सुषुम्नाया इड़ापिङ्गलात्मकचन्द्रार्कसंयोगादनुमितकालात्मकत्वात्तत्स्थानाधाराणामृत्वात्मकत्वमित्यर्थः। ग्रहर्क्षराशिचक्रेण ग्रहनक्षत्रसहितराशिचक्रेण। कालात्मा कालस्वरूपात्मा पश्चिमामुखः पश्चिमदिङ्मुख इति यावत् ज्योतिश्चक्रस्य प्रत्यङ्मुखत्वात्। तेन कारणेन। पूर्व्वाभिमुख्यं कालात्मकदेवताभिमुख्यापेक्षया पूर्व्वाभिमुख्यं साधकस्येति यावत्। अन्यत् कालस्य तात्त्विकं स्वरूपं। कथितं षट्त्रिंशे पटले काल इत्यादिना चत्वारिंशश्लोकपूर्व्वार्द्धेनेति यावत्। मिथः अत्युपह्वरं अन्यत् ते कथितं। मिथ इत्यनेनैतदुक्तं भवति इन्द्रियादीनां स्वात्मत्ववासना तत्तन्मन्त्रस्वरूपार्थस्वरूपे तव कथिते इति। अत्र कालचक्रेश्वर्य्यादीनां चत्वारिंशश्लोकेन प्रत्येकं नवधात्ववासना पञ्चमे पटले व्याख्याता ॥ ५ ॥

ज्ञाता स्वात्मा पूजक इति यावत्। ज्ञानं स्वकीयं अर्घ्यं पूजोपकरणमिति

श्रीचक्रे सिद्धयः प्रोक्ता रसा नियतिसंयुताः ।
ऊर्म्मयः पुण्यपापे च ब्राह्म्याद्या मातरः स्मृताः ॥७॥
भूतेन्द्रियमनांस्येव क्रमान्नित्याकला पुनः ।
कर्म्मेन्द्रियार्था दोषाश्च ज्ञेयाः स्युः शक्तयोष्ट वै ॥ ८ ॥
नाड्यश्चतुर्द्दश प्रोक्ताः क्षोभिण्याद्यास्तु शक्तयः ।
वायवो दश संप्रोक्ताः सर्वसिद्ध्यादिशक्तयः ॥ ९ ॥
वह्नयो दश संप्रोक्ताः सर्वज्ञाद्यास्तु शक्तयः ।
शीतोष्णसुखदुःखेच्छा गुणाः प्रोक्ताः क्रमेण वै ॥ १० ॥

यावत्। ज्ञेयं वहिःस्थितं ज्ञातुरिति शेषः। श्रीचक्र पूज्यमिति यावत्। पूजनं श्रीचक्रस्येति यावत्। तेषां ज्ञातृज्ञानज्ञेयानां एकीकरणं वोधात्मकत्वेनेति यावत्। एतदुक्तं भवति स्वात्मनो भिन्नवत् प्रतीयमानज्ञातृज्ञानज्ञेयात्मकेषु त्रिष्वपि स्वात्मस्वरूपत्वेन प्रतीयमानो ज्ञाता पूजकः स्वकीयत्वेत प्रतीयमानं ज्ञानं पूजोपकरणं अर्घ्यं स्ववाह्यत्वेन प्रतीयमानं ज्ञेयं पूज्यं श्रीचक्रं। तेषां वोधात्मकत्वेनापृथग्भावः पूजनमिति। श्रीचक्रे सिद्धय इति अणिमाद्याः। रसाः शृङ्गारादयो नव। नियतिसंयुताः नियतिसिद्ध्या शक्त्या सहिता वा सम्भूय दश शक्तय इत्यर्थः। ऊर्मयः वुभुक्षापिपासाशोकमोहजरामृतयः। पुण्यपापे कर्म्मणी सम्भूयाष्टौ। भूतेन्द्रियमनांसि भूतानि पञ्चेन्द्रियाणि दश च मनसा सहितानि षोड़श। कर्मेन्द्रियार्थाः वचनादानविहरणविसर्गानन्दाः। दोषा वातादयः। प्रोक्ताः सप्तविंशतिपटले इति यावत्। संप्रोक्ताः प्राक्पटले। अत्रातिरहस्यार्थाः मयोक्तवासनाविमर्शिन्यां द्रष्टव्याः। वह्नयो दश धातुषु सप्त दोषेषु त्रयश्च सम्भूय दशेति यावत्। संप्रोक्ताः अस्मिन् पटले उत्तरत्राग्निरित्यादिना पञ्चाशत्तमेन श्लोकेन। गुणाः सत्त्वादयः। तन्मात्राः शव्दस्पर्शरूपरसगन्धाः पञ्चतत्त्वरूपाः। तेषां पुष्पसायकत्वं प्रमुखे अभिमुखरूपतया परिणामि पुरुषरूपतया वा। मनस्तत्त्वं इक्षुधनुः विषयपरमार्थस्वरूपाणां शरसमेन्द्रियाणां तत्तद्विषयेषु प्रेरकत्वात्। इन्द्रियाणां तदर्थानां मनसश्च प्रवृत्तिरूपेण

वशिन्याद्याः शक्तयः स्युस्तन्मात्राः पुष्पसायकाः।
मनो भवेदिक्षुधनुः पाशो राग उदीरितः ॥ ११ ॥
द्वेषः स्यादङ्कुशः प्रोक्तः क्रमेण वरवर्णिनि।
अव्यक्ताहङ्कृतिमहदाकाराः प्रतिलोमतः ॥ १२ ॥
कामेश्वर्य्यादि देव्यः स्युः सम्वित् कामेश्वरः स्मृतः।
स्वात्मैव देवता प्रोक्ता ललिता विश्वविग्रहा ॥ १३ ॥
लौहित्यं तद्विमर्शः स्यादुपास्तिरिति भावना।
सिद्धिस्त्वनन्यचित्तत्वं मुद्रा वैभवभावनम् ॥ १४ ॥
उपचारास्थलत्वेपि तन्मयत्वाप्रमत्तता।
प्रयोगास्तु विकल्पानां हेतोः स्वात्मनि नाशनम् ॥ १५ ॥

वोभयक्रियात्मकत्वात्तद्द्विरुपादानं तेन न पुनरुक्तिदोषः। पाशो रागतत्त्वरूप इति यावत् तयोर्वन्धकत्वं सामान्यात् ॥ ११ ॥

द्वेषः स्यादङ्कुशः द्वेषाद्दारकत्वात्। वरवर्णिनीति सम्बुद्धिः। अव्यक्ताहङ्कृति-महदाकाराः प्रतिलोमतः महदहङ्कृतिः अव्यक्तक्रमात्तदाकारा इत्यर्थः। अत्राव्यक्तशब्देन प्रकृतितत्त्वं महच्छब्देन बुद्धितत्त्वं अहङ्कृतिशब्देनाहङ्कारतत्त्व-मुच्यते। सम्वित् कामेश्वरः सकलात्मकं चैतन्यं कामेश्वर इति यावत्। स्वात्मा विविधविश्वविकल्पात् स्वस्वरूपतया विलाप्य सद्वस्तु भासते स स्वात्मा देवता द्योतमानत्वात् ललिता निरवद्यरूपत्वात् विश्वविग्रहा ज्ञातृज्ञानज्ञेय-विग्रहा। तद्विमर्शः स्वात्मविमर्शः स्वात्मानुसन्धानमिति यावत्। एतदुक्तं भवति सर्व्वस्य स्वात्मन्यनुरागात् कस्मिंश्चिद्विषयेप्यनुरागादेव मनसः स्थित्य-भावाच्च तदनुरागो लौहित्यमिति। इति भावना स्वात्मभावनासिद्धिः। फल-मुपास्तेरिति यावत्। तुरवधारणे। अनन्यचित्तत्वं स्वात्मत्वे साधनास्थैर्य्या-दिति यावत्। मुद्राः योनिमुद्रादिसकलमुद्राः। वैभवभावनं उत्तरत्र वक्ष्य-माणप्रकारात् आत्मन इति यावत्। चलत्वेपि अननुसन्धानसमयेपि स्वप्रादाव-पीत्यर्थः। तन्मयत्वात् अप्रमत्तता स्वस्वरूपभावस्थैर्य्यं। (?) एतदुक्तं भवति। सतीति सम्बुद्धिः। असत्कारः स एवोपचार इति यत्तस्मात् सति सम्बुद्धिः सत्कारः

यन्त्राणि मन्त्राः सर्वत्र स्वात्मत्वे स्थैर्य्यसाधनम् ।
सन्ध्यासु भजनं देव्या आदिमध्यान्तमज्जनम् ॥ १६ ॥
अन्यास्तु शक्तयश्चक्रगामिन्यो याः समन्ततः ।
तास्तु विश्वविकल्पानां हेतवः समुदीरिताः ॥ १७ ॥
न्यासस्तु देवतात्वेन स्वात्मनो देहकल्पनम् ।
जपस्तन्मयतारूपभावनं सम्यगीरितम् ॥ १८ ॥
होमो विश्वविकल्पानामात्मन्यस्तमयो मतः ।
[तेषामन्योन्यसम्भेदभावनं तर्पणं भवेत् ॥ १९ ॥

स एवोपचार इति (?)। प्रयोगाः अभिमतसिद्धिकराः अनभिमतनिवारकाः क्रियाविशेषाः। तुरवधारणे। विकल्पानां हेतोः विकल्पानां हेतुरविवेकः तस्य। स्वात्मनि विमर्शरूपे। एतदुक्तं भवति स्वात्मत्ववासनया दुर्व्वासनानाशः। प्रयोगा इति यन्त्राणि मन्त्राः प्रयोगसाधनानि यन्त्राणि मन्त्राश्चेत्यर्थः। सर्व्वत्र विषये। स्वात्मत्वे स्वात्मत्ववासनायामित्यर्थः। यत् स्थैर्य्यसाधनं स्थैर्य्यकरणं। एतदुक्तं भवति स्वात्मत्ववासनास्थैर्य्यसाधनं विमर्शः। तद्वासनास्थैर्य्यपरमार्थप्रयोगसाधनभूतानां यन्त्रमन्त्राणां स्वात्मनोः विश्वात्मनोरैक्यवाक्यनिर्णीतिनिरूपणपरत्वेन विमर्शात्मकत्वात्तानि तद्वासनास्थैर्य्यसाधनानीति। तत्र सकलमन्त्रात्मिकायाः श्रीविद्यायास्तदपृथग्भावनिर्णयनिरूपणपरत्वमुत्तरत्र वक्ष्यति। सकलयन्त्रात्मकस्य श्रीचक्रस्यापि तदात्मकत्वे "कालो धामानि भूतानि नवचक्राण्यनुक्रमादिति" नित्याषोड़शिकार्णवे प्रोक्तं। आदिमध्यान्तमज्जनं (वर्जनं) अनुस्यूतरूपतया त्वपरिच्छिन्नतानुसन्धानं। एतदुक्तं भवति देव्याः सन्ध्यासु भजनं स्वात्मनः स्वपरिच्छिन्न एवेति। अन्याः गुप्तयोगिन्यः। चक्रगामिन्यः श्रीचक्रस्था या मन्त्रविभवपटलप्रोक्ताः ताः शक्तयः। तुः समुच्चये। विश्वविकल्पानां हेतवः विश्वस्य विविधविकारप्रतीतिकराः शक्तय इत्यर्थः। तुरवधारणे। स्वात्मनः स्वस्य। एतदुक्तं भवति निजदेहे देवताविग्रहभावी न्यास इति। तन्मयतारूपभावनं श्रीविद्यात्मकत्वेन मातृकामयत्वेन च स्वस्वरूपभावनं। सम्यगीरितं

मोहाज्ञानादिदुःखानामात्मन्यस्तमयो दृढम्।]
अभिषिकस्तु विद्या स्यादात्मा सर्व्वाश्रयो महान्॥ २०॥
उपाधीनान्तु राहित्यमुपदेश इतीरितः।
दक्षिणा भेदशून्यत्वं शुश्रूषा स्थैर्य्यमुच्यते॥ २१॥
तिथिरूपेण कालस्य परिणामावलोकनम्।
नित्या पञ्चदशैताः स्युरिति प्रोक्तास्तु वासनाः॥ २२॥

चतुर्थपटले कामकलारूपेण श्रीविद्यात्मकत्वं प्रथमपटले मन्त्राणां विंशति-दोषपरिहारात्मकत्वेन मातृकामयत्वं च। तच्च षड्विंशे पटले प्रोक्तोदय-विश्रान्तिस्वरूपानुसन्धानमित्यर्थः। अस्तमयः विश्रान्तिः। एतदुक्तं भवति कनकसत्तामात्रे भूषणादीनामिव स्वरूपसत्तामात्रे विश्वविकल्पानां नित्यास्थान-विलापनं होम इति। तेषां प्रोक्तानां सर्वेषां। अन्योन्यसम्भेदभावनं अन्योन्यैक-भावनं। तर्पणं स्वात्मनो विश्वाकारव्याप्त्यानुभवसञ्जाता तृप्तिरित्यर्थः। मोहा-ज्ञानादिदुःखानां कामाविष्टतया कर्त्तव्याकर्त्तव्यज्ञानाभावो मोहः विसंज्ञा-प्राप्तमज्ञानम् आदिशब्दस्त्वन्यथाज्ञानसाहसादिविषयः तदुत्पन्नदुःखानां आध्यात्मिकादीनां आत्मनि विमर्शप्रतीतिराहित्यात् तदैक्यनिर्णीतरूपे। अस्त-मयः उपशान्तिः। दृढं अपुनःप्ररोहयोग्यं। तुर्विशेषे। सर्वाश्रयः तादात्म्यात्। महान् विभुत्वात् सर्व्वशक्तित्वाच्च। उपाधीनां देहादिविकारकारणभूताः सत्त्वादि-गुणा उपाधयः तेषां। तुरवधारणे। राहित्यं स्वात्मन इति शेषः। एतदुक्तं भवति रजःपङ्कादिभिराकाशस्येव सत्त्वादिगुणैस्तदुत्पन्नविकारैश्चालेप्यत्व-भावनोपदेश इति। दक्षिणा गुरोः। भेदशून्यत्वं तस्मिन्नात्मसमर्पणात्। शुश्रूषा गुरोः स्थैर्य्यं आत्मज्ञानस्येति यावत्। तिथिरूपेण सितासितपक्षयोः परि-णामावलोकनं चन्द्रमण्डले सितासितकल्पनं। एता नित्याः पञ्चदश कामेश्वरी-नित्याद्याः। एतदुक्तं भवति चन्द्रमण्डले सितासितकलानां वृद्धिक्षयहेतुस्तिथि-कृतः काल इति यतस्तस्मात्तिथिरूपकालात्मिकाः कामेश्वर्य्यादिनित्या इति। किञ्च तिथिनित्यानामवान्तरकालात्मकत्वं ताभिरवान्तरकालात्मिकाभिश्चन्द्र-मण्डलत्वेनोपलक्षितस्य प्रपञ्चस्य कार्य्यमाणत्वं तासां महानित्यात्मकस्वरूपेणा-पृथक्त्वभावनया तदुपास्तिश्चोक्तेति सम्प्रदायार्थः। कनिष्ठाद्याः अङ्गुल्यः। तेषां

पृथिव्यादीनि भूतानि कनिष्ठाद्या क्रमान्मता ।
तेषामन्योन्यसम्भेदप्रकारैस्तत्प्रपञ्चता ॥ २३ ॥

गाँः या भि लि र्वं ता स्त्रि ल ते र्थौ धो क य ला भि स ।
न्तु दे रू षे प ण वी शे तं दि मी न रि स्या द ते ॥ २४ ॥
स्नं तो गत् शे कृत् ष ज अ रि त्म मी ह्ल प्र ख ला क ह्र ।
त: र्थं क स्या थि श्वा स्तु त त: न्त्रे गो र्वं पि त षु स ॥ २५ ॥
त्वं का मा म्ना न प्र श व्यो ना न म स ग्नि मा त्व ग्र ।
रो म ई यो का विं शं त नं त फा न्दु ल ना त्रि वि ॥ २६ ॥

अङ्गुल्यात्मकपञ्चभूतानां । अन्योन्यसम्भेदप्रकारैः अन्योन्यसम्बन्धप्रकारभेदैः । तत्प्रपञ्चता स्वात्मनो मुद्रापरमार्थरूपभेदयोगविशेषः प्रपञ्चता ॥२३॥

ललितायाः इत्यादिभिः तत्रिफालनमित्यन्तैर्व्याकुलाचरक्रमलिखितैस्त्रिभिः श्लोकैराद्यायाः ललिताविद्याया अक्षरवाच्यमर्थमुपदिशति । तत्र ललितायाः श्रीविद्यातार्त्तीयखण्डस्येति यावत् । त्रिभिः पगिमितः सकलार्थः सकलशब्दार्थः । शेषेण अक्षरेण । तुः समुच्चये । तेन प्रोक्तप्रकारावयवार्थो तार्त्तीयखण्डसमुदायभावात् । इदं अनन्तरवक्ष्यमाणार्थस्वरूपं । अशेषतो जगत् कृत्स्नं तेन समष्टिरूपं । व्यष्टिरूपं जगदिति यावत् । ह्लेखात्मकं शक्तिमयं । ईश्वरीति देवीसम्बुद्धिः । तस्याः ह्लेखायाः । चः समुच्चये । अर्थः अक्षरवाच्यः । तुरवधारणे । कथितः अनन्तरवक्ष्यमाणश्लोके । सर्व्वतन्त्रेषु एतस्मात् तन्त्रादन्येषु गोपितः अतिरहस्यत्वात् । व्योम्ना आकाशाक्षरेण प्रथमेन प्रकाशमानत्वं आकाशस्य स्फुरणात्मकत्वात् । स्वातन्त्र्येण इतरप्रकाशनैरपेक्ष्यं । ग्रासमानत्वं स्वस्वरूपतया । अग्निना अक्षरेण द्वितीयेन अग्नेरपि तादात्म्येन ग्रासात्मकत्वात् । तयोः प्रकाशग्रासरूपयोः । विमर्शः तादात्म्यपरमार्थमेलनं । निफालनं तादात्म्यविमर्शनिर्णीतिः । एतदुक्तं भवति । ह्लेखास्थेन व्योमाक्षरेण स्वात्मनः प्रकाशरूपत्वं वह्न्यक्षरेण ग्रासात्मकत्वं तदुभयपरमार्थविमर्शरूपेण शिवशक्तिसंमेलनात्मकेन चतुर्थस्वरेण तदात्मकत्वेन तस्य परमार्थस्वरूपविन्दुना तद्दैविध्यप्रतीतिराहित्यात् तदैक्यनिर्णीतिश्च क्रियत इति ॥ २६ ॥

अथ मन्त्रविनिर्म्माणविधानमभिधीयते ।
मन्त्रवीर्य्यसुसिद्धानामितरेषां विशेषकृत् ॥ २७ ॥
मन्त्रा एकाक्षराः पिण्डाः कर्त्तर्य्यो द्व्यक्षराः स्मृताः ।
वर्णत्रयं समारभ्य नवार्णावधि वीजकाः ॥ २८ ॥
ततो दशार्णमारभ्य यावद्विंशति मन्त्रकाः ।
तत ऊर्द्धं गता मालास्तासु भेदो न विद्यते ॥ २९ ॥
तथैव पिण्डकर्त्तर्य्यो र्भेदो वीजेषु वर्णतः ।
पदैर्म्मन्त्रेषु भेदः स्यात् तेषां संख्याः शृणु क्रमात् ॥ ३० ॥
षट् चतुर्विंशति तथा शतं विंशतिसंयुतम् ।
सविंशति सप्तशतं चत्वारिंशद्भिरन्वितम् ॥ ३१ ॥

अथेत्यादिभिः क्रमादित्यन्तैश्चतुर्भिः श्लोकैः पिण्डादिमालान्तानां मन्त्राणां त्रैविध्यं तेषामक्षरपदविन्यासेन वहुरूप्यञ्च तत्संख्यां प्रस्तावसहितमुपदिशति। तत्र मन्त्रवीर्य्यसुसिद्धानां अस्मिन् पटले वक्ष्यमाणमन्त्रवीर्य्यज्ञानसुसिद्धानां। इतरेषां मन्त्रवीर्य्यज्ञानसिद्धिरहितानां। पिण्डाः नाम्नेति यावत्। कर्त्तर्य्यः प्राग्वत् नाम्ना। वीजकाः वीजसंज्ञा मन्त्राः। मन्त्रकाः प्राग्वन्नाम्ना। मालाः मालामन्त्राः। तासु मालासु। तथैव न विद्यत एव इत्यर्थः। तेषां भेदानां क्रमात् त्र्यक्षरमन्त्रभेदादिनवाक्षरमन्त्रभेदान्तमिति शेषः ॥ ३० ॥

षडित्याद्दिभिः समुन्नयेदित्यन्तैस्त्रिभिः श्लोकैस्त्र्यक्षरमन्त्रमारभ्य नवाक्षरमन्त्रा-वधि सप्तविधस्य वीजाभिधानस्य मन्त्रजातस्य अक्षरसन्दर्भविकल्पजनितसंख्या-क्रममुपदिशति। तत्र षट् त्र्यक्षरमन्त्रस्य भेदाः। एतदुक्तं भवति एकस्य द्वाभ्यां त्रिभिश्च संगुणनाज्जाताः षट्संख्याः त्र्यक्षरभेदा इति। चतुर्विंशति दिव्य-त्वाच्चतुर्विंशतिरित्यर्थः। चतुरक्षरमन्त्रस्येति यावत्। त्र्यक्षरभेदषट्कं चतुर्भिः संगुणय्य चतुर्विंशतिसंख्या लब्धा इत्यर्थः। शतं विंशतिसंयुतं पञ्चाक्षरमन्त्र-भेदा इति यावत्। चतुरक्षरभेदानां पञ्चभिः संगुणनाज्जाता इत्यर्थः (१२०)। सविंशति सप्तशतं विंशत्यधिकं सप्तशतमित्यर्थः (७२०) षडक्षरमन्त्रभेदा इति

सहस्रपञ्चकं पश्चाच्चत्वारिंशत्सहस्रयुक् ।
त्रिशत विंशति ततस्त्रिलक्षेण समन्वितम् ॥ ३२ ॥
द्विषष्टिश्च सहस्राणां साशीत्यष्टशतन्विति ।
भेदसंख्येत्थं सप्तानां ताभिरन्याः समुन्नयेत् ॥ ३३ ॥
प्रस्तारक्रममेतेषां शृणु देवि यथाक्रमम् ।
एतैरेवोन्नयेन्मन्त्रपदभेदाननुक्रमात् ॥ ३४ ॥
तिर्य्यग्रेखाद्वयं कृत्वा तत्राधोर्द्धा लिखेत् क्रमात् ।
रेखाश्चतस्रः पञ्चैवमृज्वाकारा दशावधि ॥ ३५ ॥

यावत्। पञ्चाक्षरमन्त्रभेदान् षड्भिर्हृत्वा जाता इत्यर्थः। चत्वारिंशद्भिरन्वितं सहस्रपञ्चकं सप्ताक्षरमन्त्रभेदा इति यावत्। प्राग्वत् षडक्षरभेदान् सप्तभिर्हृत्वा जाता इत्यर्थः (५०४०)। पश्चात् अष्टाक्षरमन्त्रभेदसंख्येति यावत्। चत्वारिंशत्सहस्रयुक् त्रिशतं विंशति विंशत्यधिकशतत्रयोत्तरचत्वारिंशत्सहस्रमित्यर्थः (४०३२०)। प्रागवत् सप्ताक्षरभेदान् अष्टभिर्हृत्वा जाता संख्या इत्यर्थः। ततः नवाक्षरमन्त्रभेदसंख्येति यावत्। त्रिलक्षेण समन्वितं द्विषष्टिश्च सहस्राणां साशीत्यष्टशतन्विति। अशीत्युत्तराष्टशताधिकद्वाषष्टिसहस्रयुतं त्रिलक्षमित्यर्थः (३६२८८०)। प्रागवदष्टाक्षरभेदान्नवभिर्हृत्वा जाताः संख्या इत्यर्थः। इत्थं उक्तप्रकारेण। सप्तानां त्र्यक्षरादिनवाक्षरान्तानां। ताभिः संख्याभिः। अन्या दशाक्षरादिभेदसंख्याः ॥ ३३ ॥

प्रस्तारेत्यादिभिश्चोदिता इत्यन्तैर्दशभिः श्लोकैस्तेषां मन्त्राक्षरसन्दर्भभेदानां प्रस्तारक्रमानुपदिशति। तत्र एतेषां भेदानां। देवीति सम्बुद्धिः। एतैः प्रकारैः। एवावधारणे। मन्त्रपदभेदान् मन्त्रेषु पदानां भेदान्। तिर्य्यग्रेखाद्वयं सव्यदक्षिणरेखाद्वयं। एकाङ्गुलान्तरालमिति। तत्र रेखाद्वयोर्मध्ये। अधोर्द्धाः दिव्यत्वादधजद्धरूपा इत्यर्थः। रेखाश्चतस्रः एकैकाङ्गुलान्तरालमिति यावत्। एष त्र्यक्षरभेदविन्यासयन्त्रप्रकारः। पञ्चैवमृज्वाकारा दशावधि चतुरक्षरादिभेदविन्यासे पञ्चषट्सप्ताष्टनवदशरेखाः क्रमाल्लिखेदित्यर्थः। तदधो वर्द्धयेद्रेखाः

तदधो वर्द्धयेद्रेखास्तत्तत्संख्याङ्गुलावधि ।
तिर्य्यग्रेखास्तावतीश्च कृत्वा तेष्वङ्कमालिखेत् ॥ ३६ ॥
सव्यदक्षस्थितेष्वेषु कोष्ठपंक्तिष्वनुक्रमात् ।
आद्ये द्विद्विक्रमादङ्कान् पूरयेत्तत्र चोदितान् ॥ ३७ ॥
एतेनान्यत्र सर्वत्र देयानङ्काननुक्रमात् ।
द्वितीयपंक्तौ प्रथमे खण्डे शेषांस्तु पूरयेत् ॥ ३८ ॥

तदूर्द्धाधोरेखा: अधो वर्द्धयेत् । तत्तत्संख्याङ्गुलावधि तत्तद्भेदसंख्याङ्गुलावधि तत्तद्भेदसंख्याङ्गुलिभि: । तिर्य्यग्रेखास्तावतीश्च कृत्वा पूर्व्वलिखितद्वितीयतिर्य्यग्रेखाग्रे स्तावतीश्च कृत्वा पूर्व्वलिखितद्वितीयतिर्य्यग्रेखादितत्तद्भेदसंख्यास्तिर्य्यग्रेखाश्चैकैकाङ्गुलान्तरालं लिखित्वेत्यर्थ: । तेषु कोष्ठेषु अङ्कं प्रथमाक्षरस्य प्रथममङ्कं द्वितीयाक्षरस्य द्वितीयमङ्कमेवमेवमुत्तरत्राप्यक्षरसंख्यमङ्कमिति यावत् । एतदुक्तं भवति । प्राक्प्रत्यगदक्षिणोदक् च सूत्रचतुष्टयं समक्रमेणास्फालनात्तिर्य्यग्रूपेण कोष्ठत्रयकोष्ठत्रयोपेता: षट् पंक्तयो जाता: । तासु पंक्तिषु त्र्यक्षरभेदषट्कं विलिखेत् । एवमुत्तरत्रापि तिर्य्यग्रूपतत्तदक्षरसंख्यकोष्ठोपेतास्तत्तद्भेदसंख्यपंक्तीरधोध: परिकल्प्य तत्र तत्र तद्भेदान् विलिखेदिति । सव्यदक्षस्थितेष्वेषु कोष्ठेष्विति यावत् । कोष्ठपंक्तिषु कोष्ठानां पंक्तिषु । अनुक्रमात् ऊर्द्धाद्यधोध: । आद्ये कोष्ठे प्रतिपंक्तिष्विति यावत् । द्विद्विक्रमात् द्विद्विपंक्तिक्रमात् एकमेकं खण्डं परिकल्प्येति यावत् । चोदितान् अक्षरसंख्योपलक्षणभूतानिति यावत् । एतदुक्तं भवति । तिर्य्यग्रूपत्रित्रिकोष्ठात्मिकासु पंक्तिषु षट्(सु)सूत्राधरद्विद्विपंक्तिक्रमात् एकमेकं खण्डं परिकल्प्य प्रथमखण्डपंक्त्योराद्ये त्वाद्ये कोष्ठे प्रथमप्रथममङ्कं द्वितीयखण्डपंक्तिद्वयस्याद्ये त्वाद्ये कोष्ठे द्वितीयं द्वितीयमङ्कं तृतीयखण्डपंक्तिद्वयस्याद्ये त्वाद्ये कोष्ठे तृतीयं तृतीयमङ्कं चैवं अक्षरभेदषट्कन्यासे न्यसेदिति । एतेन क्रमेण । अन्यत्र सर्व्वत्र चतुरक्षरादि नवाक्षरान्ततत्तद्भेदन्यासे इति यावत् । एतदुक्तं भवति चतुरक्षरादिनवाक्षरान्तभेदप्रस्तारे तत्तद्भेदसंख्यास्तत्तदक्षरभेदसंख्यया विभज्य तत्तत्फलसंख्याभि: पंक्तिभिरेकमेकं खण्डं परिकल्प्य प्रथमखण्डस्य पंक्तिष्वाद्ये त्वाद्ये कोष्ठे प्रथमं प्रथममङ्कमेवं द्वितीयादिषु खण्डपंक्ति

द्वितीयादिष्वपि तथा शेषान् खण्डेषु पूरयेत् ।
[तृतीयपंक्तौ तु शेषैस्त्वेवमेव समालिखेत् ॥ ३९ ॥
चतुर्थादिष्वपि तथा नवमान्तं समालिखेत् ।]
तिर्य्यक्पंक्तिष्वनभ्यास्तक्रममङ्कास्तु सर्वतः ॥ ४० ॥

ष्वाद्ये त्वाद्ये कोष्ठे द्वितीयाद्यङ्कमिदं क्रमादाद्याद्यकोष्ठाकारेणोर्द्धाधःक्रमपंक्त्यां चोदितानङ्कान् पूरयेदिति। द्वितीयपंक्तौ प्रतिपंक्तिकं द्वितीयकोष्ठात्मकोर्द्धाधःक्रमपंक्तौ। प्रथमे खण्डे शेषांस्तु पूरयेत् आद्यखण्डलिखितं व्यतिरिक्तैरङ्कैः प्रागवदवान्तरखण्डानि च परिकल्प्य तत्तदवान्तरात्मकैकैकखण्डे त्वेकाङ्कक्रमात् शेषाङ्कान् पूरयेदिति यावत्। द्वितीयादिष्वपि तथा शेषान् खण्डेषु पूरयेत्। द्वितीयादिखण्डेष्वपि प्रागवदवान्तरखण्डानि च परिकल्प्य तत्तदाद्यपंक्तिविलिखिताङ्कादनन्तरा(ङ्का)द्याङ्कान् लिखितान् सर्व्वांस्तत्तत्खण्डेष्वेव पूरयेदित्यर्थः। तृतीयपंक्तौ प्रतिपंक्तिक तृतीयतृतीयकोष्ठात्मकोर्द्धाधःक्रमपंक्तौ। तुः समुच्चये। शेषैः आद्यद्वितीयकोष्ठयोः प्रतिखण्डप्रलिखिताङ्कैः। तुरवधारणे। एतदुक्तं भवति तृतीयतृतीयकोष्ठात्मकोर्द्धाधःक्रमपंक्त्यामपि तत्तत्खण्डपंक्तिषु लिखिताङ्कसंख्या भागहारेण परिकल्पिततत्तदवान्तरावान्तरखण्डानि लिखेत् शेषाङ्कैः पूरयेदिति। चतुर्थादिषु प्रतिखण्डचतुर्थपञ्चमादिकोष्ठात्मकोर्द्धाधःक्रमरूपपंक्तिष्वित्यर्थः। तथा तत्तच्छिष्टाङ्कानुगुण तत्तदवान्तरखण्डानि परिकल्प्य तत्तत्खण्डानि तत्तच्छिष्टाङ्कैः पूरयेदित्यर्थः। नवमान्तं एवं क्रमात् प्रागुक्तनवमकोष्ठात्मकपंक्तिपर्य्यन्तं। अनभ्यस्तक्रमं विभिन्नक्रमं। अयमत्र प्रस्तारक्रमः। आदिनवाक्षराभीष्टाक्षरसंख्याकोष्ठात्मकात्मकांस्तत्तद्भेदसंख्याः पंक्तीस्तिर्य्यग्रूपेण निष्पाद्य तत्तत्पंक्तिसंख्यां तत्तदभीष्टाक्षरसंख्यया विभज्य तत्तल्लब्धसंख्याभिः पंक्तिभिरेकैकखण्डक्रमात्तत्तदक्षरसंख्यानि खण्डानि परिकल्प्य तत्तत्खण्डपंक्तिष्वाद्ये त्वाद्ये कोष्ठे प्रथमाद्यङ्कानक्षरसंख्योपलक्षितान् विन्यस्य पुनस्तत्तत्खण्डपंक्तिसंख्यामपि तत्तच्छिष्टाङ्कसंख्यया विभज्य तल्लब्धसंख्यया तत्तदवान्तरतत्तदवान्तरादिखण्डानि चैवं क्रमादूर्द्धाधः क्रमरूपोपान्त्यकोष्ठपंक्त्यामेकैकतिर्य्यक्पंक्त्यैकखण्डं यथा तथा परिकल्प्य तेष्वङ्कान्

विन्यस्य तत्तत्पंक्तिषु परिशिष्टे अन्यकोष्ठे तत्तत्पंक्तिषु लिखितमङ्कं न्यसेदिति। अत्र षड्भेदप्रस्तारे उदाहरणं अक्षरत्रयस्य भेदषट्कत्वं तिसृभिः संख्याभिः षट्कं विभज्य लब्धे द्वे तस्मात् द्वाभ्यां द्वाभ्यां पंक्तिभ्या मेकं खण्डं परिकल्प्य प्रथमखण्डपंक्त्योराद्ये कोष्ठे प्रथममङ्कं द्वितीयखण्ड-पंक्त्याद्याद्यकोष्ठे द्वितीयं द्वितीयमङ्कं तृतीयखण्डाद्याद्यकोष्ठे तृतीयमङ्कं विन्यस्य पुनस्तच्छिष्टाङ्कसंख्याद्वयेन प्रतिखण्डपंक्तिद्वयं विभज्य लब्धमेकं तस्मादवान्तर-खण्डमेकैकपंक्त्या परिकल्प्य तत्तत्प्रथमखण्डशेषभूतद्वितीयं तृतीयं तत्तद्वितीय-खण्डशेषं तृतीयं प्रथमञ्च तत्तत्तृतीयखण्डशेषं प्रथमं द्वितीयं च तत्तद्वितीय-कोष्ठे क्रमाद्विन्यस्य तत्तदन्यकोष्ठात्मकोर्द्धाधःपंक्तिकोष्ठषट्के तत्तत्तिर्य्यग्रूप-पंक्तिशेषमङ्कं तृतीयं द्वितीयं प्रथमे प्रथमं तृतीयं द्वितीये तृतीये द्वितीयं प्रथमञ्च विन्यसेत्। अङ्कतोप्यूर्द्धादिषट्पंक्तिषु न्यासः। एवमुत्तरत्रापि कल्पनीयः। अभीष्टाक्षरसंख्याभेदेषु उद्दिष्टभेदसंख्याक्रमोयं लिख्यते। अभीष्ट-संख्याक्षराणि क्वचिदङ्करूपेण पंक्तिशः स्थापयित्वा तत्तद्भेदेषूद्दिष्टसंख्याखण्ड-गतपंक्तिसंख्यया शेषमशून्यं यथा तथा विभज्य तदशक्यं चेत् फलं शून्यं परिकल्प्य तत्तत्फलं शून्यफलञ्च क्वचित् स्थापयित्वा भूयो भूयस्तत्तदवान्तरा-दिखण्डगतपंक्तिसंख्यया यावदेक पंक्त्या खण्डं तावत् प्राग्वदशून्यं शेषं विभज्य तत्फलं तदधोधः संस्थाप्य तत्तत्फलं सेकं कृत्वा भागहाराभावे शिष्टमेकं तत्फलपंक्त्यामधः संस्थाप्य पंक्तिशेषस्थापिताभीष्टसंख्याक्षराङ्केषु प्रथम-स्थानादिप्रथमफलसंख्यस्थानगताङ्कमाहृत्य क्वचिदुद्दिष्टसंख्यभेदस्य प्रथमस्थान-गतमङ्कं संस्थाप्यानन्तरं तदन्तराद्यङ्केष्वपि तत्तद्वितीयादिफलसंख्यस्थानगताङ्कं क्रमादाहृत्याहृत्य तदनन्तरपंक्तिशः स्थापनादुद्दिष्टभेदात्मिका विद्या भवतीति। पञ्चाक्षरसंख्याभेदेष विंशत्यधिकशतेष्वेकोनाशीतितमभेदस्य स्वरूपानयने उदाहरणं। अक्षरपञ्चकस्य पंक्तिरूपेणाङ्कन्यासः १२३४५। उद्दिष्टसंख्याता तत्खण्डपंक्तिसंख्या २४। तया विभजत्र लब्धानि फलानि ३ तच्छिष्टात् ७ तदवान्तर खण्डपंक्तिसंख्यया विभजत्र लब्धं १ शिष्टं फलं १ तदवान्तरखण्डपंक्ति-संख्यया २ विभजत्र लब्धं फलं ० फलशून्यञ्च सेकं कृत्वा तदवशिष्टञ्च संस्थाप्य न्यासः ४५१२३। क्वचित् स्थापिताक्षरसंख्यातिष्वङ्केषु प्रथमफलोपात्तच(न्तश्च)तुर्थस्थाने त्वेकाङ्कः द्वितीयफलोपात्त(न्त)द्वितीयस्थाने द्वितीयोङ्कः तृतीयफलोपात्त(न्तत)दनं-तरस्थाने तृतीयोङ्कः प्रथमफलोपात्त(न्त)चतुर्थस्थानाङ्कः तदनन्तरस्थानाङ्कः तदधःस्था-

एवं कृते भवेद्विद्या सर्व्वोर्द्ध्वा वीरवन्दिते ।
सर्व्वाधस्ताद्विलोमा सा मध्यस्था व्याकुलक्रमाः ॥ ४१ ॥
ताभिः सर्व्वाभिरप्याशु सिध्यत्येवाभिवाञ्छितम् ।
ललिताभेदजातानि तद्यन्त्रोक्तान्यशेषतः ॥ ४२ ॥

वशिष्टोपात्ता(त्त)ङ्कस्तदधःस्थानङ्क एवं क्रमाल्लब्धैकोनाशीतितमविद्याभेदस्वरूपन्यासः। ४१२३५। अनन्तरमभीष्टसंख्याक्षरेषु उद्दिष्टभेदस्य संख्यानयनक्रमो लिख्यते। अभीष्टसंख्याक्षराण्येकद्वित्र्यादिक्रमादङ्करूपेण पंक्तिशः क्वचित् संस्थाप्य १२३४५ तेषु प्रथमस्थानादि यावतिस्थानेषूद्दिष्टभेदस्य द्वितीयादिस्थानगतं यावति स्थानेन तत्तदङ्कं परित्यज्य तत्तदङ्कगतस्थानसंख्यामप्यधोधः संस्थाप्य तेषु सर्व्वाधःस्थमङ्कं मुक्त्वा तदुपरिगताङ्केष्वेकमेकं परित्यज्य उर्द्ध्वादितत्तच्छिष्टैस्तत्तत्खण्डतदवान्तरादिखण्डगतपंक्तिसंख्यां हत्वा संयोज्य सर्व्वाधःस्थाङ्कसंयोजनाच्चोद्दिष्टविद्याभेदस्य संख्या भवतीति। उदाहरणं यथा पञ्चाक्षरन्यासः १२३४५। उद्दिष्टभेदन्यासः ४२१३५। उद्दिष्टभेदस्य प्रथमस्थानेद्वितस्य तच्चतुर्थस्थानगताङ्क १ तदधस्थानानन्तरादि द्वितीयस्थानेष्वित्यन्तं परित्यज्य तत्स्थानसंख्याङ्कस्तदधः स्थापितः। तदनन्तरस्थाने तृतीयाङ्कस्थित्या तमपहृत्य तत्स्थानसंख्याङ्कस्तदधः स्थापितः। तदनन्तरस्थाने तच्चतुर्थाङ्कस्य स्थित्या तत्स्थानस्थः तदधः स्थापितः। तदनन्तरे तत्पञ्चमस्थानाङ्कस्य स्थित्या तत्स्थानसंख्याङ्कस्तदधः स्थापितः। तेष्वेव संस्थाङ्कात् अनेन तदुपरिगताङ्केष्वेकमेकं परित्यज्याङ्कन्यासः २३१। तदधःस्थितमङ्कं मुक्त्वा तैरुर्द्ध्वाधोङ्कैः खण्डगतसंख्यापंक्तिः तदवान्तरादिखण्डगतपंक्तिश्च तैरुर्द्ध्वादिक्रमेण न्यस्ताङ्कैर्हत्वा हत्वा संयोज्य तदधःस्थमङ्कमेकञ्च संयोज्य लब्धसंख्यास्तदुद्दिष्टभेदत्वे एकोनाशीतितमसंख्याभेदो भवति। एवं सर्व्वत्र परिकल्पनीयं। एवं कृते प्रस्तार इति यावत्। विद्या उपदिष्टक्रमस्वरूपेति यावत्। सर्वोर्द्ध्वा प्रथमखण्डे प्रथमपंक्तिस्थेति यावत्। वीरवन्दिते इति देवीसम्बुद्धिः। सर्व्वाधस्तात् चरमखण्डे चरमपंक्त्यामिति यावत्। विलोमा प्रतिलोमक्रमा। सा विद्या। मध्यस्था सर्व्वाद्यसर्व्वचरमपंक्त्योर्मध्यस्थ मध्यस्थाः व्याकुलक्रमाः भिन्नक्रमाः। ताभिर्विद्याभिः। ललिताभेदजातानि खण्डस्वरूपाणीति यावत्। तद्यन्त्रोक्तानि तद्यन्त्रपटल-

नित्यानित्याभिदाश्चापि तद्‌यन्त्रपटलोदिताः ।
अन्यास्तु तत्र तत्रैव द्रष्टव्या यत्र चोदिताः ॥ ४३ ॥
एषां पञ्चप्रकाराणामर्थाः कोष्टग्विधा मताः ।
सम्यक्त्वमेषां केन स्यात् सर्वेषामप्ययत्नतः ॥ ४४ ॥
असम्यक्त्वञ्च केन स्यात्तत्सम्यक्करणं कथम् ।
कानि सिद्धस्य चिह्नानि का वा सिद्धिरुदाहृता ॥ ४५ ॥
रेखाः षड़ालिखेत्तिर्य्यक्तेष्वधोर्द्धा लिखेत् क्रमात् ।
एकादश ततश्चक्रं पञ्चाशत्कोष्ठकं भवेत् ॥ ४६ ॥

प्रोक्तानि त्रयस्त्रिंशे पटले प्रोक्तानीत्यर्थः । नित्यानित्याभिदास्तद्‌यन्त्रपटलोदिताः नित्यानित्यापूजापटले षोड़शे तद्‌यन्त्रप्रस्तारे प्रोक्ताः । अन्या इतरनित्याविद्याभिदाः । तुः समुच्चये ॥ ४३ ॥

एषामित्यादिनोदाहृतेत्यन्तेन श्लोकद्वयेन षड्‌विधं देवीप्रश्नमुपदिशति । तत्र एषां पञ्चप्रकाराणां मन्त्राणां पिण्डकर्त्तरीवीजमन्त्रमालारूपाणां । अर्थाः स्थूलसूक्ष्मपररूपा इति यावत् । एषां मन्त्राणां । सर्वेषां पिण्डादिपञ्चविधानां । तत्सम्यक्करणं मन्त्राणां सम्यक्करणं । सिद्धस्य मन्त्रविद्यादिषु । वा समुच्चये ॥ ४५ ॥

रेखा इत्यादिभिः शिवात्मन इत्यन्तैस्त्रिभिः श्लोकैर्मन्त्राणामक्षरवाक्यार्थज्ञानार्थमकारादिक्षकारान्तानां मातृकाक्षराणां पञ्चभूतात्मकत्वप्रतिपादनपरं पञ्चाशत्कोष्ठं चक्रं तत्र तेषां लेखनक्रमं भूतात्मकक्रमञ्चोपदिशति । तत्र तिर्य्यगद्क्षिणसव्यमित्यर्थः । तेषु दिव्यत्वात् तास्वित्यर्थः । रेखास्विति यावत् । अधोर्द्धं दिव्यत्वादधऊर्द्धा इत्यर्थः । रेखा इति यावत् । ततस्तेन लेखनेनेति यावत् । तत्र चक्रे । सव्यादिदक्षान्तं सव्यकोष्ठमारभ्य दक्षिणकोष्ठान्तं । अर्णान् तत्तद्वर्णान् भूताक्षराणीति यावत् । अनुक्रमादेकैकपंक्त्यामेकैकभूताक्षरदशकक्रमादिति यावत् । मायाशक्त्यभिधः मायेति शक्तिरिति च संज्ञितः । सर्गःविसर्गः विसर्जनीयस्य मूलाधारादविवक्षितपूर्व्वमुत्पत्तेः । तस्मात् कारणात्तस्य विसर्जनीयस्य । अत्र चक्रे । शिवात्मनः शिवस्वरूपस्य शक्त्यात्मन इति

तत्र सव्यादिदक्षान्तं लिखेद्वर्णाननुक्रमात् ।
प्राणाग्नीलाम्बुखात्मानः पंक्तयः पञ्च कीर्त्तिताः ॥ ४७ ॥
मायाशक्त्यभिधः सर्गः सर्वभूतात्मकः प्रभुः ।
तस्मात्तस्यात्र विन्यासो नैकदेशः शिवात्मनः ॥ ४८ ॥
वा रु रः तो प्रा म त्व वा वी दो यो यु ज र्ना र वा ।
नि र्श ना प्तः मा स्प श्व व्या श्व म तां र्णा द नां रु त्र ॥४९॥
जः स्त्रिः चि ग्नि स्ते र्वै शु च तिः वः खी भा दुग्र दा शि प्र ।
नि स ना हो मा या स्व दा पि तै सा र्णा म नां ज व ॥५०॥
कूः भूः रा रा ज्या क्ष्मा स्थि ध ला मी सा वा द्रू भू र गो ।
नां ता व मा र्णा न्ये नि ना मं स्यु था मा क्र नां र्य भौ ॥५१॥
कं रि नं लं वाः वा व ज हृत् यं सो थ म्बु स्तो र पा ।
ना ता व मा र्णा न्ये नि ना मं स्यु था प्या क्र नां र्य्य मा ॥५२॥
च स्व र भ्र ुः भ्र ं ख दुग्र वि यत् न्यं भो म वि शू न व्यो ।
नि ना न्ये स ता स्व मा हं र्णां व्यो रू मे पि णा म क्र ॥ ५३ ॥

यावत् । अयमत्र विरचनाक्रमः । प्राक्प्रत्यग्दक्षिणोदक् च क्रमात् समान्तरालमेकादशषट्सूत्रास्फालनात् पञ्चाशत्कोष्ठात्मकं चक्रं विधाय प्रतिपंक्तिकं दक्षिणसव्यरूपकोष्ठदशके प्रागुक्तक्रमात् प्राणाग्नीलाम्बुखाक्षराणि सविन्दुकानि दशदशोर्द्ध्वपंक्त्याधःपंक्तिपर्य्यन्तं क्रमाद्विलिखेदिति ॥ ४८ ॥

वात इत्यादिभि र्व्योमरूपिणामित्यन्तैर्व्याकुलाक्षरक्रमलिखितैः पञ्चभिः श्लोकैः अस्मिंस्तन्त्रे समस्तमन्त्रविद्यास्वरूपाभिधानसङ्केतरूपाणि भूतनामानि प्रत्येकं क्रमेण दश दशोपदिशति । तत्र वर्णानां मरुतां वायव्यानामक्षराणां दशानामित्यर्थः । वर्णानां तैजसानामिति दिश्यत्वात्तैजसानामित्यर्थः । आग्नेयानां दशानामक्षराणां । रसाद्वला दिश्यत्वात् न सन्धिः कृतः । भौमानां भूमिसम्बन्धिनां वर्णानां अक्षराणां । आप्यानामप्सम्बन्धिनां वर्णानां । व्योमरूपिणां प्राग्वत् व्योमानां वर्णानां आकाशात्मकानां ॥ ५३ ॥

एतैर्नामभिरेवात्र मन्त्रोद्धारः कृतः शिवे ।
तस्मादतीव गोप्यानि नामान्येतानि सर्वदा ॥ ५४ ॥
उक्तनिह्नवयोगेन लिखेत्तत्र तु पुस्तके ।
पद्यमेकं वदेत् कर्णे शिष्यस्यैवोक्तरूपिणः ॥ ५५ ॥
ङ्कै र्णान् खे त्त द जा लि वृ तः क्र यो त्य ग स्त म व्यं ।
र्य्यात् यो मे भें कु द ज ते तर्णाशेषर्भामसं (?) ॥ ५६ ॥

एतैरित्यादिना रूपिण इत्यन्तेन श्लोकद्वयेन प्रोक्तानामेषां नाम्नामस्मिंस्तन्त्रे मन्त्रोद्धारकथनपरत्वेन गोप्यत्वादस्य मन्त्रस्य च परमार्थाभिधायित्वे गोप्यत्वाच्च परमेश्वरेणैवायोग्यविषयत्वासिद्धेश्र श्लोकाक्षराणां व्याकुलक्रमलेखनप्रकारः प्रस्तूयते। तत्र एवावधारणे। अत्र तन्त्रे। शिवे इति देवीसम्बुद्धिः। तस्मात् कारणात्। उक्तनिह्नवयोगेन अनन्तरवक्ष्यमाणश्लोकोक्तनिह्नवप्रकारेण। तुः समुच्चये। पद्यं निह्नवरूपार्थगर्भमिति यावत्। एवावधारणे। उक्तरूपिणः प्रथमपटले "चतुर्भिराद्यैः संयुक्तः" इत्यादिना त्रयोविंशादिश्लोकद्वयेनेति यावत् ॥ ५५ ॥

वृत्तेत्यादिना व्याकुलाक्षरक्रमालिखितेन श्लोकेन गद्यपद्यभाषात्मनां सकल-सन्दर्भाणामिष्टरूपं व्याकुलीकरणसमग्रकरणयोरेकाकारमुपायमुपदिशति। तत्र वृत्तजार्णान् अनुष्टुवादिवृत्तोत्पन्नाक्षराणि। अङ्कैः अक्षरसंख्यासमान-संख्यैः। व्यत्यस्तक्रमयोगतः परस्परमिति यावत्। तैरङ्कैः। भेदयोजने व्याकुली-करणसमग्रकरणे। एतदुक्तं भवति अभीष्टाभीष्टवृत्तश्लोकस्य पादाक्षरपादाक्षर-संख्यानुगुणमेकद्वित्र्याद्यङ्कान् पंक्तिरूपेण विलिख्य तेषु द्वौ द्वावङ्कौ परस्परसर्व्व-मङ्कं भिन्नक्रमं यथा तथा विन्यस्य तत्तत्क्रमाङ्कगर्भं पद्यं कृत्वा तेन व्याकुली-करणं समग्रकरणञ्च कुर्य्यादिति। तस्योदाहरणमनुष्टुवतेति लिख्यते। अनुष्टुभः पादाक्षराण्यष्टौ तत्संख्याङ्काः पंक्तिरूपेण लिखिताः। १२३४५६७८। तेष्वङ्केषु प्रथमाष्टमौ द्वितीयचतुर्थौ तृतीयषष्ठौ पञ्चमसप्तमौ च परस्परं व्यत्यस्य जाताः क्रमाङ्काः पंक्तिरूपेण लिखिताः कटपयादिक्रमेण तत्तत्क्रमाङ्कगर्भश्लोके:।

श्लोकेनानेन जनयेदनन्तान् सम्प्रदायतः ।
नानावृत्तानभीष्टार्थान्निह्नवाय तु देशिकः ॥ ५७ ॥
अनुष्णाशीते विजने सुसमे रम्यविग्रहे ।
गृहे वा मण्डपे स्थित्वा पीठं धवलितोदरम् ॥ ५८ ॥
विन्यस्य तस्मिन् पूर्णायां शुभर्चे वा शुभोदये ।
कुचन्दनैः कुङ्कुमैर्वा दरदैर्वोपदेशतः ॥ ५९ ॥
कृत्वोक्तं मण्डलं सार्णं तत्रावाह्य यजेच्छिवाम् ।
नित्यशो मातृकां जप्यात् सम्प्रदायानुसारतः ॥ ६० ॥

देवीतत्त्वार्थगामी यस्तत्पदाम्बुजशेखरः ।
तस्मै ऽस्मिन् व्याकुलान् श्लोकान्वाचयेन्नैव केवलः ॥ इति ॥ ५६ ॥

श्लोकेनेत्यादिना श्लोकेन तस्य श्लोकस्य सम्प्रदायबलानुभावात् सर्व्वच्छन्दःसु वृत्तेषु इच्छानुरूपानर्थान् तत्तत्श्लोकान् सन्दर्भव्याकुलीकरणपरमार्थान् कर्त्तुं देशिकानां सामर्थ्यमुपदिशति। तत्र अनेन अन्योन्यव्यत्यासभेदक्रमेण। अनन्तान् श्लोकान् व्याकुलीकरणक्रमभेदगर्भानिति यावत्। अभीष्टार्थान् निह्नवाय व्याकुलीकरणक्रमनिह्नवार्थमर्थान्तरद्योतकानित्यर्थः ॥ ५७ ॥

अनुष्णाशीतेत्यादिभिर्योगत इत्यन्तैश्चतुर्भिः श्लोकैर्नित्याविद्यासिद्धस्य तन्त्रनिष्णातस्य मनीषितदेवतात्मत्वसिद्ध्यै तत्तद्देवतानामिच्छानुरूपाणां मन्त्राणां निर्म्माणप्रकारमुपदिशति। तत्र अनुष्णाशीते। उष्णशीतद्वयरहिते। रम्यविग्रहे हृदयङ्गमे। एतद्विशेषणचतुष्टयं मनःस्थिरीकरणापेक्षया देवतानिवासयोग्यापेक्षया च। वा विकल्पे। स्थित्वा प्राङ्मुखः इति सम्प्रदायार्थः। पीठमित्यस्यानन्तरवक्ष्यमाणश्लोके विन्यस्येत्यनेन सम्बन्धः। धवलितोदरं श्वेतवर्णानुलेपनेनेति यावत्। तस्मिन् पीठे। पूर्णायां पौर्णमास्यां। वा विकल्पे। शुभोदये शुभराश्युदये शुभग्रहोदये च। अस्य सम्प्रदायार्थो लिख्यते। इडायामेव प्रवहतः श्वासस्य प्रवेशावस्थायामिति। कुचन्दनैः रक्तचन्दनैः। वा विकल्पे। दरदैः जातिलिङ्गैः। वा विकल्पे। उपदेशतः उपदेशक्रमात् श्रीभूतलिपीनामिति यावत्। कृत्वोक्तं मण्डलं पञ्चा-

एवमब्द तु सम्पूर्णमभीष्टदेवाय मन्त्रवित् ।
कुर्य्यान्मन्त्रमभीष्टार्थगमकं प्रोक्तयोगतः ॥ ६१ ॥
नभोग्निवायुप्रायार्णाः क्रूराः क्षोभकरा मताः ।
भूतोयप्रचुराः सौम्याः सेव्याः सिद्धिकरा मताः ॥ ६२ ॥
एषामन्योन्यसम्भेदवाहुल्याद्बहवोऽर्णवाः ।
तैः तथा भजनात् सिद्धाः फलन्ति स्वैक्ययोगतः ॥ ६३ ॥
मन्त्रार्थास्त्रिविधा ज्ञेया ज्ञातव्याः सिद्धिकाङ्क्षिभिः ।
पूजापटलसंप्रोक्तास्त्रिविधाः स्वरूपासकाः ॥ ६४ ॥

शतकोष्ठात्मकमुक्तमण्डलं कृत्वेत्यर्थः। सार्णमित्यस्य पूर्व्वश्लोके उपदेशत इत्यनेन सम्बन्धः। एतदुक्तं भवति प्रागुक्तं पञ्चाशत्कोष्ठात्मकं चक्रं विधाय तत्रोर्द्धादिपंक्तिपञ्चके तिर्य्यग्रूपेण दशकोष्ठेषु यथोपदेशं श्रीभूतलिपीन् क्रमाद्विन्यस्य देवीमर्च्चयेदिति। सम्प्रदायानुसारतः सविन्दुकमकारादिचकारान्तमनुलोमक्रममक्षरं सविसर्जनीयं ऊकाराद्यकारान्तं चकारं चैवं क्रमात् प्रतिलोमक्रमश्चेत्यर्थः। एवं प्रतिदिन भजनजपादिनेत्यर्थः। कुर्य्यान्मन्त्रं मन्त्रं रचयेदित्यर्थः। अभीष्टार्थगमकं व्युत्पत्त्यादिसिद्धमार्गेणेति यावत्। प्रोक्तयोगतः वक्ष्यमाण मन्त्रवीर्य्यस्वरूपानुसन्धान योगतः ॥ ६१ ॥

नभ इत्यादिना स्वैक्ययोगत इत्यन्तेन श्लोकद्वयेन सकलमन्त्रव्यापकं क्रूरत्वं सौम्यत्वं मिश्रत्वञ्चोपदिशति। तत्र नभोऽग्निवायुप्रायार्णाः आकाशाक्षराग्नेयाक्षर वायुक्षरप्रचुरा मन्त्राः क्षोभकरा विश्वस्येति यावत्। भूतोयप्रचुराः भूम्यक्षरतोयाक्षरप्रचुरा मन्त्रा इति यावत्। सेव्या उपास्याः सर्वैः सर्व्वदा सर्व्वत्रेति यावत्। सिद्धिकराः अभिमतार्थस्येति यावत्। एषां क्रूरभूताक्षराणां सौम्यभूताक्षराणाञ्च अन्योन्यसम्भेदवाहुल्यात् अन्योन्यसंयोगप्रकारभेदवाहुल्यात्। अर्णवा मन्त्राः। तैः अर्णवैः। तथा निजनिजक्रूरसौम्यमिश्रादिस्वभावानुगुणं। एतदुक्तं भवति क्रूराक्षराणां सौम्याक्षराणाञ्च न्यूनाधिकयोगवशाद्बहुविधभेदा मन्त्राः स्वैक्ययोगतो भजनात् सिद्धाः स्वस्वक्रूरसौम्यमिश्रादि स्वभावानुगुणं फलन्तीति ॥ ६३ ॥

मन्त्रार्था इत्यादिभिः इष्टसिद्धिदा इत्यन्तैस्त्रिभिः श्लोकै मन्त्राणां सर्वेषा-

वर्णस्योदयविश्रान्तिपदे बुद्धिनिवेशनम्।
एकोन्यः सर्वतः सिद्धव्युत्पत्त्यर्थाभिवीक्षणम् ॥ ६५ ॥
वाच्यवाचक संभेदभावनादिभिरीरिताः।
एषां पञ्चप्रकाराणामशेषेणेष्टसिद्धिदाः ॥ ६६ ॥
मन्त्रवीर्य्यं शृणु प्राज्ञे कथयामि सुखास्पदम्।
येन ज्ञानानुभूतेन जीवन्मुक्तो भवेन्नरः ॥ ६७ ॥

मर्थालोचने प्रकारत्रैविध्यं तत्त्रैविध्येन त्रिविधानामर्थानामुपासकानामर्थालोचनं तत्तत् फलञ्चोपदिशति। तत्र त्रिविधाः सिद्धाद्यधिकारिभेदादिति यावत्। ज्ञातव्याः मन्त्रार्था इति शेषः। सिद्धिकांक्षिभिः मन्त्रविद्यादीनामिति यावत्। त्रिविधा सिद्धसाध्यसाधका इति यावत्। वर्णस्य प्रत्येकं मन्त्राक्षरस्येत्यर्थः। उदयविश्रान्तिपदे उदयविश्रान्तिस्थाने परास्वरूपे इति यावत्। बुद्धिनिवेशनं तदनुसन्धानात् तादात्म्यादिति यावत्। एकः अर्थ इति शेषः। एतदुक्तं भवति सर्व्वमन्त्राणामक्षरसमुदायात्मकत्वात् तत्तदक्षराणामपि प्रत्येकं परास्वरूपादितः पश्यन्त्यादिक्रमेणोदयं तेषां पुनस्तादात्म्येन तस्मिन्नेव विश्रान्त्या च सर्व्वमन्त्राणां परास्वरूपमेव स्वरूपमिति सिद्धैरनुसन्धेयमिति। अन्यः अर्थ इति यावत्। सर्व्वतः सिद्धव्युत्पत्त्यर्थाभिवीक्षणं व्याकरणप्रोक्तप्रकृतिप्रत्ययादिविभेदेन सिद्धव्युत्पत्त्या तत्तन्मन्त्रार्थानुसन्धानं। एतत् साध्यविषय इत्यर्थः। वाच्यवाचकसम्भेदभावनं वाच्यरूपाणां पञ्चभूतानामव्यक्तात्मकतया वाचकरूपाणामक्षरात्मनां तदव्यक्तात्मकनाद परमार्थशक्तित्वाच्च तादात्म्यभावनमित्यर्थः। एततु साधकविषय इत्यर्थः। ईरिता इतीरिताः श्रीविद्याया अर्था इति यावत्। एषां मन्त्राणां पञ्चप्रकाराणां पिण्डकर्त्तरीबीजमन्त्रमालासंज्ञानां इष्टसिद्धिदाः तदनुसन्धानेन यथोदितेनेति यावत् ॥ ६६ ॥

मन्त्रवीर्य्यमित्यादिभिः ईरित इत्यन्तैस्त्रिभिः श्लोकैः सकलमन्त्रविद्यागणस्य बीजभूतस्य (जीवभूतस्य) मन्त्रवीर्य्याभिधानस्य परमार्थस्य स्वरूपं तत्तज्ज्ञानेन

तेजसां शक्तिमूर्त्तीनां प्रपञ्चस्यापि कारणम् ।
गुणत्रयममीषाञ्च यत् कारणमुदाहृतम् ॥ ६८ ॥
तत्स्वरूपानुसन्धानसिद्धिः सम्यक्त्वमीरितम् ।
तन्मन्त्रवीर्य्यमुद्दिष्टं मन्त्राणां जीव ईरितः ॥ ६९ ॥

तेषां सर्वेषां समयकरणञ्चोपदिशति । तत्र मन्त्रवीर्य्यं मन्त्राणां परमार्थस्वरूपं । प्राज्ञे इति देवीसम्बुद्धिः । सुखास्पद परमार्थस्वरूपलाभात् । येन मन्त्रवीर्य्येण । ज्ञानानुभूतेन केवलं ज्ञानमात्रमन्तरेणानुभवपर्य्यवसायिना चेत्यर्थः । जीवन्मुक्तः जीवन्नेव मुक्तः । याथात्म्यज्ञानादसङ्कोच एव मुक्तिरित्यर्थः । तेजसां सोमसूर्य्याग्निमूर्त्तीनां । शक्तिमूर्त्तीनां मूर्त्तिकारणशक्तीनां मूर्त्तीनाञ्च वामेच्छाज्येष्ठाज्ञानक्रियारौद्रीणां ब्रह्मविष्णुरुद्राणामित्यर्थः । प्रपञ्चस्य ज्ञातृज्ञानज्ञेयरूपस्य । अपिशब्दः समुच्चये । कारणं भूतत्रैविध्यस्येति शेषः । गुणत्रयं सत्त्वरजस्तमांसि ते यस्मिन् । मूर्त्तीनां प्रपञ्चस्य च त्रैविध्यगुणत्रयादिवत् स्वरूप इत्यर्थः । अमीषां गुणानां । चः समाहारे । अनेन गुणानां तेजःशक्तिमूर्त्तीनाञ्चेत्यर्थः । कारणं प्राग्वत् । उदाहृतं अष्टाविंशे पटले "कारणं परमेशानि तवेच्छैव तु केवलमिति ।" तत्स्वरूपानुसन्धानसिद्धिः सकलकारणभूतेच्छाशक्त्यात्मना विद्यया स्वस्य चापृथक्त्वेनानुसन्धानसिद्धिः । समयत्वं आभिमुख्यकरणं । जीवः प्राणः । अनभिमुखमन्त्राणामकार्य्यकरत्वात् मन्त्रवीर्य्ययोगज्ञानमन्तरेण मन्त्रविद्यानामकार्य्यकरत्वात् । सम्प्रदायाविच्छित्त्यर्थं तत्प्रकारो नाथाज्ञया लिख्यते । प्रथमं कामकलाध्यानेन योगेन षट्त्रिंशे पटले वक्ष्यमाणपरमार्थतया स्वयं शक्तिर्भूत्वा श्रीविद्यावयवभूतसकलतेजःशक्तिमूर्त्तिगुणैरिदन्तानि तत्सकलानि तद्वदेकीकृत्य तदुभयमनुष्णाशीतं वाह्यदाभ्यन्तरमाभ्यन्तराद्वाह्यमिति क्रमात् स्वबुद्ध्या कृष्णीकृत्य तदात्मना भजनं मन्त्रवीर्य्ययोजनप्रकार इति । इतरनित्याभजने केवलहृल्लेखावयवभूतैरितरमन्त्रभजने प्रणवावयवभूतैरपि प्राग्वदेकीकुर्य्यादिति सम्प्रदायः ॥ ६८ ॥

असम्यक्त्वन्तु मन्त्राणामयोग्यकथनेन वै ।
सदा प्रयोगाद्भजनादकाले संशयाद्भवेत् ॥ ७० ॥
गुरोरवज्ञया पापान्निषिद्धाचारयोगतः ।
देवताद्रोहतः सर्व्वपरिवादानवस्थया ॥ ७१ ॥
असम्प्रदायादज्ञानादनेकभजनादपि ।
तत्समाप्तं येन भवेत् कार्य्यं तत् पूर्व्वमीरितम् ॥ ७२ ॥
नातिद्वेषो नातिरागो नातिभोगेषु सङ्गतिः ।
नातिशोको नातिहर्षो नातिस्नेहो न मत्सरः ॥ ७३ ॥
नातिव्यसनवर्त्तित्वं सुखिता क्लिष्टकारिता ।
स्वदेहमात्रयात्रेच्छा परचिन्ताविवर्जनम् ॥ ७४ ॥

असमाप्तमित्यादिभिरीरितमित्यन्तैस्त्रिभिः श्लोकैर्मन्त्रविद्यादीनां त्रयोदशविधासमाप्तिकारणं प्रागुक्तसमाप्तिनिगमनसहितमुपदिशति । तत्र असमाप्तं अकार्य्यकरणत्वमन्यथाफलत्वं वा । मन्त्राणां मन्त्रविद्यानां । अयोग्यकथनेन प्रथमपटलप्रोक्तलक्षणरहितशिष्योपदेशेन । सदा प्रयोगात् नित्यनैमित्तिकपुरश्चरणभजनक्रममुपेक्ष्य कामतोऽनवरतप्रयोगात् । भजनादकाले नित्यनैमित्तिककाम्येषु प्रोक्तकालमुपेक्ष्य इतरकालभजनात् । संशयात् उक्तकरत्वे स्वाभिमतफलप्रदत्वे च । गुरोरवज्ञया गुरोरनभिमतानुष्ठानात् । पापात् प्रथमपटले विद्यत्वादिश्लोकत्रयोक्ताचारविपरीतानुष्ठानात् । निषिद्धाचारयोगतः तत्तत्पटलोक्तमिथ्याचारस्यान्यथानुष्ठानात् । देवताद्रोहतः देवताभेदप्रतिपत्तेः । सर्व्वपरिवादानवस्थया सर्व्वजनपरिवादेन जपादिष्वनवस्थया वा । असम्प्रदायात् अनभिज्ञस्य गुरोर्वा पत्रादिषु निरीक्षणाद्वा लब्धमात्रस्वरूपात् । अज्ञानाद्देवतागुरुमन्त्राणां परमार्थस्वरूपस्य । अनेकभजनान्मन्त्रविद्यादीनां । तत्समाप्तं प्रोक्तदोषैरनभिमुखमन्त्रविद्यानामाभिमुख्यकरणं । कार्य्यं तत्तन्मन्त्रविद्यानुसन्धानमित्यर्थः ॥ ७२ ॥

नातिद्वेष इत्यादिभिर्लक्षणमित्यन्तैस्त्रिभिः श्लोकैर्मन्त्रसिद्धानां षोडशलक्षणान्युपदिशति । तत्र नातिद्वेष इत्यादिना श्लोकेन सप्त सिद्धचिह्नानि । नाति-

एकरूप्यं लाभहान्योः सदा सन्तुष्टचित्तता ।
भोक्तृत्वं शक्तितो दानमिति सिद्धस्य लक्षणम् ॥ ७५ ॥
मनोरथानामक्लेशसंसिद्धिः सिद्धिरीरिता ।
राज्ञः प्रसादः सर्वेषां मान्यत्वं पुण्यसिद्धयः ॥ ७६ ॥
ख्यातिर्वाहनभूषादिलाभः सुचिरजीवितम् ।
आरोग्यमविसंवादः सच्छिष्यत्वं कृतज्ञता ॥ ७७ ॥
विषाणां जरणं ज्ञानं स्वस्थस्यावेदनं तथा ।
प्रत्यक्षाः सिद्धयः प्रोक्ता मनोः सिद्धस्य सर्वतः ॥ ७८ ॥
एताः स्युः सिद्धयः प्रोक्ताः सिद्धमन्त्रस्य सूचकाः ।
सिद्धमन्त्रेण कर्त्तव्याः प्रयोगा नान्यथा प्रिये ॥ ७९ ॥
नराणामिव मन्त्राणां देवतानाञ्च पार्वति ।
अन्योन्यवैरमस्त्येव गुणभूतसमन्वयात् ॥ ८० ॥
आग्नेयानाञ्च भौमानामाप्या मन्त्रास्तु वैरिणः ।
वायव्यानां जलानाञ्च भौमानां स्यात् परस्परम् ॥ ८१ ॥

व्यसनवर्त्तित्वमित्यादिना श्लोकेन पञ्च सिद्धचिह्नानि। एकरूप्यमित्यादिना श्लोकेन चत्वारि चिह्नानि प्रोक्तानिगमनञ्च ॥ ७५ ॥

मनोरथानामित्यादिभिः प्रिये इत्यन्तैश्चतुर्भिः श्लोकैर्मन्त्रसिद्धेश्चतुर्द्दशविधत्वं प्रयोगेषु गुणविधानादिकं चोपदिशति। तत्र पुण्यसिद्धयः चिरकालस्थायीनि परप्रयोजनानि यानि कर्म्माणि तानि पुण्यानि तेषां सिद्धयः। वाहनभूषादीत्यत्रादिशब्दो महार्हवस्त्रादिविषयः। अविसंवादः दृष्टादृष्टयोरिति यावत्। सच्छिष्यत्वं स्वस्येति यावत्। विषाणां जङ्गमस्थावरकृत्रिमादीनां। ज्ञानं चात्मन इति यावत्। मनोर्मन्त्रविद्यादेरित्यर्थः। सर्व्वतः सर्व्वा इत्यर्थः। नान्यथा असिद्धमन्त्रेण न कर्त्तव्या इति यावत्। प्रिये इति देवीसम्बुद्धिः ॥ ७९ ॥

नराणामित्यादिभिस्त्वन्नत इत्यन्तैश्चतुर्भिः श्लोकैर्मन्त्रविद्यादीनामन्योन्यं सकारणं वैरमुपदिशति। तत्र चः समुच्चये। पार्व्वतीति देवीसम्बुद्धिः। एवाव

स्त्रीदैवत्या वैरिणः स्युः पुंदैवत्यस्य भूयसा ।
स्त्रीदैवत्येषु सौम्यानां क्रूराणां स्यात् परस्परम् ॥ ८२ ॥
तथैव पुंदेवतानां त्वरितानरसिंहयोः ।
शस्त्रानुयच्छिणीनां स्यादघोरास्त्रस्य चक्रतः ॥ ८३ ॥
मन्त्राणां देवतानाञ्च वैरीकरणमीश्वरि ।
कथयामि शृणु प्राज्ञे येन लोकोऽतिसीदति ॥ ८४ ॥
वैषम्यभजनं पुंसामज्ञानादाशयाथवा ।
तेन मन्त्रा देवताश्च क्रुद्धा घ्नन्त्युपासकम् ॥ ८५ ॥
तस्मात् सर्वस्य लोकस्य मन्त्रवीर्य्यं हि जीवितम् ।
यन्निष्ठानाममी दोषा न स्पृशन्ति कदाचन ॥ ८६ ॥

धारणे। गुणभूतसमन्वयात् सत्त्वादिगुणानां भूतानाञ्च समन्वयात्। आग्नेयानां आग्नेयाक्षरप्रचुराणां अग्निदेवतानामित्यर्थः। मन्त्रविद्यादीनामिति यावत्। चः समुच्चये। भौमानां प्राग्वत्। आप्याः प्राग्वत्। तुरगधारणे। वायव्यानां प्राग्वत्। चः समुच्चये। भौमानां प्राग्वत् भौमाक्षरप्रचुराणां भूमिदेवतानाञ्च। स्यात् वैरमिति यावत्। स्त्रीदैवत्या मन्त्रविद्यादय इति यावत्। पुंदैवत्यस्य मन्त्रविद्यादेरिति यावत्। स्त्रीदैवतेषु मन्त्रविद्यास्विति यावत्। सौम्यानां प्राग्वन्मन्त्रादीनां। क्रूराणां प्राग्वत्। स्यात् वैरमिति यावत्। तथा क्रूराणां सौम्यानाञ्च परस्परं वैरं स्यादिति यावत्। एवावधारणे। त्वरितानरसिंहयोः परस्परं वैरं स्यादिति यावत्। शस्त्रानुयच्छिणीनां वैरमिति। चक्रतः सुदर्शनेनेति यावत् ॥ ८३ ॥

मन्त्राणामित्यादिभिः कदाचनेत्यन्तैस्त्रिभिः श्लोकैरुपासकदोषैर्मन्त्राणां देवतानां च वैरीकरणं तेषामनर्थप्राप्तिं तत्परिहारोपायञ्चोपदिशति। तत्र प्राज्ञे इति देवीसम्बुद्धिः। येन वैरीकरणेन। वैषम्यभजनं अनुदिनभजनक्रमभेदादधिकन्यूनादिभावभेदादेति यावत्। अज्ञानात् परमार्थस्वरूपस्येति यावत्। आशया फलेष्विति यावत्। तेन वैषम्यभजनेन। चः समुच्चये। तस्मात् कारणात् जीवितं अधिष्ठानमिति यावत्। यन्निष्ठानां दिव्यत्वाद्यन्मन्त्रवीर्य्यनिष्ठानामित्यर्थः ॥ ८६ ॥

गुरोः शुश्रूषया काले दीक्षया लब्धमादरात् ।
तदाज्ञया भजेदेकरूपं मन्त्रं स्वसिद्धये ॥ ८७ ॥
अन्यथा साधकं हन्याच्छस्त्रेण रिपुतो भयात् ।
दारिद्र्याद्यैर्घोरोगाद्वा व्यसनैर्व्वातिसर्जनात् ॥ ८८ ॥
यो यो मन्त्रस्तस्य तस्य वर्णौषधिविनिर्म्मिता ।
तत्तद्वर्णोत्थसंख्याभिर्गुलिका मन्त्रसिद्धिदा ॥ ८९ ॥
तयाभिषेकस्तद्धारणं तत्स्वादस्तद्विलेपनम् ।
तत्पूजा च तथा सिद्धिलाभाय स्यान्न चान्यथा ॥ ९० ॥

गुरोरित्यादिनातिसर्जनादित्यन्तेन श्लोकद्वयेन गुरुमन्त्रदेवतानां सम्यग्भजनक्रममुपदिशति । तत्र गुरोः सत इत्यर्थः । काले द्वितीयपटले स्थिरे इत्यादिना चत्वारिंशादिश्लोकद्वयेन प्रोक्ते इति यावत् । दीक्षया अभिषेककटाक्षादिप्रकारेण इति यावत् । आदरात् गुरुशिष्ययोरित्यर्थः । तदाज्ञया नाथाज्ञया । एकरूपं अनुदिनमिति यावत् । हन्याद्देवतेति यावत् । रिपुतः रिपोः भयात् । येन केनचिद्व्याजेन हन्यात् नवा केवलभयात् । वा विकल्पे । व्यसनेषु स्त्र्यादिषु सप्तस्वित्यर्थः ॥ ८८ ॥

यो य इत्यादिना श्लोकेन सकलतन्त्रोक्तमन्त्रविद्यादीनां सम्यक् सिद्धिकरमक्षरौषधिगुलिकारूपं प्रस्तौति । तत्र तस्य मन्त्रस्येति यावत् । वर्णौषधिविनिर्मिता गुलिकेति यावत् स्यादित्यर्थः ॥ तत्तद्वर्णोत्थसंख्याभिः तत्तन्मन्त्रेष्वेकैकाक्षरस्य यावत्यो यावत्यः परिवृत्तयस्तावन्तोभिस्तदक्षरौषधीनां अंशसंख्याभिरिति यावत् । गुलिका मन्त्रसिद्धिदा तत्तन्मन्त्रसिद्धिदा इत्यर्थः ॥ ८९ ॥

तयेत्यादिना श्लोकेन गुलिकाविनियोगक्रममुपदिशति । तत्र तया गुलिकया । तद्धारणं गुलिकाधारणं । तत्स्वादः तद्गुलिकाभक्षणं । तद्विलेपनं तद्गुलिकाविलेपनं । तत्पूजा तस्यां पूजा तया पूजा च । तथा सिद्धिलाभाय प्रागुक्तलक्षणसिद्धिलाभाय । न चान्यथा न संशय इत्यर्थः । अस्मिन् श्लोके प्रथमपादे लेकाक्षराधिक्यकारणं दिव्यत्वात् ॥ ९० ॥

सितरक्ते चन्दने च मांसी पिप्पलकस्तथा ।
लज्जातुका शिखिशिखा दर्भाः पाटलभृङ्गकौ ॥ ९१ ॥
श्रीदेवीति समुद्दिष्टा वायुवर्णौषधानि वै ।
क्रमाद्दशानां वर्णानां तैः कुर्य्यात्तत्तदर्च्चनम् ॥ ९२ ॥
लघुश्चन्द्रो मुरो विल्वोदुम्बरः प्लक्षकस्तथा ।
कृष्णशङ्खप्रसूनञ्च चित्राफान्ता इति क्रमात् ॥ ९३ ॥
वह्निवर्णौषधानि स्युः एवं सर्गस्य कीर्त्तितम् ।
तैस्तेषामर्चनं कुर्य्याद्गुरुपादार्च्चने रतः ॥ ९४ ॥
उशीरकुष्ठौ चौरगुह्ये अश्मरीकाग्निमन्थकौ ।
रोहिषस्तुलसी पोची सदाभद्रेति च क्रमात् ॥ ९५ ॥
भूमेर्वर्णौषधान्युक्तान्येभिस्तेषां समर्च्चयेत् ।
तत्तत्कार्य्यार्थसंसिद्ध्यै कुर्य्यात् सद्गुरुदक्षिणाम् ॥ ९६ ॥
सलिलं घुसृणं ग्रन्थिपर्णौ शोणाटणं तथा ।
कुशो वृहती द्रुलता दूर्व्वा लक्ष्मीरिति क्रमात् ॥ ९७ ॥
श्रीदेवीति जलार्णानामौषधानि क्रमेण वै ।
तेषां समर्च्चनं कुर्य्यादोषधैरेभिरादरात् ॥ ९८ ॥

सितेत्यादिभिः सिद्धयः इत्यन्तैर्दशभिः श्लोकैरकारादिक्षकारान्तानाम क्षराणामेतत्तन्त्रोदितपञ्चभूतक्रमेण वर्णानां दशदशौषधविधानान्युपदिशति । तत्र सितरक्ते चन्दने सितचन्दनं रक्तचन्दनं च । पिप्पलः अश्वत्थः । लज्जातुका कुम्भिचन्दनी । तैरौषधैः तत्तदर्च्चनं तत्तदक्षराणां तत्तद्देवतानाञ्चार्च्चनमेतत् । लघुः अगुरुः । विल्वोदुम्बरः अत्र दिव्यत्वात् विल्व उदुम्बर इति पदच्छेदः । सर्गस्य विसर्जनीयस्य अस्य भूताक्षरानन्तर्भूतत्वात् पृथग्ग्रहणं । क्षकारस्य ककारषकार योगात्मकत्वात् पृथगौषधमनुक्तं च । तेषां प्राग्वत् । पोची वाराही मुग्धलोत्यर्थः । एभिरौषधैः । तेषां प्राग्वत् । तत्तत्कार्य्यार्थसंसिद्ध्यै तत्तत्कार्य्यार्थसिद्ध्यर्थं ।

* कक्कोलश्च तथा रोचनाकलकिङ्कक (?) ।
सिंही दुन्दूकयुगलमपामार्गाञ्जलिः सह ॥ ९९ ॥
इत्युक्तानि खवर्णानामौषधानि क्रमेण वै ।
तैस्तेषामर्च्चनं कुर्य्यात्तत्तत्कार्य्यार्थसिद्धये ॥ १०० ॥
सदाशिवमयी व्याप्तिरिति सम्यक् समीरिता ।
अस्या निफालनाच्चित्ते तत्तत्त्वं स्वात्मसात् कृतम् ॥
इति षोड़शनित्यातन्त्रेषु श्रीकादिमते पञ्चत्रिंशत्
पटलम् परिपूर्णम्॥ ३५ ॥

---

* कक्कोल रोचनया लवङ्गोदरपुष्पिका इति वा ।

अञ्जलिः अञ्जलिकरी प्रसारिणी । तैरौषधैः । तेषां प्रागवत् । कक्कोलेत्यादि श्लोकस्यान्तपादस्याक्षराधिक्यकरणं दिव्यत्वात् । अत्रौषधानामव्याख्यातानि नामान्याराध्यमुखादवगन्तव्यानि । तत्र यथासिद्धि प्रागुक्तविधानेनेत्यर्थः ॥१००॥

इति षोड़शनित्यातन्त्रेषु श्रीकादिमताख्यस्य परिपूर्णस्य तन्त्रस्य प्रपञ्चसारसिंहराजप्रकाशाभिधानेन सुभगानन्दनाथेन विरचितायां मनोरमाख्यायां व्याख्यायां नित्यानां स्वात्मत्ववासनायास्तत्तद्विद्यास्वरूपभेद प्रकारप्रस्तारादिकस्य स्वरूपप्रकाशनपरं पञ्चत्रिंशपटलं परिपूर्णं परामृष्टम् ॥ ३५ ॥ ॐतत्सत् ॥

व्याख्यान ग्रन्थसंख्याः—पञ्चत्रिंशे तु पटले यन्त्राष्टकमुदीरितम् ।
सप्ताधिका च नवतिः व्याख्याग्रन्थाः शतत्रयम् ॥

षट्त्रिंशपटलम् ।

अथ षोडशनित्यानां विधानानि त्वयाधुना ।
कथितानि मया तानि श्रुतानि च महेश्वर ॥ १ ॥
तासां ते मे* तथान्येषां दैवतानां यथार्थतः ।
स्वरूपं किं कथं विश्वं किमाकारञ्च दृश्यते ॥ २ ॥

पूर्व्वस्मिन् पञ्चत्रिंशे पटले षोडशनित्यानां सपरिवाराणां स्वात्मत्वे वासनादिकमुपदिश्यानन्तरं षोडशनित्याविद्यासिद्धानां तत्तत् परमार्थस्वरूपादिकमुपदिशति । अथ षोडशेत्यादिमदं शक इत्यन्तश्लोकशतरूपेण षट्त्रिंशेन पटलेन । तत्र अथ षोडशेत्यादिभिः सदा इत्यन्तैर्दशभिः श्लोकैस्तन्त्रोक्तार्थनिगमनपुरःसरं विंशतिविधं प्रश्नं तदुत्तरस्य वक्ष्यमाणस्य स्तवनं स्वस्वरूपतस्तस्योपकारत्वञ्चोपदिशति । अथ षोडशेत्यादिना श्लोकेन तन्त्रोक्तार्थान् देवी निगमयति । तत्र तानि विधानानि । चः समुच्चये । महेश्वरेतीश्वर सम्बुद्धिः ॥ १ ॥

तासामित्यादिना श्लोकेन परमार्थस्वरूपं तत्स्वरूपप्रकाशोपायं परमार्थस्वरूपस्य प्रकाशकारणञ्च देवो पृच्छति । तत्र तासां षोडशनित्यानां । ते तव शिवस्य । अत्र तच्छब्देन नित्यानुग्रहात्मकत्वं गुरुं मच्छब्देनानादिमायाकल्पितत्वादनुग्राह्यं शिष्यं प्रत्युपलक्षयतीति । [यत् यस्मात् गुरोरिति यावत् ?] मे मम देव्याः शिष्यभूतायाः । अन्येषां सकलवेदागमेषूपदिष्टस्वरूपाणां । यथार्थतः स्वरूपाङ्गं परमार्थस्वरूपं किमिति यावत् । एषः प्रथमः प्रश्नः । अनन्तरं परमार्थस्वरूपप्रकाशोपायं पृच्छति । कथमिति द्वितीयः प्रश्नः । विश्वं किमाकारञ्च दृश्यते इत्यनेनैतदुक्तं भवति । परमार्थस्वरूपस्यैव प्रकाशो युज्यते तथाप्यपरमार्थस्वरूपं विश्वं गगनकुसुमादिवत् संज्ञामात्रमन्तरेणैव दृश्यते तत् किमाकारमिति । एष तृतीयः प्रश्नः ॥ २ ॥

---

* ते मे इत्यत्र तव इति पाठो दृश्यते ।

प्राणिनां पुण्यपापानि किंरूपाणि च कैस्तथा ।
तेषां जन्मानि केन स्युः का मुक्तिः संसृतिश्च का ॥३॥
कस्य मुक्तिः कथं बन्धः केन तस्य च मोचनम् ।
किं मूलं संसृतेरस्याः कानि तत्त्वानि का च धीः ॥४॥
कानीन्द्रियाणि के प्राणाः को जीवः कः परस्तथा ।
कः कालः के ग्रहाः सर्वं यथावन्मे वद प्रभो ॥५॥
येन वेदैश्च शास्त्रैश्च पुराणैरागमैरपि ।
कथ्यते तत् स्फुटं ब्रूहि नातिसङ्कोचविस्तरम् ॥ ६ ॥

प्राणिनामित्यादिना श्लोकेन प्राणिनां पुण्यपापैरसम्बन्धं तत् पुण्यपापस्वरूपं जन्मकारणं मुक्तिस्वरूपं जन्मकारणस्वरूपं संसृतिस्वरूपञ्च पृच्छति। तत्र प्राणिनां सम्बन्धे षष्ठी। किंरूपाणि किंरूपेणेति यावत्। एतदुक्तं भवति प्राणिनां पुण्यपापात्मकत्वं केन युज्यते इति चतुर्थः प्रश्नः। कैः कर्मभिरिति शेषः। तथा पुण्यपापत्वमिति यावत्। इति पञ्चमः प्रश्नः। तेषां प्राणिनां। केन कारणेनेति षष्ठः प्रश्नः। का मुक्तिरिति सप्तमः प्रश्नः। संसृतिश्च का इत्यष्टमः प्रश्नः ॥ ३ ॥

कस्येत्यादिना श्लोकेन प्रश्नषट्कं। तत्र तस्य बन्धस्य। चः समुच्चये ॥४॥

कानीत्यादिना श्लोकेन प्रश्नषट्कं। तत्र कः परस्तथा वस्तुतो जीवपदाधिकः कः पर इति यावत्। सर्वं विंशतिविधान् पृष्टानर्थानिति यावत्। यथावत् यथार्थतः मे नित्यानुग्राह्याया अन्तेवासिन्या इति यावत्। प्रभो इतीश्वर सम्बुद्धिः ॥ ५ ॥

येनेत्यादिना श्लोकेन दृष्टार्थानां वेदशास्त्रैरपि सम्वादि स्फुटकथनं प्रार्थयति। तत्र येन प्रकारेणेति यावत् कथ्यते। यदि विशेषः तत् स्वरूपं स्फुटं अनुभव-योग्यं नातिसङ्कोचविस्तरं अतिसङ्कोचातिविस्ताराभ्यां ज्ञातुमशक्यत्वात् ॥६॥

यत्त्वया विंशतिविधः क्रृतः प्रश्नः शिवेऽधुना।
तेषामुक्तक्रमेणैव कथयामि तवोत्तरम् ॥ ७ ॥
यैरुत्तरैः स्वस्वरूपं ज्ञायते सम्यगञ्जसा।
यद्गितोऽन्यत्र सर्वत्र प्रोक्तं निह्नवचक्रतः ॥ ८ ॥
अत्राञ्जसा प्रोच्यते तद्दुर्वचं तु निदर्शनैः *।
तैर्मयोक्तक्रमाज्जित्वा दुर्जयां वासनां शनैः। ९ ॥
सत्यशुद्धस्फुटाशेषस्फुरत्तात्मा भवेद्ध्रुवम्।
गुह्यं रहस्यं परमं गोपयेत् सर्वतः सदा ॥ १० ॥

यत्त्वयेत्यादिभिः सदा इत्यन्तैश्चतुर्भिः श्लोकैः पृष्टार्थकथनपीठिकापुरःसरं तदनुभावं तदुपकरत्वञ्चोपदिशति। तत्र यत् इति हेतोः। शिवे इति देवीसम्बुद्धिः। तेषां प्रश्नानां। एवावधारणे। कथयामि तस्मादिति शेषः। यैरुत्तरैर्वक्ष्यमाणैरिति यावत्। स्वस्वरूपं परमार्थस्वरूपं। लभ्यते प्रकाशते। सम्यक् अनुभवयोग्यं। अञ्जसा यथावत्। यत् हेतोः। इतस्तस्मादिति शेषः। अन्यत्र सर्व्वत्र इतरेषु तन्त्रेषु वेदेषु चेति यावत्। निह्नवचक्रतः अतिरहस्यत्वादिति यावत्। अत्र अस्मिंस्तन्त्रे। अञ्जसा प्राग्वत् यथावत्। तत् स्वरूपं। दुर्व्वचं वाचामविषयम्। तुर्व्विशेषे। निदर्शनैः तत्तत्प्रकाशनपरैरिति यावत्। तैरुत्तरत्वेनोपदेष्टव्यैरर्थैः। उक्तक्रमाद्वक्ष्यमाणोपाययोरन्यतरेणेति यावत्। दुर्जयां अनादिसिद्धत्वात्। शनैः कालक्रमात् अभ्यासबलादित्यर्थः। सत्यशुद्धस्फुटाशेषस्फुरत्तात्मा सत्यत्वं परमार्थतया शुद्धत्वमलेपकत्वात् अशेषस्फुरत्तात्वं तत्तदात्मकत्वेन भासमानत्वात्। अत्रात्मशब्दश्चतुर्ष्वपि योजनीयः। एतदुक्तं भवति। साधको द्वितीयप्रश्नस्योत्तरत्वेन वक्ष्यमाणोपाययोरन्यतरेण दुर्जयां वासनां शनैर्जित्वा सत्यशुद्धस्फुटाशेषस्फुरत्तात्मा भवेदिति। गुह्यं गुहायां निहितं अन्तःप्रकाशमानत्वात्। रहस्यं केवलं गुरुकटाक्षादेव लभ्यत्वात्। परमं स्वव्यतिरिक्ताभावात्। गोपयेत् अभक्तेभ्य इत्यर्थः। सर्व्वतः प्रकारत इति यावत् ॥ १० ॥

* भूरिदर्शनैरिति वा।

यज्ज्ञानमिदमो ज्ञानं यज्ज्ञानमहमस्तथा ।
द्वयोरपि च यज्ज्ञानं तज्ज्ञानं विद्धि मे वपुः ॥ ११ ॥
तासां तव तथान्येषां चैतन्यात्म यथार्थतः ।
लाभादेवं वासनाया विनाशादन्यथा तथा ॥ १२ ॥
स्थिरः स्वात्मप्रकाशः स्यान्नित्योऽप्रतिभटो महान् ।
नित्याहृदयसंप्रोक्तस्फुटोपायेन वा भवेत् ॥ १३ ॥

यज्ज्ञानमित्यादिना यथार्थत इत्यन्तेनाध्यर्धेन श्लोकेन प्रथमप्रश्नस्योत्तरत्वेन परमार्थतः स्वरूपमुपदिशति। तत्र यज्ज्ञानं वाङ्मनसयोरविषयं चैतन्यं। इदमो ज्ञानं इदमः प्रतीतिर्यज्ज्ञानं प्राग्वत्। अहमस्तथा अहमः प्रतीतिरिति यावत्। अत्र तथा इत्यस्य काकाक्षिन्यायेन पूर्वत्र परत्र च सम्बन्धः। तथा तस्माद्द्वयोरिदन्ताहन्तयोर्ममेदमस्याहं इदमेवाहमहमेवेदमित्यादि प्रतीतिसम्बन्ध इति यावत्। अपि च किञ्चेति यावत्। तज्ज्ञानं वाङ्मनसयोरविषयं ज्ञानं विद्धि विजिज्ञासस्व इति यावत्। मे शिवस्य गुरोः। यथार्थतः यथास्वरूपत इति यावत्। एतदुक्तं भवति प्रतप्तलोहे निरवयववत् व्याप्तविश्वस्य चैतन्यस्य भूतेन्द्रियादियोगात्मकेषु देहेषु बुद्ध्यात्मनोपलब्धिस्थानात्मकं तद्देहमात्रमहमिति तदिति तद्व्याप्तिज्ञानं विश्वमिदमिति। किञ्च ममेदमित्याद्याकारेण तयोर्द्वयोरन्योन्यसम्बन्धं चानुसन्धाति। तत्र तत्र तत्तदाकारज्ञानतया यच्चैतन्यमात्रमेव स्फुरति तच्चैतन्यं यथार्थतो मे वपुर्विद्धीति। तासां षोडशनित्यानां। अन्येषां देवतानामिति यावत्। चैतन्यात्म चैतन्यस्वरूपं वपुरिति शेषः ॥ ११ ॥

लाभादित्यादिना भवेदित्यन्तेनार्धाद्येन श्लोकेन द्वितीयप्रश्नस्योत्तरत्वेन परमार्थस्वरूपप्रकाशस्योपायं तन्त्रान्तरप्रोक्तोपायान्तरञ्च निगमनसहितमुपदिशति। तत्र एवं वासनाप्रोक्तप्रकारेण समस्तभेदेषु चैतन्यस्वरूपमात्रानुसन्धानं। वासनायाः विनाशादन्यथा तथा अत एव दुर्वासनाया विनाशादिति यावत्। स्थिरः कटकमुकुटादिविकारेषु कनकसत्तामात्रप्रकाशवदिति यावत्। नित्यः कालानवच्छेदात्। अप्रतिभटः सत्यत्वात्। महान् देशानवच्छेदात्। नित्याहृदयसंप्रोक्तस्फुटोपायेन नित्याहृदयमिति षोडशनित्यातन्त्रेषु कस्य-

शब्दस्य बुद्धेर्द्वैरूप्यात् प्रपञ्चस्य च दृश्यते ।
द्वैरूप्यमनयोरुक्तं सत्यासत्यसम[मय]त्वतः ॥ १४ ॥
तेनैव प्राणिनां पुण्यपापकर्म्मसु वर्त्तनम् ।
यथात्मजानतोऽर्थेषु व्यापारः पुण्यसंज्ञकः ॥ १५ ॥
अनर्थेष्वर्थसङ्कल्पः पापाख्यो मनसा तथा ।
जन्मानि नानारूपाणि यैर्नित्यं क्लेशभाजनम् ॥ १६ ॥

चित्तन्वस्य नाम तस्मिन् प्रोल्लस्फुटापायेन । वा विकल्पे । भवेत् स्वात्मप्रकाश इति यावत् । एतदुपायस्याद्युपस्करत्वात् आराध्यमुखादवगन्तव्यम् ॥ १३ ॥

शब्दस्येत्यादिना श्लोकेन तृतीयप्रश्नोत्तरत्वेन प्रपञ्चप्रकाशस्य कारणादिकमुपदिशति । तत्र द्वैरूपात् उभयात्मकत्वात् । इत्यनेनोत्तरत्र द्विशप्रश्नस्योत्तरकथनप्रसङ्गात् प्रपञ्चस्य वक्ष्यमाणस्वरूपं स्मारयति । चः समुच्चये । अनयोः शब्दबुद्ध्योः परमार्थरूपे अपरमार्थरूपे च समप्रवृत्तित्वात् । एतदुक्तं भवति परमार्थवदपरमार्थोऽपि शब्दबुद्ध्योः प्रवृत्तस्यैव प्रपञ्चो नामरूपाभ्यां प्रकाशते इति ॥ १४ ॥

तेनैवेत्यादिनार्द्धेन चतुर्थप्रश्नस्योत्तरत्वेन प्राणिनां पुण्यपापात्मकप्रकारं तदपरमार्थकथन पुरःसरमुपदिशति । तत्र तेन शब्दबुद्ध्योर्द्वैरूप्येण । एवावधारणे । प्राणिनां सम्बन्धे षष्ठी । वर्त्तनं व्यापारः । एतदुक्तं भवति शब्दबुद्ध्योर्द्वैरूप्येण पुण्यपापकर्मसु वर्त्तनमेव प्राणिनां पुण्यपापात्मकत्वमिति ॥ १५ ॥

यथेत्यादिना भाजनमित्यन्तेनार्द्धद्वयेन श्लोकेन पञ्चमषष्ठप्रश्नयोरुत्तरत्वेन पुण्यपापकर्मस्वरूपं प्राणिनां जन्मकारणञ्चोपदिशति । तत्रार्थेषु शब्दादितन्मात्रासु । व्यापारः इन्द्रियाणामिति यावत् । एतदुक्तं भवति याथार्थ्यविदो विषयेषु तन्मात्रास्वरूपमात्राङ्गीकारात्तेनैवासङ्गाच्च तस्य तत्तद्विषयेष्विन्द्रियाणां व्यापारः पुण्यसंज्ञो भवतीति । अनर्थेषु अर्थाः शब्दादयः तेषु तन्मात्राप्रतिपत्तिमात्रमन्तरेण पुत्रादिभावा अनर्थास्तेषु । अर्थसंकल्पः याथात्म्यबुद्धिः । मनसा इत्यस्य अर्थसंकल्प इत्यनेन पूर्ववत् सम्बन्धः । एतदुक्तं भवति विषयेषु शब्दादितन्मात्रामात्रप्रतिपत्तिमन्तरेण पुत्रमित्रकलत्रादित्वेन तेषु मनःसंयोग एव पापसंज्ञो भवतीति । तथा अयथात्म्यज्ञानेनेति यावत् । नानारूपाणि जरायु-

याथार्थ्ये ज्ञानमर्थानां मुक्तिस्तद्विपरीतता ।
संसृतिर्मोचनं बुद्धेर्व्वासना बन्ध ईरितः ॥ १७ ॥
कर्म्मक्षयात् सद्गुरोस्तु कटाक्षोक्तिविमर्शतः ।
मोचनं सर्वजन्तूनां नेतरैश्च कदाचन ॥ १८ ॥

जादिरूपाणि। यैः रूपभेदैः। नित्यक्लेशभाजनं तत्तद्रूपेष्वहं मित्रमहं शत्रुरित्यादिभाववत्। एतदुक्तं भवति यथा श्रोत्रेन्द्रियस्य शब्द एव विषयः त्वगिन्द्रियस्य स्पर्शः चक्षुरिन्द्रियस्य रूपं रसनेन्द्रियस्य रसः घ्राणेन्द्रियस्य गन्धः आकाशस्य गुणः शब्दः वायोः शब्दस्पर्शौ अग्नेः शब्दस्पर्शरूपाणि जलस्य शब्दस्पर्शरूपरसाः भूमेः शब्दस्पर्शरूपरसगन्धाः तस्मात् शब्दादितन्मात्रा एव भूतानि भूतान्येवान्योन्यसंयोगविशेषात् जरायुजाण्डजस्वेदजोद्भिज्जात्मकत्वेनोत्पत्तिपरिणामक्षयविकारनाशात्मकानि रूपाणि तान्येव नानारूपाणि जन्मानि भवन्ति। तत्तद्रूपेषु स्वात्मत्वाभिमानात्तत्स्वभावसिद्धैर्विकारैर्दुःखान्यनुभवन्तीति ॥ १६ ॥

याथार्थ्येत्यादिना श्लोकेन सप्तमादिदशमान्तानां चतुर्णां प्रश्नानामुत्तरत्वेन मुक्तेः संसृतेः बुद्धेर्मोचनस्य बन्धस्य च स्वरूपाण्युपदिशति। तत्र याथार्थ्ये ज्ञानमर्थानां मुक्तिः घटशरावादिविकारेषु मृत्स्नामात्रज्ञानवद्दृश्यमानविविधरूपेषु चित्सत्तामात्रप्रतिपत्तिर्मुक्तिरिति यावत्। तद्विपरीतता अयथात्मज्ञानमिति यावत्। मोचनं बुद्धेः अयथात्मज्ञानस्य बुद्धिधर्मत्वात्। वासना बन्धः अयथात्मज्ञानमनादिदुर्व्वासनयैवेति यावत् ॥ १७ ॥

कर्म्मक्षयादित्यादिना श्लोकेनैकादशप्रश्नस्योत्तरत्वेन मुक्तिप्रदातारं मुक्तिप्रकारं चोपदिशति। तत्र कर्म्मक्षयात् अज्ञानकार्य्यत्वात् कर्म्मणः कारणकार्य्ययोरभेदोपचारात् अज्ञानक्षयादिति यावत्। सद्गुरोरित्यत्र सत्त्वमस्मिंस्तन्त्रे द्वितीयपटले विरच्येत्यादिभिरेकषष्टितमाद्येकादशभिः श्लोकैः प्रोक्तविधानात् कृतपूर्णाभिषेकत्वमस्मिन् पटले प्रोक्तपरमार्थस्वरूपे स्थैर्य्यञ्च। गुरुत्वं प्रथमे पटले सुन्दर इत्यादिनैकोनविंशच्छ्लोकेन प्रोक्तलक्षणसम्पूर्णत्वं। तुरवधारणे। कटाक्षोक्तिविमर्शतः कटाक्षा विंशे पटले सर्व्वासामित्यादिभिरेकचत्वारिंशादिनवभिः श्लोकैः प्रोक्तत्रिविधप्रकारेष्वन्यतमः उक्तिः श्रीविद्यायाश्चास्मिन् पटले प्रोक्तपरमार्थस्वरूपस्योपदेशः विमर्शस्तु प्रोक्तप्रश्नोत्तरप्रकारेण शिवस्वरूपानुसन्धानं तस्मात् कटाक्षोक्तिविमर्शैरिति यावत्। [प्रोक्तप्रश्नो-

संसृतेः कन्दमुदितमविवेकः परो महान् ।
यदायत्तमिदं जीवभुवनं परिवर्त्तते ॥ १९ ॥
तत्त्वानि तत्त्वान्युक्तानि सर्वैःसर्वत्र सर्वदा ।
ज्ञातृज्ञानज्ञेयमयान्यन्यथान्यानि सर्वदा ॥ २० ॥
का च धीरिति यत् पृष्टं तद्दुर्वचमपि स्फुटम् ।
कथयामि शृणु प्राज्ञे यदायत्ता च विंशतिः ॥ २१ ॥

त्तरप्रकारेण शिष्ये या स्वरूपानुसन्धानं तस्मात् कटाक्षोक्तिविमर्शैरिति यावत् ।] एतदुक्तं भवति भूतयोगविशेषमात्रदेहेषु चित्स्फुरणवशादेव जन्तुत्व-बुद्धिः । तद्विकारादेव देहगताहन्ता अवस्था बुद्धीन्द्रियाणां व्यापाराः पुण्य-पापानि मनःप्राणदेहानां धर्म्मास्तत्फलानि । एतस्य सर्व्वस्य सद्गुरुकटाक्षो-पदेशविमर्शैरपरमार्थत्वात् सर्व्वजन्तूनां मोचनं सम्भवतीति । इतरैरुपायै-रिति यावत् । कदाचन यावदाभूतसंप्लवमिति यावत् ॥ १८ ॥

संसृतेरित्यादिना श्लोकेन द्वादशप्रश्नस्योत्तरत्वेन संसृतेः परमकारणं तत्स्वरूपं तद्वैभवञ्चोपदिशति । तत्र कन्दं दिव्यत्वात् कन्दः परमकारण-मित्यर्थः । अविवेकः देहात्मविवेकाभावः । परो दिव्यत्वात् । महान् ब्रह्मादि-स्तम्बान्तेषु सकलजन्तुषु संतन्यमानत्वात् । यदायत्तं यत् यस्य पराधीनं अविवेक-पराधीनमिति यावत् । जीवभुवनं जीवलोकः । परिवर्त्तते जन्मजरामरणाद्या-वृत्तिभ्रान्तिरूपिणीति यावत् ॥ १९ ॥

तत्त्वानीत्यादिना श्लोकेन त्रयोदशप्रश्नस्योत्तरत्वेन स्वरूपविमर्शसाधनभूतानां ज्ञातृज्ञानज्ञेयानां त्रयाणां तत्त्वात्मकं तदितरस्वरूपाणां अतत्त्वात्मकत्वञ्चोप-दिशति । तत्र तत्त्वान संज्ञयेति यावत् । तत्त्वानि सत्यानि चैतन्यस्य तादात्म्येन स्फुरणत्वात् । सर्वैः रागमार्दिभिरिति यावत् । सर्व्वत्र सर्व्वदेहेष्विति यावत् । ज्ञातृज्ञानज्ञेयमयानि ज्ञातृज्ञानज्ञेयात्मकानि । अन्यथा अन्यानि तदितरात्मकत्वेन प्रतीतानि अन्यानि असत्यानीति यावत् ॥ २० ॥

का च धीरित्यादिभिर्विंशत्यन्तैः सप्तदशभिः श्लोकैश्चतुर्दशप्रश्नस्योत्तरत्वेन बुद्धेः सप्ताधिकशतगुणांस्तदनुभावञ्चोपदिशति । तत्र तत्रस्त्विति शेषः ।

मनोबुद्धिरहङ्कारचित्तमित्यादि नामभिः ।
वस्तुभेदादभेदाच्च यदुक्तं सर्वतः सदा ॥ २२ ॥
तदेकमचयं स्थूलं सूक्ष्मं दुर्ज्ञमतिस्फुटम् ।
विषमञ्च समं विश्वं विश्वातीतमनामयम् ॥ २३ ॥
अरूपं सर्वरूपञ्च सर्वक्लेशकरं हरम् ।
सर्वतृष्णाकरहरं सर्वेषां सर्वतः सदा ॥ २४ ॥
सत्त्वरूपं रजोरूपं तमोरूपमतन्मयम् ।
संसाररूपमुत्तीर्णविग्रहं सुस्थिरं चलम् ॥ २५ ॥
अपापं पापरूपञ्च जीवरूपं परात्मकम् ।
अतीन्द्रियं चेन्द्रियात्मानिर्देश्यं (वं) सर्वदैवतम् ॥ २६ ॥

दुर्व्वचं वाचामविषयत्वात्। स्फुटं अनुभवयोग्यं। प्राज्ञे इति देवीसम्बुद्धिः। विंशतिः प्रश्नानामिति यावत्। इत्यादीत्यत्रादिशब्देन प्रोक्तनामचतुष्टयस्य धीप्रज्ञादिवत् पर्य्यायमात्रत्वं कथयति। यदित्यस्य वस्त्वित्यनेनान्वयः। सर्व्वत आगमादितः ॥ २२ ॥

तदित्यादिना श्लोकेनैकादशगुणाः। तत्र तद्वस्तु एकं स्वरूपमिति यावत्। अचयं चिदुपलब्धात्मकत्वात्। स्थूलं विश्वव्याप्तेः। सूक्ष्मं पिपीलिकादिसूक्ष्म-देहेष्वप्यत्यन्तस्फुरद्रूपत्वात्। दुर्ज्ञं दुर्ज्ञेयं अतीन्द्रियत्वात्। अतिस्फुटं ज्ञान-स्वरूपत्वात्। विषमं वक्ष्यमाणवैविध्यात्। समं सकलजन्तुषु वैविध्यसाम्यात्। विश्वं तादात्म्यात्। विश्वातीतं यथार्थत इति यावत्। अनामयं अशरीर-त्वात् ॥ २३ ॥

अरूपमित्यादिना श्लोकेन षड्गुणाः। तत्र सर्व्वक्लेशकरं हरं दिव्यत्वात् सर्व्वक्लेशकरं सर्व्वक्लेशहरमिति च। सर्व्वतृष्णाकरहरं सर्व्वतृष्णाकरं सर्व्व-तृष्णाहरञ्च। सर्वेषां प्राणिनामिति यावत्। सर्व्वतः प्रकारत इति यावत् ॥ २४ ॥

सत्त्वेत्यादिना श्लोकेन दश गुणाः। तत्र अतन्मयं निर्गुणमिति यावत् ॥२५॥

अपापमित्यादिना श्लोकेनाष्टगुणाः। तत्र अपापं पुण्यरूपमिति यावत ॥२६॥

सर्वक्षोभात्मकं सर्वशान्तिरूपञ्च निर्दयम् ।
सदयञ्चाविवेकात्म विवेकपरमार्थकम् ॥ २७ ॥
उत्तारकं पातनकृद्भङ्गरूपं जयात्मकम् ।
शोकात्मकञ्च निःशोकं सकौतुकमकौतुकम् ॥ २८ ॥
निरुद्यमं सदोद्युक्तं सावलेपमगर्वकम् ।
अमर्शरूपमक्षोभ्यं सर्वक्षोभ्यं सुखासुखम् ॥ २९ ॥
क्रोधलोभमदद्रोहमात्सर्य्यकामविग्रहम् ।
अस्पृष्टषड्‌गुणं षण्डः वनिता पूरुषस्तथा ॥ ३० ॥
अपकृष्टं तथोत्कृष्टं स्वच्छाकारं तथाविलम् ।
अगाधमतिगम्भीरमुदारं कृपणन्तथा ॥ ३१ ॥
भाग्यरूपमभाग्यात्म निर्भयं सभयं तथा ।
अनिच्छमिच्छारूपञ्च कातरं वीरविग्रहम् ॥ ३२ ॥
निर्दोषः सर्वदोषात्मा सर्वविन्मूढविग्रहः ।
सङ्कोचरूपः सर्वेषां तथा सर्वप्रकाशकः ॥ ३३ ॥

सर्वेत्यादिना श्लोकेन षड्‌गुणाः । तत्र विवेकपरमार्थकं विवेकपरमार्थस्वरूपम् ॥ २७ ॥

उत्तारकमित्यादिना श्लोकेनाष्टगुणाः । तत्र भङ्गरूपं पराजयरूपम् ॥ २८ ॥

निरुद्यममित्यादिना श्लोकेनाष्टगुणाः । तत्र सुखासुखं सुखरूपं दुःखरूपञ्चेति ॥ २९ ॥

क्रोधमित्यादिना श्लोकेन पञ्चदश गुणाः । तत्र अस्पृष्टषड्‌गुणं क्रोधादिषड्‌गुणरहितम् ॥ ३० ॥

अपकृष्टमित्यादिना श्लोकेनाष्टगुणाः । तत्र अगाधं दुरवगाहं ॥ ३१ ॥

भाग्येमित्यादिना श्लोकेनाष्टगुणाः ॥ ३२ ॥

निर्दोष इत्यादिना श्लोकेनाष्टगुणाः । तत्र सर्व्वदोषात्मा वातादित्रिदोषात्मा । सर्वेषां प्राणिनामिति यावत् ॥ ३३ ॥

अस्तेयरूपस्तेयात्मा वश्योऽवश्यस्वरो मृदुः ।
सरसं विरसं क्रूरं सौम्यं तैर्वैर्गुणैभिस्तु किम् ॥ ३४ ॥
त्वन्मयी धीः समाख्याता मन्मयी चिदुदीरिता ।
उभयैक्याद्विवेकात्मा जीवोऽन्यस्तद्विवेकवान् ॥ ३५ ॥
तस्यास्तु बुद्धेर्यो वेत्ति याथात्म्यं विकृतीरपि ।
सामर्थ्यं स्वाविभेदित्वं सिद्धे प्राप्यफलानि च ॥ ३६ ॥
योगी ज्ञो ब्रह्मविज्ञानी शिवयोगी तथात्मवित् ।
तेनैव विहितं सर्वं प्रपञ्चात्मैक्यविग्रहम् ॥ ३७ ॥
स्वात्मनस्तु मनो वृत्त्या विषयग्रहणाय वै ।
सृष्टानि भूतशक्त्यात्मविग्रहाणीन्द्रियाणि तु ॥ ३८ ॥

अस्तेयमित्यादिना श्लोकेन दश गुणाः । तत्र अवश्यः स्वतन्त्रः । तैर्गुणैः ॥३४॥

त्वन्मयी शक्तिमयीति यावत् । एतदुक्तं भवति चित्स्वरूपस्य स्वेच्छयाप-लब्धिर्बुद्धिरिति । मन्मयी शिवमयी स्वात्मिकेति यावत् । एतदुक्तं भवति उपलब्धिस्वरूपमन्तरेण तद्गतवह्निवत् सैव यदा स्थिता तदा चिदिति संज्ञेति । उभयैक्याद्विविवेकात्मा धीचित्स्वरूपयोरपृथक्त्वात् चिदात्मानं विमृशतीति यावत् । अन्यः परः तद्विवेकवान् धीचित्स्वरूपयोरपृथक्त्वं विमृशतीति यावत् । स्वाविभेदित्वं स्वात्मापृथग्भावत्वं । सिद्धे याथात्म्यस्वरूपे । प्राप्यफलानि अवाप्तव्यफलानि । चः समुच्चये । ज्ञः बुद्धेर्याथात्म्यवेत्ता । योगीत्यादिनाम-पञ्चकं वेदेष्वागमेषु च परमार्थविदस्तत्तन्मतानुगुणं प्रोक्तमनेन तत्सर्वं बुद्ध्यधीन-मिति यावत् । तेन बुद्धेर्याथात्म्यविदा । एवावधारणे ॥ ३७ ॥

स्वात्मन इत्यादिना श्लोकेन पञ्चदशप्रश्नस्योत्तरत्वेनेन्द्रियाणां स्वरूपमुप-दिशति । तत्र स्वात्मनः स्वस्य मनोवृत्त्या मनोव्यापारेण सृष्टानि उपलब्धानीति यावत् । भूतशक्त्यात्मविग्रहाणि पञ्चभूतशक्तिस्वरूपाणि । तुरवधारणे । एतदुक्तं भवति स्वस्य मनोवृत्त्या स्वस्वविषयग्रहणार्थमुपलब्धानि भूतशक्तिस्वरूपा-णीन्द्रियाणीति ॥ ३८ ॥

भूतात्मबुद्धिसंघातशक्तिचैतन्यजृम्भणम् ।
प्राणास्तत्साक्षिभूतो हि जीवस्तत्त्वात्मकः परः ॥ ३९ ॥

कालस्तु पूर्वं बुद्ध्येर्यदुक्तं गुणसमस्तवान् ।
काल इत्यक्षरद्वन्द्वाद्ग्यद्वाच्यं तद्वपुर्मम ॥ ४० ॥

न शक्यतेऽञ्जसा वक्तुं तथा दर्शयितुं तव ।
तथापि तव यत्किञ्चिद्व्याकरोमि समञ्जसा ॥ ४१ ॥

अहोरात्रादिभेदस्तु चन्द्रार्कादिसमन्वयात् ।
तेन तन्मयतारूपकथनं नोचितं ततः ॥ ४२ ॥

लवत्रुट्यादयो यत्तद्व्याप्यन्ते खण्डकास्तु तत् ।
कालस्य रूपं तत् प्रोक्तं यदनाद्यन्तविग्रहम् ॥ ४३ ॥

भूतात्मेत्यादिना श्लोकेन षोडशसप्तदशाष्टादशानां प्रश्नानां त्रयाणां उत्तरत्वेन प्राणानां जीवस्य च स्वरूपमुपदिशति। तत्र भूतात्मबुद्धिसंघातशक्तिचैतन्यजृम्भणं प्राणा इत्यनेनैतदुक्तं भवति पञ्चभूतस्वरूपाणां बुद्धेश्च संघातसामर्थ्येन चैतन्यस्य विजृम्भणभेदाः प्राणा इति। तत्साक्षिभूतो देहेन्द्रियादिस्वरूपानुसन्धानप्रवृत्तः। एतदुक्तं भवति चिदुपलब्धिस्वरूपा बुद्धिः स्वाविवेकावस्थायां देहादिरूपतयानुसन्धानप्रवृत्तेर्निवृत्ता जीवसंज्ञां लभत इति। तत्त्वात्मकतः तद्याथात्म्येन। एतदुक्तं भवति यदा चिदुपलब्धिस्वरूपिणी बुद्धिः स्वस्वरूपपरामर्शेन देहेन्द्रियादीनामयाथात्म्यात्तदात्मकत्वेनानुसन्धानप्रवृत्तेर्निवृत्ता दाह्याभावाद्वह्निरिव स्वस्वरूपेण विश्राम्यति तदा परसंज्ञां लभत इति ॥ ३९ ॥

काल इत्यादिभिरत्र वै इत्यन्तैरष्टभिः श्लोकैरेकोनविंशत्प्रश्नस्योत्तरत्वेन कालस्वरूपादिकमुपदिशति। तत्र तुरवधारणे। पूर्वं चतुर्दशप्रश्नस्योत्तरे तदेकमित्यादिभिरिति यावत्। यतो गुणवैविध्यं ततः गुणसमस्तवान् समस्तगुणवान्। तथापि अशक्यमपीति यावत्। समञ्जसा उद्देशत इति यावत्। अहोरात्रादीत्यत्रादिशब्दः पूर्णमण्डलादिविषयः। तुः समुच्चये। चन्द्रार्कादीत्यत्रादिशब्दो भौमादिविषयः। तेन कारणेन। तन्मयतारूपकथनं अहोरात्रादिरूपतया

लवत्रुट्यादिकं ब्रूहि यैः कालो ज्ञायते मया ।
नलिन्या पत्रनिचये सूचीविद्धेऽथ तस्य वै ॥ ४४ ॥
एकैकदलभेदोत्थावस्था लव उदाहृतः ।
तत्त्रिंशद्गुणितं प्रोक्तं त्रुटीत्यादिशरीरवान् ॥ ४५ ॥
काल इत्युदितं तस्य स्वरूपं किं कथं भवेत् ।
इति पृष्टेन तद्वक्तुं शक्यते सुस्फुटं मया ॥ ४६ ॥
स्वबुद्ध्या प्रोक्तमात्रस्य भावनाद्यत्तु लभ्यते ।
तत्तस्य वपुरुद्दिष्टं नान्यास्ति गतिरत्र वै ॥ ४७ ॥

कालस्वरूपकथनं । एतदुक्तं भवति चन्द्रार्कादिग्रहगतिवशात् कल्पिताहोरात्रादिविषयः कालस्य तत्त्वतो वपुर्न भवतीति । ततः तस्मात् । लवत्रुट्यादीत्यत्रादिशब्दः कलाकाष्ठादिविषयः । यत् तत्स्वरूपं भाष्यन्ते अतन्मयत्वात् खण्डकाः परिच्छेदकाः विशस्येति यावत् । तुरवधारणे । तत् कालस्य रूपं कालस्य तत्रूपमित्यन्वयः । अत्र तच्छब्देन तन्त्रादौ प्रोक्तं कालस्यानुभावं स्मारयति । तत् चिद्रूपं । एतदुक्तं भवति अनाद्यन्तविग्रहं तच्चित्स्वरूपं यत्तदेव कालस्य स्वरूपमिति । लवत्रुट्यादीत्यत्रादिशब्दः प्राग्वत् कलाकाष्ठादिविषयः । यैः लवत्रुट्यादिभिर्ज्ञायते अनुमीयते । तस्य नलिनीपत्रनिचयस्य लव इति संज्ञा । तत्त्रिंशद्गुणितं लवादिस्वरूपं त्रिंशत्त्रिंशद्गुणितमिति यावत् । त्रुटीत्यादिशरीरवान् त्रुटिकलाकाष्ठादिसंज्ञावान् इति यावत् । एतदुक्तं भवति त्रिंशद्भिर्लवैः त्रुटिः त्रिंशत्त्रुटिभिः कला त्रिंशत्कलाभिः काष्ठा त्रिंशत्काष्ठाभिर्निमिषः अष्टभिर्निमिषैर्मात्रा सा मात्रा एकः श्वास इति । एकश्वासमारभ्य दिवसान्तस्वरूपं सप्तविंशे पटले कथितं दिवसादिचतुर्युगान्तस्वरूपं पञ्चविंशे पटले कथितं तस्मादिह नोच्यते । इति उक्तप्रकारेण । तस्य कालस्य । तत् स्वरूपं प्रोक्तमात्रस्य तन्त्रादावस्मिन् पटले वा स्वरूपस्येति शेषः । भावनाद्विमर्शतः । यत् स्वरूपं तत्तस्य कालस्य स्वरूपमिति यावत् । अत्र कालस्वरूपकथने ॥ ४७ ॥

ग्रहास्तु चिन्मयाः काले क्वापि चक्रभ्रमात् पुनः ।
भूतादीनि समस्तानि विकृतानि वितन्वते ॥ ४८ ॥
नानाविधास्तथाकाराः प्रपञ्चो दृश्यते सदा ।
तैरेव तेषां नाशश्च मरुतेव हविर्भुजः ॥ ४९ ॥
प्रश्नानामुत्तरं देव त्वया च कथितं विभो ।
तथापि मे प्रपञ्चात्मविवेकोऽभून्न मेऽधुना ॥ ५० ॥
जननं मरणञ्चेति द्वयं कस्य कथं भवेत् ।
अरूपस्य विभोस्तस्य जीवस्येत्तत् कथं स्थितिः ॥ ५१ ॥

ग्रहा इत्यादिना विभो इत्यन्तेनाध्यर्द्धेन श्लोकद्वयेन विंशप्रश्नस्योत्तरत्वेन ग्रहाणां स्वरूपाद्युपदेशपुरःसरमुक्तनिगमनं करोति। तत्र तु चिन्मयाः कालापृथग्रूपचिद्रूपाः। काले क्वापि क्वापि काले क्वापि देश इति यावत्। चक्रभ्रमात् स्वस्वगतिवशात् इति शेषः। पुनः पुनः पुनरिति यावत्। भूतादिनीत्यत्रादिशब्दो बुद्धीन्द्रियप्राणादिविषयः। तद्विकारा भूतादिविकाराः प्रपञ्चसंज्ञयेति शेषः। एतदुक्तं भवति अत्र ज्योतिश्चक्रे ग्रहगतिवशात् भूतादीनां नानाविधविकारः प्रपञ्चसंज्ञया दृश्यत इत्यत्र प्रसङ्गात् तृतीयप्रश्नस्योत्तरशेषं प्रपञ्चस्वरूप मुपदिष्टं। तैः ग्रहैः। एवावधारणे। तेषां भूतादिविकाराणां। देव विभो इति द्वयमपीश्वरसम्बुद्धिः॥ ४८ ॥

तथापीत्यादिनोत्तरार्द्धेन प्रश्नान्तरावतारस्य पीठिकाबन्धं करोति। तत्र तथापि मे कथितमपि। अधुनापीति शेषः। अद्यापीति यावत्॥ ५० ॥

जननमित्यादिभिरुपदेशत इत्यन्तैश्चतुर्भिः श्लोकैर्द्वादशविधप्रश्नस्वरूपादिकमुपदिशति। तत्र जननमित्यादिना श्लोकार्द्धेन प्रश्नचतुष्टयं। अरूपस्येत्यादिनार्द्धद्वयेन प्रश्नत्रयं। तस्य स्वात्मन इति यावत्। कुतो हेतोः। तत्कालपरमात्मनोः अनाद्यन्तविग्रहयोः कालपरमात्मनोः। मुक्ता इत्यादिनोत्तरार्द्धेन प्रश्नद्वयं। तत्र मुक्ताः जीव इति शेषः। परे जीवा इति शेषः। वा विकल्पे। एतदुक्तं भवति एते जीवाः प्रतिमेकैकमुक्ता (?) यद्यपि कालस्यानादित्वात् प्रपञ्चभावो युज्यते तथापीदानीं प्रारब्धवत् प्रपञ्चः प्रसरतीति यत्तस्मात् प्रसरणार्थं

कुतः स्थितिः कथं वा स्यात्तत्कालपरमात्मनोः।
मुक्तो वा जायते किन्तु परे वा सम्भवन्ति किम् ॥ ५२ ॥
कथं वा पञ्चभूतानां स्थितिर्देहेषु वान्यतः।
देहेषु जीवसंप्राप्तिः कीदृशीत्यादि मे वद ॥ ५३ ॥
येन श्रुतेन चित्ते मे शुश्रूषान्यस्य नो भवेत्।
तथा मे सर्वसन्देहांश्छिन्धि पूर्णोपदेशतः ॥ ५४ ॥
प्रागुक्तवृद्धिवैविध्यारब्धकर्मविपाकतः।
जननं मरणश्चेति द्वयं देहपरिग्रहात् ॥ ५५ ॥
प्रतप्तलोहपिण्डेऽग्निस्थितिवत् परविश्वयोः।
अवस्था कालपरयोस्तादात्म्यादेव वर्त्तनम् ॥ ५६ ॥

मुक्ता एव जीवाः पुनर्जाताः किमथवा परे जीवाः सम्भवन्तीति किमिति। कथमित्यादिना श्लोकार्द्धेन प्रश्नद्वयं। तत्र अन्यतः देहाद्बहिरिति यावत्। देहेष्वित्यादिना उपदेशत इत्यन्तेनार्द्धाधेन श्लोकेनैकः प्रश्नः। तत्र कीदृशी कस्यां अवस्थायां केन प्रकारेणेति यावत्। इत्यादीत्यत्रादिशब्दो जीवदेहेभ्यो विनिर्गमनप्रकारस्य तत्तत्सुगतित्वात् श्रानकालस्य च प्रश्नविषयः। येन श्रुतेनोत्तरेण। अन्यस्य प्रश्नस्येति शेषः ॥ ५४ ॥

प्रागुक्तेत्यादिना श्लोकेन प्रश्नचतुष्टयस्योत्तरं कथयति। तत्र प्रागुक्तवृद्धिवैविध्यारब्धकर्मविपाकतः भूतादियोगात्मके देहे प्रागुक्तवृद्धिवैविध्येन जीवस्याविर्भावः। प्रारब्धकर्मतस्तद्विपाकस्तद्विश्रान्तिः ततश्च। एतदुक्तं भवति प्रागुक्तवृद्धिवैविध्येनारब्धजीवोपलब्धिकर्मतस्तद्विपाकतश्च। जननं मरणश्चेति इति द्वयं देहपरिग्रहात्। इत्येतद्द्वयं देहे स्वात्माभिमानात्। एतदुक्तं भवति जीवस्य जननमरणकारणं देहाभिमानमात्रमेवेति ॥ ५५ ॥

प्रतप्तेत्यादिना श्लोकेन पञ्चमादिप्रश्नस्योत्तरं कथयति। तत्र अवस्थेत्यस्य काकाक्षिन्यायेन पूर्वत्रोत्तरत्र च सम्बन्धः। एतदुक्तं भवति प्रतप्तलोहपिण्डेऽग्निस्थितिवत् परविश्वयोरवस्थानमिति पञ्चमस्योत्तरं कथितं। जड़विषये परस्यावस्थानकारणं कुत इति प्रोक्तस्य षष्ठप्रश्नस्योत्तरं तादात्म्या-

मुक्तास्तु जीवा न कदाप्याविर्भूयुः कुतश्चन ।
न वापूर्व्वाः सम्भवन्ति बुद्धेः कृत्यमशेषतः ॥ ५७ ॥

मुद्रिकारूपमुद्रेव मधूच्छिष्टादिविग्रहम् ।
जीवादिरूपतो बुद्धिर्विशेषयति तत्परम् ॥ ५८ ॥

भूमेरेवास्फुटं स्थानं कुतश्चित् सुस्थिरं सदा ।
जलाग्न्योस्तत्र चान्यत्र व्यक्ताव्यक्तस्थितिः सदा ॥ ५९ ॥

देवेति कथितं । कालपरयोरन्योन्यावस्थानं कथमिति प्रोक्तस्य सप्तमप्रश्नस्योत्तरं तादात्म्यादेव वर्त्तनमिति कथितमिति ॥ ५६ ॥

मुक्ता इत्यादिना तत्परमित्यन्तेन श्लोकद्वयेनाष्टमनवमप्रश्नयोरुत्तरं कथयति । तत्र जीवा जन्तवः । तुरवधारणे । आविर्भूयुः दिव्यत्वादाविर्भूयासुरित्यर्थः । कुतश्चन हेतोरिति शेषः । अपूर्वाः जीवा इति यावत् । बुद्धेः कृत्यं अन्यथाप्रतिपत्तिरिति यावत् । अशेषतः जन्मादितत्सर्वमिति यावत् । मुद्रिकारूपमुद्रा मुद्रिकासमानरूपा मुद्रा मधूच्छिष्टमृदादिष्वारोपितेति शेषः । मधूच्छिष्टादिविग्रहं मधूच्छिष्टमृदादिस्वरूपं विग्रहं । स्वविग्रहं जीवादिरूपतः तेजोरूपतः स्वजन्तुरूपतश्चेति यावत् । बुद्धिः चित्स्वरूपस्य भूतयोगविशेषेषु उपलब्धिरिति यावत् । विशेषयति भेदयति । तत्परं तस्मादन्यं उपादानस्वरूपादन्यमित्यर्थः । एतदुक्तं भवति मधूच्छिष्टाद्यधिकरणे स्वारोपितया मुद्रिकया समानविग्रहा मुद्रा स्वाधिकरणात्मकतन्मधूच्छिष्टादिना स्वरूपात् स्वविग्रहकारणभूतमुद्रिकास्वरूपार्थं स्वस्वरूपमित्यविशेषयतीव भूतयोगविशेषेषु चित्स्वरूपस्योपलब्धिस्वरूपात्मिका बुद्धिः स्वाधिकरणात्मकभूतसमवायात् स्वकीयोपादानात्मकं चित्स्वरूपाच्च स्वस्वरूपमन्यं विशेषयतीति यत्तस्मादेतत् सर्वं बुद्धेः कृत्यमिति ॥ ५८ ॥

भूमेरित्यादिना सदेत्यन्तेन श्लोकद्वयेन दशमप्रश्नस्योत्तरादिकं कथयति । तत्र कुतश्चित् इच्छाशक्तिवैभवादिति यावत् । तत्र भूम्यां । चः समुच्चये । अन्यत्र भूमेरिति शेषः । व्यक्ताव्यक्तस्थितिः व्यक्तरूपेण चाव्यक्तरूपेण च स्थितिः । एतदुक्तं भवति भूमध्यमव्यक्तरूपं जलं खननान्तरं दृश्यते वहिरपि व्यक्तरूपं जलं कर्षणाद्दृश्यते । भूमध्यमव्यक्तरूपोऽग्निः सूर्य्यकान्ते काष्ठादिषु मथनादिना दृश्यते

वायोः सर्वं च सततमवस्थानं त्वनेकधा ।
व्योम सर्वगमेव स्यात् कालताद्रूप्यतः सदा ॥ ६० ॥
देहेषु सस्फुटं तेषामवस्थानन्तु पञ्चधा ।
जीवानामागतिर्देहे मातापित्रोस्तु वीर्य्यतः ॥ ६१ ॥
तादात्म्यं सङ्गतं तत्र जृम्भते सा चिदात्मना ।
तत्र प्रारब्धविरमान्मरणं निद्रया समम् ॥ ६२ ॥
सिद्धानां सर्वदा देहत्यागे भेदो न विद्यते ।
प्रागेव तस्य देहात्मविवेकान्मनसि स्वगे ॥ ६३ ॥

वह्निरशनाद्याकारेण च दृश्यते। अनेकधा गत्यादिभेदादिति शेषः। कालताद्रूप्यतः कालात्मकत्वेनेति यावत् ॥ ६० ॥

देहेष्वित्यादिनाद्यार्द्धेन श्लोकेनैकादशप्रश्नस्योत्तरं कथयति। तत्र तेषां पञ्चभूतानां पञ्चधा तत्तदाकारेणेति शेषः। एतदुक्तं भवति देहेषु घनरूपं भूमिः द्रवरूपं जलं उष्णरूपमग्निः प्राणो वायुः सुषिराणि नभ इति। जीवानामित्यादिनार्द्धद्वयेन द्वादशप्रश्नस्योत्तरं कथयति। तत्र आगतिः प्राप्तिः। तुरवधारणे। वीर्य्यतः शुक्रशोणितयोगादित्यर्थः। आरब्धेति शेषः। एतदुक्तं भवति मातापित्रोः शुक्रशोणितयोगादारब्धेव देहे जीवस्य प्राप्तिरिति। तादात्म्यं जीवात्मभावं सङ्गतं दिव्यत्वात् संगतेति यावत्। तत्र देहे। जृम्भते उपलभ्यते। सा आगतिरिति शेषः। आत्मना स्वेन स्वातन्त्र्यादिति यावत्। एतदुक्तं भवति मातापित्रोः शुक्रशोणितसंयोगादारब्धे देहे तत्र देहे त्वनवच्छिन्नरूपा चित् स्वातन्त्र्याज्जीवात्मभावमुपगता उपलभ्यत इति यावत्। देहे जीवानामागतिः सेति ॥ ६१ ॥

तत्रेत्यादिभिः अयमित्यन्तैरर्द्धैश्चतुर्भिः श्लोकैर्द्वादशप्रश्नावसानप्रोक्तादिशब्दस्य तात्पर्य्यप्रश्नयोरुत्तरद्वयं कथयति। तत्र तत्र देहे। प्रारब्धविरमादहमित्युपलब्धिः प्रारब्धकर्म तद्विरमात् तदभावात्। मरणं जीवानां देहान्निष्क्रान्तिप्रकार इति यावत्। मरणं निद्रया सममित्यस्योत्तरत्र श्लोके सिद्धानामित्यनेन सम्बन्धः। एतदुक्तं भवति अनवच्छिन्नस्य चित्स्वरूपस्य स्वेच्छया देहेषूप

नेतरेषां स साध्यानां साधकानाञ्च कालतः ।
पुष्यादिषु तु मासेषु षट्सु राकोपकण्ठतः ॥ ६४ ॥
मरणं सुगतित्वस्य ज्ञापकं सुगतिस्फुटम् ।
सिद्धस्तु पूर्वतो मुक्तो देहेन्द्रियमनःस्थिरः ॥ ६५ ॥

लब्धिस्वरूपा जीवभावमुपगता बुद्धिरिन्द्रियद्वारा वहिर्गता व्याप्य विश्वं यदा विषयाननुभवति तदा जाग्रदवस्था यदा पुनः सा तत्तदिन्द्रियेभ्यो निवृत्ता हृत्प्रदेशस्था तत्तद्विषयान् स्मरति तदा स्वप्नावस्था यदा पुनरसौ हृदयादपि निवृत्ता स्वपरमार्थचैतन्यस्वरूपे विश्राम्यति तदा सुषुप्तवस्थेति । तत्तस्मात् चित्स्वरूपस्य बुद्धिस्वरूपतया देहादिष्वनुपलब्धिसामग्रात् मरणं निद्रया सममित्यवैतन्मात्रमन्तरेण परमार्थतो जीवस्य देहप्राप्तिनिर्गमनादि-प्रतीतिरपां पात्रे चन्द्रस्येवेति सिद्धा कृतनिश्चया भवतीति । भेदः पूर्वावस्थाया इति शेषः । प्राक् सद्गुरुकटाक्षसमये । एवावधारणे । तस्य सिद्धस्य । देहात्म-विवेकाद्देहात्मनोः स्वरूपविमर्शात् । स्वगी स्वस्वरूपं गते सति पश्चात् कालतो देहत्यागे पूर्व्वावस्थाया भेदो न विद्यत इति न देहात्मविवेकाद्देहात्मविवेक-भावात् देहविश्लेषत एव देहाभिमानत्यागः देहाभिमानरहित्यमिति यावत् । इतरेषां पामराणां । सः देहाभिमानत्यागः । अस्य कालत इत्यने-नोत्तरत्र सम्बन्धः । साध्यानां सद्गुरुकटाक्षे सत्यप्यनादिदुर्व्वासनावलाज्जड़-क्रियातात्पर्य्येण देहात्मविवेकविमुखानां । साधकानां सद्गुरुकटाक्षादुपलब्ध-परमार्थस्वरूपानुभूत्यां सत्यां अपि निःशेषापरिमुक्तदुर्व्वासनानाञ्च । चः समुच्चये । कालतः कालधर्म्मतः शरीरविनाशादिति यावत् । एतदुक्तं भवति पामराणां साध्यानां साधकानाञ्च देहात्मविवेकाभावाद्देहविश्लेषत एव देहाभिमानत्यागो भवति । पुष्यादिषु तु मासेषु षट्सु उत्तरायण इति यावत् । राकोपकण्ठतः शुक्लपक्षाष्टम्युत्तरार्द्धादारभ्य कृष्णपक्षाष्टमीपूर्व्वार्द्धान्ततिथिष्विति यावत् । सुगतित्वस्य ज्ञापकमित्यने दक्षिणायने कृष्णाष्टम्युत्तरार्द्धादारभ्य शुक्लाष्टमी पूर्व्वार्द्धान्ततिथिषु च मरणाद्दुर्गतित्वस्य ज्ञापकमिति कथितं । सिद्धः ज्ञातपरमार्थः । तुर्विशेषे । पूर्व्वतो मुक्तः तेन हेतुना अस्य सिद्धस्य निधनं देहविश्लेषः । सर्व्वदा सर्व्वतः देशतः प्रकारतश्चेति शेषः । तथा यथोत्तरायणे

यतस्तेनास्य निधनं सर्वदा सर्वतस्तथा।
सुगतित्वं व्यनक्त्येव जीवन्मुक्तो यतस्त्वयम् ॥ ६६ ॥
देहवत्त्वे समानेऽपि प्राणिनां सर्वतः सदा।
बुद्धेर्वैविध्यरूपस्य कारणं किं वद प्रभो ॥ ६७ ॥
भूमिष्ठत्वे समानेपि तोयानां रसभेदवत्।
जायते त्वाश्रयवशात् स च कर्म्मभिरेव वै ॥ ६८ ॥
यथाश्वत्थगतो वह्निरुपायैरितरैः क्वचित्।
नोपलभ्यो भवेत् शुष्कमथनव्यापृतिं विना ॥ ६९ ॥

राकोपकण्ठे काले च वाराणस्यादिषु चेत्रेषु भृगुपतनादिप्रकारतश्चेति यथा तथेत्यर्थः। एवावधारणे। तुर्विशेषे। अयं सिद्धः ॥ ६६ ॥

देहवत्त्वे इत्यादिना श्लोकेन प्राणिनां बुद्धेर्वैविध्यकारणं सोपपत्तिकं देवी पृच्छति। तत्र सर्व्वतः प्रकारतः इति शेषः। प्रभो इतीश्वरसम्बुद्धिः ॥ ६७ ॥

भूमिष्ठत्व इत्यादिना श्लोकेन तदुत्तरं सनिदर्शनं कथयति। तत्र आश्रयवशात् दृष्टान्तस्थलविशेषवशात् दार्ष्टान्तिके प्रकृतिविशेषवशादिति यावत्। एतदुक्तं भवति भूमिष्ठत्वे समाने आश्रयवशात्तोयानां रसभेदवद्देहवत्त्वे समाने प्याश्रयप्रकृतिविशेषवशाद्बुद्धेर्गुणवैविध्यं जायत इति। अनन्तरमाश्रयविशेषः केन जायत इत्यादिशङ्कायामाह स च कर्म्मभिरेव वे तत्र स च आश्रयविशेषश्च जायत इति शेषः। कर्म्मभिः कर्मदृष्टान्ते तोयकार्य्यैः रसादिभिरिति यावत्। दार्ष्टान्तिके बुद्धिकार्य्यैरिति यावत्। एतदुक्तं भवति तोयानां रसादिभिरेव स्थलविशेषवशाद्बुद्धेः कार्य्यैरेव प्रकृतिविशेषो भवतीति ॥ ६८ ॥

यथेत्यादिभिः स्वस्वरूपकमित्यन्तैस्त्रिभिः श्लोकैर्गुरुमुखादेव प्राप्यं विद्यादिकमपि सनिदर्शनं प्रतिज्ञामुपदिशति। तत्र अश्वत्थगत इति तरुसामान्यग्रहण मन्तरेण विशेषग्रहणात् गुरोरप्यधिकारिविशेषमुपलक्षयति। इतरैः छेदनाद्यैः। क्वचित् देशे काले चेति शेषः। शुष्कमथनव्यापृतिमित्यत्र शुष्कशब्देन देहात्मविवेकात् गुरोर्देहादिषु तात्पर्य्यं। मथनव्यापृतिशब्देन शिष्यस्य तदुपास्त्या-

तथात्मज्ञानसंप्राप्तिः सद्गुरुप्राप्तितो विना ।
न कस्यापि भवेदेषा प्रतिज्ञा विश्वतोऽनिशम् ॥ ७० ॥

खननाद्भूगतं तोयं यथा समुपलभ्यते ।
तथा सद्गुरुसंसेवां संप्राप्य स्वस्वरूपकम् ॥ ७१ ॥

सद्गुरोः पादसेवातः सम्प्राप्तात्मस्वरूपिणः ।
विशेषः को*भवेदन्यदुर्लभः सत्यविग्रहः ॥ ७२ ॥

आभिरूप्यमसन्देहः सन्तोषः परिपूर्णता ।
दयार्द्रचित्तता रागद्वेषाविषयचित्तता ॥ ७३ ॥

सुलभत्वमगर्वित्वं सदा नियतशीलता ।
कृतज्ञता सत्यता†च परचिन्तानिवर्त्तनम् ॥ ७४ ॥

दिषु तात्पर्य्यञ्चोपलक्षयति। कस्यापि प्रथमे पटले चतुर्भिराद्यैरित्यादिना प्रोक्तलक्षणसम्पूर्णस्येति यावत्। प्रतिज्ञा ममेति शेषः। ईश्वरस्य प्रतिज्ञेति यावत्। विश्वतः हेतोः। स्वस्वरूपकं आत्मज्ञानं ॥ ७१ ॥

सद्गुरोरित्यादिना श्लोकेन सद्गुरुसेवाप्राप्तस्वरूपस्य विशेषं देवी पृच्छति। अत्र अन्यदुर्लभः यथावदलब्धज्ञानानां दुर्लभः ॥ ७२ ॥

आभिरूप्यमित्यादिभिः प्रवर्त्तते इत्यन्तैर्नवभिः श्लोकैस्तदुत्तरत्वेनात्मवतां सप्तचत्वारिंशल्लक्षणानीतरेषां तद्राहित्यादिकञ्चोपदिशति। तत्र आभिरूप्यमित्यादिना श्लोकेन लक्षणसप्तकम्। तत्र आभिरूप्यं अभितः स्वरूपभावः सर्व्वात्मभाव इति यावत्। सौन्दर्य्यं वा। असन्देहः विकल्पश्रुति‡भिरपीति यावत्। सन्तोषः स्वानुभूत्या परिपूर्णतास्वरूपतया नैरपेक्ष्याञ्च। दयार्द्रचित्तता रागद्वेषयोरनास्पदचित्तता। अपृथगभावादिति यावत् ॥ ७३ ॥

सुलभत्वमित्यादिना श्लोकेन लक्षणषट्कम् ॥ ७४ ॥

---

* विशेषतो ।

† स्वपत्या

‡ शुद्धि ।

आर्जवञ्चावित्तलौल्यं विषयानतिसङ्गिता ।
अदैर्घ्यसूत्रमक्षौद्र्यं नात्यगाधाशयात्मता ॥ ७५ ॥
वृथालापेष्वशक्तिश्च वृथाव्यापारवर्जनम् ।
वृथाविनोदराहित्यं जिह्मचित्तैरसङ्गतिः ॥ ७६ ॥
पुरुषार्थार्थकथनचिन्ताकरणकौतुकम् ।
अस्तेयशक्तिरास्तिक्यं परलोकानुचिन्तनम् ॥ ७७ ॥
देवतापूजनस्तोत्रवैभवालापशीलता ।
पापानां वर्जनं पुण्यकरणे कौतुकं सदा ॥ ७८ ॥
परस्तवननिन्दासु विरतिर्वीतरागिता ।
निस्पृहत्वमलोलत्वमनाक्षेपोऽजडात्मता ॥ ७९ ॥

आर्जवमित्यादिना श्लोकेन लक्षणषट्कं । तत्र अवित्तलौल्यं अर्थार्थमपारतन्त्र्यम् । विषयानतिसङ्गिता शरीररक्षणमात्रमन्तरेण विषयेषु रागतः प्रवृत्तिः सिद्धस्य न स्यादिति यावत् । अदैर्घ्यसूत्रं अचिरक्रियत्वं । नात्यगाधाशयात्मता सौलभ्यादिति यावत् ॥ ७५ ॥

वृथेत्यादिना श्लोकेन लक्षणचतुष्टयं । तत्र वृथाशब्देन दृष्टादृष्टानुपयोगित्वमुक्तं । जिह्मचित्तैः कपटहृदयैः ॥ ७६ ॥

पुरुषार्थेत्यादिना श्लोकेन लक्षणषट्कम् । तत्र पुरुषार्थार्थकथनचिन्ताकरणकौतुकं पुरुषार्थार्थकथनं पुरुषार्थचिन्ताकरणं पुरुषार्थकौतुकञ्चेत्यन्वयः । अस्तेयशक्तिः स्तेयकर्मण्यशक्तिः । आस्तिक्यं शास्त्रार्थेष्विति यावत् । परलोकानुचिन्तनं परस्वरूपावलोकनगुणचिन्तनं । आगमाभ्यास इति यावत् ॥ ७७ ॥

देवतेत्यादिना श्लोकेन लक्षणपञ्चकं । तत्र देवतापूजनस्तोत्रवैभवालापशीलता देवतानां पूजनालापशीलता देवतानां वैभवालापशीलता चेति ग्रन्थयोजना । पापानां निषिद्धकर्मणामभिचाराद्युत्पन्नकर्मणां च स्वस्य च परेषां चाहितानामिति यावत् । पुण्यकरणे स्वस्य च परेषाञ्च हितकरणे । प्राणिनां संसारक्लेशनिवृत्त्यर्थं स्वरूपसिद्ध्यर्थञ्चेति यावत् ॥ ७८ ॥

परस्तवनेत्यादिना श्लोकेन लक्षणषटकम् । तत्र परस्तवननिन्दासु परस्तवनेषु परनिन्दासु च ॥ ७९ ॥

अगोपनं स्वभक्तानामभक्तानाञ्च गोपनम् ।
गुरुविद्यागमाचारस्तवनं तत्प्रवर्त्तनम् ॥ ८० ॥
सिद्धचिह्नानि चैतानि भवन्त्यात्मवतां ध्रुवम् ।
न भवन्तीतरेषान्तु प्रद्विषन्त्येव तांश्च ते ॥ ८१ ॥
तत्कृत्यं शृणु वक्ष्येऽहं यो लब्धस्वात्मवैभवः ।
निरस्ताशेषसंसारमौर्ख्याज्ञानाविवेकवान् ॥ ८२ ॥
देशकालकुलाचारान् गुरुराजादिकल्पितान् ।
पालयन् सुस्मितमुखः पूजापूजनकौतुकी ॥ ८३ ॥
देहास्थैर्य्यं तथाज्ञानं व्यापारान् कालतः क्षणात् ।
पतितान्बन्धुचित्ताज्ञादुर्लङ्घ्यान् स्वचयस्थितीन् ॥ ८४ ॥
स्वेन्द्रियाणाञ्च सामर्थ्यं स्वकर्म्माणि कृतानि च ।
मुहुर्मुहुश्च विमृशेद्विरमेदशुभात्मनः ॥ ८५ ॥

अगोपनमित्यादिना श्लोकेन लक्षणसप्तकं । तत्र अगोपनं आगमादीनामिति यावत् । गोपनं प्रागवदागमादीनां । गुरुविद्यागमाचारस्तवनं गुरोर्विद्याया आगमानामाचाराणाञ्च स्तवनं ॥ ८० ॥

एतानि प्रोक्तानि सप्तचत्वारिंशल्लक्षणानि । तुर्विशेषे । एवावधारणे । तान् आत्मज्ञानवतः । ते आत्मज्ञानरहिताः ॥ ८१ ॥

तदित्यादिभिः सदेत्यन्तैर्नवभिः श्लोकैरात्मज्ञानवतां समाचारक्रममुपदिशति । तत्र तत्कृत्यं आत्मज्ञानवतां कृत्यं । निरस्ताशेषसंसारमौर्ख्याज्ञानाविवेकवान् निरस्ताशेषसंसारवान् । निरस्ताशेषमौर्ख्यवान् । निरस्ताशेषाज्ञानवान् । निरस्ताशेषाविवेकवान् । इति ग्रन्थयोजना । अतस्मिंस्तद्बुद्धिः संसारः । अतस्मिंस्तदभिमानो मौर्ख्यं । तस्मिन्नतद्बुद्धिरज्ञानं । तद्विमर्शहानिरविवेकः । देशकालकुलाचारानित्यत्र देशाचारः कालाचारोऽवस्थानुगुणाचारः कुलाचारस्तानिति यावत् । गुरुराजादिकल्पितान् । गुरुराजादीत्यत्रादिशब्दः प्रथमे पटले "गुरुं तदग्रतः" इत्यादिना श्लोकेन प्रोक्तपूज्यविषयः । राजादीत्यत्रादिशब्दः तत्समानपुरुषविषयः । देहास्थैर्य्यं स्वभावत इति यावत् । अत्र

वृथा न कालं गमयेद्द्यूतस्त्रीस्वापवादतः ।
गमयेद्देवतापूजाजपयोगस्तवादिना ॥ ८६ ॥
गुरोः कृपालापकथास्तोत्रागमविलोकनैः ।
गमयेदनिशं कालं न वदेत् परदूषणम् ॥ ८७ ॥
प्रत्यक्षे च परोक्षे च स्तुवीत प्रणमेद्गुरुम् ।
तद्गुणैस्तत्कृपाधिक्यैः पुण्यैश्वर्य्यैश्च सत्यतः ॥ ८८ ॥
रागलोभमदक्रोध*पापपैशुन्यवर्जनैः ।
†सन्तोषाचारनियमशान्तिज्ञानादिभिस्तथा ॥ ८९ ॥
मिताहारो मितालापो विविक्तसमवर्त्तिता ‡ ।
नित्याचिन्ता स्वात्मशुद्धिः कृत्यमात्मवतां सदा ॥ ९० ॥

द्वितीयान्तानां पदानामुत्तरत्र श्लोके विसृजेदित्यनेनान्वयः। अन्यान् व्यापारान् दृष्टादृष्टानुपयुक्तानिति यावत्। कालतः क्षणात् पतितान् बन्धुचित्ताद्यादुर्लङ्घ्यान् बन्धुभिः चित्तैः राजादिभिरपि दुर्लङ्घ्यान् कालतः क्षणात् पतितान् पुरुषादीनिति यावत्। अशुभात्मनः अशुभस्वभावान्। द्यूतस्त्रीस्वापवादत इत्यत्र द्यूतशब्दो निर्जीवद्यूतसजीवद्यूतविषयः। स्त्रीशब्दस्तु धर्म्मपत्नीव्यतिरिक्तविषयः। स्वापशब्दः प्रात्तेतरविषयः। वादशब्दो जल्पवितण्डादिविषयः। स्तवादिना इत्यत्रादिशब्दः प्रदक्षिणनमस्कारादिविषयः। गुरोः कृपालापकथास्तोत्रागमविलोकनैः गुरोः कृपायाः गुरोरालापानां च गुरोः कथाभिः गुरोः स्तोत्रैः गुरोर्लब्धागमविलोकनैश्च। तद्गुणैः गुरुगुणैः। अस्मिन् श्लोके चोत्तरश्लोके च तृतीयान्तानां पदानां स्तुवीतेत्यनेनान्वयः। तत्कृपाधिक्यैः गुरुकृपाधिक्यैः। तद्गुणैरित्यादि तृतीयान्तेषु त्रिषु चानन्तरश्लोके तृतीयान्तयोः पदयोः च गुरोरित्यध्याहार्य्यं। तत्र सत्यतः सत्येन वाङ्मनःकर्म्मणामेकरूपेणेति यावत्। ज्ञानादिभिरित्यत्रादिशब्दो दानादिविषयः। नित्याचिन्ता षोड़शनित्यानां स्वरूपचिन्ता। स्वात्मशुद्धिः स्ववाङ्मनःकायानां शुद्धिरिति यावत् ॥ ९० ॥

---

* क्रौर्य्य। † सन्तोषज्ञान। ‡ विविक्ता सर्ववर्त्तिता।

पूर्व्वोक्तद्वादशास्रस्य मध्ये कृत्वा यथाविधि ।
योनिं तन्मध्यतो देवीं ललितां पृष्ठतो गुरून् ॥ ६१ ॥
पार्श्वयोरायुधान्यष्टौ कोणेषु परितः क्रमात् ।
कामेश्वर्य्यादिकास्तत्र तद्वहिर्द्वादशस्वपि ॥ ६२ ॥
द्वादशान्या यजेत्तत्तन्नित्याविद्याभिरेव वा ।
तन्नामविद्याभिर्वा ताः पूजयेत् सार्घकल्पनम् ॥ ६३ ॥
सन्ध्यात्रयं षष्टिसंख्यं जपेत्तद्दिनविद्यया ।
नान्यत् कृत्यं भवेत्तस्य नित्यनैमित्तिकादिकम् ॥ ६४ ॥

पूर्वोक्तेत्यादिभिरभूदित्यन्तैः षड्भिः श्लोकैः आत्मवतां जीवन्मुक्तानां ललितापूजाक्रममुपदिशति । तत्र पूर्वोक्तद्वादशास्रस्य एकोनविंशपटलप्रोक्तद्वादशास्रस्य मध्ये सर्व्वमध्यस्थवृत्तमध्ये अन्यूनाधिकमानमिति यावत् । योनिं स्वाभिमुखाग्रत्रिकोणं । तन्मध्यतः योनेर्मध्ये । पृष्ठतः योनेः प्राग्रेखावृत्तरेखयोरन्तराले । गुरून् देवीरूपतयेति यावत् । पार्श्वयोः पार्श्वरेखाद्वयवृत्तरेखान्तरालद्वये । आयुधान्यष्टौ पूजापटलोक्तवाण्यादिप्रातिलोम्येनेति यावत् । कोणेषु मध्ययोनेरग्रादिषु त्रिकोणेषु । परितः क्रमात् प्रदक्षिणक्रमात् । कामेश्वर्य्यादिकाः कामेश्वरीं भगमालिनीं वज्रेश्वरीं च । तद्वहिर्द्वादशसु अस्रेष्विति यावत् । अन्याः कामेश्वरीभगमालिनीवज्रेश्वरीव्यतिरिक्ताः । तत्तन्नित्याविद्याभिः तृतीयपटलप्रोक्ताभिरिति यावत् । एवावधारणे । वा विकल्पे । तन्नामविद्याभिः एकोनविंशपटले प्रोक्ताभिरिति यावत् । ताः नित्याः । एतदुक्तं भवति एकोनविंशपटलप्रोक्तविधानेन द्वादशास्रचक्रं विलिख्य तन्मध्यवृत्तमध्ये स्वाभिमुखं समत्रिरेखं त्रिकोणं विलिख्य तन्मध्ये ललितां तन्मध्ये त्रिकोणप्राग्रेखावृत्तरेखान्तराले नाथशक्तीः तदुभयपार्श्वरेखाद्वयवृत्तरेखान्तरालद्वये वाय्वाद्यप्रादक्षिण्येन हेतीर्मध्ययोनेरग्रादिषु त्रिषु कोणेषु कामेश्वरीभगमालिनीवज्रेश्वरीश्च तद्वहिर्द्वादशास्रेषु अन्या द्वादश नित्याश्च प्रादक्षिण्येन तत्तन्नित्याविद्याभिर्नामविद्याभिर्वा यजेदिति । तस्य आत्मवतः । नित्यनैमित्तिकादिकमित्यत्रादिशब्दः काम्यविषयः । तन्मध्ये द्वादशास्रस्य मध्ये । नवयोनिं

तन्मध्ये नवयोनिं वा विधायावस्थशक्तिभिः।
पूजयेत् प्राग्वदुभयप्रकारादेकयोगतः॥ ९५॥
यावज्जीवं विधिस्त्वेष गदितः सिद्धये सदा।
सिद्धानामपि सर्वेषां येनासौ स्वात्मवानभूत्॥ ९६॥
समस्तमेतत्तन्त्रन्ते कथितं परमेश्वरि।
यत्परामर्शतो भावस्त्वावयोरैक्यमश्नुते॥ ९७॥
तद्द्यात्तन्त्रमेतत्तु नाभक्ताय कदाचन।
नाशिष्याय न दम्भाय प्रच्छन्नानयशीलिने॥ ९८॥
नायाचते नास्तिकाय न लुब्धाय न मानिने।
न पापाय न वित्ताय नादत्ताय च भेदिने॥ ९९॥

पञ्चदशपटले प्रोक्तामिति शेषः। वा विकल्पे। अवस्थशक्तिभिः सहेति शेषः। प्राग्वत् अग्न्याद्यप्रादक्षिण्येन उभयप्रकारादेकयोगतः द्वादशास्त्रमध्ये केवलं योनिं नवयोनिं वा लिखेदिति यावत्। सिद्धये आत्मज्ञानस्येति शेषः। सर्वेषां आत्मज्ञानसिद्धानां श्रीविद्यासिद्धानामिति यावत्। योगसिद्धानामाज्ञासिद्धानामिति यावत्। येन विधानेन। असौ सिद्धेषु चतुर्थ्वन्यतमः। स्वात्मवान् स्वरूपज्ञानवान्॥ ८६॥

समस्तमित्यादिभिर्भेदिन इत्यन्तैस्त्रिभिः श्लोकैस्तन्त्रार्थवेदिनः फलं तन्त्रदाने सम्प्रदानभूतस्य वर्जनीयस्य त्रयोदशदोषांश्चोपदिशति। तत्र परमेश्वरीति देवीसम्बुद्धिः। यत्परामर्शतो भावः तन्त्रार्थविद इति शेषः। आवयोरैक्यमश्नुते शिवशक्त्योरभेदस्वरूपो भवति। तच्छब्देन तन्त्रस्यानुभाव उच्यते। तुरवधारणे। कदाचन आपत्स्वपीत्यर्थः। दम्भाय मिथ्याचाराय। प्रच्छन्नानयशीलिने प्रच्छन्नाय अनयशीलिने चेति यावत्। नायाचते नास्तिकाय चेति यावत्। वित्ताय धर्मार्थमिति यावत्। अदत्ताय जड़ाय। भेदिने द्विधाभावशीलाय॥ ८८॥

यस्तन्त्रमेतत् सकलं नित्याविद्यास्तु षोडश ।
शक्त्या संगृह्य विधिवद्भजते स मदंशकः ॥ १०० ॥
शिवतत्त्वमयी व्याप्तिरिति सम्यक् समीरिता ।
अस्या निष्कालनाच्चित्ते तत्तत्त्वं स्वात्मसात् कृतम् ॥

इति षोडशनित्यातन्त्रेषु श्रीकादिमते तन्त्रराजे
स्वात्मकथनं नाम षट्त्रिंशत् पटलम्
परिपूर्णम् परामृष्टम् ॥ ॐतत्सत् ॥
॥ ३६ ॥ ॐ तत्सत् ॥

यस्तन्त्रमित्यादिना श्लोकेन यथाविधि प्राप्ततन्त्रार्थवतः फलमुपदिशति। तत्र विधिवत् नित्यनैमित्तिकादिप्रोक्तक्रमात् स भजनपरः। मदंशकः चित्स्वरूप ईश्वर इति यावत् ॥ १०० ॥

इति षोडशनित्यातन्त्रेषु श्रीकादिमताख्यस्य परिपूर्णस्य तन्त्रस्य प्रपञ्चसार-
सिंहराजप्रकाशाभिधानेन सुभगानन्दनाथेन विरचितायां मनोरमा-
ख्यायां व्याख्यायां देवतादेशिकशिष्यप्रपञ्चादीनां परमार्थ-
स्वरूपप्रकाशनपरं षट्त्रिंशत्पटलं परिपूर्णं
परामृष्टम् ॥ ३६ ॥ ॐतत्सत् ॥

ग्रन्थसंख्याः—षट्त्रिंशे पटले ज्ञेयाः शिवतत्त्वमयेऽत्र च ।
सार्धसप्तषष्टिश्च व्याख्याग्रन्थाः शतत्रयम् ॥ २६७ ॥
तन्त्रे प्रकरणान्यत्र श्रीमत्कादिमताह्वये ।
शतानां नवकं त्वेकत्रिंशता च समन्वितम् ॥ ८३१ ॥

भुक्तिभूमानमाधुर्य्यभाग्यगन्धेर्हसिद्धिगाः ।
संसत् सुरस्त्रोरित्येकविंशत्यक्षरसंख्यया ॥
२२७७७१९८७९८८३११५११९८५०५४६४ ।
यन्त्राणि स्युः कादिमते तन्त्रे प्रोक्तानि तत्र तु ।
दक्षिणापथपुण्यौघपरिणामाश्रयोदधिः ॥
कोष्ठयन्त्राख्यनन्तानि क्षादिवर्णोक्षितानि च ।
सम्भूय श्रीकादिमते तन्त्रे व्याख्यानसंख्यया ॥
सहस्राणां द्वादशकं न्यूनं पञ्चाशतेरितम् ।
काश्मीरराजस्य गुरुः श्रीकण्ठेशो द्विजेश्वरः ॥
कदाचिदागतो द्रष्टुं रामसेतुं स्वलीलया ।
तेनैवानुगृहीतोभूत्तन्मध्ये मार्गे नृसिंहराट् ॥
मन्त्राण्यधीतवांस्तस्मान्नित्यानां तेषु निर्म्मिता ।
व्याख्या मनोरमाभिख्या तेन कादिमतस्य तु ॥
शुभगानन्दनाथेन द्वाविंशपटलावधि ।
तदाज्ञयावशिष्टानां पटलानां विनिर्ममे ॥
चतुर्द्दशानां तच्छिष्यः प्रकाशानन्ददेशिकः ।
तां सुन्दरवरश्चाभ्रगाख्यां प्राक् सम्प्रदायतः ॥
समाप्ता चेयं तन्त्रराजटोका मनोरमा ॥ ॐ ॥
